HANDBOOK OF PSYCHOLOGY

HANDBOOK OF PSYCHOLOGY

VOLUME 5: PERSONALITY AND SOCIAL PSYCHOLOGY

Second Edition

Volume Editors

HOWARD TENNEN AND JERRY SULS

Editor-in-Chief

IRVING B. WEINER

WILEY

John Wiley & Sons, Inc.

Library of Congress Cataloging-in-Publication Data:

Handbook of psychology / Irving B. Weiner, editor-in-chief. — 2nd ed.
    v. cm.
  Includes bibliographical references and index.
  ISBN 978-0-470-61904-9 (set)
  ISBN 978-0-470-64776-9 (cloth : v.5)
  ISBN 978-1-118-28376-9 (e-bk.)
  ISBN 978-1-118-28192-5 (e-bk.)
  ISBN 978-1-118-28530-5 (e-bk.)
  1. Psychology. I. Weiner, Irving B.
  BF121.H213 2013
  150—dc23

                               2012005833

Printed in the United States of America
10 9 8 7 6 5 4 3 2 1

Editorial Board

Contents

Handbook of Psychology Preface

The first edition of the 12-volume *Handbook of Psychology* was published in 2003 to provide a comprehensive overview of the current status and anticipated future directions of basic and applied psychology and to serve as a reference source and textbook for the ensuing decade. With 10 years having elapsed, and psychological knowledge and applications continuing to expand, the time has come for this second edition to appear. In addition to well-referenced updating of the first edition content, this second edition of the *Handbook* reflects the fresh perspectives of some new volume editors, chapter authors, and subject areas. However, the conceptualization and organization of the *Handbook*, as stated next, remain the same.

Psychologists commonly regard their discipline as the science of behavior, and the pursuits of behavioral scientists range from the natural sciences to the social sciences and embrace a wide variety of objects of investigation. Some psychologists have more in common with biologists than with most other psychologists, and some have more in common with sociologists than with most of their psychological colleagues. Some psychologists are interested primarily in the behavior of animals, some in the behavior of people, and others in the behavior of organizations. These and other dimensions of difference among psychological scientists are matched by equal if not greater heterogeneity among psychological practitioners, who apply a vast array of methods in many different settings to achieve highly varied purposes. This 12-volume *Handbook of Psychology* captures the breadth and diversity of psychology and encompasses interests and concerns shared by psychologists in all branches of the field. To this end, leading national and international scholars and practitioners have collaborated to produce 301 authoritative and detailed chapters covering all fundamental facets of the discipline.

Two unifying threads run through the science of behavior. The first is a common history rooted in conceptual and empirical approaches to understanding the nature of behavior. The specific histories of all specialty areas in psychology trace their origins to the formulations of the classical philosophers and the early experimentalists, and appreciation for the historical evolution of psychology in all of its variations transcends identifying oneself as a particular kind of psychologist. Accordingly, Volume 1 in the *Handbook*, again edited by Donald Freedheim, is devoted to the *History of Psychology* as it emerged in many areas of scientific study and applied technology.

A second unifying thread in psychology is a commitment to the development and utilization of research methods suitable for collecting and analyzing behavioral data. With attention both to specific procedures and to their application in particular settings, Volume 2, again edited by John Schinka and Wayne Velicer, addresses *Research Methods in Psychology*.

Volumes 3 through 7 of the *Handbook* present the substantive content of psychological knowledge in five areas of study. Volume 3, which addressed *Biological Psychology* in the first edition, has in light of developments in the field been retitled in the second edition to cover *Behavioral Neuroscience*. Randy Nelson continues as editor of this volume and is joined by Sheri Mizumori as a new co-editor. Volume 4 concerns *Experimental Psychology* and is again edited by Alice Healy and Robert Proctor. Volume 5 on *Personality and Social Psychology* has been reorganized by two new co-editors, Howard Tennen and Jerry Suls. Volume 6 on *Developmental Psychology* is again edited by Richard Lerner, Ann Easterbrooks, and Jayanthi Mistry. William Reynolds and Gloria Miller continue as co-editors of Volume 7 on *Educational Psychology*.

Volumes 8 through 12 address the application of psychological knowledge in five broad areas of professional practice. Thomas Widiger and George Stricker continue as co-editors of Volume 8 on *Clinical Psychology*. Volume 9 on *Health Psychology* is again co-edited by Arthur Nezu, Christine Nezu, and Pamela Geller. Continuing to co-edit Volume 10 on *Assessment Psychology* are John Graham and Jack Naglieri. Randy Otto joins the Editorial Board as the new editor of Volume 11 on *Forensic Psychology*. Also joining the Editorial Board are two new co-editors, Neal Schmitt and Scott Highhouse, who have reorganized Volume 12 on *Industrial and Organizational Psychology*.

The *Handbook of Psychology* was prepared to educate and inform readers about the present state of psychological knowledge and about anticipated advances in behavioral science research and practice. To this end, the *Handbook* volumes address the needs and interests of three groups. First, for graduate students in behavioral science, the volumes provide advanced instruction in the basic concepts and methods that define the fields they cover, together with a review of current knowledge, core literature, and likely future directions. Second, in addition to serving as graduate textbooks, the volumes offer professional psychologists an opportunity to read and contemplate the views of distinguished colleagues concerning the central thrusts of research and the leading edges of practice in their respective fields. Third, for psychologists seeking to become conversant with fields outside their own specialty and for persons outside of psychology seeking information about psychological matters, the *Handbook* volumes serve as a reference source for expanding their knowledge and directing them to additional sources in the literature.

The preparation of this *Handbook* was made possible by the diligence and scholarly sophistication of 24 volume editors and co-editors who constituted the Editorial Board. As Editor-in-Chief, I want to thank each of these colleagues for the pleasure of their collaboration in this project. I compliment them for having recruited an outstanding cast of contributors to their volumes and then working closely with these authors to achieve chapters that will stand each in their own right as valuable contributions to the literature. Finally, I would like to thank Brittany White for her exemplary work as my administrator for our manuscript management system, and the editorial staff of John Wiley & Sons for encouraging and helping bring to fruition this second edition of the *Handbook*, particularly Patricia Rossi, Executive Editor, and Kara Borbely, Editorial Program Coordinator.

Irving B. Weiner
Tampa, Florida

Volume Preface

This volume of the *Handbook* is devoted to the fields of personality and social psychology. The first 10 chapters capture the breadth and depth, achievements and promise of personality psychology. Six of the chapters in this section cover topics addressed in the *Handbook*'s first edition: the genetics of personality, the biological bases of personality, psychodynamic models, Cognitive-Experiential Self-Theory, self-regulatory perspectives on personality, and interpersonal theory of personality. The four other section chapters cover topics new to the *Handbook*: the Five-Factor Model, the Cognitive-Affective Processing System, personality trait development in adulthood, and personality strengths. Together, these chapters convey the vitality and rigor of modern personality psychology.

This section opens with a sweeping overview by Susan South, Ted Reichborn-Kjennerud, Nicholas Eaton, and Robert Krueger of the state of the science in the application of quantitative behavior genetics and molecular genetics to the study of personality. Their review of twin and adoption studies conveys forcefully that variation in personality is due to both genetic and environmental sources. The second half of this chapter introduces the reader to the relatively young field of the molecular genetics of personality, including its most popular methods, candidate gene analysis, linkage analysis, and genome-wide association studies. South, Reichborn-Kjennerud, Eaton, and Krueger demonstrate how these methods are informing our understanding of gene-gene interactions, the interplay of genes and environment, and the role of genetic influences across the lifespan, and they make a compelling case for the continued application of twin and adoption studies and molecular genetic methods in personality psychology.

Expanding the logic of genetic underpinnings of personality to the neurochemical and physiological domains, Marvin Zuckerman presents in exquisite detail evidence from genetic, electrophysiological, and brain imaging investigations. Zuckerman reviews extensive evidence from animal and human studies to demonstrate how extraversion, sensation seeking/impulsivity, and aggression are associated with approach behavior, whereas neuroticism is associated with withdrawal-avoidance. He traces the study of the biological foundations of personality from Eysenck's "top-down" approach to Gray's "bottom-up" approach, while revealing the biological mechanisms of behavioral approach and inhibition underlying human personality.

In their chapter on psychodynamic models of personality, Robert Bornstein, Christy Denckla, and Wei-Jean Chung remind us that there are various psychodynamic models, including Freud's topographic and structural models, object relations theory and self-psychology, neo-analytic frameworks, and several contemporary perspectives. In reviewing these models, Bornstein and colleagues underscore that despite differences, psychodynamic models share three core assumptions: the primacy of the unconscious, the importance of early experiences, and psychic causality. While acknowledging that psychodynamic theorists' devotion to idiographic methods and evidence derived in the treatment context has prompted criticism, they also point to the recent rigorous empirical testing of psychoanalytic constructs and the development and continued refinement of empirically validated psychoanalytic treatments. These recent scientifically based efforts by psychodynamic investigators deserve the attention of skeptics. Empirically guided refinements to psychodynamic theory have, as Bornstein and colleagues note, strengthened its ties to cognitive psychology, health psychology, and attachment theory, as psychodynamic models of personality continue to evolve.

Psychoanalytic theory has a long tradition in literary criticism, but as Robert McCrae, James Gaines, and Marie Wellington note in their chapter on the Five-Factor Model

(FFM), literary critics have typically not kept abreast of advances in psychological theory and investigation. McCrae and colleagues offer compelling evidence that literary critics would do well by applying the methods and findings of contemporary trait psychology to questions about genres, literary periods, individual authors, and the interpretation of literary characters, and they offer stimulating illustrations of FFM personality profiles applied to the protagonists from works of Goethe, Molière, and Voltaire. In making their case, McCrae and colleagues provide an enlightening overview of the FFM, including commonly held misconceptions, they summarize what is known about how FFM traits function in people's lives, and they offer McCrae and Costa's Five-Factor Theory to organize the FFM empirical literature.

Cognitive-experiential self-theory (CEST) substitutes an adaptive unconscious for the Freudian unconscious. Seymour Epstein, who developed and elaborated CEST over the past three decades, explains with great clarity how the unconscious of CEST, referred to as the *experiential system*, is an associative learning processing system, whereas CEST's *rational system* allows people to process information through verbal reasoning. Although the systems usually operate in harmony, Epstein reveals the many ways they can conflict. Through evocative examples, he argues convincingly that although people show a remarkable ability to solve impersonal problems, the influence of the experiential system on the rational system can account for our widely acknowledged irrationality when attempting to solve relationship problems. Epstein concludes this chapter by documenting the wide-ranging implications of CEST for important issues within and beyond personality psychology, including intuition, heuristics, emotional intelligence, the relation of personality to physical disease, the meaning of dreams, psychobiography, and the ability to think objectively.

In their far-reaching chapter on self-regulatory perspectives, Charles Carver and Michael Scheier bring concepts of cybernetics to the study of personality, with a focus on the self-regulation of action and emotion. Their self-regulation model provides a perspective on questions such as how people create actions from their intentions and desires, how they persist until they achieve their goals, how they decide whether to work for a longer-term goal, and how goal progress relates to emotional experience. A provocative feature of Carver and Scheier's self-regulatory perspective is that valence is not the determinant of the dimensional structure of affects. Rather, the nature of the motivational process determines the dimensional structure, with affects arrayed as related to approach of incentives or to avoidance of threats. The dual process models of self-regulation depicted by Carver and Scheier involve a relatively reflexive and automatic set of processes producing one understanding of reality, and a deliberative and planful set of processes that yields a separate understanding of reality. As in Epstein's CEST, described above, these two understandings of reality can lead to different and even conflicting action tendencies. Carver and Scheier's ideas drawn from dynamic systems and catastrophe theories hold great promise for the future elaboration of self-regulatory models of personality.

Interpersonal theory now provides a context in which psychologists study psychotherapy, psychopathology, and behavioral contributions to health, as well as personality. Moving beyond the individual as the focus of study, interpersonal theory, as elaborated by Aaron Pincus and Emily Ansell in their conceptually rich chapter, stipulates that personality expresses itself in phenomena involving more than one person, that interpersonal situations occur both between individuals as well as in the minds of those individuals, that agency and communion provide a heuristic structure in which to conceptualize interpersonal situations, and that chronic deviations from complementarity in interpersonal situations may indicate psychopathology. Pincus and Ansell articulate the key thematic and dynamic concepts and the central developmental, motivational, and regulatory concepts of contemporary interpersonal theory, and they demonstrate how the interpersonal circumplex model provides a descriptive map of interpersonal constructs, and how interpersonal theory is poised to advance research on personality, psychopathology, and psychotherapy.

Mischel and Shoda's Cognitive Affective Processing System (CAPS) is the centerpiece among current "social-cognitive" personality theories. Lara Kammrath and Abigail Scholer review the functional utility of the CAPS perspective, and its unique ability to provide three critical aspects of personality information—prediction, explanation, and interpersonal influence. They distinguish CAPS from trait models of personality, and demonstrate how in CAPS theory, *if ... then ...* situation-behavior signatures provide a singular opportunity to understand the perceptions, goals, and feelings that motivate an individual's characteristic behaviors. Kammrath and Scholer illustrate how other current approaches to personality, including attachment theory, mindset theory, and regulatory focus theory are consistent with the CAPS framework, and they document the implications of a functionalist approach to CAPS for understanding behavior and the nature of behavior change.

Although trait theories rest on the assumption that people have relatively enduring patterns of thinking, feeling, and behaving that distinguish one person from another, only relatively recently has an evidence base been established to evaluate this assumption. In their chapter on personality trait development in adulthood, Brent Roberts, M. Brent Donnellan, and Patrick Hill review the evidence indicating that personality traits are both consistent over time and yet change systematically in adulthood. They review the evidence pointing to at least moderate-sized test-retest coefficients for personality traits across the life span, and they make a convincing case that on average, individuals become more confident, warm, responsible, and emotionally stable as they grow older. Roberts, Donnellan, and Hill also document the importance of individual differences in this general pattern of change over the life span. They posit intriguing mechanisms that may promote personality consistency, and a different set of mechanisms that may explain how personality changes occur. The implications of personality change processes are striking because they suggest, as Roberts and colleagues demonstrate, that relatively small changes in a trait may produce significant changes in people's lives.

With the recent renewed interest in positive psychology, there is now an increasingly strong evidence base on which to consider the issue of personality strengths. In the final chapter of this section, Laura King and Jason Trent address the topic of personality strengths by grappling with whether it makes sense to think of personality characteristics as strengths. King and Trent define personality strengths as situation-specific assets that promote adjustment, and they demonstrate a number of unanticipated challenges associated with approaching personality characteristics as strengths. In questioning the wisdom of thinking about personality from a strengths perspective, King and Trent traverse a broad and stimulating expanse of personality psychology, including motivation, goal pursuit, self-regulation, ego development, and person-situation fit.

These 10 chapters reflect both the vitality of today's personality psychology and its challenges. What is clear and encouraging for personality psychology is that these chapters are not conceptual and empirical silos, and they do not pit one perspective against another. Rather, the reader will be struck by the cross-cutting themes and attention to related literatures. Unconscious processes, though not Freud's dynamic unconscious, are highlighted in several of these chapters, as is self-regulation, and the idea that people not only respond to situations, but help create the situations to which they respond. Advances in

behavior genetics and neurobiology have become clearly welcomed contributions rather than reductionistic threats. These chapters reveal that personality psychology has reached a level of maturity that allows it to borrow concepts and methods from cybernetics, genetics, neurobiology, and from diverse areas of investigation within the field of personality. They also demonstrate that more than ever, personality psychology is moving beyond the study of variables to the study of people in their life contexts.

The second section of Volume 5 consists of 14 chapters authored by some of the most respected contemporary researchers who present a wide-ranging survey of empirical and theoretical accomplishments of social psychology. Eleven of the chapters in this section cover topics addressed in the *Handbook*'s first edition: social cognition, attitudes, the social self, persuasion, social influence, close relationships, altruism and prosocial behavior, social conflict and harmony, prejudice, justice, and aggression. Three other chapters represent topics that are new to the *Handbook*, but which have become prominent in recent years: cultural social psychology, emotional regulation, and evolutionary social psychology. Altogether, these chapters provide a comprehensive picture of social psychology past and present with glimmers of the future!

In Chapter 11, Galen Bodenhausen and Javier R. Morales contribute a concise overview of social cognition and perception—the psychological processes through which individuals construct a meaningful understanding of their social environment. The authors explain why construal of the social world, rather than the objective circumstances, controls much of a person's behavior and why social cognition probably evolved from early pressures in human history experienced by living in complex social communities. The core mental representations and processes contributing to these construals are described and reasons why they often emerge rapidly, automatically and unconsciously. The theme of automaticity and unconscious, or implicit, processes arises in several other chapters and represents one of the key features of contemporary social psychology. Four topics with implications for social impressions are given special attention: attribution processes, automatic inferences based on social cues (e.g., physical appearance), projection, and stereotyping. The authors also discuss how person perception is manifested and shaped by the types of relationships formed with others and the culture in which one resides, thus emphasizing the "social" in social cognition.

In their chapter on the self, Roy Baumeister, E. J. Masicampo, and Jean Twenge describe the reciprocal forces operating between self and others; in fact, they argue that the self scarcely has meaning except in the context of other people. For example, self-esteem primarily reflects the degree to which one feels accepted by others. Feeling excluded can provoke aggression, self-defeating behaviors (e.g., substance use), and cognitive impairment, and so on, but may also increase the motivation to reconnect with other people. Empirical evidence is reviewed that shows the lengths to which people adopt cognitive, affective and behavioral strategies to protect or enhance their sense of self. High self-esteem, however, can have a "dark-side"; if someone disputes this inflated sense of self, the person may lash out. Several factors contribute to self-esteem, including reflected appraisal (i.e., what the person thinks others think of them), interpersonal expectancies, and self-fulfilling prophecies. Beyond intrapsychic causes, people are motivated to present a public self to obtain receive social approval or other gains. Several strategies of self-presentation that have been experimentally shown to accomplish these goals are described. In the concluding section, the authors emphasize that the sense of the self is significantly affected by both the era and culture in which the person lives. For example, society's current focus on high self-esteem and individualism, as evidenced by survey and experimental results, seems connected to the "Generation Me" milieu.

As Gregory Maio, James Olson, and Irene Cheung observe in their chapter, attitudes are central to social psychological research. Attitudes refer to tendencies to evaluate a particular target with favor or disfavor. Although attitudes share features with constructs like values, attitudes are distinct in their scope, origin, and consequences. Different types of approaches to assess attitudes have been developed over the decades, with the most recent innovations (and controversy) focusing on the distinction between explicit (e.g., verbal self-report scales) and implicit (unconscious) measures (reaction-time based tasks) of attitude. The authors also devote attention to the content, structure, and function of attitudes, interrelations among attitudes, and the relations with values and ideologies, the latter two concepts recently receiving renewed interest from social psychologists. The chapter concludes with a lucid discussion of the relation between attitudes and behavior, a persistent and challenging question about the social psychology implications of application.

Social influence is pervasive although sometimes it is "hidden in plain sight." In Chapter 14, Donelson R. Forsyth describes social influence as a foundational social psychological concept operating via the actual, imagined, or even implied presence of others. Inspired by early research on the psychology of crowds, norms, reference groups, and leadership, three categories of influence are usually distinguished: conformity, compliance, and obedience. Experimental studies confirm that both the need for social approval and the need to reduce uncertainty prompt people to conform to others' standards, but dissenting individuals, under special circumstances, can eventually inspire large opinion changes in the majority. Compliance, like conformity, involves a change in opinions, judgments, or actions, but in response to deliberate influence attempts that are often quite subtle, such as the "foot in the door" tactic or the "that's-not-all" tactic (often employed by salespeople). Obedience, in contrast, involves direct commands from someone in a position of greater social power. Milgram's classic research on destructive obedience illustrates how problematic social influence can be. However, as Forsyth observes, "Social influence . . . is neither morally suspect nor commendable, but instead a highly functional interpersonal process that provides humans with the means to coordinate their actions, to identify solutions to communal problems that require a collective response . . ." (p. 324).

In Chapter 15, Margaret Clark and Nancy Grote selectively survey the social psychology of close relationships. Although relationships between spouses and between parents and children probably first come to mind, in fact, there are many other kinds of relationships that can be described in this way. Benefits in such relationships include help, supporting pursuit of goals, celebrating a partner's accomplishments and not taking actions that might harm the other, and communicating support symbolically. The authors discuss factors that facilitate the need for, initiation of, and development of close relationships. Certain intra- and interpersonal processes seem to characterize established close relationships, but providing noncontingent benefits is one of the primary features. Nonetheless, the degree of responsibility one assumes for the other may vary and the nature of other close relationships also figures into the complex dynamics. One of the most intriguing features about close relationships is observed when the needs of the other take precedence over one's own needs. In light of the complexity of this reciprocal "dance," it should not be surprising that some close relationships experience dissolution, a topic also considered by the authors.

In Chapter 16, Monica Biernat and Kelly Danaher describe theories, findings, and societal implications of research on prejudice—negative attitudes toward a group and its members. Several approaches for understanding the origins of prejudice have been advanced—intergroup, normative, evolutionary, and motivational—but there is overlap among them. It is observed that most views center on an antipathy view of prejudice, but more recent conceptions propose that "out of role" behavior also engenders prejudice. Different explanations suggest distinct approaches to reducing prejudice, which include intergroup contact, common ingroup identity or dual identity, perspective taking and empathy, and explicit debiasing approaches—all of which have had some efficacy in research. The chapter also considers how prejudice is perceived and its consequences, such as the effects on performance (via stereotype threat).

Persuasion has been a preoccupation of social psychologists for several decades and continues to lead to new conceptual and empirical insights with significant societal applications. In Chapter 17, Richard Petty, S. Christian Wheeler, and Zakary Tormala survey this vast literature using the distinction between effortful thinking versus reliance on less cognitively demanding processes, such as heuristics, as a framework. The dual-process perspective, for which the senior author was one of the pioneers, accomplishes several things: it predicts what variables should affect attitudes and in what situations, and it identifies in which domains different specific theories of attitude change, such as cognitive dissonance versus self-perception, most appropriately apply.

Chapter 18, authored by Gal Sheppes and James Gross, introduces a new topic, emotional regulation, to the *Handbook*. The authors explain how emotional regulation emphasizes the ways individuals directly affect what, when, and how they experience and express emotions. The generation of affect is proposed to occur in a series of stages that are subject to different regulatory strategies. The authors review recent data demonstrating that regulation strategies that intervene early on are likely to be more effective than strategies that intervene later on, after emotional response tendencies are activated. Furthermore, the success of any particular emotion regulation attempt is a joint function of the underlying operation of different regulation strategies, emotional intensity, and goals.

Chapter 19, by Linda Skitka and Daniel Wisneski, describes psychological factors implicated in the perception of fairness and justice from the earliest conceptions to recent theories. The authors observe that the social psychology of justice has been guided by five functionalist metaphors: people as lay or intuitive economists, politicians, scientists, prosecutors, and theologians. Justice research inspired by these metaphors is systematically reviewed to understand, What is fair? In the conclusion, the authors propose their functional pluralism framework, which accounts for diverse results because it posits that people reason about fairness as economists, politicians, scientists, prosecutors, or theologians, depending on their frame of reference and goals.

John Dovidio, Samuel Gaertner, Elena Wright Mayville, and Sylvia Perry, authors of Chapter 20, introduce a brief history of the study of intergroup relations, followed by a survey about how cognitive, motivational, interpersonal, and social processes can contribute to the development of intergroup bias and social conflict. The authors then explain how understanding of these processes has guided the development of functional and common group identity interventions, and has had some success in reducing intergroup bias and facilitating social integration between previously hostile groups. Acknowledging the complexities associated with achieving social harmony, Dovidio and colleagues acknowledge no single perspective can suffice, but argue convincingly that taking into account both psychological and structural factors provides a more comprehensive view of intergroup relations with implications for laypeople and policy makers.

In Chapter 21, Nathan DeWall, Craig Anderson, and Brad Bushman survey classic and contemporary aggression research. They begin by providing a definition of aggression distinguishing it from related constructs, such as anger, antisocial behavior and violence. Then five theoretical perspectives are described (along with empirical research) from the earliest, frustration-aggression theory, learning theory, excitation-transfer theory, information processing theories, cognitive neo-association theory, and finally the general aggression model, which integrates the best insights of preceding models. Individual differences in aggressive predisposition, the development of aggression and situational factors increasing aggression also are described, followed by a discussion of promising methods to prevent aggression.

Chapter 22, authored by Mark Snyder and Patrick Dwyer, is concerned with altruism and prosocial behavior. The original research in this area inquired about the factors that discourage bystanders from intervening to help other in emergencies (i.e., one-to-one helping). The authors discuss the (sometimes subtle) psychological factors, revealed by experimental research, that inhibit people from helping, such as diffusion of responsibility. However, since then, researchers also have considered collective forms of prosocial behavior, such as volunteerism and participation in social movements. Several factors instigate prosocial behavior, but one that is controversial is the existence of altruism as a truly selfless motivation that improves another person's welfare. Snyder and Dwyer explain that whether the helper is motivated by self- or other-oriented concerns, or both, prosocial action proves to be beneficial to the recipients and to society.

In Chapter 23, Jon Maner and Andrew Menzel write about evolutionary social psychology, another new topic for the *Handbook of Psychology*. Its inclusion is more than appropriate as the advocates of the evolutionary perspective in the past decade and a half have illuminated almost every domain in social psychology, from close relationships and persuasion to social influence and social cognition. Evolutionary social psychologists posit that social behaviors represent adaptations or mechanisms designed through natural and sexual selection to serve specific functions related to reproductive success. For example, cooperative behavior in animals and humans is more likely to occur among individuals who are genetically related. This is because benefits shared with kin members imply indirect genetic benefits to oneself. Maner and Menzel describe how an evolutionary perspective can elucidate and provide new insights about the nature of coalition formation, social status hierarchies, self-protection from threat, mating relationships, and parental care. In their final section, they discuss the intriguing relationships between evolution and shifts in culture.

Joan Miller and Patrick Boyle, in Chapter 24, review developments in cultural social psychology, a topic currently receiving intense interest from social psychologists and the lay public. Although this has been an area of inquiry for decades, it has had a resurgence, perhaps prompted by increasing globalization. The central question of cultural psychology is how different social practices, attitudes and feelings emerge and operate in different cultures. Rather than conceiving of culture as simply *adding on* to foundational and universal psychological processes (the conventional perspective), culture plays a major role in the *emergence* of all higher order psychological processes. The authors elaborate on the latter viewpoint by describing how cultural meanings and practices affect the form of psychological processes in the areas of self-processes, attribution, cognition, motivation, emotion, morality, attachment, and relationships with empirical examples drawn from cultures all over the globe. The chapter concludes with a discussion of the challenges and future promise of cultural social psychology.

As in the Personality section, these chapters attest to the high level of activity, rigor, diversified methods and increased sophistication in the field of social psychology. Also, the chapters reflect several cross-cutting themes. These include the role of implicit processes and automaticity, recognition of the vital role of culture, and contribution of biology and evolution to social behavior. Finally, it is clear that social psychology as a discipline has provided many insights and practical suggestions to help improve well-being and facilitate the development of a productive and humane society.

Howard Tennen

Jerry Suls

Contributors

Craig A. Anderson, PhD
Department of Psychology
Iowa State University
Ames, Iowa

Emily B. Ansell, PhD
Department of Psychiatry
Yale University School of Medicine
New Haven, Connecticut

Roy F. Baumeister, PhD
Department of Psychology
Florida State University
Tallahassee, Florida

Monica Biernat, PhD
Department of Psychology
University of Kansas
Lawrence, Kansas

Galen V. Bodenhausen, PhD
Department of Psychology
Northwestern University
Evanston, Illinois

Robert F. Bornstein, PhD
Derner Institute of Advanced Psychological Studies
Adelphi University
Garden City, New York

Patrick J. Boyle, PhD
Department of Psychology
New School for Social Research
New York, New York

Brad J. Bushman, PhD
Department of Communication
Ohio State University
Columbus, Ohio

Charles S. Carver, PhD
Department of Psychology
University of Miami
Coral Gables, Florida

Irene Cheung
Department of Psychology
University of Western Ontario
London, Ontario, Canada

Wei-Jean Chung, MA
Derner Institute of Advanced Psychological Studies
Adelphi University
Garden City, New York

Margaret S. Clark, PhD
Department of Psychology
Yale University
New Haven, Connecticut

Kelly Danaher, MA
Department of Psychology
Iowa Wesleyan College
Mt. Pleasant, Iowa

Christy A. Denckla, MA
Derner Institute of Advanced Psychological Studies
Adelphi University
Garden City, New York

C. Nathan DeWall, PhD
Department of Psychology
University of Kentucky
Lexington, Kentucky

M. Brent Donnellan, PhD
Department of Psychology
Michigan State University
East Lansing, Michigan

John F. Dovidio, PhD
Department of Psychology
Yale University
New Haven, Connecticut

Patrick C. Dwyer, PhD
Department of Psychology
University of Minnesota
Minneapolis, Minnesota

Nicholas R. Eaton, MA
Department of Psychology
University of Minnesota and
    Hennepin County Medical Center
Minneapolis, Minnesota

Seymour Epstein, PhD
Department of Psychology
University of Massachusetts
Amherst, Massachusetts

Donelson R. Forsyth, PhD
Department of Psychology
University of Richmond
Richmond, Virginia

Samuel L. Gaertner, PhD
Department of Psychology
University of Delaware
Newark, Delaware

James F. Gaines, PhD
Department of Modern Foreign Languages
University of Mary Washington
Fredericksburg, Virginia

James J. Gross, PhD
Department of Psychology
Stanford University
Stanford, California

Nancy K. Grote, PhD
School of Social Work
University of Washington
Seattle, Washington

Patrick L. Hill, PhD
Department of Psychology
University of Illinois, Urbana-Champaign
Champaign, Illinois

Lara K. Kammrath, PhD
Department of Psychology
Wake Forest University
Winston-Salem, North Carolina

Laura A. King, PhD
Department of Psychological Sciences
University of Missouri, Columbia
Columbia, Missouri

Robert F. Krueger, PhD
Department of Psychology
University of Minnesota
Minneapolis, Minnesota

Robert R. McCrae, PhD
Baltimore, Maryland

Gregory R. Maio, PhD
School of Psychology
Cardiff University
Cardiff, Wales, United Kingdom

Jon K. Maner, PhD
Department of Psychology
Florida State University
Tallahassee, Florida

E. J. Masicampo, PhD
Department of Psychology
Tufts University
Medford, Massachusetts

Elena Wright Mayville, BA
Department of Psychology
Yale University
New Haven, Connecticut

Andrew J. Menzel, PhD
Department of Psychology
Florida State University
Tallahassee, Florida

Joan G. Miller, PhD
Department of Psychology
New School for Social Research
New York, New York

Javior R. Morales, PhD
Department of Psychology
Northwestern University
Evanston, Illinois

James M. Olson, PhD
Department of Psychology
University of Western Ontario
London, Ontario, Canada

Sylvia Perry, PhD
Department of Psychology
Yale University
New Haven, Connecticut

Richard E. Petty, PhD
Department of Psychology
Ohio State University
Columbus, Ohio

Aaron L. Pincus, PhD
Department of Psychology
The Pennsylvania State University
University Park, Pennsylvania

Ted Reichborn-Kjennerud, MD, Dr. Med
Norwegian Institute of Public Health
University of Oslo
Oslo, Norway

Brent W. Roberts, PhD
Department of Psychology
University of Illinois, Urbana-Champaign
Champaign, Illinois

Michael F. Scheier, PhD
Department of Psychology
Carnegie Mellon University
Pittsburgh, Pennsylvania

Abigail A. Scholer, PhD
Department of Psychology
University of Waterloo
Waterloo, Ontario, Canada

Gal Sheppes, PhD
Department of Psychology
Stanford University
Stanford, California

Linda J. Skitka, PhD
Department of Psychology
University of Illinois, Chicago
Chicago, Illinois

Mark Snyder, PhD
Department of Psychology
University of Minnesota
Minneapolis, Minnesota

Susan C. South, PhD
Department of Psychological
    Sciences
Purdue University
West Lafayette, Indiana

Zakary L. Tormala, PhD
Department of Psychology
Stanford University
Stanford, California

Jean M. Twenge, PhD
Department of Psychology
San Diego State University
San Diego, California

Jason Trent, MA
Department of Psychological
    Sciences
University of Missouri, Columbia
Columbia, Missouri

Marie A. Wellington, PhD
Department of Modern Foreign
    Languages
University of Mary Washington
Fredericksburg, Virginia

S. Christian Wheeler, PhD
Department of Psychology
Stanford University
Stanford, California

Daniel C. Wisneski, MA
Department of Psychology
University of Illinois, Chicago
Chicago, Illinois

Marvin Zuckerman, PhD
Department of Psychology
University of Delaware
Newark, Delaware

PART I

Personality

CHAPTER 1

Genetics of Personality

SUSAN C. SOUTH, TED REICHBORN-KJENNERUD, NICHOLAS R. EATON,
AND ROBERT F. KRUEGER

INTRODUCTION

In this current chapter, we review findings from an important approach to understanding the etiology of personality—behavior genetics. Behavior genetics encompasses a series of methods for disentangling the relative influence of genes and environment on the variation in a phenotype (observed variable). Personality, or the characteristic ways that people think, feel, and behave, varies considerably within and between different populations. There are people who are more or less aggressive, more or less modest, more or less sociable, more or less humorous, and so on. It is the variation in personality that defines us and makes us distinct from every other individual on the planet. There are certainly those who have questioned the existence of consistent personality dispositions (Mischel, 1968), or theorized as to why any variation in personality exists (Penke, Denissen, & Miller, 2007). Behavior genetics is vitally important in showing that personality does exist, that it does vary in meaningful ways between people, and that this variation is due, in part, to genetic influences.

Indeed, the field of behavior genetics, particularly the use of genetically informative family data, was a driving force in establishing the importance of both nature and nurture in the development of personality. Quantitative behavior genetic methods, which parse out the relative influence of genes, family environment, and unique environmental experiences, have consistently demonstrated the importance of genetic influences. Biometric modeling with twin data reveal one of the most reliable findings in behavior genetics and in the personality literature—heritability, or proportion of variance due to genetic influences, for most major personality traits is approximately 40 to 50%. A robustly replicated finding, this has caused consternation in the molecular genetic field of personality research, where scientists have been largely stymied in their attempts to find measured genes that explain a significant portion of the variance in personality traits. Why, they have asked, is it so difficult to replicate measured gene-measured personality findings, if we know that genetic influences explain 50% of personality variation? In the current chapter, we review what has been found, and how improving technology may partly solve the problem. We also note that part of the difficulty for molecular genetics is the complex interactions that might be occurring, not only between different genes but also between genes and the environment. Gene-environment interaction, or the impact the environment has on the expression of genetic influences, may be important in our search for the etiology of personality. It might be a return to quantitative genetic methods, which can provide estimates of gene-environment interplay, which best informs our understanding of personality development. Thus, the field of behavior genetics comes full circle, from an early reliance on quantitative methods that set the stage for molecular work, which again must now rely on statistical modeling of family data to move forward. In the current chapter, our goal is to present a general conceptual overview of behavior genetics methodology, including both biometric models and molecular genetics techniques, as well as a snapshot of seminal work from the past, current issues and controversies, and recommendations for future research.

BEHAVIOR GENETICS OF PERSONALITY

We begin by briefly reviewing the major biometric modeling approaches and the assumptions underlying them, before turning to a broad overview of findings from univariate and multivariate twin studies and adoption studies.

Biometric Modeling Approaches

Much of the classic work in the behavior genetics of personality has been conducted with biometric modeling of twin data. These statistical models are *biological* in that they utilize known genetic relationships among individuals, and *metric* because they attempt to provide estimates of genetic and environmental influences based on careful observed measurement of a phenotype. Biometric modeling of personality data is based on certain assumptions about the etiology of personality. As with other types of individual difference phenotypes (e.g., psychopathology), the etiology of personality is probably best explained by a multifactoral polygenic model of inheritance. According to this model, there is a continuum of liability throughout the general population resulting from genetic and environmental influences that act in an additive manner (Falconer, 1965; Gottesman & Shields, 1967). Given that behavior genetic models generally assume there are multiple gene systems, or quantitative trait loci (QTLs), underlying complex behavioral phenotypes like personality, quantitative genetic research (i.e., biometric modeling) is therefore appropriate for examining the etiology of personality. The method most commonly used for examining genetic and environmental influences on the variation in personality is the twin study, therefore much of our review will spotlight this method and the findings from twin studies; adoption methods have also been utilized and we discuss findings from this work later in the chapter.

Twin pairs are a fascinating form of natural experiment, allowing researchers to disentangle the relative influence of genetics and environment on a phenotype, like personality. Identical (monozygotic, MZ) twins are the result of one fertilized egg splitting in two while in utero. Fraternal (dizygotic, DZ) twins are the result of two separate eggs being fertilized at the same time, and are no more alike (genetically) than two nontwin siblings. MZ twins thus share 100% of their genes, while DZ twins share an average of 50% of their segregating genes. When using a sample of MZ and DZ twin pairs in which both members of the pair are raised in the same home, the degree of genetic *and* shared family environment is known. Biometric modeling can then use the concordance (agreement) between twins on a phenotype of interest to decompose the variance in that phenotype into genetic and environmental components. As a first step, one can estimate correlations between twin pairs and compare differences in the magnitude of correlations between MZ and DZ twins to obtain a general indication of the size of genetic and environmental influences. For instance, when the MZ correlation is greater than the DZ correlation, this indicates the presence of genetic influences on the trait. Formal biometric modeling of twin data is done using structural modeling software (e.g., Mx; Neale, Boker, Xie, & Maes, 2003), by comparing the similarity (i.e., the covariance) within MZ and DZ twin pairs on the phenotype, resulting in estimates for genetic and environmental influences. In this section, we focus on univariate twin studies, which decompose the variance of one phenotype (i.e., one personality trait); however, structural modeling is readily extended to the multivariate case (e.g., the structure of multiple personality traits considered together, discussed below).

A univariate ("one variable") biometric model with twin pairs is used to separate the variation in a phenotype into three sources that collectively account for the total variance in the population (Plomin, DeFries, McClearn, & McGuffin, 2008). This is an important point, and often lost when discussing biometric models; these models explain variation in the population from which the sample is drawn, not the relative influence of genes and environment on any one person's outcome. The first source of influence on variation is heritability (abbreviated h^2), which reflects how much of the variation in a personality phenotype is due to genetic differences between people in a population. The heritability estimate is actually a ratio, or a proportion of genetic variation over total variation (the sum of genetic and environmental variation). Importantly, the heritability statistic and the commensurate estimates for environmental influences are population parameters; when we conclude that the heritability of a personality trait is 50%, what we are actually saying is that genetic differences *among people in the sample drawn from that population* account for 50% of the variance in that trait; again, we are not saying that genes account for 50% of any one individual's personality. In other words, among any population of individuals, some will be more extroverted and some will be more introverted and most will cluster around the mean, and 50% of the reason for this variation is that genetic influences also vary among people. Most biometric models of personality assume that genetic influences are additive, meaning that personality variation is due to the influence of many genes of small effect size located at different places (loci) on the genome. There is evidence for nonadditive genetic effects on normal personality traits (e.g., Keller, Coventry, Heath, & Martin, 2005) as well.

Beyond genetic influences, a second source of variation in a phenotype is the effect of the shared or common environment, abbreviated c^2. This component of variance captures the extent to which twins are similar by virtue of growing up in the same household. Examples of the shared environment include neighborhood influences, socioeconomic status, having similar friends or peer groups, customs, habits, and the extent to which siblings have similar interactions with their parents. A final source of phenotypic variance is the unique or nonshared environment, abbreviated e^2. This component of variance indexes the extent to which twins are different from each other despite having grown up in the same household and sharing genes. Examples of nonshared environmental experience include traumatic events and stressors, having different friends and life experiences from one's sibling, events in utero, and the extent to which each sibling has a unique experience with their parents. It is important to note that measurement errors are included in the estimate of nonshared environmental influences, so any imprecision or bias in measurement among individuals will result in inflated estimates of e^2. The distinction between the two environmental sources of variance can often be subtle. As noted above, neighborhoods are often thought of as shared environmental influences, working to make siblings within the family more similar to each other; however, one sibling's experience or perception of the environment may be quite unique to him or her and thus work to make siblings growing up within the same family less similar to each other (and this would be accounted for under the nonshared environmental component of variance).

Findings From Univariate Twin Studies of Personality

For decades, researchers, the media, and the lay public debated the relative influence of nature versus nurture on the development of individual differences in human behavior. Thanks to decades of work from the field of behavior genetics, we can now definitely say that *both* nature and nurture are at work when we consider the etiology of almost any phenotype that differs between people and would be of interest to psychologists. Indeed, virtually every phenotype that can be said to differ in meaningful ways between individuals in the population has a detectable genetic component, a finding so well-replicated that it has been called the "First Law" of behavior genetics (Turkheimer, 2000). This is certainly true for almost every

major personality trait or domain, as research across different populations, cultures, and personality measures has found heritability estimates of approximately 50%, with the rest of the variance primarily attributed to nonshared environmental influences. Given the prominence of trait models of personality in general and the Five-Factor Model/Big Five Model in particular (McCrae, Gaines, & Wellington, this volume), it is not surprising that behavior genetic modeling has focused on these personality domains (extraversion, openness, agreeableness, conscientiousness, and neuroticism). The heritability of all five domains range from 40 to 50%, with a majority of the rest of the variance accounted for by nonshared environmental influences (Bouchard & Loehlin, 2001). It is compelling that parameter estimates of genetic and environmental influences are so consistent across these major personality domains, which obviously differ widely in the aspects of human behavior that they capture.

There are several aspects of these key findings that bear further discussion. First, all biometric models with twin data are built on the equal environments assumption (EEA). This assumption derives from the following logic: biometric modeling compares the similarities between MZ twin pairs to the similarities between DZ twin pairs to arrive at estimates of genetic and environmental components of variance. We infer that greater similarities between MZ twin pairs is due to greater genetic similarity, since in both MZ and DZ pairs, twins are raised in the same environment (if they are not reared apart). But what if MZ twin pairs are more similar because their parents impose more similar treatment on them, compared with parents of DZ twin pairs, in ways that do not reflect the contributions of the MZ twins' genes to parental treatment? If this were true, it could result in biased estimates of genetic effects. However, there is now substantial evidence supporting the EEA (Goodman & Stevenson, 1991; Loehlin & Nichols, 1976; Scarr & Carter-Saltzman, 1979); even when the environment does seem biased to making MZ twins more similar (i.e., they are dressed the same by their parents), this does not appear to have a major influence on phenotypic similarity for individual difference phenotypes like personality.

Second, there is a great deal of consistency in the heritability estimates for a wide range of personality traits. As noted above, the domains of the Five-Factor Model (FFM) of personality, which encompass very different and nonoverlapping aspects of personality, show robustly similar levels of genetic influences (Jang, Livesley, Angleitner, Riemann, & Vernon, 2002; Jang, Livesley, & Vernon, 1996; Jang, McCrae, Angleitner, Riemann, & Livesley,

1998; Yamagata et al., 2006). Further, significant estimates of genetic influence have been found in both adults (Livesley & Jang, 2008) and children (Coolidge, Thede, & Jang, 2001) for dimensional measures of pathological personality and categorical personality disorder diagnoses, It is important to note that most heritability estimates of personality traits are "additive," that is the contributions of many genes of small effect "add up" in their influence on phenotypic variation. Certainly it is possible that more complex nonadditive genetic effects (such as the interaction of measured genes with each other) are at work, and may in part explain the difficulty with finding measured genes for personality.

Third, estimates of shared environment influences are often negligible, which would suggest that one's family has little to no impact on personality above and beyond shared genetics. Many have concluded from this finding that the family a person grows up in has no influence on personality, or even that it serves to make siblings from the same family less similar, not more. There are some exceptions to this finding, including evidence of significant shared environment on the personality trait of altruism (Krueger, Hicks, & McGue, 2001) or when personality traits are rated by previously unacquainted observers (as opposed to self-report or report by knowledgeable informants; Borkenau, Riemann, Angleitner, & Spinath, 2001). Further, it is possible that elements of the environment that might look shared from the outside actually have an interactive influence on personality, such that family-level factors (e.g., the kinds of relationships people have with their parents) either enhance or suppress genetic effects on personality. With standard biometric models, these interactive effects would be captured in heritability or nonshared environmental estimates; newer biometric moderation models have started to capture greater levels of shared environment at extreme ends of certain environments (a topic we return to later, below).

Finally, it is important to remember that most of the work thus far on the behavior genetics of personality has utilized self-report methods of personality in adult twin samples. The reliance on self-report, in particular, has methodological implications for estimates of heritability. Reliance on a single observer enhances measurement error; when self-reports are supplemented by peer or observer reports, heritability estimates increase (e.g., Wolf, Angleitner, Spinath, Riemann, & Strelau, 2004). This work is now being extended to child and adolescent samples, where both self- and observer report of personality is collected. Isen, Baker, Raine, and Bezdjian (2009) reported substantial heritability estimates for only two (self-directedness and harm avoidance) of the scales from the Junior Character and Temperament Inventory, using a sample of 9- to 10-year-old twins. What was also striking about their findings was the presence of substantial shared environmental effects for two other scales—novelty seeking and cooperativeness. In a different study that utilized a sample of toddlers, the authors found that variation in the temperament dimension of inhibitory control (IC) was 38% genetic and 62% nonshared environment when observer ratings were used, but 58% genetic, 26% shared environment, and 16% nonshared environment when parent ratings were used in the analyses (Gagne & Saudino, 2010). It remains to be seen whether these effects of rater and developmental period on estimates of genetic and environmental influences will replicate in future studies.

Multivariate and Longitudinal Twin Studies

Establishing the relative influence of genetics, shared environment, and nonshared environment on different kinds of personality traits was an important contribution of behavior genetics. However, the utility of this method does not stop once we establish heritability for a personality trait. The univariate biometric model can be readily extended to encompass multiple phenotypes, or personality traits, a technique known as *multivariate* biometric modeling. Multivariate biometric modeling has many uses, which we will discuss in more depth below. First, it can be used to examine the etiological structure of the architecture of multivariate personality space. That is, just as univariate biometric modeling decomposes the variance of a trait into genetic and environmental components, multivariate biometric modeling can decompose the covariance between two or more personality traits. This type of modeling results in estimates of the genetic and environmental contributions to each individual phenotype and the amount of overlap between these sources of variance. Typically, this overlap is represented by a correlation; for instance, a genetic correlation (varying from -1.0 to $+1.0$) indexes the degree to which the genetic influences on Personality Trait A overlap with the genetic influences on Personality Trait B. Similar correlations are computed for shared and nonshared environmental influences. Of note, these correlations can be subjected to factor analysis in the same way that phenotypic correlations between personality variables can, and resulting analysis provide insights into the structure of etiological influences.

The second extension of multivariate modeling would be to include an environmental variable in this multivariate modeling, so that it is possible to determine the etiological overlap between personality and putatively causal environmental variables. This type of modeling has important implications for finding the nonshared environmental factors that make up approximately 50% of personality variance. Third, the etiology of personality over time can be examined by including measures of the same personality traits collected over multiple points in time. If, for instance, the genetic correlations among personality traits assessed at different ages were high, this would suggest that stability of personality is due to genetic influences. Finally, there are relatively new extensions of multivariate modeling that allow for examination of not just etiological overlap between personality traits, but interactive effects between personality and the environment.

There are several multivariate models that researchers can utilize for this work, discussed below in order of increasing complexity (Neale & Cardon, 1992). The simplest model is a Cholesky decomposition, which decomposes the genetic and environmental variance shared in common between two or more phenotypes. Figure 1.1 presents an illustration of a Cholesky model for three phenotypes (e.g., three different personality traits). For simplicity, only the genetic (A) and nonshared environmental (E) components of variance are presented in Figure 1.1, but shared environmental (C) influences are easily incorporated as well. This model is most useful for estimating the amount of shared influences between multiple phenotypes (i.e., the genetic and environmental correlations), but tells us relatively little about why those influences might be shared, in the sense of delineating latent constructs

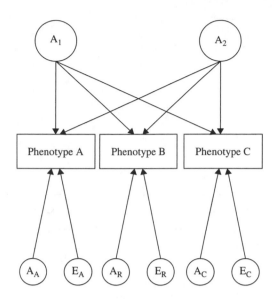

Figure 1.2 An independent pathways model

that connect multiple manifest phenotypes. For that, we turn to an additional multivariate model, the *independent pathways* (IP) model (see Figure 1.2), which differs from a Cholesky by positing direct paths from a common latent genetic factor to all of the observed variables, as well as allowing for specific genetic influences that are unique to each variable. There are commensurate general and specific factors for shared and nonshared environmental influences as well. Both the IP model and the Cholesky model are able to estimate shared etiological influences among multiple personality traits. The IP model, however, imposes a greater amount of structure on the etiological influences on personality, allowing each observed personality variable to have both general and specific genetic and environmental influences. The final multivariate model, the *common pathways* (CP) model (see Figure 1.3), goes even farther than the IP model in positing a known structure for the etiology of multiple personality domains. The CP model suggests that there is a single latent construct that accounts for the covariance among multiple personality traits, and the variance in this latent factor can be decomposed into additive genetic, shared environmental, and nonshared environmental influences. The strictest of the three models, the CP model is the closest biometric extension of a phenotypic factor analysis, and should provide the best fit to the data if the personality domain is truly an etiologically coherent underlying dimension.

Covariation Among Personality Traits

One of the most important uses of multivariate biometric models is to investigate the etiological structure of personality. On a phenotypic level, factor analysis has been

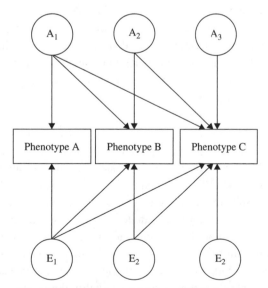

Figure 1.1 Path model for a bivariate (Cholesky) decomposition of variance into additive genetic (A) and nonshared environmental (E) sources

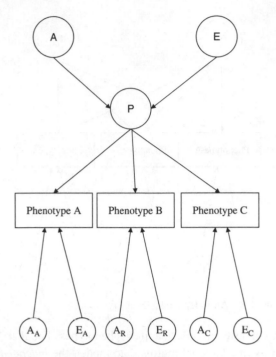

Figure 1.3   A common pathways model

widely used to examine how many and which personality traits are needed to capture all of the multivariate space. Multivariate biometric modeling can be used to determine if the genetic structure of personality parallels the phenotypic structure. The FFM, for example, is often posited to represent basic biological tendencies that account for all of the variation in normal and pathological personality. If multivariate biometric modeling found that the genetic and environmental structure of the FFM facets and domains was best represented by a biometric common pathways model, this would be strong support for Costa and McCrae's conceptualization of the FFM domains as biologically based unitary latent constructs (McCrae & Costa, 2008). Although multivariate biometric modeling has been applied to other models of personality structure, the FFM has certainly dominated this work so we concentrate our review on biometric modeling applied to the FFM.

The results from this work suggest that the etiological influences on the structure of personality are quite complex. Jang and colleagues (2002) used a combined German and Canadian adult twin sample to compare the IP and CP models when applied to lower-order personality traits subsumed under the FFM domains. They found that the lower-order facets of the NEO-PI-R (Costa & McCrae, 1992) did not load cleanly onto five genetic factors (i.e., one for each of the FFM domains, as would be expected for the CP model). Instead, the IP model provided the best fit to the data, and each of the FFM higher-order domains required

two genetic and two nonshared environmental factors. This led the authors to conclude that the FFM domains "do not exist as veridical psychological entities per se, but rather they exist as useful heuristic devices" (Jang et al., 2002, p. 99). Johnson and Krueger (2004) later examined the multivariate structure of the Big Five domains in a nationwide sample of American twins using adjectives taken from existing trait inventories. They found that the CP model best fit the data for extraversion and neuroticism, suggesting that of the FFM domains these two come closest to being unitary latent personality constructs. In contrast, the IP model best fit conscientiousness and openness, while the Cholesky model provided the best fit to the data for Agreeableness, perhaps reflecting a looser organizational etiological structure for these domains. However, in contrast to these earlier findings, a later study supported the robustness of the etiological structure of the FFM. The authors found that factor analysis of genetic and environmental correlations among the NEO-PI-R facets resulted in five, genetically robust domains that paralleled the FFM higher-order traits (Yamagata et al., 2006).

One possible interpretation of these somewhat contradictory findings is that the FFM does not completely capture the true nature of multivariate personality space. However, the FFM does exhibit greater etiological coherence than other personality models. For instance, Ando and colleagues (2004) found that there was little correspondence between the phenotypic and genetic structure of the Temperament and Character Inventory (TCI; Cloninger, Svrakic, & Przybeck, 1993), challenging the distinction between temperament and character as posited by Cloninger's model of personality. A more optimistic interpretation of these findings is that personality is truly hierarchically structured, and that the facet-level traits of the FFM are innate tendencies that have specific genetic and environmental influences of their own (Jang et al., 1998). A consequence of this conclusion is that current personality inventories may not adequately capture etiologically coherent personality constructs. In fact, when a multiple-rater model is used to explicitly account for rater-bias in measurement, greater genetic variance is found in NEO-PI-R domains and facets (Kandler, Riemann, Spinath, & Angleitner, 2010b). In future research, it may be necessary to use an iterative process whereby the results of biometric modeling are used to inform personality inventories and assessment instruments that can then capture and identify more etiologically "pure" personality traits. Only by better refining personality domains and the measures used to assess them will it be possible to identify "genetically crisp categories" (Farone, Tsuang, & Tsuang,

1999) of personality variation that may finally solve the problem that molecular geneticists face of identifying replicable measured gene-personality trait associations (Ebstein, 2006).

Etiological Links Between Personality and Psychopathology and Other Outcomes of Public Health Relevance

A second important use of multivariate biometric modeling is to examine the shared etiology between personality and important health-relevant outcomes. One of the most important of these outcomes is psychopathology. There is strong phenotypic evidence of associations between various personality traits and many different forms of psychopathology. For instance, the personality trait of neuroticism is a correlate of many different disorders, particularly mood and anxiety disorders (e.g., Griffith et al., 2010). Biometric models are an important method for determining whether these links are the result of shared genetic or environmental influences between personality and psychopathology.

There are several different models that attempt to explain the association between personality and psychopathology (for a recent review, see South, 2011, p. 509). Briefly, these models differ in the causal ordering of the associations between personality and psychopathology syndromes. The vulnerability model, for instance, presumes that certain personality traits convey vulnerability toward certain types of mental illness. However, the model that has been arguably most well supported in both the child and adult literatures posits that different psychopathology syndromes and personality traits are related by virtue of being components of a higher-order spectrum. Research is now converging on a model that posits that mood and anxiety disorders are indicators of a higher-order spectrum of Internalizing pathology, while antisocial, conduct-disordered behavior and substance use syndromes are indicators of a higher-order Externalizing spectrum (see Krueger & Markon, 2006). With regard to personality, neuroticism can be included in the internalizing factor, while disinhibtion fits well within the externalizing spectrum.

Importantly, multivariate biometric models can determine whether the phenotypic structure found for the Internalizing-Externalizing model of psychopathology extends to the etiological structure. Krueger and colleagues (2002) used a twin sample of more than 600 adolescents and concluded that a CP model best explained the covariation among adolescent antisocial behavior, conduct disorder, alcohol dependence, drug dependence, and the personality trait of constraint (reverse scored). Singh and Waldman (2010) examined the structure of externalizing phenotypes (i.e., negative emotionality and childhood externalizing disorders) in a sample of 4- to 17-year-old twins. In contrast to Krueger et al., they found that the IP model provided a better fit to the data than the CP model. Differences in findings between these two studies have important implications for the changing etiology of externalizing psychopathology over time. Finally, an analysis of the internalizing spectrum including the trait of neuroticism found two overlapping genetic factors: one factor accounted for the covariation among major depression, generalized anxiety, and panic disorder, independent of neuroticism, while the second factor explained the variation between neuroticism, major depression, generalized anxiety, panic disorder, and the phobias (Hettema, Neale, Myers, Prescott, & Kendler, 2006).

In addition to further elucidating the relationship between personality and psychopathology, multivariate biometric models can also inform the etiology of the associations between personality and its well-known correlates. The basic Cholesky decomposition model can be used with one or more personality traits and an environmental variable that is phenotypically correlated with those specific personality variables. It is then possible to examine *why* a personality trait is associated with a certain outcome variable—is the correlation mediated genetically or environmentally? That is, we can ask whether the overlap between environment and personality is due to genetic influences or environmental influences shared between the two. This type of modeling is possible because evidence now shows that what we think of as putatively "environmental" variables often have a heritable component (Kendler & Baker, 2007; Rowe, 1981, 1983). That is, an adolescent's report of the quality of their relationship with one or both parents is partly heritable (Krueger, South, Johnson, & Iacono, 2008), possibly because genetically influenced personality traits influence the way in which people perceive, or experience, the environment. This is a question that can be directly tested using biometric models, in which a sizeable genetic correlation would suggest that personality and environment are related because of genetic variance shared between personality and the environmental measure. Indeed, there are now many examples of findings in this vein in the literature. For example, Spotts and colleagues (2005) showed that 32% of the total variance in wives' marital satisfaction was shared in common with a personality composite of aggression and optimism. Other work has found links between personality and measures of the current family environment

(Chipuer, Plomin, Pedersen, McClearn, & Nesselroade, 1993) and childhood family environment recalled by adults (Kandler, Riemann, & Kampfe, 2009; Krueger, Markon, & Bouchard, 2003), life events (Saudino, Pedersen, Lichtenstein, McClearn, & Plomin, 1997), parenting behaviors (Spinath & O'Connor, 2003), job satisfaction (Ilies & Judge, 2003), propensity to marry (Johnson, McGue, Krueger, & Bouchard, 2004), and leadership style (Johnson, Vernon, Harris, & Jang, 2004).

Longitudinal Modeling of Personality Over Time

Another important extension of multivariate biometric modeling is the ability to examine genetic and environmental influences on personality over time. Longitudinal biometric modeling can help in understanding whether the stability (or instability) of personality is due to genetic influences that stay constant over important developmental stages. A longitudinal behavior genetic study using a child sample studied from age 3 to 12 examined how genetic and environmental influences contributed to the stability and change in withdrawn behavior (Hoekstra, Bartels, Hudziak, Van Beijsterveldt, & Boomsma, 2008). The authors reported substantial heritability at all ages, particularly at age 3 and age 7; further, genetic correlations between personality traits measured at different ages indicated that similar genetic influences were operating across time. As is usually the case, only modest shared environmental influences were found at every age, but when present they better explained the stability of withdrawn behavior over time in girls (14%) as compared to boys (4%). The estimates of nonshared environment were large and increased from earlier to later ages, but the decreasing size of the nonshared environmental correlations indicated that new unique environmental effects were "coming on-line" at the different ages. Using an older adolescent and adult sample (age 16 and above at baseline), a recent study compared several different models of genetic and environmental influences on developing personality traits (Kandler et al., 2010a). Similar to prior studies (McGue, Bacon, & Lykken, 1993), they found that genetic influences primarily contributed to the stability of personality over time. Further, long-term changes in personality over young and middle adulthood were attributable to environmental factors. Finally, one longitudinal biometric study decomposed the variance in latent growth curves modeled from data available on twins from average age 17 to 29 (Hopwood et al., 2011). The authors found substantial genetic and nonshared environmental influences on the overall level (i.e., intercept factor) of higher-order personality constructs of negative emotionality and constraint;

significant genetic influences were also found for change (i.e., slope growth factor) in constraint but not negative emotionality. This type of work is an exciting example of the possibilities for combining longitudinal and biometric models to explain the etiology of developmental phenomenon.

Biometric Moderation Models of Gene-Environment Interplay

As noted above, there is now abundant evidence of shared genetic overlap between personality and various measures of the environment. This invaluable finding was beneficial in demonstrating that people "make" their own environments; as such, the nature of parent-child, sibling, and marital relationships, for instance, can be explained, at least in part, by the genetically influenced traits of the individuals who comprise those relationships. This phenomenon is known as *gene-environment correlation* (rGE), or the degree to which a person's genotype influences a person's exposure to and experience of certain environments. The direct test of rGE is the magnitude of the genetic correlation between a personality trait and an environmental variable that is estimated in a multivariate biometric model. The presence of a significant and at least moderate genetic correlation from a biometric model would be evidence for rGE.

However, this is only one form of gene-environment interplay between personality and the environment. A different form of gene-environment interplay that has long been posited and studiedis known as *gene X* environment interaction (GxE), or the idea that different environments moderate (that is, enhance or suppress) the genetic and environmental influences on personality (Rutter, Moffitt, & Caspi, 2006). Influential adoption studies of conduct disorder were the first to suggest that pathogenic rearing environments may have a particularly detrimental effect on individuals possessing a genetic vulnerability (e.g., Cadoret, Yates, Troughton, Woodworth, & Stewart, 1995). That is, a person might inherit genetic propensity toward certain personality traits, but the expression of those genetic influences would depend on the context or experience of certain environmental influences. Several well-known examples have now appeared in the literature reporting instances of measured gene X measured environment interactions, including Caspi and colleagues (2002) finding that a variant of the MAO-A gene is linked to antisocial behavior in boys only if they experienced maltreatment as children. Since the publication of a new, elegant biometric model for examining GxE in the presence of rGE (Purcell, 2002), there has been an explosion of interest in research examining latent gene X environment interaction, or what also called heritability X environment interaction to differentiate it from measured GxE. These new biometric models are also called biometric moderation models, because they specifically allow for moderation of the ACE variance estimates. That is, they test for GxE by allowing heritability (and estimates for shared and nonshared environment) within a population to differ depending on a person's standing on an environmental variable of interest. If we think about a typical univariate biometric model, the resulting heritability statistic that we estimate is constant and specific to the population from which we sampled. In the same way that a mean value averages over differences within the population, a heritability estimate glosses over possible variations that might exist in subsamples of the population. The simplest example of this is gender—when gender is not accounted for, then heritability estimates are the same for men and women; both univariate and multivariate biometric models have been developed to explicitly test for quantitative and qualitative differences in heritability estimates by sex. Biometric moderation models are a logical and practical extension of this design, as they direct testing whether the presence of genetic and environmental influences on a personality trait depend on a person's level of experience of an environmental correlate.

The use of these moderation models for the study of psychopathology is growing. For instance, research has shown that genetic influences on internalizing psychopathology are increased for people with extremely poor marital relationships (South & Krueger, 2008) or decreased for people living in extremely high SES levels (South & Krueger, 2011). The use of moderation models for personality is still relatively new but increasing. For example, in a recent study using a sample of adolescent twins, the authors found that the genetic and environmental influences on higher-order domains of personality (i.e., positive and negative emotionality) varied depending on parent-adolescent relationship quality (Krueger et al., 2008). These results suggest that the etiological influences on personality differ as a function of the context of the family. In similar work, researchers found that genetic and environmental influences on emotional instability (akin to neuroticism) were impacted by perceived level of family conflict and maternal indulgence (Jang, Dick, Wolf, Livesley, & Paris, 2005). Not only did heritability differ depending on level of family variables, but moderation was also found for shared environmental effects, offering the possibility that the lack of c^2 found in many studies may partly result from the effect of GxE. That is not

to say that moderation models are a panacea that will always explain the variation in personality. Kendler and colleagues (2003a), for example, found that the genetic and environmental effects on neuroticism were not moderated by aspects of the family environment. Again, this work is relatively new, and more will need to be done and replicated before we can conclude that gene-environment interactions are vital part of understanding the developmental etiology of personality. However, it does offer the possibility of better modeling the richness and complexity of personality; it also may explain why the robust 50% heritability of personality has failed to generate replicable and reliable associations between specific alleles and personality traits.

Adoption Studies of Personality

As noted earlier, a large portion of behavior genetic research on personality has utilized biometric modeling with twin samples. Adoption studies, however, are also an excellent way of taking advantage of genetically informative samples to understand the etiology of personality. Like the twin design, families with an adopted child (or children) are a natural experiment by which it is possible to tease apart genetic and environmental influences on variation in personality. As an example, consider a family that consists of one or more biological children of the parents as well as one or more adopted, nonbiologically related children (i.e., not a kinship adoption). The parents and nonbiological adopted siblings share 100% of the rearing environment, but 0% of their genes, while the parents and biological siblings share 100% of environment and approximately 50% of their genes. As with the twin design, these known degrees of genetic and environmental relatedness can be used to calculate estimates of genetic and environmental influences on personality.

The findings from adoption studies are commensurate with the results of twin studies in finding little influence of the shared environment and substantial nonshared environmental effects; where they differ, however, is that adoption studies generally find smaller heritability estimates than twin studies (Loehlin, Willerman, & Horn, 1987; Plomin, Corley, Caspi, Fulker, & DeFries, 1998). Generally two explanations have been proposed to explain the disconnect in findings between adoption and twin studies. First, it is possible that too much faith is placed in the equal environments assumption (EEA), and that in fact identical twins reared together are more similar to each other because environmental influences encourage it. However, the powerful twins reared apart design has found heritability estimates generally comparable in magnitude to those found with samples of twins reared together (Bouchard, 1994; Pedersen, Plomin, McClearn, & Friberg, 1988), further refuting possible violation of the EEA.

A more likely possibility to explain the difference between findings from these two different methods is the relative influence of nonadditive genetic effects on personality. Most biometric modeling of twin data operates under the assumption that genetic effects are additive, and among those who test for dominant (nonadditive) genetic effects there are few significant findings. Twin-only designs may in fact be limited in their ability to identify nonadditive genetic effects (i.e., effects due to dominant genetic effects or interactions among specific genes). Keller and colleagues (2005), for instance, found evidence of nonadditive genetic effects using a twin-plus-sibling design. The Nonshared Environment in Adolescent Development (NEAD) study went even further, combining information from MZ and DZ twins, full siblings, half siblings, and genetically unrelated children in the same family resulting from remarriage. When examining broad domains of adjustment, the authors found high heritability estimates, significant shared environmental estimates, and little effect of nonshared environment (Reiss, Neiderhiser, Hetherington, & Plomin, 2000). A later follow-up study from the same sample reported slightly lower heritabilities than were found in the original study, but again reported significant nonadditive genetic effects (Loehlin, Neiderhiser, & Reiss, 2003). In fact, extensions of twin-only or adopted-only family designs may reveal more than just nonadditive influences. A recent adoption study took advantage of a large sample of families consisting of parents and two adolescent siblings, either all biologically related or, in the adoptive families, two adopted siblings or one adopted sibling and one biological sibling (Buchanan, McGue, Keyes, & Iacono, 2009). The authors found that variation in negative emotionality was largely due to nonshared environment and genetic effects; however, when examining the variance in disinhibition, the authors found evidence of significant shared environmental effects (20%). Thus, large samples that include siblings of varying genetic relatedness may be invaluable in finding systematic family influences on personality.

Biometric Modeling of Pathological Personality

Next, we review findings from biometric modeling of pathological personality, including both dimensional measures of pathological traits from different assessment instruments and *DSM*-defined personality disorders.

Univariate Studies

So far, our review has focused primarily on "normative" personality traits; in this section we review behavior genetic findings with regard to more maladaptive personality. Pathological personality traits are incorporated into the formal diagnostic nomenclature through personality disorder (PD) diagnoses on Axis II of the *Diagnostic and Statistical Manual of Mental Disorders* (*DSM-IV-TR*; American Psychiatric Association, 2000). The *DSM* system specifies 10 PDs grouped into three clusters, A, B, and C, called the odd/eccentric, dramatic/emotional and the anxious/fearful, respectively. Behavior genetic studies have been conducted with the *DSM* PDs using both categorical and dimensional approaches. Heritability estimates vary considerably depending on methodological differences, including population sampled (e.g., clinical versus general population), method of assessment (e.g., questionnaire versus structured interview), and how broadly the disorder is defined. A strong genetic influence on all *DSM-IV* PDs was found in the only twin study of children that has been published (Coolidge et al., 2001). Heritability estimates ranged from 50% (paranoid) to 81% (schizotypal, dependent), and there were no substantial shared environmental effects found for any of the disorders. In a twin study of categorical PD diagnoses based on structured interview in clinical samples of adults, most of whom had severe mental disorders, heritability estimates ranged from 28% (paranoid, avoidant) to 77% (narcissistic and obsessive-compulsive; Torgersen et al., 2000). Again, the best-fitting models did not include shared environmental effects, a finding consistent with behavior genetic work with normal personality traits.

Antisocial PD was not analyzed in any of these studies. However, this disorder has been examined in a number of studies using different phenotypes, and two meta-analytic studies have been published (Ferguson, 2010; Rhee & Waldman, 2002). In both analyses, genetic influences were found to play a major role (heritability 41% and 56%, respectively). Interestingly, both reviews found that shared environmental influences contributed significantly, 16% and 11% respectively. Nonadditive effects explained 9% of the variance in the Rhee and Waldman study.

The heritabilities of dimensional representations of *DSM-IV* PD traits, based on structured interviews, have also been estimated in a population-based study of young adult Norwegian twins. These estimates may be a closer parallel to the behavior genetic findings from models using dimensional ratings of normal personality. Genetic influences were found to be modest to moderate, ranging from 21% (paranoid) to 28% (schizoid) in Cluster A

(Kendler et al., 2006a), from 38% (antisocial) to 24% (narcissistic) in Cluster B (Torgersen et al., 2008), and from 27% (obsessive-compulsive) to 35% (avoidant) in Cluster C (Reichborn-Kjennerud et al., 2007b). No shared environmental effects were identified, and all genetic effects were additive. Thus, heritability of dimensional PD scores tend to be lower, on average, than heritability estimates for broad domains of normal personality.

The studies reviewed above primarily used data from diagnostic clinical interviews. Other studies have also used self-report data. For example, one study using self-report questionnaire data found that schizotypal personality traits had a heritability of approximately 50%, and the role played by shared environmental factors was negligible (Linney et al., 2003). Distel and colleagues studied the heritability of borderline PD traits using questionnaire data in both a twin and a twin-family design. In the twin study, additive genetic factors explained 42% of the variance (Distel et al., 2008), and in the extended twin model additive and nonadditive genetic factors each explained 24% of the variance (Distel, Rebollo-Mesa, et al., 2009). Kendler, Myers, Torgersen, Neale, and Reichborn-Kjennerud, (2007) directly compared data from both questionnaire and structured interview at different points in time to estimate the heritability of the latent liabilities to Cluster A PDs. Heritabilities were substantially higher using both methods (55 to 72%) than when structured interview data alone was utilized. Another method that can reduce measurement error is to use a model in which a common latent factor influences lower order traits of a PD. This has been done for borderline PD by two groups using different self-report data (Distel et al., 2010; Kendler, Myers, & Reichborn-Kjennerud, 2010). As expected, heritability estimates were higher, 51% and 60% respectively.

In addition to the *DSM* categorical system of classification, a number of dimensional classification systems have been proposed for abnormal personality traits, including models which integrate personality disorders with general personality structure (Widiger & Simonsen, 2005). Biometric modeling of pathological personality traits has primarily been conducted with the Dimensional Assessment of Personality Pathology-Basic Questionnaire (DAPP-BQ; Livesley & Jackson, 2001), which includes 18 primary traits and 69 defining facets. The heritability estimates of the primary traits range from 56 to 35%, with the rest of the variance primarily attributable to nonshared environmental effects and no evidence of common environmental effects (Jang, Livesley, Vernon, & Jackson, 1996; Livesley & Jang, 2008). These results resemble those found for normal personality traits (see above).

Few behavior genetic studies investigating the genetic overlap between dimensional measures of pathological personality and normal personality traits as defined by the FFM have been conducted. In a twin study of the 18 DAPP-BQ traits and the FFM traits, the largest genetic correlations were observed with *neuroticism* (median = 0.48), and the lowest with *openness* (median −0.04; Jang & Livesley, 1999). Two more recent studies have examined the etiological overlap between dimensional measures of Borderline PD and the FFM (Distel, Trull, et al., 2009; Kendler, Myers, & Reichborn-Kjennerud, 2010). Both found strong genetic correlations with the FFM traits. Indeed Distel, Trull, et al. concluded that "all genetic variation for Borderline PD is shared with normal personality traits." Further studies are needed to clarify the genetic overlap between the *DSM-IV* PDs and normal personality traits.

Multivariate Studies

As with normal personality traits, behavior genetic modeling can be used with pathological personality traits to achieve several goals, including determining the etiological structure of pathological personality, the genetic and environmental overlap between pathological personality, normal personality, and psychopathology, and the stability of pathological traits over time.

Phenotypic analyses of pathological personality traits assessed by different systems typically identify four factors (Livesley & Jang, 2008). Using principal component analyses, Livesley and colleagues (1998) identified four components in the DAPP-BQ: *emotional dysregulation*, *dissocial behavior*, *inhibitedness*, and *compulsivity*. These higher-order traits strongly resemble dimensions of normal personality. Emotional dysregulation is a broad domain with substantial loadings on 11 of the 18 primary traits. It resembles the normal personality trait neuroticism but is more extensive, including primary traits like identity problems, cognitive dysregulation, oppositionality, suspiciousness, and narcissism. Dissocial behavior resembles the negative pole of agreeableness in the five-factor approach, inhibitedness is similar to introversion, and compulsivity resembles the conscientiousness domain of the five-factor model. Multivariate genetic analyses yielded four genetic and four environmental factors that were remarkably similar to the phenotypic factors. The heritability of the secondary domains were 53%, 50%, 51%, and 38% for emotional dysregulation, dissocial behavior, inhibitedness, and compulsivity, respectively.

There has been only one population-based multivariate twin study including all 10 *DSM-IV* PDs (Kendler et al.,

2008). The best fitting model included three common additive genetic and three common individual-specific environmental factors in addition to disorder-specific genetic and environmental factors. The first common genetic factor had high loadings (> +0.28) on PDs from all three clusters, including histrionic, borderline, narcissistic, dependent, obsessive-compulsive, and paranoid, PD. One interpretation of this factor is that it reflects a broad vulnerability to PD pathology and/or negative emotionality; as such it is likely related to genetic liability to the normal personality trait *neuroticism*. In meta-analytic reviews of the phenotypic relationship between *DSM-IV* PDs and the FFM of personality, three of the five PDs with high loadings on this factor (paranoid, borderline, and dependent) were found to be closely linked phenotypically to neuroticism (Samuel & Widiger, 2008; Saulsman & Page, 2004). This factor also resembles the genetic factor reflecting the higher-order trait emotional dysregulation in the DAPP-BQ (Livesley et al., 1998). The second common genetic factor was quite specific, with substantial loadings only on borderline and antisocial PD. This suggests genetic liability to a broad phenotype for impulsive/aggressive behavior. It resembles the second genetic factor identified by Livesley et al., 1998, dissocial behavior. From the perspective of the FFM, our second factor primarily reflects genetic risk for low conscientiousness and low agreeableness (Samuel & Widiger, 2008). Of interest, in a hierarchical analysis of normal and abnormal personality, Markon, Krueger, and Watson (2005) argue that the traits of agreeableness and conscientiousness—those that are indexed by the second genetic factor—are both reflections of a high-order construct they term *disinhibition*.

The third factor had high loadings only on schizoid and avoidant PD. There are several possible interpretations. This factor might, in part, reflect genetic risk for schizophrenia spectrum pathology (see below). From the perspective of the FFM, it reflects genetic liability for introversion (low extraversion). Indeed, avoidant and schizoid PDs are the two PDs most negatively associated with *extraversion* (Samuel & Widiger, 2008; Saulsman & Page, 2004). Obsessive-compulsive PD had the highest disorder-specific genetic loading, which is consistent with prior work demonstrating that this disorder shares little genetic and environmental liability with the other Cluster C PDs (Reichborn-Kjennerud et al., 2007b). These results again parallel findings from the Livesley et al. (1998) twin study, where the fourth genetic factor reflected their higher-order factor compulsivity, which had by far the strongest loading on the lower order trait of the

same name, and which resembles the conscientiousness domain of the FFM. In sum, these findings indicate that genetic risk factors for *DSM-IV* PDs do not reflect the Cluster A, B, and C typology; however, the *DSM* cluster structure was well represented by the structure of the environmental risk factors, suggesting that the comorbidity of PDs within clusters is due to environmental experiences (Kendler et al., 2008).

Several lines of evidence indicate that common genetic or environmental liability factors might predispose to several disorders within clusters that transcend the Axis I/ Axis II division (Andrews et al., 2009; Krueger & Markon, 2006; Siever & Davis, 1991). A number of family and adoption studies have found significantly increased risk for paranoid, schizoid, and schizotypal PDs in relatives of schizophrenic and control probands. These results suggest that schizotypal PD has the closest familial relationship to schizophrenia, followed by paranoid and schizoid PD. This is consistent with the hypothesis that a common genetic risk factor for Cluster A PDs reflects the liability to schizophrenia in the general population (Kendler et al., 2006a). The term *schizophrenia spectrum* is often used to describe the extended phenotype believed to reflect this genetic liability to (e.g., Siever & Davis, 2004). In a recent family study, Fogelson and colleagues (2007) showed that avoidant PD, currently classified in *DSM* Cluster C, also occurred more frequently in relatives of probands with schizophrenia even after controlling for schizotypal and paranoid PD, suggesting that avoidant PD could also be included in this spectrum. This finding is also in accordance with the results from the multivariate twin study described above, in which avoidant and schizoid PD share genetic liability (Kendler et al., 2008).

As noted above, mood and anxiety disorders, often grouped under the internalizing spectrum of psychopathology, share genetic and environmental liability factors with each other (Kendler, Prescott, Myers, & Neale, 2003b), and with normal personality traits (Hettema et al., 2006; Kendler, Gatz, Gardner, & Pedersen, 2006b). In a population-based multivariate twin study of major depression and *DSM-IV* PDs, Reichborn-Kjennerud and colleagues (2010) found that dimensional representations of borderline PD from Cluster B, avoidant PD from Cluster C, and paranoid PD from Cluster A were all independently and significantly associated with increased risk for major depression. Multivariate biometric modeling indicated that one common latent factor accounted for the genetic covariance between major depression and the three PDs. The genetic correlations between major depression and borderline, avoidant, and paranoid PD were

+0.56, +0.22, and +0.40, respectively. This indicates that vulnerability to general PD pathology and/or negative emotionality and major depression are closely related, consistent with results from a number of studies showing that the genetic liability factors for major depression and the personality trait neuroticism are strongly correlated (Kendler et al., 2006b). At the phenotypic level, neuroticism is also closely related to depressive PD, listed in the *DSM-IV* Appendix B. In a bivariate twin study, Ørstavik and colleagues (2007) found that a substantial part of the covariation between major depressive disorder and depressive PD was accounted for by genetic factors, with a genetic correlation of 0.56. Results from another population-based twin study, investigating the sources of co-occurrence between social phobia and of avoidant PD in females, indicated that the two disorders were influenced by identical genetic factors, whereas the environmental factors were uncorrelated (Reichborn-Kjennerud et al., 2007a). This suggests that whether an individual develops avoidant PD or social phobia is entirely the result of environmental risk factors unique to each disorder, which is in accordance with the hypothesis of underlying psychobiological dimensions cutting across the Axis I/Axis II classification system.

Numerous family, twin, and adoption studies have demonstrated that antisocial PD, conduct disorder, and substance use disorders (externalizing disorders) share a common genetic liability (e.g., Kendler et al., 2003b; Krueger et al., 2002). In a family-twin study, Hicks and colleagues (2004) found that a highly heritable (80%) general vulnerability to all the externalizing disorders accounted for most of the familial resemblance. Disorder-specific vulnerabilities were found for conduct disorder, drug dependence, and alcohol dependence, but not for antisocial PD. The same research group has reported an association between externalizing disorders and reduced amplitude of the P3 component of the brain event-related potential, suggesting that this could be a common biological marker for vulnerability to these disorders (Hicks et al., 2007).

Expanding earlier efforts that have provided consistent evidence that common Axis I disorders can be divided into the two broad categories, internalizing and externalizing disorders (e.g., Krueger & Markon, 2006), a recent study used data from the Norwegian Twin Panel to investigate the underlying genetic and environmental structure of 12 syndromal and subsyndromal common *DSM-IV* Axis I disorders and dimensional representations of all 10 Axis II PDs (Kendler et al., 2011). Four correlated genetic factors were identified: Axis I internalizing, Axis II internalizing, Axis I externalizing, and Axis II externalizing. From a genetic point of view, these results provide some support for the decision in *DSM* to distinguish between Axis I and Axis II disorders. The correlation between the two internalizing factors was 0.49 and between the two externalizing factors 0.38, supporting the internalizing-externalizing distinction. Consistent with results from previous studies, antisocial PD was strongly influenced by the Axis I externalizing factor. From a genetic perspective, it may therefore be placed with the Axis I disorders. Two Axis I disorders, dysthymia and social phobia, were included in the Axis II internalizing cluster, suggesting that from a genetic perspective they may be better placed with the PDs. Borderline PD loaded on both Axis I and Axis II externalizing genetic factors in addition to an environmental liability factor common to Axis I internalizing disorder, consistent with results from factor analytic studies showing associations with both the internalizing and externalizing dimension (Eaton et al., in press). Paranoid and dependent PD had substantial loadings on both the internalizing and externalizing Axis II factors. An important limitation in this study is that it only comprised common Axis I disorders and therefore did not include schizophrenia and other psychotic disorders.

Most of the genetic studies that have investigated changes in genetic influences on PDs and PD traits over time have used measures related to antisocial PD. For example, Lyons and colleagues (1995) demonstrated that the genetic influence on symptoms of *DSM-III-R* antisocial PD was much more prominent in adulthood than in adolescence. In another study, Eley, Lichtenstein, and Moffitt (2003) studied a large number of twin pairs at ages 8 to 9 years and again at 13 to 14 years. They found that genetic influences mediate the continuity in aggressive antisocial behavior from childhood to adolescence, whereas continuity in nonaggressive antisocial behavior was mediated by both shared environment and genetic influences. Results from a study of twins between 10 and 17 years of age demonstrated that a single genetic factor influenced antisocial behavior from age 10 through young adulthood, a shared environmental effect was present beginning in adolescence, there was a transient genetic effect at puberty, and there were genetic influences specific to adult antisocial behavior (Silberg, Rutter, Tracy, Maes, & Eaves, 2007). Finally, another recent twin study of externalizing disorders reported increasing genetic variation and heritability for men but a trend toward decreasing genetic variation and increasing environmental effects for women over the course of adolescence and young adulthood (Hicks et al., 2007b).

MOLECULAR GENETICS OF PERSONALITY

As we have seen, behavior genetic methods, such as twin and family studies, provide an excellent means by which to examine the heritability of personality. These investigations have consistently pointed to sizeable genetic influences on the variance of personality traits, thus largely resolving the question of "nature versus nurture" with an answer of "both." Behavior genetic analyses, however, can only provide broad estimates of genetics effects; they do not identify particular genes that contribute to this variation. To characterize the effects of individual genes—alone or in combination—molecular genetic methods must be used.

The past few decades have seen a major expansion of molecular genetic methods as well as increasingly frequent application of these approaches. In particular, molecular genetic methods have been used to investigate the genetic substrates of a number of medical disorders, sometimes yielding remarkable insights. For instance, molecular genetic studies have identified five gene variants that together account for more than half of the total risk for age-related macular degeneration in siblings (Manolio, 2010). Compelling findings such as this have raised awareness of these methods, and they are currently finding greater traction outside of medicine. Their application has also been bolstered by decreases in cost and continuous technological innovations. As such, psychological scientists have begun using molecular genetic approaches to clarify the role of particular genes in the development of phenotypes of interest and to address precisely which genes contribute to the total heritability of phenotypes identified by behavior genetic investigations.

The molecular genetics of personality is a broad and rapidly changing area of inquiry. In addition to the complexities of molecular genetic approaches, this field is further complicated by the nature of the phenotypes: Personality is a latent construct and thus not directly observable or definitively measurable. Further, the presence of multiple trait models, and associated assessment instruments, means that various constructs are being studied. Even when multiple studies focus on the same personality construct, findings frequently fail to replicate across samples. Thus, this section should be viewed as a snapshot of the current state of a field in flux. In addition, it should be noted that there is a growing literature on the molecular genetics of personality *disorder* as well (e.g., Tadic et al., 2008). Although beyond the scope of this chapter, interested readers are referred to this literature for a deeper understanding of the genes that might underlie variation in personality, whether normal or pathological.

We have organized this section around broad themes of the molecular genetics of personality. We begin with a simplified explication of three popular molecular genetic methods for studying personality: (1) candidate gene analysis, (2) linkage analysis, and (3) genome-wide association studies (GWAS). A full exposition of these methods is beyond the scope of this chapter, but a basic understanding is necessary to digest findings from molecular genetic studies; readers seeking more detail are referred to one of a number of excellent texts on statistical methods for molecular genetics (e.g., Neale, Ferreira, Medland, & Posthuma, 2008; Sham, 1997). Further, it should be noted that the boundaries separating these methods are somewhat artificial, so this tripartite organization serves as a basic explanatory rubric rather than as a representation of three fully distinct methods. After our methodological discussion, we go on to highlight some general findings from molecular genetic studies of personality as well as several novel approaches that may further our understanding of the genetic substrates underlying personality variation.

Three Methods of Molecular Genetic Analysis

We now turn to describing the methods used to examine the molecular genetic basis of personality.

Candidate Genes

The level of focus in molecular genetic studies ranges widely. Some studies focus on the entirety of the human genome, while others focus at the level of the chromosome or at specific points along the chromosome. At a finer level, an individual gene (or a handful of individual genes) may serve as the target of interest. In this latter sort of analysis, researchers typically evaluate the relation between a phenotype and alleles of a specific gene. Alleles are different sequences of DNA that occur at the same physical location on the genome, and can be conceptualized, on a basic level, as representing different forms of a gene, each of which may have a unique impact on the phenotype.

Let us consider eye color in the commonly studied animal model *Drosophila melanogaster*, better known as the fruit fly. These flies typically have red eyes in the wild, although some have unpigmented white eyes. Eye color variation in *Drosophila* is dictated by an allele for a particular gene located on the X chromosome. One allele, the dominant "wild type," produces red eyes; another allele, a mutation, produces white eyes. Thus, in this example, the gene for eye color has two alleles. Similarly, candidate gene studies in humans typically investigate whether alleles of a particular gene are differentially associated with some phenotype of interest. This picture is complicated by the complexity of psychological phenotypes, which almost certainly result from the interplay of multiple genetic and environmental influences.

How are genes selected to serve as worthwhile "candidates" for study? There is no single method to identify candidate genes; rather, genes are typically selected as candidates for inquiry by several means ranging from the theoretical to the empirical. One common theoretical method is to focus on genes associated with brain-related variables, and particularly with neurotransmitters, as they seem likely to relate to psychological phenotypes such as personality. Some typical candidate genes for psychological and psychiatric genetic studies include those related to dopaminergic functioning (e.g., *DRD3* and *DRD4* genes) and to serotonergic functioning (e.g., *5HTTLPR* and *SLC6A4* genes). Enzymes that modulate the effects of neurotransmitters, such as monoamine oxidase A (MAOA) and catechol-*O*-methyltransferase (COMT), are another logical area of focus, and genes relating to these enzymes (e.g., *MAOA*, *COMT*) frequently serve as candidates for study.

Another means by which candidate genes are identified is through the animal literature. The genomes of many animals have been mapped and, as they frequently contain fewer genes than the human genome, the impact of particular genes on a phenotype is often comparatively easier to determine. Studies of naturally occurring mutations and rare alleles have led researchers toward a better understanding of particular genes in animal models, and analogous genes in humans can then serve as candidates for inquiry. Outside of naturally occurring mutations, experimental methods can be used in candidate gene studies to examine the effects of genes. For instance, geneticists often employ the "knock out" technique of gene modification to test hypotheses about specific gene functions. In this approach, animal models—frequently mice, due to their relatively fast development, low cost, and minimal required upkeep—are bred such that targeted genetic mutations have rendered specific genes inactive. The effects of deactivated genes, which are said to have been "knocked out," are then inferred from phenotypic differences observed between animals with and without the mutations.

A final common means by which candidate genes can be identified is through statistical genetic studies of humans. This is somewhat analogous to an atheoretical multiple regression, in which numerous variables can be used simultaneously to predict Y (the dependent variable) in a general sense; the significance of individual predictors, however, is a different, more specific question. The significance of individual predictors can be assessed, and it may be worthwhile to study the association between a single predictor and Y. Similarly, through the use of more broadband statistical molecular genetic methods, such as linkage and GWAS methods that examine large areas of the genome, researchers can uncover reasonable candidate genes for further, more direct investigation.

Candidate gene studies are an excellent means by which to tease apart genetic effects and identify the impact of an individual gene on a phenotype. However, for complex phenotypes such as personality traits, which certainly arise from the effects of multiple genes (i.e., personality traits are "polygenic") in addition to environmental influences, the relatively few reasonable candidate genes so far identified are inadequate. As such, methods that can take a more atheoretical approach to polygenic phenotypes and test multiple genes simultaneously hold a great deal of promise. We will now turn our attention to explication of two such methods: linkage analysis and GWAS.

Linkage Analysis

Candidate gene analysis examines the relations between a particular gene (or small set of genes) and a phenotype. To investigate multiple genes simultaneously, however, different approaches must be taken. One such method is linkage analysis. The results of linkage analyses indicate where on a chromosome genes possibly related to the phenotype may be located. Thus, linkage analysis suggests a *region* on a chromosome that seems probabilistically associated with the phenotype. In this way, linkage analysis has a broader focus than candidate gene analysis, but this focus comes at a cost: Resolution is lost to some degree. Within a given region of the chromosome, there can be numerous genes comprising thousands, or millions, of base pairs. Base pairs are pairs of nucleotides that code for the genetic information found in DNA; they are adenine-thymine and guanine-cytosine, often abbreviated as A-T and G-C, respectively. Ultimately, the sequence of these base pairs determines which allele of a gene an individual has. While linkage analysis yields areas of interest on the chromosome, researchers frequently are more concerned with the allelic status of individuals, defined at the level of base pairs (i.e., the genotype). As such, more fine-grained investigation, such as candidate gene analysis, of this chromosomal region can then be conducted to determine precisely which genes are associated with the phenotype of interest.

Linkage analysis is technically more complex than candidate gene analysis in many ways, and understanding it requires a basic knowledge of molecular biology. Briefly, linkage analysis relies on the principles of DNA recombination to identify regions of the chromosome likely associated with a phenotype. When human sex cells—that is eggs and sperm, known as *gametes*—are produced, they contain 23 chromosomes. (The union of the egg and sperm at fertilization yields the full complement of 46 human chromosomes.) However, the 23 chromosomes in a gamete are not simply copies of half of an individual's set of chromosomes. Rather, in the production of gametes, the genetic information from a pair of chromosomes is exchanged (i.e., "recombined"), producing two unique chromosomes. It is this DNA recombination that ensures that two same-sex siblings from the same parents do not have the same genotype. During recombination, *sections* of genetic material from each chromosome "crossover" to the other chromosome, the result of which is a swapping of swaths of physically adjacent genes. Genes that are physically close ("linked") to one another are more likely to remain together on the chromosomal section, as their proximity decreases the probability that the movement of a DNA section to the other chromosome will separate them. For instance, two genes that are immediately adjacent will likely remain on the same section of DNA, because their separation would require a break in the chromosome precisely between them; two genes separated by multiple genes are more likely to be separated during recombination, because segmentation of the chromosome occurring at any of those genes would result in them being on different DNA sections.

Because DNA recombination involves the exchange of segments of DNA comprising multiple genes (rather than, say, the exchange of individual genes), researchers can draw inferences about the physical proximity of genes—and about regions of the chromosome that seem associated with phenotypes. Researchers using linkage analysis study members of families with a given phenotype and sequence marker genes throughout the genome. Then, statistical analysis of physical proximity of genes results in identification of chromosomal areas that appear associated with phenotypic status. In this way, linkage analysis draws on what we know about DNA recombination to permit inferences about which relatively broad chromosomal regions might contain genes that affect the phenotype of interest.

GWAS

GWAS (pronounced "GEE-wahz") is a third means to find how genes are associated with phenotypes and has recently risen to prominence in many areas of medicine, and is beginning to impact psychological science. Unlike candidate gene analysis, which focuses on one or a few genes of interest, and linkage analysis, which identifies chromosomal regions for further study, GWAS examines the entire genome at a very fine-grained level, thus combining breadth with resolution. GWAS evaluates the base pairs of the genetic code and determines if substitutions of one base pair for another in a gene is associated with an expressed phenotype. These substitutions of one nucleotide base for another (e.g., TAGCAT as compared with TAGCGT) are known as single-nucleotide polymorphisms (SNP, pronounced "snip"). GWAS characterizes each individual's genotype for many SNPs—some GWAS analysis microarray chips can sequence millions of SNPs from across the genome—and then compares the SNP frequencies of individuals with different forms of the phenotype (e.g., those high in neuroticism and those low in neuroticism) to determine if any SNP is significantly associated with phenotypic status. In this way, GWAS analysis essentially involves computing thousands, or millions, of *t*-tests to determine if different SNPs are associated with different phenotypes at a level higher than one would expect based on chance alone.

GWAS balances the broad focus inherent in genome-wide analysis with the precise focus of SNP-level analysis. For all its promise, however, GWAS does have limitations. First, it is often expensive to genotype individuals at the level necessary to conduct fine-grained GWAS (although costs of genotyping are decreasing steadily with improvements in technology). Second, it is often computationally intensive and is methodologically complex. Third, it typically requires large samples, both for identification of potential SNPs and for cross-validation purposes. Finally, it is atheoretical, so even replicable results can be ambiguous: It is unclear why a gene known to be expressed in foot development, for example, would reliably relate to personality phenotypes and by what biological mechanisms this association might occur. This being said, GWAS holds great promise as a means to atheoretically identify genes of interest, and in future studies, other methods, such as candidate gene analysis, can be used to explore promising genes with high precision.

Molecular Genetic Studies of Personality

The molecular genetics of personality present a complicated and quickly changing picture. New studies are published with increasing frequency, and it is not uncommon for previous findings to fail subsequent tests of replication by independent research groups. Indeed, the state of the field is now beginning to shift from individual studies of candidate genes to more widespread use of GWAS, and the compatibility of the results from these different methodologies is not always completely clear. As such, many investigators have found it beneficial to focus at the level of literature review and meta-analysis, and several excellent reviews and meta-analyses of the molecular genetics of personality have been published. Rather than attempting to review the findings of this rapidly evolving and expanding field, we will instead focus our discussion on these reviews and meta-analytic results.

Theories and Measures

Numerous theories of personality have been proposed, each of which posits a unique set of traits and/or mechanisms to describe patterns of behavior and inner experience. Because the primary focus of molecular genetic studies of personality is personality *trait* models, our discussion will focus on personality traits as well. Many of the constructs elaborated in trait models of personality are operationalized in specific personality measures such that the theory and assessment are closely linked; however, notable areas of overlap exist, such as the inclusion of similar traits in some models (see Widiger & Simonsen, 2005). As such, the specific personality traits investigated in molecular genetic studies is often less a function of theoretical interest than of which personality assessment measure—and thus which personality model—was most available, convenient, and en vogue at the time of data collection. (It is noteworthy that some molecular genetic studies of personality resulted from personality data collected many years ago on participants who were more recently genotyped.)

An examination of reviews and meta-analyses (notably Ebstein, 2006; Munafò et al., 2003; Reif & Lesch, 2003; Sen, Burmeister, & Ghosh, 2004) indicates that two of the most commonly used measures in molecular genetic studies of personality are the Tridimensional Personality Questionnaire (TPQ) and the Temperament and Character Inventory (TCI), which operationalize personality theories proposed by Cloninger. The focus on these instruments might be surprising, given personality psychology's general shift toward the traits of the Big Five in the past decades. Cloninger's personality model is built on suggested links between the constructs of these models and biological systems (e.g., Cloninger et al., 1993); therefore, it is likely that such biologically oriented personality theories appeal to more biologically minded investigators (e.g., geneticists, researchers in medical school environments), who themselves went on to conduct many of the molecular genetic studies of personality. Regardless of

the rationale, the constructs operationalized in the TPQ and/or TCI—most notably harm avoidance and novelty seeking—have received relatively more molecular genetic attention than many of the other major personality constructs. Of the studies that did not use the TPQ or TCI, most focused on the traits of the Five-Factor Model, operationalized in the NEO-PI-R or NEO-FFI (Costa & McCrae, 1992), the Eysenck Personality Questionnaire (EPQ) and Eysenck Personality Inventory (EPI; H. Eysenck & Eysenck, 1968, 1975), or the Multidimensional Personality Questionnaire (MPQ; Tellegen & Waller, in press).

The multiplicity of personality constructs and measures investigated has proved somewhat problematic for integrating molecular genetic results. For instance, if a study of NEO-PI-R extraversion were to indicate an association with gene X, while another study failed to find an association between EPQ extraversion and gene X, several possible explanations exist. One explanation, of course, is that the original finding simply failed to replicate—a common finding in the molecular genetic literature on personality and in the molecular genetics literature broadly as well. Another possible explanation is that the NEO-PI-R and EPQ operationalizations of trait extraversion are sufficiently dissimilar such that gene X is indeed related to NEO-PI-R extraversion and not significantly related to EPQ extraversion.

The use of different assessment instruments is a real and nontrivial complication in the molecular genetics literature on personality. As highlighted by one meta-analysis (Sen et al., 2004), a major source of variation in studies of the relation between anxiety-related personality traits and a serotonergic gene (*5-HTTLPR*) is the measure used. For instance, NEO-PI-R neuroticism showed a significant association with *5-HTTLPR* ($p = .000016$) while TCI/TPQ harm avoidance did not ($p = .166$). Findings such as these draw into question why some results fail to replicate and the extent to which imperfectly related personality constructs may have different molecular correlates.

Unfortunately, the number of similar, but nonisomorphic, traits considered in molecular genetic studies often precludes the drawing of strong inferences and the quick accumulation of congruent findings. This confound is not fatal, however, and researchers have developed ways to synthesize findings in a logical and defensible way. One method has been to aggregate studies focusing on putatively similar traits and to meta-analyze their results. While necessarily imperfect, reviews and meta-analyses taking this approach have proved informative, and they are often sufficiently large to parse out the effects of measurement instruments on findings (e.g., Sen et al., 2004).

Indeed, some clarity has been found using this approach, especially when the trait groupings seem to represent major sources of variation. For example, Munafò and colleagues (Munafò et al., 2003) parsed different traits into three groups reflecting basic personality constructs: approach behaviors, avoidance behaviors, and fight-or-flight/aggressive behaviors. When statistical control of variance contributed by different measures cannot be accomplished, this sorting approach appears to hold promise for establishing molecular genetic links with broadly defined individual differences in behavioral tendencies.

Candidate Gene Findings

We will now turn our attention to discussing basic trends in the molecular genetics of personality literature. Most molecular genetic studies of personality have relied upon candidate gene analysis, which has had significant implications for the genes investigated (but see Ebstein, 2006, for discussion of other approaches). Notably, candidate gene analysis in psychiatric and psychological genetics has tended to focus on neurotransmitter-related genes, and molecular genetic personality research is no exception.

The first studies of the molecular genetics of personality, appearing in the literature in the mid-1990s, found associations between dopaminergic gene *DRD4* and extraversion/novelty seeking (see Ebstein, 2006, for a historical perspective). Subsequent studies then linked a promoter region of the serotonin transporter gene (i.e., *5-HTTLPR*) to harm avoidance. However, replication attempts of these findings by independent research groups frequently failed, leading to uncertainty about their accuracy. A set of recent meta-analyses, however, has settled these issues somewhat. For instance, two meta-analyses have supported significant associations between *5-HTTLPR* and avoidance-related traits (Munafò et al., 2003; Sen et al., 2004). Associations between *5-HTTLPR* and aggression traits, and between dopaminergic genes (e.g., *DRD3* and *DRD4*) and approach and avoidance traits, were significant ($p < .05$) in a meta-analysis of 46 studies, but most associations were reduced to nonsignificance when the effects of age, ethnicity, and sex were considered simultaneously in a multivariate context (Munafò et al., 2003). Indeed, it is worth noting that across many molecular genetic studies, ethnicity continues to be a complicating factor due to, for example, ethnicity differences in polymorphism occurrence rates, which can obscure subtle genetic effects. Thus, many studies sample only one ethnicity (typically white individuals), while others use statistical techniques, such as principal components analysis, to remove variation associated with ethnicity.

Outside of dopaminergic and serotonergic genetic links, other neurotransmitters and related enzymes have been associated with personality as well. Reviews of the literature by Reif and Lesch (2003) and Ebstein (2006) illustrate how multiple genes and traits have been investigated by researchers with varying results. In general, it has not been uncommon to find associations with genes relating to MAOA and brain-derived neurotrophic factor (BDNF). Thus, while investigation of genes regulating neurotransmitters and related enzymes has been profitable in identifying potentially important associations, the literature will remain something of a hodgepodge until more high-quality reviews and meta-analyses appear.

Gene-Gene and Gene-Environment Interactions

The effects of candidate genes on personality are further obscured by complex gene-gene interactions and epistasis. Epistasis is the phenomenon by which the effect of one gene is modulated by one or more other genes. As reviewed by Ebstein (2006), studies of interactions between candidate genes have proved somewhat fruitful. For instance, interactions have been observed between the serotonin transporter *SLC6A4* and genes relating to dopamine (e.g., *DRD4*) and to GABA (e.g., *GABA[A]*). Even more complex interactions, such as *DRD4* × *5-HTTLPR* × *COMT*, have been observed. These interactions highlight the intricate interplay between the effects of multiple genes.

Genes do not operate in a vacuum, and, as mentioned above, their effects can be modulated by those of other genes. Genetic effects may also be affected by environmental factors, a phenomenon known as gene X environment interaction and abbreviated GxE. For example, Caspi and colleagues (2002) investigated the interplay between a polymorphism in the *MAOA* gene, childhood maltreatment, and antisocial behaviors (e.g., disposition toward violence, antisocial personality disorder). The researchers found that *MAOA* genotype status moderated the impact of childhood maltreatment on subsequent antisocial behaviors, such that one genotype appeared protective against the deleterious effects of maltreatment. Numerous attempts at replicating this finding have been attempted with varying results, and a meta-analysis of these studies determined that *MAOA* status moderated the effect of maltreatment on mental health problems across studies (although moderation of the effect on antisocial behavior did not reach significance; Kim-Cohen et al., 2006). Gene X environment studies of this nature thus allow investigators to parse apart the main effects of, and interactions between, genes and environmental factors.

GWAS

In addition to candidate gene studies, some researchers have focused on genome-wide studies of personality. Similar to candidate gene analysis, GWAS attempts have produced varied results. To clarify this topic, researchers have recently completed a meta-analysis of GWAS analyses of the Five-Factor Model domains, bringing together data from around 2.4 million SNPs and more than 20,000 participants (de Moor et al., in press). The results suggested the presence of significant associations between SNPs and both openness to experience and conscientiousness, although these results failed to replicate completely across samples. Thus, the results of GWAS studies have yielded a similar picture to those of candidate gene studies, which appears simultaneously promising and ambiguous.

Novel Approaches

The failure of more "traditional" molecular genetic methods to further our understanding of personality has prompted some researchers to attempt novel approaches. Recent research that has combined molecular genetic investigations with functional neuroimaging—an approach referred to as "imaging genomics"—has produced some remarkable results, especially given the small sample sizes involved (e.g., Hariri & Holmes, 2006; Munafò, Brown, & Hariri, 2008). Other approaches are being explored as well, such as focusing on gene systems rather than individual genes. For example, Derringer and colleagues (2010) combined information from 273 SNPs, residing within eight dopaminergic genes, to test for associations between dopaminergic genes and sensation seeking. The development and use of methods such as these will likely lead to a clearer understanding of the molecular genetics of personality in the coming decades.

SUMMARY AND FUTURE DIRECTIONS

We finish our review of behavioral genetics of personality by considering why the twin method is still relevant for our understanding of the etiology of personality, and how it can inform molecular genetics as the field moves forward.

Why Twin Studies Remain Relevant: Drawing Causal Inferences

Personality genetics is a complex and constantly evolving field. Initial hopes that new technology will yield clear

and lasting breakthroughs consistently encounter the reality that identifying the numerous specific polymorphisms associated with personality will be very challenging at best. A system for classifying personality variants based on specific molecular polymorphisms is in the distant future because molecular genetic research on personality is in an early phase of development. The first major international genome-wide effort to identify SNPs associated with the Five-Factor Model of personality yielded little in terms of the number of loci identified and the size of the corresponding effects (de Moor et al., in press). This result is not unique to personality, and is commonly encountered in the study of complex medical and behavioral phenotypes. Some have perhaps seen recent technical breakthroughs in human molecular genetics as a reason that twin studies are passé. This would be an unfortunate conclusion because, as we described throughout this chapter, twin research is valuable for many reasons that go well beyond the estimation of heritability. One recent realization, for example, has been the extent to which the classical twin study design provides a handle on establishing causality in nonexperimental design, that is, in situations where variables cannot be manipulated directly for practical or ethical reasons. McGue, Osler, and Christensen (2010) provide an excellent discussion of the potential for twin research to contribute to establishing specific exposures as causally linked to specific outcomes. Briefly, twin pairs discordant on exposure to an environmental risk factor are matched for both genetic background (if MZ pairs) and rearing environment. As a result, the difference between the twins on exposure may predict a difference in outcome, and such an effect is consistent with a direct causal impact of the exposure. This would be akin to a "counterfactual," that is, it allows one to ask the question "What would have happened to this person in the absence of the exposure?" The cotwin of the exposed twin provides the counterfactual example by virtue of being matched to the exposed twin on a host of relevant factors, allowing for this kind of inference. The reader is encouraged to consult the excellent paper by McGue and colleagues (2010) for a more thorough discussion of these important ideas, illustrating why twins continue to be central to inquiry in behavioral science.

Molecular Inquiry Is Hard But We Should Keep at It and Focus It on Personality

Throughout this chapter we have discussed how challenging it has been to link specific genetic polymorphisms with specific personality dispositions. One potential conclusion is that the situation is nearly hopeless, such that further effort may be a poor use of time and resources. As with the idea that twin studies have outlived their usefulness, this is another situation where a pessimistic conclusion would be unfortunate. Human molecular genetic inquiry focused on disease is likely to continue, and our suggestion is that this kind of inquiry will be fundamentally assisted by a focus on personality assessment. The reason, as we have described throughout, is that personality is so fundamentally interwoven with so many outcomes of high public health relevance. For example, Lahey (2009) makes a very compelling case that neuroticism is probably the most important single variable in behavioral public health. Essentially, efforts to identify genetic polymorphisms associated with the numerous manifestations of neuroticism (e.g., specific mood or anxiety disorders) are likely less useful than efforts to identify the polymorphisms associated with neuroticism per se—particularly if those efforts are fragmented among different investigators. Our argument is that we need a comprehensive and highly collaborative endeavor designed to understand the genetics and psychobiology of neuroticism (and other trait domains of high public health relevance), as opposed to the fragmented approach of studying putatively distinct disorders that may be better conceived of as aspects of a broad spectrum of neuroticism-linked or "internalizing" disorders (Griffith et al., 2010; Krueger & Markon, 2006). We look forward to seeing whether the field can be galvanized around such a theme. We are optimistic that this kind of broad collaborative focus is possible because the GWAS literature has evolved in exactly this fashion, with large-scale consortia having formed to tackle the limitations of what is possible with specific studies. This kind of collaborative and cooperative approach to the psychobiology of personality is certain to ultimately yield findings that can help us to understand the dispositions underlying problem behavior, and thereby improve public health in transformative ways.

REFERENCES

American Psychiatric Association. (2000). *Diagnostic and statistical manual of mental disorders* (4th ed., text rev.). Washington, DC: American Psychiatric Association.

Ando, J., Suzuki, A., Yamagata, S., Kijima, N., Maekawa, H., Ono, Y., & Jang, K. L. (2004). Genetic and environmental structure of Cloninger's temperament and character dimensions. *Journal of Personality Disorders, 18*, 379–393.

Andrews, G., Goldberg, D. P., Krueger, R. F., Carpenter, W. T. J., Hyman, S. E., Sachdev, P., & Pine, D. S. (2009). Exploring the feasibility of a meta-structure for *DSM-V* and ICD-11: Could it improve utility and validity? *Psychological Medicine, 39*, 1993–2000.

Borkenau, P., Riemann, R., Angleitner, A., & Spinath, F. M. (2001). Genetic and environmental influences on observed personality: Evidence from the German Observational Study of Adult Twins. *Journal of Personality and Social Psychology, 80*, 655–668.

Bouchard, T. J. Jr., & Loehlin, J. C. (2001). Genes, evolution, and personality. *Behavior Genetics, 31*, 243–273.

Bouchard, T. J. J. (1994). Genes, environment, and personality. *Science, 264*, 1700–1701.

Buchanan, J. P., McGue, M., Keyes, M., & Iacono, W. (2009). Are there shared environmental influences on adolescent behavior? Evidence from a study of adopted siblings. *Behavior Genetics, 39*, 532–540.

Cadoret, R. J., Yates, W., Troughton, E., Woodworth, G., & Stewart, M. A. (1995). Genetic-environmental interaction in the genesis of aggressivity and conduct disorders. *Archives of General Psychiatry, 52*, 916–924.

Caspi, A., McClay, J., Moffitt, T., Mill, J., Martin, J., Craig, I. W., et al. (2002). Role of genotype in the cycle of violence in maltreated children. *Science, 297*, 851–854.

Chipuer, H. M., Plomin, R., Pedersen, N. L., McClearn, G. E., & Nesselroade, J. R. (1993). Genetic influence on family environment: The role of personality. *Developmental Psychology, 29*, 110–118.

Cloninger, C., Svrakic, D., & Przybeck, T. (1993). A psychobiological model of temperament and character. *Archives of General Psychiatry, 50*, 975–990.

Coolidge, F. L., Thede, L. L., & Jang, K. L. (2001). Heritability of personality disorders in childhood: A preliminary investigation. *Journal of Personality Disorders, 15*, 33–40.

Costa, P. T., & McCrae, R. R. (1992). *Revised NEO personality inventory (NEO-PI-R) and NEO five-factor inventory (NEO-FFI) professional manual*. Odessa, FL: Psychological Assessment Resources.

de Moor, M. H. M., Costa, P. T., Terracciano, A., Krueger, R. F., de Geus, E. J. C., Toshiko, T., . . . Boomsma, D. I. (in press). Meta-analysis of genome-wide association studies for personality. *Molecular Psychiatry*.

Derringer, J., Krueger, R. F., Dick, D. M., Saccone, S., Grucza, R. A., . . . Agrawal, A. Gene Environment Association Studies (GENEVA) Consortium. (2010). Predicting sensation seeking from dopamine genes: A candidate-system approach. *Psychological Science, 21*, 1282–1290.

Distel, M. A., Rebollo-Mesa, I., Willemsen, G., Derom, C. A., Trull, T. A., Martin, N. G., & Boomsma, D. I.. (2009). Familial resemblence of borderline personality disorder features: Genetic or cultural transmission? *PLoS ONE, 4*.

Distel, M. A., Trull, T. J., Derom, C. A., Thiery, E. W., Grimmer, M. A., Martin, N. G., Willemsen, G., & Boomsma, D. I. (2008). Heritability of borderline personality disorder features is similar across three countries. *Psychological Medicine, 38*, 1219–1229.

Distel, M. A., Trull, T. J., Willemsen, G., Vink, J. M., Derom, C. A., Lynskey, M., . . . Boomsma, D. I. (2009). The five-factor model of personality and borderline personality disorder: A genetic analysis of comorbidity. *Biological Psychiatry, 66*, 1131–1138.

Distel, M. A., Willemsen, G., Ligthart, L., Derom, C. A., Martin, N. G., Neale, M. C., . . . Boomsma, D. I. (2010). Genetic covariance structure of the four main features of borderline personality disorder. *Journal of Personality Disorders, 24*, 427–444.

Eaton, N., Krueger, R. F., Keyes, K. M., Skodol, A. E., Markon, K. E., Grant, B. F., & Hasin, D. S. (in press). Borderline personality disorder co-morbidity: Relationship to the internalizing-externalizing structure of common mental disorders. *Psychological Medicine*.

Ebstein, R. P. (2006). The molecular genetic architecture of human personality: Beyond self-report questionnaires. *Molecular Psychiatry, 11*, 427–445.

Eley, T. C., Lichtenstein, P., & Moffitt, T. E. (2003). A longitudinal behavioral genetic analysis of the etiology of aggressive and nonaggressive antisocial behavior. *Development and Psychopathology, 15*, 383–402.

Eysenck, H. J., & Eysenck, S. B. G. (1968). *Manual for the Eysenck personality inventory*. San Diego, CA: Educational and Industrial Testing Service.

Eysenck, H. J., & Eysenck, S. B. G. (1975). *Manual of the Eysenck personality questionnaire*. San Diego, CA: Educational and Industrial Testing Service.

Falconer, D. S. (1965). The inheritance of liability to certain diseases, estimated from the incidence among relatives. *Annals of Human Genetics, 29,* 51–76.

Farone, S. V., Tsuang, M. T., & Tsuang, D. W. (1999). *Genetics of mental disorders*. New York, NY: Guilford Press.

Ferguson, C. J. (2010). Genetic contributions to antisocial personality and behavior: A meta-analytic review from an evolutionary perspective. *Journal of Social Psychology, 150,* 160–180.

Fogelson, D. L., Nuechterlein, K. H., Asarnow, R. A., Payne, D. L., Subotnik, K. L., Jacobson, K. C., . . . Kendler, K. S. (2007). Avoidant personality disorder is a separable schizophrenia-spectrum personality disorder even when controlling for the presence of paranoid and schizotypal personality disorders—The UCLA family study. *Schizophrenia Research, 91,* 192–199.

Gagne, J. R., & Saudino, K. J. (2010). Wait for it! A twin study of inhibitory control in early childhood. *Behavior Genetics, 40,* 327–337.

Goodman, R., & Stevenson, J. (1991). Parental criticism and warmth towards unrecognized monozygotic twins. *Behavior and Brain Sciences, 14,* 394–395.

Gottesman, I. I., & Shields, J. (1967). A polygenic theory of schizophrenia. *Proceedings of the National Academy of Sciences, 58,* 199–205.

Griffith, J. W., Zinbarg, R. E., Craske, M. G., Mineka, S., Rose, R. D., Waters, A. M., & Sutton, J. M. (2010). Neuroticism as a common dimension in the internalizing disorders. *Psychological Medicine, 40,* 1125–1136.

Hariri, A. R., & Holmes, A. (2006). Genetics of emotional regulation: The role of the serotonin transporter in neural function. *TRENDS in Cognitive Sciences, 10,* 182–191.

Hettema, J. M., Neale, M. C., Myers, J. M., Prescott, C., & Kendler, K. S. (2006). A population-based twin study of the relationship between neuroticism and internalizing disorders. *American Journal of Psychiatry, 163,* 857–864.

Hicks, B. M., Bernat, E., Malone, S. M., Iacono, W. G., Patrick, C. J., Krueger, R. F., & McGue, M. (2007). Genes mediate the association between P3 amplitude and externalizing disorders. *Psychophysiology, 44,* 98–105.

Hicks, B. M., Blonigen, D. M., Kramer, M. D., Krueger, R. F., Patrick, C. J., Iacono, W. G., & McGue, M. (2007). Gender differences and developmental change in externalizing disorders from late adolescence to early adulthood: A longitudinal twin study. *Journal of Abnormal Psychology, 116,* 433–447.

Hicks, B. M., Krueger, R. F., Iacono, W. G., Mcgue, M., & Patrick, C. J. (2004). Family transmission and heritability of externalizing disorders—A twin-family study. *Archives of General Psychiatry, 61,* 922–928.

Hoekstra, R. A., Bartels, M., Hudziak, J. J., Van Beijsterveldt, T. C. E. M., & Boomsma, D. I. (2008). Genetic and environmental influences on the stability of withdrawn behavior in children: A longitudinal, multi-informant twin study. *Behavior Genetics, 38,* 447–461.

Hopwood, C. J., Donnellan, M. B., Blonigen, D. M., Krueger, R. F., McGue, M., Iacono, W. G., & Burt, S. A. (2011). Genetic and environmental influences on personality trait stability and growth during the transition to adulthood: A three wave longitudinal study. *Journal of Personality and Social Psychology, 100,* 545–556.

Ilies, R., & Judge, T. A. (2003). On the heritability of job satisfaction: The mediating role of personality. *Journal of Applied Psychology, 88,* 750–759.

Isen, J. D., Baker, L. A., Raine, A., & Bezdjian, S. (2009). Genetic and environmental influences on the junior temperament and character inventory in a preadolescent twin sample. *Behavior Genetics, 39,* 36–47.

Jang, K. L., Dick, D. M., Wolf, H., Livesley, W. J., & Paris, J. (2005). Psychosocial adversity and emotional instability: An application of gene-environment interaction models. *European Journal of Personality, 19,* 359–372.

Jang, K. L., & Livesley, W. J. (1999). Why do measures of normal and disordered personality correlate? A study of genetic comorbidity. *Journal of Personality Disorders, 13,* 10–17.

Jang, K. L., Livesley, W. J., Angleitner, A., Riemann, R., & Vernon, P. A. (2002). Genetic and environmental influences on the covariance of facets defining the domains of the five factor model of personality. *Personality and Individual Differences, 33,* 83–101.

Jang, K. L., Livesley, W. J., & Vernon, P. A. (1996). Heritability of the big five personality dimensions and their facets: A twin study. *Journal of Personality, 64,* 577–591.

Jang, K. L., Livesley, W. J., Vernon, P. A., & Jackson, D. N. (1996). Heritability of personality disorder traits: A twin study. *Acta Psychiatrica Scandinavica, 94,* 438–444.

Jang, K. L., McCrae, R. R., Angleitner, A., Riemann, R., & Livesley, W. (1998). Heritability of facet-level traits in a cross-cultural twin sample: Support for a hierarchical model of personality. *Journal of Personality and Social Psychology, 74,* 1556–1565.

Johnson, A. M., Vernon, P. A., Harris, J. A., & Jang, K. L. (2004). A behavior genetic investigation of the relationship between leadership and personality. *Twin Research, 7,* 27–32.

Johnson, W., & Krueger, R. F. (2004). Genetic and environmental structure of adjectives describing the domains of the big five model of personality: A nationwide US twin study. *Journal of Research in Personality, 38,* 448–472.

Johnson, W., McGue, M., Krueger, R. F., & Bouchard, T. J. Jr. (2004). Marriage and personality: A genetic analysis. *Journal of Personality and Social Psychology, 86,* 285–294.

Kandler, C., Bleidorn, W., Riemann, R., Spinath, F. M., Thiel, W., & Angleitner, A. (2010a). Sources of culumative continuity in personality: A longitudinal multiple-rater twin study. *Journal of Personality and Social Psychology, 98,* 995–1008.

Kandler, C., Riemann, R., & Kampfe, N. (2009). Genetic and environmental mediation between measures of personality and family environment in twins reared together. *Behavior Genetics, 39,* 24–35.

Kandler, C., Riemann, R., Spinath, F. M., & Angleitner, A. (2010b). Sources of variance in personality facets: A multiple-rater twin study of self-peer, peer-peer, and self-self (dis)agreement. *Journal of Personality, 78,* 1565–1594.

Keller, M. C., Coventry, W. L., Heath, A. C., & Martin, N. G. (2005). Widespread evidence for non-additive genetic variation in Cloninger's and Eysenck's personality dimensions using a twin plus sibling design. *Behavior Genetics, 35,* 707–721.

Kendler, K., Aggen, S. H., Czajkowski, N., Roysamb, E., Tambs, K., Torgersen, S., . . . Reichborn-Kjennerud, T. (2008). The structure of genetic and environmental risk factors for *DSM-IV* personality disorders. *Archives of General Psychiatry, 65,* 1438–1446.

Kendler, K., & Baker, J. H. (2007). Genetic influences on measures of the environment: A systematic review. *Psychological Medicine, 37,* 615–626.

Kendler, K. S., Aggen, S. H., Jacobson, K. C., & Neale, M. C. (2003a). Does the level of family dysfunction moderate the impact of genetic factors on the personality trait of neuroticism? *Psychological Medicine, 33,* 817–825.

Kendler, K. S., Aggen, S. H., Knudsen, G. P., Roysamb, E., Neale, M. C., & Reichborn-Kjennerud, T. (2011). The structure of genetic and environmental risk factors for syndromal and subsyndromal common *DSM-IV* axis I and all axis II disorders. *American Journal of Psychiatry, 168,* 29–39.

Kendler, K. S., Czajkowski, N., Tambs, K., Torgersen, S., Aggen, S. H., Neal, M. C., & Reichborn-Kjennerud, T. (2006a). Dimensional representation of *DSM-IV* cluster A personality disorders in a population-based sample of Norweigen twins: A multivariate study. *Psychological Medicine, 36*, 1583–1591.

Kendler, K. S., Gatz, M., Gardner, C. O., & Pedersen, N. L. (2006b). Personality and major depression—A Swedish longitudinal, population-based twin study. *Archives of General Psychiatry, 63*, 1113–1120.

Kendler, K. S., Myers, J., & Reichborn-Kjennerud, T. (2010). Borderline personality disorder traits and their relationship with dimensions of normative personality: A web-based cohort and twin study. *Acta Psychiatrica Scandinavica*, epub ahead of print.

Kendler, K. S., Myers, J., Torgersen, S., Neale, M. C., & Reichborn-Kjennerud, T. (2007). The heritability of Cluster A personality disorders assessed by both personal interview and questionnaire. *Psychological Medicine, 37*, 655–665.

Kendler, K. S., Prescott, C. A., Myers, J., & Neale, M. C. (2003b). The structure of genetic and environmental risk factors for common psychiatric and substance use disorders in men and women. *Archives of General Psychiatry, 60*, 929–937.

Kim-Cohen, J., Caspi, A., Taylor, A., Williams, B., Newcombe, R., Craig, I. W., & Moffitt, T. E. (2006). MAOA, maltreatment, and gene-environment interaction predicting children's mental health: New evidence and a meta-analysis. *Molecular Psychiatry, 11*, 903–913.

Krueger, R. F., Hicks, B. M., & McGue, M. (2001). Altruism and antisocial behavior: Independent tendencies, unique personality correlates, distinct etiologies. *Psychological Science, 12*, 397–402.

Krueger, R. F., Hicks, B. M., Patrick, C. J., Carlson, S. R., Iacono, W. G., & McGue, M. (2002). Etiologic connections among substance dependence, antisocial behavior, and personality: Modeling the externalizing spectrum. *Journal of Abnormal Psychology, 111*, 411–424.

Krueger, R. F., & Markon, K. (2006). Reinterpreting comorbidity: A model-based approach to understanding and classifying psychopathology. *Annual Review of Clinical Psychology, 2*, 111–133.

Krueger, R. F., Markon, K., & Bouchard, G. (2003). The extended genotype: The heritability of personality accounts for the heritability of recalled family enviornments in twins reared apart. *Journal of Personality, 71*, 809–833.

Krueger, R. F., South, S. C., Johnson, W., & Iacono, W. (2008). The heritability of personality is not always 50%: Gene-environment interactions and correlations between personality and parenting. *Journal of Personality, 76*, 1485–1522.

Lahey, B. B. (2009). Public health significance of neuroticism. *American Psychologist, 64*(4), 241–256.

Linney, Y. M., Murray, R. M., Peters, E. R., Macdonald, A. M., Rijsdijk, F., & Sham, P. C. (2003). A quantitative genetic analysis of schizotypal personality traits. *Psychological Medicine, 33*, 803–816.

Livesley, W. J., & Jackson, D. N. (2001). *Manual for the dimensional assessment of personality pathology-basic questionnaire*. Port Huron, MI: Sigma Press.

Livesley, W. J., & Jang, K. L. (2008). The behavioral genetics of personality disorder. *Annual Review of Clinical Psychology, 4*, 247–274.

Livesley, W. J., Jang, K. L., & Vernon, P. A. (1998). Phenotypic and genetic structure of traits delineating personality disorder. *Archives of General Psychiatry, 55*, 941–948.

Loehlin, J. C., Neiderhiser, J. M., & Reiss, D. (2003). The behavior genetics of personality and the NEAD study. *Journal of Research in Personality, 37*, 373–387.

Loehlin, J. C., & Nichols, R. C. (1976). *Heredity, environment and personality*. Austin: University of Texas Press.

Loehlin, J. C., Willerman, L., & Horn, J. M. (1987). Personality resemblance in adoptive families: A 10-year follow-up. *Journal of Personality and Social Psychology, 53*, 961–969.

Lyons, M. J., True, W. R., Eisen, S. A., Goldberg, J., Meyer, J. M., Faraone, S. V.,... Tsuang, M. T. (1995). Differential heritability of adult and juvenile antisocial traits. *Archives of General Psychiatry, 52*, 906–915.

Manolio, T. A. (2010). Genomewide association studies and assessment of the risk of disease. *New England Journal of Medicine, 363*, 166–176.

Markon, K. E., Krueger, R. F., & Watson, D. (2005). Delineating the structure of normal and abnormal personality: An integrative hierarchical approach. *Journal of Personality and Social Psychology, 88*, 139–157.

McCrae, R. R., & Costa, P. T., Jr. (2008). The five-factor theory of personality. In O. P. John, R. W. Robins, & L. A. Pervin (Eds.), *Handbook of personality psychology: Theory and research* (3rd ed., pp. 159–181). New York, NY: Guilford Press.

McGue, M., Bacon, S., & Lykken, D. T. (1993). Personality stability and change in early adulthood: A behavioral genetic analysis. *Developmental Psychology, 29*, 96–109.

McGue, M., Osler, M., & Christensen, K. (2010). Causal inference and observational research: The utility of twins. *Perspectives on Psychological Science, 5*, 546–556.

Mischel, W. (1968). *Personality and assessment*. New York, NY: Wiley.

Munafò, M. R., Brown, S. M., & Hariri, A. R. (2008). Serotonin transporter (5-HTTLPR) genotype and amygdala activation: A meta-analysis. *Biological Psychiatry, 63*, 852–857.

Munafò, M. R., Clark, T. G., Moore, L. R., Payne, E., Walton, R., & Flint, J. (2003). Genetic polymorphisms and personality in healthy adults: A systematic review and meta-analysis. *Molecular Psychiatry, 8*, 471–484.

Neale, B. M., Ferreira, M. A. R., Medland, S. E., & Posthuma, D. (Eds.). (2008). *Statistical genetics: Gene mapping through linkage and association*. London, UK: Taylor & Francis.

Neale, M. C., Boker, S. M., Xie, G., & Maes, H. H. (2003). *Mx: Statistical modeling* (6th ed.). Richmond, VA: Department of Psychiatry, Virginia Commonwealth University.

Neale, M. C., & Cardon, L. R. (1992). *Methodology for genetic studies of twins and families*. Dordrecht, The Netherlands: Kluwer.

Ørstavik, R. E., Kendler, K. S., Czajkowski, N., Tambs, K., & Reichborn-Kjennerud, T. (2007). The relationship between depressive personality disorder and major depressive disorder: A population-based twin study. *American Journal of Psychiatry, 164*, 1866–1872.

Pedersen, N. L., Plomin, R., McClearn, G. E., & Friberg, L. (1988). Neuroticism, extraversion, and related traits in adult twins reared apart and reared together. *Journal of Personality and Social Psychology, 55*, 950–957.

Penke, L., Denissen, J. J. A., & Miller, G. F. (2007). The evolutionary genetics of personality. *European Journal of Personality, 21*, 549–587.

Plomin, R., Corley, R., Caspi, A., Fulker, D. W., & DeFries, J. C. (1998). Adoption results for self-reported personality: Evidence for nonadditive genetic effects? *Journal of Personality and Social Psychology, 75*, 211–218.

Plomin, R., DeFries, J. C., McClearn, G. E., & McGuffin, P. (2008). *Behavioral genetics* (5th ed.). New York, NY: Worth.

Purcell, S. (2002). Variance components models for gene-environment interaction in twin analysis. *Twin Research, 5*, 554–571.

Reichborn-Kjennerud, T., Czajkowki, N., Roysamb, E., Orstavik, R. E., Neale, M. C., Torgersen, S., & Kendler, K. S. (2010). Major depression and dimensional representations of *DSM-IV* personality disorders: A population-based twin study. *Psychological Medicine, 40*, 1475–1484.

Reichborn-Kjennerud, T., Czajkowki, N., Torgersen, S., Neale, M. C., Orstavik, R. E., Tambs, K., & Kendler, K. S. (2007a). The relationship between avoidant personality disorder and social phobia: A population-based twin study. *American Journal of Psychiatry, 164*, 1722–1728.

Reichborn-Kjennerud, T., Czajkowski, N., Neale, M. S., Ørstavik, R. E., Torgersen, S., Tambs, K.,...Kendler, K. S. (2007b). Genetic and environmental influences on dimensional representations of *DSM-IV* Cluster C personality disorders: A population-based multivariate twin study. *Psychological Medicine, 37,* 645–653.

Reif, A., & Lesch, K.-P. (2003). Toward a molecular architecture of personality. *Behavioural Brain Research, 139,* 1–20.

Reiss, D., Neiderhiser, J. M., Hetherington, E. M., & Plomin, R. (2000). *The relationship code: Deciphering genetic and social influences on adolescent development*. Cambridge, MA: Harvard University Press.

Rhee, S., & Waldman, I. D. (2002). Genetic and environmental influences on antisocial behavior: A meta-analysis of twin and adoption studies. *Psychological Bulletin, 128,* 490–529.

Rowe, D. C. (1981). Environmental and genetic influences on dimensions of perceived parenting: A twin study. *Developmental Psychology, 17,* 203–208.

Rowe, D. C. (1983). A biometrical analysis of perceptions of family environment: A study of twin and singleton sibling kinships. *Child Development, 54,* 416–423.

Rutter, M., Moffitt, T. E., & Caspi, A. (2006). Gene-environment interplay and psychopathology: Multiple varieties but real effects. *Journal of Child Psychology and Psychiatry, 47,* 226–261.

Samuel, D. B., & Widiger, T. A. (2008). A meta-analytic review of the relationships between the five-factor model and *DSM-IV-TR* personality disorders: A facet level analysis. *Clinical Psychology Review, 28,* 1326–1342.

Saudino, K. J., Pedersen, N. L., Lichtenstein, P., McClearn, G. E., & Plomin, R. (1997). Can personality explain genetic influences on life events? *Journal of Personality and Social Psychology, 72,* 196–206.

Saulsman, L. M., & Page, A. C. (2004). The five-factor model and personality disorder empirical literature: A meta-analytic review. *Clinical Psychology Review, 23,* 1055–1085.

Scarr, S., & Carter-Saltzman, L. (1979). Twin method: Defense of a critical assumption. *Behavior Genetics, 9,* 527–542.

Sen, S., Burmeister, M., & Ghosh, D. (2004). Meta-analysis of the association between a serotonin transporter promoter polymorphism (5-HTTLPR) and anxiety-related personality traits. *American Journal of Medical Genetics Part B, 127B,* 85–89.

Sham, P. (1997). *Statistics in human genetics*. Hoboken, NJ: Wiley.

Siever, L., & Davis, K. L. (2004). The pathopysiology of schizophrenia disorders: Perspectives from the spectrum. *American Journal of Psychiatry, 161,* 398–413.

Siever, L. J., & Davis, K. L. (1991). A psychobiological perspective on the personality disorders. *American Journal of Psychiatry, 148,* 1647–1658.

Silberg, J. L., Rutter, M., Tracy, K., Maes, H. H., & Eaves, L. J. (2007). Etiological heterogeneity in the development of antisocial behavior: The Virginia twin study of adolescent behavioral development and the young adult follow-up. *Psychological Medicine, 37,* 1193–1202.

Singh, A. L., & Waldman, I. D. (2010). The etiology of associations between negative emotionality and childhood externalizing disorders. *Journal of Abnormal Psychology, 119,* 376–388.

South, S. C., Eaton, N. R., & Krueger, R. F. (2011). The connections between personality and psychopathology. In T. Millon, R. F. Krueger, & E. Simonsen (Eds.), *Contemporary directions in psychopathology: Toward the DSM-5, ICD-11, and beyond*. New York, NY: Guilford Press.

South, S. C., & Krueger, R. F. (2008). Marital quality moderates genetic and environmental influences on the internalizing spectrum. *Journal of Abnormal Psychology, 117,* 826–837.

South, S. C., & Krueger, R. F. (2011). Genetic and environmental influences on internalizing psychopathology vary as a function of economic status. *Psychological Medicine, 41,* 107–118.

Spinath, F. M., & O'Connor, T. G. (2003). A behavioral genetic study of the overlap between personality and parenting. *Journal of Personality, 71,* 785–808.

Spotts, E. L., Lichtenstein, P., Pedersen, N., Neiderhiser, J. M., Hansson, K., Cederblad, M., & Reiss, D. (2005). Personality and marital satisfaction: A behavioural genetic analysis. *European Journal of Personality, 19,* 205–227.

Tadic, A., Baskaya, O., Victor, A., Lieb, K., Hoppner, W., & Dahmen, N. (2008). Association analysis of SCN9A gene variants with borderline personality disorder. *Journal of Psychiatric Research, 43,* 155–163.

Tellegen, A., & Waller, N. G. (in press). *Exploring personality through test construction: Development of the multidimensional personality questionnaire (MPQ)*. Minneapolis: University of Minnesota Press.

Torgersen, S., Czajkowski, N., Jacobson, K., Reichborn-Kjennerud, T., Røysamb, E., Neale, M. S., & Kendler, K. S.. (2008). Dimensional representations of DSM-IV cluster B personality disorders in a population-based sample of Norwegian twins: A multivariate study. *Psychological Medicine, 38,* 1617–1625.

Torgersen, S., Lygren, S., Oien, P. A., Skre, I., Onstad, S., Edvardsen, J., Tambs, K., & Kringlen, E. (2000). A twin study of personality disorders. *Comprehensive Psychiatry, 41,* 416–425.

Turkheimer, E. (2000). Three laws of behavior genetics and what they mean. *Current Directions in Psychological Science, 9,* 160–164.

Widiger, T. A., & Simonsen, E. (2005). Alternative dimensional models of personality disorder: Finding a common ground. *Journal of Personality Disorders, 19,* 110–130.

Wolf, H., Angleitner, A., Spinath, F. M., Riemann, R., & Strelau, J. (2004). Genetic and environmental influences on the EPQ-RS scales: A twin study using self- and peer reports. *Personality and Individual Differences, 37,* 579–590.

Yamagata, S., Suzuki, A., Ando, J., Ono, Y., Kijima, N., Yoshimura, K.,...Jang, K. L. (2006). Is the genetic structure of human personality universal? A cross-cultural twin study from North America, Europe, and Asia. *Journal of Personality and Social Psychology, 90,* 987–998.

CHAPTER 2

Biological Bases of Personality

MARVIN ZUCKERMAN

One of the broadest behavioral differences between species is the tendency to approach or withdraw from stimuli. As Schneirla (1959) pointed out, the intensity of the stimulus is a major determinant of the reaction of the observer. Low intensities tend to elicit approach whereas high intensities tend to elicit withdrawal reactions. Unconditioned stimuli as well as conditioned stimuli associated with reward or punishment may determine the direction of the reaction. In higher-level organisms, approach may become a motivated seeking, and withdrawal a passive or active avoidance (Schneirla, 1959).

Intensity is not the only characteristic that affects the strength of approach or withdrawal and seeking or avoidance. Novelty is another, eliciting interest and approach in some individuals and withdrawal and avoidance in others. Both novelty and intensity are the basis for approach and avoidance in the trait I call *sensation seeking* (Zuckerman, 1979, 1994, 2011). Others have called this trait novelty seeking, excitement seeking, thrill seeking, and fun seeking. Although some investigators have classified sensation seeking as a facet or subtrait of extraversion, extraversion is primarily a specifically social type of seeking, whereas sensation or novelty seeking is a more generalized type of reaction to novel objects or unfamiliar members of the species (Zuckerman, 1984). Approach has been recognized as a major form of temperament or basic personality dimension in children (Buss & Plomin, 1975; Rothbart, Derryberry, & Posner, 1994; Thomas & Chess, 1977), and adults (Cloninger, 1987; Zuckerman, 1979, 1994, 1995, 2007).

Gray (1991) described the Behavioral Approach System (BAS) with a special sensitivity to signals of reward, corresponding to a trait of impulsivity in humans, and the Behavioral Inhibition System (BIS), which is sensitivity to signals of punishment or threat. At the human level it is described as an anxiety system with a strong relationship to the personality trait of neuroticism. In the revised theory (Gray & McNaughton, 2000), the BIS is instigated in conflict situations that contain cues for reward and punishment. The BIS tends to slow or inhibit approach. Similarly, Kagan (1989) described an *inhibited temperament* expressed as timidity and fearfulness in unfamiliar situations or in the presence of strangers. In fact, every adult system of personality has included a withdrawal-related factor referred to as neuroticism, neuroticism-anxiety, negative affectivity, or harm avoidance.

Gray's third system, the Fight/Flight System (FFS), is based on unconditioned responses to punishment or withdrawal of reward. The fight (aggression) option and intolerance of frustration suggests a clinical expression in psychopathic personality, or Eysenck's third dimension of personality, psychoticism (P). However, in Gray's revised theory, the FFS adds freezing as a possible response to unconditioned or conditioned stimuli of threat or punishment, making the FFS more comparable to fear or fearfulness.

The lack of connection between Gray's FFS and the dimensions of other major personality theories illustrates the difficulties of connecting "bottom-up" and "top-down" approaches to personality. Human and animal behavioral traits may show similarities, but unless we can show that they are regulated by shared genetic and biological bases, the comparisons may be specious. Our first task, however, is to demonstrate that there is more than minimal connections between the human personality traits described in different systems. Without this type of convergent/discriminant validity one would have to search separately for biological connections for each dimension in each system.

Most studies of convergent/discriminant relationships deal with only two systems in the same sample. For example, Zuckerman, Kuhlman, Joireman, Teta, and Kraft (1993) examined the correlations and emergent factors among Eysenck's (1967; Eysenck & Eysenck, 1975) Big Three, Costa and McCrae's (1992) Big Five, and Zuckerman and Kuhlman's Alternative Five (Zuckerman et al., 1993). Although the latter two systems proposed five factors, the results of a factor analysis of the primary factors showed that four factors were sufficient to account for 74% of the variance among the 13 scales involved in the analysis and a fifth factor added little to the variance. The results are shown in Table 2.1.

The first factor was clearly Extraversion. Scales from all three systems loaded highly on this factor despite the fact that sociability from the Alternative Five is a narrower construct than the broader ones in the Big Three and Big Five. Activity in the Alternative Five also loaded on this factor.

The second factor was Neuroticism, with loadings over .90 from the N scales in all three systems. The third factor was less predictable from the labels and content of the scales involved. One pole was formed by the Big-Three Psychoticism (PP) scale and the Alternative Five Impulsive Sensation Seeking (ImpSS) scale, and the other pole was the Conscientiousness (C) scale from the Big Five. The three scales are quite different in content. In a

previous factor analysis, that did not include the Big-Five, this factor was called "P-Impulsive Unsocialized Sensation Seeking (P-ImpUSS)" (Zuckerman, Kuhlman, & Camac, 1988). Apparently C represents the socialization aspect of P-ImpUSS. In addition to its primary loading on this factor, ImpSS had a secondary but much weaker loading on the E factor.

The fourth factor was clearly Big-Five Agreeableness versus Alternative-Five Aggression. There is practically no overlap in the content of these two scales because the first represents the positive pole and the second the negative pole of the dimension. Openness from the Big-Five loaded on the positive end. In a three-factor analysis, a broader P dimension included Agreeableness, C, ImpSS, and Aggression-Hostility.

These four broad factors formed the basis for the organization of my books on the psychobiology of personality (Zuckerman, 1991, 2005) and in my chapter in the previous edition of this handbook (Zuckerman, 2003), and they guide the organization of the current chapter. This is not to say that there may be some specific biological factors or genetic factors underlying subtraits of the major factors. I believe, however, that it is better to start at the broader trait level, working down to the more specific trait biology, and seeking common biological factors, which may account for their correlations at the trait level. This chapter examines some of the genetic and biological similarities and differences between the four broad trait factors similar in most trait systems. Openness to experience in the Big Five and activity in the Alternative Five will not be covered.

GENETICS OF PERSONALITY

Biological basis of personality begins with the study of genetic determinants of behavioral and personality traits. However, it must be emphasized that we do not directly inherit the phenomenal expressions of personality. Genes code for the proteins that make the biological traits underlying the individual differences in personality. Gene expression is limited by gene and gene-environment interaction. Nearly all personality traits are polygenetic. Behavioral genetics is a method for determining a quantitative index of the relative roles of genes and environment in the variance of a trait by comparing the level of the trait as a function of biological relatedness of family members.

Behavior Genetics

In older theories of personality, distinctions were made between genetically and environmentally produced traits.

TABLE 2.1 Four-Factor Analysis of NEO, ZKPQ, and EPQ Personality Scales Factor Loadings

Scale	Factor 1	Factor 2	Factor 3	Factor 4
NEO Extraversion	**.88**	−.14	−.05	.17
EPQ Extraversion	**.79**	−.32	.17	−.08
ZKPQ Sociability	**.76**	−.16	.10	−.07
ZKPQ Activity	**.60**	.01	−.18	.02
ZKPQ N-Anxiety	−.13	**.92**	−.01	.08
NEO Neuroticism	−.15	**.90**	.10	−.11
EPQ Neuroticism	−.16	**.91**	−.04	−.08
NEO Conscientious	.15	−.07	**−.86**	−.02
EPQ Psychoticism	−.09	−.08	**.80**	−.28
ZKPQ ImpSS	.48	.08	**.74**	−.02
NEO Agreeableness	−.04	−.07	−.31	**.81**
ZKPQ Agg-Host	.35	.34	.24	**−.72**
NEO Openness	.27	.14	.18	**.67**

Note. Loadings for defining scales are in boldface.
From "A Comparison of Three Structural Models for Personality: The Big Three, the Big Five, and the Alternative Five," by M. Zuckerman, D. M. Kuhlman, J. Joireman, P. Teta, and M. Kraft (1993). *Journal of Personality and Social Psychology, 65*, p. 762. Copyright 1993 by the American Psychological Association.

For instance, Murray (1938) classified traits as either "viscerogenic" or "psychogenic." If nothing else, biometric studies of personality traits have shown that such a classification is specious because genetic and environmental influences are present in all basic personality traits. Furthermore, all personality traits are polygenetic, involving a number of genes usually in an additive combination. For a detailed discussion of the genetic bases of personality, see the chapter by Susan South and colleagues in this volume.

Johnson, Vernon, and Feiler (2008) provide the most complete summary of the results of behavior genetic studies over the previous 50 years. Their results are organized around the Big Five. Table 2.2 summarizes the median heritabilities of related trait measures for four of the five Big Five factors (omitting openness). Table 2.2 also includes findings from studies of aggression and sensation seeking, components of the Alternative 5. Zuckerman (2005) provide the trait categories that were not included in the Johnson et al. (2008) review.

There is a remarkably limited range for the median heritabilities for different traits, most falling in the range of .40 to .50. Sensation seeking and extraversion are at the high end of heritability, whereas agreeableness and aggression are at the low end. But overall the range is limited. Even the heritabilities of the subtraits within the major traits have a limited range. For instance, the median heritabilities of three of the four subtraits of sensation seeking range between .51 and .57, with the fourth trait, boredom susceptibility, lower (.41) because of the lower reliability of that subscale. When Johnson et al. (2008)

applied model-fitting methods that divided the variance into genetic, shared environment and nonshared environment (a residual term that includes measurement error), hereditary estimates were close to those derived from measures of heritability.

The proportion of trait variance due to shared environment (such as parents, home, and school) is surprisingly low, averaging only .07. Most of the remaining environmental variance is nonshared, including the differential experience with siblings and peers outside the home and unique experiences specific to one child in the family but not shared with another. Nonshared environment accounts for slightly more than 50% of the variance. Even allowing for the error included in the residual measure, this is a sizeable proportion of the variance.

These kinds of model-fitting methods rely primarily on the correlations of identical and fraternal twins and rarely assess the home environment. A study conducted in the Netherlands directly assessed the role of religion on genetic and environment effects on the sensation seeking subtrait of disinhibition (Boomsma, de Geus, van Baal, & Koopmans, 1999). Disinhibition is sensation seeking in social relationships, as often expressed in partying, drinking, drugs, and sexual behavior. In several twin studies, including Boomsma et al., investigators have found a high degree of genetic and specific environment influence but no effect of shared environment. However, Boomsma et al. found strong genetic and nonshared environment effects among twins raised in nonreligious homes, with little or no effect of shared environment. Among twins raised in religious homes, however, there was no genetic effect for men and only a weak effect for women. For men growing up in religious homes there was a very strong effect of shared environment, and a significant but weaker effect for women. The effects of nonshared environment were the same as those in men and women raised in nonreligious homes. This kind of interaction has also been found in molecular genetic studies, to which we now turn.

Molecular Genetics

From the late 1980s new methods made it possible to identify specific genetic variations associated with rare single gene severe neurological disorders or multigenetic common disorders, and normally distributed cognitive and personality traits. Progress has been slow in the latter because such complex traits are influenced by many genes, some of which are not detectable by current methods. However, a few genes of stronger effect sizes have been found, accounting for 5 to 10% of the variance of a personality trait.

TABLE 2.2 Median Heritabilities and Components of Variance for Personality Traits

	Heritability (h^2)	Genetic (a^2)	Shared Environment (c^2)	Nonshared Environment (e^2)
E-Type Scales	.49	.48	.15	.48
N-Type Scales	.45	.44	.13	.51
C-Type Scales	.46	.41	.27	.59
A-Type Scales	.40	.47	.15	.48
Aggression*	.44			
Sensation Seeking**	.58–59			

NEO Scales: E = Extraversion; N = Neuroticism, C = Conscientiousness; A = Agreeableness: Data from Johnson et al. (2008).
*From Tellegen and Waller (2008).
**From Fulker, Eysenck, and Zuckerman (1980), and Hur and Bouchard (1997). The Hur and Bouchard article included only the subscales of the SSS. The results for the total score were conveyed in a personal communication by David Lykken (1992). The correlations between identical twins separated near birth and raised in different environments was .54 and for separated fraternal twins was .32. This yielded an estimated heritability of .59.

One of the first genes associated with a personality trait was the D4 dopamine receptor gene (D4DR). Ebstein et al. (1996) found that individuals with the long form (most commonly seven repeats of the base sequence in Western populations) scored higher on novelty seeking. Not all replication attempts have captured this association, but a recent meta-analysis based on 48 studies indicated that the relationship between novelty or sensation seeking and D4DR is a reliable one (Munafo, Yalcin, Willis-Owen, & Flint, 2008). The relationship was also found between D4DR and impulsivity, but not with extraversion.

Apart from its association with sensation seeking and impulsivity, the long form of D4DR has been linked to forms of psychopathology and behavior involving one or both of these traits (Ebstein, 2006). In humans, D4DR is related to heroin and alcohol abuse, pathological gambling and, in a meta-analysis of 14 studies, to attention deficit hyperactivity disorder (Faraone, Doyle, Mick, & Biederman, 2001). It has also been associated with sexual desire, function, and arousal (Ben Zion et al., 2006). The relationship with sexual arousal and behavior (also correlated with sensation seeking) could explain the selection of the gene allele in humans during the Paleolithic era. The older form of the gene, with only four repeats of the base sequence, is associated with low to average sensation seeking, but also to altruism or selflessness (Bachner-Melman et al., 2005).

Serotonin (5-hydroxytryptamine, 5-HT) is a neurotransmitter that is a major modulator of emotional behavior, generally functioning as an inhibitor. The reuptake, modulation, and transcription of 5-HT is regulated by the 5-HT transporter (5-HTT). Human and simian 5-HTT is modulated at a gene-linked promoter region on the chromosome (5-HTTLPR). Lesch et al. (1996) found that persons with one or two copies of the short form of 5-HTTLPR scored higher on neuroticism and lower on agreeableness than those with the long form of the gene. Individuals with the short version of the gene scored higher than those with the long form on the anxiety, angry hostility, depression, and impulsiveness facets of N. It is clear that the long form of the gene is associated with aggression-hostility as well as neuroticism. Although replication of associations between traits and stress sensitivity have not all been successful (for reviews see Caspi, Hariri, Holmes, Uher, & Moffitt, 2010; Lesch, Greenberg, Higley, Bennett, & Murphy, 2002), Caspi et al. (2010) noted that all nonreplications used brief self-report measures of life stress whereas successful replications used objective indicators or interviews, the gold standard in life events assessment. Studies of the effects of separation from mothers in rhesus monkeys have revealed an interactive effect of the gene form in behavioral response during the initial separation. Separated monkeys with the short form showed less evidence of a coping response and more anxiety, agitation, and stereotyped responses than those with the long form of the gene (Spinelli et al., 2007).

Monoamine oxidase type A (MAO-A) is an enzyme that regulates the monoamines, particularly serotonin and norepinephrine (Shih & Chen, 1999). Mice with the MAO-A gene "knocked out" show increased aggressiveness and decreased freezing (fear) in response to other mice. A longitudinal study of boys followed from ages 3 to 26 showed an interaction between the gene for MAO-A and childhood maltreatment in producing adult aggressiveness and psychopathy (Caspi et al., 2002). Children with the variant of the MAO-A gene associated with low activity of the enzyme and who were subjected to maltreatment as children were more likely as adults to develop antisocial personalities and tendencies toward violence. However, study participants who inherited the same gene allele but did not experience childhood maltreatment had no more aggressive or antisocial personality than those without that gene form. Conversely, participants who experienced severe maltreatment during childhood did not develop aggressive antisocial personalities unless they had the form of the gene associated with aggression. Neither nature nor nurture alone, but rather the interaction of nature and nurture, determined the outcome.

Psychopharmacology and Neuropsychology

The genes thus far connected with personality traits are those that control the production or regulation of brain neurotransmitters, particularly the monoamines. As a consequence, there is a tendency for some psychobiological model builders to construct simplistic theories assigning one neurotransmitter to one trait (ONOT). ONOT theories are a vestige of the pseudoscience of phrenology that designated one part of the cortical brain to each trait or temperament. This tendency is seen even today in theories that assign a personality trait to one brain locus, for example, anxiety to the amygdala. Psychoneurology actually identifies circuits with multiple loci activated by threat, and a balance between inhibitory and excitatory systems, sometimes mediated by the same neurotransmitter activating different systems.

Consider the following example. Most psychobiological theories hypothesize that dopaminergic reactivity in the nucleus accumbens (NA) or ventral striatum underlies impulsive approach behavior in traits like extraversion or sensation seeking. A group of French investigators used a rat model to define two extreme groups, those highly "novelty seeking," or high reactives (HRs), and those who were low reactives (LRs), and they exposed these two groups of rats to a variety of experimental situations (Dellu, Piazza, Mayo, Le Moal, & Simon, 1996). The HRs self-administered higher levels of amphetamine. In contrast, the LRs preferred familiar environments and did not ingest much amphetamine. Autopsy showed higher levels of dopamine activity in the NA in the HRs than in the LRs, but opposite results for dopamine in the prefrontal cortex. Dopamine activity in the NA correlated positively with novelty seeking behaviors, whereas dopamine activity in the prefrontal cortex correlated negatively with these behaviors. Dopamine release in the prefrontal cortex actually inhibited its release in the NA.

Preferences for amphetamine and positive arousal reactions to this drug that releases catecholamines (dopamine and norepinephrine) in the brain are related to sensation seeking (Stoops et al., 2007). Leyton et al. (2007), using Positron Emission Tomography (a brain-imaging method), found that novelty seeking was related to dopaminergic reactions to amphetamine in the ventral striatum (in the reward-sensitive nucleus accumbens) but not to another dopamine center, the dorsal striatum (including putamen and caudate). This again suggests why overall measures of neurotransmitter activity are unreliable—these indicators lack neurological specificity. We cannot assume that such measures reflect what is happening in the brain. Another problem is that most measures of monoamines are indirect, based on metabolites of the neurotransmitters or enzymes that regulate their production or disposal. Autopsy is not a viable method for determining neurochemical specificity in humans. With these caveats in mind, we now examine some of the results of studies using such indirect measures.

Monoamine oxidase type B (MAO-B), assayed in blood platelets, is an enzyme that regulates dopamine by catabolic degradation. It is primarily involved in the reduction of dopamine in human and primate brains, whereas MAO-type A preferentially oxidizes serotonin and norepinephrine. Monkeys in a colony with low MAO-B were more sociable, dominant, aggressive, playful, aggressive, and sexually active than monkeys with high levels of this enzyme (Redmond, Murphy, & Baulu, 1979). In humans, this behavior suggests the agentic type of extraversion described by Depue and Collins (1999). However, Depue (1995) did not find a correlation between the enzyme and a measure of positive emotionality (extraversion). A more consistent negative relationship has been repeatedly found between sensation seeking and

low MAO-B. Low levels of MAO-B are also found in clinical disorders characterized by loss of control and impulsivity, like attention deficit hyperactivity, antisocial and borderline personality, alcohol and drug abuse, and bipolar disorders. In the latter three it is also found among relatives and offspring, suggesting genetic sources of the correlation. It may be hypothesized that low MAO-B dysregulates dopamine pathways in the ventral striatum, allowing strong dopamine responses to novel stimuli or drugs that release dopamine in the systems. Relationships between sensation seeking subtraits and indirect biochemical indices of dopaminergic responses to dopamine agonists have provided mixed results (Depue, 1995; Gerra et al., 2000; Netter, Hennig, & Roed, 1996; Wiesbeck et al., 1996).

Absence of MAO-A is related to aggression in mice. MAO-A is not found in the blood of humans, but their brain MAO-A has been studied using the MAO-A gene. As noted previously, Caspi et al. (2002) reported an interaction between the genetic variants producing high or low MAO-A activity and childhood maltreatment in producing antisocial and aggressive adults. A rare genetic mutation in a Dutch family produced an absence of the gene comparable to its absence in mice produced experimentally (Brunner, Nelen, Breakefield, Ropers, & Van Oost, 1993). The absence of the gene in both mice and humans resulted in aggressive behavior, and antisocial behavior in the unfortunate human family. The association may be mediated by the lack of regulation of serotonin, related to the capacity for impulse inhibition.

The metabolite of serotonin, 5-HIAA, is low in aggressive human subjects (Coccaro, 1998; Zalsman & Apter, 2002) and the response to serotonin agonists tends to be blunted in sensation seeking individuals (Depue, 1995; Hennig et al., 1998; Netter et al., 1996). Low levels of serotonin are found in individuals with impulse disorders, but also among people with major depression. In fact, serotonin uptake-inhibitors (SSRIs) are a class of drugs used to treat depression. Low serotonin levels are found in persons who commit impulsive and violent homicides as well as those who attempt or commit impulsive and violent suicides. Apparently, low serotonin levels are related to impulsiveness and aggression whether directed inward or outward.

The dorsal ascending noradrenergic system (DANB) originating in the locus coeruleus (LC) ascends through the limbic system to the entire neocortex, where it has a general arousing effect. Destruction of the system in rats impairs passive avoidance learning and conditioned inhibition, suggesting an anxiogenic role in humans. In humans, drugs that increase anxiety increase activation of the system as estimated from increases in the norepinephrine (NE) metabolite MHPG. Anti-anxiety drugs, such as benzodiazepines and opiates, reduce LC activity and NE release. Electrical stimulation of the LC in monkeys produces facial and behavioral expressions normally associated with threat-induced fear. Actual external threatening stimuli increase LC activity. These results and others led Gray (1982, 1987) and Redmond (1985, 1987) to propose that this NE system is the basis of a trait of fearfulness or neuroticism in humans. Redmond (1987) suggested that the mechanism has the form of an "alarm system" at the lower level and a panic system at the higher level of activation. Activation of the DANB by drugs produces panic attacks in high proportions of patients with panic disorder but much more rarely in normal controls.

In summary, animal models show specificity for the behavioral effects of neurotransmitters depending upon their locus in the brain. Therefore, it is unlikely that overall measures of their activity, as used in most studies of humans, will reveal much of an association between neurotransmitters and either behavior or personality traits. Despite these limitations, some replicable findings have emerged in animal and human models.

Low MAO-B has been associated with sensation seeking, impulsivity, and disorders associated with impulsivity and lack of behavioral control in humans. MAO-A is related to aggression in mice and its genetic variant in humans is associated with antisocial and aggressive behavior. Activation of norepinephrine in the locus coeruleus is a reaction to threatening stimuli and associated with fearfulness in monkeys and humans. These cross-species models suggest a neuropsychopharmacological basis for personality traits with evolutionary origins.

Hormones

Testosterone in men is associated with approach traits including extraversion (and its facets of sociability, dominance and activity), and is inversely related to introversion and socialization (Daitzman & Zuckerman, 1980). Windle (1994) described the cluster of traits related to testosterone as "behavioral activation" including boldness, sociability, pleasure seeking, and rebelliousness. Dabbs (2000) found that testosterone is related to traits of high energy and activity but low responsibility. Testosterone is associated with behavioral aggression in normals (Archer, 1991, 2006) and prisoners, men (Aluja, & Garcia, 2005; Dabbs, Carr, Frady, & Riad, 1995) and women (Dabbs, Ruback, Frady, Hopper, & Sgoritas, 1988).

The evolutionary selection for high testosterone in men and its correlated traits is a promising hypothesis. Daitzman and Zuckerman (1980) found that an extraversion/sensation seeking factor included heterosexual experience and number of sexual partners. In this study the low sensation seeking young men had average levels of testosterone, but the high sensation seekers had high levels relative to their age group. A study of a polygynous African society found that extraversion was related to both high testosterone and polygynous marriage and number of offspring in men (Alvergne, Jokela, Faurie, & Lummaa, 2010; Alvergne, Jokela, & Lummaa, 2010). Apart from a high sexual drive, physical risk-taking in men may be attractive to women (Ronay & von Hippel, 2010). Young men performing skateboarding in front of an attractive female observer performed more successfully but also had more crash landings than when doing their stunts in front of male observers (Ronay & von Hippel, 2010). Apparently the men were using physical risk-taking as a sexual display strategy.

Cortisol is a hormone produced by the adrenal cortex. It is the end product of hormones produced in the hypothalamus and pituitary gland (HYPAC) system, and is reactive to stress both as trait and state. For instance, monkeys reared with peers have higher cortisol levels than those reared by their biological mothers. Cortisol rises in these monkeys when they are briefly separated from their peers or mothers. Cortisol is elevated in depression in humans, and rises in anxiety disorder patients given anxiogenic drugs. Cortisol is related to neuroticism as a trait in some but not all studies (Zobel et al., 2004). Early morning levels of salivary cortisol were higher among individuals high in neuroticism than for those low in neuroticism (Portella, Harmer, Flint, Cowen, & Goodwin, 2005). High levels of cortisol in the cerebrospinal fluid have been found among individuals scoring at the low end of a factor defined at the high end by sensation seeking, antisocial personality, and hypomania in normals (Ballenger et al., 1983; Zuckerman, 1984). Low cortisol is common among individuals high on these traits. Both testosterone and cortisol are part trait and part state in that they are moderately reliable over time but are influenced by immediate experiences. Stress tends to lower testosterone and raise levels of cortisol. Victory in competitive contests and sexual stimulation raises testosterone (Archer, 2006). These kinds of state effects can confound trait studies, particularly if testosterone or cortisol levels are assessed on only one occasion or day.

The neuropeptide oxytocin (OXT) regulates a wide range of behavior related to social interaction, including sexual arousal and behavior, pair bonding, maternal care, defensive aggression, anxiety, and coping with stress (Neumann, 2008). Although most of the research has been done with nonhuman species, preliminary work with humans suggests similar kinds of behavioral effects to those found in animals, and possible relationships with basic personality traits (Insel, 1997). Little work has been done on direct correlations between OXT and personality traits, but some ingenious experiments have observed the effects of OXT on behaviors suggestive of the traits.

Sociability in pair bonding in monogamous species, like prairie voles, is related to OXT production. In females OXT facilitates the birth process and lactation, vital functions in infant survival. OXT shows little effect on sexual arousal in men, although some effect on orgasm (Krüger et al., 2003). However, high reported spousal support in cohabiting couples has been related to higher plasma OXT in men and women during baseline and following warm physical and emotional contact between them (Grewen, Girdler, Amico, & Light, 2005). Warm contact has been shown to increase OXT in women and decrease cortisol in both men and women (Grewen et al., 2005). Among women, the period of warm contact lowered systolic blood pressure, and this decrease showed a positive association with spousal support assessed before the experiment.

Men who receive OXT intranasally appear to manifest less increase in cortisol and anxiety in response to psychosocial stress compared to their counterparts who receive placebo (Heinrichs, Baumgarten, Kirschbaum, & Ehlert, 2003). This stress reduction effect of OXT interacts with social support, so that men who received social support and OXT had the least cortisol and anxiety reactions to stress. At least one fMRI study has shown that OXT reduces activation of the amygdala and autonomic and behavioral manifestation of fear in response to fearful or angry faces (Kirsch et al., 2005).

Two different studies investigated the influence of OXT on trust and risk-taking, using decision making in a trust game with monetary stakes (Kosfeld, Heinrichs, Zak, Fischbacher, & Fehr, 2005). In the trust experiment, money was invested using an intermediary, whereas in the risk experiment, there was no intermediary and investment depended only on the subject's risk-taking proclivity. OXT increased the fund transfer in the trust experiment but not in the risk study. Trust is a subtrait of agreeableness in the Big Five (Costa & McCrae, 1992), whereas risk-taking, including financial risk-taking (Harlow & Brown, 1990; Sciortino, Huston, & Spencer, 1987), is an expression of sensation seeking (Zuckerman, 1994, 2007) in the Alternative Five.

Extrapolating from these experimental studies, we might predict that OXT is involved in extraversion or sociability, neuroticism (less anxiety and stress response), and agreeableness (trust), but not in sensation seeking, activity, conscientiousness, or openness to experience. However, at this time it is difficult to predict from the specific experimental situations to the broader traits that may be related to OXT.

Psychophysiology

Eysenck's (1967) early theory proposed that extraversion was based on low arousal of the reticulocortical system, and neuroticism was based on high arousal of the "limbic system" and its efferents in the autonomic nervous system. Extraverts and introverts were thought to differ in their "optimal levels" of stimulation and arousal. Introverts feel and function better at low levels of arousal, whereas extraverts feel and function better at high levels of arousal. Before the 1980s, brain arousal in humans was measured by the EEG from scalp electrodes and cortical response from evoked potentials (EPs) derived from averaging EEG potentials in reaction to stimuli. Beginning in the 1980s new methods of brain imaging were developed. Zuckerman (1969; Zuckerman, Kolin, Price, & Zoob, 1964) independently adopted a theory similar to Eysenck's to explain individual differences in sensation seeking. However, in subsequent revisions of the theory, the biological basis of sensation seeking was attributed to an optimal level of arousability rather than tonic arousal (Zuckerman, 1979), and then to a more specific optimal level of catecholamine system activity (Zuckerman, 1994).

Reviews of studies using EEG to measure arousal conclude that extraversion is only very weakly or inconsistently related to arousal when the EEG is measured under resting conditions, that is with eyes closed and minimal external stimulation (De Pascalis, 2004; Gale, 1983; Stelmack, 1990; Stelmack & Rammsayer, 2008; Zuckerman, 2005, 2011). Most of the studies reviewed used relatively small samples, but two studies that relied on larger samples found small yet significant correlations between extraversion and slow-wave delta activity (Matthews & Amelang, 1993; Tran et al., 2006). These effects were found only for the delta activity and were not found in the alpha band most frequently used as an index of arousal in other studies.

Gale (1983) hypothesized that the relationship between low cortical arousal and extraversion would be found only in conditions of "moderate arousal," operationalized as a condition requiring opening and closing of eyes on command as contrasted with eyes closed. Zuckerman (2011) compared results in more recent studies comparing eyes closed conditions with those alternating eyes open and closed. Three studies supported the hypothesis and two did not. Most other studies have used more complex situations to define moderate arousal, such as positive and negative affect pictures (Gale, Edwards, Morris, Moore, & Forrester, 2001).

With the advent of brain-imaging technology in the 1980s it was hoped that the new methods would yield less equivocal data on the arousal hypothesis. The first study using brain-imaging technology (Mathew, Weinman, & Barr, 1984) using 33 female participants and measuring cerebral blood flow (CBF) found relatively strong evidence for Eysenck's prediction. Extraversion was negatively correlated with CBF in all cortical brain areas, and neuroticism correlated with none. Subsequent studies, for example, Haier (2004), Haier, Sokolski, Katz, and Buchsbaum (1987), found the CBF measure of arousal correlated with extraversion in more specific cortical areas including the frontal and temporal lobes. But Haier et al., as well as some others, also found relationships between extraversion and brain activation in striate and limbic areas like the cingulate gyrus and the amygdala. Studies using the advanced fMRI technology found a relationship between extraversion and amygdaloid response to pictures of happy faces but not to angry or fearful faces (Canli, Sivers, Whifield, Giotlib, & Gabriel, 2002). Extraversion is related to general positive affect, and a trait of positive emotions is included as a facet of extraversion in both the Costa and McCrae (1992) Big Five and the recent factor/facet measure of the Alternative Five (Aluja, Kuhlman, & Zuckerman, 2010). Gray's reinforcement sensitivity theory (Corr, 2008) specifies that sensitivity to signals of reward is characteristic of extraversion or impulsivity, in contrast to Eysenck's theory of extraversion and general arousal. A meta-analysis of studies of performance in reinforced tasks showed that high impulsivity is related to stronger effects of reward, whereas trait anxiety is related to stronger effects of punishment (Leue & Beauducel, 2008).

The problem with the concept of cortical arousal is that it is based on a presumably resting or nonstimulating situation, whereas there is always some kind of internal stimulation in the waking state. The experimental situation of sitting or lying down while one's brain waves are recorded is novel for most people, and may be either anxiety provoking or boredom inducing, either producing some kind of arousal. Arousal levels may vary with these internal states, producing more or less arousal.

The differences due to personality may depend on some particular level of arousal, as Gale (1983) pointed out for extraversion.

The event-related potential (ERP) is a measure of arousability that allows us to specify and control stimulus intensity. The stimulus is usually a tone or light flash whose intensity may be constant or varied. Variation of stimulus intensity allows for measure of the interaction effects, if any. The EEG is averaged over many events to provide an average EP for a particular stimulus. Averaging cancels out the "noise" and provides a clear EP amplitude specific to the stimulus. Typical peaks at different times after the stimulus presentation identify different levels of brain processing. There is some individual variation in the latency of peaks, with shorter latencies indicative of more sensitive response. Peaks prior to 50 msecs after the stimulus originate in subcortical processing, starting in the brain stem and moving up to the thalamus. A peak at about 100 msec poststimulus (N1) represents the first cortical impact of the stimulus related to stimulus intensity. A later peak at 300 msec (P3) is related to qualitative features like the novelty of the stimulus or how frequently it has been presented in a series.

Stelmack and Wilson (1982) first observed that introverts had shorter latency brainstem auditory evoked potentials than introverts and this finding has been replicated several times by other investigators (e.g., Cox-Fuenzalida, Gilliland, & Swickert, 2001). Introverts have also been found to have higher amplitude auditory ERs, peaks developing 100 to 200 msec (cortical) after the stimulus, particularly when the tones are of moderate intensity and lower frequency (Stelmack & Rammsayer, 2008).

Introverts and extraverts differ in response to auditory "oddball effects." P3 is amplified in response to stimuli infrequently presented ("odd balls") within a series of standard stimuli. Introverts typically have stronger amplitude responses to such stimuli. However, the P3 amplitude may also vary in response to intense stimuli (Gonsalvez, Barry, Rushby, & Polich, 2007). Background noise may also affect personality variations of P3 response. Brocke, Tasche, and Beauducel (1997) found that intensity of white noise backgrounds to a visual vigilance task interacted with extraversion: Introverts had stronger P3 amplitudes at lower noise intensities, whereas at higher intensities the extraverts had stronger P3 responses. A stimulus intensity interaction with personality has also been found for EPs and sensation seeking.

The augmenting-reducing function of the ERP represents the interaction between stimulus intensity and the amplitude of the EP as an individual difference measure.

EP reactions to a range of auditory or visual stimuli are recorded and the relationship between the intensity of the stimulus and the EP response may be expressed as the slope (Buchsbaum, 1971). Augmenters are characterized by a positive slope, that is, the ER amplitude rises steadily with the increase in stimulus intensity. However, some individuals, referred to as reducers, show little increase of EP amplitude with increase in intensity, and even a reduction in EP at the higher intensities.

Zuckerman, Murtaugh, and Siegel (1974) showed that augmenters on a visual ERP tended to be high sensation seekers, whereas reducers tended to be low sensation seekers. This finding has been fairly replicable, particularly for the auditory EP (Zuckerman, 1990). The relationship was found for an early cortical component of the EP (P1/N1), but Brocke (2004) found that both the experience seeking subscale of the Sensation Seeking Scale (SSS; Zuckerman, Eysenck, & Eysenck, 1978) and the impulsive sensation seeking subscale of the Zuckerman-Kuhlman Personality Questionnaire (ZKPQ; Zuckerman, Kuhlman, Joireman, Teta, & Kraft, 1993) correlated positively with the slope of the auditory EP for N1 and P2 at several cortical locations (Brocke, Beauducel, & Tasche, 1999). Other studies have related the ER-stimulus intensity slope to impulsivity (Barratt, Pritchard, Faulk, & Brandt, 1987; Carillo-de-la-Pena, & Barratt, 1993).

The Augmenter-Reducer (A-R) model has also been used in cats and rats. In cats, EP augmenters are more exploratory, active, and reactive to novel stimuli (Saxton, Siegel, & Lukas, 1987). In operant conditioning studies the augmenter cats performed more poorly than reducer cats on a schedule requiring a low rate of response for reward. Augmenter cats were less able to inhibit a maximal rate of response. An augmenter strain of rats was more exploratory, aggressive, willing to drink alcohol, and more active in seeking high intensity rewards by hypothalamic self-stimulation (Siegel & Driscoll 1996; Siegel, Sisson, & Driscoll, 1993).

Eysenck (1967) linked cortical arousal primarily to extraversion, and arousal in limbic system structures to neuroticism, but conceded that collaterals from the limbic system to the reticulocortical ascending tracts could activate some cortical arousal secondary to limbic arousal. Gray's theory (1982) suggested that this kind of cortical arousal would happen only when stimulated by negative stimuli or conditions. Early EEG studies showed no significant associations between EEG and neuroticism (Gale, 1981). Later studies, however, using improved EEG methodology, found an association between beta wave (fast waves associated with anxiety, and stress)

arousal and neuroticism in the frontal and temporal cortex (Ivashenko, Berus, Zhuravlev, & Myamlim, 1999; Knyazen, Slobodskaya, & Wilson, 2002).

Using fMRI responses to negative and positive emotionally provoking pictures, Canli et al. (2001) found that neuroticism was associated with greater activation by negative stimulation relative to positive stimulation in left frontal and temporal brain regions. These results support Gray's theory, although the activation did not occur in limbic areas postulated to be the source of anxiety in both Eysenck's and Gray's theories. Canli (2006) found that negative emotional reactions, but not trait neuroticism, were associated with anterior cingulate response to negative emotional stimuli, thus underscoring the importance of the distinction between trait and state anxiety.

Because trait neuroticism is associated with anxiety, peripheral measures of the sympathetic branch of the autonomic nervous system, like heart rate, blood pressure and skin conductance, were expected to correlate with trait neuroticism. Indeed, these measures are usually elevated in patients with some types of anxiety disorders (Insel, Zahn, & Murphy, 1985; Kelly, 1980). In nonpatients, however, neuroticism is not associated with physiological measures, either in basal states or in stressful conditions (Fahrenberg, 1987; Myrtek, 1984; Naveteur & Baque, 1987). The absence of a connection between neuroticism and autonomic arousal in nonpatients may reflect a difference between two types of anxiety disorders, panic disorder (PD) and generalized anxiety disorder (GAD). PD is characterized by periodic attacks of autonomic hyperarousal, where the cognitive fear that develops is a consequence rather than a cause of the panic attacks. The person with PD fears the unpleasant sensations during panic attacks and develops catastrophic fears in anticipation of their consequences. In contrast, the person with GAD is bothered by anticipations of more general negative events (worries) and does not show intense autonomic arousal, except for a chronic high level of muscle tension. GAD is also highly associated with depression. High levels of neuroticism are found in both disorders. The nonpatient who scores high in neuroticism is more like the person with GAD, that is, more in cognitive dysfunction than autonomic dyscontrol.

Anger and hostility are considered part of neuroticism in the Big Five, whereas aggression is regarded as the obverse of another major factor, agreeableness. In the Alternative Five, anger, hostility, and verbal and physical aggression are all part of one common factor: aggression-hostility (Zuckerman, 2002; Zuckerman et al., 1993). Physical aggression and threat are important traits in other social species maintaining dominance, social rank, and sexual selection. The "top dog" fights off competitors and maintains dominance through aggression or threat of aggression. In some species he accounts for most of the reproduction in a band, as in the "harem" of dominant male gorillas.

Direct expression of aggression is a function of areas in the amgdala and hypothalamus. Inhibition of aggression is mediated by the prefrontal and orbitofrontal cortex and anterior cingulate cortex (Davidson, Putnam, & Larson, 2000; Emery & Amaral, 2000). Within aggressive human groups, some are impulsively aggressive whereas others are characterized by premeditative aggression. The former have weaker executive control or capacity to inhibit aggression, reflected in weaker orbitofrontal activity (Lijf-fijt, Swann, & Moeller, 2008). Aggressive persons in general have less activity than controls in the anterior cingulate cortex. The P3 amplitude of the ERP is lower in aggressive persons than controls, and is weaker in impulsive compared with premeditated aggressive individuals. The serotonin metabolite 5-HIAA is negatively related to impulsive aggression in free-ranging monkeys (Higley, Suomi, & Linnoila, 1992) and humans (Coccaro, 1998). The norepinephrine (NE) metabolite MHPG is positively related to aggression in monkeys (Higley et al., 1992) possibly because of the role of NE in emotional arousal.

As with sensation seeking, aggression is an approach motive in which the outcome reflects the relationship between instigators and inhibitory factors. The sensitivity to instigation is associated with the lack of inhibition in the impulsive aggressive individual, although the premeditated aggressive individual also shows some weakness of inhibition in brain and neurotransmitters.

In summary, the modern period of biological approaches to personality began with Eysenck's (1967) arousal theory of extraversion based on individual differences in optimal levels of arousal in the reticulocortical feedback system. Behavioral and psychophysiological research conducted to test the theory yielded largely inconsistent findings. Subsequently, the augmenting-reducing paradigm incorporated stimulus intensities into a combined measure dependent on individual differences in the magnitude of the EP in relation to increases in stimulus intensity. The main difference between high and low sensation seekers occurred at the higher intensities of stimulation, where individuals high on sensation seeing (particularly in the form of disinhibition or impulsivity) tended to respond more strongly whereas more behaviorally restrained low sensation seekers tended to reduce, demonstrating a cortical inhibition effect. Major advances

have been made by Gray (1982, 1987, 1991) using a "bottom-up" rather than Eysenck's "top-down" approach. Working from neuropsychological experimental studies of rats, Gray has proposed behavioral approach and inhibition mechanisms underlying human personality and psychopathology. As documented in Corr's (2008) edited volume, recent developments have included questionnaires based on the basic behavioral trait mechanisms and their influences in sensitivities to stimuli associated with positive and negative reinforcement and punishment.

CONSILIENCE

The term *consilience* was used by Wilson (1998) to describe the combination of knowledge across disciplines to create a common background of explanation. He viewed the goal of science as the reduction of complex to simple explanation. Can complex personality description be reduced to explanation at the biological level? There are many obstacles to such reductionism. For one thing there is often a two-way causal effect. Even at the most basic genetic level, environmental or internal biological events can influence the release of genetic action. Although we may establish correlations between behavior and brain traits, the direction of causation is not clear. Moreover, there is no simple one-to-one correspondence between personality traits and the biological mechanisms that underlie them. Evolution did not result in personality traits but in differences in complex biological systems.

There is unlikely to be one gene, brain area, neurotransmitter, enzyme, hormone, or physiological reaction that is specific to one personality trait. Each biological or brain usually has more than one function and more than one biological system operates in one behavioral trait function. For instance, approach behavior is determined not only by systems controlling approach but by other systems determining inhibition.

This is not to say the whole brain is involved in all personality traits and the behavior traits on which they are based. That would lead us back to the nihilism of Skinner, who viewed the brain as a locked "black box" whose functions were irrelevant to stimulus-response science. We now have the tools to open the box in humans and observe the circuits in action (fMRIs). "Bottom-up" studies based on experiments in nonhuman species cannot be assumed to reflect the same mechanisms as in humans, but they can tell us where to look when we have the tools to do so. Evolution and genetic changes move slowly, but it is reasonable to assume that changes are built on older but still operative functions.

SUMMARY AND INTEGRATION

To this point we have reviewed correlative results from one level of biological function to four basic personality traits. The time has come to see if there are patterns among the diverse findings. Not all of the findings discussed thus far are based on sufficiently replicated results, unless one considers analogous results using nonhuman species as replication. Even when consistent, biological traits account for only a small part of the variance of human personality traits.

Table 2.3 summarizes the more replicable results with primary attention to the findings for humans. Many of the results are based on preliminary brain imaging findings. Some, like those for oxytocin, are based primarily on animal experiments, although there is a growing experimentation on humans suggestive of possible personality trait associations. Other findings, like those for MAO-B, are based on assumed relationships between peripheral measures and brain measures, although there is not yet evidence for such relationships. Still other findings, like the findings for MAO-B, are based on an assumed relationship between genetic markers (polymorphisms) and the biological function they are assumed to control. Given the limitations of this shaky structure, let us see what we can build upon it.

The four broad personality traits have been divided into three approach traits, and one withdrawal trait (neuroticism/anxiety). Wilson, Barrett, and Gray (1989)

constructed a questionnaire for Gray's three dimensions based on the specific behavioral traits in Gray's "bottom-up" theory. Fight (aggression) and approach were positively correlated, contrary to the theory, which hypothesized separate factors. Gray's theory also suggested a distinction between passive and active avoidance, but Wilson et al.'s (1989) results showed a positive correlation between flight (active avoidance) and passive avoidance, and a negative correlation between approach and active avoidance. Therefore the withdrawal-avoidance dimension, here identified with neuroticism, is closer to Schneirla's (1959) concept than to Gray's Behavioral Inhibition System. This shows the problems in applying systems based on animals to humans.

In this chapter I have questioned the idea that each personality trait is associated with a distinctive biological trait. This is seen most clearly with testosterone, which correlates with all four traits, positively with the three approach traits and negatively with the withdrawal-avoidance trait. In the public mind testosterone is most closely associated with aggression, but it would be more correct to describe the high testosterone male as extraverted, impulsively sensation seeking, nonconscientious, but emotionally stable. The aggression connection is clearest in criminals and psychopaths.

As previously noted (see Table 2.2) there is a remarkable consistency in heritabilities of the four major traits in three different systems. The extremes are sensation seeking and extraversion at the high end, and agreeableness

TABLE 2.3 Biological Levels for Four Traits

	Approach			Withdrawal
Personality Traits	Extraversion	Conscientiousness/ Impulsivity/ Sensation Seeking	Agreeableness/Aggression	Neuroticism Anxiety
Heritability*	.49	.46/.49/.58	.40/.42	.45
Enzymes		MAO/B (-Imp/SS)	MAO-A (-Agg)	
Neurotransmitters	Dopamine	Dopamine Serotonin (−)	Norepinephrine Serotonin (−)	Norepinephrine
Hormones	Testosterone Oxytocin (?)	Testosterone Cortisol (−)	Testosterone Oxytocin (Aggression-) (?)	Testosterone (−) Cortisol Oxytocin (Anxiety-)
Psychophysiology/ Neuropsychology	EP Arousability Prefrontal, Temporal Cortex (−)	EP Augmenting-Reducing (A-R) Cortex (A- Impulsivity/ Sensation Seeking)	R Amygdala and Hippocampus, Prefrontal and Orbitofrontal cortex (−)	Arousability Prefrontal and Temporal Cortex in response to negative stimuli

*Heritabilities for extraversion, conscientiousness, agreeableness, and neuroticism based on median values in Johnson et al. (2008). Those for impulsivity, sensation seeking, and aggression based on median values in Zuckerman (2007).
A minus (−) sign indicates a negative relationship between the personality trait and the biological trait. In the absence of the minus sign the relationship is a positive one. A "?" indicates that the association is one inferred from behavioral correlates rather than a direct one with personality trait measures.

and aggression at the low end of the .4 to .6 range. This is what might be expected if personality traits are polygenetic and based upon many genes.

Some specificity is also obvious. Impulsivity and sensation seeking are related to low MAO-B, possibly a cause of dopaminergic dysregulation, whereas aggression is related to low MAO-A, probably due to dysregulation of serotonin and norepinephrine. The fact that norepinephrine has some role in both aggression and neuroticism may be due to the fact that the emotional components of aggression (anger and hostility) are actually facets of neuroticism in systems other than the Alternative Five.

Weak serotonergic system reactivity may be a factor in disinhibited and impulsive sensation seeking and aggression. The involvement of serotonin in neuroticism or trait anxiety is more problematic. Cloninger (1987) regards serotonin as the main neurotransmitter in harm avoidance, his version of neuroticism/anxiety. Gray, however, sees the role of serotonin as secondary to that of norepinephrine. Norepinephrine is involved in the sensitization to signals of punishment and the experience of anxiety, whereas serotonin is involved in the output of the BIS, resulting in behavioral inhibition.

Cortisol is a hormone that is increased in neuroticism, particularly under stress. However, sensation seekers show a weakened cortisol system even in response to stress. This is another case where too much of a biochemical is associated with anxious arousal, and too little with disinhibition or impulsivity. Oxytocin release is stimulated by warm social contact between mother and child and between spousal partners. Its effects are opposite to those of cortisol, reducing cortisol, amygdala activity, autonomic arousal and anxiety in stressful situations. Its behavioral effects suggest involvement in extraversion (warm emotions), agreeableness, and reduced trait anxiety.

Older psychophysiological work was largely done using EEG for cortical arousal, and peripheral measures like heart rate, blood pressure, and skin conductance for autonomic arousal. Although theories were based on the idea of a generalized arousal factor, studies tended to show less generality of such measures and functions specific to areas of brain and subcortical loci. Much of the more recent work uses brain imaging methods rather than the EEG. Using either method, a common conclusion is that brain arousability is a function of stimuli varying in intensity, novelty and emotional valence, interacting with personality.

Sensation seeking is related to the functional relationship of stimulus intensity to strength of the visual or auditory EP, or "augmenting-reducing." This is particularly true for disinhibition. The A-R function itself is related to impulsive and novelty seeking behavior in other species. The locus of the A-R function is the cortex itself, and not in lower centers like the thalamus that regulate stimulus input (Siegel & Driscoll, 1996). Both correlational and experimental studies link augmenting of the EP to low levels of serotonin or its metabolite (von Knorring & Johansson, 1980; von Knorring & Perris, 1981). This suggests that we might look for serotonergic pathways in the cortex regulating arousal. Dopaminergic reactivity is strong in both extraversion and sensation seeking, and could account for some of the minor relationship between these two personality traits. Evidence from studies of humans is less conclusive, but the findings from studies of rats suggest that the dopaminergic connection with novelty seeking lies in the nucleus accumbens, the reward center in the ventral striatum.

Studies of cats find specific nuclei in the amygdala where aggressive "rage" reactions may be triggered by stimulation, whereas other amygdala nuclei inhibit these reactions. Lesions of the amygdala reduce aggression, rage, and emotional reactions in general. Stimulation of septal areas and prefrontal cortex also inhibit aggressive reactions. Neuroimaging studies of humans find some confirmation of results in studies of other species. Aggressive individuals are higher than controls on activity of the amygdala and show lower activity in the orbitofrontal cortex and anterior cingulate cortex (Lijffijt et al., 2008). They are also lower on amplitudes of the N2 and P3 components of the ERP. Aggressive individuals have many of these indicators in common with extraverts or impulsive sensation seekers.

The idea of a general approach trait finds some justification in terms of personality trait characteristics with some common biological bases. These traits include extraversion, sensation seeking, impulsivity, agreeableness and aggression. The opposing tendency, withdrawal-avoidance, includes primarily neuroticism and its associated negative emotions, particularly anxiety and depression. The conflict between risky approach and caution or withdrawal is a primary source of individual differences for all species. Human memory and foresight based on unique cognitive capacities extend these further into the past and forward into the future. The forebrain, most highly developed in the human species, is the source of executive control, although subcortical areas also participate.

The basic emotions were encoded in brain structures early in the mammalian line of evolution and formed the basis for more complex traits. Anger is a basis for impulsive aggression, fear for the anxious anticipations of neuroticism, depression for the protective withdrawal of mood disorder, and joy for the positive anticipations of reward leading to approach behavior. As Gray (1991) noted, sensitivities or biases in stimulus evaluation are the initial expressions of personality differences. However, it is not just sensitivities to stimuli associated with reward and punishment, but reactions to differences in intensity and novelty that determine approach, inhibition, or withdrawal. Psychophysiology explores these differences. Intensity and novelty of stimulation are important qualities influencing approach or preferences in behavior. Valence of stimuli or emotional association is more crucial in neuroticism.

One can study personality without regard for its biological bases just as one may drive an automobile without an understanding of the engine that transmits your mechanical instructions to the motor mechanisms. Most of us leave the latter to our mechanics. But just as a science of automobiles requires more than a driver's manual, personality science requires an understanding at all levels and the significance of their connections.

REFERENCES

Aluja, A., & Garcia, L. F. (2005). Sensation seeking, sexual curiosity and testosterone in inmates. *Neuropsychobiology, 51*, 28–33.

Aluja, A., Kuhlman, M., & Zuckerman, M. (2010). Development of the Zuckerman-Kuhlman-Aluja personality questionnaire (ZKA-PQ): A factor/facet version of the Zuckerman-Kuhlman personality questionnaire (ZKPQ). *Journal of Personality Asssessment, 92*, 416–431.

Alvergne, A., Jokela, M., Faurie, C., & Lummaa, V. (2010). Personality and testosterone in men from a high fertility population. *Personality and Individual Differences, 49*, 840–844.

Alvergne, A., Jokela, M., & Lummaa (2010). Personality and reproductive success in a high fertility human population. *Proceedings of the National Academy of Sciences, 107*, 11745–11750.

Archer, J. (1991). The influence of testosterone on human aggression. *British Journal of Psychology, 82*, 1–28.

Archer, J. (2006). Testosterone and human aggression: An evaluation of the challenge hypothesis. *Neuroscience and Biobehavioral Reviews, 30*, 319–345.

Bachner-Melman, R., Zohar, A. H., Bacon-Shnoor, N., Elizur, Y., Nemanov, L., Elizur, Y.,...Ebstein, R. P. (2005). Link between vasopressin receptor AVPR1A promoter region microsatellite and measures of social behavior in humans. *Journal of Individual Differences, 26*, 2–10.

Ballenger, J. C., Post, R. M., Jimerson, D. C., Lake, C. R., Murphy, D. L., Zuckerman, M., & Cronin, C. (1983). Biochemical correlates of personality traits in normals: An exploratory study. *Personality and Individual Diffferences, 4*, 615–625.

Barratt, E. S., Pritchard, W. S., Faulk, D. M., & Brandt, M. E. (1987). The relationship between impulsiveness subtraits, trait anxiety, and visual N100-augmenting-reducing: A topographic analysis. *Personality and Individual Differences, 8*, 43–51.

Ben Zion, I. Z., Tessler, R., Cohen, L., Lerer, E., Raz, Y., Bachner-Melman, R.,...Ebstein, R. P. (2006). Polymorphisms in the dopamine D4 receptor gene (DRD4) contribute to individual differences in sexual behavior: desire, arousal, and sexual function. *Molecular Psychiatry, 11*, 782–786.

Boomsma, D. I., de Geus, E. J. C., van Baal, G. C. M., & Koopmans, J. R. (1999). A religious upbringing reduces the influence of genetic factors on disinhibition: Evidence for interaction between genotype and environment on personality. *Twin Research, 2*, 115–125.

Brocke, B. (2004). The multilevel approach in sensation seeking: Potentials and findings of a four level research program. In R. M. Stelmack (Ed.), *On the psychobiology of personality: Essays in honor of Marvin Zuckerman* (pp. 267–293). Amsterdam, The Netherlands: Elsevier.

Brocke, B., Beauducel, A., & Tasche, K. G. (1999). Biopsychological bases and behavioral correlates of sensation seeking: Contributions to a multilevel validation. *Personality and Individual Differences, 26*, 1103–1123.

Brocke, B., Tasche, K. G., & Beauducel, A. (1997). Biopsychological foundations of extraversion: Differential effort reactivity and state control. *Personality and Individual Differences, 22*, 447–458.

Brunner, H. G., Nelen, M., Breakefield, X. O., Rogers, H. H., & Van Oost, B. A. (1993). Abnormal behavior associated with a point mutation in the structural gene for monoamine oxidase-A. *Science, 262*, 578–580.

Buchsbaum, M. S. (1971). Neural events and the psychophysical law. *Science, 172*, 502.

Buss, A. H., & Plomin, R. (1975). *A temperament theory of personality development.* New York, NY: Wiley.

Canli, T. (2006). Genomic imaging of extraversion. In T. Canli (Ed.), *Biology of personality* (pp. 116–132). New York, NY: Guilford Press.

Canli, T., Sivers, H., Whitfield, S. L., Gotlib, I. H., & Gabrieli, J. D. E. (2002). Amygdala response to happy faces as a function of extraversion. *Science, 296*, 2191.

Canli, T., Zhao, Z., Desmond, J. E., Kang, E., Gross, J., & Gabrieli, J. D. E. (2001). An fMRI study of personality influences on brain reactivity to emotional stimuli. *Behavioral Neuroscience, 115*, 33–42.

Carillo-de-la-Pena, M. T., & Barratt, E. S. (1993). Impulsivity and the ERP augmenting/reducing. *Personality and Individual Differences, 15*, 25–32.

Caspi, A., Hariri, A. R., Holmes, A., Uher, R., & Moffitt, T. E. (2010). Genetic sensitivity to the environment: The case of the serotonin transporter gene and its implications for studying complex diseases and traits. *American Journal of Psychiatry, 167*, 509–527.

Caspi, A., McClay, J., Moffitt, T. E., Mill, J., Martin, J., Craig, I. W., ...Poulton, R. (2002). Role of genotype in the cycle of violence in maltreated children. *Science, 297*, 851–854.

Cloninger, C. R. (1987). A systematic method for clinical description and classification of personality variants. *Archives of General Psychiatry, 44*, 573–588.

Coccaro, E. F. (1998). Central neurotransmitter function in human aggression and impulsivity. In M. Maes & E. F. Coccro (Eds.), *Neurobiology and clinical views on aggression and impulsivity* (pp. 143–168). Chichester, UK: Wiley.

Corr, P. J. (2008) (Ed.). *The reinforcement sensitivity theory of personality.* Cambridge, UK: Cambridge University Press.

Costa, P. T. Jr., & McCrae, R. R. (1992). *Revised NEO Personality Inventory (NEO-PI-R).* Odessa, FL: Psychological Assessment Resources.

Cox-Fuenzalida, L.-E, Gilliland, K., & Swickert, R. J. (2001). Congruency of the relationship between extraversion and the brain-stem auditory evoked response based on the EPI versus the EPQ. *Journal of Research in Personality, 35*, 117–126.

Dabbs, J. M. Jr. (2000). *Heroes, rogues, and lovers.* New York, NY: McGraw-Hill.

Dabbs, J. M. Jr., Carr, T. S., Frady, R. I., & Riad, J. F. (1995). Testosterone, crime and misbehavior among 692 prison inmates. *Personality and Individual Differences, 18,* 627–633.

Dabbs, J. M. Jr., Ruback, R. B., Frady, R. L., Hopper, C. H., & Sgoritas, D. S. (1988). Saliva testosterone and criminal violence among women. *Personality and Individual Differences, 9,* 269–275.

Daitzman, R. J., & Zuckerman, M. (1980). Disinhibitory sensation seeking, personality, and gonadal hormones. *Personality and Individual Differences, 1,* 103–110.

Davidson, R. J., Putnam, K. M., & Larson, C. L. (2000). Dysfunction in the neural circuitry of emotion regulation: A possible prelude to violence. *Science, 289,* 591–594.

Dellu, F., Piazza, P. V., Mayo, W., Le Moal, M., & Simon, H. (1996). Novelty-seeking in rats-Biobehavioral characteristics and possible relationship with the sensation seeking trait in man. *Neuropsychobiology, 34,* 136–145.

De Pascalis, V. (2004). On the psychophysiology of extraversion. In R. M. Stelmack (Ed.), *On the psychobiology of personality: Essays in honor of Marvin Zuckerman* (pp. 205–327). Oxford, UK: Elsevier.

Depue, R. A. (1995). Neurobiological factors in personality and depression. *European Journal of Personality, 9,* 413–439.

Depue, R. A., & Collins, P. F. (1999). Neurobiology of the structure of personality: Dopamine facilitation of incentive motivation and extraversion. *Behavioral and Brain Sciences, 22,* 491–569.

Ebstein, R. P. (2006). The molecular genetic architecture of human personality. *Molecular Psychiatry, 11,* 427–445.

Ebstein, R. P., Novick, O., Umansky, R., Priel, B., Osher, Y., Blaine, D., ... Belmaker, R. H. (1996). Dopamine D4 receptor (D4DR) exon III polymorphism associated with the human personality trait of novelty seeking. *Nature Genetics, 12,* 78–80.

Emery, N. J., & Amaral, D. G. (2000). The role of the amaydala in primate social cognition. In P. D. Lane & L. Nadal (Eds.), *Cognitive neuroscience of emotion* (pp. 156–191). New York, NY: Oxford University Press.

Eysenck, H. J. (1967). *The biological basis of personality.* Springfield, IL: Charles C. Thomas.

Eysenck, H. J., & Eysenck, S. B. G. (1975). *Manual of the Eysenck Personality Questionnaire.* London, UK: Hodder & Stoughton.

Fahrenberg, J. (1987). Concepts of activation and arousal in the theory of emotionality (neuroticism). A multivariate conceptualization. In J. Strelau & H. J. Eysenck (Eds.), *Personality dimensions and arousal* (pp. 99–120). New York, NY: Plenum Press.

Faraone, S. V., Doyle, A. E., Mick, E., & Biederman, J. (2001). Meta-analysis of the association between the 7-repeat allele of the dopamine D4 receptor gene and the attention-deficit hyperactivity disorder. *American Journal of Psychiatry, 158,* 1052–1057.

Fulker, D. W., Eysenck, S. B. G., & Zuckerman, M. (1980). A genetic and environmental analysis of sensation seeking. *Journal of Research in Personality, 14,* 261–281.

Gale, A. (1981). EEG studies of extraversion-introversion: What is the next step? In R. Lynn (Ed.) *Dimensions of personality: Papers in honour of H. J. Eysenck* (pp. 181–207). Oxford: Permagon.

Gale, A. (1983). Electroencephalographic studies of extraversion-introversion: A case study in the psychophysiology of individual differences. *Personality and Individual Differences, 4,* 371–380.

Gale, A., Edwards, J., Morris, P., Moore, R., & Forrester, D. (2001). Extraversion-introversion, neuroticism-stability, and EEG indicators of positive and negative empathic mood. *Personality and Individual Differences, 30,* 449–461.

Gerra, G., Zaimovic, A., Timpano, M., Zambelli, U., Begarani, M., Marzocchi, G. F., ... Brambilla, F. (2000). Neuroendocrine correlates of the temperament traits in abstinent opiate addicts. *Journal of Substance Abuse, 11,* 337–354

Gonsalvez, C. J., Barry, R. J., Rushby, J. A., & Polich, J. (2007). Target-target interval, intensity and P300 from an auditory single-stimulus task. *Psychophysiology, 44,* 245–250.

Gray, J. A. (1982). *The neuropsychology of anxiety: An enquiry into the functions of the septohippocampal systems.* New York, NY: Oxford University Press.

Gray, J. A. (1987). The neuropsychology of emotion and personality. In S. M. Stahl, S. D. Iverson, & E. C. Goodman (Eds.), *Cognitive neurochemistry* (pp. 171–190). Oxford, UK: Oxford University Press.

Gray, J. A. (1991). The neuropsychology of temperament. In J. Strelau & A. Angleitner (Eds.), *Explorations in temperament: International perspectives on theory and measurement* (pp. 105–128). London, UK: Plenum Press.

Gray, J., & McNaughton, N. (2000). *The neuropsychology of anxiety* (2nd ed.). Oxford, UK: Oxford Univerity Press.

Grewen, K. M., Girdler, S. S., Amico, J., & Light, K. C. (2005). Effects of partner support on resting oxytocin cortisol, norepinephrine, and blood pressure before and after warm partner contact. *Psychosomatic Medicine, 67,* 531–538.

Haier, R. J. (2004). Brain imaging studies of personality: The slow revolution. In R. M. Stelmack (Ed.), *On the psychobiology of personality: Essays in honor of Marvin Zuckerman* (pp. 329–340). Oxford, UK: Elsevier.

Haier, R. J., Sokolski, K., Katz, M., & Buchsbaum, M. S. (1987) The study of personality with positron emission tomography. In J. Strelau & H. J. Eysenck (Eds.), *Personality dimensions and arousal* (pp. 251–267). New York, NY: Plenum.

Hariri, A. R., Mattay, V. S., Tessitore, A., Kolachana, B., Fera, F., Goldman, D., ... Weinberger, D. R. (2002). Serotonin transporter genetic variation and the response of the human amgdala. *Science, 297,* 400–403.

Harlow, W. V., & Brown, K. C. (1990). *The role of risk-tolerance in the asset allocation process: A new perspective.* Charlottesville, VA: Research Foundation of the Institute of Chartered Financial Analysis.

Heinrichs, M., Baumgarten, T., Kirschbaum, C., & Ehlert, U. (2003). Social support and oxytocin interact to suppress cortisol and subjective responses to psychosocial stress. *Biological Psychiatry, 54,* 1389–1398.

Hennig, J., Kroeg, A., Meyer, B., Prochaska, H., Krien, P., Huwe, S., & Netter, P. (1998). Personality correlates of +/− pinodal induced decreases in prolacatin. *Psychopharmacopsychiatry, 31,* 19–24.

Higley, J. D., Suomi, S. J., & Linnoila, M. (1992). A longitudinal study of CSF monoamine metabolite and plasma cortisol concentrations in young rhesus monkeys. *Biological Psychiatry, 32,* 127–145.

Hur, Y.-M., & Bouchard, T. J. Jr. (1997). The genetic correlation between impulsivity and sensation seeking traits. *Behavior Genetics, 27,* 455–463.

Insel, T. R. (1997). A neurobiological basis of social attachment. *American Journal of Psychiatry, 154,* 726–735.

Insel, T. R., Zahn, T., & Murphy, D. L. (1985). Obsessive-compulsive disorder: An anxiety disorder? In A. H. Tuma & J. Maser (Eds.), *Anxiety and the anxiety disorders* (pp. 577–589). Hillsdale, NJ: Erlbaum.

Ivashenko, O. V., Berus, A. V., Zhuravlev, A. B., & Myamlim, V. V. (1999). Individual and typological features of basis personality traits in norms and their EEG correlates. *Human Physiology, 25,* 162–170.

Johnson, A. M., Vernon, P. A., & Feiler, A. R. (2008). Behavior genetic studies of personality: An introduction and review of the results of 50+ years of research. In G. J. Boyle, G. Matthews, & D. H. Saklofske (Eds.), *Personality theory and assessment, Vol. 1 Personality theory and assessment* (pp. 145–173). Los Angeles, CA: Sage.

Kagan, J. (1989). Temperamental contributions to social behavior. *American Psychologist, 44*, 668–674.

Kelly, D. (1980). *Anxiety and emotions*. Springfield, IL: Thomas.

Kirsch, P., Esslinger, C., Chen, Q., Mier, D., Lis, S., Siddhanti, S.,...Meyer-Lindenberg, A. (2005). Oxytocin modulates neural circuitry for social cognition. *Journal of Neuroscience, 25*, 11489–11493.

Knyazen, G. C., Slobodskaya, H. R., & Wilson, G. D. (2002). Psychophysiological correlates of behavioural inhibition and activation. *Personality and Individual Differences, 33*, 647–660.

Kosfeld, M., Heinrichs, M. Zak, P. H., Fischbacher, U., & Ehlert, V. (2005). Ocytocin increases trust in humans. *Nature, 435*, 673–676.

Krüger, T. H. C., Haake, P., Chereath, D., Knapp, W., Janssen, O. E., Exton, N. S.,...Hartmann, U. (2003). Specificity of the neuroendocrine response to orgasm during sexual arousal in men. *Journal of Endocrinology, 177*, 57–64.

Lesch, K. P., Greenberg, B. D., Higley, J. D., Bennett, A., & Murphy, D. L., (2002). Serotonin transporter, personality, and behavior: Toward dissection of gene-gene and gene-environment interaction. In J. Benjamin, R. P. Epstein, & R. H. Belmaker (Eds.). *Molecular genetics and the human personality* (pp. 109–135). Washington, DC: American Psychiatric Publishing.

Lesch, K. P., Bengel, D. Heils, A., Sabol, S. Z., Greenberg, B. D., Petri, S.,...Murphy, D. L. (1996). Association of anxiety-related traits with a polymorphism in the serotonin transporter gene regulatory region. *Science, 274*, 1527–1531.

Leue, A., & Beauducel, A. (2008). A meta-analysis of reinforcement sensitivity theory: On performance parameters. *Personality and Social Psychology Review, 12*, 353–369.

Leyton, M., aan het Rot, M., Booij, L., Beker, G. B., Young, S. N., & Benkelfat, C. (2007). Mood-elevating effects of d-amphetamine and incentive salience: The effect of acute dopamine precursor depletion. *Journal of Psychiatry and Neuroscience, 32*, 129–136.

Lijffijt, M., Swann, A. C., & Moeller, F. G. (2008). Biological substrate of personality traits associated with aggression. In G. J. Boyle, G. Matthews, & D. H. Saklofske (Eds.), *Personality theory and assessment* (Vol. 1, pp. 334–356). Los Angeles, CA: Sage

Lykken, D. T. (1992). Personal communication.

Mathew, R. J., Weinman, M. L., & Barr, D. L. (1984). Personality ad regional cerebral blood flow. *British Journal of Psychiatry, 144*, 529–532.

Matthews, G., & Amelang, M. (1993). Extraversion, arousal theory and performance: A study of individual differences in the EEG. *Personality and Individual Differences, 14*, 347–363.

Munafo, M. R., Yalcin, B., Willis-Owen, S. A., & Flint, J. (2008). Association of the D4 receptor (DRD4) and approach related personality traits: Meta-analysis and new data. *Biological Psychiatry, 63*, 197–206.

Murray, H. A. (1938). *Explorations in personality*. New York, NY: Oxford University Press.

Myrtek, M. (1984). *Constitutional psychophysiology*. London, UK: Academic Press.

Naveteur, J., & Baque, E. F. (1987). Individual differences in electrodermal activity as a function of subject's anxiety. *Personality and Individual Differences, 8*, 615–626.

Netter, P., Hennig, J., & Roed, I. S. (1996). Serotonin and dopamine as mediators of sensation seeking behavior. *Neuropsychobiology, 34*, 155–165.

Neumann, I. D. (2008). Brain oxytocin: A key regulator of emotional and social behaviours in both females and males. *Journal of Nueroendocrinoloy, 20*, 858–865.

Portella, M. J., Harmer, C. J., Flint, J., Cowen, P., & Goodwin, G. M. (2005). Enhanced early morning salivary cortisol in neuroticism. *American Journal of Psychiatry, 162*, 807–809.

Redmond, D. E. Jr. (1985). Neurochemical basis for anxiety disorders: Evidence from drugs which decrease human fear or anxiety. In A. H. Tuma & J. D. Maser (Eds.), *Anxiety and the anxiety disorders* (pp. 533–535). Hillsdale, NJ: Erlbaum.

Redmond, D. E. Jr. (1987). Studies of locus coeruleus in monkeys and hypotheses for neuropsychopharmacology. In H. Y. Meltzer (Ed.), *Psychopharmacology: The third generation of progress* (pp. 967–975). New York, NY: Raven Press.

Redmond, D. E. Jr., Murphy, D. L., & Baulu, J. (1979). Platelet monoamine oxidase activity correlates with social affiliative and agonistic behaviors in normal rhesus monkeys. *Psychosomatic Medicine, 41*, 87–100.

Ronay, R., & von Hippel, W. (2010). The presence of an attractive woman elevates testosterone and physical risk-taking in young men. *Social Psychological and Personality Science, 1*, 57–64.

Rothbart, M. K., Derryberry, D., & Posner, M. I. (1994). A psychobiological approach to the development of temperament. In J. E. Bates & T. D. Wachs (Eds.), *Temperament: Individual differences at the interface of biology and behavior* (pp. 83–116). Washington, DC: American Psychological Association.

Saxton, P. M., Siegel, J., & Lukas, J. H. (1987). Visual evoked potential augmenting-reducing slopes in cats-2. Correlations with behavior. *Personality and Individual Differences, 8*, 511–519.

Schneirla, T. C. (1959). An evolutionary and developmental theory of biphasic processes underlying approach and withdrawal. In M. J. Jones (Ed.), *Nebraska symposium on motivation* (Vol. 7, pp. 1–42). Lincoln, NE: University of Nebraska Press.

Sciortino, J. J., Huston, J. H., & Spencer, R. W. (1987). Perceived risk and the precautionary demand for money. *Journal of Economic Psychology, 8*, 339–346.

Shih, J. C., & Chen, K. (1999). MAO-A and −B gene knock-out mice exhibit distinctly different behavior. *Neurobiology, 7*, 235–246.

Siegel, J., & Driscoll, P. (1996). Recent developments in an animal model of visual evoked potential augmenting/reducing and sensation seeking behavior. *Neuropsychobiology, 34*, 130–135.

Siegel, J., Sisson, D. F., & Driscoll, P. (1993). Augmenting and reducing of visual evoked potentials in Roman high- and low-avoidance rats. *Physiology and Behavior, 54*, 707–711.

Spinelli, S., Schwandt, M. L., Lindell, S. G., Newman, T. K., Heilig, H., Suomi, S. J.,...Barr, C. S. (2007). Association between the recombinant human serotonin transporter linked promoter region polymorphism and behavior in rhesus macaques during a separation paradigm. *Development and Psychopathology: Special Issue, 19*, 977–987.

Stelmack, R. M. (1990). Biological bases of extraversion: Psychophysiological evidence. *Journal of Personality, 58*, 293–311.

Stelmack, R. M., & Rammsayer, T. H. (2008). Psychophysiological and biochemical correlates of personality. In G. J. Boyle, G. Mathews, & D. H. Saklofske (Eds.), *The Sage handbook of personality and assessment* (Vol. 1, pp. 33–55). Los Angeles, CA: Sage.

Stelmack, R. M., & Wilson, K. G. (1982). Extraversion and the effects of frequency and intensity on the auditory brainstem evoked response. *Personality and Individual Differences, 3*, 373–380.

Stoops, W. W., Lile, J. A., Robbins, C. G., Martin, C. A., Rush, C. R., & Kelly, T. H. (2007). The reinforcing, subject rated performance, and cardiovascular effects of d-amphetamine: Influence of sensation seeking status. *Addictive Behaviors, 32*, 1177–1188.

Tellegen, A., & Waller, N. G. (2008). Exploring personality through test construction: Development of the multidimensional personality questionnaire. In G. J. Boyle, G. Mathews, & D. H. Saklofske (Eds.), *Personality theory and assessment* (Vol. 2, pp. 261–292). Los Angeles, CA: Sage.

Thomas, A., & Chess, S. (1977). *Temperament and development.* New York, NY: Bruner/Mazel.

Tran, Y., Craig, A., Boord, P., Connell, K., Cooper, N., & Gordon, E. (2006). Personality traits and their association with resting brain activity. *International Journal of Psychophysiology, 60*, 215–224.

von Knorring, L., & Johansson, F. (1980). Changes in the augmenter-reducer tendency and in pain measures as a result of treatment with a serotonin reuptake inhibition zimelidine. *Neuropsychobiology, 6*, 313–318.

von Knorring, L., & Perris, C. (1981). Biochemistry of the augmenting-reducing response in visual evoked potentials. *Neuropsychobiology, 7*, 1–8.

Wiesbeck, G. A., Wodarz, N., Mauerer, C., Thorne, J., Jakob, F., & Boening, J. (1996). Sensation seeking, alcoholism, and dopamine activity. *European Psychiatry, 11*, 87–92.

Wilson, E. O. (1998). *Consilience: The unity of knowledge*. New York, NY: Vintage Books.

Wilson, G. D., Barrett, P. T., & Gray, J. A. (1989). Human reactions to reward and punishment: A questionnaire examination of Gray's personality theory. *British Journal of Psychology, 80*, 509–515.

Windle, M. (1994). Temperamental inhibition and activation: Hormonal and psychosocial correlates and associated psychiatric disorders. *Personality and Individual Differences, 17*, 61–70.

Zalsman, G., & Apter, A. (2002) Serotonergic metabolism and violence/aggression. In J. Glicksohn (Ed.), *Neurobiology of criminal behavior* (pp. 231–250). Boston, MA: Kluwer.

Zobel, A., Borkow, K., Schulze-Rauschenback, S., von Widdern, O., Metten, M., Pfieffer, U., . . . Maier, W. (2004). High neuroticism and depressive temperament are associated with dysfunctional regulation of the hypothalamic-pituitary-adrenocortical system in healthy volunteers. *Acta Psychiatrica Scandinavica, 109*, 392–399.

Zuckerman, M. (1969). Theoretical formulations: I. In J. P. Zubek (Ed.), *Sensory deprivation: Fifteen years of research* (pp. 407–432). New York, NY: Appleton Century Crofts.

Zuckerman, M. (1979). *Sensation seeking: Beyond the optimal level of arousal*. Hillsdale, NJ: Erlbaum.

Zuckerman, M. (1984). Sensation seeking: A comparative approach to a human trait. *Behavioral and Brain Sciences, 7*, 413–434.

Zuckerman, M. (1990). The psychophysiology of sensation seeking. *Journal of Personality, 58*, 313–345.

Zuckerman, M. (1991). *Psychobiology of personality*. Cambridge, UK: Cambridge University Press.

Zuckerman, M. (1994). *Behavioral expressions and biosocial bases of sensation seeking*. New York, NY: Cambridge University Press.

Zuckerman, M. (1995). Good and bad humors: Biochemical bases of personality and its disorders. *Psychological Science, 6*, 325–332.

Zuckerman, M. (2002). Zuckerman-Kuhlman Personality Questionnaire (ZKPQ): An alernative five-factorial model. In B. De Raad & M. Perugini (Eds.). *Big five assessment* (pp. 277–396). Seattle, WA: Hogrefe & Huber.

Zuckerman, M. (2003). Biological bases of personality. In T. Millon & M. J. Lerner (Eds.), *Handbook of psychology* (Vol. 5, pp. 85–116). Hoboken, NJ: Wiley.

Zuckerman, M. (2005). *Psychobiology of personality, second edition, revised and updated*. New York, NY: Cambridge University Press.

Zuckerman, M. (2007). *Sensation seeking and risky behavior*. Washington, DC: American Psychological Association.

Zuckerman, M. (2011). *Personality science: Three approaches and their applications to the causes and treatment of depression*. Washington, DC: American Psychological Association.

Zuckerman, M., Eysenck, S. B. G., & Eysenck, H. J. (1978). Sensation seeking in England and America: Cross-cultural, age, and sex comparisons. *Journal of Consulting and Clinical Psychology, 46*, 139–149.

Zuckerman, M., Kolin, I., Price, L., & Zoob, I. (1964). Development of a sensation seeking scale. *Journal of Consulting Psychology, 28*, 477–482.

Zuckerman, M., Kuhlman, D. M., & Camac, C. (1988). What lies beyond E and N? Factor analyses of scales believed to measure basic dimensions of personality. *Journal of Personality and Social Psychology, 54*, 96–107.

Zuckerman, M., Kuhlman, D. M., Joireman, J., Teta, P., & Kraft, M. (1993). A comparison of three structural models for personality: The big three, the big five and the alternative five. *Journal of Personality and Social Psychology, 65*, 757–768.

Zuckerman, M., Murtaugh, T. T., & Siegel, J. (1974). Sensation seeking and cortical augmenting-reducing. *Psychophysiology, 11*, 535–542.

CHAPTER 3

Psychodynamic Models of Personality

ROBERT F. BORNSTEIN, CHRISTY A. DENCKLA, AND WEI-JEAN CHUNG

No intellectual discipline exists in a vacuum, but evolves in response to events taking place in other, neighboring fields. As philosophers of science have pointed out, new concepts and findings not only reflect accumulating knowledge within a particular area of inquiry, but also the impact of the broader cultural milieu that helps shape the thinking of theorists and researchers in subtle, often unrecognized ways (see Kuhn, 1970; Spence, 1982). Thus, it is probably not a coincidence that Freud's (1900/1953a) *The Interpretation of Dreams*, Einstein's (1905) specific theory of relativity, and Picasso's (1907) painting *Les Demoiselles D'Avignon* all appeared within a 7-year period. All three works arose from the same turn-of-the-century European *zeitgeist*, and although ostensibly quite different, all three works had a common theme: The uniqueness of individual perspective.

Freud's (1900/1953a) *The Interpretation of Dreams* was a landmark event in the evolution of psychoanalysis. In it Freud described his first comprehensive model of the mind, discussed the dynamics of dream symbolism and the process of dream analysis, and argued persuasively that unconscious mental processes affect a broad array of behaviors, both normal and pathological. Freud's monograph helped establish psychoanalysis as a viable theory and method of treatment, and in this book Freud made a strong case that for psychoanalysis, perspective is crucial. Both patient and therapist viewpoints are essential, Freud argued, and if psychoanalytic treatment goes well the more dispassionate observer (the analyst) can see patterns in patients' behavior that the patients themselves cannot see.

In 1905 Einstein published his specific theory of relativity (the general theory of relativity came a decade later, in 1915). Although Einstein's (1905, 1915) ideas initially met with some resistance, they eventually turned out to have profound scientific and philosophical implications. Einstein's model suggested, for example, that the mass of objects changes as they accelerate and approach the speed of light. It pointed out that apparent motion is relative, and depends not only on the trajectory of the object itself, but also on the position and movement of the observer. In short, Einstein's theory explained why nothing in the universe is absolute, and everything is relative, even the physical world.

In 1907 Picasso exhibited *Les Demoiselles D'Avignon*. It was among the artist's first serious attempts at cubism. Aside from the primitive, primordial quality that pervades Picasso's painting, one of the image's most notable features is its internal inconsistency: Different parts of the scene are deliberately depicted from different, conflicting perspectives. This sort of internal incongruity was a theme that came to dominate Picasso's work, and over time he placed increasing emphasis on presenting an image from multiple vantage points simultaneously. Eventually color and content were lost altogether, replaced with a near-exclusive focus on multiplicity of perspective.

Freud's psychoanalysis is like Einstein's relativity and Picasso's cubism in its emphasis on uniqueness of individual perspective, but Freud's theory aligns with the work of Einstein and Picasso in another way as well. Like psychoanalytic theory, Einstein's concept of relativity was not readily accepted by colleagues, but eventually became a key intellectual component of the discipline; no physicist today can remain unaware of the implications of Einstein's thinking. Picasso's cubism was also controversial from the outset, enchanting some and alienating others, but every 20th-century artist has responded to it in some way. And so it is with Freud's psychoanalytic theory: Some psychologists love it, others hate it, but every psychologist has reacted to it—deliberately or inadvertently, consciously or unconsciously—in his or her own work.

Evaluating the validity and utility of a theory of personality is never easy, but it is particularly challenging for a theory as complex and far-reaching as psychoanalysis. Psychoanalytic theory touches on virtually every aspect of human mental life, from motivation and emotion to memory and information processing. Embedded within this larger model is a theory of personality, but it is not always obvious where the personality portion of psychoanalysis begins and other aspects of the model leave off. Because of this, one cannot assess the psychoanalytic theory of personality without examining psychoanalytic theory *in toto*, with all its complexity, intricacy, and controversy.

This chapter reviews psychodynamic models of personality and their place in contemporary psychology. The chapter begins with a brief discussion of the core assumptions of psychoanalytic theory, followed by an overview of the evolution of the theory from Freud's classical model to today's integrative psychodynamic frameworks. We then discuss the common elements in different psychodynamic models and the ways that these models have grappled with key questions regarding personality development and dynamics. Finally, we discuss the place of psychoanalysis within contemporary psychology and the relationship of psychoanalytic theory to other areas of the discipline.

THE CORE ASSUMPTIONS OF PSYCHOANALYSIS

Given the complexity of psychoanalytic theory and the myriad incarnations that the model has assumed over the years, the core assumptions of the psychodynamic framework are surprisingly simple. Moreover, the three core assumptions of psychoanalysis are unique to the psychodynamic framework: No other theories of personality accept these three premises in their purest form.

Primacy of the Unconscious

Psychodynamic theorists contend that the majority of psychological processes take place outside conscious awareness. In psychoanalytic terms, the activities of the mind (or *psyche*) are presumed to be largely unconscious, and these unconscious processes are particularly revealing of personality dynamics (Brenner, 1973; Fancher, 1973). Although aspects of the *primacy of the unconscious* assumption remain controversial, research on implicit learning, memory, motivation, and cognition has converged to confirm this basic premise of psychoanalysis (albeit in a slightly modified form). Many mental activities are only imperfectly accessible to conscious awareness—including those associated with emotional responding, as well as more mundane, affectively neutral activities such as the processing of linguistic material, and various aspects of procedural memory (see Bargh & Morsella, 2008; Bornstein, 2010; Huprich, 2011; Wilson, 2009). Whether unconscious processes are uniquely revealing of personality dynamics is a different matter entirely, and psychologists remain divided on this issue.

It is ironic that the existence of mental processing outside awareness—so controversial for so long—has become a cornerstone of contemporary experimental psychology. In fact, in summarizing the results of cognitive and social research on automaticity, Bargh and Morsella (2008) concluded that evidence for mental processing outside of awareness is so pervasive and compelling that the burden of proof has actually reversed: Rather than demonstrate unconscious influences, researchers must now go to considerable lengths to demonstrate that a given psychological process is at least in part under conscious control (see Erdelyi, 2004). This conclusion represents a rather striking (and counterintuitive) reversal of prevailing attitudes regarding the conscious-unconscious relationship throughout much of the 20th century.

Critical Importance of Early Experiences

Psychoanalytic theory is not alone in positing that early developmental experiences play a role in shaping personality, but the theory is unique in the degree to which it emphasizes childhood events as determinants of personality development and dynamics. In its strongest form, psychoanalytic theory hypothesizes that early experiences—even those occurring during the first weeks or months of life—set in motion personality processes that are to a great extent immutable. In other words, the events of early childhood are thought to create a trajectory that almost invariably culminates in a predictable set of adult character traits (Emde & Robinson, 2000). This is especially true of experiences that are outside the normal range of experience, either very positive or very negative.

The psychodynamic hypothesis that the first weeks or months of life represent a critical period in personality development contrasts with those of alternative theories (e.g., the cognitive model), which contend that many key events in personality occur somewhat later, after the child has acquired a broad repertoire of verbal and locomotive skills (Pretzer & Beck, 2005). Freud's notion of a critical early period in personality development—coupled with his corollary hypothesis that many of the most important early experiences involve sexual frustration or gratification—was (and is) highly controversial. It helped create a decades-long divergence of psychoanalysis from mainstream developmental psychology, which has only recently begun to narrow (see Bornstein, 2005, for a discussion of this issue).

Psychic Causality

The third core assumption of psychodynamic theory is that nothing in mental life happens by chance—that there is no such thing as a random thought, feeling, motive, or behavior (Brenner, 1973). This has come to be known as the principle of *psychic causality*, and it too has become less controversial over the years. Few psychologists accept the principle of psychic causality precisely as psychoanalysts conceive it, but most theorists and researchers agree that cognitions, motives, emotional responses, and expressed behaviors do not arise randomly, but always stem from some combination of identifiable biological and psychological processes.

Although few psychologists would argue for the existence of random psychological events, researchers do disagree regarding the underlying processes that account for such events, and it is here that the psychodynamic view diverges from those of other perspectives. Whereas psychoanalysts contend that unconscious motives and affective states are key determinants of ostensibly random psychological events, psychologists with other theoretical orientations attribute such events to latent learning, cognitive bias, motivational conflict, chemical imbalances, or variations in neural activity (see Buss, 2008, 2009; Danzinger, 1997). The notion that a seemingly random event (e.g., a slip of the tongue) reveals something important about an individual's personality is, in its purest form, unique to psychoanalysis.

THE EVOLUTION OF PSYCHOANALYSIS: GAZING ACROSS THREE CENTURIES

Many psychodynamic ideas—including the core assumptions just discussed—predated Freud's work and were anticipated by 18th- and 19th-century philosophers (see Ellenberger, 1970; Hilgard, 1987). Nonetheless, psychoanalytic theory as an independent school of thought was conceived just over 100 years ago, with the publication of Breuer and Freud's (1895/1955b) *Studies on Hysteria*. Since that time, the history of psychoanalysis can be divided into four overlapping phases: classical psychoanalytic theory, neo-analytic models, object relations theory, and self-psychology, and contemporary integrative models. Each phase introduced a novel approach to human development and personality.

Classical Psychoanalytic Theory

Given Freud's background in neurology, it is not surprising that the first incarnation of psychoanalytic theory was avowedly biological. In his early writings, Freud (1895/1966, 1900/1958a) set out to explain psychological phenomena in terms that could be linked to extant models of neural functioning (an ironic goal to say the least, given that psychoanalysis developed in part to explain "neurological" symptoms that had no identifiable neurological basis, such as hysterical blindness and hysterical paralysis). Because the core principles of classical psychoanalytic theory developed over more than 40 years, there were numerous revisions along the way. Thus, it is most accurate to think of classical psychoanalytic theory as a set of interrelated models, which were often (but not always) consistent with and supportive of each other: the drive model, the topographic model, the psychosexual stage model, and the structural model.

The Drive Model

One consequence of Freud's determination to frame his theory in quasi-biological terms is that the earliest version of psychoanalytic *drive theory* was for all intents and purposes a theory of energy transformation and tension reduction (Breuer & Freud, 1895/1955; Freud, 1896/1955c). Inborn (presumably inherited) instincts were central to the drive model, and most prominent among these was the sex drive, or libido. Freud's interest in (some might say obsession with) sexual impulses as key determinants of personality development and dynamics was controversial during his lifetime, and has remained so ever since (e.g., see Torrey, 1992). At any rate, during the earliest phase of psychoanalytic theory, personality was seen as a by-product of the particular way in which sexual impulses were expressed in an individual.

Freud never fully renounced the drive concept, even after he shifted the emphasis of psychoanalytic theory from inborn instincts to dynamic mental structures with no obvious biological basis (Greenberg & Mitchell, 1983). The concept of cathexis—investment of libidinal (or psychic) energy in an object or act—remained central to psychoanalytic theory even as the drive model waned in influence. As his career drew to a close during the 1930s, Freud (1933/1964a, 1940/1964b) continued to use the concept of cathexis to account for a wide range of psychological processes, from infant-caregiver bonding and infantile sexuality to group behavior and parapraxes (i.e., "Freudian slips"). As the concept of cathexis became reified in classical psychoanalytic theory, so did the companion concepts of fixation (i.e., lingering investment of psychic energy in objects and activities from an earlier developmental period), and regression (i.e., reinvestment of psychic energy in an earlier stage of development, usually under stress). The concept of cathexis gradually faded from view, but the concepts of fixation and regression continue to be used to explain a wide range of issues related to personality development and dynamics.

The Topographic Model

At the same time as Freud was refining the drive theory, he was elaborating his now-famous *topographic model* of the mind, which contended that the mind could be divided into three regions: conscious, preconscious, and unconscious (Freud, 1900/1958a, 1911/1958b). Whereas the conscious part of the mind was thought to hold only information that demanded attention at the moment, the preconscious contained material that was capable of becoming conscious but was not because attention (in the form of psychic energy) was not invested in it at that time. The unconscious contained anxiety-producing material (e.g., sexual impulses, aggressive wishes) that were deliberately repressed (i.e., held outside of awareness as a form of self-protection). Because of the affect-laden nature of unconscious material, the unconscious was (and is) thought to play a more central role in personality than are the other two elements of Freud's topographic model. In fact, numerous theories of personality ascribe to the notion that emotion-laden material outside of awareness plays a role in determining an individual's personality traits and coping style (Higgins & Pittman, 2008; Morf, 2006; Pyszczynski, Greenberg, & Solomon, 2000).

The terms *conscious, preconscious,* and *unconscious* continue to be used today in mainstream psychology, and research has provided considerable support for this tripartite approach in the areas of memory and information processing (Bucci, 2000, 2002). Consciousness is indeed linked with attentional capacity, and studies show that a great deal of mental processing (including perceptual processing) occurs preconsciously (Bornstein, 1999b; Erdelyi, 1985, 2004). As noted earlier, the existence of a dynamic unconscious remains controversial, with some researchers arguing that evidence favoring this construct is compelling (Bargh & Morsella, 2008; Westen, 1999), and others contending that "unconscious" processing can be accounted for without positing the existence of a Freudian repository of repressed wishes and troubling urges and impulses (Kihlstrom, 2008).

Perhaps the most troubling aspect of the topographic model—for Freud and for contemporary experimentalists as well—concerns the dynamics of information flow (i.e., the mechanism through which information passes among different parts of the mind). Freud (1900/1958a, 1915/1957, 1933/1964a) used a variety of analogies to describe information movement among the conscious, preconscious, and unconscious, the most well-known of these being his *gatekeeper* (who helped prevent unconscious information from reaching conscious awareness), and *anteroom* (where preconscious information was held temporarily before being stored in the unconscious). Contemporary researchers (e.g., Baddeley, 2007) have coined terms that are ostensibly more scientific than those Freud used (e.g., *central executive, visuospatial scratch pad*), but in fact they have not been much more successful than Freud was at specifying the psychological and neurological mechanisms that mediate information flow (see Bornstein, 2005, for a discussion of these and other psychodynamic concepts that have reemerged in modified form in other fields).

The Psychosexual Stage Model

Freud remained devoted to the drive model (and its associated topographic framework) for several decades, in part because of his neurological background, but also because the drive model helped him bridge the gap between biological instincts and his hypothesized stages of development. By 1905, Freud had outlined the key elements of his *psychosexual stage model*, which argued that early in life humans progress through an invariant sequence of developmental stages, each with its own unique challenge and its own mode of drive (i.e., sexual) gratification (Freud, 1905/1953b, 1918/1955a). Freud's psychosexual stages—oral, anal, Oedipal, latency, and genital—are well known even to nonanalytic psychologists. So are the oral, anal, and Oedipal (or phallic) character types associated with fixation at these stages (Fisher & Greenberg, 1996). From a personality perspective, the psychosexual stage model marked a turning point in the history of

TABLE 3.1 The Psychosexual Stage Model

Stage	Age Range	Developmental Task	Associated Traits
Oral	0–18 months	Moving from infantile dependency toward autonomy and self-sufficiency	Dependency
Anal	18–36 months	Learning to exercise control over one's body, one's impulses, and other people	Obsessiveness
Oedipal	5–6 years	Mastering competitive urges and acquiring gender-role-related behaviors	Competitiveness
Latency	6 years–puberty	Investing energy in conflict-free tasks and activities	—
Genital	Puberty onward	Mature sexuality (sexuality blended with intimacy)	—

Note. Dashes indicate that no associated character traits exist for that stage (fixation in the latency and genital periods does not play a role in classical psychoanalytic theory).

psychoanalysis because it was only with the articulation of this model that personality moved from the periphery to the center of psychoanalytic theory.

Table 3.1 illustrates the basic organization of Freud's (1905/1953b) psychosexual stage model. Frustration or overgratification during the infantile, oral stage was hypothesized to result in oral fixation, and an inability to resolve the developmental issues that characterize this period (e.g., conflicts regarding dependency and autonomy). The psychosexual stage model further postulated that the orally fixated (or oral dependent) person would (a) remain dependent on others for nurturance, protection, and support; and (b) continue to exhibit behaviors in adulthood that reflect the oral stage (i.e., preoccupation with activities of the mouth, reliance on food and eating as a means of coping with anxiety). Research supports the former hypothesis, but has generally failed to confirm the latter (Bornstein, 2006; Perry, Silvera, Rosenvinge, & Holte, 2002).

A parallel set of dynamics (i.e., frustration or overgratification during toilet training) were assumed to produce anal fixation and the development of an anal character type. Because toilet training was viewed by Freud as a struggle for control over one's body and impulses, the anally fixated individual was thought to be preoccupied with issues of control, and his or her behavior characterized by a constellation of three traits, sometimes termed the *anal triad*: obstinacy, orderliness, and parsimony. Fixation during the Oedipal stage was presumed to result in a

personality style marked by aggressiveness, competitiveness, and a concern with status and influence. Empirical studies have yielded mixed results with respect to the anal and Oedipal stages. Findings support the existence of an anal triad, but they do not support the critical role of toilet training in the ontogenesis of these traits. Similarly, research offers only mixed support for the concept of an Oedipal personality type and offers little evidence for the Oedipal dynamic as Freud conceived it (see Fisher & Greenberg, 1996; Masling & Schwartz, 1979; Perry et al., 2002).

The Structural Model

Ultimately, Freud recognized certain explanatory limitations in the topographic model (e.g., the model's inability to account for certain forms of psychopathology), and as a result he developed an alternative, complementary framework to account for normal and abnormal personality development. Although the *structural model* evolved over a number of years, the theoretical shift from topography to structure is most clearly demarcated by Freud's (1923/1961b) publication of *The Ego and the Id,* wherein he described in detail the central hypothesis underlying the structural model: the notion that intrapsychic dynamics could be understood with reference to three interacting mental structures called the id, ego, and superego. The *id* was defined as the seat of drives and instincts (a throwback to the original drive model), whereas the *ego* represented the logical, reality-oriented part of the mind, and the *superego* was akin to a conscience, or set of moral guidelines and prohibitions (Brenner, 1973). Figure 3.1 illustrates the sequence of development of the id, ego, and superego in Freud's structural model.

According to the structural model, personality is derived from the interplay of these three psychic structures, which differ across individuals in relative power and influence (Freud, 1933/1964a, 1940/1964b). When the id predominates, an impulsive, stimulation-seeking personality style results. When the superego is strongest, moral prohibitions inhibit impulses, and a restrained, overcontrolled personality ensues. When the ego (which serves in part to mediate id impulses and superego prohibitions) is dominant, a more balanced set of personality traits develop. Table 3.2 summarizes the psychodynamic conceptualization of personality in Freud's structural model, as well as within the drive, topographic, and psychosexual stage models.

From 1923 until his death in 1939, Freud spent much of his time elaborating the key principles and corollaries of the structural model, and he extended the model to

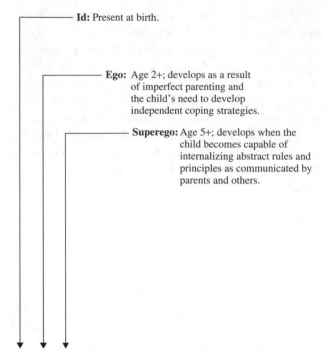

Figure 3.1 Development of the id, ego, and superego in classical psychoanalytic theory

TABLE 3.2   **Conceptions of Personality Within Classical Psychoanalytic Theory**

Model	Conception of Personality
Drive	Personality traits as drive (instinct) derivatives
Topographic	Unconscious (repressed) material is a primary determinant of personality
Psychosexual	Fixation at a particular psychosexual stage leads to an associated character type
Structural	Id-ego-superego dynamics determine personality traits and coping/defense strategies

various areas of individual and social life (e.g., humor, mental errors, cultural dynamics, religious beliefs). He also made numerous efforts to link the structural model to his earlier work to form a more cohesive psychodynamic framework. For example, Freud (and other psychoanalysts) hypothesized that oral fixation was characterized in part by a prominent, powerful id, whereas Oedipal fixation was characterized by strong investment in superego activities. At the time of his death Freud was actively revising aspects of the structural model (Fancher, 1973; Gay, 1988), and it is impossible to know how the model would have developed had Freud continued his work. This much is certain: During the decades wherein Freud explicated details of his structural model of the mind he altered it in myriad ways, and in doing so he laid the foundation

for several concepts that—many years later—became key elements of modern psychoanalytic theory.

Neo-Analytic Models

Following Freud's 1909 Clark University lectures, psychoanalysis attracted large numbers of adherents from within the medical and lay communities. At first, these adherents followed Freud's ideas with little questioning and minimal resistance. By the early 1920s, however, competing schools of psychoanalytic thought were beginning to emerge. At first, the growth of these alternative psychodynamic frameworks was inhibited by Freud's strong personality and by the immense international popularity of psychoanalytic theory (Hilgard, 1987; Torrey, 1992). It was only upon Freud's death in 1939 that competing psychoanalytic perspectives blossomed into full-fledged theories in their own right. By the mid-1940s, the discipline had splintered into an array of divergent theoretical perspectives. This splintering process, which has continued to the present day, is summarized graphically in Figure 3.2. As Figure 3.2 shows, each post-Freudian psychodynamic model was rooted in classical psychoanalytic

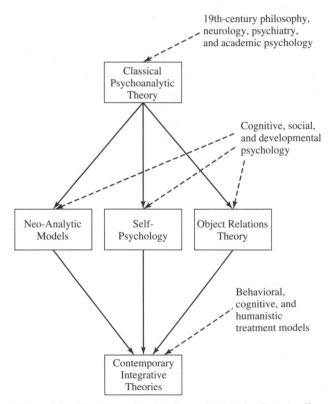

Figure 3.2 Evolution of psychodynamic models of personality; arrows indicate the influence of earlier theories/perspectives on later ones

theory, but each drew upon ideas and findings from other areas as well.

Several neo-analytic theories became particularly influential in the decades following Freud's death. Among the most important of these were Jung's (1933, 1961) analytical psychology, Erikson's (1963, 1968) psychosocial theory, Sullivan's (1947, 1953) interpersonal theory, and the quasi-dynamic models of Adler (1921, 1923), Fromm (1941, 1947), Klein (1932, 1964), and Horney (1937, 1945). These theories shared a Freudian emphasis on intrapsychic dynamics, childhood experiences, and unconscious processes as determinants of personality and psychopathology. However, each neo-analytic theorist rejected the classical psychoanalytic emphasis on sexuality as a key component of personality, and each sought to supplant sexuality with its own unique elements. Key features of the most prominent neo-analytic models are summarized in Table 3.3. Each neo-analytic model in Table 3.3 attained a loyal following during its heyday, but with the exceptions of Erikson and Sullivan, these neo-analytic theories have comparatively few adherents today outside of psychoanalytic training institutes, and they do not receive much attention within the broader clinical and research communities.

Erikson's (1963, 1968) psychosocial approach continues to have a wide-ranging impact on personality and

developmental research (Schwartz, 2001), and has garnered considerable empirical support from studies of life-span development (Miner-Rubino, Winter, & Stewart, 2004). Sullivan's (1953, 1956) interpersonal theory not only helped lay the groundwork for object relations theory and self-psychology (described later in this chapter), but continues to influence developmental research on adolescence, as well as psychodynamic writing on treatment of personality pathology (McWilliams, 2004).

Object Relations Theory and Self-Psychology

Although the influence of most neo-analytic models has waned, two other psychodynamic frameworks that evolved from Freud's work—*object relations theory* and *self-psychology*—remain very much a part of mainstream psychoanalytic theory and practice. Both frameworks developed out of early work in *ego psychology*, an offshoot of the classical model, which updated Freud's thinking on the role of the ego in personality development. Where Freud had conceptualized the ego primarily in terms of its reality-testing and defensive functions, ego psychologists posited that the ego plays an equally important role in setting goals, seeking challenges, striving for mastery, and actualizing potential (Hartmann, 1964). Within this line of thinking, the ego was seen as an autonomous, conflict-free structure, rather than an entity that simply responded to the demands of id, superego, and the external world. Ego psychologists' reconceptualization of the ego set the stage for object relations theory and self-psychology.

Object Relations Theory

Although there are several distinct variants of object relations theory (see Greenberg & Mitchell, 1983), they share a core belief that personality can be analyzed most usefully by examining mental representations of significant figures (especially the parents) that are formed early in life in response to interactions taking place within the family (Gill, 1995; Winnicott, 1971). These mental representations (sometimes called *introjects*) are hypothesized to serve as templates for later interpersonal relationships, allowing the individual to anticipate the responses of other people and draw reasonably accurate inferences regarding others' thoughts, feelings, goals, and motivations (Sandler & Rosenblatt, 1962). Mental representations of the parents—parental introjects—also allow the individual to carry on an inner dialogue with absent figures. This inner dialogue helps modulate anxiety and enables the person to

TABLE 3.3   Neo-Analytic Models of Personality

Theorist	Key Assumption	Key Terms/Concepts
Adler	Family dynamics (especially birth order) are primary determinants of personality	Striving for superiority, Inferiority complex
Erikson	Social interactions between the person and significant others are key in personality development	Psychosocial stages, Developmental crises
Fromm	Personality is best understood with reference to prevailing social and political (as well as intrapsychic) forces	Authoritarianism
Horney	Infantile dependency/powerlessness is key to personality	Basic anxiety
Jung	Personality is shaped by spiritual forces as well as biological and social variables	Archetypes, Collective unconscious
Klein	Aggressive impulses and fears regarding annihilation play a prominent role in personality development	Depressive position, Paranoid-schizoid position
Sullivan	Personality can only be conceptualized within the context of an individual's core relationships	Personifications, Developmental epochs

make decisions consistent with values and beliefs acquired early in life (Fairbairn, 1952; Jacobson, 1964).

One of the most prominent object relations models of personality today is Blatt's (1974, 1991) anaclitic-introjective framework (see Besser, Guez, & Priel, 2008; Blatt, 2008). Blending psychoanalytic theory with research in cognitive development, Blatt postulated that the structure of an individual's parental introjects play a key role in personality development and dynamics. When introjects are weak (or even absent), an anaclitic personality configuration results, characterized by dependency, insecurity, and feelings of helplessness and emptiness. When introjects are harsh and demanding, an introjective personality configuration is produced, characterized by feelings of guilt, failure, worthlessness, and self-loathing. Studies have shown that Blatt's anaclitic-introjective distinction helps predict risk for psychopathology and physical illness, the form that psychopathology and illness will take, the kinds of stressful events that are likely to be most upsetting to the individual, and the types of interventions that will effect therapeutic change most readily (Besser et al., 2008; Besser & Priel, 2011; Blatt, 2004, 2008).

Self-Psychology

Self-psychologists share object relations theorists' emphasis on mental representations as building blocks of personality, but contend that the key introjects are those associated with the self, including *selfobjects* (i.e., representations of self and others that are to varying degrees merged, undifferentiated, and imperfectly articulated). Self-psychology developed in part as a response to analysts' interest in treating severe personality disorders and other treatment resistant forms of psychopathology (Kernberg, 1984; Kohut, 1971; McWilliams, 1994). The development of self-psychology was also aided by recognition that the knowledge base of analytic theory could be enriched if greater attention were paid to the ontogenesis of the self in the context of early child-caregiver relationships (see Mahler, Pine, & Bergman, 1975).

The most widely known self-psychology framework was first described by Kohut (1971, 1977). Kohut postulated that empathic and supportive early interactions resulted in the construction of a secure, cohesive *autonomous self,* with sufficient resources to deal with the stresses and challenges of intimacy. In contrast, disturbances in infant-caregiver interactions were hypothesized to result in damage to the self along with impairments in evocative constancy (i.e., the ability to generate stable mental images of self and absent others) and an inability

to tolerate true intimacy. Difficulties within the infant-caregiver dyad are often first manifested during *mirroring*, a phenomenon wherein infant and caregiver each mimic the body language, facial expressions, breathing tempo, and behaviors exhibited by the other (Mayes, Fonagy, & Target, 2007). Kohut (1977) postulated that infant-caregiver mirroring represents the prototypical reciprocal relationship in which the infant's sense of self is initially defined, and templates for self-other interaction patterns are formed. Consistent with Kohut's (1977) view, studies have shown that failures in mirroring within the infant-caregiver dyad predict later difficulties in self-concept and affect regulation, as well as increasing risk for certain forms of personality pathology (e.g., borderline personality disorder, narcissistic personality disorder; see McWilliams, 2004; Ronningstam, 2009; Silverstein, 2007).

One of the most influential perspectives to emerge from the self-psychology tradition has been the concept of a *two-person psychology*, discussed in detail by Gill (1995) in his proposal for a shift in the traditional psychoanalytic conceptualization of patient and analyst roles (see also Mitchell, 2000). In contrast to the longstanding view of patient as subject of scrutiny and analyst as dispassionate observer, within the two-person framework patient and analyst were seen as bringing their own unique perspectives to treatment, co-creating meaning in the analytic situation. As Aron (1990) noted, implicit in the concept of two-person psychology is a relational theory of mind (in contrast to the monadic theory of mind that underlies the traditional perspective), as well as an emphasis on inter-subjectivity in psychoanalysis. The notion of two-person psychology has opened new avenues for debate regarding the dynamics of empathy, the impact of analysts' self-disclosure on treatment process, and the potential uses of countertransference as a tool for therapeutic insight (Blum, 2010; Eagle, 2000).

Contemporary Integrative Models

Object relations theory and self-psychology have revived academic psychologists' interest in psychodynamic ideas during the past several decades, in part because they represent natural bridges between psychoanalytic theory and research in other areas of psychology (e.g., cognitive, social, developmental; see Bornstein, 2005; Cramer, 2000; Masling & Bornstein, 1994; Midgley, Anderson, Grainger, Nesic-Vuckovic, & Urwin, 2009; Shapiro & Emde, 1995). While object relations theory and self-psychology continue to flourish, a parallel stream of theoretical work has developed that focuses on integrating psychodynamic models of personality with ideas and findings from competing clinical frameworks.

As Figure 3.2 shows, contemporary integrative psychodynamic models draw from both object relations theory and self-psychology (and to some extent, from classical psychoanalytic theory as well). Unlike most earlier psychodynamic theories, however, these integrative frameworks utilize concepts and findings from other schools of clinical practice (e.g., cognitive, behavioral, humanistic) to refine and expand their ideas. Some integrative models have gone a step further, drawing upon ideas from neuropsychology and psychopharmacology in addition to other, more traditional areas.

There are almost as many integrative psychodynamic models as there are alternative schools of psychotherapeutic thought. Among the most influential models are those that link psychodynamic thinking with concepts from cognitive therapy (Book, 1998; Luborsky & Crits-Christoph, 1990), behavioral therapy (Wachtel, 1997), and humanistic-existential psychology (Pyszczynski et al., 2000). Other integrative models combine aspects of psychoanalysis with ideas and findings from developmental psychology (Fraley, 2002; Shaver & Mikulincer, 2002) and neuroscience (Gerber, 2007; Roffman & Gerber, 2009). Not all analytically oriented psychologists agree that these integrative efforts are productive, and the question of whether these integrative frameworks are truly psychoanalytic or have incorporated so many nonanalytic principles as to be something else entirely is a matter of considerable debate within the psychoanalytic community.

Approaching the integration challenge from a different perspective, a number of theorists have combined psychodynamic concepts with feminist principles to widen the explanatory reach of the psychoanalytic framework and fill theoretical gaps that resulted from a longstanding emphasis on male psychosexual development as normative, and gender differences as reflecting departures from optimal adjustment (Bornstein & Masling, 2002). In a pioneering contribution in this area, Mitchell (1974) argued that a key limitation of traditional psychodynamic models was a failure to appreciate the importance of lateral relationships (i.e., relationships with peers, siblings, and romantic partners) in intrapersonal dynamics and interpersonal behavior. Along somewhat different lines, Chodorow (1978), building on the work of Klein (1964) and Horney (1945), hypothesized that women experience a sense of self-in-relation that differs fundamentally from men's sense of self as separate from others. Chodorow's work helped pave the way for Gilligan's (1982) influential model of moral development, which postulated fundamentally different premises for moral judgment and reasoning in women and men (see Tangney & Dearing, 2002, for evidence bearing on this issue).

PSYCHOANALYTIC PERSONALITY THEORIES: BRINGING ORDER TO CHAOS

Given the burgeoning array of disparate theoretical perspectives, a key challenge confronting psychodynamic theorists involves finding common ground among contrasting viewpoints (see McWilliams, 2004, and Weiner & Bornstein, 2009, for discussions of this issue). Although there are dozens of psychodynamically oriented models of personality in existence today, all these models have had to grapple with similar theoretical and conceptual problems. In the following sections we discuss how contemporary psychodynamic models have dealt with three key questions common to all personality theories.

Personality Processes and Dynamics

Three fertile areas of common ground among psychodynamic models of personality involve motivation, mental structure and process, and personality stability and change.

Motivation

With the possible exception of the radical behavioral approach, every personality theory has addressed in detail the nature of human motivation—that set of unseen internal forces that impel the organism to action (Higgins & Pittman, 2008). Although classical psychoanalytic theory initially conceptualized motivation in purely biological terms, the history of psychoanalysis has been characterized by increasing emphasis on psychological motives that are only loosely based in identifiable physiological needs (Custers & Aarts, 2010). This shift was initiated in part by evidence from laboratory studies of contact-deprived monkeys (Harlow & Harlow, 1962) and observational studies of orphaned infants from World War II (Spitz, 1945, 1946), which converged to confirm that humans and infrahumans have a fundamental need for *contact comfort* and sustained closeness with a consistent caregiver. Around this time, developmental researchers were independently formulating theories of infant-caregiver attachment that posited a separate need to relate to the primary caregiver of infancy and specified the adverse consequences of disrupted early attachment relationships (Ainsworth, 1969, 1989; Bowlby, 1969, 1973).

Object relations theorists and self-psychologists integrated these developmental concepts and empirical findings into their emerging theoretical models, so that by the late 1960s most psychodynamic psychologists assumed the existence of one or more psychological drives related to contact comfort (e.g., Kohut, 1971; Winnicott, 1971). Theorists also emphasized the critical importance of interactions that take place within the early infant-caregiver relationship because positive interactions with a nurturing caregiver were deemed necessary for the construction of a cohesive sense of self (Banai, Mikulincer, & Shaver, 2005; Donenberg, Emersen, & Mackesy-Amiti, 2011; Mahler et al., 1975); stable, benevolent introjects (Skowron, Kozlowski, & Pincus, 2010); and flexible mental models of self-other interactions (Main, Kaplan, & Cassidy, 1985; Shaver & Mikulincer, 2002).

Mental Structure and Process

Along with psychoanalysts' recognition that mental images of self and others were key building blocks of personality came a change in the way the structures and processes of personality were conceptualized. Terms like *introject*, *schema*, and *object representation* gradually took their place alongside those of Freud's structural model as cornerstones of psychoanalytic theory and therapy (Greenberg & Mitchell, 1983; McWilliams, 1994). Analysts recognized that in addition to mental images of self and others, a key derivative of early relationships was the formation of *internal working models* (sometimes identified as *scripts*) that form blueprints—or templates—for future relationships. This alternative conceptualization of the nature of mental structure not only enabled psychodynamic theorists to derive new treatment approaches (especially for working with character-disordered patients), but also helped connect psychodynamic models with research in attachment theory and social cognition (Blatt & Levy, 2003; Dykas & Cassidy, 2011; Galatzer-Levy, Bachrach, Skolnikoff, & Waldron, 2000).

This language shift not only reflected theoretical innovations, but also a need to develop a psychoanalytic terminology that was closer to the day-to-day experience of analytic patients. In this context, Mayman (1976) noted that at any given time, a psychoanalytic theorist or practitioner may use several different levels of discourse to communicate theoretical concepts. At the top of this framework is psychoanalytic metapsychology—the complex network of theoretical concepts and propositions that form the infrastructure of psychoanalysis. Metapsychological terms are often abstract, rarely operationalizable, and typically used in dialogue with other theorists and practitioners. The concepts of libido and selfobject are examples of language most closely associated with psychoanalytic metapsychology.

The middle-level language of psychoanalysis incorporates the constructs used by theorists and practitioners in their own day-to-day work. It is the language with which psychoanalysts conceptualize problems and communicate informally—the kind of language likely to turn up in the heart of a case study or in a set of clinical notes. The terms *oral dependent* and *sublimation* are examples of the middle-level language of psychoanalysis.

The bottom level of psychoanalytic language centers on the experience-near discourse that characterizes therapist-patient exchanges within an analytic session. Less formal than Mayman's (1976) middle-level language, this experience-near discourse is intended to frame psychoanalytic concepts in a way that resonates with a patient's personal experience without requiring that he or she have any formal understanding of psychoanalytic metapsychology. When an analyst discusses a patient's "aggressive impulses" or "sibling rivalry," that analyst has translated an abstract concept into experience-near terms.

Personality Stability and Change

The conceptualization of psychoanalytic concepts in relational terms introduced a fundamentally new paradigm for thinking about continuity and change in personality development and dynamics. In addition to being understood in terms of a dynamic balance among id, ego, and superego, stability in personality was now seen as stemming from continuity in the core features of key object representations, including the self-representation. In this context, personality change was presumed to occur in part because internalized representations of self and other people changed as a result of ongoing inter- and intrapersonal experiences (Schafer, 2009), or targeted therapeutic interventions (Weiner & Bornstein, 2009).

This alternative framework influenced psychoanalytic theories of normal personality development and led to a plethora of studies examining the intrapsychic processes involved in therapeutic resistance, transference, and cure (Blatt & Ford, 1994; Luborsky & Crits-Christoph, 1990). It also called theorists' attention to the critical importance of present-day events in moderating long-term psychodynamic processes. As Eagle (2000) pointed out, one important consequence of these newfound concepts of personality stability and change was a continuing shift from past to present in the study of psychodynamics (see also Roberts, Donnellan & Hill, this volume, for a wide-ranging discussion of personality stability and change).

Insight, Self-Awareness, and Coping

As noted earlier, a key tenet of all psychodynamic models is that unconscious processes are primary determinants of thought, emotion, motivation, and behavior. To the degree that people have limited introspective access to these underlying causes, they have only limited control over these processes as well. In part as a consequence of their emphasis on unconscious processes, psychodynamic theorists are unanimous in positing that a certain degree of self-deception is characteristic of both normal and abnormal functioning: Not knowing why we are driven to behave in a certain way, but needing to explain our behavior to ourselves, we generate explanations that may or may not have anything to do with the real causes of behavior (Bornstein, 1999b, 2007). Moreover, when feelings, thoughts, and motivations produce anxiety (including guilt), we invoke coping strategies called *ego defenses* to minimize these negative reactions and to hide them from ourselves (Cramer, 2000, 2006).

The once-radical notion of defensive self-deception is now widely accepted among psychoanalytic and nonanalytic psychologists alike. Research in social cognition confirms that systematic, predictable distortions in our perceptions of self and others are a part of everyday life (Baumeister, Masicampo, & Vohs, 2011; Berka, & Andersen, 2008; Kwan, John, Robins, & Kuang, 2008). Researchers have begun to bridge the gap between these ostensibly divergent theoretical perspectives, uncovering a surprising degree of overlap (Bargh & Morsella, 2008; Bornstein, 2009); one area in which psychodynamic models of defensive self-deception diverge from social psychological models of this phenomenon is in the explanations of why these distortions occur. Although both models agree that these distortions stem largely (but not entirely) from self-protective processes, only psychoanalytic theories explicitly link these distortions to an identifiable set of unconsciously determined strategies termed ego defenses. Research in terror management theory represents a potential bridge between psychodynamic and social-cognitive work in this area (see Pyszczynski et al., 1999; Pyszczynski, Henthorn, Motyl, & Gerow, 2010).

Ironically, the concept of ego defense—now central to psychodynamic models of personality—did not receive much attention during the theory's formative years. Janet (1907) paid greater attention to the defense concept than Freud did, and in certain respects Janet's position regarding this issue has turned out to be more accurate than Freud's (Bowers & Meichenbaum, 1984). Evidence suggests that a conceptualization of defensive activity as

narrowing of consciousness may be more valid and heuristic than is the classic psychoanalytic conceptualization of defense in terms of exclusion (or *barring*) of material from consciousness (Cramer, 2000, 2006; cf. Erdelyi, 2004, 2010).

Although Freud discussed certain ego defenses (e.g., repression, projection, sublimation) in his theoretical and clinical writings, it was not until Anna Freud's (1936) publication of *The Ego and the Mechanisms of Defense* that any effort was made to create a comprehensive listing of these defensive strategies. Most of the ego defenses discussed by A. Freud continue to be discussed today, although some have fallen out of favor, and new ones have been added as empirical research on defenses began to appear following A. Freud's (1936) seminal work (see Cramer, 2006, for a discussion of this issue).

In the decades following A. Freud's (1936) publication, several alternative methods for conceptualizing ego defenses were offered; the most influential are summarized in Table 3.4. As Table 3.4 shows, differences among the individual defense, defense style, and defense cluster models have less to do with the way that specific defensive processes are conceptualized and more to do with how these processes are organized and relate to one another. Each approach to conceptualizing and organizing ego defenses has its own associated measurement technique, its own research base, and its own adherents within the discipline.

TABLE 3.4   Perspectives on Ego Defenses

Perspective	Major Contributors	Key Terms
Individual defenses	S. Freud, A. Freud	Specific defenses: Repression Projection Denial Sublimation Displacement
Defense style approach	Ihilevich and Gleser	Defense styles: Reversal Projection Principalization Turning against object Turning against self
Defense levels/clusters	Bond, Vaillant	Defense levels/clusters: Adaptive/mature Maladaptive/immature Image-distorting Self-sacrificing

Note. Discussions of these three perspectives are provided by Cramer (2000), Ihilevich and Gleser (1986, 1991), and Vaillant (1986).

The combined influences of unconscious processes and ego defenses raise the unavoidable question of whether within the psychodynamic framework humans are seen as inherently irrational creatures. Like most questions in psychoanalysis, this one has more than one answer. On the one hand, humans are indeed irrational—driven by forces they do not understand, their thoughts and feelings distorted in ways they cannot control. On the other hand, humans are as rational as can be expected given the constraints of their information-processing skills, their need to manage anxiety, and the adaptations necessary to survive in an unpredictable, threatening world. Within the psychodynamic framework, all humans are irrational, but most are irrational in a rational way.

Normal and Pathological Functioning

As any psychologist knows, all humans may be irrational, but some are more irrational than others. Like most personality theorists, psychoanalysts see psychopathology as reflected in a greater-than-expected degree of self-destructive, self-defeating behavior (McWilliams, 1994; Millon, 2011). In most psychodynamic frameworks, psychopathology is also linked with increased self-deception, decreased insight into the underlying causes of one's behavior, and concomitant limitations in one's ability to modify dysfunctional interaction patterns and alter self-defeating responses (Eagle, 1984; Silverstein, 2007).

Psychodynamic models conceptualize psychopathology in terms of three general processes: (1) low ego strength, (2) maladaptive ego defenses, and (3) dysfunctional introjects (Bornstein, 2006). Low ego strength contributes to psychopathology because the ego cannot execute reality testing functions adequately; intra- and interpersonal distortions increase, and planning and decision-making are impaired. Maladaptive defenses prevent the individual from managing stress and anxiety adequately leading to higher levels of self-deception, increased perceptual bias, and decreased insight. Dysfunctional introjects (including a distorted or deficient self-representation) similarly lead to inaccurate perceptions of self and others, but they also foster dysfunctional interaction patterns and propagate problematic interpersonal relationships.

A key premise of the psychoanalytic model of psychopathology is that psychological disorders can be divided into three broad levels of severity, a concept that has been formalized in the *Psychodynamic Diagnostic Manual* (PDM; Alliance of Psychoanalytic Organizations [APO], 2006). The classic conceptualization of this three-level framework invokes the well-known terms *neurosis,*

TABLE 3.5   Levels of Psychopathology in Psychodynamic Theory

Level	Ego Strength	Ego Defenses	Introjects
Neurosis	High	Adaptive/mature (displacement, sublimation)	Articulated, differentiated, and benign
Character disorder	Variable	Maladaptive/immature (denial, projection)	Quasi-articulated, malevolent, or both
Psychosis	Low	Maladaptive/immature or nonexistent	Unarticulated, undifferentiated, and malevolent

character disorder, and *psychosis.* In most instances, neuroses are comparatively mild disorders, which affect only a few areas of functioning (e.g., phobias). Character disorders are more pervasive, long-standing disorders associated with problematic social relationships, distorted self-perception, and difficulties with impulse control (e.g., borderline personality disorder). Psychoses are characterized by severely impaired reality testing and low levels of functioning in many areas of life (e.g., schizophrenia).

Although this tripartite model is both heuristic and clinically useful, it is important not to overgeneralize regarding differences across the three levels of functioning. There are great variations in both severity and chronicity within a given level (e.g., certain neuroses may be more debilitating than an ostensibly more severe personality disorder). In addition, there is substantial comorbidity—both within and between levels—so that a disordered individual is likely to show multiple forms of psychopathology (Bornstein & Huprich, 2011; Kim & Tyrer, 2010).

As Table 3.5 shows, all three dimensions of intrapsychic dysfunction—low ego strength, maladaptive defenses, and dysfunctional introjects—can be mapped onto the tripartite psychopathology model. In this respect, the model represents an integrative framework that links different psychodynamic processes and connects the psychoanalytic model with contemporary diagnosis (APO, 2006; Bornstein, 2010). Although the term *neurosis* is rarely used today in mainstream psychopathology research, perusal of contemporary diagnostic frameworks confirms that the tripartite model has had a profound influence on the way practitioners conceptualize and classify psychological disorders (see McWilliams, 1994, 2004).

PSYCHOANALYSIS AND CONTEMPORARY PSYCHOLOGY: RETROSPECT AND PROSPECT

Psychodynamic models of personality occupy a unique place in contemporary psychology. On the one hand, they continue to be roundly criticized—perceived by those within and outside the discipline as untested and untestable, and denigrated by skeptics as a quasi-phrenological pseudoscience that has hindered the progress of both scientific and clinical psychology. On the other hand, Freud's theory continues to fascinate many, occupying a central place in undergraduate and graduate psychology texts and influencing in myriad ways our understanding of ourselves and our culture. In these final sections, we discuss the place of psychoanalysis in contemporary psychology and speculate about its future.

Testing Psychoanalytic Theories

Within the psychoanalytic community, few issues are as controversial as the nature of evidence in psychoanalysis (see Grunbaum, 1984, for a discussion of this issue). Because psychoanalysis focuses on the in-depth understanding of individuals, many of the theory's adherents argue that research aimed at confirming general principles of human functioning is of little value (e.g., Gedo, 1999; Mitchell, 2000). Others maintain that without a strong nomothetic research base, psychodynamic theory can never be refined and updated based on our evolving understanding of brain, mind, and behavior (Bornstein, 2005; Luyten, Blatt, & Corveleyn, 2006). The controversy regarding the nature of psychoanalytic evidence dates almost to the inception of the theory itself. Although Freud started his career as a researcher, his attitude toward traditional scientific methods became increasingly dismissive as time went on, and by the 1920s, psychoanalytic theory had become quite distant from its roots in the natural sciences. With this distancing came an increasing discomfort with traditional nomothetic research procedures and a shift toward idiographic data, which most theorists and practitioners saw as being ideally suited to testing and refining psychoanalytic hypotheses via close analysis of clinical material.

Psychoanalytic theories of personality continue to be strongly influenced by data obtained in the treatment setting. The case reports of psychoanalytic practitioners are still used to formulate general principles of psychopathology, after which these case-derived general principles are reapplied to new cases. Although psychoanalytic psychologists continue to accept the heuristic value of case studies, contemporary theorists and researchers have begun to question the longstanding near-exclusive emphasis on case material in psychoanalytic theory-building (Bornstein, 2001; Huprich, 2009; Josephs, Anderson, Bernard, Fatzer, & Streich, 2004; Luyten et al., 2006).

Although psychodynamic theorists have tended to place the greatest value on material derived from the psychoanalytic treatment session, other forms of idiographic evidence (e.g., anthropological findings, literary records) have also been used to assess psychoanalytic ideas. Needless to say, psychodynamic theorists' devotion to idiographic methods has led to widespread criticism from within and outside psychology. Proponents of the nomothetic approach maintain that idiographic data—especially those obtained behind closed doors—are neither objective nor replicable, and provide little compelling evidence for the validity of psychoanalytic concepts or the efficacy of psychoanalytic treatment (Crews, 1998; Macmillan, 2007). Recent conceptual frameworks that provide a conceptual context for contrasting and integrating idiographic and nomothetic data (e.g., Molenaar & Campbell, 2009) may ultimately prove useful in bridging this gap.

Divergent Researcher-Practitioner Perspectives

A noteworthy difference between psychoanalysis and other models of personality becomes apparent when one contrasts the theoretical orientations of practitioners with those of academics. Although there are relatively few practicing psychoanalysts outside large metropolitan centers, a sizable portion of clinical psychologists acknowledge the impact of psychodynamic principles on their day-to-day clinical work (Norcross, Hedges, & Castle, 2002). In contrast, few personality researchers are openly psychodynamic despite the fact that many concepts in contemporary nonanalytic models of personality are rooted to varying degrees in psychodynamic ideas (Bornstein, 2001; Morf, 2006), and some of these concepts have actually been co-opted from psychoanalysis, renamed and reinvented by researchers in other fields (see Bornstein, 2005, for examples).

This researcher-practitioner divide is in part political. During the 1960s and 1970s, behavioral, cognitive, and humanistic personality theorists deliberately distanced themselves from psychoanalytic theory. For behaviorists, this distancing was a product of their core assumptions and beliefs, which clearly conflict with those of psychoanalysis. For cognitivists and humanists, however, the split with psychoanalysis was necessary so that these burgeoning models could distinguish themselves from long-standing psychoanalytic principles and assert the uniqueness of their perspectives. Even when parallel concepts arose in these models, theorists tended to emphasize differences from psychoanalysis rather than focusing on their common elements.

The situation has changed somewhat in recent years: Now that the cognitive and humanistic perspectives are well-established, there has been a slow and subtle reconciliation with Freudian ideas. In the case of humanistic psychology, there has even been some explicit acknowledgment of the discipline's Freudian roots. Even contemporary trait approaches—which have historically been strongly bound to the biological and psychometric traditions—have begun to integrate psychodynamic principles into their models and methods.

Freud's Cognitive Revolution

The theory that upended mainstream neuroscience a century ago has had a significant impact on cognitive psychology within the past several decades. Although the synergistic interchange between these two fields dates back at least to the 1960s, the impact of Freud's cognitive revolution became widely accepted with the publication of Erdelyi's (1985) landmark analysis of the interface between cognitive psychology and psychoanalysis. Erdelyi's work demonstrated that many psychoanalytic concepts dovetailed well with prevailing models of perception, memory, and information processing, and set the stage for an increasingly productive interchange between psychodynamic researchers and cognitive psychologists (see Erdelyi, 2004, 2010, for additional evidence bearing on these issues).

The language of the topographic model—conscious, unconscious, and preconscious—continues to be used to a surprising degree, even by researchers unaffiliated with (and often unsympathetic to) Freudian ideas. Moreover, recent research in perception without awareness, implicit learning, and implicit memory draws heavily from psychodynamic concepts (Bornstein, 1999b; Erdelyi, 2004; Ghinescu, Schachtman, Stadler, Fabiani, & Gratton, 2010). Despite psychoanalysts' long-standing resistance to nomothetic research methods, psychoanalytic principles have undeniably been affected by laboratory research in these other related areas.

Although it was largely unacknowledged at the time, the integration of psychoanalysis and cognitive psychology was central to the development of object relations theory and resulted in substantive reconceptualization of such traditional psychoanalytic concepts as transference, repression, and screen (or false) memories (Bornstein, 1993; Eagle, 2000). As cognitive psychology continues to integrate findings from research on attitudes and emotion, the psychodynamic aspects of perception, memory, and information processing have become increasingly apparent. A likely consequence of this ongoing integration will be the absorption of at least some psychodynamic principles into models of problem solving, concept formation, and heuristic use. Studies confirm that systematic distortions and biases in these mental processes are due in part to constraints within the human information-processing system (Dawson, Gilovich, & Regan, 2002; Wilson, 2009), but this does not preclude the possibility that motivational factors (including unconscious need states) may also influence psychological processes that were once considered largely independent of personality and psychopathology factors (Custers & Aarts, 2010; McClelland, Koestner, & Weinberger, 1989).

Mentalization, Reflective Functioning, and Theory of Mind

One of the areas wherein the convergence of psychodynamic and cognitive concepts has been particularly fruitful is in understanding *mentalization*—the capacity to understand one's own and others' behavior in terms of underlying mental states and intentions (Slade, 2005). The concept of mentalization has been used by psychoanalytically oriented researchers to understand the processes that link dysfunctional attachment patterns with increased risk for psychopathology (Blatt & Levy, 2003; Luyten, 2011). Mentalization has been widely studied and operationalized in myriad ways, most prominently as a dimension of the Adult Attachment Interview labeled *reflective functioning* (Fonagy, Gergely, Jurist, & Target, 2002; Fonagy, Target, Steele & Steele, 1998). In clinical settings, mentalization-based treatment has shown promise in treating borderline personality disorder and other severe forms of personality pathology (Allen & Fonagy, 2006; Clarkin, Fonagy, & Gabbard, 2010; Fonagy & Bateman, 2006).

The related construct *theory of mind* initially developed outside psychoanalysis, at the intersection of primatology, philosophy, social cognition, and neuroscience. The term was first used by Premack and Woodruff (1978), who defined it as "the ability to impute mental states to oneself or to others" (p. 15). More broadly, the term theory of mind has been used to describe an individual's recognition that others have thoughts and feelings which differ from one's own. In recent years interest in the construct has blossomed, particularly as a way of conceptualizing pervasive developmental disorders. For example, Baron-Cohen (1995) proposed that children with autism spectrum disorders lack theory of mind and therefore experience "mind-blindness" (see also Baron-Cohen, 2009, for recent findings in this area).

Attachment and Life-Span Development

As several writers have noted, there is a natural affiliation between developmental psychology and the psychodynamic emphasis on stages of growth, familial influences, and the formation of internal mental structures that shape and guide behavior (Eagle, 1996; Emde, 2007). Theorists in both areas have built upon this natural affiliation, and—in contrast to cognitive psychology—the exchange between psychoanalysis and developmental psychology has been openly acknowledged from the outset (see Ainsworth, 1969, 1989). Moreover, the psychoanalysis–developmental psychology interface is synergistic: Just as models of child and adolescent development have been affected by psychodynamic concepts, psychoanalytic models of personality formation and intrapsychic dynamics have been affected by developmental research on attachment, emotions, and cognitive development (Bruschweiler-Stern et al., 2010; Cramer, 2006; Silverstein, 2007).

Following Bowlby's (1969, 1973) pioneering work on the effect of attachment on infants' social and emotional development, and Ainsworth's empirical demonstration of distinct attachment patterns in children (see Ainsworth, 1969, 1989), Hazan and Shaver (1987) proposed four styles of adult attachment in romantic relationships, which roughly correspond to the attachment classifications identified by Ainsworth and others: secure, anxious-preoccupied, dismissive-avoidant, and fearful-avoidant. Along somewhat similar lines, Bartholomew and Horowitz (1991) proposed a four-category model in which adult attachment styles are categorized according to the individual's sense of self (dependence-autonomy) and interpersonal goals (closeness-avoidance). Contemporary researchers stress the importance of viewing attachment relationships as reciprocal, with characteristics of the attachment seeker and attachment figure both contributing to the quality of the relationship (e.g., Mikulincer, Shaver, Bar-On, & Ein-Dor, 2010). In this context Robbins and Zacks (2007) suggested that attachment theory may also contribute to our understanding of mentalization and theory of mind insofar as certain attachment styles lead children to become more or less capable of interpreting others' feelings and modulating their own internal states.

Thus, attachment research has not only contributed to psychoanalysts' understanding of infant-caregiver dynamics, but has also helped set the stage for the study of life-span development within the psychodynamic framework. Although Freud denied the existence of personality development postadolescence, there has been a surprising

amount of empirical research in this area; beginning with Goldfarb's (1963) work, theoreticians and researchers have explored myriad aspects of the psychodynamics of late-life development (e.g., Miner-Rubino et al., 2004; Waldinger & Schulz, 2010). With the advent of more sophisticated multistore models of memory, the links between psychodynamic processes and injury- and illness-based dementia have also been delineated.

Psychoanalytic Health Psychology

Over the years, psychoanalysis has had an ambivalent relationship with health psychology (Duberstein & Masling, 2000). In part, this situation reflects Freud's own ambivalence regarding the mind-body relationship. After all, the great insight that led Freud to develop his topographic and structural models of the mind—in many ways, the *raison d'être* of psychoanalysis itself—was the idea that many physical symptoms are the product of psychological conflicts rather than of organic disease processes (Bowers & Meichenbaum, 1984). Freud's early interest in conversion disorders and hysteria set the stage for a psychoanalytic psychology that emphasized mental—not physical—explanations for changes in health and illness states.

Beginning in the 1920s, however, Deutsch (1922, 1924) and others argued that underlying psychodynamic processes could have direct effects on the body's organ systems. The notion that unconscious dynamics could influence bodily functioning directly was extended and elaborated by Alexander (1950, 1954), who developed a detailed theoretical framework linking specific psychodynamic processes with predictable physiological sequelae and illness states. When Sifneos (1972) articulated his empirically grounded, psychoanalytically informed model of alexithymia (an inability to verbalize emotions), the stage was set for the development of a truly psychoanalytic health psychology. The key hypotheses of Sifneos's approach—that unverbalized emotions can have destructive effects on the body's organ systems—helped lay the groundwork for several ongoing health psychology research programs that are to varying degrees rooted in psychodynamic concepts. Research on stress and coping (Pennebaker & O'Heeron, 1984), chronic pain and depression (Schattner & Shahar, 2011), emotional disclosure and recovery from illness (Niederhoffer & Pennebaker, 2009), health and hardiness (Kobasa, 1979), and the "Type C" (cancer-prone) personality (Temoshok, 1987) have all been based in part on psychodynamic models of health and illness (however, see Lopez, Ramirez, Esteve, & Anarte,

2002, for a critique of research on the concept of a cancer-prone personality).

Recent research in this area has also helped shift the focus of psychoanalytic health psychology from a near-exclusive focus on deficit and disease to a more balanced perspective, which recognizes the critical role of psychodynamic processes in coping and resilience. For example, while a repressive coping style (i.e., a defensive style characterized by avoidance of disturbing cognitions and denial of negative affect states) has long been linked with increased incidence of cancer and cardiovascular disease, studies also suggest that repressive coping may be associated with improved adjustment to trauma (Bonanno, Brewin, Kaniasty, & La Greca, 2010). J. H. Block and Block's (1980) construct of ego resiliency (i.e., the dynamic capacity of an individual to modify his or her characteristic level of ego control to accommodate environmental demands) has led to research demonstrating that resilient individuals show better psychological adjustment and more adaptive coping strategies when confronted by stressful circumstances (Block & Kremen, 1996: Denckla, Mancini, Bornstein, & Bonanno, 2011; Genet & Siemer, 2011).

Evidence-Based Psychodynamic Treatment

Although psychoanalysts were initially reluctant to test the efficacy of psychodynamic treatment empirically using traditional nomothetic research methods, in recent years considerable research has accumulated supporting the efficacy of psychoanalysis and psychodynamic therapy (*see* Diener, Hilsenroth, & Weinberger, 2007; Leichsenring & Rabung, 2008; Luborsky & Barrett, 2006). Psychodynamic interventions have proved useful in diminishing symptom severity, enhancing overall psychological adjustment, and increasing life satisfaction (Huprich, 2009; Summers & Barber, 2010). Studies confirm that the positive effects of psychoanalytic treatment generalize across different contexts (e.g., social, work), and relationship domains (e.g., friendships, romantic relationships), and are effective for patients with a broad range of ethnic and socioeconomic backgrounds (Gottdiener, 2006; Weiner & Bornstein, 2009).

A seminal study in this area was conducted by Shedler (2010), who reviewed a large number of studies of psychoanalytic treatment and systematically compared effect sizes across treatment modalities. Shedler found that (a) effect sizes for psychodynamic therapy were comparable to or larger than those associated with many evidence-based treatments (e.g., cognitive behavioral therapy; see

also Diener et al., 2007); and (b) in contrast to other treatment methods, therapeutic gains in psychodynamic therapy were maintained after treatment was terminated. Shedler's review further suggested that a number of psychodynamic concepts have been integrated into other forms of therapy without being explicitly acknowledged, a situation echoed in the empirical research literature, wherein psychodynamic concepts have been shown to re-emerge in other field without citation of their psychoanalytic roots (Bornstein, 2005).

Psychoanalysis and Culture

Given Freud's interest in using psychoanalytic principles to understand the dynamics of culture and intergroup relations (e.g., Freud, 1930/1961a), it is ironic that throughout much of the 20th century there was relatively little empirical work addressing this issue. This situation has changed within the past several decades, and one area wherein psychoanalysts have been particularly active in incorporating ideas and findings regarding cultural influences involves self-construal (see Markus & Kitayama, 2010). Myriad studies have shown that individuals raised in individualistic, independence-focused cultures (e.g., United States, Great Britain) tend to define the self primarily in terms of internal attributes and individual differences, whereas individuals raised in more sociocentric, interdependent cultures (e.g., Japan, India) are more likely to describe the self in terms of interpersonal relations and connections with others (Oyserman, Coon, & Kemmelmeier, 2002). Consistent with this pattern, Sedikides, Gaertner, and Toguchi (2003) found that self-enhancement involves different pathways in independent and interdependent individuals, with independent people focusing on individualistic attributes/traits (i.e., independent, unique) and interdependent people focusing on collectivistic attributes/traits (i.e., agreeable, respectful). Following this line of research, Brown and Cai (2010) demonstrated how these different foci moderate cultural differences in self-evaluations.

A second domain where psychoanalysts have been active in incorporating information regarding culture has been in the area of psychotherapy. Although initial writing in this area tended to emphasize the challenges that arise in psychodynamic treatment when patient and therapist come from different cultural backgrounds, evidence has not supported the contention that therapist-patient cultural differences invariably have a deleterious impact on psychotherapy process or outcome (see Weiner & Bornstein, 2009, for a review of research in this area). Several research programs are underway assessing the moderating impact of culture and ethnicity on psychodynamic treatment (e.g., Chessick, 2004; Rodriguez, Cabaniss, Arbuckle, & Oquendo, 2008), and initial findings suggest that divergences in therapist-patient cultural background can have positive effects, negative effects, or negligible effects depending upon the ways that issues regarding culture and ethnicity are addressed during treatment.

The Opportunities and Challenges of Neuroscience

More than 20 years ago, Kandel (1988) articulated a vision for an empirically oriented psychoanalysis firmly embedded within the assumptions, principles, and findings of cognitive psychology and neuroscience. Kandell's vision, coupled with the contributions of Panksepp (1998) and others, ultimately led to the development of *neuropsychoanalysis*, a systematic integration of psychodynamic and neuropsychological concepts that has increased researchers' understanding of implicit memory, unconscious conflict, defense and coping, and mental representations of self and others (Farb et al., 2007; Roffman & Gerber, 2009). Some of the first contemporary efforts to integrate psychoanalytic principles with findings from neuroscience involved sleep and dreams (Hobson, 1988; Winson, 1985), and contemporary integrative models of dream formation now incorporate principles from both domains, setting the stage for extension of this integrative effort to other aspects of mental life (Levin & Nielsen, 2007). Neuroimaging techniques such as functional magnetic resonance imaging (fMRI) have begun to play an increasingly central role in this ongoing psychoanalysis-neuroscience integration (see Gerber, 2007; Schiff, 1999; Slipp, 2000).

Two psychodynamically relevant issues now being studied via fMRI and other neuroimaging techniques are the neurological underpinnings of transference, and cortical activation patterns associated with various psychological defenses (Schiff et al., 2005; Walla, Greiner, Duregger, Deecke, & Thurner, 2007). Evidence regarding the cortical regions involved in these and other implicit processes support many of Freud's hypotheses regarding unconscious mental activity (Carhart-Harris & Friston, 2010; Roffman & Gerber, 2009). Neuroimaging studies of defensive mental operations are still in their infancy, but preliminary findings suggest that the process of biasing and distorting previously encoded information also involves predictable patterns of cortical (and possibly subcortical) activation.

CONCLUSION: THE PSYCHOLOGY OF PSYCHODYNAMICS AND THE PSYCHODYNAMICS OF PSYCHOLOGY

Despite their limitations, psychodynamic models of personality have survived for more than a century, reinventing themselves periodically in response to new empirical findings, theoretical shifts in other areas of psychology, and changing social and economic forces. Stereotypes notwithstanding, psychodynamic models have evolved considerably during the 20th century and will continue to evolve throughout the 21st century as well. For better or worse, psychoanalytic theory may be the closest thing to an overarching field theory in all of psychology (Bornstein, 2010). It deals with a broad range of issues—normal and pathological functioning, motivation and emotion, childhood and adulthood, individual and culture—and although certain features of the model have not held up well to empirical testing, the model does have tremendous heuristic value and great potential for integrating ideas and findings in disparate areas of social and neurological science.

More than a century ago, Freud (1895/1955b) speculated that scientists would be resistant to psychoanalytic ideas because of the uncomfortable implications of these ideas for their own functioning. Whether he was correct in this regard, it is true that psychodynamic models of personality provide a useful framework for examining ourselves and our beliefs. Clinical psychologists have long used psychoanalytic principles to evaluate and refine their psychotherapeutic efforts. Scientists have not been as open to this sort of self-scrutiny. There is, however, a burgeoning literature on the biases and hidden motivations of the scientist (Bornstein, 1999a; D'Este & Perkmann, 2011), and psychodynamic models of personality may eventually contribute a great deal to this literature.

REFERENCES

Adler, A. (1921). *Understanding human nature.* New York, NY: Fawcett.

Adler, A. (1923). *The practice and theory of individual psychology.* London, UK: Routledge & Kegan Paul.

Ainsworth, M. D. S. (1969). Object relations, dependency, and attachment: A theoretical review of the infant-mother relationship. *Child Development, 40,* 969–1025.

Ainsworth, M. D. S. (1989). Attachments beyond infancy. *American Psychologist, 44,* 709–716.

Alexander, F. (1950). *Psychosomatic medicine.* New York, NY: Norton.

Alexander, F. (1954). *The scope of psychoanalysis.* New York, NY: Basic Books.

Allen, J. G., & Fonagy, P. (2006). *Handbook of mentalization-based treatment.* Chichester, UK: Wiley.

Alliance of Psychoanalytic Organizations. (2006). *Psychodynamic diagnostic manual.* Silver Spring, MD: Author.

Aron, L. (1990). One person and two person psychologies and the method of psychoanalysis. *Psychoanalytic Psychology, 7*, 475–485.

Baddeley, A. (2007). *Working memory, thought, and action.* New York, NY: Oxford University Press.

Banai, E., Mikulincer, M., & Shaver, P. R. (2005). "Selfobject" needs in Kohut's self psychology: Links with attachment, self-cohesion, affect regulation, and adjustment. *Psychoanalytic Psychology, 22*, 224–260.

Bargh, J. A., & Morsella, E. (2008). The unconscious mind. *Perspectives on Psychological Science, 3*, 73–79.

Baron-Cohen, S. (1995). *Mindblindness: An essay on autism and theory of mind.* Boston, MA: MIT Press.

Baron-Cohen, S. (2009). Autism: The empathizing–systemizing (E-S) theory. *Annals of the New York Academy of Science, 1156*, 68–80.

Bartholomew, K., & Horowitz, L. M. (1991). Attachment styles among young adults: A test of a four-category model. *Journal of Personality and Social Psychology, 61*, 226–244.

Baumeister, R. F., Masicampo, E. J., & Vohs, K. D. (2011). Do conscious thoughts cause behavior? *Annual Review of Psychology, 62*, 331–361.

Berka, M. S., & Andersen, S. M. (2008). The sting of lack of affection: Chronic goal dissatisfaction in transference. *Self and Identity, 7*, 393–412.

Besser, A., Guez, J., & Priel, B. (2008). The associations between self-criticism and dependency and incidental learning of interpersonal and achievement words. *Personality and Individual Differences, 44*, 1696–1710.

Besser, A., & Priel, B. (2011). Dependency, self-criticism and negative affective responses following imaginary rejection and failure threats: Meaning-making processes as moderators or mediators. *Psychiatry, 74*, 31–40.

Blatt, S. J. (1974). Levels of object representation in anaclitic and introjective depression. *Psychoanalytic Study of the Child, 29*, 107–157.

Blatt, S. J. (1991). A cognitive morphology of psychopathology. *Journal of Nervous and Mental Disease, 179*, 449–458.

Blatt, S. J. (2004). *Experiences of depression: Theoretical, clinical, and research perspectives.* Washington, DC: American Psychological Association.

Blatt, S. J. (2008). *Polarities of experience: Relatedness and self-definition in personality development, psychopathology, and the therapeutic process.* Washington, DC: American Psychological Association.

Blatt, S. J., & Ford, R. Q. (1994). *Therapeutic change.* New York, NY: Plenum Press.

Blatt, S. J., & Levy, K. N. (2003). Attachment theory, psychoanalysis, personality development, and psychopathology. *Psychoanalytic Inquiry, 23*, 104–152.

Block, J. H., & Block, J. (1980). The role of ego-control and ego-resiliency in the origination of behavior. In W. A. Collings (Ed.), *The Minnesota symposia on child psychology* (Vol. 13, pp. 39–101). Hillsdale, NJ: Erlbaum.

Block, J., & Kremen, A. M. (1996). IQ and ego-resiliency: Conceptual and empirical connections and separateness. *Journal of Personality and Social Psychology, 70*, 349–361.

Blum, H. P. (2010). Object relations in contemporary psychoanalysis: Contrasting views. *Contemporary Psychoanalysis, 46*, 32–47.

Bonanno, G. A., Brewin, C. R., Kaniasty, K., & La Greca, A. M. (2010). Weighing the costs of disaster: Consequences, risks, and resilience in individuals, families, and communities. *Psychological Science in the Public Interest, 11*, 1–49.

Book, H. E. (1998). *How to practice brief psychodynamic psychotherapy.* Washington, DC: American Psychological Association.

Bornstein, R. F. (1993). Implicit perception, implicit memory, and the recovery of unconscious material in psychotherapy. *Journal of Nervous and Mental Disease, 181*, 337–344.

Bornstein, R. F. (1999a). Objectivity and subjectivity in psychological science: Embracing and transcending psychology's positivist tradition. *Journal of Mind and Behavior, 20*, 1–16.

Bornstein, R. F. (1999b). Source amnesia, misattribution, and the power of unconscious perceptions and memories. *Psychoanalytic Psychology, 16*, 155–178.

Bornstein, R. F. (2001). The impending death of psychoanalysis. *Psychoanalytic Psychology, 18*, 3–20.

Bornstein, R. F. (2005). Reconnecting psychoanalysis to mainstream psychology: Challenges and opportunities. *Psychoanalytic Psychology, 22*, 323–340.

Bornstein, R. F. (2006). A Freudian construct lost and reclaimed: The psychodynamics of personality pathology. *Psychoanalytic Psychology, 23*, 339–353.

Bornstein, R. F. (2007). Might the Rorschach be a projective test after all? Social projection of an undesired trait alters Rorschach Ooral Ddependency scores. *Journal of Personality Assessment, 88*, 354–367.

Bornstein, R. F. (2009). Heisenberg, Kandinsky, and the heteromethod convergence problem: Lessons from within and beyond psychology. *Journal of Personality Assessment, 91*, 1–8.

Bornstein, R. F. (2010). Psychoanalytic theory as a unifying framework for 21st century personality assessment. *Psychoanalytic Psychology, 27*, 133–152.

Bornstein, R. F., & Huprich, S. K. (2011). Toward a multidimensional model of personality disorder diagnosis: Implications for DSM-5. *Journal of Personality Disorders, 25*, 331–337.

Bornstein, R. F., & Masling, J. M. (2002). The psychodynamics of gender and gender role. In R. F. Bronstein & J. M. Masling (Eds.), *The psychodynamics of gender and gender role* (pp. xiii–xxix). Washington, DC: American Psychological Association.

Bowers, K. S., & Meichenbaum, D. (1984). *The unconscious reconsidered.* New York, NY: Basic Books.

Bowlby, J. (1969). *Attachment.* New York, NY: Basic Books.

Bowlby, J. (1973). *Separation: Anxiety and anger.* New York, NY: Basic Books.

Brenner, C. (1973). *An elementary textbook of psychoanalysis.* New York, NY: Anchor Books.

Breuer, J., & Freud, S. (1955). Studies on hysteria. In J. Strachey (Ed. & Trans.), *The standard edition of the complete psychological works of Sigmund Freud* (Vol. 2, pp. 1–305). London: Hogarth. (Original work published 1895)

Brown, J. D., & Cai, H. (2010). Self-esteem and trait importance moderate cultural differences in self-evaluations. *Journal of Cross-Cultural Psychology, 41*, 116–123.

Bruschweiler-Stern, N., Lyons-Ruth, K., Morgan, A. C., Nahum, J. P., Sander, L. W., Stern, D. N., . . . Tronick, E. Z. (2010). *Change in psychotherapy: A unifying paradigm.* New York, NY: Norton.

Bucci, W. (2000). The need for a "psychoanalytic psychology" in the cognitive science field. *Psychoanalytic Psychology, 17*, 203–224.

Bucci, W. (2002). The referential process, consciousness, and the sense of self. *Psychoanalytic Inquiry, 22*, 766–793.

Buss, D. M. (2008). Human nature and individual differences: Evolution of human personality. In O. P. John, R. W. Robins, & L. A. Pervin (Eds.), *Handbook of personality psychology: Theory and research* (3rd ed., pp. 29–60). New York, NY: Guilford Press.

Buss, D. M. (2009). How can evolutionary psychology successfully explain personality and individual differences? *Perspectives on Psychological Science, 4*, 359–366.

Carhart-Harris, R. L., & Friston, K. J. (2010). The default-mode, ego-functions and free-energy: A neurobiological account of Freudian ideas. *Brain, 133*, 1265–1283.

Chessick, R. D. (2004). The Freud encyclopedia: Theory, therapy, and culture. *American Journal of Psychiatry, 161*, 1138–1140.

Chodorow, N. (1978). *The reproduction of mothering: Psychoanalysis and the sociology of gender*. London, UK: University of California Press.

Clarkin, J. F., Fonagy, P., & Gabbard, G. O. (Eds.) (2010). *Psychodynamic psychotherapy for personality disorders: A clinical handbook*. Arlington, VA: American Psychiatric.

Cramer, P. (2000). Defense mechanisms in psychology today: Further processes for adaptation. *American Psychologist, 55*, 637–646.

Cramer, P. (2006). *Protecting the self: Defense mechanisms in action*. New York, NY: Guilford Press.

Crews, F. C. (Ed.). (1998). *Unauthorized Freud: Doubters confront a legend*. New York, NY: Viking Press.

Custers, R., & Aarts, H. (2010). The unconscious will: How the pursuit of goals operates outside of conscious awareness. *Science, 329*, 47–50.

Danzinger, K. (1997). *Naming the mind*. Beverly Hills, CA: Sage.

Dawson, E., Gilovich, T., & Regan, D. T. (2002). Motivated reasoning and performance on the Wason selection task. *Personality and Social Psychology Bulletin, 28*, 1379–1387.

Denckla, C. A., Mancini, A. D., Bornstein, R. F., & Bonanno, G. A. (2011). Adaptive and maladaptive dependency in bereavement: Distinguishing prolonged and resolved grief trajectories. *Personality and Individual Differences, 51*, 1012–1017.

D'Este, P., & Perkmann, M. (2011). Why do academics engage with industry? The entrepreneurial university and individual motivations. *Journal of Technology Transfer, 36*, 316–339.

Deutsch, F. (1922). Psychoanlayse und Organkrankheiten. *International Journal of Psychoanalysis, 8*, 290–306.

Deutsch, F. (1924). Zur Bildung des Konversions Symptoms. *International Journal of Psychoanalysis, 10*, 380–392.

Diener, M. J., Hilsenroth, M. J., & Weinberger, J. (2007). Therapist affect focus and patient outcomes in psychodynamic psychotherapy: A meta-analysis. *American Journal of Psychiatry, 164*, 936–941.

Donenberg, G. R., Emersen, E., & Mackesy-Amiti, M. E. (2011). Sexual risk among African American girls: Psychopathology and mother–daughter relationships. *Journal of Consulting and Clinical Psychology, 79*, 153–158.

Duberstein, P. R., & Masling, J. M. (Eds.). (2000). *Psychodynamic perspectives on sickness and health*. Washington, DC: American Psychological Association.

Dykas, M. J., & Cassidy, J. (2011). Attachment and the processing of social information across the life span: Theory and evidence. *Psychological Bulletin, 137*, 19–46.

Eagle, M. N. (1984). *Recent developments in psychoanalysis*. New York, NY: McGraw-Hill.

Eagle, M. N. (1996). Attachment research and psychoanalytic theory. In J. M. Masling & R. F. Bornstein (Eds.), *Psychoanalytic perspectives on developmental psychology* (pp. 105–149). Washington, DC: American Psychological Association.

Eagle, M. N. (2000). A critical evaluation of current conceptions of transference and countertransference. *Psychoanalytic Psychology, 17*, 24–37.

Einstein, A. (1905). On the electrodynamics of moving bodies. *Annalen der Physik, 17*, 891–921.

Einstein, A. (1915). On the general theory of relativity. *Preussische Akademie der Wissenschaften Sitzungsberichte* (Part 2, pp. 778–786, 799–801). Berlin, Germany: Akadamie der Wissenschaften.

Ellenberger, H. (1970). *The discovery of the unconscious*. New York, NY: Basic Books.

Emde, R. N. (2007). Engaging imagination and the future: Frontiers for clinical work. *Attachment and Human Development, 9*, 295–302.

Emde, R. N., & Robinson, J. (2000). Guiding principles for a theory of early intervention: A developmental-psychoanalytic perspective. In J. P. Shonkoff & S. J. Meisels (Eds.), *Handbook of early childhood intervention* (pp. 160–178). New York, NY: Cambridge University Press.

Erdelyi, M. H. (1985). *Psychoanalysis: Freud's cognitive psychology*. New York, NY: Freeman.

Erdelyi, M. H. (2004). Subliminal perception and its cognates: Theory, indeterminacy, and time. *Consciousness and Cognition, 13*, 73–91.

Erdelyi, M. H. (2010). The ups and downs of memory. *American Psychologist, 65*, 623–633.

Erikson, E. H. (1963). *Childhood and society*. New York, NY: Norton.

Erikson, E. H. (1968). *Identity: Youth and crisis*. New York, NY: Norton.

Fairbairn, W. R. D. (1952). *An object relations theory of the personality*. New York, NY: Basic Books.

Fancher, R. E. (1973). *Psychoanalytic psychology: The development of Freud's thought*. New York, NY: Norton.

Farb, N. A., Segal, Z. V., Mayberg, H., Bean, J., McKeon, D., Fatima, Z., & Anderson, A. K. (2007). Attending to the present: Mindfulness meditation reveals distinct neural modes of self-reference. *Social Cognitive Affective Neuroscience, 2*, 313–322.

Fisher, S., & Greenberg, R. P. (1996). *Freud scientifically reappraised*. New York, NY: Wiley.

Fonagy, P., & Bateman, A. (2006). Mechanisms of change in mentalization-based treatment of borderline personality disorder. *Journal of Clinical Psychology, 62*, 411–430.

Fonagy, P., Gergely, G., Jurist, E., & Target, M. (2002). *Affect regulation, mentalization and the development of the self*. New York, NY: Other Press.

Fonagy, P., Target, M., Steele, H., & Steele, M. (1998). *Reflective functioning manual, version 5.0, for application to adult attachment interviews*. Unpublished manual, University College London.

Fraley, R. C. (2002). Attachment stability from infancy to adulthood: Meta-analysis and dynamic modeling of developmental mechanisms. *Personality and Social Psychology Bulletin, 6*, 123–151.

Freud, A. (1936). *The ego and the mechanisms of defense*. New York, NY: International Universities Press.

Freud, S. (1953a). The interpretation of dreams. In J. Strachey (Ed. & Trans.), *The standard edition of the complete psychological works of Sigmund Freud* (Vols. 4–5). London, UK: Hogarth. (Original work published 1900)

Freud, S. (1953b). Three essays on the theory of sexuality. In J. Strachey (Ed. & Trans.), *The standard edition of the complete psychological works of Sigmund Freud* (Vol. 7, pp. 125–245). London, UK: Hogarth. (Original work published 1905)

Freud, S. (1955a). From the history of an infantile neurosis. In J. Strachey (Ed. & Trans.), *The standard edition of the complete psychological works of Sigmund Freud* (Vol. 17, pp. 3–122). London, UK: Hogarth. (Original work published 1918)

Freud, S. (1955b). A reply to criticisms of my paper on anxiety neurosis. In J. Strachey (Ed. & Trans.), *The standard edition of the complete psychological works of Sigmund Freud* (Vol. 3, pp. 119–139). London, UK: Hogarth. (Original work published 1895)

Freud, S. (1955c). Further remarks on the neuro-psychoses of defense. In J. Strachey (Ed. & Trans.), *The standard edition of the complete psychological works of Sigmund Freud* (Vol. 3, pp. 159–185). London, UK: Hogarth. (Original work published 1896)

Freud, S. (1957). Instincts and their vicissitudes. In J. Strachey (Ed. & Trans.), *The standard edition of the complete works of Sigmund Freud* (Vol. 14, pp. 117–140). London, UK: Hogarth. (Original work published 1915)

Freud, S. (1958a). The interpretation of dreams. In J. Strachey (Ed. & Trans.), *The standard edition of the complete psychological works of Sigmund Freud* (Vols. 4 & 5). London, UK: Hogarth. (Original work published 1900)

Freud, S. (1958b). Formulations on the two principles of mental functioning. In J. Strachey (Ed. & Trans.), *The standard edition of the complete psychological works of Sigmund Freud* (Vol. 12, pp. 218–226). London, UK: Hogarth. (Original work published 1911)

Freud, S. (1961a). Civilization and its discontents. In J. Strachey (Ed. & Trans.), *The standard edition of the complete psychological works of Sigmund Freud* (Vol. 21, pp. 59–145). London, UK: Hogarth. (Original work published 1930)

Freud, S. (1961b). The ego and the id. In J. Strachey (Ed. & Trans.), *The standard edition of the complete psychological works of Sigmund Freud* (Vol. 19, pp. 1–66). London, UK: Hogarth. (Original work published 1923)

Freud, S. (1964a). New introductory lectures on psycho-analysis. In J. Strachey (Ed. & Trans.), *The standard edition of the complete psychological works of Sigmund Freud* (Vol. 22, pp. 1–182). London, UK: Hogarth. (Original work published 1933)

Freud, S. (1964b). An outline of psycho-analysis. In J. Strachey (Ed. & Trans.), *The standard edition of the complete psychological works of Sigmund Freud* (Vol. 23, pp. 139–207). London, UK: Hogarth. (Original work published 1940)

Freud, S. (1966). Project for a scientific psychology. In J. Strachey (Ed. & Trans.), *The standard edition of the complete psychological works of Sigmund Freud* (Vol. 1, pp. 283–387). London, UK: Hogarth. (Original work published 1895)

Fromm, E. (1941). *Escape from freedom*. New York, NY: Avon.

Fromm, E. (1947). *Man for himself*. New York, NY: Holt, Rinehart, and Winston.

Galatzer-Levy, R., Bachrach, H., Skolnikoff, A., & Waldron, S. (2000). *Does psychoanalysis work?* New Haven, CT: Yale University Press.

Gay, P. (1988). *Freud: A life for our time*. New York, NY: Norton.

Gedo, P. M. (1999). Single case studies in psychotherapy research. *Psychoanalytic Psychology, 16*, 274–280.

Genet, J. J., & Siemer, M. (2011). Flexible control in processing affective and non-affective material predicts individual differences in trait resilience. *Cognition and Emotion, 25*, 380–388.

Gerber, A. (2007). Whose unconscious is it anyway? *The American Psychoanalyst, 41*, 11, 28.

Ghinescu, R., Schachtman, T. R., Stadler, M. A., Fabiani, M., & Gratton, G. (2010). Strategic behavior without awareness? Effects of implicit learning in the Eriksen flanker paradigm. *Memory and Cognition, 38*, 197–205.

Gill, M. (1995). Classical and relational psychoanalysis. *Psychoanalytic Psychology, 12*, 89–107.

Gilligan, C. (1982). *In a different voice: Psychological theory and women's development*. Cambridge, MA: Harvard University Press.

Goldfarb, A. (1963). Psychodynamics and the three-generation family. In E. Shanas & G. Streib (Eds.), *Social structure and the family* (pp. 10–45). Englewood Cliffs, NJ: Prentice-Hall.

Gottdiener, W. H. (2006). Individual psychodynamic psychotherapy of schizophrenia: Empirical evidence for the practicing clinician. *Psychoanalytic Psychology, 23*, 583–589.

Greenberg, J. R., & Mitchell, S. J. (1983). *Object relations in psychoanalytic theory*. Cambridge, MA: Harvard University Press.

Grunbaum, A. (1984). *The foundations of psychoanalysis*. Berkeley: University of California Press.

Harlow, H. F., & Harlow, M. K. (1962). Social deprivation in monkeys. *Scientific American, 207*, 136–146.

Hartmann, H. (1964). *Essays on ego psychology*. New York, NY: International Universities Press.

Hazan, C., & Shaver, P. (1987). Romantic love conceptualized as an attachment process. *Journal of Personality and Social Psychology, 52*, 511–524.

Higgins, E. T., & Pittman, T. S. (2008). Motives of the human animal: Comprehending, managing, and sharing inner states. *Annual Review of Psychology, 59*, 361–385.

Hilgard, E. (1987). *Psychology in America: An historical survey*. New York, NY: Harcourt Brace Jovanovich.

Hobson, J. A. (1988). *The dreaming brain*. New York, NY: Basic Books.

Horney, K. (1937). *The neurotic personality of our time*. New York, NY: Norton.

Horney, K. (1945). *Our inner conflicts*. New York, NY: Norton.

Huprich, S. K. (2009). *Psychodynamic therapy: Conceptual and empirical foundations*. New York, NY: Taylor & Francis.

Huprich, S. K. (2011). Reclaiming the value of assessing unconscious and subjective psychological experience. *Journal of Personality Assessment, 93*, 151–160.

Ihilevich, D., & Gleser, G. C. (1986). *Defense mechanisms*. Owosso, MI: DMI Associates.

Ihilevich, D., & Gleser, G. C. (1991). *Defenses in psychotherapy*. Owosso, MI: DMI Associates.

Jacobson, E. (1964). *The self and object world*. New York, NY: International Universities Press.

Janet, P. (1907). *The major symptoms of hysteria*. New York, NY: Macmillan.

Josephs, L., Anderson, E., Bernard, A., Fatzer, K., & Streich, J. (2004). Assessing progress in analysis interminable. *Journal of the American Psychoanalytic Association, 52*, 1185–1214.

Jung, C. G. (1933). *Modern man in search of a soul*. New York, NY: Harcourt Brace Jovanovich.

Jung, C. G. (1961). *The collected works of Carl Jung*. Princeton, NJ: Princeton University Press.

Kandel, E. R. (1988). A new intellectual framework for psychiatry. *American Journal of Psychiatry, 155*, 457–469.

Kernberg, O. (1984). *Severe personality disorders*. New Haven, CT: Yale University Press.

Kihlstrom, J. F. (2008). The psychological unconscious. In O. John, R. Robins, & L. Pervin (Eds.), *Handbook of personality: theory and research* (3rd ed., pp. 583–602). New York, NY: Guilford Press.

Kim, Y. R., & Tyrer, P. (2010). Controversies surrounding classification of personality disorder. *Psychiatry Investigations, 7*, 1–8.

Klein, M. (1932). *The psycho-analysis of children*. London, UK: Hogarth.

Klein, M. (1964). *Contributions to psychoanalysis, 1921–1945*. New York, NY: McGraw-Hill.

Kobasa, S. C. (1979). Stressful life events, personality, and health: An inquiry into hardiness. *Journal of Personality and Social Psychology, 37*, 1–11.

Kohut, H. (1971). *The analysis of the self*. New York, NY: International Universities Press.

Kohut, H. (1977). *The restoration of the self*. New York, NY: International Universities Press.

Kuhn, T. S. (1970). *The structure of scientific revolutions* (2nd ed., enlarged). Chicago, IL: University of Chicago Press.

Kwan, V. S. Y., John, O. P., Robins, R. W., & Kuang, L. (2008). Conceptualizing and assessing self-enhancement bias: A componential approach. *Journal of Personality and Social Psychology, 94*, 1062–1077.

Leichsenring, F., & Rabung, S. (2008). Effectiveness of long-term psychodynamic psychotherapy: A meta-analysis. *Journal of the American Medical Association, 300*, 1551–1565.

Levin, R., & Nielsen, T. A. (2007). Disturbed dreaming, posttraumatic stress disorder, and affect distress: A review and neurocognitive model. *Psychological Bulletin, 133*, 482–528.

Lopez, A. E., Ramirez, C., Esteve, R., & Anarte, M. T. (2002). The personality Tupe C construct: A contribution to its definition based on empirical data. *Psychological Research, 10*, 229–249.

Luborsky, L., & Barrett, M. S. (2006). The history and empirical status of key psychoanalytic concepts. *Annual Review of Clinical Psychology, 2*, 1–19.

Luborsky, L., & Crits-Christoph, P. (1990). *Understanding transference: The core conflictual relationship theme method*. New York, NY: Basic Books.

Luyten, P. (2011). Review of mind to mind: Infant research, neuroscience, and psychoanalysis. *Clinical Social Work Journal, 39,* 116–118.

Luyten, P., Blatt, S. J., & Corveleyn, J. (2006). Minding the gap between positivism and hermeneutics in psychoanalytic research. *Journal of the American Psychoanalytic Association, 54,* 572–609.

Macmillan, M. B. (2007). Inhibition and Phineas Gage: Repression and Sigmund Freud. *Neuropsychoanalysis, 6,* 181–192.

Mahler, M. S., Pine, F., & Bergman, A. (1975). *The psychological birth of the human infant.* New York, NY: Basic Books.

Main, M., Kaplan, M., & Cassidy, J. (1985). Security in infancy, childhood, and adulthood. *Monographs of the Society for Research in Child Development, 50,* 66–104.

Markus, H. R., & Kitayama, S. (2010). Culture and selves: A cycle of mutual constitution. *Perspectives on Psychological Science, 5,* 420–430.

Masling, J. M., & Bornstein, R. F. (Eds.). (1994). *Empirical perspectives on object relations theory.* Washington, DC: American Psychological Association.

Masling, J. M., & Schwartz, M. A. (1979). A critique of research in psychoanalytic theory. *Genetic Psychology Monographs, 100,* 257–307.

Mayes, L., Fonagy, P. & Target, M. (Eds.). (2007). *Developmental science and psychoanalysis: Integration and innovation (development in psychoanalysis)* (pp. 45–88). London, UK: Karnac Books.

Mayman, M. (1976). Psychoanalytic theory in retrospect and prospect. *Bulletin of the Menninger Clinic, 40,* 199–210.

McClelland, D. C., Koestner, R., & Weinberger, J. (1989). How do self-attributed and implicit motives differ? *Psychological Review, 96,* 690–702.

McWilliams, N. (1994). *Psychoanalytic diagnosis.* New York, NY: Guilford Press.

McWilliams, N. (2004). *Psychoanalytic psychotherapy: A practitioner's guide.* New York, NY: Guilford Press.

Midgley, N., Anderson, J., Grainger, E., Nesic-Vuckovic, T., & Urwin, C. (Eds.). (2009). *Child psychotherapy and research: New approaches, emerging findings.* New York, NY: Routledge/Taylor & Francis.

Mikulincer, M., Shaver, P. R., Bar-On, N., & Ein-Dor, T. (2010). The pushes and pulls of close relationships: Attachment insecurities and relational ambivalence. *Journal of Personality and Social Psychology, 98,* 450–468.

Millon, T. (2011). *Disorders of personality: Introducing a DSM/ICD spectrum from normal to abnormal.* New York, NY: Wiley.

Miner-Rubino, K., Winter, D. G., & Stewart, A. J. (2004). Gender, social class, and the subjective experience of aging: Self-perceived personality change from early adulthood to late midlife. *Personality and Social Psychology Bulletin, 30,* 1599–1610.

Mitchell, J. (1974). *Psychoanalysis and feminism: A radical reassessment of Freudian psychoanalysis.* New York, NY: Basic Books.

Mitchell, S. J. (2000). Response to Silverman (2000). *Psychoanalytic Psychology, 17,* 153–159.

Molenaar, P. C. M., & Campbell, C. G. (2009). The new person-specific paradigm in psychology. *Current Directions in Psychological Science, 18,* 112–117.

Morf, C. C. (2006). Personality reflected in a coherent idiosyncratic interplay of intra- and interpersonal self-regulatory processes. *Journal of Personality, 74,* 1527–1556.

Niederhoffer, K. G., & Pennebaker, J. W. (2009). Sharing one's story: On the benefits of writing or talking about emotional experience. In S. J., Lopez & C. R. Snyder (Eds.), *Oxford handbook of positive psychology* (2nd ed., pp. 621–632). New York, NY: Oxford University Press.

Norcross, J. C., Hedges, M., & Castle, P. H. (2002). Psychologists conducting psychotherapy in 2001: A study of the division 29 membership. *Psychotherapy: Theory, Research, Practice, Training, 39,* 97–102.

Oyserman, D., Coon, H. M., & Kemmelmeier, M. (2002). Rethinking individualism and collectivism: Evaluation of theoretical assumptions and meta-analyses. *Psychological Bulletin, 128,* 3–72.

Panksepp, J. (1998). *Affective neuroscience: The foundations of human and animal emotions.* New York, NY: Oxford University Press.

Pennebaker, J. W., & O'Heeron, R. C. (1984). Confiding in others and illness rate among spouses of suicide and accidental death victims. *Journal of Abnormal Psychology, 93,* 473–476.

Perry, J., Silvera, D., Rosenvinge, J. H., & Holte, A. (2002). Are oral, obsessive, and hysterical personality traits related to disturbed eating patterns? A general population study of 6,313 men and women. *Journal of Personality Assessment, 78,* 405–416.

Picasso, P. (1907). *Les Demoiselles D'Avignon* [The Young Ladies of Avignon]. New York, NY: Museum of Modern Art.

Premack, D., & Woodruff, G. (1978). Does the chimpanzee have a theory of mind? *Behavioral and Brain Sciences, 4,* 515–526.

Pretzer, J. L., & Beck, A. T. (2005). A cognitive theory of personality disorders. In M. F. Lenzenweger & J. F. Clarkin (Eds.), *Major theories of personality disorder* (2nd ed., pp. 114–156). New York, NY: Guilford Press.

Pyszczynski, T., Greenberg, J., & Solomon, S. (1999). A dual process model of defense against conscious and unconscious death-related thoughts. *Psychological Review, 106,* 835–845.

Pyszczynski, T., Greenberg, J., & Solomon, S. (2000). Proximal and distal defense: A new perspective on unconscious motivation. *Current Directions in Psychological Science, 9,* 156–160.

Pyszczynski, T., Henthorn, C., Motyl, M., & Gerow, K. (2010). Is Obama the Anti-Christ? Racial priming, extreme criticisms of Barack Obama, and attitudes toward the 2008 US presidential candidates. *Journal of Experimental Social Psychology, 46,* 863–866.

Robbins, P., & Zacks, J. M. (2007). Attachment theory and cognitive science: Commentary on Fonagy and Target. *Journal of the American Psychoanalytic Association, 55,* 457–467.

Rodriguez, C. I., Cabaniss, D. L., Arbuckle, M. R., & Oquendo, M. A. (2008). The role of culture in psychodynamic psychotherapy: Parallel processes resulting from cultural similarities between patient and therapist. *American Journal of Psychiatry, 165,* 1402–1406.

Roffman, J. L., & Gerber, A. (2009). Neural models of psychodynamic concepts and treatments: Implications for psychodynamic psychotherapy. In R. A. Levy & J. S. Ablon (Eds.), *Handbook of evidence-based psychodynamic psychotherapy.* New York, NY: Humana Press.

Ronningstam, E. (2009). Narcissistic personality disorder. In P. H., Blaney & T. Millon (Eds.), *Oxford textbook of psychopathology* (2nd ed., pp. 752–771). New York, NY: Oxford University Press.

Sandler, J., & Rosenblatt, B. (1962). The concept of the representational world. *Psychoanalytic Study of the Child, 17,* 128–145.

Schafer, R. (2009). *Tragic knots in psychoanalysis: New papers on psychoanalysis.* London, UK: Karnac Books.

Schattner, E., & Shahar, G. (2011). Role of pain personification in pain-related depression: An object relations perspective. *Psychiatry: Interpersonal and biological processes, 74,* 14–20.

Schiff, N. D. (1999). Neurobiology, suffering, and unconscious brain states. *Journal of Pain Management, 17,* 303–304.

Schiff, N., Rodriguez-Moreno, D., Kamal, A., Kim, K. H., Giacino, J., Plum, F., & Hirsch, J. (2005). fMRI reveals large-scale network activation in minimally conscious patients. *Neurology, 64,* 514–523.

Schwartz, S. J. (2001). The evolution of Eriksonian and neo-Eriksonian identity theory and research: A review and integration. *Identity, 1,* 7–58.

Sedikides, C., Gaertner, L., & Toguchi, Y. (2003). Pancultural self-enhancement. *Journal of Personality and Social Psychology, 84,* 60–79.

Shapiro, T., & Emde, R. N. (Eds.). (1995). *Research in psychoanalysis: Process, development, outcome.* Madison, CT: International Universities Press.

Shaver, P. R., & Mikulincer, M. (2002). Attachment related psychodynamics. *Attachment and Human Development, 4,* 133–161.

Shedler, J. (2010). The efficacy of psychodynamic psychotherapy. *American Psychologist, 65,* 98–109.

Sifneos, P. (1972). *Short-term psychotherapy and emotional crisis.* Cambridge, MA: Harvard University Press.

Silverstein, M. L. (2007). *Disorders of the self: A personality-guided approach.* Washington, DC: APA Books.

Skowron, E. A., Kozlowski, J. M., & Pincus, A. L. (2010). Differentiation, self–other representations, and rupture–repair processes: Predicting child maltreatment risk. *Journal of Counseling Psychology, 57,* 304–316.

Slade, A. (2005). Parental reflective functioning: An introduction. *Attachment and Human Development, 7,* 269–281.

Slipp, S. (Ed.). (2000). Neuroscience and psychoanalysis [Special Issue]. *Journal of the American Academy of Psychoanalysis, 28,* 191–395.

Spence, D. P. (1982). *Narrative truth and historical truth: Meaning and interpretation in psychoanalysis.* New York, NY: Norton.

Spitz, R. A. (1945). Hospitalism. *Psychoanalytic Study of the Child, 1,* 53–74.

Spitz, R. A. (1946). Hospitalism: A follow-up report on investigation described in Volume 1, 1945. *Psychoanalytic Study of the Child, 2,* 113–117.

Sullivan, H. S. (1947). *Conceptions of modern psychiatry.* New York, NY: Norton.

Sullivan, H. S. (1953). *The interpersonal theory of psychiatry.* New York, NY: Norton.

Sullivan, H. S. (1956). *Clinical studies in psychiatry.* New York, NY: Norton.

Summers, R., & Barber, J. (2010). *Psychodynamic therapy: A guide to evidence based practice.* New York. NY: Guilford Press.

Tangney, J. P., & Dearing, R. L. (2002). Gender differences in morality. In R. F. Bornstein & J. M. Masling (Eds.), *The psychodynamics of gender and gender role* (pp. 251–269). Washington, DC: APA Books.

Temoshok, L. (1987). Personality, coping style, emotion, and cancer: Toward an integrative model. *Cancer Surveys, 6,* 545–567.

Torrey, E. F. (1992). *Freudian fraud: The malignant effect of Freud's theory on American thought and culture.* New York, NY: HarperCollins.

Vaillant, G. E. (Ed.). (1986). *Empirical studies of ego mechanisms of defense.* Washington, DC: American Psychiatric Press.

Wachtel, P. L. (1997). *Psychoanalysis, behavior therapy, and the relational world.* Washington, DC: American Psychological Association.

Waldinger, R. J., & Schulz, M. S. (2010). What's love got to do with it? Social functioning, perceived health, and daily happiness in married octogenarians. *Psychology and Aging, 25,* 422–431.

Walla, P., Greiner, K., Duregger, C., Deecke, L., & Thurner, S. (2007). Self awareness and the subconscious effect of personal pronouns on word encoding: A magnetoencephalographic (MEG) study. *Neuropsychologia, 45,* 796–809.

Weiner, I. B., & Bornstein, R. F. (2009). *Principles of psychotherapy* (3rd ed.). New York, NY: Wiley.

Westen, D. (1999). The scientific status of unconscious processes: Is Freud really dead? *Journal of the American Psychoanalytic Association, 47,* 1061–1106.

Wilson, T. D. (2009). Know thyself. *Current Directions in Psychological Science, 4,* 384–389.

Winnicott, D. W. (1971). *Playing and reality.* Middlesex, UK: Penguin.

Winson, J. (1985). *Brain and psyche: The biology of the unconscious.* New York, NY: Doubleday.

CHAPTER 4

The Five-Factor Model in Fact and Fiction

ROBERT R. McCRAE, JAMES F. GAINES, AND MARIE A. WELLINGTON

Whether this story was true or not does not matter. Fantasy is the beloved of reason.

—*Envy* (Olesha, 1927/1967, p. 61)

Science and art have different criteria for truth. For science, it is seen in the conformity of ideas with observations—ideally, precise observations, made repeatedly, in telling circumstances. For art, truth is manifest through the experience of insight and a sense of deepened understanding. What is true for science is sometimes—but only sometimes—true in art, and vice versa. In this chapter we outline the facts about the Five-Factor Model (FFM) of personality as psychologists understand them today after decades of empirical research. We then consider personality traits in characters from literature, in particular Molière's Alceste and Voltaire's Candide. We are concerned both with what psychologists can learn from the study of personality in fiction and with how students of the humanities can benefit from an understanding of contemporary trait psychology.

Psychologists in general have ambivalent feelings about these issues (Oatley, 1999). Personality psychologists may swell with proprietary pride when Harold Bloom writes

that "the representation of human character and personality remains always the supreme literary value" (Bloom, 1998, pp. 3–4), but they are likely to take umbrage at his assertion that our greatest psychologist is Shakespeare. Although Henry Murray, one of the uncontested giants of personality psychology, devoted years to an examination of *Moby Dick*, analyses of personality in fictional characters (e.g., Johnson, Carroll, Gottschall, & Kruger, 2011) are rarely found in psychology journals today, and when they appear, may be disparaged as mere "prescientific literary allusions" (Goldberg, 1994, p. 353). One task of this chapter will be to define the conditions under which an examination of fictional characters can usefully contribute to scientific psychology.

Shakespeare was a keen observer of human nature, but he never had the opportunity to read the *Journal of Personality*. Can today's playwrights and novelists benefit in some way from a consideration of scientific insights into personality? For a century literary criticism has been influenced by Freudian thought, but Freud's stature in contemporary personality psychology has diminished markedly. Can critics gain new insights from recent research on the origins and effects of personality traits? Can an understanding of the FFM contribute to the general reader's appreciation of literature? These questions will also be addressed here.

We thank Corinna E. Löckenhoff for rating Faust; Pat Brennan, Janet McCrae, Steven Nordfjord, Richard Oloizia, Matt Scally, and Alex Weiss for suggestions of literary examples; and the late Prof. Frank L. Ingram for his infectious enthusiasm for Russian literature.

Robert R. McCrae receives royalties from the NEO Inventories.

THE FIVE-FACTOR MODEL

The FFM provides a basic description of individual differences in personality traits. Research using the FFM as a guide has yielded a substantial body of findings about how traits function, and new theories have been developed to integrate these findings into a coherent theory of personality. We turn first to the description.

An Overview

The FFM (Digman, 1990; John, Naumann, & Soto, 2008) is a taxonomy, or grouping, of personality traits that, in the past 30 years, has come to be adopted by most psychologists. Traits are "dimensions of individual differences in tendencies to show consistent patterns of thoughts, feelings, and actions" (McCrae & Costa, 2003, p. 25), and trait concepts are universally used to describe oneself and others. Laypersons use words like *nervous, enthusiastic, original, affable*, and *careful*, whereas psychologists have technical terms such as dysthymia, surgency, tolerance for ambiguity, need for abasement, and superego strength. The great advance that the FFM offered the field of personality psychology was the demonstration that almost all these lay terms and most of the concepts proposed by a wide range of personality theories could be understood in terms of just five very broad factors or trait dimensions, usually labeled *Neuroticism, Extraversion, Openness to Experience, Agreeableness*, and *Conscientiousness* (McCrae & John, 1992). The characteristics that Murray (1938) called *needs* turn out to resemble Gough's (1987) folk concepts and Lorr's (1986) interpersonal styles, as well as Jung's (1923/1971) psychological types, and all of them can be understood in terms of the FFM. This simple and powerful scheme for organizing ideas led to dramatic advances in personality psychology (McCrae & Costa, 2008a).

Because the factors are so broad, they are correspondingly rich and difficult to convey in a single label or brief definition. Neuroticism encompasses tendencies to experience distressing emotions such as fear, resentment, and guilt, and to show associated patterns of behavior, including inabilities to resist impulses or cope with stressful situations. Extraversion includes sociability and leadership, but also cheerfulness, energy, and a love of fun. Openness, the least familiar of the factors, concerns such traits as need for variety, aesthetic sensitivity, and an open-mindedness that the poet John Keats described famously, if somewhat cryptically, as "negative capability." Agreeableness refers to prosocial traits such as generosity and

cooperation; Conscientiousness denotes strength of will, organization, and purposefulness.

One way to convey the nature of traits is by pointing to examples. Psychologists frequently use case studies to illustrate their concepts—often psychotherapy patients (McCrae, Harwood, & Kelly, 2011) or historical figures (Costa & McCrae, 1998). It is also possible to use characters from fiction as case studies (McCrae, 1994b). Indeed, Levitas (1963) claimed that literature "offers us a profound psychological knowledge that transcends our intellectual awareness of meaning and offers us an emotional experience of truth" (Vol. 1, p. vii). Table 4.1 has a more modest intent: It provides brief factor definitions along with some proposed exemplars from Western literature simply as a way to familiarize the reader with the five factors.[1] For each factor, the table first describes high scorers and gives examples from fiction; the next row of the table describes and illustrates low scorers on the same factor—that is, people with the opposite or absence of the designated characteristic. Readers are invited to ponder the distinctive features of personality that the high scorers share, and that distinguish them from the low scorers for that factor.

To understand the table, it must be recalled that fictional characters, like real people, have more than one trait. Falstaff, for example, is listed as an extravert, but he is also decidedly low in Conscientiousness. His wit, vitality, and sociability make him an exemplar of Extraversion; his sloth, gluttony, and lax morals are irrelevant to that trait.

The directions of the factors, and thus the terms *high* and *low,* are arbitrary; extraverts could just as well be described as being low on the factor of Introversion. In particular, readers should not assume that it is better or psychologically healthier to score high on a trait. The value of a trait depends on the requirements of the situation: Loving-kindness is admirable in a mother, but perhaps not in a prosecuting attorney. In fact, some evolutionary psychologists have argued that individual differences are preserved precisely because both poles of all traits have adaptive value in some circumstances (Figueredo et al., 2005).

Because traits are descriptive, not evaluative, a psychological understanding of personality requires a certain detached objectivity; outright villains may have traits normally considered desirable. In Milton's *Paradise Lost*, for example, Satan has a very high aspiration level and persists tenaciously in his bid to thwart God's purposes; he is

---

[1] These examples are "proposed" because their personality profiles have not yet been formally assessed, as described in a later section.

TABLE 4.1   Factor Descriptions and Examples of High and Low Scorers from Literature

Description	Character	Source
Neuroticism		
High scorers experience many forms of emotional distress, have unrealistic ideas and troublesome urges: *anxious, irritable, gloomy, self-conscious, impulsive, fragile.*	Blanche DuBois	Williams, *A Streetcar Named Desire*
	Chip Lambert	Franzen, *The Corrections*
	J. Alfred Prufrock	Eliot, "The Lovesong"
	Miss Havisham	Dickens, *Great Expectations*
Low scorers are emotionally stable, do not get upset easily, and are not prone to depression: *calm, even-tempered, contented, confident, controlled, resilient.*	James Bond	Fleming, *Casino Royale*
	The Mother	Wyss, *Swiss Family Robinson*
	Portia	Shakespeare, *Merchant of Venice*
	Sancho Panza	Cervantes, *Don Quixote*
Extraversion		
High scorers prefer intense and frequent interpersonal interactions and are energized and optimistic: *warm, sociable, dominant, active, fun-loving, cheerful.*	Mame	Dennis, *Auntie Mame*
	Rhett Butler	Mitchell, *Gone With the Wind*
	Sir John Falstaff	Shakespeare, *Henry IV*
	The Wife of Bath	Chaucer, *The Canterbury Tales*
Low scorers are reserved and tend to prefer a few close friends to large groups of people: *distant, solitary, unassertive, slow-paced, unadventurous, somber.*	Bartleby	Melville, *Bartleby, the Scrivener*
	Beth March	Alcott, *Little Women*
	Boo Radley	Lee, *To Kill a Mockingbird*
	Elinor Dashwood	Austen, *Sense and Sensibility*
Openness to Experience		
High scorers seek out new experience and have a fluid style of thought: *imaginative, artistic, empathic, novelty-seeking, curious, liberal.*	Des Esseintes	Huysmans, *Against the Grain*
	Huck Finn	Twain, *The Adventures of Huckleberry Finn*
	Lisa Simpson	Groening, *The Simpsons*
	Little Alice	Carroll, *Through the Looking Glass*
Low scorers are traditional, conservative, and prefer familiarity to novelty: *down-to-earth, philistine, unemotional, old-fashioned, concrete, dogmatic.*	Aunt Em	Baum, *The Wonderful Wizard of Oz*
	Miss Pross	Dickens, *A Tale of Two Cities*
	The Pastor	Gide, *La Symphonie Pastorale*
	Tom Buchanan	Fitzgerald, *The Great Gatsby*
Agreeableness		
High scorers regard others with sympathy and act unselfishly: *trusting, honest, generous, forgiving, humble, merciful.*	Alexei Karamazov	Dostoyevsky, *Brothers Karamazov*
	Dorothea Brooke	Eliot, *Middlemarch*
	The Duchess	Browning, "My Last Duchess"
	The Vicar	Goldsmith, *The Vicar of Wakefield*
Low scorers are not concerned about other people and tend to be antagonistic and hostile: *suspicious, manipulative, selfish, stubborn, arrogant, cold-blooded.*	Cousin Bette	Balzac, *Cousin Bette*
	Heathcliff	Brontë, *Wuthering Heights*
	Medea	Euripides, *Medea*
	Alex	Burgess, *A Clockwork Orange*
Conscientiousness		
High scorers control their behavior in the service of their goals: *efficient, organized, scrupulous, ambitious, self-disciplined, careful.*	Antigone	Sophocles, *Antigone*
	John Henry	American folklore
	King Arthur	Tennyson, *Idylls of the King*
	Mildred Pierce	Cain, *Mildred Pierce*
Low scorers have a hard time keeping to a schedule, are disorganized, and can be unreliable: *inept, untidy, lax, lazy, weak-willed, hasty.*	Ignatius J. Reilly	Toole, *A Confederacy of Dunces*
	Oscar Madison	Simon, *The Odd Couple*
	Sadie Thompson	Maugham, "Rain"
	Uncle's Wife	Buck, *The Good Earth*

Note. Factor descriptions are adapted from McCrae and Sutin (2007).

clearly high in Conscientiousness (and all the more dangerous for it). Accurate personality assessments must give the Devil his due.

A Brief History of the FFM

Perhaps because they sensed that something momentous was happening in the emergence of the FFM, several writers offered histories of the research that had led to it (Digman, 1990; John, Angleitner, & Ostendorf, 1988; McCrae & John, 1992). Briefly, the model arose in the context of a recurring problem in trait psychology: How can individual differences be systematically studied? Throughout the middle of the 20th century some of the greatest minds in psychology had contemplated the distinctive ways in which people behaved and reacted to events, and they proposed concepts to capture these differences, often based on complete theories of personality (e.g., Murray, 1938; Reich, 1945). Other researchers created instruments—including the Minnesota Multiphasic Personality Inventory (Hathaway & McKinley, 1943), the Personality Research Form (Jackson, 1974), and the Multidimensional Personality Inventory (Tellegen, 1982)—to assess these features of personality. Hundreds of other scales had been developed for specialized purposes.

All these scales had demonstrated scientific merit, but the sheer number of them was bewildering. Another group of researchers therefore attempted to systematize them by the use of factor analysis. Despite differing labels, many of the constructs assessed by personality scales overlapped. Measures of anxiety and depression, for example, were strongly correlated, because people who are anxious are often depressed. Factor analysis is a statistical procedure for recognizing clusters of related variables—in this case, personality traits—allowing researchers to organize different scales into groups that all assessed related, if not identical, traits (Goldberg & Digman, 1994).

The problem for factor analysts was to determine which scales to include in their analyses. It was not feasible to ask research volunteers to complete each and every one of the thousands of personality scales available—nor was it possible to analyze so many variables in the days before computers. Researchers had to make a selection of traits, and there seemed to be no way to know if their results were biased by their choices. For decades, debate raged about which model—the 16 factors of Cattell, the 10 of Guilford, the 2 of Eysenck, to name only the most prominent candidates—was correct. Worse yet, the possibility remained that none of the models was correct, because psychologists may have overlooked important traits when creating their scales. How could one guarantee that a trait model was comprehensive?

Ultimately, the solution came from a somewhat different tradition. Beginning with Sir Francis Galton in the 19th century, some psychologists had been impressed by the richness and precision of the lay vocabulary of personality traits (John et al., 1988). In 1936 Gordon Allport assigned his student, Henry Odbert, to extract all the trait descriptive adjectives—some 18,000 of them—from an unabridged English dictionary (Allport & Odbert, 1936).[2]

---

[2]Odbert left the field of personality research shortly after completing this task; fifty years later, however, he was "quite impressed" by the subsequent work leading to the FFM, and thought that "Gordon Allport would have been very much interested" (H. S. Odbert, personal communication, August 19, 1991).

The rationale behind this work was the *lexical hypothesis*: Because personality traits are important in human life, people will have invented words to describe all of them. In principle, then, a factor analysis of the trait lexicon should reveal the structure of human personality. From today's perspective, this hypothesis is only roughly true, but it was an excellent beginning.

Cattell (1946) combined synonyms and distilled the list of traits down to 35 scales, and subsequent researchers, including Fiske (1949), Tupes and Christal (1961/1992), and Norman (1963) factored these scales and consistently found five factors. Twenty years later, Goldberg (1983) began again with the dictionary and again found five factors strongly resembling those of Tupes and Christal. It had become clear that the FFM was the optimal model for representing the structure of trait adjectives in English. (Subsequent lexical studies in other languages have suggested more [Ashton et al., 2004] or fewer [De Raad et al., 2010] factors, but all are closely related to the FFM factors.)

McCrae and Costa (1987), whose previous research had led them to a three-factor model based on analyses of questionnaire scales (Costa & McCrae, 1980), showed that their Neuroticism, Extraversion, and Openness factors corresponded to three of the five lexical factors, and they argued that all five were necessary and more-or-less sufficient for a comprehensive taxonomy of personality traits. In a series of studies, they showed that factors derived from the most prominent alternative personality models could be understood in terms of the FFM (McCrae, 1989), and they developed and published a new instrument that assessed the FFM and a number of its constituent traits, the NEO Personality Inventory (Costa & McCrae, 1985; McCrae & Costa, 2010).

Together with the work of many others (e.g., Angleitner & Ostendorf, 1994; John, 1990; Markon, Krueger, & Watson, 2005), this research led to the widespread adoption of the FFM as an adequate taxonomy of personality traits. It enabled researchers to address a whole range of problems systematically: Instead of having to choose from among hundreds of available trait measures, researchers needed only to sample each of the five factors. Further, existing studies could be reinterpreted in literature reviews and meta-analyses, because most of the scales used in personality research could be classified and organized using the FFM as a framework (e.g., Barrick & Mount, 1991; Steel, Schmidt, & Shultz, 2008). Personality research flourished.

The Problem of Specificity

The FFM offers tremendous economy, summarizing a host of specific traits in just five factors. The downside is that these descriptions are correspondingly superficial. One early critique (McAdams, 1992) called it a "psychology of the stranger," because it fails to provide the "contextualized and nuanced...attributions" (p. 353) we would expect in a description of someone we knew well (including ourselves). In part this criticism calls attention to the fact that there is more to personality than traits; in part, it points to the fact that the five factors themselves do not provide sufficient detail even on the level of traits. A biological taxonomy that distinguished mammals from birds but did not recognize the difference between bats, dolphins, and elephants would be of limited utility.

Psychologists usually refer to this as the *bandwidth problem*: Broad traits (like the FFM factors) predict a wide range of criteria but lack the specificity of narrow traits. Neuroticism, for example, includes both fearfulness and chronic dejection, and global measures of Neuroticism are useful predictors of a wide range of psychopathology, including anxiety and mood disorders. But to determine the optimal treatment, clinical psychologists need to know if their patients are phobic or depressed (or both), and a global measure of Neuroticism cannot provide that differential diagnosis. Instead, they need separate measures of anxiety and depression. These are traits that are both closely related to Neuroticism, but that also assess qualitatively different aspects, or facets, of that broad factor.

Surely literary scholars would raise the same objection to the use of the five factors to describe fictional characters: The assessments would be too crude to do justice to the contextualized behaviors and nuanced emotional reactions that skilled writers use to bring their creations to life. Personality psychologists would have to concede the merit of that argument, in part because they know the meaningful distinctions between facets within each factor.

The FFM is based on the observation that sets of traits covary: For example, people who are sociable are also generally cheerful and dominant—these are prototypical extraverts. But this is a generalization; some people are sociable but not cheerful, some people are cheerful but not dominant. Goethe's Faust, whose personality we discuss below, is a clear instance of this: He is active and assertive (like the typical extravert) but interpersonally cold and fond of solitude (like the typical introvert). One would be technically correct in describing him as an ambivert (average on the Extraversion factor), but this description would not adequately capture his personality.

Fortunately, there is no need to choose between the broad and economical factors and the narrow but precise facets: Personality assessment can include both. Where all facets defining a factor are at a similar level, the individual can conveniently be described by a summary factor label; where there is marked divergence among facets, a more detailed account of personality is possible at the level of facets. Different readings of characters can sometimes be resolved by adopting this approach. Is Sherlock Holmes high or low on Neuroticism? If one focuses on his periods of depression (and perhaps on his drug use), one might pronounce him high. If instead one notes his steel nerves in moments of crisis, one would conclude that he is very low. These global judgments may subtly color—and distort—perceptions of the character as a whole. Readers informed by the FFM would distinguish between Holmes's depressive tendencies and his low anxiety and vulnerability to stress.

The only problem with this hierarchical strategy is that of identifying the specific traits. After all, the FFM arose precisely because the thousands of lay adjectives and hundreds of psychological constructs that refer to specific traits were unmanageable. Is it possible to find a middle ground, to classify traits at a level one step below the five factors, as biologists divide broad classes (birds, mammals) into somewhat narrower orders (waterfowl and parrots, carnivores and primates)?

Costa and McCrae (1995) offered one such classification. They reviewed the personality literature and attempted to identify six distinct facets that represented the most important traits for each of the five factors, and they developed the NEO Inventories to assess them (McCrae & Costa, 2010). A substantial literature is now available that describes the heritability, longitudinal stability, and developmental course of these 30 facets, and they have been used to describe national stereotypes (Terracciano et al., 2005) and features of culture (McCrae, 2009) as well as traits in individuals. Although this classification has been criticized as rational rather than purely empirical (Roberts, Chernyshenko, Stark, & Goldberg, 2005), it provides a taxonomy of specific traits that has repeatedly proven to be useful (McCrae & Costa, 2008a). Assessing personality at the level of the 30 NEO facets can give a detailed portrait of literary characters.

Common Fictions About the FFM

Introductory psychology texts now routinely mention the FFM, and most psychologists and psychology students have some familiarity with it. But there are several common misconceptions that should be corrected.

- The FFM is not identical with the "Big Five." That label originated in studies of lay trait adjectives

(Goldberg, 1992) and has become a popular way to designate the five factors themselves as very broad traits. By contrast, the FFM refers to a classification of many traits in terms of the five factors. Conceptually, the Big Five refers only to the highest level of a hierarchy of traits, whereas the FFM encompasses the full hierarchy. The practical difference between these two is that one uses only five scores to characterize an individual in Big Five terms, whereas many more scores may be needed to describe a person's FFM profile. Big Five descriptions are broad-brush; FFM descriptions may be exquisitely fine-grained.

- Historically, the FFM factors were first identified from analyses of the trait adjectives used by laypersons and conveniently codified in dictionaries (McCrae & John, 1992). Studies of lay trait vocabularies in different languages are called *lexical studies*, and they are a source of useful information about personality and about cultural differences in the conceptualization of personality. But the FFM is not itself a lexical model, because the same five factors have also been found in a wide variety of scientific instruments for the assessment of personality (Markon et al., 2005). Sometimes languages lack terms for important traits—English, for example, has no single word for "sensitivity to aesthetic impressions" or "need for variety" (McCrae, 1990)—and sometimes they overrepresent narrow constructs and thus seem to define new factors (see McCrae & Costa, 2008b). The lexical approach provides one source of evidence on personality structure, but it is not a privileged perspective.

- The FFM, and traits themselves, have sometimes been criticized as being merely descriptive—that is, lacking a theoretical basis (Block, 1995) or failing to provide real explanations for behavior (Cervone, 2004). But in fact trait theory is one of the oldest theories of personality, and the FFM traits have been viewed from a variety of theoretical perspectives (Wiggins, 1996). Traits also provide a kind of explanation for behavior, although it is distal rather than proximal (McCrae & Costa, 1995). It is meaningful to say that Horatio Alger's heroes prospered *because they were hardworking*, although the details of how they translated this trait into success vary with the novel.

- Conversely, it is also an error to believe that the FFM is a complete theory of personality. Even if it carries with it an implicit trait theory, a classification of traits in itself does not account for how people act on a specific occasion or how their lives develop over time. Fortunately, new theories of personality have been proposed that put the FFM into the context of a dynamic model of personality functioning. We will return to one of these below.

THE FACTS: FINDINGS FROM FFM RESEARCH

Merely as a description of personality, the FFM might be of use to art historians who study portrait painting. But the characters of fiction are not static portraits; they are dynamic figures who go about their lives, interact with others, and often grow up or grow old. Application of the FFM to the study of fiction requires that one consider what is known about how FFM traits function in the lives of men and women. A great deal has been learned in the past two decades; we will briefly review the chief findings here. In the next section we discuss one of a new generation of personality theories that attempt to work these findings into a coherent story (McCrae & Costa, 1996).

Consensual Validation

Most personality research is conducted using self-reports: Individuals are presented with a questionnaire and asked to indicate how well they are described by a standard series of statements ("I have a very active imagination," "I am easily frightened"). This method is clearly not applicable to literary figures, so it is fortunate that there is an alternative, in which knowledgeable informants are asked to describe the target ("She has a very active imagination," "He is easily frightened"). Observer ratings of personality have been widely used to describe historical figures who, like fictional characters, cannot describe themselves (Cassandro & Simonton, 2010; Rubenzer, Faschingbauer, & Ones, 2000).

This practice is based on the premise that both self-reports and observer ratings are sufficiently accurate as to be more-or-less interchangeable, which is not a trivial assumption. The poet Robert Burns had immortalized the view that how we "see oursels" may be delusional, and that we must ask how "ithers see us" for an objective account of our traits. Psychoanalysts endorsed this view and explained the delusions as a result of defense mechanisms. Social cognitive psychologists later suggested that the trait concept itself was a delusion, and that both self-reports and observer ratings were groundless; agreement among different sources of information was therefore not to be expected (Fiske, 1974).

Many subsequent studies, however, clearly and consistently showed that external observers do agree substantially among themselves on ratings of all five factors, and that observer ratings corroborate self-reports (e.g., Funder, 1980; McCrae et al., 2004). Those findings made this chapter possible, because they established that traits are not a myth, that the FFM and its operation can be studied using either method of personality assessment, and that it is legitimate to assess the personality of individuals who cannot describe themselves.

Personality Development

By definition, traits are enduring dispositions, not transient moods, but longitudinal research was needed to determine exactly how long traits endured. In these studies, the same individuals are assessed two or more times across a period of years or decades. Keeping track of a large pool of respondents (or relocating them years later) is an arduous task, so longitudinal studies are relatively rare; it was only in the 1970s that their results began to accumulate. The findings astonished researchers: The rank-order of individuals' trait levels was strongly preserved over periods of 10 years and longer (Block, 1981; Costa, McCrae, & Arenberg, 1980). Most psychologists had assumed that intervening life events (marriage, divorce, health problems, retirement) would profoundly alter personality traits; instead, personality profiles remained largely unchanged for the great majority of people.

Subsequent studies led to a more precise statement of the stability of individual differences (Roberts & DelVecchio, 2000; Terracciano, Costa, & McCrae, 2006): There is some continuity of FFM traits from early childhood throughout old age; stability increases with age, at least until age 30; and perhaps as much as 80% of the variance in personality traits is stable over the adult lifetime. Neurological disorders such as Alzheimer's disease do alter personality traits, but personality stability is the rule for almost everyone else. The most agreeable and introverted 30-year-olds are likely to become the most agreeable and introverted 80-year-olds; 80-year-olds who are anxious and reactionary had probably been anxious and reactionary as 30-year-olds.

The stability of individual differences is logically independent of change in mean level: It is possible for everyone to change while maintaining the same order. Individual differences in height, for instance, are relatively stable between age 5 and age 15, but the average height increases dramatically over those 10 years. Something like the same phenomenon is seen in personality development, where maturational trends are seen for all five factors. Neuroticism and Extraversion decline with age, whereas Agreeableness and Conscientiousness increase (Terracciano, McCrae, Brant, & Costa, 2005); in most studies,

Openness increases from adolescence until the early 20s, and then declines (McCrae, Terracciano, & 78 Members, 2005). Moderately large changes are found between age 18 and age 30, as people settle into adulthood; thereafter, changes are very gradual and the net effect is quite subtle. Note that most changes are in the direction of greater psychological maturity: Both men and women become calmer, less excitable, kinder, and more responsible. These changes are found around the world, perhaps because all societies encourage these trends, or perhaps because evolution selected for this developmental pattern.

Do creative writers depict long-term stability and gradual maturation in their characters? Yes and no. The protagonists of serial novels, like Fleming's James Bond and Chandler's Philip Marlowe, are obliged to stay in character across episodes, although it is not clear that they actually age. A few novelists have depicted the lifecourse of their characters (Balzac's Eugénie Grandet, Mann's Thomas Buddenbrooks), and continuity is the rule in these instances. The most notable examples of personality stability occur despite dramatic life events: Scarlett O'Hara remains vivacious and egocentric through war and peace; Ilya Ilyich Oblomov rises briefly from his lethargy under the spell of love, but soon sinks back into it.

But stability is less interesting than change, and writers tend to depict life- and soul-changing events. Novels of the *Bildungsroman* genre, in which adolescents achieve adulthood, are generally consistent with the observed pattern: The largest changes in personality do occur in the decade of the 20s, and the overall direction is usually toward psychological maturity, from personal doubt and conflict to a more stable and altruistic integration with society. Other novels, however, have less empirical support. Midlife crises (like that of Bellows's Herzog) are common in literature, but rare in real life (McCrae & Costa, 2003). Radical transformations of personality, although they may occur (or may be perceived to have occurred), are usually transient in nature (Herbst, McCrae, Costa, Feaganes, & Siegler, 2000). Had Dickens been striving for verisimilitude, he would have ended his fable on Christmas day; a year later, a real Ebenezer Scrooge would likely have reverted to his prototypically disagreeable self.

Heritability

Behavior genetic studies (see South, Reichbom, Eaton, & Krueger, this volume) compare traits in people with known genetic relationships in an attempt to determine whether and to what extent traits are influenced by genes and by the environment (and, occasionally, their interaction). Hundreds of studies have now been reported, using different instruments, different kinship designs, and different samples (e.g., Japanese, German, Canadian). The results are easy to summarize, because virtually all studies come to the same conclusions, and they are the same for each of the five factors (Bouchard & Loehlin, 2001): (1) About half of the variance in personality traits in any given population is determined by genes; (2) the shared environment—what children raised in the same family all experience, such as diet, discipline, parental role models, neighborhood and schools, religious training—has almost no effect on adult personality traits (although it likely has an effect on behaviors, especially in adolescence; see Burt, McGue, & Iacono, 2010); and (3) the rest of the variance is currently unaccounted for. It may include idiosyncratic experiences of different children in the same family, peer influences, the prenatal environment, specific illnesses, or simple error of measurement in assessing the traits.

As adults, monozygotic (identical) twins strongly resemble each other on all five factors (and on the specific facets they summarize; Jang, McCrae, Angleitner, Riemann, & Livesley, 1998), whether they were raised together or separated at birth and raised in different households (Tellegen et al., 1988). By contrast, adoptive siblings raised by the same parents in the same environment do not resemble each other beyond chance. These well-replicated results are perhaps the most surprising discovery of modern personality psychology, because they run counter to almost all classic theories of personality, which attributed personality development to interactions with parents or traumatic events experienced in childhood (Scarr, 1987).

They also run counter to conventional wisdom, which holds parents responsible for their children's character (McCrae & Costa, 1988). This collective error is understandable for two reasons. First, parents do have great influence over some aspects of their children's behavior—their religious beliefs, their dietary preferences, their native language. It is easy to see why one would assume they also determine their children's chronic levels of anxiety or need for achievement—though this assumption is wrong (McCrae & Costa, 1994). Second, it is impossible to tease apart the influences of nature versus nurture when looking at any single child, or indeed at any single family. The story is told of identical twins raised apart who were both high in Conscientiousness. The first attributed it to his mother's example and her rigid insistence on order and discipline; the second to *his* mother's sloth and disorganization, which compelled him to develop self-discipline and order in compensation. Both twins provided plausible environmental explanations, but considered together, a genetic account is more likely. Scientific research sometimes gathers data that are simply not available to lay observers.

It is not surprising, therefore, that the twins of literature are not accurately portrayed. In *The Comedy of Errors*, the plot revolves around the fact that the twins, separated at birth, show a confusingly similar physical appearance, but quite distinct personalities. Although Bardolators may imagine he is an infallible guide to psychology, Shakespeare either did not understand the heritability of personality traits, or chose to ignore it for comedic purposes. The evil twins of much lesser literature are also better understood as useful plot devices than as insightful psychology.

Gender Differences

All societies assign different roles to men and women, and almost all literature portrays women and men differently. Are these groundless stereotypes? If there are real differences in personality traits, how large are they? And where do they come from—are they the creation of patriarchal social institutions, or a feature of human nature? Personality psychologists have answered most of these questions. Certainly there are gender stereotypes—assumptions about how men and women differ—and they are shared around the world (Williams & Best, 1982). By and large, however, these beliefs have a basis in fact. Using self-report personality inventories, women (on average; there are of course many exceptions) describe themselves as higher in both Neuroticism and Agreeableness than do men; women are warmer, men more assertive; women are especially open to aesthetics, men to ideas (Costa, Terracciano, & McCrae, 2001). Much the same pattern of results is seen when knowledgeable informants describe the personality traits of men and of women, and this is so whether the informants are themselves male or female (McCrae, Terracciano, & 78 Members, 2005). These findings have been replicated around the world (Schmitt, Realo, Voracek, & Allik, 2008). All these results point to the likely conclusion that there are real gender differences that are characteristic of the human species. Lay stereotypes, as a general rule, reflect this reality.

However, stereotypes tend to exaggerate differences ("men are from Mars, . . .") whereas contemporary research shows that the magnitude of gender differences in personality traits is rather small. Some women are more assertive than most men; some men are warmer than most women. Table 4.1 includes examples of both men and women at each pole of each factor, but a much more detailed examination of gender portrayals would be needed to determine whether the traits novelists and playwrights ascribe to men and to women show stereotypically large or realistically small differences—or no differences at all.

Universality

Until recently, almost all psychological research was conducted in Western nations, and it was an open question how well findings generalized to other cultures. A small group of psychological anthropologists and cross-cultural psychologists raised the possibility that Western conceptions of the self and the whole of Western psychology might not be applicable to individuals from traditional cultures, where the group—family, clan, community—was the locus of psychology (Markus & Kitayama, 1991; Shweder & Sullivan, 1990).

With the rise of the Internet, it became possible to test these ideas on a large scale, and the results, at least in the case of personality psychology, were clear. The FFM was found in cultures ranging from India to Iceland to Burkina Faso (McCrae, Terracciano, & 78 Members, 2005); gender and age differences were universal (Costa et al., 2001; McCrae et al., 1999); the heritability, reliability, and cross-observer validity of scales were much the same in all cultures examined (McCrae, Kurtz, Yamagata, & Terracciano, 2011). In a series of studies comparing cultural and trait perspectives on the operation of traits in predicting beliefs and behaviors, Church and Katigbak (2012) concluded that culture modifies the expression of traits, but that trait psychology itself is transcultural.

These conclusions probably come as no surprise to those who have read widely in world literature, or to aficionados of foreign films. Reading is often recommended as a way to broaden one's perspective and transcend the narrow boundaries of one's own culture, but it also implicitly teaches the "psychic unity of mankind." Universal motives of love, greed, and revenge are shown, but so are universal patterns of individual differences. Scheherazade outlived her predecessors because her exceptionally high level of Openness to Experience gave her a fertile imagination. Kurosawa's seven samurai have distinctive personalities that are readily intelligible to Westerners.

Animal Analogues

In the mid-20th century, when Behaviorism was the dominant school of psychology, researchers were warned against the intellectual sin of anthropomorphism: attributing human characteristics to nonhuman animals (radical behaviorists didn't even attribute them to humans). However, research on animal personality, using the same observer rating techniques that can be used on fictional humans, clearly demonstrates that there are consistent and enduring individual differences in dogs and cats (Gosling & John, 1999) as well as in primates (King, Weiss, & Sisco, 2008). The structure of personality is not identical across species—for example, Dominance appears to be a separate factor for some species (King, Weiss, & Farmer, 2005)—but factors resembling Neuroticism and Extraversion are found in many species (Gosling, 2001).

Pet owners have always believed that their companion animals have distinct personalities, as species, breeds, and individuals. Animal characters have also figured prominently in literature, from Aesop's fables to Self's *Great Apes*. In part, this illustrates the ability of literature to transcend mundane reality, but current research confirms that it may also demonstrate the psychological acumen of storytellers. It is sheer fantasy to attribute literary aspirations to a cockroach, but it is within the bounds of scientific plausibility to suppose that a cat might share personality traits with Marquis's (1927) Mehitabel.

Utility

Most research on personality traits concerns their correlates: Beliefs, interests, aptitudes, habits, and activities that are associated with, and thus predictable from, personality traits. Virtually every aspect of human existence is affected by traits, from sex (Costa, Fagan, Piedmont, Ponticas, & Wise, 1992) to drugs (Brooner, Schmidt, & Herbst, 2002) to rock-and-roll (Rentfrow & Gosling, 2003). It is because traits have pervasive and significant impacts on people's lives that trait psychology has become an essential part of the study of industrial/organizational, clinical, developmental, and health psychology.

It would therefore be extraordinary if personality traits were not also useful in understanding literary styles and reader's tastes. Such topics, however, are rarely researched, and the literature offers only a miscellaneous assortment of findings. Pennebaker and King (1999) reported small but interpretable correlations between writing styles in student essays and FFM traits; for example, writers high in Openness used longer words; those high in Neuroticism expressed negative emotions. Writers high in Neuroticism also referred more often to themselves and avoided the words *ought* and *should* (Argamon, Koppel, Pennebaker, & Schler, 2009). Djikic, Oatley, Zoeterman, and Peterson (2009) reported an experiment in which a Chekhov story (temporarily) changed readers' self-perceptions of FFM traits. Thomas and Duke (2007) found evidence of more cognitive distortions in the works of depressed writers (presumably high in Neuroticism) than of nondepressed writers. Pexman, Glenwright, Hala, Kowbel, and Jungen (2006) found that children, especially older children, use trait information to interpret verbal irony: Mean (i.e., disagreeable) people make sarcastic remarks.

These are intriguing findings, but it would be fair to say that a systematic study of the relations between personality traits and literature (fiction and nonfiction) has not yet been undertaken. In particular, scholars in the tradition of Reader-Response Criticism (Jauss, 1982) might profitably investigate how FFM traits affect the ways in which readers understand and appreciate literature (Miall & Kuiken, 1995).

THE STORY: A THEORY OF TRAITS IN OPERATION

In isolation, the FFM is simply an organized list of characteristics. Even knowledge about heritability, universality, and other trait characteristics does not in itself give a coherent sense of what people are like and how traits fit into a conception of human nature. For that, a theory is needed, and personality psychology has no lack of theories.

To put this topic in perspective, it may be helpful to begin by pointing out that the conceptions of personality commonly held by contemporary psychologists form a fairly narrow slice of the possibilities that have been entertained by human thought. Some metaphysical views (e.g., Tagore, 1917; Weil, 1986) see personality as an ineffable entity that defies scientific analysis. In classical Indian views, personality exists beyond the boundaries of the present life, carrying with it accumulated karma. At the other extreme, personality can hardly be said to exist at all for poststructuralist theorists, who reduce the person "to an intersection of discourses and a constellation of subject positions" (Falmagne, 2004, p. 835).

Many contemporary writers within the humanities seem to have adopted the notion that personality is somehow a recent creation (c.f. Gemin, 1999). Historian Michael Wood (2001) warned of "the danger of anachronism in trying to make 'modern' judgements about medieval personality" (p. 148). And Bloom (1998) has boldly declared (without much explanation) that Shakespeare so transformed consciousness as to have invented "the human."

Such chronocentric views are not shared by most personality psychologists. Research on other species shows that personality traits evolved before human beings, and there is every reason to think that the FFM characterized people in Homer's day as much as today. It is surely possible that people's conscious understanding of themselves has evolved over time, just as the language of traits has (Piedmont & Aycock, 2007)—perhaps even because of the insights of great writers. But if we used H. G. Wells' time machine to visit our ancient human ancestors, we would probably have little trouble understanding them in terms of our own psychology.

Classical and Popular Personality Theories

Psychological accounts of personality, human nature, and individuality are given by the personality theorists familiar to any college psychology student—Freud, Skinner, Maslow, Cattell, and the rest. Traditionally, these theorists are grouped into schools, usually psychoanalytic (or more broadly, psychodynamic), behaviorist, humanistic, and trait psychologies. Because these classic theories continue to be taught (as Latin and Greek were routinely taught until the 20th century), most educated laypeople—including most specialists in the humanities—assume that they are still accepted models of personality. In fact, they have been selectively abandoned or transformed in contemporary personality psychology.

Three of the schools—behaviorist, humanistic, and trait—have flourishing descendents. Behaviorism, which emphasized the experimental analysis of behavior and the conditions that shaped it, reemerged as the social-cognitive perspective (Cervone & Shoda, 1999), in which people are seen to learn from life experiences and to shape their lives through plans, goals, and self-management. Social-cognitive personality theory is, in a sense, a humanized form of behaviorism; and humanistic concerns with personal growth and psychological well-being have been taken up by positive psychologists (Sheldon, Kashdan, & Steger, 2011). Trait psychology has given rise to the FFM, research establishing a body of facts about how traits function, and a new generation of personality theories that account for these facts (McCrae & Costa, 1996). We outline one of them below.

Psychoanalytic theories also have modern-day descendants (see Bornstein Denckla, & Chung, this volume), including self-psychology, object relations theory, and especially attachment theory (Shaver & Mikulincer, 2005), where much current research is focused on trait-like attachment styles (Shaver & Brennan, 1992). However, modern psychodynamic approaches are far removed from the orthodox psychoanalytic theories of Freud and Jung that remain influential in literary theory (e.g., *PsyArt: An Online Journal for the Psychological Study of the Arts*; www .clas.ufl.edu/ipsa/journal/index.shtml). Full-scale psychoanalysis, with daily sessions on the couch, is rarely used as psychotherapy today (see Shedler, 2010, and the subsequent Comments in *American Psychologist, 66* [2], for the status of psychodynamic psychotherapy more broadly). Research has shown that dreams are not the products of unconscious conflicts (Domhoff, 1999). Bornstein and colleagues noted that there is "little evidence for the Oedipal dynamic as Freud conceived it" (Chapter 3, this volume, p. 47), and the term "Oedipus complex" does not appear in the index to the thousand-page *Handbook of Attachment* (Cassidy & Shaver, 2008). *Oedipus Rex* is great literature, but it is no longer considered a sound basis for psychiatry.

Freud (like many other thinkers before and since) was correct in pointing out that sexuality is an important part of human life, that human beings are not purely rational in their decision-making, that most psychological problems are manifested in disruptions of interpersonal relations, and that a supportive relationship in which individuals can reflect on their behavior can be very helpful. To the extent that modern clinical psychology incorporates these insights, it can be called psychodynamic. But those views are also compatible with many other, nonpsychoanalytic theoretical perspectives.

Vaguely psychodynamic thinking permeates popular psychology. Although the details naturally vary from best seller to best seller, the gist of most popular psychology is that people's problems come from a life history of stressful events or suboptimal environments, and that understanding the origins of one's problems, or changing one's circumstances, or adopting new attitudes can dramatically alter one's psychological health and happiness. Certainly, traumatic events often have psychological consequences, some of which endure for years: Posttraumatic stress disorder is now a familiar diagnosis. But popular psychologies typically neglect the facts that most psychological problems are deeply rooted in the nature of the person him- or herself, and that most therapeutic interventions bring modest improvements only after long and arduous work (McCrae, 2011).

An Evidence-Based Theory of Personality

Recently, several personality psychologists have formulated new theories of personality that are informed by what has been learned about traits (McAdams & Pals, 2006; Roberts & Wood, 2006). In particular, Five-Factor Theory (FFT; McCrae & Costa, 2008b) proposes that personality should be construed as a system, with inputs from biology (*Biological Bases*) and from the social environment (*External Influences*), and an output stream of action and experience (the *Objective Biography*). There are two major components within the system: The set of psychological proclivities, including FFM personality traits (*Basic Tendencies*), and the set of acquired features, such as skills, habits, tastes, and interpersonal relationships (*Characteristic Adaptations*). A particularly important subset of the latter is composed of beliefs, feelings, and stories about oneself (the *Self-Concept*). These components and their organization are diagramed in Figure 4.1.

The details of FFT and the supporting evidence are presented elsewhere (McCrae & Costa, 2003, 2008b). For the present purpose, it suffices to point out that personality traits themselves are hypothesized to be features of the organism, not results of life experience. In this respect, they resemble the phlegmatic, choleric, sanguine, and melancholic temperaments of antiquity. FFT, however, holds that they are shaped by genes, not humors, and by other conditions that affect the brain (e.g., drugs, neurological disorders). Personality changes, according to FFT, mainly because the brain matures, mostly in adolescence. Isolating traits from external influences—although it runs counter to classic theories as well as much folk psychology—explains why individual differences are so stable across the vicissitudes of life, and how the same traits can be found in radically different cultural settings.

This certainly does not mean that the environment is irrelevant to personality. Traits are the psychological raw material that must be expressed in culture- and situation-specific ways. Life experience interacts with personality traits to shape the beliefs, values, and routines that form the lifestyle we observe in ourselves and others; these beliefs, values, and routines interact with the immediate situation to produce the actions and reactions of any given moment. Behavior is thus an indirect reflection of personality traits in a social context, just as plot is the expression of character in a given dramatic situation.

Among the most important Characteristic Adaptations are those that involve the self, designated in Figure 4.1 as the Self-Concept. This includes the beliefs about ourselves that that we rely on when completing personality questionnaires; discrete autobiographical memories (say, drinking tea and eating madeleines as a child); and self-esteem or self-loathing. McAdams (1993) and other students of the life narrative have argued that people do not think of

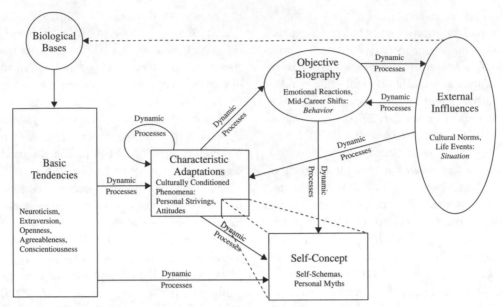

Figure 4.1 A representation of the Five-Factor Theory personality system. Core components are in rectangles; interfacing components are in ellipses. Adapted from McCrae and Costa (2008b)

themselves merely as an abstract list of traits or past behaviors, but by way of a life story that summarizes and gives meaning and purpose to their lives. Life narratives can be analyzed just as fictional narratives are, in terms of character, plot, tone, theme, and so on. Literature may help shape the individual's personal narrative, just as the life story of a novelist may be reflected more or less transparently in his or her work. It is at this level of personality, one step removed from FFM traits, that the connection between psychological fact and literary fiction is perhaps most direct.

Figure 4.1 is strewn with arrows labeled "dynamic processes," which is FFT's acknowledgment of the fact that personality is not a static entity, but a functioning system. For example, people high in Conscientiousness somehow eventually come to have a self-concept that incorporates the view that they are hardworking, competent, and organized. This might happen in many different ways: by observing their own behavior and comparing it to that of others; by introspecting on their goals and strivings; by hearing it from friends or reading it in job evaluations. By and large, trait psychologists do not study these dynamic processes; they are chiefly concerned with the end result. In contrast, social-cognitive personality psychologists and social and clinical psychologists focus on the details of these dynamic processes, often in the hope of finding ways to modify them and produce more adaptive and satisfying outcomes. The essence of the psychological novels of Dostoyevsky, Stendhal, and Conrad is the exploration

of these ongoing processes by which ideas are formed, sentiments grow and fade, and relationships alter—how personality functions in time.

THE VALUE OF LITERATURE FOR PSYCHOLOGY

Keith Oatley, himself a novelist (*A Natural History; Therefore Choose*) as well as a psychologist, has argued that fiction serves an important psychological function for the reader by simulating social experiences (Mar & Oatley, 2008; Oatley, 1999). Readers can learn vicariously from the experience of characters, develop empathy and an understanding of emotional responses in themselves and others, and broaden their appreciation of individual differences.

To be useful in this way, fiction (at least some fiction) must provide a relatively accurate portrayal of persons and their reactions to events, and there is reason to believe that it does. To survive, social animals must understand at some level why they act as they do and how others will respond to their actions, so humans must have evolved the capacity to think psychologically and to communicate their insights to others (Oatley & Mar, 2005). As lexical studies show, human languages have developed words for a great many scientifically documented personality traits, and laypersons have an intuitive, if imperfect, grasp of the FFM (Sneed, McCrae, & Funder, 1998). If all humans have some facility in understanding and communicating psychological truths, it is reasonable to suppose that a small group of exceptional individuals may excel in divining and portraying human nature, and that the intuitions of these great writers may at times outstrip current scientific knowledge. This view is widely held in the humanities, and occasionally shared by social scientists (e.g., Levitas, 1963).

Sometimes, however, the intuitions of even the greatest writers are wrong or are sacrificed to other artistic goals—as in Shakespeare's portrayal of identical twins in the *Comedy of Errors*. Casual readers are easily misled in these cases, often believing whatever a good storyteller says, unless it flatly contradicts their personal knowledge (Gerrig, 1998, cited in Oatley, 1999). If fiction is to be used not as a means of personal growth, but as a resource for scientific psychology, it seems clear that the insights of novelists must be considered simply as hypotheses to be tested, and that the portrayals of personality in fiction must be construed as a fallible, albeit potentially useful, source of information. One can, and must, ask about the construct validity of data derived from this literary method.

Psychologists already use fiction for some purposes. Todd (2008) studied group discussions of novels to investigate the psychology of reading. Pennebaker and Ireland (2008) used computerized text analysis to study psychological states in characters and authors. Emotion researchers often show Hollywood films to evoke specific affects they wish to study. Students of person perception routinely devise vignettes to serve as standard stimuli for the judgments of their experimental subjects. (These ministories are, strictly speaking, fiction, although of dubious literary merit.) Some social psychologists believe that the content of literature merits study: Contarello and Vellico (2003) examined cultural concepts of the self by analyzing a novel by Indian author Anita Desai.

Personality psychologists can also benefit from a consideration of personality in literature. Studies of the life narrative—an aspect of the self-concept—have been powerfully influenced by literary theory (McAdams, 1993), and research in this field provides a model of how aspects of fictional stories—plot, theme, tone—might be related to the personality traits of authors or characters (McAdams et al., 2004). Social-cognitive personality psychologists concerned about the mechanisms by which personality is expressed might test hypotheses based on the minutely described sequence of feelings and ideas so compellingly portrayed in great novels. Directly after confessing her affair to her husband, Anna Karenina experiences only a sense of relief that the secret is out. But the next morning in quick succession she feels shock, shame, despair, and terror; she envisions her life as an outcast, doubts that her lover's devotion will last, and becomes disoriented: "She felt as if everything were beginning to be double in her soul, just as objects sometimes appear double to over-tired eyes. She hardly knew at times what it was she feared, and what she hoped for" (Tolstoy, 1877/1950, p. 342). Are these in fact common responses to a disclosure of guilt? Is the time course and order of reactions realistic? Are such experiences universal, or are they limited to individuals with particular personality traits, such as high Neuroticism or Openness? Such questions are of more than academic interest to clinical psychologists, especially in view of the ultimate outcome depicted in *Anna Karenina*.

Personality Assessment for Fictional Characters

Judgment of characterization is admittedly a subjective business. For what my opinion is worth, I would say that Odysseus, Nestor, Agamemnon, Menelaos, Helen, and Achilleus are the same "people" in both poems. Those qualities that mark the Odysseus of the *Odyssey*—strength and courage, ingenuity, patience and self-control—all characterize the same hero in the *Iliad*.

—Lattimore, 1975, p. 19

Trait psychology has an obvious entrée into the study of fiction: Literary figures have character. The problem, which is faced by both psychologists and literary critics, is how characters' personality is to be conceptualized and assessed. Literary scholars typically use their own intuition to formulate descriptions. A few psychologists have used empirical, but ad hoc, methods. Nencini (2007) used text analysis to identify dimensions of the self (emotions, material self, relationships) for the protagonist of Tabucchi's *Sostiene Pereira*. Dotson (2009) provided his own judgments about several characteristics (e.g., obsessive, withdrawn, timid, too career-focused) in 80 fictional portrayals of physicists. These methods are not readily generalizable.

What is needed is a standard set of personality traits that encompass the full range of characteristics found not only in fictional physicists, but in all characters in literature, and the obvious choice is the FFM. One might argue that, in principle, the men and women of fiction might have more or fewer personality trait factors than real men and women, just as dogs and chimpanzees have more or fewer factors than humans (Gosling & John, 1999; King & Figueredo, 1997). But surely the FFM is the most reasonable place to start in assessing personality in fiction.

One landmark project has adopted this approach. In an Internet study, Johnson, Carroll, Gottschall, and Kruger

(2008, 2011) recruited 519 individuals with interest or expertise in 19th-century British literature (32% had doctorates, presumably in English). Respondents were asked to select one or more characters from 143 Victorian novels (from Jane Austin to E. M. Forster) and to complete an online questionnaire to describe each character; the survey included a ten-item measure of the FFM (Gosling, Rentfrow, & Swann, 2003). A total of 435 different characters were rated, some by multiple raters. Results appeared sensible. For example, Jane Eyre was rated as being conscientious and introverted; Catherine Earnshaw (from *Wuthering Heights*) was thought to be low on Agreeableness and high on Neuroticism.

These studies provide some answers to the most basic questions about personality in fictional characters. First, a factor analysis of the 10 personality items showed the five expected factors (Johnson et al., 2008). It appears that the FFM does indeed describe the personality of literary figures, at least those in Victorian novels. Second, a comparison of scores for the 206 characters with two or more raters showed cross-observer agreement for all five factors: Neuroticism (intraclass correlation = .50), Extraversion (.60), Openness (.44), Conscientiousness (.56), and especially Agreeableness (.74; J. A. Johnson, personal communication, November 19, 2010). These values substantially exceed what is typically found for peer ratings of real persons: In a study of undergraduate friends using a version of the same brief instrument (Vazire, 2010), the corresponding correlations were .36, .40, .26, .33, and .37 (S. Vazire, personal communication, November 27, 2010). In one sense this is unremarkable, because two readers of a novel have identical information about the character, information that typically includes not only overt behavior, but also private feelings and motives revealed by the author. In another sense, this is an important finding, because psychologists (and some reader-response critics) have often focused on the idiosyncratic responses of different readers to the same text. These data underscore the common perceptions of readers (Nencini, 2010); they show that personality traits in fictional characters can be consensually validated.

Johnson and colleagues (2008, 2011) also gathered data on other attributes of the characters—their role in the novel, their personal goals, their romantic styles. In a series of analyses, the authors related these attributes to FFM factors and compared their findings to patterns found in the empirical literature. For example, they reported that, as in real life, characters high in Openness to Experience were motivated by interests in creativity and discovery; those low in Agreeableness had a strong need for power.

They concluded that "authors' depiction of the workings of personality…largely mirrors the view…as revealed by modern research. Victorian authors do seem to be good intuitive psychologists" (Johnson et al., 2011, p. 56).

There were, however, some differences. In most research, there are reliable gender differences in personality, with the largest effects found for Neuroticism and Agreeableness; women score about one-half standard deviation higher than men on both factors (Costa et al., 2001). Feminist literary critics might have anticipated that Victorian novels, reflecting sexist stereotypes, would exaggerate these differences, but instead Johnson and colleagues (2011) found very small gender differences, with women only marginally more agreeable than men. The authors speculated that this finding was part of a pattern in which protagonists, including men, were portrayed as being cooperative and egalitarian. From a Darwinian point of view (Gottschall & Wilson, 2005), the function of fiction may have been to model the kind of group solidarity that had been essential for the survival of our hunter-gatherer ancestors.

Clearly, other interpretations are possible, and we do not yet know if these results would be replicated in other samples of fiction (say, Latin-American novels or Chinese films). It is also possible that the 10-item personality measure was not sufficiently sensitive to capture the relatively small differences between men and women. But even if longer measures of the five factors had been used (e.g., the Big Five Inventory; Benet-Martínez & John, 1998), the results of this study would have been chiefly valuable for making generalizations about groups. Individual characters, the focus of interest for most literary scholars, can only be crudely sketched by five scores. A more nuanced picture is needed, such as that provided by the 30 facets of the NEO Inventories.

That system is of value first in conceptualizing at a relatively fine-grained level the full range of personality traits. Raters who understand the concepts embodied in the NEO facets ought to be able to apply them to fictional characters. As a demonstration project, two personality psychologists well acquainted with the traits assessed by the NEO Inventories (RRM and C. E. Löckenhoff) estimated the standing of Goethe's Faust on each of the 30 NEO facets. RRM had recently read *Faust* in English translation; CEL had studied it in German some years before. Both gave T-score estimates for each facet comparing Faust to adult males in general; scores below 35 are considered very low; 35 to 44 low, 45 to 55 average, 56 to 65 high, and scores over 65, very high. RRM averaged the six facet scores for each factor to

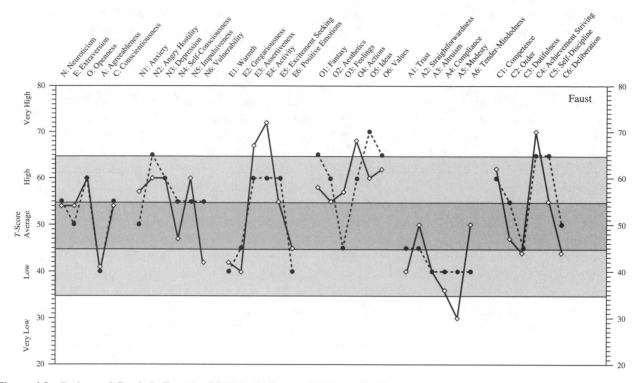

Figure 4.2   Ratings of Goethe's Faust by RRM (solid line) and CEL (dashed line)

Profile form reproduced by special permission of the publisher, Psychological Assessment Resources, Inc., 16204 North Florida Avenue, Lutz, FL 33549, from the *NEO Personality Inventory-3* by Paul T. Costa, Jr., PhD, and Robert R. McCrae, PhD. Copyright 1978, 1985, 1989, 1991, 1992, 2010 by Psychological Assessment Resources, Inc. (PAR). Further reproduction is prohibited without permission of PAR.

estimate the factor T-score; CEL estimated the factors directly.

Figure 4.2 shows the results, plotted on a NEO Inventories profile sheet. In the figure, the five factor scores are given on the left, followed toward the right by the 30 facet scales, grouped by factor. Factor and facet labels are given at the top of the figure. It is clear from the figure that there is quite substantial agreement between the two raters.[3] Both see Faust as high in Openness to Experience and low in Agreeableness, but average, on the whole, in the other factors. Looking only at these five factors, it would be hard to imagine that this is the profile of one of the most arresting figures in world literature, one who inspired symphonies by Liszt and Mahler, operas by Berlioz and Gounod. The fascination of the character is more understandable when specific facets are examined. Faust's arrogant impatience with others is seen in his high N2: Angry Hostility, low E1: Warmth, and low A5: Modesty; his restless striving for some higher level of being is seen in his high E4: Activity, O5: Ideas, and C4: Achievement

Striving. Faust as alienated seeker becomes a prototype of Romantic heroes.

From the perspective of personality assessment, perhaps the most important fact about Figure 4.2 is the convergence of two independent raters. Both raters could, of course, have written essays describing Faust's personality, and they could have compared notes to see if they agreed or disagreed. But such discussions are "a subjective business," as Lattimore noted. An important advantage of assessment on standard criteria (here, the 30 NEO facets) is that agreement can be quantified. A simple Pearson correlation across the 30 facet scales shows profile agreement of .76, a value that is not only statistically significant ($p < .001$), but is in fact higher than the agreement seen between about 90% of cases when real self-reports are compared to the ratings of knowledgeable observers (e.g., spouses; McCrae, 2008).

Further, profile agreement statistics (McCrae, 1993) make it possible to identify specific areas of disagreement. In Figure 4.2, the two raters essentially agreed on 28 of the facets (the best guess assessment would therefore be the average of the two ratings), but disagreed on N6: Vulnerability and O3: Feelings. In clinical assessment, the recommended course here is to ask informants to reconsider

---

[3]Apparently Faust's personality is preserved in translation—a fact that might surprise poets, but not personality psychologists, who understand the universality of personality traits.

the areas of disagreement. In this case, CEL recalled the famous lines expressing Faust's emotional ambivalence ("*Zwei Seelen wohnen, ach! in meiner Brust...*" ["Two souls, alas! reside within my breast..."]) and raised her estimate of his Openness to Feelings (C. E. Löckenhoff, personal communication, July 11, 2010).

An obvious limitation of this case study is that neither of the raters can claim to be an expert on Faust, and those scholars who could make that claim would probably not understand the traits assessed by the NEO facet scales well enough to make meaningful *T*-score ratings. Fortunately, there is an available technology for translating lay views of personality into standardized scores: the personality inventory. This method has been used to describe historical figures (Cassandro & Simonton, 2010; Rubenzer, et al., 2000), and was used by Johnson and colleagues (2011) to describe characters in British novels. In this case, Faust scholars might be asked to complete the 240-item NEO Personality Inventory-3 (NEO-PI-3; McCrae & Costa, 2010). Below, we will illustrate its use on two figures from French literature.

The Uses of Literature in Trait Psychology

Fictional characters are of use to trait psychologists first as illustrations. Whether writing for professional colleagues, teaching psychology students, or addressing the general public, psychologists must be able to convey their basic constructs to others, and literary figures provide widely known and often striking examples of personality traits: This is, of course, the rationale for Table 4.1.[4] Openness to Experience is the least easily grasped of the five factors, so McCrae (1994b) used the protagonists of Hesse's *Narcissus and Goldmund* as exemplars. Certain peculiarities of Goldmund's perceptual experience—such as seeing printed words morph into people and animals—vividly illustrate the permeable boundaries of consciousness found in highly open individuals, and probably convey much more to most readers than the phrase "permeable boundaries of consciousness."

Case studies, real or fictive, move beyond an abstract definition by showing how traits play out in real situations. Novelists are usually intuitive psychologists; they select actions for their characters not by consulting a list of personality correlates, but by imagining how such a person would react in such a situation. These intuitions can be considered hypotheses, and, if confirmed, can add to the store of scientific knowledge. Consider Alexei Arsenyev, the narrator of Bunin's *Lika*. He is a young poet and romantic who embodies many of the characteristics of high Openness (McCrae, 1990). He is prone to impetuous travels, sometimes inspired by nothing more than the sound of the place-name. When the NEO Personality Inventory was revised (Costa, McCrae, & Dye, 1991), a new openness to feelings item was tested, suggested by Alexei's reactions: "Odd things—like certain scents or the names of distant places—can evoke strong moods in me." Item analyses confirmed that this is in fact a good indicator of openness to feelings, and it is included in the NEO Personality Inventory-3.

If characters in novels behave like ordinary human beings, researchers could use them as subjects in studies of any aspect of personality psychology. Johnson and colleagues (2008) in fact used data on the characters in Victorian novels to test hypotheses from evolutionary psychology. It is unlikely that this kind of study will become common, because it is usually simpler to collect data from live subjects. However, studies of personality psychology using literary surrogate samples may prove invaluable in dealing with populations that are otherwise inaccessible. One could, for example, ask about age differences in personality traits in Ancient Greece or pre-Islamic India—a kind of psychoarchaeology.

Studies of literature could also throw light on some of the most vexing questions faced by students of personality and culture. When personality questionnaires are administered to members of different cultures, consistent differences are found—for example, American and European cultures usually score higher on Extraversion than do Asian or African cultures (McCrae, Terracciano, & 79 Members, 2005). It is not clear, however, that these differences are real, because a score in one language may not be strictly comparable to the same score in another language. Assessed national differences are not, in fact, supported by common national character stereotypes (Terracciano, Abdel-Khalak et al., 2005). Most people believe that the British are reserved, but they actually score higher in Extraversion than most other cultures in the world. It is not clear which kind of data should be believed (although the weight of evidence is currently against national stereotypes; McCrae, Terracciano, Realo., & Allik, 2007). Analyses of national literatures might help resolve this issue.

At least one study has addressed that possibility. Allik and colleagues (2011) informally reviewed depictions of Russians in novels (and in scholarly works), and compared

---

[4]Condon (1999) illustrated concepts from a popular personality typology with characters from films; B. F. Skinner created his own characters in *Walden Two* to illustrate his psychological ideas.

the personality profile they inferred from these sources to questionnaire scores of 7,065 Russians on FFM personality traits. They found little resemblance. However, there was also little resemblance between the literary profile and ratings of national stereotypes from 3,705 Russian respondents (Allik et al., 2009). As the authors of these studies acknowledged, a limitation was the impressionistic summary of Russian literature. A stronger test of the hypotheses would use formal personality assessments of a much larger sample of Russian novels and characters—the sort of design Johnson and colleagues (2011) used with British novelists.

It is possible, however, that each national literature is more a reflection of the social values and customs—the national ethos (McCrae, 2009)—than of the people themselves. In fact, one of the classic studies of personality and literature attempted to infer culturally-prescribed need for achievement from the stories selected for use in grade school primers (McClelland, 1961). As yet, the only assessments of ethos in terms of the NEO facets are for the United States and Japan (McCrae, 2009), but studies of the personality traits of fictional characters in American and Japanese literature would make a fascinating comparison possible.

Trait psychologists need to use the materials of fiction very cautiously. There are legitimate reasons to doubt that fictional characters are faithful representations of human personality. Novelists rely on their own observations (and on what they have read), but their personal acquaintances are likely to be even further from a truly random sample than the college sophomores typically surveyed by psychologists. Relatively few novels were written by older men or women, but younger novelists cannot have had firsthand experience with lifespan development. The characters found in historical novels or science fiction may tell us something about the creative imagination, but it is impossible to know if they accurately reflect the operation of personality traits in situations we can never study directly.

Some limitations of fiction (from the perspective of a trait researcher) have to do with the nature of the art form. The dramatic tension of struggles between heroes and villains is central to much fiction, but it means that people strikingly high and low in Agreeableness are likely to be vastly overrepresented—which might explain the exceptionally high cross-observer agreement on this factor in the studies of Johnson and colleagues (2008, 2011). Characters high in Neuroticism (like the suicidal Laura Brown in Cunningham's *The Hours* or Goethe's sorrowful young Werther) will be preferred by novelists over those who

are low in Neuroticism, because terror, despair, and rage are more interesting than equanimity. Novelists and poets themselves are usually high in Openness (e.g., McCrae, 1993–1994), which is why literature is so rich a source of illustrations of that trait. In real life, people are usually more prosaic.

Writers must create characters who are understandable and with whom readers can somehow identify, but this does not necessarily imply psychological realism—magical realism works equally well. Even authors operating in the naturalistic tradition are guided by artistic as well as scientific considerations, and the accuracy of their portrayals is not subject to empirical test. Psychologists might understandably wish to avoid the ambiguities of this source of data on human personality.

However, fiction remains of interest and of value. It provides striking illustrations of traits, suggests testable hypotheses about how they are expressed in the world, and may, under some circumstances, provide data on otherwise inaccessible topics. Proponents of literary genius would go further: They would suggest that great writers have insights into human nature that may transcend any existing theories of personality and point to entirely new schools of thought. The possibility that this is so is one reason to include literature in the education of psychologists.

THE USES OF TRAIT PSYCHOLOGY IN THE HUMANITIES

The humanities—history, philosophy, and particularly literary studies—ought to take into account whatever is known about human nature, and personality psychology is surely an important contributor to that knowledge. In this section we outline some reasons why the humanities should focus on trait psychology, and illustrate its application to the analysis of characters from French literature.

Insight, Mystification, and Psychoanalysis

> The voices of stones. The wall of a church and the wall of a prison. The mast of a ship and a gallows. The shadow of a hangman and of an ascetic. The soul of a hangman and of an ascetic. The different combinations of known phenomena in higher space.
>
> —Ouspensky, 1920, Argument, Chapter XIV, *Tertium organum*

Oatley (1999) argued that whereas science sees truth in the correspondence between idea and fact, literature sees it in the internal coherence of the story and in its personal impact, an emotionally charged insight. If we are to consider the possible value of trait psychology for understanding literature, it is useful to begin with an overview of the experience of truth in art.

Psychologists, like writers, are familiar with the concept of insight: the sudden understanding of a problem or the recognition of a previously overlooked pattern. Insight is an important feature of everyday problem-solving, but it is also a specialty of artistic creations, sometimes inducing chills, that hallmark of aesthetic experience (McCrae, 2007). Writers have long cultivated techniques designed to produce the experience of insight, including recognition scenes, epiphanies, and acute psychological observations (such as Anna Karenina's experience of a doubled soul).

Writers in fact deliberately create problems for the reader whose solutions can then be appreciated as insights. The whole genre of the mystery story is a transparent instance of this, one that requires no effort on the part of the reader beyond turning pages. More demanding are literary devices like classical references that require knowledge on the part of the reader, or metaphor and allegory, that the reader must make some kind of effort to grasp. In general, greater effort yields a stronger experience of insight.

By extension of this artistic strategy, authors may try to lure readers into ever deeper mysteries—Captain Ahab's "little lower layer"—with ambiguous symbolism or arcane allusions à la T. S. Eliot. If insight gives truth, and difficult insight gives greater truth, then the most profound truths must be those that can hardly be grasped at all (such as, according to devout Christians, the mysteries of the Trinity and the Incarnation). By *mystification* we mean the experience of truth as an anticipation of profound insight induced by artful obscurity. As a literary device, mystification is dangerous, because the effect falls flat when readers come to suspect that there is at bottom no real message. The quote from Ouspensky's argument given above (which, of course, he intended as mysticism, not mystification) is immensely evocative, but many readers would find that the chapter does not deliver a great new vision of the world. And yet literature as art is not required to deliver profound truths; if we suspend disbelief, we can be enthralled by sheer mystification. Truth, after all, is only one of many goals of literature, often less important than humor, social commentary, or moral persuasion.

The disciplinary familiarity that literary critics have with mystification may help explain the enormous attraction psychoanalytic theory has had for them. Aside from the drama of incestuous yearnings and murderous impulses, the most distinctive feature of classical psychoanalysis is its mystery. The theory postulates that people's real motives and feelings are not only unconscious, but actively disguised. More than simple objectivity (such as one might get from a knowledgeable informant) is needed to penetrate these disguises; many years of decoding symbols may be required. Such a system has an obvious appeal to literary critics, who are accustomed to the patient unraveling of hidden meanings. What a boon to interpretation if the "little lower layer" could be located on the (allegedly) well-charted maps of the unconscious mind!

But Freud's seminal writings on the unconscious mind are more than a century old, and it would be extraordinary if psychological science had made no progress since then. It is perfectly appropriate for novelists and playwrights deliberately to incorporate Freudian ideas into their work, as many 20th-century authors did (e.g., surrealist poet André Breton, dramatist Eugene O'Neill)—they are, after all, primarily concerned with telling a good story. And where they have done so, it is of course incumbent on the critic to expound on this, just as scholars of the *Divine Comedy* must understand and explain Ptolemaic astronomy. But to interpret, say, the plays of Ibsen or stories of Poe in classic Freudian terms is to write fiction about fiction. Real scholarship requires a more current conception of psychology.[5] For those with a taste for psychodynamic approaches, this means learning contemporary versions of psychoanalysis (Bornstein et al., this volume), as some critics have done (e.g., Benzon, 2003). Modern trait psychology provides another option.

Trait Psychology and Literary Criticism

Literary scholars can (and, we believe, should) familiarize themselves with FFM traits and the way they function in people's lives as a background to the understanding of any fictional character. FFM traits provide a convenient way to describe characters that is easily shared with other scholars and general readers. Because it is comprehensive, it permits a systematic approach that can call attention to aspects of the character's personality that might otherwise have been overlooked. Conformity of characters' actions to what is known about the operation of traits provides a way to assess the realism of the work and the psychological sophistication of the author.

But for many purposes, more than a general acquaintance with the FFM is needed; formal assessments of personality traits are required—a task that requires collaboration with psychologists versed in the administration, scoring, and interpretation of personality measures

---

[5]McAdams (2011) has made a parallel case for the need for up-to-date psychology in biographies.

(e.g., Johnson et al., 2011). Many literary scholars contribute to their discipline by conducting detailed studies of the chronology or geography of a novel, or the historical background of an author's work. It would also be a useful service to catalog the personality profiles of major characters. Selecting expert raters, comparing their ratings, and relating these objective assessments to conventional (sometimes conflicting) characterizations are worthy scholarly activities. Because the number of important literary figures is finite, one can envision the ultimate compilation of an encyclopedia of personality profiles from fiction as a resource for future scholars.

Personality researchers typically make generalizations based on samples of respondents, whereas clinical psychologists usually apply these generalizations to understand specific individuals. Literary studies might also operate on these two levels. The first, nomothetic, level consists of large-scale studies, based on new samples or summarizing existing data; they might examine such questions as:

- How are traits distributed in a given genre? Is it true, as suggested above, that novels overrepresent exceptionally open and highly disagreeable people in comparison to real-life samples?
- Can literary movements be characterized by the distribution of characters' traits? Is openness to ideas more salient in Enlightenment literature, with confrontations between the open- and closed-minded? Is openness to feelings more often emphasized in the Romantic period? Do novels of the 20th century, in W. H. Auden's phrase, depict an age of anxiety?
- How can the personality palette of an author be characterized? Does Thomas Hardy specialize in introverts? Mark Twain in extraverts? Do reputedly universal authors like Chaucer and Balzac in fact depict the full range of human traits?
- How do authors (or genres, or periods) differ in the *dimensionality* of their creations? A character whose personality can be summed up in a single trait term (and who is thus merely average on all other traits) is called "one-dimensional." Use of the FFM, and particularly a consideration of specific facets within each factor, could lead to a quantifiable measure of the multi-dimensionality of characters that could be used to address this question.
- How does an author's personality affect his or her portrayal of characters? Provided sufficient data are available about their lives and their relations to other people, authors can be rated on personality traits in the same way as characters are, and the profiles of authors can be compared to the profiles of their creations. How often are protagonists autobiographical in this sense? How close are the resemblances in personality, and what distortions, if any, are common?

Johnson and colleagues (2011) asked the general question of whether trait psychology in fiction mirrors trait psychology in fact, and many more studies along those lines could be conducted, examining the stability or heritability or correlates of traits in the world of fiction. Whether the results would be of more interest to personality psychologists or to literary scholars may depend on the specific questions asked, but a body of findings would help define the relations between these two fields. Johnson and colleagues also noted that the kinds of studies mentioned here differ from most literary scholarship in providing quantified results that can be subjected to statistical test. Whether that will advance our understanding of literature remains to be seen.

Two Cases From French Literature

Only a few literary scholars are likely to be interested in such systematic studies of personality in fiction, but most will be concerned about characterizing individual figures. Case studies (corresponding to the second, idiographic, level of psychological studies, clinical interpretations) thus provide the most direct way for critics to use the FFM. Here we present as examples studies of two notable figures from French literature: Molière's Alceste and Voltaire's Candide. Clinicians may find this approach to understanding individual cases—in particular, the integration of assessments from multiple informants—useful for their work, too.

In *The Misanthrope*, Alceste repeatedly tries to present an ultimatum to the coquette Celimene, with whom he is smitten: If she wishes to continue to have his love, she must abandon her dizzying social life, empty her popular salon of suitors, and eventually follow him into a kind of exile in the far provinces. She deftly puts off the showdown by fobbing Alceste off time and again on other interlocutors, such as the would-be poet Oronte, the fops Acaste and Clitandre, the prudish Arsinoe, and her own cousin Eliante, who prefers the company of Alceste's best friend, Cleante. The latter is faithful and unselfish, offering to sacrifice his own feelings for Eliante in hopes of finding a more suitable match for his prickly friend than a deceiving social butterfly like Celimene. After the two friends discuss the diverse implications of misanthropy in the early modern world, Alcest must confront a series of pesky interruptions: judge Oronte's insipid sonnet, read poison pen letters Arsinoe claims to have intercepted, and attend to legal affairs involving a potentially disastrous law suit that he refuses to take seriously. Alceste finally corners Celimene to explain the damning letters Arsinoe has shown him, only to have the lady escape his criticism and leave him begging for forgiveness. The clownish Acaste and Clitandre precipitate a crisis by publicly exposing duplicitous letters they have received from Celimene. Even *in extremis*, with her reputation destroyed, Celimene is unable to accept Alceste's final harsh offer of imposed isolation with him. In bitter spite, the misanthrope storms off stage, pursued by Eliante and Cleante, who will keep trying somehow to reconcile him with the human race.

Candide is a satire confronting philosophic optimism with harsh realities. Expulsed from his adoptive home in a shabby German castle because of his sexual curiosity about the baron's daughter, young Candide is shanghaied into the army and brutalized in a senseless war. As he falls into further misadventures, he is helped by the altruistic Anabaptist Jacques and reunited with his Leibnizian tutor Pangloss, who has instilled in him the view that this is the best of possible worlds. In Lisbon, Candide is nearly turned into a human sacrifice after the famous earthquake, but is saved by his erstwhile girlfriend, Cunegonde. Candide runs off with her to Argentina, but the unexpected intervention of Cunegonde's hostile brother ruins their New World refuge, forcing Candide into a duel and subsequent flight into the jungle, where he encounters first savages and then utopian natives who have fashioned a perfect civilization in the remote interior. Leaving this ideal world in search of his beloved, Candide discovers the horrors of colonial slavery in Surinam. After returning to Europe, Candide's entourage swells with the motley rejects of a dysfunctional society. As he reunites at last with a by-now frumpy Cunegonde, he finds himself in Turkey, where they establish a sort of pragmatist commune in an attempt finally to achieve some measure of order in their chaotic lives.

As a prelude to their FFM profiles, it would be worthwhile to consider how these characters have historically been viewed. Consider Alceste. Nicolas Boileau in his *Art poetique* epitomized *The Misanthrope* as the very best of the author's work. Boileau seems to have admired Molière's ability to create a central character who could exhibit the foibles of human nature while still maintaining an overall air of dignity. The bilious lover (subtitle to the play) was seen as a paragon of wit, possessed of a mind capable of being fooled only by itself. Alceste's good-bye

to the cruel world at the conclusion of the play eloquently expresses a common theme of 17th-century French lyric poetry, the flight to simple solitude away from the troubles and hypocrisy of civilized life. Boileau's opinion of the play became iconic through much of the following century.

However, by the time of the revolution, Alceste was taking on different colors. His disdain for society was translated into a disdain for the ancient regime. It was Jean-Jacques Rousseau who led the charge for this assessment, notably in his "Letter to D'Alembert" on the theater. Rousseau actually accused Molière of maligning his own protagonist by conspiring against Alceste's passion for honesty and frankness.[6]

Alceste was interpreted by the Romantic generations as a figure of sadness. Sainte-Beuve, Musset, and Hugo were among those who took this position. Indeed, the image of Alceste, plagued with *Weltschmerz* and precocious *mal de siecle*, came to dominate Molière's works in a way never before possible. The Molièriste movement of the late 19th century sought to return to a more naturalistic interpretation of Alceste, pointing out, for instance, that his character demonstrated similarity to some actual figures of Louis XIV's court.

Twentieth-century ideas about Alceste have enriched upon many of these early reactions. Rene Jasinski links Alceste to Jansenism, one of the dominant religious movements of 17th-century France. This view shows the possibility of associating Alceste's personality with deep philosophical and spiritual feelings, rather than just attributing his behavior to a quirky imbalance of humors.

Paul Bénichou, on the other hand, saw Alceste as a key figure in Molière's elaboration of a neo-aristocratic aesthetic. Alceste's impatience with modernity, his nostalgia for better times, his refusal to bribe judges in the despicable courts, all reflect an identification with chivalric honor of a bygone (or perhaps nonexistent) age.

North American sociocritics (Gaines, 1984) such as Larry Riggs, Ralph Albanese, and Max Vernet, also apply other approaches to the character of Alceste. Several have evoked an anthropological perspective on Alceste's relations both with the salon in the play and with the opposite sex. The play is structured around Alceste's desire to present and enforce an ultimatum to assure Celimene's absolute fidelity to him; his preoccupation with unfaithfulness goes to the heart of a drive for hegemony found in a

---

[6]Rousseau's sympathy for Alceste is understandable: Rousseau himself was high in Neuroticism and low in Agreeableness (McCrae, 1996).

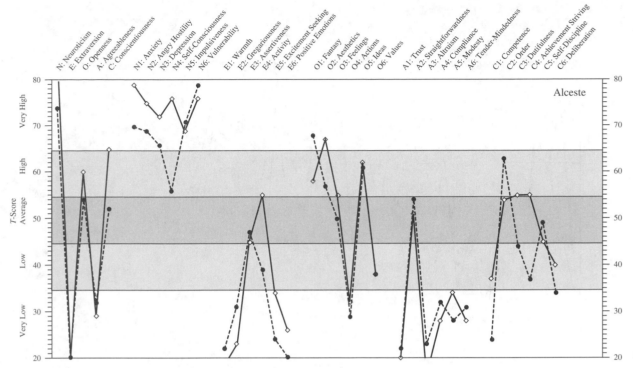

Figure 4.3 Personality profile for Molière's Alceste. NEO-PI-3 ratings by JFG (solid line) and MAW (dashed line) are plotted against adult male norms.

whole range of 17th-century institutions. At the same time, it is linked to an uncertainty of identity that constantly reverberates in his relationships with other characters in the play. Alceste seems extremely reluctant to assume an identity contingent upon the evaluation or recognition of others and is willing to accept complete solipsism as an alternative.

An FFM Perspective

Two expert raters (JFG and MAW) independently described Alceste and Candide using the NEO-PI-3.[7] Both are professors of French literature, familiar with the works in both French and English translation; they have taught them in a variety of courses. JFG has published extensively on Molière (Gaines, 1984, 2002); MAW is a Voltaire scholar (Wellington, 1987). Their ratings comparing Alceste to adult men in general are shown in Figure 4.3. The two raters agreed very closely indeed: The correlation across the 30 facet scales was .91, and

ratings were essentially the same for 27 of the facets. Agreement was somewhat lower for Candide, whose profile, compared to adolescent males, is given in Figure 4.4. The correlation across the 30 facets was .66, $p < .001$, but the two raters disagreed on eight scales, most notably Extraversion and its gregariousness, activity, and positive emotions facets.

These ratings are surely sensible. Alceste, the bilious misanthrope, is very high in angry hostility, and very low in warmth, gregariousness, and all the facets of Agreeableness except straightforwardness. Candide, the gullible optimist-in-training, is very high in trust and low in anxiety; the wild adventures he embarks on are expectable from someone very high in openness to actions and very low in deliberation. As his name suggests, he is very high in straightforwardness.

These profiles thus demonstrate first of all that literary characters can be meaningfully portrayed by modern personality assessment methods. Further, the results show enough distinctiveness to be of use to researchers. Alceste and Candide are, of course, in many respects polar opposites, which is reflected in a correlation of $r = -.42$, $p < .05$, between the two adjusted mean profiles. Figures 4.3 and 4.4 are perhaps most interesting

---

[7]Some of the NEO-PI-3 items are anachronistic when applied to 17th-century personalities, but raters usually find it easy to imagine how the targets would have responded.

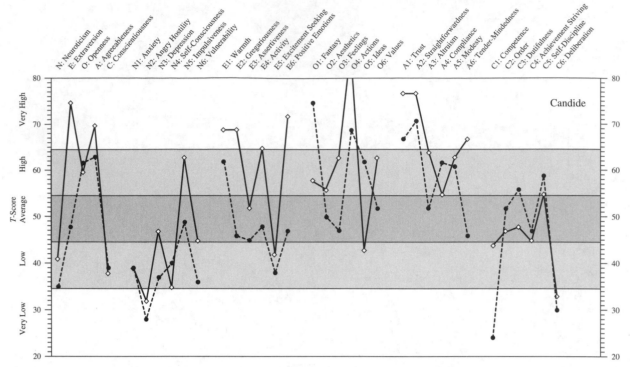

Figure 4.4 Personality profile for Voltaire's Candide. NEO-PI-3 ratings by JFG (solid line) and MAW (dashed line) are plotted against adolescent male norms.

Profile form reproduced by special permission of the publisher, Psychological Assessment Resources, Inc., 16204 North Florida Avenue, Lutz, FL 33549, from the NEO Personality Inventory-3 by Paul T. Costa, Jr., PhD, and Robert R. McCrae, PhD. Copyright 1978, 1985, 1989, 1991, 1992, 2010 by Psychological Assessment Resources, Inc. (PAR). Further reproduction is prohibited without permission of PAR.

in showing the respects in which these characters are similar: Both are high in overall Openness and especially openness to fantasy; both are low (with tragi-comic results) in competence and deliberation.

It is of interest to reexamine critical views of Alceste in light of his FFM portrait. Boileau perhaps focused on Alceste's high Openness and Conscientiousness. Rousseau admired his straightforwardness (although we might style it brutal frankness). The Romantic critics sympathized with his high Neuroticism, especially depression, and low positive emotions; Bénechou noted his reactionary tendencies, seen in low openness to actions and values. Together, these comparisons suggest that individual critics tend to overemphasize selected aspects of Alceste's personality; the comprehensive FFM gives a fuller and more balanced picture.

Different raters often see individuals somewhat differently (McCrae, 1994a), and the same is predictably true of expert opinions about fictional characters. All readers have access to the same text, but in the course of an extended work like *Candide*, personality is revealed in a wide variety of situations, and different moments will seem iconic to different readers. Raters will also likely differ in their attributions of specific behaviors to traits in the character or to

the demands of the situation. Structured personality assessment can assist criticism by pinpointing areas of differing perceptions. Figure 4.4, for example, shows notable disagreement on Candide's Extraversion, and JFG and MAW exchanged views on this discrepancy. MAW regards Candide as a rather passive figure who merely reacts to the situations in which he finds himself—an object of satire in an age that valued independent action inspired by Reason. JFG, in contrast, ascribes more vitality to Candide himself, seeing his voyage as a proactive attempt to find his way in this not-the-best of possible worlds. Both assessments are worth pondering; both can enrich the reader's understanding of the work.

THE VALUE OF CONTEMPORARY PERSONALITY PSYCHOLOGY FOR WRITERS AND READERS

Since the Renaissance, painters have studied human anatomy in preparation for their work. These lessons allowed them to produce images that were admirably lifelike. Knowing the underlying structure of muscles and bones made them more perceptive observers of the outwardly visible forms of their models, and led them to imagine plausible unseen forms, such as angels and demons. Even when they chose to ignore anatomical correctness—an in Ingres's *Grande Odalisque* or the work of the Cubists—a grounding in the scientific basis of their subject matter gave painters a basis for communication with an audience accustomed to seeing real human beings.

Surely the same argument can be applied to personality psychology. Novelists, playwrights, and poets who depict human characters draw on their own life experience, but they can and should avail themselves of whatever is known through scientific observation. The teachings of personality psychology are, of course, not prescriptive for writers. It would be absurd to insist that twins have near-identical traits, or that gender differences between heroes and heroines mirror those found in real life, or even to suggest that each of the five factors should be illustrated in one character or another.[8] But training in the FFM may help writers notice traits and behaviors that they would otherwise have overlooked, and these observations can feed their creative imaginations.

Contemporary theories of personality can contribute to artistic vision at a more philosophical level. FFT, illustrated in Figure 4.1, suggests a view of the world that is both essentialist and existentialist. In one sense, people and their lives are an expression of their enduring basic tendencies—traits that define a kind of essence. In another sense, individuals create themselves as a collection of characteristic adaptations—beliefs, relationships, courses of action—that reflect both life experience and their own personal choices. Such ideas could find expression in a variety of themes. Emerson lamented that people "are all creatures of given temperament" whose life "turns out to be a certain uniform tune which the revolving barrel of the music-box must play" (Emerson, 1844/1990). But another author might see the same phenomenon as continual self-actualization, the endless striving to become what we are destined to be. Both tragedians and comedians can find much to grapple with in the notion that, whatever we are in essence, we are inevitably confronted by changing life circumstances to which we must somehow adapt. This is perhaps the central dramatic conflict of life.

Readers, too, should benefit from research on the FFM. Readers' own personalities surely influence the books they choose to read. Those high in Openness are more likely to prefer fiction in general (Mar, Oatley, & Peterson, 2009),

---

[8]Although Dürer, in the *Four Apostles*, managed to turn the temperamental psychology of his day into high art.

and one NEO-PI-3 item shows that more open readers prefer "poetry that emphasizes feelings and images more than story lines." Additional research on this topic would probably show that other factors also affect choice: It is hard to imagine that highly agreeable people, kind and sympathetic in their dealings with others, would avidly read violent graphic novels. Reviewers might guide readers by noting the kinds of people who will be most likely to enjoy a book.

Some knowledge of the FFM ought to be part of an education in literature, introduced perhaps in high school. Students who are expected to read *The Scarlet Letter* or *The Crucible* are surely capable of understanding and profiting from the basic principles of trait psychology. All readers might develop a deeper appreciation of literary portraiture—Bloom's "supreme literary value"—if their commonsense intuitions about people are sharpened by knowledge of traits and their manifestations in people's lives.

EPILOGUE

Some 50 years ago, C. P. Snow (1961) famously lamented the rift between scientists and literary intellectuals. This gap has remained. Some contemporary literary theory is ideologically anti-scientific, but the major obstacle is the sheer remoteness of the two kinds of expertise: It is unrealistic to expect a student of 17th-century kabuki theater to have any real understanding of quantum chromodynamics (or vice versa).

Personality psychology, however, is a science within the grasp of any educated person, and there are signs that literary theory and personality psychology may be on the point of fruitful engagement. Invoking E. O. Wilson's notion of consilience, Kruger, Fisher, and Jobling (2003) argued that Darwinian literary criticism could bridge the perspectives of the sciences and humanities. The FFM, whose traits are familiar to both laypersons and trait psychologists, provides another, natural link between readers, writers, and psychologists. Literary scholars are invited to join this conversation.

But personality psychology is not a one-sided gift from science to literature; it is the product of human thought in many forms over many centuries. Oatley (1999) reminded us that "novels contain distillations of folk theory" (p. 115), and psychologists implicitly rely on such commonsense intuitions about people—for example, in writing items for personality questionnaires. Oatley argued that both psychology and literature can benefit from the cross-fertilization of scientific and folk psychologies.

Nor is this exchange limited to academics. One of the characters in Franzen's *The Corrections* is a professor of textual artifacts; another has a family that lives by the maxims of pop psychology. The many readers of this best-selling novel are participants in a grand dialogue between criticism, psychology, and literature that is reshaping human consciousness about human nature. The FFM will be central to it.

REFERENCES

Allik, J., Mõttus, R., Realo, A., Pullmann, H., Trifonova, A., McCrae, R. R., ... 55 Members of the Russian Character and Personality Survey. (2009). How national character is constructed: Personality traits attributed to the typical Russian [in Russian]. *Cultural and Historical Psychology* (1), 2–18.

Allik, J., Realo, A., Mõttus, R., Pullmann, H., Trifonova, A., McCrae, R. R., ... Korneeva, E. E. (2011). Personality profiles and the "Russian soul": Literary and scholarly views evaluated. *Journal of Cross-Cultural Psychology, 42*, 372–389.

Allport, G. W., & Odbert, H. S. (1936). Trait names: A psycho-lexical study. *Psychological Monographs, 47*, (1 Whole No. 211).

Angleitner, A., & Ostendorf, F. (1994). Temperament and the Big Five factors of personality. In C. F. Halverson, G. A. Kohnstamm, & R. P. Martin (Eds.), *The developing structure of temperament and personality from infancy to adulthood* (pp. 69–90). Hillsdale, NJ: Erlbaum.

Argamon, S., Koppel, M., Pennebaker, J. W., & Schler, J. (2009). Automatically profiling the author of an anonymous text. *Communications of the Association for Computing Machinery*. doi: 10.1145/1461928.1461959

Ashton, M. C., Lee, K., Perugini, M., Szarota, P., De Vries, R. E., Di Blass ,... De Raad, B. (2004). A six-factor structure of personality descriptive adjectives: Solutions from psycholexical studies in seven languages. *Journal of Personality and Social Psychology, 86*, 356–366.

Barrick, M. R., & Mount, M. K. (1991). The Big Five personality dimensions and job performance: A meta-analysis. *Personnel Psychology, 44*, 1–26.

Benet-Martínez, V., & John, O. P. (1998). *Los cinco grandes* across cultures and ethnic groups: Multitrait multimethod analyses of the Big Five in Spanish and English. *Journal of Personality and Social Psychology, 75*, 729–750.

Benzon, W. L. (2003). *"Kubla Khan" and the embodied mind*. Downloaded June 10, 2011, from www.psyartjournal.com/article/show/l_benzon-kubla_khan_and_the_embodied_mind

Block, J. (1981). Some enduring and consequential structures of personality. In A. I. Rabin, J. Aronoff, A. M. Barclay, & R. A. Zucker (Eds.), *Further explorations in personality* (pp. 27–43). New York, NY: Wiley-Interscience.

Block, J. (1995). A contrarian view of the five-factor approach to personality description. *Psychological Bulletin, 117*, 187–215.

Bloom, H. (1998). *Shakespeare: The invention of the human*. New York, NY: Riverhead Books.

Bouchard, T. J., & Loehlin, J. C. (2001). Genes, evolution, and personality. *Behavior Genetics, 31*, 243–273.

Brooner, R. K., Schmidt, C. W., & Herbst, J. H. (2002). Personality trait characteristics of opioid abusers with and without comorbid personality disorders. In P. T. Costa, Jr. & T. A. Widiger (Eds.), *Personality disorders and the five-factor model of personality* (2nd ed., pp. 249–268). Washington, DC: American Psychological Association.

Burt, A., McGue, M., & Iacono, W. G. (2010). Environmental contributions to the stability of antisocial behavior over time: Are they shared or non-shared? *Journal of Abnormal Child Psychology, 38*, 327–337.

Cassandro, V. J., & Simonton, D. K. (2010). Versatility, openness to experience, and topical diversity in creative products: An exploratory historiometric analysis of scientists, philosophers, and writers. *Journal of Creative Behavior, 44*, 1–18.

Cassidy, J., & Shaver, P. R. (Eds.). (2008). *Handbook of attachment: Theory, research, and clinical applications* (2nd ed.). New York, NY: Guilford Press.

Cattell, R. B. (1946). *The description and measurement of personality*. Yonkers, NY: World Book.

Cervone, D. (2004). The architecture of personality. *Psychological Review, 111*, 183–204.

Cervone, D., & Shoda, Y. (Eds.). (1999). *The coherence of personality: social-cognitive bases of consistency, variability, and organization*. New York, NY: Guilford Press.

Church, A. T., & Katigbak, M. S. (2012). Culture and personality. In M. J. Gelfand, C.-y. Chiu, & Y.-y. Hong (Eds.), *Advances in culture and psychology* (Vol. 2, pp. 139–204). New York, NY: Oxford University Press.

Condon, T. (1999). *The Enneagram movie & video guide: How to see personality styles in the movies* (2nd ed.). Portland, OR: Metamorphous Press.

Contarello, A., & Vellico, E. (2003). Social psychology and literary texts: An empirical analysis of a contemporary Indian novel. *Empirical Studies of the Arts, 21*, 21–49.

Costa, P. T., Jr., Fagan, P. J., Piedmont, R. L., Ponticas, Y., & Wise, T. (1992). The five-factor model of personality and sexual functioning in outpatient men and women. *Psychiatric Medicine, 10*, 199–215.

Costa, P. T., Jr., & McCrae, R. R. (1980). Still stable after all these years: Personality as a key to some issues in adulthood and old age. In P. B. Baltes & O. G. Brim, Jr. (Eds.), *Life span development and behavior* (Vol. 3, pp. 65–102). New York, NY: Academic Press.

Costa, P. T., Jr., & McCrae, R. R. (1985). *The NEO personality inventory manual*. Odessa, FL: Psychological Assessment Resources.

Costa, P. T., Jr., & McCrae, R. R. (1995). Domains and facets: Hierarchical personality assessment using the Revised NEO Personality Inventory. *Journal of Personality Assessment, 64*, 21–50.

Costa, P. T., Jr., & McCrae, R. R. (1998). Six approaches to the explication of facet-level traits: Examples from conscientiousness. *European Journal of Personality, 12*, 117–134.

Costa, P. T., Jr., McCrae, R. R., & Arenberg, D. (1980). Enduring dispositions in adult males. *Journal of Personality and Social Psychology, 38*, 793–800.

Costa, P. T., Jr., McCrae, R. R., & Dye, D. A. (1991). Facet scales for agreeableness and conscientiousness: A revision of the NEO Personality Inventory. *Personality and Individual Differences, 12*, 887–898.

Costa, P. T., Jr., Terracciano, A., & McCrae, R. R. (2001). Gender differences in personality traits across cultures: Robust and surprising findings. *Journal of Personality and Social Psychology, 81*, 322–331.

De Raad, B., Barelds, D. P. H., Levert, E., Ostendort, F., Mlačić, B., De Blas, L., ... Katigbak, M. S. (2010). Only three factors of personality description are fully replicable across languages: A comparison of 14 trait taxonomies. *Journal of Personality and Social Psychology, 98*, 160–173.

Digman, J. M. (1990). Personality structure: Emergence of the five-factor model. *Annual Review of Psychology, 41*, 417–440.

Djikic, M., Oatley, K., Zoeterman, S., & Peterson, J. B. (2009). On being moved by art: How reading fiction transforms the self. *Creativity Research Journal, 21*, 24–29.

Domhoff, G. W. (1999). Drawing theoretical implications from descriptive empirical findings on dream content. *Dreaming: Journal of the Association for the Study of Dreams, 9,* 201–210.

Dotson, D. (2009). Portrayal of physicists in fictional works. *CLCWeb: Comparative literature and culture, 11,* http://docs.lib.purdue.edu/clcweb/vol11/iss12/15

Emerson, R. W. (1990). Experience. In *Essays: First and second series.* New York, NY: Vintage. (Original work published in 1844)

Falmagne, R. J. (2004). On the constitution of "self" and "mind": The dialectic of the system and the person. *Theory & Psychology, 14,* 822–845.

Figueredo, A. J., Sefcek, J. A., Vasquez, G., Brumbach, B. H., King, J. E., & Jacobs, W. J. (2005). Evolutionary personality psychology. In D. M. Buss (Ed.), *Handbook of evolutionary psychology* (pp. 851–877). Hoboken, NJ: John Wiley & Sons.

Fiske, D. W. (1949). Consistency of the factorial structures of personality ratings from different sources. *Journal of Abnormal and Social Psychology, 44,* 329–344.

Fiske, D. W. (1974). The limits for the conventional science of personality. *Journal of Personality, 42,* 1–11.

Funder, D. C. (1980). On seeing ourselves as others see us: Self-other agreement and discrepancy in personality ratings. *Journal of Personality, 48,* 473–493.

Gaines, J. F. (1984). *Social structures in Molière's theater.* Columbus, OH: Ohio State University Press.

Gaines, J. F. (2002). *The Molière encyclopedia.* Westport, CT: Greenwood Press.

Gemin, J. (1999). The dissolution of the self in unsettled times: Postmodernism and the creative process. *Journal of Creative Behavior, 33,* 45–61.

Gerrig, R. J. (1998). *Experiencing narrative worlds: On the psychological activities of reading.* New Haven, CT: Yale University Press.

Goldberg, L. R. (1983, June). *The magical number five, plus or minus two: Some considerations on the dimensionality of personality descriptors.* Paper presented at a Research Seminar, Gerontology Research Center, Baltimore, MD.

Goldberg, L. R. (1992). The development of markers for the Big Five factor structure. *Psychological Assessment, 4,* 26–42.

Goldberg, L. R. (1994). Resolving a scientific embarrassment: A comment on the articles in this special issue. *European Journal of Personality, 8,* 351–356.

Goldberg, L. R., & Digman, J. M. (1994). Revealing structure in the data: Principles of exploratory factor analysis. In S. Strack & M. Lorr (Eds.), *Differentiating normal and abnormal personality* (pp. 216–242). New York, NY: Springer.

Gosling, S. D. (2001). From mice to men: What can we learn about personality from animal research? *Psychological Bulletin, 127,* 45–86.

Gosling, S. D., & John, O. P. (1999). Personality dimensions in nonhuman animals: A cross-species review. *Current Directions in Psychological Science, 8,* 69–75.

Gosling, S. D., Rentfrow, P. J., & Swann, W. B. Jr. (2003). A very brief measure of the Big Five personality domains. *Journal of Research in Personality, 37,* 504–528.

Gottschall, J., & Wilson, D. S. (Eds.). (2005). *The literary animal: Evolution and the nature of narrative.* Evanston, IL: Northwestern University Press.

Gough, H. G. (1987). *California Psychological Inventory administrator's guide.* Palo Alto, CA: Consulting Psychologists Press.

Hathaway, S. R., & McKinley, J. C. (1943). *The Minnesota Multiphasic Personality Inventory* (Rev. ed.). Minneapolis, MN: University of Minnesota Press.

Herbst, J. H., McCrae, R. R., Costa, P. T., Jr., Feaganes, J. R., & Siegler, I. C. (2000). Self-perceptions of stability and change in personality at midlife: The UNC Alumni Heart Study. *Assessment, 7,* 379–388.

Jackson, D. N. (1974). *Personality Research Form manual* (Rev. ed.). Port Huron, MI: Research Psychologists Press.

Jang, K. L., McCrae, R. R., Angleitner, A., Riemann, R., & Livesley, W. J. (1998). Heritability of facet-level traits in a cross-cultural twin sample: Support for a hierarchical model of personality. *Journal of Personality and Social Psychology, 74,* 1556–1565.

Jauss, H.-R. (1982). *Toward an aesthetic of reception* (T. Bahti, Trans.). Minneapolis, MN: University of Minnesota Press.

John, O. P. (1990). The "Big Five" factor taxonomy: Dimensions of personality in the natural language and in questionnaires. In L. A. Pervin (Ed.), *Handbook of personality theory and research* (pp. 66–100). New York, NY: Guilford Press.

John, O. P., Angleitner, A., & Ostendorf, F. (1988). The lexical approach to personality: A historical review of trait taxonomic research. *European Journal of Personality, 2,* 171–203.

John, O. P., Naumann, L., & Soto, C. J. (2008). Paradigm shift to the integrative Big Five taxonomy: Discovery, measurement, and conceptual issues. In O. P. John, R. W. Robins, & L. A. Pervin (Eds.), *Handbook of personality: Theory and research* (3rd ed., pp. 114–158). New York, NY: Guilford Press.

Johnson, J. A., Carroll, J., Gottschall, J., & Kruger, D. (2008). Hierarchy in the library: Egalitarian dynamics in Victorian novels. *Evolutionary Psychology, 6,* 715–738.

Johnson, J. A., Carroll, J., Gottschall, J., & Kruger, D. (2011). Portrayal of personality in Victorian novels reflects modern research findings but amplifies the significance of agreeableness. *Journal of Research in Personality, 45,* 50–58.

Jung, C. G. (1971). *Psychological types* (H. G. Baynes, Trans., rev. by R. F. C. Hull). Princeton, NJ: Princeton University Press. (Original work published 1923)

King, J. E., & Figueredo, A. J. (1997). The five-factor model plus dominance in chimpanzee personality. *Journal of Research in Personality, 31,* 257–271.

King, J. E., Weiss, A., & Farmer, K. H. (2005). A chimpanzee (*Pan troglodytes*) analogue of cross-national generalization of personality structure: Zoological parks and an African sanctuary. *Journal of Personality, 73,* 389–410.

King, J. E., Weiss, A., & Sisco, M. M. (2008). Aping humans: Age and sex effects in chimpanzee (*Pan troglodytes*) and human (*Homo sapiens*) personality. *Journal of Comparative Psychology, 122,* 418–427.

Kruger, D. J., Fisher, M., & Jobling, I. (2003). Proper and dark heroes as DADS and CADS: Alternative mating strategies in British Romantic literature. *Human Nature, 14,* 305–317.

Lattimore, R. (1975). Introduction. In *The Odyssey of Homer* (pp. 1–24). New York, NY: Harper Colophon Books.

Levitas, G. B. (Ed.). (1963). *The world of psychology* (Vol. 1–2). New York, NY: George Braziller.

Lorr, M. (1986). *Interpersonal Style Inventory (ISI) manual.* Los Angeles, CA: Western Psychological Services.

Mar, R. A., & Oatley, K. (2008). The function of fiction is the abstraction and simulation of social experience. *Perspectives on Psychological Science, 3,* 173–192.

Mar, R. A., Oatley, K., & Peterson, J. B. (2009). Exploring the link between reading fiction and empathy: Ruling out individual differences and examining outcomes. *Communications, 34,* 407–428.

Markon, K. E., Krueger, R. F., & Watson, D. (2005). Delineating the structure of normal and abnormal personality: An integrative hierarchical approach. *Journal of Personality and Social Psychology, 88,* 139–157.

Markus, H. R., & Kitayama, S. (1991). Culture and the self: Implications for cognition, emotion, and motivation. *Psychological Review, 98,* 224–253.

Marquis, D. (1927). *archy and mehitabel.* New York, NY: Doubleday.

McAdams, D. P. (1992). The five-factor model *in* personality: A critical appraisal. *Journal of Personality, 60,* 329–361.

McAdams, D. P. (1993). *The stories we live by: Personal myths and the making of the self*. New York. NY: Morrow.

McAdams, D. P. (2011). *George W. Bush and the redemptive dream: A psychological portrait*. New York, NY: Oxford University Press.

McAdams, D. P., Anyidoho, N. A., Brown, C., Huang, Y. T., Kaplan, B., & Machado, M. A. (2004). Traits and stories: Links between dispositional and narrative features of personality. *Journal of Personality, 72*, 761–784.

McAdams, D. P., & Pals, J. L. (2006). A new big five: Fundamental principles for an integrative science of personality. *American Psychologist, 61*, 204–217.

McClelland, D. C. (1961). *The achieving society*. Princeton, NJ: Van Nostrand.

McCrae, R. R. (1989). Why I advocate the five-factor model: Joint analyses of the NEO-PI and other instruments. In D. M. Buss & N. Cantor (Eds.), *Personality psychology: Recent trends and emerging directions* (pp. 237–245). New York, NY: Springer-Verlag.

McCrae, R. R. (1990). Traits and trait names: How well is openness represented in natural languages? *European Journal of Personality, 4*, 119–129.

McCrae, R. R. (1993). Agreement of personality profiles across observers. *Multivariate Behavioral Research, 28*, 13–28.

McCrae, R. R. (1993–1994). Openness to experience as a basic dimension of personality. *Imagination, Cognition and Personality, 13*, 39–55.

McCrae, R. R. (1994a). The counterpoint of personality assessment: Self-reports and observer ratings. *Assessment, 1*, 159–172.

McCrae, R. R. (1994b). Openness to experience: Expanding the boundaries of Factor V. *European Journal of Personality, 8*, 251–272.

McCrae, R. R. (1996). Social consequences of experiential openness. *Psychological Bulletin, 120*, 323–337.

McCrae, R. R. (2007). Aesthetic chills as a universal marker of openness to experience. *Motivation and Emotion, 31*, 5–11.

McCrae, R. R. (2008). A note on some measures of profile agreement. *Journal of Personality Assessment, 90*, 105–109.

McCrae, R. R. (2009). Personality profiles of cultures: Patterns of ethos. *European Journal of Personality, 23*, 205–227.

McCrae, R. R. (2011). Personality traits and the potential of positive psychology. In K. M. Sheldon, T. Kashdan, & M. F. Steger (Eds.), *Designing positive psychology: Taking stock and moving forward* (pp. 193–206). New York, NY: Oxford University Press.

McCrae, R. R., & Costa, P. T., Jr. (1987). Validation of the five-factor model of personality across instruments and observers. *Journal of Personality and Social Psychology, 52*, 81–90.

McCrae, R. R., & Costa, P. T., Jr. (1988). Recalled parent-child relations and adult personality. *Journal of Personality, 56*, 417–434.

McCrae, R. R., & Costa, P. T., Jr. (1994). The paradox of parental influence: Understanding retrospective studies of parent-child relations and adult personality. In C. Perris, W. A. Arrindell, & M. Eisemann (Eds.), *Parenting and psychopathology* (pp. 107–125). New York, NY: John Wiley & Sons.

McCrae, R. R., & Costa, P. T., Jr. (1995). Trait explanations in personality psychology. *European Journal of Personality, 9*, 231–252.

McCrae, R. R., & Costa, P. T., Jr. (1996). Toward a new generation of personality theories: Theoretical contexts for the five-factor model. In J. S. Wiggins (Ed.), *The five-factor model of personality: Theoretical perspectives* (pp. 51–87). New York, NY: Guilford Press.

McCrae, R. R., & Costa, P. T., Jr. (2003). *Personality in adulthood: A five-factor theory perspective* (2nd. ed.). New York, NY: Guilford Press.

McCrae, R. R., & Costa, P. T., Jr. (2008a). Empirical and theoretical status of the five-factor model of personality traits. In G. Boyle, G. Matthews, & D. Saklofske (Eds.), *Sage Handbook of personality theory and assessment* (Vol. 1, pp. 273–294). Los Angeles, CA: Sage.

McCrae, R. R., & Costa, P. T., Jr. (2008b). The five-factor theory of personality. In O. P. John, R. W. Robins, & L. A. Pervin (Eds.), *Handbook of personality: Theory and research* (3rd ed., pp. 159–181). New York, NY: Guilford Press.

McCrae, R. R., & Costa, P. T., Jr. (2010). *NEO Inventories professional manual*. Odessa, FL: Psychological Assessment Resources.

McCrae, R. R., Costa, P. T., Jr., Lima, M. P., Simões, A., Ostendorf, F., Angleitner, A.,...Piedmont, R. L. (1999). Age differences in personality across the adult life span: Parallels in five cultures. *Developmental Psychology, 35*, 466–477.

McCrae, R. R., Costa, P. T., Jr., Martin, T. A., Oryol, V. E., Rukavishnikov, A. A., Senin,...Urbánek, T. (2004). Consensual validation of personality traits across cultures. *Journal of Research in Personality, 38*, 179–201.

McCrae, R. R., Harwood, T. M., & Kelly, S. L. (2011). The NEO Inventories. In T. M. Harwood, L. E. Beutler, & G. Groth-Marnat (Eds.), *Integrative assessment of adult personality* (3rd ed., pp. 252–275). New York, NY: Guilford Press.

McCrae, R. R., & John, O. P. (1992). An introduction to the five-factor model and its applications. *Journal of Personality, 60*, 175–215.

McCrae, R. R., Kurtz, J. E., Yamagata, S., & Terracciano, A. (2011). Internal consistency, retest reliability, and their implications for personality scale validity. *Personality and Social Psychology Review, 15*, 28–50.

McCrae, R. R., & Sutin, A. R. (2007). New frontiers for the five-factor model: A preview of the literature. *Social and Personality Psychology Compass, 1*. doi:10.1111/j.1751–9004.2007.00021.x

McCrae, R. R., Terracciano, A., & 78 Members of the Personality Profiles of Cultures Project. (2005). Universal features of personality traits from the observer's perspective: Data from 50 cultures. *Journal of Personality and Social Psychology, 88*, 547–561.

McCrae, R. R., Terracciano, A., & 79 Members of the Personality Profiles of Cultures Project. (2005). Personality profiles of cultures: Aggregate personality traits. *Journal of Personality and Social Psychology, 89*, 407–425.

McCrae, R. R., Terracciano, A., Realo, A., & Allik, J. (2007). On the validity of culture-level personality and stereotype scores. *European Journal of Personality, 21*, 987–991.

Miall, D. S., & Kuiken, D. (1995). Aspects of literary response: A new questionnaire. *Research in the Teaching of English, 29*, 37–58.

Murray, H. A. (1938). *Explorations in personality*. New York, NY: Oxford University Press.

Nencini, A. (2007). The reader at work: The role of the text and text-receiver in the construction of the protagonist of a novel. *Empirical Studies of the Arts, 25*, 97–115.

Nencini, A. (2010). *A matter of shared knowledge: Possible theoretical integrations in the study of literary reception*. Unpublished manuscript, University of Padova.

Norman, W. T. (1963). Toward an adequate taxonomy of personality attributes: Replicated factor structure in peer nomination personality ratings. *Journal of Abnormal and Social Psychology, 66*, 574–583.

Oatley, K. (1999). Why fiction may be twice as true as fact: Fiction as cognitive and emotional simulation. *Review of General Psychology, 3*, 101–117.

Oatley, K., & Mar, R. A. (2005). Evolutionary pre-adaptation and the idea of character in fiction. *Culture and Evolutionary Psychology, 3*, 181–196.

Olesha, Y. (1967). Envy. In *Envy and other works* (A. R. MacAndrew, Trans., pp. 1–121). Garden City, NY: Doubleday. (Original work published 1927)

Ouspensky, P. D. (1920). *Tertium organum: The third canon of thought, a key to the enigmas of the world*. Rochester, NY: Manas Press.

Pennebaker, J. W., & Ireland, M. (2008). Analyzing words to understand literature. In J. Auracher & W. van Peer (Eds.), *New beginnings in literary studies* (pp. 24–48). Newcastle, UK: Cambridge Scholars.

Pennebaker, J. W., & King, L. A. (1999). Linguistic styles: Language use as an individual difference. *Journal of Personality and Social Psychology, 77*, 1296–1312.

Pexman, P. M., Glenwright, M., Hala, S., Kowbel, S. L., & Jungen, S. (2006). Children's use of trait information in understanding verbal irony. *Metaphor and Symbol, 21*, 39–60.

Piedmont, R. L., & Aycock, W. (2007). An historical analysis of the lexical emergence of the Big Five personality adjective descriptors. *Personality and Individual Differences, 42*, 1059–1068.

Reich, W. (1945). *Character analysis*. New York, NY: Orgone Institute.

Rentfrow, P. J., & Gosling, S. D. (2003). The do re mi's of everyday life: The structure and personality correlates of music preferences. *Journal of Personality and Social Psychology, 84*, 1236–1256.

Roberts, B. W., Chernyshenko, O. S., Stark, S. E., & Goldberg, L. R. (2005). The structure of conscientiousness: An empirical investigation based on seven major personality questionnaires. *Personnel Psychology, 58*, 103–139.

Roberts, B. W., & DelVecchio, W. F. (2000). The rank-order consistency of personality traits from childhood to old age: A quantitative review of longitudinal studies. *Psychological Bulletin, 126*, 3–25.

Roberts, B. W., & Wood, D. (2006). Personality development in the context of neo-socioanalytic theory. In D. K. Mroczek & T. D. Little (Eds.), *Handbook of personality development* (pp. 11–39). Mahwah, NJ: Erlbaum.

Rubenzer, S. J., Faschingbauer, T. R., & Ones, D. S. (2000). Assessing the U.S. presidents using the Revised NEO Personality Inventory. *Assessment, 7*, 403–420.

Scarr, S. (1987). Distinctive environments depend on genotypes. *Behavioral and Brain Sciences, 10*, 38–39.

Schmitt, D. P., Realo, A., Voracek, M., & Allik, J. (2008). Why can't a man be more like a woman? Sex differences in Big Five personality traits across 55 cultures. *Journal of Personality and Social Psychology, 94*, 168–182.

Sheldon, K. M., Kashdan, T., & Steger, M. F. (Eds.). (2011). *Designing positive psychology: Taking stock and moving forward*. New York, NY: Oxford University Press.

Shaver, P. R., & Brennan, K. A. (1992). Attachment styles and the "Big Five" personality traits: Their connection with each other and with romantic relationship outcomes. *Personality and Social Psychology Bulletin, 18*, 536–545.

Shaver, P. R., & Mikulincer, M. (2005). Attachment theory and research: Resurrection of the psychodynamic approach to personality. *Journal of Research in Personality, 39*, 22–45.

Shedler, J. (2010). The efficacy of psychodynamic psychotherapy. *American Psychologist, 65*, 98–109.

Shweder, R. A., & Sullivan, M. A. (1990). The semiotic subject of cultural psychology. In L. A. Pervin (Ed.), *Handbook of personality: Theory and research* (pp. 399–416). New York, NY: Guilford Press.

Sneed, C. D., McCrae, R. R., & Funder, D. C. (1998). Lay conceptions of the five-factor model and its indicators. *Personality and Social Psychology Bulletin, 24*, 115–126.

Snow, C. P. (1961). *The two cultures and the scientific revolution*. New York, NY: Cambridge University Press.

Steel, P., Schmidt, J., & Shultz, J. (2008). Refining the relationship between personality and subjective well-being. *Psychological Bulletin, 134*, 138–161.

Tagore, R. (1917). *Personality*. New York, NY: Macmillan.

Tellegen, A. (1982). *Brief manual for the Multidimensional Personality Questionnaire*. Unpublished manuscript, University of Minnesota.

Tellegen, A., Lykken, D. T., Bouchard, T. J. Jr., Wilcox, K. J., Segal, N. L., & Rich, S. (1988). Personality similarity in twins reared apart and together. *Journal of Personality and Social Psychology, 54*, 1031–1039.

Terracciano, A., Abdel-Khalak, A. M., Ádámm, N., Adamovová, L., Ahn, C.-k., Ahn, H.-n., . . . McCrae, R. R. (2005). National character does not reflect mean personality trait levels in 49 cultures. *Science, 310*, 96–100.

Terracciano, A., Costa, P. T., Jr., & McCrae, R. R. (2006). Personality plasticity after age 30. *Personality and Social Psychology Bulletin, 32*, 999–1009.

Terracciano, A., McCrae, R. R., Brant, L. J., & Costa, P. T., Jr. (2005). Hierarchical linear modeling analyses of NEO-PI-R scales in the Baltimore Longitudinal Study of Aging. *Psychology and Aging, 20*, 493–506.

Thomas, K. M., & Duke, M. (2007). Depressed writing: Cognitive distortions in the works of depressed and nondepressed poets and writers. *Psychology of Aesthetics, Creativity, and the Arts, 1*, 204–218.

Todd, Z. (2008). Talking about books: A reading group study. *Psychology of Aesthetics, Creativity, and the Arts, 2*, 256–263.

Tolstoy, L. (1950). *Anna Karenina* (C. Garnett, Trans.). New York, NY: Modern Library. (Original work published 1877)

Tupes, E. C., & Christal, R. E. (1992). Recurrent personality factors based on trait ratings. *Journal of Personality, 60*, 225–251. (Original work published 1961)

Vazire, S. (2010). Who knows what about a person? The self-other knowledge asymmetry (SOKA) model. *Journal of Personality and Social Psychology, 98*, 281–300.

Weil, S. (1986). Human personality. In S. Miles (Ed.), *Simone Weil: An anthology* (pp. 49–78). New York, NY: Grove Press. (Original work published 1950)

Wellington, M. A. (1987). *The art of Voltaire's theater*. New York, NY: Lang.

Wiggins, J. S. (Ed.). (1996). *The five-factor model of personality: Theoretical perspectives*. New York, NY: Guilford Press.

Williams, J. E., & Best, D. E. (1982). *Measuring sex stereotypes: A thirty nation study*. Newbury Park, CA: Sage.

Wood, M. (2001). *In search of the Dark Ages*. New York, NY: Checkmark Books.

CHAPTER 5

Cognitive-Experiential Self-Theory:
An Integrative Theory of Personality

SEYMOUR EPSTEIN

Cognitive-experiential self-theory (CEST) is a global theory of personality that integrates significant aspects of self/phenomenological theory, learning theory, cognitive theory, psychoanalytic theory, and emotions theory. It includes important aspects of self/phenomenological theory by assuming that everyone automatically constructs an implicit theory of reality in the course of living because such an implicit theory is rewarding as it is necessary for effective adaptation. An implicit theory of reality includes subtheories about the self, others, the inanimate world, and beliefs regarding their interactions. People's implicit theories of reality automatically and effortlessly direct people's everyday behavior and also influence their interpretation of events, feelings, and conscious thinking. Thus, people's implicit theories of reality determine in large measure their performance and the quality of their lives.

Learning theory plays a critical role in CEST because of the assumption that the implicit beliefs in people's theories of reality are acquired by automatically learning from experience according to the principles and attributes of associative learning. The experiential system in humans is assumed to be the same system with which nonhuman animals have successfully adapted to their environments

This chapter includes material from several of my articles published elsewhere including in the first edition of the *Handbook of Psychology*. The research reported here was supported by a National Institute of Mental Health (NIMH) Research Grant MH 01293 and NIMH Research Scientist Award 5 KO5 MH 00363.

over millions of years of evolution. The automatic learning of this system because of its adaptive significance can be assumed to be intrinsically highly compelling, as life itself has depended on it. It follows that people's deliberative conscious reasoning cannot easily override the influence of experiential processing. Learning theory is extended in CEST by regarding the attributes of associative learning as important as its operating principles in determining its manner of its operation. The attributes refer to the following kinds of characteristics of associative learning: It operates in a manner that is automatic, effortless, rapid, primarily nonverbal, holistic, concrete, minimally demanding of cognitive resources, and it normally operates outside of awareness. The operating rules of associative learning include association, contiguity, reinforcement, extinction, and spontaneous recovery.

Although the operating rules and attributes of associative learning evolved because of their adaptive significance once having evolved, the same principles and attributes can be used for other purposes than learning from experience by a process referred to in evolutionary theory as preadaptation. This assumption greatly expands the explanatory power of experiential processing, as it makes it possible for its rules and attributes to account for responses to entirely new information, as in implicit learning, unconscious pattern identification, and intuitive responses to situations never before experienced.

Important aspects of cognitive theory are assimilated in CEST by the assumption that people learn cognitions in the form of internal representations of events, schemas, or implicit beliefs that are the building blocks of people's implicit theories of reality. The learning of such schemas is considered much more important for personal theories of reality than the learning of behavioral/motor responses. In agreement with cognitive theory and in contrast to Freudian theory, most information processing is assumed to occur outside of awareness, not because of repression as Freud believed, but because it is a more efficient, less effortful way of processing information in everyday life than by conscious reasoning. CEST is also similar to cognitive science in its views of how schemas, or implicit beliefs, are encoded, stored, and retrieved. CEST differs from cognitive theory by its much greater emphasis on the importance of emotions, psychodynamics, self/phenomenological concepts, and learning theory.

Important aspects of psychoanalytic theory are incorporated into CEST by the importance attributed to unconscious processing, psychodynamics, and transference reactions, which are viewed more generally in CEST in terms of generalization. CEST differs from psychoanalytic theory by its view of unconscious processing, its de-emphasis on psychosexual stages, and its assumption that unconscious rather than conscious processing is primarily (not exclusively) the default condition in everyday life. A particularly important difference between the two theories is that CEST replaces the Freudian maladaptive unconscious, which is indefensible from an evolutionary perspective, with an adaptive unconscious that is consistent with evolutionary principles.

Affect and emotion are considered to be a significant aspect of almost all, if not all, associative networks in the experiential system. According to CEST they are particularly important because of their critical role in reinforcement and motivation and therefore of the acquisition of the implicit beliefs and networks in the experiential system. They are also important as they provide a royal road to the identification of the schemas in people's implicit theories of reality.

In the remainder of this chapter, I review the basic assumptions of CEST and summarize the research my associates and I have conducted to test and extend its assumptions. I further consider the implications of CEST for elucidating a few topics of particular interest, such as the nature of intuition, an evaluation of the accuracy and value of the concept of emotional intelligence, the relation of the operation of the experiential system to physical disease, psychobiography, and the meaning of dreams.

THE EXISTENCE OF TWO INFORMATION-PROCESSING SYSTEMS

According to CEST, people process information with two information-processing systems, *rational* and *experiential*. The two systems are assumed to operate in parallel and to interact bidirectionally simultaneously and sequentially. CEST has nothing new to say about the rational system, other than to emphasize the degree to which it is influenced outside of awareness by experiential processing. CEST does have a great deal to say about the experiential system. In effect, CEST introduces a new system of unconscious processing in its proposal of an experiential adaptive system that is scientifically defensible in ways in which the Freudian unconscious system is not.

Before proceeding further, a caveat is in order about the term *rational* as referred to in the rational system of CEST. Unfortunately the word *rational* has two meanings. One meaning is *reasonable,* whereas the other refers to a *logical* process of reasoning. According to CEST a logical manner of reasoning can only occur in the rational system as it is dependent on the use of grammatical language. Experiential processing can never be rational as the term is used in CEST, but it can be reasonable and therefore rational according to the alternative meaning of rational.

As previously noted, according to CEST everyone automatically constructs an implicit personal theory of reality that includes sub-theories concerning the self, others, and the inanimate world, as well as beliefs about their interactions. Personal theories of reality consist of a hierarchical organization of schemas, or implicit beliefs, that are organized into cognitive-affective networks. Toward the apex of the organization are highly general implicit beliefs, such as that the self is worthy, people are generally trustworthy, and the world is mainly orderly and benevolent. Because of their high level of generality these beliefs and networks of beliefs have widespread connections with other schemas and cognitive-affective networks. As a result, they are normally highly stable and not easily invalidated. However, should they be invalidated, it would tend to destabilize the overall conceptual system. Evidence that such destabilization actually occurs is provided by the profound disorganization following unassimilable experiences in acute schizophrenic reactions (e.g., Bleuler, 1978; Bowers, 1974; Epstein, 1979a; Kaplan, 1964; Perry, 1974). At the opposite end of the hierarchy are narrow, situation-specific schemas. The narrower schemas are readily susceptible to change, and their changes have little effect on the overall stability of the organization of the conceptual system. Thus, the hierarchic structure of implicit personal theories of reality allows the theory to be stable in the vicinity of its apex and flexible at the more specific levels. It is important to recognize, in this respect, that the experiential system is an organized, adaptive system, rather than a collection of unrelated implicit cognitions and networks, like tools in a cognitive tool box as some have proposed (e.g., Tversky & Kahneman, 1974). As it is assumed in CEST that the experiential system in humans is essentially the same system with which nonhuman animals adapt to their environments, it follows that nonhuman animals also have an organized model of the world that is subject to disorganization. Support for this assumption is provided by the widespread dysfunctional behavior exhibited in animals exposed to emotionally significant unassimilable stimuli (e.g., Pavlov, 1941).

Unlike nonhuman animals, humans in addition to having an implicit experiential system also have an explicit rational system. The degree to which people's implicit and explicit theories of reality are discrepant is considered in CEST to be an important source of stress and psychopathology.

The Operating Principles of the Two Systems

The experiential system adapts to reality by empirically learning from experience in a manner that is automatic, preconscious, rapid, effortless, holistic, concrete, associative, primarily nonverbal, and minimally demanding of cognitive resources. It encodes information in two ways: as memories of specific events, particularly those that were emotionally arousing, and in an abstract, more general way. The abstract representations are in the form of generalizations, prototypes, and as representations that include a significant, subordinate rational component as in metaphors, narratives, and scripts.

The implicit beliefs in a personal theory of reality are assumed always to be associated with affect, which may vary from negligible to very strong. As previously noted, affect is extremely important in CEST as it plays critical important roles in reinforcement in learning, in affect-driven motivation, and in providing a royal road to identifying the beliefs in people's implicit theories of reality. It follows that CEST is as much an emotional as a cognitive theory, as without affect there would be no associative learning and therefore no experiential system. The primary motive of the experiential system is to operate according to the hedonic principle. It is noteworthy that, although emotions and affect are often

sources of irrational behavior in humans, they also serve a critically important role in the development of an implicit model of reality (Epstein, 1984, 1993a, 1998b). Thus, by pursuing positive affect and avoiding negative affect organisms, including humans, automatically empirically construct an adaptive working theory of reality.

In contrast to the experiential system, the rational system is a reasoning system that operates according to an individual's understanding of the rules of reasoning including the importance and evaluation of evidence. The rational system operates in a manner that is conscious, primarily verbal, analytic, relatively effortful, relatively slow, affect-free, and demanding of cognitive resources. Unlike the experiential system, the rational system has a very brief evolutionary history. The primary motive of the rational system is to operate according to the reality principle, the desire to be realistic and logical. A comparison of the operation of the two systems is provided in Table 5.1.

TABLE 5.1   Comparison of Attributes of Experiential and Rational Information-Processing Systems

Experiential System	Rational System
1. Holistic	1. Analytic
2. Emotional: Pleasure-pain oriented. Operates by hedonic principle.	2. Logical: Reason- and accuracy-oriented. Operates by reality principle.
3. Associative relations	3. Cause-and-effect relations
4. More outcome-oriented	4. More process-oriented
5. Behavior mediated by "vibes" and emotions from past experience	5. Behavior mediated by conscious appraisal of events
6. Encodes reality in concrete images, primary generalization, metaphors, and narratives	6. Encodes reality in abstract symbols, words, and numbers
7. More rapid processing: Oriented toward immediate action	7. Slower processing: Capable of long-delayed action
8. Slower to change: Changes with repetitive or intense experience	8. Changes more rapidly: Can change with speed of thought
9. More crudely differentiated: Broad generalization gradient; categorical thinking	9. More highly differentiated: Dimensional and nuanced thinking
10. More crudely integrated: Dissociative, organized in part by emotional complexes (cognitive-affective modules)	10. More highly integrated: Organized according to cross-situational generalizations.
11. Experienced passively and preconsciously: We feel seized by our emotions	11. Experienced actively and consciously: We believe we are in control of our conscious thoughts
12. Self-evidently valid: "Experiencing is believing"	12. Requires justification via logic or evidence

Which system is superior? At first thought, it might seem that it must be the rational system. After all, with its ability to solve problems with the use of grammatical language, the rational system is a recent very high level of evolutionary development that is unique to the human species. It is capable of much higher levels of abstract thinking and complexity than the experiential system, and it makes possible planning, long-term delay of gratification, cross-situational, conceptually determined generalizations, high levels of stimulus and response discrimination, comprehension of cause-and-effect relations, and communication over great distances and across generations. These attributes of the rational system have made it possible for the remarkable accomplishments of humans in science, technology, mathematics, medicine, and the arts.

The experiential system also has some extremely important abilities, some never before recognized, which will be discussed shortly. For now, it will suffice to note that it's most important ability is one that no animal, including humans, could live without, namely the ability to effortlessly, rapidly, and efficiently direct everyday behavior.

The widespread belief in the superiority of the rational system is supported by research that examined people's ability to solve normative problems. However, increasing evidence is emerging that the experiential system is superior to the rational system in several other ways (e.g., Norris & Epstein, 2011; Wilson, 2002) and even in some kinds of complex information-processing (e.g., Dijksterhuis, 2004; Reber, 1993). Research my associates and I have conducted has identified several important previously unrecognized ways in which the experiential system is superior to the rational system. For example, in a study by Norris and Epstein (2011) it was found that the experiential system is more strongly associated than the rational system with creativity, empathy, favorable interpersonal relationships, intuition, sense of humor, and aesthetic judgment. A more detailed comparison of the virtues and limitations of the two systems will be presented in the section on research.

Returning to the question of which system is superior, the only reasonable conclusion is that neither system is generally superior as each has equally important advantages and limitations. It is therefore encouraging to realize that as the two systems are independent, improvement in one does not have to be obtained at the expense of improvement in the other. It is therefore to people's advantage to cultivate the desirable attributes of both systems. Moreover, even if people wished to suppress the operation of the experiential system in order to become more rational, it would no more be possible to accomplish this than to stop breathing because the air is polluted. Rather than attempting in vain to suppress its influence, the only way effectively to control the experiential system it is to identify, understand, and influence its operation, particularly with regard to controlling its biasing influence on conscious reasoning (Epstein, 1998a).

How the Experiential System Operates

As previously noted, the operation of the experiential system is intimately associated with affect in the form of "vibes" as well as full-blown emotions. Vibes refer to vague feelings that are experienced only dimly, if at all, in a person's consciousness. Stating that vibes often operate outside of awareness is not meant to imply that people cannot become aware of them, but only that people usually make no attempt to do so. Examples of negative vibes are unarticulated feelings of agitation, irritation, tension, disquietude, and apprehension. Examples of positive vibes are unarticulated feelings of wellbeing, affection, gratification, positive anticipation, calmness, and light-heartedness.

When a person responds to an emotionally arousing event, the sequence of reactions is normally as follows: The experiential system automatically and instantaneously searches its memory banks for related events. If the memories are pleasant, the person has thoughts, images, and impulses that promote behaving in ways anticipated to reproduce the feelings. If the memories are unpleasant, the person has thoughts, images, and impulses to behave in ways anticipated to avoid experiencing the feelings. As this sequence of events occurs automatically, people are usually unaware of its operation. Seeking consciously to understand their behavior, people under the influence of the hedonic principle of the experiential system and the reality principle of the rational system construct the most favorable compromise they can think of. In other words, they rationalize, meaning according to CEST that they attribute primarily experientially determined behavior to a rational cause. According to CEST, such rationalization is a routine process that occurs far more often than is recognized and helps to maintain the undetected influence of experiential on rational processing. It should be noted that the experiential system in the above explanation biases the operation of the rational system outside of awareness at two points in time, once at the beginning of the response sequence and again at the end of the sequence. Such influence of experiential on rational processing is considered particularly important in CEST because it helps to explain why, despite their remarkable intelligence, people often think irrationally in ways that are destructive to others and even to themselves.

Basic Needs

Most major theories of personality propose a single basic need. CEST achieves an integration of their positions by regarding four proposed needs as equally basic according to criteria shortly to be noted.

Identification of Basic Needs

In classical Freudian theory, the one most basic need before the introduction of a death instinct was the pleasure principle, which refers to the pursuit of pleasure and the avoidance of pain (Freud, 1924/1960). Some learning theorists such as Thorndike (1927) make a similar assumption in their view of the importance of affective reinforcement. For object-relations theorists, most notably Bowlby (1988), the most fundamental need is the need for relatedness. For Rogers (1951) and other phenomenological psychologists, it is the need to maintain the stability and coherence of a person's conceptual system. For Allport (1961) and Kohut (1971), it is the need to enhance self-esteem. (For a more thorough discussion of these proposals see Epstein, 1993a, 1998b.) From the perspective of CEST, the four proposed basic needs all meet the following criteria for a basic need: the need is universal; the need can dominate the other basic needs; and a failure to fulfill the need can destabilize the overall conceptual system.

Recently the view in CEST regarding basic needs was modified as follows. Two superordinate basic needs were added, the need to behave according to the hedonic principle and the need to maintain cortical excitation within homeostatic limits (Epstein, in press a). The previous basic needs were accordingly reclassified as subordinate basic needs. The reason why the two superordinate basic needs were added is that both are important aspects of all the subordinate basic needs. Thus, all the subordinate basic needs are assumed to vary along two dimensions, a bipolar dimension of positive versus negative affect and a unipolar dimension of degree of cortical excitation. It follows from this assumption that each subordinate basic need is associated with some kind of positive and negative affect. For example, the pleasure and pain associated with the sensory pleasure principle are qualitatively different from the pride and displeasure experienced by increases and decreases in self-esteem. That is, although all basic needs involve experiencing positive and negative affect, the kind of positive and negative affect is different for different basic needs.

Interactions Among Basic Needs

Given two superordinate basic needs and four subordinate basic needs that operate simultaneously, it follows that behavior is determined by the degree of activation of all of the needs in a particular situation at a particular time. An important adaptive consequence of such behavior is that the needs normally serve as checks and balances against each other. Thus, if a basic need is fulfilled at the expense of fulfilling other basic needs, the fulfillment of the other basic needs becomes increasingly insistent. However, under certain circumstances the motivation to fulfill a particular need may be so great that frustration of the other needs is disregarded. Such a condition is assumed to be a source of different kinds of pathology, shortly to be discussed.

The finding that normal people characteristically have unrealistic self-enhancing and optimistic biases (Taylor & Brown, 1988) has evoked considerable interest because it appears to contradict the widely held assumption that reality awareness is an important criterion of mental health. From the perspective of CEST, rather than indicating that reality awareness is a false criterion of mental health, all it indicates is that it is not the only relevant criterion. According to CEST, a compromise commonly occurs between the fulfillment of different needs. Unrealistic self-enhancement can be understood as a compromise between the need for self-enhancement (in the experiential system) and the need to be realistic (in the rational system). The result is a modest self-enhancing bias that is not seriously unrealistic. It suggests that normal individuals tend to give themselves the benefit of the doubt in situations in which the cost of a modest degree of inaccuracy is outweighed by the gain in positive feelings about the self.

There are important individual differences in how people fulfill a specific basic need in relation to fulfilling other basic needs. Poorly adjusted people tend to fulfill their basic needs in a conflicted manner, whereas well-adjusted people tend to do so in a harmonious manner by fulfilling each of their basic needs in a manner that is compatible with, and where possible, even synergistic with fulfilling their other basic needs. For example, a well-adjusted person is likely to fulfill the need for relatedness in a manner that enhances the person's self-esteem whereas a poorly adjusted person may fulfill the need for relatedness by ingratiating himself with others and feeling diminished for having done so.

Imbalances in the Fulfillment of Basic Needs as Sources of Psychopathology

As previously noted, specific imbalances among the basic needs are associated with particular mental disorders. For present purposes, it will suffice to present a few such examples. Paranoia with delusions of grandeur can be understood as an extreme compensatory response to a threat to self-esteem. The cost of doing so is a failure to fulfill other basic needs. Thus, being incarcerated in a mental institution for a delusion of grandeur results in a failure to fulfill the need for a favorable sensory pleasure-pain balance, as such incarceration does not provide for a happy existence. Fulfilling the need for self-esteem with a delusion of grandeur also sacrifices the need to maintain favorable relationships with others, who are not likely to appreciate being treated as inferiors, and who are repelled by unrealistic views and inappropriate behavior. The need to maintain a coherent, realistic conceptual system is obviously sacrificed because a delusion of grandeur is unrealistic.

Paranoia with delusions of persecution can be understood as a desperate attempt to defend the stability of a person's conceptual system and, to a lesser extent, to enhance self-esteem. Attributing problems in living to persecution by others can provide an increase in the stability of a conceptual system that is threatened with disorganization. Another source of stability is provided by the mobilization of efforts to defend or retaliate against perceived persecutors. In other words, such focus and mobilization against threat provide a unifying state of cognitive organization that serves as a defense against disorganization. Delusions of persecution contribute to self-esteem as well as to stability as the perception of persecutors as powerful or important people implies that the targets of their persecution must also be somewhat important or the persecutors would not bother with them. The basic need for the fulfillment of the sensory pleasure principle is sacrificed as a delusion of persecution is a terrifying experience. Fulfillment of the need for relationships is sacrificed as others are perceived as threatening and are repelled by the paranoid individual's unrealistic beliefs.

Schizophrenic disorganization is understood in CEST as the best bargain in need-fulfillment available to a person in a particular situation at a particular time. Given the threat of disorganization and the intense anxiety it produces, it can be a relief for a schizophrenic individual to succumb to total disorganization and with it a loss of the conceptual system that has been the source of great anxiety and misery (Jefferson, 1974). Thus, what is gained is a net improvement in the superordinate pleasure-pain balance from a negative to a zero value and an improvement in the fulfillment of the superordinate need for maintaining cortical excitation within homeostatic limits by reducing it to a more acceptable level. What is sacrificed are all the subordinate basic needs, namely the need to maintain the stability and coherence of the conceptual system, to achieve a positive sensory pleasure-pain balance, to maintain relatedness, and to maintain self-esteem.

It is hypothesized that disorganization of a conceptual system developed in the course of evolution, as it provided for the possible correction of a conceptual system that has failed to fulfill basic needs and for the possible reconstruction of a more effective conceptual system (Epstein, 1979a; Laing, 1965; Perry, 1974; Silverman, 1970). Menninger observed, "Some patients have a mental illness and then get well and then get weller! I mean they get better than they ever were.... This is an extraordinary and little realized truth" (in Silverman, 1970, p. 63). Lara Jefferson (1974), who recovered from a prolonged state of complete disintegration of her conceptual system, stated the following: "Remember that when a soul sets out on that unmarked sea called Madness, they have gained release much greater than your loss—and more important. Though the need which brought it cannot well be known by those who have not felt it. For what the sane call "ruin"—because they do not know—those who have experienced what I am speaking of, know the wild hysteria of Madness means salvation" (p. 199).

Basic Beliefs

The four subordinate basic needs are sources of four corresponding basic beliefs. These basic beliefs, along with the four basic needs, are considered among the most important constructs in an implicit theory of reality. Because of their dominant and central position and their corresponding influence on an extensive network of lower order beliefs, should any of the subordinate basic beliefs be invalidated, the entire conceptual system would be subject to destabilization and the person would experience intense anxiety. The disorganization, should it occur for psychological reasons, as previously noted, would correspond to an acute schizophrenic reaction.

According to CEST people acquire implicit basic beliefs based on their experiences regarding the fulfillment and frustration of their basic needs. When a basic need is fulfilled it is accompanied by positive affect, and when its fulfillment is frustrated it is accompanied by negative affect. Because of the super-ordinate hedonic principle, people automatically attend to whatever is associated with the fulfillment and frustration of their basic needs. As a result, they develop basic beliefs corresponding to each of the basic needs. Let us examine this in greater detail.

Depending on a person's reinforcement history, the person will tend to develop superordinate basic beliefs about the self, others, and the inanimate world as being sources of positive and negative feelings and therefore of being sources of favorable or unfavorable beliefs. Thus, if a person had predominantly favorable experiences concerning the self, others, and the inanimate world, the person will tend to represent the experiences in terms of implicit basic beliefs reflecting these experiences. This will occur at both the superordinate and subordinate levels of belief. For example, at the superordinate level of belief a person may have very general implicit beliefs about the self, others, and the inanimate world located along a dimension varying from highly favorable to highly unfavorable beliefs. The basic implicit belief about the overall favorability of a person's experiences will be reflected in a person's general optimism or pessimism. The process just described for the acquisition of superordinate favorable or unfavorable beliefs can be extended to all other basic beliefs. Given space constraints, it is not possible here to describe the development of each of the basic belief dimensions from the fulfillment of their corresponding basic needs. The interested reader can find such information in a book on CEST (Epstein, in press a).

Interactions Between the Experiential and Rational Systems

As previously noted, according to CEST the experiential and rational systems operate in parallel and are interactive. The interactions occur bi-directionally, both simultaneously and sequentially.

The Influence of the Experiential System on the Rational System

As the experiential system is the more rapidly reacting system, it is in a favorable position for influencing the subsequent processing of the rational system. Such a relation is particularly important because, as previously noted, it can help to explain why humans, despite their unique intelligence, in many circumstances, particularly in those that involve human relationships, think and behave irrationally.

The influence of the experiential system on the rational system can also be positive, such as by providing associations that can contribute to creativity that would not otherwise be available to the linear-processing rational system. Because the experiential system is an empirical learning system, it can also be a source of useful empirically derived information that can be incorporated into the rational system. In addition, the experiential system can provide a source of infused passion for the rational system that the rational system otherwise lacks. The result is that intellectual pursuits can be passionately pursued. Experiential processing can also contribute to rational processing by having a synergistic effect when the two systems operate in a harmonious manner. Thus problem-solving can be facilitated by using procedures that harmoniously engage both systems, such as by the use of metaphors, narratives, and the use of concrete examples of abstract principles (e.g., Epstein, Denes-Raj, & Pacini, 1995).

The Influence of the Rational System on the Experiential System

As the slower reacting system, the rational system is in an advantageous position for correcting the experiential system. It is common for people to reflect on their immediate thoughts and impulses, suppress those they consider inappropriate, and substitute more constructive thoughts and impulses. For example, in a flash of anger an employee may have the thought that he would like to tell off his boss, but, on further reflection, he decides it would be most unwise to do so. To investigate this process, we conducted an experiment in which people listed their first three thoughts in response to a variety of provocative vignettes (reported in Epstein, 1993b; Epstein & Morling, 1995; Epstein & Pacini, 1999). The first thought was often an inappropriate, emotional response consistent with the operation of the experiential system, whereas the third thought was usually more reasonable and in the mode of the rational system.

The rational system can also influence the experiential system by identifying and understanding its operation and deciding whether to express or suppress its promptings. Understanding of the principles and attributes of experiential processing can also be used by the rational system to train the experiential system, so that its prompting are more constructive (Epstein, 1998a).

The rational system may influence the experiential system in unintentional ways. As the experiential system is an associative system, conscious thoughts in the rational system can trigger associations and emotions in the experiential system that influence behavior. For example, a student attempting to solve a mathematics word-problem that requires calculating the arrival times at a destination of two speeding automobiles travelling from different starting points is reminded of a near fatal car crash he experienced when driving too fast. The memory produces emotional reactions that interfere with his performance. We have here an interesting cycle of the rational system influencing the experiential system, which then influences the performance of the rational system.

Another unintentional way in which the rational system influences the experiential system is through the effect of repeatedly responding in a way that was initially controlled by the rational system. As the result of continued replication, the behavior becomes increasingly automated, or "experientialized." An obvious advantage to this shift in control is that it allows the behavior to be conducted with minimal cognitive effort. A disadvantage is that it makes the behavior difficult to change. Although this is desirable for constructive thoughts and behaviors, it can be problematic when the thoughts and behavior are counterproductive, or if circumstances change so that what was once adaptive is now maladaptive. Under such circumstances, the person has developed a bad habit that is difficult to break.

The Lower and Higher Reaches of the Experiential System

The experiential system, often with various degrees of contribution by the rational system, operates over a wide range of complexity.

Conditioning

Classical conditioning is an example of the operation of the experiential system at its simplest level. In classical conditioning, a neutral stimulus, such as a tone, precedes an unconditioned stimulus (the UCS), such as food. Over several trials, a relation is established between the conditioned and unconditioned stimuli so that the animal salivates on hearing the tone in anticipation of receiving the food. Thus, the neutral stimulus becomes a conditioned stimulus (CS) that elicits a conditioned response (CR), which in this case is salivation. With a failure to provide reinforcement, the CR gradually extinguishes, but spontaneously recovers after a while. This process illustrates the operation of several attributes of experiential processing, including forming associative connections between stimuli, outcomes, and responses; the role of affective reinforcement; the increasing strength of the associations as a function of the number of reinforced trials; the occurrence of the extinction of the associations as a function of number of unreinforced trials; and the occurrence of spontaneous recovery. It is noteworthy that the CS is responded to holistically, which is an attribute of the experiential

system, as the animal reacts not only to the CS and the UCS but to the overall laboratory situation. Through such classical conditioning animals, including humans, automatically obtain information about relations between stimuli with each other and with outcomes that are important building blocks in the construction of a model of the environment including its effects on themselves (Hollis, 1997; Rescorla, 1988).

Through operant conditioning animals learn about the relation between their responses to stimuli and the outcomes that follow, which expands their model of reality as it now includes the consequences of their behavior. Through observational learning organisms learn vicariously about relations among stimuli, responses, and outcomes. All these associations allow animals to construct a working model of their environments, its influence on themselves, and their influence on it that has allowed higher order organisms to adapt successfully to their environments by automatically learning from experiences over millions of years of evolution. Note that the essence of such adaptation is that it is based on automatic, empirical learning from experience and not on reasoning. The point I wish to emphasize is that building a working model of the environment and its effect on the organism and the organism's effect on it by empirically automatically learning from experience is no inconsequential feat and should not be dismissed as simply a crude form of adaptation that is inferior to adaptation by reasoning.

Heuristics

Tversky and Kahneman (1974) defined heuristics as cognitive shortcuts that people use when making decisions. They and other cognitive psychologists consider heuristic responses to be adequate for making decisions in situations where a high level of accuracy is unnecessary, but that it can be a source of serious irrational decisions in situations in which greater accuracy is required. For example, people typically report that protagonists in situations described in vignettes would become more upset following arbitrary outcomes preceded by acts of commission than by acts of omission, by near than by far misses, by free than by constrained behavior, and by unusual than by usual acts. As they respond in all these situations as if the protagonist's behavior is responsible for arbitrary outcomes, their thinking is clearly irrational. If people thought that way when investigating in the stock market they would lose a lot of money, and as Tversky and Kahneman and others indicate, this is what actually happens because people do think that way. They do tend to sell when prices go down and buy when prices go up.

Psychologists such as Kahneman and Tversky (1973), Nisbett and Ross (1980), and others regarded heuristics as "cognitive tools" that are employed within a single conceptual system that includes deliberative processing. This is very different from the view in CEST according to which there are two kinds of heuristics, one that corresponds to cognitive shortcuts and the other to the use of an entirely different system of information processing that operates by different rules and has different attributes from rational processing. Of particular interest, the outcome of such processing unlike the other kind of processing is often preferred to the outcome of deliberative processing even when the latter is available without requiring additional effort or resources (e.g., Denes-Raj & Epstein, 1994), and it is even sometimes superior to deliberative reasoning (e.g., Dijksterhuis, 2004; Norris & Epstein, 2011; Reber, 1993; Wilson, 2002).

In conclusion, the assumption that all heuristic processing can be attributed to the use of cognitive shortcuts is an overgeneralization that has resulted in a failure to recognize an alternative mode of information processing in the experiential system that operates automatically and effortlessly and is inherently highly compelling and sometimes more effective than rational processing. It is noteworthy that Kahneman (2003) has more recently acknowledged the limitations of his previous view of heuristics and now endorses a dual-process explanation of heuristics that is similar to the position of CEST.

Experiential Processing in More Complex Decision Making

The experiential system is able to generalize, discriminate, integrate, and direct behavior in more complex ways than by classical and operant conditioning and heuristics. It often does so with a subordinate contribution by the rational system, as in its use of prototypes, metaphors, symbols, and narratives. Representations in the experiential system are also associated and generalized through their relations with emotions. It is perhaps through processes such as these that the experiential system is able to make its contributions to empathy, creativity, the establishment of rewarding interpersonal relationships, the appreciation of art, and a sense of humor (Norris & Epstein, 2011).

Can the Experiential System Reason?

Is it is possible for nonhuman animals to reason without the use of language? If so, it can be assumed that the experiential system in humans can also do so. The answer to the question is that it can be done with the use of imagery. All that is necessary is for an animal to imagine alternative solutions to a problem and to select the image associated with the most favorable affect. This, of course, is solving a problem by trial and error. However, as the trial and error occurs in imagination it qualifies as reasoning if reasoning is defined as solving problems by mental operations.

Psychodynamics and Maladaptive Needs and Beliefs

Psychodynamics, as used in CEST, refers to the interaction of implicit and explicit motives, defenses, and beliefs and their influence on conscious thinking and behavior. The influence of experiential processing on conscious thinking and on behavior is assumed in CEST to be mediated by feelings, including vibes and emotions. A major source, but not the only one, of maladaptive behavior, is the implicit beliefs acquired in childhood when individuals are most dependent on others and have limited cognitive resources.

The beliefs in people's implicit theories of reality consist primarily of generalizations from emotionally significant experiences. These affect-laden implicit beliefs, or schemas, indicate how people tend automatically to view themselves, others, and the impersonal world. Particularly important sources of such beliefs are emotionally significant early experiences with parents, siblings, peers, and authority figures. These schemas exist at varying levels of generality. Implicit beliefs at a more general level are about what the self and other people in general are like, for examples whether the self is considered love-worthy and competent or the opposite and whether others are considered helpful and trustworthy or the opposite. At a more specific level are views about categories of people, such as authority figures, parental figures, siblings, and peers. At a yet more specific level are beliefs about how categories of people behave in particular kinds of situations. Such implicit beliefs at all levels influence how people relate to others, particularly to those who provide cues that are reminders of their important generalization figures.

An important question is why people maintain maladaptive negative beliefs that are sources of distress. Why are such beliefs not simply abandoned because of the ubiquitous influence of the hedonic principle? There are three reasons why people maintain beliefs that are a source of distress. First, people's biased perceptions and interpretations are usually consistent with and therefore support their maladaptive beliefs. For example, an offer by someone to be helpful may be interpreted as condescending or as an attempt to gain trust that can be used to exploit others, and an expression of affection can be viewed as manipulative. Second, people often engage in self-verifying behavior, such as by provoking responses in others that confirm their view that other people are unfriendly, aggressive, or rejecting. For example, a person who fears rejection in intimate relationships may behave with aggression or withdrawal whenever threatened by intimacy. This provokes the other person to react with aggression or withdrawal, which is interpreted as evidence that the other person is rejecting. Third, people often fail to recognize the influence of their implicit beliefs and the behavior it promotes, which prevents them from identifying and correcting their biased interpretations and self-verifying behavior. As a result, they tend to attribute the consequences of their maladaptive behavior to the behavior of others.

Returning to the presumed ubiquitous influence of the hedonic principle in maladaptive behavior, the question remains as to whether people's behavior that is a source of distress is consistent with or violates the operation of the hedonic principle. It will be recalled that one of the four subordinate basic needs is the need to maintain the stability and coherence of people's conceptual systems and that the hedonic principle, as a superordinate motive, is involved in all behavior and the fulfillment of all needs. Thus, fulfilling any basic need is a source of positive affect and a failure to fulfill any basic need is a source of negative affect. It follows that behaving in a way that fulfills the need to maintain the stability and coherence of people's belief systems is a source of positive affect and behaving in ways that conflict with fulfilling this need is a source of negative affect. Thus maintaining behaviors that are maladaptive and produce distress is consistent with the hedonic principle in a very fundamental way, namely the affective consequences of maintaining or failing to maintain the stability and coherence of one's belief system, which can override the negative affective consequences of people's maladaptive behavior. In other words, it is assumed that people automatically tend to behave in a manner that produces the best affective bargain possible under the circumstances as perceived by the person, which may result in an unhappy state, but at least less unhappy than any perceived alternative.

Psychoanalysts have emphasized the importance of transference relationships in psychotherapy. They often encourage the development of maladaptive transference relations in psychotherapy with the aim of interpreting to their patients a presumed tendency to establish similar maladaptive relationships with others. Although this procedure is well-intended and may often be effective, it is fraught with danger, as patients may become overly dependent on their therapists. Moreover, an emphasis on maladaptive transference relationships may cause the analyst to overlook other important reasons for people's maladaptive behavior than the influence of early relationships with their parents as the source of their difficulties. Moreover, working through a transference relationship, even when successful, may not be the most efficient way of treating inappropriate generalizations about relationships. Nevertheless, it illustrates how generalizations from early childhood experiences are often reproduced in later relationships, including those with therapists, and how correcting such maladaptive generalizations can be therapeutic.

Although there are obvious similarities between the concepts of transference in psychoanalysis and of generalization in CEST, there are also important differences. Generalization is a much broader concept, which, unlike transference, is not restricted to the formative influence of relationships with parents. Rather, it refers to the generalization of all significant relationships, including relationships with siblings, other children, teachers, and authority figures.

Schemas derived from early childhood experiences are emphasized in CEST because later experiences are assimilated into extant cognitive-affective networks. Also, schemas derived from early childhood experiences are likely to be poorly articulated and therefore exert an unconscious influence on maladaptive behavior that, in the absence of identification may be overlooked in certain therapeutic approaches, such as cognitive-behavioral therapy, or may be considered untreatable with such an approach.

Important as early relationships are, a caveat is in order regarding an overemphasis on such relationships at the cost of recognizing other sources of maladaptive behavior. Psychoanalytically oriented therapists often search for maladaptive parenting as the sole or major source of their clients' difficulties. They therefore may convince their patients that their problems are the result of destructive childhood relationships with their parents, which may then operate as a self-fulfilling prophecy. Such an expectancy about maladaptive parenting may then selectively influence recall in a manner that falsely confirms the expectancy. This may result in an apparent improvement in the patient because of the general effectiveness of scapegoating as a way of increasing self-esteem. That is, the self-esteem of patients can be elevated by their construction of narratives in which the origin of their problem is attributed to dysfunctional parenting and not at all to fortuitous events or their own behavior. Unfortunately,

I have observed such a development all too often in acquaintances whom I know well and with whom I have discussed their psychotherapeutic experiences. In some cases, I believe the therapist completely missed the mark by emphasizing poor parenting and failing to recognize that the origin of the patient's maladaptive behavior was initiated by circumstances in which, as a child, the patient was fortuitously rewarded for a maladaptive belief that had nothing to do with the child's parents. For example, maladaptive beliefs and behavior can be reinforced by providing a short-term advantage despite a long-term disadvantage. That is, a person may be seduced by the short-term time perspective of the experiential system into making a pact with the devil, who later claims his long-term price. As the results of such observations, I believe that Freud's views that all neurosis is the result of repression and maladaptive relationships with parents has been far more influential than is warranted and has resulted in the neglect by many psychoanalytically oriented therapists of other important sources of their patients' difficulties in living. Such behavior contributes to my belief that there is nothing more destructive than a strong, wrong hypothesis. It has been the source of lost battles, wars, and empires, and, not surprisingly, it is no less forgiving in psychotherapy.

SUPPORT FOR CEST IN AN EXTENSIVE RESEARCH PROGRAM

The following kinds of research are reviewed: research on the operating principles of the experiential system, research on the interactions within and between the two processing systems, and research on individual differences, including individual differences in the "intelligence," or efficacy, of the experiential system, individual differences in the degree to which people engage in processing in each of the two systems, and individual differences in basic beliefs.

Research on the Operating Principles of the Experiential System

My associates and I have conducted an extensive research program for testing the operating principles and attributes of the experiential system. One approach consisted of adapting procedures used by Tversky and Kahneman and other cognitive and social-cognitive psychologists to study heuristic information processing through the use of specially constructed vignettes.

As previously noted, in most of the research on heuristic processing there is a failure to distinguish between two different kinds of heuristic processing. Thus, some researchers interpret all their results on heuristics as indicative of cognitive shortcuts within a single system that includes deliberative processing, whereas others attribute all their results on heuristics to a different system of information processing. This latter approach has been criticized by noting that the results claimed to report a different kind of information processing from deliberative processing could just as well be attributed to cognitive shortcuts in a single processing system (Kruglansky, Thompson, & Spiegel, 1999). The only way to establish a different system of processing is to demonstrate that it operates by different principles, has different attributes from analytical processing, and may even conflict with the latter.

Irrational Reactions to Unfortunate Arbitrary Outcomes

People in everyday life often react to arbitrary outcomes as if they or others are responsible for the outcomes. Thus, they reward the proverbial bearer of good tidings and punish the conveyer of unwelcome news. Such rational reactions are readily explained by the attributes of the experiential system.

We investigated people's reactions to arbitrary unfavorable outcomes by adding some questions to the usual one concerning the protagonists' reactions to the situations in the vignettes. We asked the participants to indicate in addition to how most people would behave, how the participant would behave in real life, and how a completely logical person would behave (e.g., Epstein, Lipson, Holstein, & Huh, 1992). To investigate the effect of degree of emotional consequences of the outcomes, one group was given a version of the vignette with a very unfortunate outcome and another group was given a version with a less unfavorable outcome. As an example, one of the vignettes described a situation in which two people dawdled at home for 10 minutes before driving to the airport. Both missed their flights because of unanticipated heavy traffic and both arrived at the airport 30 minutes after the scheduled departure of their flights. One learned that the flight left on time, and the other learned that the flight was delayed and left only a few minutes ago. Who felt more foolish about having dawdled at home? Participants were asked to respond from three perspectives, how most people would react in the situation, how they themselves would react, and how a completely logical person would react. Tversky and Kahneman (1982) reported that their participants indicated that the protagonist who barely missed the flight would be more upset than the other protagonist. We replicated this finding, and we also found that most participants reported that a logical person would feel much less foolish about having dawdled than the participant or others would feel. The significance of the consequences of missing the flight also influenced the protagonists' responses. When the outcomes were very unfortunate the respondents were said to feel more foolish for having dawdled than when the outcomes were less unfortunate. The results supported the following hypotheses based on CEST:

- People are aware of two different modes of thinking, one that determines how people normally behave, which corresponds to the operation of the experiential system, and the other that determines how people would behave if they were logical, which corresponds to the operation of the rational system.
- The more people are emotionally involved in an outcome the more they tend to think and behave in the mode of the experiential system.
- People regard themselves as similar to others in processing information primarily in the experiential mode, but they consider themselves more than others like a completely logical person, indicating that they explicitly (not necessarily implicitly) value rational over experiential processing.
- The experiential system can co-opt the rational system as indicated by a substantial minority of participants rating heuristic responses as the way a completely logical person would respond. Such co-option of the rational system by the experiential system is considered in CEST to be an important source of the prevalence of human irrationality despite the capacity of humans for extraordinary levels of rational thinking.

The Ratio-Bias Phenomenon

The ratio-bias (RB) experimental paradigm is of particular interest for dual-process theories as it pits experiential against rational processing in a situation in which the two modes of processing are equally accessible and in which both require equally negligible cognitive effort.

Imagine that you are told that on every trial in which you blindly draw a red jellybean from a bowl containing red and white jellybeans you will receive two dollars. You are given a choice of drawing from either of two bowls, both of which offer a 10% probability of obtaining a red jellybean. One bowl contains 1 red and 9 white jellybeans and the other contains 10 red and 90 white jellybeans.

When people are asked which bowl they would draw from and how much they would be willing to pay to draw from the bowl of their choice, almost all say they would have no preference and would not pay a cent to have a choice between two equal probabilities. Yet, an interesting thing happens when they are placed in a real situation in which they can win a significant amount of money over trials. Most then willingly part with small sums of money from an amount given to them to keep at the beginning of the experiment for the privilege of drawing from the bowl of their choice, which is almost always from the bowl that contains more red jellybeans (Kirkpatrick & Epstein, 1992). The preference for the bowl with more red jellybeans despite its having no probability advantage has been labeled the ratio-bias (RB) phenomenon.

Even more impressive than the irrational behavior of paying for the privilege of choosing between bowls that offer the same probabilities are the results that are obtained when the bowl with the larger number of red jellybeans offers a lower probability of obtaining one. In one study, a probability-advantaged bowl always contained 1 in 10 red jellybeans, and a frequency-advantaged bowl contained 5 to 9 red jellybeans out of 100 jellybeans, depending on the trial (Denes-Raj & Epstein, 1994). Most participants preferred to draw from the slightly frequency-advantaged bowl despite it being probability-disadvantaged. Some participants volunteered that although they knew such behavior was irrational, they had a feeling that they had a better chance of getting a red jellybean when there were more of them. Although a substantial minority consistently made optimal choices, some acknowledged that they had to overcome a temptation to pick from the bowl with more red jellybeans.

In a study in which equal probabilities were presented in the two bowls, one bowl always containing 100 jellybeans and the other always containing 10 jellybeans, with the probabilities of drawing a red jellybean being varied randomly over trials (e.g., 10%, 30%, 50%, 70%, 90%), a strong RB effect in the 10% condition became increasingly weaker as the probability of drawing a red jellybean increased until the RB effect was no longer significant at the 70% probability condition and even exhibited a slight non-significant reverse RB effect in the 90% probability condition (Pacini & Epstein, 1999a). The results were attributed to the combined influence of two different effects, a small-numbers effect, according to which small numbers are better comprehended by the experiential system than large numbers, and a frequency effect according to which the comprehension of frequencies is greater than that of ratios or probabilities, as frequencies are more concrete and therefore more comprehensible as indicated by the behavior of young children and nonhuman animals (Gallistel & Gelman, 1992). The combined influence of these two effects can explain the results we obtained as their influence operates in the same direction in the 10% condition and in the opposite direction in the 90% condition. In the 10% condition, 10 in 100 red jellybeans is preferred over 1 in 10 red jellybeans because it is frequency advantaged and because 1 in 10 red jellybeans is a more compelling losing condition than 10 in 100 red jellybeans because of the small numbers effect. In the 90% probability condition the frequency effect favors the bowl with 90 out of 100 red jellybeans but the small numbers effect favors the bowl with 9 out of 10 red jellybeans as it is a more compelling winning condition.

The overall conclusions from the many studies we conducted on the RB phenomenon (Denes-Raj & Epstein, 1994; Denes-Raj, Epstein, & Cole, 1995; Epstein et al., 1996; Epstein & Pacini, 1999; Kirkpatrick & Epstein, 1992; Pacini & Epstein, 1999a, 1999b; Pacini, Muir, & Epstein, 1998; Yanko & Epstein, 2000) can be summarized as follows:

- The RB effect in low probability conditions can be attributed to the frequency effect and the small-numbers effect operating in the same direction. Both of these effects are consistent with the concrete attribute of experiential processing (e.g., Pacini & Epstein, 1999).
- An absence of the RB effect under high probability conditions can be attributed to the frequency effect and the small-numbers effect operating in opposite directions. Both effects are consistent with the concrete operation of the experiential system (Pacini & Epstein, 1999).
- The two systems can respond together in the following ways: Either system can be dominant depending on the situation and the person. Thus, most participants preferred nonoptimal, slightly frequency-advantaged responses but a substantial number consistently made optimal, probability-advantaged responses. The two processing systems usually produced compromises as indicated by the most common response being a frequency-advantaged response that was only slightly probability disadvantaged. For example, most participants preferred a 9% frequency-advantaged response over a 10% probability-advantaged response but only a few preferred a 5% frequency-advantaged response over a 10% probability-advantaged response (e.g., Denes-Raj & Epstein, 1994).

- The two systems sometimes conflict with each other as indicated by some participants reporting a conflict between frequency-advantaged and probability-advantaged choices.
- The experiential system is more responsive than the rational system to real situations and to vividly imagined situations, whereas the rational system is more responsive to abstract, verbal presentations (Epstein & Pacini, 2000–2001).
- With increasing maturation from childhood to adulthood, the balance of influence between the two systems shifts increasingly in the direction of rational dominance (Yanko & Epstein, 2000).
- Priming the rational system in young children before they have formal knowledge of ratios by asking them to give the reasons for their responses interferes with their intuitive understanding of ratios. This indicates that processing in the rational system can interfere with processing in the experiential system (Yanko & Epstein, 2000; see also Wilson, 2002).
- An increase in incentive produces an increase in optimal, rational responses in some participants and an increase in experiential, non-optimal responses in an approximately equal number of participants (Pacini & Epstein, 1999b).
- Research with subclinically depressed participants verified the depressive-realism phenomenon (Alloy & Abramson, 1988), which refers to depressed people being more realistic than others as indicated by their making more optimal responses than their nondepressed counterparts. However, we found this only occurred in conditions in which the consequences were minimal. When the consequences were increased, the depressed participants responded more non-optimally and the extremely nondepressed participants responded more optimally, which canceled out the depressive-realism effect. The phenomenon of depressive realism was explained as a compensatory reaction by depressed people for their awareness of their more general tendency to respond irrationally. They are presumably unable to maintain this compensatory control in more consequential, emotionally engaging situations (Pacini et al., 1998).

The Global-Evaluation Heuristic

The global-evaluation heuristic refers to evaluating people holistically as either good or bad people, rather than restricting evaluations more accurately to specific behaviors. As the global-evaluation heuristic is consistent with the assumption that holistic evaluation is a fundamental attribute of experiential processing (see Table 5.1), it follows that global evaluations tend to be automatic, compelling, and difficult to overcome. This heuristic is particularly important because of its prevalence in causing serious problems, as in stereotyping and in the influence of the appearance of a defendant on jurors' decisions.

My associates and I investigated the global-evaluation heuristic (reported in Epstein, 1994) by having participants respond to a vignette adapted from a study by Miller and Gunasegaram (1990). According to the vignette, a rich benefactor tells three friends that if each throws a coin that comes up heads, he will give each $100. The first two throw a heads, but Smith, the third, throws a tails. When asked to rate how each of the protagonists feels, most participants report that Smith feels guilty and the others are angry at him. In an alternative version of the vignette in which we reduced the stakes to a more modest sum, the ratings of guilt and anger were reduced. When asked if the other two would be willing, as they previously had intended, to invite Smith to join them on a gambling vacation in Las Vegas, where they would share their wins and losses, most participants said they would no longer invite him "because he is a loser." These responses were made both from the perspective of how the participants reported they themselves would react in real life and how they believed most people would behave. When responding from the perspective of how a completely logical person would behave, most said a logical person would recognize that the outcome of coin tosses are completely arbitrary, and they therefore would not resent Smith and they would invite him to join them on their gambling adventure.

This study indicates that people are aware of two systems of information-processing that operate in a manner consistent with the operating principles and attributes of the experiential and rational systems of CEST. It also supports the hypotheses that experiential processing becomes increasingly dominant with an increase in emotional engagement and that people over-generalize broadly and associatively by judging others on the basis of outcomes over which the person has no control, despite knowing better in their rational system.

Conjunction Problems

The Linda conjunction problem is probably the most researched vignette in the history of psychology. It has evoked a great deal of interest because of its paradoxical results. Although the solution to the Linda problem requires the application of one of the simplest and most fundamental rules of probability theory, almost everyone, including many who are highly sophisticated about statistics, make a conjunction error (CE) when responding to it. Linda is described as a 31-year-old woman who is single, outspoken, and very bright. In college she was a philosophy major who participated in anti-nuclear demonstrations and was concerned about social justice. We asked participants to rank-order the following alternatives: Linda is a feminist, Linda is a bank teller, and Linda is a feminist and a bank teller. Most ranked Linda as being a feminist and a bank teller ahead of Linda just being a bank teller. In doing so, they made what Tversky and Kahneman (1982) labeled a "conjunction fallacy," and that we refer to as a CE. It is an error or fallacy because, according to the conjunction rule, the occurrence of two events cannot be more likely than the occurrence of just one of them.

The usual explanation of the high rate of CEs elicited by the Linda problem is that people do not know the conjunction rule or they do not think of it in the context of the Linda vignette. According to Tversky and Kahneman (1982), they make CEs because they respond by the representativeness heuristic, according to which being both a bank teller and a feminist is more representative of Linda's personality than being just a bank teller.

In a series of studies on conjunction problems, including several on the Linda problem (Donovan & Epstein, 1997; Epstein, Denes-Raj, & Pacini, 1995; Epstein, Donovan, & Denes-Raj, 1999), we demonstrated that the major reason for the difficulty of the Linda problem is that it provides a concrete representation of a problem in an unnatural manner. As a result, people tend not to view the Linda problem as a probability problem no matter what they are told about how they should view it, including as a probability problem.

Following is a summary of the conclusions we arrived at about the Linda problem based on all the studies we conducted:

• The difficulty of the Linda problem cannot be fully accounted for by the misleading manner in which it is presented as a personality problem, for even with full disclosure about the nature of the problem and the request to treat it as a probability problem most participants made CEs. However when responding to a conceptually equivalent problem presented in a concrete, natural manner, as in a problem concerning winning one or two lotteries or one or two bets on horse races, almost no one made CEs (Epstein, Denes-Raj, & Pacini, 1995). This is particularly interesting from the perspective of CEST because it indicates that the experiential system knows the conjunction rule, at least when it is presented in a natural context, but it is easily led astray when it is presented in an unnatural context. This is consistent with the view in CEST that the experiential system is very context-oriented and, unlike the rational system, resistant to cross-situational generalizations.

- Making a CE to the Linda problem is so compelling that even when presented with the correct conjunction rule (i.e., "two events are less like to occur than just one of them") among several incorrect rules simultaneously with the Linda problem, thereby circumventing the problem of whether people think of the conjunction rule, most participants selected a wrong rule that was consistent with making a CE. In other words, they made the rule correspond to their response to the Linda problem, rather than making their response to the Linda problem correspond to the correct rule and then using it to respond correctly to the Linda problem. This result demonstrates the highly compelling nature of experiential processing and its ability to co-opt rational processing.
- The difficulty of the Linda problem can be explained by the operating rules and attributes of the experiential system, which is apparently the mode employed by most people when responding to it. Thus, the Linda problem demonstrates that people tend to process information associatively, concretely, holistically and in a narrative manner, rather than abstractly and analytically when responding to the Linda problem. For example, a few participants justified their CEs by stating that Linda is more likely to be a bank teller and a feminist than just a feminist because she has to make a living.
- The essence of the difficulty of the Linda problem is that it involves an unnatural, concrete presentation of a problem, where an unnatural presentation of a problem refers to a presentation in a different context from how such problems are normally experienced in real life. Concrete representations facilitate performance in natural representations, in which case the two processing systems operate harmoniously, whereas they conflict with each other when problems are presented in a concrete, an unnatural form.
- Processing in the experiential mode is intrinsically highly compelling and can over-ride processing in the rational mode even when the latter does not require more effort or resources. Thus, many participants, despite knowing and thinking of the conjunction rule, simply find an experiential response more compelling than a rational response. As a result of their experiential

processing, context for them is given precedence over abstract generalizations.
- Priming intuitive knowledge in the experiential system can facilitate the solution of problems in the rational system that people are otherwise unable to solve.

Interactions

In this section I discuss research on two kinds of interaction, interactions between the two systems and interactions among basic needs.

Interactions Between the Two Processing Systems

An important assumption in CEST is that the two systems are simultaneously and sequentially interactive. Simultaneous interaction was demonstrated in the compromises between the two systems in the RB studies. Sequential interaction was demonstrated in studies on conjunction problems in which presenting concrete, natural problems first facilitated solutions to subsequently presented conceptually similar abstract problems, which illustrates how experiential processing can prime the effective operation of rational processing.

There is also considerable evidence that priming the experiential system subliminally can influence subsequent responses in the rational system (see review in Bargh, 1989). Other research indicates that the form, independent of the content, of processing in the rational system can be influenced by priming the experiential system. Thus, when processing in the experiential mode is followed by attempts to respond rationally, the operation of the rational processing can be compromised (Chaiken & Maheswaren, 1994; Denes-Raj et al., 1995; Epstein et al., 1992).

Sequential interactions occur not only in the direction of the experiential system influencing the rational system but also in the opposite direction. A common example is suppression of the expression of unacceptable thoughts and impulses.

Interactions Among Basic Needs

A basic assumption in CEST is that behavior often represents a compromise among basic needs. This processt provides checks and balances against the excessive investment in the fulfillment of a particular need. It occurs because fulfilling any need at the expense of fulfilling other needs increases the strength of the other frustrated needs. To test this assumption about compromises among needs, we examined the combined influence of the needs for self-enhancement and self-verification. Swann and associates had previously demonstrated that the needs for enhancement and verification tend to operate sequentially, with the former preceding the latter (e.g., Hixon & Swann, 1993; Swann, 1990). We wished to demonstrate that the interaction also occurs simultaneously in the form of compromises between these two needs. Our procedure consisted of varying the favorableness of evaluative feedback and observing whether participants had a preference for feedback that either matched or was more favorable to a different extent than their self-assessments (Epstein & Morling, 1995; Morling & Epstein, 1997). In support of hypothesis, participants preferred feedback that was only slightly more favorable than their self-assessments, consistent with a compromise between fulfilling the needs for verification and self-enhancement.

Individual Differences in Experiential and Rational Information Processing

In this section I discuss several measures of individual differences and the research that was conducted with them. Included are measures of individual differences in the intelligence of the experiential system, individual differences in the extent to which people report they engage in experiential and rational thinking styles, and individual differences in basic beliefs.

Individual Differences in the Intelligence of the Experiential System

If there are two different processing systems for adapting to the environment it is reasonable to suspect that there may also be important individual differences in the intelligence of both systems. It is therefore assumed in CEST that each system has its own form of intelligence and that it would be useful to have ways of measuring such individual differences. Fortunately, there are many tests that provide excellent measures of individual differences in the intelligence of the rational system. Such tests are fairly good predictors of academic performance and to a somewhat lesser extent of performance in the real world, including performance in the workplace, particularly in situations that require complex operations (see reviews in Gordon, 1997; Gottfredson, 1997; Hunter, 1983, 1986; J. Hunter & R. Hunter, 1984). However, there were no tests that measured experiential intelligence. Thus, if we wanted such a test, it was necessary to construct it. We named the test the Constructive Thinking Inventory (CTI; Epstein, 2001).

People respond to the CTI by reporting the degree to which they have certain adaptive and maladaptive

behavior and automatic or spontaneous thoughts. An example of an item is, "I spend a lot of time thinking about my mistakes, even if there is nothing I can do about them" (reverse scored). The CTI provides a Global Constructive Thinking scale and six main scales, all but one of which has subscales. The six main scales are Emotional Coping, Behavioral Coping, Categorical thinking, Esoteric Thinking, Naïve Optimism, and Personal Superstitious Thinking. The main scales all have high internal-consistency reliability coefficients and evidence of validity from numerous studies. The CTI has been translated into 14 languages and research with it has been conducted in many of these countries as well as in the United States. The CTI is predictive of a wide variety of criteria related to success in living. A review of the extensive literature supporting the validity of the CTI is beyond the scope of this chapter, but is available in the manual for the CTI (Epstein, 2001). For present purposes, it will suffice to note that it is related to performance in the workplace, superior achievement by managers, superior academic performance, social competence, leadership ability, ability to cope with stress, emotional adjustment, physical well-being, and an absence of drug and alcohol abuse.

The relation of constructive thinking to intellectual intelligence is of special interest for theoretical as well as practical reasons. As the experiential and rational systems process information by different rules and have different attributes (see Table 5.1), it was found in several studies that scores on the Global CTI scale are either unrelated or negligibly related to IQ (see review in Epstein, 2001). Of additional interest, constructive thinking and intellectual intelligence exhibit a nearly opposite course of development across the life span. It can be seen in Figure 5.1 that constructive thinking is at its nadir in adolescence when intellectual intelligence is at its peak and gradually increases throughout most of the adult years when mental age is gradually declining.

Although constructive thinking is less strongly related to academic achievement than intellectual intelligence, it contributes significant variance beyond that of intellectual intelligence to performance in the classroom, as indicated by grades received and class rank (Epstein, 2001). Apparently, good constructive thinkers are able to behave in ways that gain them recognition for their intellectual ability, whereas poor constructive thinkers are less able to do so.

A finding of particular importance is that there is a general factor of experiential intelligence that is measured by the CTI Global Constructive Thinking Scale. As this

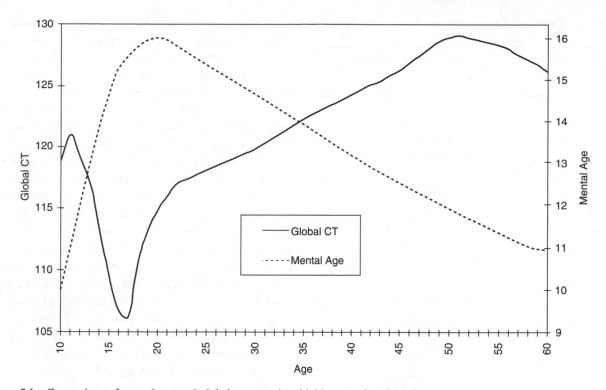

Figure 5.1 Comparison of mental age and global constructive thinking as a function of age

Note: Mental age was measured by the Wechsler-Bellevue Intelligence Test. Constructive thinking was measured by the CTI. The curve for mental age was adapted from D. Wechsler, *The Measurement of Adult Intelligence* (Baltimore, MD: Williams & Wilkins, 1939).

factor includes a wide variety of favorable non-intellective abilities and attributes, it is suggestive of a general factor of nonintellective ability comparable in generality to a global factor of intellectual ability.

Individual Differences in Rational and Experiential Thinking Styles

The Rational/Experiential Inventory (REI) was constructed to measure individual differences in the extent to which people process information in each of the two processing modes. The REI includes two main scales that measure the extent of processing information in rational and in experiential thinking styles. Each of the main scales has subscales of the degree of processing in the subscale and of the self-assessed ability to use it effectively. A summary of the major findings from studies conducted by my research team with the REI (Epstein, 2001; Epstein et al., 1996; Norris & Epstein, 2011; Pacini & Epstein, 1999b; Pacini, Muir, & Epstein, 1998) is presented in Table 5.2, in which it can be seen that a rational thinking style is more strongly positively associated than an experiential thinking style with intellectual performance and a variety of measures related to good adjustment, including low

anxiety, low depression, low stress, low neuroticism, high self-esteem, and high meaningfulness of life. An experiential/intuitive thinking style is more strongly associated than a rational thinking style with measures of creativity, empathy, aesthetic judgment, intuitive ability, and establishing satisfactory interpersonal relationships. It follows that no statement can be made about the general superiority of either thinking style, as each is superior in some important ways and inferior in other equally important ways than the other thinking style.

It is important, when introducing a new measure, to demonstrate that it provides information that is unavailable from existing instruments. In order to determine whether the REI meets this standard we conducted a study (Pacini & Epstein, 1999b) in which we compared the REI to several other personality inventories, including the NEO Five Factor Inventory (NEO-FI; Costa & McCrae, 1992), the most popular measure of the "Big Five" personality traits (see the chapter by McCrae, Gaines, & Wellington in this volume). The REI contributed independent variance to the prediction of many of the same variables as the NEO and unique variance to the prediction of other variables. When scores on the five NEO-FFI scales were entered into a regression equation as

TABLE 5.2   Correlates of Experiential and Rational Thinking Styles

Rational Thinking Style	Experiential Thinking Style
Positive Attributes	**Positive Attributes**
High level of intellectual performance	Favorable interpersonal relationships
High meaningfulness in life	High social popularity
Realistic thinking	Imaginative thinking
Low stress in living	High agreeableness
High self-esteem	High empathy
Positive world view	High spontaneity
Low neuroticism	Emotionally expressive
Low anxiety	Good esthetic sense
Low depression	Good sense of humor
Conscientious	Creative
Open-minded	Open-minded
High personal growth	High personal growth
Negative Attributes	**Negative Attributes**
Weak tendency of a dismissive relationship style	Naïve optimism
	Polyanna-ish thinking
	Stereotyped thinking
	Unrealistic beliefs
	Superstitious beliefs

predictors of scores on the REI scales, they accounted for less than half (e.g., 37%) of the variance of the rationality scale and considerably less (e.g., 11%) of the variance of the Experiential scale. This demonstrates that the REI scales are mainly independent of the NEO-FFI and that the NEO-FFI mainly measures attributes associated with the rational system and is comparatively deficient in measuring attitudes and behavior associated with the experiential system.

Individual Differences in Basic Beliefs Concerning the Self, Others, and the Impersonal World

A major assumption in CEST is that people's implicit beliefs about themselves, others, and the impersonal world are derived primarily from emotionally significant experiences and that such beliefs are important determinants of people's feelings, behavior, adjustment, and overall quality of life. Based on this assumption, a measure of basic beliefs, the Basic Beliefs Inventory (BBI; Catlin & Epstein, 1992), was constructed. The BBI is a self-report questionnaire that includes a global scale of individual differences in the overall favorability of basic beliefs and scales for measuring the favorability of the following more specific beliefs: self-esteem, love-worthiness, competence, meaningfulness of life, views about relationships, and views

about the world. A study with the BBI was conducted that tested the hypotheses that two important sources of basic beliefs are extreme life-events, as in the loss of a loved one or experiencing a transforming love relationship, and relationships with parents during early childhood.

In support of the hypotheses, both kinds of experiences were related to individual differences in basic beliefs. People who reported favorable relationships with their parents and those who obtained high scores on overall favorableness of extreme life-events based on both positive and negative events obtained higher scores than others on the BBI scales of self-esteem, meaningfulness of life, favorable view of others, and an optimistic view about the world. Those who reported unfavorable relationships with their parents or who reported predominantly unfavorable extreme life events, such as the death of a beloved pet or a significant failure in an important event, obtained less favorable scores than others on all basic beliefs.

The more recently an extreme negative event occurred, the less favorable a person's current basic beliefs. Over time, the effect of extremely unfavorable life events became less unfavorable and sometimes even favorable. This is consistent with other research on extreme life events in which several participants reported that they gained strength in the long run from coping with adversity (Epstein, 1979b).

Parental relationships and life events often made supplementary contributions to the same basic belief. Also the quality of childhood relationships with parents moderated the influence of extreme life events. For those who reported favorable childhood relationships with parents there was a strong positive relation between the basic belief in the meaningfulness of life and the overall favorableness of extreme life events, whereas for those who reported poor relationships with parents there was a near zero relation between these two variables. This suggests that those who felt most secure in their relationships with their parents were able to assimilate their favorable life events, whereas those who reported poor childhood relationships with parents were more resistant to assimilating the implications of extremely favorable life events. It is as if they did not trust viewing life as meaningful because such a belief could make them vulnerable to destabilizing changes in their belief system.

Summary and Conclusions Regarding Research on the Basic Assumptions in CEST

An extensive research program provided support for the validity of all the assumptions in CEST that were tested, which consists of most of the assumptions in CEST. In summary, the following basic assumptions in CEST received research support: There are two independent information-processing systems that operate in parallel and are simultaneously and sequentially bi-directionally interactive. The influence of experiential processing on rational processing is of particular importance, as it identifies a process by which people's automatic, pre-conscious, experiential processing operating most often outside of awareness biases their deliberative, conscious rational thinking. The influence of experiential process-ing is intrinsically highly compelling and can override rational processing and influence people to behave against their better judgment (e.g., Denes-Raj & Epstein, 1994). However, when people are aware of their experientially determined maladaptive thoughts and beliefs, they may be able to control or correct them through their rational processing.

There are reliable individual differences in the effi-cacy, or "intelligence," of the experiential system. As hypothesized based on CEST, experiential intelligence is independent of intellectual intelligence and is more strongly associated than intellectual intelligence with a variety of nonintellectual desirable attributes and abilities, whereas rational intelligence is more strongly associated with intellectual performance and emotional adjustment. With respect to the latter, people apparently can be well adjusted within a wide range of an experiential thinking style so long as it is not irrational. There are also reli-able individual differences in the degree to which people report they engage in experiential and in rational process-ing. Rational and experiential thinking styles exhibited different relations with a variety of important criterion variables. It was concluded that neither mode of infor-mation processing can be considered generally superior to the other mode. The hypothesis was supported that there are reliable individual differences in self-reported basic beliefs. Other hypotheses that received support are that two important sources of basic beliefs are early rela-tionships with parents and the occurrence of extremely favorable and unfavorable life events.

IMPLICATIONS OF CEST FOR DIVERSE TOPICS

As a broadly integrative global theory of personality, CEST provides a useful perspective for elucidating a wide variety of psychological phenomena. In this section I describe research based on CEST regarding the following topics: the nature of intuition, the limitations and need for extension of the concept of emotional intelligence, the meaning of dreams, Hitler's rabid anti-Semitism, and the existence of a cancer-prone personality.

Implications of CEST for Understanding Intuition: What It Is, What It Does, and How It Does It

Intuition has been a most confusing topic in psychology. There is not even agreement on what it is, let alone on how it operates. In a survey by Abernathy and Hamm (1995), 20 different definitions of intuition were identified. Although many psychologists believe there is something of importance captured by the idea of intuition, there are others who doubt it is a useful construct, and yet others who consider it as simply a lazy form of cogni-tion (e.g., Simon, 1992). Interestingly, most authorities define intuition in terms of what it is not rather than by what it is. For example, Bruner (1961) defines intu-ition as "the intellectual technique of arriving at plausible but tentative conclusions without going through the ana-lytic steps by which such formulations would be found to be valid or invalid conclusions" (p. 13). Others iden-tify intuition with unconscious processing, which is only a slight improvement in the absence of describing its operating principles and attributes. In contrast, CEST is explicit about what intuition is, what it does, and how it does it. According to CEST, intuition is nothing more and somewhat less than the operation of the experien-tial system (Epstein, 2010). It is a subset of experien-tial processing that operates according to the rules and attributes of experiential processing. It thereby arrives at impressions automatically and by procedures that occur outside of awareness. However, unlike the very broad domain of experiential processing it has a narrower range of content and does not include fundamentalist religious beliefs, superstitious thinking, irrational fears and the motor and sensory coordination that occur in activities such as catching a ball. It follows that intuition consists primarily of tacit information acquired by automatically learning from experience outside of awareness. Thus intu-ition can be valid or invalid depending on the relation of past experience to present circumstances. Although mainly based on past learning, intuition can also be exhib-ited in completely new situations by a process referred to in evolutionary theory as preadaptation. According to preadaptation, a process acquired for one purpose may then be used for other purposes. Thus, intuitive reactions can occur in entirely new situations by processing infor-mation according to the principles and attributes of the experiential system.

Implications of CEST for Emotional Intelligence

More than two decades ago Salovey and Mayer (1990) introduced the idea that there is an important nonintellectual form of intelligence that is related to emotions. They and their associates constructed a performance test of what they referred to as emotional intelligence, the MSCEIT V2.0. This test includes a global scale of emotional intelligence (EI) with subscales of managing emotions, understanding emotions, using emotions to facilitate thinking, and the accurate perception of emotions (Mayer, Salovey, Caruso, & Sitarenios, 2003). The authors note that theirs is the only test of EI that is a performance test, and that it is specifically restricted to aspects of coping with emotions. All other tests of EI are self-report tests that measure many attributes different from emotions, such as assertiveness, self-regard, problem solving, and social responsibility.

Although the construction of a performance test for measuring EI would be a notable achievement, the test is not a measure of emotional intelligence from the perspective of CEST but rather a test of intelligence about emotions. It is one thing to know what adaptive emotional responses are and another to have them. A proper test of EI that remains to be constructed would include items that refer to the degree to which people have adaptive rather than maladaptive, emotions in a variety of situations (Epstein, in press b). A person who had emotions such as anger, fear, sadness, joy, and affection appropriately would obtain a high score on such a test, whereas a person who reacted emotionally inappropriately would obtain a low score. It is uncertain how such scores would be related to scores on a test of intelligence about emotions. I suspect the relation would not be strong because the former is the result of automatic experiential processing whereas the latter is the result primarily of rational processing.

Among the various self-report tests purported to measure of EI, the most thoroughly researched one is the Bar-On Emotional Quotient Inventory (Bar-On EQ-i, Bar-On, 1997). The test has impressive evidence of factorial and empirical validity. However, all the self-report tests, including the Bar-On, that have been constructed are open to the criticism that they are not actually tests of EI as they include a variety of other abilities and attributes that are not emotional (see Daus & Ashkanasy, 2003; Locke, 2005).

From the perspective of CEST, although criticisms that such tests as not valid measures of emotional intelligence are correct, they make the mistake of throwing out the baby with the bathwater. What these tests unintentionally and importantly demonstrate is that there is a global factor of nonintellectual ability that is broader than EI. That is, just as there is a global factor of intellectual intelligence, there is also a global factor of nonintellectual intelligence, which includes abilities and attributes such as ego-strength, assertiveness, independence, empathy, flexibility, and social facility, among others. The existence of such a broad global, nonintellectual ability is consistent with the operation of the experiential system of CEST. It would include the following abilities and attributes of the experiential system identified in Table 5.2: empathy, social ability, sense of humor, creativity, and intuitive ability. Thus, the global nonintellectual factor would accurately have to be referred to as experiential intelligence rather than as emotional intelligence (Epstein, in press b).

Implications of CEST for Psychobiography

Two basic principles of CEST particularly relevant to psychobiography are: wherever there is grossly irrational behavior it is likely to be the result of the biasing influence of experiential on rational processing, and there is likely to have been an intense negative life experience. The operation of both of these principles is well illustrated in Hitler's rabid and irrational hostility toward Jews. For example, he stated that if Jews were not eliminated from the world they would destroy all humanity and therefore exterminating them should be regarded as is a humanitarian act.

An interesting hypothesis about the source of Hitler's hostility to Jews was proposed by Gertrud Kurth (1947), a psychoanalytically oriented psychologist. The hypothesis was later expanded on by Rudolph Binion (1976), a psychoanalytically oriented psychohistorian. According to the hypothesis, Hitler's hostility to Jews was the result of the displacement of repressed hostility to Dr. Bloch, the family physician, who was a Jew who treated Hitler's mother for terminal cancer.

Hitler's mother had experienced a prolonged period of intense suffering because of her treatment with iodoform, a form of chemotherapy used at the time. Dr. Bloch warned Hitler against this treatment as he said it would cause his mother great suffering and provide only a negligible possibility of remission. Hitler nevertheless insisted on using it if it offered any hope at all. Dr. Bloch later reported that he had never seen anyone exhibit as intense empathy in response to the suffering of another as he witnessed in Hitler's reaction to his mother's suffering. It is noteworthy in this respect that Hitler was so deeply devoted to his mother that he kept a photograph of her with him at all times until his death.

It is noteworthy that Hitler expressed his appreciation to Dr. Bloch in a postcard he wrote after his mother's death. He also gave Dr. Bloch a note granting his request to immigrate to the United States and ordering any readers of the note to treat Dr. Bloch very favorably.

The question may be raised as to why Hitler was not hostile to Dr. Bloch. The answer is that Dr. Bloch was carrying out Hitler's orders and to condemn him would mean condemning himself, which would probably arouse more guilt than Hitler could bear. Moreover, Hitler was never one to accept responsibility for any of his poor decisions.

To test the hypothesis concerning the displacement of Hitler's repressed hostility to a Jewish physician, I had an undergraduate research assistant, Lisa Sirop, tally the number of paragraphs in the first volume of *Mein Kampf* (Hitler, 1925) in a 2 × 2 table with divisions according to the presence and absence of a reference to Jews and the presence and absence of a disease-metaphor (Epstein, 2003). There were 223 paragraphs that included one or more references to Jews. On average, Hitler made a reference to Jews 1.6 times in every 10 paragraphs, or more than once in every two pages. Clearly, Hitler was obsessed with Jews.

The number of disease-related metaphors was also very large, with 194 such references. Thus Hitler was almost as obsessed with disease-related metaphors as he was with Jews. The critical question is whether there is a statistical relation between the two obsessions. To determine whether there is such an association, I calculated a chi-square and obtained a value of 57.82, 1 *df, p* < .0001. Apparently, in Hitler's mind there was a strong association between disease-metaphors and Jews. Examining the data in greater detail, in 33% of Hitler's use of a disease-related metaphor it was used with reference to Jews as "poisoners," which is consistent with an association to iodoform, the chemical treatment that caused his mother great suffering. Following is an example of a metaphor that expresses Hitler's rage and wish for retribution against Jews for their "poisonous" influence: "But now the time has come to take steps against the whole of the treacherous brotherhood of the Jewish poisoners of the people. Now was the time to deal with them summarily without the slightest consideration for any screams and complaints that might arise. It would have been the duty of a serious government—to exterminate mercilessly the agitators who were misleading the nation" (p. 169). It is also of interest that in 16% of Hitler's use of a disease-related metaphor for Jews, he refers to them as parasites. Cancers are, of course, parasites that destroy their hosts, a relation often noted by Hitler.

In conclusion, the present study of Hitler's extremely irrational, rabid thinking about Jews supports the hypothesis that Hitler's hatred of Jews is at least in part related to displaced hostility to a Jewish physician who, under the direction of Hitler, treated Hitler's mother with a form of chemotherapy that caused her great suffering. Although the experience concerning the death of his mother may seem an insufficient explanation for Hitler's wish to exterminate all Jews, this is only true from a rational perspective. From an unconscious, associative, experiential, psychodynamic perspective a much more viable case can be made for such a relation.

IMPLICATIONS OF CEST FOR THE EXISTENCE OF A CANCER-PRONE PERSONALITY

Is there any validity to the concept of a cancer-prone personality (CPP)? Alice Epstein (1989) in a book describing her very unusual recovery from a terminal stage of cancer stated that she believes there is a relation between a cancer-prone personality and vulnerability to and recovery from cancer based on her own experience. She has now been free for more than two decades of all signs of a kidney cancer from which the likelihood of remission, let alone cure, according to actuarial data at the time of her disease was less than 4 in 1,000 (DeVita, Hellman, & Rosenberg, 1985). She believes that the reason for her recovery was the transformation of her cancer-prone personality that was a source of self-negation and depression into a happier and more adaptive personality, so that now it is even difficult for her to remember how she used to feel.

According to CEST there is good reason to suspect that there is a relation between certain personality characteristics and a proneness to certain diseases as well as the course of recovery from them. This is because the experiential system is intimately related to emotions, and emotions have physiological as well as psychological components and therefore can serve as a mediating link between personality characteristics and physical disorders. An association between a particular personality characteristic and disease has been demonstrated in the relation between the suppressed anger component of the Type A personality and hypertension as well as by our own findings of a relation between poor constructive thinking and psychosomatic disorders (e.g., Epstein & Katz,

1992; Valach & Epstein, 1995). In the same research we demonstrated that negative emotions are a mediating link between personality characteristics and physical ailments. When we entered emotions into a regression equation in which there had been a significant relation between constructive thinking and physical ailments, emotions completely displaced constructive thinking as a predictor of physical ailments.

Alice Epstein's book inspired one of my graduate students, Laurie Katz, to conduct a study under my supervision in which she investigated whether there is an unusual incidence of other cases like that of Alice Epstein in which transforming a CPP to a more adaptive personality resulted in an extremely unusual remission from a terminal stage of cancer (Katz & Epstein, 2005).

In the study, the scores on a Cancer-prone Personality Inventory (CPPI) of an exceptional cancer-recovered group were compared with the scores of two unexceptional recovered groups, an unexceptional cancer-recovered group, and an unexceptional heart-disease recovered group. The CPPI was constructed by creating a pool of items from the psychological and medical literature on a proposed CPP. The final items in the CPPI were those that most strongly contributed to the alpha reliability of the scale and were minimally redundant. The CPPI has 27 items and an alpha internal-consistency reliability coefficient of .90 to .95. The items in the CPPI describe someone who is reluctant to express emotions, who feels helpless, hopeless and lacking in commitment to an important goal, who is unassertive and unable to fulfill her own needs, yet eager to please others and fulfill their needs, who feels unwanted or unloved, who maintains a stoic façade of well-being despite her underlying misery, and who has a very negative self-image despite being reasonably successful. Such a person tends to be liked by everyone but herself.

In support of the hypothesis that mitigation of a cancer-prone personality is associated with unusual recoveries from cancer, the exceptional cancer-recovered group obtained higher CPPI scores for the reporting period preceding diagnosis and a greater decrease in CPPI scores from before to after recovery than the other recovered groups. After recovery the CTI scores of the two cancer groups no longer differed.

Of additional interest, both cancer groups reported more frequent and more intense stressful life events in the two-year period preceding diagnosis than the heart-disease group reported. This occurred to the greatest extent for stressful events concerning a loss or threatened loss of a close relationship. It is noteworthy that this is a condition widely considered likely to produce feelings of depression.

Implications of CEST for the Meaning of Dreams

The experiential system of CEST provides a different view about the nature of dreams than the Freudian unconscious. Freud regarded his book, *The Interpretation of Dreams* (1900/1950), as his most important achievement as in it he believed he had unlocked the secret of dreams and the operation of the unconscious mind.

As previously noted, according to CEST there is one thing wrong with Freud's understanding of the unconscious mind; he had the wrong unconscious. Freud's view of an unconscious mind that unrealistically operates according to primary process thinking is indefensible from an evolutionary perspective. This is because it is highly unlikely that the foundation of mental activity would be maladaptive and would require the addition of a conscious, rational mind for people to behave adaptively. Moreover, as nonhuman animals do not have a verbal, conscious, reasoning system, they would be left with only a wish-fulfilling, unrealistic unconscious mind that is incapable of adaptive action by itself. In contrast to Freud's conception of a maladaptive unconscious mind, the unconscious mind of CEST is in the form of an experiential system that is highly adaptive. This raises the question of how, if at all, the experiential system can account for the strangeness of dream content that is anything but realistic? It can do so by recognizing that the dream-mind operations in the manner of a degraded form of experiential processing as the result of the altered state of consciousness produced by sleep.

Based on principles in CEST and a research program, shortly to be described, CEST is in agreement with the following principles of dream formation proposed by Freud: association, displacement, symbolic representation, and condensation. However, there remain important differences between the two theories. CEST rejects wish fulfillment as the underlying motive for all and even most dreams. As previous noted, according to CEST, dreams simply reflect the degraded operation of experiential processing in the altered state of consciousness produced by sleep. If there is one major motivation that influences dream representations according to CEST, it is the superordinate need to control cortical excitation, which is consistent with Freud's view that the dream-work operates in a manner that normally protects sleep.

Dreams according to CEST are assumed to be influenced by the implicit and explicit thoughts of the day, including thoughts about the past and the future. For evolutionary considerations regarding the need to be alert to danger, fear-fulfillment in dreams is probably more prevalent than wish-fulfillment. Accordingly, most anxiety dreams are considered to be produced by thoughts related to real or imagined threats rather than to guilt reactions because of unacceptable wishes.

Displacement is extremely important in dreams according to CEST because cortical excitatory level can be controlled in most situations by displacement. That is, whatever level of displacement is necessary for managing a particular level of cortical excitation can be achieved by an appropriate level of displacement for maintaining sleep, with one exception. The exception is the occurrence of anxiety dreams that awaken the dreamer. In that case, the biological need to control cortical excitation within a homeostatic limit is maintained by aborting the dream and awakening the dreamer. Thus, according to CEST, the reason why displacement is extremely prevalent in dreams is not because it prevents awareness of taboo wishes, as Freud believed, and which is accepted in CEST as sometimes occurring, but more generally because it is considered to be a highly effective way of controlling cortical excitation in almost all situations.

According to CEST dreams are constructed in the following manner. Certain events and thoughts of the day, depending on their excitatory level as a result of their personal and emotional significance as well as the attention they automatically received for a variety of reasons including how surprizing they were become potential items for inclusion in dreams. The selection from this item-pool of candidates for inclusion in a dream is then determined by the combined influence of several variables including an item's excitatory strength, the strength of its associations with other relevant potential dream items, condensation, preference for certain symbolic representations based on past experience, and cohesion with other items in the construction of a narrative. In constructing the narrative, the dream work simply does the best it can to assimilate a variety of disparate potential dream representation into a story that has some coherence.

To investigate the operation of dreams in everyday life, I conducted a 10-year study of my own dreams by recording what I considered to be highly transparent dreams whose meaning was self-evident to me (Epstein, 1999).

Following is an example of the interpretation of a transparent dream and what I believe it reveals about the nature of dreams: I dreamed I was at a very expensive restaurant. I asked the waiter why no prices were on the menu. He said if I had to know the prices I did not belong in that restaurant. I tried to select something very modest. I chose a salad with a side dish of brains. The bill came to $69. I asked the waiter why it was so expensive. He said the salad is $4 and the brains are $65.

The day before the dream I was honored for my "scholarly achievements" by receiving the "Chancellors Medal," which is the highest award bestowed by the University of Massachusetts for academic achievement. I was surprised to receive the honor because I did not believe I was in the same league as others who had previously received it. While working on the lecture I had to give the next day, I received a call from a colleague who said he had discovered a wonderful place for trout fishing, and he asked me to go fly-fishing with him that evening. I would have loved to go, but I declined the invitation because I had to prepare my lecture. I had the fleeting thought that it was a mixed blessing to have achieved some measure of success. It further occurred to me that if I were even more successful, it could mean a change in lifestyle that would not necessarily be more attractive.

After awakening from the dream, I remembered my thought about being honored as a mixed blessing, which was followed by another thought that made me burst into laughter as the meaning of the dream became apparent to me. The thought was: "It may be too costly to have brains."

This dream is particularly interesting because of its creative use of metaphors. The very expensive restaurant that is beyond my means represents the thought that the honor bestowed on me is more than I deserve or can afford. The use of the brain metaphor appears to be a clever joke, but the apparent humor can be explained by a fortuitous association between the price of a meal and the price of success.

CONCLUSIONS

Cognitive-experiential self-theory (CEST) is an integrative global theory of personality that substitutes an adaptive unconscious processing system for the Freudian maladaptive unconscious system. The unconscious system of CEST is an associative learning system that humans share with other higher order animals. Because it adapts primarily by empirically learning from experience, the system is referred to in CEST as an "experiential system." Humans also uniquely process information with a "rational system," which is primarily a verbal reasoning system.

The influence of the experiential system on the rational system is considered particularly important in CEST, as it can account for the irrationality in the thinking of humans particularly when they attempt to solve problems concerning interpersonal relationships between individuals and between societies. According to CEST, the reason for this is that, despite their extraordinary ability to solve impersonal problems, humans are often poor at solving relationship problems because such problems are primarily in the domain of the experiential system whereas impersonal problems are primarily in the domain of the rational system. Thus, even when people attempt to reason logically and objectively about interpersonal relationships their reasoning is often biased by the influence of their experiential on their rational processing. This has had disastrous consequences throughout the course of history, as indicated by the prevalence of warfare. It also has ominous implications for the future, as the rational system has made it possible for humans to develop weaponry that can destroy all life on earth. The hope for the future is that humans will use their remarkable intelligence to solve the problems created by the interaction of their two processing systems.

REFERENCES

Abernathy, C. M. & Hamm, R. M. (1995). *Surgical intuition: What it is and how to get it*. Philadelphia, PA: Hanley & Belfus.

Alloy, L. B., & Abramson, L. Y. (1988). Depressive realism: Four theoretical perspectives. In L. B. Alloy (Ed.), *Cognitive processes in depression* (pp. 167–232). New York, NY: Guilford Press.

Allport, G. W. (1961). *Pattern and growth in personality*. New York, NY: Holt, Rinehart & Winston.

Bargh, J. A. (1989). Conditional automaticity: Varieties of automatic influence in social perception and cognition. In J. S. Uleman & J. A. Bargh (Eds.), *Unintended thought* (pp. 3–51). New York, NY: Guilford Press.

Bar-On, R. (1997). *Bar-On Emotional Quotient Inventory: Technical manual*. Toronto, Ontario, Canada: Multi-Health Systems.

Binion, R. (1976). *Hitler among the Germans*. DeKalb, H: Northern Illinois University Press.

Bleuler, M. (1978). *The schizophrenic disorders: Long-term patient and family studies*. S. M. Clemens (Trans.). New Haven CT: Yale University Press.

Bowers, M. B. Jr. (1974). *Retreat from sanity*. New York, NY: Human Sciences Press.

Bowlby, J. (1988). *A secure base*. New York, NY: Basic Books.

Bruner, J. (1961). *The process of education*. Cambridge, MA: Harvard University Press.

Catlin, G., & Epstein, S. (1992). Unforgettable experiences: The relation of life-events to basic beliefs about the self and world. *Social Cognition, 10*, 189–209.

Chaiken, S., & Maheswaren, D. (1994). Heuristic processing can bias systematic processing: Effects of source credibility, argument ambiguity, and task importance on attitude judgment. *Journal of Personality and Social Psychology, 66*, 460–473.

Costa, P. T., & McCrae, R. R. (1992). *NEO-PI-R: The revised NEO personality inventory*. Odessa, FL: Psychological Assessment Resources.

Denes-Raj, V., & Epstein, S. (1994). Conflict between experiential and rational processing: When people behave against their better judgment. *Journal of Personality and Social Psychology, 66*, 819–829.

Denes-Raj, V., Epstein, S., & Cole, J. (1995). The generality of the ratio-bias phenomenon. *Personality and Social Psychology Bulletin, 10*, 1083–1092.

Dijksterhuis, A. (2004). Think different: The merits of unconscious thought in preference development and decision making. *Journal of Personality and Social Psychology, 87*, 586–598.

Donovan, S., & Epstein, S. (1997). The difficulty of the Linda conjunction problem can be attributed to its simultaneous concrete and unnatural representation, and not to conversational implicature. *Journal of Experimental Social Psychology, 33*, 1–20.

Daus, C. S., & Ashkanasy, N. M. (2003). Will the real emotional intelligence stand up? On deconstructing the emotional intelligence "debate." *The Industrial-Organizational Psychologist, 41*, 69–72.

DeVita, V. T. Jr., Hellman, D., & Rosenberg, S. A. (1985). *Cancer: Principles and practice of oncology*. Philadelphia, PA: Lippincott.

Epstein, A. (1989). *Mind, fantasy, and healing*. New York: Delacorte. (This book is out of print. Copies can be obtained from Amazon.com or from Alice Epstein, 37 Bay Road, Amherst, MA 01002 by enclosing a check for $15, which includes postage).

Epstein, S. (1979a). Natural healing processes of the mind: I. Acute schizophrenic disorganization. *Schizophrenia Bulletin, 5*, 213–321

Epstein, S. (1979b). The ecological study of emotions in humans. In P. Pliner, K. R. Blankstein, & I. M. Spigel (Eds), *Advances in the study of communication and affect, Vol. 5: Perception of emotions in self and others* (pp. 47–83). New York, NY: Plenum Press.

Epstein, S. (1984). Controversial issues in emotion theory. In P. Shaver (Ed.), *Annual review of research in personality and social psychology* (pp. 64–87). Beverly Hills, CA: Sage.

Epstein, S. (1993a). Emotion and self-theory. In M. Lewis & J. Haviland (Eds.), *The handbook of rmotions*. New York, NY: Guilford Press.

Epstein, S. (1993b). Implications of cognitive-experiential self-theory for personality and developmental psychology. In D. Funder, R. Parke, C. Tomlinson-Keasey, & K. Wideman (Eds.), *Studying lives through time: Personality and development* (pp. 399–438). Washington, DC: American Psychological Association.

Epstein, S. (1994). Integration of the cognitive and the psychodynamic unconscious. *American Psychologist, 49*, 709–724,

Epstein, S. (1998a). *Constructive thinking: The key to emotional intelligence*. Westport, CT: Praeger.

Epstein, S. (1998b). Emotions and psychopathology from the perspective of cognitive-experiential self-theory. In W. E. Flack & J. D. Laird (Eds.), *Emotions and psychopathology: Theory and Research* (pp. 57–69). New York, NY: Oxford University Press.

Epstein, S. (1999). The interpretation of dreams from the perspective of cognitive-experiential self-theory. In J. A. Singer, & P. Salovey (Eds), *At play in the fields of consciousness: Essays in honor of Jerome L. Singer* (pp. 59–82). Mahway, NJ: Erlbaum.

Epstein, S. (2001). *Manual for the constructive thinking inventory*. Odessa, FL: Psychological Assessments Resources.

Epstein, S. (2003). Unconscious roots of Hitler's anti-Semitism. In J. A. Winer (Ed.), *The Annual of Psychoanalysis* (Vol. 31, pp. 47–61). Hillsdale, NJ: Analytic Press.

Epstein, S. (2010). Demystifying intuition: What it is, what it does, and how it does it. *Psychological Inquiry, 21*, 295–312.

Epstein, S. (in press a). *Cognitive-experiential self theory: An integrative theory of personality*. Oxford Press.

Epstein, S. (in press b). Emotional intelligence from the perspective of cognitive-experiential self-theory. *The International Journal of Transformative Emotional Intelligence.*

Epstein, S., Denes-Raj, V., & Pacini, R. (1995). The Linda problem revisited from the perspective of cognitive-experiential self-theory. *Personality and Social Psychology Bulletin, 21,* 1124–1138.

Epstein, S., Donovan, S., & Denes-Raj, V., (1999). The missing link in the paradox of the Linda conjunction problem: Beyond knowing and thinking of the conjunction rule, the intrinsic appeal of hueristic processing. *Personality and Social Psychology Bulletin, 25,* 204–214.

Epstein, S., & Katz, L. (1992). Coping ability, stress, productive load, and symptoms. *Journal of Personality and Social Psychology, 62,* 813–825.

Epstein, S., Lipson, A., Holstein, C., & Huh, E. (1992). Irrational reactions to negative outcomes: Evidence for two conceptual systems. *Journal of Personality and Social Psychology, 62,* 328–339.

Epstein, S., & Morling, B. (1995). Is the self motivated to do more than enhance and verify itself? In M. H. Kernis (Ed.), *Efficacy, agency, and self-esteem* (pp. 9–29). New York, NY: Plenum Press.

Epstein, S., & Pacini, R. (1999). Some basic issues regarding dual-process theories from the perspective of cognitive-experiential self-theory. In S. Chaiken & Y. Trope (Eds.), *Dual-process theories in social psychology* (pp. 462–482). New York, NY: Guilford Press.

Epstein, S., & Pacini., R. (2000–2001). The influence of visualization on intuitive and analytical information processing. *Imagination, Cognition, and Personality, 20,* 195–216.

Epstein, S., Pacini, R., Denes-Raj, V., & Heier, H. (1996). Individual differences in intuitive-experiential and analytical-rational thinking styles. *Journal of Personality and Social Psychology, 71,* 390–405.

Freud, S. (1900/1950). *The interpretation of dreams* (Brill, Trans.). New York, NY: Random House.

Freud, S. (1924/1960). *A general introduction to psychoanalysis* (Joan Riviere, Trans.). New York, NY: Washington Square Press.

Gallistel, C. R., & Gelman, R. (1992). Preverbal and verbal counting and computation. *Cognition, 44,* 43–74.

Gordon, R. A. (1997). Everyday life as an intelligence test. In D. K. Detterman (Ed.), *Intelligence, a multidisciplinary journal. Special issue: Intelligence and social policy.* (Guest editor: L. S. Gottfredson), *24,* 203–320.

Gottfredson, L. S. (1997). Why g matters: The complexity of everyday life. In D. K. Detterman (Ed.), *Intelligence, a multidisciplinary journal. Special issue: Intelligence and social policy.* (Guest editor: L. S. Gottfredson), *24,* 79–132.

Hitler, A. (1925/1971). *Mein Kampf* (Vol. I, R. Anheim, Trans.). Boston, MA: Houghton Mifflin.

Hixon, J. G., & Swann, W. B. (1993). When does introspection bare fruit? Self-reflection, self-insight, and interpersonal choices. *Journal of Personality and Social Psychology, 64,* 35–43.

Hollis, K. L. (1997). Contemporary research on Pavlovian conditioning, *American Psychologist, 52,* 956–965.

Hunter, J. E. (1983). Overview of validity generalization for the U.S. Employment Service. *USES Test Research Report, No. 43.* Washington, DC: U.S. Department of Labor, Employment, and Training Administration.

Hunter, J. E. (1986). Cognitive ability, cognitive aptitudes, job knowledge, and job performance. *Journal of Vocational Behavior, 29,* 340–362.

Hunter, J. E., & Hunter, R. F., (1984). Validity and utility of alternative predictors of job performance. *Psychological Bulletin, 96,* 72–98.

Jefferson, L. (1974). *These are my sisters.* Garden City, NY: Anchor Press.

Kahneman, D. (2003). A prospective on judgment and choice. Mapping bounded rationality. *American Psychologist, 58,* 697–720.

Kahneman, D., & Tversky, (1973). On the psychology of prediction. *Psychological Review, 80,* 237–251.

Kaplan, B. (1964). *The inner world of mental illness.* New York, NY: Harper & Row.

Katz, L., & Epstein, S. (2005). The relation of cancer-prone personality to exceptional recovery from cancer. *Advances in Mind Body Medicine, 21,* 1–15.

Kirkpatrick, L. A., & Epstein, S. (1992). Cognitive-experiential self-theory and subjective probability: Further evidence for two conceptual systems. *Journal of Personality and Social Psychology, 63,* 534–544.

Kohut, H. (1971). *The analysis of the self.* New York, NY: International Universities Press.

Kruglansky, A. W., Thompson, E. P., & Spiegel, S. (1999). Separate or equal? Bimodal notions of persuasion and a single process "uni-model." In S. Chaiken & E. Trope (Eds.), *Dual- process theories in social psychology* (pp. 293–313). New York, NY: Guilford Press.

Kurth, G. (1947). The Jew and Adolf Hitler. *Psychoanalytic Review, 16,* 11–32.

Laing, R. D. (1965). *The divided self.* Baltimore, MD: Penguin Books.

Locke, E. A., (2005). Why emotional intelligence is an invalid concept. *Journal of organizational behavior, 26,* 425–431.

Mayer, J. D., Salovey, P., Caruso, E. R., & Sitarenios, G. (2003). Measuring emotional intelligence with the MSCEIT V2.0. *Emotion, 3,* 97–105.

Miller, D. T., & Gunasegaram, S. (1990). Temporal order and the perceived mutability of events: Implications for blame assignment. *Journal of Personality and Social Psychology, 59,* 1111–1118.

Morling, B., & Epstein, S. (1997). Compromises produced by the dialectic between self-verification and self-enhancement. *Journal of Personality and Social Psychology, 73,* 1268–1283.

Nisbett, R., & Ross, L. (1980). *Human inference: Strategies and shortcomings of social judgment.* Englewood Cliffs, NJ: Prentice Hall.

Norris, P., & Epstein, S. (2011). An intuitive-experiential thinking style: Its facets and relations with objective and subjective criterion-measures. *Journal of Personality, 79,* 1043–1079.

Pacini, R., & Epstein, S. (1999a). The interaction of three facets of concrete thinking in a game of chance. *Thinking and reasoning, 5,* 303–325.

Pacini, R., & Epstein, S. (1999b). The relation of rational and experiential information processing styles to personality, basic beliefs, and the ratio-bias phenomenon. *Journal of Personality and Social Psychology, 76,* 972–987.

Pacini, R., Muir, F., & Epstein, S. (1998). Depressive realism from the perspective of cognitive-experiential self-theory. *Journal of Personality and Social Psychology, 74,* 1056–1068.

Pavlov, I. P. (1941). *Conditioned reflexes in psychiatry* (W. H. Gannt, Trans.). Madison, CT: International Universities Press.

Perry, J. W. (1974). *The far side of madness.* Englewood Cliffs, NJ: Prentice-Hall.

Reber, A. S. (1993). *Implicit learning and tacit knowledge.* New York, NY: Oxford University Press.

Rescorla, R. A., (1988). Pavlovian conditioning: It's not what you think it is. *American Psychologist, 43,* 151–160.

Rogers, C. R. (1951). *Client-centered therapy: Its current practice, applications, and theory.* Boston, MA: Houghton-Mifflin.

Salovey, P., & Mayer, J. D. (1989–1990). Emotional Intelligence. *Imagination, Cognition, and Personality, 9,* 185–211.

Silverman, J., (1970). When schizophrenia helps. *Psychology Today, 4,* 63–65.

Simon, H. A. (1992). What is an "explanation" of behavior? *Psychological Science, 3,* 150–161.

Swann, W. B. Jr. (1990). To be known or to be adored: The interplay of self-enhancement and self-verification. In R. M. Sorrentino & E. T. Higgins (Eds.), *Handbook of motivation and cognition: Foundations of social behavior* (Vol. 2, pp. 408–448). New York, NY: Guilford Press.

Taylor, S. E., & Brown, J. D. (1988). Illusion and wellbeing: A social psychological perspective on mental health. *Psychological Bulletin, 103,* 193–210.

Thorndike, E. L. (1927). The law of effect. *American Journal of Psychology, 29,* 212–222.

Tversky, A., & Kahneman, D. (1974). Judgment under uncertainty: Heuristics and biases. *Science, 185,* 1124–1131.

Tversky, A., & Kahneman, D. (1982). Judgments of and by representativeness. In D. Kahneman, P. Slovic, & A. Tversky (Eds.), *Judgment under uncertainty: Heuristics and biases.* New York, NY: Cambridge University Press.

Valach, L., & Epstein, S. (1995). *The relation of constructive thinking to mental and physical wellbeing in a middle-aged sample.* (Unpublished analyzed data)

Weschler, D. (1939). The measurement of adult intelligence. Baltimore, MD: Williams & Wilkins.

Wilson, T. D. (2002). *Strangers to ourselves: Discovering the adaptive unconscious.* Cambridge, MA: Harvard University Press.

Yanko, J., & Epstein, S. (2000). *The intuitive knowledge of ratios in children and interference by explanations.* (Unpublished analyzed data)

CHAPTER 6

Self-Regulatory Perspectives on Personality

CHARLES S. CARVER AND MICHAEL F. SCHEIER

Personality is a hard concept to pin down. It obviously is a broad concept, because personality impinges on almost all aspects of human behavior. This breadth is viewed differently by different theorists, of course. As a result, various people have devised many approaches to conceptualizing personality. The diversity in focus displayed by the chapters in Part I of this volume attests very clearly to that fact.

We were both trained as personality psychologists, but our background is relatively unusual for this field. Throughout our careers, a good part of our research interest has focused on a set of issues regarding the structure of behavior. These issues link the concept of personality and how it functions to a set of themes that might be regarded as belonging to the psychology of motivation. Our interest in how behavior occurs has taken us into a number of specific research domains—including studies of health-related behavior and coping with stress (e.g., Carver & Connor-Smith, 2010; Carver & Scheier, 2001; Carver, Scheier, & Segerstrom, 2010; Rasmussen, Scheier, & Greenhouse, 2009; Scheier, Carver, & Bridges, 2001) and studies of the dynamics underlying mood disorders (e.g., Carver, Johnson, & Joormann, 2008; Johnson, Carver, & Fulford, 2010). However, these explorations into specific

topics have almost always reflected a more general interest in the structure of behavior.

What we mean by "the structure of behavior" is reflected in questions such as these: What is the most useful way to think about how people create actions from their intentions, plans, and desires? Once people decide to do something, how do they stay on course until they finish? What is the relationship between people's values and their actions? What processes account for the existence of feelings, as people make their way through the world? How do people decide whether to enjoy the moment versus work for a longer-term goal?

As we have tried to work on such questions, we have consistently returned to the idea that people are self-regulatory beings. That is, most human behavior is an attempt to make something occur in action that is already held in mind. Similarly, the prime function of emotions is to serve as self-regulatory controls on what actions take place and with how much urgency. We did not invent the concepts of self-regulation ourselves, by any means, but we have found them compelling.

The self-regulatory principles we emphasize in our writings were not conceived as being a model of personality, and we do not claim that they cover the full range of phenomena covered by the word *personality*. However, we believe the principles do provide a useful *perspective* on personality. They suggest some implications about how personality is organized and expressed in people's actions. The principles also highlight some of the issues involved in successfully getting around in the

Preparation of this chapter was facilitated by grants from the National Cancer Institute (CA64710), the National Science Foundation (BCS0544617), and the National Heart, Lung, and Blood Institute (HL65111, HL65112, HL076852, and HL076858).

world. The principles we emphasize deal most explicitly with the "process" aspect of personality—the core functions that make everyone a little bit alike—but they also have implications for the individual differences that form a part of personality psychology.

This chapter is organized as a series of conceptual themes that reflect this self-regulatory perspective on personality. We start with basic ideas about the nature of behavior and some of the processes by which we believe behavior is regulated. We then turn to emotion—how we think it arises and a way in which two classes of affects differ from each other. This leads to a discussion of the fact that people sometimes are unable to do what they set out to do, and what follows from that problem. The next sections are more speculative and reflect emerging themes in thinking about behavior. The first deals with dual process models of self-regulation and how they embellish and complicate the picture presented earlier in the chapter. The second deals with dynamic systems and catastrophe theory as models for behavior and how such models may influence how people such as ourselves view self-regulation.

BEHAVIOR AS GOAL-DIRECTED AND FEEDBACK-CONTROLLED

The view we take on behavior begins with the process of feedback control. One of the roots of this idea is the broad conception of homeostatic mechanisms, which regulate diverse aspects of the body's physiological functioning (Cannon, 1932). Wiener (1948) coined the term *cybernetic* (from the Greek word meaning steersman) to characterize the overall functioning of this type of system. Cybernetic systems (whether mechanical, electronic, or living systems) regulate some current condition so as to stay "on course." These principles were applied to behavior by a number of writers in the 1960s and 70s (e.g., MacKay, 1966; Miller, Galanter, & Pribram, 1960; Powers, 1973).

The idea that the structure that underlies homeostasis may also underlie overt action is not very intuitive. An easy way to approach this idea, however, is to start with the more intuitive concept of goal. Everyone knows more or less what a goal is: a mental representation of a state the person is trying to attain. People have many goals at any given time, at varying levels of abstraction and importance. Most can be reached in many ways, and a given action can create movement toward very different goals.

Feedback Processes

Goals provide us an entry point into the application of feedback principles to behavior. More specifically, the processes entailed in approaching a goal illustrate the elements of feedback control. A feedback loop involves several sub-functions (MacKay, 1966; Miller et al., 1960; Powers, 1973; Wiener, 1948): an input, a reference value, a comparison, and an output (Figure 6.1). Think of the input as perception. Input is information about present circumstances. A reference value is a goal. The input is compared to the reference value. Any discrepancy detected is called an *error signal*. We treat the output here as a behavior, but sometimes the behavior is internal.

If the comparison detects no discrepancy, the output remains as it was. If a discrepancy is detected, the output changes. How detection of a discrepancy affects output depends on what kind of loop it is. In a discrepancy-reducing loop, the output acts to reduce the discrepancy, diminishing the error signal. Such an effect is seen in people's attempts to reach a valued goal, maintain a desired condition, or conform to a standard. There also are discrepancy-enlarging loops, in which movement occurs away from the reference value rather than toward it. The value in this case acts as a threat or an "anti-goal." In human behavior, a feared or disliked possible self would work in this way (Carver, Lawrence, & Scheier, 1999; Ogilvie, 1987). A discrepancy-enlarging loop senses existing conditions, compares them to the anti-goal, and enlarges the discrepancy.

Effects of discrepancy-enlarging processes in living systems are typically limited in some way or other. In some cases there may be a natural endpoint (e.g., sexual

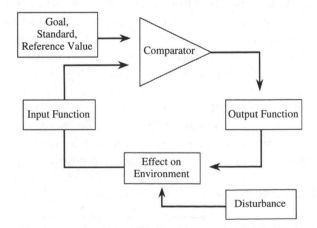

Figure 6.1   Schematic depiction of a feedback loop, the basic unit of cybernetic control. In such a loop, a sensed value is compared to a reference value or standard, and adjustments are made in an output function (if necessary) to shift the sensed value in the appropriate direction.

arousal prompts further increase in arousal to the point of orgasm, which ends the increase). Another possibility is that the discrepancy-enlarging process is constrained by discrepancy reducing processes. Put differently, acts of avoidance often lead into acts of approach. Imagine a person escaping a threat. Initially this is purely an escape. There may be a goal to approach, however, that simultaneously keeps the person distant from the threat. Thus, the tendency to avoid the threat is joined by the tendency to approach that goal. This pattern of dual influence defines active avoidance: An organism facing a feared stimulus picks a safer location to escape to, and approaches that location.

Feedback loops are ubiquitous in living systems. The feedback concept is most often applied to physiological systems, such as the homeostatic systems that maintain blood pressure and body temperature. We have adopted the view, however, that the same structural elements underlie the kinds of behaviors that are of interest to personality psychologists (Miller et al., 1960; Powers, 1973). Remember that personality emerges from a body that stays alive through feedback processes. Nature is a miser. If the same structure that keeps life moving forward can also yield more complex phenomena, there is no need to evolve a new kind of structure—the existing one will likely be used.

A few more points: It is easy to portray the elements of a feedback loop conceptually. In some cases (e.g., in electronic systems), it is also easy to point to each element. In other cases, this is harder. In some cases, feedback processes exist with no explicit representation of a reference value. The system regulates around a value, but no value is represented as a goal (Berridge, 2004; Carver & Scheier, 2002).

Another point concerns the use of homeostasis as an illustration of feedback processes. It is a convenient illustration, and it links the feedback concept to something that is understood about the body. Some people infer from this example, however, that feedback loops act only to create and maintain steady states. This is a misinference. Some goals *are* static end states. But others are dynamic and evolving (e.g., the goal of taking a week's vacation, the goal of raising a child to become a good citizen). In such cases, the "goal" is not the endpoint, but rather the entire process of traversing the changing trajectory of the activity. The feedback concept applies perfectly well to moving targets (Beer, 1995).

Finally, goals vary in abstractness. You may have the goal of being a good citizen, but you can also have the goal of recycling refuse, a narrower goal that contributes to being a good citizen. To recycle entails concrete goals: placing newspapers into containers and moving them to a pick-up location. Thus it is often said that goals form a hierarchy (Carver & Scheier, 1998; Powers, 1973; Toates, 2006; Vallacher & Wegner, 1987). Abstract goals are attained by the attaining of the concrete goals that help to define them.

Hierarchy of Goals and Action Qualities

It may be useful to consider some of these levels of abstraction in a bit more detail, as was portrayed some time ago by Powers (1973). Some kinds of relatively low-level goals are defined by brief *sequences* of action (Powers, 1973): for example, picking up a pen or walking across the room. Such sequences are fairly simple (though each can also be broken down into even simpler subcomponents of motor control, e.g., Rosenbaum, Meulenbroek, Vaughan, & Jansen, 2001). Sequences have something of a self-contained quality about them, and they require little monitoring once they are triggered.

Such sequences can be organized into more elaborate strings of actions, which Powers (1973) called *programs*. These strings of action are more planful and more effortful. They often require choices to be made at various points along the way, which depend on conditions that are encountered at those points. Programs thus follow the sort of logic one expects of a computer program. There is some blurring between these levels, however. Given repetition, programs can become quite familiar. If they become so familiar that they are executed all-at-a-piece without much monitoring, they probably are no longer programs, but instead have become sequences.

Programs are sometimes enacted in the service of broader guiding *principles*. These are more abstract qualities. Principles can provide a basis for making decisions at choice points within programs, and they can suggest that particular programs be undertaken or be refrained from. The term *principle* refers to the sorts of qualities that social psychologists often call values (Schwartz & Bilsky, 1990; Schwartz & Rubel, 2005). What defines a principle as a principle is its abstractness and broad applicability to diverse behaviors. Being a principle does not in itself imply anything about the direction of the resulting behavior. For example, one principle leads people to support affirmative action, a different principle leads people to oppose it (Reyna, Henry, Korfmacher, & Tucker, 2006).

Even values are not the end of potential complexity and abstraction, though. Patterns of values coalesce to form the essence of a person's sense of desired (and undesired) self, or a person's sense of desired (and undesired) community. These properties are very broad points of reference (goals) for behavioral conformity.

From the point of view of personality-social psychology, goals from the ideal self down through sequences can be thought of as common starting points for self-regulation. All of them serve as classes of values to try to approximate (or sometimes to deviate from). Any of them might be taken as the focal point for a given behavior (that is, the person could try to self-regulate at any of these levels). Once that value is adopted as a guide, lower levels are engaged automatically by the engagement of that one.

Thus, it is easy to imagine cases in which a person is behaving according to a principle (e.g., a moral or ethical value); it is easy to imagine cases in which the person is behaving according to a plan or program. It is also easy, however, to imagine cases in which the person acts impulsively and spontaneously, without regard to either principle or plan. In all of these cases, the physical movements involved in the act are being managed by systems that are automatically engaged by whichever level of control is in charge. Later in the chapter we reexamine this idea, and consider some potentially important differences among these various levels of abstraction.

Goals and the Self

It will be apparent from the foregoing that goals are not equivalent in their importance. The higher you go into the person's organization among goals and values, the more fundamental to the overriding sense of self are the qualities encountered. Thus, goal qualities at higher levels would appear to be intrinsically more important than those at lower levels.

Goals at a given level are not necessarily equivalent to one another in importance, however. In a hierarchical arrangement there are at least two ways in which importance accrues to a goal. First, the more directly an action contributes to attainment of some highly valued goal at a more abstract level, the more important is that action. Second, an act that contributes to the attainment of several goals at once is thereby more important than an act that contributes to the attainment of only one goal.

Considering the relative importance of goals brings up the concept of self. In contemporary theory the self-concept has several aspects. One is the structure of knowledge a person has about his or her personal history. Another is a set of beliefs about who one is now. Another

is the plans or images of potential selves that are used to guide movement from the present into the future. A broad implication of the self-regulatory view on personality is that the self—indeed, personality—consists partly of a person's goals.

Approach and Avoidance

The distinction made a little earlier in the chapter between discrepancy reducing and discrepancy enlarging loops echoes a distinction made in other literatures between approach behavior and avoidance behavior. Incentives are approached by systems that close discrepancies between current conditions and the incentives. Threats are avoided by systems that enlarge discrepancies between current conditions and the threats. The logic of feedback self-regulatory processes thus provides a way to think about this fundamental dichotomy among motivations, a dichotomy that plays a key role in many other ideas about motivation.

This dichotomy has become prominent again in recent times (e.g., Elliot, 2008). One literature that emphasizes this dichotomy stems from a group of theories that are biological in focus, with research bases that ranges from animal conditioning and behavioral pharmacology (Gray, 1987b) to studies of human brain activity (Davidson, 1992). These theories assume that two core biological systems (or more) are involved in regulating behavior.

A system managing approach behavior in response to incentives has been called the behavioral activation system (Cloninger, 1987; Fowles, 1980), behavioral approach system (Gray, 1987a, 1990), behavioral engagement system (Depue, Krauss, & Spoont, 1987), the behavioral facilitation system (Depue & Iacono, 1989), and sometimes the incentive system. Another, dealing with withdrawal or avoidance in response to threats, has been called behavioral inhibition system (Cloninger, 1987; Gray, 1987a, 1990), withdrawal system (Davidson, 1992), and sometimes threat system. The incentive system and the threat system are often regarded as relatively independent, with different areas of the cortex being differentially involved in their functioning.

FEEDBACK PROCESSES AND ORIGINS OF AFFECT

We turn now to another aspect of self-regulation: emotion. Here we add a layer of complexity that differs greatly from the complexity represented by a hierarchical structure of action. Again the organizing principle is feedback control. But now the control is over a different quality.

What are feelings, and what makes them exist? Many theorists have analyzed the information that feelings provide and the situations in which affect arises (see, e.g., Frijda, 1986; Lazarus, 1991; Ortony, Clore, & Collins, 1988; Roseman, 1984; Scherer & Ekman, 1984). The question we address here is slightly different from those concerns: Our question is what is the internal mechanism by which feelings arise?

Many different kinds of answers to this question have been offered, ranging from neurobiological (e.g., Davidson, 1992) to cognitive (Ortony et al., 1988). We have proposed an answer that focused on what appear to be some of the functional properties of affect (Carver & Scheier, 1990, 1998, 1999a, 1999b).

Velocity Control

We suggest that feelings arise as a consequence of a feedback process that operates simultaneously with the behavior-guiding process and in parallel to it. It operates automatically and without supervision. The easiest characterization of what this second process is doing is that it is checking on how well the first process is doing. The input for this second loop thus is the *rate of progress in the action system over time*. (We focus first on discrepancy-reducing loops, then consider enlarging loops.)

Consider a physical analogy. Action implies a change between states. Thus, behavior is analogous to distance. If the action loop controls distance, and if the affect loop assesses the action loop's progress, then the affect loop is controlling the psychological analog of velocity, the first derivative of distance over time. If this analogy is meaningful, the perceptual input to the affect loop would be the first derivative over time of the input used by the action loop.

Input alone does not create affect; a given rate of progress has different affective effects in different contexts. We argue that this input is compared to a reference value (cf. Frijda, 1988), as in other feedback systems. In this case, the reference is an acceptable or expected rate of behavioral discrepancy reduction. As in other feedback loops, the comparison checks for deviation from the standard. If there is a discrepancy, the output function changes.

We believe that the error signal in this loop is manifest as affect, a positive or negative valence. A rate of progress below the criterion creates negative affect. A rate exceeding the criterion creates positive affect. In essence, feelings with a positive valence mean you are doing better at something than you need to, and feelings with a negative valence mean you are doing worse than you need to (for detail, see Carver & Scheier, 1998, Chapters 8 and 9). The absence of affect means being neither ahead nor behind.

The plausibility of this idea is suggested indirectly by resemblances between it and findings from research in two bodies of work in neuropsychology and related fields. One of these bodies of work concerns the existence of timing devices in the nervous system. Our view is predicated on the existence of an ability to monitor change over time. This requires a representation of time, and it is important to know that neural structures do exist that represent time in some manner or other (e.g., Handy, Gazzaniga, & Ivry, 2003; Ivry & Richardson, 2002; Ivry & Spencer, 2004).

A second source of indirect support concerns the detection of discrepancies between actual and expected events. Our affect model assumes that discrepancies above and below a velocity criterion are detected in some manner. Recent views of the function of dopaminergic circuits appear to point to an analogous function. Specifically, dopaminergic neurons respond to rewards, but they respond more intensely when a reward occurs unexpectedly than when it is expected. Their responses diminish when an expected reward fails to occur (Schultz, 2000, 2006). This pattern appears to indicate that dopaminergic neurons are involved in detecting when things are going better than expected and worse than expected (see also Holroyd & Coles, 2002). Though this is not precisely the point of our view (which deals with progress rather than outcome), it has a strong parallelism to it.

What determines the criterion value for the velocity loop? There surely are many influences. The criterion may depend on how one frames the action to oneself (Brendl & Higgins, 1996). If the activity is unfamiliar, what is used as a velocity criterion probably is quite tentative and easily changed. If the activity is familiar, however, the criterion is likely to reflect accumulated experience, in the form of an expected rate. Sometimes the criterion is more likely to be a "desired" or "needed" rate.

The criterion can also change. We think that change in rate criterion in a relatively familiar behavior domain occurs relatively slowly. Still, repeated overshoot of the criterion automatically yields an upward drift of the criterion (e.g., Eidelman & Biernat, 2007); repeated undershoots yield a downward drift. Repeated overshoots result automatically in an upward drift, repeated undershoots result in a downward drift (see Carver & Scheier, 2000, for greater detail). A somewhat ironic consequence of such a recalibration would be to keep the balance of a person's emotional experience (positive to negative, aggregated across a span of time) relatively similar, even when the rate criterion has changed considerably over time.

Research Evidence

This line of thought is also supported directly by research evidence. Here are a few examples. Hsee and Abelson (1991), who came independently to the velocity hypothesis, studied velocity and satisfaction. In one example, participants read descriptions of paired hypothetical scenarios and indicated which they would find more satisfying. For example, would they be more satisfied if their class standing had gone from the 30th percentile to the 70th over the past 6 weeks, or if it had done so over the past 3 weeks? For positive outcomes, they preferred improving to a high outcome over a constant high outcome; they preferred a fast velocity over a slow one; and they preferred fast small changes to slower larger changes. When the change was negative (e.g., salaries got worse) they preferred a constant low salary to a salary that started high and fell to that same low level; they preferred slow falls to fast falls; and they preferred large slow falls to small fast falls.

We conducted a study that conceptually replicates aspects of these findings, but with an event that was personally experienced rather than hypothetical (Lawrence, Carver, & Scheier, 2002). We manipulated success feedback on an ambiguous task over an extended period. The patterns of feedback converged, such that Block 6 was identical for all subjects at 50% correct. Subjects in a neutral condition had 50% on the first and last block, and 50% average across all blocks. Others had positive change in performance, starting poorly and gradually improving. Others had negative change, starting well and gradually worsening. All rated their mood before starting and again after Block 6 (which they didn't realize ended the session). Those whose performances were improving reported mood improvement, those whose performances were deteriorating reported mood deterioration, compared to those with a constant performance.

Another study that appears to bear on this view of affect, although not having this purpose in mind, was reported by Brunstein (1993). It examined subjective well-being among college students over the course of an academic term, as a function of several perceptions, including perception of progress toward goals. Of particular interest at present, perceived progress at each measurement point was strongly correlated with concurrent well being.

Cruise Control Model

Although the idea described above may sound complex, the system we are arguing for acts much the same as another device that is well known to most readers: the cruise control on a car. To recap the idea, if you are moving too slowly toward a goal, negative affect arises. You react by putting more effort into your action, trying to speed up. If you're going faster than you need to, positive affect arises, and you pull back effort and coast. A car's cruise control is very similar. You come to a hill, which slows you down. The cruise control responds by delivering more gas to the engine, to bring the speed back up. If you come across the crest of a hill and roll downhill too fast, the system restricts the gas, which eventually drags the speed back down.

This analogy is intriguing, because it concerns regulation of the very quality we believe the affect system is regulating: velocity. It's also intriguing that the analogy incorporates a similar asymmetry in the consequences of deviating from the set point. That is, both in a car's cruise control and in human behavior, going too slow calls for investing greater effort and resources. Going too fast does not. It calls only for pulling back on resources. That is, the cruise control doesn't apply the brakes, it just cuts back on the gasoline. In this way it permits the car to coast gradually back to its velocity set point. In the same fashion, people don't respond to positive affect by trying to make it go away, but just by easing off.

The idea that people increase effort when they are lagging behind is not controversial. In contrast, the idea that people reduce effort when they are doing unexpectedly well is not very intuitive. Does positive affect actually lead people to withdraw effort? What limited information exists on this question suggests that it does. Melton (1995) found that people in a good mood performed worse than control subjects on syllogisms. A variety of ancillary data led him to conclude that the people in good moods did worse because they were expending less effort. In another study, Mizruchi (1991) found that professional basketball teams in playoffs tend to lose games immediately after winning games, but it is unclear whether the initially winning team slacked off, the initially losing team tried harder, or both.

In a series of studies that were far less ambiguous, Louro, Pieters, and Zeelenberg (2007) explicitly examined the role of positive feelings resulting from surging ahead in multiple-goal pursuit. Across three studies, they found that when people were relatively close to a goal, positive feelings prompted a decrease in effort toward that goal and a shift of effort toward an alternate goal. As a final example, Fulford, Johnson, Llabre, and Carver (2010) conducted an experience-sampling study in which participants reported on three different goals three times a day for 21 consecutive days. Overall, unexpectedly high progress with respect to a given goal in a given time block led to reduced effort toward that goal in the following time block.

Affect From Discrepancy-Enlarging Loops

Thus far discussion has been restricted to the context of approach. Now we turn to attempts to avoid, attempts to not-be or not-do something, what we characterized previously as discrepancy-enlarging loops. The view just outlined rests on the idea that positive affect results when a behavioral system is making rapid progress in doing what it is organized to do. The systems we have considered thus far are organized to reduce discrepancies. There is no obvious reason, though, why the logic should not apply as well to systems organized to enlarge discrepancies. If that kind of a system is making rapid progress doing what it is organized to do, there should be positive affect. If it is doing poorly, there should be negative affect.

Thus, in our view both approach and avoidance have the potential to induce positive feelings (by doing well), and both have the potential to induce negative feelings (by doing poorly). But doing well at moving *toward an incentive* is not quite the same as doing well at moving *away from a threat*. Thus, the two positives may not be quite the same, nor may the two negatives.

Drawing in part on insights from Higgins (e.g., 1987, 1996) and his collaborators, we posit two sets of affects, one relating to approach, the other to avoidance (Carver & Scheier, 1998). Approach gives rise to such positive affects as eagerness, excitement, and elation, and also to such negative affects as frustration, anger, and sadness (Carver, 2004; Carver & Harmon-Jones, 2009a). Avoidance gives rise to such negative affects as fear, guilt, and anxiety, and also to such positive affects as relief and contentment (Carver, 2009).

Affect and Action: Two Facets of a Single Event in Time

This two-layered viewpoint implies a natural connection between affect and action. That is, if the input function of the affect loop is a sensed rate of progress in action, the output function of the affect loop must be a change in the rate of progress in that action. Thus, the affect loop has a direct influence on what occurs in the action loop.

What does adjust the rate of progress mean? In some cases it means literally change velocity. If you are behind, go faster. Some adjustments are less straightforward. The rates of many behaviors in which personality–social psychologists are interested are not defined in terms of literal motion. Rather, they're defined in terms of choices among actions, even potential programs of action. For example, increasing your velocity on a reading assignment may mean choosing to spend a weekend working rather than playing. Increasing your rate of manifestation of kindness means choosing to perform an action that reflects that value. Thus, adjustment in rate must often be translated into other terms, such as concentration or reallocation of time and effort.

Despite this complexity in implementing changes in rate, it should be apparent from this description that the action system and the velocity system must work in concert with one another. Both are involved in the flow of action. The regulation provided by these systems thus forms a two-layered array (Carver & Scheier, 1998, 1999a, 1999b), analogous to position and velocity controls in a two-layered engineering control system (e.g., Clark, 1996). Such a system in engineering has the quality of responding both quickly and accurately (without undue oscillation). The simultaneous functioning of the two layers likely has the same broad consequence for human behavior.

The combination of quickness and stability in responding is desirable in many of the devices engineers deal with. It is also desirable in people. A person with highly reactive emotions is prone to overreact, and oscillate behaviorally. A person who is emotionally unreactive is slow to respond even to urgent events. A person whose reactions are between those extremes responds quickly but without overreaction and oscillation.

For biological entities, being able to respond quickly yet accurately confers a clear adaptive advantage. We believe this combination of quick and stable responding is a consequence of having both behavior-managing and affect-managing control systems. Affect causes people's responses to be quicker (because this control system is time sensitive); as long as the affective system is not overresponsive, the responses are also stable.

AFFECT ISSUES

There are several ways in which this model of the origins of affect differs from other viewpoints bearing on emotion. At least two of the differences are worth noting explicitly.

Dimensions of Affective Experience

One difference concerns dimensionality in the structure of affect. Some theories (though surely not all) treat affects as aligning along dimensions. Theories differ, however, in what the basis for the dimensionality is. One popular view holds that valence is the determinant of the dimensional structure. That is, some affects form a dimension of positive emotionality and others form a dimension of negative emotionality (Cacioppo, Gardner, & Berntson, 1999; Lang, Bradley, & Cuthbert, 1990; Watson, Wiese, Vaidya, & Tellegen, 1999).

Our view, in contrast, is that the nature of the underlying motivational process is the determinant of dimensional structure. Thus, affects are arrayed as pertaining to approach of incentives or as pertaining to avoidance of threats. Though this view may be less known, we are not the only ones to have taken this position. Roseman (1984) argued similarly that joy and sadness are related to appetitive (moving-toward) motives, whereas relief and distress are related to aversive (moving-away-from) motives. Rolls (2005) arrayed emotions in terms of occurrence versus omission of either reward or punishment. We have elsewhere (Carver & Harmon-Jones, 2009) suggested that this array is most easily viewed in terms of two dimensions of variability pertaining to two classes of event (reward, punishment). Each dimension then would range from highest probability (occurrence) to lowest probability (omission).

Is there any evidence linking positive affects to the threat avoidance system or negative affects to the incentive approach system? Yes. For example, there is evidence, albeit limited, that positive feelings of calmness and relief (as situationally relevant) relate to avoidance motivation (Carver, 2009; Higgins, Shah, & Friedman, 1997). There is far more evidence that links sadness to failure of approach (for reviews see Carver, 2004; Higgins, 1996). There is also a good deal of evidence linking the approach system to the negative affect of anger (Carver & Harmon-Jones, 2009). Although it is clear that diverse kinds of negative feeling qualities coalesce with one another in mood states (Watson, 2009), the evidence does not make that case with regard to situation-specific affective responses.

This issue is an important one, because it has implications for any attempt to identify a conceptual mechanism underlying the creation of affect. The view that argues for two unipolar dimensions assumes that greater activation of a system translates to more affect of that valence (or more potential for affect of that valence). If the approach system relates both to positive and to negative feelings, however, this direct transformation of system activation to affect is not tenable. A conceptual mechanism is needed that naturally addresses both valences within the approach function (and, separately, within the avoidance function). The mechanism described here does so.

Counterintuitive Effect of Positive Affect

A second issue also differentiates this model from most other views (Carver, 2003; Carver & Scheier, 2009). Recall our argument that affect reflects the error signal from a comparison in a feedback loop. If it reflects an error signal, affect is a signal to adjust rate of progress. This would be true whether the rate is above the criterion or below it—that is, whether affect is positive or negative. For negative feelings, this is quite intuitive. The first response to negative feelings about something is usually to try harder. If the person tries harder—and if more effort (or better effort) increases progress—the negative affect diminishes or ceases.

For positive feelings, prediction is counterintuitive. In this model, positive feelings arise when things are going better than they need to. But the feelings still reflect a discrepancy (albeit a positive one), and the function of a negative feedback loop is to keep discrepancies small. Such system is organized in such a way that it "wants" to see neither negative nor positive affect. Either quality (deviation from the standard in either direction) would lead to change in output that would eventually reduce it.

This view holds that people who exceed the criterion rate of progress (and who thus have positive feelings) will automatically tend to reduce subsequent effort in this domain. They will "coast" a little—ease back. This prediction derived from a consideration of feedback principles, but a similar argument was made on other grounds by Izard (1977, p. 257; Izard & Ackerman, 2000, p. 258). Earlier in the chapter we described several sources of evidence that offer support for this view.

We should be clear that our position is that expending greater effort to catch up when behind, and coasting when ahead, are both specific to the goal domain to which the affect is attached, which is usually the goal from which the affect arises in the first place. We do not argue that positive affect creates a tendency to coast *in general,* but rather with respect to the activity producing the positive feelings. We should also be clear that we are talking about the current, ongoing episode of action. We are *not* arguing that positive affect makes people less likely to do the behavior later on.

Skepticism about the idea that positive affect (or getting ahead) leads to coasting stems in part from the fact that it is hard to see why a process would be built into the organism that limits positive feelings—indeed, dampens them. We see at least two bases for this. The first lies in a basic biological principle: it is adaptive not to spend energy needlessly. Coasting prevents this. Indeed, Brehm built an entire motivational theory around the argument that people engage only as much effort as is needed to accomplish a given task, and no more (e.g., Brehm & Self, 1989; Wright & Kirby, 2001).

A second basis for the existence of such a function stems from the fact that people have multiple simultaneous concerns. Given multiple concerns, people do not optimize their outcome on any one of them, but "satisfice" (Simon, 1953)—do a good enough job on each concern to deal with it satisfactorily. This permits them to handle the many concerns adequately, rather than just any one of them. Coasting facilitates satisficing. A tendency to coast with respect to some goal virtually defines satisficing regarding that particular goal. A tendency to coast also fosters satisficing for a broader set of goals, by allowing easy shift to other domains at little or no cost (see Carver, 2003, for detail).

RESPONDING TO ADVERSITY: PERSISTENCE AND GIVING UP

In earlier descriptions of the origin of affect, we typically suggested that a single process yields two subjective experiences as readouts: one is affect, the other is a sense of confidence versus doubt. We turn now to confidence and doubt—expectancies for the immediate future—focusing on their behavioral and cognitive manifestations.

One likely consequence of momentary doubt is a search for more information. We have often suggested that when people experience adversity in trying to move toward goals, they periodically interrupt efforts, to assess in a more deliberative way the likelihood of a successful outcome (e.g., Carver & Scheier, 1990, 1998). In effect, people suspend the behavioral stream, step outside it, and evaluate in a more deliberated way. This may happen once, or often. It may be brief, or it may take a long time. In making this assessment people presumably depend heavily on memories of prior outcomes in similar situations. They may also consider additional resources

they might bring to bear, alternative approaches that they might take, and social comparison information (Wills, 1981; Wood, 1989).

These thoughts sometimes influence the expectancies with which people move forward. When people retrieve relatively "chronic" expectancies from memory, the information already *is* expectancies, summaries of outcomes of previous behavior. In some cases, however, the process is more complex. People bring to mind possibilities for changing the situation and evaluate their consequences, perhaps by playing the possibility through mentally as a behavioral scenario (cf. Taylor & Pham, 1996). Doing this can lead to conclusions that influence expectancies. ("If I try doing it this way instead of that way, it should work better." "This is the only thing I can see to do, and it will just make the situation worse.")

It seems reasonable that this mental simulation engages some of the same processing mechanism as handles affect creation during overt behavior. When your progress is temporarily stalled, playing through a confident and optimistic scenario yields a higher rate of progress than is currently being experienced. The affect loop thus yields a more optimistic outcome assessment than is being derived from current action. If the scenario is negative and hopeless, it indicates a further reduction in progress, and the loop yields further doubt.

Behavioral Manifestations

Whether stemming from the immediate flow of experience or from a more thorough introspection, people's expectancies are reflected in their behavior. This general theme is fully embedded in contemporary psychology (e.g., Bandura, 1986; Carver & Scheier, 1990, 1998, 1999a; Klinger, 1975; Wortman & Brehm, 1975). If people expect a successful outcome, they continue exerting effort toward the goal. If doubts are strong enough, the result is an impetus to disengage from effort, and potentially from the goal itself. This theme—divergence in behavioral response as a function of expectancies—clearly is an important one, applying to a surprisingly broad range of literatures (see Chapter 11 of Carver & Scheier, 1998).

Sometimes the disengagement that follows from doubt is overt. Sometimes disengagement instead takes the form of mental disengagement—off-task thinking, daydreaming, and so on. Although this can sometimes be useful (self-distraction from a feared stimulus may permit anxiety to abate temporarily), it can also create problems. Under time pressure, mental disengagement can impair performance, as time is spent on task-irrelevant thoughts.

Often mental disengagement cannot be sustained, as situational cues force the person to re-confront the problematic goal. In such cases, the result is a phenomenology of repetitive negative rumination, which often focuses on self-doubt and perceptions of inadequacy. This cycle is both subjectively unpleasant and performance-impairing.

Is Disengagement Good or Bad?

Is the disengagement tendency good or bad? Both and neither (Miller & Wrosch, 2007; Wrosch, Miller, Scheier, & Brun de Pontet, 2007). On the one hand, disengagement (at some level, at least) is an absolute necessity. Disengagement is a natural and indispensable part of self-regulation (cf. Klinger, 1975). If people are ever to turn away from unattainable goals, to back out of blind alleys, they must be able to disengage, to give up and start over somewhere else.

The importance of disengagement is particularly obvious with regard to concrete, low-level goals: People must be able to remove themselves from literal blind alleys and wrong streets, give up plans that have become disrupted by unexpected events, even spend the night in the wrong city if they miss the last plane home. Disengagement is also important, however, with regard to more abstract and higher-level goals. It can be important to disengage and move on with life after the loss of close relationships (e.g., Orbuch, 1992; Stroebe, Stroebe, & Hansson, 1993). People sometimes must even be willing to give up values that are deeply embedded in the self, if those values create too much conflict and distress in their lives.

However, there are many ways in which adaptive functions can become problems (Carver & Scheier, 1998). Sometimes people stop trying too soon. A complete lack of persistence can create serious problems, as the person rarely accomplishes anything. It is also possible to hold onto goals too long, thereby preventing oneself from taking adaptive steps toward new goals. Both continued effort and giving up are necessary parts of the experience of adaptive self-regulation. Each plays an important role in the flow of behavior.

Importance Can Impede Disengagement

Disengagement sometimes is precluded by situational constraints. However, another, broader aspect of this problem stems from the idea that behavior is hierarchically organized, with goals increasingly important higher in the hierarchy, and thus harder to disengage from.

Presumably disengaging from concrete values is often easy. Lower-order goals vary, however, in how closely they link to values at a higher level, and thus how important they are. To disengage from low-level goals that are tightly linked to higher-level goals causes discrepancy enlargement at the higher level. These higher order qualities are important, even central to one's life. One cannot disengage from them, or disregard them, or tolerate large discrepancies between them and current reality, without reorganizing one's value system (Greenwald, 1980; Kelly, 1955; McIntosh & Martin, 1992; Millar, Tesser, & Millar, 1988). In such a case, disengagement from even very concrete behavioral goals can be quite difficult.

Now recall again the affective consequences of being in this situation. The desire to disengage was prompted by unfavorable expectancies. These expectancies are paralleled by negative affect. In this situation, then, the person experiences negative feelings (because of an inability to make progress toward the goal) and is unable to do anything about the feelings (because of an inability to give up). This kind of situation—continued commitment to unattainable goals—is a sure prescription for distress.

Watersheds, Disjunctions, and Bifurcations Among Responses

An issue that bears some further mention is the divergence of the behavioral and cognitive responses to favorable versus unfavorable expectancies in this model. We have long argued for a psychological watershed among responses to adversity (Carver & Scheier, 1981). One set of responses consists of continued comparisons between present state and goal, and continued efforts. The other set consists of disengagement from comparisons and quitting. Just as rainwater on a mountain ridge ultimately flows to one side of the ridge or the other, so do behaviors ultimately flow to one of these sets or the other.

Our initial reason for taking this position stemmed largely from several demonstrations that self-focused attention creates diverging effects on information seeking and behavior as a function of expectancies of success. We are not the only ones to have emphasized a disjunction among responses, however. A number of others have also done so, for reasons of their own. Perhaps the best known is the reactance–helplessness integration of Wortman and Brehm (1975). They made the argument that threat to control produces attempts to regain control and that perceptions of lost control produce helplessness. Brehm and his collaborators (Brehm & Self, 1989; Wright & Brehm,

1989) subsequently went on to embellish this view. Not all theories about persistence and giving up yield this dichotomy among responses. The fact that some do, however, is interesting. It becomes more so a bit later on in the chapter.

TWO-MODE MODELS OF SELF-REGULATION

Earlier in the chapter we distinguished between sequences of action that seem to occur more or less all-at-a-piece when begun, and programs and principles of action that appear to require more decision making and planning. At that time, we noted the boundary between the more automatic and the less automatic as a matter of differences in level of abstraction of the action goal. Now we look at this boundary in a somewhat different way. First, however, we need to take an excursion into some additional issues, issues that at first seem quite unrelated to anything discussed thus far.

During the past two decades, a variety of changes have occurred in how people view cognition and action. The implicit assumption that behavior is generally managed in a top-down, directive way has been challenged. Questions have been raised about the role of consciousness in many kinds of action. Interest has arisen in the idea that the mind has both explicit and implicit representations. These various issues have also influenced how we think about some of the ideas we have been using.

Dual Process Models

Several literatures have developed around the idea that there are two partially distinct ways of experiencing the world (Carver et al., 2008), which result in different patterns of learning (Daw, Niv, & Dayan, 2005) and different sorts of action. In personality psychology, Epstein (e.g., 1973, 1994, this volume) has long advocated such a view. He argues that people experience reality via two systems. What he calls a *rational* system operates mostly consciously, uses logical rules, is verbal and deliberative, and thus is fairly slow. In contrast, the *experiential* system is intuitive and associative in nature. It provides a quick and dirty way of assessing and reacting to reality. It relies on salient information and uses shortcuts and heuristics. It functions automatically and quickly. It is considered to be emotional (or at least very responsive to emotions) and nonverbal.

The experiential system is presumably older and more primitive neurobiologically. It dominates when speed is needed (as when a situation is emotionally charged) or when the behavior is well learned. The rational system evolved later, providing a more cautious, analytic, planful way of proceeding. Operating in that way has important advantages, provided there is sufficient time to think things through. Both systems are presumed to be always at work, jointly determining behavior. The extent of each one's influence varies according to both situational and dispositional variables.

A model in many ways similar to this was proposed by Metcalfe and Mischel (1999), drawing on decades of work on delay of gratification. Metcalfe and Mischel proposed that two systems influence self-restraint. One they called a *hot* system: emotional, impulsive, and reflexive. The other they called a *cool* system: strategic, flexible, slower, and unemotional. How people respond to difficult situations depends on which system is in charge.

There are also several two-mode theories in social psychology (Chaiken & Trope, 1999). The essence of such a view has existed for a long time in the literature of persuasion. Strack and Deutsch (2004) have recently extended this reasoning more broadly into the range of behavioral phenomena of interest to social psychologists. They proposed that overt behavior is a joint output of two simultaneously operating systems that they termed *reflective* and *impulsive*. Again, there are differences in the operating characteristics of the systems, which lead to differences in behavior. The reflective system anticipates the future, makes decisions on the basis of those anticipations, and forms intentions. It is planful and wide-ranging in its search for relevant information. It is restrained and deliberative. The impulsive system acts spontaneously when its schemas or production systems are sufficiently activated. It acts without consideration for the future or for broader implications or consequences of the action.

Two-mode thinking has also been influential in developmental psychology. Rothbart and her colleagues have argued for the existence of three temperament systems: two for reactive approach and reactive avoidance, and a third termed *effortful control* (e.g., Derryberry & Rothbart, 1997; Rothbart, Ahadi, & Evans, 2000; Rothbart & Posner, 1985; see also Nigg, 2000). Effortful control is reflected in being able to suppress approach when approach is situationally inappropriate. Effortful control is superordinate to approach and avoidance temperaments. The label *effortful* conveys the sense that this is an executive, planful activity, entailing the use of cognitive resources beyond those needed to react impulsively.

Hierarchical Structure Reexamined

Thus, several theorists suggest that the mind functions in two modes (indeed, the views described here are far from being an exhaustive list). All promote the view that a deliberative mode of functioning uses symbolic and sequential processing and thus is relatively slow; all suggest that a more impulsive or reactive mode of functioning uses associationist processing and is relatively fast. Many of the theories suggest that the two modes are semi-autonomous in their functioning, competing with each other to influence actions. Indeed, many point to situational variables that influence which mode dominates at a given time.

These kinds of ideas have begun to influence our own thinking about the hierarchy of control proposed by Powers (1973) that we have for years used as a conceptual heuristic. We said earlier that programs of action entail decisions. They seem to be managed top-down, using effortful processing. Planfulness, an element of programs, is also a common characterization of behavior managed by the reflective system. It seems reasonable to map program-level control onto the deliberative, reflective mode of functioning.

In contrast to this deliberative quality, well-learned *sequences* occur in a relatively automatic stream once they are triggered. Sequences (along with lower levels of control) are necessarily evoked during the execution of programs. That is, programs cannot be carried out without the involvement of all lower levels of control. However, perhaps sequences can also be triggered more autonomously, without being linked in any way to efforts toward a higher-level goal. Sequences may be triggered merely by the activation of strong associations in memory by cues of the moment. In such cases, the operating characteristics of sequence execution would seem akin to those of the reactive mode of functioning.

In the past we have often noted that the level of control that is functionally superordinate can vary by situations and persons (e.g., Carver & Scheier, 1998, 1999a). As we said earlier, it is easy to imagine cases in which a person is behaving according to a principle (e.g., a moral or ethical value), and it is easy to imagine cases in which the person is behaving according to a plan or program. It is also easy, however, to imagine cases in which the person is acting impulsively and spontaneously, without regard to either principle or plan.

In making this case in the past, we simply focused on how sequences and programs differ. Now we are inclined to wonder if this particular differentiation is not perhaps more important than we had realized. Perhaps we have under-appreciated the extent to which lower levels of self-regulatory structures can be triggered autonomously and their outputs enter the stream of ongoing action, without oversight from higher levels, and potentially even in conflict with values at higher levels.

Self-Control: Impulse and Restraint

Part of what makes the two modes of functioning different from each other descriptively is that the reflective mode tends to take longer-term and broader goals into account, whereas the reflexive mode does not. The idea that there can be conflicts between longer-term and shorter-term goals is also part of the literature on self-control and self-control failure (e.g., Baumeister, Heatherton, & Tice, 1994). This literature focuses on cases in which a person is both motivated to act and motivated to restrain that action. This is essentially the same case as is examined by work on children's effortful control, and it is also the same structure of competing forces as in the delay of gratification paradigm. A difference is that in the self-control literature the intent often is to delay indefinitely rather than temporarily.

Although the self-control situation is often seen as pitting longer- and shorter-term goals against each other, a somewhat different view also seems plausible. Specifically, the self-control situation may pit the two modes of processing against each other. This interpretation would be consistent in many ways with the literature on self-control failure, which tends to portray such failures as involving a relatively automatic tendency to act in one way, being opposed by a planful effort to restrain that act. The action being inhibited is often characterized as an impulse, a desire that automatically yields action unless it is controlled (often because the action is habitual). The restraint is presumed to be effortful, and to depend on limited resources. If the planful part of the mind is able to attend adequately to the conflict, the person can resist the impulse. If not, the impulse is more likely to be expressed. This portrayal seems quite consonant with the two-mode view of functioning.

DYNAMIC SYSTEMS AND SELF-REGULATION

At this point we shift to a very different set of themes. The last part of the 20th century saw the emergence in the psychological literature of some new (or at least newly prominent) ideas about how to conceptualize natural systems.

Several labels attach to these ideas: chaos, dynamic systems theory, complexity, catastrophe theory. A number of introductions to this body of thought have been written, some of which include applications to psychology (e.g., Brown, 1995; Gleick, 1987; Thelen & Smith, 1994; Vallacher & Nowak, 1994, 1997; Waldrop, 1992). These themes are of growing interest in several areas of psychology, including personality–social psychology. In this section we sketch some of the themes of this way of thinking.

Nonlinearity

Dynamic systems theory holds that the behavior of a system reflects all the forces operating on (and within) it. It also emphasizes that the behavior of a complex system over any period but a brief one is very hard to predict. One reason for this difficulty in prediction is that these forces may affect the system's behavior in nonlinear ways. Thus, the behavior of the system—even though highly determined—can appear random.

Many people are used to thinking of relationships between variables as linear. But some relationships clearly are not. Familiar examples of nonlinear relationships are step functions (ice turning to water and water turning to steam as temperature increases), threshold functions, and floor and ceiling effects. Other examples of nonlinearity are interactions. In an interaction the effect of one predictor on the outcome differs as a function of the level of a second predictor. Thus the effect of the first predictor on the outcome is not linear.

Many personality psychologists think in terms of interactions much of the time. Threshold effects and interactions are nonlinearities that most of us take for granted, though perhaps not labeling them as such. Looking intentionally for nonlinearities, however, reveals others. For example, many psychologists now think many developmental changes are dynamic rather than linear (Goldin-Meadow & Alibali, 1995; Ruble, 1994; Siegler & Jenkins, 1989; Thelen, 1992, 1995; van der Maas & Molenaar, 1992).

Sensitive Dependence on Initial Conditions

Nonlinearity is one reason for the difficulty in predicting complex systems. Two more reasons why prediction over any but the short term is difficult is that you never know all the influences on a system, and the ones you do know are never known with total precision. What you think is going on may not be quite what's actually going on. That difference, even if it's small, can be very important.

This theme is identified with the phrase "sensitive dependence on initial conditions." This phrase means that a very small difference between two states of affairs can lead to divergence, and ultimately an absence of relation between the paths that follow later on. The idea is (partly) that a small initial difference between systems causes a difference in what they encounter next, which produces slightly different outcomes (Lorenz, 1963). Through repeated iterations of slightly different situations and slightly different outcomes, the systems diverge, eventually moving on very different pathways. After a surprisingly brief period they no longer have any noticeable relation to one another.

How does the notion of sensitive dependence on initial conditions relate to human behavior? Most generally, it suggests that a person's behavior will be hard to predict over a long period except in general terms. For example, although you might be confident that Howard usually eats lunch, you won't be able to predict as well what time, where, or what he'll eat on the second Friday of next month. This doesn't mean Howard's behavior is random or unlawful (cf. Epstein, 1979). It just means that small differences between the influences you think are affecting him and the influences that are actually taking place will ruin the predictability of moment-to-moment behavior.

This principle also holds for prediction of your own behavior. People apparently don't plan very far into the future most of the time (Anderson, 1990, pp. 203–205)—not even experts (Gobet & Simon, 1996). People seem to have goals in which the general form of the goal is sketched out, but only a few steps toward it have been planned. Even attempts at relatively thorough planning appear to be recursive and "opportunistic," changing—sometimes drastically—when new information becomes known (B. Hayes-Roth & Hayes-Roth, 1979).

The notion of sensitive dependence on initial conditions fits these tendencies. It's pointless (and maybe even counterproductive) to plan too far ahead too fully, because chaotic forces in play (which are hard to predict because of nonlinearities and sensitive dependence) can render much of the planning irrelevant. Thus, it makes sense to plan in general terms, chart a few steps, get there, reassess, and plan the next bits. This seems a perfect illustration of how people implicitly take chaos into account in their own lives.

Phase Space, Attractors, and Repellers

Another set of concepts important in dynamic-systems thinking are variations on the terms phase space and attractor (Brown, 1995; Vallacher & Nowak, 1997). A phase diagram is a depiction of the behavior of a system over time. Its states are plotted along two (sometimes three) axes, with time displayed as the progression of the line of the plot, rather than on an axis of its own. A phase space is the array of states that the system occupies across a period of time. As the system changes states from one moment to the next, it traces a trajectory within its phase space—a path of the successive states it occupies across that period.

Phase spaces often contain regions called *attractors*. Attractors are areas the system approaches, occupies, or tends toward more frequently than other areas. Attractors exert a metaphorical gravitational pull on the system, bringing the system into proximity to them. Each attractor has a basin, the attractor's region of attraction. Trajectories that enter the basin tend to move toward that attractor (Brown, 1995).

There are several kinds of attractors, some simple, others more complex. In a point attractor, all trajectories converge onto some point in phase space, no matter where they begin (e.g., body temperature). Of greater interest are chaotic attractors. This term refers to an irregular and unpredictable movement around two or more attraction points. An example is the Lorenz attractor, named for the man who first plotted it (Lorenz, 1963). This one has two attraction zones (Figure 6.2). Plotting the behavior of this system over time yields a tendency to loop around both attractors, but to do so unpredictably. Shifts from one basin to the other seem random.

The behavior of this system displays sensitivity to initial conditions. A small change in starting point changes the specific path of motion entirely. The general tendencies remain the same—that is, the revolving around both attractors. But details such as the number of revolutions around one before deflection to the other, form an entirely different pattern. The trajectory over many iterations shows this same sensitivity to small differences. As the system continues, it often nearly repeats itself, but never quite does, and what seem nearly identical paths sometimes diverge abruptly, with one path leading to one attractor and the adjacent path leading to the other.

A phase space also contains regions called repellers, regions that are hardly ever occupied. Indeed, these regions seem to be actively avoided. That is, wandering into the basin of a repeller leads to a rapid escape from that region of phase space.

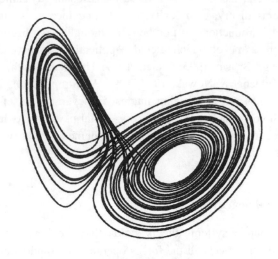

Figure 6.2 The Lorenz attractor, an example of what is known as a chaotic attractor or strange attractor

From C. S. Carver and M. F. Scheier, *On the Self-Regulation of Behavior*, copyright 1998, Cambridge University Press; reprinted with permission.

Another Way of Picturing Attractors

The phase-space diagram gives a vivid visual sense of what an attractor "looks like" and how it acts. Another common depiction of attractors is shown in Figure 6.3. In this view, attractor basins are basins or valleys in a surface (more technically called *local minima*). Repellers are ridges. This view assumes a metaphoric "gravitational" drift downward in the diagram, but other forces are presumed to be operative in all directions. (For simplicity, this portrayal usually is done in two dimensions, sometimes three, but keep in mind that the diagram often assumes the merging of a large number of dimensions into the horizontal axis.)

The behavior of the system at a given moment is represented as a ball on the surface. If the ball is in a valley (Point 1 or Point 2 in Figure 6.3A), it's in an attractor basin and will tend to stay there unless disturbed. If it's on a hill (between 1 and 2), any slight movement in either direction will cause it to escape its current location and move to an adjacent attractor.

A strength of this portrayal is that it does a good job of creating a sense of how attractors vary in robustness. The breadth of a basin indicates the diversity of trajectories in phase space that are drawn into it. The broader the basin (B-1, in Figure 6.3), the more trajectories drawn in. The narrower the basin (B-2), the closer the ball has to come to its focal point to be drawn to it. The steepness of the valley indicates how abruptly a trajectory is drawn into it.

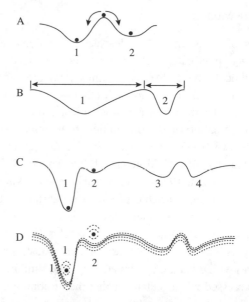

(A) Attractor basins as valleys in a surface (local minima). Behavior of the system is represented as a ball. If the ball is in a valley (Point 1 or 2), it's in an attractor basin and will tend to stay there unless disturbed. If the ball is on a ridge (between 1 and 2), it will tend to escape its current location and move to an attractor. (B) A wider basin (1) attracts more trajectories than a narrower basin (2). A steeply sloping basin (2) attracts more *abruptly* any trajectory that enters the basin than does a more gradually sloping basin (1). (C) A system in which attractor 1 is very stable, the others are less stable. It will take more energy to free the ball from attractor 1 than from the others. (D) The system's behavior is energized, much as the shaking of a metaphoric tambourine surface, keeping the system's behavior in flux and less than completely captured by any particular attractor. Still, more shaking will be required to escape from attractor 1 than attractor 2.

Figure 6.3 Another way to portray attractors

From C. S. Carver and M. F. Scheier, *On the Self-Regulation of Behavior*, copyright 1998, Cambridge University Press; reprinted with permission.

The steeper the slope of the wall (B-2), the more sudden is the entry of a system that encounters that basin.

The depth of the valley indicates how firmly entrenched the system is, once drawn into the attractor. Figure 6.3C represents a system of attractors with fairly low stability (the valleys are shallow). In Figure 6.3C, one attractor represents a stable situation (Valley 1), whereas the others are less so. It will take a lot more "energy" to free the ball from Valley 1 than from the others.

There's a sense in which both breadth and depth suggest that a goal is important. Breadth does so because the system is drawn to the attractor from widely divergent trajectories. Depth does so because the system that's been drawn into the basin tends to stay there.

A weakness of this picture, compared to a phase-space portrait, is that it isn't as good at giving a sense of the

erratic motion from one attractor to another in a multiple-attractor system. You can regain some of that sense of erratic shifting, however, if you think of the surface in Figure 6.3 as a tambourine, with continuous shaking going on (Figure 6.3D). Even a little shaking causes the ball to bounce around in its well, and may jostle it from one well to another, particularly if the attractors are not highly stable. An alternative would be to think of the ball as a jumping bean. These two characterizations would be analogous to jostling that comes from situational influences and jostling from internal dynamics, respectively.

Goals as Attractors

The themes of dynamic systems thinking outlined here have had several applications in personality–social and even clinical psychology (Hayes & Strauss, 1998; Mahoney, 1991; Nowak & Vallacher, 1998; Vallacher & Nowak, 1997). Perhaps the easiest application of the attractor concept to self-regulatory models is to link it with the goal concept. As we said earlier in the chapter, goals are values around which behavior is regulated. People spend much of their time doing things that keep their behavior in close proximity to their goals. It seems reasonable to suggest, then, that a goal represents a kind of attractor. Further, if a goal is an attractor, it seems reasonable that an anti-goal would represent a repeller.

This functional similarity between the goal construct and the attractor basin is interesting. However, the similarity exists only regarding the end product—that is, maintaining proximity to a value (or remaining distant from a value). The two views make radically different assumptions about the presence or absence of structure underlying the functions. The feedback model assumes a structure of processes underlying and supporting the maintenance of proximity to a value, whereas the dynamic systems model does not necessarily incorporate such an assumption.

Self-Organization and Self-Regulation

Another term that goes along with the dynamic systems view is *self-organization* (e.g., Prigogine & Stengers, 1984). The idea behind this label is that multiple causal forces that have no intrinsic relation to each other can cause the spontaneous emergence of some property of the system as a whole that does not otherwise exist. The term is used to describe emergent qualities in a variety of scientific disciplines. A number of people have begun to invoke it as a basis for emergent properties in dynamic systems (Nowak & Vallacher, 1998; Prigogine & Stengers, 1984).

Some would argue that models of self-organization in dynamic systems represent a serious challenge to the viability of the type of self-regulatory model with which we began. That is, it might be asserted that behavior only *seems* to be self-regulated—that behavior instead self-organizes from among surrounding forces, like foam appearing on roiling surf.

Do feedback processes actually reflect self-organization—a haphazard falling together of disparate forces? Or are there structures in the nervous system (and elsewhere) in living systems that carry out true feedback functions? In considering the relation between the two sets of ideas, it is of interest that the principle of self-organization was anticipated many years ago by MacKay (1956), who described a system of feedback processes that could evolve its own goals (see also Beer, 1995; Maes & Brooks, 1990). Thus, MacKay (1956) found the principle of self-organization to be useful, but he found it useful explicitly within the framework of a self-regulatory model.

Our view, similarly, is that the concepts of attractors and trajectories within phase space complement the idea that behavior is guided by feedback processes, but do not replace it. There do appear to be times and circumstances in which forces converge—unplanned—and induce acts to occur that were not intended beforehand (as reflected in the dual process models discussed in the previous section). However, there also seem to be clear instances of intentionality in behavior and its management.

Even when the focus is on planful behavior, the two kinds of models seem to complement each other in some ways. The feedback model provides a mechanism by which goal-directed action is managed, which the phase-space model lacks. The phase-space model suggests ways of thinking about how multiple goals exist and how people shift among those multiple goals over time, an issue that isn't dealt with as easily in terms of feedback processes.

That is, think of the landscape of chaotic attractors, but with many different basins rather than just two or three. This seems to capture rather well the sense of human behavior. No basin in this system ever becomes a point attractor. Behavior tends toward one goal then another, never being completely captured by any goal. The person does one thing for a while, then something else. The goals are all predictable—in the sense that they all influence the person—and the influence is highly predictable when aggregated across time. But the shifts from one to another occur unpredictably (thus being chaotic).

Catastrophe Models

Another set of ideas that resembles aspects of dynamic systems thinking is catastrophe theory, though the two bodies of thought have different origins (and are seen by some as quite different from each other—e.g., Kelso, 1995). Catastrophe theory is a mathematical model that examines the creation of discontinuities, bifurcations, or splittings (Brown, 1995; Saunders, 1980; Stewart & Peregoy, 1983; van der Maas & Molenaar, 1992; Woodcock & Davis, 1978; Zeeman, 1977). A catastrophe occurs when a small change in one variable produces an abrupt (and usually large) change in another variable.

An abrupt change implies nonlinearity. This focus on nonlinearity is one of several themes that catastrophe theory shares with dynamic systems theory. The similarity is nicely expressed in the statement that the discontinuity in catastrophe theory reflects "the sudden disappearance of one attractor and its basin, combined with the dominant emergence of another attractor" (Brown, 1995, p. 51).

Though several types of catastrophe exist (Brown, 1995; Saunders, 1980; Woodcock & Davis, 1978), the one best known is the cusp catastrophe, in which two variables influence an outcome. Figure 6.4 portrays its three-dimensional surface. Variables x and z are predictors, y is the outcome. At low values of z, the surface of the figure shows a roughly linear relationship between x and y. As x increases, so does y. As z increases, the relationship between x and y becomes less linear. It first

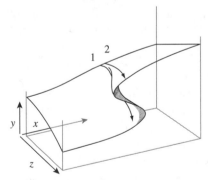

Variables x and z are predictors, y is the system's "behavior," the dependent variable. The catastrophe shows sensitive dependence on initial conditions. Where z is low, points 1 and 2 are nearly the same on x. If these points are projected forward on the surface (with increases in z), they move in parallel until the cusp begins to emerge. The lines are then separated by the formation of the cusp, and project to completely different regions of the surface.

Figure 6.4   Three-dimensional depiction of a cusp catastrophe

From C. S. Carver and M. F. Scheier, *On the Self-Regulation of Behavior*, copyright 1998, Cambridge University Press; reprinted with permission.

shifts toward something like a step function. With further increase in z, the x–y relationship becomes even more clearly discontinuous—the outcome is either on the top surface or on the bottom. Thus, changes in z cause a change in the way x relates to y.

Another theme that links catastrophe theory to dynamic systems is the idea of sensitive dependence on initial conditions. The cusp catastrophe displays this characteristic nicely. Consider the portion of Figure 6.4 where z has low values and x has a continuous relation to y (the system's behavior). Points 1 and 2 on x are nearly identical, but not quite. Now track these points across the surface, as z increases. For a while the two paths track each other closely, until suddenly they begin to be separated by the fold in the catastrophe. At higher levels of z, one track ultimately projects to the upper region of the surface, the other to the lower region. Thus, a very slight initial difference results in a substantial difference farther along.

The preceding description also hinted at an important feature of a catastrophe known as hysteresis. A simple characterization of what this term means is that at some levels of z, there's a kind of foldover in the middle of the x–y relationship. A region of x exists in which more than one value of y exists. Another way to characterize hysteresis is that two regions of this surface are attractors and one is a repeller (Brown, 1995). This unstable area is illustrated in Figure 6.5. The dashed-line portion of Figure 6.5

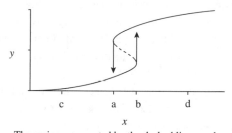

The region represented by the dashed line repels trajectories, whereas the stable regions (those surrounding values c and d on the x axis) attract trajectories. Traversing the zone of hysteresis from the left of this figure results in an abrupt shift (at value b on the x axis) from the lower to the upper portion of the surface (right arrow). Traversing the zone of hysteresis from the right of this figure results in an abrupt shift (at value a on the x axis) from the upper to the lower portion of the surface (left arrow). Thus, the disjunction between portions of the surface occurs at two different values of x, depending on the starting point.

Figure 6.5 A cusp catastrophe exhibits a region of hysteresis (between values a and b on the x axis), in which x has two stable values of y (the solid lines) and one unstable value (the dotted line that cuts backward in the middle of the figure).

From C. S. Carver and M. F. Scheier, *On the Self-Regulation of Behavior*, copyright 1998, Cambridge University Press; reprinted with permission.

that lies between values a and b on the x axis—the region where the fold is going backward—repels trajectories (Brown, 1995), whereas the areas near values c and d attract trajectories. To put it more simply, you can't *be* on the dashed part of this surface.

Yet another way of characterizing hysteresis is captured by the statement that the system's behavior depends on the system's recent history (Brown, 1995; Nowak & Lewenstein, 1994). That is, as you move into the zone of variable x that lies between Points a and b in Figure 6.5, it matters which side of the figure you're coming from. If the system is moving from Point c into the zone of hysteresis, it stays on the bottom surface until it reaches Point b, where it jumps to the top surface. If the system is moving from d into the zone of hysteresis, it stays on the top surface until it reaches Point a, where it jumps to the bottom surface.

How might catastrophe theory apply to the human behaviors of most interest to personality and social psychologists? Several applications of these ideas have been made in the past decade or so, and others seem obvious candidates for future study (for broader discussion, see Carver & Scheier, 1998, Chapter 16).

One interesting example concerns the bifurcation between effort and giving up. Earlier we pointed to a set of theories that assume such a disjunction (Brehm & Self, 1989; Wortman & Brehm, 1975). In all those models (as in ours), there's a point at which effort seems fruitless and the person stops trying. Earlier we simply emphasized that the models all assume a discontinuity. Now we look at the discontinuity more closely and suggest that the phenomena addressed by these theories may embody a catastrophe.

Figure 6.6 shows a slightly relabeled cross section of a cusp catastrophe, similar to that in Figure 6.5. This figure displays a region of hysteresis in the engagement versus disengagement function. In that region, where task

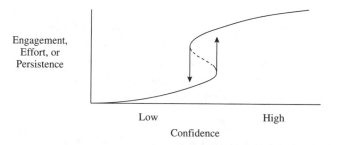

Figure 6.6 A catastrophe model of effort versus disengagement

From C. S. Carver and M. F. Scheier, *On the Self-Regulation of Behavior*, copyright 1998, Cambridge University Press; reprinted with permission.

demands are close to people's perceived limits to perform, there should be greater variability in effort or engagement, as some people are on the top surface of the catastrophe, others on the bottom surface. Some people would be continuing to exert efforts, at the same point where others would be exhibiting a giving-up response.

Recall that the catastrophe figure also conveys the sense that the history of the behavior matters. A person who enters the region of hysteresis from the direction of high confidence (who starts out confident but confronts many contradictory cues) will continue to display engagement and effort, even as the situational cues imply less and less basis for confidence. A person who enters that region from the direction of low confidence (who starts doubtful but confronts contradictory cues) will continue to display little effort, even as the cues imply more basis for confidence.

This model helps indicate why it can be so difficult to get someone with strong and chronic doubts about success in some domain of behavior to exert real effort and engagement in that domain. It also suggests why a confident person is so rarely put off by encountering difficulties in the domain where the confidence lies. To put it in terms of broader views about life in general, it helps show why optimists tend to stay optimistic and pessimists tend to stay pessimistic, even when the current circumstances of the two sorts of people are identical (i.e., in the region of hysteresis).

It's important to keep in mind that the catastrophe cross section (Figure 6.6) is the picture that emerges under catastrophe theory *only once a clear region of hysteresis has begun to develop*. Farther back, the model is more of a step function. An implication is that to see the foldover it's important to engage the variable that's responsible for bringing out the bifurcation in the surface (that is, axis z in Figure 6.4).

What is the variable that induces the bifurcation? We think that in the motivational models under discussion— and perhaps more broadly—the control parameter is importance. Importance arises from several sources, but there's a common thread among events seen as important. They demand mental resources. We suspect that almost any strong pressure that demands resources (time pressure, self-imposed pressure) will induce bifurcating effects.

CONCLUDING COMMENT

This chapter sketched a depiction of a set of ideas that we believe are useful in thinking about human self-regulation.

We believe that behavior is goal-directed and feedback-controlled, and that the goals underlying behavior form a hierarchy of abstractness. We believe that experiences of affect (and of confidence versus doubt) also arise from a process of feedback control, but a feedback process that takes into account temporal constraints. We believe that confidence and doubt yield patterns of persistence versus giving up, and that these two responses to adversity form a dichotomy in behavior. These ideas have been embedded in our self-regulatory viewpoint for some time.

We have also recently begun to consider some newer ideas, addressed in the latter parts of the chapter. In one of those sections we described dual-process models of self-regulation, in which a relatively reflexive, automatic, associative set of processes computes one understanding of reality and a deliberative, linear, planful set of processes computes a separate understanding of reality. These two understandings sometimes promote different action tendencies that can conflict with each other. An interesting set of questions is how those conflicts are resolved.

Another set of ideas is drawn from dynamic systems theory and catastrophe theory. These ideas come from a systems viewpoint, but one that is very different in some of its characteristics than the feedback view. We suggest that these ideas represent useful tools for the analysis and construal of behavior, though much of their promise is yet to be achieved. Our view is that they supplement rather than replace the tools now in use (though not everyone will agree on this point). We see many ways in which those ideas mesh with the ideas presented earlier, though space constraints limited us to discussing that integration only briefly.

In thinking about the structure of self-regulation, we have tried to draw on ideas from disparate sources, while continuing to follow the thread of the logical model from which we started. The result is an aggregation of principles that we think have a good deal to say about how behavioral self-regulation takes place. In so doing, they also say something about personality and how it is manifested in people's actions.

The conceptual model presented here is surely not complete, and many avenues exist for further discussion and indeed further conceptual development. For example, this chapter included little attention to the issue of how new goals are added to people's hierarchies, or how to think about growth and change over time (though see Carver & Scheier, 1998, 1999a, 1999b). Similarly, the concepts addressed here bear in several ways on problems in behavior and behavior change, though space constraints prevent us from describing them in detail. We suspect that many problems in people's lives are, at their core, problems of disengagement versus engagement and the failure to disengage adaptively (Carver & Scheier, 1998). As another example, it may be useful to conceptualize problems as less-than-optimal adaptations in a multidimensional phase space, which require some jostling to bounce the person to a new attractor (Hayes & Strauss, 1998). These are all areas in which more work remains to be done.

These are just some of the ways in which we think the family of ideas described here will likely be explored in the near future. Further analyses of the self-regulation of behavior are likely to produce insights that transform the models from which the insights grew. As the models change, so will our understanding of motivational processes and of how human beings function as coherent, autonomous units. This we take to be one of the core pursuits of personality psychology.

REFERENCES

Anderson, J. R. (1990). *The adaptive character of thought.* Hillsdale, NJ: Erlbaum.

Bandura, A. (1986). *Social foundations of thought and action: A social cognitive theory.* Englewood Cliffs, NJ: Prentice-Hall.

Baumeister, R. F., Heatherton, T. F., & Tice, D. M. (1994). *Losing control: Why people fail at self-regulation.* San Diego, CA: Academic Press.

Beer, R. D. (1995). A dynamical systems perspective on agent-environment interaction. *Artificial Intelligence, 72,* 173–215.

Berridge, K. C. (2004). Motivation concepts in behavioral neuroscience. *Physiology and Behavior, 81,* 179–209.

Brehm, J. W., & Self, E. A. (1989). The intensity of motivation. *Annual Review of Psychology, 40,* 109–131.

Brendl, C. M., & Higgins, E. T. (1996). Principles of judging valence: What makes events positive or negative? *Advances in Experimental Social Psychology, 28,* 95–160.

Brown, C. (1995). *Chaos and catastrophe theories* (Quantitative applications in the social sciences, no. 107). Thousand Oaks, CA: Sage.

Brunstein, J. C. (1993). Personal goals and subjective well-being: A longitudinal study. *Journal of Personality and Social Psychology, 65,* 1061–1070.

Cacioppo, J. T., Gardner, W. L., & Berntson, G. G. (1999). The affect system has parallel and integrative processing components: Form follows function. *Journal of Personality and Social Psychology, 76,* 839–855.

Cannon, W. B. (1932). *The wisdom of the body.* New York, NY: Norton.

Carver, C. S. (2003). Pleasure as a sign you can attend to something else: Placing positive feelings within a general model of affect. *Cognition and Emotion, 17,* 241–261.

Carver, C. S. (2004). Negative affects deriving from the behavioral approach system. *Emotion, 4,* 3–22.

Carver, C. S. (2009). Threat sensitivity, incentive sensitivity, and the experience of relief. *Journal of Personality, 77,* 125–138.

Carver, C. S., & Connor-Smith, J. (2010). Personality and coping. *Annual Review of Psychology, 61,* 679–704.

Carver, C. S., & Harmon-Jones, E. (2009). Anger is an approach-related affect: Evidence and implications. *Psychological Bulletin, 135,* 183–204.

Carver, C. S., Johnson, S. L., & Joormann, J. (2008). Serotonergic function, two-mode models of self-regulation, and vulnerability to depression: What depression has in common with impulsive aggression. *Psychological Bulletin, 134,* 912–943.

Carver, C. S., Lawrence, J. W., & Scheier, M. F. (1999). Self-discrepancies and affect: Incorporating the role of feared selves. *Personality and Social Psychology Bulletin, 25,* 783–792.

Carver, C. S., & Scheier, M. F. (1981). *Attention and self-regulation: A control-theory approach to human behavior.* New York, NY: Springer-Verlag.

Carver, C. S., & Scheier, M. F. (1990). Origins and functions of positive and negative affect: A control-process view. *Psychological Review, 97,* 19–35.

Carver, C. S., & Scheier, M. F. (1998). *On the self-regulation of behavior.* New York, NY: Cambridge University Press.

Carver, C. S., & Scheier, M. F. (1999a). Themes and issues in the self-regulation of behavior. In R. S. Wyer Jr. (Ed.), *Advances in social cognition* (Vol. 12, pp. 1–105). Mahwah, NJ: Erlbaum.

Carver, C. S., & Scheier, M. F. (1999b). Several more themes, a lot more issues: Commentary on the commentaries. In R. S. Wyer Jr. (Ed.), *Advances in social cognition* (Vol. 12, pp. 261–302). Mahwah, NJ: Erlbaum.

Carver, C. S., & Scheier, M. F. (2000). Autonomy and self-regulation. *Psychological Inquiry, 11,* 284–291.

Carver, C. S., & Scheier, M. F. (2001). Optimism, pessimism, and self-regulation. In E. C. Chang (Ed.), *Optimism and pessimism: Implications for theory, research, and practice* (pp. 31–51). Washington, DC: American Psychological Association.

Carver, C. S., & Scheier, M. F. (2002). Control processes and self-organization as complementary principles underlying behavior. *Personality and Social Psychology Review, 6,* 304–315.

Carver, C. S., & Scheier, M. F. (2009). Action, affect, multi-tasking, and layers of control. In J. P. Forgas, R. F. Baumeister, & D. Tice (Eds.), *The psychology of self-regulation: Cognitive, affective, and motivational processes* (pp. 109–126). New York, NY: Psychology Press.

Carver, C. S., Scheier, M. F., & Segerstrom, S. C. (2010). Optimism. *Clinical Psychology Review, 30,* 879–889.

Chaiken, S. L., & Trope, Y. (Eds.). (1999). *Dual-process theories in social psychology.* New York, NY: Guilford Press.

Clark, R. N. (1996). *Control system dynamics.* New York, NY: Cambridge University Press.

Cloninger, C. R. (1987). A systematic method for clinical description and classification of personality variants. *Archives of General Psychiatry, 44,* 573–588.

Davidson, R. J. (1992). Anterior cerebral asymmetry and the nature of emotion. *Brain and Cognition, 20,* 125–151.

Daw, N. D., Niv, Y., & Dayan, P. (2005). Uncertainty-based competition between prefrontal and dorsolateral striatal systems for behavioral control. *Nature Neuroscience, 8,* 1704–1711.

Depue, R. A., & Iacono, W. G. (1989). Neurobehavioral aspects of affective disorders. *Annual Review of Psychology, 40,* 457–492.

Depue, R. A., Krauss, S. P., & Spoont, M. R. (1987). A two-dimensional threshold model of seasonal bipolar affective disorder. In D. Magnusson & A. Öhman (Eds.), *Psychopathology: An interactional perspective* (pp. 95–123). Orlando, FL: Academic Press.

Derryberry, D., & Rothbart, M. K. (1997). Reactive and effortful processes in the organization of temperament. *Development and Psychopathology, 9,* 633–652.

Eidelman, S., & Biernat, M. (2007). Getting more from success: Standard raising as esteem maintenance. *Journal of Personality and Social Psychology, 92,* 759–774.

Elliot, A. J. (Ed.) (2008). *Handbook of approach and avoidance motivation.* New York, NY: Psychology Press.

Epstein, S. (1973). The self-concept revisited: Or a theory of a theory. *American Psychologist, 28,* 404–416.

Epstein, S. (1979). The stability of behavior: I. On predicting most of the people much of the time. *Journal of Personality and Social Psychology, 37,* 1097–1126.

Epstein, S. (1994). Integration of the cognitive and the psychodynamic unconscious. *American Psychologist, 49,* 709–724.

Fowles, D. C. (1980). The three arousal model: Implications of Gray's two-factor learning theory for heart rate, electrodermal activity, and psychopathy. *Psychophysiology, 17,* 87–104.

Frijda, N. H. (1986). *The emotions.* Cambridge, UK: Cambridge University Press.

Frijda, N. H. (1988). The laws of emotion. *American Psychologist, 43,* 349–358.

Fulford, D., Johnson, S. L., Llabre, M. M., & Carver, C. S. (2010). Pushing and coasting in dynamic goal pursuit: Coasting is attenuated in bipolar disorder. *Psychological Science, 21,* 1021–1027.

Gleick, J. (1987). *Chaos: Making a new science.* New York, NY: Viking Penguin.

Gobet, F., & Simon, H. A. (1996). The roles of recognition processes and look-ahead search in time-constrained expert problem solving: Evidence from grand-master-level chess. *Psychological Science, 7,* 52–55.

Goldin-Meadow, S., & Alibali, M. W. (1995). Mechanisms of transition: Learning with a helping hand. In D. Medin (Ed.), *The psychology of learning and motivation* (Vol. 33, pp. 115–157). San Diego, CA: Academic Press.

Gray, J. A. (1987a). Perspectives on anxiety and impulsivity: A commentary. *Journal of Research in Personality, 21,* 493–509.

Gray, J. A. (1987b). *The psychology of fear and stress.* Cambridge, UK: Cambridge University Press.

Gray, J. A. (1990). Brain systems that mediate both emotion and cognition. *Cognition and Emotion, 4,* 269–288.

Greenwald, A. G. (1980). The totalitarian ego: Fabrication and revision of personal history. *American Psychologist, 35,* 603–618.

Handy, T., Gazzaniga, M., & Ivry, R. B. (2003). Cortical and subcortical contributions to the representation of temporal information. *Neuropsychologia, 41,* 1461–1473.

Hayes, A. M., & Strauss, J. L. (1998). Dynamic systems theory as a paradigm for the study of change in psychotherapy: An application to cognitive therapy for depression. *Journal of Consulting and Clinical Psychology, 66,* 939–947.

Hayes-Roth, B., & Hayes-Roth, F. (1979). A cognitive model of planning. *Cognitive Science, 3,* 275–310.

Higgins, E. T. (1987). Self-discrepancy: A theory relating self and affect. *Psychological Review, 94,* 319–340.

Higgins, E. T. (1996). Ideals, oughts, and regulatory focus: Affect and motivation from distinct pains and pleasures. In P. M. Gollwitzer & J. A. Bargh (Eds.), *The psychology of action: Linking cognition and motivation to behavior* (pp. 91–114). New York, NY: Guilford Press.

Higgins, E. T., Shah, J., & Friedman, R. (1997). Emotional responses to goal attainment: Strength of regulatory focus as moderator. *Journal of Personality and Social Psychology, 72,* 515–525.

Holroyd, C. B., & Coles, M. G. H. (2002). The neural basis of human error processing: Reinforcement learning, dopamine, and the error-related negativity. *Psychological Review, 109,* 679–709.

Hsee, C. K., & Abelson, R. P. (1991). Velocity relation: Satisfaction as a function of the first derivative of outcome over time. *Journal of Personality and Social Psychology, 60,* 34347.

Ivry, R. B., & Richardson, T. (2002). Temporal control and coordination: The multiple timer model. *Brain and Cognition, 48,* 117–132.

Ivry, R. B., & Spencer, R. (2004). The neural representation of time. *Current Opinion in Neurobiology, 14,* 225–232.

Izard, C. E. (1977). *Human emotions.* New York, NY: Plenum Press.

Izard, C. E., & Ackerman, B. P. (2000). Motivational, organizational, and regulatory functions of discrete emotions. In M. Lewis & J. M. Haviland-Jones (Eds.), *Handbook of emotions* (2nd ed., pp. 253–264). New York, NY: Guilford Press.

Johnson, S. L., Carver, C. S., & Fulford, D. (2010). Goal dysregulation in the affective disorders. In A. M. Kring & D. M. Sloan (Eds.), *Emotion regulation and psychopathology: A transdiagnostic approach to etiology and treatment* (pp. 204–228). New York, NY: Guilford Press.

Kelly, G. A. (1955). *The psychology of personal constructs.* New York, NY: Norton.

Kelso, J. A. S. (1995). *Dynamic patterns: The self-organization of brain and behavior.* Cambridge, MA: MIT Press.

Klinger, E. (1975). Consequences of commitment to and disengagement from incentives. *Psychological Review, 82,* 25.

Lang, P. J., Bradley, M., & Cuthbert, B. (1990). Emotion, attention, and the startle reflex. *Psychological Review, 97,* 377–395.

Lawrence, J. W., Carver, C. S., & Scheier, M. F. (2002). Velocity toward goal attainment in immediate experience as a determinant of affect. *Journal of Applied Social Psychology, 32,* 788–802.

Lazarus, R. S. (1991). *Emotion and adaptation.* New York, NY: Oxford University Press.

Lorenz, E. N. (1963). Deterministic nonperiodic flow. *Journal of Atmospheric Science, 20,* 130–141.

Louro, M. J., Pieters, R., & Zeelenberg, M. (2007). Dynamics of multiple-goal pursuit. *Journal of Personality and Social Psychology, 93,* 174–193.

MacKay, D. M. (1956). Towards an information-flow model of human behaviour. *British Journal of Psychology, 47,* 30–43.

MacKay, D. M. (1966). Cerebral organization and the conscious control of action. In J. C. Eccles (Ed.), *Brain and conscious experience* (pp. 422–445). Berlin, Germany: Springer-Verlag.

Maes, P., & Brooks, R. A. (1990). Learning to coordinate behaviors. *Proceedings of the American Association of Artificial Intelligence* (pp. 796–802). Los Alto, CA: Morgan Kaufmann.

Mahoney, M. J. (1991). *Human change processes: The scientific foundations of psychotherapy.* New York, NY: Basic Books.

McIntosh, W. D., & Martin, L. L. (1992). The cybernetics of happiness: The relation of goal attainment, rumination, and affect. In M. S. Clark (Ed.), *Review of personality and social psychology: Volume 14. Emotion and social behavior* (pp. 222–246). Newbury Park, CA: Sage.

Melton, R. J. (1995). The role of positive affect in syllogism performance. *Personality and Social Psychology Bulletin, 21,* 788–794.

Metcalfe, J., & Mischel, W. (1999). A hot/cool-system analysis of delay of gratification: Dynamics of willpower. *Psychological Review, 106,* 3–19.

Millar, K. U., Tesser, A., & Millar, M. G. (1988). The effects of a threatening life event on behavior sequences and intrusive thought: A self-disruption explanation. *Cognitive Therapy and Research, 12,* 44458.

Miller, G. A., Galanter, E., & Pribram, K. H. (1960). *Plans and the structure of behavior.* New York, NY: Holt, Rinehart, & Winston.

Miller, G. E., & Wrosch, C. (2007). You've gotta know when to fold 'em: Goal disengagement and systemic inflammation in adolescence. *Psychological Science, 18,* 773–777.

Mizruchi, M. S. (1991). Urgency, motivation, and group performance: The effect of prior success on current success among professional basketball teams. *Social Psychology Quarterly, 54,* 181–189.

Nigg, J. T. (2000). On inhibition/disinhibition in developmental psychopathology: Views from cognitive and personality psychology as a working inhibition taxonomy. *Psychological Bulletin, 126,* 220–246.

Nowak, A., & Lewenstein, M. (1994). Dynamical systems: A tool for social psychology. In R. R. Vallacher & A. Nowak (Eds.), *Dynamical systems in social psychology* (pp. 17–53). San Diego, CA: Academic Press.

Nowak, A., & Vallacher, R. R. (1998). *Dynamical social psychology.* New York, NY: Guilford Press.

Ogilvie, D. M. (1987). The undesired self: A neglected variable in personality research. *Journal of Personality and Social Psychology, 52,* 379–385.

Orbuch, T. L. (Ed.). (1992). *Close relationship loss: Theoretical approaches.* New York, NY: Springer-Verlag.

Ortony, A., Clore, G. L., & Collins, A. (1988). *The cognitive structure of emotions.* Cambridge, UK: Cambridge University Press.

Powers, W. T. (1973). *Behavior: The control of perception.* Chicago, IL: Aldine.

Prigogine, I., & Stengers, I. (1984). *Order out of chaos: Man's new dialogue with nature.* New York, NY: Random House.

Rasmussen, H. N., Scheier, M. F., & Greenhouse, J. B. (2009). Optimism and physical health: A meta-analytic review. *Annals of Behavioral Medicine, 37,* 239–256.

Reyna, C., Henry, P. J., Korfmacher, W., & Tucker, A. (2006). Examining the principles in principled conservatism: The role of responsibility stereotypes as cues for deservingness in racial policy decisions. *Journal of Personality and Social Psychology, 90,* 109–128.

Rolls, E. T. (2005). *Emotion explained.* Oxford, UK: Oxford University Press.

Roseman, I. J. (1984). Cognitive determinants of emotions: A structural theory. In P. Shaver (Ed.), *Review of personality and social psychology* (Vol. 5, pp. 136). Beverly Hills, CA: Sage.

Rothbart, M. K., Ahadi, S. A., & Evans, D. E. (2000). Temperament and personality: Origins and outcomes. *Journal of Personality and Social Psychology, 78,* 122–135.

Rothbart, M. K., & Posner, M. (1985). Temperament and the development of self-regulation. In L. C. Hartlage & C. F. Telzrow (Eds.), *The neuropsychology of individual differences: A developmental perspective* (pp. 93–123). New York, NY: Plenum Press.

Rosenbaum, D. A., Meulenbroek, R. G. J., Vaughan, J., & Jansen, C. (2001). Posture-based motion planning: Applications to grasping. *Psychological Review, 108,* 709–734.

Ruble, D. N. (1994). A phase model of transitions: Cognitive and motivational consequences. In M. Zanna (Ed.), *Advances in experimental social psychology* (Vol. 26, pp. 163–214). San Diego, CA: Academic Press.

Saunders, P. T. (1980). *An introduction to catastrophe theory.* Cambridge, UK: Cambridge University Press.

Scheier, M. F., Carver, C. S., & Bridges, M. W. (2001). Optimism, pessimism, and psychological well-being. In E. C. Chang (Ed.), *Optimism and pessimism: Implications for theory, research, and practice* (pp. 189–216). Washington, DC: American Psychological Association.

Scherer, K. R., & Ekman, P. (Eds.). (1984). *Approaches to emotion.* Hillsdale, NJ: Erlbaum.

Schultz, W. (2000). Multiple reward signals in the brain. *Nature Reviews, 1,* 199–207.

Schultz, W. (2006). Behavioral theories and the neurophysiology of reward. *Annual Reviews of Psychology, 57,* 87–115.

Schwartz, S. H., & Bilsky, W. (1990). Toward a theory of the universal content and structure of values: Extensions and cross-cultural replications. *Journal of Personality and Social Psychology, 58,* 878–891.

Schwartz, S. H., & Rubel, T. (2005). Sex differences in value priorities: Cross-cultural and multimethod studies. *Journal of Personality and Social Psychology, 89,* 1010–1028.

Siegler, R. S., & Jenkins, E. A. (1989). *How children discover new strategies.* Hillsdale, NJ: Erlbaum.

Simon, H. A. (1953). *Models of man.* New York, NY: Wiley.

Stewart, I. N., & Peregoy, P. L. (1983). Catastrophe theory modeling in psychology. *Psychological Bulletin, 94,* 336–362.

Strack, F., & Deutsch, R. (2004). Reflective and impulsive determinants of social behavior. *Personality and Social Psychology Review, 8,* 220–247.

Stroebe, M. S., Stroebe, W., & Hansson, R. O. (Eds.). (1993). *Handbook of bereavement: Theory, research, and intervention.* Cambridge, UK: Cambridge University Press.

Taylor, S. E., & Pham, L. B. (1996). Mental stimulation, motivation, and action. In P. M. Gollwitzer & J. A. Bargh (Eds.), *The psychology of action: Linking cognition and motivation to behavior* (pp. 219–235). New York, NY: Guilford Press.

Thelen, E. (1992). Development as a dynamic system. *Current Directions in Psychological Science, 1,* 189–193.

Thelen, E. (1995). Motor development: A new synthesis. *American Psychologist, 50,* 79–95.

Thelen, E., & Smith, L. B. (1994). *A dynamic systems approach to the development of cognition and action.* Cambridge, MA: MIT Press.

Toates, F. (2006). A model of the hierarchy of behaviour, cognition, and consciousness. *Consciousness and Cognition: An International Journal, 15,* 75–118.

Vallacher, R. R., & Nowak, A. (Eds.). (1994). *Dynamical systems in social psychology.* San Diego, CA: Academic Press.

Vallacher, R. R., & Nowak, A. (1997). The emergence of dynamical social psychology. *Psychological Inquiry, 8,* 73–99.

Vallacher, R. R., & Wegner, D. M. (1987). What do people think they're doing? Action identification and human behavior. *Psychological Review, 94,* 3–15.

van der Maas, H. L. J., & Molenaar, P. C. M. (1992). Stagewise cognitive development: An application of catastrophe theory. *Psychological Review, 99,* 395–417.

Waldrop, M. (1992). *Complexity: The emerging science at the edge of order and chaos.* New York, NY: Simon & Schuster.

Watson, D. (2009). Locating anger in the hierarchical structure of affect: Comment on Carver and Harmon-Jones (2009). *Psychological Bulletin, 135,* 205–208.

Watson, D., Wiese, D., Vaidya, J., & Tellegen, A. (1999). The two general activation systems of affect: Structural findings, evolutionary considerations, and psychobiological evidence. *Journal of Personality and Social Psychology, 76,* 820–838.

Wiener, N. (1948). *Cybernetics: Control and communication in the animal and the machine.* Cambridge, MA: MIT Press.

Wills, T. A. (1981). Downward comparison principles in social psychology. *Psychological Bulletin, 90,* 245–271.

Wood, J. V. (1989). Theory and research concerning social comparisons of personal attributes. *Psychological Bulletin, 106,* 23248.

Woodcock, A., & Davis, M. (1978). *Catastrophe theory.* New York, NY: Dutton.

Wortman, C. B., & Brehm, J. W. (1975). Responses to uncontrollable outcomes: An integration of reactance theory and the learned helplessness model. In L. Berkowitz (Ed.), *Advances in experimental social psychology* (Vol. 8, pp. 277–336). New York, NY: Academic Press.

Wright, R. A., & Brehm, J. W. (1989). Energization and goal attractiveness. In L. A. Pervin (Ed.), *Goal concepts in personality and social psychology* (pp. 169–210). Hillsdale, NJ: Erlbaum.

Wright, R. A., & Kirby, L. D. (2001). Effort determination of cardiovascular response: An integrative analysis with applications in social psychology. In M. P. Zanna (Ed.), *Advances in experimental social psychology* (Vol. 33, pp. 255–307). New York, NY: Academic Press.

Wrosch, C., Miller, G. E., Scheier, M. F., & Brun de Pontet, S. (2007). Giving up on unattainable goals: Benefits for health? *Personality and Social Psychology Bulletin, 33,* 251–265.

Zeeman, E. C. (1977). *Catastrophe theory: Selected papers 1972–1977.* Reading, MA: Benjamin.

CHAPTER 7

Interpersonal Theory of Personality

AARON L. PINCUS AND EMILY B. ANSELL

INTERPERSONAL THEORY OF PERSONALITY

In this chapter we outline the major assumptions and key concepts of the interpersonal theory of personality (Pincus & Ansell, 2003), which provides the foundational underpinnings for interpersonal psychology more generally (Horowitz & Strack, 2010a). Many overviews of the 60-year history of interpersonal theory and research are available for interested readers (e.g., Pincus, 1994; Strack & Horowitz, 2010; Wiggins, 1996). The origins are found in Harry Stack Sullivan's (1953a, 1953b, 1954, 1956, 1962, 1964) highly generative interpersonal theory of psychiatry, which defined personality as "the relatively enduring pattern of recurrent interpersonal situations which characterize a human life" (Sullivan, 1953b, p. 110–111); and, the Berkeley/Kaiser Group's (LaForge, 2004; Leary, 1957) empirical operationalization of Sullivan's ideas in an elegant mathematical and measurement model, the interpersonal circumplex (IPC). Here, we emphasize the theoretical and empirical advances that create a highly integrative and interdisciplinary "interpersonal nexus" for the study of the whole person via individual differences, psychological processes, and relational dynamics (Pincus, 2005b; Pincus, Lukowitsky, & Wright, 2010; Pincus, Lukowitsky, Wright, & Eichler, 2009), with implications for understanding normality, psychopathology and psychotherapy (Pincus, 2010).

The interpersonal legacy that emerged from Sullivan's work is now in its fourth generation and has dramatically advanced over the decades, increasing in level of theoretical integration, methodological sophistication, and scope.

Whether referred to as the "interpersonal paradigm" (Wiggins, 2003), the "interpersonal system" (LaForge, 2004), or the "interpersonal tradition" (Pincus & Gurtman, 2006), this approach to personality and social functioning is evolving into a meta-theory for psychological science. Interpersonal theory provides a nomological net for the study of personality (e.g., Fournier, Moskowitz, & Zuroff, 2010; Hopwood et al., 2011; Wiggins & Broughton, 1985), personality assessment (e.g., Hopwood, 2010; Pincus, 2010), psychotherapy (e.g., Anchin & Pincus, 2010; Pincus & Cain, 2008), symptom syndromes (e.g., Ansell, Grilo, & White 2012; Hopwood, Clarke, & Perez, 2007; Horowitz, 2004), personality disorders (e.g., Benjamin, 1996; Pincus, 2005a; Pincus & Hopwood, in press), and health psychology and behavioral medicine (e.g., Gallo, Smith, & Cox, 2006; Smith & Cundiff, 2010). These advances are ongoing, yet Sullivan's commitment to the study of interpersonal phenomena remains at the forefront of current developments. This allows the diverse efforts in the interpersonal nexus to be interconnected and reciprocally influential.

The interpersonal nexus has evolved, in large part, due to the integrative nature of contemporary interpersonal theory itself, which can accommodate findings from a number of research traditions that bear on personality and relational functioning (Horowitz & Strack, 2010b; Pincus & Ansell, 2003). This was best described by Horowitz and colleagues, who stated, "Because the interpersonal approach harmonizes so well with all of these theoretical approaches, it is integrative: It draws from the wisdom of all major approaches to systematize our understanding of interpersonal phenomena. Although it is integrative, however, it is also unique, posing characteristic questions of its own" (Horowitz et al., 2006, p. 82). Interpersonal models have been integrated conceptually and empirically with attachment (Bartholomew & Horowitz, 1991; Benjamin, 1993; Florsheim & McArthur, 2009; Gallo, Smith, & Ruiz, 2003; Ravitz, Maunder, & McBride, 2008), psychodynamic (Blatt, 2008; Blatt & Luyten, 2010; Heck & Pincus, 2001; Lukowitsky & Pincus, 2011; Luyten & Blatt, 2011), social-cognitive (Locke & Sadler, 2007; Safran, 1990a, 1990b), evolutionary (Fournier, Zuroff, & Moskowitz, 2007; Hoyenga, Hoyenga, Walters, & Schmidt, 1998; Zuroff, Moskowitz, & Côté, 1999), and neurobiological (aan het Rot, Moskowitz, Pinard, & Young, 2006; Depue, 2006) theories of personality, psychopathology, and psychotherapy. The breadth of interpersonal theory and its applications promote the "interpersonal situation" (Pincus & Ansell, 2003) as a uniquely valuable unit of analysis for studying psychological phenomena at multiple levels.

Contemporary Assumptions of Interpersonal Theory

Virtually all theories of personality touch upon interpersonal functioning. The interpersonal perspective proposes that in examining personality or its substrates, our best bet is to look at personality processes in relation to interpersonal functioning. Four assumptions undergird contemporary interpersonal theory, which both facilitate its integrative nature and define its unique characteristics. The contemporary assumptions of the interpersonal tradition are presented in Table 7.1.

The Interpersonal Situation

> I had come to feel over the years that there was an acute need for a discipline that was determined to study not the individual organism or the social heritage, but the interpersonal situations through which persons manifest mental health or mental disorder.
>
> —Sullivan, 1953b, p. 18

> An interpersonal situation can be defined as the experience of a pattern of relating self with other associated with varying levels of anxiety (or security) in which learning takes place that influences the development of self-concept and social behavior.
>
> —Pincus & Ansell, 2003, p. 210

Sullivan's emphasis on the interpersonal situation as the focus for understanding both personality and psychopathology set an elemental course for psychiatry, clinical psychology, and personality psychology. Contemporary

TABLE 7.1   Contemporary Assumptions and Corollaries of the Interpersonal Tradition

Assumption 1: The most important expressions of personality and psychopathology occur in phenomena involving more than one person (i.e., interpersonal situations).
- An interpersonal situation can be defined as, "the experience of a pattern of relating self with other associated with varying levels of anxiety (or security) in which learning takes place that influences the development of self-concept and social behavior" (Pincus & Ansell, 2003, p. 210).

Assumption 2: Interpersonal situations occur between proximal interactants *and* within the minds of those interactants via the capacity for perception, mental representation, memory, fantasy, and expectancy.

Assumption 3: Agency and communion provide an integrative meta-structure for conceptualizing interpersonal situations.
- Explicatory systems derived from agency and communion can be used to describe, measure, and explain normal and pathological interpersonal motives, traits, and behaviors.
- Such systems can be applied to both proximal interpersonal situations *and* internal interpersonal situations.

Assumption 4: Interpersonal complementarity is most helpful if considered a common baseline for the field regulatory pulls and invitations of interpersonal behavior.
- Chronic deviations from complementary reciprocal patterns may be indicative of psychopathology.

interpersonal theory thus begins with the assumption that the most important expressions of personality and psychopathology occur in phenomena involving more than one person (see Table 7.1). Sullivan (1953a, 1953b) suggested that persons live in communal existence with the social environment and individuals express integrating tendencies which bring them together in the mutual pursuit of satisfactions (generally a large class of biologically grounded needs), security (i.e., anxiety-free functioning), and self-esteem. These integrating tendencies develop into increasingly complex dynamisms, or patterns of interpersonal experience. From infancy throughout the life span, these dynamisms are encoded in memory via age-appropriate social learning. According to Sullivan, interpersonal learning of self-concept and social behavior is based on an anxiety gradient associated with interpersonal situations. All interpersonal situations range from rewarding (highly secure, esteem-promoting) through various degrees of anxiety (insecurity, low self-esteem) and end in a class of situations associated with such severe anxiety that they are dissociated from experience. The interpersonal situation underlies genesis, development, maintenance, and mutability of personality and psychopathology through the continuous patterning and repatterning of interpersonal experience in an effort to increase security and self-esteem (positively reinforcing) while avoiding anxiety (negatively reinforcing). Over time, this gives rise to schematic representations of self and others (Sullivan's personifications) as well as to enduring patterns of adaptive or disturbed interpersonal relating.

Individual variation in learning occurs due to the interaction between the developing person's level of cognitive maturation and the characteristics of the interpersonal situations encountered. Interpersonal experience is understood differently depending on the developing person's grasp of cause and effect logic and the use of consensual symbols such as language. This affects how one makes sense of the qualities of significant others (including their "reflected appraisals" which communicate approval or disapproval of the developing person), as well as the ultimate outcomes of interpersonal situations characterizing a human life. Pincus and Ansell (2003) summarized Sullivan's concept of the interpersonal situation as "the experience of a pattern of relating self with other associated with varying levels of anxiety (or security) in which learning takes place that influences the development of self-concept and social behavior" (p. 210). In one way or another, all perspectives on personality, psychopathology, and psychotherapy within the interpersonal tradition address elements of the interpersonal situation. These elements include individual differences, reciprocal interpersonal patterns of behavior, internal psychological processes, and the transactional and contextual frameworks for understanding interpersonal relations that we review in this chapter.

A potential misinterpretation of the term *interpersonal* is to assume it refers to a limited class of phenomena that can be observed only in the immediate interaction between two proximal people. In contemporary interpersonal theory, "The term *interpersonal* is meant to convey a sense of primacy, a set of fundamental phenomena important for personality development, structuralization, function, and pathology. It is not a geographic indicator of locale: It is not meant to generate a dichotomy between what is inside the person and what is outside the person" (Pincus & Ansell, 2003, p. 212). Interpersonal functioning occurs not only between people, but also inside people's minds via the capacity for mental representation of self and others (e.g., Blatt, Auerbach, & Levy, 1997). This allows the contemporary interpersonal tradition to incorporate important pantheoretical representational constructs such as cognitive interpersonal schemas, internalized object relations, and internal working models (Lukowitsky & Pincus, 2011). Contemporary interpersonal theory does suggest that the most important personality and psychopathological phenomena are relational in nature, but it does not suggest that such phenomena are limited to contemporaneous, observable behavior. Interpersonal situations

occur in perceptions of contemporaneous events, memories of past experiences, and fantasies or expectations of future experiences. Regardless of the level of distortion or accuracy in these perceptions, memories, and fantasies, the ability to link internal interpersonal situations and proximal interpersonal situations was crucial to the maturation of the contemporary interpersonal tradition (Lukowitsky & Pincus, 2011; Safran, 1992). Both proximal and internal interpersonal situations continuously influence an individual's learned relational strategies, regulatory functioning, and self-concept. A primary pathway by which psychopathology is inherently expressed is via the disturbed interpersonal relations that characterize dysfunction (Pincus & Wright, 2010).

Agency and Communion as Integrative Metaconcepts

In a seminal review and integration of the interpersonal nature and relevance of Bakan's (1966) metaconcepts of "agency" and "communion," Wiggins (1991, 1997a, 2003) argued that these two superordinate dimensions have propaeduetic explanatory power across scientific disciplines. "Agency" refers to the condition of being a differentiated individual, and it is manifested in strivings for power and mastery, which can enhance and protect one's differentiation. "Communion" refers to the condition of being part of a larger social or spiritual entity, and is manifested in strivings for intimacy, union, and solidarity with the larger entity. Bakan (1966) noted that a key issue for understanding human existence is to comprehend how the tensions of this duality in our condition are managed. Wiggins (2003) proposed that agency and communion are most directly related to Sullivan's theory in terms of the goals of human relationship: security (communion) and self-esteem (agency). As can be seen in Figure 7.1, these metaconcepts form a superordinate structure used to derive explanatory and descriptive concepts at different levels of specificity. At the broadest and most interdisciplinary level, agency and communion classify the interpersonal motives, strivings, and values of human relations (Horowitz, 2004). In interpersonal situations, motivation can reflect the agentic and communal nature of the individual's personal strivings or current concerns, or more specific agentic and communal goals (e.g., to be in control; to be close) that specific behaviors are enacted to achieve (Grosse Holtforth, Thomas, & Caspar, 2010; Horowitz et al, 2006).

At more specific levels, the structure provides conceptual coordinates for describing and measuring interpersonal dispositions and behaviors (Wiggins, 1991). The

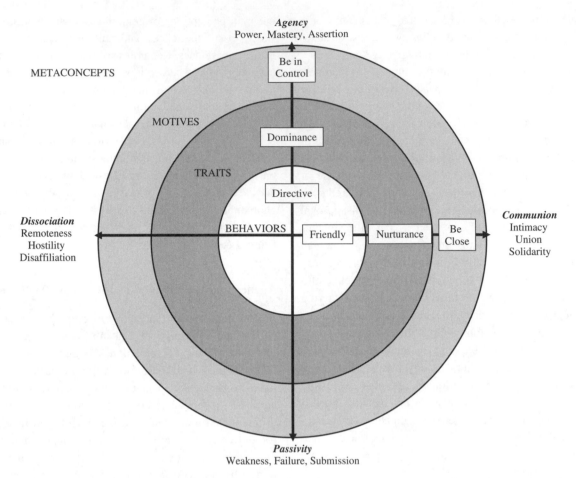

Figure 7.1   Agency and communion: Metaconcepts for the integration of interpersonal motives, dispositions, and behaviors

From Pincus, Lukowitsky, & Wright (2010). The interpersonal nexus of personality and psychopathology. In T. Millon, R. F. Krueger, & E. Simonsen (Eds.), *Contemporary directions in psychopathology: Scientific foundations for DSM-5 and ICD-11* (p. 529). New York, NY: Guilford Press. Reprinted with permission of Guilford Press.

intermediate level of dispositions includes an evolving set of interpersonal constructs (Hopwood et al., 2011; Locke, 2006, 2010). Agentic and communal dispositions imply enduring patterns of perceiving, thinking, feeling, and behaving that are probabilistic in nature, and describe an individual's interpersonal tendencies aggregated across time, place, and relationships. At the most specific level, the structure can be used to classify the nature and intensity of specific interpersonal behaviors (Moskowitz, 1994, 2005, 2009). Wiggins' theoretical analysis simultaneously allows for the integration of descriptive levels within the interpersonal tradition as well as expansion of the conceptual scope and meaning of interpersonal functioning. Contemporary interpersonal theory proposes that (a) agency and communion are fundamental metaconcepts of personality, providing a superordinate structure for conceptualizing interpersonal situations; (b) explicatory systems derived from agency and communion can be used to understand, describe, and measure interpersonal motives,

dispositions, and behaviors; and (c) such systems can be applied equally well to the objective description of contemporaneous interactions between two or more people (e.g., Sadler, Ethier, Gunn, Duong, & Woody, 2009) and to interpersonal situations within the mind evoked via perception, memory, fantasy, and mental representation (e.g., Lukowitsky & Pincus, 2011).[1]

KEY CONCEPTS OF INTERPERSONAL THEORY: I. DESCRIBING INTERPERSONAL THEMES AND DYNAMICS

In this section we articulate the key thematic and dynamic concepts of contemporary interpersonal theory, which are briefly summarized in Table 7.2.

---

[1]The fourth contemporary assumption in Table 7.1 is discussed in a later section.

TABLE 7.2 Description of Interpersonal Themes and Interpersonal Dynamics

Interpersonal Themes

Extremity	Maladaptive behavioral intensity (rarely situationally appropriate or successful)
Rigidity	Limited behavioral repertoire (often inconsistent with the situational pulls or norms)
Pathoplasticity	Interpersonal subtypes within a diagnostic category with differential expression, course, or outcome

Interpersonal Dynamics
Intraindividual Variability

Flux	Variability about an individual's mean behavioral score on dominance and nurturance dimensions
Pulse	Variability of the overall extremity of the emitted behavior
Spin	Variability of the range of behaviors emitted

Interpersonal Signatures

Complementarity	Reciprocity on Dominance and Correspondence on Nurturance
	Example: Arrogant Vindictiveness (BC) → Social Avoidance (FG)
Acomplementarity	Reciprocity on Dominance or Correspondence of Nurturance
	Example: Arrogant Vindictiveness (BC) → Arrogant Vindictiveness (BC)
Anticomplementarity	Neither Reciprocity on Dominance nor Correspondence on Nurturance
	Example: Warm Gregariousness (NO) → Arrogant Vindictiveness (BC)

Transaction Cycles

Person X's covert reaction to Person Y (input)
Person X's overt behavior toward Person Y (output)
Person Y's covert reaction to Person X (input)
Person Y's overt behavior toward Person X (output)

Parataxic Distortions

Chronic distortions of interpersonal input leading to increased interpersonal insecurity, self and emotion dysregulation, interbehavioral noncontingency, and disrupted interpersonal relations.

The Interpersonal Circumplex

The emphasis on interpersonal functioning in Sullivan's work led to efforts to develop orderly and lawful conceptual and empirical models describing interpersonal behavior (for reviews of these developments, see LaForge, 2004; LaForge, Freedman, & Wiggins, 1985; Leary, 1957; Pincus, 1994; Wiggins, 1982, 1996). The goal of such work was to obtain an interpersonal taxonomy of dispositions and behaviors, that is, "to obtain categories of increasing generality that permit description of behaviors according to their natural relationships" (Schaefer, 1961, p. 126). In contemporary terms, these systems are referred to as

structural models, which can be used to conceptually systematize observation and covariation of variables of interest. When seen in relation to the metaconcepts of agency and communion, such models become part of an illuminating nomological net.

Empirical research into diverse interpersonal taxa including traits (Wiggins, 1979), problems (Alden, Wiggins, & Pincus, 1990); sensitivities (Hopwood et al., 2011), values (Locke, 2000), impact messages (Kiesler, Schmidt, & Wagner, 1997), strengths (Hatcher & Rogers, 2009), efficacies (Locke & Sadler, 2007), and behaviors (Benjamin, 1974, 2010; Di Blas, Grassi, Luccio, & Momenté, in press; Gifford, 1991; Moskowitz, 1994; Trobst, 2000) converge in suggesting the structure of interpersonal functioning takes the form of a circle or "circumplex" (Gurtman & Pincus, 2000; Wiggins & Trobst, 1997). An exemplar of this form based on the two underlying dimensions of dominance-submission (agency) on the vertical axis and nurturance-coldness (communion) on the horizontal axis is the most common instantiation of the IPC (see Figure 7.2). The geometric properties of circumplex models give rise to unique computational methods for assessment and research (Gurtman & Balakrishnan, 1998; Gurtman & Pincus, 2003; Wright, Pincus, Conroy, & Hilsenroth, 2009) that will not be reviewed here. In this chapter, we use the IPC to anchor description of theoretical concepts. Blends of dominance and nurturance can be located along the 360-degree perimeter of the circle. Interpersonal qualities close to one another on the perimeter are conceptually and statistically similar, qualities at 90 degrees are conceptually and statistically independent, and qualities 180 degrees apart are conceptual and statistical opposites. Although the circular model itself is a continuum without beginning or end (Carson, 1996; Gurtman & Pincus, 2000), any segmentalization of the IPC perimeter to identify lower-order taxa is potentially useful within the limits of reliable discriminability. The IPC has been segmentalized into sixteenths (Kiesler, 1983), most commonly octants (Wiggins, Trapnell, & Phillips, 1988), and quadrants (Carson, 1969).

Intermediate-level structural models derived from agency and communion focus on the description of the individual's interpersonal dispositions that, when understood in relation to their motives and goals, are assumed to give rise to adaptive and maladaptive behavior that is generally consistent across interpersonal situations (Horowitz & Wilson, 2005; Wiggins, 1997b). Thus, we can use circumplex models to describe a person's typical ways of relating to others and refer to their interpersonal style or theme. At the level of specific behaviors, interpersonal description

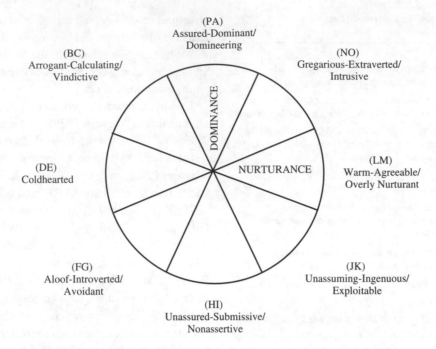

Figure 7.2 The interpersonal circumplex (traits/problems)

permits microanalytic, or transactional, analyses of interpersonal situations. Because interpersonal situations also occur within the mind, these models can also describe the person's typical ways of encoding new interpersonal information and their consistent mental representations of self and others (i.e., social-cognitive schemas). Using IPC models to classify individuals in terms of their agentic and communal characteristics is often referred to as "interpersonal diagnosis" (Pincus & Wright, 2010; Wiggins, Phillips, & Trapnell, 1989). Importantly, however, there are not one to one relationships between traits and behaviors, leaving the interpersonal meaning of a given behavior ambiguous without consideration of the person's interpersonal motives or goals (Horowitz et al., 2006). Thus a certain trait or behavior (whether adaptive or maladaptive) may not necessarily be expressed in a particular interpersonal situation or relationship, or dictate a particular emergent process. For this level of specificity, contemporary interpersonal theory relies on additional theoretical constructs.

Behavioral Extremity and Interpersonal Rigidity

When referenced to the IPC, extremity (i.e., intense expressions of behaviors) and rigidity (i.e., displaying a limited repertoire of interpersonal behaviors) are critical variables for conceptualizing adaptive and maladaptive functioning within the interpersonal tradition. Although the two are assumed to co-occur, they are conceptually

distinct (O'Connor & Dyce, 2001). In the context of IPC models, extremity reflects a specific behavior's intensity on a particular dimension, and is represented linearly, by the behavior's distance from the origin of the circle. Behaviors can vary from relatively mild expressions of a trait dimension close to the origin (e.g., *asks for what is wanted*) to extreme versions at the periphery of the circle (e.g., *insists/demands getting one's way*). Extreme behaviors that populate the circle's periphery are likely to be undesirable for both self and others, as their lack of moderation rarely render them appropriate or adaptive (Carson, 1969; Horowitz, 2004; Kiesler, 1996).

As Pincus (1994) pointed out, whereas extremity (or intensity) is a property of an individual's single *behavior*, rigidity is a characteristic of a whole *person* over time or more specifically, a summary of his or her limited behavioral repertoire across various interpersonal situations. Following Leary (1957), interpersonalists have argued that disordered individuals tend to enact or rely on a restricted range of behaviors, failing to adapt their behaviors to the particular demands of a given situation. From an IPC perspective, they tend to draw from a small segment of the circle, rather than draw broadly as the situation requires. In contrast, interpersonally flexible individuals are capable of adjusting their behaviors to the cues of others in order to act effectively (Carson, 1991), and are more likely to engage in and sustain behavior patterns that are mutually satisfying to both relational partners (Kiesler, 1996).

Although rigidity and extremity are important for describing interpersonal behavior, the explanatory power of these concepts is too limited and their scope is insufficient to anchor a theory of personality and psychopathology. Research indicates that trait-like consistency is probabilistic (Fournier, Moskowitz, & Zuroff, 2008; Mischel & Shoda, 2008) and clearly even very rigid individuals such as those with severe personality disorders vary in how consistently they behave and in what ways consistency is exhibited (e.g., Lenzenweger, Johnson, & Willett, 2004; Russell, Moskowitz, Zuroff, Sookman, & Paris, 2007). It is certainly informative to examine interpersonal themes associated with prominent personality features and psychiatric diagnoses. However, evidence is accumulating that individuals with a specific mental disorder or prominent disposition do not always present with a single, prototypic interpersonal theme both between and within persons (Pincus et al., 2010). Thus, to fully apply interpersonal diagnosis, interpersonal theory must move beyond basic descriptions founded on the covariation of personality and psychopathology in which interpersonal characteristics are assessed as static individual differences and investigate other conceptualizations of psychopathology. Next, we focus on two such conceptualizations: pathoplastic associations and dynamic processes.

Interpersonal Pathoplasticity

The contemporary interpersonal tradition assumes a pathoplastic relationship between interpersonal functioning and many individual differences and forms of psychopathology. Pathoplasticity is characterized by a mutually influencing nonetiological relationship between two psychological systems (Klein, Wonderlich, & Shea, 1993; Widiger & Smith, 2008). Initially conceptualized as a model identifying personality-based subtypes of depression—dependent/sociotropic/anaclitic versus self-critical/autonomous/introjective (e.g., Beck, 1983; Blatt, 2004; see also Klein, Kotov, & Bufferd, 2011 for a contemporary review)—its scope has been broadened to personality, adjustment, and psychopathology in general. Pathoplasticity assumes that the expression of certain maladaptive behaviors, symptoms, and mental disorders tend to occur in the larger context of an individual's personality (Millon, 2005). Likewise, it is assumed that personality has the potential for influencing the content and focus of symptoms and will likely shape the responses and coping strategies individuals employ when presented with psychological and social stressors (Millon, 2000). Therefore, pathoplasticity is observed when there is

diversity of interpersonal traits, problems, or behaviors within psychopathology that is meaningful in understanding the heterogeneity of symptom etiology, expression, course, or treatment outcome.

Interpersonal pathoplasticity (Pincus et al., 2010; Pincus & Wright, 2010) can describe the observed heterogeneity in phenotypic expression of psychopathology (e.g., Ansell et al., 2012; Przeworski et al., 2011), predict variability in response to psychotherapy within a disorder (e.g., Cain, Pincus, & Grosse Holtforth, 2010; Salzer, Pincus, Winkelbach, Leichsenring, & Leibing, 2011), and account for a lack of uniformity in regulatory strategies displayed by those who otherwise are struggling with similar issues (e.g., Wright, Pincus, Conroy, & Elliot, 2009). The identification of interpersonal subtypes within a singular psychiatric diagnosis allows clinicians to anticipate and understand differences in patients' expressions of distress and their typical bids for the type of interpersonal situation they feel is needed to regulate their self, affect, and relationships. A number of empirical investigations find that interpersonal problems exhibit pathoplastic relationships with personality features, symptoms, and mental disorders, including patients with depression (Cain et al., 2012), generalized anxiety disorder (Przeworski et al., 2011; Salzer et al., 2008), social phobia (Cain et al., 2010; Kachin, Newman, & Pincus, 2001), and disordered eating (Ambwani & Hopwood, 2009; Ansell et al., 2012; Hopwood et al., 2007), as well as individuals exhibiting maladaptive perfectionism (Slaney, Pincus, Uliaszek, & Wang, 2006) and fear of failure (Wright et al., 2009).

Some *Diagnostic and Statistical Manual of Mental Disorders* (*DSM-IV-TR*; APA, 2000) personality disorders also exhibit interpersonal pathoplasticity, although research is only beginning in this area. Similar to research on social phobia, warm-submissive and cold-submissive interpersonal subtypes of avoidant personality disorder exhibited differential responses to interventions emphasizing habituation and intimacy training respectively (Alden & Capreol, 1993). Leihener and colleagues (2003) found two interpersonal clusters of patients diagnosed with borderline personality disorder (BPD), a primary cluster with dependency problems (exploitable) and a secondary group with autonomy problems (domineering). These clusters were replicated in a student sample exhibiting strong borderline features (Ryan & Shean, 2007). Leichsenring, Kunst, and Hoyer (2003) examined associations between interpersonal problems and borderline symptoms that may inform interpersonal pathoplasticity of BPD. They found that primitive defenses and object relations were associated with controlling, vindictive, and cold interpersonal problems while identity diffusion was associated with overly affiliative interpersonal problems. New conceptualizations of pathological narcissism including both grandiosity and vulnerability (Pincus & Lukowitsky, 2010) may also exhibit interpersonal pathoplasticity. Narcissistic grandiosity is similar to the diagnostic criteria for narcissistic personality disorder enumerated in the *DSM*, and focuses on arrogance, exploitativeness, and inflated self-importance. In contrast, narcissistic vulnerability is characterized by self- and affect-dysregulation in response to self-enhancement failures and lack of needed recognition and admiration. Therefore, these two very different interpersonal expressions of motives and regulatory functioning (one domineering, the other avoidant) share the same core narcissistic pathology (Dickinson & Pincus, 2003; Miller et al., 2011; Pincus & Roche, 2011).

It is notable that pathoplasticity is also an implicit feature of the *DSM-5* proposal for personality and personality disorders (Skodol et al., 2011). We would argue strongly that interpersonal theory and the IPC would augment such an approach for all diagnosis, and recommend that *DSM-5* include assessment of agentic and communal personality features in order to provide additional clinically relevant information beyond identifying the disorder itself (Pilkonis, Hallquist, Morse, & Stepp, 2011; Pincus, 2011; Pincus & Hopwood, in press; Wright, 2011).

Intraindividual Variability

The addition of pathoplasticity greatly extends the empirical and practical utility of interpersonal diagnosis. However, describing psychopathology using dispositional personality concepts implying marked consistency of relational functioning is still insufficient and does not exhaust contemporary interpersonal diagnostic approaches (Pincus & Wright, 2010). Even patients described by a particular interpersonal style do not robotically emit the same behaviors without variation. Recent advances in the measurement and analysis of intraindividual variability (e.g., Erickson, Newman, & Pincus, 2009; Ram & Gerstorf, 2009) converge to suggest that dynamic aspects of interpersonal behavior warrant further investigations and clinical assessment. This accumulating body of research indicates that individuals are characterized not only by their stable individual differences in trait levels of behavior, but also by stable differences in their variability in psychological states (Fleeson, 2001), behaviors (Moskowitz, Russell, Sadikaj, & Sutton, 2009), and affect (Kuppens, Van Mechelen, Nezlek, Dossche, & Timmermans, 2007) across time and situations.

Moskowitz and Zuroff (2004, 2005) introduced the terms *flux*, *pulse*, and *spin* to describe the stable levels of intraindividual variability in interpersonal behaviors sampled from the IPC. *Flux* refers to variability about an individual's mean behavioral score on agentic or communal dimensions (e.g., dominant flux, submissive flux, friendly flux, hostile flux). *Pulse* refers to variability of the overall extremity of the emitted behavior. And *spin* refers to variability of the angular coordinates about the individual's mean interpersonal theme. Low spin would thus reflect a narrow repertoire of interpersonal behaviors enacted over time. Low pulse reflects little variability in behavioral intensity, and if it were associated with a high mean intensity generally, it would be consistent with the enactment of consistently extreme interpersonal behaviors. This dynamic lexicon has important implications for the assessment of normal and abnormal behavior. Theory and research suggest that the assessment of intraindividual variability offers unique and important new methods for the description of personality and psychopathology (Côté, Moskowitz, & Zuroff, in press; Ram, Conroy, Pincus, Hyde, & Molloy, in press).

Russell and colleagues (2007) differentiated individuals with BPD from nonclinical control participants based on intraindividual variability of interpersonal behavior over a 20-day period. Specifically, individuals with BPD reported a similar mean level of agreeable (communal) behavior as compared to their nonclinical counterparts but BPD participants displayed greater flux in their agreeable behaviors suggesting that control participants demonstrated consistent agreeable behavior across situations while individuals with BPD varied greatly in their agreeable behaviors, vacillating between high and low levels. Results also suggested elevated mean levels of submissive behaviors in conjunction with low mean levels of dominant behavior coupled with greater flux in dominant behaviors for individuals with BPD relative to the control participants. However, the groups did not differ in the variability of submissive behaviors. In other words, individuals with BPD were consistently submissive relative to normal controls but also demonstrated acute elevations and declines in their relatively low level of dominant behavior. As predicted, individuals with BPD endorsed higher mean levels of quarrelsome (low communal) behavior and higher levels of flux in quarrelsome behavior when compared to controls. Finally, individuals with BPD also demonstrated greater spin than their nonclinical counterparts suggesting greater behavioral lability. The contemporary interpersonal theory of personality includes flux, pulse, and spin as constructs of behavioral variability that can differentiate phenomenological expression of individual differences and psychopathology.

Interpersonal Signatures

Interpersonal behavior is not emitted in a vacuum; rather it is reciprocally influential in ongoing human transaction. Temporally dynamic interpersonal processes that are contextualized within the social environment (i.e., transactional processes and mechanisms) must be examined in order to fully model social functioning (Ebner-Priemer, Eid, Kleindienst, Stabenow, & Trull, 2009; Mischel & Shoda, 2010). Advances in the study of intraindividual variability have stimulated a major reconceptualization of personality consistency (Fleeson & Noftle, 2008; Funder, 2006). Moving beyond traditional conceptions of cross-situational consistency, personality is considered to reflect stability of behavior within situations and variability of behavior across situations. This increases the salience of contextual factors without losing the essence of personality itself. Assessing personality consistency via the identification of stable if-then behavioral signatures (Kammrath & Scholer, this volume; Shoda, Mischel, & Wright, 1993, 1994) has thus become an important arena of personality research (Mischel & Shoda, 2008). In this approach, the stability of personality and core patterns of psychopathology are anchored to consistent contingent if-then structures of behavioral, emotional, and symptomatic responses (thens) in situations the individual experiences as functionally equivalent (ifs).

Conceptualizing and measuring patterns of variability and stability of interpersonal behavior over time and across situations is an important development for interpersonal theory, as a key implication of situation–behavior contingencies is the need to identify the psychologically salient features of situations, and this requires an organizing psychological theory. Recent work in personality, social, and clinical psychology converges in emphasizing the salience of interpersonal features of situations (Anderson & Thorpe, 2009; Pincus & Ansell, 2003; Pincus et al., 2009, 2010; Pincus & Wright, 2010; Reis, 2008). Importantly, this is directly incorporated into interpersonal theory by the assessment of interpersonal behavior contextualized within interpersonal situations both described on the common metric of agentic and communal dimensions, that is, interpersonal signatures (Moskowitz, 2009). Empirical tests demonstrate that the stability and variability of interpersonal signatures can be modeled in both normal samples (Fournier, Moskowitz, & Zuroff, 2009) and in samples diagnosed with personality pathology (Sadikaj,

Russell, Moskowitz, & Paris, 2010). That is, patterns of interpersonal functioning can be contextualized by linking the perceived agentic and communal characteristics of the other person(s) in an interpersonal situation (ifs) with the behavioral, emotional, and symptomatic responses (thens) of the target person (Roche, Pincus, Conroy, Hyde, & Ram, under review). Consistent with the nature of interpersonal theory, these interpersonal signatures can be conceptualized at a variety of descriptive levels ranging from molar dispositional profiles (e.g., Pincus & Wiggins, 1990; Wiggins & Pincus, 1989) to highly articulated behavioral patterns (e.g., Benjamin, 1996) to the structure of social-cognitive schemas (e.g., Horowitz & Wilson, 2005) and articulations of internal object-relations (Pincus, 2005a).

Interpersonal Complementarity

Within the interpersonal tradition, the framework to examine contextualized dynamic social processes is referred to in terms of adaptive and maladaptive transaction cycles (Kiesler, 1991), self-fulfilling prophecies (Carson, 1982), and vicious circles (Millon, 1996). Reciprocal relational patterns create an interpersonal field (Sullivan, 1948; Wiggins & Trobst, 1999) in which various transactional influences impact both interactants as they resolve, negotiate, or disintegrate the interpersonal situation. Within this field, interpersonal behaviors tend to pull, elicit, invite, or evoke "restricted classes" of responses from the other, and this is a continual, dynamic if-then transactional process. Thus, interpersonal theory emphasizes "field regulatory" processes in addition to "self regulatory" or "affect regulatory" processes (Pincus, 2005a). Carson (1991) referred to this as an interbehavioral contingency process where, "there is a tendency for a given individual's interpersonal behavior to be constrained or controlled in more or less predictable ways by the behavior received from an interaction partner" (p. 191).

The IPC provides conceptual anchors and a lexicon to systematically describe interpersonal signatures (see Table 7.2). The most basic of these processes is referred to as interpersonal *complementarity* (Carson, 1969; Kiesler, 1983). Interpersonal complementarity occurs when there is a match between the field regulatory goals of each person. That is, reciprocal patterns of activity evolve where the agentic and communal needs of both persons are met in the interpersonal situation, leading to stability and likely recurrence of the pattern. Carson (1969) first proposed that complementarity could be defined via the IPC based on the social exchange of status (agency) and love (communion) as reflected in reciprocity for the vertical dimension (i.e., dominance pulls for submission; submission pulls for dominance) and correspondence for the horizontal dimension (friendliness pulls for friendliness; hostility pulls for hostility). Kiesler (1983) extended this by adapting complementarity to the geometry of the IPC model such that the principles of reciprocity and correspondence could be employed to specify complementary points along the entire IPC perimeter. Thus, beyond the cardinal points of the IPC, hostile dominance pulls for hostile submission, friendly dominance pulls for friendly submission, and so on. Although complementarity is neither the only reciprocal interpersonal pattern that can be described by the IPC nor proposed as a universal law of interaction, empirical studies consistently find support for its probabilistic predictions (e.g., Markey, Funder, & Ozer, 2003; Sadler et al., 2009; Sadler et al., 2010). The final contemporary assumption of interpersonal theory (Table 7.1) is that complementarity should be considered a common baseline for the field regulatory influence of interpersonal behavior. Deviations from complementary interpersonal signatures are more likely to disrupt interpersonal relations and may be indicative of pathological functioning (Fournier et al., 2009; Pincus, 2005a; Pincus et al., 2009; Pincus & Hopwood, in press; Roche et al., under review).

The two other broad classes of interpersonal signatures anchored by the IPC model are referred to as acomplementary and anticomplementary patterns (Kiesler, 1983, 1996). When interpersonal signatures meet one of the two rules of complementarity, this is referred to as an acomplementary pattern. In such a case, interactants may exhibit correspondence with regard to nurturance or reciprocity with regard to dominance, but not both. When interactants exhibit neither reciprocity on dominance nor correspondence on nurturance, this is referred to as an anticomplementary pattern. Interpersonal patterns in human transaction directly impact the outcomes of interpersonal situations. Complementary signatures are considered to promote relational stability, that is, such interpersonal situations are resolved, mutually reinforcing, and recurring. Acomplementary signatures are less stable and instigate negotiation towards or away from greater complementarity. Finally, anticomplementary signatures are the most unstable and lead to avoidance, escape, and disintegration of the interpersonal situation (i.e., disrupted interpersonal relations).

Transaction Cycles and Field Regulation

Complementarity is the interpersonal signature that anchors most theoretical discussions of interpersonal interaction. If interpersonal behavior is influential or "field regulatory," there must be some basic goals toward which

behaviors are directed. Social learning underlying one's self-concept and interpersonal relations becomes relatively stable over time due to self-perpetuating influences on awareness and organization of interpersonal experience (input), and the field regulatory influences of interpersonal behavior (output). When we interact with others, a proximal interpersonal field is created where behavior serves to present and define our self-concept and negotiate the kinds of interactions and relationships we seek from others. Sullivan's (1953b) theorem of reciprocal emotion and Leary's (1957) principle of reciprocal interpersonal relations have led to the formal view that we attempt to regulate the responses of the other within the interpersonal field. "Interpersonal behaviors, in a relatively unaware, automatic, and unintended fashion, tend to invite, elicit, pull, draw, or entice from interactants restricted classes of reactions that are reinforcing of, and consistent with, a person's proffered self-definition" (Kiesler, 1983, p. 201; see also Kiesler, 1996). To the extent that individuals can mutually satisfy needs for interaction that are congruent with their self-definitions (i.e., complementarity), the interpersonal situation remains integrated. To the extent this fails, negotiation or disintegration of the interpersonal situation is more probable.

Interpersonal complementarity (or any other interpersonal signature) should not be conceived of as some sort of stimulus-response process based solely on overt actions and reactions (Pincus, 1994). A comprehensive account of the contemporaneous interpersonal situation must bridge the gap between the proximal interpersonal situation and the internal interpersonal situation (e.g., Safran, 1992). Kiesler's (1991) "Interpersonal Transaction Cycle" is the most widely applied framework to describe the relations among proximal and internal interpersonal behavior within the interpersonal tradition. He proposes that the basic components of an interpersonal transaction are (1) Person X's covert experience of Person Y, (2) Person X's overt behavior toward Person Y, (3) Person Y's covert experience in response to Person X's action, and (4) Person Y's overt behavioral response to Person X. These four components are part of an ongoing transactional chain of events cycling toward resolution, further negotiation, or disintegration. Within this process, overt behavioral output serves the purpose of regulating the proximal interpersonal field via elicitation of complementary responses in the other. The IPC specifies the range of descriptive taxa, while the motivational conceptions of interpersonal theory give rise to the nature of regulation of the interpersonal field. For example, dominant interpersonal behavior (e.g., "You have to call your mother") communicates a bid for status (e.g., "I am in charge here") that impacts the other in ways that elicit either complementary (e.g., "You're right, I should do that now") or noncomplementary (e.g., "Quit bossing me around!") responses in an ongoing cycle of reciprocal causality, *mediated by internal subjective experience*.

Although there are a number of proposed constructs related to the covert mediating step in interpersonal transaction cycles (see Pincus, 1994; Pincus & Ansell, 2003, for reviews), contemporary interpersonal theory formally proposes that covert reactions reflect internal interpersonal situations, which can be described using the same agentic and communal constructs that have been applied to the description of proximal interpersonal situations. Normality may reflect the tendency or capacity to perceive proximal interpersonal situations and their field regulatory influences in generally undistorted forms. That is, healthy individuals are generally able to accurately encode the agentic and communal "bids" proffered by the others. Thus, all goes well, the interpersonal situation is resolved, and the relationship is stable. However, this is clearly not always the case, such as in psychotherapy with personality disordered patients. Therapists generally attempt to work in the patient's best interest and promote a positive therapeutic alliance. Patients who are generally free of personality pathology typically enter therapy hoping for relief of their symptoms and are capable of experiencing the therapist as potentially helpful and benign. Thus, the proximal and internal interpersonal situations are consistent with each other and the behavior of therapist and patient is likely to develop into a complementary reciprocal pattern (i.e., a therapeutic alliance). Despite psychotherapists taking a similar stance with personality disordered patients, the beginning of therapy is often quite rocky as the patients tend to view the therapists with suspicion, fear, contempt, intense neediness, idealized expectations, and so on. When the internal interpersonal situation is not consistent with the proximal interpersonal situation the patient may distort the agentic and communal behavior of the therapist (Pincus, 2005a; Pincus & Hopwood, in press). Thus treatment often starts with noncomplementary patterns requiring further negotiation of the therapeutic relationship.

The covert experience of the other is influenced to a greater or lesser degree by enduring tendencies to elaborate incoming interpersonal data in particular ways. Interpersonal theory can accommodate the notion that individuals exhibit tendencies to organize their experience in certain ways (i.e., they have particular interpersonal schemas, expectancies, memories, fantasies), and proposes that the best way to characterize these internal interpersonal

situations is in terms of their agentic and communal characteristics. There are now converging literatures that suggest mental representations of self and other are central structures of personality that significantly affect perception, emotion, cognition, and behavior (Blatt, et al., 1997; Bretherton & Munholland, 2008; Lukowitsky & Pincus, 2011). The fundamental advantage of integrating conceptions of dyadic mental representation into interpersonal theory is the ability to import the proximal interpersonal field (Wiggins & Trobst, 1999) into the intrapsychic world of the interactants (Heck & Pincus, 2001) using a common metric. Thus, an interpersonal relationship is composed of the ongoing participation in proximal interpersonal fields in which overt behavior serves important communicative and regulatory functions, as well as ongoing experiences of internal interpersonal fields that reflect enduring individual differences in covert experience through the elaboration of interpersonal input. The unique and enduring organizational influences that people bring to relationships contribute to their covert feelings, impulses, interpretations, and fantasies in relation to others, and interpersonal theory proposes that overt behavior is mediated by such covert processes. Psychodynamic, attachment, and cognitive theories converge with this assertion, and suggest that dyadic mental representations are key influences on the subjective elaboration of interpersonal input. Integrating pantheoretical representational constructs enhances the explanatory power of interpersonal theory by linking a developmental account of individuals' enduring tendencies to organize interpersonal information in particular ways. The developmental propositions of interpersonal theory describe mechanisms that give rise to such tendencies as well as their functional role in personality.

Parataxic Distortions

Sullivan (1953a) proposed the concept of "parataxic distortion" to describe the mediation of proximal relational behavior by internal subjective interpersonal situations, and suggested that these occur "when, beside the interpersonal situation as defined within the awareness of the speaker, there is a concomitant interpersonal situation quite different as to its principle integrating tendencies, of which the speaker is more or less completely unaware" (p. 92). The effects of parataxic distortions on interpersonal relations can occur in several forms, including chronic distortions of new interpersonal experiences (input): generation of rigid, extreme, and/or chronically non-normative interpersonal behavior (output): and dominance of self-protective motives (Horowitz, 2004; Horowitz et al., 2006) leading to the disconnection of interpersonal input and output (see also Eaton, South, & Krueger, 2009).

Normal and pathological personalities may be differentiated by their enduring tendencies to organize interpersonal experience in particular ways, leading to integrated or disturbed interpersonal relations. Interpersonal theory proposes that healthy relations are promoted by the capacity to organize and elaborate incoming interpersonal input in generally undistorted ways, allowing for the agentic and communal needs of self and other to be mutually satisfied. That is, the proximal interpersonal field and the internal interpersonal field are relatively consistent (i.e., free of parataxic distortion). Maladaptive interpersonal functioning is promoted when the proximal interpersonal field is encoded in distorted or biased ways, leading to increased interpersonal insecurity, and behavior (output) that disrupts interpersonal relations due to noncontingent field regulatory influences. To account for the development and frequency of such distortions in personality, key developmental, motivational, and regulatory principles must be articulated.

KEY CONCEPTS OF INTERPERSONAL THEORY: II. DEVELOPMENT, MOTIVATION, AND REGULATION

An interpersonal theory of personality can only be comprehensive if, beyond description of interpersonal themes and interpersonal dynamics based on the metaconcepts of agency and communion, it also accounts for the development and maintenance of healthy and disordered self-concepts and patterns of interpersonal relating. Key developmental, motivational, and regulatory concepts of contemporary interpersonal theory are briefly summarized in Table 7.3.

Attachment and the Internalization of Interpersonal Experience

The first interpersonal situations occur during infancy. Horowitz (2004) proposed that the two fundamental tasks associated with the infant attachment system (staying close/connecting to caregivers, separating and exploring) are the first communal and agentic motives, respectively. According to attachment theory (Bowlby, 1969, 1973; Cassidy, 1999), repeated interactions become schematized interpersonal representations, or internal working models,

TABLE 7.3 Developmental, Motivational, and Regulatory Concepts of Contemporary Interpersonal Theory

Copy Processes	
Identification	Treat others as you were treated by attachment figures.
Recapitulation	Act as if attachment figures are still present and in control.
Introjection	Treat self as you were treated by attachment figures.
Catalysts of Internalization	
Developmental Achievements	Attachment, Security, Separation-Individuation, Positive Affects, Gender Identity, Resolution of Oedipal Dynamics, Self-Esteem, Self-Confirmation, Mastery of Unresolved Conflicts, Adult Identity
Traumatic Learning	Early Loss of Attachment Figure, Childhood Illness or Injury, Physical Abuse, Sexual Abuse, Emotional Abuse, Parental Neglect
Interpersonal Motives	
Agentic	Individuation, Power, Mastery, Assertion, Autonomy, Status
Communal	Attachment, Intimacy, Belongingness, Love
Self-Protective	Regulatory strategies to cope with feelings of vulnerability arising from relational experience
Regulatory Metagoals	
Self Regulation	Esteem, Cohesion, Control, Focus, Confidence
Affect Regulation	Negative Affectivity, Positive Affectivity
Field Regulation	Behavior/Feelings of Proximal Other(s), Behavior/Feelings of Internalized Other(s)

that guide perception, emotion, and behavior in relationships. These processes lead to the development of secure or insecure attachment, which has significant implications for personality and psychopathology (Shorey & Snyder, 2006). Over time, these generalize via adult attachment patterns associated with agentic and communal motives, traits, and behaviors (Bartholomew & Horowitz, 1991; Gallo et al., 2003). Horowitz (2004) also suggested that insecure attachment leads to significant self-protective motivations that can interfere with healthy agentic and communal functioning, an important issue we take up later.

Interpersonal Copy Processes

Similarly, Benjamin's (1993, 2003) Developmental Learning and Loving Theory argues that attachment itself is the fundamental motivation that catalyzes social learning processes. She proposed and empirically examined (Critchfield & Benjamin, 2008, 2010) three developmental "copy processes" that describe the ways in which early interpersonal experiences are internalized as a function of achieving attachment, be it secure or insecure (see

Table 7.3). The first is identification, which is defined as "treating others as one has been treated." To the extent that individuals strongly identify with attachment figures, there will be a tendency to act toward others in ways that copy how important others have acted toward the developing person. When doing so, such behaviors are associated with positive reflected appraisals of the self from the internal working model of the attachment figure. This mediates the selection of interpersonal output and may lead to repetition of such behavior regardless of the field regulatory pulls of the actual other, that is, noncomplementary reciprocal patterns. The second copy process is recapitulation, which is defined as "maintaining a position complementary to an internalized other." This can be described as reacting "as if" the internalized other is still there and in control of things. In this case, new interpersonal input is likely to be elaborated in a distorted way such that the proximal other is experienced as similar to the internalized other, or new interpersonal input from the proximal other may simply be ignored and field regulation is focused on the dominant internalized other. This again may lead to noncomplementary reciprocal patterns in the proximal interpersonal situation while complementary interpersonal patterns are played out in the internal interpersonal situation. The third copy process is introjection, which is defined as "treating the self as one has been treated." By treating the self in introjected ways, the internal interpersonal situation may promote security and esteem (see Loevinger's [1966] first principle and Benjamin's [1996] concept of psychic proximity) even while generating noncomplementary behavior in the proximal interpersonal situation.

Catalysts of Internalization and Social Learning

Pincus and Ansell (2003) extended the catalysts of social learning beyond attachment motivation by proposing that "Reciprocal interpersonal patterns develop in concert with emerging motives that take developmental priority" (p. 223). These developmentally emergent motives may begin with the formation of early attachment bonds and felt security; but later, separation-individuation and the experiences of self-esteem and positive emotions may become priorities. Later still, adult identity formation and its confirmation from the social world, as well as mastery of continuing unresolved conflicts may take precedence. In addition to the achievement of emerging developmental goals, influential interpersonal patterns are also associated with traumatic learning that leads to self-protective motives and requirements to cope with impinging events such as early loss of an attachment figure, childhood

illness or injury, and neglect or abuse. Individuals internalize such experiences in the form of consistent interpersonal themes and dynamics. These themes and dynamics become the basis for the recurrent interpersonal situations that characterize a human life. If we are to understand the relational strategies individuals employ when such developmental motives or traumas are reactivated, we must learn what interpersonal behaviors and patterns were associated with achievement or frustration of particular developmental milestones or were required to cope with stressors and to regulate emotions and the self in the first place. Table 7.3 presents a list of probable catalysts.

Identifying the developmental and traumatic catalysts for internalization and social learning of interpersonal themes and dynamics allows for greater understanding of current behavior. For example, in terms of achieving adult attachment relationships, some individuals have developed hostile strategies like verbally or physically fighting in order to elicit some form of interpersonal connection, while others have developed submissive strategies like avoiding conflict and deferring to the wishes of the other in order to be liked and elicit gratitude. A person's social learning history will significantly influence their ability to accurately organize new interpersonal experiences. In a toxic early environment, behavior will be non-normative, but will mature in the service of attachment needs, self-protection, and developmental achievements, and be maintained via internalization. This may lead to a strong tendency to be dominated by self-protective motives and parataxic distortions of new interpersonal experience.

Generalized Social Learning: Self-Protective Motives, Parataxic Distortion, and Regulatory Metagoals

For individuals with notable personality problems, the experience of others is often distorted by strong identifications, recapitulations of relationships with parents and other attachment figures, and the dominance of introjected, often self-destructive, behaviors (Benjamin, 2003; Pincus & Hopwood, in press). This, in turn, leads to parataxic distortions of the proximal interpersonal situation and frequent noncomplementary reciprocal interpersonal patterns that disrupt relationships. Why does this occur? Beyond agentic and communal motives, contemporary interpersonal theory identifies a third class of interpersonal motives referred to as "self-protective motives," which can be described as arising "as a way of defending oneself from feelings of vulnerability that are related to relational schemas" that often take the form of "strategies people use to reassure themselves that they possess desired communal (e.g., likeable) and agentic (e.g., competent) self-qualities" (Horowitz et al., 2006, pp. 75–76). To the extent that a person has strongly copied internalized interpersonal themes and dynamics associated with a toxic developmental environment, difficulties with developmental achievements, and insecure attachment, the more likely they are to exhibit parataxic distortions of interpersonal situations, feel threatened and vulnerable due to their characteristic ways of organizing interpersonal experience, and engage in self-protective interpersonal behavior that is noncontingent with the behavior of others or the normative situational press. The severity of personality pathology could be evaluated in terms of the pervasiveness of parataxic distortions over time and situations. Severe personality pathology is often reflected in pervasive chronic or chaotic parataxic distortions. The former render the experience of most interpersonal situations functionally equivalent (and typically anxiety provoking and threatening to the self); while the latter render the experience of interpersonal situations highly inconsistent and unpredictable (commonly oscillating between secure and threatening organizations of experience).

We propose that when self-protective motives are strong, they are linked with one or more of three superordinate regulatory functions or metagoals (Pincus, 2005a): self-regulation, emotion regulation, and field regulation (see Table 7.3). The concept of regulation is ubiquitous in psychological theory, particularly in the domain of human development. Most theories of personality emphasize the importance of developing mechanisms for emotion-regulation and self-regulation (Carver & Scheier, this volume). Interpersonal theory is unique in its added emphasis on field-regulation, that is, the processes by which the behavior of self and other transactionally influence each other. The emerging developmental achievements and the coping demands of traumas listed in Table 7.3 all have significant implications for emotion-, self-, and field-regulation. Pervasive, socially learned and self-perpetuating internalized self-protective interpersonal patterns render many interpersonal situations functionally equivalent. This contributes to the generalization of interpersonal learning by providing a small number of superordinate psychological triggers (e.g., other's coldness or other's control) to guide psychological functioning, for example, motives, schemas, expectancies, and behavior choice.

The importance of distinguishing these three regulatory metagoals is most directly related to understanding the shifting priorities that may be associated with interpersonal behavior, giving rise to unique patterns of intraindividual variability and interpersonal signatures. At any given time, the most prominent metagoal may be proximal field regulation. However, the narcissistic person's derogation of others to promote self-esteem demonstrates that interpersonal behavior may also be associated with self-regulation, and the histrionic person's use of sexual availability in order to feel more emotionally secure and stable shows the application of interpersonal behavior for emotion regulation. Although healthy relationships may (and do) serve as appropriate regulators of self and affect, interpersonal behavior chronically motivated solely in the service of regulating the self or emotion is likely to reduce the contingencies associated with the behavior of the other person and situational norms, and promote further parataxic distortion.

Development of Normal and Abnormal Personality

Contemporary interpersonal theory suggests that normality and psychopathology can be differentiated via the relative success or impairment in calibrating interpersonal relations to facilitate the mutual satisfaction of agentic and communal motives and goals. The key processes involve the capacity to enter into new proximal interpersonal situations without parataxic distortion (Pincus, 2005a; Pincus & Hopwood, in press). In other words, the wider the range of proximal interpersonal situations that can be entered in which the person exhibits anxiety-free functioning (little effort required for emotion regulation) and maintains self-esteem (little effort required for self-regulation), the more adaptive the individual. When this is the case, self-protective motives are not evoked and there is no need to activate mediating interpersonal schemas, or competing regulatory needs. The person can focus on the proximal situation, encode incoming interpersonal input without distortion, respond in adaptive ways that facilitate interpersonal relations (i.e., meet the agentic and communal needs of self and other), and establish complementary patterns of reciprocal behavior by fully participating in the relationship. The individual's current behavior will exhibit relatively strong contingency with the proximal behavior of the other and the normative contextual press of the situation. Adaptive interpersonal functioning is promoted by relatively trauma-free development in a culturally normative facilitating environment that has allowed the person to achieve most developmental milestones in normative ways, leading to full capacity to encode and elaborate incoming interpersonal input without bias from competing psychological needs.

However, when the individual develops in a traumatic or non-normative environment, significant non-normative interpersonal learning around basic motives such as attachment, individuation, gender identity, and so on, may be internalized and associated with difficulties in self-regulation, emotion-regulation, and field-regulation. In contrast to normality, psychopathology is reflected in a large range of proximal interpersonal situations that elicit anxiety, threaten self-esteem, and promote dysregulation. This, in turn, evokes self-protective motives, activating specific self- and emotion-regulation strategies and eliciting dysfunctional behaviors that disrupt interpersonal relations (non-normative field-regulation strategies). When this is the case, internal interpersonal situations dominate the organization of experience and the individual is prone to exhibit various forms of parataxic distortion as his or her interpersonal learning history dictates. Thus the perception of the proximal interpersonal situation is mediated by internal experience, incoming interpersonal input is distorted, behavioral responses (output) disrupt interpersonal relations (i.e., fail to meet the agentic and communal needs of self and other), and relationships tend toward maladaptive patterns of reciprocal behavior. The individual's current behavior will exhibit relatively weak contingency with the proximal behavior of the other.

CONCLUSION

The contemporary interpersonal theory of personality is a robust, interdisciplinary, and integrative nomological framework that continues to evolve both conceptually and methodologically, incorporating advances that keep pace with psychological science. Some theories fade with time, but interpersonal theory is growing more sophisticated, precise, rigorous, and generalizeable (Horowitz & Strack, 2010a). Although empirical investigations of interpersonal dispositions as assessed by IPC-based measures are abundant, research on interpersonal pathoplasticity, intraindividual variability of interpersonal behavior, and interpersonal signatures has only emerged in the last decade, taking advantage of new developments in psychological science. Although it is too early to provide definitive, empirically validated interpersonal models that integrate dispositions and dynamic personality processes, we conclude by highlighting three fruitful interrelated areas for future research. First, personality research should continue efforts to establish and clarify the nature of normal and pathological interpersonal patterns (prototypic, pathoplastic, situationally contingent). Second, empirical

tests of the within-person dynamics of behavior using multilevel modeling and latent growth curve frameworks can examine associations between social processes and changes in affects, well-being, and symptoms. Finally, clinical research should aim to demonstrate the incremental utility of interpersonal diagnostic information for treatment planning, treatment effectiveness, and treatment efficacy.

REFERENCES

aan het Rot, M., Moskowitz, D. S., Pinard, G., & Young, S. N. (2006). Social behaviour and mood in everyday life: The effects of tryptophan in quarrelsome individuals. *Journal of Psychiatry and Neuroscience, 31,* 253–262.

Alden, L. E., & Capreol, M. J. (1993). Avoidant personality disorder: Interpersonal problems as predictors of treatment response. *Behavior Therapy, 24,* 357–376.

Alden, L. E., Wiggins, J. S., & Pincus, A. L. (1990). Construction of circumplex scales for the Inventory of Interpersonal Problems. *Journal of Personality Assessment, 55,* 521–536.

Ambwani, S., & Hopwood, C. J. (2009). The utility of considering interpersonal problems in the assessment of bulimic features. *Eating Behaviors, 10,* 247–253.

American Psychiatric Association. (2000). *Diagnostic and statistical manual for mental disorders DSM-IV-TR* (4th ed.). Washington, DC: American Psychiatric Association.

Anchin, J. C., & Pincus, A. L. (2010). Evidence-based interpersonal psychotherapy with personality disorders: Theory, components, and strategies. In J. J. Magnavita (Ed.), *Evidence-based treatment of personality dysfunction: Principles, methods, and processes* (pp. 113–166). Washington, DC: American Psychological Association.

Anderson, S. M., & Thorpe, J. S. (2009). An IF-THEN theory of personality: Significant others and the relational self. *Journal of Research in Personality, 43,* 163–170.

Ansell, E. B., Grilo, C. M., & White, M. E. (2012). Examining the interpersonal model of binge eating and loss of control over eating in women. *International Journal of Eating Disorders, 45,* 43–50.

Bakan, D. (1966). *The duality of human existence: Isolation and communion in Western man.* Boston: Beacon Press.

Bartholomew, K., & Horowitz, L. M. (1991). Attachment styles among young adults: A test of a four-category model. *Journal of Personality and Social Psychology, 61,* 226–244.

Beck, A. T. (1983). Cognitive therapy of depression: New perspectives. In P. J. Clayton & J. E. Barrett (Eds.), *Treatment of depression: Old controversies and new approaches* (pp. 265–290). New York, NY: Raven.

Benjamin, L. S. (1974). Structural analysis of social behavior. *Psychological Review, 81,* 392–425.

Benjamin, L. S. (1993). Every psychopathology is a gift of love. *Psychotherapy Research, 3,* 1–24.

Benjamin, L. S. (1996). *Interpersonal diagnosis and treatment of personality disorders* (2nd ed.). New York, NY: Guilford Press.

Benjamin, L. S. (2003). *Interpersonal reconstructive therapy: Promoting change in nonresponders.* New York, NY: Guilford Press.

Benjamin, L. S. (2010). Structural analysis of social behavior: Studying the nature of nature. In L. M. Horowitz & S. Strack (Eds.), *Handbook of interpersonal psychology* (pp. 325–342). Hoboken, NJ: Wiley.

Blatt, S. J. (2004). *Experiences of depression: Theoretical, clinical, and research perspectives.* Washington, DC: American Psychological Association.

Blatt, S. J. (2008). *Polarities of experience: Relatedness and self-definition in personality development, psychopathology, and the therapeutic process.* Washington, DC: American Psychological Association.

Blatt, S. J., Auerbach, J. S., & Levy, K. N. (1997). Mental representations in personality development, psychopathology, and the therapeutic process. *Review of General Psychology, 1*, 351–374.

Blatt, S. J., & Luyten, P. (2010). Relatedness and self-definition in normal and disrupted personality development. In L. M. Horowitz & S. Strack (Eds.), *Handbook of interpersonal psychology* (pp. 37–56). Hoboken, NJ: Wiley.

Bowlby, J. (1969). *Attachment and loss: Vol 1. Attachment.* New York, NY: Basic Books.

Bowlby, J. (1973). *Attachment and loss: Separation: Anxiety and Anger.* New York, NY: Basic Books.

Bretherton, I., & Munholland, K. A. (2008). Internal working models in attachment relationships: Elaborating a central construct in attachment theory. In J. Cassidy & P. Shaver (Eds.), *Handbook of attachment: Theory, research and clinical application* (2nd ed., pp. 102–127). New York, NY: Guilford Press.

Cain, N. M., Ansell, E. B., Wright, A. G. C., Hopwood, C. J., Thomas, K. M., Pinto, A., . . . Grilo, C. M. (2012) Interpersonal pathoplasticity in the course of major depression. *Journal of Consulting and Clinical Psychology, 80*, 78–86.

Cain, N. M., Pincus, A. L., & Grosse Holtforth, M. (2010). Interpersonal subtypes in social phobia: Diagnostic and treatment implications. *Journal of Personality Assessment, 92*, 514–527.

Carson, R. C. (1969). *Interaction concepts of personality.* Chicago, IL: Aldine.

Carson, R. C. (1982). Self-fulfilling prophecy, maladaptive behavior, and psychotherapy. In J. C. Anchin & D. J. Kiesler (Eds.), *Handbook of interpersonal psychotherapy* (pp. 64–77). New York, NY: Pergamon Press.

Carson, R. C. (1991). The social-interactional viewpoint. In M. Hersen, A. Kazdin, & A. Bellack (Eds.), *The clinical psychology handbook* (2nd ed., pp. 185–199). New York, NY: Pergamon Press.

Carson, R. C. (1996). Seamlessness in personality and its derangements. *Journal of Personality Assessment, 66*, 240–247.

Cassidy, J. (1999). The nature of the child's ties. In J. Cassidy & P. Shaver (Eds.), *Handbook of attachment: Theory, research, and clinical applications* (pp. 3–20). New York, NY: Guilford Press.

Côté, S., Moskowitz, D. S., & Zuroff, D. C. (in press). Social relationships and intraindividual variability in interpersonal behavior: Correlates of interpersonal spin. *Journal of Personality and Social Psychology.*

Critchfield, K. L., & Benjamin, L. S. (2008). Internalized representations of early interpersonal experience and adult relationships: A test of copy process theory in clinical and non–clinical settings. *Psychiatry, 71*, 71–92.

Critchfield, K. L., & Benjamin, L. S. (2010). Assessment of repeated relational patterns for individual cases using the SASB-based Intrex Questionnaire. *Journal of Personality Assessment, 92*, 480–589.

Depue, R. A. (2006). Interpersonal behavior and the structure of personality: Neurobehavioral foundation of agentic extraversion and affiliation. In T. Canli (Ed.), *Biology of personality and individual differences* (pp. 60–92). New York, NY: Guilford Press.

Di Blas, L., Grassi, M., Luccio, R., & Momenté, S. (in press). Assessing the interpersonal circumplex model in late childhood: The interpersonal behavior for questionnaire for children. *Assessment.*

Dickinson, K. A., & Pincus, A. L. (2003). Interpersonal analysis of grandiose and vulnerable narcissism. *Journal of Personality Disorders, 17*, 188–207.

Eaton, N. R., South, S. C., & Krueger, R. F. (2009). The cognitive–affective processing system (CAPS) approach to personality and the concept of personality disorder: Integrating clinical and social-cognitive research. *Journal of Research in Personality, 43*, 208–217.

Ebner-Priemer, U. W., Eid, M., Kleindienst, N., Stabenow, S., & Trull, T. J. (2009). Analytic strategies for understanding affective (in)stability and other dynamic processes in psychopathology. *Journal of Abnormal Psychology, 118*, 195–202.

Erickson, T. M., Newman, M. G., & Pincus, A. L. (2009). Predicting unpredictability: Do measures of interpersonal rigidity/flexibility and distress predict intraindividual variability in social perceptions and behavior? *Journal of Personality and Social Psychology, 97*, 893–912.

Fleeson, W. (2001). Toward a structure- and process-integrated view of personality: Traits as density distributions of states. *Journal of Personality and Social Psychology, 80*(6), 1011–1027.

Fleeson, W., & Noftle, E. E. (2008). Where does personality have its influence? A supermatrix of consistency concepts. *Journal of Personality, 76*, 1355–1386.

Florsheim, P., & McArthur, L. (2009). An interpersonal approach to attachment and change. In J. H. Obegi & E. Berent (Eds.), *Attachment theory and research in clinical work with adults* (pp. 379–409). New York, NY: Guilford Press.

Fournier, M. A., Moskowitz, D. S., & Zuroff, D. C. (2008). Integrating dispositions, signatures, and the interpersonal domain. *Journal of Personality and Social Psychology, 94*, 531–545.

Fournier, M., Moskowitz, D. S., & Zuroff, D. (2009). The interpersonal signature. *Journal of Research in Personality, 43*, 155–162.

Fournier, M. A., Moskowitz, D. S., & Zuroff, D. C. (2010). Origins and applications of the interpersonal circumplex. In L. M. Horowitz & S. Strack (Eds.), *Handbook of interpersonal psychology* (pp. 57–73). Hoboken, NJ: Wiley.

Fournier, M. A., Zuroff, D. C., & Moskowitz, D. S. (2007). The social competition theory of depression: Gaining from an evolutionary approach to losing. *Journal of Social & Clinical Psychology, 26*, 786–790.

Funder, D. C. (2006). Towards a resolution of the personality triad: Persons, situations, and behaviors. *Journal of Research in Personality, 40*, 21–34.

Gallo, L. C., Smith, T. W., & Cox, C. M. (2006). Socioeconomic status, psychosocial processes, and perceived health: An interpersonal perspective. *Annals of Behavioral Medicine, 31*, 109–119.

Gallo, L. C., Smith, T. W., & Ruiz, J. M. (2003). An interpersonal analysis of adult attachment style: Circumplex descriptions, recalled developmental experiences, self-representations, and interpersonal functioning in adulthood. *Journal of Personality, 71*, 141–181.

Gifford, R. (1991). Mapping nonverbal behavior on the interpersonal circle. *Journal of Personality and Social Psychology, 61*, 279–288.

Grosse Holtforth, M., Thomas, A., & Caspar, F. (2010). Interpersonal motivation. In L. M. Horowitz & S. Strack (Eds.), *Handbook of interpersonal psychology* (pp. 107–122). Hoboken, NJ: Wiley.

Gurtman, M. B., & Balakrishnan, J. D. (1998). Circular measurement redux: The analysis and interpretation of interpersonal circle profiles. *Clinical Psychology: Science and Practice, 5*, 344–360.

Gurtman, M. B., & Pincus, A. L. (2000). Interpersonal adjective scales: Confirmation of circumplex structure from multiple perspectives. *Personality and Social Psychology Bulletin, 26*, 374–384.

Gurtman, M. B., & Pincus, A. L. (2003). The circumplex model: Methods and research applications. In J. A. Schnika & W. F. Velicer (Eds.), *Comprehensive handbook of psychology, Vol. 2: Research methods in psychology* (pp. 407–428). Hoboken, NJ: Wiley.

Hatcher, R. L., & Rogers, D. T. (2009). Development and validation of a measure of interpersonal strengths: The inventory of interpersonal strengths. *Psychological Assessment, 21*, 554–569.

Heck, S. A., & Pincus, A. L. (2001). Agency and communion in the structure of parental representations. *Journal of Personality Assessment, 76*, 180–184.

Hopwood, C. J. (2010). An interpersonal perspective on the personality assessment process. *Journal of Personality Assessment, 92*, 471–479.

Hopwood, C. J., Ansell, E. B., Pincus, A. L., Wright, A. G. C., Lukowitsky, M. R., & Roche, M. J. (2011). The circumplex structure of interpersonal sensitivities. *Journal of Personality, 79*, 707–740.

Hopwood, C. J., Clarke, A. N., & Perez, M. (2007). Pathoplasticity of bulimic features and interpersonal problems. *International Journal of Eating Disorders, 40*, 652–658.

Horowitz, L. M. (2004). *Interpersonal foundations of psychopathology*. Washington, DC: American Psychological Association.

Horowitz, L. M., & Strack, S. (2010a). *Handbook of interpersonal psychology*. Hoboken, NJ: Wiley.

Horowitz, L. M., & Strack, S. (2010b). Summary and concluding remarks. In L. M. Horowitz & S. N. Strack (Eds.), *Handbook of interpersonal psychology* (pp. 579–592). Hoboken, NJ: Wiley.

Horowitz, L. M., & Wilson, K. R. (2005). Interpersonal motives and personality disorders. In S. Strack (Ed.), *Handbook of personology and psychopathology* (pp. 495–510). Hoboken, NJ: Wiley.

Horowitz, L. M., Wilson, K. R., Turan, B., Zolotsev, P., Constantino, M. J., & Henderson, L. (2006). How interpersonal motives clarify the meaning of interpersonal behavior: A revised circumplex model. *Personality and Social Psychology Review, 10*, 67–86.

Hoyenga, K. B., Hoyenga, K. T., Walters, K., & Schmidt, J. A. (1998). Applying the interpersonal circle and evolutional theory to gender differences in psychopathological traits. In L. Ellis & L. Ebertz (Eds.), *Males, females, and behavior: Toward biological understanding* (pp. 213–240). Westport: Praeger/Greenwood.

Kachin, K. E., Newman, M. G., & Pincus, A. L. (2001). An interpersonal problem approach to the division of social phobia subtypes. *Behavior Therapy, 32*, 479–501.

Kiesler, D. J. (1983). The 1982 interpersonal circle: A taxonomy for complementarity in human transactions. *Psychological Review, 90*, 185–214.

Kiesler, D. J. (1991). Interpersonal methods of assessment and diagnosis. In C. R. Snyder & D. R. Forsyth (Eds.), *Handbook of social and clinical psychology* (pp. 438–468). New York, NY: Pergamon Press.

Kiesler, D. J. (1996). *Contemporary interpersonal theory and research: Personality, psychopathology, and psychotherapy*. Hoboken, NJ: Wiley.

Kiesler, D. J., Schmidt, J. A., & Wagner, C. C. (1997). A circumplex inventory of impact messages: An operational bridge between emotion and interpersonal behavior. In R. Plutchik & H. Contes (Eds.), *Circumplex mdels of personality and emotions* (pp. 221–244). Washington, DC: American Psychological Association.

Klein, D. N., Kotov, R., & Bufferd, S. J. (2011). Personality and depression: Explanatory models and review of the evidence. *Annual Review of Clinical Psychology, 7*, 269–295.

Klein, M. H., Wonderlich, S., & Shea, M. T. (1993). Models of relationships between personality and depression: Toward a framework for theory and research. In M. Klein, D. Kupfer, & M. Tracie (Eds.), *Personality and depression: A current view* (pp. 1–54). New York, NY: Guilford Press.

Kuppens, P., Van Mechelen, I., Nezlek, J. B., Dossche, D., & Timmermans, T. (2007). Individual differences in core affect variability and their relationship to personality and psychological adjustment. *Emotion, 7*, 262–274.

LaForge, R. (2004). The early development of the interpersonal system of personality (ISP). *Multivariate Behavioral Research, 39*, 359–378.

LaForge, R., Freedman, M. B., & Wiggins, J. S. (1985). Interpersonal circumplex models: 1948–1983. *Journal of Personality Assessment, 49*, 613–631.

Leary, T. (1957). *Interpersonal diagnosis of personality*. New York, NY: Ronald Press.

Leichsenring, F., Kunst, H., & Hoyer, J. (2003). Borderline personality organization in violent offenders: Correlations of identity diffusion and primitive defense mechanisms with antisocial features, neuroticism, and interpersonal problems. *Bulletin of the Menninger Clinic, 67*, 314–327.

Leihener, F., Wagner, A., Haff, B., Schmidt, C., Lieb, K., Stieglitz, R., & Bohus, M. (2003). Subtype differentiation of patients with borderline personality disorder using a circumplex model of interpersonal behavior. *Journal of Nervous and Mental Disease, 191*, 248–254.

Lenzenweger, M. F., Johnson, M. D., & Willett, J. B. (2004). Individual growth curve analysis illuminates stability and change in personality disorder features: The longitudinal study of personality disorders. *Archives of General Psychiatry, 61*, 1015–1024.

Locke, K. D. (2000). Circumplex scales of interpersonal values: Reliability, validity, and applicability to interpersonal problems and personality disorders. *Journal of Personality Assessment, 75*, 249–267.

Locke, K. D. (2006). Interpersonal circumplex measures. In S. Strack (Ed.), *Differentiating normal and abnormal personality* (2nd ed., pp. 383–400). New York, NY: Springer.

Locke, K. D. (2010). Circumplex measures of interpersonal constructs. In L. M. Horowitz & S. Strack (Eds.), *Handbook of interpersonal psychology* (pp. 313–324). Hoboken, NJ: Wiley.

Locke, K. D., & Sadler, P. (2007). Self-efficacy, values, and complementarity in dyadic interactions: Integrating interpersonal and social-cognitive theory. *Personality and Social Psychology Bulletin, 33*, 94–109.

Loevinger, J. (1966). The meaning and measurement of ego development. *American Psychologist, 21*, 195–206.

Lukowitsky, M. R., & Pincus, A. L. (2011). The pantheoretical nature of mental representations and their ability to predict interpersonal adjustment in a nonclinical sample. *Psychoanalytic Psychology, 28*, 48–74.

Luyten, P., & Blatt, S. J. (2011). Integrating theory-driven and empirically-derived models of personality development and psychopathology: A proposal for DSM V. *Clinical Psychology Review, 31*, 52–68.

Markey, P. M., Funder, D. C., & Ozer, D. J. (2003). Complementarity of interpersonal behaviors in dyadic interactions. *Personality and Social Psychology Bulletin, 29*, 1082–1090.

Miller, J. D., Hoffman, B. J., Gaughan, E. T., Gentile, B., Maples, J., & Campbell, W. K. (2011). Grandiose and vulnerable narcissism: A nomological network analysis. *Journal of Personality, 79*, 1013–1042.

Millon, T. (1996). *Disorders of personality: DSM-IV and beyond*. New York, NY: Wiley.

Millon, T. (2000). Reflections on the future of DSM axis II. *Journal of Personality Disorders, 14*, 30–41.

Millon, T. (2005). Reflections on the future of personology and psychopathology. In S. Strack (Ed.), *Handbook of personology and psychopathology* (pp. 527–546). Hoboken, NJ: Wiley.

Mischel, W., & Shoda, Y. (2008). Toward a unified theory of personality: Integrating dispositions and processing dynamics within the cognitive–affective personality system. In O. John, R. Robbins & L. Pervin (Eds.), *Handbook of personality: Theory and research* (3rd ed., pp. 208–241). New York, NY: Guilford Press.

Mischel, W., & Shoda, Y. (2010). The situated person. In B. Mesquita, L. Feldman-Barrett, & E. R. Smith (Eds.), *The mind in context* (pp. 149–173). New York, NY: Guilford Press.

Moskowitz, D. S. (1994). Cross-situational generality and the interpersonal circumplex. *Journal of Personality and Social Psychology, 66*, 921–933.

Moskowitz, D. S. (2005). Unfolding interpersonal behavior. *Journal of Personality, 73*, 1607–1632.

Moskowitz, D. S. (2009). Coming full circle: Conceptualizing the study of interpersonal behaviour. *Canadian Psychology/Psychologie Canadienne, 50*, 33–41.

Moskowitz, D. S., Russell, J. J., Sadikaj, G., & Sutton, R. (2009). Measure people intensively. *Canadian Psychology/Psychologie Canadienne, 50*, 131–140.

Moskowitz, D. S., & Zuroff, D. C. (2004). Flux, pulse, and spin: Dynamic additions to the personality lexicon. *Journal of Personality and Social Psychology, 86*, 880–893.

Moskowitz, D. S., & Zuroff, D. C. (2005). Robust predictors of flux, pulse, and spin. *Journal of Research in Personality, 39*, 130–147.

O'Connor, B. P., & Dyce, J. A. (2001). Rigid and extreme: A geometric representation of personality disorders in five-factor model space. *Journal of Personality and Social Psychology, 81*, 1119–1130.

Pilkonis, P. A., Hallquist, M. N., Morse, J. Q., & Stepp, S. D. (2011). Striking the (im)proper balance between scientific advances and clinical utility: Commentary on the DSM-5 proposal for personality disorders. *Personality Disorders: Theory, Research, and Treatment, 2*, 68–82.

Pincus, A. L. (1994). The interpersonal circumplex and the interpersonal theory: Perspectives on personality and its pathology. In S. Strack & M. Lorr (Eds.), *Differentiating normal and abnormal personality* (pp. 114–136). New York, NY: Springer.

Pincus, A. L. (2005a). A contemporary integrative interpersonal theory of personality disorders. In J. Clarkin & M. Lenzenweger (Eds.), *Major theories of personality disorder* (2nd ed., pp. 282–331). New York, NY: Guilford Press.

Pincus, A. L. (2005b). The interpersonal nexus of personality disorders. In S. Strack (Ed.), *Handbook of personology and psychopathology* (pp. 120–139). New York, NY: Wiley.

Pincus, A. L. (2010). Introduction to the special series on integrating personality, psychopathology, and psychotherapy using interpersonal assessment. *Journal of Personality Assessment, 92*, 467–470.

Pincus, A. L. (2011). Some comments on nomology, diagnostic process, and narcissistic personality disorder in the DSM-5 proposal for personality and personality disorder disorders. *Personality Disorders: Theory, Research, and Treatment, 2*, 41–53.

Pincus, A. L., & Ansell, E. B. (2003). Interpersonal theory of personality. In T. Millon & M. Lerner (Eds.), *Personality and social psychology* (pp. 209–229). Vol. 5 in I. B. Weiner (Ed.-in-Chief), *Handbook of psychology*. Hoboken, NJ: Wiley.

Pincus, A. L., & Cain, N. M. (2008). Interpersonal psychotherapy. In D. C. S. Richard & S. K. Huprich (Eds.), *Clinical psychology: Assessment, treatment, and research* (pp. 213–245). San Diego, CA: Academic Press.

Pincus, A. L., & Gurtman, M. B. (2006). Interpersonal theory and the interpersonal circumplex: Evolving perspectives on normal and abnormal personality. In S. Strack (Ed.), *Differentiating normal and abnormal personality* (2nd ed., pp. 83–111). New York, NY: Springer.

Pincus, A. L., & Hopwood, C. J. (in press). A contemporary interpersonal model of personality pathology and personality disorder. In T. A. Widiger (Ed.), *Oxford handbook of personality disorders*. New York, NY: Oxford University Press.

Pincus, A. L., & Lukowitsky, M. R. (2010). Pathological narcissism and narcissistic personality disorder. *Annual Review of Clinical Psychology, 6*, 421–446.

Pincus, A. L., Lukowitsky, M. R., & Wright, A. G. C. (2010). The interpersonal nexus of personality and psychopathology. In T. Millon, R. F. Krueger, & E. Simonsen (Eds.), *Contemporary directions in psychopathology: Scientific foundations of the DSM-5 and ICD-11* (pp. 523–552). New York, NY: Guilford Press.

Pincus, A. L., Lukowitsky, M. R., Wright, A. G. C., & Eichler, W. C. (2009). The interpersonal nexus of persons, situations, and psychopathology. *Journal of Research in Personality, 43*, 264–265.

Pincus, A. L., & Roche, M. J. (2011). Narcissistic grandiosity and narcissistic vulnerability. In W. K. Campbell & J. D. Miller (Eds.), *Handbook of narcissism and narcissistic personality disorders* (pp. 31–40). Hoboken, NJ: Wiley.

Pincus, A. L., & Wiggins, J. S. (1990). Interpersonal problems and conceptions of personality disorders. *Journal of Personality Disorders, 4*, 342–352.

Pincus, A. L., & Wright, A. G. C. (2010). Interpersonal diagnosis of psychopathology. In L. M. Horowitz & S. Strack (Eds.), *Handbook of interpersonal psychology* (pp. 359–381). Hoboken, NJ: Wiley.

Przeworski, A., Newman, M. G., Pincus, A. L., Kasoff, M. B., Yamasaki, A. S., Castonguay, L. G., & Berlin, K. S. (2011). Interpersonal pathoplasticity in individuals with generalized anxiety disorder. *Journal of Abnormal Psychology, 120*, 286–298.

Ram, N., Conroy, D. E., Pincus, A. L., Hyde, A. L., & Molloy, L. (in press). Tethering theory to method: Using measures of intraindividual variability to operationalize individuals' dynamic characteristics. In G. Hancock & J. Harring (Eds.), *Advances in longitudinal modeling in the social and behavioral sciences*. New York, NY: Routledge.

Ram, N., & Gerstorf, D. (2009). Time-structured and net intraindividual variability: Tools for examining the development of dynamic characteristics and processes. *Psychology and Aging, 24*, 778–791.

Ravitz, P., Maunder, R., & McBride, C. (2008). Attachment, contemporary interpersonal theory and IPT: An integration of theoretical, clinical, and empirical perspectives. *Journal of Contemporary Psychotherapy, 38*, 11–21.

Reis, H. T. (2008). Reinvigorating the concept of situation in social psychology. *Personality and Social Psychology Review, 12*, 311–329.

Roche, M. J., Pincus, A. L., Conroy, D. E., Hyde, A. L., & Ram, N. (2012). Interpersonal signatures associated with pathological narcissism. Manuscript under review.

Russell, J. J., Moskowitz, D. S., Zuroff, D. C., Sookman, D., & Paris, J. (2007). Stability and variability of affective experience and interpersonal behavior in borderline personality disorder. *Journal of Abnormal Psychology, 116*, 578–588.

Ryan, K., & Shean, G. (2007). Patterns of interpersonal behaviors and borderline personality characteristics. *Personality and Individual Differences, 42*, 193–200.

Sadikaj, G., Russell, J. J., Moskowitz, D. S., & Paris, J. (2010). Affect dysregulation in individuals with borderline personality disorder: Persistence and interpersonal triggers. *Journal of Personality Assessment, 92*, 490–500.

Sadler, P., Ethier, N., & Woody, E. (2010). Interpersonal complementarity. In L. M. Horowitz & S. Strack (Eds.), *Handbook of interpersonal psychology* (pp. 123–142). Hoboken, NJ: Wiley.

Sadler, P., Ethier, N., Gunn, G. R., Duong, D., & Woody, E. (2009). Are we on the same wavelength? Interpersonal complementarity as shared cyclical patterns during interactions. *Journal of Personality and Social Psychology, 97*, 1005–1020.

Safran, J. D. (1990a). Towards a refinement in cognitive therapy in light of interpersonal theory: I. Theory. *Clinical Psychology Review, 10*, 87–105.

Safran, J. D. (1990b). Towards a refinement of cognitive therapy in light of interpersonal theory: II. Practice. *Clinical Psychology Review, 10*, 107–121.

Safran, J. D. (1992). Extending the pantheoretical applications of interpersonal inventories. *Journal of Psychotherapy Integration, 2*, 101–105.

Salzer, S., Pincus, A. L., Hoyer, J., Kreische, R., Leichsenring, F., & Leibling, E. (2008). Interpersonal subtypes within generalized anxiety disorder. *Journal of Personality Assessment, 90*, 292–299.

Salzer, S., Pincus, A. L., Winkelbach, C., Leichsenring, F., & Leibing, E. (2011). Interpersonal subtypes and change of interpersonal problems in the treatment of patients with generalized anxiety disorder: A pilot study. *Psychotherapy: Theory, Research, Practice, & Training, 48*, 304–310.

Schaefer, E. S. (1961). Converging conceptual models for maternal behavior and child behavior. In J. C. Glidwell (Ed.), *Parental attitudes and child behavior* (pp. 124–146). Springfield, IL: Thomas.

Shoda, Y., Mischel, W., & Wright, J. C. (1993). The role of situational demands and cognitive competencies in behavior organization and personality coherence. *Journal of Personality and Social Psychology, 65*, 1023–1035.

Shoda, Y., Mischel, W., & Wright, J. C. (1994). Intraindividual stability in the organization and patterning of behavior: Incorporating psychological situations into the idiographic analysis of personality. *Journal of Personality and Social Psychology, 67*, 674–687.

Shorey, H. S., & Snyder, C. R. (2006). The role of adult attachment styles in psychopathology and psychotherapy outcomes. *Review of General Psychology, 10*, 1–20.

Skodol, A. E., Clark, L. A., Bender, D. S., Krueger, R. F., Morey, L., Verheul, R.,...Oldham, J. M. (2011). Proposed changes in personality and personality disorder assessment and diagnosis for DSM-5. Part I: Description and rationale. *Personality Disorders: Theory, Research, and Treatment, 2*, 4–22.

Slaney, R. B., Pincus, A. L., Uliaszek, A. A., & Wang, K. T. (2006). Conceptions of perfectionism and interpersonal problems: Evaluating groups using the structural summary method for circumplex data. *Assessment, 13*, 138–153.

Smith, T. W., & Cundiff, J. M. (2010). An interpersonal perspective on risk for coronary heart disease. In L. M. Horowitz & S. Strack (Eds.), *Handbook of interpersonal psychology* (pp. 471–489). Hoboken, NJ: Wiley.

Strack, S., & Horowitz, L. M. (2010). Introduction. In L. M. Horowitz & S. Strack (Eds.), *Handbook of interpersonal psychology* (pp. 1–13). Hoboken, NJ: Wiley.

Sullivan, H. S. (1948). The meaning of anxiety in psychiatry and in life. *Psychiatry: Journal for the Study of Interpersonal Processes, 11*, 1–13.

Sullivan, H. S. (1953a). *Conceptions of modern psychiatry*. New York, NY: Norton.

Sullivan, H. S. (1953b). *The interpersonal theory of psychiatry*. New York, NY: Norton.

Sullivan, H. S. (1954). *The psychiatric interview*. New York, NY: Norton.

Sullivan, H. S. (1956). *Clinical studies in psychiatry*. New York, NY: Norton.

Sullivan, H. S. (1962). *Schizophrenia as a human process*. New York, NY: Norton.

Sullivan, H. S. (1964). *The fusion of psychiatry and social science*. New York, NY: Norton.

Trobst, K. K. (2000). An interpersonal conceptualization and quantification of social support transactions. *Personality and Social Psychology Bulletin, 26*, 971–986.

Widiger, T. A., & Smith, G. T. (2008). Personality and psychopathology. In O. P. John, R. Robins, & L. A. Pervin (Eds.), *Handbook of personality: Theory and research* (3rd ed., pp. 743–769). New York, NY: Guilford Press.

Wiggins, J. S. (1979). A psychological taxonomy of trait descriptive terms: The interpersonal domain. *Journal of Personality and Social Psychology, 37*, 395–412.

Wiggins, J. S. (1982). Circumplex models of interpersonal behavior in clinical psychology. In P. C. Kendall & J. N. Butchner (Eds.), *Handbook of research methods in clinical psychology* (pp. 183–221). New York, NY: Wiley.

Wiggins, J. S. (1991). Agency and communion as conceptual coordinates for the understanding and measurement of interpersonal behavior. In D. Cicchetti & W. M. Grove (Eds.), *Thinking clearly about psychology: Essays in honor of Paul E. Meehl, Vol. 2: Personality and psychopathology* (pp. 89–113). Minneapolis: University of Minnesota Press.

Wiggins, J. S. (1996). An informal history of the interpersonal circumplex tradition. *Journal of Personality Assessment, 66*, 217–233.

Wiggins, J. S. (1997a). Circumnavigating Dodge Morgan's interpersonal style. *Journal of Personality, 65*, 1069–1086.

Wiggins, J. S. (1997b). In defense of traits. In R. Hogan, J. A. Johnson, & S. R. Briggs (Eds.), *Handbook of personality psychology* (pp. 95–141). San Diego, CA: Academic Press.

Wiggins, J. S. (2003). *Paradigms of personality assessment*. New York, NY: Guilford Press.

Wiggins, J. S., & Broughton, R. (1985). The interpersonal circle: A structural model for the integration of personality research. In R. Hogan & W. H. Jones (Eds.), *Perspectives in personality* (Vol. 1, pp. 1–47). Greenwich, CT: JAI Press.

Wiggins, J. S., Phillips, N., & Trapnell, P. (1989). Circular reasoning about interpersonal behavior: Evidence concerning some untested assumptions underlying diagnostic classification. *Journal of Personality and Social Psychology, 56*, 296–305.

Wiggins, J. S., & Pincus, A. L. (1989). Conceptions of personality disorders and dimensions of personality. *Psychological Assessment, 1*, 305–316.

Wiggins, J. S., Trapnell, P., & Phillips, N. (1988). Psychometric and geometric characteristics of the revised interpersonal adjective scales (IAS-R). *Multivariate Behavioral Research, 23*, 517–530.

Wiggins, J. S., & Trobst, K. K. (1997). When is a circumplex an "interpersonal circumplex"? the case of supportive actions. In R. Plutchik & H. R. Conte (Eds.), *Circumplex models of personality and emotions* (pp. 57–80). Washington, DC: American Psychological Association.

Wiggins, J. S., & Trobst, K. K. (1999). The fields of interpersonal behavior. In L. Pervin and O. P. John (Eds.), *Handbook of personality: Theory and research* (2nd ed., pp. 653–670). New York, NY: Guilford Press.

Wright, A. G. C. (2011). Qualitative and quantitative distinctions in personality disorder. *Journal of Personality Assessment, 93*, 370–379.

Wright, A. G. C., Pincus, A. L., Conroy, D. E., & Elliot, A. J. (2009). The pathoplastic relationship between interpersonal problems and fear of failure. *Journal of Personality, 77*, 997–1024.

Wright, A. G. C., Pincus, A. L., Conroy, D. E., & Hilsenroth, M. J. (2009). Integrating methods to optimize circumplex description and comparison of groups. *Journal of Personality Assessment, 91*, 311–322.

Zuroff, D. C., Moskowitz, D. S., & Côté, S. (1999). Dependency, self-criticism, interpersonal behaviour and affect: Evolutionary perspectives. *British Journal of Clinical Psychology, 38*, 231–250.

CHAPTER 8

The Cognitive-Affective Processing System

LARA K. KAMMRATH AND ABIGAIL A. SCHOLER

Personality is a topic that is inherently interesting to both laypeople and behavioral scientists. Humans start making judgments about what other people are like from the first "thin slices" of information we get about them (Ambady & Rosenthal, 1993; Zebrowitz & Collins, 1997). We revise and enrich our representations of others as new information comes in, through direct behavioral observation, conversation and self-disclosure, gossip and second-hand information, etc. (Berg & Archer, 1982; Blackman & Funder, 1998; Gilovich, 1987; Kammrath, Ames, & Scholer, 2007). We take in information about personality not just through naturalistic means, but also through personality assessments conducted by experts. Companies spend lots of money hiring consultants to come in and do personality assessments of team members. Dating websites highlight their use of personality assessments as a way to lure members. Given all of the attention and resources devote to obtaining information about people's personalities, it begs the question: What good *is* personality information for navigating our social worlds?

When discussing and evaluating the merits of different scientific theories of personality, it may be helpful to consider the purposes for which people typically use and seek personality information, and to examine the extent to which a given personality theory offers tools and constructs that advance these purposes. Of the many possibilities, we'd like to highlight three primary purposes for which people use personality information. The first is *prediction*. How is a person likely to act, especially as their behaviors might impact my own outcomes? People are interested in predicting others' behavior at both general and specific levels. On the one hand, it is good to get

a general sense of a person's global behavior base rates. How frequently will interactions with a certain person be pleasant and agreeable versus unpleasant and disagreeable? What percent of tasks that the person pursues will be completed in a timely and high-quality manner? On the other hand, people frequently want to be able to make more specific predictions—if I introduce my new dating partner to my mother at Thanksgiving dinner, will she be welcoming to him? (And what about on a different day?) If I assign this faculty member to this committee, will he keep up with the committee responsibilities at the end of the semester when committee tasks are highly urgent but teaching demands are also high? Having the ability to predict another person's behavior, both in terms of general base-rates and specific likelihoods for specific situations, is extremely useful, particularly for person selection (who to hire, who to marry) and person placement (who to assign this task, or this role).

The second useful purpose of personality information is *explanation*. We may learn that someone frequently expresses anger by shouting, or that another person consistently procrastinates starting unpleasant tasks, information which may satisfy our general goal of prediction, but we still want an answer to the question of why: What are the underlying reasons that this person does the characteristic behaviors that they do? When people behave in ways that noticeably differ from how others behave, or when they engage in characteristic actions that impact our own outcomes, we often want to go beyond mere description of those behaviors to an understanding of the causal reasons behind those behaviors (Kelley, 1967). Does the angry shouter shout because her anger is very extreme? Is it because she expects shouting to result in getting what she wants? Is it because she doesn't think that shouting is inappropriate or hurtful? Causal explanations for characteristic behaviors can lead to enhanced predictions, and they give us a window into what life might be like for a person with a different personality than our own.

The third useful purpose of personality information, *influence,* draws on and applies the previous two purposes. Once we are in committed interdependent relationships with others, we need to coordinate our behaviors to create positive relational and instrumental outcomes. Because of the high interdependence of humans with those in their social groups, we influence other people all the time, for better or for worse, and we are frequently looking to use personality information to enhance the "for better" and minimize the "for worse." Will a particular colleague be more likely to comply with a request framed as a threat or as an opportunity? Would it be better in a certain friendship to disclose a hard truth, or maintain a white lie? People don't just look to personality information when they are selecting persons and placing them in tasks and roles, they also hope to use this information to learn how to maximize interpersonal harmony and/or effectiveness in their committed relationships. Research on influence and persuasion offers generalized advice on the topic of how to influence others, but people often seek more specific information. If one wants to get a procrastinator to start working sooner, for example, it is not enough to know that it might be effective to increase the penalty for lateness or to increase the perceive likelihood of success, or any of a number of other cognitive-behavioral interventions. We need to know what will motivate this *particular* procrastinator. When we get to know one another's personalities well, we can customize our influence strategies to the specific person and the current situation.

A good scientific personality theory should, we believe, offer tools to advance all three of the above concerns: prediction, explanation, and influence. Mischel and Shoda's (1995, 1998, 2008) Cognitive Affective Personality System (CAPS) theory, described in this chapter, is one such theory. In the first half of the chapter, we review the development and major tenets of CAPS theory, highlighting its distinctive contribution to a scientific understanding of personality, and we describe recent research in this metatheoretical tradition. In the second half of the chapter, we turn our attention to a new generation of theories emerging on the scene of personality research—functionalist approaches—and discuss how this new perspective can be fruitfully integrated to advance existing CAPS theoretical principles.

A PARADIGM SHIFT IN PERSONALITY PSYCHOLOGY: CAPS THEORY FROM 1968, 1973, 1995, TO BEYOND

Mischel and Shoda's work on CAPS theory (Mischel, 1968, 1973; Mischel & Shoda, 1995, 2008) introduced an important new paradigm in the field of personality psychology, which inspired a new subgroup of personality theories, known as *social-cognitive* theories. To highlight the contributions of CAPS theory, we begin by contrasting an alternative type of personality theory: dispositional essentialism.

Dispositional Essentialism

In simplest form, dispositional essentialist theories posit that individual differences in behavior result from a set of essential internal qualities that function to modulate the probability of behavior occurrence (Kagan, 2007; Shweder, 2007). Such theories take the form "this person frequently/infrequently engages in behavior X because s/he has a low/high disposition to engage in behavior X." Dispositional essentialist theories are arguably highly circular, but likely feel familiar to most readers, as laypeople commonly use this kind of language to explain one another's behavior. When a manager asks why an employee is not working hard at assigned tasks, a fellow employee might answer, "It's because he is lazy," which in effect simply says, "it's because he has a fixed internal essence that gives him a tendency to not work hard." As another example, one might similarly say that people who frequently perform friendly behaviors are high in dispositional friendliness, whereas people who rarely perform friendly behaviors are low in dispositional friendliness.

It is important to point out that we all are likely to be dispositional essentialists, at least some of the time, in our lay explanations of individual differences. Although people will sometimes engage in much richer personality explanations than the examples above (Idson & Mischel, 2001; Malle & Hodges, 2005), we are often content, in everyday explanations for behavior, to locate the source of the behavior somewhere inside the person as a stable, internal force, without providing much further explanation (Jones et al., 1987; Kelley, 1967). Within the landscape of scientific theories of personality, trait theories have most frequently been described as dispositional essentialist theories (Mischel, 1968; Shweder, 2007), because the same terms—trait adjectives—are frequently used to describe a behavior and the internal dispositions believed to give rise to the behavior, such as a friendly trait causing friendly behavior. Moreover, modern trait theories of personality rely heavily on factor analytic techniques to extract "latent traits" (John & Srivastava, 1999), which are theoretical, unobserved causal essences posited to cause behavior, but which are estimated and described primarily in terms of the indicator variables they are supposed to explain (Borsboom, Mellenbergh, & van Heerden, 2003; Wood & Hensler, 2011).[1]

The first thing to note about dispositional essentialism is that it provides tools for only one of the three previously identified purposes of personality information: prediction. A description of dispositional essences allows one to make predictions about someone's behavior frequencies, but it offers no insight about the nature of the underlying causes of these behavior tendencies and no insights as to how one might strategically interact with another person to alter their behavior and/or interpersonal outcomes. Describing a person as "lazy," for example, does not help one learn anything about the reasons why the person fails to effortfully pursue assigned tasks or provide any insight into ways to motivate the person to work hard on particular important goals.

A further problem with dispositional essentialism came to light when a plethora of research throughout the 20th century discovered that behavior prediction on the basis of dispositional assessments—the one function this type of theory was supposed to reliably accomplish—was surprisingly elusive. A person who scored as honest, friendly, or self-disciplined on dispositional assessment might or might not display correspondent behavior in a particular occasion where such behavior was afforded by the situation and recorded by the researcher (Mischel, 1968). At first researchers concluded that the problem must be located in the unreliability of their existing personality assessment measures, but mounting evidence led several investigators in the 1960s to conclude that human behavior was simply more variable than initially expected (Mischel, 1968; Peterson, 1968; Vernon, 1964).[2]

In fact, Fleeson and colleagues (Fleeson, 2001, 2004; Fleeson & Leicht, 2006; Noftle & Fleeson, 2010) have

persuasively shown that in daily life, nearly all individuals regularly display behaviors from both poles of any given dispositional dimension: from friendly to unfriendly, honest to dishonest, and so on. Given the tremendous flexibility and variability of human behavior, it has become clear that information about global dispositional tendencies can provide only a probabilistic prediction of behavior in any specific instance. The typical global unconditional probability of a behavior (i.e., dispositional tendency) may indeed differ from person to person, but these probabilities on the whole tend to be low rather than high, as might have originally been expected. For small probabilities, large samples of accumulated occasions are necessary for regularities in behavior to reliably manifest (Epstein, 1979).

Once this fact was recognized, trait theorists were able to reorient their search for valid personality prediction, and subsequently the hypothesis that people reliably differ in their behavior base-rates has been widely supported. Thus, when dispositional assessments are used to predict global behavior averages over a large enough sample of occasions (Epstein, 1979; Fleeson & Gallagher, 2009), or to predict cumulative outcomes, such as the judgments of close others (Funder, 1995), the quality of relationships (Ozer & Benet-Martinez, 2006), overall job satisfaction and motivation (Judge, Heller, & Mount, 2002; Judge & Ilies, 2002), long-term health or well-being (T. W. Smith & MacKenzie, 2006; Steel, Schmidt, & Shultz, 2008), then substantial predictive validity is achieved. Nevertheless, the goal of situation-specific prediction from dispositional assessments has continued to prove challenging (Mischel & Shoda, 2008).

The Cognitive-Affective Personality System (CAPS) Theory

When Walter Mischel undertook a systematic review of the field of personality in 1968, he uncovered a great deal of evidence that people display much higher variability in behavior from situation to situation than previously assumed. In his own work, for example, he demonstrated that a child who was capable of a high degree of self-discipline in one lab situation where she or he was required to delay gratification might be utterly unable to display similar self-discipline in a slightly modified lab situation, and vice versa (Mischel, 1974). In his 1968 book, *Personality and Assessment,* Mischel made the case that individuals frequently display behaviors that deviate from their "dispositional tendency," and that indeed, strong evidence for the existence of global behavior tendencies was currently lacking in the empirical literature.

---

[1] It should be noted, however, that there is substantial variability among trait theories in the extent to which they fit the prototype of a dispositional essentialist theory. Many modern trait theories go beyond simple dispositional essentialist principles to postulate more specific psychological processes involved in behavior production (Fleeson, in press).

[2] Research on social perception has since uncovered a variety of reasons that lay perceivers maintain the intuition that individuals behave more consistently than they actually do (Srull & Wyer, 1989).

Many personality theorists perceived this argument as one that undermined the very foundations of a scientific study of personality. If a person's behavior was highly dependent on the specific situation in which she or he found him- or herself, perhaps personality consistency and dispositional person factors were a myth. Thus, the "person-situation debate" was born. Although Mischel's 1968 critique sparked this debate, Mischel was not an active participant in it; in fact, in 1973 he actively tried to end the debate by changing the terms of the discussion (Mischel, 1973). Rather than perceiving the evidence of behavioral variability as a paradigm crisis, Mischel used it as an opportunity for a paradigm shift.

It is now recognized that people's behavior is best described by a distribution of variable actions with a particular central tendency (Fleeson, 2001; Fleeson & Noftle, 2009). From the perspective of dispositional essentialism, the central tendency is what reveals personality, and any deviations from that central tendency might be attributed to situations or to randomness, but do not reflect the person. Thus, if person is typically not hardworking, but does occasionally perform bursts of high-intensity effort, a dispositional essentialist would focus on the average behavior frequency and characterize the person as lazy (or low in conscientiousness). A dispositional essentialist would deal with the inconsistent behaviors by simply averaging them in with the rest. Thus, nothing special would be done with the information that this person is sometimes capable of showing high effort.

In contrast to this averaging approach, in Mischel's 1973 "Towards a Cognitive Social Learning Reconceptualization of Personality" article, he turned the "problem" of behavior variability on its head, by suggesting that the very fact that people are capable of such flexibility in behavior suggests that we need a new theory of behavior generation, one that can simultaneously encompass the central tendency (Why is this person non-hardworking so much of the time?) and the deviations from this tendency (Why does this person exert high effort on those occasions that she or he does?). Mischel argued that personality is revealed both in those situations where the average tendency is manifested and in those situations where behavior deviates, and that by examining the conditions that elicit one behavior versus another, personality psychologists could gain a deeper understanding of the psychological processes underlying the person's characteristic behavior patterns (for a similar argument, see Fleeson, in press).

Imagine two glasses, each filled with a clear liquid. Both are translucent. Both are wet. Both are frequently consumed at bars and restaurants. One, however, is flammable whereas the other is used to put out fires. Vodka and water look similar most of the time, but their different response to flame is one way to determine that they are fundamentally different compounds. Mischel (1973) proposed that like chemical compounds, human beings reveal the basic units of their personalities in the flexible ways they respond to their situations and environments. To fully understand a person, it is not enough to observe his or her current steady state, or to extract a decontextualized behavior base-rate from multiple observations—one must come to know the specific situations in which the person characteristically dials his or her behavior up or down, left or right (e.g., what does and does not provoke aggression, what leads to persistence versus withdrawal).

Mischel (1973) specifically proposed that the fundamental explanatory variables for personality should not be "dispositional tendencies" to engage in particular behaviors, but rather, psychological process variables that explain how people give meaning to situations and actively pursue their goals within them. Individuals are not seen as passive emitters of behavior, but rather as active agents that flexibly respond to perceived situational contingencies. Thus, the basic units of personality should be those that explain how people interpret, experience, and respond to situations. Mischel highlighted five types of psychological process variables—called *cognitive-affective units* or CAUs—that causally explain a person's characteristic responses to situations: (1) encodings, (2) expectancies and beliefs, (3) affects, (4) goals and values, and (5) competencies and self-regulatory plans (Mischel, 1973; Mischel & Shoda, 2008). These five variables are summarized in Table 8.1.

In their 1995 articulation of CAPS theory, Mischel and Shoda proposed that a person's personality is actually a "system" or network of CAUs, characterized by the

TABLE 8.1   Types of Cognitive-Affective Units in the Personality Mediating System

Encodings: Categories (constructs) for the self, people, events, and situations (external and internal).

Expectancies and Beliefs: About the social world, about outcomes for behavior in particular situations, about self-efficacy.

Affects: Feelings, emotions, and affective responses (including physiological reactions).

Goals and Values: Desirable outcomes and affective states, aversive outcomes and affective states, goals, values, and life projects.

Competencies and Self-Regulatory Plans: Potential behaviors and scripts, and plans and strategies for organizing action and for affecting outcomes and one's own behavior and internal states.

Note. From Mischel and Shoda (2008, p. 211). Copyright 2008 by Guilford Press. Adapted by permission.

chronic accessibilities of the CAUs, the interconnections among the CAUs, and links between CAUs and features of psychological situations (Mischel & Shoda, 1995). When a person enters a situation, key psychological features of the situation are encoded and interpreted by the person, in light of his or her active goals, affects, expectancies, and so on. Activation spreads among linked CAUs as through an associationist network (see Figure 8.1). For example, a person might hear his romantic partner say, "Why didn't you go to the grocery store on the way home from work?" and encode this as a criticism and a rejection, and might subsequently feel heightened anxiety and a goal to defend the self, leading to the activation of argument scripts. Another person might hear the same statement from a romantic partner and might encode it as a friendly reminder, and might subsequently feel heightened guilt and a goal to meet the other person's needs, leading to the activation of a grocery shopping script. Importantly, the *same* person might experience either pattern depending on the state of the CAU network at the time the situation was encountered—if thoughts of rejection were accessible at the time of encoding, one response might be provoked, but if thoughts of security and affiliation were accessible at the time of encoding, another might emerge.

People differ, according to CAPS theory, in (a) the *accessibility* of particular CAUs (e.g., encoding rejection, feeling anger, experiencing a goal to protect the self), (b) in the psychologically *active ingredients of situations* that activate the CAUs, and (c) in the *patterns of connection* among CAUs (Mischel & Shoda, 2008). One person, for example, might be chronically vigilant for rejection cues, and as a result, might encode a wide variety of ambiguous interpersonal situations as rejecting, and subsequently experience strong arousal of fear and anger emotions in those situations, emotions that quickly activate aggression scripts (e.g., a high rejection sensitive person; Pietrzak, Downey, & Ayduk, 2005). Another person, on the other hand, might be less on-guard for rejections from others, and thus encode rejection less frequently. Moreover, this other person might also have a weaker connection between feelings of anger and activation of hostile behavior scripts, because of strong self-regulatory plans that become active when anger is aroused (e.g., a highly agreeable person; Graziano & Tobin, 2009).

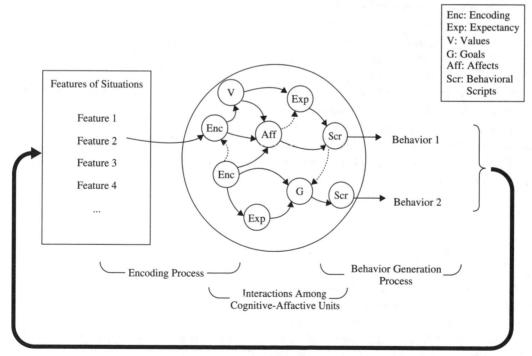

Situational features activate a given mediating unit, which activates specific subsets of other mediating units through a stable network of relations that characterizes an individual, generating a characteristic pattern of behavior in response to different situations. The relation may be positive (solid line), which increases the activation, or negative (dashed line), which decreases the activation.

Figure 8.1 The cognitive-affective processing system (CAPS)

From Mischel and Shoda (1995, p 254). Copyright 1995 by the American Psychological Association. Adapted by permission.

This type of personality system is able to generate many different types of behavior patterns (Bolger & Romero-Canyas, 2007; Mischel & Shoda, 1998). To the extent that a person encounters many situations that he encodes in similar psychological units, the person will manifest a higher global act-frequency of the behavior linked to those encodings. For example, a person who sees provocation in many interpersonal interactions is likely to display higher global act-frequencies of aggressive behavior. On the occasions that the person encounters situations that he encodes in different psychological units, however, the person will manifest behaviors that vary from this global act frequency, revealing a predictable *if... then...* profile, for example, "if provoked, then aggressive; if praised, then benevolent."

In CAPS theory, these *if... then...* situation-behavior signatures (*if* situation A... *then* behavior X; *if* situation B... *then* behavior Y) provide the clearest view of the perceptions, goals, and feelings that drive the person's characteristic behaviors (Mischel & Shoda, 1995, 1998, 2008). Two people might avoid hard work with equal frequency, but they might be doing so for different reasons. Person A, for example, might be regulating a frequent fear of failure, whereas Person B may simply rarely see compelling rewards to motivate goal pursuit. In this perspective, the behavior variation, rather than the central tendency, provides the insight into the underlying process variables. Person A is likely to occasionally deviate from her global trend and engage in high effort specifically in those situations where expectations of success are especially high, whereas Person B is likely to occasionally deviate and engage in high effort specifically in those situations where the expected rewards are highly valued. As this example illustrates, a person's *if... then...* profile, rather than global act-frequency, provides the most information about the underlying explanatory CAUs guiding the person's behavior.

Modeling If... Then... Profiles

One of the first challenges for CAPS theory was to demonstrate that the variation in people's behavior across situations really does form stable *if... then...* profiles, and is not just random fluctuation. The first empirical assessment of *if... then...* profiles took place in the early 1990s at the Wediko summer camp for boys. Under the research direction of Shoda, Wright, and Mischel (1994), camp counselors used event-contingent diaries to code the interpersonal situations encountered by each camper (e.g., the camper was approached by a peer, or warned by an

adult) and the presence or absence of aggressive response by the child. This yielded a rich dataset full of repeated situation-behavior observations for each child. From the data, Shoda and colleagues were able to construct for each child an *if... then...* profile of aggressive behavior across the interpersonal situations (see Figure 8.2). Some children were most aggressive when teased by a peer; other children were most aggressive when warned by an adult, or when approached by a peer to play. These *if... then...* aggression profiles were highly stable and reliable (Shoda et al., 1994), and showed systematic links to the personality inferences of the camp counselors (Shoda, Mischel, & Wright, 1993).

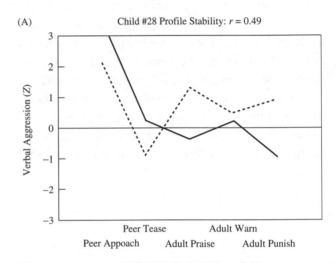

(A)

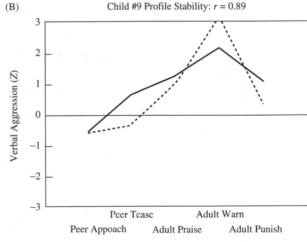

(B)

Illustrative intra-individual, situation-behavior profiles for verbal aggression in relation to five situations in two time samples (solid and dotted lines). Data are shown in standardized scores (*z*) relative to the normative levels of verbal aggression in each situation.

Figure 8.2 Examples of situation-behavior profiles for verbal aggression

From Shoda, Mischel, and Wright (1994, p. 678). Copyright 1994 by the American Psychological Association. Reprinted by permission.

This method of collecting *if...then...* profile data was highly laborious, both from a data collection and a data analysis perspective, and in the next several years, little research followed in the footsteps of Wediko to document and investigate *if...then...* profiles. Subsequently, however, a statistical approach to handling repeated measures data—multilevel modeling—gained popularity in psychological research (Bickel, 2007; Bryk & Raudenbush, 2002; Hox, 2002, 2010), making it more feasible to model and study *if...then...* profiles. The Wediko approach relied on the researcher's categorical identification of important classes of situations. A multilevel modeling approach allows researchers to use either categorical or continuous assessments of situations. Participants can be asked to rate their psychological situation on key dimensions themselves, or the researcher can generate situational ratings from qualitative information, such as written reports or video recordings. For example, in a recent study, Kammrath and colleagues (Kammrath, McCarthy, Friesen, & Cortes, 2011) asked participants to read 72 potentially aversive interpersonal behaviors and to indicate how important they perceived it to be to confront someone about each kind of behavior (situation rating), and the likelihood that they would actually confront a person about the behavior (response rating). Scatterplots from two participants in this study are shown in Figure 8.3. The figure shows that both participants indicated they would be more likely to assert themselves when the issue was more important; nevertheless, the slope between perceived importance and behavior assertiveness was steeper for Participant B than for Participant A, indicating that perceived importance is a stronger active psychological ingredient for assertive behavior for the former participant.

In multilevel modeling, situation variables can be used to predict the outcome variable of interest: expectancies, feelings, behaviors, and so on. The multilevel model fits a fixed slope for the situational predictor for the whole sample, but then additionally fits a deviation from this fixed slope (a random slope) for each person in the dataset. The model thus describes the normative effect of the situation (the fixed slope) as well as individual differences in responses to the situation (the random slope). For example, in the assertiveness study described above, perceived importance was a significant predictor of assertive behavior across the entire sample. Nevertheless, participants significantly differed in their random slopes—some participants showed slopes just barely above zero, whereas other participants showed slopes close to 1. Such multilevel models are easy to run in commonly available

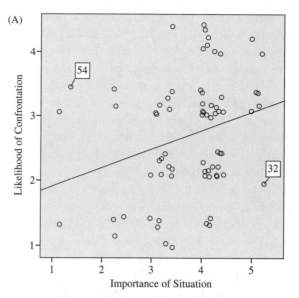

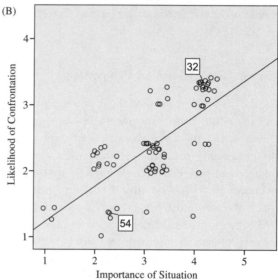

If . . . then . . . situation-behavior profiles for two participants (Kammrath et al., 2011), plotting each person's likelihood of confrontation as a function of perceived situational importance. Participant A demonstrates a weak slope of the situational predictor: she is less confrontational in Situation 32 than in Situation 54, even though she perceives Situation 32 as much more important than Situation 34. Participant B shows a strong slope of the situational predictor, and is typically more confrontational as the situation has greater perceived importance. Thus, situational importance is a stronger "active ingredient of situations" for Participant B than for Participant A.

Figure 8.3 The role of situational importance in situation-behavior profiles for confrontation

statistical packages, such as SPSS and SAS, and they allow researchers to model multiple situational predictors simultaneously, uncovering the different active ingredients of situations important for different individuals (Fleeson, 2007; Shoda & LeeTiernan, 2002; Zayas & Shoda, 2009).

Researchers have used multilevel modeling to explore many aspects of participants' CAPS dynamics. Multilevel analyses have demonstrated reliable differences in how people weight various aspects of persons and behaviors (e.g., attractiveness, degree of prosociality) in their evaluative judgments (Kammrath & Scholer, 2011; Wood & Brumbaugh, 2009), how people form expectancies for interpersonal behaviors (Kammrath, 2011), people's emotional reactivity to event appraisals (Bolger & Zuckerman, 1995; Cote & Moskowitz, 1998; Rhodewalt & Morf, 1998; Suls & Martin, 2005; Zautra, Affleck, Tennen, Reich, & Davis, 2005), and their behavioral responses to the actions of others (Fleeson, 2007; Fournier, Moskowitz, & Zuroff, 2008; R. E. Smith, Shoda, Cumming, & Smoll, 2009). Several researchers have recently called for greater use of multilevel modeling to explore individual differences in response to situations (Bolger & Romero-Canyas, 2007; Fleeson, 2007; Shoda & LeeTiernan, 2002; Zayas & Shoda, 2009).

CAPS as a Meta-Theoretical Perspective

CAPS, like dispositional essentialism, is a meta-theory of personality, rather than a specific theory of a particular set of personality processes. Numerous theories of more specific personality patterns fall nicely within the CAPS meta-theoretical perspective; most of these are from a tradition known as *social-cognitive* theories of personality. Two such theories are frequently cited as prototypes of the CAPS meta-theoretical perspective: the hot-cool theory of self-regulation (Metcalfe & Mischel, 1999) and the rejection-sensitivity model (Romero-Canyas, Anderson, Reddy, & Downey, 2009). These theories will not be reviewed here, as they have been extensively discussed in other CAPS chapters (Mischel & Shoda, 1998, 1999, 2008), but the reader is directed to these chapters as excellent summaries.

Another prominent personality theory that sits comfortably within the CAPS meta-theoretical tradition is attachment theory (Collins, Guichard, Ford, & Feeney, 2004; Feeney, 2006; Mikulincer, Shaver, Cassidy, & Berant, 2009; Shaver & Mikulincer, 2009). Rather than viewing attachment styles as essential dispositions (e.g., for interpersonal anxiety or avoidance), anxious and avoidant attachment styles are understood at the level of CAUs: They are believed to arise from different mental models of the interpersonal world. People with high attachment anxiety expect caregiving to be inconsistent and unreliable, leading them to vigilantly watch for signs of rejection and neglect, to experience anxiety when such signs are

detected, and to cope using a variety of tactics, including ingratiation and pre-emptive hostility (Shaver & Mikulincer, 2007). People with high attachment avoidance expect caregiving to be simply unavailable, leading them to vigilantly watch for signs of interdependence and attachment to others, and to experience threat when such signs are detected, and to cope using a variety of tactics, including hyper-independence and suppression of the attachment system (Edelstein & Shaver, 2004). Thus, attachment anxiety and attachment avoidance are associated with monitoring systems that are tuned to different situational "threats": rejection versus interdependence, respectively. When key activating situations are encountered, these two personality styles are linked to different expectancies, goals, affects, and they manifest in different patterns of self-regulation and goal pursuit.

Dweck's mind-set theory (Dweck, 2006, 2008; Dweck & Grant, 2008; Dweck & Leggett, 1988), a social cognitive personality theory from the achievement literature, provides another excellent example of a theory within the CAPS meta-theoretical tradition. According to this theory, variation in effort and persistence on achievement tasks is often best explained not by dispositional essences (e.g., an internal tendency to be lazy or to be conscientious), but rather by the goals and beliefs a person brings to a particular achievement situation. Two personality styles, arising from two "mind-sets," are described in this theory. People who have "fixed" mind-sets believe that intelligence is an immutable internal quality that manifests in the world with high performances on achievement tasks. When people with fixed mind-sets encounter an achievement task that is within their current skill level, they adopt a goal to perform with distinction and they put in effort to achieve this goal. If, however, they encounter an achievement task that is a stretch for their current skill level, or if they have recently experienced failure, they adopt a goal to avoid future failed efforts, and they self-handicap and disengage from the task. Thus, a person with a fixed mind-set may appear highly conscientious in one setting but low in conscientiousness in another, depending on the perceived risk of failure. Individuals who have "growth" mind-sets, on the other hand, believe that intelligence is an internal quality that can grow in capacity with challenge and practice. If these people encounter an achievement task that is a stretch for their current skill level and where there is a risk of failure, they adopt a goal to learn from the experience and to grow their skill level through trial and error, and they work effortfully toward that end. Thus, people with growth mind-sets appear most conscientious when they are the most, rather than the least, challenged.

A final theory consistent with the CAPS approach that we will mention here is Higgins's regulatory focus theory (Higgins, 1997, 2001; Molden, Lee, & Higgins, 2008; Scholer & Higgins, 2010). According to this theory, there are two independent motivational systems: the promotion system is concerned with advancement, whereas the prevention system is concerned with safety. When people's promotion systems have been activated, their attention is drawn toward opportunities, and they approach gains and avoid nongains with an eagerness self-regulatory strategy. If they achieve their desired gains, they experience emotions of elation, but if they fail to achieve these ends, they experience emotions of dejection. When people's prevention systems have been activated, on the other hand, their attention is drawn toward dangers, and they avoid losses and approach nonlosses with a vigilance self-regulatory strategy. If they successfully avoid a loss, they experience emotions of relief, but if they fail to avoid the loss, they experience emotions of anxiety. This theory highlights that although the features of the external situation influence a person's CAU activation in that situation, the current state of the system itself when the situation is encountered (e.g., whether the person's promotion or prevention system is more strongly activated) is also highly important in determining the encodings, meanings, and responses that the person will pursue in the situation.

The three social cognitive theories summarized above, attachment theory (Shaver & Mikulincer, 2009), mind-set theory (Dweck, 2008), and regulatory focus theory (Higgins, 1997), all focus on CAUs as the core explanatory variables for their specific personality processes. The three theories also heavily emphasize the situational contexts that activate characteristic personality dynamics, and they emphasize how a person's behavior is likely to vary in predictable, meaningful ways depending on the situation. It is these features that situate the theories in the CAPS meta-theoretical tradition. We will return to these theories in the second half of the chapter, when we discuss functional approaches to personality and behavior variation.

Building Bridges Between CAPS and Trait Theories of Personality

For many years, research in the CAPS tradition and trait tradition continued on independent tracks. Trait researchers were focused on the challenge of identifying the best number of latent trait factors to capture the co-variation of natural language trait adjectives (John & Srivastava, 1999), and on finding rigorous evidence that individual differences in global act frequencies do indeed

exist (Fleeson & Gallagher, 2009). Once these questions were satisfactorily answered, however, many trait researchers turned their attention to questions of psychological processes and mechanisms. Research has uncovered, for example, that extraversion is associated with enjoyment of risk, high positive emotionality, positive perceptions of others, and a number of other process variables (Fleeson, in press; Matthews, 2008; Wood & Hensler, 2011).[3] Further bridging the gap between trait and CAPS personality approaches, research has linked each of the Big Five trait constructs to *if . . . then . . .* behavior profiles (Bolger & Zuckerman, 1995; Cote & Moskowitz, 1998; Fleeson, 2007; Kammrath, 2011; Kammrath et al., 2011; Kammrath, Mendoza-Denton, & Mischel, 2005; Kammrath & Peetz, 2011; Kammrath & Scholer, 2011). This research suggests that the kinds of traits studied in the trait tradition may manifest in highly contextualized ways.

Thus, it now appears that at the level of psychological process variables and contextualized behavioral manifestations, there are many similarities between trait personality constructs and CAPS personality constructs. A likely reason for these similarities sits in the head of the lay perceiver (Kammrath et al., 2005). It is true that perceivers identify behaviors in trait terms very quickly (Winter & Uleman, 1984). Nevertheless, perceivers use all kinds of information about the situation and the person to disambiguate the "meaning" of the behavior before they identify the correct trait designation (Reeder, Vonk, Ronk, Ham, & Lawrence, 2004; Trope, 1986). Trait adjectives often connote not only a behavior tendency, but also a set of CAUs that give rise to the behavior (e.g., friendly behavior isn't friendly if it is done for selfish reasons), and a set of characteristic situations in which the behavior should be more or less likely to occur (e.g., friendly people should be more outgoing with peers than with high-status others; unfriendly people should be more outgoing with high-status others than with peers). Thus, when a layperson explains a friendly behavior by saying "she's a friendly person," this explanation may not be as close to dispositional essentialism as it first appears (Kammrath et al., 2005).

---

[3]Most trait theorists would agree with Mischel and Shoda that cognitive-affective process variables are theoretically important personality constructs, although there is disagreement among trait researchers as to whether these process variables are simply mediators of the more causally central latent traits, or whether, as Mischel and Shoda argue, the process variables are indeed the core of personality (Fleeson, in press; Lucas & Donnellan, 2009; Wood & Hensler, 2011).

The Functional Utility of a CAPS Perspective

To examine the functional utility of CAPS as a personality theory, we will first examine the issue of *prediction*. Unlike dispositional essentialism, CAPS does not allow one to make behavior predictions in the absence of situational information. If personality is expressed in the way people interpret and respond to situations, information about the situation is crucial to making a prediction about a person's behavior. To predict the effort of a person with a fixed mind-set, for example, one must first know whether the person perceives a high or low risk of failure on the task. It is readily apparent that CAPS lends itself to situation specific predictions, but CAPS can also generate global ones. To make global behavior predictions, one must simply know something about the global distribution of situations the person regularly encounters (Bolger & Romero-Canyas, 2007). For example, is the person in an environment that rarely provides tasks that threaten failure, or is the person in an environment that regularly tests the limits of his/her current skills?

Importantly, CAPS theory cautions us from making predictions about one set of psychological situations based on observations from a meaningfully different set of psychological situations. A person who is quiet and reserved with co-workers might be able to light up a stage on performance night, or be uninhibited and emotionally expressive with a romantic partner, or fiercely aggressive in a competition. According to CAPS, behavior will generalize across situations only to the extent that situations have similar active ingredients for the individual (Mischel, 1973; Shoda & LeeTiernan, 2002). This perspective raises fascinating questions about situational equivalence and "diagnostic situations." Many times when we are given the task of person selection and/or person placement (e.g., Should I have children with this person? Should I promote this person to manager?), we must try to predict their behavior in a set of situations the person has not previously encountered. CAPS theory would argue that past global base-rates will be less useful for such predictions than information about the person's characteristic behaviors in diagnostic situations—that is, situations with similar psychological ingredients to those upcoming in the new role.

To further evaluate the functional utility of CAPS theory, we will next examine the issue of *explanation*. One of the greatest strengths of CAPS is that the explanatory variables (i.e., CAUs) are different from the behaviors they are intended to explain. Rather than explaining a person's characteristic friendliness with new acquaintances using the construct "a friendly disposition," CAPS might explain it using the person's positive perceptions of others, goals to affiliate, feelings of enjoyment and confidence during social interactions, and so on. Rather than explaining a person's viciously harmful actions as the result of an "evil disposition," CAPS might point to the person's poorly regulated anger reactivity, to her failure to take the other person's perspective, or to her perception that her actions served a greater good.

These explanatory variables are located at an especially meaningful level of analysis. When people explain their own behavior, they are likely to discuss their goals, feelings, and expectancies with respect to the opportunities and constraints offered by the situation (Jones & Nisbett, 1987). One could certainly build a personality theory in which the core explanatory units are neural firings or genetic codes. However, by seating the explanatory variables at the level of psychological processes, CAPS theory gives individuals tools to understand one another better through perspective-taking and mental simulation. Learning that someone has a particular variant of an allele or an abundance of a certain neurotransmitter does not help us imagine life in that person's shoes. Explaining a person's behavior in terms of his or her CAUs, however, allows individuals to access their own memories of times when they may have experienced similar thoughts, feelings, or motivations, and enables people to take more fully the perspective of others (Epley & Waytz, 2010).

CAUs are also valuable as explanatory units because they can be used to explain many different kinds of behavior consistency: between-person differences in base-rates of behavior, normative effects of situations on people's behavior, and idiographic within-person variation from situation to situation. They also work extremely well as experiential mediators of a wide variety of causal antecedents of personality, from idiographic social learning history, to cultural influences, to genetic or biological influences. If men are more aggressive, on average than women (Feingold, 1994), or if people with more reactive amygdalas are more prone to depression than people with less reactive amygdalas (Kagan, 2007), it is likely that there will always be found psychological process variables that mediate these effects (e.g., men might focus more on situational cues signaling status, or high amygdala-reactive individuals might experience more feelings of fear in response to threats). Because of the usefulness of psychological process variables for human perspective-taking, we imagine that CAUs will always have their place in theories of personality, even if a fuller mapping of distal causes comes about.

A final utility of the CAPS model is that it provides a clear map for *influence and change*. In fact, CAPS suggests several routes by which people can influence their own behavior and the behavior of others. One route is though situation selection/avoidance. By approaching some situations and avoiding others, one can influence the frequency that particular processing dynamics get activated. A recent study found, for example, that close friends who had an accurate understanding of one another's *if...then...* trigger profiles (i.e., how negatively each person typically feels about each of 72 potentially aversive interpersonal behaviors) also reported less conflict in the relationship, presumably because they were able to avoid, to some extent, engaging in one another's strong triggers (Friesen & Kammrath, 2011). Many popular parenting and business management books encourage people to think about the situations their own behavior creates for those around them, and to recognize how one can alter a child's or employee's psychological situation by changing the approach one takes toward them (from threatening to autonomy-supportive, from permissive to authoritative, etc.). Thus, influencing the situation is one of the most powerful ways to influence behavior, changing the perceptions, goals, and feelings that the person is likely to experience.

Another route to interpersonal influence and behavior change is through CAU intervention. Such interventions are a key part of cognitive-behavior therapy, in which maladaptive cognitions are identified and modified. Social cognitive personality researchers frequently attempt to directly manipulate the encodings, beliefs, expectancies, goals, feelings, and so on, of participants, in order to demonstrate the causal centrality of these psychological variables to the personality behaviors of interest (Bartz & Lydon, 2008; Cassidy, Shaver, Mikulincer, & Lavy, 2009; Higgins, 1999a). Their success in doing so suggests that indeed, a person with a fixed mind-set about intelligence can be led to use a growth mind-set instead (Blackwell, Trzesniewski, & Dweck, 2007), or that a person with a promotion goal of advancement can be led to adopt a prevention goal of security (Liberman, Molden, Idson, & Higgins, 2001), or that a person who vigilantly guards against rejection can be trained to attend to acceptance cues (Dandeneau, Baldwin, Baccus, Sakellaropoulo, & Pruessner, 2007). Thus, by changing the accessibility of key CAUs involved in maintaining a personality pattern, the pattern itself may transform into something new.

A FUNCTIONALIST APPROACH TO CAPS THEORY

CAPS theory was developed just as the cognitive revolution was sweeping the field of psychology, and its emphasis on associationist principles (i.e., spreading activation from situations to encodings to mental and behavioral responses) reflects that tradition. On the rise, however, is a new school in psychology, the "functionalist" approach (Buss, 2009a; Schaller & Murray, 2008; Wood & Hensler, 2011). Researchers with a functionalist approach to personality highlight not only the content of mental and behavioral associations activated by situations, but also the *functions* served by any particular set of associations (Kenrick, Neuberg, Griskevicius, Becker, & Schaller, 2010; Simpson, Beckes, & Weisberg, 2008; Tamir, 2009). That is, a functionalist approach examines the response output of the associationist system with an eye to understanding the instrumentality of the response for the active goals of the person. Thus, when a person is assessed as characteristically anxious, a functionalist asks: What functions does anxiety serve for this individual (Norem, 2008; Tamir & Ford, 2009)? If a person is frequently aggressive, a functionalist would focus on how aggressive behavior functions to help the person meet key goals (McMurran, Jinks, Howells, & Howard, 2010).

In a functionalist approach, people's traits and behaviors are seen as imperfect-yet-functional solutions to the challenges of pursuing goals in imperfect environments (Buss, 2009b). The word "functional" does not, in this context, imply that all characteristic behavior is adaptive or healthy, but simply that the behavior serves a strategic function in the person's motivational system. Functionalist personality researchers come from a variety of perspectives, including evolutionary, social-cognitive, and trait psychology. They point to research highlighting the central role of motivation in organizing thought, feelings, and behavior (Bargh, Gollwitzer, & Oettingen, 2010; Gross, 2008; Kenrick, et al., 2010). Fiske famously said, "thinking is for doing" (Fiske, 1992), a sentiment since echoed by many others (e.g., "liking is for doing," Ferguson & Bargh, 2004; "feeling is for doing," Neuberg, Kenrick, & Schaller, 2010). Bargh has provided decades of evidence for the "remarkable transformational power of currently active goals over the rest of the cognitive and affective machinery of the mind" (Bargh et al., 2010, p. 289).

To a functionalist, "behavior can be understood only by identifying the goals to which it is addressed" (Carver, Scheier, & Fulford, 2008, p. 727). Specifically, to understand the function behind a person's characteristic behaviors, it is important to know (1) the goals, conscious or unconscious, that are active when the behavior is enacted, and (2) the perceptions, conscious or unconscious, that support the enactment of this particular behavior rather than other behaviors that could also serve one's active goals. These correspond to the why (what are the desired ends?) and the how (what are the preferred means?) of behavior.

Many fascinating programs of research have examined specific personality processes from a functional perspective. Norem and Cantor (1986) showed, for example, that defensive pessimists actively harness feelings of anxiety to motivate themselves to work hard, and that if this anxiety-boosting strategy is disrupted, their performance is undermined. Tamir (2009) has further explored the ways in which a variety of personality traits lead individuals to harness negative emotions for their motivational properties, such as people using angry emotions to motivate assertive behavior or anxious emotions to motivate achievement striving (Tamir, 2005; Tamir, Mitchell, & Gross, 2008). In the clinical domain, researchers have shown that many negative behaviors, such as self-injurious acts and acts of aggression toward others, serve functions for the individuals who enact them, helping them to regulate emotions and pursue valued goals (McMurran et al., 2010; Niedtfeld et al., 2010). Big Five researchers with a functional perspective have begun to uncover the functions served by the behaviors on the five dimensions of extraversion, agreeableness, conscientiousness, neuroticism, and openness (Wood & Hensler, 2011). On a larger scale, evolutionary psychologists have begun to uncover how the distribution of personality traits in specific populations varies by properties of the local environment, such as openness being less common in regions of high disease prevalence (Schaller & Murray, 2008). Presumably, if traits are characteristic adaptations to goal-pursuit challenges, environmental factors that affect goal pursuit would also affect personality development (Neuberg et al., 2010).

Hierarchical Models of Motivation and *If . . . Then . . .* Profiles

Many theories of motivation point out that goals can be arranged in a hierarchy, ranging from abstract high-level goals (e.g., "be a good person") to concrete low-level goals (e.g., "give $5 to the child at the door asking for a donation"). Theories that focus on this hierarchical aspect of goals (Carver & Scheier, 1998, this volume; Kruglanski et al., 2002; Miller, Galanter, & Pribram, 1960; Powers, 1973; Scholer & Higgins, 2008; Vallacher & Wegner, 1987) vary in the number of levels they highlight and the terms used to describe these levels, but they agree that high-level goals capture the "why" (ends) whereas low-level goals describe the "how" (means). Lower-level goals

are systematically linked to higher-level goals, following two principles (Kruglanski et al., 2002). The *principle of multifinality* posits that the same lower-level means can be in service of different higher-level ends (e.g., hiding the truth to protect the self, hiding the truth to protect someone else). An implication of this principle is that information about outward behavior (e.g., lying) is not sufficient to know the function behind the behavior, as any given behavior might be serving a wide variety of functions. The *principle of equifinality* posits that the same higher-level end can be attained by multiple lower-level means (e.g., graduating with a high GPA can be accomplished by studying hard in registered classes, by only registering for easy classes, or by cheating on graded assessments). An implication of this principle is that a person may switch from one lower-level means to another, when perceptions of the situation change. This flexibility in strategies and tactics in response to shifting situations provides a direct link to CAPS notions of *if . . . then . . .* profiles.

In this chapter, we use Scholer and Higgins's (Scholer & Higgins, 2008, 2010) tri-level theory of self-regulation to demonstrate the potential usefulness of an integration of functionalist and CAPS approaches to personality. Scholer and Higgins identify three levels of goals in a person's goal hierarchy. *System level goals* are the highest level and they describe the abstract, ultimate aims the person hopes to realize (e.g., self-protection, self-advancement). *Strategic goals* are the middle level, and they describe a general means for pursuing the system level goal (e.g., eagerly approach success, vigilantly avoid failure). *Tactical goals* are the third and most concrete level, and they describe an even more specific means within the larger strategy. For example, one can try to avoid failure by working very hard or by avoiding challenging tasks, two tactics that on the surface look quite different but that serve the same higher-level strategy.

By linking Scholer and Higgins's tri-level theory of regulation to CAPS ideas of *if . . . then . . .* profiles, we propose that situation-behavior variation can be classified into two types: tactical profiles (or tactical *shifts*) and strategic profiles (shifts). Tactical shifts are low-level shifts in the specific means of goal-pursuit from one class of situations to another. Tactical shifts can yield dramatic changes in observed behavior (e.g., working hard versus avoiding challenging tasks), but these shifts are organized by a higher-level strategic consistency (e.g., vigilantly avoiding failure). Strategic shifts, in comparison, are higher-level shifts in the general preferred method of pursuing the system goal (e.g., vigilantly avoiding failure versus eagerly approaching successes). Strategic shifts can activate a host of new tactical responses to situations and can also change the links between previously associated tactics and situations (e.g., deciding to approach challenging tasks versus avoid challenging tasks). Unlike tactical shifts, strategic shifts typically reflect a profoundly different orientation of system level goals (e.g., a prevention versus a promotion system goal orientation). Thus, although tactical shifts may sometimes appear more dramatic at the behavioral level than strategic shifts, strategic shifts reflect a more profound change in the pattern of activated CAUs throughout all levels of the goal hierarchy.

To illustrate the difference between tactical shifts and strategic shifts, we will use Regulatory Focus Theory (Higgins, 1999b), applying it to the domain of financial goals (see Figure 8.4). At the system level, a person may have an abstract goal to be on strong financial footing. This system goal might be in one of two orientations: either promotion or prevention. A promotion-focused system goal is oriented toward the pursuit of advancement whereas a prevention-focused system goal is oriented toward the pursuit of security. To begin pursuing this system-level goal in the world, it needs to be translated into a general strategy for satisfying the goal. Thus, the person might adopt a "vigilance" strategy, which involves avoiding financial losses and approaching financial non-losses, or the person might adopt an "eagerness" strategy, which involves approaching financial gains and avoiding financial non-gains. These strategies, in turn, must be further specified into tactics, such as risky or conservative financial decision-making in a particular class of situations (Scholer, Zou, Fujita, Stroessner, & Higgins, 2010).

According to Scholer and Higgins (2008), the factor that is the driving force in strategy selection is *regulatory fit*, that is, how well the strategy fits with the orientation of the system goal (Higgins, 2009). If the system goal is in a promotion orientation, for example, then an eagerness strategy will be preferred. If, however, the system goal is in a prevention orientation, then a vigilance strategy will be preferred. The same system goal may be in a different orientation under different environmental contingencies

(Molden et al., 2008), and changes in goal orientation at the system level will manifest in strategic shifts. Thus, strategic shifts reveal information about the orientation of the system at the highest level. A naturalistic shift in strategy from vigilance to eagerness, for example, is a cue that the person may have shifted at the system level from a prevention to a promotion orientation.

A strategy has many different tactics linked to it. Although Scholer and Higgins (2008) have not as yet fully outlined the principles that influence tactic selection, some likely candidates are expectancies and automaticity (Bargh et al., 2010). To the extent that a tactic is under deliberate control, its selection should be influenced by perceived feasibility (i.e., "How likely is it that I can successfully execute this tactic?") and perceived instrumentality (i.e., "What is the likelihood that the successful execution of this tactic will lead to the desired outcome?"). To the extent that the tactic is not under deliberate control, it should be influenced by the history of conditioned links between the situation, the tactic, and outcomes: Tactics that are frequently activated in the situation and followed by desired outcomes should have high accessibility for subsequent activation in similar situations (and undoubtedly, these conditioned links developed, in part, because of the feasibility and instrumentality of the tactic).

Tactical shifts will occur naturalistically in response to environmental changes that impact either the feasibility of enacting the tactic or the likelihood that the tactic will produce the desired outcomes. Research has shown, for example, that prevention-focused people pursuing a vigilance strategy will make conservative financial choices when they are financially "up" but risky financial choices when they are financially "down" (Scholer et al., 2010). When the status quo is a state of gain, a vigilance strategy requires cautious avoidance of danger, but when the status quo is a state of loss, a vigilance strategy requires approaching safety by any means necessary. The driving principle behind tactical shifts, therefore, might best be termed *strategic functionality*—people should shift tactics when the current tactic is no longer functional for meeting the active strategic goal.[4]

Figure 8.4 A tri-level model of sample goals, strategies, and tactics as applied to Regulatory Focus Theory

---

[4]The important dimension here is the functionality of the tactic for the active goal, not the overall functionality of the tactic for the person. Thus, one might argue that the self-injurious behavior of someone with borderline personality disorder ceases to be functional for the person overall when it puts the person's life or health in danger, but as long as it continues to function to help the person regulate emotion in the moment, the tactic is still functional for the currently active goal (Niedtfeld et al., 2010).

CAPS theory can encompass both types of shifts, tactical and strategic, within the more general category of situation-behavior profiles. CAPS does not, however, currently highlight the distinction between these lower-level and higher-level shifts within the self-regulation hierarchy. We believe that the distinction between tactics and strategies provides a valuable addition to the CAPS approach, suggesting that not all "if...then..." shifts are functionally equivalent. Furthermore, the tri-level theory of self-regulation provides a framework to disentangle lower-level and higher-level shifts, but has not yet been widely applied as a meta-theory of personality, as has CAPS. In the sections that follow, we apply the tactical/strategic distinction to two social cognitive personality theories in the CAPS meta-theoretical tradition reviewed previously: mind-set theory (Dweck & Molden, 2008) and attachment theory (Shaver & Mikulincer, 2009).

If...Then... **Profile Variation: Tactical Shifts**

We define *tactical shifts* as *if...then...* profiles that result from a consistent strategy that is manifested in different tactics depending on the situation. Information about tactical shifts, we argue, is especially useful for disambiguating the strategic function of a given observed behavior. Any given behavior, such as making a risky financial decision, effortfully striving on a task, or displaying hostile rejection, can be described at the level of base-rates, but because of the principles of multifinality and equifinality, two people could exhibit the same behavior for different strategic reasons, or two people could exhibit opposite behaviors for the same strategic reason. Thus, the behavior alone cannot typically disambiguate the strategy behind the behavior (e.g., Is this person making a risky financial choice because he is eagerly approaching success or because he is vigilantly avoiding failure?). By seeing how a person switches tactics in response to different situational contingencies, however, the underlying strategy is often revealed. For example, the following pattern: *"if* situation of loss, *then* risky decision, but *if* situation of gain, *then* conservative decision" is a tactical *if...then...* profile that strongly suggests a consistent vigilance strategy.

In an achievement goal hierarchy, an observed tactic might be effortful striving (see Figure 8.5). According to Dweck (2006), a person might effortfully strive on tasks as a result of performance goal strategies or as a result of learning goal strategies. Thus, observing that a person works hard on tasks is not sufficient to identify the strategic function of hard work in the person's goal system. To understand which strategy is driving the behavior, it

Figure 8.5 A tri-level model of sample goals, strategies, and tactics as applied to Dweck's mind-set theory

is useful to examine the situations that produce tactical shifts. In a performance goal strategy, effortful striving is functional when such striving has a high likelihood of leading to performance success, but not when it has a high likelihood of leading to performance failure. Thus, a person pursuing a performance strategy should shift from an effortful striving tactic to a disengagement tactic as expectancies for performance outcomes change (*"if* expect success, *then* effort; *if* expect failure, *then* disengagement"). In a learning goal strategy, effortful striving is functional when such striving has a high likelihood of revealing new insights and growing one's skills, but not when it has a low likelihood of doing so. Thus, a person pursuing a learning goal strategy should shift from an effortful striving tactic to a disengagement tactic as expectancies for learning and growth opportunities change (*"if* there is challenge or even failure, *then* effort; *if* there is no challenge or easy success, *then* disengagement"). Indeed, research suggests that performance and learning strategies are manifested in these kinds of tactical shifts (Dweck & Grant, 2008; Dweck & Leggett, 1988; Dweck & Master, 2009).

In a relatedness goal hierarchy (see Figure 8.6), observed tactics might include both friendly approach (pulling close) and hostile rejection (pushing away), as people try to keep relationships at an optimal level of closeness, responsiveness, and autonomy (Murray, Derrick, Leder, & Holmes, 2008). People who have anxious, avoidant, and secure attachment styles are likely to use both friendly and hostile tactics to meet their goals, but in different situations, according to changes in the tactics' strategic functionality (Feeney, 2006; Mikulincer et al., 2009). People with an anxious attachment style pursue a vigilance strategy and strive to avoid painful rejection. When there is a potential threat of rejection, anxiously attached people will engage in friendly, ingratiating behaviors to ward off the rejection, but when rejection is inevitable, anxiously attached people will engage in preemptive rejection of the other person, to minimize rejection's sting (*"if* acceptance is threatened, *then* engage in friendly repair; *if* rejection is certain,

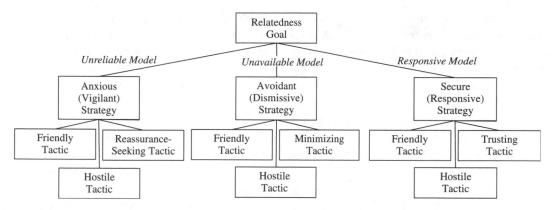

Figure 8.6   A tri-level model of sample goals, strategies, and tactics as applied to attachment theory

then engage in hostile defensiveness"). People with an avoidant attachment style pursue a dismissive strategy and strive to minimize emotional or instrumental dependence in relationships. When there is a high level of autonomy, avoidantly attached people will engage in friendly approach behavior, but when the other person shows signs of neediness, avoidantly attached people will display hostile unfriendliness ("*if* autonomy is secure, *then* engage in friendly approach; *if* autonomy is threatened, *then* engage in hostile pushing away"). Thus, both anxious and avoidant individuals are capable of friendly and hostile behavior, but they use these behaviors in different situations to advance their different strategic goals. By identifying the situational factors that catalyze the shift from friendly to unfriendly tactics (rejection versus dependence, respectively), the strategic function of the tactics is revealed.

As these examples illustrate, sometimes dramatic changes in behavior are driven by a strong consistency at the strategic level. An anxiously attached person can shift from friendly approach to hostile rejection, all in pursuit of a strategy of protecting acceptance. In this case, a friendly tactic does not necessarily imply a shift to a secure attachment strategy and a hostile tactic does not necessarily imply a change to an avoidant attachment strategy. Indeed, it is *precisely* situational shifts at the tactical level that reveal the consistent strategic functions of the tactics. Tactical shifts are thus driven by strong higher-level consistency; the active goal and the state of the system has not changed, but the opportunities and constraints that the person perceives in the situation leads them to switch tactics to continue working toward their strategic goal using different means.

If . . . Then . . . Profile Variation: Strategic Shifts

We define *strategic shifts* as *if . . . then . . .* profiles that result when a person switches from one strategy to another

in their pursuit of valued goals (e.g., a strategy of eagerly approaching success versus a strategy of vigilantly avoiding failure). Strategic shifts allow a person to react to old situations in new ways, as various tactics will have new strategic functionalities under the new strategy (e.g., approaching risky opportunities for advancement would be functional under an eagerness strategy but not functional under a vigilance strategy). Unlike tactical shifts, which are likely to be observed when the situation affects the strategic functionality of the tactic without affecting variables at higher levels in the goal system, strategic shifts are most likely to occur when the situation has reoriented goals at the system level. For example, a situation might change the system-level goal from a focus on desired end states to a focus on undesired end states (Carver & White, 1994), from a concern with advancement to a concern with security (Higgins, 1999b), from a focus on internal experiences to a focus on external contingencies (Deci & Ryan, 2009), and so on. When a person's system level goal is in a different orientation, an entirely different strategy with a host of new tactics may quite naturally emerge from the person, even if these tactics would rarely be seen in other circumstances (e.g., "*if* advancement concerns are most accessible, *then* activate an eagerness strategy and its associated tactics; *if* security concerns are most accessible, *then* activate a vigilance strategy and its associated tactics").

Research in the achievement domain suggests that implicit theories are system variables that influence the adoption of performance versus learning strategies (Dweck, 2008; Dweck & Grant, 2008; see Figure 8.5). When people focus on the possibility that intelligence can be improved (a "growth" or incremental theory), their achievement system goal becomes oriented around improvement concerns, which activates a learning strategy. When people focus on the possibility that intelligence may be fixed (a "fixed" or entity theory), their achievement goal becomes oriented around demonstration concerns, which activates a performance strategy. Situations that draw attention to the opposing theory (e.g., reading an article about environmental versus genetic contributions to intelligence, Dweck & Leggett, 2000) can change the accessibility of these two viewpoints enough to shift the achievement goal strategy ("*if* I think about how intelligence is fixed, *then* I pursue a performance strategy; *if* I think about how intelligence can grow, *then* I activate a learning strategy"). The achievement subdomain itself can be a situation that changes the accessibility of a growth or fixed theory. A person may, for example, pursue a performance strategy with its associated tactics in school, but may pursue a learning strategy with its associated tactics in music or art lessons, if a person holds a different theory of ability for the two domains. How would this strategic shift be manifested in behavior? The person should display a noticeably different response to failure in the two domains, and this is not a surface inconsistency but rather a deep one—the orientation of the person's system goal is quite different from one domain to the other.

Turning to attachment theory, research suggests that mental models of others are system variables that influence the activation of secure, anxious, or avoidant strategies in a relational goal system (Shaver & Mikulincer, 2009). When people believe that others will not be responsive to their needs, their relatedness goal orients toward autonomy-protection concerns, which activates the dismissive strategy. When people believe that others will be inconsistently responsive to their needs, their relatedness goal orients toward connection-protection concerns, which activates the vigilance strategy. When people believe that others will be responsive to their needs, their relatedness goal orients toward advancement concerns, which activates the trusting strategy. Individual differences in the chronic accessibility of each mental model lead to individual differences in chronic goal orientation and strategic preference.

Nevertheless, particular situations may activate any one of the three mental models, which can shift the goal orientation and the pursuant strategy. Thus, someone who typically pursues anxious strategies may activate trusting strategies in a particular relationship with a person who they perceive to be consistently responsive, and someone who typically pursues secure strategies may activate anxious strategies in a particular relationship with a person who they perceive to be inconsistently responsive (Bartz & Lydon, 2008; Davila & Kashy, 2009; Fraley, Heffernan, Vicary, & Brumbaugh, 2011). These strategic shifts reflect pervasive changes in the state of the motivational system and the associated spreading activation to strategies and tactics ("*if* I perceive that a relationship partner is inconsistently responsive, *then* I activate an anxious strategy; *if* I perceive that a relationship partner is reliably responsive, *then* I activate a secure strategy"). Thus, the same individual may appear to be "a different person" in one relationship versus another, and this perception is in some sense entirely accurate, in that the individual's behavior is coming from a fundamentally different place at the system level.

The tri-level theory of self-regulation (Scholer & Higgins, 2008) draws attention to the distinction between tactical and strategic shifts in behavior. Tactical shifts represent changes in the low-level selection of means given the perceived opportunities and constraints of the situation, whereas strategic shifts represent more pervasive changes at all three levels of the goal hierarchy. Thus, tactical versus strategic *if...then...* profile variation in response to situations represents differing amounts of change in the goal system as a whole: Tactical shifts illustrate low-level variation with underlying strategic consistency, and strategic shifts illustrate variation that is produced by meaningful and pervasive changes in the activation of goals and related cognitions from the highest to lowest hierarchical level.

Implications of a Functionalist CAPS Framework

Our approach suggests that when one takes seriously the idea that behaviors serve functions, superficial and simple evaluations of behavior are not sufficient for capturing personality. What looks similar on the surface can actually be quite different. And superficial differences may reveal deep similarity. This is true both within and between people; acknowledging these dynamics provides a framework for thinking about how to better understand persons. Echoing others, we believe that a behavior cannot be understood without knowing the strategy that drives it. Likewise, knowing an individual's strategic orientation is critical for discerning higher-level system variables. Is a risky choice a reflection of creativity or desperation? Is withdrawal a signal of anger or reflection? Personality is involved at all levels; comprehensive person perception must involve all three.

This does not simply lead to more accurate person perception, but has significant implications for personality change. Trying to change a behavior without considering the function the behavior serves is likely a futile effort. If you take away an avoidant person's hostile responses to neediness, how will that person protect autonomy? Is a rejection sensitive person really going to be able to just "let go" of their anxious expectations of rejection? Probably not. However, some tactics are more effective for general well-being and growth than others. Hostility may be functional for avoidant individuals because it protects their autonomy, but it is not functional for all goals—certainly not for building close relationships. By introducing a new tactic that serves the same strategy in a more optimal way (e.g., trying to get an avoidant person to offer a needy romantic partner autonomy support rather than trying to get them to offer instrumental support), individuals may be more open and able to adopt new behaviors. For the avoidant individual, for instance, this more adaptive tactic may be less likely to sabotage relationships. Over time, such tactical changes may profoundly influence people's well-being.

It is also possible to consider a top-down approach to personality change, using system changes that will themselves pull for a corresponding and cascading set of strategies and tactics. An individual who continually disengages from challenging situations may be doing so because of their concerns with demonstrating their abilities. Recognizing that their disengagement stems from system level beliefs that intelligence is immutable suggests the possibility of an intervention at the highest level. If an individual can be shown that abilities are mutable, they are likely to focus on improvement, with disengagement giving way to engagement. We don't suggest that such changes are always (or ever) easy. We do suggest, however, that understanding where in the hierarchy to target an intervention—and how that intervention will affect other levels—is critical.

We began by suggesting that a comprehensive personality theory should serve three goals, providing insight into personality prediction, explanation, and dynamics of interpersonal influence. From its inception, CAPS made great strides in advancing all of these goals and in so doing, fundamentally changed the way personality itself was conceptualized. The functionalist approach to CAPS, we believe, is an even more powerful tool. Early work in CAPS focused on understanding psychological meaningful "ifs." The functionalist approach we have taken here highlights differences in psychologically meaningful "thens" as well. Not all "thens" are equal; tactical shifts may in fact highlight strong strategic consistency, whereas strategic shifts may reveal high-level changes. Continued exploration of these dynamics has the potential to deepen and broaden our understanding of personality.

REFERENCES

Ambady, N., & Rosenthal, R. (1993). Half a minute: Predicting teacher evaluations from thin slices of nonverbal behavior and physical attractiveness. *Journal of Personality & Social Psychology*, *64*, 431–441.

Bargh, J. A., Gollwitzer, P. M., & Oettingen, G. (2010). Motivation. In S. T. Fiske, D. T. Gilbert, & G. Lindzey (Eds.), *Handbook of social psychology* (Vol. 1, 5th ed., pp. 268–316). Hoboken, NJ: Wiley.

Bartz, J. A., & Lydon, J. E. (2008). Relationship-specific attachment, risk regulation, and communal norm adherence in close relationships. *Journal of Experimental Social Psychology, 44*, 655–663. doi: http://dx.doi.org/10.1016/j.jesp.2007.04.003

Berg, J. H., & Archer, R. L. (1982). Responses to self-disclosure and interaction goals. *Journal of Experimental Social Psychology, 18*, 501–512. doi: http://dx.doi.org/10.1016/0022–1031%2882%2990069–5

Bickel, R. (2007). *Multilevel analysis for applied research: It's just regression!* New York, NY: Guilford Press.

Blackman, M. C., & Funder, D. C. (1998). The effect of information on consensus and accuracy in personality judgment. *Journal of Experimental Social Psychology, 34*, 164–181.

Blackwell, L. S., Trzesniewski, K. H., & Dweck, C. S. (2007). Implicit theories of intelligence predict achievement across an adolescent transition: A longitudinal study and an intervention. *Child Development, 78*, 246–263. doi: http://dx.doi.org/10.1111/j.1467–8624.2007.00995.x

Bolger, N., & Romero-Canyas, R. (2007). Integrating personality traits and processes: Framework, method, analysis, results. In Y. Shoda, D. Cervone, & G. Downey (Eds.), *Persons in context: Building a science of the individual* (pp. 201–210). New York, NY: Guilford Press.

Bolger, N., & Zuckerman, A. (1995). A framework for studying personality in the stress process. *Journal of Personality and Social Psychology, 69*, 890–902.

Borsboom, D., Mellenbergh, G. J., & van Heerden, J. (2003). The theoretical status of latent variables. *Psychological Review, 110*, 203–219. doi: http://dx.doi.org/10.1037/0033–295X.110.2.203

Bryk, A. S., & Raudenbush, S. W. (2002). *Hierarchical linear models: Applications and data analysis methods* (2nd ed.). Thousand Oaks, CA: Sage.

Buss, D. M. (2009a). An evolutionary formulation of person-situation interactions. *Journal of Research in Personality, 43*, 241–242. doi: http://dx.doi.org/10.1016/j.jrp.2008.12.019

Buss, D. M. (2009b). How can evolutionary psychology successfully explain personality and individual differences? *Perspectives on Psychological Science, 4*, 359–366. doi: http://dx.doi.org/10.1111/j.1745–6924.2009.01138.x

Carver, C. S., & Scheier, M. F. (1998). *On the self-regulation of behavior*. New York, NY: Cambridge University Press.

Carver, C. S., Scheier, M. F., & Fulford, D. (2008). Self-regulatory processes, stress, and coping. In O. P. John, R. W. Robins, & L. A. Pervin (Eds.), *Handbook of personality psychology: Theory and research* (3rd ed., pp. 725–742). New York, NY: Guilford Press.

Carver, C. S., & White, T. L. (1994). Behavioral inhibition, behavioral activation, and affective responses to impending reward and punishment: The BIS/BAS Scales. *Journal of Personality and Social Psychology, 67*, 319–333. doi: http://dx.doi.org/10.1037/0022–3514.67.2.319

Cassidy, J., Shaver, P. R., Mikulincer, M., & Lavy, S. (2009). Experimentally induced security influences responses to psychological pain. *Journal of Social and Clinical Psychology, 28*, 463–478. doi: http://dx.doi.org/10.1521/jscp.2009.28.4.463

Collins, N. L., Guichard, A. C., Ford, M. B., & Feeney, B. C. (2004). Working models of attachment: New developments and emerging themes. In W. S. Rholes & J. A. Simpson (Eds.), *Adult attachment: Theory, research, and clinical implications* (pp. 196–239). New York, NY: Guilford.

Cote, S., & Moskowitz, D. S. (1998). On the dynamic covariation between interpersonal behavior and affect: Prediction from neuroticism, extraversion, and agreeableness. *Journal of Personality and Social Psychology, 75*, 1032–1046.

Dandeneau, S. D., Baldwin, M. W., Baccus, J. R., Sakellaropoulo, M., & Pruessner, J. C. (2007). Cutting stress off at the pass: Reducing vigilance and responsiveness to social threat by manipulating attention. *Journal of Personality and Social Psychology, 93*, 651–666. doi: http://dx.doi.org/10.1037/0022–3514.93.4.651

Davila, J., & Kashy, D. A. (2009). Secure base processes in couples: Daily associations between support experiences and attachment security. *Journal of Family Psychology, 23*, 76–88. doi: http://dx.doi.org/10.1037/a0014353

Deci, E. L., & Ryan, R. M. (2009). Self-determination theory: A consideration of human motivational universals. In P. J. Corr & G. Matthews (Eds.), *The Cambridge handbook of personality psychology* (pp. 441–456). New York, NY: Cambridge University Press.

Dweck, C. S. (2006). *Mindset: The new psychology of success*. New York, NY: Random House.

Dweck, C. S. (2008). Can personality be changed? The role of beliefs in personality and change. *Current Directions in Psychological Science, 17*, 391–394. doi: http://dx.doi.org/10.1111/j.1467–8721.2008.00612.x

Dweck, C. S., & Grant, H. (2008). Self-theories, goals, and meaning. In J. Y. Shaw & W. L. Gardner (Eds.), *Handbook of motivation science* (pp. 405–416). New York, NY: Guilford Press.

Dweck, C. S., & Leggett, E. L. (1988). A social-cognitive approach to motivation and personality. *Psychological Review, 95*, 256–273. doi: http://dx.doi.org/10.1037/0033–295X.95.2.256

Dweck, C. S., & Leggett, E. L. (2000). A social-cognitive approach to motivation and personality. In E. T. Higgins & A. W. Kruglanski (Eds.), *Motivational science: Social and personality perspectives* (pp. 394–415). New York, NY: Psychology Press.

Dweck, C. S., & Master, A. (2009). Self-theories and motivation: Students' beliefs about intelligence. In K. R. Wenzel & A. Wigfield (Eds.), *Handbook of motivation at school* (pp. 123–140). New York, NY: Routledge/Taylor & Francis.

Dweck, C. S., & Molden, D. C. (2008). Self-theories: The construction of free will. In J. Baer, J. C. Kaufman, & R. F. Baumeister (Eds.), *Are we free? Psychology and free will* (pp. 44–64). New York, NY: Oxford University Press.

Edelstein, R. S., & Shaver, P. R. (2004). Avoidant attachment: Exploration of an oxymoron. In D. J. Mashek & A. P. Aron (Eds.), *Handbook of closeness and intimacy* (pp. 397–412). Mahwah, NJ: Erlbaum.

Epley, N., & Waytz, A. (2010). Mind perception. In S. T. Fiske, D. T. Gilbert, & G. Lindzey (Eds.), *Handbook of social psychology*, (Vol. 1, 5th ed., pp. 498–541). Hoboken, NJ: Wiley.

Epstein, S. (1979). The stability of behavior: I. On predicting most of the people much of the time. *Journal of Personality & Social Psychology, 37*, 1097–1126.

Feeney, B. C. (2006). An Attachment theory perspective on the interplay between intrapersonal and interpersonal processes. In K. D. Vohs & E. J. Finkel (Eds.), *Self and relationships: Connecting intrapersonal and interpersonal processes* (pp. 133–159). New York, NY: Guilford Press.

Feingold, A. (1994). Gender differences in personality: A meta-analysis. *Psychological Bulletin, 116*, 429–456. doi: http://dx.doi.org/10.1037/0033–2909.116.3.429

Ferguson, M. J., & Bargh, J. A. (2004). Liking is for doing: The effects of goal pursuit on automatic evaluation. *Journal of Personality*

and Social Psychology, 87, 557–572. doi: http://dx.doi.org/10.1037/0022–3514.87.5.557

Fiske, S. T. (1992). Thinking is for doing: Portraits of social cognition from daguerreotype to laserphoto. *Journal of Personality and Social Psychology, 63*, 877–889. doi: http://dx.doi.org/10.1037/0022–3514.63.6.877

Fleeson, W. (2001). Toward a structure- and process-integrated view of personality: Traits as density distributions of states. *Journal of Personality and Social Psychology, 80*, 1011–1027. doi: http://dx.doi.org/10.1037/0022–3514.80.6.1011

Fleeson, W. (2004). Moving personality beyond the person-situation debate: The challenge and the opportunity of within-person variability. *Current Directions in Psychological Science, 13*, 83–87. doi: http://dx.doi.org/10.1111/j.0963–7214.2004.00280.x

Fleeson, W. (2007). Situation-based contingencies underlying trait-content manifestation in behavior. *Journal of Personality, 75*, 825–862. doi: http://dx.doi.org/10.1111/j.1467–6494.2007.00458.x

Fleeson, W. (in press). Perspectives on the person: Rapid growth and opportunities for integration. In K. Deaux & M. Snyder (Eds.), *Oxford Handbook of Personality and Social Psychology*. New York, NY: Oxford University Press.

Fleeson, W., & Gallagher, P. (2009). The implications of big five standing for the distribution of trait manifestation in behavior: Fifteen experience-sampling studies and a meta-analysis. *Journal of Personality and Social Psychology, 97*, 1097–1114. doi: http://dx.doi.org/10.1037/a0016786

Fleeson, W., & Leicht, C. (2006). On delineating and integrating the study of variability and stability in personality psychology: Interpersonal trust as illustration. *Journal of Research in Personality, 40*, 5–20. doi: http://dx.doi.org/10.1016/j.jrp.2005.08.004

Fleeson, W., & Noftle, E. E. (2009). In favor of the synthetic resolution to the person-situation debate. *Journal of Research in Personality, 43*, 150–154. doi: http://dx.doi.org/10.1016/j.jrp.2009.02.008

Fournier, M. A., Moskowitz, D., & Zuroff, D. C. (2008). Integrating dispositions, signatures, and the interpersonal domain. *Journal of Personality and Social Psychology, 94*, 531–545. doi: http://dx.doi.org/10.1037/0022–3514.94.3.531

Fraley, R., Heffernan, M. E., Vicary, A. M., & Brumbaugh, C. C. (2011). The experiences in close relationships–relationship structures questionnaire: A method for assessing attachment orientations across relationships. *Psychological Assessment, 23*, 615–625. doi: http://dx.doi.org/10.1037/a0022898

Friesen, C., & Kammrath, L. K. (2011). What it pays to know about a close other: The value of contextualized "if-then" personality knowledge in close relationships. *Psychological Science, 22*, 567–571.

Funder, D. C. (1995). On the accuracy of personality judgment: A realistic approach. *Psychological Review, 102*, 652–670.

Gilovich, T. (1987). Secondhand information and social judgment. *Journal of Experimental Social Psychology, 23*, 59–74. doi: http://dx.doi.org/10.1016/0022–1031%2887%2990025–4

Graziano, W. G., & Tobin, R. M. (2009). Agreeableness. In M. R. Leary & R. H. Hoyle (Eds.), *Handbook of individual differences in social behavior* (pp. 46–61). New York, NY: Guilford Press.

Gross, J. J. (2008). Emotion and emotion regulation: Personality processes and individual differences. In O. P. John, R. W. Robins, & L. A. Pervin, *Handbook of personality psychology: Theory and research* (3rd ed., pp. 701–724). New York, NY: Guilford Press.

Higgins, E. (1997). Beyond pleasure and pain. *American Psychologist, 52*, 1280–1300. doi: http://dx.doi.org/10.1037/0003–066X.52.12.1280

Higgins, E. (1999a). Persons or situations: Unique explanatory principles or variability in general principles? In D. Cervone & Y. Shoda (Eds.), *The coherence of personality: Social-cognitive bases of consistency, variability, and organization* (pp. 61–93). New York, NY: Guilford Press.

Higgins, E. (1999b). Promotion and prevention as a motivational duality: Implications for evaluative processes. In S. Chaiken & Y. Trope (Eds.), *Dual-process theories in social psychology* (pp. 503–525). New York, NY: Guilford Press.

Higgins, E. (2001). Promotion and prevention experiences: Relating emotions to nonemotional motivational states. In J. P. Forgas (Ed.), *Handbook of affect and social cognition* (pp. 186–211). Mahwah, NJ: Erlbaum.

Higgins, E. (2009). Regulatory fit in the goal-pursuit process. In G. B. Moskowitz & H. Grant, *The psychology of goals* (pp. 505–533). New York, NY: Guilford Press.

Hox, J. J. (2002). *Multilevel analysis techniques and applications*. Mahwah, NJ: Erlbaum.

Hox, J. J. (2010). *Multilevel analysis: Techniques and applications* (2nd ed.). New York, NY: Routledge/Taylor & Francis.

Idson, L. C., & Mischel, W. (2001). The personality of familiar and significant people: The lay perceiver as a social-cognitive theorist. *Journal of Personality and Social Psychology, 80,* 585–596. doi: http://dx.doi.org/10.1037/0022–3514.80.4.585

John, O. P., & Srivastava, S. (1999). The big five trait taxonomy: History, measurement, and theoretical perspectives. In L. A. Pervin & O. P. John (Eds.), *Handbook of personality: Theory and research* (2nd ed., pp. 102–138). New York, NY: Guilford Press.

Jones, E. E., Kanouse, D. E., Kelley, H. H., Nisbett, R. E., Valins, S., & Weiner, B. (Eds.). (1987). *Attribution: Perceiving the causes of behavior*. London, UK: Erlbaum.

Jones, E. E., & Nisbett, R. E. (1987). The actor and the observer: Divergent perceptions of the causes of behavior. In E. E. Jones, D. E. Kanouse, H. H. Kelley, R. E. Nisbett, S. Valins, & B. Weiner (Eds.), *Attribution: Perceiving the causes of behavior* (pp. 79–94). London, UK: Erlbaum.

Judge, T. A., Heller, D., & Mount, M. K. (2002). Five-factor model of personality and job satisfaction: A meta-analysis. *Journal of Applied Psychology, 87,* 530–541. doi: http://dx.doi.org/10.1037/0021–9010.87.3.530

Judge, T. A., & Ilies, R. (2002). Relationship of personality to performance motivation: A meta-analytic review. *Journal of Applied Psychology, 87,* 797–807. doi: http://dx.doi.org/10.1037/0021–9010.87.4.797

Kagan, J. (2007). The power of context. In Y. Shoda, D. Cervone, & G. Downey (Eds.), *Persons in context: Building a science of the individual* (pp. 43–61). New York, NY: Guilford Press.

Kammrath, L. K. (2011). What we think we do (to each other): How the same relational behaviors mean different things to people with different personality profiles. *Journal of Personality and Social Psychology, 101,* 754–770.

Kammrath, L. K., Ames, D. R., & Scholer, A. A. (2007). Keeping up impressions: Inferential rules for impression change across the big five. *Journal of Experimental Social Psychology, 43,* 450–457. doi: http://dx.doi.org/10.1016/j.jesp.2006.04.006

Kammrath, L. K., McCarthy, M., Friesen, C., & Cortes, K. (2011). Picking one's battles: The personality predictors of discriminative assertiveness. *Manuscript under review*.

Kammrath, L. K., Mendoza-Denton, R., & Mischel, W. (2005). Incorporating if...then...personality signatures in person perception: Beyond the person-situation dichotomy. *Journal of Personality and Social Psychology, 88,* 605–618. doi: http://dx.doi.org/10.1037/0022–3514.88.4.605

Kammrath, L. K., & Peetz, J. (2011). The limits of love: Predicting immediate versus sustained caring behaviors in close relationships. *Journal of Experimental Social Psychology, 47,* 411–417. doi: http://dx.doi.org/10.1016/j.jesp.2010.11.004

Kammrath, L. K., & Scholer, A. A. (2011). The Pollyanna myth: How agreeable people judge positive and negative relational acts. *Personality and Social Psychology Bulletin, 37,* 1172–1184.

Kelley, H. H. (1967). Attribution theory in social psychology. In D. Levine (Ed.), *Nebraska symposium on motivation* (Vol. 15, pp. 192–238). Lincoln: University of Nebraska Press.

Kenrick, D. T., Neuberg, S. L., Griskevicius, V., Becker, D., & Schaller, M. (2010). Goal-driven cognition and functional behavior: The fundamental-motives framework. *Current Directions in Psychological Science, 19,* 63–67. doi: http://dx.doi.org/10.1177/0963721409359281

Kruglanski, A. W., Shah, J. Y., Fishbach, A., Friedman, R., Chun, W. Y., & Sleeth-Keppler, D. (2002). A theory of goal systems. In M. P. Zanna (Ed.), *Advances in experimental social psychology* (Vol. 34, pp. 331–378). San Diego, CA: Academic Press.

Liberman, N., Molden, D. C., Idson, L. C., & Higgins, E. (2001). Promotion and prevention focus on alternative hypotheses: Implications for attributional functions. *Journal of Personality and Social Psychology, 80,* 5–18. doi: http://dx.doi.org/10.1037/0022–3514.80.1.5

Lucas, R. E., & Donnellan, M. (2009). If the person-situation debate is really over, why does it still generate so much negative affect? *Journal of Research in Personality, 43,* 146–149. doi: http://dx.doi.org/10.1016/j.jrp.2009.02.009

Malle, B. F., & Hodges, S. D. (2005). *Other minds: How humans bridge the divide between self and others*. New York, NY: Guilford Press.

Matthews, G. (2008). Personality and information processing: A cognitive-adaptive theory. In G. J. Boyle, G. Matthews, & D. H. Sakofske, *The SAGE handbook of personality theory and assessment, Vol 1: Personality theories and models* (pp. 56–79). Thousand Oaks, CA: Sage.

McMurran, M., Jinks, M., Howells, K., & Howard, R. C. (2010). Alcohol-related violence defined by ultimate goals: A qualitative analysis of the features of three different types of violence by intoxicated young male offenders. *Aggressive Behavior, 36,* 67–79. doi: http://dx.doi.org/10.1002/ab.20331

Metcalfe, J., & Mischel, W. (1999). A hot/cool-system analysis of delay of gratification: Dynamics of willpower. *Psychological Review, 106,* 3–19. doi: http://dx.doi.org/10.1037/0033–295X.106.1.3

Mikulincer, M., Shaver, P. R., Cassidy, J., & Berant, E. (2009). Attachment-related defensive processes. In J. H. Obegi & E. Berant (Eds.), *Attachment theory and research in clinical work with adults* (pp. 293–327). New York, NY: Guilford Press.

Miller, G. A., Galanter, E., & Pribram, K. H. (1960). *Plans and the structure of behavior*. New York, NY: Holt.

Mischel, W. (1968). *Personality and assessment*. Hoboken, NJ: Wiley.

Mischel, W. (1973). Toward a cognitive social learning reconceptualization of personality. *Psychological Review, 80,* 252–283. doi: http://dx.doi.org/10.1037/h0035002

Mischel, W. (1974). Processes in delay of gratification. *Advances in Experimental Social Psychology, 7,* 249–292.

Mischel, W., & Shoda, Y. (1995). A cognitive-affective system theory of personality: Reconceptualizing situations, dispositions, dynamics, and invariance in personality structure. *Psychological Review, 102,* 246–268. doi: http://dx.doi.org/10.1037/0033–295X.102.2.246

Mischel, W., & Shoda, Y. (1998). Reconciling processing dynamics and personality dispositions. *Annual Review of Psychology, 49,* 229–258. doi: http://dx.doi.org/10.1146/annurev.psych.49.1.229

Mischel, W., & Shoda, Y. (1999). Integrating dispositions and processing dynamics within a unified theory of personality: The cognitive-affective personality system. In L. A. Pervin & O. P. John (Eds.), *Handbook of personality: Theory and research* (2nd ed., pp. 197–218). New York, NY: Guilford Press.

Mischel, W., & Shoda, Y. (2008). Toward a unified theory of personality: Integrating dispositions and processing dynamics within the cognitive-affective processing system. In O. P. John, R. W. Robins, & L. A. Pervin (Eds.), *Handbook of personality psychology: Theory and research* (3rd ed., pp. 208–241). New York, NY: Guilford Press.

Molden, D. C., Lee, A. Y., & Higgins, E. (2008). Motivations for promotion and prevention. *Handbook of motivation science* (pp. 169–187). New York, NY: Guilford Press.

Murray, S. L., Derrick, J. L., Leder, S., & Holmes, J. G. (2008). Balancing connectedness and self-protection goals in close relationships: A levels-of-processing perspective on risk regulation. *Journal of Personality and Social Psychology, 94*, 429–459. doi: http://dx.doi.org/10.1037/0022-3514.94.3.429

Neuberg, S. L., Kenrick, D. T., & Schaller, M. (2010). Evolutionary social psychology. In S. T. Fiske, D. T. Gilbert, & G. Lindzey, *Handbook of social psychology* (Vol. 2, 5th ed., pp. 761–796). Hoboken, NJ: Wiley.

Niedtfeld, I., Schulze, L., Kirsch, P., Herpertz, S. C., Bohus, M., & Schmahl, C. (2010). Affect regulation and pain in borderline personality disorder: A possible link to the understanding of self-injury. *Biological Psychiatry, 68*, 383–391. doi: http://dx.doi.org/10.1016/j.biopsych.2010.04.015

Noftle, E. E., & Fleeson, W. (2010). Age differences in big five behavior averages and variabilities across the adult life span: Moving beyond retrospective, global summary accounts of personality. *Psychology and Aging, 25*, 95–107. doi: http://dx.doi.org/10.1037/a0018199

Norem, J. K. (2008). Defensive pessimism, anxiety, and the complexity of evaluating self-regulation. *Social and Personality Psychology Compass, 2*, 121–134. doi: http://dx.doi.org/10.1111/j.1751-9004.2007.00053.x

Norem, J. K., & Cantor, N. (1986). Defensive pessimism: Harnessing anxiety as motivation. *Journal of Personality and Social Psychology, 51*, 1208–1217. doi: http://dx.doi.org/10.1037/0022-3514.51.6.1208

Ozer, D. J., & Benet-Martinez, V. (2006). Personality and the prediction of consequential outcomes. In S. T. Fiske, A. E. Kazdin, & D. L. Schachter, *Annual review of psychology* (Vol. 57, pp. 401–421). Palo Alto, CA: Annual Reviews.

Peterson, D. R. (1968). *The clinical study of social behavior*. East Norwalk, CT: Appleton-Century-Crofts.

Pietrzak, J., Downey, G., & Ayduk, O. (2005). Rejection sensitivity as an interpersonal vulnerability. In M. W. Baldwin (Ed.), *Interpersonal cognition* (pp. 62–84). New York, NY: Guilford Press.

Powers, W. T. (1973). *Behavior: The control of perception*. Oxford, UK: Aldine.

Reeder, G. D., Vonk, R., Ronk, M. J., Ham, J., & Lawrence, M. (2004). Dispositional attribution: Multiple inferences about motive-related traits. *Journal of Personality & Social Psychology, 86*, 530–544.

Rhodewalt, F., & Morf, C. C. (1998). On self-aggrandizement and anger: A temporal analysis of narcissism and affective reactions to success and failure. *Journal of Personality and Social Psychology, 74*, 672–685. doi: http://dx.doi.org/10.1037/0022-3514.74.3.672

Romero-Canyas, R., Anderson, V. T., Reddy, K. S., & Downey, G. (2009). Rejection sensitivity. In M. R. Leary & R. H. Hoyle (Eds.), *Handbook of individual differences in social behavior* (pp. 466–479). New York, NY: Guilford Press.

Schaller, M., & Murray, D. R. (2008). Pathogens, personality, and culture: Disease prevalence predicts worldwide variability in sociosexuality, extraversion, and openness to experience. *Journal of Personality and Social Psychology, 95*, 212–221. doi: http://dx.doi.org/10.1037/0022-3514.95.1.212

Scholer, A. A., & Higgins, E. (2008). Distinguishing levels of approach and avoidance: An analysis using regulatory focus theory. In A. J. Elliot (Ed.), *Handbook of approach and avoidance motivation* (pp. 489–503). New York, NY: Psychology Press.

Scholer, A. A., & Higgins, E. (2010). Regulatory focus in a demanding world. In R. Hoyle (Ed.), *Handbook of personality and self-regulation.* (pp. 291–314). Malden, MA: Blackwell.

Scholer, A. A., & Higgins, E. (2010). Promotion and prevention systems: Regulatory focus dynamics within self-regulatory hierarchies. In R. F. Baumeister & K. D. Vohs (Eds.), *Handbook of self-regulation: Research, theory, and applications* (2nd ed., pp. 143–161). New York, NY: Guilford Press.

Scholer, A. A., Zou, X., Fujita, K., Stroessner, S. J., & Higgins, E. (2010). When risk seeking becomes a motivational necessity. *Journal of Personality and Social Psychology, 99*, 215–231. doi: http://dx.doi.org/10.1037/a0019715

Shaver, P. R., & Mikulincer, M. (2007). Adult attachment strategies and the regulation of emotion. In J. J. Gross (Ed.), *Handbook of emotion regulation* (pp. 446–465). New York, NY: Guilford Press.

Shaver, P. R., & Mikulincer, M. (2009). Attachment styles. In M. R. Leary & R. H. Hoyle (Eds.), *Handbook of individual differences in social behavior* (pp. 62–81). New York, NY: Guilford Press.

Shoda, Y., & LeeTiernan, S. (2002). What remains invariant?: Finding order within a person's thoughts, feelings, and behaviors across situations. In D. Cervone & W. Mischel (Eds.), *Advances in personality science* (pp. 241–270). New York, NY: Guilford Press.

Shoda, Y., Mischel, W., & Wright, J. C. (1993). Links between personality judgments and contextualized behavior patterns: Situation-behavior profiles of personality prototypes. *Social Cognition, 11*(4), 399–429.

Shoda, Y., Mischel, W., & Wright, J. C. (1994). Intraindividual stability in the organization and patterning of behavior: Incorporating psychological situations into the idiographic analysis of personality. *Journal of Personality and Social Psychology, 67*, 674–687. doi: http://dx.doi.org/10.1037/0022-3514.67.4.674

Shweder, R. A. (2007). From persons and situations to preferences and constraints. In Y. Shoda, D. Cervone, & G. Downey (Eds.), *Persons in context: Building a science of the individual* (pp. 84–94). New York, NY: Guilford Press.

Simpson, J. A., Beckes, L., & Weisberg, Y. J. (2008). Evolutionary accounts of individual differences in adult attachment orientations. In J. V. Wood, A. Tesser, & J. G. Holmes (Eds.), *The self and social relationships* (pp. 183–206). New York, NY: Psychology Press.

Smith, R. E., Shoda, Y., Cumming, S. P., & Smoll, F. L. (2009). Behavioral signatures at the ballpark: Intraindividual consistency of adults' situation-behavior patterns and their interpersonal consequences. *Journal of Research in Personality, 43*, 187–195. doi: http://dx.doi.org/10.1016/j.jrp.2008.12.006

Smith, T. W., & MacKenzie, J. (2006). Personality and risk of physical illness. *Annual Review of Clinical Psychology, 2*, 435–467. doi: http://dx.doi.org/10.1146/annurev.clinpsy.2.022305.095257

Srull, T. K., & Wyer, R. S. (1989). Person memory and judgment. *Psychological Review, 96*, 58–83. doi: http://dx.doi.org/10.1037/0033-295X.96.1.58

Steel, P., Schmidt, J., & Shultz, J. (2008). Refining the relationship between personality and subjective well-being. *Psychological Bulletin, 134*, 138–161. doi: http://dx.doi.org/10.1037/0033-2909.134.1.138

Suls, J., & Martin, R. (2005). The daily life of the garden-variety neurotic: Reactivity, stressor exposure, mood spillover, and maladaptive coping. *Journal of Personality, 73*, 1485–1510. doi: http://dx.doi.org/10.1111/j.1467-6494.2005.00356.x

Tamir, M. (2005). Don't worry, be happy? Neuroticism, trait-consistent affect regulation, and performance. *Journal of Personality and Social Psychology, 89*, 449–461. doi: http://dx.doi.org/10.1037/0022-3514.89.3.449

Tamir, M. (2009). What do people want to feel and why?: Pleasure and utility in emotion regulation. *Current Directions in Psychological Science, 18*, 101–105. doi: http://dx.doi.org/10.1111/j.1467-8721.2009.01617.x

Tamir, M., & Ford, B. Q. (2009). Choosing to be afraid: Preferences for fear as a function of goal pursuit. *Emotion, 9*(4), 488–497. doi: http://dx.doi.org/10.1037/a0015882

Tamir, M., Mitchell, C., & Gross, J. J. (2008). Hedonic and instrumental motives in anger regulation. *Psychological Science, 19*, 324–328.

Trope, Y. (1986). Identification and inferential processes in dispositional attribution. *Psychological Review, 93*(3), 239–257.

Vallacher, R. R., & Wegner, D. M. (1987). What do people think they're doing? Action identification and human behavior. *Psychological Review, 94*, 3–15.

Vernon, P. E. (1964). *Personality assessment: A critical survey*. Oxford, UK: Wiley.

Winter, L., & Uleman, J. S. (1984). When are social judgments made? Evidence for the spontaneousness of trait inferences. *Journal of Personality & Social Psychology, 47*, 237–252.

Wood, D., & Brumbaugh, C. C. (2009). Using revealed mate preferences to evaluate market force and differential preference explanations for mate selection. *Journal of Personality and Social Psychology, 96*, 1226–1244. doi: http://dx.doi.org/10.1037/a0015300

Wood, D., & Hensler, M. (2011). How a functionalist understanding of behavior can explain trait variation and covariation without the use of latent factors. *Manuscript under review.*

Zautra, A. J., Affleck, G. G., Tennen, H., Reich, J. W., & Davis, M. C. (2005). Dynamic approaches to emotions and stress in everyday life: Bolger and Zuckerman reloaded with positive as well as negative affects. *Journal of Personality, 73*, 1511–1538. doi: http://dx.doi.org/10.1111/j.0022-3506.2005.00357.x

Zayas, V., & Shoda, Y. (2009). Three decades after the personality paradox: Understanding situations. *Journal of Research in Personality, 43*, 280–281. doi: http://dx.doi.org/10.1016/j.jrp.2009.03.011

Zebrowitz, L. A., & Collins, M. A. (1997). Accurate social perception at zero acquaintance: The affordances of a Gibsonian approach. *Personality & Social Psychology Review, 1*, 204–223.

CHAPTER 9

Personality Trait Development in Adulthood

BRENT W. ROBERTS, M. BRENT DONNELLAN, AND PATRICK L. HILL

Gordon Allport (1961) defined personality as "the dynamic organization within the individual of those psychophysical systems that determine [her or his] characteristic behavior and thought" (1961, p. 28). A critical element of Allport's definition is the idea that the psychological attributes of the individual account for specific patterns of thoughts, feelings, and behavior. Personality psychology is therefore about individuality, and the study of personality development largely concerns the degree of consistency and change in individual differences from infancy to old age. Where do individual differences come from? How stable are they across the life span? What processes explain personality stability and personality change?

As it stands, there have been lengthy debates over the most appropriate ways of conceptualizing and classifying individual differences. After all, individuals differ in terms of their temperamental proclivities, cognitive abilities, underlying motives, central identities, political ideologies, self-defining autobiographical memories, and life stories (Roberts & Wood, 2006). Integrative approaches like the ones proposed by McAdams and Pals (2006) and Roberts and Wood (2006) distinguish domains of analysis and organize these various ways that personality scholars have conceptualized human individuality. McAdams and his colleagues (e.g., McAdams & Olson, 2010; McAdams & Pals, 2006) recently indentified three hierarchical levels of individuality: personality traits, characteristic adaptations to the world, and life stories. Traits are the relatively enduring, automatic patterns of thinking, feeling, and behavior

that make one person different from another that are elicited in trait-relevant situations (Roberts, 2009). Characteristic adaptations encompass constructs like goals, motives, and internal representations of others (as in attachment theory; see Mikulincer & Shaver, 2007). Life stories are the narratives that individuals construct about their own lives that serve as the core of their sense of identity. Roberts and Wood (2006) add abilities to these three domains, as individual differences in cognitive, physical, and social abilities are clearly important to individual functioning and relatively independent of the remaining three domains of individual differences. Researchers have accumulated more systematic knowledge about the development of personality traits than these other levels of individuality and therefore traits are the focus of this chapter. Nonetheless, constructs in all four domains are important elements of an integrative science of personality and we anticipate more will be learned about these aspects of individuality as additional longitudinal studies on these domains are initiated.

Traits are relatively enduring dispositions that reflect characteristic patterns of emotionality, self-regulation, and general orientations to the social and physical environment. Traits are basically what people think, feel, and do. Moreover, it is not only what people think, feel, and do, but what people *automatically* think, feel, and do. Although traits can be reflected on in consciousness and reported on via self-report inventories, they reflect highly habituated patterns that are nonconscious rather than deliberate.

Researchers have proposed different ways of categorizing personality traits and the Big Five (see John, Naumann, & Soto, 2008) have proven to be an especially influential

This research was supported by grants R01 AG21178 and R01 AG1846 from the National Institute of Aging.

approach (e.g., Roberts, Kuncel, Shiner, Caspi, & Goldberg, 2007). This popular taxonomy parses personality traits into the domains of extraversion (assertive, energetic, and sociable), agreeableness (cooperative, kind, and trusting), conscientiousness (hardworking, norm-abiding, and self-controlled), neuroticism (easily distressed, tense, and moody), and openness (curious, inventive, and open-minded). Much of the research described in this chapter investigates one or more of the Big Five domains.

A key component of the definition of personality traits is that they are "relatively enduring" dispositions. Consistency is thus considered to be the defining and essential feature of a psychological trait and therefore personality researchers have devoted considerable attention to studying personality stability and change. Research over the past few decades has examined multiple indices of stability and change and shown that personality traits are consistent over time, but also that traits change throughout adulthood (e.g., Lucas & Donnellan, 2011; Mroczek & Spiro, 2003; Roberts & DelVecchio, 2000; Roberts & Mroczek, 2008; Roberts, Walton, & Viechtbauer, 2006; Soto, John, Gosling, & Potter, 2011; Srivastava, Gosling, John, & Porter, 2003).

In short, the same body of developmental research that affirms the idea that there are relatively enduring psychological qualities also provides compelling evidence that personality traits change over time. The emerging view is that personality traits change in concert with enduring environmental or intrapsychic presses that give rise to particular patterns of thought, feeling, and behavior. This body of research has therefore motivated researchers to change their conceptualizations of the trait construct (Roberts, 2009). The goal of this chapter is to provide an overview of the field of personality trait development and to summarize the existing evidence for these different kinds of continuity and change. In addition to identifying processes that underlie stability and change, we describe the practical and theoretical implications of the developmental perspective on personality traits. We begin, however, by describing the relevant methodological considerations that arise when studying personality trait development.

METHODOLOGICAL ISSUES IN PERSONALITY TRAIT DEVELOPMENT

Longitudinal studies are the preferred research design for studying personality development. Using this approach, the same set of individuals is assessed repeatedly over a substantial length of time. This method allows researchers to track how an individual changes over time. It is impossible to achieve this goal using a cross-sectional design. Although two waves are the minimum number required for a longitudinal study, there is increasing recognition that two wave studies have limitations for addressing important questions about development (Roberts, Wood, & Caspi, 2008; Rogosa, Brandt, & Zimowski, 1982). Multiple waves of longitudinal data provide researchers with a more precise understanding of the pattern of personality changes and provide more reliable estimates of change (Roberts et al., 2008).

Beyond issues of study design, researchers have to consider how they will assess personality traits in any developmental study. There are generally three methods for measuring traits: self-reports, informant reports, and behavioral data. Self-reports are the most common technique used in studies of adult personality development (Roberts & Mroczek, 2008). The basic strategy is to have individuals complete the same personality measure at multiple time points. Self-report studies are commonly used because the data are relatively easy to collect and it is assumed that individuals have a unique and important perspective when it comes to reporting on their own inner thoughts and feelings (see Lucas & Baird, 2006). It is also the case that self-reports of personality have criterion-related validity. For example, self-reports of conscientiousness predict risky health behaviors (Bogg & Roberts, 2004) and even mortality (Hill et al., 2011; Kern & Friedman, 2008). Thus, although there are limitations associated with self-reports (as is true of any single approach to measuring a psychological construct), self-reports of personality traits have demonstrated their reliability and validity in countless studies.

A concern, however, with using self-reports in longitudinal studies of trait development is the possibility that the properties of the personality measures change over time. For example, individuals might become more or less willing to disclose certain kinds of information about themselves as they become more accustomed to participating in an ongoing study. Likewise, individuals might use scale response options differently across different waves of a longitudinal study. These kinds of issues can be evaluated by statistically testing for measurement invariance (see Schmitt & Kuljanin, 2008). Although formal tests of measurement invariance are not always conducted and reported in the literature, existing studies using these techniques do not find that psychometric properties change dramatically in longitudinal studies (e.g., Allemand, Zimprich, & Hertzog, 2007; Lucas & Donnellan, 2011). Thus, the kinds of personality changes observed in longitudinal studies are unlikely to be solely a consequence of methodological artifacts.

Although researchers investigating personality development often rely on self-reports of personality, researchers do not typically use self-reports of personality change to study personality development. At first blush, it would seem useful to directly ask individuals how much their personality attributes have changed over time as this would obviate the need for longitudinal studies. One concern with such a strategy is that individuals might not be good reporters of how much they have actually changed (e.g., Herbst, McCrae, Costa, Feaganes, & Siegler, 2000), and this concern may apply more strongly to older adults than younger adults (Robins, Noftle, Trzesniewski, & Roberts, 2005). Individuals have cognitive biases and limitations to self-insight that can compromise self-reports of change (Robins et al., 2005). For example, individuals might draw on stereotypes when reporting on personality change (such as the idea that the college years are a time of exceptional growth). In short, developmental researchers are more comfortable inferring the existence of personality change from evaluating differences in assessments taken at multiple time points. This is not to say that an individual's perceptions of personality change are not psychologically interesting and important, rather the point is that such an approach might not be the most optimal way to evaluate actual personality changes.

Informant report studies of personality development are also possible (e.g., Vazire, 2006; Watson & Humrichouse, 2006). This approach involves obtaining an "outsider" perspective from someone knowledgeable about the personality of the target individual at multiple time points. The informant could be a parent, a romantic partner, a work supervisor, or a friend. It is critical to obtain reports from the same informant at multiple time points to avoid confounding changes in personality with changes in informants. Different informants have different biases and they have different vantage points to observe the target individual. Informant report studies can therefore pose practical problems because close friends, romantic partners, and supervisors sometimes change over time. Informant ratings may also suffer from halo effects (Thorndike, 1920), or tendencies for the perception of one trait to affect the report of others, and other rating biases and these may change systematically with time. This complication might occur, for example, using personality ratings taken from a spouse right after the couple married and comparing those with ratings made later in the marital relationship (Watson & Humrichouse, 2006). It is possible that the positively

biased perceptions that newlyweds hold of their spouse subside, to some extent, as the marriage progresses.

The last approach to assessing personality involves laboratory tasks and behavioral observations. This approach is often used to study attributes of temperament in children (e.g., Durbin, 2010) and analogues of these tasks could be used to assess adult personality. However, this approach is used relatively infrequently in the adult personality development literature. In contrast, behavioral tests of cognitive ability (e.g., IQ test) are used frequently when studying the development of intellectual abilities of adults (e.g., Salthouse, Schroeder, & Ferrer, 2004). Data about adult personality trait development using behavioral tasks are exceedingly scarce and this represents an important direction for future study. The first steps toward this aim though are being taken, as researchers have begun to pursue the behavioral signatures of different personality traits (e.g., Holtzman, Vazire, & Mehl, 2010; Jackson et al., 2010). Now that we have described basic methodological issues, we turn to a discussion of the different types of continuity and change described in the literature.

Definitions of Personality Trait Continuity and Change

Questions about whether personality traits change over time are deceptively simple to pose. Indeed, one reason for the confusion over personality continuity and change is that researchers fail to clarify what they mean when they pose such questions. Part of the difficulty arises from the multiple ways to track continuity and change, such as rank-order consistency, mean-level change, structural consistency, and individual differences in change. A complete understanding of personality continuity and change can only come from a thorough examination of multiple indices of continuity and change as they are often provide complementary information. Different ways of conceptualizing and assessing personality change can provide different perspectives on personality development (Caspi & Bem, 1990; De Fruyt et al., 2006; Donnellan & Robins, 2009; Roberts et al., 2008; Robins, Fraley, Roberts, & Trzesniewski, 2001). Accordingly, it is essential that questions about personality development are framed and answered in specific ways.

In this chapter, we review rank-order (or differential) consistency, mean-level change, and individual differences in change because these ways of framing questions about personality development reflect the most direct indicators of continuity and change. These are also the most commonly investigated kinds of developmental questions in the field. Other types include ipsative continuity and measurement continuity and those are described in detail in Donnellan and Robins (2009) or Roberts et al. (2008).

Rank-order consistency and mean-level change answer questions about personality development at the level of the sample or population. Rank-order consistency refers to the maintenance of rank on a trait relative to others in the sample or population. For example, an investigation about the rank-order consistency of shyness can answer the question as to whether extremely shy adolescents develop into extremely shy adults. Mean-level change refers to absolute increases or decreases (gains or losses) in specific personality traits over a prespecified period of time and age for a population of individuals. In other words, a question as to whether adolescents have more or less self-control than middle-aged adults falls under the domain of mean-level change as does the question of whether there are average increases in self-control during the transition from adolescence to adulthood. In contrast to a focus on stability and change at the aggregate level, investigations into individual differences in change focus on patterns of personality development at the level of the person. Questions about individual differences in change ask how well individuals either conform or deviate from the overall population patterns of mean-level change. That is, some people change much more or less than the average patterns of increase or decrease.

Rank-Order Consistency/Change

Researchers have been finding the same two findings since the earliest review of rank-order consistency (i.e., Crook, 1941): Personality traits demonstrate modest to high rank-order consistency (e.g., retest correlations or stability coefficients between .4 and .6) over reasonably long periods of time (e.g., 4 to 10 years) and the longer one tracks rank-order consistency, the lower it gets (e.g., Fraley & Roberts, 2005), with the evidence zeroing in on a long-term level of about .2 over 40 years. Five meta-analyses on the topic have come to similar conclusions (Ardelt, 2000; Bazana & Stelmack, 2004; Ferguson, 2010; Roberts & DelVecchio, 2000; Schuerger, Zarrella, & Hotz, 1989).

The findings of these meta-analyses on the rank-order consistency of personality traits provide a clear picture. Across hundreds of studies, test-retest correlations over time for personality are at least moderate in magnitude, even from childhood to early adulthood. Furthermore, rank-order consistency across appreciable intervals increases as people age and then reaches a plateau around .70 between ages 50 and 70 (or even higher if additional controls for measurement unreliability are applied to the correlations; Ferguson, 2010). Personality traits demonstrate a clear pattern of increasing continuity across the life course.

In terms of the overall levels of test-retest consistency, personality psychologists can find solace in the fact that the magnitude of rank-order consistency, although not high enough to argue for absolute stability, is still remarkably high. The only psychological constructs that seem to generate larger stability coefficients are measures of cognitive ability (Conley, 1984; Schuerger, Tait, & Tavernelli, 1982). Vocational interests and self-esteem are just about equal to personality traits in their consistency (Low, Yoon, Roberts, & Rounds, 2005; Trzesniewski, Donnellan, & Robins, 2003). All in all, a number of psychological qualities show an impressive level of consistency across the life span. Moreover, the level of continuity in childhood and adolescence is much higher than originally expected especially after age three. Although childhood character is by no means fate, there are striking continuities that point to the importance of childhood temperament and the effects of cumulative continuity from childhood through adulthood (Moffitt et al., 2011; Nave, Sherman, Funder, Hampson, & Goldberg, 2010).

One of the most conspicuous aspects of the increase in rank-order consistency is the fact that it is linear for much of the life course. Given developmental depictions of adolescence and young adulthood, one might expect to see marked decreases in rank-order consistency in these age periods, especially if environmental changes result in a drastic reconstruction of one's personality. For example, adolescence is often characterized as a time of psychological, if not social tumult (Arnett, 1999). If dynamic and difficult life experiences translate one-to-one into personality trait change, then we would expect a marked decrease in continuity during these periods of the life course. This implies that the relationship between life experiences and personality trait development is neither simple nor direct. Despite psychological and demographic shifts, personality consistency marches in a linear fashion toward a peak in adulthood in seeming concert with depictions of increased agency from childhood to adulthood (Scarr & McCartney, 1983). This pattern is referred to as the cumulative continuity principle of personality development—traits become more consistent with age (Caspi, Roberts, & Shiner, 2005).

A recent and relatively unexplored issue is whether stability coefficients begin to decline in old age. A curvilinear pattern for stability coefficients was found for global self-esteem (Trzesniewski et al., 2003), but evidence of this pattern for personality traits has been inconsistent. One reason is that few longitudinal studies have followed large numbers of older participants to fully evaluate this possibility (Lucas & Donnellan, 2011). The Lucas and Donnellan report also provides a concrete example of how researchers evaluate rank-order consistency in practice. More than 14,000 participants in the German Socio-Economic Panel Study completed a measure of the Big Five (i.e., extraversion, agreeableness, conscientiousness, emotional stability, and openness to experience) attributes twice across a four-year interval. Lucas and Donnellan estimated the association between the two measures of each Big Five trait across the four-year interval for individuals of different ages (e.g., the correlation between extraversion scores in 2005 and extraversion scores in 2009 for those between the ages of 20 to 24 in 2005). The stability coefficients were typically above .50 for all age groups and all Big Five domains. However, Lucas and Donnellan found that four-year stability coefficients for measures of several of the Big Five domains declined after around age 70 even correcting for measurement unreliability. Additional research is needed to fully evaluate whether the inverted U-shape curve for personality stability is robust; however, this inverted U pattern is plausible given that biological and social changes at the end of the life span may generate personality changes that are unique to individuals.

Mean-Level Changes in Personality Traits

Mean-level changes in personality traits can be investigated using longitudinal designs and age differences in mean-levels of personality can be studied using cross-sectional designs. Both kinds of studies attempt to estimate the typical trait level at different points in the life span. Roberts, Caspi, and Moffitt (2001) provide a paradigmatic example of a longitudinal investigation of mean-level change. More than 900 participants in an ongoing longitudinal study of a birth cohort in New Zealand completed a personality inventory when they were 18 (late adolescence) and again when they were 26 (young adulthood). Roberts et al. found that average levels of negative emotionality (akin to neuroticism in the Big Five scheme) decreased during this interval, which covered the transition to adulthood. This kind of study therefore suggests that individuals develop more functional personalities as they mature.

Indeed, mean-level investigations complement the studies showing an increase in continuity from childhood to adulthood by generally finding that personality traits show reliable mean-level changes well into adulthood. Specifically, cross-sectional research has shown that middle-aged individuals tend to score higher than young adults on agreeableness and conscientiousness and lower on extraversion, neuroticism, and openness (Lucas & Donnellan, 2009; Soto et al., 2011; Srivastava et al., 2003). Changes in mean-levels of personality traits were summarized in a meta-analysis of 92 longitudinal studies covering the life course from age 10 to 101 (Roberts et al., 2006). Like the cross-sectional studies, significant mean-level change in all trait domains was found at some point in the life course and statistically significant change in 75% of personality traits in middle (age 40 to 60) and old age (age 60-plus). Clearly, personality traits continue to develop in adulthood. The fact that the mean-level findings continue to be replicated across several decades (e.g., Soto et al., 2011) also provides strong evidence against the argument that age differences in personality traits are due to cohort effects (cultural/historical factors unique to individuals born during a particular year). Different longitudinal studies, mostly of Western cultures, have found generally similar results.

Several important conclusions about personality development can be drawn from the Roberts et al. (2006) meta-analysis. First, most mean-level personality trait change occurs between the ages of 20 and 40. This contradicts the widely held perspective that the most interesting years for studying personality development are either early or late in life. In contrast, young adulthood appears to be the most important period for mean-level personality trait change. The mechanisms responsible for personality trait change in young adulthood have received little empirical or theoretical attention.

Second, personality traits continue to change, even in old age. This finding contradicts that often quoted passage from William James that personality is set like plaster by age 30. One of the precepts of a life span orientation is that humans are open systems (e.g., Baltes & Nesselroade, 1973). That is, people retain the capacity to change at all ages. The changes in personality traits in middle and old age are by no means dramatic, but nonetheless they show that the life span orientation applies to personality traits and that personality is not set like plaster at any point in the life course.

Third, time has a positive effect on personality trait change. Studies that follow people for a longer period of time show larger mean-level changes (Roberts et al., 2006). The positive association between time and mean-level change is important for theoretical models of human nature. A common assumption is that personality traits act like metabolic set points. People may stray briefly from their biological propensity, but they will then tend to drift back to their genetically driven set point (see Kandler et al., 2010, for a review). Under these types of models, one would expect to find a negative or null association between time and mean-level change because any change will represent short-term fluctuations that disappear as people return to their biologically driven set point. However, time is positively associated with personality trait change, which indicates that a strong set-point model does not apply to personality trait development. That is, when people change they tend to retain the changes in personality traits for the remainder of their lives.

Fourth, the direction of change is generally in the positive direction. People become more confident, warm, responsible, and calm with age, or what some have described as socially mature (Roberts & Wood, 2006). Social maturity is equated with the capacity to become a productive and involved contributor to society. Accordingly, most people do become more socially mature with age, and those who develop the cardinal traits of psychological maturity earliest are more effective in their relationships and work, and lead healthier and longer lives (Roberts et al., 2007). Mean-level trends are in the direction of personality changes that seemingly facilitate the fulfillment of the roles played by mature members of the social group. This notion has even been formalized into the maturity principle of personality development (Caspi et al., 2005; Roberts et al., 2001).

All in all, existing research on mean-level personality trait change has mapped out the "normative" trends and generated important insights about the times in the life span that are the most active periods for personality development. Personality traits change more in young adulthood than any other period of the life course but they also continue to change in old age. Moreover, most of the normative change is positive, at least until the very end of the life span. These findings motivate a new generation of questions concerning why personality traits change more in young adulthood than other periods of the life course, and what the implications of the mostly positive trend in personality trait change might be. Of course, one of the realities of any generalization is that it does not apply to all people. Much of this research needs to be replicated in non-Western cultures before firm conclusions are drawn. More importantly, some people even within Western cultures fail to conform to the general trends by either not changing at all, being more accelerated in their change patterns with time, or changing in ways that contradict normative trends. These deviations are captured with the concept of individual differences in personality trait change.

Individual Differences in Personality Trait Change in Adulthood

The concept of individual differences in change, a major tenet of lifespan developmental theory (Baltes & Nesselroade, 1973), refers to the observation that individuals may show different patterns of increases or decreases in absolute levels of a personality trait over time. These person-specific patterns may deviate from the population mean-level pattern of change. This perspective holds that personality change (and stability) is yet another individual differences variable—people have different patterns of personality development. More broadly, this perspective asserts that a complete understanding of personality development is only possible if individual differences in personality trait change are examined alongside more traditional indices like retest stability and mean-level change. The irony is that many individual difference researchers fail to appreciate the existence of individual differences in change.

The key empirical hurdle that needs to be addressed is whether individual differences in change are real or simply represent error in measurement (Watson, 2004). This has drawn many personality development researchers toward techniques to gauge the amount and pattern of change over time at the level of the individual, such as the Reliable Change Index (RCI; Roberts et al., 2001) or the variance in slopes from growth models (Vaidya, Gray, Haig, Mroczek, & Watson, 2008). These methods range from fairly simple to complex and numerous studies using these methods have established that personality traits show variability across individuals in both the direction and rate of change.

The use of the RCI can be illustrated by returning to the Roberts et al. (2001) longitudinal study of New Zealanders. Recall that each participant completed the same personality measure at age 18 and 26. Roberts et al. therefore computed a difference score for all sample members to estimate how much she or he absolutely changed on each personality attribute during the transition to adulthood. Consider, for example, an individual who scored 100 on negative emotionality (akin to neuroticism) at age 18 and scored 80 at age 26. This individual would have declined 20 points in absolute terms. The RCI is a statistical tool for judging whether the amount of absolute change exhibited by an individual exceeded what would be expected due to measurement error. Using this approach, Roberts et al. found that 21% of the sample "reliably" declined in negative emotionality whereas only 7% "reliably" increased, thereby leaving 72% of the sample as showing no evidence of "reliable" change. This perspective complements the mean-level finding of an average decline in negative emotionality from age 18 to 26.

The RCI has proven useful for showing that there are individual differences in personality change. However, the RCI is limited in at least two respects (see Roberts et al., 2008). The first limitation is that the RCI sets a high standard for judging whether an individual actually increased or decreased in an attribute. Individuals often have to show absolute increases or decreases amounting to more than two standard deviations of a measure in the metric of the original scale to surmount the RCI thresholds. Second, the RCI views change from the perspective of a two-wave study and this design provides an imprecise estimate of change and is a generally impoverished method for studying personality development. More sophisticated approaches for identifying individual differences in change therefore capitalize on longitudinal studies with three or more waves using growth curve methods (Roberts & Mroczek, 2008).

An example of how growth modeling is used to identify individual differences in change is found in Vaidya et al. (2008). These authors measured the Big Five domains (among other constructs) at three time points during the transition to adulthood (participants were 24 years of age at the last assessment). In mean-level terms, there was a substantial increase in the domain of conscientiousness during the transition to adulthood (approximately .75 of a standard deviation from the first wave to the last wave). Using growth curve methods, Vaidya et al. (2008) found that there were individual differences in the linear rate of change in conscientiousness. Some individuals increase more than others in the domain of conscientiousness and some even declined.

Once the existence of reliable individual differences in personality trait change has been established, the compelling question becomes why these changes occur. A number of studies have shown that life experiences are associated with changes in personality traits (reviewed in Roberts et al., 2008). For example, people who experience more successful and satisfying careers in young adulthood increase disproportionately on measures of emotional stability and conscientiousness (Roberts, Caspi, & Moffitt, 2003). Similarly, initiating and staying in a committed relationship in young adulthood is associated with increases in conscientiousness and decreases in neuroticism (Lehnart, Neyer, & Eccles, 2010; Robins, Caspi, & Moffitt, 2002). Furthermore, men who get remarried in middle age show decreases in neuroticism (Mroczek & Spiro, 2003).

Not all life experiences are for the better. Personality maturity is not achieved by all individuals, perhaps because individuals do not randomly assort themselves into situations. People who conduct problematic, counterproductive activities at work, such as theft, aggression, and malingering are prone to decrease on measures of conscientiousness and emotional stability (Roberts et al., 2006). Similarly, people who continue to abuse drugs and alcohol tend to decrease in conscientiousness and neuroticism in young adulthood (see Littlefield, Sher, & Wood, 2010). Interestingly, seeing a psychotherapist is associated with increases in neuroticism in college students regardless of whether the experience is a good one (Luedtke et al., 2011).

The corresponsive principle of personality development (Caspi et al., 2005; Roberts et al., 2003) offers a compelling way to explain the observed connections between many life events and personality trait development. The basic idea is that life events and circumstances often accentuate and reinforce the personality attributes that are associated with initial selection into situations that lead to particular life events. For example, low conscientiousness is generally associated with problematic health behaviors including heavy drinking (Bogg & Roberts, 2004). Thus, low conscientiousness may increase the likelihood that an individual will abuse drugs and alcohol, behaviors, which in turn, may further diminish conscientiousness (Littlefield et al., 2010). As another example, consider that neuroticism is a robust correlate of relationship dissatisfaction and instability (e.g., Karney & Bradbury, 1995; Malouff, Thorsteinsson, Schutte, Bhullar, & Rooke, 2010) and thus low neuroticism may increase the likelihood that individuals will be involved in satisfying and stable relationships. Involvement in such high-quality relationships may further reduce neuroticism (Robins et al., 2002). Both of these cases illustrate the fact that both social selection and social influence processes are relevant for understanding personality development.

The corresponsive principle has broad implications for understanding individual development by generating predictions about the likely consequences of many person-environment transactions. The existing evidence suggests that non-normative life paths might be consequential as they might result in personality changes that deviate from the maturity principle. Individuals who chronically abuse drugs and alcohol, habitually engage in counterproductive work behaviors, and find themselves in dissatisfying romantic partnerships may not increase in functional maturity during adulthood. Such individuals may actually become less conscientious and agreeable and more emotionally unstable. If true, this means that the coupling of personality attributes and life circumstances may have profound consequences for understanding the dynamics of human development across the life span. Corresponsive patterns may also explain why intervention efforts aimed at the earlier portions of the life span may prove to be particularly effective.

Processes Promoting Personality Stability and Change

An important theme of contemporary studies of personality development is that stability and change are produced by the dynamic interplay between individuals and social environments. In other words, stability and change are the result of person-environment transactions. An important insight offered by earlier reviews of the literature is that different kinds of person-environment transactions serve as the mechanisms that produce personality stability as opposed to personality change (Caspi & Roberts, 2001; Roberts, 2006; Roberts et al., 2008; Roberts & Pomerantz, 2004).

Several categories of processes underlie the corresponsive principle of personality development and seem to be particularly relevant for understanding personality consistency (e.g., Buss, 1987; Caspi & Roberts, 2001; Roberts & Pomerantz, 2004; Scarr & McCartney, 1983). Specifically, as part of the ASTMA model, Roberts (2006) identified attraction, selection, manipulation and attrition as processes most relevant to maintaining individual differences in personality traits over time. Attraction effects reflect the fact that people sort themselves into life paths in a nonrandom fashion. Individuals gain agency and the ability to select, shape, and otherwise create their own environments during the transition from childhood to adulthood. Individuals with particular kinds of personal characteristics select certain kinds of friends and romantic partners. Different individuals choose different career paths that match, to some extent, their personal characteristics. For example, people who score higher on measures of creativity are more likely to enter into and excel at artistic careers (Helson, Roberts, & Agronick, 1995). Of course, the sorting process is seldom exclusively under the control of individuals. Organizations and societal institutions attempt to select people who are perceived to possess the qualities necessary to succeed in specific occupations. Many people lament the general lack of "bedside manner" that doctors possess. Their lack of interpersonal skills is likely a reflection of the fact that doctors are selected predominantly for technical and academic skills, which may be somewhat negatively correlated with people skills.

Two additional mechanisms, reactive and evocative transactions, fall into the attraction and selection categories respectively. Reactive transactions occur as different people construe the same objective social environment differently because of their personalities. Life events such as starting a new job or starting a relationship with potential romantic partners are construed differently by those high versus low in neuroticism. Individuals often interpret ambiguous social situations differently and these interpretations and information processing differences can set in motion self-fulfilling prophecies. For instance, an individual low in agreeableness may interpret a neutral social cue as an indicator of disrespect and respond with hostility. This response will set in motion a chain of events that will likely reinforce the initial disposition toward hostility and alienation. Accordingly, reactive person-environment transactions tend to reinforce dispositions and behavioral tendencies.

Evocative person-environment transactions occur when individuals elicit characteristic responses from the social environment because of their underlying dispositions. Shy children elicit different levels of attention from classroom teachers when compared to their more outgoing peers. Individuals with hostile and aggressive personalities evoke aggressive responses from others including even unacquainted partners in a laboratory-based game designed to study aggressive responses in a controlled setting (Anderson, Buckley, & Carnagey, 2008). Many of the responses individuals elicit from others tend to promote personality consistency because of the positive correspondence between the personality attribute and the features of the social situation. Thus, evocative person-environment transactions may also reinforce personality attributes.

Two additional categories of mechanisms that are thought to contribute to consistency are manipulation and attrition. Manipulation (Buss, 1987) reflects attempts to shape environments so that they fit better with one's personality. People can employ passive strategies, such as trying to outlast policy changes or subtly undermine change agents, or employ active strategies where they pursue different positions in an organization or community that better suits their personality. For example, disagreeable people may simply avoid their neighbors, thus contributing to a decline of communitarian climate in a neighborhood. In contrast, a friendlier person may invite neighbors over for dinner or host barbecues for the entire neighborhood, thus fostering a different culture. Finally, people can leave environments that do not fit their personality, thus avoiding any environmental pressures for change.

All in all, four of the five kinds of mechanisms high-lighted by the ASTMA contribute to personality continuity rather than change via corresponsive processes. Attraction, selection, manipulation, and attrition seem to promote personality consistency because these processes generate a positive match between the characteristics of the individual and the features of her or his social environment. In terms of strategies, it appears the opportunities for maintaining consistency far outweigh those for change.

The "Transformation" category of the ASTMA model is the only one dedicated to identifying change mechanisms. Perhaps the most important mechanism accounting for personality change stems from the cornerstone of behaviorism and learning approaches to personality: Individuals respond to situational contingencies and likewise individuals can learn from others who are rewarded and punished for particular behaviors. The law of effect (e.g., Thorndike, 1933) holds that behaviors that produce satisfying, pleasant, or positive consequences will tend to be repeated whereas behaviors that generate distressing, annoying, or negative consequences will be less likely to be repeated. New situations with new reward structures can change behavior, especially when previous ways of thinking, feeling, and behaving are actively discouraged and new ways of behaving are made salient (Caspi & Moffitt, 1993). These tenets of personality development are why some major life transitions such as entering a marriage, becoming a parent, entering the military, or assuming an important job may change personality.

Additional processes coupled with a motivation to change may also explain personality changes. First, deliberate self-reflection may promote change especially when accompanied by therapeutic interventions designed to change thoughts, feelings, and behaviors (such as cognitive behavioral therapy). Smith, Glass, and Miller (1980) conducted a classic meta-analysis on the efficacy of psychotherapy and documented that therapy changed personality traits in addition to many other outcomes. In particular, cognitive-behavioral therapy changed measures of personality traits more than a standard deviation. Thus, personality change seems to be possible if individuals are motivated and provided with the necessary tools. We should note, however, that current evidence for the effectiveness of therapy is tempered by the recognition that the time frame for psychotherapy treatment studies is often short term. For example, Gi, Egger, Kaarsemaker, and Kreutzkamp (2010) evaluated changes in the Big Five in a treatment sample. Although individuals receiving treatment for anxiety disorder appeared to increase in extraversion and decrease in neuroticism, the time frame of the

study was only three to six months. Long-term follow-up studies are badly needed to establish whether changes are maintained over substantial intervals of time.

Second, changes in expectancies and perceptions of important others that occur as individuals assume new identities and social roles may create personality changes. One concern, however, is the seemingly pervasive existence of information processing mechanisms that tend to confirm preexisting views of the self (Swann, 1997). Once again, a strong motivation to change is a seemingly important ingredient for certain mechanisms of personality change. An important task for intervention efforts is to find ways to motivate individuals to want to change and to help sustain their motivation through challenges. For example, motivational interviewing techniques could be used to enhance people's interest in changing themselves (Miller & Rose, 2009). Similarly, behavioral activation approaches, which not only rely on motivational interviewing approaches, but also positive reinforcement of behaviors that directly reflect the goal to change could be employed (Lejuez, Hopko, & Hopko, 2001).

Theoretical Implications

Research and theorizing concerning personality development is rapidly expanding as this is one of the more vibrant strands of personality research. Developmental research on traits also has some clear theoretical implications for personality psychology in general. One of the most significant implications of the fact that personality traits show both stability and change across the life span is the need to revise prominent models of personality and personality traits. For a variety of reasons, most theoretical perspectives on the nature of personality traits fall into one of two extreme camps (Roberts, 2009). On one side is the view that personality traits are intrinsically biologically-based entities that are largely unchanging across time. This essentialist perspective is manifest explicitly in some theoretical systems (e.g., McCrae & Costa, 2008) and manifest implicitly in most research utilizing personality traits. Consider that most research invoking personality assumes that traits cause outcomes and therefore are used solely as predictors. Based on these assumptions, personality traits need not be assessed more than once because they do not change. Alternatively, some theoreticians minimize the significance and consistency of personality traits, typically by emphasizing the context-dependency and state-like nature of behavior (Mischel, 2009). Those sympathetic to this perspective often take the fact that behaviors change across time or situation as support for a completely contextual model of personality.

The reality of life course dynamics is uncomfortably different from either of these essentialist or contextualist viewpoints. Personality traits are, in fact, quite consistent over time, but not absolutely consistent. Accordingly, personality traits are best considered to be *relatively* enduring psychological constructs and that they can and often do change with time. What emerges from the existing developmental data is a unique perspective that combines opposing views on the nature of traits (Roberts, 2009). Personality traits are consistent, and consistent enough to be considered causal forces. Importantly, personality traits also change and change enough to consider personality change itself a phenomenon of interest and key feature of human functioning.

The observation that traits change and that trait changes may even occur in middle and old age for some individuals invites some challenging questions. Why would human beings remain open systems in which modifications are capable of being made late in life? Many developmental models assume that childhood is the critical period of personality development and that little of interest happens thereafter. However, the majority of personality trait change appears to occur in adulthood, which begs the question of why?

One of the unique aspects of the study of individual differences in change is that personality traits are considered dependent variables rather than solely independent variables, as they are typically viewed. For example, in some studies, such as Roberts (1997), personality traits are seen as the consequence of work experiences. One reason to consider personality traits as dependent variables is that personality trait change may be quite consequential for people. Mroczek and Spiro (2007) demonstrated that long-term increases in neuroticism were predictive of mortality in an 18-year survival analysis. Those who started high on neuroticism (above the sample median) and increased over 10 years had higher mortality, controlling for age, depression, and physical health.

Conceptualizing traits as outcomes necessitates a fundamental shift in the defining theoretical models of personality and personality development. Future theoretical systems will, by necessity, have to handle the empirical facts that personality traits are important and consistent, yet also dynamic. To date, too many researchers have fallen into the easy paths of seeing traits as static causes or as immaterial because of their variability. Moving beyond these two immature perspectives will necessitate more than compromise.

Practical and Applied Considerations—Personality Change and Social Policy

Research in personality development attracts the attention of those outside of academic psychology for the simple reason that there is enormous interest in improving society by changing the behaviors of individuals. The fact that personality trait changes may bring about positive outcomes, such as greater success in work and better health and longevity, leads naturally to questions about deliberate efforts to change personality.

A smattering of studies has now reported on the changeability of personality traits through direct intervention across a number of domains. For example, after a 20-week cognitive behavior therapy intervention aimed to treat depression, patients changed on a number of personality traits, most notably in extraversion and neuroticism (Clark, Vittengl, Kraft, & Jarrett, 2003). Evidence also exists that personality traits change in response to a combination of therapy and medication (Santor, Bagby, & Joffe, 1997). For example, DeFruyt, Van Leeuwen, Bagby, Rolland, and Rouillon (2006) found that individuals treated with a combination of either tianeptine or fluoxetine (the active drug in Prozac) and therapy showed significant positive increase in all Big Five personality traits. Similarly, a recent study also found that both cognitive therapy and medication (SSRIs) were associated with changes in neuroticism and extraversion compared to a control group (Tang et al., 2009). As we noted, a concern with these studies is the limited time frame used to evaluate personality change. The DeFruyt et al. (2006) study was based on a six-month follow-up whereas Tang et al. (2009) used an eight-week follow-up. Another point that these studies highlight is the need for more thorough theorizing about the mechanisms that promote personality change. The majority of mechanisms identified to date emerged out of passive longitudinal studies in which people were not being pressed to change. One relevant question is whether the changes imparted by therapy, drugs, or training work through the same mechanisms identified above. To date, few efforts have been made to examine this issue.

In addition to clinical interventions, a number of other types of intervention studies demonstrate that personality traits are amenable to change. Training programs where the participant learns some type of skill appear to be especially effective in changing personality traits. For example, a recent intervention trained medical students to become more mindful. The mindfulness intervention resulted in personality trait changes in the traits of conscientiousness, agreeableness, empathy, and emotional stability that were evident across the 15-month follow-up period (Krasner et al., 2009). Similarly, a social skills training program for recovering substance abusers led to increases in agreeableness, conscientiousness, and emotional stability sustained over a 15-month span (Piedmont, 2001). Moreover, a cognitive training intervention for older adults was also associated with changes in a personality trait. Across 16 weeks elder adults learned inductive reasoning skills and completed 10 hours a week of crossword and Sudoku puzzles. Compared to a control condition, the intervention increased participants' levels of openness to experience (Jackson et al., in press).

Based on these studies it is clear that personality traits can be changed through a variety of interventions over a relatively short period of time. These findings raise several issues. First, as none of these studies was embedded in an ongoing longitudinal study, it is unclear whether the changes will persist over long periods of time. It is quite possible that people change for the better in the short run only to regress back to where they were at earlier times in the absence of some active intervention. If, however, positive changes in personality traits are sustained over time, it generates some interesting issues. For example, most interventions focus on specific proximal thoughts, feelings, attitudes, and behaviors that are linked to outcomes deemed important by societies. Studies intervening to increase the efficacy for specific outcomes, such as achievement and health behaviors are legion. Unfortunately, specific attitudes and expectancies may not generalize to different context or to be negatively related to separate domains. For example, in the education domain, efficacy in a topic such as mathematics is often negatively correlated with efficacy in language arts (Trautwein, Lüdtke, Roberts, Schnyder, & Niggli, 2009). In contrast, conscientiousness is positively related to effort and achievement across domains. Therefore, intervening to increase conscientiousness might prove much more efficient and effective than intervening to change domain-specific attitudes. Enhancing conscientiousness may also result in positive effects across domains and not adversely affect other important outcomes.

The fact that personality traits can be changed through concerted effort opens up interesting and provocative policy implications. Instead of hewing to the prevailing ethos that change efforts should be focused on narrow constructs, policy makers may want to contemplate the potential benefits of focusing on a broad domain such as personality traits. The initial research not only points to the potential for this approach, but also the fact that changing something like a personality trait may leverage positive outcomes across numerous domains. Thus, relatively small changes in a trait like conscientiousness may not have huge effects on any one particular domain, but it may result in a cumulative positive effect on people's lives because it ranges in effect from the simple, such as health behaviors and academic achievement, to the structural, such as stable marriages.

Summary

The major point stressed in this chapter is that personality traits are relatively enduring psychological constructs that are both stable and changeable at the same time. In the first portion of this chapter, we described basic methodological issues and then defined different types of stability and change and reviewed the existing research evidence on these topics. With respect to the rank-order stability, the existing evidence indicates that personality consistency increases with age. In terms of mean-level changes, it appears that average levels of traits associated with performance of adult roles like conscientiousness and agreeableness increase over the life span. In general, levels of extraversion, neuroticism, and openness decline from adolescence to old age. In contrast to the information about sample or population level trends in personality development, researchers have a relatively impoverished understanding of individual differences in change. Nonetheless, there is accumulating evidence that different individuals follow different trajectories of personality development, in part, because of different life events and circumstances.

In addition to the point that personality traits show both stability and change across the life span, we stressed the proposition that stability and change are the outcome of a dynamic process involving individuals and their social contexts. We described mechanisms that may account for personality stability and a different set of mechanisms that may account for personality change. Many life events and social settings serve to accentuate and deepen the personality attributes that were seemingly correlated with selection into those social situations in the first place. Nonetheless, change is possible especially when social environments are changed and individuals are given the tools and motivation needed to change their thoughts, feelings, and behaviors.

Last, we described the theoretical and practical implications of personality development research in light of the importance of personality traits for a number of consequential life outcomes (e.g., Ozer & Benet-Martínez, 2006; Roberts et al., 2007). In particular, we briefly reviewed provocative evidence that personality traits can be changed by receiving medication, psychological therapy, and cognitive interventions. With these findings in mind, we need to move on the next steps on personality research. One possible future direction of personality psychology is to explore the pragmatic questions raised by the existence of personality trait change. For example, how can personality trait change be used to promote better health and economic outcomes; are personality traits appropriate candidates as an epidemiological risk factor that predicts the development of physical diseases (Roberts, 2009), and how we should develop our personality traits to live as a sound members of human society (Heckman, 2007).

REFERENCES

Allemand, M., Zimprich, D., & Hertzog, C. (2007). Cross sectional age differences and longitudinal age changes of personality in middle adulthood and old age. *Journal of Personality, 75*, 323–358.

Allport, G. W. (1961). *Pattern and growth in personality*. New York, NY: Holt, Rinehart, and Winston.

Anderson, C. A., Buckley, K. E., & Carnagey, N. L. (2008). Creating your own hostile environment: A laboratory examination of trait aggressiveness and the violence escalation cycle. *Personality and Social Psychology Bulletin, 34*, 462–473.

Ardelt, M. (2000). Still stable after all these years? Personality stability theory revisited. *Social Psychology Quarterly, 63*, 392–405.

Arnett, J. J. (1999). Adolescent storm and stress, reconsidered. *American Psychologist, 54*, 317–326.

Baltes, P. B., & Nesselroade, J. R. (1973). The developmental analysis of individual differences on multiple measures. In J. R. Nesselroade & H. W. Reese (Eds.), *Life-span developmental psychology: Methodological issues* (pp. 219–251). New York, NY: Academic Press.

Bazana, P. G., & Stelmack, R. M. (2004). Stability of personality across the life span: A meta-analysis. In R. M. Stelmack (Ed.), *On the Psychobiology of Personality* (pp. 113–144). Oxford: UK: Elsevier.

Bogg, T., & Roberts, B. W. (2004). Conscientiousness and health-related behaviors: A meta-analysis of the leading behavioral contributors to mortality. *Psychological Bulletin, 130*, 887–919.

Buss, D. M. (1987). Selection, evocation, and manipulation. *Journal of Personality and Social Psychology, 53*, 1214–1221.

Caspi, A., & Bem, D. J. (1990). Personality continuity and change across the life course. In L. Pervin (Ed.), *Handbook of personality: Theory and research* (pp. 549–575). New York, NY: Guilford Press.

Caspi, A., & Moffitt, T. E. (1993). When do individual differences matter? A paradoxical theory of personality coherence. *Psychological Inquiry, 4*, 247–271.

Caspi, A., & Roberts, B. W. (2001). Personality development across the life course: The argument for change and continuity. *Psychological Inquiry, 12*, 49–66.

Caspi, A., Roberts, B. W., & Shiner, R. L. (2005). Personality development: Stability and change. *Annual Review of Psychology, 56*, 453–484.

Clark, L. A., Vittengl, J., Kraft, D., & Jarrett, R. J. (2003). Separate personality traits from states to predict depression. *Journal of Personality Disorders, 17*, 152–172.

Conley, J. J. (1984). Longitudinal consistency of adult personality: Self-reported psychological characteristics across 45 years. *Journal of Personality and Social Psychology, 47*, 1325–1333.

Crook, M. N. (1941). Retest correlations in neuroticism. *Journal of General Psychology, 24*, 173–182.

De Fruyt, F., Bartels, M., Van Leeuwen, K. G., De Clerq, B., Decuyper, M., & Mervielde, I. (2006). Five types of personality continuity in childhood and adolescence. *Journal of Personality and Social Psychology, 91*, 538–552.

DeFruyt, F., Van Leeuwen, K., Bagby, R. M., Rolland, J. P., & Rouillon, F. (2006). Assessing and interpreting personality change and continuity in patients treated for major depression. *Psychological Assessment, 18*, 71–80.

Donnellan, M. B., & Robins, R. W. (2009). The development of personality across the life span. In P. J. Corr & G. Matthews (Eds.), *Cambridge handbook of personality* (pp. 191–204). New York, NY: Cambridge University Press.

Durbin, C. E. (2010). Modeling temperamental risk for depression using developmentally sensitive laboratory paradigms. *Child Development Perspectives, 4*, 168–173.

Ferguson, C. J. (2010). A meta-analysis of normal and disordered personality across the life span. *Journal of Personality and Social Psychology, 98*, 659–667.

Fraley, C., & Roberts, B. W. (2005). Patterns of continuity: A dynamic model for conceptualizing the stability of individual differences in psychological constructs across the life course. *Psychological Review, 112*, 60–74.

Gi, S. T. P., Egger, J., Kaarsemaker, M., & Kreutzkamp, R. (2010). Does symptom reduction after cognitive behavioural therapy of anxiety disorderd patients predict personality change? *Personality and Mental Health, 4*, 237–245.

Heckman, J. J. (2007). The economics, technology, and neuroscience of human capability formation. *Proceedings of the National Academy of Sciences, 104*, 13250–13255.

Helson, R., Roberts, B. W., & Agronick, G. (1995). Enduringness and change in creative personality and the prediction of occupational creativity. *Journal of Personality and Social Psychology, 69*, 1173–1183.

Herbst, J. H., McCrae, R. R., Costa, P. T. Jr., Feaganes, J. R., & Siegler, I. C. (2000). Self-perceptions of stability and change in personality at midlife: The UNC alumni heart study. *Assessment, 7*, 379–388.

Hill, P. L., Turiano, N. A., Hurd, M. D., Mroczek, D. K., & Roberts, B. W. (2011). Conscientiousness and longevity: An examination of possible mediators. *Health Psychology, 30*, 536–541.

Holtzman, N. S., Vazire, S., & Mehl, M. R. (2010). Sounds like a narcissist: Behavioral manifestations of narcissism in everyday life. *Journal of Research in Personality, 44*, 478–484.

Jackson, J. J., Hill, P. L., Payne, B. R., Roberts, B. W., & Stine-Morrow, E. A. L. (in press). Can an old dog learn (and want to experience) new tricks? Cognitive training increases openness to experience in older adults. *Psychology and Aging*.

Jackson, J. J., Wood, D., Bogg, T., Walton, K., Harms, P. & Roberts, B. W. (2010). What do conscientious people do? Development and validation of the behavioral indicators of conscientiousness scale (BICS). *Journal of Research in Personality, 44*, 501–511.

John, O. P., Naumann, L. P., & Soto, C. J. (2008). Paradigm shift to the integrative big five trait taxonomy: History, measurement, and conceptual issues. In O. P. John, R. W. Robins, & L. A. Pervin (Eds.), *Handbook of personality: Theory and Research* (3rd ed., pp. 114–158). New York, NY: Guilford Press.

Kandler, C., Bleidorn, W., Riemann, R., Spinath, F. M., Thiel, W., & Angleitner, A. (2010). Sources of cumulative continuity in personality: A longitudinal multiple-rater twin study. *Journal of Personality and Social Psychology, 98*, 995–1008.

Karney, B. R., & Bradbury, T. N. (1995). The longitudinal course of marital quality and stability: A review of theory, method, and research. *Psychological Bulletin, 118*, 3–34.

Kern, M. L., & Friedman, H. S. (2008). Do conscientious individuals live longer? A quantitative review. *Health Psychology, 27*, 505–512.

Krasner, M. S., Epstein, R. M., Beckman, H., Suchman, A. L., Chapman, B., Mooney, C. J., & Quill, T. E. (2009). Association of an educational program in mindful communication with burnout, empathy, and attitudes among primary care physicians. *Journal of the American Medical Association, 302*, 1284–1293.

Lehnart, J., Neyer, F. J., & Eccles, J. (2010). Long-term effects of social investment: The case of partnering in young adulthood. *Journal of Personality, 78*, 639–670.

Lejuez, C. W., Hopko, D. R., & Hopko, S. D. (2001). A brief behavioral activation treatment for depression: Treatment manual. *Behavioral Modification, 25*, 255–286.

Littlefield, A. K., Sher, K. J., & Wood, P. K. (2010). A personality-based description of maturing out of alcohol problems: Extension with a five-factor model and robustness to modeling challenges. *Addictive Behaviors, 35*, 948–954.

Low, D. K. S., Yoon, M., Roberts, B. W., & Rounds, J. (2005). The stability of interests from early adolescence to middle adulthood: A quantitative review of longitudinal studies. *Psychological Bulletin, 131*, 713–737.

Lucas, R. E., & Baird, B. M. (2006). Global self-assessment. In M. Eid & E. Diener (Eds.), *Handbook of multimethod measurement in psychology* (pp. 29–42). Washington, DC: American Psychological Association.

Lucas, R. E., & Donnellan, M. B. (2009). Age differences in personality: Evidence from a nationally representative sample of Australians. *Developmental Psychology, 45*, 1353–1363.

Lucas, R. E., & Donnellan, M. B. (2011). Personality development across the life span: Longitudinal analyses with a national sample from Germany. *Journal of Personality and Social Psychology, 101*, 847–861.

Luedtke, O., Roberts, B. W., Trautwein, U., & Nagy, G. (2011). A random walk down university avenue: Life paths, life events, and personality trait change at the transition to university life. *Journal of Personality and Social Psychology, 101*, 620–637.

Malouff, J. M., Thorsteinsson, E. B., Schutte, N. S., Bhullar, N., & Rooke, S. E. (2010). The five-factor model of personality and relationship satisfaction of intimate partners: A meta-analysis. *Journal of Research in Personality, 44*, 124–127.

McAdams, D. P., & Olson, B. D. (2010). Personality development: Continuity and change over the life course. *Annual Review of Psychology, 61*, 517–542.

McAdams, D. P., & Pals, J. L. (2006). A new big five: Fundamental principles for an integrative science of personality. *American Psychologist, 61*, 204–217.

McCrae, R. R., & Costa, P. T. Jr. (2008). The five-factor theory of personality. In O. P. John, R. W. Robins, & L. A. Pervin (Eds.), *Handbook of personality: Theory and research* (3rd ed., pp. 157–180). New York, NY: Guilford Press.

Mikulincer, M., & Shaver, P. R. (2007). *Attachment in adulthood: Structure, dynamics, and change.* New York, NY: Guilford Press.

Miller, W. R., & Rose, G. S. (2009). Toward a theory of motivational interviewing. *American Psychologist, 104*, 883–893.

Mischel, W. (2009). From personality and assessment (1968) to personality science, 2009. *Journal of Research in Personality, 43*, 282–290.

Moffitt, T. E., Arseneault, L., Belsky, D., Dickson, N., Hancox, R. J., Harrington, H., . . . Caspi, A. (2011). A gradient of childhood self-control predicts health, wealth, and public safety. *Proceedings of the National Academy of Sciences, 108*, 2693–2698.

Mroczek, D. K., & Spiro, A. (2003). Modeling intraindividual change in personality traits: Findings from the normative aging study. *Journals of Gerontology: Psychological Sciences, 58B*, 153–165.

Mroczek, D. K., & Spiro, A. (2007). Personality change influences mortality in older men. *Psychological Science, 18*, 371–376.

Nave, C. S., Sherman, R. A., Funder, D. C., Hampson, S. E., & Goldberg, L. R. (2010). On the contextual independence of personality: Teachers' assessments predict directly observed behavior after four decades. *Social Psychological and Personality Science, 1*, 327–334.

Ozer, D. J., & Benet-Martínez, V. (2006). Personality and the prediction of consequential outcomes. *Annual Review of Psychology, 57*, 401–421.

Piedmont, R. L. (2001). Cracking the plaster cast: Big five personality change during intensive outpatient counseling. *Journal of Research in Personality, 35*, 500–520.

Roberts, B. W. (2009). Back to the future: Personality and assessment and personality development. *Journal of Research in Personality, 43*, 137–145.

Roberts, B. W. (2006). Personality development and organizational behavior (Chap. 1, pp. 1–41). In B. M. Staw (Ed.), *Research on organizational behavior*. New York, NY: Elsevier Science/JAI Press.

Roberts, B. W. (1997). Plaster or plasticity: Are work experiences associated with personality change in women? *Journal of Personality, 65*, 205–232.

Roberts, B. W., Bogg, T., Walton, K., & Caspi, A. (2006). De-investment in work and non-normative personality trait change in young adulthood. *European Journal of Personality, 20*, 461–474.

Roberts, B. W., Caspi, A., & Moffitt, T. (2001). The kids are alright: Growth and stability in personality development from adolescence to adulthood. *Journal of Personality and Social Psychology, 81*, 670–683.

Roberts, B. W., Caspi, A., & Moffitt, T. (2003). Work experiences and personality development in young adulthood. *Journal of Personality and Social Psychology, 84*, 582–593.

Roberts, B. W., & DelVecchio, W. F. (2000). The rank-order consistency of personality from childhood to old age: A quantitative review of longitudinal studies. *Psychological Bulletin, 126*, 3–25.

Roberts, B. W., Kuncel, N., Shiner, R. N., Caspi, A., & Goldberg, L. (2007). The power of personality: A comparative analysis of the predictive validity of personality traits, SES, and IQ. *Perspectives in Psychological Science, 2*, 313–345.

Roberts, B. W., & Mroczek, D. (2008). Personality trait change in adulthood. *Current Directions in Psychological Science, 17*, 31–35.

Roberts, B. W., & Pomerantz, E. M. (2004). On traits, situations, and their integration: A developmental perspective. *Personality and Social Psychology Review, 8*, 402–416.

Roberts, B. W., Walton, K., & Viechtbauer, W. (2006). Patterns of mean-level change in personality traits across the life course: A meta-analysis of longitudinal studies. *Psychological Bulletin, 132*, 1–25.

Roberts, B. W., & Wood, D. (2006). Personality development in the context of the neo-socioanalytic model of personality (Chap. 2, pp. 11–39). In D. Mroczek & T. Little (Eds.), *Handbook of personality development*. Mahwah, NJ: Erlbaum.

Roberts, B. W., Wood, D, & Caspi, A. (2008). Personality development. In O. P. John, R. W. Robins, & L. A. Pervin (Eds.), *Handbook of personality: Theory and research* (3rd ed., Chap. 14, pp. 375–398). New York, NY: Guilford Press.

Robins, R. W., Caspi, A., & Moffitt, T. (2002). It's not just who you're with, it's who you are: Personality and relationship experiences across multiple relationships. *Journal of Personality, 70*, 925–964.

Robins, R. W., Fraley, R. C., Roberts, B. W., & Trzesniewski, K. H. (2001). A longitudinal study of personality change in young adulthood. *Journal of Personality, 69*, 617–640.

Robins, R. W., Noftle, E. E., Trzesniewski, K. H., & Roberts, B. W. (2005). Do people know how their personality has changed? Correlates of perceived and actual personality change in young adulthood. *Journal of Personality, 73*, 489–522.

Rogosa, D., Brandt, D., & Zimowski, M. (1982). A growth curve approach to the measurement of change. *Psychological Bulletin, 92*, 726–748.

Salthouse, T. A., Schroeder, D. H., & Ferrer, E. (2004). Estimating retest effects in longitudinal assessments of cognitive functioning in adults between 18 and 60 years of age. *Developmental Psychology, 40,* 813–822.

Santor, D. A., Bagby, R. M., & Joffe, R. T. (1997). Evaluating stability and change in personality and depression. *Journal of Personality and Social Psychology, 73,* 1354–1362.

Scarr, S., & McCartney, K. (1983). How people make their own environments: A theory of genotype → environment effects. *Child Development, 54,* 424–435.

Schmitt, N., & Kuljanin, G. (2008). Measurement invariance: Review of practice and implications. *Human Resource Management Review, 18,* 210–222.

Schuerger, J. M., Tait, E., & Tavernelli, M. (1982). Temporal stability of personality by questionnaire. *Journal of Personality and Social Psychology, 43,* 176–182.

Schuerger, J. M., Zarrella, K. L., & Hotz, A. S. (1989). Factors that influence the temporal stability of personality by questionnaire. *Journal of Personality and Social Psychology, 56,* 777–783.

Smith, M. L., Glass, G. V., & Miller, T. I. (1980). *The benefits of psychotherapy.* Baltimore, MD: Johns Hopkins University Press.

Soto, S. J., John, O. P., Gosling, S. D., & Potter, J. (2011). Age differences in personality traits from 10 to 65: Big five domains and facets in a large cross-sectional sample. *Journal of Personality and Social Psychology, 100,* 330–348.

Srivastava, S., John, O. P., Gosling, S. D., & Potter, J. (2003). Development of personality in early and middle adulthood: Set like plaster or persistent change? *Journal of Personality and Social Psychology, 84,* 1041–1053.

Swann, W. B. Jr. (1997). The trouble with change: Self-verification and allegiance to the self. *Psychological Science, 8,* 177–180.

Tang, T. Z., DeRubeis, R. J., Hollon, S. D., Amsterdam, J., Shelton, R., & Schalet, B. (2009). Personality change during depression treatment: A placebo-controlled trial. *Archives of General Psychiatry, 66,* 1322–1330.

Thorndike, E. L. (1920). A constant error in psychological ratings. *Journal of Applied Psychology, 4,* 25–29.

Thorndike, E. L. (1933). A proof of the law of effect. *Science, 77,* 173–175.

Trautwein, U., Lüdtke, O., Roberts, B. W., Schnyder, I., & Niggli, A. (2009). Different forces, same consequence: Conscientiousness and competence beliefs are independent predictors of academic effort and achievement. *Journal of Personality and Social Psychology, 97,* 1115–1128.

Trzesniewski, K. H., Donnellan, M. B., & Robins, R. W. (2003). Stability of self-esteem across the life span. *Journal of Personality and Social Psychology, 84,* 205–220.

Vaidya, J. G., Gray, E. K., Haig, J. R., Mroczek, D. K., & Watson (2008). Differential stability and individual growth trajectories of big five and affective traits during young adulthood. *Journal of Personality, 76,* 267–304.

Vazire, S. (2006). Informant reports: A cheap, fast, and easy method for personality assessment. *Journal of Research in Personality, 40,* 472–481.

Watson, D. (2004). Stability versus change, dependability versus error: Issues in the assessment of personality over time. *Journal of Research in Personality, 38,* 319–350.

Watson, D., & Humrichouse, J. (2006). Personality development in emerging adulthood: Integrating evidence from self-ratings and spouse ratings. *Journal of Personality and Social Psychology, 91,* 959–974.

CHAPTER 10

Personality *Strengths*

LAURA A. KING AND JASON TRENT

When the positive psychology movement burst onto the scene of academic psychology at the turn of the century, one of its calls was for enhanced scholarly attention to human strengths and virtues. Seligman and Csikszentmihalyi (2000) declared that the science of psychology was far too dominated by research on psychological disorders and human failings and should turn its attention instead to the valuable capacities that contribute to high levels of human functioning. Since that time, even the most casual perusal of the literature would suggest that psychological strengths have developed a considerable bandwagon. Perhaps, then, it was inevitable that a chapter such as this one would one day be written, nominally focused on the ambiguous topic of personality strengths.

One way to tackle the question of personality strengths would be to catalogue the associations between personality variables and outcomes and then separate those outcomes into "good" (e.g., well-being, physical health, occupational success) and "bad" things (e.g., psychological disorders, physical illness, criminality). Thorough reviews of the relations of personality to various important outcomes provide fodder for such a catalog (e.g., Carver & Connor-Smith, 2010; Ozer & Benet-Martinez, 2006) and we attempt such an overview here, eventually. Rest assured that there are few surprises in store: Self-efficacy, optimism, personal control are generally "good" as are, generally, extraversion, emotional stability, agreeableness, conscientiousness, and openness to experience. Anyone with the slightest familiarity with modern personality psychology knows these essential truisms already. Nevertheless, we forge relentlessly onward. In doing so, our goals differ from an exhaustive review of individual

differences that may be considered strengths (or weaknesses). Instead, we hope to demonstrate the particular challenges associated with approaching *personality* characteristics as strengths. Further, we hope to show how asking whether personality characteristics may be viewed as strengths opens up a host of important lessons for basic personality science. Before jumping in, it may be helpful to contemplate thoughtfully the implications of the question itself, the notion of thinking about personality characteristics as strengths.

STRENGTHS, PERSONALITY, AND ADJUSTMENT

When applied to physical objects, the meaning of strength is obvious. A strong wind possesses unusual power and force. A strong tree limb withstands that force. A strong metal is difficult to bend. When applied to persons, however, the meaning of strength is more ambiguous. An individual who stubbornly refuses to budge from a position might be viewed as strong-willed. Such resoluteness of spirit characterizes a host of individuals, some of whom we might view as heroic (e.g., a person standing firm on egalitarian principles in the face of prejudice), profoundly mistaken (e g., if the defended principle is, instead, one of prejudice), or dysfunctional (e.g., if the person resolutely espouses a delusional belief system). When we talk about a strong person, we can mean a number of quite different things. Strength of character often refers to someone who is morally courageous, who resists selfish impulses or expedience to do the right thing. We might view a person who has overcome adversity as *strong* if he or she demonstrates the capacity to engage with life energetically despite those difficult times. A mourner who fights the urge to cry while delivering a eulogy might be viewed as demonstrating enormous strength. A person who strives mightily to achieve a difficult goal, persisting in the face of obstacles, may be described as strong. Finally, we might consider specific characteristics as strengths or assets—as particular capacities or skills that enhance the likelihood of success in a specific life domain—in the way that height is a particular strength in basketball. In this chapter, we rely primarily on this latter notion and explore the question of whether personality characteristics can serve, in some ways, as assets associated with particularly good outcomes.

Considering any psychological quality as a strength readily invites associations to muscular strength. Bodily muscles have features that implicate four conceptual questions that should be considered in a discussion of psychological strengths. First, muscles can, through exercise, become stronger. Thus, in examining personality strengths, we must consider whether and how these characteristics can be changed (or strengthened) through experience or intentional effort. Second, there is no obvious downside to strong muscles: Strong muscles are, generally speaking, simply better than weak ones. In this sense, strengths are typically thought of in an explicitly evaluative way that is somewhat unusual for personality psychologists. We may think of honesty as a character strength (e.g., Peterson & Seligman, 2004) and the trait of agreeableness is linked to honesty (Hall, Park, Song, & Cody, 2010), but we rarely think of agreeableness as inherently morally good. Thinking about personality characteristics as strengths invites us to think (perhaps rather uncomfortably) about their ultimate usefulness (and, perhaps even more uncomfortably, their potential uselessness as well). The term *strength* is inherently evaluative, while personality characteristics are not typically considered in such an explicitly value-laden light.

Third, we note the cliché, "I didn't know my own strength," which refers to moments when a person misjudges the force needed for a particular act (e.g., intending to tap someone on the shoulder but poking them hard instead). Even when using our physical muscles, we may not be aware of their strength. Similarly, psychological characteristics may not be well understood by the person who possesses them. Awareness of psychological strengths might emerge in the aftermath of coping with a traumatic life event, when individuals might note that they did not realize how strong they really were. In the words of Jonathan Swift, "It is in men as in soils, where sometimes there is a vein of gold which the owner knows not of." Of course, individuals may be equally unaware of their own weaknesses. Individuals may enter a situation feeling well suited to its demands only to find out that they lack its requisite strengths.

Finally, muscular strength is proven in specific behavioral enactment, not in indirect measures such as bicep circumference. A person who can lift 100 pounds is *stronger* than one who can lift only 50. If the musclebound 50-pound lifter wants to argue the case, he or she will have to lift the next set of dumb bells. Strength ought to be demonstrable in some objective way, suggesting that thinking about personality variables as strengths implicates a central dilemma in personality psychology: the extent to which individual differences predict behavior.

Defining Personality

Before exploring the question at the center of this chapter, it behooves us to define personality. Here, we rely on Allport's (1937, p. 48) classic definition of personality as, "the dynamic organization within the person of those psychophysical systems that determine his (or her) unique adjustment to the environment." Personality is a system of interconnected variables and processes located inside the person that connects the person to the environment. The quality of this connection, in turn, defines adjustment. The inclusion of adjustment implies the possibility of strengths. The outcome of the interaction of personality with the environment can be evaluated in terms of its relative functional (versus dysfunctional) nature. A personality strength, then, is a characteristic that *promotes adjustment*. Further, adjustment is conditional on the environment in which the person is situated. Whether a characteristic is a strength depends on its match to the person's context, suggesting that a strength in one situation may be a weakness in another, a theme we revisit throughout this chapter.

Defining Adjustment

A challenge in examining personality characteristics as strengths is that the outcomes of interest are, themselves, inherently value-laden. Whether a characteristic is a strength depends on the value we place on its consequences or correlates. If a trait predisposes someone to deep, complex introspection, we might not consider that trait a strength unless we lived in a social context in which such introspection "counts" as a good in life. In the United States, happiness is highly valued, so characteristics that are associated with happiness might be considered strengths (e.g., Fulmer et al., 2010). However, in other cultural contexts such characteristics might be viewed as patently irrelevant to the outcomes that matter.

Evolutionary approaches to personality have the advantage of very specific definitions of what matters. From this approach, fitness is defined as the extent to which a characteristic enhances one's success at the two main challenges for any organism, survival, and reproduction. Characteristics can be considered adaptive to the extent that they enhance the chances of an organism succeeding at these two challenges. Clearly, as a more general rule, the outcomes that psychologists view as "adaptive" are a more general class of "good things" (Ryff & Singer, 1998). These might include a person's capacity for meaningful relationships with others, accomplishments in the work domain, and overall psychological and physical health. The difference between these notions of adaptation is clear when one considers, for instance, a teenager whose plans are disrupted by an unwanted pregnancy. Although from an evolutionary perspective this individual can check off a key accomplishment of adaptation, many would view this outcome as potentially maladaptive. Thus, in this chapter we consider the relationships of various personality characteristics to a general class of functional outcomes that may or may not represent the evolutionary notion of adaptation.

From this perspective, a characteristic can be viewed as a strength if it is reliably associated with outcomes such as psychological and physical health, satisfying interpersonal relationships, and occupational success. Although these many goods of life may exist in harmony in some fantasy of the best human life, clearly there may be trade-offs among them. Given that human beings occupy many roles in life (e.g., scholar, parent, romantic partner, advisor, teacher) and that these might sometimes conflict, it may be the case that in the connection between the person and his or her situation some outcomes are optimized and others less so. Which of these roles wins out may or may not have much to do with their *adaptive* significance. In any case, there is an important lesson to take from evolutionary approaches to personality, the fact that the adaptive significance of personality characteristics is likely to be found in their variation and that what "works" depends on the situation, as we now consider.

Tooby and Cosmides (1990) expressed great skepticism that individual differences could be viewed as products of natural selection because these differences, by definition,

represent variation not invariants within our species. Put simply, evolutionary arguments can be posited for features that are shared by members of a species (e.g., why we have two eyes, or two arms), but not for characteristics on which species members vary widely. More recently, the notion that characteristics can be selected *for variation* has received wider attention and acceptance (e.g., Buss, 2009; Nettle, 2006; Nichols, Sheldon, & Sheldon, 2008). Such selection for variation can be seen in nonhuman species, such that those who possess the less optimal set of features may be well-suited to an unusual niche or may be "kept around" to ensure species survival in case the environment changes (e.g., Nettle, 2006). To the extent that the world we see around us is at least in part a product of natural selection, the fact that most broad psychological variables are normally distributed suggests that, on the species level, variation is adaptive. Evolutionary accounts of the reliable individual differences we see in human personality focus on the adaptive significance of variation on these and the costs and benefits they represent relative to specific environmental features (e.g., Nettle, 2006).

Just as the relative adaptiveness of personality characteristics depends on environmental factors, whether a characteristic is a strength depends on situational demands and the fit of the characteristic with these (Cronbach, 1957). This conclusion may be less satisfying than the notion that specific characteristics are unconditionally "good." Nevertheless, the function of personality characteristics (i.e., their relations to adjustment) likely and inevitably *depends*. It may be the case that psychological swords are often double-edged (e.g., Chang & Sanna, 2003) and their value is likely determined by their fit with the environment, as Allport's definition of personality implies.

Even within the positive psychology movement, strengths and virtues are often considered stable aspects of the person that must be uncovered in order for the person to seek out situations (e.g., occupations, activities) that capitalize on these. For example, strengths-based management is built around the notion of matching a person's strengths with particular tasks and roles (e.g., Hodges & Clifton, 2004). The value of a particular ability, capacity, or *virtue* depends on its fit with particular situational demands. These issues are particularly relevant to personality characteristics. To the extent that some characteristics may resist change (or *strengthening*), we might say that these could emerge as strengths if the person is able to find the appropriate situation. As noted (perhaps optimistically) by Cronbach (1957, p. 679), "if for each environment there is a best organism, for every organism there must a best environment."

Is Adjustment a Strength?

Before concluding this overview of the notion of adjustment, we broach one final question, whether aspects of this broad notion of adjustment are themselves strengths. Surely, outcomes such as career success and satisfying relationships might also be considered strengths or resources on which a person might rely in difficult times. Lyubomirsky, King, and Diener (2005) review evidence suggesting that well-being (another of our candidate adjustment indices) may be a strength. Although happiness has often been viewed as an outcome of life experiences, Lyubomirsky et al. cite correlational, experimental, and longitudinal evidence in support of the contention that happiness precedes many of the goods of life. They suggest that happiness may set the social and cognitive stage for a variety of valued outcomes and life experiences. For our purposes, we will focus on aspects of adjustment as outcomes but caution the reader to bear in mind that these outcomes may facilitate other positive consequences in the lives of individuals who enjoy them.

With these general considerations on the table, in the rest of this chapter we turn to a discussion of personality characteristics as strengths. We begin with a discussion of the concept of resilience and briefly review emotional regulation and coping strategies, and psychological resources associated with resilience. We then consider broader dispositional factors as potential strengths, including traits and motivational variables. Next, we examine experience itself as a potential strength or strengthening process. Finally, we conclude by considering, first, the implications of the question of personality strengths for basic research in personality and, second, the ultimate value of asking that question.

As noted above, the positive psychology movement included among its calls to action increased scholarly focus on human strengths. The movement has fostered a taxonomy of virtues that are thought to represent broad band, socially desirable, universal human strengths (Peterson & Seligman, 2004). This Virtues in Action (or VIA) approach proposes a hierarchical structure characterized at the highest level by six virtues—wisdom, humanity, courage, justice, temperance, and transcendence (Dahlsgaard, Peterson, & Seligman, 2005; Peterson & Seligman, 2004). Each of these virtues includes lower level character strengths (e.g., the strengths included within humanity include social intelligence, kindness, and love), with a total of 24 such strengths being posited. These virtues were produced essentially out of whole cloth, without the typical psychometric practices that define one of the strengths of personality psychology itself (see Shryack, Steger, Krueger, & Kallie, 2010). In this chapter, we are centrally concerned with established personality variables, although we refer to these virtues and the research surrounding them as warranted.

RESILIENCE AND COPING

Resilience refers to a person's ability to recover from or adapt to difficult times. Resilience means that even in the face of adversity, a person shows signs of positive functioning (Ong, Bergeman, & Boker, 2009; Vetter et al., 2010). Resilience can refer to factors that compensate for difficulties, buffering the individual from the effects of these, or to the fact that moderate difficulties may themselves help to promote development (Masten, 2001). Resilience has been studied as a trait-like construct (e.g., Block, 1971; Ong, Bergeman, Bisconti, & Wallace, 2006). This individual difference refers specifically to individuals who report themselves (or who are judged by observers) to be likely to recover easily from disruptions and setbacks.

Although resilience would seem an ideal candidate for the discussion of personality strengths, most resilience researchers view the construct as either a process (e.g., Luthar, Cicchetti, & Becker, 2000; Richardson, 2002; Tugade & Fredrickson, 2004; Waugh, Fredrickson, & Taylor, 2008) or outcome (Bonanno, 2004, 2005; Bonanno, Wortman, & Nesse, 2004; Mancini & Bonanno, 2009; Masten, 2001; Silver, 2009), and several speak out specifically against the idea of viewing resilience as a trait (e.g., Fergus & Zimmerman, 2005; Luthar et al., 2000). In addition, particularly within developmental psychology, resilience has been conceptualized as a host of protective factors contributing to positive outcomes (e.g., Garmezy, 1991; Masten, 2001), some of which do not fall within the purview of personality (e.g., particularly helpful or caring adults in an otherwise difficult environment). Certainly, these differences have led to confusion in the literature, leading to calls for greater clarity in the definition of resilience itself (e.g., Davydov, Stewart, Ritchie, Chaudieu, 2010; Luthar et al., 2000). To the extent the resilience may be viewed as the capacity to maintain functioning in the presence of a stressor, we can examine individual differences in affective and coping processes that contribute to resilience.

Resilient Coping

To the extent that resilience involves a lack of emotional disruption in the face of traumatic events, it may be supported by emotional experiences and particularly effective emotion regulation strategies. For instance, the experience of positive emotions has been shown to support resilience (Fredrickson, Tugade, Waugh, & Larkin, 2003). Resilient individuals centrally differ from their less resilient counterparts not so much in the level of negative affect they experience, but in their abilities to capitalize on pleasurable experiences when they occur, even in the midst of difficulty (Cohn, Fredrickson, Brown, Mikels, & Conway, 2009; Fredrickson, Cohn, Coffey, Pek, & Finkel, 2008).

In this sense, resilient coping entails bolstering positive affect in the aftermath of a negative event. As such, emotion regulation strategies that promote such experiences may be particularly associated with resilience. Emotion regulation refers to behavioral and cognitive strategies used to change the duration and intensity of one's emotional experience (Gross & Thompson, 2007). To the extent that such strategies alter affective experience, we can say that regulation has been successful. Individual differences in two specific emotion regulation strategies have been the focus of much research, suppression and cognitive reappraisal (Gross & John, 2003). Suppression involves dampening emotional experience by not expressing the emotion. Cognitive reappraisal refers to construing an emotionally evocative situation in a different, less threatening way. Note that these strategies here refer to a person's characteristic style of regulating affect. Generally, research has supported the prediction that reappraisal is superior to suppression when it comes to changing one's emotions, as well as in terms of its relations to emotional experience, well-being, and interpersonal functioning (Gross & John, 2003; Srivastava, Tamir, McGonigal, John, & Gross, 2009). Cognitive reappraisal ability has been shown to serve as a buffer against depression in the face of stress (Troy, Wilhelm, Shallcross, & Mauss, 2010). Resilient individuals may reappraise negative events in a particular way—by focusing on their potential positive consequences. Positive reappraisal involves changing one's take on a potentially negative experience by looking on the bright side or finding benefits in the experience (e.g., Ong, Fuller-Rowell, & Bonanno, 2010). One form of benefit-finding involves attributions of personal growth as a result of a negative life event, a topic we take up later in this chapter.

A variety of social cognitive skills have been linked to greater resilience as well as more general positive life

outcomes. Scholars have suggested that an array of such psychological characteristics can be considered "Psychological Capital" (PsyCaps) or resources that can be called upon during stressful times (Luthans, Youssef, & Avolio, 2007; Schaubroeck, Riolli, Peng, & Spain, 2011). A litany of these constructs and their concomitant literatures would occupy a handbook unto itself. We briefly note three resources associated with particularly good outcomes—self-efficacy, optimism, and personal control.

Self-efficacy, the belief that one has the competence to accomplish a given goal or task, is associated with a number of positive outcomes in people's lives (e.g., Bandura, 2001). Self-efficacy influences coping, stress, and physical health (Sarkar, Ali, & Whooley, 2009). Beyond these outcomes, self-efficacy has been linked with successful job interviewing and job performance (Tay, Ang, & Van Dyne, 2006).

Optimism involves general expectations that good things will happen in the future. Such an outlook has been found to relate to more engaged coping (Carver & Connor-Smith, 2010), as well as a variety of indicators of psychological and physical health (Carver, Scheier, & Segerstrom, 2010). A sense of personal control has also been suggested as a potentially crucial factor in well-being and health (Baumeister & Alquist, 2009). Overall, across a wide range of studies, a sense of personal control has been related to emotional well-being, successful coping with a stressful event, healthy behavior change, and good health (Frazier et al., 2011; Stanton, Revenson, & Tennen, 2007).

Given the associations between particular coping strategies, and the promise of change that is implied in self-efficacy, optimism, and sense of control, it is tempting to focus on a simple "bottom line": The "strongest" person is one who is high in self-efficacy and control, possesses an optimistic perspective, and a tendency to use positive reappraisal. All of these potential characteristics must be considered in the context of a person's life, the trauma itself, and the emotions it has produced. Further, we might consider how these strategies are brought to bear flexibly in response to immediate demands. These issues are well represented in a recent model of individual differences in resilience.

Hidden Ambiguities in Resilience

Mancini and Bonanno (2009) proposed an individual difference model of resilience that highlights the ambiguities inherent in thinking about resilience as a strength and points to the potential trade-offs that likely exist in the ways that individuals achieve resilience. These scholars begin by defining resilience specifically as an outcome to stressful experience, manifested in the lack of disruption of a person's everyday functioning in the aftermath of traumatic loss. Resilience can be distinguished from recovery. The resilient pattern is characterized by acute grief followed by a rapid return to previous levels of adjustment (e.g., Bonanno, 2004). Recovery, in contrast, is characterized by more prolonged grief and a more gradual return to previous functioning. Mancini and Bonanno point out that, rather than being an unusual outcome demonstrating enormous strength, resilience is relatively commonplace. Indeed, in one study of bereaved spouses, nearly half showed the resilient pattern (Mancini, Pressman, & Bonanno, 2006). Further, Mancini and Bonanno point out that low threat appraisals, engaged coping, and reappraisals that lead to resilience can emerge from surprising sources.

In their analysis of the coping processes that facilitate resilient outcomes, Mancini and Bonanno articulate a compelling case for the likely trade-offs that characterize resilience. As one example, repressive coping (i.e., the tendency to automatically avoid negative emotional information), has generally been considered maladaptive (Bonanno & Singer, 1990). Yet, repressive coping, in the face of a potentially calamitous personal loss, may allow the person to avoid threat appraisals, to reduce the burden of negative emotions, and engage in problem-focused coping (Mancini & Bonanno, 2009). In fact, in one study, following the death of a loved one, bereaved repressors reported fewer health problems and were rated as better adjusted by their friends, compared to bereaved individuals who did not use this coping strategy (Coifman, Bonanno, Ray, & Gross, 2007).

The lesson of the apparent temporary benefits of repressive coping can also be applied to suppression. Suppression may have its place as the individual seeks to accomplish goals in a social world. For instance, a person who is angered by an offhand remark might simply suppress the expression of that anger, as a socially expeditious way to handle an unwanted emotion. Indeed, it is the chronic reliance on suppression that appears to be especially problematic (Srivastava et al., 2009). One prospective study of emotional expression and suppression found that capacity for flexibility was the key to later adjustment (Bonanno, Papa, Lalande, Westphal, & Coifman, 2004).

The notion that *flexibility* is key to resilience has implications for potential personality strengths. Generally personality dispositions are considered chronic aspects of the person. Overuse or the indiscriminate application of a particular behavioral or affective strategy would seem to be problematic, but at least as it is often defined (e.g., by Allport), personality may implicate precisely this tendency.

This consideration of resilience reveals a problem in thinking about even this seemingly obvious "psychological strength" as an unmitigated good in people's lives. Some might note, for instance, that resilience may represent an overemphasis on immediate psychological adjustment over and above other potentially valuable outcomes. For instance, some scholars have argued that coping with difficult life circumstances can propel positive changes in the self or personality development (Aldwin & Gilmer, 2004; Janoff-Bulman, 1992; King & Hicks, 2007; Tedeschi & McNally, 2011). Yet those who report little distress after a traumatic loss are also those who report *less* self-change in response to that loss (Galatzer-Levy, Bonanno, & Mancini, 2009). Individuals who show a resilient pattern to loss might have pointedly avoided self-reflective, accommodative, or meaning-focused coping (Folkman, 2008). Such individuals may be well-adjusted in some ways, but they may also lack the possible benefits or strengths that may accrue as a result of suffering (Janoff-Bulman, 1992; King & Hicks, 2007).

Clearly, more general personality dispositions may undergird some of the more proximal and contextualized social cognitive processes involved in coping. Although some have argued against broad and relatively stable characteristics as a valuable focus for the science of personality (Kammrath & Scholer, this volume; Mischel, 1968, 2004, 2009), personality psychologists have persisted in their attempts to understand personality through such broad variables. We now turn to the more challenging question of whether broad dispositions may be considered strengths.

BROAD DISPOSITIONS AS STRENGTHS

A central question in considering personality characteristics as strengths, then, is whether these can be viewed as resources on which the resilient person might have relied to successfully cope with difficulties. Are individual differences potential sources of resilience? May they be considered as protective (or risk) factors in the person's capacity to survive or thrive during stressful times? More broadly, can broader dispositions be viewed as assets that lead to positive outcomes? We address this question in two categories of individual differences, traits and motivation.

Traits as Strengths

Given the dominance of the trait approach to personality, it makes sense to consider personality strengths within the dominant trait approach, the Five-Factor Model (FFM; Costa & McCrae, 1988; McCrae, Gaines, & Wellington, this volume; McCrae & John, 1992). Importantly, traits have not been conceptualized as strengths, per se. Rather these constructs have emerged as general descriptions (or explanations) of the enduring characteristics that have been observed in people. If we entertain the notion that personality traits can be viewed as situational strengths, we might consider their relationships to valued outcomes to understand the contexts in which various traits might be considered strengths. The five traits include neuroticism (or emotional stability), extraversion, openness to experience, agreeableness, and conscientiousness.

Before reviewing the potential status of these traits as strengths, a few key points bear mention. All of these traits have relatively substantial heritability estimates (e.g., Bouchard & Loehlin, 2001). These traits are also generally thought to be relatively stable over the life span (Costa & McCrae, 2006). Thus, in considering traits as strengths, we might note that they may not hold great promise of change. Although they may be strengths, they might not be expected to show evidence of *strengthening* (though we review evidence in this regard toward the end of this section). Thus, for these traits, situational factors may be especially important to their manifestation in adjustment to the environment. Making a trait a strength, we might say, involves finding its optimal setting. In this brief overview, we offer research that implicates these traits as strengths (or weaknesses) and, where needed offer unsupported conjecture in this regard (inspired in large part by Block, 2010).

The dilemma of thinking about personality characteristics as strengths is captured best in neuroticism. Neuroticism (versus emotional stability) is defined as a susceptibility toward worry, distress, lingering negative emotions (Widiger, 2009), and viewing the world as threatening (Watson & Casillas, 2003). Neuroticism has been shown as well to relate to more health complaints (Carver & Connor-Smith, 2010), and in one longitudinal study of older adults spanning nearly seven years, neuroticism was associated with dying during the study (Fry & Debats, 2009). Elevated levels of neuroticism are incorporated into most personality pathologies in dimensional approaches to personality disorders (Trull & Widiger, 2008). Neuroticism is associated with potentially maladaptive coping strategies (including wishful thinking and avoidance), and is negatively associated with engaged coping and positive reappraisal (e.g., Carver & Connor-Smith, 2010; Watson, David, & Suls, 1999). Finally, in terms of VIA strengths, neuroticism is strongly negatively correlated with hope/optimism and valor/courage (Mac-Donald, Bore, & Munro, 2008). Even this brief sketch does not paint a promising picture in terms of the notion that neuroticism might ever serve as a strength. What possible use might it have?

Evolutionary explanations for the existence of neuroticism typically rely on the notion that, for our species, it is adaptive to have some members who are highly sensitive to potential threats and vigilant for negative information in the environment (Nettle, 2006). Is this hypothetical species-level adaptiveness a domain-specific strength at the individual level? A key stumbling block for this intuitively appealing idea is that neuroticism does not relate to performance on tasks requiring vigilance (Finomore, Mathews, Shaw, & Warm, 2009; Shaw et al., 2010). Further, neuroticism is not necessarily associated with observable behavior (Vazire, 2010). Apparently, neurotics are not generally sending out alarm calls. So, it does not appear likely that neuroticism's strength value will be found in vigilance.

It might be that the frequent negative affect experienced by the neurotic person (e.g., Zelenski & Larsen, 1999) leads to attention to detail or analytical processing (Clore & Palmer, 2009), which might be handy in particular settings. Neurotic individuals might also be motivated by negative affect to continue to work on a problem. To the extent that negative mood provides information to the person that things are not yet "quite right" (Martin, 2001), neuroticism may relate to task persistence.

Another possibility is that trait neuroticism offers an adaptive counterweight to the strong incentive value of pleasure-and-approach motivation. Embedding neuroticism in an overarching motivational framework (e.g., Gray, 1982) allows us to locate the value of neuroticism not in the group but the individual. Flexibly balancing the motivations to approach and avoid stimuli in the environment (e.g., Corr, 2008) requires a system that is capable not only of joy and anticipation but also misery and dread.

Finally, in the absence of data, one also might note that there appear to be social roles and occupational settings where neuroticism is tolerated or even celebrated. For instance, one can readily think of examples of neurotic playwrights, novelists, actors, artists, and musicians. Such a thought experiment suggests, at least, an illusory correlation between neuroticism and eminence in some domains.

Importantly, despite the considerable literature surrounding personality traits, and the almost reflexive demand to "control for neuroticism" in any study of personality, the nature of neuroticism is somewhat ambiguous. Neuroticism, as currently defined, may not be as central to conceptions of personality as its current standing in the literature suggests. For instance, lexical approaches to personality traits have not strongly supported the cross-cultural occurrence of neuroticism in the natural language of a variety of cultures (de Raad et al., 2010). This is not to say that neuroticism does not exist, but rather that, apparently, in many cultures, people are not talking about how neurotic people are.

Neuroticism is often equated with the negative affective states or vulnerability to anxious mood (e.g., Carver & Connor-Smith, 2010). This equation occurs even in self-report measures of neuroticism. For example, the NEO-PIR (Costa & McCrae, 1985) contains the item, "When I'm under a great deal of stress, sometimes I feel like I'm going to pieces." Finding out that neuroticism when measured with such an item relates to feeling like one is falling to pieces under stress is not terribly illuminating. Further, such items suggest that neuroticism is defined, operationally, in terms of proximal responses to negative events rather than as a trait that is present in the person's life, in good times and bad, and potentially influencing behavior even when things are going well.

Recent theory and research on the genetic correlates of neuroticism suggest a potentially different view of this variable. Like many other aspects of human misery (e.g., depression, alcohol dependence), neuroticism has been linked to a particular feature of the serotonin transporter gene (Brummett, Boyle, Kuhn, Siegler, & Williams, 2008; Middeldorp et al., 2007; Vinberg, Mellerup, Andersen, Bennike, & Kessing, 2010). The allele of interest here is 5-HTTLPR, a location on the gene on which a person can have two long alleles, a long and a short allele, or two short alleles. Short alleles are associated with neuroticism (Pluess et al., 2010).

Research on 5-HTTPLR suggests that the private torment we associate with neuroticism is not the inevitable outcome of those short alleles. Rather, the short alleles have been identified as moderators of the effect of context on the person (e.g., Way & Gurbaxani, 2008), with individuals with two short alleles being relatively more influenced by the environment (e.g., Manuck, Flory, Ferrell, & Muldoon, 2004). For instance, having high levels of social support plays a stronger role in the moods of those with these alleles compared to those with two long (Kaufman et al., 2005). Individuals who possess the short/short pattern are at a *decreased* risk for depression if they are also in a warm, positive environment (Eley et al., 2004). From this perspective, the affective life of an individual with these short alleles depends more on the quality of his or her interaction with the environment. That is, the very meaning of the trait of neuroticism may depend on the situation. In this sense, neuroticism may represent, at its base, a tendency to have one's affect finely tuned to events of life (Pluess et al., 2010). Such fine-tuning may well have its uses. To the extent that models of personality (and self-regulation) generally assume that behavior, thoughts, and feelings are, in part, a function of situational factors, neurotic individuals may best represent that model. Further, these findings suggest that the function of neuroticism in people's lives may depend more on social situations, and perhaps social traits (as we consider later).

No such mental acrobatics are required with the second big dimension of the FFM, extraversion, the tendencies to be outgoing, sociable, and energetic. Extraversion is strongly related to subjective well-being (DeNeve & Cooper, 1998; Diener & Lucas, 1999; Steel, Schmidt, & Shultz, 2008), engaged coping (Carver & Connor-Smith, 2010), marital satisfaction (Stroud, Durbin, Saigal, & Knobloch-Fedders, 2010), and a strong sense of meaning in life (King, Hicks, Krull, & Del Gaiso, 2006). Extraverts are particularly susceptible to positive affective experiences (e.g., Zelenski & Larsen, 1999) and appear to carry a bit of positive affect with them wherever they go (Lucas & Baird, 2004). Extraversion is strongly correlated with the self-reports of VIA strengths including teamwork, capacity for love, hope, optimism, humor, zest and leadership (MacDonald et al., 2008). Evidence for a straightforward main effect of extraversion on success in the work domain is less strong (Barrick & Mount, 2005). Extraversion appears to share a weak positive relationship to work success and may be particularly associated with success in sales-related occupations (Vinchur, Schippman, Switzer, & Roth, 1998).

Can extraversion be viewed as a domain-specific weakness? Extraversion may be irrelevant to success in domains that do not involve social interaction and may be a liability in settings in which social traits are less relevant to the overarching goals of a situation. For example, extraversion has been found to be irrelevant (Higgins, Peterson, Pihl, & Lee, 2007) or to correlate negatively with academic performance (Bratko, Chamoro-Premuzic, & Saks, 2006) and research productivity (Rushton, Murray, & Paunonen, 1987). Finally, in terms of health behavior, extraversion is associated with sexual risk-taking, particularly for men (Miller et al., 2004).

Openness to experience refers to sophistication in thought, interest in art and culture, open-mindedness, tolerance (McCrae & Sutin, 2009) and creativity (Silvia, Nusbaum, Berg, Martin, & O'Connor, 2009). Openness to experience is associated with superior cognitive functioning (Sharp, Reynolds, Pedersen, & Gatz, 2010), to more engaged coping (Carver & Connor-Smith, 2010), and with creative accomplishments (King, McKee-Walker, & Broyles, 1996). Individuals who rate themselves as open to experience are more likely to pursue entrepreneurial goals (for instance, starting their own business), and to experience success in those pursuits (Zhao, Seibert, & Lumpkin, 2010). Openness is associated with accruing wisdom from life experience (Baltes & Smith, 2008). Within the VIA taxonomy of strengths, openness to experience is strongly correlated of intellect, love of learning, curiosity, originality, creativity, wisdom (MacDonald et al., 2008). On the negative side, high openness to experience appears to be a distinctive feature of marijuana smokers (Terracciano, Lockenhoff, Crum, Bienvenu, & Costa, 2008).

Agreeableness (Graziano & Tobin, 2009)—the tendency to be gentle, kind, and trusting—is related to generosity and altruism (Caprara et al., 2012), to religious faith (Saroglou, 2010), and to more satisfying romantic relationships (Donnellan, Larsen-Rife, & Conger, 2005). Though unrelated to engaged coping, agreeableness is negatively related to more disengaged coping (Carver & Connor-Smith, 2010). Agreeableness relates strongly to VIA virtues, such as modesty, humility, fairness, kindness, and mercy (MacDonald et al., 2008).

The HEXACO model proposes a sixth factor, separated out from FFM agreeableness, honesty/humility (Ashton & Lee, 2007). This factor, like FFM agreeableness would seem to represent a potentially unmitigated strength and it has been associated with a number of positive outcomes, particularly workplace integrity, citizenship, and low levels of toxic behaviors, such as sexual harassment (Ashton & Lee, 2007). More generally, scholars have argued that humility is a psychological strength (Exline & Geyer, 2004; Exline, Single, Lobel, & Geyer, 2004).

Agreeable, honest, and humble people are, in essence, nice. Considering niceness as a strength prompts the question of whether one can be "too nice." Niceness may be a liability when the situation is adversarial. For instance, individuals might wish for a divorce lawyer or book agent who treats them kindly but prefer one who is less than agreeable at the bargaining table. Agreeable individuals may be conflict averse, conforming, or overly compliant (Block, 2010).

Conscientiousness, the broad tendency to be reliable, responsible, and planful can be viewed as a strength in a variety of life domains. Conscientiousness is related to engaged coping (Carver & Connor-Smith, 2010), health, healthy living, and longevity (Roberts, Jackson, Fayard, Edmonds, & Meints, 2009; Roberts & Mroczek, 2008). Longitudinal studies demonstrate that conscientious individuals are at lower risk for mortality than their counterparts who are less conscientious (Fry & Debats, 2009; Iwasa et al., 2008, 2009; Kern & Friedman, 2008; Martin, Friedman, & Schwartz, 2007). A variety of studies show that conscientiousness is associated with dutifully performing the mundane behaviors that are vital to good health, such as getting regular exercise, avoiding drinking and smoking, and wearing seatbelts (O'Connor, Conner, Jones, McMillan, & Ferguson, 2009; Rush, Becker, & Curry, 2009).

Conscientiousness is associated with high school and college students' grade point averages (Noftle & Robins, 2007), and academic performance, even controlling for IQ and cognitive ability (Higgins et al., 2007). It is positively related to better-quality friendships (Jensen-Campbell & Malcolm, 2007), religious faith (Saroglou, 2010), and a forgiving attitude (Balliet, 2010). In the work domain, conscientiousness has been linked to entrepreneurial success (Zhao et al., 2010) and work performance (e.g., Higgins et al., 2007). Low levels of conscientiousness are associated with criminal behavior (Wiebe, 2004) and substance abuse (Walton & Roberts, 2004). Factor analytic work has identified conscientiousness as a major component underlying the VIA strengths of self-regulation, self-control, prudence, judgment, and integrity. Indeed, conscientiousness correlated .71 with these values (MacDonald et al., 2008).

Clearly there is a large body of evidence suggesting the value of conscientiousness. Might it have a downside? Conscientiousness might be a situation-specific weakness in contexts where variety and change are common. Conscientious individuals might be considered risk averse, and less successful in situations involving some risk taking (Block, 2010). Although (along with extraversion) conscientiousness predicts serving in leadership positions in college fraternities and sororities (Harms, Roberts, & Wood, 2007), childhood experiences with some small-time rule-breaking has also been linked to leadership (Avolio, Rotundo, & Walumbwa, 2009).

Trait Interactions

Although straightforward "main effects" of traits are most easily digested, it is important to bear in mind that traits combine within the persons who possess them and these combinations may have important consequences for behavior. Examining the ways that traits interact to produce positive outcomes in people's lives is necessary to understanding when and for whom traits might be strengths. Research that has examined such interactions suggests the promise of such an approach.

Industrial and organizational (I/O) psychologists have examined interactions among traits as predictors of work performance (Tett & Burnett, 2003). Witt, Burke, Barrick, and Mount (2002) found, for instance, that conscientiousness, though generally considered a strong predictor of work performance, interacted with agreeableness to predict work outcomes. Specifically, they found that when coupled with high agreeableness, conscientiousness was strongly related to superior performance ratings. However, low agreeable conscientious individuals were characterized as difficult micromanagers.

A study by Judge and Erez (2007) found that extraversion was strongly related to work performance only when neuroticism was taken into account. In this study, in fact, for relatively neurotic individuals, extraversion was essentially irrelevant to performance. Neurotic individuals received relatively *high* work performance ratings regardless of their extraversion. In contrast, extraversion was strongly correlated with work performance only for those low on neuroticism. In fact, those who were low on both extraverion *and neuroticism* were likely to receive the worst evaluations, suggesting, perhaps, a withdrawn, laissez faire attitude toward work. Highly extraverted individuals received high-performance evaluations only if they were also low on neuroticism. Judge and Erez suggest that this profile of high extraversion and low neuroticism may represent a particularly buoyant personality, which was, perhaps, particularly valuable in the specific workplace examined, a fitness center.

Furthermore, research provides tantalizing evidence that interactions may be especially important to the relation of neuroticism to psychological well-being. Extraversion appears to play a particularly strong role in well-being specifically for highly neurotic individuals. For example, research has shown that neurotic individuals may be likely to enjoy high levels of well-being as a function of their extraversion (Hotard, McFatter, McWhirter, & Stegall, 1989; Pavot, Diener, & Fujita, 1990). In addition, extraverted neurotic individuals' daily moods may be more strongly driven by their extraversion than their neuroticism (McFatter, 1994).

In addition, researchers have examined trait *profiles* as predictors of risky outcomes. For instance, alcohol abuse is associated with a pattern of high extraversion and low conscientiousness, while marijuana abuse is characterized by high openness to experience and low extraversion (Flory, Lynam, Milich, Leukefeld, & Clayton, 2002). Smokers tend to show high neuroticism coupled with low conscientiousness and marijuana users show a pattern of high openness, low agreeableness, and low conscientiousness and mid-range neuroticism (Terracciano et al., 2008).

Higher-Level Traits

Although the dispositions that occupy the most commonly studied level of the trait construct (i.e., the five or six factors) are conceptually distinct, empirically there is shared variance among them. Two higher order factors have been identified, with the first factor (sometimes called *alpha* or *stability*) including (low) neuroticism, conscientiousness, and agreeableness and the second (sometimes called *beta* or *plasticity*) including extraversion and openness to experience (De Young, 2006; Digman, 1990). Digman suggested that these two factors represent the requirements for adjustment in human society, with alpha/stability representing socialization or conformity and beta/plasticity representing openness to change or exploration. Clearly, either of these two broad impulses can be viewed as strengths, once again, depending on the situation. If the social world is rigidly structured, high alpha would seem to be a good way to succeed in that world. Coping within a context that is changing might require, instead the flexibility that is represented in high beta. Of course, we might also consider, with the normal curve looming large, that those in the mid range of these broad traits represent most of us, and extremes are not only unusual but probably not the key to adaptation or functioning.

Before leaving the trait domain, we review a controversial literature that has emerged in trait psychology, suggesting that a single factor may help to explain the shared variance in the FFM traits. From this perspective, a single General Factor of Personality (GFP; Musek, 2007; Rushton & Irwing, 2008, 2009) occupies the highest level of abstraction and represents a supertrait that is defined at one end by the "positive" traits of extraversion, agreeableness, conscientiousness, and openness to experience, and is defined at the opposite end by high neuroticism (or low emotional stability). Some scholars view this high level trait as primarily an artifact of social desirability (McCrae et al., 2008), the relatively spurious result of incidental item overlap across traits (Ashton, Lee, Goldberg, & de Vries, 2009), or partially a function of the halo effect (Anusic, Schimmack, Pinkus, & Lockwood,

2009). Others have taken a more substantive view of the GFP, suggesting that it represents a kind of optimal personality (Rushton & Irwing, 2008, 2009). The GFP has, for instance, been found to relate to supervisor ratings of work performance (van der Linden, te Nijenhuis, & Bakker, 2010).

Drawing on the relatively high heritability estimates for this supertrait, Rushton and colleagues (e.g., Rushton, Bons, & Hur, 2008) argue that the GFP represents a product of selection pressures. This line of reasoning implies that millions of years from now we might expect *Homo sapiens* to converge on this optimal trait (the apparent reproductive success of neurotic individuals in traditional societies notwithstanding, Alvergne, Jokela, & Lummaa, 2010). Regardless of how one views such a possibility, we would note a few cautions. First, correlations between the GFP and valued outcomes might well be best explained by relations among its specific constituent traits (and their lower-order facets). Even strong evidence for the GFP as a personality strength may mask more specific action at the lower level of organization. Second, although conceiving of personality as one big latent factor may seem to simplify things, the GFP is generally measured using the long forms of the various traits it comprises. Third, and most importantly, moving to ever more general levels of analysis, as the GFP necessarily implies, renders less likely the research on trait interactions that we have suggested is vital to understanding the potential for personality characteristics to serve as strengths.

Can Traits Be Strengthened?

Although trait theories generally assume these characteristics to be stable over the life span, research points to reliable changes in traits over time. Longitudinal studies of the FFM traits (Edmonds, Jackson, Fayard, & Roberts, 2008; Roberts, Jackson, Fayard, Edmonds, & Meints, 2009; Roberts, Walton, & Viechtbauer, 2006; Roberts, Wood, & Caspi, 2008) provide evidence for patterns of increases in social dominance (a facet of extraversion), conscientiousness, and emotional stability between the ages of 20 and 40. Social vitality, another facet of extraversion, and openness to experience increase most during adolescence but then decline in old age. Agreeableness shows a steady rise over the life course. To the extent that agreeableness, conscientiousness, and emotional stability are considered strengths, we might say that normative increases show evidence of strengthening on these dimensions. In addition, experience may play a role in facilitating "strengthening" in personality. Scollon and

Diener (2006) examined changes in extraversion and neuroticism as a function of life experiences and found that increases in work and relationship satisfaction predicted changes increases in extraversion and decreases in neuroticism over time.

Motivational Strength

Although traits are the most commonly studied level of personality, we note that within the dynamic organization of personality lies motivation. Some trait psychologists ascribe a motivational component to traits (McCrae & Costa, 1999, 2008). Nevertheless, there are empirical and conceptual reasons for examining motivation apart from traits. Although research supports the notion that the content of goals can be partially explained by traits (e.g., Bleidorn et al., 2010; Roberts, O'Donnell, & Robins, 2004; Romero, Villar, Luengo, & Gómez-Fraguela, 2009), these relations are not of such a magnitude as to suggest redundancy. Conceptually, motivation and traits are clearly separable. Roberts and Robins (2000) have suggested that traits are who people are, while goals are who they want to become. Thus, we might consider motivational aspects of personality as strengths. In this section, we describe two broad approaches to motivation, classic social motivation theory (McClelland, 1987) and self-determination theory (SDT), as well a more circumscribed approach, personalized goals, and finally, self-regulatory strength. These approaches differ from the trait approach in one important way: In all of these, the motivational variables considered were hypothesized, at the outset, to serve the function of promoting adjustment. In each case, the variables considered were conceptualized as serving as domain-specific or general strengths.

Social Motives

Social motives (or implicit motives) are defined as enduring concerns for a particular class of goal states (McClelland, 1987). These motives were introduced by Henry Murray (1938) and are generally measured using the Thematic Apperception Test (more recently called the Picture Story Exercise, or PSE), in which imaginative stories are reliably coded for motive relevant imagery (Smith, 1992). Conceptually, these motives are thought to represent nonconscious motivational tendencies that specifically influence spontaneous (as opposed to self-conscious) behavior (McClelland, Koestner, & Weinberger, 1989; Spangler, 1992). Although Murray initially posited a long list of such needs, the three that have garnered the most empirical attention are the need for Achievement (*n*Ach), the need for Power (*n*Pow), and the need for Affiliation (*n*Aff). We focus our discussion here on *n*Ach and *n*Pow.

McClelland (1987) described the social motives as serving three functions. First, these motives are thought to *orient attention,* such that a person high on a particular motive should be more likely to notice motive-relevant cues in the environment. The second function of social motives is to *drive behavior,* indicating that individuals high on a given motive ought to persist longer at motive-relevant tasks. Finally, social motives function to facilitate *selecting behavioral strategies* in a motive-relevant context. An implication of this selecting function is that individuals who are high on a particular implicit need should enjoy greater success in motive-relevant contexts. That is, individuals who possess a high level of a particular motive ought to be able to choose the optimal strategy for success in a particular domain. In this way, we could think of social motives as domain-specific strengths (i.e., as leading to positive outcomes in motive-relevant contexts).

A case in point is provided by research on *n*Ach, the enduring concern for striving for excellence. Does *n*Ach predict actual achievement? When considered in a straightforward way the answer is a rather weak "yes" (e.g., Spangler, 1992). Importantly, this predicted association is stronger when moderators are taken into account. Specifically, a meta-analysis suggested that *n*Ach was most strongly associated with performance, particularly on tasks that carried intrinsic achievement incentives (rather than extrinsic social incentives) (Spangler, 1992).

Similarly, *n*Pow, the enduring concern for having impact on the social world, was expected to be a strength in the domain of leadership (McClelland, 1987), and some research supported this prediction (Winter, 1987, 1991). Yet, research also suggested that *n*Pow had a number of potentially problematic correlates (such as heavy drinking, promiscuous sexual behavior, exploitativeness, Winter, 1988). In striving to understand when and for whom *n*Pow might be a strength (or a weakness), scholars examined the role of socialization experiences and found that the outcomes associated with *n*Pow depend on the degree to which early experiences had instilled a sense of responsibility (Hofer et al., 2010; Winter & Berenbaum, 1985).

This research, presented in a limited way here, demonstrates important insights with regard to personality strengths. Understanding personality characteristics as strengths is facilitated when the characteristics themselves are conceptualized as strengths, per se. Such a

conceptualization can dictate specific theoretically relevant outcomes. In such a context, potential moderators can be readily specified and tested.

Self-Determination Theory

SDT (e.g., Deci & Ryan, 1991, 2000) is a broad theory of human motivation. Rooted in humanistic perspectives on personality, SDT views motives as largely available to awareness and as providing the essential nutriments for psychological growth. SDT suggests that we, as a species, have evolved to strive for three basic needs, autonomy, competence, and relatedness. Theoretically, these needs underlie intrinsic motivation. The satisfaction of these needs contributes, individually and additively, to well-being (e.g., Baard, Deci, & Ryan, 2004; Reis, Sheldon, Gable, Roscoe, & Ryan, 2000; Ryan, 1995).

Even though the desire to fulfill these needs is hypothesized to be universal (Deci & Ryan, 1991, 2000), research demonstrates variability in the degree to which people strive for them (e.g., Kasser & Ryan, 1993, 1996). A key reason for this variability is that external influences, such as societal values, parenting, and the media (Kasser, 2002), may convince people to strive for goals that do not satisfy these basic needs. Motivational tendencies that align with striving for and achieving these needs can be conceptualized as strengths. SDT would suggest that a person who seeks out intrinsic (versus extrinsic) goals would be more likely to experience positive outcomes, and there have been numerous studies to support this hypothesis (e.g., Kasser & Ryan, 1993, 1996; Ryan et al., 1999; Sheldon & Kasser, 1998).

Just as research has examined interactions among traits, interactions within the motivational realm have also been explored. For example, Schüler, Sheldon, and Fröhlich (2010) found that implicit *n*Ach interacted with SDT competence to predict motivational persistence. Researchers have also examined the interaction between explicit (or consciously avowed) and implicit motivation as a predictor of well-being (e.g., Hofer, Chasiotis, & Campos, 2006), and self-knowledge (Schultheiss, Patalakh, Rawolle, Liening, & MacInnes, 2011).

Personalized Goals

Psychologists have referred to goals by various names, including *personal projects, best possible selves, life tasks,* and *personal strivings* (King, 2008). All of these terms reflect the goals a person is trying to accomplish in everyday life. Having valued goals and making progress on them is certainly related to heightened well-being (Brunstein, 1993; Emmons, 1986). Optimal goal pursuit would seem to include striving for goals that are personally valued, specific, and moderately challenging. Further, these goals should share an instrumental relationship with each other—so that the pursuit of one goal facilitates the accomplishment of another (Emmons & King, 1988). Goal striving is particularly associated with enhanced psychological and physical well-being when goals are stated in an approach rather than avoidance manner (Elliot & Thrash, 2010).

Within any context, personally valued goals may provide a through line in life experience, a kind of idiosyncratic structure even in the face of chaos. This capacity of goals to give structure to life is explicitly acknowledged in Hope Theory (e.g., Snyder, 2004). Embedding the experience of hope in the language of goals, Snyder suggested that hope can be viewed as a strength that involves thinking of the self as the agent of goal-directed action combined with belief that one can generate many pathways to the achievement of particular goals.

The self-concordance model (Sheldon & Elliot, 1999) integrates daily goals in the context of the motivational framework proposed by SDT. This model suggests that although broad needs may be universal, optimal functioning requires that conscious daily goals serve the core needs of competence autonomy and relatedness and be enacted for intrinsic reasons. Research demonstrates that self-concordant goal strivers are ultimately more successful and experience greater levels of well-being as a result of that success (e.g., Judge, Bono, Erez, & Locke, 2005; Sheldon & Elliot, 1999; Sheldon & Houser-Marko, 2001). Cross-cultural research supports the role of self-concordance in well-being in the United States, China, South Korea, and Taiwan (Sheldon et al., 2004).

No matter how well chosen or doggedly pursued, goals are not a panacea for happiness or any other life good (see King & Burton, 2003, for a review). Setting a goal includes not only the promise of fulfillment but also the potential for failure. Investing in goals may mean experiencing worry over whether one will succeed (Pomerantz, Saxon, & Oishi, 2000) and experiencing disappointment when things do not go well (Kernis, Paradise, Whitaker, Wheatman, & Goldman, 2000). These feelings are part and parcel of self-regulation. Goal approaches to motivation typically place goals in the larger context of self-regulation. These perspectives stress the importance of monitoring progress, the role of naturally occurring affect as providing feedback in a system that governs goal directed activity. Recently, the notion that self-regulation

itself may be viewed as a strength has received a great deal of attention.

Self-Regulatory Strength

The ability to exert self-control over our impulses is vital to survival and the ability to thrive. Research has shown self-control to be linked to a number of important life outcomes, from mental health to personal relationships (for an overview, see Baumeister & Vohs, 2004; Carver & Scheier, this volume). One line of research views self-control, which has also been referred to as self-regulation or willpower, as a strength of finite capacity (Muraven, Tice, & Baumeister, 1998). From this theory self-control is a limited resource that can become temporarily depleted, which then requires rest (e.g., Tyler & Burns, 2008) or energy (e.g., Gailliot, Plant, Butz, & Baumeister, 2007) to build up again. Baumeister and colleagues liken this to a physical muscle, such that after exertion there is a period of fatigue with the self-control resource eventually returning to its prior strength. A wide variety of activities, from suppressing emotions to physical stamina, can be hindered by depleting this resource (e.g., Muraven et al., 1998; Tyler, 2008; Wright, Martin, & Bland, 2003). As the muscle metaphor would suggest, research has shown that *exercising* this self-control resource can strengthen it, buffering the effects of future exertion (e.g., Gailliot et al., 2007; Oaten & Cheng, 2007). In its simplest version, this model of self-regulatory strength does not incorporate individual differences, focusing instead on task-specific demands and depletion (or repletion) as general processes.

However, a recent meta-analysis on the strength model of self-control suggests that *trait* self-control may act as a moderator of the more circumstance-focused self-control (Hagger, Wood, Stiff, & Chatzisarantis, 2009). For instance, in one study high-trait self-control was associated with better grades, less psychopathological symptoms, higher self-esteem, and more secure interpersonal relationships (Tangney, Baumeister, & Boone, 2004). Similar findings have emerged around delay of gratification, another indicator of self-control (e.g., Funder, Block, & Block, 1983; Funder & Block, 1989; Mischel, Shoda, & Peake, 1988; Shoda, Mischel, & Peake, 1990).

It seems clear, then, that too little self-control can be problematic in numerous areas of life. But can someone have too much self-control? The answer depends on whether self-control is viewed as an outcome or a resource. When discussed as an outcome, too much self-control, or "overcontrolled behavior," can indicate poor self-regulation (e.g., Block, 2002; Funder & Block, 1989; King, 1996). The relative merits of engaging one's self-control muscle can only be truly evaluated in terms of the consequences of that engagement. Tangney et al. (2004) suggest that negative life outcomes do not arise from an abundance of the self-control but from the *misuse* of it.

STRENGTHENING EXPERIENCES

A final individual difference that might be considered a strength is experience itself. The notion that coping with difficulties can propel personality development has long been recognized (Aldwin & Gilmer, 2004; Loevinger, 1976). Erik Erikson's (1959/1980) theory of psychosocial development implies that grappling with particular crises leads to the development of strengths. For each of his crises, Erikson noted a basic virtue or strength that could emerge on its resolution. For instance, resolving the crisis of intimacy versus isolation, the young adult emerges with the sense of love and affiliation. The notion that actively grappling with life difficulties can be strengthening is represented in the very notion of positive reappraisal. The good that comes from negative life events may often be a sense of growth through that experience. In this section, we first examine the notion that adversity itself can be strengthening. Then we briefly touch on two potential strengths that might emerge from that experience, personal growth and ego development.

Adversity and Strength

Although generally experiences with adversity are considered stressors, theory and research have addressed the ways that adversity can lead to heightened resilience in the face of later stress. Dienstbier (1989, 1992) proposed that the experience of some adversity early in life could lead to a "toughening" against the effects of subsequent stressors. Constructs similar to toughness include "stress inoculation" (e.g., Lyons & Parker, 2007), "steeling" (e.g., Rutter, 2007), or immunization (e.g., Basoglu et al., 1997). All of these constructs share the notion that limited exposure to adversity can lead to toughening when that exposure is not prolonged and when there is an opportunity to recover. Toughening is thought to render the person less reactive to stressful circumstances, more emotionally stable, and to influence the appraisal of later stressors, such that these are viewed as less threatening to the individual. From Dienstbier's perspective, while prolonged and accumulated stress is certainly likely to take a toll, complete sheltering from any adversity might leave an organism unable to develop toughness or any sense of mastery over stressful circumstances. A recent study provides provocative support for these ideas.

Seery, Holman, and Silver (2010) examined lifetime adversity in a national longitudinal study spanning 4 years. Participants were asked about various life experiences at each wave, along with their psychological and physical well-being. The result showed the predicted U-shape curve for the association between accumulated life adversity and distress (as well as an inverted U-shape curve for early adversity and well-being). That is, those who reported no adversity were worse off than those who reported a small amount of adversity. Further, in prospective analyses, these researchers found that individuals who reported moderate amounts of lifetime adversity were less affected by a recent stressor than those who reported no adversity or a great deal of adversity.

These results are particularly notable for a few reasons. First, those who reported no lifetime adversity would seem unlikely to be demonstrating response bias (such as not wanting to admit negative things about their lives because they did so on the outcome measures). Further, the prospective analyses suggest that those who reported no stressful events early on did report some adverse events, eventually, suggesting that retrospective bias cannot wholly account for these effects.

What processes might account for the salubrious effects of early adversity? These might include a sense of mastery and efficacy in terms of dealing with stressful events. Individuals might gain a sense of control over coping and garner a more optimistic perspective engendered by the survival of previous bad times. Although this study examined early adversity as a potentially strengthening experience, other research has examined how difficult times at any point in life may promote strengths, including personal growth and personality development.

The processes underlying the contribution of negative life experiences to growth or personality development may be understood within the larger framework of personality development presented by Block (1982). Block applied the Piagetian processes of assimilation and accommodation to characterize personality development. In assimilation, existing cognitive structures are used to make sense out of the current environment. When experience is incongruent with existing cognitive structures, it is necessary to modify current ways of thinking. In accommodation, existing cognitive structures are modified or new structures are developed.

Among the benefits that individuals are thought to attain in grappling actively with a traumatic event are strength accrued through suffering, existential reevaluation, and a sense of psychological preparedness (Janoff-Bulman, 1992; Calhoun & Tedeschi, 2006). These are the difficult rewards of accommodation that, presumably, leave the person better suited to coping with future challenges. There are at least two potential psychological resources that have been suggested to emerge subsequent to life stressors and we review these in turn: personal growth and ego development.

Personal Growth or Posttraumatic Growth

In the aftermath of some negative life event, people commonly report having grown through the experience. Tedeschi and McNally (2011) define posttraumatic growth as positive personal change as the result of struggling with a trauma, and note that people report such growth in a variety of life domains in response to various traumatic events. Posttraumatic growth or personal growth can be thought of as a type of benefit-finding, in which the person sees the good that has come from a negative event, specifically because it has made him or her "a better person." As noted previously, resilience itself may not promote these growth processes. Resilient individuals may be less likely to appraise a traumatic event as, indeed, traumatic. The actual experience of an event as threatening and possibly overwhelming one's ability to cope would appear to be required for the experience of growth through that event (Levine, Laufer, Stein, Hamama-Raz, & Solomon, 2009). Self-reports of growth through stressful life events are related to heightened intrusive thoughts and appraisals of events as more severe, threatening, and stressful (Helgeson, Reynolds, & Tomich, 2006). At the same time, such reports are strongly related to psychological well-being (though not typically physical health) (Helgeson et al., 2006).

Whether individuals who report growing from life experiences have actually changed in some objective way remains an open and somewhat controversial question. Personal growth may be an inherently subjective variable. Perhaps because of this subjectivity (and its consequent reliance on self-report) studies of personal growth may always be open to a variety of alternative explanations, including positive illusions, cognitive dissonance, and response biases (Bonanno, 2004; Coyne & Tennen, 2010; Taylor et al., 2000; Tennen & Affleck, 2009). Certainly, feeling like one has grown through life events is a strong predictor of subsequent well-being. We might think

of such personal benefit-finding as a form of positive reappraisal which is a healthy way to cope, whether or not it reflects "actual" change.

There are outcomes or strengths that emerge from negative experiences that are quite apart from well-being. After some traumatic life event, a person might embrace more bittersweet conclusions, for instance that he or she understands his or her own limitations better, has realized the fragile nature of the human experience of meaning itself. Such realizations (though feeling like growth and seeming on the face to represent something like maturity) are not likely to lead to enhanced happiness. Nevertheless, these realizations may have value. To gain a sense of these potential strengths, researchers have turned to Jane Loevinger's (1976) construct of ego development.

Ego Development

Ego development refers to the level of complexity with which one experiences oneself and the world (Loevinger, 1976). The essence of the ego is "the striving to master, to integrate, and make sense of experience" (Loevinger, 1976, p. 59). As ego level increases, the individual's organismic frame of reference becomes more complex. At the earliest stages of ego development, individuals are dominated by impulses and engage in simplistic thinking. With development come the abilities to control and channel impulses. Ego development involves an increasing capacity to recognize conflict and experience ambivalence. People at the higher stages of ego development view the world through eyes that recognize the relative and contextualized nature of life's lessons. Research has shown that ego development is related to experiencing a variety of life events (e.g., Helson, 1992; Helson & Roberts, 1994). Ego development has also been linked to accommodative processing, as coded in stories of life transition. Such processing predicts ego development prospectively over two years (King, Scollon, Ramsey, & Williams, 2000).

Ego development differs from personal growth in a few notables ways, and indeed the two variables are not related (King et al., 2000). That is, people who say they have grown through a difficult life experience are not more likely to show ego development over time (King et al., 2000). Unlike posttraumatic growth, ego development is not measured using self-report but with a sentence completion task that assesses the complexity and sophistication with which individuals respond to various stems (Hy & Loevinger, 1996). Although personal growth may be relatively common, high levels of ego development are unusual (e.g., King et al., 2000). Moreover, unlike measures of personal growth, ego development is patently unrelated to well-being or psychological adjustment (Helson & Wink, 1987; King et al., 2000; Noam, 1998; Vaillant & McCullough, 1987).

Although it does not relate to well-being, ego development may relate to other strengths. Ego development is related to the capacity to acknowledge loss, to elaborate deeply on one's lost longings (King & Hicks, 2007). It relates to compassion, intellectuality, and tolerance (Helson & Roberts, 1994; Helson & Wink, 1987); articulateness, intuition and sublimation (Vaillant & McCullough, 1987); empathy, and the capacity for interpersonal connectedness (Carlozzi, Gaa, & Liberman, 1983; Pals & John, 1998). If it is a strength, ego development would appear to be a strength that "happens" to people, a strength of which they may not be aware, and a strength that emerges out of actively engaging with difficult life experiences (King, 2011).

WHAT HAVE WE LEARNED?

In this final section, we confront the question: Is there value in thinking about personality characteristics as strengths? We answer this question in two ways. First, we consider the implications of this examination of personality strengths for basic personality science, particularly in terms of the kinds of research questions that have not received sufficient attention to answer the question itself. Second, we consider more specifically, once again, the very notion of personality strengths.

Asking More Than Whether Personality Matters

Considering personality characteristics as strengths highlights compelling gaps in the literature. One might say that personality psychology has, perhaps as a result of Mischel's (1968) attack, developed a feverish dedication to one specific goal: demonstrating that personality, per se, matters to important outcomes (e.g., Ozer & Benet-Martinez, 2006; Roberts, Kuncel, Shiner, Caspi, & Goldberg, 2007). In their efforts to establish the fact of personality's important place in the science of human behavior, researchers may have missed important and more nuanced research questions that come to the fore in thinking about personality characteristics as strengths. These questions center around five issues: (1) individual difference moderators; (2) situational moderators; (3) the importance of situation selection; (4) specifying

mediators; and finally (5) the usefulness of null results. We discuss each of these issues in turn.

Individual Differences as Moderators

First, generally speaking, research has not examined the ways that personality characteristics combine to contribute to valued outcomes. With some notable exceptions reviewed previously, studies relating personality to outcomes have focused on straightforward "main effects." Here we echo calls by scholars from diverse perspectives for greater attention to potential interactions (Barrick & Mount, 2005; Carver & Connor-Smith, 2010; John & Srivastava, 1999; Winter, John, Stewart, Klohnen, & Duncan, 1998). Understanding the ways that individual differences, within and across levels of abstraction, combine to influence the quality of the connection between a person and his or her environment is crucial to understanding whether (and for whom) these might be considered strengths.

In addition, personality characteristics may interact with less global characteristics, skills, and abilities to serve as strengths (e.g., Witt & Ferris, 2003). For example, a recent study of car salespeople found that the relationship between extraversion and sales was moderated by sensitivity to interpersonal cues, such that extraverts who were more successful only if they were especially skilled at picking up on social cues (Blickle, Wendel, & Ferris, 2010).

Similarly, in a study of creative accomplishments, researchers measured creative ability and each of the FFM traits (King et al., 1996). Traits and ability contributed to self-reported accomplishments in unexpected ways. Although both creative ability and openness were positively correlated with accomplishments, these straightforward relations were qualified by interactions between openness to experience and creative ability as well as conscientiousness and creative ability. Only at high levels of openness did creative ability share a positive relation with accomplishments. Ability without the added level of interest in or valuing of creativity carried by high openness to experience led to few creative activities. Perhaps more interestingly, conscientiousness was related to heightened accomplishments by those low in creative talent (King et al., 2000), suggesting that hard work might compensate for lack of ability in the creative domain.

Situational Moderators

The contextual factors that might help to provide information about the conditional nature of the associations between personality variables and outcomes (informing their potential status as strengths) have not received sufficient attention. Research should focus on the situational factors that are associated with particularly good fit for various traits. Something beyond thought experiments ought to be available providing evidence for the potential usefulness of traits that have not been explored as such (e.g., introversion).

On a larger scale, sociocultural context may also moderate the expression of personality traits as strengths. For instance, Helson, George, and John (2011) have demonstrated that conscientiousness, openness to experience, and extraversion relate positively to women's work lives in the Mills Sample only in the years *after* the advent of the women's movement. In early adulthood, these traits were irrelevant to work-related variables, but when the larger social context changed, they emerged as significant predictors of occupational success.

Situation Selection

A third important issue to be addressed in examining the ways that traits may be viewed as strengths is understanding how people get into situations that make the best of their personalities. Research has shown at least modest relations between traits and occupational interests that make conceptual sense (Woods & Hampson, 2010). In a prospective study examining the association of adolescent personality traits with adult occupations, openness to experience was associated with artistic or investigative interests, conscientiousness with investigative interests, agreeableness with social occupations, and extraversion with enterprising interests (Judge, Higgins, Thoresen, & Barrick, 1999). These associations suggest that individuals may well seek out occupational roles that fit with their traits. Whether this fit relates to actual success in those settings remains an open question. Furthermore, we note again that traits do not exist in a psychological vacuum and that constellations of traits (and other characteristics) may determine the ultimate fit with any environment.

Indeed, as the research on creative accomplishments noted above would indicate, sometimes individuals succeed in domains that are not in keeping with this simple mapping of traits onto interests. How does a conscientious person wind up in a creative setting? Understanding how individuals select situations that are well suited to their personalities may require attention to a variety of variables at different levels of analysis in personality. For example, self-efficacy in particular domains may influence whether a person brings his or her personality to bear on a task, role, or occupation (Walsh, 2007). Hartman and Betz (2007) found that extraversion and conscientiousness were associated with a generalized self-efficacy applied across various occupational domains. In contrast, openness to experience showed more specific relationships to self-efficacy in artistic and intellectual pursuits. Neuroticism related to broad levels of low self-efficacy across all domains. It is not clear whether the "can do" spirit of extraverts and conscientious individuals (or the more pessimistic view of neurotic individuals) translates into actual work success (or failure).

Of course, once in a situation individuals may *alter* them. A set of studies by Geen (1984) examined how introverts and extraverts adjusted their environments to optimize their own performance. In those studies, performance on a cognitive task was measured while individuals were exposed to varying levels of noise. In the first study, participants were given the opportunity to adjust the volume of the noise they would experience while completing the tasks. Extraverts tended to turn the volume up, while introverts turned it down. For our purposes, the key finding is that in subsequent studies, extraverts performed better on the tasks when they were assigned to "average" extravert level of noise, whereas the introverts performed better when they were assigned to the "average" introvert level of noise. These results suggest an uncanny wisdom that might characterize the ways that traits lead individuals to adjust their own environments to suit these enduring characteristics in the service of task performance.

Within I/O psychology, Wrzesniewski (2003) introduced the notion of *job crafting,* which refers to the changes individuals can make within the constraints of a particular work role to transform a task into one that optimizes personal strengths. Job crafting implies that even within a particular situation, individuals can capitalize on whatever freedom they have to express their particular characteristics (Berg, Wrzesniewski, & Dutton, 2010). This discussion suggests that we might consider the ways that individuals differ in how they occupy life roles to optimize their performance as, for instance, an extraverted librarian, an agreeable divorce lawyer, or a neurotic romantic partner.

A final point in this regard is that in addition to selecting and altering situations, people actively create situations. It may be ironic that in a chapter entitled "Personality Strengths" so much has depended on the situation. And in some ways this focus may have led to the unfortunate perception that situations are simply "out there" waiting to be happened on by people with variously well-suited dispositions. Cultures and societies certainly play a large role in defining the situations or roles that individuals might occupy; nevertheless, people can *create situations*. They make homes, host parties, hold gatherings. They start businesses and create the culture of those businesses. They call meetings. They initiate activism. Sometimes they even design experiments. Understanding the role of personality in situation creation remains a broad topic for research.

Specifying Mediators

Personality variables do not magically promote adjustment in any domain. Rather their impact is mediated through the patterns of thoughts, feelings, and behaviors they foster. Understanding the specific mediators that underlie the links between personality and outcomes is clearly important. Self-perceptions may play an important role in channeling personality characteristics into situation selection. For example, in a study examining the leadership roles occupied by undergraduates in Greek organizations, the contributions of traits (i.e., extraversion and conscientiousness) and motivation (i.e., power motivation) on leadership positions was mediated by self-perceptions or personal identity as a leader (Harms et al., 2007).

The Informational Value of the Null Hypothesis

Finally, in any study of personality and behavior, three outcomes are possible. Personality can relate to behavior in a positive way, a negative way, or be entirely irrelevant. Each of these conclusions provides important information for understanding personality characteristics as potential strengths. Irrelevance may be the most dreaded outcome for the field, a kind of scholarly white flag, surrendering to the situation in the war over explained variance (Mischel, 2004). (Certainly, such results might be quite difficult to publish.) Nevertheless, evidence in favor of the null hypothesis might be helpful in understanding the conditions under which a proposed strength such as extraversion might not matter or when a proposed weakness such as neuroticism, might not carry a liability. (Personality psychology might curse the null result, but neurotics everywhere might celebrate.) Although not a conclusion that can be broached using null hypothesis significance testing, identifying outcomes in which personality *does not matter* must be recognized as an important path to scientific truth (Gallistel, 2009).

Is There Value in Thinking About Personality Characteristics as Strengths?

Although wrestling with the question of personality strengths, at the very least, helps to highlight these important potential questions for future research, it might be a simple exercise in cognitive dissonance that suggests that this was a worthwhile endeavor. As we come toward the end of this chapter, we note a number of problems inherent in thinking about personality characteristics in this way.

To begin, in some ways, treating personality characteristics as strengths seems to represent a kind of functionalism on steroids. Writing this chapter, we have grappled with the question of whether personality characteristics *should* be expected to be strengths. We have struggled as well with the notion that finding some strength value in a characteristic somehow promotes that characteristic to a higher place in the pantheon of personality psychology. Further it seems to imply the disturbing conclusion that some personalities are simply better than others. Apart from evolutionary notions of adaptiveness, *why should* personality characteristics have specific situational purposes? In some ways, thinking about personality characteristics as even domain-specific strengths has placed the onus on the wrong entity. If we assume (which some, of course, do not) that some aspects of the person are stable, why should we look at those stable, enduring aspects in the evaluative context of strengths? Perhaps a different question might be posed, one that takes seriously the existence of the broad and enduring characteristics that are typically thought of as personality: Given that we have these personalities in our world, what sorts of situations should we be creating to optimize human adjustment?

The goals that underlie the hunt for strengths in psychology would seem to concern two issues, facilitating self-improvement and improving the match between personalities and situations. Each of these goals seems either poorly suited to personality psychology or simply ill fated as applied to the relationship between personality and adjustment, as we now consider.

Self-Improvement

With regard to the first goal, personality variables would seem to be odd places to focus one's self-improvement goals. Some of these variables may be changeable and others quite a bit less so. Certainly, the dominant approach to personality (traits) would seem to be an unfortunate focus for any self-improvement program. Even if one focused only on social cognitive variables that might be more amenable to change, we offer a note of caution. The idea that one might psychologically "strengthen" oneself in a frenzy of self-improvement to some unequivocally optimal person seems to lurk in some research inspired by positive psychology. Conceptualizations of strengths that reflect unconditional goods would seem to be less nuanced than the likely reality of psychological dispositions would require. Human beings must always be open to bad news and negative emotions. That life will include both good and bad experiences is simply one of the invariants of human existence, like gravity. Until such time as this ceases to be the case, in order to function, human personality must maintain a capacity for responsiveness to life events. A functional human being is not an invulnerable fortress. It is, perhaps, a guarantee that no matter how strong one becomes, one can look forward to both joy and pain in human life.

There may be strength, indeed, in learning to live with these inevitabilities. Similarly, strength may come from learning to live with who we are, with all of the costs and benefits of those things about us that make up our personalities. Like attendees at an AA meeting, those interested in strengthening their personalities, might wish to be granted "the serenity to accept the things they cannot change, the courage to change the things they can, and the wisdom to know the difference."

Person-Situation Fit

Identifying personality characteristics as strengths might facilitate matching individuals with the optimal situations. This is a key goal of vocational testing and certainly a worthy circumscribed goal in some ways. In retrospect, however, it seems limiting and even trivializing to think about the relations of the broad range of personality characteristics to adjustment in this way.

We might consider, first, the ultimate value of person-situation fit. Is the optimal life one in which a person compulsively avoids situations that do not seem to "fit" his or her personality? Would we remove the misfits from their various ill-fitting situations? In families, groups, teams, occupational settings, and societies, there may be those who seem particularly poorly suited to the context. Nevertheless, they may add to the emotional richness, the diversity of opinion, the quality work, or contribute to their settings (however ill fitting) in vital ways. Thinking about the quality of a person-situation "fit" in terms of broad adjustment, we note that such outcomes typically depend on time. Whether a particularly good match has

been achieved may not be an outcome that we can assess until many years down the line (at a 50th wedding anniversary, a retirement ceremony, or a eulogy). Only then might we be able to say, in a sense like Aristotle, judging the Goodness of a life, "That really did work out pretty well."

Although the notion of optimizing the fit between personality characteristics and situational demands to benefit adjustment sounds straightforward, it may far underestimate the complexity of both sides of the equation. Even knowing all that we do about personality, and all that we could about situations, we might find it difficult to predict with any confidence the particular outcome of a particular person-environment interaction.

Perhaps this leads us to the crux of the problem with thinking about personality characteristics as strengths. Personality psychologists know very well that personality predicts behavior but we also know that it does so probabilistically and sometimes weakly. We may know a great deal about a person when we know their personalities, but we do not know, exactly, *what they are going to do* (not precisely, certainly not yet, and perhaps not ever).

Personality psychologists study a person's *typical* behavior. But what a person typically does and what he or she *is capable of doing* may be quite different things. What people are capable of may be a better demonstration of strengths than their typical behavior. Indeed, strength might be best demonstrated when one goes against one's natural impulses, those moments when the person "swims upstream": when an introvert gives a public speech, when an agreeable person rises up in righteous anger, or when a neurotic person plunges into a stressful task. At these moments, people might say, "This is not like me, but . . ." or "I am not this kind of person, however . . . ." These are fascinating moments for personality psychologists (though they are largely missing from the science of personality). These are moments when the people we study acknowledge that they have personalities and (to our delight) make it clear that those personalities, generally, direct their behavior. But these moments also tell us that people have the capacity to step outside of their typical patterns and behave in ways that are not so typical. In this sense, personality may not be so much a strength, as an obstacle to be overcome by the strong. The goal of fitting people to situations would seem to be the easiest life path possible. Ironically, then, we might identify our strengths so that we can pursue a life course that *requires little* in terms of actual strength.

Here we note, at last, that Allport's definition of personality cited at the beginning of this chapter included the word *unique* as a descriptor of adjustment. Here is where the modern approach to personality, perhaps, falls short in truly capturing the notion of personality strength. One might say we know a great deal about variables and how variables relate but we do not know nearly as much about persons (Lamiell, 2007). The kinds of research we have reviewed here tell us a great deal about how personality variables relate to adjustment "on average." That research cannot be "specified" down to the single case any more than a single case can be generalized to the wider population. Within an individual and his or her interaction with the environment, strengths, although constituted by constructs such as motives, traits, or skills, may be found in *unique adjustments* to the environment.

Is There a "Best Environment" for Every Organism?

We close this chapter by revisiting Cronbach's quote (1957, p. 679), "if for each environment there is a best organism, for every organism there must a best environment." This statement implies that life is a puzzle and that every personality is a puzzle piece, in need only of a perfectly fitting spot in that puzzle. If there is a best environment for every organism, then every constellation of characteristics can, indeed, be viewed as a strength (in that environment). This idea has an undeniable appeal. It has, as well, a sense of comforting fairness that, frankly, implies it is unlikely to be true. At the very least, if "a best environment" does exist for every organism, we note that organisms may differ in terms of the patience and effort required to locate that context.

In contrast to Cronbach, Kluckhohn and Murray (1953, p. 19) rather grimly observed, "the most difficult and painful function of personality (is) that of accommodating its expressions, needs, choice of goal-objects, methods, and time programs, to the patterns that are conventionally sanctioned by society." Clearly, Kluckhohn and Murray saw no such inevitable, serendipitous fit for most personalities. Indeed, given that the person is embedded in layers of social context, the outlook would not seem bright for finding one's ideal setting in whatever local environment one finds oneself.

We might claim a middle ground that for every person there is, at least, a "best possible" environment. That best possible or good enough environment might involve some jamming of the puzzle piece of personality in, wedging it tightly, even trimming some of its edges. Certainly, good lives can emerge out of the difficult compromise between personality and situations. Within those imperfectly suited situations are opportunities for fine-tuning. The possibility of creating situations that fit better looms as well, on the horizon.

REFERENCES

Aldwin, C. M., & Gilmer, D. F. (2004). *Health, illness, and optimal aging*. Thousand Oaks, CA: Sage.

Allport, G. W. (1937). *Personality: A psychological interpretation*. New York, NY: Holt, Rinehart & Winston.

Alvergne, A., Jokela, J., & Lummaa, V. (2010). Personality and reproductive success in a high-fertility human population. *Proceedings of the National Academy of Sciences, 107*, 11745–11750

Anusic, I., Schimmack, U., Pinkus, R. T., & Lockwood, P. (2009). The nature and structure of correlations among big five ratings: The halo-alpha-beta model. *Journal of Personality and Social Psychology, 97*, 1142–1156.

Ashton, M. C., & Lee, K., (2007). Empirical, theoretical, and practical advantages of the HEXACO model of personality structure. *Personality and Social Psychology Review, 11*, 150–166.

Ashton, M. C., Lee, K., Goldberg, L. R., & de Vries, R. E. (2009). Higher order factors of personality: Do they exist? *Personality and Social Psychology Review, 13*, 79–91.

Avolio, B. J., Rotundo, M., & Walumbwa, F. O. (2009). Early life experiences as determinants of leadership role occupancy: The importance of parental influence and rule breaking behavior. *The Leadership Quarterly, 20*(3), 329–342.

Baard, P. P., Deci, E. L., & Ryan, R. M. (2004). Intrinsic need satisfaction: A motivational basis of performance and well-being in two work settings. *Journal of Applied Social Psychology, 34*, 2045–2068.

Balliet, D. (2010). Communication and cooperation in social dilemmas: A meta-analytic review. *Journal of Conflict Resolution, 54*, 39–57.

Baltes, P. B., & Smith, J. (2008). The fascination of wisdom: Its nature, ontogeny, and function. *Perspectives on Psychological Science, 3*, 56–64.

Bandura, A. (2001). Social cognitive theory: An agentic perspective. *Annual Review of Psychology, 52*, 1–26.

Barrick, M. R., & Mount, M. K. (2005). Yes, personality matters: Moving on to more important matters. *Human Performance, 18*, 359.

Basoglu, M., Mineka, S. S., Paker, M. M., Aker, T. T., Livanou, M. M., & Gök, S. S. (1997). Psychological preparedness for trauma as a protective factor in survivors of torture. *Psychological Medicine: A Journal of Research in Psychiatry and the Allied Sciences, 27*, 1421–1433.

Baumeister, R., & Alquist, J. (2009). Is there a downside to good self-control? *Self and Identity, 8*, 115–130.

Baumeister, R. F., & Vohs, K. D. (Eds.). (2004). *The handbook of self-regulation: Research, theory, and applications*. New York, NY: Guilford Press.

Berg, J. M., Wrzesniewski, A., & Dutton, J. E. (2010). Perceiving and responding to challenges in job crafting at different ranks: When proactivity requires adaptivity. *Journal of Organizational Behavior, 31*, 158–186.

Bleidorn, W., Kandler, C., Hülsheger, U. R., Riemann, R., Angleitner, A., & Spinath, F. M. (2010). Nature and nurture in the interplay of personality traits and major life goals. *Journal of Personality and Social Psychology, 99*, 366–379.

Blickle, G., Wendel, S., & Ferris, G. R. (2010). Political skill as moderator of personality-job performance relationships in socioanalytic theory: Test of the getting ahead motive in automobile sales. *Journal of Vocational Behavior, 76*, 326–335.

Block, J. (1971). *Lives through time*. Berkeley, CA: Bancroft Books.

Block, J. (1982). Assimilation, accommodation, and the dynamics of personality development. *Child Development, 53,* 281–295.

Block, J. (2002). *Personality as an affect-processing system.* Mahwah, NJ: Erlbaum.

Block. J. (2010). The five-factor framing of personality and beyond: Some ruminations. *Psychological Inquiry, 21,* 2–25.

Bonanno, G. A. (2004). Loss, trauma, and human resilience: Have we underestimated the human capacity to thrive after extremely aversive events? *American Psychologist, 59,* 20–28.

Bonanno, G. A. (2005). Resilience in the face of potential trauma. *Current Directions in Psychological Science, 14,* 135–138.

Bonanno, G. A., Papa, A., Lalande, K., Westphal, M., & Coifman, K. (2004). The importance of being flexible: The ability to both enhance and suppress emotional expression predicts long-term adjustment. *Psychological Science, 15,* 482–487.

Bonanno, G. A., & Singer, J. L. (1990). Repressor personality style: Theoretical and methodological implications for health and pathology. In J. L. Singer (Ed.), *Repression and Dissociation* (pp. 435–440). Chicago, IL: University of Chicago Press.

Bonanno, G. A., Wortman, C. B., & Nesse, R. M. (2004). Prospective patterns of resilience and maladjustment during widowhood. *Psychology and Aging, 19,* 260–271.

Bouchard, T. J. Jr., & Loehlin, J. C. (2001). Genes, evolution, and personality. *Behavior Genetics, 31,* 243–273.

Bratko, D., Chamorro-Premuzic, T., & Saks, Z. (2006). Personality and school performance: Incremental validity of self-and peer-ratings over intelligence. *Personality and Individual Differences, 41,* 131–142.

Brummett, B. H., Boyle, S. H., Kuhn, C. M., Siegler, I. C., & Williams, R. B. (2008). Associations among central nervous system serotonergic function and neuroticism are moderated by gender. *Biological Psychology, 78,* 200–203.

Brunstein, J. C. (1993). Personal goals and subjective well-being: A longitudinal study. *Journal of Personality and Social Psychology, 65*(5), 1061–1070.

Buss, D. M. (2009). How can evolutionary psychology successfully explain personality and individual differences? *Perspectives on Psychological Science, 4,* 359–366.

Calhoun, L. G., & Tedeschi, R. G. (2006). The foundations of posttraumatic growth: An expanded framework. In L. G. Calhoun, R. G. Tedeschi, L. G. Calhoun, R. G. Tedeschi (Eds.), *Handbook of posttraumatic growth: Research & practice* (pp. 3–23). Mahwah, NJ: Erlbaum.

Caprara, G. V., Allessandri, G., & Eisenberg, N. (2012). Prosociality: The contribution of traits, values, and self-efficacy beliefs. *Journal of Personality and Social Psychology,* (in press at time of publication).

Caprara, G. V., Fagnani, C., Alessandri, G., Steca, P., Gigantesco, A., Sforza, L. L. C., & Stazi, M. A. (2009). Human optimal functioning: The genetics of positive orientation towards self, life, and the future. *Behavior Genetics, 39,* 277–284.

Carlozzi, A. F., Gaa, J. P., & Liberman, D. B. (1983). Empathy and ego development. *Journal of Counseling Psychology, 30,* 113–116.

Carver, C. S., & Connor-Smith, J. (2010). Personality and coping. *Annual Review of Psychology, 61,* 679–704.

Carver, C. S., Scheier, M. F., & Segerstrom, S. C. (2010). Optimism. *Clinical Psychology Review*. doi: 10.1016/j.cpr.2010.01.006

Chang, E. C., & Sanna, L. J. (Eds.). (2003). *Virtue, vice and personality: The complexity of behavior.* Washington, DC: APA.

Clore, G. L., & Palmer, J. (2009). Affective guidance of intelligent agents: How emotion controls cognition. *Cognitive Systems Research, 10,* 21–30.

Cohn, M. A., Fredrickson, B. L., Brown, S. L., Mikels, J. A., & Conway, A. M. (2009). Happiness unpacked: Positive emotions increase life satisfaction by building resilience. *Emotion, 9,* 361–368.

Coifman, K. G., Bonanno, G. A., Ray, R. D., & Gross, J. J. (2007). Does repressive coping promote resilience? Affective-autonomic response discrepancy during bereavement. *Journal of Personality and Social Psychology, 92,* 745–758.

Corr, P. J. (2008). Reinforcement sensitivity theory (RST): Introduction. In P. J. Corr (Ed.), *The reinforcement sensitivity theory of personality* (pp. 1–43). Cambridge, UK: Cambridge University Press.

Costa, P. T., & McCrae, R. R. (1988). From catalogue to classification: Murray's needs and the five factor model. *Journal of Personality and Social Psychology, 55,* 258–265.

Costa, P., & McCrae, R. R. (1985). *The NEO personality inventory manual.* Odessa, FL: Psychological Assessment Resources.

Costa, P., & McCrae, R. R. (2006). Age changes in personality and their origins: Comment on Roberts, Walton, and Viechtbauer (2006). *Psychological Bulletin, 132,* 26–28.

Coyne, J. C., & Tennen, J. H. (2010). Positive psychology in cancer care: Bad science, exaggerated claims, and unproven medicine. *Annals of Behavioral Medicine, 39,* 16–26.

Cronbach, L. J. (1957). The two disciplines of scientific psychology. *American Psychologist, 12,* 671–684.

Dahlsgaard, K., Peterson, C., & Seligman, M. E. P. (2005). Shared virtue: The convergence of valued human strengths across culture and history. *Review of General Psychology, 9,* 203–213.

Davydov, D. M., Stewart, R., Ritchie, K., & Chaudieu, I. (2010). Resilience and mental health. *Clinical Psychology Review, 30,* 479–495.

Deci, E. L., & Ryan, R. M. (1991). A motivational approach to self: Integration in personality. In R. Dienstbier (Ed.), *Nebraska symposium on motivation* (Vol. 38, pp. 237–288). Lincoln: University of Nebraska Press.

Deci, E. L., & Ryan, R. M. (2000). The "what" and "why" of goal pursuits: Human needs and the self-determination of behavior. *Psychological Inquiry, 11,* 227–268.

DeNeve, K. M., & Cooper, H. (1998). The happy personality: A meta-analysis of 137 personality traits and subjective well-being. *Psychological Bulletin, 124,* 197–229.

De Raad, B., Barelds, D. P, Levert, E., Ostendorf, F., Mlacić, B., Di Blas, L.,... Katigbak, M. S. (2010). Only three factors of personality description are fully replicable across languages: A comparison of 14 trait taxonomies. *Journal of Personality and Social Psychology, 98,* 160–173.

De Young, C. G. (2006). Higher-order factors of the big five in a multi-informant sample. *Journal of Personality and Social Psychology, 91,* 1138–1151.

Diener, E., & Lucas, R. E. (1999). Personality and subjective well-being, In D. Kahneman, E. Diener, & N. Schwarz (Eds.), *Well-being: The foundations of hedonic psychology* (pp. 213–229). New York, NY: Sage.

Dienstbier, R. A. (1989). Arousal and physiological toughness: Implications for mental and physical health. *Psychological Review, 96,* 84.

Dienstbier, R. A. (1992). Mutual impacts of toughening on crises and losses. In L. Montada, S. Filipp, M. J. Lerner, L. Montada, S. Filipp, & M. J. Lerner (Eds.), *Life crises and experiences of loss in adulthood* (pp. 367–384). Hillsdale, NJ: Erlbaum.

Digman, J. M. (1990). Personality structure: Emergence of the five factor model. *Annual Review of Psychology, 41,* 417–440.

Donnellan, M. B., Larsen-Rife, D., & Conger, R. D. (2005). Personality, family history, and competence in early adult romantic relationships. *Journal of Personality and Social Psychology, 88,* 562–576.

Edmonds, G. W., Jackson, J. J., Fayard, J. V., & Roberts, B. W. (2008). Is character fate, or is there hope to change my personality yet? *Social and Personality Psychology Compass, 2,* 399–413.

Eley, T. C., Sugden, K., Corsico, A., Gregory, A. M., Sham, P., McGuffin, P.,... Craig, I. W. (2004). Gene-environment interaction analysis of serotonin system markers with adolescent depression. *Molecular Psychiatry, 9,* 908–915.

Elliot, A. J., & Thrash, T. M. (2010). Approach and avoidance temperaments as basic dimensions of personality. *Journal of Personality, 78,* 865–906.

Edmonds, G. W., Jackson, J. J., Fayard, J. V., & Roberts, B. W. (2008). Is character fate, or is there hope to change my personality yet? *Social and Personality Psychology Compass, 2,* 399–413.

Emmons, R. A. (1986). Personal strivings: An approach to personality and subjective well-being. *Journal of Personality and Social psychology, 51,* 1058–1068.

Emmons, R. A., & King, L. A. (1988). Conflict among personal strivings: Immediate and long-term implications for psychological and physical well-being. *Journal of Personality and Social Psychology, 54,* 1040–1048.

Erikson, E. H. (1959/1980). *Identity and the life cycle.* New York, NY: Norton.

Exline, J. J., & Geyer, A. (2004). Perceptions of humility: A preliminary study. *Self and Identity, 3,* 95–114.

Exline, J. J., Single, P. B., Lobel, M., & Geyer, A. L. (2004). Glowing praise and the envious gaze: Social dilemmas surrounding the public recognition of achievement. *Basic and Applied Social Psychology, 26,* 119–130.

Fergus, S., & Zimmerman, M. A. (2005). Adolescent resilience: A framework for understanding healthy development in the face of risk. *Annual Review of Public Health, 26,* 399–419.

Finomore, V. S., Mathews, G., Shaw, T., & Warm, J. S. (2009). Predicting vigilance: A fresh look at an old problem. *Ergonomics, 52,* 791–808.

Flory, K., Lynam, D., Milich, R., Leukefeld, C., & Clayton, R. (2002). The relations among personality, symptoms of alcohol and marijuana abuse, and symptoms of comorbid psychopathology: Results from a community sample. *Experimental and Clinical Psychopharmacology, 10,* 425–434.

Folkman, S. (2008). The case for positive emotions in the stress process. *Anxiety, Stress & Coping, 21,* 3–14.

Frazier, P., Keenan, N., Anders, S., Perera, S., Shallcross, S., & Hintz, S. (2011). Perceived past, present, and future control and adjustment to stressful life events. *Journal of Personality and Social Psychology, 100,* 749–765.

Fredrickson, B. L., Cohn, M. A., Coffey, K., Pek, J., & Finkel, S. M. (2008). Open hearts build lives: Positive emotions, induced through meditation, build consequential personal resources. *Journal of Personality and Social Psychology, 95,* 1045–1062.

Fredrickson, B. L., Tugade, M. M., Waugh, C. E., & Larkin, G. (2003). What good are positive emotions in crises. *Journal of Personality and Social Psychology, 84,* 365–376.

Fry, P. S., & Debats, D. L. (2009). Perfectionism and the five-factor personality traits as predictors of mortality in older adults. *Journal of Health Psychology, 14,* 513–524.

Fulmer, A. C., Gelfand, M. J., Kruglanski, A. W., Kim-Prieto, C., Diener, E., Pierro, A., & Higgins, E. T. (2010). On "feeling right" in cultural contexts: How person-culture match affects self-esteem and subjective well-being. *Psychological Science, 21,* 1563–1569.

Funder, D. C., & Block, J. (1989). The role of ego-control, ego-resiliency, and IQ in delay of gratification in adolescence. *Journal of Personality and Social Psychology, 57,* 1041–1050.

Funder, D. C., Block, J. H., & Block, J. (1983). Delay of gratification: Some longitudinal personality correlates. *Journal of Personality and Social Psychology, 44,* 1198–1213.

Gailliot, M. T., Plant, E. A., Butz, D. A., & Baumeister, R. F. (2007). Increasing self-regulatory strength can reduce the depleting effect of suppressing stereotypes. *Personality and Social Psychology Bulletin, 33,* 281–294.

Galatzer-Levy, I., Bonanno, G. A., & Mancini, A. D. (2009). Reexamining identity continuity and complexity in adjustment to loss. *Self and Identity, 8,* 162–175.

Gallistel, C. R. (2009). The importance of proving the null. *Psychological Review, 116,* 439.

Garmezy, N. (1991). Resilience and vulnerability to adverse developmental outcomes associated with poverty. *American Behavioral Scientist, 34,* 416–430.

Geen, R. (1984). Preferred stimulation levels in introverts and extraverts: Effects on arousal and performance. *Journal of Personality and Social Psychology, 46,* 1303–1312.

Gray, J. A. (1982). *The neuropsychology of anxiety.* New York, NY: Oxford University Press.

Graziano, W. G., & Tobin, R. M. (2009). Agreeableness. In M. R. Leary & R. H. Hoyle (Eds.), *Handbook of individual differences in social behavior* (pp. 46–61). New York, NY: Guilford Press.

Gross, J. J., & John, O. P. (2003). Individual differences in two emotion regulation processes: Implications for affect, relationships and well-being. *Journal of Personality and Social Psychology, 85,* 348–362.

Gross, J. J., & Thompson, R. A. (2007). Emotion regulation: Conceptual foundations. In J. J. Gross (Ed.), *Handbook of emotion regulation* (pp. 3–24). New York, NY: Guilford Press.

Hagger, M. S., Wood, C., Stiff, C., & Chatzisarantis, N. L. D. (2009). The strength model of self-regulation failure and health-related behavior. *Health Psychology Review, 3,* 208–238.

Hall, J. A., Park, N., Song, H., & Cody, M. J. (2010). Strategic misrepresentation in online dating: The effects of gender, self-monitoring, and personality traits. *Journal of Social and Personal Relationships, 27,* 117–135.

Harms, P. D., Roberts, B. W., & Wood, D. (2007). Who shall lead? An integrative personality approach to the sudy of the antecedents of status in informal social organizations. *Journal of Research in Personality, 41,* 689–699.

Hartman, R. O., & Betz, N. E. (2007). The five-factor model and career self-efficacy. *Journal of Career Assessment, 15,* 145–161.

Helgeson, V. S., Reynolds, K. A., & Tomich, P. L. (2006). A meta-analytic review of benefit finding and growth. *Journal of Consulting and Clinical Psychology, 74,* 797–816.

Helson, R. (1992). Women's difficult times and the rewriting of the life story. *Psychology of Women Quarterly, 16,* 331–347.

Helson, R., George, L., & John, O. P. (2011). The "CEO" of women's work lives: How big five extraversion, conscientiousness, and openness predict 50 years of work experiences in a changing sociocultural context. *Journal of Personality and Social Psychology, 101,* 812–830.

Helson, R., & Roberts, B. W. (1994). Ego development and personality change in adulthood. *Journal of Personality and Social Psychology, 66,* 911–920.

Helson, R., & Wink, P. (1987). Two conceptions of maturity examined in the findings of a longitudinal study. *Journal of Personality and Social Psychology, 53,* 531–541.

Higgins, D. M., Peterson, J. B., Pihl, R. O., & Lee, A. G. M. (2007). Prefrontal cognitive ability, intelligence, big five personality, and the prediction of advanced academic and workplace performance. *Journal of Personality and Social Psychology, 93,* 298–319.

Hodges, T. D., & Clifton, D. O. (2004). Strengths-based development in practice. In A. Linley & S. Joseph (Eds.), *Handbook of positive psychology in practice* (pp. 256–268). Hoboken, NJ: Wiley.

Hofer, J., Busch, H., Bond, M. H., Campos, D., Li, M., & Law, R. (2010). The implicit power motive and sociosexuality in men and women: Pancultural effects of responsibility. *Journal of Personality and Social Psychology, 99,* 380–394.

Hofer, J., Chasiotis, A., & Campos, D. (2006). Congruence between social values and implicit motives: Effects on life satisfaction across three cultures. *European Journal of Personality, 20,* 305–324.

Hotard, S. R., McFatter, R. M., McWhirter, R. M., & Stegall, M. E. (1989). Interactive effects of extraversion, neuroticism, and social relationships on subjective well-being. *Journal of Personality and Social Psychology, 57,* 321–331.

Hy, L. X., & Loevinger, J. (1996). *Measuring ego development* (2nd ed.). Mahwah, NJ: Erlbaum.

Iwasa, H., Masui, Y., Gondo, Y., Inagaki, H., Kawaai, C., & Suzuki, T. (2008). Personality and all-cause mortality among older adults dwelling in a Japanese community: A five-year population-based prospective cohort study. *American Journal of Geriatric Psychology, 16,* 399–405.

Iwasa, H., Masui, Y., Gondo, Y., Yoshida, Y., Inagaki, H., Kawai, C., ... Suzuki, T. (2009). Personality and participation in mass health checkups among Japanese community-dwelling elderly. *Journal of Psychosomatic Research, 66*(2), 155–159.

Janoff-Bulman, R. (1992). *Shattered assumptions: Towards a new psychology of trauma.* New York, NY: Free Press.

Jensen-Campbell, L. A., & Malcolm, K. T. (2007). The importance of conscientiousness in adolescent interpersonal relationships. *Personality and Social Psychology Bulletin, 33,* 368.

John, O. P., & Srivastava, S. (1999). The big five trait taxonomy: History, measurement, and theoretical perspectives. In L. A. Pervin & O. P. John (Eds.), *Handbook of personality: Theory and research* (2nd ed., pp. 102–138). New York, NY: Guilford Press.

Judge, T. A., Bono, J. E., Erez, A., & Locke, E. A. (2005). Core self-evaluations and job and life satisfaction: The role of self-concordance and goal attainment. *Journal of Applied Psychology, 90,* 257–268.

Judge, T. A., & Erez, A. (2007). Interaction and intersection: The constellation of emotional stability and extraversion in predicting performance. *Personnel Psychology, 60,* 573–596.

Judge, T. A., Higgins, C. A., Thoresen, C. J., & Barrick, M. R. (1999). The big five personality traits, general mental ability, and career success across the life span. *Personnel Psychology, 52,* 621–652.

Kasser, T. (2002). *The high price of materialism.* Cambridge, MA: MIT Press.

Kasser, T., & Ryan, R. M. (1993). A dark side of the American dream: Correlates of financial success as a central life aspiration. *Journal of Personality and Social Psychology, 65,* 410–422.

Kasser, T., & Ryan, R. M. (1996). Further examining the American dream: Differential correlates of intrinsic and extrinsic goals. *Personality and Social Psychology Bulletin, 22,* 80–87.

Kaufman, J., Yang, B. Z., Douglas-Palumberi, H., Houshyar, S., Lipschitz, D., Krystal, J. H., & Gelernter, J. (2005). Social supports and serotonin transporter gene moderate depression in maltreated children. *Proceedings of the National Academy of Sciences, 101,* 17316–17321.

Kern, M. L., & Friedman, H. S. (2008). Do conscientious individuals live longer? A quantitative review. *Health Psychology, 27,* 505–512.

Kernis, M. H., Paradise, A. W., Whitaker, D. J., Wheatman, S. R., & Goldman, B. N. (2000). Master of one's psychological domain? Not likely if one's self-esteem is unstable. *Personality and Social Psychology Bulletin, 26,* 1297–1305.

King, L. A. (1996). Who is regulating what and why? The motivational context of self-regulation. *Psychological Inquiry, 7,* 57–61.

King, L. A. (2008). Personal goals and life dreams: Positive psychology and motivation in daily life. In W. Gardner & J. Shah (Eds.), *Handbook of Motivation Science* (pp. 518–532). New York, NY: Guilford Press.

King, L. A. (2011). The challenge of ego development: Intentional vs. active development. In A. Combs, A. H. Pfaffenberger, & P. W. Marko (Eds.), *The postconventional personality: Perspectives on higher development* (pp. 163–174). Albany: State University of New York Press.

King, L. A., & Burton, C. M. (2003). The hazards of goal pursuit. In E. Chang & L. Sanna (Eds.), *Virtue, vice and personality: The complexity of behavior* (pp. 53–70). Washington, DC: APA.

King, L. A., & Hicks, J. A. (2007). Whatever happened to "what might have been"? Regret, happiness, and maturity. *American Psychologist, 62,* 625–636.

King, L. A., Hicks, J. A., Krull, J. L., & Del Gaiso, A. K. (2006). Positive affect and the experience of meaning in life. *Journal of Personality and Social Psychology, 90,* 179–196.

King, L. A., McKee-Walker, L., & Broyles, S. (1996). Creativity and the five factor model. *Journal of Research in Personality, 30,* 189–203.

King, L. A., Scollon, C. K., Ramsey, C. M., & Williams, T. (2000). Stories of life transition: Happy endings, subjective well-being, and ego development in parents of children with Down Syndrome. *Journal of Research in Personality, 34,* 509–536.

Kluckhohn, C., & Murray, H. A. (1953). Outline of a conception of personality. In H. A. Murray & C. Kluckhohn (Eds.), *Personality, in nature, society and culture,* (2nd ed., pp. 3–32). New York, NY: Knopf.

Lamiell, J. T. (2007). On sustaining critical discourse with mainstream personality psychology. *Theory and Psychology, 17,* 169–185.

Levine, S. Z., Laufer, A., Stein, E., Hamama-Raz, Y., & Solomon, Z. (2009). Examining the relationship between resilience and posttraumatic growth. *Journal of Traumatic Stress, 22,* 282–286.

Loevinger, J. (1976). *Ego development: Conceptions and theories.* San Francisco, CA: Jossey-Bass.

Luthans F., Youssef, C. M., & Avolio, B. J. (2007). *Psychological capital.* New York, NY: Oxford University Press.

Lyons, D. M., & Parker, K. J. (2007). Stress inoculation-induced indications of resilience in monkeys. *Journal of Traumatic Stress, 20*(4), 423–433.

Lucas, R. E., & Baird, B. (2004). Extraversion and emotional reactivity. *Journal of Personality and Social Psychology, 86,* 473–485.

Luthar, S. S., Cicchetti, D., & Becker, B. (2000). The construct of resilience: A critical evaluation and guidelines for future work. *Child Development, 71,* 543–562.

Lyubomirsky, S., King, L. A., & Diener, E. (2005). The benefits of frequent positive affect: Does happiness lead to success? *Psychological Bulletin, 131,* 803–855.

MacDonald, C., Bore, M., & Munro, D. (2008). Values in action scale and the big 5: An empirical indication of structure. *Journal of Research in Personality, 42,* 787–799.

Mancini, A. D., & Bonanno, G. A. (2009). Predictors and parameters of resilience to loss: Toward an individual difference model. *Journal of Personality, 77,* 1805–1832.

Mancini, A. D., Pressman, D. L., & Bonanno, G. A. (2006). Clinical interventions with the bereaved: What clinicians and counselors can learn from the CLOC study. In D. Carr, R. M. Nesse, & C. B. Wortman (Eds.), *Spousal bereavement in late life* (pp. 255–278). New York, NY: Springer.

Manuck, S. B., Flory, J. D., Ferrell, R. E., & Muldoon, M. F. (2004). Socioeconomic status covaries with central nervous system serotogenic responsivity as a function of allelic variation on the serotonin transporter gene-linked polymorphic region. *Psychoneuroendocrinology, 29,* 651–668.

Martin, L. L. (2001). Mood as input: A configural view of mood effects. In L. L. Martin & G. L. Clore (Eds.), *Theories of mood and cognition: A user's guidebook* (pp. 135–157). Mahwah, NJ: Erlbaum.

Martin, L. R., Friedman, H. S., & Schwartz, J. E. (2007). Personality and mortality risk across the life span: The importance of conscientiousness as a biopsychosocial attribute. *Health Psychology, 26,* 428–436.

Masten, A. S. (2001). Ordinary magic: Resilience processes in development. *American Psychologist, 56,* 227–238.

McClelland, D. C. (1987). *Human motivation*. Cambridge, MA: Cambridge University Press.

McClelland, D. C., Koestner, R., & Weinberger, J. (1989). How do implicit and self-attributed motives differ? *Psychological Review, 96,* 690–702.

McCrae R. R. and Costa P. T., Jr. (1999). A Five-Factor Theory of personality. In L. A. Pervin & O. P. John (Eds.), *Handbook of personality psychology* (pp. 139–153). New York, NY: Guilford Press.

McCrae, R. R., & Costa, P. T., Jr. (2008). Empirical and theoretical status of the five-factor model of personality traits. In G. J. Boyle, G. Matthews, & D. H. Saklofske (Eds.), *The SAGE Handbook of Personality Theory and Assessment, Vol 1: Personality theories and models* (pp. 273–294). Thousand Oaks, CA: Sage.

McCrae, R. R., & John, O. P. (1992). An introduction to the five-factor model and its applications. *Journal of Personality, 60,* 175–215.

McCrae, R. R., & Sutin, A. R. (2009). Openness to experience and its social consequences. In M. R. Leary & R. H. Hoyle (Eds.), *Handbook of individual differences in social behavior* (pp. 257–273). New York, NY: Guilford Press.

McCrae, R. R., Yamagata, S., Jang, K. L., Riemann, R., Ando, J., Ono, Y., & Spinath, F. M. (2008). Substance and artifact in the higher-order factors of the big five. *Journal of Personality and Social Psychology, 95,* 442–455.

McFatter, R. M. (1994). Interactions in predicting mood from extraversion and neuroticism. *Journal of Personality and Social Psychology, 66,* 570–578.

Middeldorp, C. M., de Geus, E. J. C., Beem, A. L., Lakenberg, N., Hottenga, J. J., Slagboom, P. E., & Boomsma, D. I. (2007). Family based association analyses between the serotonin transporter gene polymorphism (5-HTTLPR) and neuroticism, anxiety and depression. *Behavior genetics, 37,* 294–301.

Miller, J. D., Lynam, D., Zimmerman, R. S., Logan, T. K., Leukefeld, C., & Clayton, R. (2004). The utility of the five factor model in understanding risky sexual behavior. *Personality and individual differences, 36,* 1611–1626.

Murray, H. A. (1938). *Explorations in personality*. New York, NY: Oxford University Press.

Mischel, W. (1968). *Personality and assessment*. New York, NY: Wiley.

Mischel, W. (2004). Toward an integrative science of the person. *Annual Review of Psychology, 55,* 1–22.

Mischel, W. (2009). From personality and assessment (1968) to personality science, 2009. *Journal of Research in Personality, 43,* 282–290.

Mischel, W., Shoda, Y., & Peake, P. K. (1988). The nature of adolescent competencies predicted by preschool delay of gratification. *Journal of Personality and Social Psychology, 54,* 687–696.

Muraven, M., Tice, D. M., & Baumeister, R. F. (1998). Self-control as a limited resource: Regulatory depletion patterns. *Journal of Personality and Social Psychology, 74,* 774–789.

Musek, J. (2007). A general factor of personality: Evidence for the big one in the five-factor model. *Journal of Research in Personality, 41,* 1213–1233.

Nettle, D. (2006). The evolution of personality variations in humans and other animals. *American Psychologist, 61,* 622–631.

Nichols, C., Sheldon, K., & Sheldon, M. (2008). Evolution and personality: What should a comprehensive theory address and how? *Social and Personality Psychology Compass, 2,* 968–984.

Noam, G. (1998). Solving the ego development–mental health riddle. In P. Westenberg, A. Blasi, L. D. Cohn, P. Westenberg, A. Blasi, & L. D. Cohn (Eds.), *Personality development: Theoretical, empirical, and clinical investigations of Loevinger's conception of ego development* (pp. 271–295). Mahwah, NJ: Erlbaum.

Noftle, E. E., & Robins, R. W. (2007). Personality predictors of academic outcomes: Big five correlates of GPA and SAT scores. *Journal of Personality and Social Psychology, 93,* 116–130.

Oaten, M., & Cheng, K. (2007). Improvements in self-control from financial monitoring. *Journal of Economic Psychology, 28,* 487–501.

O'Connor, D. B., Conner, M., Jones, F., McMillan, B., & Ferguson, E. (2009). Exploring the benefits of conscientiousness: An investigation of the role of daily stressors and health behaviors. *Annals of Behavioral Medicine, 37,* 184–196.

Ong, A. D., Bergeman, C. S., Bisconti, T. L., & Wallace, K. A. (2006). Psychological resilience, positive emotions, and successful adaptation to stress in later life. *Journal of Personality and Social Psychology, 91,* 730–749.

Ong, A. D., Bergeman, C. S., & Boker, S. M. (2009) Resilience comes of age: Defining features and dynamic conceptions. *Journal of Personality, 77,* 2–28.

Ong, A. D., Fuller-Rowell, T. E., & Bonanno, G. A. (2010). Prospective predictors of positive emotion following spousal loss. *Psychology and Aging, 25,* 653–660.

Ozer, D., & Benet-Martinez, V. (2006). Personality and the prediction of consequential outcomes. *Annual Review of Psychology, 57,* 401–421.

Pals, J. L., & John, O. P. (1998). How are dimensions of adult personality related to ego development? An application of the typological approach. In P. M. Westenberg, A. Blasi, & L. D. Cohn (Eds.), *Personality development: Theoretical, empirical, and clinical investigations of Loevinger's conception of ego development* (pp. 113–131). Mahwah, NJ: Erlbaum.

Pavot, W., Diener, E., & Fujita, F. (1990). Extraversion and happiness. *Personality and Individual Differences, 11,* 1299–1306.

Peterson, C., & Seligman, M. E. P. (2004). *Character strengths and virtues: A classification and handbook*. New York, NY: Oxford University Press/Washington, DC: American Psychological Association.

Pluess, M., Belsky, J., Way, B. M., & Taylor, S. E. (2010). 5-HTTLPR moderates effects of current life events on neuroticism: Differential susceptibility to environmental influences. *Progress in Neuro-Psychopharmacology & Biological Psychiatry, 34,* 1070–1074.

Pomerantz, E. M., Saxon, J. L., & Oishi, S. (2000). The psychological trade-offs of goal investment. *Journal of Personality and Social Psychology, 79,* 617–630.

Reis, H. T., Sheldon, K. M., Gable, S. L., Roscoe, R., & Ryan, R. (2000). Daily well being: The role of autonomy, competence, and relatedness. *Personality and Social Psychology Bulletin, 26,* 419–435.

Richardson, G. E. (2002). The metatheory of resilience and resiliency. *Journal of Clinical Psychiatry, 58,* 307–321.

Roberts, B. W., Jackson, J. J., Fayard, J. V., Edmonds, G., & Meints, J. (2009). Conscientiousness. In M. Leary & R. Hoyle (Eds.), *Handbook of individual differences in social behavior* (pp. 369–381). New York, NY: Guilford Press.

Roberts, B. W., Kuncel, N. R., Shiner, R., Caspi, A., & Goldberg, L. R. (2007). The power of personality: The comparative validity of personality traits, socioeconomic status, and cognitive ability for predicting important life outcomes. *Perspectives on Psychological Science, 2,* 313–345.

Roberts, B. W., & Mroczek, D. (2008). Personality trait change in adulthood. *Current Directions in Psychological Science, 17,* 31–35.

Roberts, B. W., O'Donnell, M., & Robins, R. W. (2004). Goal and personality trait development in emerging adulthood. *Journal of Personality and Social Psychology, 87,* 541.

Roberts, B. W., & Robins, R. W. (2000). Broad dispositions, broad aspirations: The intersection of personality traits and major life goals. *Personality and Social Psychology Bulletin, 26,* 1284–1296.

Roberts, B., Walton, K. E., & Viechtbauer, W. (2006). Patterns of mean level change in personality traits across the life course: A meta-analysis of longitudinal studies. *Psychological Bulletin, 132,* 1–25.

Roberts, B. W., Wood, D., & Caspi, A. (2008). Personality development. In O. P. John & R. W. Robins (Eds.), *Handbook of personality: Theory and research* (3rd ed., pp. 375–398). New York, NY: Guilford Press.

Romero, E., Villar, P., Luengo, M., & Gómez-Fraguela, J. A. (2009). Traits, personal strivings and well-being. *Journal of Research in Personality, 43,* 535–546.

Rush, C. C., Becker, S. J., & Curry, J. F. (2009). Personality factors and styles among college students who binge eat and drink. *Psychology of Addictive Behaviors, 23,* 140–145.

Rushton, J. P., Bons, T. A., & Hur, Y. (2008). The genetics and evolution of a general factor of personality. *Journal of Research in Personality, 42,* 1173–1185.

Rushton, J. P., & Irwing, P. (2008). A general factor of personality (GFP) from two meta-analyses of the big five: Digman (1997) and Mount, Barrick, Scullen, and Rounds (2005). *Personality and Individual Differences, 45,* 679–683.

Rushton, J. P., & Irwing, P. (2009). A general factor of personality in the Comrey personality scales, Minnesota multiphasic personality inventory-2, and the multicultural personality questionnaire. *Personality and Individual Differences, 46,* 437–442.

Rushton, J. P., Murray, H. G., & Paunonen, S. V. (1987). Personality characteristics associated with high research productivity. In D. N. Jackson & J. P. Rushton (Eds.), *Scientific excellence: Origins and assessment* (pp. 129–148). Newbury Park, CA: Sage.

Rutter, M. (2007). Resilience, competence, and coping. *Child Abuse and Neglect, 31,* 205–209.

Ryan, R. M. (1995). Psychological needs and the facilitation of integrative processes. *Journal of Personality, 63,* 397–427.

Ryan, R. M., Chirkov, V. I., Little, T. D., Sheldon, K. M., Timoshina, E., & Deci, E. L. (1999). The American dream in Russia: Extrinsic aspirations and well-being in two cultures. *Personality and Social Psychology Bulletin, 25,* 1509–1524.

Ryff, C. D., & Singer, B. H. (1998). The contours of positive human health. *Psychological Inquiry, 9,* 1–28.

Sarkar, U., Ali, S., & Whooley, M. A. (2009). Self-efficacy as a marker of cardiac function and predictor of heart failure hospitalization and mortality in patients with stable coronary heart disease: findings from the Heart and Soul Study. *Health Psychology, 28,* 166–173.

Saroglou, V. (2010). Religiousness as a cultural adaptation of basic traits: A five-factor model perspective. *Personality and Social Psychology Review, 14,* 108–125.

Schaubroeck, J. M., Riolli, L. T., Peng, A. C., & Spain, E. S. (2011). Resilience to traumatic exposure among soldiers deployed in combat. *Journal of Occupational Health Psychology, 16,* 18–37.

Schüler, J., Sheldon, K. M., & Fröhlich, S. M. (2010). Implicit need for achievement moderates the relationship between competence need satisfaction and subsequent motivation. *Journal of Research in Personality, 44,* 1–12.

Schultheiss, O., Patalakh, M., Rawolle, M., Liening, S., & MacInnes, J. J. (2011). Referential competence is associated with motivational congruence. *Journal of Research in Personality, 45,* 59–70.

Scollon, C. N., & Diener, E. (2006). Love, work, and changes in extraversion and neuroticism over time. *Journal of Personality and Social Psychology, 91,* 1152–1165.

Seery, M. D., Holman, E., & Silver, R. (2010). Whatever does not kill us: Cumulative lifetime adversity, vulnerability, and resilience. *Journal of Personality and Social Psychology, 99,* 1025–1041.

Seligman, M. E. P., & Csikszentmihalyi, M. (2000). Positive psychology: An introduction. *American Psychologist, 55,* 5–14.

Sharp, E. S., Reynolds, C. A., Pedersen, N. L., & Gatz, M. (2010). Cognitive engagement and cognitive aging: Is openness protective? *Psychology and aging, 25,* 60–73.

Shaw, T. H., Matthews, G., Warm, J. S., Finomore, V. S., Silverman, L., & Costa, P. T. (2010). Individual differences in vigilance: Personality, ability, and states of stress. *Journal of Research in Personality, 44,* 297–308.

Sheldon, K. M., & Elliot, A. J. (1999). Goal striving, need satisfaction, and longitudinal well-being: The self-concordance model. *Journal of Personality and Social Psychology, 76,* 546–557.

Sheldon, K. M., Elliot, A. J., Ryan, R. M., Chirkov, V., Kim, Y., Wu, C. . . . Sun, Z. (2004). Self-concordance and subjective well-being in four cultures. *Journal of Cross-Cultural Psychology, 35,* 209–223.

Sheldon, K. M., & Houser-Marko, L. (2001). Self-concordance, goal attainment, and the pursuit of happiness: Can there be an upward spiral? *Journal of Personality and Social Psychology, 80,* 152–165.

Sheldon, K. M., & Kasser, T. (1998). Pursuing personal goals: Skills enable progress but not all progress is beneficial. *Personality and Social Psychology Bulletin, 24,* 1319–1331.

Shoda, Y., Mischel, W., & Peake, P. K. (1990). Predicting adolescent cognitive and self-regulatory competencies from preschool delay of gratification. *Developmental Psychology, 26,* 978–986.

Shryack, J., Steger, M. F., Krueger, R. F., & Kallie, C. S. (2010). The structure of virtue: An empirical investigation of the dimensionality of the virtues in action inventory of strengths. *Personality and Individual Differences, 48,* 714–719.

Silver, R. C. (2009). Resilience. In D. Sander & K. Scherer (Eds.), *The Oxford companion to emotion and the affective sciences* (p. 343). New York, NY: Oxford University Press.

Silvia, P. J., Nusbaum, E. C., Berg, C., Martin, C., & O'Connor, A. (2009). Openness to experience, plasticity, and creativity: Exploring lower-order, high-order, and interactive effects. *Journal of Research in Personality, 43,* 1087–1090.

Smith, C. (Ed.). (1992). *Handbook of thematic content analysis for motivation and personality research.* New York, NY: Cambridge University Press.

Snyder, C. R. (2004). Hope and other strengths: Lessons from *The Animal Farm*. *Journal of Social and Clinical Psychology, 23,* 624–627.

Spangler, W. D. (1992). Validity of questionnaire and TAT measures of need for achievement: Two meta-analyses. *Psychological Bulletin, 112,* 140–154.

Srivastava, S., Tamir, M., McGonigal, K. M., John, O. P., & Gross, J. J. (2009). The social costs of emotional suppression: A prospective study of the transition to college. *Journal of Personality and Social Psychology, 96,* 883–897.

Stanton, A. L., Revenson, T. A., & Tennen, H. (2007). Health psychology: Psychological adjustment to chronic disease. *Annual Review of Psychology, 58,* 565–592.

Steel, P., Schmidt, J., & Shultz, J. (2008). Refining the relationship between personality and subjective well-being. *Psychological Bulletin, 134*(1), 138.

Stroud, C. B., Durbin, C. E., Saigal, S. D., & Knobloch-Fedders, L. M. (2010). Normal and abnormal personality traits are associated with marital satisfaction for both men and women: An actor-partner interdependence model analysis. *Journal of Research in Personality, 44,* 466–477.

Tangney, J. P., Baumeister, R. F., & Boone, A. L. (2004). High self-control predicts good adjustment, less pathology, better grades, and interpersonal success. *Journal of Personality, 72,* 271–324.

Tay, C., Ang, S., & Van Dyne, L. (2006). Personality, biographical characteristics, and job interview success: A longitudinal study of the mediating effects of interviewing self-efficacy and the moderating effects of internal locus of causality. *Journal of Applied Psychology, 91,* 446–454.

Taylor, S. E., Kemeny, M. E., Reed, G. M., Bower, J. E., & Gruenewald, T. L. (2000). Psychological resources, positive illusions, and health. *American Psychologist, 55,* 99–109.

Tedeschi, T. G., & McNally, R. J. (2011). Can we facilitate posttraumatic growth in combat veterans? *American Psychologist, 66,* 19–24.

Tennen, H., & Affleck, G. (2009). Assessing positive life change: In search of meticulous methods. In C. L. Park, S. C. Lechner, M. H. Antoni, A. L. Stanton, C. L. Park, S. C. Lechner, . . . A. L. Stanton (Eds.), *Medical illness and positive life change: Can crisis lead to personal transformation?* (pp. 31–49). Washington, DC: APA.

Terracciano, A., Lockenhoff, C. E., Crum, R. M., Bienvenu, J., & Costa, P. T. (2008). Five factor model personality profiles of drug users. *BMC Psychiatry, 8. Online open access journal.* doi: 10.1186/1471–244X-8–22

Tett, R. P., & Burnett, D. D. (2003). A personality trait-based interactionist model of job performance. *Journal of Applied Psychology, 88,* 500–517.

Tooby, J., & Cosmides, L. (1990). On the universality of human nature and the uniqueness of the individual: The role of genetics and adaptation. *Journal of Personality, 58,* 17–67.

Troy, A. S., Wilhelm, F. H., Shallcross, A. J., & Mauss, I. B. (2010). Seeing the silver lining: Cognitive reappraisal ability moderates the relationship between stress and depression. *Emotion, 10,* 783–795.

Trull, T., & Widiger, T. (2008). Geology 102: More thoughts on a shift to a dimensional model of personality disorders. *Social and Personality Psychology Compass, 2,* 949–967.

Tugade, M. M., & Fredrickson, B. L. (2004). Resilient individuals use positive emotions to bounce back from negative emotional experiences. *Journal of Personality and Social Psychology, 86,* 320–333.

Tyler, J. M. (2008). In the eyes of others: Monitoring for relational value cues. *Human Communication Research, 34,* 521–534

Tyler, J. M., & Burns, K. C. (2008). After depletion: The replenishment of the self's regulatory resources. *Self and Identity, 7,* 305–321.

Vaillant, G. E., & McCullough, L. (1987). The Washington University sentence completion test compared with other measures of adult ego development. *American Journal of Psychiatry, 144,* 1189–1194.

van der Linden, D., te Nijenhuis, J., & Bakker, A. B. (2010). The general factor of personality: A meta-analysis of big five intercorrelations and a criterion-related validity study. *Journal of Research in Personality, 44,* 315–327.

Vazire, S. (2010). Who knows what about a person? The self-other knowledge asymmetry (SOKA) model. *Journal of Personality and Social Psychology, 98,* 281–300.

Vetter, S., Dulaev, I., Mueller, M., Henley, R. R., Gallo, W. T., & Kanukova, Z. (2010). Impact of resilience enhancing programs on youth surviving the Beslan school siege. *Child and Adolescent Psychiatry and Mental Health, 4,* 1–11.

Vinberg, M., Mellerup, E., Andersen, P. K., Bennike, B., & Kessing, L. V. (2010). Variations in 5-HTTLPR: Relation to familiar risk of affective disorder, life events, neuroticism and cortisol. *Progress in Neuro-Psychopharmacology and Biological Psychiatry, 34,* 86–91.

Vinchur, A. J., Schippmann, J. S., Switzer III, F. S., & Roth, P. L. (1998). A meta-analytic review of predictors of job performance for salespeople. *Journal of Applied Psychology, 83,* 586.

Walsh, B. (2007). Introduction: Special issue on self-efficacy, interests, and personality. *Journal of Career Assessment, 15,* 143–144.

Walton, K. E., & Roberts, B. W. (2004). On the relationship between substance use and personality traits: Abstainers are not maladjusted. *Journal of Research in Personality, 38,* 515–535.

Watson, D., & Casillas, A. (2003). Neuroticism: Adaptive and maladaptive features. In E. C. Chang & L. J. Sanna (Eds.), *Virtue, vice, and personality: The complexity of behavior* (pp. 145–161). Washington/DC: American Psychological Association.

Watson, D., David, J. P., & Suls, J. (1999). Personality, affectivity, and coping. In C. R. Snyder (Ed.), *Coping: The psychology of what works* (pp. 119–140). Oxford, UK: Oxford University Press.

Waugh, C. E., Fredrickson, B. L., & Taylor, S. F. (2008). Adapting to life's slings and arrows: Individual differences in resilience when recovering from an anticipated threat. *Journal of Research in Personality, 42,* 1031–1046.

Way, B. M., & Gurbaxani, B. M. (2008). A genetics primer for social health research. *Social and Personality Psychology Compass, 2,* 785–816.

Widiger, T. A. (2009). Neuroticism. In M. Leary & R. Hoyle (Eds.), *Handbook of individual differences in social behavior* (pp. 129–146). New York, NY: Guilford Press.

Wiebe, R. P. (2004). Delinquent behavior and the five factor model: Hiding in the adaptive landscape. *Individual Differences Research, 2,* 38–62.

Winter, D. G. (1987). Leader appeal, leader performance, and the motive profiles of leaders and followers: An exploratory study of U.S. presidents and elections. *Journal of Personality and Social Psychology, 52,* 196–202.

Winter, D. G. (1988). The power motive in women—and men. *Journal of Personality and Social Psychology, 54,* 510–519.

Winter, D. G. (1991). A motivational model of leadership: Predicting long-term management success from TAT measures of power motivation and responsibility. *The Leadership Quarterly, 2,* 67–80.

Winter, D. G., & Berenbaum, N. B. (1985). Responsibility and the power motive in men and women. *Journal of Personality, 53,* 335–355.

Winter, D. G., John, O. P., Stewart, A. J., Klohnen, E. C., & Duncan, L. E. (1998). Traits and motives: Toward an integration of two traditions in personality research. *Psychological Review, 105,* 230–250.

Witt, L. A., Burke, L. A., Barrick, M. R., & Mount, M. K. (2002). The interactive effects of conscientiousness and agreeableness on job performance. *Journal of Applied Psychology, 87,* 164–169.

Witt, L. A., & Ferris, G. R. (2003). Social skill as a moderators of the conscientiousness-performance relationships: Convergent results across four studies. *Journal of Applied Psychology, 88,* 809–821.

Woods, S. A., & Hampson, S. E. (2010). Predicting adult occupational environments from gender and childhood personality traits. *Journal of Applied Psychology, 95,* 1045–1057

Wright, R. A., Martin, R. E., & Bland, J. L. (2003). Energy resource depletion, task difficulty, and cardiovascular response to a mental arithmetic challenge. *Psychophysiology, 40,* 98–105.

Wrzesniewski, A. (2003). Finding positive meaning in work. In K. S. Cameron, J. E. Dutton, & R. E. Quinn (Eds.), *Positive organizational scholarship: Foundations of a new discipline* (pp. 327–347). San Francisco, CA: Berrett–Koehler.

Zelenski, J. M., & Larsen, R. J. (1999). Susceptibility to affect: A comparison of three personality taxonomies. *Journal of Personality, 67,* 761–791.

Zhao, H., Seibert, S. E., & Lumpkin, G. T. (2010). The relationship of personality to entrepreneurial intentions and performance: A meta-analytic review. *Journal of Management, 36,* 381–404.

PART II

Social Psychology

CHAPTER 11

Social Cognition and Perception

GALEN V. BODENHAUSEN AND JAVIER R. MORALES

STEREOTYPING

Social cognition consists of the ensemble of mental processes that are specifically attuned to perceiving, understanding, and interacting with other people. These capacities are central to human psychology and have likely enabled our phenomenal success as a species. Comparative psychologists have advanced a "social intelligence hypothesis," which asserts that relatively sophisticated and flexible forms of cognition emerge within the context of social pressures associated with group living (Whiten & Byrne, 1997). Among primates (and also other mammals), there is clear evidence that brain size is correlated with social group size and with the complexity of the social relations that exist within a group (Byrne & Bates, 2007), consistent with the conclusion that bigger, smarter brains emerged from the selection pressures imposed by sociality (Cheney, Seyfarth, & Smuts, 1986; Cummins, 1998). As an intensely social species, humans have always survived and thrived via effective interpersonal coordination and cooperation (Leakey, 1978). The human mind emerged within social contexts defined by a complex fission-fusion structure in which individuals participate in multiple, nonoverlapping cooperative coalitions that arise and dissolve on a variety of time scales (Kummer, 1971). Exactly these sorts of dynamic social pressures are thought to have given rise to special capacities of social cognition (and, quite possibly, set the stage for more general forms of intelligence to emerge). To capitalize on the opportunities afforded by interdependence, as well as to avoid the potential dangers of exploitation

and abuse that social living imposes, individuals would profit immensely from the capacity to evaluate others in terms of their current intentions and goals, as well as their more enduring dispositions (e.g., trustworthiness, aggressiveness). Understanding the states and traits of others is perhaps the most central capacity at the heart of social cognition.

The vital importance of social coordination for an individual's survival and reproductive success has led some scholars to propose that the human mind contains a specific module (or set of modules) specifically devoted to social cognition (e.g., Adolphs, 1999; Cosmides & Tooby, 1992; Jackendoff, 1992). Cognitive modules are domain-specific, encapsulated, innate structures that have been selected by evolution because of the functional advantages they afforded ancestral humans (e.g., Barrett & Kurzban, 2006; Fodor, 1983). Jackendoff (1992) proposed the existence of a social cognition module that is fundamentally concerned with the identity of other actors and the nature of their relationship with the self, which he contrasted with a spatial cognition module that is fundamentally concerned with the identity of objects and their localization in space. Both modules could operate when we encounter another person, but they would have different concerns; the spatial cognition module would be concerned with locating the person in space and defining her physical dimensions, while the social cognition module would be concerned with the psychological aspects of the individual (what kind of person she is, how she is related to the perceiver). In line with the proposition that these processes unfold separately and can be dissociated from one another,

Macrae, Bodenhausen, Milne, Thorne, and Castelli (1997) showed that when people encountered others in a context in which perceivers' processing goals activated the spatial cognition module, relevant psychological characteristics (gender stereotypes) were not activated; however, when these same targets were encountered in a context in which processing goals activated the social cognition module, then gender stereotypes associated with the targets were indeed activated (thereby addressing the question "what kind of person is this?" that is of central concern to the module). The question of whether there is a specific, anatomically encapsulated brain structure responsible for social cognition remains controversial. However, it is certainly clear that attending to, thinking about, and understanding others is a central preoccupation of human beings, and our behavior is influenced in countless ways, for better or worse, by the social cues that we encounter throughout daily life.

The obvious starting point for an analysis of social cognition lies in the informational cues that are present in the social environment (e.g., the appearance and behavior of other persons, the characteristics of the social setting). However, the forms of social understanding that underlie social cognition rely not only on the informational cues that are momentarily present in the immediate context but also require the retrieval of relevant prior experiences from memory (e.g., Hastie et al., 1980). The rich legacy of past experiences with a relationship partner, for example, provides a wealth of context for interpreting the partner's current behavior. However, the impact of these past experiences depends entirely on how they have been encoded, stored, and retrieved from memory. The influence of the past is necessarily mediated by the qualities it has been imbued with in the mental representations that endure across time. These representations are not objective or complete records of prior experience; rather, they are subjective and selective impressions. Thus, a great deal of social cognition research has been concerned with understanding how mental representations of the social

world are constructed, stored, and later retrieved. A foundational assumption of this perspective is that social cognition involves a dynamic process integrating bottom-up, stimulus-driven input with top-down, memory-based representations. A simple schematic model of this perspective is provided in Figure 11.1.

As Figure 11.1 makes clear, social cognition research assumes that any impact of the social environment on behavior is mediated by intervening cognitive processes (for some noteworthy exceptions, see Dijksterhuis, Chartrand, & Aarts, 2007). As such, researchers in this tradition have built theoretical models that focus on the infamous "black box" that was so vigorously eschewed by behaviorism, postulating particular forms of mental representation and various processes governing their creation and use. Figure 11.1 provides some common examples of the mental structures and processes that have been invoked in social-cognitive theory. Although social cognition researchers have not hesitated to venture into the black box, they have generally done so with the clear understanding that the hypothesized mental entities and events that are of interest are not necessarily amenable to direct introspection. As Nisbett and Wilson (1977) documented, people often make choices that are clearly influenced by situational features, yet they show no evidence of being aware of these influences. It has become abundantly clear that quite sophisticated forms of information acquisition occur in the absence of conscious awareness (Lewicki, Hill, & Czyzewska, 1992), so there is zero chance that individuals will have a complete and accurate introspective accounting of the stimulus properties and relevant mental processes underlying their behavior. Rather than regarding such evidence as proof of the irrelevance of the black box, social cognition researchers instead regarded these demonstrations as raising a challenge to identify methods for studying mental processes that go beyond a naïve faith in introspective self-reports (for a recent overview, see Klauer, Voss, & Stahl, 2011).

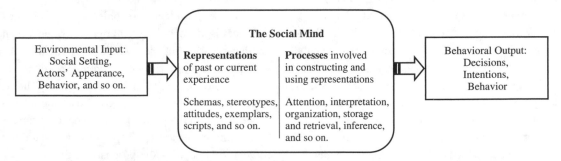

Figure 11.1   A schematic overview of the purview of social cognition research

Two broad methodological strategies have characterized the study of the social mind. The first involves the development of indirect measures of hypothesized mental structures and processes. These techniques typically involve the assessment of performance (in terms of both speed and accuracy) on a variety of cognitive tasks such as categorization, recognition, or recall. By examining memory for previously encountered information (e.g., memory omissions, intrusions of nonpresented information, the serial ordering or clustering of items; see Srull, 1984), researchers can draw inferences about both mental contents and processes (e.g., Jacoby, 1998). A wide variety of techniques have focused on simple categorization tasks (Fazio & Olson, 2003), with the Implicit Association Test (IAT; Greenwald, McGhee, & Schwartz, 1998) being perhaps the most well known. In this task, participants are asked to classify two distinct sets of stimuli by using two response buttons. For example, they might be asked to classify names (e.g., Brian, Barbara) as male or female, while also classifying trait words as being related to leaders or followers (e.g., assertive, supportive). On some trial blocks, the male names and the leadership traits require the same response (e.g., pushing the left button), while in other blocks the male names and the follower traits share the same response. If participants are slower or more error-prone in performing the task in one blocking condition versus the other, this implies that one of these response pairings is more "natural" to them—that is, there is already a mental association between the two concepts that makes it easier to perform the task when they go together. Researchers have indeed shown that many individuals exhibit automatic gender stereotypes linking men to leadership and women to followership (e.g., Dasgupta & Asgari, 2004). Techniques such as these do not require participants to have accurate insights into the workings of their own minds. In fact, they raise very interesting questions regarding how and when people's automatic mental associations in fact do align with their self-reported attitudes, stereotypes, and beliefs (see Greenwald & Nosek, 2009).

The second broad methodological strategy involves the use of experimental manipulations that activate or inhibit particular mental processes (Bargh & Chartrand, 2000). Researchers have used a variety of priming techniques to activate particular mental contents (such as stereotypes, Devine, 1989; or self-construals, Gardner, Gabriel, & Lee, 1999) or to initiate particular mental processes (such as counterfactual thinking, Galinsky & Moskowitz, 2000; or goal pursuit, Shah, 2005). These techniques exert their effects even when the priming stimuli are presented subliminally; moreover, even when supraliminally presented, experimental primes commonly exert effects that participants do not consciously intend. Thus, evidence based on priming effects is also able to document mental processes without requiring conscious, accurate self-insight. Researchers also utilize experimental manipulations to block the operation of certain types of mental processes, typically ones that are relatively conscious, verbal, and effortful. This blocking can be achieved by imposing a "cognitive load" (i.e., an additional task that must be performed). Because conscious verbal processes require attentional resources (Baddeley, 1992), they can be undermined by requiring participants to engage in a task that usurps these resources (such as counting backward from 100 by 3s). When a cognitive load is imposed, it reveals mental and behavioral processes that might otherwise be masked or controlled (e.g., for reasons of social desirability). For instance, Ward and Mann (2000) showed that imposing a cognitive load led to disinhibited eating among chronic dieters. Such findings document both the presence of an underlying impulse to act as well as the role of effortful self-regulation in controlling the impulse, albeit without relying on self-reports or assuming self-insight. Although this sampler of methodological strategies has been necessarily brief, it provides a general sense of the social-cognitive researcher's forays into the black box. By creatively developing measures and manipulations of hypothesized social-cognitive processes, researchers have been able to build empirical arguments for their theoretical conceptualizations using objective, quantitative observations rather than subjective introspections.

The methodological toolbox that we have just sketched out has been used to pursue a dizzying variety of empirical questions and theoretical models. Beyond a general commitment to understanding social behavior as being mediated by cognitive processes that link environmental input to behavioral output, there is no consensual set of core theoretical assumptions at the heart of the social cognition perspective. Debates have raged concerning the basic nature of mental representations and the fundamental processes underlying social phenomena (e.g., whether they merely involve "cold," cognitive mechanisms versus recruiting "hot," motivational ones). As one example, the hindsight bias—the tendency to think that we would have predicted a known outcome all along—has been explained via distinct motivational (e.g., M. Pezzo & Pezzo, 2007) and cognitive (e.g., Blank & Nestler, 2007) mechanisms. The diversity of substantive and theoretical concerns that fall under the rubric of "social cognition" is far too extensive to be meaningfully summarized here. Instead, in the remainder of this chapter we address a set of core issues, focusing first on core assumptions about the nature of mental representations, then on core assumptions concerning the nature of mental processes. Next, we consider the core substantive questions that are addressed by social cognition research: (a) how social perceivers construe the states and traits of other individuals, and (b) how they construe social relationships. We wrap up by discussing cross-cultural variations in social cognition and identifying some important avenues for future research.

PRINCIPLES OF MENTAL REPRESENTATION

A key idea of the social cognition perspective is the assumption that social behavior is a function of social cues *as they are represented in the mind,* rather than as they exist objectively in the social environment (e.g., Lingle & Ostrom, 1979; Srull & Wyer, 1983). Rather than functioning like a video camera, straightforwardly recording representations of experience, the mind functions in much more complex and proactive ways. As a consequence, social representations can and do deviate from veridicality. Three general processes governing these deviations have been extensively researched.

1. **Attentional filtering**. The world presents us with a wide array of stimulus input, far more than we could ever consciously process. Fortunately, much of this input is irrelevant to our goals and priorities, so it can be safely ignored. However, the selectivity of attentional processing means that our representations of social entities are always incomplete, whether in significant or merely trivial ways (for a review, see Bodenhausen & Hugenberg, 2009). Research on inattentional blindness has shown that even something as remarkable as a person in a gorilla suit walking through a basketball game can fail to be noticed if one's attention is focused intently on the basketball play (Simons & Chabris, 1999). Attentional filtering inevitably produces memory representations containing less than a full recreation of the social environment.
2. **Inference**. Perceivers routinely go beyond the information provided in stimulus input, drawing on prior experience and general world knowledge to elaborate on available cues. Inferences often arise when relevant information is missing or ambiguous (for a review, see Bodenhausen & Peery, 2009). For example, when

reading about a doctor whose gender is not specified, people often unwittingly assume that the individual is male. Indeed, unless otherwise specified, male is the default assumption made about a person's gender (Hamilton, 1991). Even when gender is specified, if it conflicts with traditional gender roles, it may later be misremembered in the traditional way (e.g., an incidentally encountered female doctor might later be misremembered as having been male; see Signorella & Liben, 1984). Inference processes can enrich social representations considerably, but they do so at the risk of misrepresenting the actual reality of the matter.

3. **Motivated distortion**. The representations that perceivers construct are subject to motivational pressures that transform objective reality into more desirable and gratifying forms. This process can occur via the previously mentioned mechanisms of attentional bias and inference, as well as others (e.g., Kunda, 1990). Perhaps the most widely studied form of motivational distortion is self-enhancement bias (Leary, 2007), in which perceivers form social representations that provide flattering images of the self. For example, people may erroneously recall having earned a higher grade point average in college than they actually did (Gramzow & Willard, 2006). When representations bear on any of a wide variety of fundamental motives (e.g., feeling safe and managing anxiety, feeling connected to others), they become vulnerable to being shaped by the distortions of wishful thinking (for a review, see Krizan & Windschitl, 2007).

The fact that two different individuals can have dramatically different representations of the same event (e.g., Hastorf & Cantril, 1954) clearly establishes that models of mental representation must accommodate mechanisms that go beyond a simple recording of the environmental input. In response to this challenge, social-cognitive theorists have proposed a variety of representational formats, including associative networks, schemas, and many others. Such constructs are metaphorical, in the sense that no strong claims are necessarily made about their literal existence in the central nervous system, which is the presumptive repository of our actual mental representations. Nevertheless, they can be quite scientifically useful to the extent that they capture important properties of how the social mind works, particularly if their implications point researchers to the discovery and specification of new phenomena. Smith (1998) provided an encompassing review of the different perspectives on mental representation taken by social cognition researchers, focusing on four principal hypothesized formats. We briefly summarize each one in turn.

Associative Network Models

Rooted in the thinking of British empiricist philosophers such as Locke and Hume, associative network models (e.g., Wyer & Carlston, 1994) assume that mental representations consist of simple associations between low-level concepts, called nodes. A target person can be mentally represented by a set of feature nodes (descriptors of the person's features, behavior, etc.) that are linked to a central target-identity node in a network, with the specific pattern and strength of the associative connections among these nodes varying to reflect the importance and centrality of different features, the extent to which the features have been experienced simultaneously, and so on. Principles of associative learning are assumed to guide the formation of the links in the network. Once established, associative networks are assumed to operate on a principle of *spreading activation* (Collins & Loftus, 1975). When a representation stored in long-term memory enters working memory (as, for example, when one encounters a neighbor), the representation is said to be activated, and the activation spreads from the central, identifying node (e.g., "my neighbor Paul") to associated features defining the person (e.g., "loud," "talkative"). Greater activation flows to those feature nodes that are more strongly linked to the central node.

Within this core set of assumptions, a variety of specific associative network models have been proposed by social cognition researchers. For example, Fazio's (1986) model of attitude representation is founded on the assumption that attitudes are defined by a simple associative connection between a node representing the attitude object and an evaluative node. The strength of the link between these nodes captures the strength of the attitude (i.e., the likelihood that it will be spontaneously activated when the attitude object is encountered). Starting from these minimal representational assumptions, Fazio constructed a model of attitude-behavior relations that has proven to provide a powerful account of much of the variance in this relationship (Fazio, 2007). Associative network models have also been used to conceptualize the process of stereotyping (e.g., Devine, 1989; Dovidio, Evans, & Tyler, 1986). In these approaches, representations of social groups are thought to consist of a central, group identity node (e.g., "Germans") that is connected to a variety of attribute nodes (e.g., "efficient") that characterize the group. The most central or prototypical characteristics of

the group have stronger connecting pathways to the central node. Thus, activation is likely to spread to these nodes, even in cases where there is no direct evidence regarding the relevance or applicability of these traits to a given person. A new German acquaintance, Heinrich, might be assumed to be efficient, without any corroborating evidence, simply because activation spreads from "Heinrich" to "German" to closely linked traits, including "efficient." In an influential demonstration, Devine (1989) showed that subliminally activating the stereotype of African Americans led to the increased accessibility of unmentioned characteristics associated with the group (e.g., hostility) that presumably came to mind via spreading activation, and which then exerted a marked influence on how a target's ambiguous behavior was interpreted. Beyond these two examples, many other specific variants of associative networks models have proven to be fruitful in social cognition theories.

Schemas

Rooted in the thinking of Continental philosophers (especially Kant), schema theories hold that simple associations are insufficient to account for the complexity of social understanding. Instead, schema models favor the view that mental representations are typically richly structured, containing more organizing constraints than would be assumed in a simple associationistic account. For example, schemas are assumed to contain information specifying spatial and causal relations among the various feature-elements comprising them, rather than merely linking these features to some central node. The structure of a given schema is assumed to be abstracted from multiple experiences with the type of entity being represented. For example, after experiencing several classical music concerts, a person may develop an "orchestra schema" that contains the generalities that were evident across these experiences. Such a schema would consist of more than just associated features (e.g., violins, woodwind instruments, conductor); it would also specify the typical spatial relationships of these elements with one another and perhaps also identifying causal connections between the orchestral elements and the music that is produced. However, it would not specify elements that vary unpredictably across instances (e.g., the height of the conductor). In essence, the elements of the schema represent the general case of a given class of entity, and a schema can be applied in understanding a specific example of that class through the process of *instantiation*. Instantiation involves the use of general, schematic expectations to structure the representation of a newly encountered, particular instance. When a schema is activated for this purpose, it is assumed to be activated in its entirety (all-or-none activation), in contrast to associative networks, which assume that different parts of the network can be activated to varying degrees, depending on how activation spreads.

Many types of social schemas have been proposed by researchers, including gender schemas, social role schemas, self-schemas, and others (see Fiske & Taylor, 1991). An emphasis of these various applications is on the use of the generic knowledge contained in the schema to fill in gaps in the informational input and clarify the meaning of ambiguous cues (Bodenhausen, 1992). Although in many circumstances these functions should aid adaptive functioning, there are certainly also well-documented cases of dysfunctional schemas. For example, Dodge (2006) argued that many juvenile delinquents possess a maladaptive interpersonal schema that tends to lock them into self-fulfilling cycles of conflict. Presumably based on their past experiences, these individuals expect interpersonal exchanges to involve hostility and disrespect being directed at themselves, and they readily construe ambiguous interactions as being an instantiation of this generalized interpersonal conflict schema. Although invoked by scholars less frequently in recent years, the schema construct has enjoyed wide currency in several domains and has been especially useful for understanding the (re)constructive aspects of social representation.

Exemplars

Whereas schema theories emphasize general cases and generic understandings, exemplar models (e.g., Smith & Zárate, 1992) assume that mental representations are grounded in specific instances. According to this approach, when the mind has cause to use any particular concept, it retrieves a set of relevant instances and extrapolates on the spot from this sample of exemplars. The key processing principle is parallel activation of multiple exemplars from memory, depending on any given exemplar's similarity to currently salient retrieval cues. For example, the category "Germans" would be represented not by some general associations with the category label or schematically organized generic knowledge, but by the set of specific category members that comes to mind when one contemplates the general category. An important emphasis of this approach is on the flexibility and context-sensitivity of mental representations, because it is assumed that one's representation of "Germans" is not some static mental entity, but rather is likely to shift,

depending on which particular exemplars of the category happen to come to mind. In keeping with this idea, past research has shown that general judgments about the category "African Americans" are influenced by the activation (or not) of thoughts about particularly well-liked members of this category in an immediately preceding, but ostensibly unrelated, context (Bodenhausen, Schwarz, Bless, & Wänke, 1995).

Exemplar theories have often been pitted against schema theories, within the context of debates about the degree of abstraction versus concreteness inherent in our stored representations of the social world. Critical tests have proven elusive, and several theorists have adopted the position that social representations can take the form of both specific instances and generic expectations. Sherman (1996) argued that new social concepts (e.g., a newly encountered social group) heavily emphasize exemplar-based representations, but over time, as a generic pattern comes to be discerned, these same concepts are more likely to be represented schematically. Park, Judd, and Ryan (1991) argued that different representational formats are likely to apply to different kinds of social concepts. In particular, they argued that representations of one's own ingroups are likely to incorporate specific, individuated exemplars, while representations of outgroups are likely to rely on schematic generalizations. These examples highlight the fact that one need not assume that the different representational formats are mutually exclusive.

Distributed Memory Models

Distributed memory models constitute the most recent of these representational models, and they espouse a view in which mental representations are conceived of as transitory states, rather than enduring entities (Smith, 1998). In this approach, familiar concepts like nodes (or units), connections, and the flow of activation are invoked, but the emphasis is on low-level units that are assumed to participate, via different patterns of activation, in multiple distinct representational states. A commonly invoked analogy is to the pixels in an image. Any given pixel conveys only very simple information, but when a large set of pixels is activated in a particular way, a very meaningful higher-order concept comes into focus. The same pixel, activated in the same way, can participate in the construction of multiple, highly diverse concepts. Many theorists find this approach—with its emphasis on the integration of input across a number of low-level processing units—to have greater plausibility as an approximation of how neural networks in the mind actually work (e.g., McLeod, Plunkett, & Rolls, 1998). As noted, these approaches are newer and have not been as widely influential in social cognition research, but they have proven to be illuminating in several domains, including trait attributions and cognitive dissonance (for a review, see Van Overwalle, 2011).

These diverse perspectives on mental representation each offer a set of insights about how the mind works, and in that sense that they have proven to be theoretically useful metaphors about the workings of the social mind. At the same time, as Smith (1998) cautioned, we can often be blinded by our representational metaphors, potentially overlooking important principles of social cognition that happen to be at odds with our starting assumptions. For this reason it is important to keep these assumptions explicitly in mind and reexamine them periodically. Although cracking the mysteries of the black box is proving to be a tractable problem, it is certainly fraught with dangers for theorists who take their conceptual metaphors too seriously.

AUTOMATIC AND CONTROLLED PROCESSES IN SOCIAL COGNITION

As an alternative to focusing on assumptions about mental structures, some theorists have focused instead on the identification of the fundamental mental processes underlying social cognition. Of course, this difference of emphasis is a matter of degree, as theories of mental representation typically incorporate a variety of assumptions about mental process. The process-focused approach has come to dominate recent theoretical developments in social cognition research. The precursors of contemporary social cognition were early research on attribution and person perception that generally assumed that social impressions emerge from the rational use of relevant informational cues. Although these approaches were typically mute with respect to the specific mental processes involved in forming attributions, they were often taken to imply that some form of effortful deliberation underlies the emergence of social impressions. The emergence of social cognition as a distinct theoretical perspective in the 1980s marked a turning point at which the specification of mediating cognitive processes underlying causal attributions, impression formation, and other social perceptions became a matter of paramount importance. Out of all the various ways one could analyze mental processes, the distinction that captured the imagination of the field

is the one between automatic and deliberative mental processes (Chaiken & Trope, 1999). We return to this issue several times throughout the remainder of this chapter; here, we briefly sketch out the basic elements of the distinction.

Bargh has championed the perspective that most mental processes occur automatically, and he has spelled out and explored the characteristics of automaticity across his influential research program (e.g., Bargh, 1994, 2006). The terms "automatic" and "controlled" define two processing poles. At the automatic end lie mental processes that are rapid, efficient, spontaneous, implicit, and hard to control, while at the controlled end are processes that are relatively slow, resource-dependent, intentional, explicit, and controllable (see Moors & De Houwer, 2006). In addition, automatic reactions can be characterized as conceptually primitive associations that are insensitive to issues of truth or falsity, while controlled, deliberate reactions consist of propositionally articulated verbal claims that are subject to logical assessment (Gawronski & Bodenhausen, 2006, 2011). Any given process may not possess all of the criteria required to be considered "fully" automatic, but relative automaticity is reflected in the extent to which any subset of the relevant criteria is present.

Different research programs have tended to emphasize different aspects of automaticity. The large literature on spontaneous trait inferences (e.g., Uleman, Saribay, & Gonzalez, 2008) has focused on the question of whether social impressions are formed without any intention on the part of the perceiver to do so. Research on subliminal priming effects (e.g., Custers & Aarts, 2010) has focused on the question of whether we need to be consciously aware of environmental stimuli in order to be influenced by them. Research on the effects of cognitive load (e.g., Macrae, Milne, & Bodenhausen, 1994) has focused on the question of whether we require attentional resources in order to perform some task, or if instead performance is unimpeded by the imposition of a secondary task. In all of these cases, ample evidence exists for automatic forms of social cognition that occur spontaneously, implicitly, and efficiently.

By clarifying the role of automatic mental processes, social cognition researchers have also been able to better circumscribe the nature and role of deliberative mental processes in social cognition. In general, the rapidity of automatic processes means that they start to unfold well before any deliberation has occurred. This head start for automatic reactions is important, because it opens the door for the possibility that subsequent deliberations will be biased by the initial reaction, as when individuals seek a rational justification for their immediate impulsive tendency (for a review, see Bodenhausen & Todd, 2010). Alternatively, deliberative processes can be used to rein in automatic impulses before they are enacted. The literature on the correspondence bias (Gilbert & Malone, 1995), which is the automatic tendency to draw dispositional inferences about an actor's behavior even when situational constraints are present, shows that this bias can be overridden—provided that perceivers have sufficient attentional resources available to make a deliberative adjustment to their initial assumptions. Research on thought suppression (Wegner, 1994) provides another window on the role of more deliberative or effortful processes in mental life. In this research, unwanted automatic thoughts and emotions are shown to be susceptible to eradication (at least temporarily) by the deployment of an *operating process* that replaces the troublesome reaction with an acceptable substitute, whenever the emergence of an unwanted thought or feeling is detected by a *monitoring process*. Unfortunately, as Wegner's research shows, these efforts to control the stream of thought can often backfire, resulting in the heightened accessibility of the unwanted thought.

In general, effortful, controlled mental processes require both (a) sufficient motivation and (b) sufficient opportunity (time, attentional capacity) to unfold. When perceivers lack either one of these ingredients, automatic reactions are likely to dictate behavioral reactions. Dual-process models founded on this general set of assumptions have been proposed in virtually every area of social psychological inquiry one might contemplate (see Chaiken & Trope, 1999; Evans, 2008). In the following sections, we return again to the question of how this distinction plays out in the specific context of person perception.

CORE PROCESSES OF PERSON PERCEPTION

What psychological processes allow us to construct meaningful mental representations of other actors? In many respects, this question has been the central preoccupation of social cognition research. In this section, we review the major approaches that have been taken in trying to answer it.

Commonsense Reasoning

One historically prominent approach to person perception is found in attribution theory. In this approach, social perceivers are thought to rely on commonsense reasoning

processes in order to make sense of the social behavior they observe. Although different theoretical approaches have emphasized different angles on this topic, the shared assumption of these approaches is the notion that individuals think like lay scientists, using informal logical principles to deduce the probable meaning of an actor's behavior. Most research in this tradition focused specifically on the question of when and how perceivers make inferences about the internal dispositions of an actor. From this perspective, lay perceivers deploy reasoning processes in order to categorize behavior as being caused by "personal dispositions" or by "situational forces" (e.g., Jaspars, 1983; Kelley, 1967). When behavior is categorized as dispositional, then the specific disposition also needs to be deduced by the application of logical analysis (e.g., Jones & Davis, 1965). Kelley's (1967) attribution model provides an example of the type of cognitive analysis that is assumed to direct these kinds of inferences. The model assumes that perceivers routinely monitor three kinds of covariation in the social environment: (1) consensus (the extent to which different actors engage in the same behavior), (2) distinctiveness (the extent to which a given actor responds in a distinctive way to a particular stimulus, compared to the response elicited from the actor by most other stimuli), and (3) consistency (the extent to which an actor responds to a particular stimulus in the same way across multiple occasions). These three factors have obvious logical relevance for inferences about the dispositionality of an actor's behavior. If a particular behavior reflects the actor's disposition, rather than just being driven by the stimulus or the situation, then the behavior would be expected to be low in consensus (not something that almost everyone would do), low in distinctiveness (something that the actor does in many different kinds of interactions), and high in consistency (something that occurs reliably in the same or similar situations).

Although attribution theory inspired extensive research, its core tenets have been radically revised in light of failed empirical predictions (e.g., Jones & Harris, 1967) as well as the increasing appreciation that it is simply unrealistic to assume that perceivers will possess the relevant information required to make meaningful covariation assessments as originally laid out by the theory (Malle, 2011). As a result, newer models have developed different kinds of assumptions about the underlying processes of commonsense reasoning. One approach has argued that people rely on general world knowledge to characterize what is normal and typical behavior, and they use this knowledge to direct their attention toward abnormal or

atypical conditions in order to derive causal attributions (Hilton & Slugoski, 1986). Other approaches argued that dispositional inferences occur automatically, by default; more effortful reasoning processes might potentially result in revising or overturning these automatic inferences, but they require attentional and motivational resources for their deployment (see Gilbert, 1998).

A more fundamental critique of attribution theory holds that it has emphasized the wrong causal dichotomy (Malle, 2004). Specifically, by focusing on the question of whether behavior is caused by dispositions versus situations, traditional attribution theory might be missing an arguably more fundamental concern of interest to social perceivers, namely whether an action is intentional versus unintentional. If behavior is perceived as intentional, then perceivers are likely to be preoccupied with the actor's *reasons* for intending that course of action. Although an actor's dispositions could have obvious bearing on his or her intentions, a more likely emphasis of reasons analysis will be on the active psychological states rather than the (latent) traits of the actor. In particular, intentional actions are perceived as arising from an actor's concurrent desires and beliefs (Malle & Knobe, 1997). Consider a man who runs over his neighbor's dog while backing out of his garage. Surely this must be an accident—but what if we know that the man has bitterly complained about the dog barking and digging in his garden *and* we discover that the man knew the dog was unleashed and had been roaming around his driveway that day? Suddenly the possibility of intentionality must be considered, given the plausible assumption that the man desired to get rid of the dog and had relevant beliefs about the dog's whereabouts. As this unhappy scenario exemplifies, we commonly use assumptions about an actor's desires and beliefs to explain meaningful social behavior.

It turns out that here, too, research suggests an automatic rather than an inherently analytic reasoning process—in this case, assuming that behavior is intentional by default (Rosset, 2008). However, when motivation and attention are in adequate supply, commonsense reasoning processes can be used to reevaluate immediate assumptions of intentionality, provided that evidence to the contrary is available (e.g., evidence that the actor in fact did not desire the obtained outcome or lacked relevant knowledge that would have been required to plan the action). This folk psychology approach to understanding lay perceptions of the causes of behavior is closely linked to research on "theory of mind" (e.g., C. Frith & Frith, 2008), which refers to the capacity to draw inferences about the mental states of others.

Although evidence of having a theory of mind emerges early in human development, it appears to be absent or extremely rudimentary, at best, in other species (Penn & Povinelli, 2007).

As we have seen, research suggests that we automatically assume that behavior is dispositional (emphasis on the actor's personal traits) and intentional (emphasis on the actor's psychological states). Regardless of which particular attributional approach one adopts, a key question remains to be addressed: How exactly do perceivers make inferences about the inner states and traits of others, if it is not by some reasoning process? A variety of mechanisms have been proposed, and we review them in the following sections.

Automatic Inferences

As we noted earlier, a great deal of social cognition research has been devoted to the relatively automatic processes that characterize much of our everyday analysis of and response to the social environment. In the realm of person perception, there is now abundant evidence that perceivers make immediate, automatic assumptions about the psychological states and traits of the actors they observe in the social environment. Actors are assumed to emit signals of their inner states, and perceivers are assumed to be quite sensitive to such signals. Emotional signaling is perhaps the best-known and most studied context in which these issues have been investigated. We can learn a great deal about the psychological states of others by attending to their emotional signals, as Darwin (1872) argued long ago. Angry displays, for example, immediately suggest the existence of hostile desires and correspondingly threatening intentions. It is logically possible that individuals must learn to associate angry displays with threatening behavior, but there is good reason to think that such inferences can arise directly, without any learning. Given the universality of the stimulus configurations that signal basic emotional states as well as the universal capacity to "read" these configurations correctly (e.g., Aronoff, Woike, & Hyman, 1992; Eibl-Eibesfeldt, 1989), it appears that perceiving others' emotions is an innate ability. In addition, recent research on mirror neurons suggests a specific mechanism through which this capacity is realized (e.g., Dapretto et al., 2005; Gallese, Keysers, & Rizzolatti, 2004). Specifically, the mere perception of emotional signals in others can trigger an ensemble of corresponding neural activations within the perceiver's brain that appear to allow an analog of the target's internal states to be simulated within the perceiver. Thus, others'

emotions can be "read" by virtue of being mirrored within one's own brain.

Interestingly, research has shown that unwitting, pseudo-affective signals in the face are also used by perceivers to judge a target's traits. Oosterhof and Todorov (2008) exposed participants to affectively neutral faces and showed that, to the extent that a target's neutrally posed facial physiognomy resembled a happy display (because the natural configuration of the target's facial features happens to resemble features of a happy display), the person was more likely to be judged to be warm and trustworthy. In contrast, to the degree that a neutral facial configuration resembled an angry display, targets were judged to be more hostile and untrustworthy. This research also showed that greater degrees of facial masculinity and maturity predicted inferences of a target's dominance. Thus, the core interpersonal dimensions of warmth/affiliation and dominance/competence are "read into" faces, based upon their physiognomic structure. Of course, the accuracy of such assumptions is limited (Oosterhof & Todorov, 2008), but there is clearly a readiness to make rapid, automatic assumptions about actors based on simple implicit rules for reading their faces (e.g., "masculine face = dominant personality").

Although emotional displays have the potential to signal actors' desires, cues regarding their attentional processes provide an important signal of their intentions and beliefs. Eye gaze is a primary source of information about an actor's attention, and social perceivers are typically quite attuned to the eye gaze of others (C. Frith & Frith, 2007). Research on the development of theory of mind shows that even young children use an actor's eye gaze to make predictions about his or her behavior (e.g., Lee, Eskritt, Symons, & Muir, 1998), reflecting their implicit understanding that attention is related to intentions.

Our capacity to rapidly infer the psychological characteristics of others is also reflected in the sizable literature on the use of "thin slices" of behavior in making judgments of others (Ambady, Bernieri, & Richeson, 2000). In contrast to classic research on attribution, in which participants were presented with often detailed descriptions a target's behavior (and the surrounding circumstances) before making judgments about the target, research on thin slices presents participants with brief (often even less than 1 second) samples of a target's nonverbal or verbal behavior before requesting judgments about him or her. Even with such a minimal evidence base, perceivers show nontrivial amounts of accuracy in their ratings of variables such as a target's personality and intelligence

(e.g., Borkenau, Mauer, Riemann, Spinath, & Angleitner, 2004).

Of course, in most everyday life contexts, we observe "thick slices" of behavior that form meaningful units, and we use this richer evidence to make assumptions about the inner forces driving the actor's behavior. Even in simply describing such naturalistic behavior, we often resort to language that already incorporates assumptions of intentionality (e.g., Malle, 2002). Research on spontaneous trait inferences has used a variety of research paradigms to show that perceivers immediately draw inferences about actors that correspond to the natural language descriptors that would commonly be used to describe the behavior (e.g., if we see Sheila give a homeless man $10, we spontaneously infer that she is kind). To understand what a given behavior means, we reflexively match its features to category prototypes stored in memory. The resulting categorization of the behavior (e.g., a kind act) is automatically extended to the actor (a kind person), without any intention on the perceiver's part to do so—even when the perceiver is actively trying *not* to do so (see Uleman et al., 2008).

The literature reviewed in this section clearly points to the existence of a range of processes that use available informational cues in a largely automatic way to make rapid assumptions about the states and traits of other actors. These mechanisms provide a rough-and-ready way of forming social impressions with minimal effort. It appears that more active forms of thinking about the meaning of others' behavior are limited to circumstances in which perceivers have sufficient motivation and free attention to engage in the commonsense reasoning processes that have been the focus of much attributional research. When this more active analysis occurs, it is assumed to increase the accuracy of interpersonal judgments, but at the cost of additional time and effort. However, there are clearly also circumstances in which thoughtful deliberation can undermine the quality of judgments (for a review, see Bodenhausen & Todd, 2010), and much more remains to be learned about the relative accuracy of automatic versus thoughtful forms of social analysis.

Social Projection

In the preceding sections we considered how individuals use available information about a social target to draw rapid inferences. However, sometimes people want or need to make judgments about a target, but there is scant relevant information available, or the available

information is ambiguous in its meaning. Under such circumstances, social perceivers must resort to inferential strategies that can fill in the gaps. One such strategy is *social projection* (e.g., Murstein & Pryer, 1959). In social projection, perceivers make use of their extensive self-knowledge in judging the psychological states and traits of others. In essence, projection involves the assumption of similarity between the self and a social target. We assume that others are likely to think and do the same things that we ourselves would think and do, if we were in their situation.

Social projection has been found in judging others' personality traits (Newman, Duff, & Baumeister, 1997) as well as their transitory states such as goals (e.g., competitive people are more likely to assume that others are competitive; Kawada, Oettingen, Gollwitzer, & Bargh, 2004) and their somatic drive states (e.g., thirsty people are more likely to assume that others are also thirsty; Van Boven & Loewenstein, 2003). Much research on social projection has focused on judgments about the attitudes and beliefs of others (Crano, 1983). For example, van der Pligt, van der Linden, and Ester (1982) asked people to estimate the proportion of the general public that shares their beliefs and attitudes regarding nuclear energy; both pro-nuclear and anti-nuclear respondents believed that their own position was more prevalent. Ambiguity fosters projection: The less that is known about a target, the more likely we are to assume that are target is similar to us. Epley, Converse, Delbosc, Monteleone, and Cacioppo (2009) examined the extent to which religious believers project their own attitudes and beliefs onto God. They found that estimates of God's beliefs about social issues such as affirmative action and capital punishment were indeed egocentrically biased, and to a greater degree than were estimates of the corresponding beliefs of other individuals (such as Bill Gates or Barry Bonds). Presumably, God constitutes a particularly ambiguous case in which direct evidence is lacking, so projection fills the gap. However, even when we do have relevant information, sometimes projection still occurs. For example, Goel, Mason, and Watts (2010) showed that people tended to overestimate the extent to which their Facebook friends agreed with their own attitudes, even when they say they have discussed the particular attitude topic(s) with their friends. The egocentric bias evident in social projection appears to be difficult to avoid (Krueger & Clement, 1994).

A variety of psychological mechanisms could underlie social projection. The effect might have a motivational basis, in that people often derive comfort from the thought that others are similar to themselves; in the domain of attitudes, for example, a perceived social consensus in support of one's own views would imply the correctness of those views. "Cold" cognitive mechanisms could also be involved; for instance, examples of other individuals who share one's own views may come more easily to mind than counterexamples, leading to their overestimation via the availability heuristic (Tversky & Kahneman, 1973). Aforementioned research on mirror neurons (e.g., Gallese et al., 2004) suggests that low-level neural processes can play a fundamental role in social projection in situations involving the online observation of others' behavior. Recall that, according to this account, when perceivers observe others, sensorimotor programs corresponding to the observed behavior are activated in the perceivers' own brains. Relevant self-knowledge can then be activated and used to make assumptions about why this (internally simulated) behavior is occurring. Whatever mechanisms are involved, they appear to operate in a relatively automatic manner, in that they can be triggered unconsciously (Kawada et al., 2004) and, as noted, they are hard to prevent (Krueger & Clement, 1994). Evidence suggests that, by default, people make egocentric projections about others, but when they have the capacity and the motivation for accuracy, they can scale back the degree of egocentricity in their judgments at least somewhat (Epley, Keysar, Van Boven, & Gilovich, 2004).

One particularly interesting moderator of social projection is social categorization. Judgments about other ingroup members are generally much more susceptible to egocentric projection biases than are judgments about outgroup members (Robbins & Krueger, 2005). In fact, people often make the assumption that members of outgroups are dissimilar to themselves (or to the ingroup more generally; see Gawronski, Bodenhausen, & Banse, 2005). Because people typically view themselves positively, seeing outgroup members as dissimilar to the self implies a relatively negative impression. However, Stathi and Crisp (2008) showed that this potentially pernicious pattern can be overcome under conditions in which people first imagine interacting with an outgroup member before making intergroup judgments. Particularly when the perceivers' (typically quite positive) personal self was salient, imagining intergroup contact was associated with projecting positive qualities onto the outgroup.

It is thus apparent that we often use ourselves as a model for understanding others, provided those others are not too dissimilar. It is easy to understand why. Each person's memory is filled with a great abundance of personal experience and self-knowledge, and these rich stores constitute a ready basis for judging the minds of others. However, when others seem too dissimilar to us, then other strategies for making inferences about them (in the absence of clearly diagnostic, available behavioral cues) must be sought out. We now turn our attention to this situation.

Social Stereotyping

Perhaps the most well-studied mechanism for making assumptions about the characteristics of others is the process of stereotyping. Stereotyping occurs when perceptually available cues are used to categorize a person in terms of a social group membership (e.g., race, sex, occupation), and then generalized beliefs about the social group are recruited from memory and applied to the individual in question. In other words, generic social knowledge is brought to bear in understanding a particular instance. There are many positive features of this process. It allows for the rapid establishment of relatively rich, structured social impressions. It reduces potentially chaotically complex kinds of social input into orderly and manageable categories. It provides a basis for behavior prediction that can guide social interactions. In many cases, this process serves the perceiver's goals well. However, it ultimately involves regarding the target individual as interchangeable with other group members, creating the potential for overgeneralizations and unwarranted assumptions. In some cases, it can result in unfair discrimination (for a review, see Bodenhausen & Richeson, 2010). Because it is a mental process affording both notable benefits as well as potentially deplorable costs, it has attracted a great deal of attention from social cognition researchers. (Also see chapter by Biernat & Danaher in this volume.)

The stereotyping process can be broken down into several component processes, the most basic of which are category selection, stereotype activation, and stereotype application. Category selection is the necessary first step. Any individual could be categorized in countless ways (by age, sex, ethnicity, religion, etc.), but stereotyping typically focuses on just one particular social identity. The choice of categories is of critical importance, because the beliefs and attitudes associated with different categories often imply very different reactions to the target. A wide range of variables can influence which of a target's social identities will be most salient to the perceiver in a given context (for a review, see Bodenhausen, Kang, & Peery, in press). Relatively distinctive, unusual, or rare categories tend to be salient, as are categories that have just recently been used in a preceding social context. The social context itself can make certain categories salient, as emphasized

by social identity theory (e.g., Oakes, 1987). One way this happens is when a person's behavior is closely aligned with expectations derived from one particular category. For instance, if we see a Chinese woman eating rice with chopsticks, her ethnicity will likely be much more salient than her gender because her behavior "fits" her ethnic category in a much more direct way than it fits her gender category; however, if we see the same person applying makeup to her face, then her gender is likely to be more salient than her ethnicity (Macrae, Bodenhausen, & Milne, 1995). Another contextual source of category salience is known as comparative fit (e.g., Wegener & Klauer, 2004), which occurs when a particular basis for categorization effectively captures the patterns of similarity and difference that are present in a social setting. For example, consider a group of college students having a group discussion. If it were the case that the men in the group voiced similar views, and these views were in contrast to an opposing point of view being consistently voiced by the women, then gender would become very salient; however, if the patterns of similarity and difference in the group opinions were aligned with a different basis for categorization (e.g., humanities versus science majors), then gender might not be at all salient. Finally, individual differences can be important. Highly prejudiced individuals are likely to chronically categorize others in terms of their prejudicial preoccupations (e.g., a White supremacist who routinely views others through the lens of race; see Stangor, Lynch, Duan, & Glass, 1992). Thus, for a number of reasons, particular social identities tend to "pop out" and suggest themselves to perceivers as bases for categorizing—and stereotyping—others.

Once a category is selected, then stereotypes associated with that category become automatically activated in working memory. These stereotypes tend to be held with a relatively high degree of consensus across perceivers (Haslam, 1997), and their fundamental role involves the specification of where a given group stands on two critically important dimensions of social evaluation: competence and warmth (Fiske, Cuddy, & Glick, 2007). Competence-related stereotypes are shaped by a group's relative status, while warmth-related stereotypes are shaped by the degree to which a group is perceived to be cooperative versus competitive with one's own group. An interesting pattern of ambivalent stereotyping seems to characterize many social groups, in that when a group is seen as high in warmth, it also tends to be seen as low in competence, whereas when a group is seen as high in competence, it is also seen as low in warmth (Fiske, Cuddy, Glick, & Xu, 2002). This pattern reflects a more general tendency toward a compensatory dynamic between perceptions of warmth and competence (Kervyn, Yzerbyt, Judd, & Nunes, 2009).

Activated stereotypes provide the basis for inferences about a social target, but interestingly, such inferences do not appear to emerge directly, in the sense that perceivers automatically assume that group-typical traits apply to a particular group member. Instead, perceivers need to feel that they have a reasonable basis for making assumptions about social targets (Yzerbyt, Schadron, Leyens, & Rocher, 1994). For this reason, stereotypic inferences often arise indirectly, through the impact of activated stereotypes on the processing of other information about the target. Bodenhausen (1988) showed that ethnic stereotypes biased the decisions of mock jurors when they were activated prior to exposure to case-related evidence, but they had no effect when they were activated after exposure to the evidence (but before judgments were rendered). This pattern strongly suggests that the impact of stereotypes on guilt judgments was mediated by their influence on the processing of case-specific evidence—and, in fact, stereotypic biases in memory for the case evidence were found when stereotypes were activated before consideration of the evidence, but not when they were activated afterward. In general, activated stereotypes tend to bias attention toward stereotype-consistent information, and they lead perceivers to interpret ambiguous information in stereotypic ways (for a review, see Bodenhausen et al., in press). Thus, the representations of others that are formed via stereotyping processes subjectively seem to be based on relevant evidence rather than mere supposition. However, this evidential base is often far from being an objective record of the target's behavior; rather, it is commonly distorted in stereotype-validating ways.

The likelihood of judging a target in stereotypic terms is known to be moderated by a range of perceiver, target, and situational variables. Targets "attract" more stereotyping and discrimination as their group prototypicality increases (Maddox, 2004). For example, Eberhardt, Davies, Purdie-Vaughns, and Johnson (2006) showed that greater physical prototypicality (i.e., phenotypicality) of Black defendants was associated with a higher likelihood of receiving a death sentence. In addition, minority group members who feel stronger ties of identification with their group tend to be the targets of greater bias (Kaiser & Pratt-Hyatt, 2009). Perceiver variables that affect the likelihood of stereotyping include any factor that bears on either (a) the motivation to form a thoughtful, accurate, individuated impression, or (b) the ability to engage in deliberative rather than automatic thinking about the target.

When motivation and ability for deliberation are sufficiently high, perceivers often go beyond merely stereotypic impressions of others and rely on more extensively bottom-up or data-driven forms of impression formation. However, if either motivation or ability for deliberation is compromised, then more automatic forms of social analysis, including stereotyping, are likely to shape person perception.

Finally, in an interesting twist, recent research has shown that stereotyping can occur even when an individual is not a member of the relevant stereotyped group. For example, a White target can be stereotyped using common African-American stereotypes. The mechanism for such unexpected effects is known as *feature-based stereotyping*. To the extent that White people possess Afrocentric facial features, they become more susceptible to being judged as having stereotypical African-American traits. For example, Blair, Judd, and Chapleau (2004) examined race biases in criminal sentencing and found that, among both Black and White defendants, persons with faces having more Afrocentric features received harsher sentences than persons with less Afrocentric features. In the same way, variations of facial masculinity/femininity within each sex are associated with gender bias. Sczesny, Spreemann, and Stahlberg (2006) found that, for both male and female targets, greater facial masculinity was associated with heightened perceptions of leadership competence. Research of this sort shows that the process of stereotyping is complex and based not just on top-down categorization processes but also on attention to specific bottom-up features of social targets.

PERCEIVING RELATIONSHIPS

Although we have focused much of our attention on the process of perceiving and understanding individual persons, it is important to recognize that individuals are embedded within social structures, and these structures also play a central role in mental representations of the social world (Smith & Semin, 2004). In particular, the nature of the relationship that exists between perceivers and targets is of paramount importance in shaping person perception processes. One testament to this importance is the previously discussed evidence that social perceptions are organized in terms of two fundamental dimensions—warmth and competence (Fiske et al., 2007; Judd, James-Hawkins, Yzerbyt, & Kashima, 2005). Each of these dimensions is imbued with deep interpersonal significance (Wiggins, 1991). The level of warmth perceived in social targets bears directly on their trustworthiness and on the affective qualities that are likely to be experienced in social interactions with them. Competence bears on targets' capacity to influence the well-being of the perceiver and signals whether alliances with targets are likely to be helpful or a burdensome. Thus, the core dimensions of social meaning are inherently oriented toward understanding likely patterns of relationship between target and perceiver. In this section, we review several theoretical approaches that have focused distinctly on the relational context of social cognition.

Interdependence Theory

Perhaps the most prominent general-purpose theory of interpersonal relationships is provided by interdependence theory (e.g., Rusbult & Van Lange, 2008). In this approach, researchers have set out to specify a basic set of recurring social situations faced in everyday life and then link the properties of these situations to personal and interpersonal functioning. These core situation configurations are built from a relative small set of basic dimensions that characterize interdependence (Kelley et al., 2003): the degree to which one person's outcomes depend on another's actions; whether social influence is mutual (both Person A and Person B have power over one another) or asymmetric (Person A has power over Person B, but not vice versa); the degree to which different actors' interests coincide or conflict; and the degree to which behavior coordination is required for successful outcomes. In their "atlas" of interpersonal situations, Kelley et al. document the most noteworthy combinations of these factors, which define the basic set of social situations that perceivers face on a regular basis.

Reis (2008) summarized research showing that basic social-cognitive processes are modified by the key variables of interdependence theory. Perhaps the most extensively studied example is the case of asymmetric power (Fiske & Dépret, 1996). One basic finding is that being in a position of low power (i.e., dependence) results in generally more thoughtful and extensive forms of interpersonal analysis than being in a position of high power. For example, high-power persons are more likely to rely on simplistic stereotypes in forming impressions of persons with lower power, while dependent persons are likely to engage in much more nuanced and individuated processes when forming impressions of persons with higher power (Dépret & Fiske, 1993). In addition, people who are high in power are much less likely than their low-power counterparts to engage in perspective taking and, thus, they are unlikely to accurately gauge how others see, think, and feel (Galinsky, Magee, Inesi, & Gruenfeld, 2006). These (and many other) findings examining the impact of asymmetric power on social cognition constitute but one of several arenas in which the importance of interdependence in shaping and constraining social cognition has been studied (see Brewer, 2004). Another example is provided by research showing that the process of social projection is moderated by the nature of the interdependence between the perceiver and the target; egocentric projection is markedly greater in cooperative than in competitive contexts (Toma, Yzerbyt, & Corneille, 2010).

Relational Models

A different approach to conceptualizing the nature of social relationships was developed by Fiske (2004) in his relational models theory. The ambition of this theory is to provide a comprehensive taxonomy of the basic, universal types of social relationships, together with an account of how these basic relationships are expressed in culturally embedded ways. Although daily life might seem to present a nearly infinite variety of social relationships, Fiske argued persuasively that there are just four basic forms of interpersonal relations.

1. *Communal sharing relationships* are characterized by a focus on strong interpersonal ties forged within a shared identity, and the primary principle of resource distribution within these relationships is need-based allocation (the individuals with the greatest need get the biggest share of the pie).
2. *Authority ranking relationships* are characterized by a focus on ordered differences between individuals and are strongly concerned with relative status; the primary principle of resource distribution within these relationships is status-based allocation (higher status individuals get a bigger share of the pie).
3. *Equality matching relationships* are characterized by a focus on additive imbalances and are concerned with reciprocity, turn-taking, and other processes that can rebalance any imbalances that emerge; the primary principle of resource distribution within these relationships is equal allocation (but equal contributions are also expected).
4. *Market pricing relationships* are characterized by a focus on relative ratios, with a strong emphasis on equity-based fairness in social exchange; the primary principle of resource distribution in these relationships is proportionality—one's allocation should be proportionate to one's contributions.

These four basic types of relationship are postulated to exist in all cultures, but cultures can vary in terms of the specific contexts within which a given form of relationship is expected to hold. Thus, for example, communal sharing might be expected to operate within an entire social group (e.g., a tribal village) in one culture, but only within the nuclear family in another. Cultural complements (which Fiske calls *preos*) are thus required to render the relational models useful to an individual; as a basic part of socialization, individuals within a given culture must learn when and how the rules governing each type of relationship are expected to apply.

According to Fiske (2004), social cognition will be directly impacted by the internalized representations of these four generic relationship models because they are routinely used throughout daily life to anticipate, understand, and remember the actions of others. Haslam (2004) reviewed a range of empirical evidence from psychological and neuroanatomical studies documenting the existence of these relational models and showing their influence on social cognition. For example, a diary study conducted by Fiske, Haslam, and Fiske (1991) showed that perceivers' attention and social memory are attuned to the expected, model-specific patterns of social exchange, and when they later misremembered details about a particular interaction, it was far more likely to involve a confusion within a particular relationship type (e.g., misremembering a market-pricing exchange that occurred with Person A as having involved Person B, with whom a market-pricing relationship also holds), compared to confusions based on many other variables such as age, race, similarity of names, and so on. Thus, memory for social experiences clearly seems to be organized around these distinct relationship models.

Collective Identities

So far, our discussion of social cognition's relationship context has focused on small-scale, interpersonal relationships. However, social cognition also unfolds in the context of large-scale collectivities; in times of war, for example, national identities play a salient role in organizing the social-cognitive processes that unfold within the minds of affected individuals. Social identity theory and self-categorization theory (e.g., Schmid, Hewstone, & Al Ramiah, 2011) have provided a powerful account of how social cognition is modified when intergroup relations become salient. A key idea of this approach is the notion that different comparative frames of reference will draw out different emphases in social cognition. In

interpersonal contexts, the individual is the frame of reference for comparisons; thus, social impressions will be oriented toward characteristics that set one person apart from others, and one's perceptions of other individuals will be heavily influenced by one's own personal, idiosyncratic goals, motives, and biases. However, when an intergroup context becomes salient, the group is the frame of reference for comparisons; thus, social impressions will be oriented toward characteristics that set one group apart from another, while also minimizing the variability that is perceived to exist within groups. Under these conditions, a process of depersonalization is said to occur (e.g., Simon & Hamilton, 1994), and perceptions of others become aligned with group norms rather than one's own personal biases. In a sense, one's view of the world comes to be defined by the ingroup's consensual reality, rather than by one's own personal outlook.

Verkuyten and Hagendoorn (1998) provided a good example of depersonalization at work. In their study, they examined how well prejudice toward immigrants could be predicted by a personality variable (authoritarianism, which is typically positively associated with prejudice) versus by perceived ingroup norms regarding prejudice. In general, there was no correlation between levels of authoritarianism and perceived ingroup norms. Prejudice was assessed under two experimental conditions. In one case, the participants' personal identity was emphasized, but in the other condition, their national identity was emphasized. As expected, when personal identity was salient, the personality measure significantly predicted prejudice, while the ingroup norms did not; however, when national identity was salient, perceived ingroup norms predicted prejudice, while the personality measure did not. Thus, evaluations of the social world were quite differently tuned, depending on whether an interpersonal or an intergroup frame of reference was salient.

The findings discussed in this section confirm that basic aspects of social cognition and person perception are acutely attuned to the relational context within which they occur. It is not sufficient to view social cognition as a process unfolding in the disconnected mind of an autonomous agent; rather, it emerges within the mind of a socially connected, interdependent agent whose goals and priorities are strongly influenced by those of the other parties involved in the situation. In this sense, important aspects of social cognition consist of emergent phenomena that are negotiated intersubjectively within the context of particular relationships (Ickes, 2002). There is still much to be discovered about the relational tuning of social understanding.

CULTURAL CONTEXTS OF SOCIAL COGNITION

Although social perception occurs in a wide diversity of contexts, psychologists have (often implicitly) assumed that the basic cognitive processes by which people understand the world around them are essentially universal. This view has steadily been changing with the rise of cross-cultural research investigating the ways in which cultural experiences affect human thinking. As we have emphasized, social perception depends not only on sensory input but is also subject to various "top-down," theory-driven processes. Appraisals of the objects of perception can be modified by values, expectations, emotional needs and other factors that arise within the perceiver (see Bodenhausen & Hugenberg, 2009). Culture is a major source of such values, experiences, and expectations; thus, cultural differences can play a potentially important role in how a stimulus is perceived. In fact, cross-cultural research suggests that cognitive processes can be greatly shaped by the cultural context in which they occur, leading to pronounced differences in the cognitive strategies used by individuals. This diversity of thought does not imply that important universals do not exist. People are likely to possess a number of basic cognitive processes regardless of their cultural origins. However, some cognitive processes normally regarded as basic are highly susceptible to change. (Also see the chapter by Miller and Boyle in this volume.)

Across cultures, preferences for one type of self-construal over another may influence how individuals perceive others in different situations and social roles. Markus and Kitayama (1991) identified independent self-construal and interdependent self-construal as two conceptualizations of the self that reflect the degree to which different cultures emphasize the individual versus relationships. In particular, the independent view is exemplified by Western cultures, which tend to focus on the separateness and uniqueness of the individual and thus emphasize autonomy and independence. Interdependent self-construals are most clearly exemplified by Eastern cultures, but are also characteristic of African cultures and Latin-American cultures. According to this view, the self is conventionally construed as a component of a broader surrounding context and understood to be inextricably linked to personal relationships and social roles. A consequence of this divergence in self-construal is that the nature of psychological processes will vary according to the organization of the self inherent in a given construal. For example, individuals with interdependent selves, more so than those with independent selves, are more likely to be guided in social and nonsocial thinking alike by a pervasive attentiveness to the relevant others in the social context. Many of the differences between Eastern cultures and Western cultures can be ascribed to the distinction between these types of self-construals, including motivations for uniqueness (Kim & Markus, 1999), self-enhancement (Heine, Lehman, Markus, & Kitayama, 1999), feelings of agency (Morling, Kitayama, & Miyamoto, 2002), and holistic versus analytic reasoning styles (Nisbett, Peng, Choi, & Norenzayan, 2001).

If cultural differences can guide these types of processes, then they may also influence psychological processes underlying person perception. Markus and Kitayama (1991) argued that different ways of seeing the self affect the degree to which social perceivers attribute behavior to dispositional or situational explanations. If the self is seen as stable, unique, and independent of context, then behavior should be seen as relatively consistent across situations. However, if the self is seen as interdependent on context, individual behavior should vary as a result of situations and social roles. According to this view, persons with a Western cultural orientation are more likely to understand and predict the behavior of others through insight gained by making dispositional attributions. On the other hand, persons from East Asian cultures should be less inclined to show a preference for explanations of behaviors in terms of traits or dispositions of the target and more likely to rely on situational characteristics. There is evidence indicating that this is the case. For example, Morris and Peng (1994) have shown that Americans exhibit a bias toward personal dispositions, whereas Chinese participants emphasize social situations. When asked about their attributions for murders, Americans rely more heavily on presumed dispositions of the individual, whereas Chinese participants explain the same events with reference to situational factors. Likewise, Lee, Hallahan, and Herzog (1996) found that attributions made while describing sports events were more situational and less dispositional for Hong Kong citizens than attributions from the United States. These patterns are different even for social events that do not involve people. Morris and Peng (1994) and Hong, Chiu, and Kung (1997) presented Chinese and American participants with animated displays of fish moving in relation to one another. Chinese participants were more likely than American participants to see the behavior of an individual fish as being produced by situational factors, whereas U.S. participants were more likely to perceive the behavior as resulting from internal attributes. These types of cultural differences, however, do not appear to be due to an absence of dispositional thinking among Eastern cultures. Korean participants are equally as willing as U.S. participants to make disposition-based predictions in the absence of contextual cues (Choi & Nisbett, 1998; Norenzayan, Choi, & Nisbett, 2002). However, Koreans are more likely to use contextual factors when making predictions about an individual's behavior, and they are also more willing than Americans to revise their mistaken inferences about dispositions. Studies among Japanese (Masuda & Kitayama, 2003; Miyamoto & Kitayama, 2002) and Chinese (Knowles, Morris, Chiu, & Hong, 2001) have also replicated these results, demonstrating that East Asians are less likely to rely on internal attributions even if they also possess tendencies toward initial dispositional judgments.

Cultural differences may also be seen in the interpretation of facial emotions. Americans see emotional expressions as manifestations of a person's inner feelings (Markus & Kitayama, 1991), and believe they can infer emotions from people's faces (Carroll & Russell, 1996). However, in Asian contexts emotions may be considered inseparable from the feelings of the larger group, as they are more likely to be seen in terms of interpersonal relationships rather than strictly reflecting internal states (Markus & Kitayama, 1994; Mesquita, 2003; Mesquita & Markus, 2004). Thus, for East Asians judgments of an actor's feelings are more likely to depend on the social context than for Westerners. Masuda et al. (2008) found that Japanese are more influenced by the social context in interpreting a facial expression than American. Compared to Americans, Japanese participants' ratings of a central figure's emotions were influenced more by whether the facial expressions of the background characters were consistent or inconsistent. This pattern suggests that Americans see emotions as individual feelings, whereas Japanese see them as inseparable from the group's feelings. These differences are a result of differences in attention as Japanese participants looked at the surrounding figures more than Americans did.

Research on individuals with multiple cultural identities has provided another powerful way to make inferences about culture-specific patterns in person perception. In a series of studies, Hong, Morris, Chiu, and Benet-Martínez (2000) presented evidence suggesting that multiple cultural meaning systems can be mentally represented and integrated by an individual and that these meaning systems are responsive to situational cues. Individuals who have successfully internalized more than one culture are able to participate in each by actively switching between cultural mental frames in response to specific social contexts; this

perspective is known as frame switching. For example, Hong and colleagues (2000) showed that biculturals are able to shift between attribution styles as a result of frame switching. In these studies, Westernized Chinese participants in Hong Kong were primed with American, Chinese, or neutral thoughts by exposing them to cultural icons (or neutral images) and asking them to write about them. Following the priming, participants were asked to complete an interpretive task that required them to make a causal attribution for the behaviors of images of fish. Biculturals were more likely to make external attributions, a characteristically East Asian attribution style, when primed with Chinese icons, and relied more on internal attributions, a characteristically Western attribution style, when primed with U.S. icons. Attributions for those primed with neutral images fell in between these two results.

In summary, culture, like other knowledge, can shape the way we perceive and understand others. Although it may not rigidly determine judgments and behavior, the preceding examples illustrate how culture acts as a lens through which we experience the world and organize our impressions of others.

CONCLUSION

The study of social cognition has become a large, interdisciplinary enterprise, with important contributions emerging from neuroscience, developmental psychology, comparative psychology, and many other fields besides social psychology. In this chapter, we have surveyed a variety of these threads and have tried to weave them together around a set of core issues that lie at the heart of social cognition and perception: How do we come to understand other persons? In what ways are our social impressions firmly grounded in available informational cues versus derived from inferential processes that go beyond the given information? How do the specific characteristics of social relationships constrain and direct basic processes of person perception? Which aspects of social cognition are universal, and which are shaped by the perceiver's cultural context? Much has already been learned about this set of rich questions, and there are many exciting new directions emerging in social cognition research. For example, much of the research we have discussed in this chapter has focused on how an individual perceiver comes to understand social targets. However, the language of "perceiver" and "target" fails to capture the dynamic nature of social cognition in real interactions, in which each individual serves simultaneously as a perceiver and a target. A more dynamic perspective on social cognition suggests that it is important to view the perceiver not as a passive recipient of informational input but as an active agent that solicits or otherwise contributes to the creation of the very cues that are used to understand the meaning of a social situation. Prior investigations have typically relegated social perceivers to a passive role in research methodology, but when they can take on a more proactive role, interesting differences emerge in the quality of social perception (Waggoner, Smith, & Collins, 2009). Recognizing the fact that each social perceiver is part of a social network through which information and influence spreads in complex and bidirectional ways further underscores the active and collaborative process of constructing social understandings (Smith & Collins, 2009). These observations clearly complicate the theoretical picture, but they do so in ways that raise important new issues for investigation. It is, in short, an exciting time for social cognition research.

REFERENCES

Adolphs, R. (1999). Social cognition and the human brain. *Trends in Cognitive Sciences, 3,* 469–479.

Ambady, N., Bernieri, F. J., & Richeson, J. A. (2000). Toward a histology of social behavior: Judgmental accuracy from thin slices of the behavioral stream. *Advances in Experimental Social Psychology, 32,* 201–271.

Aronoff, J., Woike, B. A., & Hyman, L. M. (1992). Which are the stimuli in facial displays of anger and happiness? Configural bases of emotion recognition. *Journal of Personality and Social Psychology, 62,* 1050–1066.

Baddeley, A. (1992). Working memory. *Science, 255,* 556–559.

Bargh, J. A. (1994). The four horsemen of automaticity: Awareness, intention, efficiency, and control in social cognition. In R. S. Wyer Jr. & T. K. Srull (Eds.), *Handbook of social cognition* (2nd ed., pp. 1–40). Hillsdale, NJ: Erlbaum.

Bargh, J. A. (2006). What have we been priming all these years? On the development, mechanisms, and ecology of nonconscious social behavior. *European Journal of Social Psychology, 36,* 147–168.

Bargh, J. A., & Chartrand, T. L. (2000). The mind in the middle: A practical guide to priming and automaticity research. In H. T. Reis & C. M. Judd (Eds.), *Handbook of research methods in social and personality psychology* (pp. 253–285). Cambridge, UK: Cambridge University Press.

Barrett, H. C., & Kurzban, R. (2006). Modularity in cognition: Framing the debate. *Psychological Review, 113,* 628–647.

Blair, I. V., Judd, C. M., & Chapleau, K. M. (2004). The influence of Afrocentric features in criminal sentencing. *Psychological Science, 15,* 674–679.

Blank, H., & Nestler, S. (2007). Cognitive process models of hindsight bias. *Social Cognition, 25,* 132–146.

Bodenhausen, G. V. (1988). Stereotypic biases in decision making and memory: Testing process models of stereotype use. *Journal of Personality and Social Psychology, 55,* 726–737.

Bodenhausen, G. V. (1992). Information-processing functions of generic knowledge structures and the role in context effects in social judgment. In N. Schwarz & S. Sudman (Eds.), *Context effects in social and psychological research* (267–277). New York, NY: Springer-Verlag.

Bodenhausen, G. V., & Hugenberg, K. (2009). Attention, perception, and social cognition. In F. Strack & J. Förster (Eds.), *Social cognition: The basis of human interaction* (pp. 1–22). New York, NY: Psychology Press.

Bodenhausen, G. V., Kang, S. K., & Peery, D. (in press). Social categorization and the perception of social groups. In S. T. Fiske & C. N. Macrae (Eds.), *Sage handbook of social cognition*. Thousand Oaks, CA: Sage.

Bodenhausen, G. V., & Peery, D. (2009). Social categorization and stereotyping in vivo: The VUCA challenge. *Social and Personality Psychology Compass, 3,* 133–151.

Bodenhausen, G. V., & Richeson, J. A. (2010). Prejudice, stereotyping, and discrimination. In R. F. Baumeister & E. J. Finkel (Eds.), *Advanced social psychology: The state of the science* (pp. 341–383). Oxford, UK: Oxford University Press.

Bodenhausen, G. V., Schwarz, N., Bless, H., & Wänke, M. (1995). Effects of atypical exemplars on racial beliefs: Enlightened racism or generalized appraisals? *Journal of Experimental Social Psychology, 31,* 48–63.

Bodenhausen, G. V., & Todd, A. R. (2010). Automatic aspects of judgment and decision making. In B. Gawronski & B. K. Payne (Eds.), *Handbook of implicit social cognition: Measurement, theory, and applications* (pp. 278–294). New York, NY: Guilford Press.

Borkenau, P., Mauer, N., Riemann, R., Spinath, F. M., & Angleitner, A. (2004). Thin slices of behavior as cues of personality and intelligence. *Journal of Personality and Social Psychology, 86,* 59–614.

Brewer, M. B. (2004). Taking the social origins of human nature seriously: Toward a more imperialist social psychology. *Personality and Social Psychology Review, 8,* 107–113.

Byrne, R. W., & Bates, L. A. (2007). Sociality, evolution, and cognition. *Current Biology, 17,* R714–R723.

Carroll, J. M., & Russell, J. A. (1996). Do facial expressions signal specific emotions? Judging emotion form the face in context. *Journal of Personality and Social Psychology, 70,* 205–218.

Chaiken, S., & Trope, Y. (Eds.) (1999). *Dual process theories in social psychology*. New York, NY: Guilford Press.

Cheney, D., Seyfarth, R., & Smuts, B. (1986). Social relationships and social cognition in nonhuman primates. *Science, 234,* 1361–1366.

Choi, I., & Nisbett, R. (1998). Situational salience and cultural differences in the correspondence bias and actor observer bias. *Personality and Social Psychology Bulletin, 24,* 949–960.

Collins, A. M., & Loftus E. F. (1975). A spreading-activation theory of semantic processing. *Psychological Review, 82,* 407–428.

Cosmides, L., & Tooby, J. (1992). Cognitive adaptations for social exchange. In J. H. Barkow, L. Cosmides, & J. Tooby (Eds.), *The adapted mind: Evolutionary psychology and the generation of culture* (pp. 163–228). New York, NY: Oxford University Press.

Crano, W. D. (1983). Assumed consensus of attitudes: The effect of vested interest. *Personality and Social Psychology Bulletin, 9,* 597–608.

Cummins, D. D. (1998). Social norms and other minds: The evolutionary roots of higher cognition. In D. D. Cummins & C. Allen (Eds.), *The evolution of mind* (pp. 30–50). New York, NY: Oxford University Press.

Custers, R., & Aarts, H. (2010). The unconscious will: How the pursuit of goals operates outside of conscious awareness. *Science, 329,* 47–50.

Dapretto, M., Davies, M. S., Pfeifer, J. H., Scott, A. A., Sigman, M., Bookheimer, S. Y., & Iacoboni, M. (2005). Understanding emotions in others: Mirror neuron dysfunction in children with autism spectrum disorders. *Nature Neuroscience, 9,* 28–30.

Darwin, C. (1872). *The expression of the emotions in man and animals*. London, UK: John Murray.

Dasgupta, N., & Asgari, S. (2004). Seeing is believing: Exposure to counterstereotypic women leaders and its effect on the malleability of automatic gender stereotyping. *Journal of Experimental Social Psychology, 40,* 642–658.

Dépret, E., & Fiske, S. T. (1993). Social cognition and power: Some cognitive consequences of social structure as a source of control deprivation. In G. Weary, F. Gleicher, & K. Marsh (Eds.), *Control motivation and social cognition* (pp. 176–202). New York, NY: Springer-Verlag.

Devine, P. G. (1989). Stereotypes and prejudice: Their automatic and controlled components. *Journal of Personality and Social Psychology, 56,* 5–18.

Dijksterhuis, A., Chartrand, T. L., & Aarts, H. (2007). Effects of priming and perception on social behavior and goal pursuit. In J. A. Bargh (Ed.), *Social psychology and the unconscious: The automaticity of higher mental processes* (pp. 51–131). New York, NY: Psychology Press.

Dodge, K. A. (2006). Translational science in action: Hostile attributional style and the development of aggressive behavior problems. *Development and Psychopathology, 18,* 791–814.

Dovidio, J. F., Evans, N., & Tyler, R. B. (1986). Racial stereotypes: The contents of their cognitive representations. *Journal of Experimental Social Psychology, 22,* 22–37.

Eberhardt, J. L., Davies, P. G., Purdie-Vaughns, V. J., & Johnson, S. L. (2006). Looking deathworthy: Perceived stereotypicality of Black defendants predicts capital-sentencing outcomes. *Psychological Science, 17,* 383–386.

Eibl-Eibesfeldt, I. (1989). *Human ethology.* Chicago, IL: Aldine.

Epley, N., Converse, B. A., Delbosc, A., Monteleone, G. A., & Cacioppo, J. T. (2009). Believers' estimates of God's beliefs are more egocentric than estimates of other people's beliefs. *Proceedings of the National Academy of Sciences USA, 106,* 21533–21538.

Epley, N., Keysar, B., Van Boven, L., & Gilovich, T. (2004). Perspective-taking as egocentric anchoring and adjustment. *Journal of Personality and Social Psychology, 87,* 327–339.

Evans, J. St. B. T. (2008). Dual-processing accounts of reasoning, judgment, and social cognition. *Annual Review of Psychology, 59,* 255–278.

Fazio, R. H. (1986). How do attitudes guide behavior? In R. M. Sorrentino & E. T. Higgins (Eds.), *Handbook of motivation and cognition* (pp. 204–243). New York, NY: Guilford Press.

Fazio, R. H. (2007). Attitudes as object-evaluation associations of varying strength. *Social Cognition, 25,* 603–637.

Fazio, R. H., & Olson, M. A. (2003). Implicit measures in social cognition research: Their meaning and use. *Annual Review of Psychology, 54,* 297–327.

Fiske, A. P. (2004). Relational models theory 2.0. In N. Haslam (Eds.), *Relational models theory: A contemporary overview* (pp. 3–25). Mahwah, NJ: Erlbaum.

Fiske, A. P., Haslam, N., & Fiske, S. T. (1991). Confusing one person with another: What errors reveal about the elementary forms of social relations. *Journal of Personality and Social Psychology, 60,* 656–674.

Fiske, S. T., Cuddy, A. J., & Glick, P. (2007). Universal dimensions of social cognition: Warmth and competence. *Trends in Cognitive Sciences, 11,* 77–83.

Fiske, S. T., Cuddy, A. J. C., Glick, P., & Xu, J. (2002). A model of (often mixed) stereotype content: Competence and warmth respectively follow from perceived status and competition. *Journal of Personality and Social Psychology, 82,* 878–902.

Fiske, S. T., & Dépret, E. (1996). Control, interdependence and power: Understanding social cognition in its social context. *European Review of Social Psychology, 7,* 31–61.

Fiske, S. T., & Taylor, S. E. (1991). *Social cognition* (2nd ed.). New York, NY: McGraw-Hill.

Fodor, J. A. (1983). *The modularity of mind.* Cambridge, MA: MIT Press.

Frith, C. D., & Frith, U. (2007). Social cognition in humans. *Current Biology, 17,* R724–R732.

Frith, C. D., & Frith, U. (2008). Theory of mind. *Advances in Clinical Neuroscience and Rehabilitation, 8,* 7–8.

Gallese, V., Keysers, C., & Rizzolatti, G. (2004). A unifying view of the basis of social cognition. *Trends in Cognitive Sciences, 8,* 396–403.

Galinsky, A. D., Magee, J. C., Inesi, M. E., & Gruenfeld, D. H. (2006). Power and perspectives not taken. *Psychological Science, 17,* 1068–1074.

Galinsky, A. D., & Moskowitz, G. B. (2000). Counterfactuals as behavioral primes: Priming the simulation heuristic and consideration of alternatives. *Journal of Experimental Social Psychology, 36,* 384–409.

Gardner, W. L., Gabriel, S., & Lee. A. Y. (1999). "I" value freedom but "we" value relationships: Self-construal priming mirrors cultural differences in judgment. *Psychological Science, 10,* 321–326.

Gawronski, B., & Bodenhausen, G. V. (2006). Associative and propositional processes in evaluation: An integrative review of implicit and explicit attitude change. *Psychological Bulletin, 132,* 692–731.

Gawronski, B., & Bodenhausen, G. V. (2011). The associative-propositional evaluation model: Theory, evidence, and open questions. *Advances in Experimental Social Psychology, 44,* 59–127.

Gawronski, B., Bodenhausen, G. V., & Banse, R. (2005). We are, therefore they aren't: Ingroup construal as a standard of comparison for outgroup judgments. *Journal of Experimental Social Psychology, 41,* 515–526.

Gilbert, D. T. (1998). Ordinary personology. In D. T. Gilbert, S. T. Fiske, & G. Lindzey (Eds.), *Handbook of social psychology* (Vol. 2, 4th ed., pp. 89–150). Boston, MA: McGraw-Hill.

Gilbert, D. T., & Malone, P. S. (1995). The correspondence bias. *Psychological Bulletin, 117,* 21–30.

Goel, S., Mason, W., & Watts, D. J. (2010). Real and perceived attitude agreement in social networks. *Journal of Personality and Social Psychology, 99,* 611–621.

Gramzow, R. H., & Willard, G. (2006). Exaggerating current and past performance: Motivated self-enhancement versus reconstructive memory. *Personality and Social Psychology Bulletin, 32,* 1114–1125.

Greenwald, A. G., McGhee, D. E., & Schwartz, J. L. K. (1998). Measuring individual differences in implicit cognition: The implicit association test. *Journal of Personality and Social Psychology, 74,* 1464–1480.

Greenwald, A. G., & Nosek, B. A. (2009). Attitudinal dissociation: What does it mean? In R. E. Petty, R. H. Fazio, & P. Briñol (Eds.), *Attitudes: Insights from the new implicit measures* (pp. 65–82). New York, NY: Psychology Press.

Hamilton, M. C. (1991). Masculine bias in the attribution of personhood. *Psychology of Women Quarterly, 15,* 393–402.

Haslam, N. (2004). Research on the relational models: An overview. In N. Haslam (Eds.), *Relational models theory: A contemporary overview* (pp. 27–57). Mahwah, NJ: Erlbaum.

Haslam, S. A. (1997). Stereotyping and social influence: Foundations of stereotype consensus. In R. Spears, P. J. Oakes, N. Ellemers, & S. A. Haslam (Eds.), *The social psychology of stereotyping and group life* (pp. 119–143). Oxford, UK: Blackwell.

Hastie, R., Ostrom, T. M., Ebbesen, E. B., Wyer, R. S. Jr., Hamilton, D. L., & Carlston, D. E. (1980). *Person memory: The cognitive basis of social perception.* Hillsdale, NJ: Erlbaum.

Hastorf, A. H., & Cantril, H. (1954). They saw a game: A case study. *Journal of Abnormal and Social Psychology, 49,* 129–134.

Heine, S. J., Lehman, D. R., Markus, H. R., & Kitayama, S. (1999). Is there a universal need for positive self-regard? *Psychological Review, 106*, 766–794.

Hilton, D. J., & Slugoski, B. R. (1986). Knowledge-based causal attribution: The abnormal conditions focus model. *Psychological Review, 93*, 75–88.

Hong, Y. Y., Chiu, C. Y., & Kung, T. (1997). Bringing culture out in front: Effects of cultural meaning system activation on social cognition. In K. Leung, Y. Kashima, U. Kim, & S. Yamaguchi (Eds.), *Progress in Asian social psychology* (Vol. 1, pp. 135–146). Singapore: Wiley.

Hong, Y., Morris, M. W., Chiu, C., & Benet-Martínez, V. (2000). Multicultural minds: A dynamic constructivist approach to culture and cognition. *American Psychologist, 55*, 705–720.

Ickes, W. (2002). Subjective and intersubjective paradigms for the study of social cognition. *New Review of Social Psychology, 1*, 112–121.

Jackendoff, R. S. (1992). *Languages of the mind: Essays on mental representation*. Cambridge, MA: MIT Press.

Jacoby, L. L. (1998). Invariance in automatic influences of memory: Toward a user's guide for the process-dissociation procedure. *Journal of Experimental Psychology: Learning, Memory, & Cognition, 24*, 3–26.

Jaspars, J. M. F. (1983). The process of attribution in common sense. In M. Hewstone (Ed.), *Attribution theory: Social and functional extensions* (pp. 28–44). Oxford, UK: Blackwell.

Jones, E. E., & Davis, K. E. (1965). From acts to dispositions: The attribution process in person perception. *Advances in Experimental Social Psychology, 2*, 219–266.

Jones, E. E., & Harris, V. A. (1967). The attribution of attitudes. *Journal of Experimental Social Psychology, 3*, 1–24.

Judd, C. M., James-Hawkins, L., Yzerbyt, V. Y., & Kashima, Y. (2005). Fundamental dimensions of social judgment: Understanding the relations between judgments of competence and warmth. *Journal of Personality and Social Psychology, 89*, 899–913.

Kaiser, C. R., & Pratt-Hyatt, J. S. (2009). Distributing prejudice unequally: Do Whites direct their prejudice toward strongly identified minorities? *Journal of Personality and Social Psychology, 96*, 432–445.

Kawada, C., Oettingen, G., Gollwitzer, P. M., & Bargh, J. A. (2004). The projection of implicit and explicit goals. *Journal of Personality and Social Psychology, 86*, 545–559.

Kelley, H. H. (1967). Attribution theory in social psychology. *Nebraska Symposium on Motivation, 15*, 192–238.

Kelley, H. H., Holmes, J. G., Kerr, N. L., Reis, H. T., Rusbult, C. E., & Van Lange, P. A. M. (2003). *An atlas of interpersonal situations*. New York, NY: Cambridge University Press.

Kervyn, N., Yzerbyt, V. Y., Judd, C. M., & Nunes, A. (2009). A question of compensation: The social life of the fundamental dimensions of social perception. *Journal of Personality and Social Psychology, 96*, 828–842.

Kim, H. S., & Markus, H. R. (1999). Deviance or uniqueness, harmony or conformity? A cultural analysis. *Journal of Personality and Social Psychology, 77*, 785–800.

Klauer, K. C., Voss, A., & Stahl, C. (Eds.). (2011). *Cognitive methods in social psychology*. New York, NY: Guilford Press.

Knowles, E. D., Morris, M. W., Chiu, C., & Hong, Y. (2001). Culture and the process of person perception: Evidence for automaticity among East Asians in correcting for situational influences on behavior. *Personality and Social Psychology Bulletin, 27*, 1344–1356.

Krizan, Z., & Windschitl, P. D. (2007). The influence of outcome desirability on optimism. *Psychological Bulletin, 133*, 95–121.

Krueger, J., & Clement, R. W. (1994). The truly false consensus effect: An ineradicable and egocentric bias in social perception. *Journal of Personality and Social Psychology, 67*, 596–610.

Kummer, H. (1971). *Primate societies: Group techniques of ecological adaptations*. Chicago, IL: Aldine.

Kunda, Z. (1990). The case for motivated reasoning. *Psychological Bulletin, 108*, 480–498.

Leakey, R. E. (1978). *The people of the lake: Mankind and its beginnings*. New York, NY: Avon.

Leary, M. R. (2007). Motivational and emotional aspects of the self. *Annual Review of Psychology, 58*, 317–344.

Lee, F., Hallahan, M., & Herzog, T. (1996). Explaining real life events: How culture and domain shape attributions. *Personality and Social Psychology Bulletin, 22*, 732–741.

Lee, K., Eskritt, M., Symons, L. A., & Muir, D. (1998). Children's use of triadic eye gaze information for "mind reading." *Developmental Psychology, 34*, 525–539.

Lewicki, P., Hill, T., & Czyzewska, M. (1992). Nonconscious acquisition of information. *American Psychologist, 47*, 796–801.

Lingle, J. H., & Ostrom, T. M. (1979). Retrieval selectivity in memory-based impression judgments. *Journal of Personality and Social Psychology, 37*, 180–194.

Macrae, C. N., Bodenhausen, G. V., & Milne, A. B. (1995). The dissection of selection in social perception: Inhibitory processes in social stereotyping. *Journal of Personality and Social Psychology, 69*, 397–407.

Macrae, C. N., Bodenhausen, G. V., Milne, A. B., Thorne, T. M. J., & Castelli, L. (1997). On the activation of social stereotypes: The moderating role of processing objectives. *Journal of Experimental Social Psychology, 33*, 471–489.

Macrae, C. N., Milne, A. B., & Bodenhausen, G. V. (1994). Stereotypes as energy-saving devices: A peek inside the cognitive toolbox. *Journal of Personality and Social Psychology, 66*, 37–47.

Maddox, K. B. (2004). Perspectives on racial phenotypicality bias. *Personality and Social Psychology Review, 8*, 383–401.

Malle, B. F. (2002). Verbs of interpersonal causality and the folk theory of mind and behavior. In M. Shibatani (Ed.), *The grammar of causation and interpersonal manipulation* (pp. 57–83). Amsterdam: Benjamins.

Malle, B. F. (2004). *How the mind explains behavior: Folk explanations, meaning, and social interaction*. Cambridge, MA: MIT Press.

Malle, B. F. (2011). Time to give up the dogmas of attribution: An alternative theory of behavior explanation. *Advances in Experimental Social Psychology, 44*, 297–352.

Malle, B. F, & Knobe, J. (1997). The folk concept of intentionality. *Journal of Experimental Social Psychology, 33*, 101–121.

Markus, H. R., & Kitayama, S. (1991). Culture and the self: Implications for cognition, emotion, and motivation. *Psychological Review, 98*, 224–253.

Markus, H. R., & Kitayama, S. (1994). The cultural construction of self and emotion: Implications for social behavior. In S. Kitayama & H. R. Markus (Eds.), *Emotion and culture: Empirical studies of mutual influence* (pp. 89–130). Washington, DC: American Psychological Association.

Masuda, T., Ellsworth, P. C., Mesquita, B., Leu, J., Tanida, S., & van de Veerdonk, E. (2008). Placing the face in context: Cultural differences in the perception of facial emotion. *Journal of Personality and Social Psychology, 94*, 365–381.

Masuda, T., & Kitayama, S. (2003). Perceiver-induced constraint and attitude attribution in Japan and the US: A case for the cultural dependence of the correspondence bias. *Journal of Experimental Social Psychology, 40*, 409–416.

McLeod, P., Plunkett, K., & Rolls, E. T. (1998). *Introduction to connectionist modeling of cognitive processes*. Oxford, UK: Oxford University Press.

Mesquita, B. (2003). Emotions as dynamic cultural phenomena. In R. Davidson, H. Goldsmith, & K. R. Scherer (Eds.), *The handbook of affective sciences* (pp. 871–890). New York, NY: Oxford University Press.

Mesquita, B., & Markus, H. R. (2004). Culture and emotion: Models of agency as sources of cultural variation in emotion. In N. H. Frijda, A. S. R. Manstead, & A. H. Fisher (Eds.), *Feelings and emotions: The Amsterdam symposium* (pp. 341–358). Cambridge, MA: Cambridge University Press.

Miyamoto, Y., & Kitayama, S. (2002). Cultural variation in correspondence bias: The critical role of attitude diagnosticity of socially constrained behavior. *Journal of Personality and Social Psychology, 83,* 1239–1248.

Moors, A., & De Houwer, J. (2006). Automaticity: A theoretical and conceptual analysis. *Psychological Bulletin, 132,* 297–326.

Morling, B., Kitayama, S., & Miyamoto, Y. (2002). Cultural practices emphasize influence in the United States and adjustment in Japan. *Personality and Social Psychology Bulletin, 28,* 311–323.

Morris, M., & Peng, K. (1994). Culture and cause: American and Chinese attributions for social and physical events. *Journal of Personality and Social Psychology, 67,* 949–971.

Murstein, B. I., & Pryer, R. S. (1959). The concept of projection: A review. *Psychological Bulletin, 56,* 353–374.

Newman, L. S., Duff, K. J., & Baumeister, R. F. (1997). A new look at defensive projection: Thought suppression, accessibility, and biased person perception. *Journal of Personality and Social Psychology, 72,* 980–1001.

Nisbett, R. E., Peng, K., Choi, I., & Norenzayan, A. (2001). Culture and systems of thought: Holistic versus analytic cognition. *Psychological Review, 2,* 291–310

Nisbett, R. E., & Wilson, T. D. (1977). Telling more than we can know: Verbal reports on mental processes. *Psychological Review, 84,* 231–259.

Norenzayan, A., Choi, I., & Nisbett, R. E. (2002). Cultural similarities and differences in social inference: Evidence from behavioral predictions and lay theories of behavior. *Personality and Social Psychology Bulletin, 28,* 109–120.

Oakes, P. J. (1987). The salience of social categories. In J. C. Turner, M. A. Hogg, P. J. Oakes, S. D. Reicher, & M. S. Wetherell (Eds.), *Rediscovering the social group* (pp. 117–141). Oxford, UK: Blackwell.

Oosterhof, N. N., & Todorov, A. (2008). The functional basis of face evaluation. *Proceedings of the National Academy of Sciences USA, 105,* 11087–11092.

Park, B., Judd, C. M., & Ryan, C. S. (1991). Social categorization and the representation of variability information. *European Review of Social Psychology, 2,* 211–244.

Penn, D. C., & Povinelli, D. J. (2007). On the lack of evidence that non-human animals possess anything remotely resembling a "theory of mind." *Philosophical Transactions of the Royal Society B, 362,* 731–744.

Pezzo, M. V., & Pezzo, S. P. (2007). Making sense of failure: A motivated model of hindsight bias. *Social Cognition, 25,* 147–164.

Reis, H. (2008). Reinvigorating the concept of situation in social psychology. *Personality and Social Psychology Review, 12,* 311–329.

Robbins, J. M., & Krueger, J. (2005). Social projection to ingroups and outgroups: A review and meta-analysis. *Personality and Social Psychology Review, 9,* 32–47.

Rosset, E. (2008). It's no accident: Our bias for intentional explanations. *Cognition, 108,* 771–780.

Rusbult, C. E., & Van Lange, P. A. M. (2008). Why we need interdependence theory. *Social and Personality Psychology Compass, 2,* 2049–2070.

Schmid, K., Hewstone, M., & Al Ramiah, A. (2011). Self-categorization and social identification: Making sense of us and them. In D. Chadee (Ed.), *Theories in social psychology* (pp. 211–231). Chichester, UK: Wiley-Blackwell.

Sczesny, S., Spreemann, S., & Stahlberg, D. (2006). Masculine = competent? Physical appearance and sex as sources of gender-stereotypic attributions. *Swiss Journal of Psychology, 65,* 15–23.

Shah, J. Y. (2005). The automatic pursuit and management of goals. *Current Directions in Psychological Science, 14,* 10–13.

Sherman, J. W. (1996). Development and mental representation of stereotypes. *Journal of Personality and Social Psychology, 70,* 1126–1141.

Signorella, M. L., & Liben, L. S. (1984). Recall and reconstruction of gender-related pictures: Effects of attitude, task difficulty, and age. *Child Development, 55,* 393–405.

Simon, B., & Hamilton, D. L. (1994). Self-stereotyping and social context: The effects of relative in-group size and in-group status. *Journal of Personality and Social Psychology, 66,* 699–711.

Simons, D. J., & Chabris, C. F. (1999). Gorillas in our midst: Sustained inattentional blindness for dynamic events. *Perception, 28,* 1059–1074.

Smith, E. R. (1998). Mental representation and memory. In D. T. Gilbert, S. T. Fiske, & G. Lindzey (Eds.), *Handbook of social psychology* (Vol. 1, 4th ed., pp. 391–445). New York, NY: McGraw-Hill.

Smith, E. R., & Collins, E. C. (2009). Contextualizing person perception: Distributed social cognition. *Psychological Review, 11,* 343–364.

Smith, E. R., & Semin, G. R. (2004). Situated social cognition. *Current Directions in Psychological Science, 16,* 132–135.

Smith, E. R., & Zárate, M. A. (1992). Exemplar-based model of social judgment. *Psychological Review, 99,* 3–21.

Srull, T. K. (1984). Methodological techniques for the study of person memory and social cognition. In R. S. Wyer Jr. & T. K. Srull (Eds.), *Handbook of social cognition* (Vol. 2, 1st ed., pp. 1–72). Hillsdale, NJ: Erlbaum.

Srull, T. K., & Wyer, R. S. Jr. (1983). The role of control processes and structural constraints in models of memory and social judgment. *Journal of Experimental Social Psychology, 19,* 497–521.

Stangor, C., Lynch, L., Duan, C., & Glass, B. (1992). Categorization of individuals on the basis of multiple social features. *Journal of Personality and Social Psychology, 62,* 207–218.

Stathi, S., & Crisp, R. J. (2008). Imagining intergroup contact promotes projection to outgroups. *Journal of Experimental Social Psychology, 44,* 943–957.

Toma, C., Yzerbyt, V., & Corneille, O. (2010). Anticipated cooperation vs. competition moderates interpersonal projection. *Journal of Experimental Social Psychology, 46,* 375–381.

Tversky, A., & Kahneman, D. (1973). Availability: A heuristic for judging frequency and probability. *Cognitive Psychology, 5,* 207–232.

Uleman, J. S., Saribay, S., & Gonzalez, C. M. (2008). Spontaneous inferences, implicit impressions, and implicit theories. *Annual Review of Psychology, 59,* 329–360.

Van Boven, L., & Loewenstein, G. (2003). Social projection of transient drive states. *Personality and Social Psychology Bulletin, 29,* 1159–1168.

van der Pligt, J., van der Linden, J., & Ester, P. (1982). Attitudes to nuclear energy: Beliefs, values, and false consensus. *Journal of Environmental Psychology, 2,* 221–231.

Van Overwalle, F. (2011). Connectionist simulation as a tool for understanding social cognition and neuroscience. In K. C. Klauer, A. Voss, & C. Stahl (Eds.), *Cognitive methods in social psychology* (pp. 391–419). New York, NY: Guilford Press.

Verkuyten, M., & Hagendoorn, L. (1998). Prejudice and self-categorization: The variable role of authoritarianism and in-group stereotypes. *Personality and Social Psychology Bulletin, 24,* 99–110.

Waggoner, A. S., Smith, E. R., & Collins, E. C. (2009). Person perception by active versus passive perceivers. *Journal of Experimental Social Psychology, 45,* 1028–1031.

Ward, A., & Mann, T. (2000). Don't mind if I do: Disinhibited eating under cognitive load. *Journal of Personality and Social Psychology, 78,* 753–763.

Wegener, I., & Klauer, K. C. (2004). Inter-category versus intra-category fit: When social categories match social context. *European Journal of Social Psychology, 34,* 567–593.

Wegner, D. M. (1994). Ironic processes of mental control. *Psychological Review, 101,* 34–52.

Whiten, A., & Byrne, R. W. (1997). *Machiavellian intelligence II: Extensions and evaluations.* Cambridge, UK: Cambridge University Press.

Wiggins, J. S. (1991). Agency and communion as conceptual coordinates for the understanding and measurement of interpersonal behavior. In W. Grove & D. Cicchetti (Eds.), *Thinking clearly about psychology: Essays in honor of Paul Everett Meehl* (pp. 89–113). Minneapolis, MN: University of Minnesota Press.

Wyer, R. S. Jr., & Carlston, D. E. (1994). The cognitive representation of persons and events. In R. S. Wyer Jr. & T. K. Srull (Eds.), *Handbook of social cognition* (Vol. 1, 2nd ed., pp. 41–98). Mahwah, NJ: Erlbaum.

Yzerbyt, V. Y., Schadron, G., Leyens, J.-P., & Rocher, S. (1994). Social judgeability: The impact of meta-informational cues on the use of stereotypes. *Journal of Personality and Social Psychology, 66,* 48–55.

CHAPTER 12

The Social Self

ROY F. BAUMEISTER, E. J. MASICAMPO, AND JEAN M. TWENGE

THE SOCIAL SELF

It is difficult to think about the self without referring to other people. Although the very concept of the self seems to denote individualism, the self is nevertheless incomplete without acknowledging interactions with others. People often describe themselves in terms of relationships (husband, son, mother) or as a member of a profession (and thus as a member of a social group). Even personality traits are usually conceptualized in comparison to other people (one is not extraverted per se, but extraverted compared to others). Self-esteem reflects what others think (Leary, Tambor, Terdal, & Downs, 1995). Attempts at self-control can benefit or harm others (e.g., smoking and drinking: Baumeister, Heatherton, & Tice, 1994). People's behavior can be radically affected by social rejection or exclusion (Twenge, Baumeister, Tice, & Stucke, 2001; Williams, Cheung, & Choi, 2000). Selves do not develop and flourish in isolation. People learn who and what they are from other people, and they always have identities as members of social groups. By the same token, close personal relationships are potent and probably crucial to the development of selfhood. A human being who spends an entire life in social isolation would have a stunted and deficient self.

In addition, the self is inherently interpersonal because relating to others is part of what the self is *for*. The self is constructed, used, altered, and maintained as a way of connecting the individual organism to other members of its species. If no one likes you, the odds are that you will start asking "What's wrong with me?" and will make changes to the self when you reach some answers. In this chapter, we explore how individual selves affect others and how others affect individual selves.

The interpersonal self is one of three major facets of the self (Baumeister, 1998). The other two main aspects are the experience of reflexive consciousness, which involves being aware of oneself and constructing knowledge structures (including self-concept and self-esteem) about the self, and the executive function, which controls the decisions and actions of the self. As argued above, the social self provides a crucial piece of this puzzle.

BELONGINGNESS, SOCIAL EXCLUSION, AND OSTRACISM

Meaningful human relationships are a crucial part of the self. Baumeister and Leary (1995) proposed that the need to belong is one of the most fundamental human motivations, underlying many emotions, actions, and decisions throughout life. Belongingness theory predicts that people seek to have close and meaningful relationships with others, perhaps because such relationships increase the likelihood of survival and reproduction (Shaver, Hazan, & Bradshaw, 1988). Social exclusion hampers reproductive success; it is difficult to find a mate when one is isolated from or devalued by others. In addition, exclusion often led to death during hunter-gatherer times due to lack of food sharing, the difficulty of hunting alone, and lack of protection from animal and human enemies (e.g., Ainsworth, 1989; Hogan, Jones, & Cheek, 1985; Moreland, 1987). Therefore, people form relationships readily and with minimal external impetus. In addition, people are reluctant to break off a relationship even when its practical purpose has ended. People also seem to categorize others based on their relationships (Baumeister & Leary, 1995). In general, humans are social animals, and they seek relationships with others as a fundamental need; only the need for food, clothing, and shelter is greater. But what happens when these needs are not met—when people feel disconnected from social groups and lonely from a lack of close relationships? How does the lack of interpersonal relationships affect the self and behavior?

Previous research suggests that social exclusion is correlated with a variety of negative circumstances, including poor physical and mental health (Bloom, Asher, & White, 1978; Williams, Takeuchi, & Adair, 1992), antisocial behavior and crime (Sampson & Laub, 1993), alcohol and drug abuse (Williams et al., 1992), and even reckless driving (Harano, Peck, & McBride, 1975; Harrington & McBride, 1970; Richman, 1985). People who are ostracized by others report negative emotions and a feeling of losing control (Williams et al., 2000). In general, social exclusion leads to negative emotional experiences such as anxiety, depression, loneliness, and feelings of isolation (Baumeister & Leary, 1995; Baumeister & Tice, 1990; Gardner, Pickett, & Brewer, 2000). Social rejection can also lead to considerable decreases in feelings of self-esteem. Sociometer theory (Leary et al., 1995) posits that self-esteem is primarily a measure of the health of social relationships. That is, high self-esteem comes from a sense of being liked by others. Low self-esteem arises when people experience rejection or else fear that they will end up alone in life.

A sense of belonging seems to serve as an inoculation against negative outcomes and a predictor of positive ones. An influential review by Cohen and Wills (1985) concluded that high social support is correlated with lower self-reports of anxiety and depression. Baumeister (1991), Myers (1992), and Myers and Diener (1995) reviewed the empirical literature on happiness and concluded that the strongest predictor of happiness was social connectedness. People who are relatively alone in the world are much less happy than people who have close connections with others. All other objective predictors of happiness, including

money, education, health, and place of residence, are only weakly correlated with happiness. The importance of social ties for positive life outcomes suggests that social connection carries considerable explanatory power. Conversely, social exclusion may be connected to many of the personal and social problems that trouble modern citizens. The socially excluded may comprise the more aggressive and anti-social segments of the population. Moreover, feelings of exclusion may contribute to lowered academic performance, poor self-regulation, and other self-defeating behaviors.

Aggression and Helping

During the late 1990s, a series of shootings occurred at U.S. schools, leading to the deaths of a number of young people and the serious injury of many others. In almost every case, the perpetrators were boys who felt rejected by their peers (Leary, 2000). Apparently these young men responded to rejection with violence, walking into their schools with guns and shooting their fellow students. These tragedies were consistent with the notion that antisocial, violent behavior is linked to a lack of social connections. Garbarino's (1999) studies confirmed that many perpetrators of violence are young men who feel rejected from family and peer groups (see also Leary, 2000; Walsh, Beyer, & Petee, 1987).

Prior research provides support for a connection between social exclusion and aggressive behavior. Rejected children are more physically aggressive, more disruptive, and issue more verbal threats than other children (Coie, 1990; Newcomb, Bukowski, & Pattee, 1993). Compared to married men, single men are more likely to speed and drive recklessly, two antisocial behaviors that can lead to injury and death (Harano et al., 1975; Harrington & McBride, 1970). Marital status also correlates with criminal behavior. Stable relationships in adulthood (especially a healthy spousal relationship) are connected to lower incidence of crime and delinquency (Sampson & Laub, 1990, 1993). On the other hand, Wright and Wright (1992) found no link between criminality and marital status in itself. Apparently only a happy (or reasonably happy) marriage protects against criminal behavior.

The above links between social exclusion and aggression are correlational, so the direction of causation is not clear. It is possible that aggression leads to fewer interpersonal relationships. Aggressive children may be less likely than others to keep friends. Adults with criminal tendencies may be less likely than others to marry. Hidden third variables could also explain the associations. Perhaps a lack of money makes people both more prone to criminal activity and less desirable as potential mates.

Laboratory research has examined whether there is a causal link between social exclusion and aggressive behavior. Twenge et al. (2001) manipulated social exclusion across numerous studies, either by giving participants false feedback on a personality test (in the crucial condition, participants heard they would end up alone later in life) or by manipulating peer rejection (participants heard either that everyone or no one in a group of their peers chose them as a desirable partner for further interaction). Rejected participants were consistently more aggressive toward other people than were control participants. Rejected participants aggressed toward people who provoked them (e.g., with insults) and they also aggressed against innocent parties with whom they had never interacted. Thus, these studies showed that social exclusion can indeed cause numerous forms of aggression toward others. Later work revealed that social exclusion motivates such aggressive tendencies by activating hostile thought patterns (DeWall, Twenge, Gitter, & Baumeister, 2009). After they are rejected, people view the world in aggressive and hostile ways, and that causes them to respond in an aggressive manner.

Because socially excluded people are so apt to aggress toward others, later work examined whether social exclusion could produce other antisocial tendencies. One line of work examined the effect of social exclusion on helping behavior (Twenge, Baumeister, DeWall, Ciarocco, & Bartels, 2007). Across seven studies, socially excluded people were less prosocial: they donated less money to a student fund, were less willing to volunteer for more experiments, were less helpful to the experimenter after a mishap, and were less cooperative in a Prisoner's Dilemma game. This tendency remained whether the prosocial behavior involved a cost to the self, no cost or benefit to the self, or even a benefit to the self. Thus social exclusion not only increases aggression but it also decreases prosocial behavior.

The effects described above were not due to simply hearing bad news. In many of the studies reported, a misfortune control group heard that they would be accident prone in the future. This group demonstrated significantly less aggression and more prosocial behavior compared to the social exclusion group. These manipulations of social exclusion are weak compared to real-life experiences such as romantic breakups or ostracism by friends. It is therefore not surprising that rejections outside the laboratory can sometimes lead to lethally violent reactions.

Self-Defeating Behavior

Psychologists have long been fascinated with self-defeating behavior because of its paradoxical nature (for reviews, see Baumeister, 1997; Baumeister & Scher, 1988). It seems irrational for people to act in ways that are self-defeating. Why do people do things that bring them suffering, failure, and other misfortunes? A broad range of social problems (e.g., drug addiction, overeating, underachievement, excessive risk-taking) could fairly be labeled self-defeating acts. Many of these problems are caused by self-control or self-regulation failures (Baumeister et al., 1994), which occur when people find it difficult to resist impulsive behavior. In addition, a loss of self-control can lead to taking self-defeating risks (Leith & Baumeister, 1996), which in turn may cause undesirable outcomes such as poor health, drug and alcohol abuse, and harmful accidents.

Self-control loss is detrimental for relationships. Living together with other people requires some degree of accommodation and compromise, because the self-interest of the individual is sometimes in conflict with the best interests of the group. Sharing, humility, respecting the rights and property of others, and other socially desirable acts require some degree of self-control. Few people want to live with someone who continually overeats, abuses drugs, lashes out in anger, and takes stupid risks. Yet people must use reserves of self-control to curb these impulses (Baumeister, Bratslavsky, Muraven, & Tice, 1998).

Evidence from the sociological literature suggests that marriage, one indicator of belongingness, inoculates against many self-defeating behaviors. When compared to unmarried or divorced individuals, married people are less likely to abuse alcohol and drugs (Williams et al., 1992). As mentioned earlier, married men are less likely to be arrested for speeding or reckless driving (Harrington & McBride, 1970) and are less likely to be involved in car accidents (Harano et al., 1975), especially those related to alcohol (Richman, 1985). In one of the first works of modern sociology, Durkheim (1897/1951) found that suicide (perhaps the most self-defeating of behaviors) was more common among people who were unmarried or otherwise socially unconnected. These correlational studies suggest a relationship between belongingness and self-defeating behaviors including loss of self-control and risk-taking.

In addition, married people are often mentally and physically healthier than single, divorced, or widowed individuals (Schoenborn, 2004). The correlation between marital status and health may have several causes. First, it is possible that spouses provide practical support for health behaviors, reminding their partners to keep doctors' appointments, eat right, and exercise regularly. The social interaction of a marital relationship may also directly increase mental health, which may increase physical health in turn. Third, and most relevant here, not being involved in a close relationship may encourage risky, self-defeating behaviors. Just as single and divorced people are more likely to take risks while driving, they may also take more risks with their health. We have already established that unmarried people are more likely to abuse alcohol and drugs. The same risk-taking, self-defeating tendency may also lead the unmarried to neglect their health by missing appointments, declining to seek health information, and taking a passive role toward health maintenance. It seems that many people feel that life is not worth living (or as worth living) without close relationships. However, the causation may work the other way; it is certainly plausible that unhealthy people are not as likely to marry or have as many close social relationships.

A series of experiments helped to determine the causal path between social exclusion and self-defeating behavior (Twenge, Catanese, & Baumeister, 2002). Numerous experiments manipulated social exclusion using the same methods employed in the research on aggressive and prosocial behaviors (future prediction of a life devoid of social relationships, or rejection by peers). These experiments found that excluded participants consistently displayed more self-defeating behavior. Compared to the other groups, excluded participants procrastinated longer, took irrational risks in a lottery choice, and made more unhealthy choices. These effects were not mediated by mood, no matter how mood was measured (three different mood measures were used). The misfortune control group, who heard that they would be accident prone later in life, did not show significant increases in self-defeating behavior. Thus social exclusion, more than any other kind of misfortune, causes self-defeating behavior.

Other work has examined the effects of social exclusion on self-regulation. Self-regulation involves monitoring and guiding behavior, and so good self-regulation is often necessary to avoid many self-defeating behaviors. Across six studies, social exclusion was found to impair self-regulation (Baumeister, DeWall, Ciarocco, & Twenge, 2005). Relative to accepted people, rejected people were less able to exercise restraint in eating behavior (when eating cookies), persisted for less time on a difficult problem-solving task, and were less able to control their attention. Reductions in self-regulation thus appear to contribute to many of the negative, self-defeating outcomes that are linked to being socially excluded.

Cognitive Impairment and Emotional Numbness

As reviewed above, social rejection can lead to a wide range of negative outcomes. One aim of recent research on social rejection has been to uncover why social rejection has so many negative effects. One reasonable explanation is that social rejection causes stress, anger, sadness, and other negative emotions and that these emotions can drive people to engage in self-defeating and anti-social behaviors. However, laboratory experiments have yielded little support for that view. In the research reviewed above that found effects of rejection on aggression (Twenge et al., 2001), self-defeating behavior (Twenge et al., 2002), and poor self-control (Baumeister et al., 2005), no causal role of emotion was found. Rejection rarely induced negative moods, and it usually did not mediate the effects of rejection on behavior.

If emotions do not mediate the effects of rejection on negative behavioral outcomes, then what does? One possibility is cognitive impairment. Social exclusion may impair the ability to reason effectively, and this in turn could lead to self-defeating behavior. Indeed, self-defeating behavior is often attributable to a failure to rationally consider the outcomes of one's actions (Leith & Baumeister, 1996). Cognitive impairment could also lead to antisocial behavior, as socially excluded individuals may give in to aggressive impulses without considering the consequences. This decrease in the ability to reason may result from excessive rumination about having been rejected.

Laboratory research has shown that social exclusion does indeed reduce the ability to reason effectively (Baumeister, Twenge, & Nuss, 2002). In one study, socially excluded participants obtained lower scores on timed tests of intelligence. In another study that used a reading comprehension task, social exclusion led to impairments in the ability to retrieve information. Crucially, social exclusion did not affect the storage of information or the retrieval of simple information (e.g., nonsense syllables), but when retrieval required thinking carefully about encoded information (e.g., in a story), socially rejected participants performed poorly. Social rejection therefore appears to hurt higher reasoning. That could undermine decision making and self-regulation, thereby leading to various negative outcomes.

Another possible mediator of the effects of social rejection on negative behavioral outcomes is emotional numbness. It is possible that social rejection causes a person to become emotionally numb (i.e., detached and emotionally insensitive), and that could perturb a number of adaptive self-regulatory functions (e.g., anticipating the regret that would come with harming other people). This view derives from the theory that social and physical forms of pain are linked. Theorists have suggested that evolution co-opted the physical pain system when minds encountered the need to deal with social threats and social pain (Herman & Panksepp, 1978; Panksepp, Herman, Conner, Bishop, & Scott, 1978; Panksepp, Vilberg, Bean, Coy, & Kastin, 1978). Hence, social pain is experienced by using parts of the brain that were originally designed to experience physical pain. As a result, social pain is experienced similarly to physical pain. Of relevance to the present work, one theory posits that much as physical pain can cause numbness, social pain too can cause numbness (though for an alternative interpretation, see Richman & Leary, 2009).

Laboratory experiments have supported the view that social rejection, which is a socially painful experience, can cause physical and emotional numbness. DeWall and Baumeister (2006) found that when people experience social rejection, they become physically numb so that pain threshold and pain tolerance are increased. DeWall and Baumeister also examined emotional responding. Rejected participants predicted less joy (and sorrow) at the prospect of watching a favored sports team win (or lose) an upcoming game. Rejected participants also empathized less with another person who either broke up with a significant other or had experienced a recent injury. Thus, rejected people appeared to exhibit dampened responses to emotional and physically painful situations. A meta-analysis of laboratory experiments also confirmed that people tend to become emotionally numb after social rejection. Blackhart, Nelson, Knowles, and Baumeister (2009) found that social rejection led to an emotionally neutral state characterized by low levels of both positive and negative emotions.

A lack of emotion could explain many of the negative effects of social exclusion on behavior. Empathy plays a vital role in regulating behavior. Identifying with another person's pain can motivate helping, and the anticipation of regret is often sufficient for fending off aggressive impulses. Intrapersonal behaviors may also be affected. Persisting toward achievement and avoiding self-defeat are made much more difficult when one is unable to anticipate future joys and disappointments.

Cognitive impairment and emotional numbness are two potential causes of many of the known negative effects of social exclusion. The two processes may be related. It is possible that emotional numbness contributes to cognitive impairment, particularly to the extent that thoughts and judgments depend in part on accessing one's feelings and emotions. Moreover, an inability to think reasonably about relationships and outcomes may contribute to the inability to experience many of the emotions that typically regulate behavior.

Seeking Reconnection

Despite the negative outcomes reviewed above, rejection does not always lead to dysfunction. In some cases, rejection can lead to a cascade of beneficial effects. Some work has found that social rejection can increase rather than decrease prosocial behavior. Williams, Cheung, and Choi (2000) found that people were more likely to conform to the behaviors of others after being rejected. Likewise, Maner, DeWall, Baumeister, and Schaller (2007) found that rejected people were more likely than others to express interest in making friends, to form positive impressions of another person, and to express a desire to work with others.

The above work seems to contradict research showing that rejected people act in aggressive and antisocial ways. Why are rejected people sometimes antisocial and at other times prosocial? The deciding factor is whether rejected people think that they will be able to forge new social bonds. Maner and colleagues (2007) found that rejected people did not act so prosocially toward people who rejected them, nor did they act prosocially toward people with whom they did not expect to interact. However, if rejected people expected to interact with a novel partner who had not rejected them, then they were willing to affiliate and therefore behaved in prosocial ways.

Further research supports to the view that rejected people become oriented toward reconnecting with others. Rejected people are more willing than others to alter their spending and consumption behavior so as to increase affiliation with others (Mead, Baumeister, Stillman, Rawn, & Vohs, 2011), so that rejected people are particularly willing to purchase brand name goods (but not practical items) and to try an illegal drug that they perceive to be popular. The motivation to reconnect is also apparent in how rejected people perceive others. Rejected people are better able than others to detect real (Duchenne) versus fake (non-Duchenne) smiles (Bernstein, Young, Brown, Sacco, & Claypool, 2008). Likewise, rejected people show a greater preference than other people do for working with people who exhibit real (versus fake) smiles (Bernstein, Sacco, Brown, Young, & Claypool, 2010). Thus rejected people seem especially sensitive to the potential for reconnection.

Because rejected people are so motivated to reconnect, some of the negative effects of rejection can be eliminated merely by framing a task as being relevant to reconnection. DeWall, Baumeister, and Vohs (2008) revealed that the tendency for social exclusion to undermine self-regulation can be eliminated if the self-regulation task is framed as a diagnostic indicator of one's ability to get along with others. Thus, if rejected people think that a task will help them reconnect, their ability to self-regulate on that task is restored. In contrast, DeWall and colleagues found that socially included people performed worse than others on self-regulation tasks described as diagnostic of social skills. Thus social acceptance does not lead uniformly to positive outcomes! Sometimes, social rejection more so than social acceptance can motivate people to behave in positive and prosocial ways.

THE SELF AS AN INTERPERSONAL ACTOR

Once people have social relationships, how do these relationships influence their selves, and vice versa? One reason people have selves is in order to facilitate interactions and relationships with others. For example, it is difficult to go out on a first date if one is in the middle of an identity crisis. Accordingly, Erik Erikson (1950, 1968) famously asserted that identity is a prerequisite for intimacy. People must settle the problems of identity before they are developmentally ready for intimate relations. The sequence may not be that simple, because identity and intimacy seem to develop together, but the link between the two is hard to deny (Orlofsky, Marcia, & Lesser, 1973; Tesch & Whitbourne, 1982).

Identity is also constructed out of social roles. A series of cluster analyses by Deaux, Reid, Mizrahi, and Ethier (1995) revealed five main types of social identities: relationships (husband, sibling), vocational or avocational role (coin collector, teacher), political affiliation (Republican, feminist), stigmatized identity (homeless person, fat), and religion or ethnicity (Jewish, Hispanic). As products of the culture and society, roles again reveal the interpersonal dimension of selfhood. To fulfill a relationship-oriented role (such as mother or police officer), one must make the self fit a script that is collectively defined. Each person may interpret a given role in a slightly different way, but the role is nonetheless understood by the social group and is a way of relating to others.

Reflexive consciousness itself may depend partly on interpersonal contact. Sartre's (1956) famous analysis of consciousness emphasized what he called "the look," that is, the subjective experience of looking at someone else and knowing that that person is looking at you. The rise in adolescent self-consciousness and social awkwardness is in part a result of the increased cognitive ability to understand how one appears to others. Teenagers feel self-conscious because they are beginning to fully realize how they are being judged by other people.

How do interpersonal interactions shape the self? The *tabula rasa* view of human nature holds that selves are the products of interpersonal relations. That is, people start off as blank slates, and experiences gradually produce the unique individuality of the complex adult self. Although such views are elegant and sometimes politically appealing, they may suggest too passive or simple a role of the self. The self plays an active role in how it is influenced by others. The broader issue is how selfhood is maintained in an interpersonal environment. Part of the self exists in other people's minds. Selfhood cannot be achieved or constructed in solitude.

Self-Esteem and Interpersonal Relationships

Self-esteem may be defined as a person's evaluation of self. Thus, self-esteem is a value judgment based on self-knowledge. Because much of self-knowledge concerns relations with others, it is not surprising that self-esteem is heavily influenced by interpersonal relationships.

Sociometer Theory

Leary et al. (1995) proposed that self-esteem is a sociometer: an internal measure of how one is succeeding at connecting with others (see also Leary & Downs, 1995). In their experimental studies, participants are told that no one has chosen them as a partner for further interaction. This experience causes a decline in state self-esteem. In contrast, being chosen by group members increases state self-esteem. Leary et al. (1995) compare self-esteem to a car's gas gauge. The gas gauge itself does not affect the mechanical functioning of the car, but it serves a crucial function by alerting the driver to how much fuel is in the tank. Leary et al. (1995) suggest that human drivers are strongly motivated to keep their automobile's gas gauge from reading "empty," because most people seek out relationships whenever they see the needle moving toward empty. Self-esteem lets people know when they need "refueling" in the form of human interaction.

Sociometer theory is important for an interpersonal view of the self, because it takes one of the best-known and most prominent intrapsychic variables (self-esteem) and recasts it in interpersonal terms. Concern with self-esteem can easily seem like a private, inner matter. It is easy to assume that self-esteem goes up and down in the person's own inner world with only minimal connection to the environment, and that people accept or reject environmental input according their own choices (e.g., one can either be in denial about a problem, or acknowledge and deal with the problem). Yet sociometer theory proposes that self-esteem is not purely personal but instead fundamentally relies on interpersonal connection.

There is abundant evidence that people are consistently concerned with the need to form and maintain interpersonal connections (Baumeister & Leary, 1995). As discussed previously, such a drive would have a number of evolutionary benefits. The sociometer view can also readily explain why so much emotion is linked to self-esteem, because strong emotional responses are generally associated with interpersonal relationships. In addition, people tend to derive their self-esteem from the same traits that lead to social acceptance (e.g., competence, likability, attractiveness). When people feel socially anxious, however, self-esteem suffers. A review of multiple studies concluded that the average correlation between social anxiety and self-esteem is about −.50 (Leary & Kowalski, 1995). That is, there is a substantial and robust link between worrying about social rejection and having low self-esteem.

But why do people need self-esteem to register changes in social connection, when emotion seems to serve the same purpose? Leary and Baumeister (2000) argue that self-esteem registers long-term eligibility for relationships, rather than just responding to current events. Hence someone might have low self-esteem despite being socially connected—if, for example, she believed that she has managed to deceive people about her true self and personality. If people knew what she is really like, she thinks, they might abandon her. Conversely, someone might have high self-esteem despite having no close friends at the moment, because he might attribute this dearth of friendships to the situation or to the lack of suitable people. He might believe that he will have plenty of friends as soon as there are enough people around who can appreciate his good qualities.

There are several possible objections to the sociometer view. It does seem that people can have high self-esteem without having any close relationship at that moment. There is also not a direct and simple link between one's immediate social status and self-esteem. Self-esteem seems more stable than social inclusion status. Shifting the emphasis from current relationships to perceived eligibility for such relationships is one way to address this problem, but more research is needed to verify whether that solution is correct.

Social and Interpersonal Patterns

Self-esteem is also associated with different patterns of social behavior. Indeed, such differences were one of the original sources of research interest in self-esteem. Janis (1954) hypothesized that people with low self-esteem are more easily persuaded than people with high self-esteem. One of the most influential and popular measures of self-esteem was developed specifically for use in studies of attitude change (Janis & Field, 1959). This measure, usually known as the Janis-Field Feelings of Inadequacy scale, cemented the view that low self-esteem people feel little self-confidence and are easily swayed by other people's arguments.

The view that low self-esteem is associated with greater susceptibility to persuasion was supported in those early studies, and subsequent work built upon those studies to link low self-esteem to a broad range of susceptibility to influence and manipulation. A seminal review article by Brockner (1984) concluded that low self-esteem is marked by what he called "behavioral plasticity"—that is, people with low self-esteem are broadly malleable and easily influenced by others. For example, anxiety-provoking stimuli produce stronger and more reliable effects in low self-esteem people; their reactions are more influenced by the anxiety-provoking situation than people with high self-esteem. Low self-esteem people also show stronger responses to expectancy effects and self-focus inductions.

Self-esteem also affects choices between self-enhancement and self-protection. Many self-esteem differences occur more frequently or only in interpersonal situations, and self-esteem may be fundamentally tied toward self-presentational patterns (see Baumeister, Tice, & Hutton, 1989, for review). In general, people with high self-esteem are oriented toward self-enhancement, whereas people with low self-esteem tend toward self-protection. People with high self-esteem want to capitalize on their strengths and virtues and are willing to take chances in order to stand out in a positive way. On the other hand, people with low self-esteem want to remedy their deficiencies and seek to avoid standing out in a bad way.

High self-esteem people's tendency toward self-enhancement can sometimes make them less likable to others. After receiving a negative evaluation, people high in self-esteem emphasized their independence and separateness from others, whereas low self-esteem people emphasized their interdependence and connectedness with others (Vohs & Heatherton, 2001). These self-construals had direct consequences for interpersonal perceptions. Raters saw the independence-oriented people as less likable and the interdependence-oriented people as more likable. Given the differences in behavior based on level of self-esteem, this meant that partners saw low self-esteem individuals as more likable than high self-esteem individuals. However, these differences occurred only after the high and low self-esteem individuals being rated had received a negative evaluation; presumably self-esteem moderates reactions to ego threat.

Social Identity Theory

Another way that interpersonal relationships influence self-esteem is through group memberships. Social identity theory (e.g., Tajfel, 1982; Tajfel & Turner, 1979; Turner, 1982) argues that the self-concept contains both personal and social attributes. Self-esteem usually focuses on personal attributes, but group memberships are also important. A person will experience higher self-esteem when his or her important social groups are valued and compare favorably to other groups (see also Rosenberg, 1979). Empirical research has confirmed this theory; collective self-esteem (feeling that one's social groups are positive) is correlated with global personal self-esteem (Luhtanen & Crocker, 1992). This is particularly true for members of racial or ethnic minorities (Crocker, Luhtanen, Blaine & Broadnax, 1994). This most likely occurs because minority group members identify more strongly with their ethnic group, and this group is obvious and salient to others. In addition, improving the status of one's group tends to increase personal self-esteem. For example, favoring ingroups over outgroups in allocation of points or rewards can enhance self-esteem, even when the self does not personally benefit from those allocations (e.g., Lemyre & Smith, 1985; Oakes & Turner, 1980). Thus self-esteem is not just personal: It also includes a person's evaluations of the groups to which he or she belongs.

Is High Self-Esteem Always Good?

To place the findings about self-esteem in perspective, it is useful to ask how important and beneficial high self-esteem actually is. In the United States today, many people seem to believe that high self-esteem is extremely beneficial. The strong belief in the benefits of self-esteem is a major reason why it remains a popular topic of discussion and research. By one count, there are almost 7,000 books and articles about self-esteem (Mruk, 1995). The belief that high self-esteem is a vital aspect of mental health and good adjustment is strong and widespread (e.g., Bednar, Wells, & Peterson, 1989; Mruk, 1995; Taylor & Brown, 1988). In many studies, in fact, self-esteem is measured as an index of good adjustment, so even the operational definition of healthy functioning involves self-esteem (e.g., Kahle, Kulka, & Klingel, 1980; Whitley, 1983).

However, there is a "dark side" to high self-esteem, especially concerning interactions with others. Some people with high self-esteem are more likely than most people to aggress against others and be interpersonally violent (Baumeister, Smart, & Boden, 1996). Aggression seems to be most common among people who think well of themselves but then interact with someone who disputes their favorable self-appraisal. In particular, inflated, unrealistic, or fluctuating forms of high self-esteem predict outbursts of violence and aggression. This most likely occurs because these types of self-esteem are the most vulnerable to ego threats (e.g., Blaine & Crocker, 1993; Kernis, Granneman, & Barclay, 1989). People appear to lash out at others who criticize them as a way of avoiding any decrease in their self-esteem and the accompanying negative emotion (see Tangney, Wagner, Fletcher, & Gramzow, 1992). Normally people with high self-esteem do not seem defensive, but that may be because they usually think highly of themselves and expect to succeed at most things. When they do fail or are rejected, they are very surprised and thus may respond dramatically.

Inflated self-esteem also predicts social maladjustment. In one study, researchers compared people's self-descriptions with the descriptions of their friends (Colvin, Block, & Funder, 1995). This identified a group of people who thought more highly of themselves than warranted by the opinions of their friends. When followed over time in a longitudinal design, these self-enhancing people displayed poor social skills and decreased psychological adjustment. In a laboratory study, the people in this group tended to express hostility, interrupt others, be socially awkward, irritate others, talk at people instead of talking with them, and perform a variety of other negatively evaluated behaviors. The composite picture is one of a self-centered, conceited person who lacks genuine regard for others. This picture is quite consistent with the literal meaning of high self-esteem, even though it does not fit the popular stereotype.

Narcissism and Interpersonal Relationships

Another individual difference likely to affect interpersonal relationships is narcissism, usually defined as an exaggerated view of one's importance, influence, and entitlements. People high in self-esteem are more likely to be high in narcissism, although the correlation is low to moderate rather than high. The imperfect correlation probably reflects the fact that high self-esteem is a very heterogeneous category, including plenty of arrogant, narcissistic people as well as others who simply accept themselves without assuming they are superior to others. Put another way, narcissism is a subcategory of high self-esteem; very few people score high in narcissism but low in self-esteem.

Generally, narcissists tend not only to feel good about themselves, but they also expect deference and recognition from others. Thus in some ways narcissism is more interpersonally relevant than self-esteem. Campbell (1999) found that narcissists were more interpersonally attracted to highly positive and highly admiring individuals. Narcissists were less attracted to people who offered greater amounts of emotional intimacy. This occurred because narcissists preferred partners who were more self-oriented rather than other-oriented, as part of a strategy to enhance self-esteem. Thus, narcissists found it more important to be with someone who made them look good rather than to be with someone who truly cared for them. This overall strategy for self-enhancement is linked to a noncaring, nonintimate experience of interpersonal relationships in general. Compared to non-narcissists, narcissists report lower levels of empathy (Watson, Grisham, Trotter, & Biderman, 1984), intimacy (Carroll, 1987), communion (Bradlee & Emmons, 1992), caring (Campbell, 1999), and selflessness (Campbell, Foster, & Finkel, 2002). It seems that a narcissist's first question in a relationship is "What can you do for *me*?"

Narcissists also tend to react badly when they are criticized or challenged by others. In laboratory experiments, Bushman and Baumeister (1998) found that narcissists were considerably more aggressive toward someone who had insulted them, as compared to non-narcissists. When the researchers controlled for narcissism statistically, self-esteem did not predict aggressive behavior. Thus it appears that narcissism is the better predictor of interpersonal hostility. This fits the view that aggression comes from only a subset of people with high self-esteem, while other people with high self-esteem are not aggressive.

Other research has found that narcissists are willing to derogate others after receiving threatening feedback (e.g., Kernis & Sun, 1994). They react with hostility, denigration, and aggression when they feel threatened (Rhodewalt & Morf, 1998). Thus narcissists tend to be more personally sensitive to criticism, but insensitive to how their behavior affects others. Like the research on self-esteem presented above, these results suggest that inflated self-views can often lead to poor consequences for interpersonal relationships.

Reflected Appraisals

The reflected appraisals model suggests that people learn about themselves by interacting with others. People find out what other people think of them and then internalize these opinions into their self-views. In addition, information about the self is often only meaningful in comparison to others (e.g., Festinger, 1954). One is only fat or thin, intelligent or stupid, or friendly or hostile in comparison to other people. In these cases and many others, self-knowledge can grow only when people make these implicit comparisons. Much of reflected appraisals theory stems from symbolic interactionism (e.g., Mead, 1934). Mead's theory argues that most self-knowledge comes from social interactions with other people. The process of reflected appraisals (i.e., how other people's appraisals of you shape your self-understanding) is often described with Cooley's (1902) term the *looking-glass self*. Using an antiquated term for a mirror, the looking-glass self posits that other people provide the mirror through which people see and understand themselves.

Cooley argued that the self-concept consists of "the imagination of our appearance to the other person; the imagination of his judgment of that appearance, and some sort of self-feeling, such as pride or mortification" (p. 184). Thus self-esteem is also heavily influenced by other people's impressions. Mead (1934) elaborated on this notion by suggesting that the self is also shaped by one's vision of how one is perceived by a "generalized other." The "generalized other" is basically the person's whole sociocultural environment. If a society has a negative view of children at a given time, for example, children are likely to internalize this negative view of the generalized other.

An influential literature review by Shrauger and Schoeneman (1979) concluded symbolic interactionism was partially supported by data. The review gathered data comparing self-concepts with the views of others. Although these correlations were positive, they were rather small. Subsequent studies have confirmed that symbolic interaction effects are significant but small (Edwards & Klockars, 1981; Malloy & Albright, 1990). Even some of these weak links can be questioned on methodological grounds, as noted by Felson (1989).

On the other hand, Shrauger and Schoeneman (1979) found that self-concepts were highly correlated with how people *believed* that others perceived them (and subsequent work has replicated this conclusion). Therefore there is a meaningful link between self-perceptions and other-perceptions (although the causal direction is unclear and probably bidirectional). The discrepancy arises between how people actually perceive Bob and how Bob thinks other people perceive him. But Bob's view of himself is quite similar to how he thinks others see him. Thus others do shape self-views, even though people are not always accurate about how others perceive them.

There seem to be two major reasons for these inaccuracies (see Felson, 1989). First, people do not generally tell someone precisely what they think of him or her. The exchange of interpersonal evaluations is highly distorted. People do not want to offend or distress someone by an honest, negative evaluation, and they are often afraid that the person they criticize will no longer like them. (This is a legitimate fear; most humans tend to like people who like them, and distrust those who criticize them.) When refusing a date, for example, people tend to give false and misleading explanations, often resulting in their being unable to discourage further invitations from the same person (e.g., Folkes, 1982). (Although some of these have become so popular that they are now more easily understood as a genuine brush-off: "It's not you, it's me." Translated: "It's totally you. You are the big problem. I'm fine.") Even when people are engaging in deliberate self-presentation, they are not very accurate at estimating the impression they actually make on others (e.g., DePaulo, Kenny, Hoover, Webb, & Oliver, 1987). Given the dearth of honest and precise negative feedback from others, it is not surprising that people's self-views remain blissfully unaffected by those concealed opinions and appraisals.

The other source of distortion is self-deception. People do not accept information directly into their views of themselves. Instead, they filter it, bias it, and adapt it to fit in with what they already believe and what they prefer to believe. Hence even if others do tell Bob exactly what they think of him, he may discount or ignore the unwelcome

parts of the message. Some authors have argued that some amount of optimistic self-deception is necessary for psychological adjustment (Taylor & Brown, 1988).

Influence of Others' Expectancies

Thus, it seems that people do not directly internalize others' opinions of them. However, people might still change their behavior and beliefs according to other people's expectations. For example, Rosenthal and Jacobson (1968) provided a demonstration of the effect of the self-fulfilling prophecy in a study that has become a classic. Teachers were told that certain students were about to experience a leap forward in intelligence and academic success. Although this expectancy was not true (in fact, the supposedly newly intelligent students were chosen at random), the chosen students nevertheless showed increases in academic performance. With new faith in these students' abilities, the teachers presumably provided more encouragement of the students and expected more of them. These expectancies were enough to produce results, even though they originated from outside the students.

Do self-concepts change in response to others' expectancies? Darley and Fazio (1980) argued that a self-fulfilling prophecy can produce three different types of changes: changes in the perceiver's final belief, the target's actual behavior, or the target's self-appraisal. Out of the three, the evidence for the last (the target's self-appraisal) was the weakest. Thus, perceivers see that the target changes his or her behavior and believe that their expectancies are confirmed. However, targets do not usually come to share the perceiver's initially false belief about themselves.

One of the most widely cited studies of self-fulfilling prophecies was performed by Snyder, Tanke, and Berscheid (1977). In their study, male subjects saw bogus photographs of female interaction partners and then had telephone conversations with this partner (who they believed was the woman in the photograph they saw; actually, the photographs were varied randomly). The men who saw a photograph of an attractive woman perceived their telephone partner as more attractive and socially charming than those who saw a photograph of an unattractive woman. These expectancies were confirmed when the women's responses varied depending on how the men interacted with them. However, the women did not accept the way the men treated them when it was unfavorable. When the man thought the woman was unattractive and treated her accordingly, she tended to reject and discount (as inaccurate) his view of her.

Group-level expectancies can also greatly impact a person's behavior. Steele and Aronson (1995) showed that increasing the salience of one's group membership (e.g., reminding someone of their race) can cause a person to perform in a manner stereotypic of the salient group. One common example of that phenomenon invokes the stereotype that Black Americans perform poorly on tests of intelligence. When Black Americans are reminded (versus. not reminded) of their racial group, they tend to perform more poorly on tests of intelligence. This stereotype threat effect works with a number of stereotypes. Women perform worse on math exams when reminded of their gender (Johns, Schmader, & Martens, 2005), and White men perform worse on math tests if they are told they will be compared to Asian men (Aronson et al., 1999). The effect can also work in the opposite direction. Shih, Pittinsky, and Ambady (1999) examined math performance in a sample of Asian-American women. When participants in that sample were reminded of their gender identity, their performance suffered. When their Asian identity was made salient instead, their performance was boosted. Hence, expectations about a group to which one belongs can cause one to behave in a group-consistent manner, whether for better or worse.

SELF-PRESENTATION

The most obvious and proactive way that the self-participates in social life is through self-presentation. Self-presentation is defined as people's attempts to convey information about themselves to others. Some authors have emphasized self-presentation to such an extent that they see life as an ongoing series of roles, played out like an actor on stage (Goffman, 1959).

People seem to be inherently and pervasively concerned with self-presentation. Baumeister (1982) showed that many of social psychology's classic effects only occurred because of self-presentation. For example, subjects in the Asch line-judging study conformed to others' judgments only when these other people were watching. When judgments were anonymous, the conformity effect disappeared. Cognitive and intrapsychic theories that explained many effects seemed to be missing something, because the effects depended on interpersonal contexts. Thus, aggression, helping, attitude change, emotion, attributional patterns, and other responses seemed to change when the individual's acts would be seen by others. Leary (1995) has furnished an even longer and more impressive list, showing effects of self-presentation in contexts ranging from sports teams to business meetings to the beach to mental hospitals.

Favorability of Self-Presentation

In general, people want to present themselves favorably. However, people are sometimes torn between self-enhancement and being seen as likable. The basic question is this: How favorably should one present oneself? People's answers appear to depend on several factors. In Schlenker's (1980, 1986) terms, self-presentation is often the result of a tradeoff between the opposing forces of favorability and believability. People often make positive claims about themselves in order to make a good impression. However, excessively positive claims might not be believed, and they could even be discredited. (For example, you could try to make a good impression by saying you are a good basketball player. Someone might not believe you, or, worse, you might later play basketball and perform poorly.) Boasting about one's abilities and being proved wrong leaves a bad impression.

In one of the earliest and most cited experiments on self-presentation, Schlenker (1975) gave participants moderately negative feedback about their abilities on a novel task prior to a session in which group members would perform the task. Participants were then asked to describe themselves to the group members. Schlenker wanted to see if participants would self-present in positive terms or incorporate the negative feedback they had just received. As it turned out, the favorability of self-presentation depended on whether the upcoming group performance was expected to be public or private. If it would be private, so that no one would know anyone else's performance, then participants presented themselves in rather favorable terms. But if they thought other people would be able to see how well they did, they refrained from boasting. Thus, people seemed to present themselves as favorably as they could get away with: They boasted when it was safe to do so but remained modest when it seemed likely that the truth would be found out.

The possibility of future discrediting is not the only constraint on the favorability of self-presentation. It is also limited by past actions and other socially available information. After all, people do not simply form a wholly new impression of someone with every single interaction. New information is added to old information. The self-presenter must anticipate this and know that whatever is done now will be combined, in the observer's mind, with what the observer already knows.

An early study of the effects of prior knowledge on self-presentation was conducted by Baumeister and Jones (1978). Subjects were told that their interaction partner would read their personality profile. As in Schlenker's (1975) study, people felt constrained to be consistent with independent information. In this case, they altered their self-presentations to fit the randomly assigned feedback. This occurred even when the personality profiles were unfavorable. Yet they did not leave the matter at that: They sought to compensate for the unfavorable image of themselves by presenting themselves extra favorably on other, unrelated dimensions. Thus, people felt constrained to be consistent with what the observer already knew about them, but they tried to compensate for a bad impression by balancing it with unrelated, highly favorable information.

The general trend toward favorable self-presentation may therefore have significant limits. An additional and quite important limit was identified by Tice, Butler, Muraven, and Stillwell (1995). These authors pointed out that nearly all self-presentation research had been done on first meetings between strangers. However, the vast majority of actual social interactions take place between people who already know each other. The studies they performed showed that people tend to be positive and self-enhancing when interacting with strangers, but they are more modest and neutral when presenting themselves to friends. This occurs in part because of differences in the perceivers' knowledge. Strangers know nothing about you, and so it is necessary to convey one's good traits in order to make a favorable impression on them. In addition, a stranger will not be able to dispute an overly favorable self-presentation. On the other hand, friends already have substantial information about you, and so it is not necessary to name all of one's good traits. Meanwhile, friends will know when you are exaggerating. Even if one is being honest, friends will probably not respond well to bragging and self-aggrandizement.

Cognition and Self-Presentation

Do people know what impressions they convey to others? DePaulo et al. (1987) investigated that question by having subjects interact in a round-robin pattern. Each subject interacted with three others, one at a time, in interactions structured around different tasks (e.g., a teaching task versus a competition). After each interaction, both subjects reported their impression of the partner and the impression they thought they had made on the partner. The researchers were then able to determine if there were discrepancies in perceived versus actual impressions. The answers were mixed. There was indeed significant accuracy, although most of the correlations were rather low. People could tell in a general way how the other person's impression of them changed over time. They were not effective, however, at guessing which partner liked them the most or perceived them as most competent. In other words, people cannot often tell who likes them the most. In another analysis, the authors found that people believed that they had made similar impressions on everyone in the group; in fact, different partners reported very different impressions of the same person. People seem to think that they come across the same way to everyone, but they do not.

Baumeister, Hutton, and Tice (1989) studied the cognitive processes behind self-presentation. In this study, subjects were interviewed in pairs. An experimenter instructed one member of each pair to self-present in either a modest or self-enhancing fashion. After the interview, subjects were given a surprise recall test for both their own and their partner's self-presentations, as well as for impressions of the partner. Subjects who had been instructed to be modest and self-effacing showed impaired memory for the interaction. Apparently, acting modestly (which is an unusual way to act with strangers) causes greater cognitive load and interferes with the memory storage process during the interaction. In addition, subjects seemed unaware of the influence they had on the other person (see Gilbert & Jones, 1986). Thus, for example, if Brandon presents himself by saying highly favorable things about himself, Harry may also start to boast. This might lead Brandon to conclude that Harry must be rather conceited (or at least very self-confident). In fact, Harry's self-promotion was merely a response to Brandon's.

The increase in cognitive load caused by counterinstinctual self-presentation may explain some of the findings of DePaulo et al. (1987). When people are concentrating on trying to make a certain impression, they may not be fully able to attend to how the other person is responding. After a series of interactions, people may remember merely that they tried to make roughly the same good impression on each interaction partner. However, they might not remember that the partners responded to them differently. Thus, self-presentation is not always successful because it is difficult cognitive work. Making a good impression consumes so many resources that people find it hard to attend to other people's responses and adjust that impression (e.g., Vohs, Baumeister, & Ciarocco, 2005).

Harmful Aspects of Self-Presentation

Through various means, self-presentation can lead to health risks (Leary, Tchividjian, and Kraxberger, 1994). For example, concern about the impression one is making can lead to risky and harmful behaviors; at times, the drive to impress others can outweigh self-preservation. How does this occur? Appearance concerns are a relevant example. On the one hand, people believe that having a suntan is attractive; on the other, most people have heard the warnings about skin cancer. Leary and Jones (1993) showed that the risky behaviors of sunbathing were mainly linked to concern over physical appearance and to the lack of concern about health. People sunbathe to make themselves attractive, often ignoring the physical danger involved. High-heeled and platform shoes are another example: many women wear them because they think it makes them look attractive despite the pain, back problems, and lack of coordination that such shoes often cause. Risky sexual behavior is also influenced by self-presentation. Condoms are generally regarded as the safest method for having intercourse outside of stable, monogamous relationships, but many people do not use them. People often cite self-presentational concerns when explaining their lack of protection, such as embarrassment when buying them and the fear of making a bad impression on an anticipated sexual partner (Leary, 1995). Other risks reviewed by Leary et al. (1994) include hazardous dieting and eating patterns, use of alcohol and illegal drugs, cigarette smoking, steroid use, accidental injury and even death (e.g., not wearing safety equipment), and complications from cosmetic surgery. Taken together, these provide strong evidence that self-presentational concerns often take precedence over the concerns with maintaining health and even protecting life.

Recent work has demonstrated that self-presentational risk taking is often motivated by mate seeking, particularly among men. Males have been shown to engage in risky behavior when sexually aroused and in the presence of a romantically available female (Baker & Maner, 2009). Similar work has found that men report a willingness to take extremely dangerous risks when sexually motivated. When motivated (versus not motivated) to attract mates, men report a greater willingness to confront armed burglars and to rescue a stranger who is being attacked by a grizzly bear (Griskevicius et al., 2007). People may thus be willing to put their lives on the line (or at least they will lay claim to) in order to be viewed favorably by others.

INTERPERSONAL CONSEQUENCES OF SELF-VIEWS

Clearly, characteristics of the self exert an influence on interpersonal relations. One of the best-known findings in social psychology is the link between similarity and attraction (Byrne, 1971; Smeaton, Byrne, & Murnen, 1989); that is, people like those who resemble them. (Or, at least, they avoid and dislike people who are different from them; Rosenbaum, 1986.) Similarities on important, heritable traits are especially potent bases for liking and disliking others (Crelia & Tesser, 1996; Tesser, 1993).

Self-Views Alter Person Perception

Evidence suggests that self-views affect how people understand others. Markus, Smith, and Moreland (1985; see also Fong & Markus, 1982) examined the role of self-schemas in person perception. Self-schemas are mental structures that organize and process information about the self in relation to some domain. People who have well-developed self-schemas in a particular domain are described as being schematic in that domain. Hence a record store owner and a piano teacher might both be described as schematic in the domain of music. Markus and colleagues proposed that someone who has a self-schema in a particular domain will act like an expert in that domain. For example, schematic people will spot domain-relevant information faster, integrate it into existing information better, and fill in gaps in information more thoroughly. In Markus et al.'s research, people who were schematic for masculinity tended to group more items together when judging the masculinity-relevant behavior of a stimulus person. They also saw the stimulus person as more masculine and more like themselves than did aschematic individuals.

Thus, aspects of self-concept can influence the perception of others. (However, it is also possible that greater interest in the area relevant to the self leads to the expertise.) The key point appears to be that a particularly well-developed aspect of self-knowledge makes one act like an expert in that sphere. If your view of yourself emphasizes loyalty, for example, you will probably be more sensitive to loyalty or disloyalty in others.

One mechanism driving the link between self-views and person perception is the *self-image bias* (Lewicki, 1983, 1984). According to this bias, people tend to judge others on the basis of traits in their areas of strength. Thus there is a correlation between the favorability and the centrality of self-ratings (Lewicki, 1983). That is, people's most favorable traits are also those which are most central and important for their judgments of others—people judge others by a standard that favors them (the perceiver). For example, students who did well in a computer science course tended to place more emphasis on computer skills when judging others than did students who did not perform well in the computer course (Hill, Smith, & Lewicki, 1989). Lewicki (1984) showed that the self-image bias serves a defensive function: When people receive negative feedback, the effect of self-image bias on perception of others is increased. Along these lines, Dunning, Perie, and Story (1991) found that people construct prototypes of social categories such as intelligence, creativity, and leadership in ways that emphasize their own traits. Thus, inquisitive people think inquisitiveness is a valuable aid to creativity, but noninquisitive people do not believe that inquisitiveness has any far-reaching implications for other outcomes. These prototypes then influence how people evaluate others.

Rejecting a view of self through a defensive process also affects person perception. Newman, Duff, and Baumeister (1997) proposed a new model of the Freudian defense mechanism of *projection* (basically, seeing one's faults in other people rather than in oneself). This model builds on evidence that suggests that when people try not to think about something, it instead becomes highly accessible in memory (Wegner & Erber, 1992). Newman et al. showed that when people tried to suppress thoughts about a bad trait that had been attributed to them, they then interpreted other people's behavior in terms of that bad trait. Thus, person perception can be shaped by the traits you are trying to deny in yourself, just as much as by the traits that you do see in yourself.

All of these effects can be explained by accessibility. The attributes the self emphasizes, and those the self seeks to deny, operate as highly accessible categories for interpreting others' behavior (Higgins, King, & Mavin, 1982). Social perception thus tends to be self-centered and self-biased. Still, these effects appear to be specific and limited; not all interpersonal perception is wildly distorted by self-appraisals. In particular, these effects seem to be limited to situations in which information about the target person is ambiguous (Lambert & Wedell, 1991; Sedikides & Skowronski, 1993).

Self-Evaluation Maintenance

Several important links between self-esteem and interpersonal relations have been elaborated in Tesser's (1988) self-evaluation maintenance theory. Among other

consequences, this theory explains how people may become closer to or more distant from relationship partners as a result of pressures to maintain self-esteem. According to Tesser (1988), two main processes link self-views to interpersonal outcomes. First is the process of *reflection*; one can gain esteem when a close other achieves something. People gain a boost in esteem simply because their uncle is a Congressman, their child is quarterback of the football team, they slept with a movie star, or their college basketball team wins a championship. Cialdini and his colleagues have shown how people bask in reflected glory of institutions, such as by wearing school colors more frequently following a team victory than following a defeat (Cialdini & Richardson, 1980).

The other process is one of *comparison* (see Festinger, 1954; Wills, 1981); this process can instead lead to a decrease in self-esteem when a close other achieves something. People may compare themselves with others close to them—and feel bad if the other person is outperforming them. If your sibling gets better grades than you, if your dimwit brother-in-law earns double your salary, or if your friend wins a scholarship or a job you wanted, you may lose esteem.

Thus, the reflection and comparison processes of close others produce opposite effects on self-esteem. Tesser's work has therefore gone on to look for factors that determine which process will operate in a given situation. One factor is the *relevance* of the accomplishment to one's self-concept. Thus, a friend's football victory may bring you esteem as the reflection process predicts—but only if your own football-playing ability is not highly relevant to your own self-esteem. If you played in the same football game and performed terribly, your friend's success would make you look that much worse by comparison. For this reason, people prefer to see strangers succeed rather than close friends when the domain in question is highly self-relevant, because the stranger's success does not invite such close comparison and is less humiliating. Tesser and Smith (1980) showed that people will do more to help a stranger than a friend to succeed at a task that is relevant to the person's own self-esteem.

Meanwhile, the closer the relationship is, the greater the effect. A person gains (or loses) more esteem if one's spouse wins a major award than if one's hairdresser wins it. Thus the comparison process may be especially disruptive to close relationships. If a romantic partner succeeds on something irrelevant to one's own self-esteem, one may feel closer to the romantic partner. If the partner succeeds at something highly relevant to one's own self-esteem, then one may feel jealous or threatened. The intimate relationship may be damaged (Beach, 1992). When the comparison process makes a person look bad, the only way to limit the damage may be to reduce closeness. Research confirms that people distance themselves from someone who performs too well on something that is highly relevant to their self-concepts (Pleban & Tesser, 1981).

Close Others' Views of Self

Swann (1992) advanced a simpler theory of how interpersonal relationships are shaped by self-views. The theory was based on the idea that people are motivated to seek information that confirms their self-concepts (Swann, 1990). Extending that view, Swann argued that people prefer a romantic partner who sees them as they see themselves. People are sometimes torn between a desire to see themselves favorably and a desire to confirm what they already think of themselves (as we discussed earlier). If love is truly blind, a person in love would see the beloved partner in an idealized way. Would such idealized views be helpful or harmful given the tendency for people to want to confirm their self-views?

Swann and his colleagues (Swann, Hixon, & De La Ronde, 1992) have examined such dilemmas in various relationships, ranging from roommates to spouses. On a variety of measures, they found that people prefer to be with someone who confirms their self-views over someone who sees them favorably. People choose, like, and retain partners who see them accurately. Indeed, there seems to be a powerful link between romantic relationship partners and the desire for self-verification. Recent work revealed that mere reminders of a significant other are sufficient to activate the self-verification motive (Kraus & Chen, 2009). Reminders of acquaintances did not have the same effect, and those who were reminded of significant others even preferred self-verifying feedback to positive feedback. This research might explain why some people have partner after partner who treats them badly: they somehow feel that they do not deserve to be treated well. In this view, the idealizing effects of love are dangerous and harmful to the relationship. Apparently people want their friends and lovers to see all their faults.

However, a large independent investigation found that favorability is more important than consistency with self-views. Murray, Holmes, and Griffin (1996a) found that favorable views of one's partner were associated with better relationships. Idealization was associated with greater satisfaction and happiness about the relationship. A follow-up study (Murray, Holmes, and Griffin, 1996b) found that favorable views of one's partner predicted greater stability and durability of the relationship. This research suggests that perhaps love should be blind (or at least nearsighted enough to wear rose-colored glasses when looking at the loved one). The authors argue that idealized love is not blind, but instead farsighted; partners who idealized each other created the relationships they wanted. Idealization and positive illusions about one's partner seem to strengthen the relationship, making it more pleasant and more likely to last. Seeing the real person beneath the facade is not always the beginning of real intimacy: Sometimes it is the beginning of the end.

These somewhat discrepant results do at least agree that it is quite important for people to believe that their friends and lovers appreciate their good points. It is less clear if people want their partners to also see their faults and flaws. One possible explanation for the discrepant results of the two authors is that most of Swann's self-consistency work has emphasized traits about which the person is highly certain of and committed to having. On the other hand, Murray's favorability effects tend to emphasize a broader spectrum of less certain traits. People might want their close relationship partners to recognize one or two favorite faults but otherwise maintain a highly favorable view of them.

Recent work suggests that others' views of the self can combine with self-verification motives to create self-fulfilling prophecies. A longitudinal study examined self-fulfilling prophecies in the domain of mothers' expectations about their children's alcohol intake (Madon et al., 2008). Three potential causes of self-fulfilling prophecies in that context were examined. First, children could model alcohol intake by watching their parents (e.g., a mother who thinks her kids will surely drink might exhibit drinking behavior herself). Second, children could be influenced by informational conformity (e.g., by thinking that is socially acceptable to drink based on their mothers' expectations). Third, children could adopt their parents' views about them ("If my mom thinks I am the type of kid who will drink, then she is probably right") and then seek to verify those views once they are adopted. Madon and colleagues found support for the third model. Mothers' views were adopted during an initial stage. Then self-verification motives appeared to drive drinking behavior during a second stage, thereby producing the self-fulfilling prophecy.

There is also intriguing but preliminary evidence that relationship partners can help sustain consistency. Swann and Predmore (1985) gave people feedback that was discrepant from their self-views and watched how they and their romantic partners responded. When the subject and the subject's partner agreed that the feedback was wrong, the pair then joined forces to reject it: They discussed its flaws and decided how best to refute or dismiss it. In contrast, when the partner's view of the subject differed from the subject's self-views, the discrepant feedback led to further disagreements between the subject and partner. It may be that one vital function of close relationship partners is to help maintain and defend one's self-concept against the attacks of the outer world (see also De La Ronde & Swann, 1998).

Sedikides, Campbell, Reeder, and Elliot (1998) explored another important link between self-deception and the interpersonal self. They examined the self-serving bias, a classic pattern of self-deception that occurs when people take credit for success but deny blame for failure. When people work in groups, the self-serving bias produces the tendency to hog the credit for success at joint tasks but dump the blame for failure on the other group members. However, the authors found that self-serving bias is mitigated when the group members feel a close interpersonal bond with each other. Thus, people will flatter themselves at their partner's expense—but only when they do not care much about the partner. The interpersonal context dictates whether people will display the self-serving bias.

Self-Handicapping

To self-handicap involves explaining away failure (or even possible failure) by attributing it to external causes (often external causes of his or her own making). Self-handicapping is usually studied within the context of individual performance, but it has a strong interpersonal aspect as well. One study manipulated whether several crucial aspects of the situation were public (known to others) or private (known only to the subject; Kolditz and Arkin, 1982). Self-handicapping emerged mainly in the public conditions, when the subject's handicap and subsequent performance would be seen by others. In contrast, subjects did not self-handicap when the experimenter was unaware of the handicap. Apparently, self-handicapping is primarily a self-presentational strategy used to control the impression one makes on other people. Self-handicapping rarely occurs when people are concerned only with their private self-views.

EMOTIONS AND THE INTERPERSONAL SELF

Emotions often reflect value judgments relevant to the self. Self-discrepancy theory describes the relationship between self-views and the experience of emotion (Higgins, 1987). That theory posits that people hold numerous views of the self that serve as guides, such as the ideal self (whom one aspires to be) and the ought self (whom one should be). When a person's actual self fails to meet and thus becomes discrepant from one's self guides, negative emotions are experienced. Failing to realize one's ideal self leads to disappointment and sadness, while failing to realize one's ought self leads to agitation and guilt. Recent work has also increasingly emphasized interpersonal determinants and processes of emotion (Tangney & Fischer, 1995). Various emotions and their relationships both to the self and to interpersonal relationships are described below.

Shame and Guilt

Both shame and guilt have strong interpersonal components. The difference between the two lies in how much of the self is affected: Guilt denounces a specific action by the self, while shame condemns the entire self (Lewis, 1971; Tangney, 1992, 1995).

Shame is usually the more destructive of the two emotions. Because shame signifies that the entire self is bad, simple reparations or constructive responses seem pointless. This absence of constructive solutions probably leads to many of the pathological outcomes connected with shame, such as suicide and/or major depression (Tangney, Burggraf, & Wagner, 1995). Shame also seems to produce socially undesirable outcomes such as a complete withdrawal from others. Other people, however, respond to shame with anger (Tangney et al., 1992). The shift from shame into anger may be a defensive effort to negate the global negative evaluation. There is some evidence that this shift in emotions can lead to violent outbursts (Baumeister et al., 1996). Kitayama, Markus, and Matsumoto (1995) have proposed that the movement from shame to anger reflects the independent selfhood model common to Western cultures and may not occur in cultures that emphasize more interdependent selves.

In contrast, guilt is more reparable and less socially disruptive than shame. Guilt has a strong basis in relationships even when no transgression is involved. For example, some people feel "survivor guilt" because they have survived when others have died or suffered. The term originated in studies of survivors of the Holocaust and the Hiroshima bombing (Lifton, 1967). More recently, survivor guilt emerged during episodes of corporate downsizing, when people who kept their jobs felt guilty while others were fired (Brockner, Davy, & Carter, 1985).

In general, people may feel guilty when they outperform others (Exline & Lobel, 1999).

According to Baumeister, Stillwell, and Heatherton (1994), guilt is mainly interpersonal and seems designed to strengthen relationships. People may try to avoid hurting close others because it makes them feel guilty. After a transgression, guilt makes people seek to make amends or rectify the situation in an attempt to repair the damage to the relationship. It makes people change their behavior so that they will not repeat the damaging behavior. It makes them try to live up to the expectations of others. Feeling guilty is sometimes beneficial to the relationship in and of itself, because guilty feelings confirm that the person cares about the relationship (even if the transgression made it appear that they did not care). In addition, people sometimes exaggerate how hurt or upset they are by another person's actions, in order to make that person guilty. The guilt makes the other person more willing to comply with the wishes of the person who felt hurt. This tactic can be used to redistribute power in a relationship: Guilt enables otherwise powerless people to sometimes get their way. Usually, the person who is hurt makes his or her feelings and disappointment clear. If the other person cares about your welfare, he or she will want to avoid hurting you, because hurting you will make him or her feel guilty. Hence the person will do what you want.

Baumeister, Reis, and Delespaul (1995) confirmed that guilt plays an important role in close relationships. The authors asked participants to describe their most recent experience of six different emotions, including guilt. These were then coded for the level of interpersonal connection. Guilt scored the highest of the six major emotions on interpersonal connection. That is, hardly any guilt stories referred to solitary experiences or interactions with strangers; the overwhelming majority of guilt stories involved partners in close relationships, such as family members or romantic partners.

Embarrassment

Similar to shame and guilt, embarrassment seems to be a mixture of self and interpersonal concerns. Modigliani (1971) linked embarrassment to the public self by showing that the best predictor of embarrassment was a situational, perceived loss of others' good opinion. In addition, susceptibility to embarrassment correlates more highly with public self-consciousness than with private self-consciousness (Edelmann, 1985).

In an influential review, Miller (1995) argued that two theoretical perspectives on embarrassment are predominant. The first theory emphasizes concern over being evaluated by others; to be embarrassed, you must be concerned about others' evaluations. The alternative view invokes the unpleasant nature of awkward social interactions. In one study, Parrott, Sabini, and Silver (1988) presented participants with a hypothetical scenario in which someone refused a date. People reported that they would feel less embarrassed if the rejector used an obvious excuse than if the rejector bluntly rejected them, even if the person's rejection was equally negative. However, making an excuse may itself convey a positive evaluation, such as concern for the rejected person's feelings (Miller, 1995). Miller concluded that both perspectives are valid; nevertheless, the concern over social evaluation is the more common cause of embarrassment.

Blushing is one common sign of embarrassment, but people sometimes blush even when there is no obvious social evaluation. Leary, Britt, Cutlip, and Templeton (1992) concluded that unwanted social attention is the most common cause of blushing. In general, people blush as an appeasement to others after violating social norms. People hope that looking embarrassed after a transgression will inform other people that they feel remorseful. Apparently embarrassment is effective in minimizing negative evaluations. Semin and Manstead (1982) found that subjects expressed greater liking toward someone who was embarrassed after an accidental transgression. When the target person was not embarrassed, subjects did not like the person as much.

Social Anxiety

Schlenker and Leary (1982) argued that social anxiety is directly linked to self-presentation. In their view, social anxiety arises when someone wants to make a particular, desired impression but fears that she will fail to do so. As Leary and Kowalski (1995) describe it, social anxiety is essentially a concern about controlling public impressions. Making a particular impression is important for gaining acceptance by others and for achieving status (two important interpersonal goals). Given the importance of being perceived positively by others, it is hardly surprising that some people become extremely concerned and anxious during social situations.

Happiness

Early research on emotion and the self has focused on negative emotions, but positive emotions are also relevant to selfhood and social life. Research on happiness has flourished in recent years, due in large part to the positive psychology movement. One theory about happiness that has emerged from that movement is the broaden-and-build theory (Fredrickson, 2001). That theory posits that the function of happiness is to promote a broadening of resources. Happy people are open to trying new activities and interacting with new people, and that can lead to new skills and friendships on which to draw in the future.

Broaden-and-build theory dovetails nicely with functional accounts of negative emotions. Most negative emotions incite a person to resolve a specific problem or goal. Guilt might motivate a person to make up for a past transgression, while disappointment might motivate a person to overcome some poor performance. Once the transgression is forgiven or one's performance improved, positive emotions such as joy and happiness may result. Those positive feelings can then motivate a person to acquire new skills and forge new friendships, which can prove helpful in dealing with future goals and obstacles.

Disclosing Emotion and Personal Information

So far, we have discussed the interpersonal roots of emotion. But how do interpersonal situations affect the expression of these emotions? Clark, Pataki, and Carver (1995) found that people are careful about how much happiness they express when they are concerned about the impression they are making on others. As an influential review showed, people are concerned that their success will create feelings of jealousy and dislike (Exline & Lobel, 1999). Clark et al. (1995) also found that people express anger in an attempt to get their own way. Sadness can also be used as an interpersonal lever; people show sadness when they want others to see them as dependent to help them. These strategies correspond to the self-presentational tactics of ingratiation, intimidation, and supplication (Jones & Pittman, 1982). A more general statement was provided by DePaulo (1992): People can either exaggerate or downplay their emotional reactions in order to meet their self-presentational goals. That is, sometimes it is best to pretend to be having a strong emotional reaction, and other times it is advantageous to conceal one's emotions.

Levels of self-disclosure are also affected by self-control. When people's will power is depleted by a self-control task, they are less able to maintain an appropriate level of self-disclosure. People with an avoidant attachment style withdraw too much during interactions after being depleted, while those with an anxious attachment style disclose too much (Vohs et al., 2005). Because a moderate amount of self-disclosure is best for smooth interaction, self-regulatory depletion affects the quality of interactions through disrupting self-disclosure.

CULTURAL AND HISTORICAL VARIATIONS IN SELFHOOD

Most of the research presented so far has studied North American college students at specific points in time (usually between 1975 and 2000). Although this research is informative, it also does not capture the variations in selfhood across the cultures of the world and the decades of the century. Given that the self is an inherently social construct, there should be considerable cultural and historical variation.

Culture and Society

Recent decades have brought much interest in the cultural determinants of selfhood. In way of summary, it is useful to draw from an influential review article by Triandis (1989). This review identified several key features of selfhood that vary across different cultures. First, cultures vary in conceptions of the *private self,* or how people understand themselves (e.g., self-regard, self-esteem, introspection, and individual decision making). Second, the *public self* refers to how the individual is perceived by other people, thus including issues such as reputation, specific expectations of others, and impression management. Third, the *collective self* involves memberships in various social groups, from the family to an employing organization or an ethnic group. Triandis argues that individualistic societies such as the United States emphasize the private and public selves and downplay the collective self, whereas other (e.g., Asian) societies tend to emphasize the collective self while downplaying the private self. Variation in these conceptions may also occur within a society. For example, some authors have argued that African-Americans show more collectivistic tendencies compared to white Americans (e.g., Baldwin & Hopkins, 1990).

Triandis (1989) also proposed several important cultural dimensions that have important implications for the self. One dimension is individualism versus collectivism. Individualistic societies support diversity, self-expression, and the rights of individuals, whereas collectivistic societies promote conformity and a sense of obligation to the group. As a general rule, Western societies such as the United States are more individualistic, while Asian and African societies are more collectivistic. In general, relationships are closer in collectivistic societies. The concept of an independent, individual self is not as common; rather, a person sees his- or herself as overlapping with the selves of close others.

Another dimension that varies between societies is tightness, or the amount of social pressure on individuals. Tight societies demand that individuals conform to the group's values, role definitions, and norms. In contrast, loose societies allow people more freedom to do what they want. (For that reason, tight societies tend to promote the public and collective selves, whereas loose ones allow more scope for the private self to flourish.)

A third dimension of cultural variation proposed by Triandis (1989) is societal complexity. In a complex society, an individual tends to belong to many different groups; thus it is less imperative to stay on good terms with any of these groups. The collective self is therefore not so crucially important. In addition, complex societies allow greater development of the private self (because of the greater availability of many social relationships). The public self is also quite important because it is the common feature of all one's social relations. In contrast, in a simple society people belong to relatively few groups, each of which is then quite important in defining the self. The collective self flourishes in adapting to these memberships, and the need to conform to the group tends to stifle the private self.

Triandis (1989) illustrated some of his central ideas by contrasting U.S. and Japanese societies. Japan tends to be more collectivistic and tighter than the United States, and as a result there is much greater homogeneity: Japanese citizens tend to eat the same foods, while Americans use the prerogative of the private self and choose from a broad assortment. Certain Asian traditions, such as having the oldest male order the same food for the entire table, would be unthinkable in the United States, where each individual's special preferences is honored.

Furthermore, Americans place a premium on sincerity. At its base, sincerity is the congruency between public and private selves: You are supposed to say what you mean and mean what you say. In Japan, however, public actions are more important than private sentiments. For example, Americans object to hypothetical dilemmas in which people think one thing and say another, while Japanese respondents approved of these options.

Markus and Kitayama (1991) proposed that Asian and Western cultures primarily vary in independence versus interdependence. Western cultures, they argue, emphasize the independent self: People are supposed to attend to themselves, to discover and express their unique attributes, and to try to stand out in important ways. In the West, they say, "the squeaky wheel gets the grease." In contrast, Asian cultures emphasize interdependence. Asians are expected to attend to others, to conform to group demands and role obligations, and to try to fit in to the group. In Asia, "the nail that stands out gets pounded down." To the Western mind, the self is an autonomous unit, which is essentially separate and unique, whereas the Asian view begins with an assumption of the basic and pervasiveness connectedness of people.

Multiple consequences flow from this idea. As might be expected in an interdependent culture, relationship harmony was more important to self-esteem for students in Hong Kong compared to students in the United States (Kwan, Bond, & Singelis, 1997). Because relationships are more intertwined with the self in these cultures, they are more important to self-esteem and life satisfaction.

Self-enhancing biases differ between the two types of cultures. Early work in this area found that Americans tended to self-enhance, while Japanese tended to self-criticize (Kitayama, Markus, Matsumoto, & Norasakkunkit, 1997). More recent work, however, suggests that individuals in both independent and interdependent cultures self-enhance, albeit in different ways. That work suggests that Americans tend to self-enhance on individualistic attributes, while Asians tend to self-enhance on collectivistic attributes (Sedikides, Gaertner, & Toguchi, 2003).

Emotional experiences also differ according to cultural models of the self. Early work on emotional experience argued that self-focused attention increased the intensity of emotional experience (Scheier, 1976; Scheier & Carver, 1977). More recent work, however, revealed that cultural differences predict different effects of self-focus on emotional experience (Chentsova-Dutton & Tsai, 2010). Attention to individual aspects of the self intensifies emotional experiences more among European Americans than among Asian Americans. The converse is true for relational aspects of the self, so that Asian Americans' emotional experiences are more intensely experienced than European Americans' when focused on interpersonal dimensions of the self.

People from independent cultures also tend to describe others in terms of cross-situation, person-centered traits (e.g., he is stingy). In contrast, people from interdependent cultures tend to describe others more in terms of specific contexts (e.g., "He behaves properly with guests but feels sorry if money is spent on them"; Markus & Kitayama, 1991, p. 232). Self-descriptions also vary between cultures

(Bond & Cheung, 1983; Cousins, 1989). Japanese college students asked to finish the sentence "I am..." were more likely to respond with social roles ("brother," "student at Tokyo University"), whereas American college students were more likely to respond in terms of personal attributes ("outgoing," "blonde"). Thus members of independent societies see themselves and others in terms of relatively constant personality traits, while members of interdependent societies see personality and behavior as more dependent on the situation.

In addition, interdependent societies do not emphasize consistency among private thoughts and feelings as much as independent societies. In an interdependent society, it is more important to be accommodating and kind than to be internally consistent. Among independent selves, politeness means giving the other person the maximum freedom to express unique, special, and changing wants. Among interdependent selves, however, politeness means anticipating what the other might want and showing appreciation for their actions. There are also emotional consequences, as Markus and Kitayama explain. In the West, the expression versus suppression of anger has long been a point of controversy; anger is socially disruptive, but it also expresses the needs of the individual. In Asian cultures, however, there is no controversy: anger is to be avoided at all costs.

Thus it is important to consider culture when studying the self. Most research on the self, like that on most psychological topics, has involved participants from Western countries. As a result, it may exaggerate the fundamental nature and pervasiveness of the independent self. Although cultures share many conceptions of selfhood, many others show striking differences.

Historical Evolution of Self

It is not necessary to visit multiple cultures to find variations in selfhood. There is often ample variation within a single culture, because cultural change over time modifies the society. This is the root of research on birth cohort differences (e.g., Caspi, 1987; Stewart & Healy, 1989; Twenge, 2000, 2001a, 2001b): your generation influences the culture you are exposed to and thus your individual characteristics. Western culture's dominant ideas about selfhood have changed and evolved dramatically over the past few centuries (see Baumeister, 1987; Twenge & Campbell, 2001). Thus, the special nature of the modern Western form of selfhood can be understood in a historical context as well as in the context of cross-cultural comparisons. These changes are important for the interpersonal

self because many of these trends have affected personal relationships and the independent versus interdependent nature of the self. Just as some cultures (such as the West) are more independent, so are some time periods (such as 1970 to the present). In addition, shifts in self-views due to societal trends demonstrate the inherently social nature of the self: it changes in response to the larger society and one's generational peers.

Medieval Times to the 20th Century

During medieval times, people did not have identity crises the way we do today (see Baumeister, 1987, for a review). In earlier times, age, gender, and family were the decisive determinants of life outcomes and thus of identity. There were set patterns for life depending on the constraints of these ascribed attributes; if you were born a peasant worker, you stayed a peasant worker. Upward mobility was almost nonexistent, and most men entered their father's profession or were apprenticed to a profession chosen by their parents. Religion dictated strict standards for behavior and worship. Many marriages were arranged. To put it crudely, a rigid society told our ancestors who they were, and there was not much they could do about it. In general, these societies were more collectivistic and tighter than Western societies are today.

Over the course of several centuries, Western societies became more individualistic and looser. For example, modern selves are based on changing rather than stable attributes. Gender and family background slowly became less important than more changeable attributes such as ability, diligence, and personality. The modern Western self can be defined and redefined much more than the self of earlier eras. This greater freedom has also shifted the burden of defining the self onto the individual; today everyone can choose from a wide spectrum of possible identities. This freedom can cause anxiety, however, because these choices can be overwhelming in their scope and direction. It also requires great self-knowledge, because decisions about careers and romantic partners are based on suitability (What is the best job for me? Is this man the one I'm supposed to marry?). The burden falls most heavily on adolescents, because adolescence ends with the formation of adult identity (e.g., Erikson, 1968). Hence in the 20th century, adolescence has become a period of indecision, uncertainty, experimentation, and identity crisis (see Baumeister & Tice, 1986).

The 1960s to the Present

The trend toward greater focus on the self has accelerated in recent decades. Over the past 30 years, the self has become increasingly more individualized and autonomous. During the late 1960s and 1970s, popular culture promoted self-fulfillment, self-love, and "being your own best friend" (Ehrenreich & English, 1978). Pollsters noted that "the rage for self-fulfillment" had spread everywhere (Yankelovich, 1981). At one time, duty and modesty were the most favorable traits; during the 1970s, however, self-help books advised "a philosophy of ruthless self-centeredness" that informed people that "selfishness is not a dirty word" (Ehrenreich & English, 1978, p. 303). The preoccupation with self so permeated the society that Lasch (1978) called it "The Culture of Narcissism," Jones (1980, p. 260) spoke of the decade's "orgy of self-gratification," and the young adults of the 1970s acquired the label "The 'Me' Generation." Increasingly, proclaiming that you loved, cherished, and valued yourself was no longer an immodest proposition (Jones, 1980; Rosen, 1998; Swann, 1996). By the 1980s, Whitney Houston could sing (without irony) that "the greatest love of all" was for one's self.

This emphasis on individualism had specific consequences for many interpersonal relationships. Because spouses and children necessarily hindered the expression of unfettered individualism, writers and commentators increasingly portrayed marriage and children as "a drag" (Ehrenreich & English, 1978, p. 295). For example, if there was a conflict between what is best for the marriage and what is best for the self, earlier generations often placed the obligation to marriage as the supreme duty, but more recent generations placed the self higher (Zube, 1972). "From now on, Americans would live *for themselves*," notes David Frum in his cultural history of the 1970s (2000, p. 58). "If anyone or anything else got in the way—well, so much the worse for them." It is probably not a coincidence that divorce rates began to rise substantially during the late 1960s and early 1970s, just as this new individualism was taking hold (Frum, 2000).

In addition, many authors have argued that the 1970s promoted negative attitudes toward children—what the Germans call "Kinderfeindlichkeit," or "hostility toward children" (see, e.g., Holtz, 1995; Strauss & Howe, 1991). According to some authors, the growing emphasis on individualism tended to decrease the priority parents placed on children's needs as opposed to their own (Ehrenreich & English, 1978). At the same time, the birth rate declined during the 1970s, reaching historic lows that have not been equaled since. Children did not fit into the picture of individual self-fulfillment—after all, what could they really do for their parents?

Not only did the general societal ethos promote the self, but a *self-esteem movement* (an offshoot of the "human potential" and "self-growth" movements) gained prevalence, arguing that "the basis for *everything* we do is self-esteem" (MacDonald, 1986, p. 27; quoted in Seligman, 1995). During the early 1980s, educators began actively to promote self-esteem in schoolchildren. This was partially accomplished by affirmation (children were given T-shirts that said "I'm lovable and capable" or sang songs about self-love; e.g., Swann, 1996). In addition, many schools discouraged criticism, telling teachers not to correct misspellings or grammar mistakes, so as not to harm a child's self-esteem (Sykes, 1995). Thus the culture increasingly promoted self-esteem as an end onto itself, rather than as an outcome of accomplishment or meaningful personal relationships.

This popular interest in the self also meant that young people became increasingly exposed to self-esteem as a desirable goal. Gergen (1973) argued that the popularization of psychological concepts often creates changes in the responses of the subject populations. Self-esteem is a prime candidate for changes based on popularization. Not only has self-esteem been directly trumpeted by social movements and promoters, but the concept has received wide media attention in newspapers, magazines, television programs, and popular music (Whitney Houston sings about it, and a popular song in the mid-1990s explained the singer's misguided actions as resulting from "low self-esteem"). If anything, this attention increased during the 1980s. While the self-esteem and human potential movements reached only some people in the 1970s, the 1980s and 1990s saw talk about self-esteem enter the mainstream.

Empirical searches show that coverage of self-esteem has increased substantially in the popular press (these searches were originally performed for Twenge & Campbell, 2001). In 1965, the *Reader's Guide to Periodical Literature* did not even include a listing for self-esteem (nor did it list any articles under self-respect or self-love). In 1995, the *Reader's Guide* listed 27 magazine articles devoted solely to the topic of self-esteem. In addition, a search of the Lexis-Nexus database for 1995 articles mentioning self-esteem exceeded the search limit of 1,000 articles. The 1,000-article limit was still exceeded even when the search was limited to a single month (June 1995). In the academic literature, research in psychology also shows a steady increase in articles mentioning self-esteem. From 1970 to 1974, 0.6% of all articles in the PsycLit database mentioned self-esteem. This number increased steadily, reaching 0.10% from 1975 to 1979 and

0.12% from 1980 to 1984; the number has since leveled off at 0.12% to 0.13%. Thus over the time period in question, academic publications examining self-esteem have doubled.

One consequence of these cultural changes has been increases in self-esteem as measured by popular questionnaires. College students' scores on the Rosenberg Self-Esteem scale rose more than a half a standard deviation between the late 1960s and the early 1990s (Twenge & Campbell, 2001), and that pattern continued on through the 2000s (Gentile, Twenge, & Campbell, 2010). The most common score on the Rosenberg Self-Esteem scale by 2008 was a perfect self-esteem score of 40. Steadily increasing scores in other domains such as assertiveness (Twenge, 2001b) and extraversion (Twenge, 2001a) complete the picture of a generation increasingly concerned with the self, individual rights, and self-expression. Researchers argue that much of this change can be traced to the self-esteem movement and the general emphasis on the individual self in the larger society (e.g., Twenge, 2006). Indeed, an examination of one index of cultural values, popular song lyrics, has revealed that words related to self-focus have increased in frequency over recent decades (DeWall, Pond, Campbell, & Twenge, in press). As people's self-views have become more positive, cultural artifacts have come to reflect increasing attention to the self. Cultural views and self-views are intricately connected.

In sum, the self cannot be fully understood without reference to culture, whether that culture differs with respect to region (Plaut, Markus, & Lachman, 2002), beliefs about individualism and collectivism (Triandis, 1989), treatment of the sexes (Gentile et al., 2009), or place in time (Twenge, 2006). Research on cultural differences has blossomed into an extensive and growing subfield, while research on birth cohort and change over time has just recently started to be conducted. As Caspi (1987) argued, many aspects of development and personality must be understood within the context of time, because the larger sociocultural environment changes so much from decade to decade (also see Gergen, 1973). The time period in which people are born, grow up, and discover their adolescent and adult identities has a substantial effect on how they will see the self as an entity.

REFERENCES

Ainsworth, M. D. (1989). Attachments beyond infancy. *American Psychologist, 44,* 709–716.

Aronson, J., Lustina, M. J., Good, C., Keough, K., Steele, C. M., & Brown, J. (1999). When White men can't do math: Necessary and sufficient factors in stereotype threat. *Journal of Personality and Social Psychology, 35,* 29–46.

Baker, M. D. Jr., & Maner, J. K. (2009). Male risk-taking as a context-sensitive signaling device. *Journal of Experimental Social Psychology, 45,* 1136–1139.

Baldwin, J. A., & Hopkins, R. (1990). African-American and European-American cultural differences as assessed by the worldviews paradigm: An empirical analysis. *Western Journal of Black Studies, 14,* 38–52.

Baumeister, R. F. (1982). A self-presentational view of social phenomena. *Psychological Bulletin, 91,* 3–26.

Baumeister, R. F. (1987). How the self became a problem: A psychological review of historical research. *Journal of Personality and Social Psychology, 52,* 163–176.

Baumeister, R. F. (1991). *Meanings of life.* New York, NY: Guilford Press.

Baumeister, R. F. (1997). Esteem threat, self-regulatory breakdown, and emotional distress as factors in self-defeating behavior. *Review of General Psychology, 1,* 145–174.

Baumeister, R. F. (1998). The self. In D. T. Gilbert, S. T. Fiske, & G. Lindzey (Eds.), *Handbook of social psychology* (4th ed., pp. 680–740). New York, NY: McGraw-Hill.

Baumeister, R. F., Bratslavsky, E., Muraven, M., & Tice, D. M. (1998). Ego depletion: Is the active self a limited resource? *Journal of Personality and Social Psychology, 74,* 1252–1265.

Baumeister, R. F., DeWall, C. N., Ciarocco, N. J., & Twenge, J. M. (2005). Social exclusion impairs self-regulation. *Journal of Personality and Social Psychology, 88,* 589–604.

Baumeister, R. F., Heatherton, T. F., & Tice, D. M. (1994). *Losing control: How and why people fail at self-regulation.* San Diego, CA: Academic Press.

Baumeister, R. F., Hutton, D. G., & Tice, D. M. (1989). Cognitive processes during deliberate self-presentation: How self-presenters alter and misinterpret the behavior of their interaction partners. *Journal of Experimental Social Psychology, 25,* 59–78.

Baumeister, R. F., & Jones, E. E. (1978). When self-presentation is constrained by the target's knowledge: Consistency and compensation. *Journal of Personality and Social Psychology, 36,* 608–618.

Baumeister, R. F., & Leary, M. R. (1995). The need to belong: Desire for interpersonal attachments as a fundamental human motivation. *Psychological Bulletin, 117,* 497–529.

Baumeister, R. F., Reis, H. T., & Delespaul, P. A. E. G. (1995). Subjective and experiential correlates of guilt in everyday life. *Personality and Social Psychology Bulletin, 21,* 1256–1268.

Baumeister, R. F., & Scher, S. J. (1988). Self-defeating behavior patterns among normal individuals: Review and analysis of common self-destructive tendencies. *Psychological Bulletin, 104,* 3–22.

Baumeister, R. F., Smart, L., & Boden, J. M. (1996). Relation of threatened egotism to violence and aggression: The dark side of high self-esteem. *Psychological Review, 103,* 5–33.

Baumeister, R. F., Stillwell, A. M., & Heatherton, T. F. (1994). Guilt: An interpersonal approach. *Psychological Bulletin, 115,* 243–267.

Baumeister, R. F., & Tice, D. M. (1986). How adolescence became the struggle for self: A historical transformation of psychological development. In J. Suls & A. G. Greenwald (Eds.), *Psychological perspectives on the self,* (Vol. 3, pp. 183–201). Hillsdale, NJ: Erlbaum.

Baumeister, R. F., & Tice, D. M. (1990). Anxiety and social exclusion. *Journal of Social and Clinical Psychology, 9,* 165–195.

Baumeister, R. F., Tice, D. M., & Hutton, D. G. (1989). Self-presentational motivations and personality differences in self-esteem. *Journal of Personality, 57,* 547–579.

Baumeister, R. F., Twenge, J. M., & Nuss, C. K. (2002). Effects of social exclusion on cognitive processes: Anticipated aloneness reduces intelligent thought. *Journal of Personality and Social Psychology, 83*, 817–827.

Beach, S. R. H. (1992, May). *Self-evaluation maintenance and marital functioning*. Presented at the conference of the Midwestern Psychological Association, Chicago IL.

Bednar, R., Wells, G., & Peterson, S. (1989). *Self-esteem: Paradoxes and innovations in clinical theory and practice*. Washington, DC: American Psychological Association.

Bernstein, M. J., Sacco, D. F., Brown, C. M., Young, S. G., & Claypool, H. M. (2010). A preference for genuine smiles following social exclusion. *Journal of Experimental Social Psychology, 46*, 196–199.

Bernstein, M. J., Young, S. G., Brown, C. M., Sacco, D. F., & Claypool, H. M. (2008). Adaptive responses to social exclusion: Social rejection improves detection of real and fake smiles. *Psychological Science, 19*, 981–983.

Blackhart, G. C., Nelson, B. C., Knowles, M. L., & Baumeister, R. F. (2009). Rejection elicits emotional reactions but neither causes immediate distress nor lowers self-esteem: A meta-analytic review of 192 studies of social exclusion. *Personality and Social Psychology Review, 13*, 269–309.

Blaine, B., & Crocker, J. (1993). Self-esteem and self-serving biases in reactions to positive and negative events: An integrative review. In R. Baumeister (Ed.), *Self-esteem: The puzzle of low self-regard* (pp. 55–85). New York, NY: Plenum Press.

Bloom, B. L., Asher, S. J., & White, S. W. (1978). Marital disruption as a stressor: A review and analysis. *Psychological Bulletin, 85*, 867–894.

Bond, M. H., & Cheung, T. (1983). College students' spontaneous self-concept: The effect of culture among respondents in Hong Kong, Japan, and the United States. *Journal of Cross-Cultural Psychology, 14*, 153–171.

Bradlee, P. M., & Emmons, R. A. (1992). Locating narcissism within the interpersonal circumplex and the five-factor model. *Personality and Individual Differences, 13*, 821–830.

Brockner, J. (1984). Low self-esteem and behavioral plasticity: Some implications for personality and social psychology. In L. Wheeler (Ed.), *Review of personality and social psychology* (Vol. 4, pp. 237–271). Beverly Hills, CA: Sage.

Brockner, J., Davy, J., & Carter, C. (1985). Layoffs, self-esteem, and survivor guilt: Motivational, affective and attitudinal consequences. *Organizational Behavior and Human Decision Processes, 36*, 229–244.

Bushman, B. J., & Baumeister, R. F. (1998). Threatened egotism, narcissism, self-esteem, and direct and displaced aggression: Does self-love or self-hate lead to violence? *Journal of Personality and Social Psychology, 75*, 219–229.

Byrne, D. (1971). *The attraction paradigm*. New York NY: Academic Press.

Campbell, W. K. (1999). Narcissism and romantic attraction. *Journal of Personality and Social Psychology, 77*, 1254–1270.

Campbell, W. K., Foster, C. A., & Finkel, E. J. (2002). Does self-love lead to love for others?: A story of narcissistic game playing. *Journal of Personality and Social Psychology, 83*, 340–354.

Carroll, L. (1987). A study of narcissism, affiliation, intimacy, and power motives among students in business administration. *Psychological Reports, 61*, 355–358.

Caspi, A. (1987). Personality in the life course. *Journal of Personality and Social Psychology, 53*, 1203–1213.

Chentsova-Dutton, Y. E., & Tsai, J. L. (2010). Self-focused attention and emotional reactivity: The role of culture. *Journal of Personality and Social Psychology, 98*, 507–519.

Cialdini, R. B., & Richardson, K. D. (1980). Two indirect tactics of image management: Basking and blasting. *Journal of Personality and Social Psychology, 39*, 406–415.

Clark, M. S., Pataki, S. P., & Carver, V. H. (1995). Some thoughts on self-presentation of emotions in relationships. In G. Fletcher & J. Fitness (Eds.), *Knowledge structures in close relationships: A social psychological approach* (pp. 247–274). Hillsdale, NJ: Erlbaum.

Cohen, S., & Wills, T. A. (1985). Stress, social support, and the buffering hypothesis. *Psychological Bulletin, 98*, 310–357.

Coie, J. D. (1990). Toward a theory of peer rejection. In S. R. Asher & J. D. Coie (Eds.), *Peer rejection in childhood* (pp. 365–401). New York, NY: Cambridge University Press.

Colvin, C. R., Block, J., & Funder, D. C. (1995). Overly positive evaluations and personality: Negative implications for mental health. *Journal of Personality and Social Psychology, 68*, 1152–1162.

Cooley, C. H. (1902). *Human nature and the social order*. New York, NY: Scribner's.

Cousins, S. D. (1989). Culture and self-perception in Japan and the United States. *Journal of Personality and Social Psychology, 56*, 124–131.

Crelia, R. A., & Tesser, A. (1996). Attitude heritability and attitude reinforcement: A replication. *Personality and Individual Differences, 21*, 803–808.

Crocker, J., Luhtanen, R., Blaine, B., & Broadnax, S. (1994). Collective self-esteem and psychological well-being among white, black, and Asian college students. *Personality and Social Psychology Bulletin, 20*, 503–513.

Darley, J. M., & Fazio, R. H. (1980). Expectancy confirmation processes arising in the social interaction sequence. *American Psychologist, 35*, 867–881.

Deaux, K., Reid, A., Mizrahi, K., & Ethier, K. A. (1995). Parameters of social identity. *Journal of Personality and Social Psychology, 68*, 280–291.

De La Ronde, C., & Swann, W. B. (1998). Partner verification: Restoring shattered images of our intimates. *Journal of Personality and Social Psychology, 75*, 374–382.

DePaulo, B. M. (1992). Nonverbal behavior and self-presentation. *Psychological Bulletin, 111*, 203–243.

DePaulo, B. M., Kenny, D. A., Hoover, C. W., Webb, W., & Oliver, P. V. (1987). Accuracy of person perception: Do people know what kinds of impressions they convey? *Journal of Personality and Social Psychology, 52*, 303–315.

DeWall, C. N., & Baumeister, R. F. (2006). Alone but feeling no pain: Effects of social exclusion on physical pain tolerance and pain threshold, affective forecasting, and interpersonal empathy. *Journal of Personality and Social Psychology, 91*, 1–15.

DeWall, C. N., Baumeister, R. F., & Vohs, K. D. (2008). Satiated with belongingness? Effects of acceptance, rejection, and task framing on self-regulatory performance. *Journal of Personality and Social Psychology, 95*, 1367–1382.

DeWall, C. N., Pond, R. S., Campbell, W. K., & Twenge, J. M. (in press). Tuning in to psychological change: Linguistic markers of self-focus, loneliness, anger, anti-social behavior, and misery increase over time in popular U.S. song lyrics. *Psychology of Aesthetics, Art, and Creativity*.

DeWall, C. N., Twenge, J. M., Gitter, S. A., & Baumeister, R. F. (2009). It's the thought that counts: The role of hostile cognition in shaping aggressive responses to social exclusion. *Journal of Personality and Social Psychology, 96*, 45–59.

Dunning, D., Perie, M., & Story, A. L. (1991). Self-serving prototypes of social categories. *Journal of Personality and Social Psychology, 61*, 957–968.

Durkheim, E. (1951). *Suicide*. (J. A. Spaulding & G. Simpson, Trans.) New York, NY: Free Press. (Original work published 1897)

Edelmann, R. J. (1985). Individual differences in embarrassment: Self-consciousness, self-monitoring, and embarrassability. *Personality and Individual Differences, 6*, 223–230.

Edwards, A. L., & Klockars, A. J. (1981). Significant others and self-evaluation: Relationships between perceived and actual evaluations. *Personality and Social Psychology Bulletin, 7,* 244–251.

Ehrenreich, B., & English, E. (1978). *For her own good: 150 years of the experts' advice to women.* New York, NY: Doubleday.

Erikson, E. H. (1950). *Childhood and society.* New York, NY: Norton.

Erikson, E. H. (1968). *Identity: Youth and crisis.* New York, NY: Norton.

Exline, J. J., & Lobel, M. (1999). The perils of outperformance: Sensitivity about being the target of a threatening upward comparison. *Psychological Bulletin, 125,* 307–337.

Felson, R. B. (1989). Parents and the reflected appraisal process: A longitudinal analysis. *Journal of Personality and Social Psychology, 56,* 965–971.

Festinger, L. (1954). A theory of social comparison processes. *Human Relations, 7,* 117–140.

Folkes, V. S. (1982). Communicating the reasons for social rejection. *Journal of Experimental Social Psychology, 18,* 235–252.

Fong, G. T., & Markus, H. (1982). Self-schemas and judgements about others. *Social Cognition, 1,* 191–204.

Fredrickson, B. L. (2001). The role of positive emotions in positive psychology: The broaden-and-build theory of positive emotions. *American Psychologist, 56,* 218–226.

Frum, D. (2000). *How we got here: The 1970s, the decade that brought you modern life—for better or worse.* New York, NY: Basic Books.

Garbarino, J. (1999). *Lost boys: Why our sons turn violent and how we can save them.* San Francisco, CA: Jossey-Bass.

Gardner, W. L., Pickett, C. L., & Brewer, M. B. (2000). Social exclusion and selective memory: How the need to belong influences memory for social events. *Personality and Social Psychology Bulletin, 26,* 486–496.

Gentile, B., Grabe, S., Dolan-Pascoe, B., Twenge, J. M., & Wells, B. E., & Maitino, A. (2009). Gender differences in domain-specific self-esteem: A meta-analysis. *Review of General Psychology, 13,* 34–45.

Gentile, B., Twenge, J. M., & Campbell, W. K. (2010). Birth cohort differences in self-esteem, 1998–2008: A cross-temporal meta-analysis. *Review of General Psychology, 14,* 261–268.

Gergen, K. J. (1973). Social psychology as history. *Journal of Personality and Social Psychology, 26,* 309–320.

Gilbert, D. T., & Jones, E. E. (1986). Perceiver-induced constraint: Interpretations of self-generated reality. *Journal of Personality and Social Psychology, 50,* 269–280.

Goffman, E. (1959). *The presentation of self in everyday life.* New York, NY: Anchor Books.

Griskevicius, V., Tybur, J. M., Sundie, J. M., Cialdini, R. B., Miller, G. F., & Kenrick, D. T. (2007). Blatant benevolence and conspicuous consumption: When romantic motives elicit strategic costly signals. *Journal of Personality and Social Psychology, 93,* 85–102.

Harano, R. M., Peck, R. L., & McBride, R. S. (1975). The prediction of accident liability through biographical data and psychometric tests. *Journal of Safety Research, 7,* 16–52.

Harrington, D. M., & McBride, R. S. (1970). Traffic violations by type, age, sex, and marital status. *Accident Analysis and Prevention, 2,* 67–79.

Herman, B. H., & Panksepp, J. (1978). Effects of morphine and naloxone on separation distress and approach attachment: Evidence for opiate mediation of social affect. *Pharmacology, Biochemistry, and Behavior, 9,* 213–220.

Higgins, E. T. (1987). Self-discrepancy: A theory relating self and affect. *Psychological Review, 94,* 319–340.

Higgins, E. T., King, G. A., & Mavin, G. H. (1982). Individual construct accessibility and subjective impressions and recall. *Journal of Personality and Social Psychology, 43,* 35–47.

Hill, T., Smith, N., & Lewicki, P. (1989). The development of self-image bias: A real-world demonstration. *Personality and Social Psychology Bulletin, 15,* 205–211.

Hogan, R., Jones, W. H., & Cheek, J. M. (1985). Socioanalytic theory: An alternative to armadillo psychology. In B. R. Schlenker (Ed.), *The self and social life* (pp. 175–198). Newberry Park, CA: Sage.

Holtz, G. T. (1995). *Welcome to the jungle: The why behind generation X.* New York, NY: St. Martin's Press.

Janis, I. L. (1954). Personality correlates of susceptibility to persuasion. *Journal of Personality, 22,* 504–518.

Janis, I. L., & Field, P. (1959). Sex differences and personality factors related to persuasibility. In C. Hovland & I. Janis (Eds.), *Personality and persuasibility* (pp. 55–68 and 300–302). New Haven, CT: Yale University Press.

Johns, M., Schmader, T., & Martens, A. (2005). Knowing is half the battle: Teaching stereotype threat as a means of improving women's math performance. *Psychological Science, 16,* 175–179.

Jones, E. E., & Pittman, T. S. (1982). Toward a general theory of strategic self-presentation. In J. Suls (Ed.), *Psychological perspectives on the self* (Vol. 1, pp. 231–262). Hillsdale, NJ: Erlbaum.

Jones, L. Y. (1980). *Great expectations: America and the baby boom generation.* New York, NY: Coward, McCann, & Geoghegan.

Kahle, L. R., Kulka, R. A., & Klingel, D. M. (1980). Low adolescent self-esteem leads to multiple interpersonal problems: A test of social-adaptation theory. *Journal of Personality and Social Psychology, 39,* 496–502.

Kernis, M. H., Granneman, B. D., & Barclay, L. C. (1989). Stability and level of self-esteem as predictors of anger arousal and hostility. *Journal of Personality and Social Psychology, 56,* 1013–1022.

Kernis, M. H., & Sun, C. (1994). Narcissism and reactions to interpersonal feedback. *Journal of Research in Personality, 28,* 4–13.

Kitayama, S., Markus, H. R., & Matsumoto, H. (1995). Culture, self, and emotion: A cultural perspective on "self-conscious" emotions. In J. Tangney & K. Fischer (Eds.), *The self-conscious emotions* (pp. 439–464). New York, NY: Guilford Press.

Kitayama, S., Markus, H. R., Matsumoto, H., & Norasakkunkit, V. (1997). Individual and collective processes in the construction of the self: Self-enhancement in the United States and self-criticism in Japan. *Journal of Personality and Social Psychology, 72,* 1245–1267.

Kolditz, T. A., & Arkin, R. M. (1982). An impression management interpretation of the self-handicapping strategy. *Journal of Personality and Social Psychology, 43,* 492–502.

Kraus, M. W., & Chen, S. (2009). Striving to be known by significant others: Automatic activation of self-verification goals in relationship contexts. *Journal of Personality and Social Psychology, 97,* 58–73.

Kwan, V. S. Y., Bond, M. H., & Singelis, T. M. (1997). Pancultural explanations for life satisfaction: Adding relationship harmony to self-esteem. *Journal of Personality and Social Psychology, 73,* 1038–1051.

Lambert, A. J., & Wedell, D. H. (1991). The self and social judgment: Effects of affective reaction and "own position" on judgments of unambiguous and ambiguous information about others. *Journal of Personality and Social Psychology, 61,* 884–897.

Lasch, C. (1978). *The culture of narcissism: American life in an age of diminishing expectations.* New York, NY: Norton.

Leary, M. R. (1995). *Self-presentation: Impression management and interpersonal behavior.* Madison, WI: Brown & Benchmark.

Leary, M. R. (2000, October). *Anger and aggression as responses to relational devaluation.* Symposium talk presented at the annual meeting of the Society of Experimental Social Psychology, Atlanta, Georgia.

Leary, M. R., & Baumeister, R. F. (2000). The nature and function of self-esteem: Sociometer theory. In M. Zanna (Ed.), *Advances in experimental social psychology* (Vol. 32). San Diego, CA: Academic Press.

Leary, M. R., Britt, T. W., Cutlip, W. D., & Templeton, J. L. (1992). Social blushing. *Psychological Bulletin, 112,* 446–460.

Leary, M. R., & Downs, D. L. (1995). Interpersonal functions of the self-esteem motive: The self-esteem system as a sociometer. In M. H. Kernis (Ed.), *Efficacy, agency, and self-esteem* (pp. 123–144). New York, NY: Guilford Press.

Leary, M. R., & Jones, J. L. (1993). The social psychology of tanning and sunscreen use: Self-presentational motives as a predictor of health risk. *Journal of Applied Social Psychology, 23,* 1390–1406.

Leary, M. R., & Kowalski, R. (1995). *Social anxiety.* New York, NY: Guilford Press.

Leary, M. R., Tambor, E. S., Terdal, S. K., & Downs, D. L. (1995). Self-esteem as an interpersonal monitor: The sociometer hypothesis. *Journal of Personality and Social Psychology, 68,* 518–530.

Leary, M. R., Tchividjian, L. R., & Kraxberger, B. E. (1994). Self-presentation can be hazardous to your health: Impression management and health risk. *Health Psychology, 13,* 461–470.

Leith, K. P., & Baumeister, R. F. (1996). Why do bad moods increase self-defeating behavior? Emotion, risk taking, and self-regulation. *Journal of Personality and Social Psychology, 71,* 1250–1267.

Lemyre, L., & Smith, P. M. (1985). Intergroup discrimination and self-esteem in the minimal intergroup paradigm. *Journal of Personality and Social Psychology, 49,* 660–670.

Lewicki, P. (1983). Self-image bias in person perception. *Journal of Personality and Social Psychology, 45,* 384–393.

Lewicki, P. (1984). Self-schema and social information processing. *Journal of Personality and Social Psychology, 47,* 1177–1190.

Lewis, H. B. (1971). *Shame and guilt in neurosis.* New York, NY: International Universities Press.

Lifton, R. J. (1967). *Death in life.* New York, NY: Simon & Schuster.

Luhtanen, R. K., & Crocker, J. (1992). A collective self-esteem scale: Self-evaluation of one's social identity. *Personality and Social Psychology Bulletin, 18,* 302–318.

MacDonald, S. (1986). Political priority #1: Teaching kids to like themselves. *New Opinions,* April 28.

Madon, S., Guyll, M., Buller, A. A., Scherr, K. C., Willard, J., & Spoth, R. (2008). The mediation of mothers' self-fulfilling effects on their children's alcohol use: Self-verification, informational conformity, and modeling processes. *Journal of Personality and Social Psychology, 95,* 369–384.

Malloy, T. E., & Albright, L. (1990). Interpersonal perception in a social context. *Journal of Personality and Social Psychology, 58,* 419–428.

Maner, J. K., DeWall, C. N., Baumeister, R. F., & Schaller, M. (2007). Does social exclusion motivate interpersonal reconnection? Resolving the "porcupine problem." *Journal of Personality and Social Psychology, 92,* 42–55.

Markus, H. R., & Kitayama, S. (1991). Culture and the self: Implications for cognition, emotion, and motivation. *Psychological Review, 98,* 224–253.

Markus, H., Smith, J., & Moreland, R. (1985). Role of the self-concept in the perception of others. *Journal of Personality and Social Psychology, 49,* 1494–1512.

Mead, G. H. (1934). *Mind, self, and society.* Chicago, IL: University of Chicago Press.

Mead, N. L., Baumeister, R. F., Stillman, T. F., Rawn, C. D., & Vohs, K. D. (2011). Social exclusion causes people to spend and consume in the service of affiliation. *Journal of Consumer Research, 37,* 902–919.

Miller, R. S. (1995). Embarrassment and social behavior. In J. Tangney & K. Fischer (Eds.), *The self-conscious emotions* (pp. 322–339). New York, NY: Guilford Press.

Modigliani, A. (1971). Embarrassment, facework, and eye contact: Testing a theory of embarrassment. *Journal of Personality and Social Psychology, 17,* 15–24.

Moreland, R. L. (1987). The formation of small groups. In C. Hendrick (Ed.), *Group processes: Review of personality and social psychology* (Vol. 8, pp. 80–110). Newberry Park, CA: Sage.

Mruk, C. (1995). *Self-esteem: Research, theory, and practice.* New York, NY: Springer.

Murray, S. L., Holmes, J. G., & Griffin, D. W. (1996a). The benefits of positive illusions: Idealization and the construction of satisfaction in close relationships. *Journal of Personality and Social Psychology, 70,* 79–98.

Murray, S. L., Holmes, J. G., & Griffin, D. W. (1996b). The self-fulfilling nature of positive illusions in romantic relationships: Love is not blind, but prescient. *Journal of Personality and Social Psychology, 71,* 1155–1180.

Myers, D. (1992). *The pursuit of happiness.* New York, NY: Morrow.

Myers, D. G., & Diener, E. (1995). Who is happy? *Psychological Science, 6,* 10–19.

Newcomb, A. F., Bukowski, W. M., & Pattee, L. (1993). Children's peer relations: A meta-analytic review of popular, rejected, neglected, controversial, and average sociometric status. *Psychological Bulletin, 113,* 99–128.

Newman, L. S., Duff, K., & Baumeister, R. F. (1997). A new look at defensive projection: Suppression, accessibility, and biased person perception. *Journal of Personality and Social Psychology, 72,* 980–1001.

Oakes, P. J., & Turner, J. (1980). Social categorization and intergroup behavior: Does minimal intergroup discrimination make social identity more positive? *European Journal of Social Psychology, 10,* 295–301.

Orlofsky, J. L., Marcia, J. E., & Lesser, I. M. (1973). Ego identity status and the intimacy versus isolation crisis of young adulthood. *Journal of Personality and Social Psychology, 27,* 211–219.

Panksepp, J., Herman, B. H., Conner, R., Bishop, P., & Scott, J. P. (1978). The biology of social attachments: Opiates alleviate separation distress. *Biological Psychiatry, 13,* 607–618.

Panksepp, J., Vilberg, T., Bean, N. J., Coy, D. H., & Kastin, A. J. (1978). Reduction of distress vocalization in chicks by opiate-like peptides. *Brain Research Bulletin, 3,* 663–667.

Parrott, W. G., Sabini, J., & Silver, M. (1988). The roles of self-esteem and social interaction in embarrassment. *Personality and Social Psychology Bulletin, 14,* 191–202.

Plaut, V. C., Markus, H. R., & Lachman, M. E. (2002). Place matters: Consensual features and regional variation in American well-being and self. *Journal of Personality and Social Psychology, 83,* 160–184.

Pleban, R., & Tesser, A. (1981). The effects of relevance and quality of another's performance on interpersonal closeness. *Social Psychology Quarterly, 44,* 278–285.

Rhodewalt, F., & Morf, C. C. (1998). On self-aggrandizement and anger: A temporal analysis of narcissism and affective reactions to success and failure. *Journal of Personality and Social Psychology, 74,* 672–685.

Richman, A. (1985). Human risk factors in alcohol-related crashes. *Journal of Studies on Alcohol, 10,* 21–31.

Richman, L. S., & Leary, M. R. (2009). Reactions to discrimination, stigmatization, ostracism, and other forms of interpersonal rejection: A multimotive model. *Psychological Review, 116,* 365–383.

Rosen, B. C. (1998). *Winners and losers of the information revolution: Psychosocial change and its discontents.* Westport, CT: Praeger.

Rosenbaum, M. E. (1986). The repulsion hypothesis: On the nondevelopment of relationships. *Journal of Personality and Social Psychology, 51,* 1156–1166.

Rosenberg, M. (1979). *Conceiving the self.* New York, NY: Basic Books.

Rosenthal, R., & Jacobson, L. (1968). *Pygmalion in the classroom.* New York, NY: Holt.

Sampson, R. J., & Laub, J. H. (1990). Crime and deviance over the life course: The salience of adult social bonds. *American Sociological Review, 55,* 609–627.

Sampson, R. J., & Laub, J. H. (1993). *Crime in the making: Pathways and turning points through life*. Cambridge, MA: Harvard University Press.

Sartre, J. P. (1953). *The existential psychoanalysis* (H. E. Barnes, Trans.) New York, NY: Philosophical Library.

Sartre, J. P. (1956). *Being and nothingness*. (H. E. Barnes, Trans.) Secaucus, NJ: Citadel Press. Original work published in 1943.

Scheier, M. F. (1976). Self-awareness, self-consciousness, and angry aggression. *Journal of Personality, 44,* 627–644.

Scheier, M. F., & Carver, C. S. (1977). Self-focused attention and the experience of emotion: Attraction, repulsion, elation, and depression. *Journal of Personality and Social Psychology, 35,* 625–636.

Schlenker, B. R. (1975). Self-presentation: Managing the impression of consistency when reality interferes with self-enhancement. *Journal of Personality and Social Psychology, 32,* 1030–1037.

Schlenker, B. R. (1980). *Impression management: The self-concept, social identity, and interpersonal relations*. Monterey, CA: Brooks/Cole.

Schlenker, B. R. (1986). Self-identification: Toward an integration of the private and public self. In R. Baumeister (Ed.), *Public self and private self* (pp. 21–62). New York, NY: Springer-Verlag.

Schlenker, B. R., & Leary, M. R. (1982). Social anxiety and self-presentation: A conceptualization and model. *Psychological Bulletin, 92,* 641–669.

Schoenborn, C. A. (2004). Marital status and health: United States, 1999–2002. *Advance Data,* No. 351.

Sedikides, C., Campbell, W. K., Reeder, G. D., & Elliot, A. J. (1998). The self-serving bias in relational context. *Journal of Personality and Social Psychology, 74,* 378–386.

Sedikides, C., Gaertner, L., & Toguchi, Y. (2003). Pancultural self-enhancement. *Journal of Personality and Social Psychology, 84,* 60–79.

Sedikides, C., & Skowronski, J. J. (1993). The self in impression formation: Trait centrality and social perception. *Journal of Experimental Social Psychology, 29,* 347–357.

Seligman, M. (1995). *The optimistic child.* New York, NY: Houghton Mifflin.

Semin, G. R., & Manstead, A. S. R. (1982). The social implications of embarrassment displays and restitution behavior. *European Journal of Social Psychology, 12,* 367–377.

Shaver, P., Hazan, C., & Bradshaw, D. (1988). Love as attachment: The integration of three behavioral systems. In R. J. Sternberg & M. L. Barnes (Eds.), *The psychology of love* (pp. 68–99). New Haven, CT: Yale University Press.

Shih, M., Pittinsky, T. L., & Ambady, N. (1999). Stereotype susceptibility: Identity salience and shifts in quantitative performance. *Psychological Science, 10,* 80–83.

Shrauger, J. S., & Schoeneman, T. J. (1979). Symbolic interactionist view of self-concept: Through the looking glass darkly. *Psychological Bulletin, 86,* 549–573.

Smeaton, G., Byrne, D., & Murnen, S. K. (1989). The repulsion hypothesis revisited: Similarity irrelevance or dissimilarity bias? *Journal of Personality and Social Psychology, 56,* 54–59.

Snyder, M., Tanke, E. D., & Berscheid, E. (1977). Social perception and interpersonal behavior: On the self-fulfilling nature of social stereotypes. *Journal of Personality and Social Psychology, 35,* 656–666.

Steele, C. M., & Aronson, J. (1995). Stereotype threat and intellectual test performance of African Americans. *Journal of Personality and Social Psychology, 69,* 797–811.

Stewart, A. J., & Healy, J. M. (1989). Linking individual development and social changes. *American Psychologist, 44,* 30–42.

Strauss, W., & Howe, N. (1991). *Generations: The history of America's future, 1584 to 2069*. New York, NY: Morrow.

Swann, W. B. (1990). To be adored or to be known? The interplay of self-enhancement and self-verification. In R. M. Sorrentino & E. T. Higgins (Eds.), *Motivation and cognition* (pp. 404–448). New York, NY: Guilford Press.

Swann, W. B. (1992). Seeking "truth," finding despair: Some unhappy consequences of a negative self-concept. *Current Directions in Psychological Science, 1,* 15–18.

Swann, W. B. (1996). *Self-traps: The elusive quest for higher self-esteem.* New York, NY: Freeman.

Swann, W. B., Hixon, J. G., & De La Ronde, C. (1992). Embracing the bitter "truth": Negative self-concepts and marital commitment. *Psychological Science, 3,* 118–121.

Swann, W. B., & Predmore, S. C. (1985). Intimates as agents of social support: Sources of consolation or deapair? *Journal of Personality and Social Psychology, 49,* 1609–1617.

Sykes, C. J. (1995). *Dumbing down our kids: Why American children feel good about themselves but can't read, write, or add*. New York, NY: St. Martin's Griffin.

Tajfel, H. (1982). Social psychology of intergroup relations. *Annual Review of Psychology, 33,* 1–59.

Tajfel, H., & Turner, J. C. (1979). An integrative theory of intergroup conflict. In S. Worchel & W. Austin (Eds.), *Psychology of intergroup relations* (2nd ed., pp. 7–24). Chicago, IL: Nelson-Hall.

Tangney, J. P. (1992). Situational determinants of shame and guilt in young adulthood. *Personality and Social Psychology Bulletin, 18,* 199–206.

Tangney, J. P. (1995). Shame and guilt in interpersonal relationships. In J. Tangney & K. Fischer (Eds.), *The self-conscious emotions* (pp. 114–139). New York, NY: Guilford Press.

Tangney, J. P., Burggraf, S. A., & Wagner, P. E. (1995). Shame-proneness, guilt-proneness, and psychological symptoms. In J. Tangney & K. Fischer (Eds.), *The self-conscious emotions* (pp. 343–367). New York, NY: Guilford Press.

Tangney, J. P., & Fischer, K. W. (Eds.). (1995). *The self-conscious emotions: The psychology of shame, guilt, embarrassment, and pride*. New York, NY: Guilford Press.

Tangney, J. P., Wagner, P. E., Fletcher, C., & Gramzow, R. (1992). Shamed into anger? The relation of shame and guilt to anger and self-reported aggression. *Journal of Personality and Social Psychology, 62,* 669–675.

Taylor, S. E., & Brown, J. D. (1988). Illusion and well-being: A social psychological perspective on mental health. *Psychological Bulletin, 103,* 193–210.

Tesch, S. A., & Whitbourne, S. K. (1982). Intimacy and identity status in young adults. *Journal of Personality and Social Psychology, 43,* 1041–1051.

Tesser, A. (1988). Toward a self-evaluation maintenance model of social behavior. In L. Berkowitz (Ed.), *Advances in experimental social psychology* (Vol. 21, pp. 181–227). San Diego, CA: Academic Press.

Tesser, A. (1993). The importance of heritability in psychological research: The case of attitudes. *Psychological Review, 100,* 129–142.

Tesser, A., & Smith, J. (1980). Some effects of friendship and task relevance on helping: You don't always help the one you like. *Journal of Experimental Social Psychology, 16,* 582–590.

Tice, D. M., Butler, J. L., Muraven, M. B., & Stillwell, A. M. (1995). When modesty prevails: Differential favorability of self-presentation to friends and strangers. *Journal of Personality and Social Psychology, 69,* 1120–1138.

Triandis, H. C. (1989). The self and social behavior in differing cultural contexts. *Psychological Review, 96,* 506–520.

Turner, J. C. (1982). Towards a cognitive redefinition of the social group. In H. Tajfel (Ed.), *Social identity and intergroup relations* (pp. 15–40). Cambridge, UK: Cambridge University Press.

Twenge, J. M. (2000). The age of anxiety? Birth cohort change in anxiety and neuroticism, 1952–1993. *Journal of Personality and Social Psychology, 79,* 1007–1021.

Twenge, J. M. (2001a). Birth cohort changes in extraversion: A cross-temporal meta-analysis, 1966–1993. *Personality and Individual Differences, 30,* 735–748.

Twenge, J. M. (2001b). Changes in women's assertiveness in response to status and roles: A cross-temporal meta-analysis, 1931–1993. *Journal of Personality and Social Psychology 81,* 133–145.

Twenge, J. M. (2006). *Generation me: Why today's young Americans are more confident, assertive, entitled—and more miserable than ever before.* New York, NY: Free Press.

Twenge, J. M., Baumeister, R. F., DeWall, C. N., Ciarocco, N. J., & Bartels, J. M. (2007). Social exclusion decreases prosocial behavior. *Journal of Personality and Social Psychology, 92,* 56–66.

Twenge, J. M., Baumeister, B. F., Tice, D. M., & Stucke, T. S. (2001). If you can't join them, beat them: The effects of social exclusion on aggressive behavior. *Journal of Personality and Social Psychology, 81,* 1058–1069.

Twenge, J. M., & Campbell, W. K. (2001). Age and birth cohort differences in self-esteem: A cross-temporal meta-analysis. *Personality and Social Psychology Review, 5,* 321–344.

Twenge, J. M., Catanese, K. R., & Baumeister, R. F. (2002). Social exclusion causes self-defeating behavior. *Journal of Personality and Social Psychology, 83,* 606–615.

Vohs, K. D., Baumeister, R. F., & Ciarocco, N. J. (2005). Self-regulation and self-presentation: Regulatory resource depletion impairs impression management and effortful self-presentation depletes self-regulatory resources. *Journal of Personality and Social Psychology, 88,* 632–657.

Vohs, K. D., & Heatherton, T. F. (2001). Self-esteem and threats to self: Implications for self-construals and interpersonal perceptions. *Journal of Personality and Social Psychology, 81,* 1103–1118.

Walsh, A., Beyer, J. A., & Petee, T. A. (1987). Violent delinquency: An examination of psychopathic typologies. *Journal of Genetic Psychology, 148,* 385–392.

Watson, P. J., Grisham, S. O., Trotter, M. V., & Biderman, M. D. (1984). Narcissism and empathy: Validity evidence for the narcissistic personality inventory. *Journal of Personality Assessment, 45,* 159–162.

Wegner, D. M., & Erber, R. (1992). The hyperaccessibility of suppressed thoughts. *Journal of Personality and Social Psychology, 63,* 903–912.

Whitley, B. E. (1983). Sex role orientation and self-esteem: A critical meta-analytic review. *Journal of Personality and Social Psychology, 44,* 765–778.

Williams, D. R., Takeuchi, D. T., & Adair, R. K. (1992). Martial status and psychiatric disorders among blacks and whites. *Journal of Health and Social Behavior, 33,* 140–157.

Williams, K. D., Cheung, C. K. T., Choi, W. (2000). Cyberostracism: Effects of being ignored over the Internet. *Journal of Personality and Social Psychology, 79,* 748–762.

Wills, T. A. (1981). Downward comparison principles in social psychology. *Psychological Bulletin, 90,* 245–271.

Wright, K. N., & Wright, K. E. (1992). Does getting married reduce the likelihood of criminality? A review of the literature. *Federal Probation, 56,* 50–56.

Yankelovich, D. (1981). *New rules: Searching for self-fulfillment in a world turned upside-down.* New York, NY: Random House.

Zube, M. J. (1972). Changing concepts of morality: 1948–1969. *Social Forces, 50,* 385–393.

CHAPTER 13

Attitudes in Social Behavior

GREGORY R. MAIO, JAMES M. OLSON, AND IRENE CHEUNG

Global interest in the concept of attitude may be at a record high. Nations around the world are grappling with a variety of common problems that seem to arise from widely shared attitudes. Examples of these problems include the destruction of natural resources, climate change, intergroup conflict, obesity, and the spread of disease (e.g., AIDS, flu). Although these problems have multiple causes (e.g., population growth, social structure), individual attitudes are undoubtedly important contributors. For instance, the World Health Organization has concluded that obesity is a global epidemic with multiple causes. One of these causes is the inappropriateness of people's lifestyles for an environment that features easy energy availability through high-calorie food, combined with low-energy requirements through mechanized transport and production. Put simply, many of us need to eat less and do more. To elicit such lifestyle changes, policy makers have often focused on promoting positive attitudes toward healthy options. For example, the U.K. government recently undertook a social marketing program to alter unhealthy attitudes and behavior (Change4Life), based on earlier investigations of the causes of obesity and methods to induce lifestyle change (see Maio et al., 2007). The fundamental idea of the program is that a change in attitude will create a change in behavior.

This assumption is a key reason for Gordon Allport's (1935) famous assertion that attitude is one of the most indispensable constructs in social psychology. Social psychologists study attitudes because of the deep connections between attitudes and how we think, feel, and act. In this chapter, we review social psychological research and theory about attitudes. In the first section, we define attitudes and compare this construct to other important social psychological constructs (e.g., values). Next, we briefly consider some issues related to attitude measurement and a distinction between explicit and implicit measures of attitude. We then discuss different perspectives on the psychological content, structure, and function of attitudes, focusing on the perspectives' implications for measuring attitudes and the evidence supporting or refuting them. Fourth, we discuss how attitudes are related to one another, as well as the relations between attitudes and higher-order constructs, such as ideologies. Fifth, we identify important ways that attitudes vary. Sixth, we address briefly how attitudes form. Seventh, we discuss the effects of attitudes on information processing. Finally, we consider the relation between attitudes and behavior.

WHAT ATTITUDES ARE AND WHAT ATTITUDES ARE NOT

When social psychologists define attitudes, they focus on the tendency to like or dislike an attitude object or behavior (Bohner & Wanke, 2002; Eagly & Chaiken, 1998; Fazio, 1990; Maio & Haddock, 2010; Petty, Briñol, & DeMarree, 2007). This tendency to like or dislike is a broad *evaluative* (good-bad) process, which can be applied to any identifiable object in our environment.

Thus, we have attitudes toward concrete objects (e.g., pizza), controversial issues (e.g., higher taxes on fuel), abstract ideas (e.g., freedom), specific individuals (e.g., the President), and groups of people (e.g., ethnic groups). The potentially unlimited range of attitude objects is part of what makes attitudes so central to social psychological research. At the same time, the broad array of targets that can elicit attitudes creates some conceptual overlap between attitudes and other constructs and processes in psychology. For example, attitudes toward some abstract concepts are similar to social values, which are abstract ideals that people consider to be important guiding principles in their lives (e.g., equality; Rokeach, 1973; Schwartz, 1992). The major difference between attitudes toward abstract concepts and values is that the attitudes involve judgments of favorability (good or bad), whereas values are always positive and involve judgments of importance (Feather, 1995; Maio & Olson, 1998).

ATTITUDE MEASUREMENT

Ever since the earliest discussions of the attitude concept in psychology, there have been sophisticated attempts to develop reliable and valid measures of attitude. Three measurement approaches have dominated research on attitudes: self-report scales, psychophysiological techniques, and implicit measures.

Self-Report

Past researchers have most often measured attitudes using self-report scales. The most common scales ask participants to rate their attitude on bipolar evaluative dimensions (e.g., bad-good, unfavorable-favorable, negative-positive), and responses are averaged to yield an attitude estimate. For example, respondents might be asked to rate their attitude toward rap music using 7-point scales from −3 (very unfavorable; very negative) to +3 (very favorable; very positive), with 0 (neither favorable nor unfavorable; neither positive nor negative) in between. One important limitation of self-report scales, however, is that they are affected by tendencies to respond in a socially desirable manner (Paulhus, 1991). For example, people might be reluctant to report prejudice against ethnic groups because of the social stigma attached to prejudicial attitudes.

To overcome this problem, various techniques have been developed. For example, the bogus pipeline procedure (E. Jones & Sigall, 1971) deceives participants into believing that the researcher can detect their true feelings about attitude objects, after which participants are asked to report their attitude toward particular targets. This technique has been shown to reduce social desirability in responses compared to simple self-report attitude measures (Roese & Jamieson, 1993). Also, as described below, other approaches to attitude measurement attempt to circumvent social desirability by assessing attitudes in indirect ways, so that people do not alter their responses to conform to what they perceive as being popular or desirable.

Psychophysiological Techniques

One indirect approach involves assessing participants' physiological responses to attitude objects. Unfortunately, many physiological measures (e.g., skin conductance, pupillary responses) reflect only the intensity of feeling and are incapable of distinguishing positive versus negative responses (Guglielmi, 1999; Petty & Caciopppo, 1983). Positive and negative evaluations can be distinguished, however, using facial electromyography (EMG) recordings (Cacioppo, Petty, Losch, & Kim, 1986), which detect the relative amount of electrical activity in the muscles that control smiling and frowning.

Two other psychophysiological techniques show considerable promise. One technique detects a specific pattern of electrical activity (amplitude of the late positive potential) in the centroparietal region of the brain (Cacioppo, Crites, & Gardner, 1996), whereas the other examines the frequency and latency of eye blinks during exposure to attitude objects (Ohira, Winton, & Oyama, 1998). These techniques have the potential to help identify immediate, spontaneous evaluative reactions in a way that is difficult to achieve through self-report measures (e.g., Seigle, Ichakawa, & Steinhauer, 2008).

Implicit Measures of Attitude

A second limitation of self-report measures of attitudes is that they assess only attitudes that are consciously retrievable from memory. In contrast, people's automatic or spontaneous evaluative responses to objects may sometimes be nonconscious, in that individuals may not be aware of them. Typically, though, people are probably aware of most of their spontaneous responses to objects (e.g., their spontaneous negative response to spiders). Nonetheless, it is useful to employ implicit measures of attitude to assess the spontaneous evaluative reactions (see Gawronski & Bodenhausen, 2007).

Several techniques are available to accomplish this goal. The most common techniques use reaction times as implicit measures of attitude. For example, the *Implicit Association Test* (IAT; Greenwald, McGhee, & Schwartz, 1998) requires participants to complete two sorting tasks as quickly as possible. On one sorting task, the target of the attitude (e.g., elderly people) must be sorted into the same category as some good objects (e.g., words with positive meanings, such as good, beautiful, and honest). On the second sorting task, the target must be sorted into the same category as some bad objects (e.g., words with negative meanings, such as bad, ugly, and dishonest). If participants complete the task where the target is associated with *good* things *more quickly* than the task where the target is associated with *bad* things, they are assumed to have a *positive* implicit attitude toward the target. If, on the other hand, they complete the task where the target of the attitude is associated with *bad* things *more quickly* than the task where the target of the attitude is associated with *good* things, they are assumed to have a *negative* implicit attitude toward the target. Although the IAT has been the target of some criticism (e.g., Brendl, Markman, & Messner, 2001; Fazio & Olson, 2003), it has been shown to have predictive validity for individuals' attitude-related responses (Greenwald, Poehlman, Uhlmann, & Banaji, 2009).

Another method of measuring implicit attitudes is Fazio, Jackson, Dunton, and Williams's (1995) *evaluative priming technique*. This task presents participants with a target attitude object and then asks them to classify subsequently presented adjectives as being good or bad. Given that positive affect should be activated in memory after viewing an object that evokes a positive attitude, this priming of positive affect should help participants to be faster at classifying positive adjectives (e.g., nice, pleasant) than negative adjectives (e.g., disgusting, repugnant). In contrast, after viewing an object that evokes a negative attitude, participants should be slower at classifying positive adjectives than negative adjectives. Thus, attitudes are measured by seeing whether viewing the object speeds up the respondents' classifications of positive or negative adjectives. Several studies have shown that these attitude scores predict attitude-relevant behavior toward the attitude object (e.g., Fazio et al., 1995).

THREE KEY ASPECTS OF ATTITUDES

Broad judgments of favorability or unfavorability appear simple on the surface: People have no trouble understanding what we mean when we say that we like something or dislike something. This apparent simplicity, however, belies a considerable degree of complexity within attitude judgments. These judgments may contain different thoughts, feelings, and actions. At the same time, the thoughts, feelings, and actions can be structured in different ways. In addition, the attitudes may serve different psychological functions. These three aspects—attitude content, attitude structure, and attitude function—have been metaphorically labeled the "three witches of attitude" in one text (Maio & Haddock, 2010). The metaphor suggests that it takes all three aspects to understand attitudes, in the same way as folklore suggests that it takes three witches to make a potent brew. The next sections consider each of these "witches" in turn, focusing on relevant evidence and their implications for measuring attitudes.

Attitude Content

Two theoretical perspectives have dominated research on the content of attitudes: the expectancy-value model and the three-component model. Below, we describe each model and then highlight some of the evidence used to evaluate them.

Expectancy-Value Model

The expectancy-value model describes how beliefs are linked to attitudes (Fishbein & Ajzen, 1975; Wyer & Goldberg, 1970). For example, a message might argue that it is good to reduce carbon dioxide emissions, and, therefore, people should travel by airplane less often. The message is persuasive if the message recipient accepts both the premise of the argument (i.e., reducing carbon dioxide emissions is good) and the implied link between the premise and the conclusion (i.e., taking fewer flights will reduce carbon dioxide emissions). Notice that the evaluative nature of the premise (reducing carbon dioxide emissions is good) introduces an evaluative implication of accepting the conclusion. That is, people should become less *favorable* toward traveling by air because of its undesirable implications for carbon dioxide emissions. In this manner, attitudes can be influenced by beliefs (i.e., premises) that are evaluative in nature.

The notion that attitudes reflect the acceptance or rejection of evaluative beliefs is central to the expectancy-value perspective on attitudes. A well-known example is Fishbein and Ajzen's (1975) *Theory of Reasoned Action*. According to this approach, an attitude is the sum of all of the evaluative beliefs about the attitude object. For instance, if people believe that recycling is easy and that recycling helps the environment, people should hold a positive attitude toward recycling. This attitude is positive because both beliefs link positively valued attributes to the behavior. Of course, beliefs are rarely held with absolute certainty. For example, a person may be only 70% certain that recycling is easy, but 100% certain that recycling helps the environment. According to the expectancy-value model, beliefs have less impact on attitudes when they are less certain. This reasoning is frequently summarized in a well-known equation: $A = \Sigma \ b_i e_i$, where A is the overall attitude toward the attitude object, b_i is the subjective belief that the object possesses attribute i (e.g., the probability that recycling helps the environment), and e_i is the evaluation of attribute i (e.g., the positive value attached to the environment).

Researchers using the expectancy-value model often measure attitudes by asking participants to first consider a list of potential attributes of an attitude object and then, for each attribute, rate (a) the probability that the object possesses the attribute and (b) the desirability of the attribute. In most research, the probability ratings are made using scales from -3 (very improbable) to $+3$ (very probable) or from 0 (not at all) to 1 (definitely). The evaluative ratings are made using evaluative scales from -3 (very bad) to $+3$ (very good). To derive the overall attitude, the product of the probability and evaluative ratings is computed for each attribute, and the products are summed across all of the attributes.

The Three-Component Model

The three-component model hypothesizes that attitudes are based on more than beliefs alone. This model suggests that attitudes are based simultaneously on people's beliefs, feelings, and past behaviors regarding the attitude object (Zanna & Rempel, 1988): people have positive attitudes toward an object when their beliefs, feelings, and past behaviors regarding the object are largely favorable, whereas people have negative attitudes toward an object when their beliefs, feelings, and past behaviors regarding the object are largely unfavorable. For example, people might form a positive attitude toward cycling to work because cycling feels good (affective component) and they believe that cycling is good for them (cognitive component). Moreover, through the process of self-perception (Bem, 1972; J. M. Olson, 1992), people may decide that they like cycling because they can recall doing it often as a child (behavioral component). In contrast, people might form a negative attitude toward cycling to work because cycling makes them tired (affective component),

they believe it is time consuming (cognitive component), and they have not cycled much in the past (behavior component). In the three-component view, the attitude is a net evaluation of the target. People store this evaluation in memory and can retrieve it when they encounter the attitude object (some attitudes may be activated automatically when the target is encountered).

The summative aspect of attitudes makes it possible to obtain measures of overall attitudes without attempting to assess specific attitude-relevant beliefs, feelings, or behaviors. For example, attitudes are frequently measured using an attitude thermometer, which asks people to use a thermometer-like scale from $0°$ (extremely unfavorable) to $100°$ (extremely favorable) to indicate the extent to which they feel favorable versus unfavorable toward the attitude object (Campbell, 1971; Haddock, Zanna, & Esses, 1993). This scale enables people to report a general evaluation, which presumably is derived from attitude-relevant beliefs, feelings, behaviors, or some combination of all three.

The three-component model suggests that it is also possible to assess directly the attitude-relevant beliefs, feelings, and behaviors (Breckler, 1984). One method for assessing the three components of attitudes utilizes open-ended measures. These measures ask participants to list their beliefs, feelings, and behaviors regarding the attitude object (Esses & Maio, 2002; Haddock & Zanna, 1998). Participants then rate the extent to which each response is positive or negative, using a self-report scale (e.g., from "very negative" to "very positive"). This approach elicits responses from participants that are accessible to them, rather than having participants simply rate their agreement with responses presented by the researcher.

Evidence

Research has tested the expectancy-value model by examining whether people's reports of their overall attitudes are correlated with the summed products of the attitude-relevant expectancies and values. Results indicate that there are substantial correlations between attitudes and the expectancy-value products (e.g., Budd, 1986; van der Pligt & de Vries, 1998), Although there have been statistical and methodological criticisms of the correlational findings (Sparks, Hedderley, & Shepherd, 1991), there is experimental evidence that persuasive messages can induce attitude change by changing evaluative beliefs about an object, particularly when people are motivated and able to process persuasive messages in a systematic manner (Chen & Chaiken, 1999; Petty & Wegener, 1999).

In support of the three-component model, research has found that experimental manipulations of beliefs, feelings, and behavior relevant to an object can shape attitudes toward it. For example, persuasive messages can shape attitudes by altering beliefs about an object (see below), subliminal presentations of affective images can alter attitudes toward an object (Krosnick, Betz, Jussim, & Lynn, 1992), and reminders of past behavior can lead people to infer congruent attitudes (Chaiken & Baldwin, 1981). Moreover, people's scores on indicators of their beliefs, feelings, and behaviors toward an attitude object are correlated, but distinct. For example, Breckler (1984) found that people's beliefs, feelings, and behaviors toward snakes were only moderately correlated when the components were assessed using verbal and nonverbal measures in a context where a snake was present. Further, Trafimow and Sheeran (1998) found that attitude-relevant feelings and beliefs were clustered separately in memory (e.g., we are more likely to recall feelings and beliefs in different clusters than in intermixed sets).

Given the evidence that the cognitive and affective components are distinct (though correlated), attitudes in different domains may be uniquely related to one or the other component. Consistent with this prediction, cognitive responses are strong predictors of attitudes toward a variety of controversial issues, such as capital punishment, legalized abortion, and nuclear weapons (Breckler, 1984; Crites, Fabrigar, & Petty, 1994). In contrast, affective responses are strong predictors of attitudes toward blood donation (Breckler & Wiggins, 1989a), intellectual pursuits (Crites, et al., 1994), smoking (Trafimow & Sheeran, 1998), and politicians (Glaser & Salovey, 1998).

In addition, there are differences in the importance of emotions and cognitions between individuals. In a series of studies, Huskinson and Haddock (2004, 2006) found that people differ in the degree to which their attitudes are based on affective and cognitive information. These differences may be related to individual differences in the need for affect and the need for cognition. The need for affect is the tendency to seek out and enjoy emotional experiences (Maio & Esses, 2001), whereas the need for cognition is the tendency to seek out and enjoy effortful cognitive tasks (Cacioppo & Petty, 1982). Emotional information affects attitudes more strongly among people who are high in the need for affect (rather than low in this need), whereas cognitive information affects attitudes more strongly among people who are high in the need for cognition (Haddock, Maio, Arnold, & Huskinson, 2008). In fact, similar effects of matching to personality occur even when the message is merely *framed* in a way that

highlights either feelings or thoughts (i.e., "I think..." versus "I feel..."), while the message content remains the same (Mayer & Tormala, 2010). Thus, the role of different attitude components is influenced by the personality of the attitude holder.

Attitude Structure

Thus far, we have explained that attitudes summarize beliefs, feelings, and behavior relevant to an attitude object, but we have not considered the underlying structure of these summative judgments. That is, how do our brains organize these representations of positivity and negativity? There are two prominent perspectives on this question: the unidimensional model and the bidimensional model.

Unidimensional Model

The unidimensional perspective regards attitudes as evaluations that express sentiments ranging from extreme unfavorability toward the attitude object to extreme favorability toward the attitude object. This perspective is labeled as unidimensional because it emphasizes a single dimension of evaluation. In other words, the unidimensional perspective assumes that attitudes can take the form of (a) favorability, (b) unfavorability, or (c) neither favorability nor unfavorability. Thus, a person may feel either positively or negatively about the object, but not both at the same time.

The most common measures of attitudes are based on the unidimensional perspective. These measures include bipolar semantic-differential scales, which were mentioned earlier in the discussion of self-report measures of attitudes. These scales are anchored by a negative adjective at one end (e.g., bad) and a positive adjective at the other end (e.g., good). Respondents may be given numerous semantic differential scales, anchored by different adjective pairs (e.g., good versus bad; negative versus positive). To yield an overall index of attitudes, responses are averaged across the scales.

Another common procedure uses Likert-type scales. This technique asks respondents to indicate their agreement or disagreement with several statements expressing varying degrees of favorability or unfavorability toward the attitude object. For example, a measure of attitudes toward the internet might include the items: "The internet gives people access to useful information" and "The internet makes obscene material accessible to everyone." People respond to each item on a scale from −3 (strongly disagree) to +3 (strongly agree). To yield an overall index of attitudes, responses to the items that imply unfavorability toward the attitude object are reverse-coded (e.g., +3 changes to −3), and responses to all items are averaged.

Bidimensional Model

The bidimensional model rejects the notion that attitudes exist only on a single evaluative continuum from negativity to positivity. Instead, the bidimensional model suggests that attitudes subsume two evaluative tendencies: one that varies in positivity *and* one that varies in negativity. Consequently, attitudes can take the form of (a) favorability, (b) unfavorability, (c) neither favorability nor unfavorability, or (d) both favorability and unfavorability toward the attitude object.

To measure attitudes from the bidimensional perspective, the positive and negative responses must be assessed separately. Kaplan (1972) suggested that any single semantic differential scale could be "split" to yield separate positive and negative dimensions. For example, researchers could use a semantic differential scale from −3 (very bad) to 0 (neutral) and another semantic differential scale from 0 (neutral) to +3 (very good), rather than use a single semantic differential scale from −3 (very bad) to +3 (very good). In this manner, separate negative and positive dimension scores are obtained. This approach prevents ambiguous neutral responses. That is, in single semantic differential and Likert items, neutrality may stem from an absence of both positivity and negativity toward the attitude object (a weak attitude) or from the simultaneous presence of both positivity and negativity (a mixed attitude); the split scales can differentiate between these two types of neutrality.

Split scales may be unnecessary when an attitude measure includes many items that assess both positive and negative attributes of the attitude object. For example, open-ended measures of attitudes ask participants to list their beliefs, feelings, and past behaviors regarding an attitude object (Esses & Maio, 2002; Haddock & Zanna, 1998). Participants then rate the valence of each response, using a traditional semantic differential scale. This scale enables respondents to indicate some responses that are positive and some that are negative. A positive dimension score can then be derived from the sum or average of the positive ratings, and a negative dimension score can be derived from the sum or average of the negative ratings.

Separation of the positive and negative dimensions also enables the calculation of *ambivalence*, which is the simultaneous existence of positivity and negativity toward the attitude object (Kaplan, 1972). Ambivalence is calculated using formulae that are designed to assess the extent to which there is a high amount of positivity *and* a high amount of negativity, rather than a high amount of positivity or negativity alone (Maio, Esses, & Bell, 2000; Priester & Petty, 1996; M. M. Thompson, Zanna, & Griffin, 1995; cf. Ullrich, Schermelleh-Engel, & Böttcher, 2008). Interestingly, however, the scores that are derived from these formulae exhibit only moderate correlations (approximately $r = .40$) with measures of felt ambivalence (Priester & Petty, 1996); these latter measures ask people to rate the extent to which they feel conflicted about the attitude object using a number of adjectives (e.g., divided, muddled, torn). Thus, feelings of ambivalence appear to tap psychological processes that are at least somewhat distinct from the ambivalence that is evident in people's actual evaluative responses.

Evidence

Unidimensional measures of attitude exhibit substantial criterion validity. In particular, these measures are good predictors of behavior (Ajzen & Fishbein, 1977; Kraus, 1995). Also, when people are given a chance to indicate separately their negative and positive reactions to an object, those who list more negative reactions also tend to list fewer positive reactions (e.g., Bell, Esses, & Maio, 1996; I. Katz & Hass, 1988; M. M. Thompson et al., 1995), implying some degree of trade-off between negativity and positivity.

Nonetheless, if the bidimensional view is valid, people's unfavorability toward an attitude object should at least sometimes be largely unrelated to their favorability toward the object. In contrast, the unidimensional view suggests that there should be a strong negative correlation between negativity and positivity. Researchers have typically obtained negative correlations between measures of negativity and positivity, across a variety of attitude objects, but these correlations tend to be weak-to-moderate in magnitude, and they are weaker when the time interval between the measurement of negativity and positivity is increased (M. M. Thompson et al., 1995). The low magnitude of these negative correlations suggests that negativity and positivity are not entirely in opposition; there are ways in which they might evolve independently.

Cacioppo, Gardner, and Berntson (1997) observed that positivity and negativity toward an object do not change in parallel: (1) there is a tendency for people to initially possess less negativity than positivity toward attitude objects, and (2) negativity increases more quickly than positivity. Therefore, it is plausible that negativity and positivity reflect different mental processes. Also, if these dimensions are distinct, they should exhibit somewhat different correlations with other variables. Unfortunately, to our knowledge, researchers have not yet systematically examined this issue.

Finally, if the bidimensional view is valid, the simultaneous existence of positivity and negativity (i.e., ambivalence) should have unique psychological consequences that are not predicted by the unidimensional model. And, indeed, researchers have found unique consequences of ambivalence (see the section on characteristics of attitudes later in this chapter).

Despite the empirical support for the bidimensional view, it should be noted that most researchers have not examined the correlations between positivity and negativity while simultaneously controlling random *and* systematic measurement error. Failure to control for both sources of error can artifactually decrease the magnitude of the observed correlation (Green, Goldman, & Salovey, 1993), leaving the impression that the positive and negative dimensions are less strongly related than they actually are.

Also, even if future evidence supports the bidimensional model, it is plausible that the unidimensional model and bidimensional model are valid at different psychological levels. For instance, the bidimensional model may apply to attitude formation, where people perceive the attitude object on both positive and negative dimensions; these dimensions might then be integrated to form a single, unidimensional evaluation (Cacioppo et al., 1997). But this unidimensional evaluation may lose predictive validity as knowledge about the attitude object becomes more complex, because it becomes difficult to integrate the object's positive and negative attributes.

Attitude Functions

The models of attitude content and attitude structure reveal that attitudes summarize diverse information in ways that may be complex, but they do not explain *why* attitudes exist. Theories of attitude function address this issue (Maio & Olson, 2000b). These theories elucidate the psychological motivations that attitudes fulfill and clarify why people bother to form and maintain attitudes. The theories also address how underlying motivations influence the valence and structure of attitudes.

Seminal Theories

Two early theories are the best-known models of attitude function (D. Katz, 1960; M. B. Smith, Bruner, & White, 1956). Smith et al. suggested that attitudes serve three functions: object-appraisal, social-adjustment, and externalization. Object-appraisal refers to the ability of attitudes to summarize the positive and negative attributes of objects in our environment; social-adjustment is served by attitudes that help us to identify with people whom we like and to dissociate from people whom we dislike; and externalization is fulfilled by attitudes that defend against threats to our self-concept. These functions overlap somewhat with four attitude functions independently proposed by Katz: knowledge, utility, value-expression, and ego-defense. The knowledge function represents the ability of attitudes to summarize information about attitude objects; the utilitarian function exists in attitudes that maximize rewards and minimize punishments obtained from attitude objects; the value-expressive function exists in attitudes that express the self-concept and central values; and the ego-defensive function protects self-esteem.

Since the early theoretical statements about attitude function, two central themes have emerged from relevant research. First, evidence suggests that virtually all attitudes fulfill an object-appraisal function to some extent. Second, a distinction between instrumental attitudes (serving a utilitarian function) and symbolic attitudes (serving a value-expressive function) appears to be useful. We describe the evidence regarding these observations after considering how attitude functions are measured in research.

Measurement of Attitude Functions

Researchers have attempted to identify the functions served by particular attitudes in diverse ways. Herek's (1987) Attitude Function Inventory asks participants to rate the extent to which their attitude serves different functions using a number of self-report response scales. Another approach attempts to code attitude functions from participants' responses to an open-ended question about the reasons for their attitude (Maio & Olson, 1994; Shavitt, 1989). For example, if a person's reasons for liking a brand of perfume focus on how others react to it, then the researcher might conclude that the person's attitude serves a social-adjustive function. A pitfall of these self-report approaches, however, is that people may have limited ability to infer the functions served by their attitudes, particularly when their function is ego-defensive.

These limitations can be addressed through methods that examine the role of different functions through implicit methods, which do not ask participants to say anything about the bases of their attitude. For instance, measures of attitude accessibility provide one way to operationalize the object-appraisal function (Fazio, 2000). Alternatively, dominant attitude functions can be inferred when there is a clear, easily identified purpose of the attitude object (e.g., flags are symbolic objects, Shavitt, 1990). Recently, a team of researchers has developed an approach for implicitly measuring the motivational functions of attitudes toward groups (Johnson et al., 2006), which may ultimately prove to be adaptable for other attitude targets.

Another approach infers functions from evidence that the attitude changes when particular psychological needs are met. For instance, defensiveness toward threatening health information can be reduced by an opportunity to affirm the integrity of the self, which suggests that these attitudes serve, at least in part, an ego-defensive function (Sherman, Nelson, & Steele, 2000). Similar approaches have been used to detect ego-defensive functions of prejudicial attitudes toward Blacks (Lowery, Knowles, & Unzueta, 2007) and homosexual men (Falomir-Pichastor & Mugny, 2009).

Object-Appraisal

The object-appraisal function (which combines aspects of the utilitarian and knowledge functions) perhaps best explains why people form attitudes in the first place. In their description of the object-appraisal function, Smith et al. (1956) hypothesized that attitudes are energy-saving devices, because attitudes make decisions about the attitude object faster and easier to perform. This function implies that attitudes classify objects in the environment for the purposes of action. Moreover, it can be argued that *all* attitudes simplify interaction with the environment in this way, regardless of whether the attitudes imply favorability or unfavorability toward the attitude object.

Two programs of research have directly supported this reasoning, while suggesting important caveats. First, Fazio (1995, 2000) argued that the object-appraisal function should be more strongly served by attitudes that are spontaneously activated from memory when the object is encountered than by attitudes that are not spontaneously retrieved. This prediction is based on the assumption that activated attitudes will guide relevant judgments and behavior, whereas dormant attitudes will have little effect on judgments and behavior. Consistent with this hypothesis, highly accessible attitudes (either measured via response latency or manipulated via repeated attitude expression) have been shown to increase the ease with which people make attitude-relevant judgments. For example, people who have accessible attitudes toward an abstract painting have been shown to be subsequently faster at deciding whether they prefer the painting over

another painting and to exhibit less physiological arousal during these preference decisions than people who have less accessible attitudes (see Fazio, 2000). This ability of accessible attitudes to reduce arousal may even have consequences over the longer term: there is evidence that the negative impact of stress on health is attenuated among students who possess many accessible attitudes relevant to their academic pursuits (Fazio & Powell, 1997).

Another program of research has revealed that the strength of the object-appraisal motivation is influenced by individuals' *need for closure*, which is their "desire for a definite answer on some topic, *any* answer as opposed to confusion and ambiguity" (Kruglanski, 1989, p. 14). The object-appraisal function reflects the notion that attitudes can provide such "answers," because attitudes help people to make decisions about attitude objects. Consequently, a high need for closure should increase the desire to form and maintain attitudes. Kruglanski and Webster (1996) tested this hypothesis using both an individual difference measure of need for closure and situational manipulations of the need for closure (which involve manipulating situational pressures to make rapid decisions). As expected, the effects of need for closure on attitude change depended on whether participants had already formed an attitude toward the assigned topic. If participants had already formed an attitude, those who were high in need for closure were less persuaded by new information than participants who were low in need for closure. In contrast, if participants had not yet formed an attitude, those who were high in need for closure were more persuaded by new information than participants who were low in need for closure. Thus, the need for closure was associated with tendencies both to form and to maintain attitudes.

Instrumental Versus Symbolic Attitudes

Research has frequently emphasized a distinction between instrumental (or utilitarian) and symbolic (or value-expressive) attitudes. Instrumental attitudes classify attitude objects according to their ability to promote self-interest, whereas symbolic attitudes express self-image and personal values. This distinction has been used to understand attitudes toward social groups (e.g., homosexuals, people with HIV, blacks; Herek, 2000; Reeder & Pryor, 2000; Sears & Henry, 2003), consumer objects (Ennis & Zanna, 2000; Prentice, 1987; Shavitt, 1990), altruistic behaviors (Maio & Olson, 1995; Snyder, Clary, & Stukas, 2000), and political issues (Lavine & Snyder, 2000; Nelson, 2004).

At least two lines of research support this distinction. First, some attitude *objects* elicit attitudes that are associated primarily with one or the other of these functions. For example, Shavitt (1990) found that people's thoughts about air conditioners focus on the utility of the conditioners, whereas thoughts about greeting cards focus on the cards' capacity to express the self and social values.

Second, evidence indicates that people are more persuaded by messages containing arguments that match the instrumental or symbolic functions of their attitudes than by messages containing arguments that do not match the functions of their attitudes. For example, Shavitt (1990) found that instrumental ads for instrumental products (e.g., an air conditioner) were more persuasive than symbolic ads for instrumental products. Similarly, Snyder and DeBono (1987) found that low self-monitors (who typically possess instrumental attitudes) were more persuaded by instrumental ads for various products (e.g., cigarettes, whisky) than were high self-monitors (whose attitudes typically fulfill social-adjustive functions). These and other matching effects (e.g., Murray, Haddock, & Zanna, 1996; Prentice, 1987) may have occurred because participants scrutinized arguments that matched the function of their attitude more carefully than they scrutinized arguments that did not match the function of their attitude. Consistent with this reasoning, matching effects occur only when the persuasive arguments are strong, but not when the persuasive arguments are weak (Petty & Wegener, 1998).

Multifunctional Roles

Despite the evidence distinguishing different attitude functions, attitudes also can fulfill multiple functions for the individual. For instance, a peace activist, whose attitudes initially fulfilled only a value-expressive or symbolic function, may find that his pacifism makes him more desirable to some women. In this example, his pacifist attitudes may come to fulfill both a value-expressive and an instrumental role.

This type of interplay was revealed in a clever set of experiments examining the effects of motivation for being correct (i.e., the knowledge function) on the use of others' opinions in the formation of one's own attitude (Lun, Sinclair, Whitchurch, & Glenn, 2007). In these experiments, White research participants completed an implicit measure of prejudice toward Blacks. Beforehand, the researchers manipulated whether or not the (White) experimenter was perceived to have nonracist views through a T-shirt she was wearing, which featured the word "eracism" or a nonsense string of letters. The eracism T-shirt produced lower levels of prejudice among those participants whose prior racial attitudes were low (versus high) in accessibility and among participants who were (versus were not) previously primed with uncertainty-relevant terms (e.g., uncertain, want to know, curious). Presumably, these individuals had a stronger need for an attitude fulfilling the knowledge function, which increased the impact of social information (i.e., the experimenter's T-shirt) on their implicitly measured attitude.

ATTITUDES AND HIGHER-ORDER CONSTRUCTS

Attitudes do not, of course, exist in isolation from each other or from other constructs. For example, people who favor social assistance payments to the poor may, on average, possess positive attitudes toward other social welfare programs, such as national health care and subsidized housing. The positive attitudes toward all of these programs may, in turn, arise because the person attaches high importance to the social value of helpfulness. Such relations among attitudes and values may have implications for stability and change in attitudes. In this section, we consider how attitudes are structurally and functionally related to each other and how sets of attitudes may be related to higher-order constructs, such as values and ideologies.

Interattitude Structure

Heider's (1958) balance theory is one of the earliest models of relations between attitudes. This theory examined a situation wherein a person (P) holds a positive or negative attitude toward another person (O), and both people (P and O) hold a positive or negative attitude toward a particular object (X). According to Heider, such P-O-X triads are *balanced* when P likes O and they hold the same (positive or negative) attitude toward X, or when P dislikes O and they hold different attitudes toward X. A state of *imbalance* occurs when P likes O and they hold different attitudes toward X, or when P dislikes O and they hold the same attitude toward X. In other words, balance exists when a person agrees with someone whom he or she likes, or a person disagrees with someone whom he or she dislikes.

Heider (1958) hypothesized that unbalanced states create an unpleasant tension, which motivates people to try to achieve balance. Research has documented that participants report more discomfort with hypothetical unbalanced triads than with hypothetical balanced triads (e.g., Jordan, 1953). Individuals can convert unbalanced states to balanced states in several ways: change the attitude toward either O or X (attitude change), change the belief about O's attitude (belief change), or focus on some aspect of O or X that balances the triad (differentiation). In cases where attitude change is the selected route to imbalance reduction, Heider did not indicate whether the attitude toward O or the attitude toward X is more likely to change, but later research suggested that the more extreme attitude of these two attitudes will change the least (Osgood & Tannenbaum, 1955; Tannenbaum, 1966; cf. Tannenbaum & Gengel, 1966).

Relations Between Attitudes, Values, and Ideologies

The interconnections between attitudes suggest a certain degree of organization should emerge. In theory, these patterns of organization can then be interpreted in the context of higher-order constructs, such as values and ideologies.

Attitudes and Values

The capacity of attitudes to express values is highlighted by theories describing the value-expressive function of attitudes (D. Katz, 1960; Maio & Olson, 2000a) and by measures that specifically include value-relevant beliefs in the assessment of attitude components (Haddock & Zanna, 1998). In addition, Rokeach's (1973) seminal theory of values emphasized the role of values in driving attitudes. He suggested that a relatively small set of social values underlies most attitudes. Consistent with this reasoning, the importance of specific values can predict a large variety of relevant attitudes and behavior (Bernard, Maio, & Olson, 2003; Maio, Roese, Seligman, & Katz, 1996; Verplanken & Holland, 2002). Moreover, priming a value makes accessible a variety of value-relevant attitudes, but priming value-relevant attitudes does not make accessible a variety of values (Gold & Robbins, 1979; Thomsen, Lavine, & Kounios, 1996), suggesting that values are "above" attitudes in the hierarchical network of attitudes, beliefs, and values.

The potential centrality of values is also reflected in expectancy-value perspectives on attitudes. As described earlier in this chapter, these perspectives regard attitudes as being a product of people's expectancies about the extent to which an attitude object possesses particular attributes or outcomes and the extent to which these attributes or outcomes are valued. The source of the "valuation" is explicitly held to be social values in

Rosenberg's (1968) classic elaboration of the expectancy-value perspective, and more recent evidence expands this view (Feather, 1995; Rabinovich, Morton, Postmes, & Verplanken, 2009).

Attitudes and Ideologies

Attitudes may also express ideologies, which are clusters of thematically related values and attitudes (Kinder, 1998). Liberalism and conservatism are well-known ideologies, although there are divergent views on their psychological content (Greenberg & Jonas, 2003). For instance, one perspective suggests that conservative ideologies and liberal ideologies are independent (neither opposed nor congruent) differences in value expression: conservative ideologies encompass attitudes and values that promote freedom and self-enhancement, and liberal ideologies encompass attitudes and values that promote universal rights and benevolence (Kerlinger, 1984). In contrast, another perspective suggests that "preferences for tradition, conformity, order, stability, traditional values, and hierarchy—*versus* [italics added] those for progress, rebelliousness, chaos, flexibility, feminism, and equality—are associated with conservatism and liberalism, respectively" (Jost, Nosek, & Gosling, 2008, p. 126). Not only do these perspectives differ in the specific content that they assign to liberalism and conservatism, but they also differ in whether the ideologies are viewed as independent or opposites.

If political attitudes reside on a single dimension that treats liberal and conservative as opposites, then people should tend to endorse either conservative attitudes or liberal attitudes, but not both. Yet, people's actual endorsements of liberal and conservative attitudes often document variation across subgroups of the population (Converse, 1964; Fleishman, 1986). For example, unidimensionality is evident only among people who are highly knowledgeable about political issues, but not among those who exhibit less expertise (Converse, 2000; Federico & Schneider, 2007; Lavine, Thomsen, & Gonzalez, 1997; Lusk & Judd, 1988; Sidanius & Duffy, 1988). The lack of evidence for unidimensionality in people with low expertise is problematic because they are in the majority—an issue recognized even by researchers who often utilize the liberal-conservative distinction. For example, according to Jost, Federico, and Napier (2009, p. 316), "Decades of research suggest that the majority of the population exhibits a relatively low level of knowledge about the specific discursive contents of liberal and conservative ideologies, a relative inability and/or unwillingness to understand political conflict in strictly liberal-conservative terms, and a relatively low level of ideological consistency (or constraint) in their attitudes toward many different issues."

So why do researchers persist in looking at liberalism versus conservatism? One reason is a belief that the liberal-conservative dimension does exist (Jost et al., 2009), but is more easily detectable in particular people (e.g., political experts), issues (e.g., core system challenging issues) and contexts (e.g., high public engagement in politics). Another perspective is that differences between liberals and conservatives may vary across cultures and that, where these groups are distinct (e.g., U.S.), the differences pertain to the weight that they attach to five moral principles: nonharm, fairness, group loyalty, respect for authority, and purity (Graham, Haidt, & Nosek, 2009). These views imply that, although there is variability in the extent to which this ideological dimension is valid across individuals, issues, contexts, and cultures, its average validity is sufficient to predict important judgments.

An opposing view is that there are different ideological dimensions within political attitudes. Ashton et al. (2005) found evidence for two dimensions across several Western nations: attitudes toward moral regulation versus individual freedom and attitudes toward compassion versus competition (see also Boski, 1993). These dimensions were significantly correlated with basic dimensions of cultural ideology and values, and more recent evidence indicates connections to basic dimensions of personality as well (Lee, Ashton, Ogunfowora, Bourdage, & Shin, 2010; Lee et al., 2009). Future research is needed to determine whether these dimensions help to predict related attitudes and behaviors better than the traditional liberal-conservative dimension.

The recent surge of interest in ideological dimensions of attitudes has extended beyond the study of political views. For example, researchers in the area of intergroup attitudes have examined several ideological dimensions, including multiculturalism versus color-blindness (Knowles, Lowery, Hogan, & Chow, 2009; Wolsko, Park, Judd, & Wittenbrink, 2000) and individualism versus communalism (I. Katz & Hass, 1988). Diverse ideologies have also been examined in studies of attitudes toward gender roles (Spence, 1993), body weight and obesity (Crandall et al., 2001), ways of life (de St. Aubin, 1996), and violence (Nisbett & Cohen, 1996).

Across research domains, there is relatively little evidence documenting how attitudes express broad values and ideologies (Maio, 2010; Maio, Olson, Bernard, & Luke, 2003), although some obtained patterns of correlations between values (e.g., Schwartz & Rubel, 2005) and

some documented effects of priming values on actions (Maio, Pakizeh, Cheung, & Rees, 2009) are consistent with the recent multidimensional analyses of political ideology and personality (Lee et al., 2009; Lee et al., 2010). Nonetheless, the causal direction of these connections is not yet clear. For example, values may occasionally function as post hoc justifications for attitudes, rather than as their psychological basis (Kristiansen & Zanna, 1988). When causal influences of values and ideologies do occur, the effects may be indirect or direct. In an indirect effect, values and ideologies influence a specific attitude indirectly through other attitudes, whereas a direct effect occurs when people perceive the value itself as being relevant to their attitude (Maio & Olson, 1998, 2000a). The latter, direct process may be more likely when the value and the reasons for its importance have been concretely instantiated (Maio, Hahn, Frost, & Cheung, 2009; Maio, Olson, Allen, & Bernard, 2001).

CHARACTERISTICS OF ATTITUDES

Attitudes vary along numerous dimensions, or characteristics, that have significant implications for information processing, resistance to influence, and behavior. A continuing issue in the attitudes literature has been the relations among these dimensions; some researchers have argued that the various characteristics are distinct and should be treated as independent, but other researchers have argued that many of the characteristics are interdependent and should be treated as manifestations of a smaller set of constructs. In this section, we briefly describe these dimensions and address the controversy surrounding the interrelations among them.

Valence

The valence of an attitude is its most basic property, referring to whether the attitude is favorable, unfavorable, or neutral. Favorable attitudes reflect positive evaluations of the target, whereas unfavorable attitudes reflect negative evaluations. In our earlier discussion of the object appraisal function of attitudes, we pointed out that attitudes allow rapid decisions to be made that have implications for action. For example, attitudes can spontaneously elicit approach or avoidance behavior toward the target. Of course, the critical feature of the attitude that determines whether approach or avoidance is elicited is its valence: favorable attitudes elicit approach, whereas unfavorable attitudes elicit avoidance.

Extremity

After valence, attitude extremity is the next most basic dimension of attitudes. Extremity refers to the extent to which the attitude deviates from a neutral midpoint—that is, the extent to which the individual's evaluation is strongly favorable or strongly unfavorable. Extreme attitudes, compared to moderate attitudes, are more resistant to influence (Osgood & Tannenbaum, 1955), more likely to be projected onto others (Allison & Messick, 1988), and more likely to predict behavior (Fazio & Zanna, 1978a). Attitude theorists have generally assumed that extreme attitudes develop over time, often resulting from actions that publicly commit the individual to his or her position.

Accessibility

Accessibility refers to the ease of activation, or activation potential, of a construct (Higgins, 1996). Highly accessible attitudes are evaluations that come to mind quickly and spontaneously when the attitude object is encountered. Accessibility depends, at least in part, on the frequency with which the attitude has been activated in the recent past. Researchers have found that highly accessible attitudes, compared to less accessible attitudes, are more resistant to change (Bassili, 1996), more likely to influence perceptions of attitude-relevant events (Houston & Fazio, 1989), and more likely to predict behavior (Fazio & Williams, 1986). These effects of accessibility presumably reflect that highly accessible attitudes will consistently be activated when the attitude object is encountered, so they are more likely to exert an impact than low accessibility attitudes, which may remain dormant.

Ambivalence

As described above, ambivalence refers to the simultaneous presence of conflicting positive and negative elements within an attitude (Kaplan, 1972). Ambivalence can occur between elements of the same component of an attitude, such as when people possess both positive and negative feelings about a minority group (intracomponent ambivalence), or between two components of an attitude, such as when people possess negative beliefs but positive feelings about junk food (intercomponent ambivalence).

Studies have shown that, compared to nonambivalent attitudes, ambivalent attitudes are easier to change (Armitage & Conner, 2000), less accessible from memory (Bargh, Chaiken, Govender, & Pratto, 1992), and less predictive of behavior (Lavine, Thomsen, Zanna, &

Borgida, 1998). Ambivalent attitudes also polarize judgments when one of the conflicting elements is made more salient than another. For example, MacDonald and Zanna (1998) showed that individuals with ambivalent attitudes toward feminists made either more favorable or more unfavorable judgments about a feminist job applicant, depending on whether positive or negative information was made salient, whereas individuals with nonambivalent, but equally extreme, attitudes were not affected by the salience of positive or negative information. Ambivalent attitudes are hypothesized to have these polarizing effects because such attitudes contain both positive and negative information; priming can make one or the other category of information accessible, which will then influence judgments.

Nevertheless, an important caveat to these findings is that most research on attitudinal ambivalence has occurred in Western cultures, even though, ironically, attitudinal ambivalence may be more prevalent among people from Eastern cultures (Spencer-Rodgers, Williams, & Peng, 2010). As described by Spencer-Rodgers et al., Eastern cultures are more accepting of ambivalence because of a stronger dialectic emphasis in their general styles of thinking (i.e., there is greater recognition of opposites). It remains to be seen whether this cultural difference in thinking style also entails divergent antecedents and consequences of attitudinal ambivalence.

Direct-Indirect Experience

Attitudes can be based on direct, personal experience with the attitude object or on indirect information from others about the object. For example, students' attitudes toward chemistry courses can be based on their own experiences with previous chemistry courses or on things they have heard from others who have taken chemistry courses. Researchers have found that attitudes based on direct experience, compared to those based on indirect experience, are more confidently held (Fazio & Zanna, 1978b), more stable over time (Doll & Ajzen, 1992), more resistant to influence (Wu & Schaffer, 1987), and more likely to predict behavior (Fazio & Zanna, 1981). Presumably, these effects of direct experience reflect that we trust our own senses more than others' reports, which increases confidence in attitudes based on direct experience.

Embeddedness

Attitude embeddedness, also called *working knowledge*, refers to the amount of attitude-relevant information that is linked to the attitude, such as beliefs and experiences (Pomerantz, Chaiken, & Tordesillas, 1995; Scott, 1968; Wood, Rhodes, & Biek, 1995). The more information that comes to mind when one encounters the attitude object, the more embedded is the attitude. Highly embedded attitudes are more resistant to change (Wood et al., 1995), more likely to influence perceptions of attitude-relevant stimuli (Vallone, Ross, & Lepper, 1985), and more predictive of behavior (Kallgren & Wood, 1986) than are low embeddedness attitudes. These effects of embeddedness presumably reflect that attitudes based on a lot of information are held more confidently and provide the individual with many bits of knowledge to counteract the potential influence of new information. Also, embedded attitudes can be more accessible than attitudes low in embeddedness (Wood et al., 1995).

Strength: An Integrative Concept?

The characteristics of attitudes discussed to this point are interrelated. For example, attitudes based on direct experience tend to be more extreme, more accessible, and less ambivalent; highly embedded attitudes tend to be more accessible and less ambivalent; and so on (Krosnick, Boninger, Chuang, Berent, & Carnot, 1993). Indeed, our descriptions of five of the characteristics (extremity, accessibility, ambivalence, direct-indirect experience, and embeddedness) all cited empirical evidence that attitudes at one end of the continuum of the characteristic (high or low) are more resistant to change and more predictive of behavior than are attitudes at the other end of the continuum.

Given the conceptual overlap among these various characteristics, theorists have wondered whether the variables represent more-or-less-interchangeable terms for a single characteristic; the term *attitude strength* has been offered as a label for this common quality (Krosnick & Petty, 1995). In other words, some theorists have speculated that the various characteristics may form a single dimension ranging from weak to strong attitudes. The most common way to investigate this issue has been to measure numerous characteristics and conduct a factor analysis of the data. If a single factor emerged, the unidimensional attitude strength notion would be supported, whereas if multiple factors emerged, a more complex framework would be suggested. Such studies have generally supported the multidimensional view (Abelson, 1988; Krosnick et al., 1993; Pomerantz et al., 1995; Prislin, 1996), although the precise natures of the factors emerging from the analyses have been inconsistent. Based on

these data, the most common conclusion has been that the various characteristics should be viewed as distinct, though related, constructs.

An interesting issue in research on attitude strength has been how this quality changes over the lifespan. Common stereotypes suggest that we become more fixed in our opinions as we grow older; as one cliché suggests, "You can't teach an old dog new tricks." A number of studies have found that this view is only partly correct: persuasibility on diverse topics decreases from young adulthood to middle adulthood, but rises again through the late adult years (e.g., Visser & Krosnick, 1998). Recent results have indicated that these changes are attributable to the greater social power that people assume as they reach middle age (e.g., job roles, family roles), compared to the younger and older ages (Eaton, Visser, Krosnick, & Anand, 2009). High power roles activate norms of strength and resilience, which people may internalize, making them more resistant to attempts to change their attitudes.

ATTITUDE FORMATION

Where do attitudes come from? How do they develop? As described in the earlier section on attitude structure, attitudes can be based on cognitive, affective, and/or behavioral information. Each of these possible avenues of attitude formation is discussed below, as well as a biological perspective on attitude formation.

Cognitive Processes

One crucial source of attitudes is cognitive information about the target—that is, beliefs about attributes of the target. Indeed, as discussed in the attitude structure section, belief-based models of attitudes are common. Knowledge about an object can come either from direct experience with the object or from indirect sources such as parents, peers, and the media. As already noted, attitudes based on direct experience tend to be stronger than attitudes derived from indirect information.

The best-known theory of attitude formation based on cognitive beliefs is the previously mentioned *theory of reasoned action* (Fishbein & Ajzen, 1975), which is an expectancy-value model wherein salient (i.e., highly accessible) beliefs are hypothesized to combine additively to form the overall evaluation of the target (attitude toward the target). As noted earlier in the chapter, many researchers have documented substantial relations between attitudes and expectancy-value products (Budd, 1986; van der Pligt & de Vries, 1998). This model of attitudes is based on a conception of humans as rational, deliberate thinkers who base their behavior on information about the positive and negative consequences of various actions.

A more recent approach stresses the neglected role of meta-cognitive processes in attitudes (Petty et al., 2007). The Meta-Cognitive Model acknowledges the importance of beliefs about expectancies and values in attitudes, but also points out that these expectancies and values may be accompanied by feelings of either high or low confidence (Petty, Briñol, & Tormala, 2002). For instance, a person might believe that mankind is greatly increasing the amount of carbon dioxide in the atmosphere and feel confident about this belief, but lack confidence in his or her evaluation of the presence of carbon dioxide as a bad thing. Differences in thought confidence are important because they predict differences in the way attitudes appear on explicit and implicit measures (cf. Gawronski & Bodenhausen, 2006; Petty, Tormala, Briñol, & Jarvis, 2006), as well as interesting effects on attitude change (Briñol & Petty, 2009). For instance, the model can explain the emergence of ambivalence on an implicit measure of attitudes after processing a persuasive message, whereas an explicit measure simply shows change in the direction advocated by the message (Petty et al., 2006).

Some of these effects might also be explained by Gawronski and Bodenhausen's (2007) Associative-Propositional Evaluation (APE) Model. This model suggests that evaluations of an object are shaped by two constructs: associations, which are affective responses activated by an object, and propositions, which are mental representations of the truth or falsehood of different claims that can be made about the attitude object. According to this model, conflicts between associations and propositions can lead to discrepancies between responses on implicit and explicit measures. One strength of the APE model is its explicit incorporation of affective processes, such as the impact of evaluative conditioning on attitudes. Evaluative conditioning and other affective processes are described in greater detail below. A detailed discussion of the APE model is beyond the scope of this chapter, but, as an example of its predictive power, the model predicts that evaluative conditioning will exert different effects on implicit and explicit measures of attitude when people focus on their knowledge (rather than their feelings) about the attitude object (Gawronski & LeBel, 2008).

Affective Processes

Individuals' evaluations of targets can be based on how the target makes them feel—that is, on the emotions or affect aroused by the target. Indeed, as noted in the section on structure, affect sometimes predicts attitudes better than does cognition (e.g., Esses et al., 1993). Of course, affect and cognition will often (or even usually) be consistent with one another, because these processes are mutually interdependent or synergistic (Eagly & Chaiken, 1998). That is, knowledge can influence feelings, and feelings can guide thoughts.

Although most affect toward objects probably springs from beliefs about those objects, there are a number of processes that can result in affect becoming associated with an object independently of cognition (i.e., independently of information about the characteristics of the object). A. Staats and Staats (1958) introduced the idea that attitudes can be formed through *classical conditioning*, which occurs when a stimulus comes to evoke a response that it did not previously evoke, simply by being paired with another stimulus that already evokes that response. For example, the genial receptionist at a dental office might come to evoke negative affect for patients who are very fearful of dental work.

In the attitudes literature, this process has been labeled *evaluative conditioning* (EC), and there is evidence that EC can occur without individuals' awareness of any connection between the two stimuli (De Houwer, Thomas, & Baeyens, 2001). The past decade has seen sophisticated studies documenting EC effects. There is evidence that EC occurs through an automatic process (M. A. Olson & Fazio, 2001, 2002), wherein people's affective response to the emotional stimulus is misattributed to the attitude object (C. R. Jones, Fazio, & Olson, 2009). Some studies suggest that the process can even be used to alter trenchant attitudes, such as prejudice (M. A. Olson & Fazio, 2006).

Another process through which affect can become linked to objects without necessary cognitive mediation is mere exposure. The *mere exposure effect* (Zajonc, 1968) occurs when repeated, simple exposure to an object (i.e., exposure without reinforcement feedback) leads to more favorable feelings toward the object. For example, an abstract painting that initially evokes confusion might come to be liked over time, simply because the painting is more familiar. The results of several fascinating studies have shown that conscious recognition that stimuli are familiar is not necessary for the mere exposure effect to occur (Moreland & Beach, 1992), nor, in fact, is conscious *perception* of the object: even subliminal exposures can increase liking for a stimulus (Bornstein & D'Agostino, 1992). On the other hand, perceived familiarity can also lead to liking: people tend to like an object if they merely think they have seen it many times before, even if they have not (Murphy & Zajonc, 1993). Mere exposure effects can have important practical implications. For instance, one recent investigation found that mere exposure may be an important factor in the maintenance of prejudice, because we have much more exposure to our own ethnic groups (and therefore like them more) than to other ethnic groups (P. K. Smith, Dijksterhuis, & Chaiken, 2008).

Behavioral Processes

A third potential source of attitudes is behavioral information: knowledge of our previous actions toward a target affects our attitude toward it. Importantly, this knowledge about our prior actions does not have to be accurate: the mere belief that we have performed a particular behavior (without necessarily having done so) can elicit attitudes that conform to the alleged prior action (Albarracín & Wyer, 2000). Thus, the subjective perception of our own past behavior appears to matter independently of the actual performance of the behavior.

Behavior can influence attitudes through a variety of processes, including dissonance arousal, self-perception, and embodiment processes. From the perspective of dissonance theory (Festinger, 1964), knowing that one has acted favorably or unfavorably toward a target will *motivate* an individual to evaluate the target in a manner consistent with those actions (see Harmon-Jones & Mills, 1999). Recent neurological and behavioral evidence suggests that dissonance reduction facilitates action; specifically, dissonance reduction helps people stop questioning themselves about whether a past decision or action was good or bad, so that they can move on to other decisions and actions (Harmon-Jones, Harmon-Jones, Fearn, Sigelman, & Johnson, 2008).

From the perspective of self-perception theory (Bem, 1972), individuals might logically *infer* their attitudes from their actions and the environment in which they acted (see J. M. Olson & Stone, 2005). This process entails a simple deductive inference, without motivational forces at work. If we laugh at a joke on television and do not notice that it was accompanied by recorded laughter, we may decide that the joke was funny, even though it is possible that the recorded laughter caused us to laugh because of automatic mimicry (J. M. Olson, 1992). This process is potentially quite powerful: recent evidence suggests

that we may even infer our attitudes from watching the behaviors of others with whom we identify (Goldstein & Cialdini, 2007).

Another perspective is that behavior can shape attitudes through the direct connotations of specific bodily actions. This perspective comes from research on *embodied social cognition* (Niedenthal, Barsalou, Winkielman, Krauth-Gruber, & Ric, 2005). There are many ways in which bodily actions can shape attitudes, but one mechanism worth highlighting is that actions can affect individuals' confidence in their thoughts. For instance, attitudes are more strongly influenced by thoughts that people write with their dominant hand than by thoughts they write with their nondominant hand, because people have developed more confidence in the thoughts that they have expressed with their dominant hand (Briñol & Petty, 2004). Thought confidence is also influenced by actions such as sitting upright versus slouching and head nodding versus head shaking (Briñol & Petty, 2009).

Biological Processes

Social psychological research has begun to direct more attention to biological processes in attitude formation than has historically been the case. The biological factors that have been examined include physiological indicators of attitude (Cacioppo & Petty, 1987), the impact of drugs such as alcohol (MacDonald, Zanna, & Fong, 1996) and caffeine (Martin, Hamilton, McKimmie, Terry, & Martin, 2007), and the roles of physiological arousal (Zanna & Cooper, 1974) and region-specific brain activity (Harmon-Jones et al., 2008).

One important biological perspective on attitudes concerns the role of genetic factors. Although it is unlikely that genes shape attitudes through simple one-to-one connections, they may affect other traits that lead to particular patterns of attitude. That is, genes may establish general predispositions that shape environmental experiences in ways that increase the likelihood of an individual developing specific traits and attitudes. For instance, it is unlikely that there is a gene that causes negative attitudes toward the death penalty, but there may be a variety of genes that create more forgiving or benevolent attitudes in general.

Some attitude-relevant genes may encode physical features. For example, children might pick on other children who are naturally small for their age with the result that the smaller children might develop anxieties about social interaction, with consequences for their attitudes toward social events. Other genes, as described below, may encode particular personality traits (e.g., sociability), which can affect a number of relevant social attitudes.

In an early study of these issues, Arvey, Bouchard, Segal, and Abraham (1989) found that approximately 30% of the observed variance in job satisfaction in their sample of identical twins raised apart was attributable to genetic factors. Thus, respondents' attitudes toward their jobs appeared to be partly inherited. In addition, Eaves, Eysenck, and Martin (1989) reported the results of two surveys involving almost 4,000 pairs of same-sex twins. A variety of social attitudes were assessed, including crime, religion, race, and lifestyle. Heritability estimates for individual items ranged from 1% to 62%, with a median of 39%.

But *how* do genes impact on attitudes? What are some specific, genetically influenced characteristics that can systematically bias environmental experience so as to induce particular attitudes? Tesser (1993) identified several possibilities, including intelligence, temperament, and sensory structures. Olson, Vernon, Harris, and Jang (2001) measured some potential mediators of attitude heritability in a study of more than 300 pairs of same-sex twins, including physical characteristics and personality factors. Most of these possible mediators were themselves highly heritable in the sample of twins, and multivariate analyses showed that several of the variables correlated at a genetic level with attitudes that were heritable. For example, the personality trait of sociability yielded a significant heritability coefficient and significant genetic correlations with five measures of heritable attitudes. These data suggest that the heritability of sociability might account, in part, for the heritable components of some attitudes.

Tesser (1993) hypothesized that attitudes that are highly heritable might have a biological basis that makes attitude change difficult. Individuals may develop psychological defenses to protect these attitudes. For example, niche-building might occur (Plomin, DeFries, & Loehlin, 1977), such that individuals seek out environments that are compatible with their highly heritable attitudes. Tesser (1993; Tesser & Crelia, 1994) tested this idea in several ingenious ways. In all of his studies, attitudes that had been shown by Eaves et al. (1989) to have either high or low heritability coefficients were studied. In one study, individuals were found to provide answers more quickly for high than low heritability attitudes. In another study, individuals were found to be less affected by conformity pressure when reporting high than low heritability attitudes. In a third study, interpersonal similarity on high heritability attitudes was shown to affect liking for others more than similarity on low heritability attitudes.

Finally, in two studies, individuals found agreement feedback more reinforcing when the agreement occurred for highly heritable attitudes than when it occurred for less heritable attitudes. These findings suggest that attitude strength is positively correlated with attitude heritability (see also J. M. Olson et al., 2001).

ATTITUDES AND INFORMATION PROCESSING

One of the fundamental functions of attitudes, as discussed earlier, is the *object appraisal* function, which refers to the capacity of attitudes to facilitate both the identification of objects and the rapid appraisal of the objects' implications for the self. This function underscores that attitudes influence how objects are perceived and how information about those objects is processed. In this section, we review research on the effects of attitudes on information processing. The theme of this section will be *selectivity*: Attitudes tend to facilitate the processing of information that is consistent with them and to inhibit the processing of inconsistent information.

Selective Attention

Festinger's (1957) *dissonance theory* proposed that people want to believe that their decisions and attitudes are correct. Whereas individuals will attend in an unbiased way to information *prior* to making decisions or forming attitudes, Festinger argued that, once formed, attitudes motivate people to pay attention to consistent information and avoid inconsistent information. Early tests of this *selective exposure hypothesis* yielded little support (Freedman & Sears, 1965), but researchers gradually identified boundary conditions for the effect (Frey, 1986; Holbrook, Berent, Krosnick, Visser, & Boninger, 2005). For example, the utility, novelty, and salience of consistent versus inconsistent information must be controlled in order for the effects of attitudinal consistency to be tested clearly. In addition, we are more drawn to an attitude object or related information when our attitudes toward it are highly accessible (Roskos-Ewoldsen & Fazio, 1992) or personally important (Holbrook et al., 2005). Researchers have documented selective attention in the laboratory (e.g., Frey & Rosch, 1984) and in field settings (e.g., Sweeney & Gruber, 1984), and there is evidence that individuals with repressing/avoidance defensive styles may exhibit selective attention to consistent information more than individuals with ruminative/approach defensive styles (J. M. Olson & Zanna, 1979).

Selective Perception

Many researchers have shown that attitudes influence the perception or interpretation of attitude-relevant information, with the effect generally being to interpret information as more supportive of one's attitudes than is actually the case (Vidmar & Rokeach, 1974). For example, Lord, Ross, and Lepper (1979) found that individuals' attitudes toward capital punishment predicted their assessments of the quality of two alleged scientific studies, one supporting and one questioning the deterrence value of the death penalty: Participants evaluated the study that apparently supported their own view more favorably than the study that apparently disconfirmed their view (see also Edwards & Smith, 1996). Houston and Fazio (1989) replicated this study and showed that the biasing effect of attitudes on the interpretation of information was significant only when the attitudes were highly accessible (Fazio & Williams, 1986; Schuette & Fazio, 1995). In another domain, Vallone et al. (1985) found that individuals' evaluations of the media coverage of an event were biased by their relevant attitudes (see also Giner-Sorolla & Chaiken, 1994).

If there is a general bias to perceive the world as consistent with one's attitudes, then existing attitudes might reduce the ability of perceivers to detect that the attitude object has changed. For instance, if you have a strong positive or negative attitude toward someone, you might recognize the person quickly even if the person's appearance has changed a great deal, while failing to register the differences. Indeed, Fazio, Ledbetter, and Towles-Schwen (2000) have documented such an effect and related it to attitude accessibility. Specifically, attitudes tended to interfere with participants' ability to perceive change in an attitude target, and this effect was stronger for highly accessible attitudes than for less accessible attitudes. In another set of studies, Stewart, Vassar, Sanchez, and David (2000) showed that participants' attitudes toward women's and men's societal roles influenced whether they judged male or female targets more as a function of their individual characteristics (rather than their gender): participants with traditional sex-role attitudes focused on individual characteristics more for male targets than female targets, whereas participants with nontraditional sex-role attitudes focused on individual characteristics more for female targets than male targets.

Selective Memory

Attitudes have long been thought to influence memory and learning of attitude-related information, such that information consistent with an attitude will be easier to learn and remember than information inconsistent with the attitude. A variety of processes could contribute to such selective memory, including paying more attention to attitudinally consistent information (but see Roberts, 1985), finding it easier to store attitudinally consistent information, and finding it easier to retrieve attitudinally consistent information from memory. Early studies indicated that individuals were better at learning and recalling information that was consistent with their attitudes than information that was inconsistent with their attitudes (Levine & Murphy, 1943). Subsequent researchers, however, had difficulty obtaining significant selective memory effects and questioned the reliability of the phenomenon (Greenwald & Sakamura, 1976).

In a comprehensive meta-analysis of research on attitude-memory effects, Eagly, Chen, Chaiken, and Shaw-Barnes (1999) concluded that the attitude congeniality effect (such that information congenial with one's attitudes is more memorable than uncongenial information) has been small in magnitude and inconsistent across studies. Especially worrisome was evidence that the effect has grown weaker in more recent experiments (compared to earlier experiments), because the recent studies have generally used more rigorous methods. It appears that selective memory may be a weaker phenomenon than selective attention and selective perception.

Perhaps the clearest evidence of selective memory has been obtained in studies testing whether individuals use their attitudes as clues for searching memory. Ross (1989) reviewed a number of studies showing that people used their attitudes as clues for searching memory and/or reconstructing past events. For example, Ross, McFarland, and Fletcher (1981) exposed respondents to one of two messages that had previously been shown to have reliable persuasive effects in opposite directions. In an apparently separate study, respondents provided reports of the frequency with which they had performed a number of behaviors in the past month, including some behaviors related to the target of the persuasive message. Respondents reported more frequent behaviors consistent with the attitude promoted in the message to which they were exposed than behaviors consistent with the attitude promoted in the message they did not see. Presumably, respondents used their newly formed attitudes to search memory and to reconstruct their behaviors in the previous month.

Attitude Polarization

Attitudes guide information processing in another way; namely, they guide spontaneous thinking about the attitude object. Tesser (1978) showed that simply thinking about an attitude object tended to polarize the evaluation even in the absence of any new information. For example, simply thinking about a person who was either likeable or unlikeable led to stronger evaluations (positive for the likeable target, negative for the unlikeable partner) than a control condition where participants performed a distracting task. Presumably, information in memory supporting the existing attitude led participants to generate thoughts that were consistent with it. This interpretation is supported by findings that polarization effects are stronger when the individual is knowledgeable about the attitude object (Tesser & Leone, 1977), the existing attitude is low in ambivalence (Chaiken & Yates, 1985), and the attitude does *not* put two important personal values in conflict (Liberman & Chaiken, 1991).

ATTITUDES AND BEHAVIOR

We discussed earlier how attitudes fulfill various functions for individuals, including the rapid appraisal of attitude objects (object-appraisal function) and the approach associated with rewarding objects and the avoidance associated with punishing objects (utilitarian function). These hypothesized functions are predicated, in part, on the assumption that individuals will behave in ways that are consistent with their attitudes. In other words, we tend to assume that attitudes influence action. In this final section, we review some of the evidence on attitude-behavior consistency.

The hypothesized strong relation between attitudes and behavior has sometimes proven difficult to document. For example, Wicker (1969) reviewed 30 studies that examined attitude-behavior consistency and concluded that there was little evidence to support the idea that people hold stable attitudes that influence their actions. However, he noted the need for further study of potential moderators of the relation between attitudes and behavior, and, since that time, researchers have identified several relevant factors. The appropriate conclusion now seems to be that measures of attitudes and behavior are closely related in some circumstances, but not in others. We outline these factors that affect attitude-behavior consistency in the following sections.

Nature of the Attitude and Behavior Measures

One important conceptual advance came from Fishbein and Ajzen's (1975) theory of reasoned action. These theorists distinguished between attitudes toward objects and attitudes toward behaviors. Conceptually, attitudes toward objects should predict the average favorability of a reasonably large sample of behaviors related to the object, whereas attitudes toward behaviors should predict the favorability of those specific actions. In other words, in order for there to be a strong relation between measures of attitudes and behavior, the measures must be *compatible* (or congruent) in terms of their specificity. Measures of general attitudes toward an object will best predict measures that average across a variety of relevant behaviors (called *multiple act behavioral criteria*). In contrast, measures of attitudes toward a specific behavior will best predict measures of that single, focal behavior. The measures of attitudes toward specific behaviors will be most accurate when the measures describe the behavior on four dimensions: action (e.g., giving money), target (e.g., to a homeless person), context (e.g., on the street), and time (e.g., at lunchtime today). For example, a measure of the individual's attitude toward "giving money to a homeless person on the street at lunchtime today" would be the best predictor of this specific behavior, whereas a measure of attitudes that asked only about giving money (the action dimension) or about homeless people (the target dimension) would yield weaker correlations. Many early researchers inappropriately used general attitude measures (e.g., participants' attitudes toward an ethnic group) to try to predict specific behavior measures (e.g., how participants behaved toward a particular member of the ethnic group in a particular setting at a particular time). When measures of attitudes and behavior have been highly compatible in terms of their specificity, attitude-behavior correlations have been substantial (Ajzen & Fishbein, 1977; Kraus, 1995).

There is also evidence that another feature of how attitudes are measured may be important. Typically, measures of attitudes ask participants to rate their favorability toward the attitude object. An alternative approach involves asking participants to rate their favorability *compared to other people* (e.g., compared to other university students). For example, students might be asked to rate their attitude toward recycling on a scale from 0 "less favorable than the average student" to 100 "more favorable than the average student" (J. M. Olson, Goffin, & Haynes, 2007). Across a number of studies, Olson et al. found that this type of relative measure of attitudes improved the prediction of behavior. It appeared that this effect was associated with respondents giving greater consideration to both social comparison information and behavioral information before making the relative attitude ratings (see also Goffin & Olson, in press).

Nature of the Behavior

Certain kinds of behavior are more predictable from attitudes than are other kinds of behavior. To begin, attitudes are hypothesized to guide only *volitional* actions: behaviors that individuals are free to perform or to not perform. When strong external incentives or constraints exist regarding an action, attitudes may not play much role in determining behavior. To take a simple example, politeness norms may cause people to say hello to co-workers whom they dislike. This conceptual point was recognized in the theory of reasoned action (Fishbein & Ajzen, 1975) by including *subjective norms* as a determinant of behavioral intentions that was distinct from attitudes. Subjective norms refer to individuals' perceptions that other people who are important to them want them to act in certain ways.

Norms are likely not the only variable that competes with attitudes in the prediction of behavior, however. Ajzen (1991) proposed a revision to the theory of reasoned action, which he labeled the *theory of planned behavior*. This model includes perceived behavioral control as another determinant of intentions and behavior, distinct from both attitudes and subjective norms. The construct of perceived behavioral control extends the model to behavior that is not fully under volitional control; for example, individuals who believe that they cannot easily perform a behavior might not do it even if they have a positive attitude toward the behavior and/or perceive that other people want them to perform it (see also Gollwitzer & Sheeran, 2006). Thus, the behavior's controllability or difficulty also influences the strength of the attitude-behavior relation.

Other aspects of behavior are more subtle, but no less important. Foremost among these subtle factors, the strength of the attitude-behavior relation depends on the behavior's correspondence to the mental representation of the attitude object at the time the attitude was measured. We have already noted that if the measure of the attitude is general (e.g., an attitude toward an object) but the behavior is specific, then the measures are not highly compatible, and attitude-behavior consistency will be low. Yet, a general measure of an attitude may still predict a specific measure of behavior *if the behavior mirrors the mental representation of the attitude object at the time it was measured*. The importance of this feature was articulated in *attitude representation theory* (Lord & Lepper, 1999). According to this perspective, measures of attitude will best predict behavior toward a "typical" instance of a general attitude. For example, Lord, Lepper, and

Mackie (1984) found that individuals' attitudes toward gay men predicted how they behaved toward a gay man who closely matched the stereotype better than how they behaved toward a gay man who differed substantially from the stereotype. Presumably, a stereotypic gay man better matched participants' mental representations of gay men that were salient when participants reported their attitudes, so the attitudes best predicted behavior toward stereotypic targets (see also Blessum, Lord, & Sia, 1998).

The nature of the behavior may be important in yet another way. Vallacher and Wegner's (1987) *action identification theory* proposes that any behavior can be construed at different levels of abstraction. For instance, we can regard the act of cleaning a countertop as "disinfecting" (an abstract definition) or as "rubbing the countertop with a soapy cloth" (a relatively specific, concrete definition). The latter construal can be considered more specific because it contains more elements that are unique to a particular situation. Vallacher and Wegner found that obstacles to the enaction of an abstract goal (e.g., disinfecting) cause people to shift to lower-level construals of the behavior (e.g., rubbing with a soapy cloth). For example, cleaners who cannot find a special disinfectant cleanser might change their representation of the "disinfect" goal to accommodate a different, specific behavior, such as rubbing with a soapy cloth. This finding suggests that the role of abstract and specific attitudes may depend on the obstacles to behavior enaction (cf. Rabinovich et al., 2009).

Nature of the Attitude

As noted earlier in the chapter, several characteristics of the attitude also influence the strength of the attitude-behavior relation. Indeed, we noted that better prediction of behavior is associated with attitudes that are extreme, accessible, not ambivalent, based on direct experience, and highly embedded. In the following paragraphs, we expand on three of these findings and describe one additional attitudinal characteristic that influences attitude-behavior consistency.

One of the first attitude qualities to be studied in this regard was direct versus indirect experience: attitudes that are based on direct experience with the attitude object predict behavior better than do attitudes that are based on indirect experience (Fazio & Zanna, 1981; Fazio, Zanna, & Cooper, 1978). Presumably, these findings reflected that attitudes based on direct experience are stronger, more confidently held, more stable, and so on, than attitudes based on indirect experience. Consistent with this reasoning, in a meta-analysis of the attitude-behavior consistency literature, Kraus (1995) concluded that direct experience, certainty, and stability predicted the strength of the attitude-behavior relation.

Fazio (1990) proposed that the effects of direct experience operate through another manifestation of attitude strength; namely, the accessibility of the attitude. This idea is developed elegantly in Fazio's MODE model of attitude-behavior relations. According to this model, accessible attitudes are more likely to be evoked spontaneously in the presence of the attitude object (Fazio, 2000; Fazio, Sanbonmatsu, Powell, & Kardes, 1986), which makes them more likely to serve as the basis for judgments and action concerning the object. At the same time, in order for attitudes to actually influence judgments and action, people cannot be highly motivated or cannot have the opportunity to deliberate carefully, which might lead them to override their attitudes and act in some other way. (The MODE label for the model comes from *M*otivation and *O*pportunity to *DE*liberate.)

In line with the model, highly accessible attitudes have predicted judgments (Schuette & Fazio, 1995) and behavior (Fazio & Williams, 1986) better than low accessibility attitudes in a variety of studies where motivation and opportunity to override the attitude were presumably low (Fazio, 1990). Support for the MODE model has also come from studies of the correspondence between implicit measures of attitude and behavior. Implicit measures tap evaluations that are spontaneously elicited by an attitude object—in other words, attitudes that are accessible (Fazio & Olson, 2003). From the model, these measures should be better predictors of behavior when the actors' motivation and opportunity to think about their behavior are low, and this is precisely the pattern that has occurred across a range of studies (M. A. Olson & Fazio, 2009).

A third attitude characteristic related to attitude-behavior consistency is ambivalence, which, as explained earlier, refers to evaluative conflict within or between the components of an attitude. In a review of the literature, Armitage and Conner (2000) concluded that ambivalent attitudes are generally less predictive of behavior than nonambivalent attitudes, presumably because the conflicting elements may become differentially salient at various times or in various settings, thus inducing inconsistent actions (see MacDonald & Zanna, 1998).

On the other hand, individuals who exhibit higher levels of attitudinal ambivalence also pay closer attention to information that might help to reduce their ambivalence (Clark, Wegener, & Fabrigar, 2008; Maio, Bell, & Esses, 1996), presumably because ambivalence

feels uncomfortable and aversive when individuals are trying to make a decision (van Harreveld, van der Pligt, & de Liver, 2009). Ironically, then, this motivation to reduce ambivalence may actually produce more deeply elaborated attitudes that manifest higher *subsequent* attitude-behavior consistency (Jonas, Diehl, & Bromer, 1997).

A final feature of attitudes that influences attitude-behavior consistency was not included in our earlier section on attitude characteristics. Trope and his colleagues (Ledgerwood, Trope, & Liberman, 2010; Trope, Liberman, & Wakslak, 2007) showed that, when individuals are induced to generate a "high-level" construal of an attitude object when reporting their attitude, their evaluations are less susceptible to incidental social influence and more consistent with previously reported ideological values. In contrast, when individuals are induced to generate a "low-level" construal of the object, their evaluations reflect the incidental social influence (Ledgerwood, Trope, & Chaiken, 2010). A high-level construal is one that focuses on the central and enduring features of the object (e.g., the core features of dogs, such as they are devoted to their masters, they bark, they wag their tails), whereas a low-level construal focuses on more concrete, "contextualized" features (e.g., features of a particular dog that comes to mind as an exemplar). There is obvious overlap between high-level construals of attitudes and Vallacher and Wegner's (1987) abstract construals of behavior. These concepts also overlap with "general attitudes toward an object" in Ajzen and Fishbein's (1977) discussion of the importance of compatibility between measures of attitudes and behavior. In each case, a common principle is that abstract, global construals of an attitude are more appropriate for predicting abstract, globally construed actions than actions that must be construed at a more concrete level.

Personality Variables

Over several decades, researchers have been curious about whether some people may behave in accordance with their attitudes to a greater extent than other people. That is, collapsing across attitude-behavior domains (hence, ignoring the nature of the attitude and the nature of the behavior), do personality variables predict the strength of attitude-behavior consistency?

The trait variable that has received the most attention in this regard is self-monitoring (Snyder, 1986). Self-monitoring reflects the extent to which people base their behavioral choices on internal versus external cues. Low self-monitors rely on internal cues to guide their behavior, whereas high self-monitors use external, situational cues as guides to action. Given that attitudes are an internal construct, low self-monitors should exhibit stronger attitude-behavior consistency than high self-monitors. Several studies have supported this prediction (Snyder & Kendzierski, 1982; Zanna, Olson, & Fazio, 1980).

There are probably multiple determinants of the differences in attitude-behavior consistency between low and high self-monitors. Ajzen, Timko, and White (1982) found that low self-monitors were more likely to follow through on their behavioral intentions than were high self-monitors. Presumably, high self-monitors are easily diverted from their intended courses of action by unanticipated situational demands. Related evidence indicates that the attitudes of low self-monitors are more accessible than the attitudes of high self-monitors, perhaps because low self-monitors think about their attitudes more often than do high self-monitors (Kardes, Sanbonmatsu, Voss, & Fazio, 1986). The higher accessibility of low self-monitors' attitudes may keep their attitudes in mind during unanticipated situational demands, enabling low self-monitors to "stay the course."

Another personality variable that moderates attitude-behavior consistency is private self-consciousness, which reflects the extent to which individuals are aware of their internal states, such as moods, values, and attitudes (Fenigstein, Scheier, & Buss, 1975). Individuals who are high in private self-consciousness exhibit stronger attitude-behavior correlations than those who are low in private self-consciousness (Scheier, Buss, & Buss, 1978; Wicklund, 1982). Although, to our knowledge, the mediators of this finding have not been investigated, one very plausible candidate is that people who are high in private self-consciousness have more accessible attitudes, given that they are more aware in general of their internal states.

The Role of Habits

The correspondence between attitudes and behavior can also depend on the frequency with which the behavior has been performed in the past. Past behaviors that are performed less frequently tend to be guided by attitudes and conscious intentions, whereas past behaviors that are practiced regularly can become habitual and be initiated and executed automatically without consideration of attitudes or intentions (Ji & Wood, 2007; Ouellette & Wood, 1998; Verplanken, Aarts, van Knippenberg, & Moonen, 1998). Past behaviors that are well-practiced and occur with little

intent are known as *habits* and can develop for a variety of everyday behaviors, such as wearing a seatbelt or exercising. At the outset, people have to make decisions about what actions to take in order to achieve certain outcomes, such as wearing a seatbelt in a car for safety or exercising at the gym to improve physical fitness. As these actions are repeated, people rely less on their attitudes, intentions, or decisions to perform the actions, instead being cued directly by stimuli in the environment (e.g., when people get into their car, they may put on their seatbelts without deliberation). Frequently performed behaviors, however, do not necessarily become habits (Ronis, Yates, & Kirscht, 1989). Rather, it is the repeated pairing of a behavior with specific stimuli in a stable context (e.g., time, location) that forms a habit. As such, an association in memory is formed between the behavior and the context in which the behavior occurs; the extent to which the behavior and the context are co-activated determines the *strength* of the habit. Thus, habits can be defined as repeated behaviors that have a degree of automaticity in response to specific cues in the environment and serve to fulfill certain goals or end-states (Verplanken & Aarts, 1999).

A meta-analysis conducted by Ouellette and Wood (1998) found that past behavior predicted future behavior independently of intentions, attitudes, norms, and perceived behavioral control. In addition, past behavior was a stronger predictor of future behavior in domains that were conducive to habit formation (e.g., behaviors that were performed daily or weekly in a stable context), whereas intention was a stronger predictor for future behavior in domains that were not conducive to habit formation (e.g., behaviors that are performed bi-annually or in an unstable context). These findings demonstrate the importance of habit in determining behavior.

One way in which habits are perpetuated is by limiting individuals' attention to information that might change their behavior. For example, in the domain of travel mode choices, Verplanken, Aarts, and van Knippenberg (1997) asked car owners to imagine 27 trips that involved purchasing goods at a grocery store and to choose between four travel modes (walking, bus, bicycle, and car). Prior to making their travel mode choice for each trip, participants were given the opportunity to learn more about the trip, such as weather conditions, travel time, and distance. They found that participants with stronger habits (e.g., to always use a car) acquired less information about the trip than those with weaker habits. Therefore, habit limited the amount of information required before making the behavioral choice. Verplanken and colleagues (1998) extended these findings in a field experiment in which they asked participants to keep a daily diary of their travel behavior and travel mode choices over a 7-day period. They found that among participants with strong car-use habits, intentions to use a car did not predict travel mode choices, whereas among weak and moderate car-use habit participants, intentions did predict travel mode choice. Thus, intentions are more likely to translate into behavior when strong habits are not established.

Similarly, in a meta-analysis, Webb and Sheeran (2006) found that informational interventions that were successful at changing people's intentions did not always change behaviors. Specifically, they found that interventions that changed people's intentions also changed behaviors in domains that were unlikely to become habits (e.g., getting the flu shot), but did not change behaviors in domains that were likely to elicit habits (e.g., eating behavior).

Given that habits are cued by the context, researchers have suggested that changing the context can disrupt habits. For example, Wood, Tam, and Wit (2005) examined whether college students transferring universities would maintain their habit to exercise (as well as other behaviors) at the new university. One month prior to and one month after the transfer, students completed measures of the extent to which they exercised *habitually* (i.e., frequently and in the same location) and their intentions to exercise. The researchers found that students who had strong exercise habits continued to exercise at the new university if the context was perceived to be the same as the old university, and this was independent of their intentions to exercise. When students had weak or moderate exercise habits or had strong habits but perceived change in the context, their decision to exercise at the new school was guided by their intentions.

Applications to Social Behavior

We have reviewed various theories of attitude-behavior consistency and outlined the conditions under which strong relations between attitudes and behavior can be expected. The title of this chapter is "Attitudes in Social Behavior," so we close with the consideration of some of the important social behaviors to which the concept of attitude can be applied. In each case, data support the hypothesis that attitudes facilitate attitude-consistent behaviors.

For example, research on prejudice, racism, and discrimination explores interpersonal and intergroup settings where negative attitudes toward an outgroup (prejudice) can cause conflict and violence. Prejudice is one of the oldest topics in social psychology and continues to be a vibrant research area today, with recent attention expanding to examine ways in which media can be used to alter prejudice (Maio, Haddock, Watt, & Hewstone, 2009; Paluck, 2009), the role of ideologies in prejudice (Duckitt, 2006; Knowles et al., 2009), and the role of motivations to control prejudice in interracial interactions (Plant, Devine, & Peruche, 2010; Shelton, West, & Trail, 2010). Similarly, attitudes influence individuals' responses to situations involving justice considerations (see Bobocel, Kay, Zanna, & Olson, 2009). For example, individuals are more likely to tolerate a situation where distributive or procedural justice was violated when they have positive attitudes toward the responsible authority (Tyler & Smith, 1998). Family and close relationships are built on positive attitudes, encompassing such concepts as love, trust, caring, commitment, and intimacy (e.g., Murray & Holmes, 2011). Positive attitudes encourage good communication, which is the basis of effective relationships.

A long-standing area of application of findings from attitude research has been consumer behavior. Numerous studies of persuasion and attitude-behavior connections have focused on attitudes toward consumer objects, such as razor blades (Petty, Cacioppo, & Schumann, 1983), telephone answering machines (Chaiken & Maheswaran, 1994), and kitchen appliances (Brehm, 1966). Not only are consumer objects of interest, but there is also research examining how consumption is affected by habits (Verplanken & Wood, 2006) and how the marketing of consumer objects is affected by the real-world contexts in which they are advertised (e.g., television), utilizing observations from basic research on attitude change (e.g., Mathur & Chattopadhyay, 1991). Cialdini (2008) has provided a provocative and well-known review of research on a variety of influence techniques that are often used in the consumer domain and in other areas of application (e.g., charities, organizational leadership).

There has also been a long-standing interest in application of attitude research to altruistic behaviors, such as donating blood (Breckler & Wiggins, 1989b), time (Maio et al., 2001), and money (Rabinovich et al., 2009). In each of these cases, researchers are attempting to predict a behavior that people find difficult to perform. In recent years, researchers have recognized that similar difficulties occur in two domains of growing importance: healthy lifestyles and environmental sustainability. In particular, researchers have investigated the effectiveness of campaigns that target behaviors leading to the spread of AIDS (Albarracín et al., 2005), obesity (Armitage, 2004), and damage to the environment (Cialdini, 2003). These issues share common problems that arise when there is a high degree of ambivalence in the target attitudes because of competing motives and beliefs (Maio et al., 2007).

CONCLUSIONS

There are many issues and questions that must be addressed in future research on attitudes in social behavior. One important issue is the internal structure of attitudes, including the dimensionality of attitudes and the conditions under which different components of attitudes will be more influential than other components. A related issue is the distinction between implicit and explicit measures of attitudes, including the question of which sorts of behavior are best predicted by each type of attitude (measure). The connections between attitudes and broader constructs like values and ideologies also need to be clarified. Turning to a different domain, the role of biological factors in attitude formation and change seems likely to receive more attention over the next decade. Finally, the connection between attitudes and behavior will continue to interest social psychologists, with models of attitude-behavior consistency becoming increasingly complex. For example, prediction may be improved by simultaneously taking into account attitudes toward all of the different behavioral options in a setting.

In closing, the evidence described in this chapter supports the importance of the attitude construct. Because of their broad evaluative nature, attitudes may potentially reflect diverse beliefs, feelings, and behaviors. In addition, these evaluations serve a number of important functions and vary on several characteristics (e.g., accessibility, ambivalence). Most importantly, attitudes influence a wide variety of important social behaviors. Indeed, no matter what the setting, personal evaluations play a role in information processing and behavior.

REFERENCES

Abelson, R. P. (1988). Conviction. *American Psychologist, 43,* 267–275.

Ajzen, I. (1991). The theory of planned behavior. *Organizational Behavior and Human Decision Processes, 50,* 179–211.

Ajzen, I., & Fishbein, M. (1977). Attitude-behavior relations: A theoretical analysis and review of empirical research. *Psychological Bulletin, 84,* 888–918.

Ajzen, I., Timko, C., & White, J. B. (1982). Self-monitoring and the attitude-behavior relation. *Journal of Personality and Social Psychology, 42,* 426–435.

Albarracín, D., Gillette, J. C., Earl, A. N., Glasman, L. R., Durantini, M. R., & Ho, M. H. (2005). A test of major assumptions about behavior change: A comprehensive look at the effects of passive and active HIV-prevention interventions since the beginning of the epidemic. *Psychological Bulletin, 131,* 856–897.

Albarracín, D., & Wyer, R. S. Jr. (2000). Cognitive impact of past behavior: Influences on beliefs, attitudes, and future behavioral decisions. *Journal of Personality and Social Psychology, 79,* 5–22.

Allison, S. T., & Messick, D. M. (1988). The feature-positive effect, attitude strength, and degree of perceived consensus. *Personality and Social Psychology Bulletin, 14,* 231–241.

Allport, G. W. (1935). Attitudes. In C. Murchison (Ed.), *Handbook of social psychology* (pp. 798–844). Worcester, MA: Clark University Press.

Armitage, C. J. (2004). Implementation intentions and eating a low-fat diet: A randomized controlled trial. *Health Psychology, 23,* 319–323.

Armitage, C. J., & Conner, M. (2000). Attitudinal ambivalence: A test of three key hypotheses. *Personality and Social Psychology Bulletin, 26,* 1421–1432.

Arvey, R. D., Bouchard, T. J., Segal, N. L., & Abraham, L. M. (1989). Job satisfaction: Environmental and genetic components. *Journal of Applied Psychology, 74,* 187–192.

Ashton, M. E., Danso, H. A., Maio, G. R., Bond, M. H., Esses, V., & Keung, D. K. Y. (2005). Two dimensions of political attitudes and their individual difference correlates: A cross-cultural perspective. In R. M. Sorrentino, D. Cohen, J. M. Olson, & M. P. Zanna (Eds.), *Culture and social behavior: The Ontario symposium* (Vol. 10, pp. 1–29). Mahwah, NJ: Erlbaum.

Bargh, J. A., Chaiken, S., Govender, R., & Pratto, F. (1992). The generality of the automatic attitude activation effect. *Journal of Personality and Social Psychology, 62,* 893–912.

Bassili, J. N. (1996). Meta-judgmental versus operative indexes of psychological attributes: The case of measures of attitude strength. *Journal of Personality and Social Psychology, 71,* 637–653.

Bell, D. W., Esses, V. M., & Maio, G. R. (1996). The utility of open-ended measures to assess intergroup ambivalence. *Canadian Journal of Behavioural Science, 28,* 12–18.

Bem, D. J. (1972). Self-perception theory. *Advances in Experimental Social Psychology, 6,* 1–62.

Bernard, M. M., Maio, G. R., & Olson, J. M. (2003). The vulnerability of values to attack: Inoculation of values and value-relevant attitudes. *Personality and Social Psychology Bulletin, 29,* 63–75.

Blessum, K. A., Lord, C. G., & Sia, T. L. (1998). Cognitive load and positive mood reduce typicality effects in attitude-behavior consistency. *Personality and Social Psychology Bulletin, 24,* 496–504.

Bobocel, D. R., Kay, A. C., Zanna, M. P., & Olson, J. M. (2009). *The psychology of justice and legitimacy: The Ontario symposium* (Vol. 11). New York, NY: Academic Press.

Bohner, G., & Wanke, M. (2002). *Attitudes and attitude change.* Hove, UK: Psychology Press.

Bornstein, R. F., & D'Agostino, P. (1992). Stimulus recognition and the mere exposure effect. *Journal of Personality and Social Psychology, 63,* 545–552.

Boski, P. (1993). Socio-political value orientations among Poles in presidential '90 and '91 elections. *Polish Psychological Bulletin, 20,* 551–567.

Breckler, S. J. (1984). Empirical validation of affect, behavior, and cognition as distinct components of attitude. *Journal of Personality and Social Psychology, 47,* 1191–1205.

Breckler, S. J., & Wiggins, E. C. (1989a). Affect versus evaluation in the structure of attitudes. *Journal of Experimental Social Psychology, 25,* 253–271.

Breckler, S. J., & Wiggins, E. C. (1989b). Scales for the measurement of attitudes toward blood donation. *Transfusion, 29,* 401–404.

Brehm, J. W. (1966). *A theory of psychological reactance.* New York, NY: Academic Press.

Brendl, M., Markman, A. B., & Messner, C. (2001). How do indirect measures of evaluation work? Evaluating the inference of prejudice in the implicit association test. *Journal of Personality and Social Psychology, 81,* 760–773.

Briñol, P., & Petty, R. E. (2004). Self-validation processes: The role of thought confidence in persuasion. In G. Haddock & G. R. Maio (Eds.), *Contemporary perspectives on the psychology of attitudes* (pp. 205–226). Philadelphia, PA: Psychology Press.

Briñol, P., & Petty, R. E. (2009). Persuasion: Insights from the self-validation hypothesis. *Advances in Experimental Social Psychology, 41,* 70–118.

Budd, R. J. (1986). Predicting cigarette use: The need to incorporate measures of salience in the theory of reasoned action. *Journal of Applied Social Psychology, 16,* 663–685.

Cacioppo, J. T., Crites, S. L. Jr., & Gardner, W. L. (1996). Attitudes to the right: Evaluative processing is associated with lateralized late positive event-related brain potentials. *Personality and Social Psychology Bulletin, 22,* 1205–1219.

Cacioppo, J. T., Gardner, W. L., & Berntson, G. G. (1997). Beyond bipolar conceptualizations and measures: The case of attitudes and evaluative space. *Personality and Social Psychology Review, 1,* 3–25.

Cacioppo, J. T., & Petty, R. E. (1982). The need for cognition. *Journal of Personality and Social Psychology, 42,* 116–131.

Cacioppo, J. T., & Petty, R. E. (1987). Stalking rudimentary processes of social influence: A psychophysiological approach. In M. P. Zanna, J. M. Olson, & C. P. Herman (Eds.), *Social Influence: The Ontario symposium* (Vol. 5, pp. 41–74). Mahwah, NJ: Erlbaum.

Cacioppo, J. T., Petty, R. E., Losch, M. E., & Kim, H. S. (1986). Electromyographic activity over facial muscle regions can differentiate the valence and intensity of affective reactions. *Journal of Personality and Social Psychology, 50,* 260–268.

Campbell, D. T. (1971). *White attitudes toward Black people.* Ann Arbor, MI: Institute for Social Research.

Chaiken, S., & Baldwin, M. W. (1981). Affective-cognitive consistency and the effect of salient behavioral information on the self-perception of attitudes. *Journal of Personality and Social Psychology, 41,* 1–12.

Chaiken, S., & Maheswaran, D. (1994). Heuristic processing can bias systematic processing: Effects of source credibility, argument ambiguity, and task importance on attitude judgment. *Journal of Personality and Social Psychology, 66,* 460–473.

Chaiken, S., & Yates, S. (1985). Affective-cognitive consistency and thought-induced attitude polarization. *Journal of Personality and Social Psychology, 49,* 1470–1481.

Chen, S., & Chaiken, S. (1999). The heuristic-systematic model in its broader context. In S. Chaiken & Y. Trope (Eds.), *Dual-process theories in social psychology* (pp. 73–96). New York, NY: Guilford Press.

Cialdini, R. B. (2003). Crafting normative messages to protect the environment. *Current Directions in Psychological Science, 12,* 105–109.

Cialdini, R. B. (2008). *Influence: Science and practice* (5th international ed.). Essex, UK: Pearson Education.

Clark, J. K., Wegener, D. T., & Fabrigar, L. R. (2008). Attitude ambivalence and message-based persuasion: Motivated processing of proattitudinal information and avoidance of counterattitudinal information. *Personality and Social Psychology Bulletin, 34,* 565–577.

Converse, P. E. (1964). The nature of belief systems in mass publics. In D. E. Apter (Ed.), *Ideology and discontent* (pp. 206–261). New York, NY: Free Press.

Converse, P. E. (2000). Assessing the capacity of mass electorates. *Annual Review of Political Science, 3,* 331–353.

Crandall, C. S., D'Anello, S., Sakalli, N., Lazarus, E., Wieczorkowska, G., & Feather, N. T. (2001). An attribution-value model of prejudice: Anti-fat attitudes in six nations. *Personality and Social Psychology Bulletin, 27,* 30–37.

Crites, S. L., Fabrigar, L. R., & Petty, R. E. (1994). Measuring the affective and cognitive properties of attitudes: Conceptual and methodological issues. *Personality and Social Psychology Bulletin, 20,* 619–634.

De Houwer, J., Thomas, S., & Baeyens, F. (2001). Associative learning of likes and dislikes: A review of 25 years of research on human evaluative conditioning. *Psychological Bulletin, 127,* 853–869.

de St. Aubin, E. (1996). Personal ideology polarity: Its emotional foundation and its manifestation in individual value systems, religiosity, political orientation, and assumptions concerning human nature. *Journal of Personality and Social Psychology, 71,* 152–165.

Doll, J., & Ajzen, I. (1992). Accessibility and stability of predictors in the theory of planned behavior. *Journal of Personality and Social Psychology, 63,* 754–765.

Duckitt, J. (2006). Differential effects of right wing authoritarianism and social dominance orientation on outgroup attitudes and their mediation by threat from and competitiveness to outgroups. *Personality and Social Psychology Bulletin, 32,* 684–696.

Eagly, A. H., & Chaiken, S. (1998). Attitude structure and function. In D. T. Gilbert, S. T. Fiske, & G. Lindzey (Eds.), *Handbook of Social Psychology* (4th ed., pp. 269–322). Boston, MA: McGraw-Hill.

Eagly, A. H., Chen, S., Chaiken, S., & Shaw-Barnes, K. (1999). The impact of attitudes on memory: An affair to remember. *Psychological Bulletin, 125,* 64–89.

Eaton, A. A., Visser, P. S., Krosnick, J. A., & Anand, S. (2009). Social power and attitude strength over the life course. *Personality and Social Psychology Bulletin, 35,* 1646–1660.

Eaves, L., Eysenck, H. J., & Martin, N. G. (1989). *Genes, culture, and personality: An empirical approach.* London, UK: Academic Press.

Edwards, K., & Smith, E. E. (1996). A disconfirmation bias in the evaluation of arguments. *Journal of Personality and Social Psychology, 71,* 5–24.

Ennis, R., & Zanna, M. P. (2000). Attitude function and the automobile. In G. R. Maio & J. M. Olson (Eds.), *Why we evaluate: Functions of attitude* (pp. 395–415). Mahwah, NJ: Erlbaum.

Esses, V. M., Haddock, G., & Zanna, M. P. (1993). Values, stereotypes, and emotions as determinants of intergroup attitudes. In D. M. Mackie & D. L. Hamilton (Eds.), *Affect, cognition, and stereotyping: Interactive processes in group perception* (pp. 137–166). New York, NY: Academic Press.

Esses, V. M., & Maio, G. R. (2002). Expanding the assessment of attitude components and structure: The benefits of open-ended measures. *European Review of Social Psychology, 12,* 71–102.

Falomir-Pichastor, J. M., & Mugny, G. (2009). "I'm not gay.... I'm a real man!": Heterosexual men's gender self-esteem and sexual prejudice. *Personality and Social Psychology Bulletin, 35,* 1233–1243.

Fazio, R. H. (1990). Multiple processes by which attitudes guide behavior: The MODE model as an integrative framework. *Advances in Experimental Social Psychology, 23,* 75–109.

Fazio, R. H. (1995). Attitudes as object-evaluation associations: Determinants, consequences, and correlates of attitude accessibility. In R. E. Petty & J. A. Krosnick (Eds.), *Attitude strength: Antecedents and consequences* (pp. 247–282). Mahwah, NJ: Erlbaum.

Fazio, R. H. (2000). Accessible attitudes as tools for object appraisal: Their costs and benefits. In G. R. Maio & J. M. Olson (Eds.), *Why we evaluate: Functions of attitudes* (pp. 1–36). Mahwah, NJ: Erlbaum.

Fazio, R. H., Jackson, J. R., Dunton, B. C., & Williams, C. J. (1995). Variability in automatic activation as an unobtrusive measure of racial attitudes: A bona fide pipeline? *Journal of Personality and Social Psychology, 69,* 1013–1027.

Fazio, R. H., Ledbetter, J. E., & Towles-Schwen, T. (2000). On the costs of accessible attitudes: Detecting that the attitude object has changed. *Journal of Personality and Social Psychology, 78,* 197–210.

Fazio, R. H., & Olson, M. A. (2003). Implicit measures in social cognition research: Their meaning and use. *Annual Review of Psychology, 54,* 297–327.

Fazio, R. H., & Powell, M. C. (1997). On the value of knowing one's likes and dislikes: Attitude accesibility, stress, and health in college. *Psychological Science, 8,* 430–436.

Fazio, R. H., Sanbonmatsu, D. M., Powell, M. C., & Kardes, F. R. (1986). On the automatic activation of attitudes. *Journal of Personality and Social Psychology, 50,* 229–238.

Fazio, R. H., & Williams, C. J. (1986). Attitude accessibility as a moderator of the attitude-perception and attitude-behavior relations: An investigation of the 1984 presidential election. *Journal of Personality and Social Psychology, 51,* 505–514.

Fazio, R. H., & Zanna, M. P. (1978a). Attitudinal qualities relating to the strength of the attitude-behavior relationship. *Journal of Experimental Social Psychology, 14,* 398–408.

Fazio, R. H., & Zanna, M. P. (1978b). On the predictive validity of attitudes: The roles of direct experience and confidence. *Journal of Personality, 46,* 228–243.

Fazio, R. H., & Zanna, M. P. (1981). Direct experience and attitude-behavior consistency. *Advances in Experimental Social Psychology, 14,* 161–202.

Fazio, R. H., Zanna, M. P., & Cooper, J. (1978). Direct experience and attitude-behavior consistency: An information processing analysis. *Personality and Social Psychology Bulletin, 4,* 48–51.

Feather, N. T. (1995). Values, valences, and choice: The influences of values on the perceived attractiveness and choice of alternatives. *Journal of Personality and Social Psychology, 68,* 1135–1151.

Federico, C. M., & Schneider, M. (2007). Political expertise and the use of ideology: Moderating effects of evaluative motivation. *Public Opinion Quarterly, 71,* 221–252.

Fenigstein, A., Scheier, M. F., & Buss, A. H. (1975). Public and private self-consciousness: Assessment and theory. *Journal of Applied Psychology, 43,* 522–527.

Festinger, L. (1957). *A theory of cognitive dissonance.* Evanston, IL: Row, Peterson.

Festinger, L. (1964). *Conflict, decision, and dissonance.* Stanford, CA: Stanford University Press.

Fishbein, M., & Ajzen, I. (1975). *Belief, attitude, intention, and behavior: An introduction to theory and research.* Reading, MA: Addison-Wesley.

Fleishman, J. A. (1986). Types of political attitude structure: Results of a cluster analysis. *Public Opinion Quarterly, 50,* 371–386.

Freedman, J. L., & Sears, D. O. (1965). Selective exposure. In L. Berkowitz (Ed.), *Advances in Experimental Social Psychology* (Vol. 2, pp. 57–97). San Diego, CA: Academic Press.

Frey, D. (1986). Recent research on selective exposure to information. *Advances in Experimental Social Psychology, 19,* 41–80.

Frey, D., & Rosch, M. (1984). Information seeking after decisions: The roles of novelty of information and decision reversibility. *Personality and Social Psychology Bulletin, 10,* 91–98.

Gawronski, B., & Bodenhausen, G. (2006). Associative and propositional processes in evaluation: An integrative review of implicit and explicit attitude change. *Psychological Bulletin, 132,* 692–731.

Gawronski, B., & Bodenhausen, G. V. (2007). Unraveling the processes underlying evaluation: Attitudes from the perspective of the APE Model. *Social Cognition, 25,* 687–717.

Gawronski, B., & LeBel, E. P. (2008). Understanding patterns of attitude change: When implicit measures show change, but explicit measures do not. *Journal of Experimental Social Psychology, 44,* 1355–1361.

Giner-Sorolla, R., & Chaiken, S. (1994). The causes of hostile media judgments. *Journal of Experimental Social Psychology, 30,* 165–180.

Glaser, J., & Salovey, P. (1998). Affect in electoral politics. *Personality and Social Psychology Review, 2,* 156–172.

Goffin, R. D., & Olson, J. M. (in press). Is it all relative? Comparative judgments and the possible improvement of self-ratings and ratings of others. *Perspectives on Psychological Science.*

Gold, J. A., & Robbins, M. A. (1979). Attitudes and values: A further test of the semantic memory model. *Journal of Social Psychology, 108,* 75–81.

Goldstein, N. J., & Cialdini, R. B. (2007). The spyglass self: A model of vicarious self-perception. *Journal of Personality and Social Psychology, 92,* 402–417.

Gollwitzer, P. M., & Sheeran, P. (2006). Implementation intentions and goal achievement: A meta-analysis of effects and processes. *Advances in Experimental Social Psychology, 38,* 69–119.

Graham, J., Haidt, J., & Nosek, B. A. (2009). Liberal and conservatives rely on different sets of moral foundations. *Journal of Personality and Social Psychology, 96,* 1029–1047.

Green, D. P., Goldman, S. L., & Salovey, P. (1993). Measurement error masks bipolarity in affect ratings. *Journal of Personality and Social Psychology, 64,* 1029–1041.

Greenberg, J., & Jonas, E. (2003). Psychological motives and political orientation—the left, the right, and the rigid: Comment on Jost et al. (2003). *Psychological Bulletin, 129,* 376–382.

Greenwald, A. G., McGhee, D. E., & Schwartz, J. K. L. (1998). Measuring individual differences in implicit cognition: The implicit association test. *Journal of Personality and Social Psychology, 74,* 1464–1480.

Greenwald, A. G., Poehlman, T. A., Uhlmann, E. L., & Banaji, M. R. (2009). Understanding and using the Implicit Association Test: III. Meta-analysis of predictive validity. *Journal of Personality and Social Psychology, 97,* 17–41.

Greenwald, A. G., & Sakamura, J. S. (1976). Attitude and selective learning: Where are the phenomena of yesteryear? *Journal of Abnormal and Social Psychology, 7,* 387–397.

Guglielmi, R. S. (1999). Psychophysiological assessment of prejudice: Past research, current status, and future directions. *Personality and Social Psychology Review, 3,* 123–157.

Haddock, G., Maio, G. R., Arnold, K., & Huskinson, T. (2008). Should persuasion be affective or cognitive? The moderating effects of Need for Affect and Need for Cognition. *Personality and Social Psychology Bulletin, 34,* 769–778

Haddock, G., & Zanna, M. P. (1998). On the use of open-ended measures to assess attitudinal components. *British Journal of Social Psychology, 37,* 129–149.

Haddock, G., Zanna, M. P., & Esses, V. M. (1993). Assessing the structure of prejudicial attitudes: The case of attitudes toward homosexuals. *Journal of Personality and Social Psychology, 65,* 1105–1118.

Harmon-Jones, E., Harmon-Jones, C., Fearn, M., Sigelman, J. D., & Johnson, P. (2008). Left frontal cortical activation and spreading of alternatives: Tests of the action-based model of dissonance. *Journal of Personality and Social Psychology, 94,* 1–15.

Harmon-Jones, E., & Mills, J. (1999). An introduction to cognitive dissonance theory and an overview of current perspectives on the theory. In E. Harmon-Jones & J. Mills (Eds.), *Cognitive dissonance: Progress on a pivotal theory in social psychology* (pp. 3–21). Washington, DC: American Psychological Association.

Heider, F. (1958). *The psychology of interpersonal relations.* New York, NY: Wiley.

Herek, G. M. (1986). The instrumentality of attitudes: Toward a neo-functional theory. *Journal of Social Issues, 42,* 99–114.

Herek, G. M. (1987). Can functions be measured? A new perspective on the functional approach to attitudes. *Social Psychology Quarterly, 50,* 285–303.

Herek, G. M. (2000). The social construction of attitudes: Functional consensus and divergence in the U.S. public's reactions to AIDS. In G. R. Maio & J. M. Olson (Eds.), *Why we evaluate: Functions of attitudes* (pp. 325–364). Mahwah, NJ: Erlbaum.

Higgins, E. T. (1996). Knowledge activation: Accessibility, applicability, and salience. In E. T. Higgins & A. W. Kruglanski (Eds.), *Social psychology: Handbook of basic principles* (pp. 133–168). New York, NY: Guilford Press.

Holbrook, A. L., Berent, M. K., Krosnick, J. A., Visser, P. S., & Boninger, D. S. (2005). Attitude importance and the accumulation of attitude-relevant information in memory. *Journal of Personality and Social Psychology, 88,* 749–769.

Houston, D. A., & Fazio, R. H. (1989). Biased processing as a function of attitude accessibility: Making objective judgments subjectively. *Social Cognition, 7,* 51–66.

Huskinson, T. L. H., & Haddock, G. (2004). Individual differences in attitude structure: Variance in the chronic reliance on affective and cognitive information. *Journal of Experimental Social Psychology, 40,* 82–90.

Huskinson, T. L. H., & Haddock, G. (2006). Individual differences in attitude structure and the accessibility of the affective and cognitive components of attitude. *Social Cognition, 24,* 453–468.

Ji, M. F., & Wood, W. (2007). Purchase and consumption habits: Not necessarily what you intend. *Journal of Consumer Psychology, 17,* 261–276.

Johnson, A. L., Crawford, M. T., Sherman, S. J., Rutchik, A. M., Hamilton, D. L., Ferreira, M. B., & Petrocelli, J. V. (2006). A functional perspective on group memberships: Differential need fulfillment in a group typology. *Journal of Experimental Social Psychology, 42,* 707–719.

Jonas, K., Diehl, M., & Bromer, P. (1997). Effects of attitudinal ambivalence on information processing and attitude-intention consistency. *Journal of Experimental Social Psychology, 33,* 190–210.

Jones, C. R., Fazio, R. H., & Olson, M. A. (2009). Implicit misattribution as a mechanism underlying evaluative conditioning. *Journal of Personality and Social Psychology, 96,* 933–948.

Jones, E., & Sigall, H. (1971). The Bogus Pipeline: A new paradigm for measuring affect and attitude. *Psychological Bulletin, 76,* 349–364.

Jordan, N. (1953). Behavioral forces that are a function of attitudes and cognitive organization. *Human Relations, 6,* 273–287.

Jost, J. T., Federico, C. M., & Napier, J. L. (2009). Political ideology: Its structure, functions, and elective affinities. *Annual Review of Psychology, 60,* 307–337.

Jost, J. T., Nosek, B. A., & Gosling, S. D. (2008). Ideology: Its resurgence in social, personality, and political psychology. *Perspectives on Psychological Science, 3,* 126–136.

Kallgren, C. A., & Wood, W. (1986). Access to attitude-relevant information in memory as a determinant of attitude-behavior consistency. *Journal of Experimental Social Psychology, 22,* 328–338.

Kaplan, K. J. (1972). On the ambivalence-indifference problem in attitude theory and measurement: A suggested modification of the semantic differential technique. *Psychological Bulletin, 77,* 361–372.

Kardes, F. R., Sanbonmatsu, D. M., Voss, R. T., & Fazio, R. H. (1986). Self-monitoring and attitude accessibility. *Personality and Social Psychology Bulletin, 12,* 468–474.

Katz, D. (1960). The functional approach to the study of attitudes. *Public Opinion Quarterly, 24,* 163–204.

Katz, I., & Hass, R. G. (1988). Racial ambivalence and American value conflict: Correlational and priming studies of dual cognitive structures. *Journal of Personality and Social Psychology, 55,* 893–905.

Kerlinger, F. N. (1984). *Liberalism and conservatism: The nature and structure of social attitudes.* Mahwah, NJ: Erlbaum.

Kinder, D. R. (1998). Opinion and action in the realm of politics. In D. T. Gilbert, S. T. Fiske, & G. Lindzey (Eds.), *Handbook of Social Psychology* (4th ed., pp. 778–867) Boston, MA: McGraw-Hill.

Knowles, E. D., Lowery, B. S., Hogan, C. M., & Chow, R. M. (2009). On the malleability of ideology: Motivated construals of color-blindness. *Journal of Personality and Social Psychology, 96,* 857–869.

Kraus, S. J. (1995). Attitudes and the prediction of behavior: A meta-analysis of the empirical literature. *Personality and Social Psychology Bulletin, 21,* 58–75.

Kristiansen, C. M., & Zanna, M. P. (1988). Justifying attitudes by appealing to values: A functional perspective. *British Journal of Social Psychology, 27,* 247–256.

Krosnick, J. A., Betz, A. L., Jussim, L. J., & Lynn, A. R. (1992). Subliminal conditioning of attitudes. *Personality and Social Psychology Bulletin, 18,* 152–162.

Krosnick, J. A., Boninger, D. S., Chuang, Y. C., Berent, M. K., & Carnot, C. G. (1993). Attitude strength: One construct or many related constructs? *Journal of Personality and Social Psychology, 65,* 1132–1151.

Krosnick, J. A., & Petty, R. E. (1995). Attitude strength: An overview. In R. E. Petty & J. A. Krosnick (Eds.), *Attitude strength: Antecedents and consequences* (pp. 1–24). Mahwah, NJ: Erlbaum.

Kruglanski, A. W. (1989). *Lay epistemics and human knowledge: Cognitive and motivational bases.* New York, NY: Plenum Press.

Kruglanski, A. W., & Webster, D. M. (1996). Motivated closing of the mind: "Seizing" and "freezing." *Psychological Review, 103,* 263–283.

Lavine, H., & Snyder, M. (2000). Cognitive processes and the functional matching effect in persuasion: Studies of personality and political behavior. In G. R. Maio & J. M. Olson (Eds.), *Why we evaluate: Functions of attitudes* (pp. 97–131). Mahwah, NJ: Erlbaum.

Lavine, H., Thomsen, C. J., & Gonzalez, M. H. (1997). The development of interattitudinal consistency: The shared-consequences model. *Journal of Personality and Social Psychology, 72,* 735–749.

Lavine, H., Thomsen, C. J., Zanna, M. P., & Borgida, E. (1998). On the primacy of affect in the determination of attitudes and behavior: The moderating role of affective-cognitive ambivalence. *Journal of Experimental Social Psychology, 34,* 398–421.

Ledgerwood, A., Trope, Y., & Chaiken, S. (2010). Flexibility now, consistency later: Psychological distance and construal shape evaluative responding *Journal of Personality and Social Psychology, 99,* 32–51.

Ledgerwood, A., Trope, Y., & Liberman, N. (2010). Flexibility and consistency in evaluative responding: The function of construal level. *Advances in Experimental Social Psychology, 43,* 259–297.

Lee, K., Ashton, M. C., Ogunfowora, B., Bourdage, J. S., & Shin, K. (2010). The personality bases of socio-political attitudes: The role of honesty-humility and openness to experience. *Journal of Research in Personality, 44,* 115–119.

Lee, K., Ashton, M. C., Pozzebon, J. A., Visser, B. A., Bourdage, J. S., & Ogunfowora, B. (2009). Similarity and assumed similarity in personality reports of well-acquainted persons. *Journal of Personality and Social Psychology, 96,* 460–472.

Levine, J. M., & Murphy, G. (1943). The learning and forgetting of controversial material. *Journal of Abnormal and Social Psychology, 38,* 507–517.

Liberman, A., & Chaiken, S. (1991). Value conflict and thought-induced attitude change. *Journal of Experimental Social Psychology, 27,* 203–216.

Lord, C. G., & Lepper, M. R. (1999). Attitude Representation Theory. *Advances in Experimental Social Psychology, 31,* 265–343.

Lord, C. G., Lepper, M. R., & Mackie, D. M. (1984). Attitude prototypes as determinants of attitude-behavior consistency. *Journal of Personality and Social Psychology, 46,* 1254–1266.

Lord, C. G., Ross, L., & Lepper, M. R. (1979). Biased assimilation and attitude polarization: The effects of prior theories on subsequently considered evidence. *Journal of Personality and Social Psychology, 37,* 2098–2109.

Lowery, B. S., Knowles, E. D., & Unzueta, M. M. (2007). Framing inequity safely: Whites' motivated perceptions of racial privilege. *Personality and Social Psychology Bulletin, 33,* 1237–1250.

Lun, J., Sinclair, S., Whitchurch, E. R., & Glenn, C. (2007). (Why) do I think what you think? Epistemic social tuning and implicit prejudice. *Journal of Personality and Social Psychology, 93*, 957–972.

Lusk, C. M., & Judd, C. M. (1988). Political expertise and the structural mediators of candidate evaluations. *Journal of Experimental Social Psychology, 24*, 105–126.

MacDonald, T. K., & Zanna, M. P. (1998). Cross-dimension ambivalence toward social groups: Can ambivalence affect intentions to hire feminists? *Personality and Social Psychology Bulletin, 24*, 427–441.

MacDonald, T. K., Zanna, M. P., & Fong, G. T. (1996). Why common sense goes out the window: The effects of alcohol on intentions to use condoms. *Personality and Social Psychology Bulletin, 22*, 763–775.

Maio, G. R. (2010). Mental representations of social values. *Advances in Experimental Social Psychology, 42*, 1–43.

Maio, G. R., Bell, D. W., & Esses, V. M. (1996). Ambivalence and persuasion: The processing of messages about immigrant groups. *Journal of Experimental Social Psychology, 32*, 513–536.

Maio, G. R., & Esses, V. M. (2001). The need for affect: Individual differences in the motivation to approach or avoid emotions. *Journal of Personality, 69*, 583–616.

Maio, G. R., Esses, V. M., & Bell, D. W. (2000). Examining conflict between components of attitudes: Ambivalence and inconsistency are distinct constructs. *Canadian Journal of Behavioural Science, 32*, 58–70.

Maio, G. R., & Haddock, G. (2010). *The psychology of attitudes and attitude change*. London, UK: Sage.

Maio, G. R., Haddock, G., Watt, S. E., & Hewstone, M. (2009). Implicit measures and applied contexts: An illustrative examination of anti-racism advertising. In R. E. Petty, R. H. Fazio, & P. Brinol (Eds.), *Attitudes: Insights from the new wave of implicit measures* (pp. 327–357). Mahwah, NJ: Erlbaum.

Maio, G. R., Hahn, U., Frost, J., & Cheung, W. (2009). Applying the value of equality unequally: Effects of value instantiations that vary in typicality. *Journal of Personality and Social Psychology, 97*, 598–614.

Maio, G. R., & Olson, J. M. (1994). Value-attitude behaviour relations: The moderating role of attitude functions. *British Journal of Social Psychology, 33*, 301–312.

Maio, G. R., & Olson, J. M. (1995). Relations between values, attitudes, and behavioral intentions: The moderating role of attitude function. *Journal of Experimental Social Psychology, 31*, 266–285.

Maio, G. R., & Olson, J. M. (1998). Values as truisms: Evidence and implications. *Journal of Personality and Social Psychology, 74*, 294–311.

Maio, G. R., & Olson, J. M. (2000a). What is a "value-expressive" attitude? In G. R. Maio & J. M. Olson (Eds.), *Why we evaluate: Functions of attitudes* (pp. 249–269). Mahwah, NJ: Erlbaum.

Maio, G. R., & Olson, J. M. (Eds.). (2000b). *Why we evaluate: Functions of attitudes*. Mahwah, NJ: Erlbaum.

Maio, G. R., Olson, J. M., Allen, L., & Bernard, M. M. (2001). Addressing discrepancies between values and behavior: The motivating effect of reasons. *Journal of Experimental Social Psychology, 37*(2), 104–117.

Maio, G. R., Olson, J. M., Bernard, M. M., & Luke, M. A. (2003). Ideologies, values, attitudes, and behavior. In J. DeLamater (Ed.), *Handbook of social psychology* (pp. 283–308). New York, NY: Kluwer.

Maio, G. R., Pakizeh, A., Cheung, W., & Rees, K. J. (2009). Changing, priming, and acting on values: Effects via motivational relations in a circular model. *Journal of Personality and Social Psychology, 97*, 699–715.

Maio, G. R., Roese, N. J., Seligman, C., & Katz, A. (1996). Rankings, ratings, and the measurement of values: Evidence for the superior validity of ratings. *Basic and Applied Social Psychology, 18*, 171–181.

Maio, G. R., Verplanken, B., Manstead, A. S. R., Stroebe, W., Abraham, C. S., Sheeran, P., & Conner, M. (2007). Social psychological factors in lifestyle change and their relevance to policy. *Journal of Social Issues and Policy Review, 1*, 99–137.

Martin, P. Y., Hamilton, V. E., McKimmie, B. M., Terry, D. J., & Martin, R. (2007). Effects of caffeine on persuasion and attitude change: The role of secondary tasks in manipulating systematic message processing. *European Journal of Social Psychology, 37*, 320–338.

Mathur, M., & Chattopadhyay, A. (1991). The impact of moods generated by television programs on responses to advertising. *Psychology and Marketing, 8*, 59–77.

Mayer, N. D., & Tormala, Z. L. (2010). "Think" versus "feel" framing effects in persuasion. *Personality and Social Psychology Bulletin, 36*, 443–454.

Moreland, R. L., & Beach, S. R. (1992). Exposure effects in the classroom: The development of affinity among students. *Journal of Experimental Social Psychology, 28*, 255–276.

Murphy, S. T., & Zajonc, R. B. (1993). Affect, cognition, and awareness: Affective priming with optimal and suboptimal stimulus exposures. *Journal of Personality and Social Psychology, 64*, 723–739.

Murray, S. L., Haddock, G., & Zanna, M. P. (1996). On creating value-expressive attitudes: An experimental approach. In C. Seligman, J. M. Olson, & M. P. Zanna (Eds.), *The psychology of values: The Ontario symposium* (Vol. 8, pp. 107–133). Mahwah, NJ: Erlbaum.

Murray, S. L. & Holmes, J. G. (2011). *Interdependent minds: The dynamics of close relationships*. New York: Guilford Press.

Nelson, T. E. (2004). Policy goals, public rhetoric, and political attitudes. *Journal of Politics, 66*, 581–605.

Niedenthal, P. M., Barsalou, L. W., Winkielman, P., Krauth-Gruber, S., & Ric, F. (2005). Embodiment in attitudes, social perception, and emotion. *Personality and Social Psychology Review, 9*, 184–211.

Nisbett, R. E., & Cohen, D. (1996). *Culture of honor: The psychology of violence in the South*. Boulder, CO: Westview Press.

Ohira, H., Winton, W. M., & Oyama, M. (1998). Effects of stimulus valence on recognition memory and endogenous eyeblinks: Further evidence for positive-negative asymmetry. *Personality and Social Psychology Bulletin, 24*, 986–993.

Olson, J. M. (1992). Self-perception of humor: Evidence for discounting and augmentation effects. *Journal of Personality and Social Psychology, 62*, 369–377.

Olson, J. M., Goffin, R. D., & Haynes, G. A. (2007). Relative versus absolute measures of explicit attitudes: Implications for predicting diverse attitude-relevant criteria. *Journal of Personality and Social Psychology, 93*, 907–926.

Olson, J. M., & Stone, J. (2005). The influence of behavior on attitudes. In D. Albarracín, B. T. Johnson, & M. P. Zanna (Eds.), *Handbook of attitudes* (pp. 223–272). Mahwah, NJ: Erlbaum.

Olson, J. M., Vernon, P. A., Harris, J. A., & Jang, K. L. (2001). The heritability of attitudes: A study of twins. *Journal of Personality and Social Psychology, 80*, 845–860.

Olson, J. M., & Zanna, M. P. (1979). A new look at selective exposure. *Journal of Experimental Social Psychology, 15*, 1–15.

Olson, M. A., & Fazio, R. H. (2001). Implicit attitude formation through classical conditioning. *Psychological Science, 12*, 413–417.

Olson, M. A., & Fazio, R. H. (2002). Implicit acquisition and manifestation of classically conditioned attitudes. *Social Cognition, 20*, 89–104.

Olson, M. A., & Fazio, R. H. (2006). Reducing automatically activated prejudice through implicit evaluative conditioning. *Personality and Social Psychology Bulletin, 32*, 421–433.

Olson, M. A., & Fazio, R. H. (2009). Implicit and explicit measures of attitudes: The perspective of the MODE Model. In R. E. Petty, R. H. Fazio, & P. Brinol (Eds.), *Attitudes: Insights from the new implicit measures* (pp. 19–63). Hove, UK: Psychology Press.

Osgood, C. E., & Tannenbaum, P. H. (1955). The principle of congruity in the prediction of attitude change. *Psychological Review, 62,* 42–55.

Ouellette, J. A., & Wood, W. (1998). Habit and intention in everyday life: The multiple processes by which past behavior predicts future behavior. *Psychological Bulletin, 124,* 54–74.

Paluck, E. L. (2009). Reducing intergroup prejudice and conflict using the media: A field experiment in Rwanda. *Journal of Personality and Social Psychology, 96,* 574–587.

Paulhus, D. L. (1991). Measurement and control of response bias. In J. P. Robinson, P. R. Shaver, & L. S. Wrightsman (Eds.), *Measures of personality and social psychological attitudes* (pp. 17–59). San Diego, CA: Academic Press.

Petty, R. E., Briñol, P., & DeMarree, K. G. (2007). The meta-cognitive model (MCM) of attitudes: Implications for attitude measurement, change, and strength. *Social Cognition, 25,* 657–686.

Petty, R. E., Briñol, P., & Tormala, Z. L. (2002). Thought confidence as a determinant of persuasion: The self-validation hypothesis. *Journal of Personality and Social Psychology, 82,* 722–741.

Petty, R. E., & Cacioppo, J. T. (1983). The role of bodily responses in attitude measurement and change. In J. T. Cacioppo & R. E. Petty (Eds.), *Social psychophysiology: A sourcebook* (pp. 51–101). New York, NY: Guilford Press.

Petty, R. E., Cacioppo, J. T., & Schumann, D. (1983). Central and peripheral routes to advertising effectiveness: The moderating role of involvement. *Journal of Consumer Research, 10,* 135–146.

Petty, R. E., Tormala, Z. L., Briñol, P., & Jarvis, W. B. G. (2006). Implicit ambivalence from attitude change: An exploration of the PAST Model. *Journal of Personality and Social Psychology, 90,* 21–41.

Petty, R. E., & Wegener, D. T. (1998). Matching versus mismatching attitude functions: Implications for scrutiny of persuasive messages. *Personality and Social Psychology Bulletin, 24,* 227–240.

Petty, R. E., & Wegener, D. T. (1999). The elaboration likelihood model: Current status and controversies. In S. Chaiken & Y. Trope (Eds.), *Dual process theories in social psychology* (pp. 41–72). New York, NY: Guilford Press.

Plant, E. A., Devine, P. G., & Peruche, M. B. (2010). Routes to positive interracial interactions: Approaching egalitarianism or avoiding prejudice. *Personality and Social Psychology Bulletin, 36,* 1135–1147.

Plomin, R., DeFries, J. C., & Loehlin, J. C. (1977). Genotype-environment interaction and correlation in the analysis of human behavior. *Psychological Bulletin, 84,* 309–322.

Pomerantz, E. M., Chaiken, S., & Tordesillas, R. S. (1995). Attitude strength and resistance processes. *Journal of Personality and Social Psychology, 69,* 408–419.

Prentice, D. A. (1987). Psychological correspondence of possessions, attitudes, and values. *Journal of Personality and Social Psychology, 53,* 993–1003.

Priester, J. R., & Petty, R. E. (1996). The gradual threshold model of ambivalence: Relating the positive and negative bases of attitudes to subjective ambivalence. *Journal of Personality and Social Psychology, 71,* 431–449.

Prislin, R. (1996). Attitude stability and attitude strength: One is enough to make it stable. *European Journal of Social Psychology, 26,* 447–477.

Rabinovich, A., Morton, T. A., Postmes, T., & Verplanken, B. (2009). Think global, act local: The effect of goal and mindset specificity on willingness to donate to an environmental organization. *Journal of Environmental Psychology, 29,* 391–399.

Reeder, G. D., & Pryor, J. B. (2000). Attitudes toward persons with HIV/AIDS: Linking a functional approach with underlying process. In G. R. Maio & J. M. Olson (Eds.), *Why we evaluate: Functions of attitudes* (pp. 295–323). Mahwah, NJ: Erlbaum.

Roberts, J. V. (1985). The attitude-memory relationship after 40 years: A meta-analysis of the literature. *Basic and Applied Social Psychology, 6,* 221–241.

Roese, N., & Jamieson, D. (1993). Twenty years of Bogus Pipeline research: A critical review and meta-analysis. *Psychological Bulletin, 114,* 363–375.

Rokeach, M. (1973). *The nature of human values.* New York, NY: Free Press.

Ronis, D. L., Yates, J. F., & Kirscht, J. P. (1989). Attitudes, decisions, and habits as determinants of repeated behavior. In A. R. Pratkanis, S. J. Breckler & A. G. Greenwald (Eds.), *Attitude Structure and Function* (pp. 213–239). Hillsdale, NJ: Erlbaum.

Rosenberg, M. J. (1968). Hedonism, inauthenticity, and other goads toward expansion of a consistency theory. In R. P. Abelson, E. Aronson, W. J. McGuire, T. M. Newcomb, M. J. Rosenberg, & P. H. Tannenbaum (Eds.), *Theories of cognitive consistency: A sourcebook* (pp. 73–111). Chicago, IL: Rand McNally.

Roskos-Ewoldsen, D. R., & Fazio, R. H. (1992). On the orienting value of attitudes: Attitude accessibility as a determinant of an object's attraction of visual attention. *Personality and Social Psychology Bulletin, 63,* 198–211.

Ross, M. (1989). Relation of implicit theories to the construction of personal histories. *Psychological Review, 96,* 341–357.

Ross, M., McFarland, C., & Fletcher, G. J. O. (1981). The effect of attitude on the recall of personal histories. *Journal of Personality and Social Psychology, 40,* 627–634.

Scheier, M. F., Buss, A. H., & Buss, D. M. (1978). Self-consciousness, self-report of aggressiveness, and aggression. *Journal of Research in Personality, 12,* 133–140.

Schuette, R. A., & Fazio, R. H. (1995). Attitude accessibility and motivation as determinants of biased processing: A test of the MODE model. *Personality and Social Psychology Bulletin, 21,* 704–710.

Schwartz, S. H. (1992). Universals in the content and structure of values: Theoretical advances and empirical tests in 20 countries. *Advances in Experimental Social Psychology, 25,* 1–65.

Schwartz, S. H., & Rubel, T. (2005). Sex differences in value priorities: Cross-cultural and multimethod studies. *Journal of Personality and Social Psychology, 89,* 1010–1028.

Scott, W. A. (1968). Attitude measurement. In G. Lindzey & E. Aronson (Eds.), *Handbook of social psychology* (Vol. 2, 2nd ed., pp. 204–273). Reading, MA: Addison-Wesley.

Sears, D. O., & Henry, P. J. (2003). The origins of symbolic racism. *Journal of Personality and Social Psychology, 85,* 259–275.

Seigle, G. J., Ichakawa, N., & Steinhauer, S. (2008). Blink before and after you think: Blinks occur prior to and following cognitive load indexed by pupillary responses. *Psychophysiology, 45,* 679–687.

Shavitt, S. (1989). Operationalizing functional theories of attitude. In A. R. Pratkanis, S. J. Breckler, & A. G. Greenwald (Eds.), *Attitude structure and function* (pp. 311–337). Hillsdale, NJ: Erlbaum.

Shavitt, S. (1990). The role of attitude objects in attitude functions. *Journal of Experimental Social Psychology, 26,* 124–148.

Shelton, J. N., West, T. V., & Trail, T. E. (2010). Concerns about appearing prejudiced: Implications for anxiety during daily interracial interactions. *Group Processes and Intergroup Relations, 13,* 329–344.

Sherman, D. A. K., Nelson, L. D., & Steele, C. M. (2000). Do messages about health risks threaten the self? Increasing the acceptance of threatening health messages via self-affirmation. *Personality and Social Psychology Bulletin, 26,* 1046–1058.

Sidanius, J., & Duffy, G. (1988). The duality of attitude structure: A test of Kerlinger's Criterial Referents Theory within samples of Swedish and American youth. *Political Psychology, 9,* 649–670.

Smith, M. B., Bruner, J. S., & White, R. W. (1956). *Opinions and personality.* New York, NY: Wiley.

Smith, P. K., Dijksterhuis, A., & Chaiken, S. (2008). Subliminal exposure to faces and racial attitudes: Exposure to Whites makes Whites like Blacks less. *Journal of Experimental Social Psychology, 44,* 50–64.

Snyder, M. (1986). *Public appearances/private realities: The psychology of self-monitoring.* New York, NY: Freeman.

Snyder, M., Clary, E. G., & Stukas, A. A. (2000). The functional approach to volunteerism. In G. R. Maio & J. M. Olson (Eds.), *Why we evaluate: Functions of attitudes* (pp. 365–393). Mahwah, NJ: Erlbaum.

Snyder, M., & DeBono, K. G. (1987). Appeals to image and claims about quality: Understanding the psychology of advertising. *Journal of Personality and Social Psychology, 49,* 586–597.

Snyder, M., & Kendzierski, D. (1982). Acting on one's attitudes: Procedures for linking attitudes and behavior. *Journal of Experimental Social Psychology, 18,* 165–183.

Sparks, P., Hedderley, D., & Shepherd, R. (1991). Expectancy-value models of attitudes: A note on the relationship between theory and methodology. *European Journal of Social Psychology, 21,* 261–271.

Spence, J. T. (1993). Gender-related traits and gender ideology: Evidence for a multifactorial theory. *Journal of Personality and Social Psychology, 64,* 624–635.

Spencer-Rodgers, J., Williams, M. J., & Peng, K. (2010). Cultural differences in expectations of change and tolerance for contradiction: A decade of empirical research. *Personality and Social Psychology Review, 14,* 296–312.

Staats, A. W., & Staats, C. K. (1958). Attitudes established by classical conditioning. *Journal of Abnormal and Social Psychology, 57,* 37–40.

Stewart, T. L., Vassar, P. M., Sanchez, D. T., & David, S. E. (2000). Attitude toward women's societal roles moderates the effect of gender cues on target individuation. *Journal of Personality and Social Psychology, 79,* 143–157.

Sweeney, P. D., & Gruber, K. L. (1984). Selective exposure: Voter information preferences and the Watergate affair. *Journal of Personality and Social Psychology, 46,* 1208–1221.

Tannenbaum, P. H. (1966). Mediated generalization of attitude change via the principle of congruity. *Journal of Personality and Social Psychology, 3,* 493–499.

Tannenbaum, P. H., & Gengel, R. W. (1966). Generalization of attitude change through congruity principle relationships. *Journal of Personality and Social Psychology, 3,* 299–304.

Tesser, A. (1978). Self-generated attitude change. *Advances in Experimental Social Psychology, 11,* 289–338.

Tesser, A. (1993). The importance of heritability in psychological research: The case of attitudes. *Psychological Review, 100,* 129–142.

Tesser, A., & Crelia, R. A. (1994). Attitude heritability and attitude reinforcement: A test of the niche building hypothesis. *Personality and Individual Differences, 16,* 571–577.

Tesser, A., & Leone, C. (1977). Cognitive schemas and thought as determinants of attitude change. *Journal of Experimental Social Psychology, 13,* 340–356.

Thompson, M. M., Zanna, M. P., & Griffin, D. W. (1995). Let's not be indifferent about (attitudinal) ambivalence. In R. E. Petty & J. A. Krosnick (Eds.), *Attitude strength: Antecedents and consequences* (pp. 361–386). Mahwah, NJ: Erlbaum.

Thomsen, C. J., Lavine, H., & Kounios, J. (1996). Social value and attitude concepts in semantic memory: Relational structure, concept strength, and the fan effect. *Social Cognition, 14,* 191–225.

Trafimow, D., & Sheeran, P. (1998). Some tests of the distinction between cognitive and affective beliefs. *Journal of Experimental Social Psychology, 34,* 378–397.

Trope, Y., Liberman, N., & Wakslak, C. J. (2007). Construal levels and psychological distance: Effects on representation, prediction, evaluation, and behavior. *Journal of Consumer Psychology, 17,* 83–95.

Tyler, T. R., & Smith, H. J. (1998). Social justice and social movements. In D. T. Gilbert, S. T. Fiske, & G. Lindzey (Eds.), *Handbook of social psychology* (4th ed., Vol. 2, pp. 595–629). New York, NY: McGraw-Hill.

Ullrich, J., Schermelleh-Engel, K., & Böttcher, B. (2008). The moderator effect that wasn't there: Statistical problems in ambivalence research. *Journal of Personality and Social Psychology, 95,* 774–794.

Vallacher, R. R., & Wegner, D. M. (1987). What do people think they're doing? Action identification and human behavior. *Psychological Review, 94,* 3–15.

Vallone, R. P., Ross, L., & Lepper, M. R. (1985). The hostile media phenomenon: Biased perception and perceptions of media bias in coverage of the Beirut massacre. *Journal of Personality and Social Psychology, 49,* 577–585.

van der Pligt, J., & de Vries, N. (1998). Belief importance in expectancy-value models of attitudes. *Journal of Applied Social Psychology, 28,* 1339–1354.

van Harreveld, F., van der Pligt, J., & de Liver, Y. N. (2009). The agony of ambivalence and ways to resolve it: Introducing the MAID Model. *Personality and Social Psychology Review, 13,* 45–61.

Verplanken, B., & Aarts, H. (1999). Habit, attitude, and planned behaviour: Is habit an empty construct or an interesting case of goal-directed automaticity? *European Review of Social Psychology, 10,* 101–134.

Verplanken, B., Aarts, H., & van Knippenberg, A. (1997). Habit, information acquisition, and the process of making travel mode choices. *European Journal of Social Psychology, 27,* 539–560.

Verplanken, B., Aarts, H., van Knippenberg, A., & Moonen, A. (1998). Habit versus planned behaviour: A field experiment. *British Journal of Social Psychology, 37,* 111–128.

Verplanken, B., & Holland, R. W. (2002). Motivated decision making: Effects of activation and self-centrality of values on choices and behavior. *Journal of Personality and Social Psychology, 82,* 434–447.

Verplanken, B., & Wood, W. (2006). Interventions to break and create consumer habits. *Journal of Public Policy and Marketing, 25,* 90–103.

Vidmar, N., & Rokeach, M. (1974). Archie Bunker's bigotry: A study in selective perception and exposure. *Journal of Communication, 24,* 36–47.

Visser, P. S., & Krosnick, J. A. (1998). Development of attitude strength over the life cycle: Surge and decline. *Journal of Personality and Social Psychology, 75,* 1389–1410.

Webb, T. L., & Sheeran, P. (2006). Does changing behavioral intentions engender behavior change? A meta-analysis of the experimental evidence. *Psychological Bulletin, 132,* 249–268.

Wicker, A. (1969). Attitudes versus actions: The relationship of verbal and overt behavioral responses to attitude objects. *Journal of Social Issues, 25,* 41–78.

Wicklund, R. A. (1982). Self-focused attention and the validity of self-reports. In M. P. Zanna, E. T. Higgins, & C. P. Herman (Eds.), *Consistency in social behavior: The Ontario symposium* (Vol. 2, pp. 149–172). Mahwah, NJ: Erlbaum.

Wolsko, C., Park, B., Judd, C. M., & Wittenbrink, B. (2000). Framing interethnic ideology: Effects of multicultural and color-blind perspectives on judgments of groups and individuals. *Journal of Personality and Social Psychology, 78,* 635–654.

Wood, W., Rhodes, N., & Biek, M. (1995). Working knowledge and attitude strength: An information-processing analysis. In R. E. Petty & J. A. Krosnick (Eds.), *Attitude strength: Antecedents and consequences* (pp. 283–313). Mahwah, NJ: Erlbaum.

Wood, W., Tam, L., & Wit, M. G. (2005). Changing circumstances, disrupting habits. *Journal of Personality and Social Psychology, 88,* 918–933.

Wu, C., & Schaffer, D. R. (1987). Susceptibility to persuasive appeals as a function of source credibility and prior experience with the attitude object. *Journal of Personality and Social Psychology, 52,* 677–688.

Wyer, R. S. Jr., & Goldberg, L. (1970). A probabilistic analysis of the relationships among beliefs and attitudes. *Psychological Review, 77,* 100–120.

Zajonc, R. B. (1968). Attitudinal effects of mere exposure. *Journal of Personality and Social Psychology Monograph Supplement, 9,* 1–27.

Zanna, M. P., & Cooper, J. (1974). Dissonance and the pill: An attribution approach to studying the arousal properties of dissonance. *Journal of Personality and Social Psychology, 29,* 703–709.

Zanna, M. P., Olson, J. M., & Fazio, R. H. (1980). Attitude-behavior consistency: An individual difference perspective. *Journal of Personality and Social Psychology, 38,* 432–440.

Zanna, M. P., & Rempel, J. K. (1988). Attitudes: A new look at an old concept. In D. Bar-Tal & A. Kruglanski (Eds.), *The social psychology of knowledge* (pp. 315–334). Cambridge, UK: Cambridge University Press.

CHAPTER 14

Social Influence and Group Behavior

DONELSON R. FORSYTH

Most people loudly proclaim their autonomy and independence. Like Ralph Waldo Emerson they avow "I must be myself. I will not hide my tastes or aversions.... I will seek my own" (1903/2004, p. 127). But this claim of self-determination is often overstated, for anyone who lives with other people will never be completely free from the inexorable demands of a social life. Each person influences others in myriad ways, and those others influence the individual in return. People, embedded in complex webs of reciprocal relationships, shape one another's attitudes and feelings, sway their judgments and outlooks, and convince each other to stop doing some things all the while encouraging them to do something else. The force of *social influence*—interpersonal processes that change people's feelings, thoughts, or behaviors—is undeniable. Rare is the person who is the source of influence only, and never the target.

All of the social sciences investigate influence in some form. Anthropologists, for example, study the customs of human societies and the pervasive impact of those customs on social life. Political scientists study the effects of social systems on civic engagement and governance. Economists include social factors in their analyses of the production and distribution of goods and services. Sociologists and psychologists investigate influence that flows from individuals and groups to other individuals and groups. Within psychology the subfield of social psychology is most centrally concerned with the study of social influence. Social psychologists analyze such topics as attitudes, impression formation, interpersonal attraction, altruism, and conflict, but the mutual impact of one person on another is the constant theme underlying all

their investigations. Allport highlighted this theme when he defined social psychology as "an attempt to understand and explain how the thought, feeling, and behavior of individuals are influenced by the actual, imagined, or implied presence of others" (Allport, 1985, p. 3).

This chapter examines three familiar, yet often misunderstood, forms of social influence: *conformity, compliance,* and *obedience*. Conformity occurs when individuals' opinions, judgments, or actions change to become more consistent with those manifested by other people. People rising to give a standing ovation after a performance, drivers who match, approximately, the speed of the other drivers on the roadway, adolescents who dress as their peers do, and employees who dawdle on the job because everyone else is dawdling are all conforming to the social standard set by others. Conformity can take many forms, and it often goes unnoticed as individuals gradually change until they find themselves in agreement with others. Compliance, like conformity, involves a change caused by others, but compliance suggests acquiescence rather than private acceptance, and it is also often triggered by the relatively direct intervention of others. Negotiators attempting to sway others, a salesperson speaking persuasively with a customer, and an adolescent pressuring a close friend to engage in such proscribed behaviors as underage drinking are all compliance settings, for they involve one party pressuring another party to comply with a request. Obedience is the most direct of the three: a change in response to an order from another person, often an authority. The soldier who carries out an officer's command, students who put away their cell phones because the professor tells them to, and the office worker who stays late because the boss demands it are all displaying obedience. The analysis of obedience inevitably raises questions concerning *social power*, which is the capacity to influence another person, even when that person struggles to resist that influence. *Persuasion*, or the communication of facts, arguments, and information so as to change another person's attitudes, is also a form of social influence and is examined in a separate entry of this volume.

STUDIES OF SOCIAL INFLUENCE: HISTORICAL BACKGROUND

People have long been intrigued by the possibility that individuals, despite their claims of self-regulation and personal agency, are nonetheless substantially influenced by other people. But only in the past 100 years or so have social psychologists sought to study social influence scientifically. Philosophers, poets, and sages may have offered intellectually compelling analyses of the factors that cause individuals to ignore their internal compass and turn, instead, to a social one, but social psychologists did not merely speculate; they developed theories that explained social influence and tested the adequacy of these theories through research. This section reviews that history, stressing classic studies that offered novel theoretical insights as well as those that pioneered methods that subsequent researchers used in their work (Prislin & Crano, 2012).

Crowd Psychology

The scientific study of social influence began near the end of the 19th century when, ironically, a number of scholars in a variety of fields simultaneously expressed a shared fascination with crowds, mobs, and masses. Although accounts of people exhibiting unexpected qualities and characteristics when immersed in crowds appeared as early as 1841 when MacKay wrote his *Memoirs of Extraordinary Delusions and the Madness of Crowds*, the last decade of 1800s witnessed the publication of dozens of books and monographs examining the transformative effects of crowds on their constituents (e.g., Fournial, 1892; Le Bon, 1895/1960; Sighele, 1891; Tarde, 1892). Gustave Le Bon's 1895 *The Crowd* is the best known of these works. Le Bon wove together his psychological insights, social commentary, and vivid descriptions in a forceful style that convinced readers that human beings are so attuned to the actions of others that unconscious urges can find their release in the anonymity of large gatherings. He described various kinds of social groups, including riots, street crowds, religious sects, juries, military units, and even widely distributed classes within a society (e.g., the "middle class, the peasant classes," 1895/1960, p. 157), and suggested that the members of these groups often converged to a consensus over time, as "the heterogeneous is swamped by the homogenous" (p. 29). Le Bon believed that this convergence resulted from a number of interrelated social mechanisms, including heightened suggestibility caused by the excitement of the crowd, the tendency for members to imitate one another, and contagion: the transmission of ideas and emotions from one person to another. More controversially he also suggested that in some cases groups intensified members' emotions and inhibited the intellect, with the result that a group mind emerged to guide the individuals in the group. The group mind's level of sophistication was limited by the cognitive capacity of its least capable members, and so the group mind often led them to act in socially reprehensible ways. Skilled leaders, Le Bon concluded, could easily manipulate such mobs (van Ginneken, 2007).

Researchers, intrigued by Le Bon's speculations, avidly investigated various forms of social influence in the early decades of the 20th century (Pratkanis, 2007a). Few accepted the idea of a superordinate mind that emerged in large collectives that overwhelmed the self-restraint of individual members, but these studies of crowds and mass movements did much to challenge the received view of humans as rational, self-directed actors and elevated the importance of considering social causes of actions, emotions, and cognitions. Subsequently, studies of rumor transmission, propaganda, and mass persuasion suggested individuals, in seeking information about their world, are significantly influenced by the opinions of other people (Allport & Postman, 1947; Swift, 1918). Researchers examining work groups discovered that people's productivity rises and falls depending on the output of others, with those who are most productive gradually reducing their output, and those who underproduce tend to increase their performance (Roethlisberger & Dickson, 1934). Researchers examined fads and fashions to discover why individuals tend to adopt similar styles of dress and appearances (Barr, 1934). They also turned their attention to widespread social movements, such as interpersonal bases of sweeping shifts in patriotism and nationalism in wartime (McDougall, 1920). Each one of these analyses added to the general conception that people are creatures of conformity rather than staunch individualists, for their actions, thoughts, and emotions are as often influenced by other people as they are by unseen psychological processes. These investigations also set researchers on paths of exploration that stretch, unbroken, from those first fledgling studies of social influence to contemporary—and far more theoretically sophisticated—analyses of such topics as rumor transmission (DiFonzo & Bordia, 2007), the interpersonal determinants of productivity in groups (Larson, 2010), the alignment of preferences across social networks (Raafat, Chater, & Frith, 2009), and patriotism and cultural identity (Huddy, 2003).

Norms and Social Influence

Studies of crowds, mobs, and mass movements suggest that people are often swayed in dramatic ways by social pressures, but many psychologists remained unconvinced, for this influence process had never been demonstrated under controlled, laboratory conditions. Muzafer Sherif (1936) addressed this issue directly by creating small face-to-face groups in the confines of his research laboratory, and then systematically documenting conformity within these groups. Sherif took advantage of a naturally occurring perceptual illusion called the *autokinetic effect*: the apparent movement of a stationary pinpoint of light in an otherwise completely darkened room. He recruited male volunteers and first tested them alone, repeatedly asking them to state aloud how far the dot of light seemed to move in the darkened room. These men's judgments tended to be consistent across the individual trials, as each one established a personal distance standard that varied from 1 to 10 inches. He then put people together in two- or three-man groups and had them state their estimates aloud, one at a time, and in no required order. These men, seated in the dark trying to accurately estimate the distance a stationary light moved, shifted from their own personal estimates and instead adopted a shared standard. Significantly, the process did not involve an explicit competition among the group members with one pressing his opinion on the others, but rather a gradual emergence of consensus. The process of change was also so subtle that most of the men did not think that they were influenced at all by the others' judgments. They maintained that they had made up their mind about the distance estimate before hearing what others said, and yet their judgments in the groups usually matched their fellow members' estimates rather than those they had given when they worked at the problem alone.

Sherif believed that he had succeeded in experimentally creating a social norm in the groups he studied. Social norms, in contrast to statistical norms, are frames of reference that describe what behaviors should and should not be performed in a given context. They prescribe the socially appropriate way to respond in the situation—the "normal" course of action—as well as proscribing actions to avoid if at all possible. Sherif argued that norms emerge, spontaneously, whenever people find themselves in an unstructured, ambiguous situation where they have no reference point to define their expectations, perceptions, or activities. In such situations people unwittingly use other people's actions and expressions as useful data about how they should themselves respond. Subsequent studies confirmed that once norms develop they become stable frames of reference that resist change. Sherif, for example, found that the impact of a norm on judgments was not transitory. When the men who had made decisions in a group and had tailored their estimates to that standard were asked to make estimates by themselves the men nonetheless based their estimates on the group's standard, rather than reverting back to their own estimates. Thus, even though freed from the direct pressure of the group situation, the norm continued to influence them, for they had personally accepted the group's standard as their own.

Sherif argued that a norm, once established, creates a social convention that can live on even after the individuals who established it have long departed. Researchers tested this assumption by surreptitiously planting one or more confederates into groups making distance estimates in the autokinetic situation. These confederates deliberately offered up relatively extreme distance estimates: Most groups tended toward estimates in the 4- to 8-inch range, but the confederates steadfastly maintained that the dot of light was moving about 15 inches. Once the confederates deflected the group's distance norm upward, they were removed from the group and naive newcomers took their places. The researchers continued to replace old members with new ones, but the new arrivals all shifted their estimates in the direction of the group norm. This arbitrary norm eventually disappeared, but it took several generations before a more reasonable norm emerged (Jacobs & Campbell, 1961; MacNeil & Sherif, 1976).

Influence and Attitude Change

Le Bon and other early psychologists asserted that people who find themselves in turbulent situations (e.g., mobs, riots) are sometimes influenced to an extraordinary degree by other people in that situation. Sherif's study of norm formation indicated that people who find themselves in confusing, complicated, or ambiguous situations sometimes base their own choices on the choices made by those around them. But Theodore Newcomb's (1943) study of students at Bennington College documented the ubiquity of social influence. Newcomb's work made it clear that social influence is not a rare occurrence, but an ever-present, if taken-for-granted, aspect of everyday social life.

Newcomb studied the interpersonal factors that prompt people to change their political beliefs. Political orientation—conservative or liberal—generally remains stable over time, but Newcomb noticed that many of his students' politics changed with each year they spent at Bennington. Bennington students came from politically conservative New England families, and when they first matriculated their attitudes matched their families' beliefs: They were conservative. But this attitudinal congruity dissipated the longer the students remained at Bennington, so by the time the students were seniors they expressed more liberal attitudes. Newcomb studied this shift by measuring the attitudes, social standing, and family backgrounds of an entire class of Bennington students from their entrance in 1935 to their graduation in 1939. After analyzing his data he concluded that the change in attitudes in this cohort was caused by their close association with the more liberal students at Bennington and the faculty. Although no overt attempt was made to change students' beliefs, over time most unwittingly accepted the Bennington community as their frame of reference for defining their political beliefs. Those students who conformed to the politics of the place tended to be "both capable and desirous of cordial relations with the fellow community members" (p. 149). Students who did not become more liberal were of two types: ones who did not identify with Bennington College and those who maintained very close family ties throughout their college years. The more liberal attitudes created by the group remained a part of the beliefs of many of the graduates some 25 years later (Newcomb, Koenig, Flacks, & Warwick, 1967).

Newcomb did not use the terms *reference group* and *social comparison* in his 1943 analysis, but his findings stimulated subsequent studies of these processes. Hyman (1942), in his initial statement of his theory of reference groups, posited that people use groups or social aggregates as standards or frames of reference when evaluating their abilities, attitudes, or beliefs. When students first enrolled at Bennington their family was their reference group, so their attitudes matched their families' attitudes. The longer students remained at Bennington, however, the more their attitudes changed to match the attitudes of their

new reference group: their peers and professors. Studies of reference groups indicate that any identifiable group can function as a definitional reference point, including statistical aggregations of noninteracting individuals, imaginary groups, or even groups that deny the individual membership (Singer, 1990).

Newcomb's work also foreshadowed the study of social comparison: the tendency to evaluate the accuracy of personal beliefs, attitudes, and abilities by comparing oneself to others. Leon Festinger's (1950, 1954) initial formulation of this theory maintained that people are more likely to think their opinions, beliefs, or attitudes are "correct" or "valid" if they correspond with the interpretations of appropriate others. They are, therefore, likely to respond negatively if they find others disagree with them, and they may also change their own position to decrease any discrepancy between their outlook and those of similar others. Subsequent studies have confirmed the powerful impact of this subtle, but ubiquitous, comparison process on people's preferences ("Do I like X?"), beliefs ("Is Y correct?"), evaluations of their abilities and sense of worth ("Am I more able than others?"), and even their predictions about future events ("Will I enjoy doing Z?"; Suls, Martin, & Wheeler, 2002).

The Influence of Leaders

At about the same time that Newcomb was studying the influence of groups on members' political beliefs the sociologist William Foote Whyte and a team of social psychological researchers led by Kurt Lewin, Ronald Lippitt, and Ralph White were investigating how some individuals manage to exert greater influence over their groups and communities than do others. These studies suggested that *leadership* can be considered a form of social influence, for leaders organize, direct, coordinate, and motivate others who are working together to achieve individual and collective goals.

Whyte (1943) studied the influence of various types of groups—gangs, social clubs, racketeering groups, and political associations—on their members and their communities. He was particularly intrigued by urban corner gangs: "groups of men who center their social activities upon particular street corners, with their adjoining barbershops, lunchrooms, poolrooms, or clubrooms" (p. xviii). Whyte observed one such group (the Nortons) in the late 1930s and recorded his experiences in his book *Street Corner Society*. Whyte focused on quantifying the frequencies and duration of the group interactions, and discovered complex patterns of mutual influence as well as group-level leadership. The leader of the Nortons, Doc, exerted a powerful influence over the group and community as a whole, but he was also influenced in turn by the group.

Lewin, Lippitt, and White (1939; White & Lippitt, 1968) also studied leaders' influence on their followers, but through experimentation rather than observation in the field. They put an adult male in charge of groups of boys who were working on hobby projects after school. In some groups the leader made all the decisions for the group without consulting the boys. This directive, or autocratic, leader told the boys what to do, he often criticized them, and he remained aloof from the group. Other groups were guided by a participatory, or democratic, leader who let them make decisions as he provided guiding advice. He explained long-term goals and steps to be taken to reach the goals, but he rarely criticized the boys or gave orders. Other groups were given a laissez-faire leader who allowed the boys to work in whichever way they wished. He provided information on demand, but he did not offer information, criticism, or guidance spontaneously.

Lewin et al.'s findings made it clear that leaders substantially influence their followers. Boys with directive leaders spent more time working than boys with a leader who adopted a more participatory style, and they in turn spent more time working than the boys in the laissez-faire groups—provided the leader was physically present. Boys with a participative leader continued to work when their leader left but the boys working under the direction of a directive leader did not. Boys working with a laissez-faire leader were also less aggressive than those with a directive leader. In the latter case observers noted high rates of hostility among members, more demands for attention, more destructiveness, and a greater tendency to single out one group member to serve as the target of hostile commentary. Lewin et al. also found that the boys acted differently when a new leader, using a different style of leadership, took over their group. For example, the previously unproductive boys with a laissez-faire leader began expending far more effort when a more directive leader took charge, and the previously cowed boys working for the autocrat became more expressive and cooperative under the direction of a democratic leader. Overall, the participatory leader heightened members' feelings of satisfaction and involvement in the group.

The Historical Foundations: Conclusions

The early studies of social influence demonstrated empirically the significant impact of social influence on people's

thoughts, emotions, and actions. Although some of this work explored extreme forms of influence, as when a crowd seems to transform its members, researchers also studied the types of influence that people encounter each day; friends pressuring each other, teammates recommending alternatives to one another, shifts in political beliefs, and leadership. This work illustrated that some forms of social influence are coercive and disruptive, but that in many cases influence works subtly and slowly rather than obviously and abruptly. These early investigations also set the foundation for a more fully developed science of social influence that offered conceptually sophisticated theories of interpersonal influence and then tested these theories using valid empirical procedures. In the years that followed these groundbreaking studies researchers explored many aspects of social influence, but most focused on the three areas reviewed in the remainder of this chapter: conformity, compliance, and obedience.

CONFORMITY

Individuals often change their beliefs and behaviors to conform to the beliefs and behaviors of the people around them. When alone individuals may be free to think and act as they choose, but social situations often favor consensus and uniformity rather than idiosyncrasy. Groups favor one interpretation of reality over another and encourage certain behaviors while discouraging others. Members often respond to that influence by conforming.

Asch's Studies of Conformity

Solomon Asch (1955) studied conformity by pitting single individuals against a unanimous—and incorrect—group. Asch assembled groups ranging in size from 2 to 16 members in his research laboratory. They sat in a semicircle facing Asch's experimenter, who explained that he was studying perception, and so would be asking participants to make comparative judgments about the length of lines. On each trial participants were shown two cards. One card displayed a single line that was to serve as the standard. The second card displayed three numbered test lines. Participants stated aloud which line of the three matched the test line.

Asch found that when making such judgments alone, people made few mistakes. But when part of a group that made an error, many of the participants also made mistakes. And the group made mistakes on several trials because only one group member was an actual subject.

All the others were trained confederates who deliberately made errors to see if the subject would conform to a unanimous majority's judgments. On one of the rigged trials, for example, the first confederate would glance at the cards and confidently say, "The answer is Line 1." The other confederates then repeated this wrong answer until it was the subject's turn to answer. Asch wished to see how often the subject would go along with the majority's opinion by repeating the incorrect answer.

Even though the task was an extremely easy one, Asch found people conformed on approximately one third of the trials (36.8%). Nearly all of the subjects disagreed with the majority more frequently than they agreed, but more than 75% of the participants went along with the majority at least once during the study (Hodges & Geyer, 2006). Asch (1955, p. 32) concluded that "people submit uncritically and painlessly to external manipulation by suggestion."

Asch was surprised by these high rates of conformity; he expected most would resist the group pressure and make the correct choice. He expected more *independence* (or nonconformity or dissent). So he interviewed the participants following each session, asking them why they were willing to keep silent and not confront their mistaken group mates. Those interviews indicated that many of the participants knew that the group was mistaken, yet they decided to just go along because they did not want to seem out of step with the others, anger the experimenter, or appear stupid. This type of conformity is usually labeled *compliance* (or acquiescence). But others were not simply going along with the others, because they questioned the accuracy of their own judgments. These individuals were displaying *conversion* (or private acceptance or internalization), for their personal opinions changed in response to the social influence (Nail & MacDonald, 2007).

These different types of social responses correspond to the two types of influence Asch ingenuously combined in his study: *normative influence* and *informational influence* (Deutsch & Gerard, 1955; Kelley, 1952). Norms are the formal and informal standards for action in a given situation, so normative influence is said to occur when people tailor their actions and attitudes to match those standards. Most groups look favorably on people who act in ways that match the group's norms, so people conform to avoid the negative consequences that often result from nonconformity. But norms are not simply external constraints pressed on members by the group. Members internalize group standards; they accept the legitimacy of the established norms and they recognize the importance of supporting these norms. They conform, then, not only to avoid ostracism, ridicule, and punishment, but also because they feel personally compelled to live up to their own expectations. Normative influence accounts for the transmission of religious, economic, moral, political, and interpersonal beliefs across generations.

Informational influence occurs when group members use the responses of others in the group as a source of information. When an individual thinks that other people are responding rationally to a situation after weighting their options carefully, it is wise to use their choices as an informational resource (Cialdini, 2009). When choosing a restaurant, for example, most people assume that a popular restaurant serves better food than one that is unpopular (Venkatesh & Goyal, 1998). College students' alcohol consumption rates correspond to the amount of drinking that they think is typical on their particular campus, for they drink more or less depending on how much others drink (Miller & Prentice, 1996). Users of online social networking sites, such as Facebook, install applications to their pages if many other users have also installed these applications (Onnela & Reed-Tsochas, 2010). Behavioral economists call these shifts in the direction of more popular options behavioral cascades or herding, and underscore its rational basis (Raafat et al., 2009).

Dual-process models of influence suggest that informational influence is sustained by both direct and indirect cognitive processes (Crano & Seyranian, 2009; Martin & Hewstone, 2008). Direct processes (or central, systematic processes) entail a thoughtful analysis, or elaboration, of the issues at hand. Group members, confronted with an opinion that is different from their own, review the arguments, look for weaknesses, reexamine their own ideas on the topic, and revise their position if revision is warranted. Indirect processes (or peripheral, heuristic processes), in contrast, do not require very much mental effort or elaboration. Particularly when group members' cognitive resources are limited or when they are not motivated to do the cognitive work necessary to weigh the information available to them, group members will conform because they assume "none of us is as smart as all of us" (Maio & Haddock, 2007).

Situational Influences on Conformity

Social psychologists often distinguish between strong situations and weak situations. Strong situations are ones that are structured in such a way that they leave little opportunity for people to act in unusual or idiosyncratic ways. Weak situations, in contrast, do not pressure people to act as everyone else does, and so their actions in such settings tend to be shaped more by their personal proclivities rather than by social constraints (Mischel, 1977). The pressure to conform, then, waxes and wanes across social settings. Some situational factors undercut group members' capacity to resist the group—for example, accountability, commitment to the group, and the difficulty of the task—whereas others encourage individuality and dissent (Cialdini & Goldstein, 2004; Cialdini & Trost, 1998).

Unanimity and Support

Asch (1955), in his initial work, studied people's reactions to a strong situation that made dissent very difficult. Each participant was the only dissenter in the group, and so had no ally to support him and his choice. When Asch modified his procedures by arranging for one of the confederates to disagree with the others, thereby breaking the group's consensus on a solution, conformity rates dropped to one fourth their previous levels. Even an inaccurate ally helped subjects withstand conformity pressures, as was the case when one of the confederates disagreed with the majority but still gave an incorrect answer. Another dissenting voice breaks the unanimity of the majority and reduces the risk of standing apart from the group as a solo (Sabini, Garvey, & Hall, 2001).

Group Size

Asch (1955) studied the relationship between group size and conformity by carrying out his line-judgment task with groups that varied in size from 2 to 17 members. He found that increasing the size of the majority increases its influence, but only up to a point. Subjects conformed on 3.6% of the trials when one other person disagreed with them, on 13.6% of the trials when facing two others, and a majority of three increased conformity to 31.8%. Adding even more sources of influence beyond three increased conformity to some extent, but even a majority of 16 did not raise conformity appreciably above the 31.8% level achieved with three people against one.

Bond (2005), in a meta-analytic review of studies that used Asch's task, found that when individuals state their opinions publicly, Asch's pattern is replicated: a relatively steep increase in conformity that asymptotes when one person faces a unanimous three-person majority. If, however, the other group members express their opinions publicly but the subject's response is kept private, then conformity decreases in larger groups. In such cases individuals suspect that the other group members are conforming to the bad decision offered by the first few responders, and anonymity frees them from having to follow

their example. But when individuals believe that the other group members reached their conclusions independently of one another, then their influence increases (slightly) as the number of sources increases (Wilder, 1977).

Social Impact

Social impact theory, developed by Latané (1981) and his colleagues, posits that the magnitude of social influence depends on number of source present, but also the strength and the immediacy of these sources. This theory draws on a basic law of psychophysical processes, which states that increasing the intensity of a stimulus increases the intensity of the psychological experience of that stimulus, but at an ever-decreasing rate. Hence, as Asch found, conformity pressure does not increase at a constant rate as more people unite in opposition to the individual, but instead each new members' influence is less and less; adding one person to two-person group has more impact than the 100th person added to a group of 99. Influence, however, also depends on who is present in the group, their level of skill, how near they are to one another spatially and temporally, and the presence of any barriers that influence how they communicate (Latané & Wolf, 1981; Nowak, Vallacher, & Miller, 2003). Latané and his colleagues have found support for the theory across a range of influence and performance settings. For example, their research suggests that people experience elevated levels of nervousness when performing for an audience of experts and when immediacy is increased by focusing the audience's attention on individual performers (Jackson & Latané, 1981; Latané & Harkins, 1976). They also found that when individuals were motivated to reach consensus on an issue their impact depended on the geometric configuration of the space they occupied: Close neighbors frequently agreed with each other, but those located further away (in the virtual space) were less likely to reach mutual agreement (Latané & L'Herrou, 1996).

Situational Cues

In many cases conformity is the external manifestation of automatic cognitive processes. Unlike controlled cognitive processes, which are regulated by the individual and so are initiated, monitored, and terminated at will, automatic cognitive processes are rapid, autonomous, effortless, and unintentional, and they operate outside of awareness (Bargh, 1990). These automatic processes are often instantiated by situational cues, called *primes*, that the individual may not notice, but nonetheless are causing them to react in a particular way. When, for example, one person adopts a particular nonverbal stance, such as crossing his or her arms, others nearby often mimic that display, but without realizing they are doing so (Chartrand & Bargh, 1999). Similarly, one person laughing in an audience acts as a situational prime that triggers laughter in others, as do many forms of emotional expression (Anderson, Keltner, & Oliver, 2003). Posted signs displaying rules and regulations—even if not explicitly noted by the individual—may increase conformity by activating preexisting cognitive structures pertaining to that particular situation (Aarts & Dijksterhuis, 2003).

Conformity, therefore, becomes more likely when cues in the situation prime a response that is consistent with prevailing group or cultural norms. Cialdini and his colleagues demonstrated this process by priming norms pertaining to littering (Cialdini, Kallgren, & Reno, 1991; Cialdini, Reno, & Kallgren, 1990). They deliberately created littered areas and unlittered areas, and then provided passersby with handbills that they would be tempted to dispose of carelessly. More people littered when there was already litter on the ground, particularly if they saw someone else (a member of the research team) also litter. In a second study, the researchers altered the message on the handbills, to prime or not prime a pro-environmental response. If the handbill's message stated "Please do not litter," very few people dropped it to the ground, whereas more did so if the message was a reminder to support a local museum. In a third study, the researchers manipulated the salience of norms about littering across three conditions. In one condition when participants passed by, the confederate carefully dropped a bag of trash into a garbage can. In a second condition the confederate picked up a piece of litter from the ground and disposed of it in the garbage can when the subject walked by. In the control condition, the confederate merely walked by the participant. As they predicted, no one who saw the confederate pick up trash littered, and people who saw others carefully throw away their trash were also less likely to litter themselves (Reno, Cialdini, & Kallgren, 1993, Study 3). These findings highlight the relative power of descriptive and injunctive norms. Descriptive norms describe what most people do, feel, or think in a particular situation. An area that is covered in litter implies that most people do not dispose of their trash appropriately. Injunctive norms, in contrast, define how people *ought* to act, feel, and think. People who violate descriptive norms are thought to be unusual, but people who do not conform to injunctive norms are evaluated negatively and are likely to be punished in some way. Confederates who threw away their trash primed a descriptive norm, but confederates who

picked up trash primed an injunctive norm (Cialdini et al., 1990; Miller & Prentice, 1996).

Cialdini (2003) describes well-intentioned community interventions that have mistakenly primed descriptive norms instead of injunctive ones—with unintended consequences. Public service announcements, such as the well-regarded "Iron Eyes Cody" spot that featured a Native American canoeing sadly through the littered streams of America, were created to convince the audience that littering is harmful to the environment, but at the same time it suggested that most people litter. Cialdini (2003) finds that such messages increase, rather than decrease, negative environmental actions. For example, in one study he sought to reduce the amount of petrified wood stolen by visitors to Arizona's Petrified Forest National Park. Significantly more visitors (7.9%) stole wood when they were warned, "Many past visitors have removed petrified wood from the Park, changing the natural state of the Petrified Forest," rather than "Please don't remove the petrified wood from the Park, in order to preserve the natural state of the Petrified Forest." Similarly, when households were given feedback about the average use of electricity by others in their neighborhood, residents who were above average in their consumption of electricity subsequently reduced their use, but those residents who discovered they were using less electricity than others increased their usage: Adding an injunctive element to the feedback, such as a frowny emoticon face, reduced this backlash (Schultz, Nolan, Cialdini, Goldstein, & Griskevicius, 2007).

Online Groups

Asch's procedure required participants announce their choice publicly during the face-to-face group session. In contrast, *online groups* use various computer-based technologies to communicate synchronously while remaining spatially separate. Yet, despite this lower level of social presence members of online groups display dynamics that are similar to those of offline groups. Online groups are structured groups, complete with norms, roles, and intermember relations and members identify strongly with their groups (Tanis & Postmes, 2005). In consequence, conformity rates in online groups are as high, if not higher, than those displayed by members of face-to-face, *offline groups* (Spears, Lea, & Postmes, 2007).

Individual Differences in Conformity

Just as conformity varies across situations, it also varies across individuals. Some people are more likely to conform than are others, depending on such factors as personality traits, sex, and culture of origin.

The Conforming Personality

Crutchfield (1955) carried out some of the earliest systematic studies of individual differences in conformity and nonconformity using a special procedure now known as the Crutchfield Apparatus. The subjects sat in individual cubicles containing a series of response switches and lights. When asked a multiple-choice type question—such as "Which one of the lines (A, B, or C) is the same length as the standard line?"—they answered by flipping the appropriate switch. The subjects thought that their answers were being transmitted to the experimenter and the other subjects, but in actuality the experimenter tested for conformity by telling each subject to answer last and substituting incorrect responses on critical trials.

Crutchfield concluded that some people were conformists, for they bent to social influence pressures across a range of situations. They were high in "respect to authority, submissive, compliant, and overly accepting" (1955, p. 194). Other people, in contrast, were independent types: they were "self reliant; independent in judgment; and able to think for" themselves. Other studies conducted in the years since Crutchfield's completed his work support his findings, for those who tend to conform are often authoritarians: Their conventionality, conservative values, and unwillingness to confront authority increase their willingness to accept the majority's opinion (Altemeyer, 1988). Conformists also tend to be people who let the situation and other people influence their perceptions, opinions, and outlooks. People who rely on situational cues when making perceptual judgments (field dependents), whose attention is focused more on themselves rather than others (self-consciousness individuals), and those who tend to monitor and regulate their actions to fit situations (self-monitors) are the ones who are more likely to make certain their actions match the group's standards. In general, people who show a greater interest in other people are more likely to conform more than others. They are higher in the need for social approval, more interpersonally oriented, and more fearful of social rejection (Bornstein, 1992). People who lack confidence, perhaps because they have low self-esteem or are uncertain of their competence, are more likely to conform (see Forsyth, 2010, for a review).

Men, Women, and Conformity

Meta-analytic reviews of studies of social influence that have included both women and men suggest women conform more than men, but only to a small degree and in specific kinds of situations—when, for example, in face-to-face groups discussing nonpersonal issues or stating opinions aloud (Bond & Smith, 1996; Leaper & Ayres, 2007). Eagly's social role theory traces these sex differences to sex-role stereotypes and traditions pertaining to agreement and independence. Women, for example, who adopt a traditional feminine sex role are more likely to conform than men and women who enact a less feminine or more masculine sex role, for femininity is traditionally associated with building relationships, seeking unity, and expressing support for others' views. Men, in contrast, may use dissent to compete with others in the group whereas women, instead of stressing their points of disagreement, seek consensus and cohesion (Eagly, 1987; Eagly & Carli, 1981).

Conformity Across Cultures and Eras

Conformity, as a process, is not unique to any particular cultural context or era. Asch's line-judging task has been used to study the reactions of people in dozens of different countries, and the results are consistent with those reported by Asch: People tend to conform, at surprisingly high rates, to the inaccurate choices of their fellow group members. Bond and Smith (1996), in a meta-analytic survey of those studies, concluded that Asch may actually have underestimated conformity by studying people living in the United States, which is a relatively individualistic culture. Such cultures tend to place the individual above the collective, whereas collectivistic societies stress shared goals and interdependence. As a result, people tend to conform more in collectivistic cultures, especially when the sources of influence are family members or friends. Bond and Smith (1996) also found, however, that more recently conducted studies report lower rates of conformity, suggesting that younger generations may be more resistant to influence.

Minority Influence

As consensus on an issue builds, the majority usually pressures any dissenters to join the majority by withdrawing their objections to the majority's choice. In juries, for example, the lone holdout who opposes all the other jurors usually succumbs to conformity pressure. When a majority of the jurors initially think the defendant is guilty, the jury returns a verdict of guilt 90% of the time. Most groups implicitly assume the matter is settled as soon as a significant majority of the members favor an opinion or decision (Hastie, Penrod, & Pennington, 1983).

In some cases, however, those who disagree with the majority of the group members succeed in influencing the majority—particularly when they make no concessions to the majority and maintain their own position consistently. Moscovici and his colleagues, in a study of such *minority influence*, reversed the usual Asch situation by putting a single dissenting confederate into a group of otherwise unanimous individuals. The confederate made no claim to special expertise, skill, or insight, but he or she never wavered during the discussion. Although minorities rarely convinced the majority during that session, on subsequent sessions the majority often moved in the direction advocated by the minority (e.g., Moscovici, 1985; Moscovici & Personnaz, 1980).

Conversion Theory

Moscovici's (1994) conversion theory argues that a minority's influence is different, in kind, than the majority's influence. Majorities use social pressure to convince group members to comply, and so some may publicly agree with the majority but privately they still disagree. In some cases, too, people do not think very much about an issue once they discover where most people stand—they just adopt that position as their own, without considering alternatives. In consequence, the change a majority generates sometimes dissipates over time and once the group disbands.

Minorities, in contrast, capture the group's attention, shake the confidence of the majority, and force the group to seek out new information about the situation. This conversion process takes longer than the compliance process, and so the effects of a minority on the majority sometimes do not emerge until the group has completed its initial deliberations and moved on to another task. Moreover, because this change comes about through subtle interpersonal processes rather than blatant social pressuring, Moscovici argues that the change is more permanent: true conversion to the minority's position rather than mere compliance with someone else's view (Nemeth, 1986). When majorities find that someone in their midst disagrees with the dominant view, they spend time critically examining the evidence, and in consequence process the issue more fully, causing group members to reinterpret or cognitively restructure key aspects of the issue (Martin & Hewstone, 2008).

Subsequent studies have confirmed the importance of behavioral consistency on the part of the minority, but they also suggest that minorities will not be influential if the majority perceives them to be outsiders—members of the out-group rather than the ingroup (Crano & Seyranian,

2009). An influential minority avoids threatening the integrity of the group itself. Many groups will tolerate debate and disagreement, but if the dissent creates deep divisions the majority may take steps to quash the minority or expel its members from the group. If a group is just a loose conglomeration of individuals with no clear sense of identity, then members are not threatened by disagreement. But if the group members identify strongly with their group, and they feel that the dissenter is undermining its collective identity, they are more likely to respond negatively if other members begin to take a minority's arguments seriously (Prislin, Brewer, & Wilson, 2002). In such cases, individuals who are not even members of the group may become stronger sources of influence relative to in-group members who challenge the group's unity (Phillips, 2003).

Minorities must also walk the line between appearing self-assured versus unreasonable. They are particularly influential if they offer coherent, compelling arguments that contradict the majority's position and if they seem confident in their facts and interpretations (Crano & Seyranian, 2009). As Hollander's (2006) concept of idiosyncrasy credits suggests, some successful dissenters first demonstrate their willingness to cooperate with others before challenging the majority. This initial conformity increases influencers' status within the group (their so-called idiosyncrasy credits) so that they can later take an unpopular position without fear of recrimination. Expectations states theory further suggests that early conformity must be coupled with both a record of achievement in the task domain as well as evidence of a group-oriented, rather than individualistic, motivation before the group member can influence others by expressing a moderate level of nonconformity to positions taken by the group's majority (Ridgeway, 1978, 2006).

Dynamic Social Impact Theory

Social psychological studies of conformity suggest that groups require both conformity and disagreement if they are to endure. Majority influence ensures the continuation of a group's traditions and outlook, for it requires group members recognize the wisdom of the collective and conform to its choices. Minority influence prompts the group to reexamine and possibly revise its position. Social influence, then, is not unidirectional, but a mutual process, as the majority influences the minority and the minority influences the majority.

Dynamic social impact theory, developed by Latané, Harton, Nowak, Vallacher, and their colleagues, describes the processes underlying this give-and-take between various individuals, factions, and pluralities within social groups. Social impact theory suggested that influence varies depending on the strength, immediacy, number of sources present in the situation. Dynamic social impact theory expands this analysis by describing four basic tendencies that regulate the changes that occur in groups over time: consolidation, clustering, correlation, and continuing diversity (Harton & Bullock, 2007; Latané, 1996; Vallacher & Nowak, 2007). Groups tend to be homophilous, for group members are usually similar to one another in terms of such qualities as ethnicity, age, attitudes, or values (McPherson, Smith-Lovin, & Cook, 2001). Social influence, however, leads to the consolidation of those similarities, as the opinions held by a majority of the group spread throughout the group and dissenting members either leave the group or change their position to match that of the majority. Clustering results because individuals who live or work in close proximity to one another influence each other at higher rates than individuals who are not co-located. This process was identified as early as 1950 by Festinger, Schachter, and Back in their study of attitude change among residents of two sets of housing units on a college campus. Correlation also contributes the increasing similarity of group members to one another. Cullum and Harton (2007), for example, confirmed that over time group members' opinions on a variety of issues—even ones that are not discussed openly in the group—converge, so that their opinions become correlated. Despite these pressures toward uniformity, diversity continues in the groups as individuals who disagree with the majority tend to cluster in subgroups, and use these associations to withstand the pressure brought by the majority.

Consequences of Conformity

Human groups could not form, remain intact, and achieve their goals if their members did not continually, and successfully, influence one another. Groups require coordinated action and conformity is the means to achieve that coordination. This section concludes the analysis of conformity in groups by considering its impact on such related group processes as cohesion, inclusion, and decision making.

Cohesion and Conformity

Pressures to conform increase as groups become more cohesive, where cohesion is defined as the strength of the bonds linking individuals to and in the group. Resisting social influence is difficult in groups, but members of

highly cohesive groups are particularly likely to avoid disagreement. Anecdotal accounts of highly cohesive groups—military squads, adolescent peer groups, sports teams, fraternities and sororities, and cults—often describe the strong pressures that these groups put on their members. Crandall (1988), for example, in a study of sororities found that when women joined these highly cohesive groups, the women conformed to group norms pertaining to dieting and weight regulation, and in so doing developed eating disorders. Giordano (2003) traced drug use and illegal activities of adolescents back to conformity pressures in their peer groups. Sports teams, if highly cohesive, may require complete conformity from members (Prapavessis & Carron, 1997). Members of work teams that have established a norm of high productivity are very industrious, but productivity is uniformly low in cohesive work teams with norms that sustain idleness rather than production (Seashore, 1954). When high cohesion combines with high levels of conformity such negative group processes as outgroup rejection, conflict and hostility, and scapegoating become more likely (French, 1941).

Faulty Decision Making

Many decisions are made by groups, rather than individuals, and conformity pressures can influence the wisdom of group's choices. Rather than independently reviewing evidence and then reaching a conclusion, people reflexively moderate their own position on an issue so that it is not too different from the position taken by others. Unfortunately, members' samplings of others opinions is not systematic or objective. They oversample, for example, the opinions of those in their own group rather than people outside of their group (Denrell & Le Mens, 2007). If they happen to interact more frequently with some group members rather than others, in time the opinions of those more frequent contacts will come to define their inferences about the group's overall position on issues—even if they are only a small sample of the group (Weaver, Garcia, Schwarz, & Miller, 2007). In consequence, both members of the majority and the minority display a false consensus effect: They assume that there is more support for their position than there actually is (Biernat & Eidelman, 2007).

This natural tendency to seek support for one's views frequently causes groups to display the shared information bias: spending more time discussing details that two or more group members know in common rather than unshared information. If, for example, a group is working on a problem where the shared information suggests that Alternative A is correct, but the unshared information favors Alternative B, then the group will only discover this so-called *hidden profile* if it discusses the unshared information (Stasser, 1992; Wittenbaum, Hollingshead, & Botero, 2004). Studies suggest groups can control this bias if a leader guides the discussion effectively (Larson, Christensen, Abbott, & Franz, 1996), by using an advocacy approach rather than general discussion (Greitemeyer, Schulz-Hardt, Brodbeck, & Frey, 2006), and by emphasizing the importance of dissent (Klocke, 2007).

Groupthink

Janis's studies of decision-making groups suggest that, in some cases, the members of highly cohesive groups become so concerned with conforming to the group's standards that they experience what he calls *groupthink*: "a mode of thinking that people engage in when they are deeply involved in a cohesive in group, when the members' strivings for unanimity override their motivation to realistically appraise alternative courses of action" (1982, p. 9). In groupthink situations, pressures to conform become overwhelming as each member experiences a strong reluctance to disagree with others. Even members who question the group's decision privately engage in self-censorship by hiding their misgivings when they discuss the issue openly. Group members also become increasingly intolerant of dissent. Some, Janis suggests, became "mindguards" who shield the group from information that will shake the members' confidence in themselves or their leaders. Self-censorship, pressuring dissenters, and mindguarding combine to create a false feeling of unanimity. Every person may privately disagree with what is occurring in the group, yet publicly everyone expresses total agreement with the group's policies. Janis suggests the best way to avoid groupthink is to limit premature concurrence seeking, correct misperceptions and errors, and improve the group's decisional methods.

Baron's (2005) ubiquity model of groupthink, like Janis's theory, recognizes that members of groups often strive for consensus, limit dissent, ridicule the outgroup, and misjudge their own group's competence. Baron, however, suggests that these qualities are common in most group performance situations, but that they undermine performance only if (a) the group is facing a situation where failure will significantly threaten members' social identity; (b) the group's norms constrains members' openness to alternatives; and (c) members lack self-confidence. In such cases members are likely to rush to make judgments on the basis of insufficient information.

The Bystander Effect

Studies of individuals who fail to respond to emergencies suggest that this bystander effect is due, in part, to conformity. Latané and Darley (1970), in their original work, suggested that people are less responsive when in groups because they feel reduced responsibility for helping. Social influence processes, however, also play a role in limiting helping in emergencies. First, informational influence prompts individuals to rely on the actions of the other bystanders to guide their interpretation of the situation. Unfortunately, because emergencies are sometimes ambiguous, each unresponsive bystander tells the next bystander that no help is needed. In situations that are obviously emergencies the bystander effect disappears (Clark & Word, 1974). Second, normative influence does not enjoin bystanders to help. Instead, bystanders worry about breaking norms of civil inattention. Most people prefer to appear poised and normal in social settings, and actively avoid doing anything that may lead to embarrassment. In an ambiguous emergency, people fear that they look foolish if they offer assistance to someone who does not need it, so they look the other way rather than get involved.

Psychological Reactions to Dissent

People sometimes feel very good when they disagree with their group—particularly if their dissent, while running counter to the group's norms, matches the group's aspirations or ambitions. These "different, but good" nonconformists tend to be quite vocal and are proud of their dissent (Miller & Morrison, 2009; Morrison & Miller, 2008). As deviance regulation theory explains, the need to fit in with the group is a powerful one, but so is the need to maintain one's autonomy and individuality. Hence, individuals sometimes strive to be individualists who do not follow the groups norms, but in ways that will not earn social rejection. They "try to 'stick out' from others in good ways and not in bad ways" (Blanton & Christie, 2003, p. 115).

Such cases are the exception, however, for most people report experiencing strong, negative emotional reactions when they find they have violated a group's standards. In one study participants were told to violate an everyday social norm regulating seat selection on a subway (Milgram, 1992). Even though they knew they were carrying out the action deliberately, and that they would experience no tangible consequences by breaking this informal social rule, they nonetheless reported the experience to be a wrenching one that caused them considerable anxiety, tension, and embarrassment.

Other research suggests that acting in ways that are discrepant from the group's standards may trigger a psychological condition akin to cognitive dissonance. Cognitive dissonance, as defined by Festinger (1957), occurs when individuals simultaneously hold two or more inconsistent cognitions, but researchers have confirmed that people also experience dissonance when they discover that they do not agree with other group members (Glasford, Pratto, & Dovidio, 2008; Matz & Wood, 2005). Additional evidence of the noxiousness of finding oneself in violation of a group's norms comes from studies of brain activity during dissent with others. When researchers used functional magnetic resonance imaging (fMRI) technology to study neuronal activity of participants in an Asch-like situation they found that agreement with a group—even an incorrect one—stimulated activity in the information processing areas of the brain. But when they disagreed with the group, portions of the brain that are responsible for strong emotional responses (the amygdala) showed evidence of high neuronal activity (Berns et al., 2005).

Ostracism and Coercion

Even though most groups, organizations, and cultures explicitly claim to value nonconformity and innovation, people who disagree consistently with the group are usually punished more than they are lauded. Schachter (1951) confirmed the interpersonal consequences of refusal to conform in groups by covertly inserting three kinds of confederates in a number of all-male discussion groups: the deviant who was trained to disagree with the majority; the slider who disagreed at the start of the discussion but gradually came to agreed with the majority; and the mode who consistently agreed with the majority. When the group members later rated each other in terms of liking, Schachter found that the deviant was viewed negatively by the group, and that many suggested the deviant's membership be terminated. Schachter also tracked the number of times each subject spoke to each confederate, and those measures revealed that the group consistently pressured the deviant throughout the group session—except in cases where the group was highly cohesive and discussing a topic that was very relevant to the group's purposes. The majority of the members of these groups stopped speaking to the deviant altogether (Levine, 1980).

The consequences of ostracism are so substantial and so negative that most individuals will conform rather than risk possible ostracism for dissent. As Williams (2007) reports, ostracism is associated with such negative feelings as frustration, anxiety, nervousness, and loneliness. Ostracized people evidence physiological signs of stress, including elevated blood pressure and cortisol levels (a stress-related hormone). Functional magnetic resonance imaging (fMRI) research even suggests that the pain of exclusion is neurologically similar to pain caused by physical injury (Eisenberger, Lieberman, & Williams, 2003; MacDonald & Leary, 2005).

COMPLIANCE

People often change their overtly expressed beliefs and behaviors in response to the intervention of others. The motorist who usually drives over the speed limit slows after seeing a police officer on the highway shoulder, the office manager who decides to replace the company's photocopying machine after listening to a creative, fast-paced sales pitch, and the consumer who impulsively buys a product that is described as "new and improved" illustrate compliance: public acquiesce that is (a) relatively transitory, (b) not driven by (and in some cases even inconsistent with) the individual's privately held beliefs, and (c) a response to a deliberate and/or orchestrated intervention by another person or persons (Cialdini & Griskevicius, 2010).

Compliance Tactics

In many situations—negotiations, business deals, board meetings, planning sessions, sales pitches, and so on—interacting individuals use various methods to induce others to change their position, outlook, or action and adopt one that the influencer favors. Although the naturally emerging conformity pressures present in the group context generate change, influencers supplement these processes by complaining, building coalitions, exchanging favors, making demands, manipulating moods, persisting, enacting fait accomplis, manipulations, supplications, evasion, lying, and so on (Falbo, 1977; Yukl, 2006).

A *compliance tactic*, as defined by Pratkanis (2007b, p. 17), is a "noncoercive technique, device, procedure, or manipulation capable of creating or changing the belief or behavior of a target of the influence attempt," where noncoercive suggests methods that are subtle and indirect rather than forceful or threatening. These tactics, Pratkanis suggests, work by creating a favorable cognitive response in the targets of the influence attempt, so that their thoughts when they consider the proposed course of action are positive ones, and any negative thoughts that might warn them against following the suggestion are disrupted. Falbo (1977; Falbo & Peplau, 1980), in studies that compared these various strategies, identified two key aspects that distinguished among the myriad methods of influence: rationality and directness. First, many tactics make use of reason, argument, and logic to influence (e.g., claiming expertise, persistence, restatement of arguments, bargaining, and compromise) whereas others do not require higher-order cognitive responses (e.g., hinting, mood manipulation, evasion). Second, whereas some tactics are direct ones whereby the influencer's goals are overt and acknowledged (e.g., assertion, threats, fait accompli), indirect tactics disguise the influencer's goals and intentions from the target of the influence (e.g., deceit, thought manipulation, evasion). Kipnis (1984) suggests yet a third way in which these tactics differ. In his view, some tactics are strong ones, in that they are more likely to generate influence, whereas others are relatively weak.

People use different tactics depending on the situation they face. When dealing with subordinates, for example, people vary their tactics, but when working with superiors they rely more on rational methods such as persuasion and discussion. When people are uncertain of their authority in the situation, they tend to use indirect tactics but when empowered they rely more on direct, strong tactics. A leader, for example, will more likely use demands, threats, or promises when dealing with a subordinate, but coalition tactics when trying to influence a superior. Also, when the target of the influence resists, people shift to stronger and stronger tactics (see Kipnis, 1984, for a review).

Not everyone uses the full range of tactics. People who are very concerned with being accepted and liked by their fellow group members use more indirect and rational tactics than direct and nonrational strategies, but those who enjoy manipulating others instead use indirect and nonrational as opposed to direct and rational ones. Men use more of the tactics than women do, and they are the ones who are most likely to rely on the more direct strategies (Instone, Major, & Bunker, 1983). In general, people who use more rational methods of influence, such as reasoning, compromise, expertise, bargaining, or persuasion to influence others, are better liked than those who use less rational influence tactics, such as deceit, evasion, or threats (Falbo, 1977; Yukl, 2006).

Compliance Principles

The social psychologist Robert Cialdini, to better understand why people comply with requests they should refuse, studied individuals who used compliance tactics regularly and effectively: salespersons, recruiters to alternative religious movements, con artists, fundraisers, and telemarketers. The strategies these influence masters used, Cialdini concluded, were based on a small number of psychological principles that pushed people in the direction desired by the influencer, who then took advantage of that psychological momentum to lock the target into a new position (Cialdini, 2009; Cialdini & Griskevicius, 2010; Cialdini & Trost, 1998).

Reciprocity

Many compliance tactics take advantage of the norm of reciprocity, which enjoins people to give something back (to reciprocate) when another person gives them something. The principle suggests that individuals who receive something from another person—a gift, a favor, a reward, or even a smile—tend to feel obligated to give something back in return, even if the item that was received was unsolicited and not even desired. Across a number of studies, researchers have confirmed that people are more likely to comply with another person's request—to help with a task, to make a monetary donation to a charitable cause, to serve as a volunteer—if the person making the request previously did something that provided a benefit to the target of the request (e.g., Boster, Rodriguez, Cruz, & Marshall, 1995). Individuals who are negotiating a deal are more likely to offer a concession if the other party in the negotiation has previously offered one (e.g., Burger, 1986). Individuals will disclose personal information about themselves if the person they are talking to has already engaged in disclosure of personal information (Cunningham, Strassberg, & Haan, 1986). People are more likely to cooperate with another person if that person has acted in a cooperative, rather than competitive manner, in previous interactions (Axelrod, 1984). The norm of reciprocity's impact on behavior is moderated by such factors as the extent to which the recipients' actions are public or private ones, the value of initial bequest, and the extent to which the original gift or favor was thought to be motivated by manipulative motives, but reciprocity's consistent impact across most situations suggests an evolutionary basis: homo sapiens, as a gregarious species, is genetically ready to help those that have helped in the past (e.g., Whatley, Webster, Smith, & Rhodes, 1999).

Cialdini and his colleagues have found that one particular influence strategy, the *door-in-the-face technique*, capitalizes on a form of reciprocity they term *reciprocal concession*. The door-in-the-face technique involves following up a substantial request, which will in all certainty be refused, with a smaller request. When, for example, college students were asked if they would chaperon children on a trip to the zoo, about 17% agreed. Many more, however, said yes to this request if it was prefaced with a more substantial request that they had already declined. These subjects were asked if they would be willing to work with troubled youth for 2 years, once a week or more. The students refused this request, but then 50% agreed when asked, "Well, would you be willing to chaperon a group on a trip to the zoo?" (Cialdini et al., 1975).

The *that's-not-all technique* also takes advantage of the human tendency to pay back a favor or a concession. The method is based on the strategy used in commercials that advertise a product at a high price, but before the viewer can make a decision the announcer lowers the price or explains a free gift or product is included in the original purchase price. This tactic creates a sense of indebtedness in the receiver, who then feels compel to respond to the seller's generosity by making a purchase. Burger (1986; Burger, Reed, DeCesare, Rauner, & Rozolis, 1999) confirmed this tactic's effectiveness by offering passersby an item (cupcakes) for 75¢, but as the customers pondered the purchase the seller explained that the price included a small bag of cookies. Those customers assigned to a control condition were told, when they first inquired about price, that for 75¢ they would receive a cupcake and the cookies. Burger found that 74% of the people in his study purchased the cupcake when they received a bonus of the cookies, compared to only 40% in the control condition.

Consistency and Commitment

Many theorists believe that people have a powerful need to maintain consistency across their emotions, cognitions, and behaviors. Feelings should correspond to thoughts and actions, and cognitions and emotions should match behaviors. This consistency, however, exacts a cost, and this view is perhaps best elaborated in Festinger's (1957) theory of cognitive dissonance. That theory suggests that individuals will change their cognitions to match their actions and their emotions, for the experience of dissonance is unpleasant.

Several compliance tactics take advantage of the need for cognitive consistency. The *foot-in-the-door technique*, for example, is based on the commonsense recommendation of many salespersons: Before pressing customers to buy, make some small request of them that they cannot refuse. Then follow up the initial request with the real sales pitch. Freedman and Fraser (1966) tested this tactic's effectiveness by telephoning women who were homemakers and making a small request. The caller claimed he was a pollster for a public service publication, and asked the women who answered the phone if they would be

willing to take part in a short survey. Most women said they would, and then the caller asked them a few questions before thanking them for their participation. Three days later the researchers called back and explained that the study had been expanded, and that they would like to send a team to the woman's house to enumerate and classify all her household products. The five-man team must have the run of the house, so that they could go through all her cupboards and storage places, and the information they collected would be published in their report. Only 22.2% of the women who received only the second request agreed, but more than twice as many (52.8%) who participated in the initial survey agreed to the outrageous second request. Subsequent studies have confirmed the efficacy of two requests rather than one for increasing compliance, although such factors as the sex of the influencer and the amount of time that elapses between the two requests moderate the power of the foot-in-the-door method (Beaman, Cole, Preston, Klentz, & Steblay, 1983).

A related tactic, the *low-ball technique*, begins by extracting a commitment from a person, and only then revealing the extra costs associated with that commitment. A favorite ploy in automobile sales, the tactic begins when the seller offers the customer a bargain on a car. Once the customer agrees the salesperson reveals the hidden costs in a variety of ways (a change in the agreed-on value of the trade-in, processing fees, etc.). Cialdini, Cacioppo, Bassett, and Miller (1978) tested the method when scheduling subjects for research. They telephoned college students to ask if they would be interested in participating in an experiment on thinking processes for extra credit in their psychology class. In the control condition, before asking if the subject was willing to take part the caller admitted that the sessions were scheduled for 7 A.M. In the low-ball condition the researcher omitted this key piece of information until after the subject had agreed or refused to participate. Compliance was greater in the low-ball condition (56%) than in the control condition (31%), and the low-ball subjects were more likely than the controls to keep the appointment.

OBEDIENCE

Most human societies are hierarchical ones, with some individuals commanding more respect, resources, and status than others. When these individuals are recognized by others as legitimate authorities, their capacity to influence can reach extraordinary levels.

Obedience to Authority

Social psychologist Stanley Milgram (1963) investigated the power of authorities to influence followers in his experimental studies of obedience conducted in the early 1960s. The Milgram experiment created, in a laboratory setting, a situation in which a legitimate authority ordered subordinates to do something they would usually not do—in this case, significantly harm another person who was innocent of any wrongdoing.

The participants were mostly adult men who responded to an advertisement in the local newspaper. The experimenter who conducted the sessions was trained to act in an authoritative, imposing fashion: He explained what was required of each participant, assigned them their tasks and outlined their responsibilities, set up the equipment, answered all questions, and issued orders. Each session also included a second man who posed as another subject, but in actuality he was a confederate of the research team.

The experimenter told the two men that he was studying the effects of punishment on learning. One of the participants, he explained, would be chosen at random to act as the Teacher who would read a series of paired words (*blue box, nice day, wild day,* and so on) to the Learner, who was to memorize the pairings. After the learning phase, the Teacher would test the Learner's memory for the pairs, and punish any errors by giving the Learner an electric shock. Following a rigged drawing in which the true subject was always assigned to the role of the Teacher, the experimenter immobilized the Learner by strapping him into a chair; only his right hand was left free to press a response pad that would be used to signal answers. The experimenter also connected an electrode to the Learner, who asked if the shocks were dangerous. "Oh, no," said the experimenter, "although the shocks can be extremely painful, they cause no permanent tissue damage" (Milgram, 1974, p. 19).

The experimenter then seated the actual subject in an adjacent room in front of the supposed shock generator. This bogus machine featured a row of 30 electrical switches that would seemingly send a shock to the Learner. The shock level of the first switch on the left was 15 volts (v); the next switch was 30v, the next was 45v, and so on all the way up to 450 volts. Milgram also labeled the voltage levels from "Slight Shock" to "Danger: Severe Shock" and "XXX." The rest of the face of the shock generator was taken up by dials, lights, and meters that flickered whenever a switch was pressed. The machine looked realistic, but it did not deliver any shocks to the confederate in the adjacent room.

After the experimenter administered a sample shock of 45v to each subject (supposedly to give him an idea of the punishment magnitude), the Teacher read the word pairs to the Learner using an intercom system. He then initiated the memory test that involved reading one of the words of the pair, and waited for the Learner to indicate his response using the response pad. Subjects were to deliver one shock for each mistake and increase the voltage one step each time.

Milgram set the stage for the order-giving phase by having the Learner make mistakes deliberately. Although subjects punished that first mistake with just 15v, each subsequent failure was followed by a stronger shock. At the 300v level the Learner also began to protest the shocks by pounding on the wall, and after the next shock of 315v he stopped responding altogether. Most subjects assumed that the session was over at this point, but the experimenter told them to treat a failure to respond as a wrong answer and to continue the delivery of shock. If a subject initially refused, the experimenter would use a sequence of prods to goad them into action (Milgram, 1974, p. 21), such as "Please continue," "The experiment requires that you continue," and "You have no other choice; you must go on."

The situation was a realistic one for participants, and served as a laboratory analog to real-world settings where authorities give orders to subordinates. The experimenter acted with self-assurance and poise. He gave orders crisply, and if the subject questioned these orders the experimenter seemed surprised to have his authority challenged. Yet from the participants' point of view, this authority was requiring them to act in a way that might be harmful to another person. Milgram expected few would follow the authority's orders, and that most would refuse when the shocks reached the portion of the shock generator marked "Strong Shock" or when the confederate stopped responding (Elms, 1995). Yet, Milgram found that 65% of the participants he tested were fully obedient, delivering the maximum level of shock to the helpless victim.

Harm and Obedience

After Milgram tested the first group of subjects he realized that many were confused about what was happening to the learner. So, to make it clear that the learner did not wish to continue participation, Milgram added an explicit declaration of refusal. In the voice-feedback condition the learner's shouts of pain and pleas for release (carefully rehearsed and tape-recorded) could be heard clearly. These cues did not substantially reduce the level of obedience seen in the initial study, for fully 62.5% of the participants obeyed by giving what they thought was the 450v shock. Moreover, those who did disobey seemed to be responding more to the learner's demand to be released than to his suffering. At the 120 and 135v level the learner complained about the pain, but his suffering did not deter the teachers from their task. If participants were going to disobey, they usually stopped when the learner retracted his consent to continue. At the 150v mark the learner stated, explicitly, "I refuse to go on. Let me out." Those who passed that milestone usually continued to 450v, even though the learner screamed in pain until he eventually lapsed into silence (Packer, 2008). So Milgram increased the possibility of significant harm by suggesting that the Learner had a heart condition. When he was strapped into the chair he mentioned, so that the Teacher could hear, that he had been diagnosed with a heart condition several years earlier. Then, during the shock phase, the Learner screamed out that his heart was bothering him. Even though he stopped responding after 330v, 65% of the participants administered the 450v shock. Other variations, including moving the Learner closer to the Teacher, removing the authority from the room, requiring that the Teacher touch the Learner as he pressed his hand down on a shock plate, and moving the entire experiment out of the psychology department building and into a nondescript commercial research site lowered the level of obedience, but never eliminated it.

Obedience and Conformity

The subject in the original version of the experiment was alone when he faced the authority. In many cases individuals are part of a group when they work with an authority, so Milgram also studied how people reacted when they were part of a disobedient or obedient group. In these variations subjects tended act as others in their group acted. In one condition the subject still gave the shocks, but two other subjects (actually, confederates) helped with related tasks, such as reading the questions and giving feedback. When the two confederates refused to continue at 150v and 210v, respectively, only 10% the real subjects followed the authority's orders. In contrast, 92.5% of the participants were fully obedient when they played a subsidiary role in a group that obeyed the authority's orders.

The Agentic State

Milgram concluded that aspects of the situation, and not aspects of the specific individuals in the situation, created the high level of obedience he documented. Most of the participants did not want to follow the authority's orders, but they were no longer autonomous individuals acting as they personally wished. Instead, they became agents of a higher authority than themselves, and so experienced what Milgram (1974) called the *agentic state*. In the obedience situation their role as Teacher required paying attention to instructions, avoiding making mistakes, and carrying out the orders of the authority. Although they questioned the punishment of the Learner, most accepted the authority's definition of the situation as a nonharmful one. Also, they felt little responsibility for what happened to the Learner since they are only following orders. In the agentic state obedience was easy. Disobedience, in contrast, was achieved only with great difficulty and at a considerable psychological cost (Kelman & Hamilton, 1989).

Replications and Conclusions

Milgram's results sparked theoretical, methodological, and ethical controversies that are unresolved even today (Blass, 2000). Some researchers believed that the participants were not taken in by Milgram's subterfuge, even though fewer than 20% challenged the reality of the situation when interviewed (Elms, 1995). Others have suggested that Milgram's findings were specific to the era in which he worked (the 1960s), even though subsequent studies continue to document more obedience than disobedience. A replication conducted by Burger in California in 2006, for example, found that 70% of the men and women he studied were obedient—although for ethical reasons he did not pressure them to continue past the 150v level (Burger, 2009). Field and case studies of obedience in natural settings also support the Milgram's finding, and suggest that the levels of obedience that Milgram documented in his laboratory matches levels found in medical, military, organizational, and educational settings (Fiske & Berdahl, 2007; Fiske, Harris, & Cuddy, 2004).

Bases of Power

Milgram's experimenter was influential, but not uniquely so. Few interactions advance far before elements of power and influence come into play; the coach demanding obedience from a player, the teacher ordering students to stop texting on the cell phones, and the boss telling employees to do all they can to increase their unit's sales are all relying on social power as they influence others. A powerful person can control others' actions to promote his or her own goals "without their consent, against their will, or without their knowledge or understanding" (Buckley,

1967, p. 186). They can influence others even when these others actively resist that influence.

John French and Bertram Raven (1959), in their seminal analysis of the *bases of power,* theorized that people draw their power from five key sources: rewards, punishments, status, attraction, and expertise. Individuals who control these five bases can significantly influence other people's actions, thoughts, and emotions, whereas those who cannot control these bases are uninfluential.

Reward Power

The influencer who has the capacity to control the distribution of rewards given or offered to other people has reward power. These rewards are often tangible things that people need to survive or succeed in reaching their goals, such as a raise for a worker, good grades for students, promotions for the rising executive, or shelter for the homeless (Raven, 1992). In other instances, an individual may use intangible, personal types of rewards, such as approval, compliments, intimacy, agreement, and love, to influence other people. Ironically, rewards distributed by an authority are viewed as more valuable, and hence are more sought after, than the same reward when distributed by those with less power. The boss, by smiling, influences others in a more powerful way than does a smiling co-worker (Thye, 2000).

Coercive Power

The influencer who has the capacity to threaten and punish those who do not comply with his or her requests or demands has coercive power. Tangible threats and punishments include noxious physical events, such as abuse, fines, low grades, and firings, whereas intangible, social threats and punishments include disapproval, insults, and expressions of contempt. Some leaders, for example, rely heavily on coercive power to influence their followers, for they monitor their actions closely, penalize them for any mistakes, and generally subject them to constant criticism. Bullies, both in schools and in the workplace, also make use of coercive power to psychologically and physically harm relatively powerless targets. The experimenter in the Milgram study had little coercive power, but the participants perceived him to be threatening when he announced, "The experiment requires that you continue," and "You have no other choice, you must go on" (Blass, 2000).

Coercive power is most effective in changing behaviors when it is applied immediately and without emotion, but even then it tends to trigger negative side-effects. People who use coercive influence methods evoke negative emotions and actions in others, leading to increased hostility

and conflict. In consequence, authorities tend to avoid coercive influence, turning to it only as a last resort. Parents and teachers, for example, recognize that they have more authority in the home and in school, yet they may feel that their children and students do not recognize that authority. In consequence, such individuals often turn, in contentious situations, to the use coercive threats, punishments, and abuse more than do empowered authorities (Bugental & Lewis, 1999). In contrast, when individuals who are equal in coercive power interact, they often learn over time to avoid the use of their power (Lawler, Ford, & Blegen, 1988; Lawler & Yoon, 1996).

Legitimate Power

Unlike reward and coercive power, legitimate power stems from the influencer's recognized right to require and demand the performance of certain behaviors. The employer has a legitimate right to demand a certain level of productivity because of the contractual relationship between employer and employee. Similarly, the teacher can insist that students refrain from using cell phones in class if both the students and the teacher recognize that this demand is among the teacher's prerogatives. Like normative social influence—one of the causes of conformity examined earlier—legitimate power arises from an internalized sense of duty, loyalty, obedience, or normative obligation rather than a desire to gain rewards or avoid punishments. Many subjects in the Milgram study felt that when they agreed to participate in the study they had entered into an oral contract that obliged them to obey. In consequence, the experimenter had a legitimate right to control their actions and the learner had no right to quit the study. Unlike reward or coercive power, which diminishes when the authority loses control over the resources, authorities who achieve their position through methods that the group considers fair or proper generally find that their decisions are accepted, without resistance, by others in the group (Tyler, 2005).

Referent Power

Individuals who are well liked or admired possess referent power, for others look to them to define their beliefs and behavior. Bosses who enjoy the unswerving loyalty of their employees may be able to increase productivity simply by looking at a worker. Teachers who are high in referent power—the friendly teacher who all the students like and the tough but well-respected teacher—may be able to maintain discipline in their classes with little apparent effort because the students obey every request. The participants in Milgram's study respected the experimenter, because he worked at a major university (Yale) and was conducting scientific research. He was not particularly likable, however, so this source of referent power was likely relatively weak (Blass, 2000).

Leaders with high levels of referent power are often said to be charismatic. The sociologist Max Weber (1921/1946) used this term to describe the powerful emotional impact that some leaders have on their followers. Charismatic leaders were, in earlier times, thought to have special power that allowed them to perform extraordinary, miraculous feats, but Weber suggested that such leaders are successful if they only convince their followers that they have these powers. People sometimes refer to a charming leader as charismatic, but Weber reserved the term to describe the tremendous referent and legitimate power of leaders.

Expert Power

When followers believe that their leader is an expert—perhaps because of his or her special training, experience, or aptitude—then that leader enjoys expert power. An employee may refuse to follow the suggestion of a younger supervisor, but comply with the same request made by someone who is older and thought to be more experienced. Similarly, students may be reluctant to disagree with a teacher who seems to be an expert in his or her field. Milgram's experiment, because it involved electricity, placed many subjects at a disadvantage in terms of expertise, since few understood the effect of high voltage on humans. Because they considered the experimenter to be an expert, they believed him when he said, "Although the shocks may be painful, there is no permanent tissue damage" (Milgram, 1974, p. 21).

The Metamorphic Effects of Influence

Power and influence are adaptive processes that help groups deal with situations that vary from the cooperative and collaborative to those rife with conflict, tension, and animosity. As an evolutionary account of human gregariousness would suggest, people accept influence from others because such behavioral responses are adaptive (Keltner, Van Kleef, Chen, & Kraus, 2008). When people join forces to achieve an outcome, individuals must step forward and guide the group toward its goals and others must accept that guidance. So long as those in power are motivated by group-level goals and not seeking their own selfish ends, then those lower in the status hierarchy will benefit if they follow their leaders' orders (Tiedens, Unzueta, & Young, 2007). As Milgram (1974, p. 124)

explained, "Each member's acknowledgement of his place in the hierarchy stabilizes the pack."

Power, however, generates consequences for both those it influences and those who exercise it (Kipnis, 1974, 1984). Targets of influence attempts may conform and comply, change and adapt, or resist and rebel. Kelman (1958) identified three basic reactions that people display in response to influence. Much influence generates only compliance: The individual complies with the authority's demands, but does not personally agree with them. If the influencer is not present, the target disobeys. Influence can, however, cause people to identify so strongly with the influencer that they adopt his or her actions, characteristics, and attitudes. This identification, if prolonged and unrelenting, can lead to complete acceptance of the influencer's message: internalization. When internalization occurs, the individual "adopts the induced behavior because it is congruent with his value system" (Kelman, 1958, p. 53).

But authorities do not always succeed. In some cases the targets of influence do not obey, but instead escape the power holder's region of control or apply influence in return. They may, for example, form revolutionary coalitions that oppose the power holder's demands (Lawler, 1975). Rebellion also becomes more likely when the authority lacks referent power, relies on nonrational influence methods, and asks the group members to carry out unpleasant assignments (Yukl, Kim, & Falbe, 1996). Such conditions can generate reactance in group members. When reactance occurs, individuals strive to reassert their sense of freedom by reaffirming their autonomy (Brehm, 1976).

Power also influences those who wield it. When individuals acquire power, they tend to make use of it to influence others. And once power has been used to influence others, changes in power holders' perceptions of themselves and of the target of influence may also take place. These changes are described by Keltner and his colleagues in their approach/inhibition theory of power. This theory suggests that having power, using power, even thinking about power leads to psychological and interpersonal changes for both those who have power, and those who do not. Power tends to increase one's level of activity, augments energy levels, and increases awareness of environmental constraints and resources. The lack of power, in contrast, triggers inhibition and is associated with reaction, self-protection, vigilance, loss of motivation, and an overall reduction in activity. In consequence, powerful people tend to be active group members whose increased drive, energy, motivation, and emotion help the group overcome difficulties and reach its goals (Keltner, Gruenfeld, & Anderson, 2003; Keltner, Gruenfeld, Galinsky, & Kraus, 2010).

Power even alters cognitive functioning by enhancing executive functioning. People who feel powerful plan, make decisions, set goals, and monitor information flow more effectively and efficiently. When distracted by irrelevant information, powerful individuals make better decisions than less powerful group members, apparently because they can think in more abstract terms (Smith, Dijksterhuis, & Wigboldus, 2008). Powerful people also tend to be happier group members. Their moods are elevated, they report higher levels of such positive emotions such as happiness and satisfaction, and they are more optimistic and enthusiastic (Keltner et al., 2010).

But these positive consequences of power are counterbalanced by power's liabilities. Powerful people are proactive, but in some cases their actions are risky, inappropriate, or unethical ones. Simply being identified as the leader of a group prompts individuals to claim more than the average share of the resources, as members believe the leadership role entitles them to take more than others (De Cremer & Van Dijk, 2005). When individuals gain power, their self-evaluations grow more favorable, whereas their evaluations of others grow more negative. If they believe that they have a mandate from their group or organization, they may do things they are not empowered to do. When individuals feel powerful, they sometimes treat others unfairly, particularly if they are more self-centered rather than focused on the overall good of the group (Russell & Fiske, 2010). Eventually, too, power holders may become preoccupied with seeking power, driven by a strong motivation to acquire greater and greater levels of interpersonal influence (Winter, 2010).

The challenge, then, for those who are the recipients of influence: to recognize when the requests put to them are reasonable ones; motivated not by the selfishness of the source of influence but by a legitimate desire to promote the welfare and outcomes of the group and its members. Recipients of influence must know when to stand fast and not abandon their interests, outlooks, and appraisals and when they should accept the recommendations of others. The challenge for those who seek to influence others: to capitalize on the psychological and interpersonal gains that power yields, while at the same time resisting its corruptive effects. As Lord Acton so famously warned: "Power tends to corrupt, and absolute power corrupts absolutely."

CONCLUSIONS

Philosophers and political theorists since the time of Aristotle and Sun Tzu have puzzled over the way people are changed by other people, but only in the past century have those scholars been joined by social psychologists who took a scientific approach to the study of social influence. The theories they have developed, the studies they have carried out, and the results they have reported all combine to explain when and why people conform to match other's actions, comply with their requests, and obey their orders (even when they should resist). The study of social influence is a defining feature of the field of social psychology, for as Crano and Seyranian conclude, "Almost all that is considered worthy of study in social psychology is linked in one way or another to questions of influence" (2009, p. 354).

Social psychological studies of conformity, compliance, and obedience underscore the key role that social influence processes play in building and sustaining productive interpersonal relations. Although those who conform are sometimes thought to be weak or insecure and those who remain resolute even when challenged to change are lionized, conformity is required to insure the continued existence and functioning of groups over time. Although some people make use of compliance-gaining tactics to take advantage of others, compliance can as easily be used for a good cause as for a suspect one. And even though people sometimes fail to disobey the orders of a malevolent authority, the tendency to accept direction from a powerful person provides leaders with the means to organize their followers in the pursuit of commonly accepted joint outcomes. Social influence, then, is neither morally suspect nor commendable, but is instead a highly functional interpersonal process that provides humans with the means to coordinate their actions, to identify solutions to communal problems that require a collective response, and change, as needed, in response to new ideas and novel inputs from others. Homo sapiens, as a gregarious species, survives through the skilled use of, and judicious response to, social influence.

REFERENCES

Aarts, H., & Dijksterhuis, A. (2003). The silence of the library: Environment, situational norm, and social behavior. *Journal of Personality and Social Psychology, 84,* 18–28.

Allport, G. W. (1985). The historical background of modern social psychology. In G. Lindzey & E. Aronson (Eds.), *Handbook of social psychology* (Vol. 1, 3rd ed., pp. 1–46). New York, NY: Random House.

Allport, G. W., & Postman, L. (1947). *The psychology of rumor.* New York, NY: Holt.

Altemeyer, B. (1988). *Enemies of freedom: Understanding right-wing authoritarianism.* San Francisco, CA: Jossey-Bass.

Anderson, C., Keltner, D., & Oliver J. (2003). Emotional convergence between people over time. *Journal of Personality and Social Psychology, 84,* 1054–1068.

Asch, S. E. (1955). Opinions and social pressures. *Scientific American, 193,* 31–35.

Axelrod, R. (1984). *The evolution of cooperation.* New York, NY: Basic Books.

Bargh, J. A. (1990). Auto-motives: Preconscious determinants of social interaction. In E. T. Higgins & R. M. Sorrentino (Eds.), *Handbook of motivation and cognition: Foundations of social behavior* (Vol. 2, pp. 93–130). New York, NY: Guilford Press.

Baron, R. S. (2005). So right it's wrong: Groupthink and the ubiquitous nature of polarized group decision making. *Advances in Experimental Social Psychology, 37,* 219–253.

Barr, E. D. (1934). A psychological analysis of fashion motivation. *Archives of Psychology, 171,* 100.

Beaman, A. L., Cole, C. M., Preston, M., Klentz, B., & Steblay, N. M. (1983). Fifteen years of foot-in-the door research: A meta-analysis. *Personality and Social Psychology Bulletin, 9,* 181–196.

Berns, G. S., Chappelow, J., Zink, C. F., Pagnoni, G., Martin-Skurski, M. E., & Richards, J. (2005). Neurobiological correlates of social conformity and independence during mental rotation. *Biological Psychiatry, 58,* 245–253.

Biernat, M., & Eidelman, S. (2007). Standards. In A. W. Kruglanski & E. T. Higgins (Eds.), *Social psychology: Handbook of basic principles* (2nd ed., pp. 308–333). New York, NY: Guilford Press.

Blanton, H., & Christie, C. (2003). Deviance regulation: A theory of action and identity. *Review of General Psychology, 7,* 115–149.

Blass, T. (2000). The Milgram paradigm after 35 years: Some things we now know about obedience to authority. In T. Blass (Ed.), *Obedience to authority: Current perspectives on the Milgram paradigm* (pp. 35–59). Mahwah, NJ: Erlbaum.

Bond, R. (2005). Group size and conformity. *Group Processes & Intergroup Relations, 8,* 331–354.

Bond, R., & Smith, P. B. (1996). Culture and conformity: A meta-analysis of studies using Asch's (1952b, 1956) line judgment task. *Psychological Bulletin, 119,* 111–137.

Bornstein, R. F. (1992). The dependent personality: Developmental, social, and clinical perspectives. *Psychological Bulletin, 112,* 3–23.

Boster, F. J., Rodriguez, J. I., Cruz, M. G., & Marshall, L. (1995). The relative effectiveness of a direct request message and a pregiving message on friends and strangers. *Communication Research, 22,* 475–484.

Brehm, J. W. (1976). Responses to loss of freedom: A theory of psychological reactance. In J. W. Thibaut, J. T. Spence, & R. C. Carson (Eds.), *Contemporary topics in social psychology* (pp. 51–78). Morristown, NJ: General Learning Press.

Buckley, W. (1967). *Power.* Englewood Cliffs, NJ: Prentice-Hall.

Bugental, D. B., & Lewis, J. C. (1999). The paradoxical misuse of power by those who see themselves as powerless: How does it happen? *Journal of Social Issues, 55,* 51–64

Burger, J. M. (1986). Increasing compliance by improving the deal: The that's-not-all technique. *Journal of Personality and Social Psychology, 51,* 277–283.

Burger, J. M. (2009). Replicating Milgram: Would people still obey today? *American Psychologist, 64,* 1–11.

Burger, J. M., Reed, M., DeCesare, K., Rauner, S., & Rozolis, J. (1999). The effects of initial request size on compliance: More about the that's-not-all technique. *Basic and Applied Social Psychology, 21,* 243–249.

Chartrand, T. L., & Bargh, J. A. (1999). The chameleon effect: The perception–behavior link and social interaction. *Journal of Personality and Social Psychology, 76,* 893–910.

Cialdini, R. B. (2003). Crafting normative messages to protect the environment. *Current Directions in Psychological Science, 12,* 105–109.

Cialdini, R. B. (2009). *Influence: Science and practice* (6th ed.). Boston, MA: Allyn & Bacon.

Cialdini, R. B., Cacioppo, J. T., Bassett, R., & Miller, J. A. (1978). Low-ball procedure for producing compliance: Commitment then cost. *Journal of Personality and Social Psychology, 36,* 463–476.

Cialdini, R. B., & Goldstein, N. J. (2004). Social influence: Compliance and conformity. *Annual Review of Psychology, 55,* 591–621.

Cialdini, R. B., & Griskevicius, V. (2010). Social influence. In R. F. Baumeister & E. J. Finkel (Eds.), *Advanced social psychology: The state of the science* (pp. 385–417). New York, NY: Oxford University Press.

Cialdini, R. B., Kallgren, C. A., & Reno, R. R. (1991). A focus theory of normative conduct: A theoretical refinement and reevaluation of the role of norms in human behavior. *Advances in Experimental Social Psychology, 24,* 201–234.

Cialdini, R. B., Reno, R. R., & Kallgren, C. A. (1990). A focus theory of normative conduct: Recycling the concept of norms to reduce littering in public places. *Journal of Personality and Social Psychology, 58,* 1015–1026.

Cialdini, R. B., & Trost, M. R. (1998). Social influence: Social norms, conformity and compliance. In D. T. Gilbert, S. T. Fiske, & G. Lindzey (Eds.), *The handbook of social psychology* (Vol. 2, 4th ed., pp. 151–192). New York, NY: McGraw-Hill.

Cialdini, R. B., Vincent, J. E., Lewis, S. K., Catalan, J., Wheeler, D., & Darby, B. L. (1975). Reciprocal concessions procedure for inducing compliance: The door-in-the-face technique. *Journal of Personality and Social Psychology, 31,* 206–215.

Clark, R. D., & Word, L. E. (1974). Where is the apathetic bystander? Situational characteristics of the emergency. *Journal of Personality and Social Psychology, 29,* 279–287.

Crandall, C. S. (1988). Social contagion of binge eating. *Journal of Personality and Social Psychology, 55,* 588–598.

Crano, W. D., & Seyranian, V. (2009). How minorities prevail: The context/comparison-leniency contract model. *Journal of Social Issues, 65,* 335–363.

Crutchfield, R. S. (1955). Conformity and character. *American Psychologist, 10,* 191–198.

Cullum, J., & Harton, H. C. (2007). Cultural evolution: Interpersonal influence, issue importance, and the development of shared attitudes in college residence halls. *Personality and Social Psychology Bulletin, 33,* 1327–1339.

Cunningham, J. A., Strassberg, D. S., & Haan, B. (1986). Effects of intimacy and sex-role congruency of self-disclosure. *Journal of Social and Clinical Psychology, 4,* 393–401.

De Cremer, D., & Van Dijk, E. (2005). When and why leaders put themselves first: Leader behaviour in resource allocations as a function of feeling entitled. *European Journal of Social Psychology, 35,* 553–563.

Denrell, J., & Le Mens, G. (2007). Interdependent sampling and social influence. *Psychological Review, 114,* 398–422.

Deutsch, M., & Gerard, H. B. (1955). A study of normative and informational social influences upon individual judgment. *Journal of Abnormal and Social Psychology, 51,* 629–636.

DiFonzo, N., & Bordia, P. (2007). *Rumor psychology: Social and organizational approaches.* Washington, DC: American Psychological Association.

Eagly, A. H. (1987). *Sex differences in social behavior: A social-role interpretation.* Mahwah, NJ: Erlbaum.

Eagly, A. H., & Carli, L. L. (1981). Sex of researchers and sex-typed communications as determinants of sex differences in influenceability: A meta-analysis of social influence studies. *Psychological Bulletin, 90,* 1–20.

Eisenberger, N. I., Lieberman, M. D., & Williams, K. D. (2003). Does rejection hurt? An fMRI study of social exclusion. *Science, 302,* 290–292.

Elms, A. C. (1995). Obedience in retrospect. *Journal of Social Issues, 51,* 21–31.

Emerson, R. W. (2004). *Essays and poems by Ralph Waldo Emerson.* New York, NY: Barnes & Noble. (Originally published 1903)

Falbo, T. (1977). The multidimensional scaling of power strategies. *Journal of Personality and Social Psychology, 35,* 537–548.

Falbo, T., & Peplau, L. A. (1980). Power strategies in intimate relationships. *Journal of Personality and Social Psychology, 38,* 618–628.

Festinger, L. (1950). Informal social communication. *Psychological Review, 57,* 271–282.

Festinger, L. (1954). A theory of social comparison processes. *Human Relations, 7,* 117–140.

Festinger, L. (1957). *A theory of cognitive dissonance.* Stanford, CA: Stanford University Press.

Festinger, L., Schachter, S., & Back, K. (1950). *Social pressures in informal groups.* New York, NY: Harper.

Fiske, S. T., & Berdahl, J. (2007). Social power. In A. W. Kruglanski & E. T. Higgins (Eds.), *Social psychology: Handbook of basic principles* (2nd ed., pp. 678–692). New York, NY: Guilford Press.

Fiske, S. T., Harris, L. T., & Cuddy, A. J. C. (2004). Why ordinary people torture enemy prisoners. *Science, 306,* 1482–1483.

Forsyth, D. R. (2010). *Group dynamics* (5th ed.). Belmont, CA: Wadsworth Cengage Learning.

Fournial, H. (1892). *Essai sur la psychologie des foules. Considérations medico-judiciares sur les responsabilites collectives.* Lyon/Paris, France: Storck/Masson.

Freedman, J. L., & Fraser, S. C. (1966). Compliance without pressure: The foot-in-the-door technique. *Journal of Personality and Social Psychology, 4,* 195–202.

French, J. R. P. Jr. (1941). The disruption and cohesion of groups. *Journal of Abnormal and Social Psychology, 36,* 361–377.

French, J. R. P. Jr., & Raven, B. (1959). The bases of social power. In D. Cartwright (Ed.), *Studies in social power* (pp. 150–167). Ann Arbor, MI: Institute for Social Research.

Giordano, P. C. (2003). Relationships in adolescence. *Annual Review of Sociology, 29,* 257–281.

Glasford, D. E., Pratto, F., & Dovidio, J. F. (2008). Intragroup dissonance: Responses to ingroup violation of personal values. *Journal of Experimental Social Psychology, 44,* 1057–1064.

Greitemeyer, T., Schulz-Hardt, S., Brodbeck, F. C., & Frey, D. (2006). Information sampling and group decision making: The effects of an advocacy decision procedure and task experience. *Journal of Experimental Psychology: Applied, 12,* 31–42.

Harton, H. C., & Bullock, M. (2007). Dynamic social impact: A theory of the origins and evolution of culture. *Social and Personality Psychology Compass, 1,* 521–540.

Hastie, R., Penrod, S. D., & Pennington, N. (1983). *Inside the jury.* Boston, MA: Harvard University Press.

Hodges, B. H., & Geyer, A. L. (2006). A nonconformist account of the Asch experiments: Values, pragmatics, and moral dilemmas. *Personality and Social Psychology Review, 10,* 2–19.

Hollander, E. P. (2006). Influence processes in leadership-followership: Inclusion and the idiosyncrasy credit model. In D. A. Hantula (Ed.), *Advances in social & organizational psychology: A tribute to Ralph Rosnow* (pp. 293–312). Mahwah, NJ: Erlbaum.

Huddy, L. (2003). Group identity and political cohesion. In D. O. Sears, L. Huddy, & R. Jervis (Eds.), *Oxford handbook of political psychology* (pp. 511–558). New York, NY: Oxford University Press.

Hyman, H. (1942). The psychology of status. *Archives of Psychology, 38*(269).

Instone, D., Major, B., & Bunker, B. B. (1983). Gender, self confidence, and social influence strategies: An organizational simulation. *Journal of Personality and Social Psychology, 44,* 322–333.

Jackson, J. M., & Latané, B. (1981). All alone in front of all those people: Stage fright as a function of number and type of co-performers and audience. *Journal of Personality and Social Psychology, 40,* 73–85.

Jacobs, R. C., & Campbell, D. T. (1961). The perpetuation of an arbitrary tradition through several generations of a laboratory microculture. *The Journal of Abnormal and Social Psychology, 62,* 649–658.

Janis, I. L. (1982). *Groupthink: Psychological studies of policy decisions and fiascos* (2nd ed.). Boston, MA: Houghton Mifflin.

Kelley, H. H. (1952). Two functions of reference groups. In G. E. Swanson, T. M. Newcomb, & E. L. Hartley (Eds.), *Readings in social psychology* (2nd ed., pp. 410–414). New York, NY: Holt.

Kelman, H. C. (1958). Compliance, identification, and internalization: Three processes of attitude change. *Journal of Conflict Resolution, 2,* 51–60.

Kelman, H. C., & Hamilton, V. L. (1989). *Crimes of obedience: Toward a social psychology of authority and responsibility.* New Haven, CT: Yale University Press.

Keltner, D., Gruenfeld, D. H., & Anderson, C. (2003). Power, approach, and inhibition. *Psychological Review, 110,* 265–284.

Keltner, D., Gruenfeld, D., Galinsky, A., & Kraus, M. W. (2010). Paradoxes of power: Dynamics of the acquisition, experience, and social regulation of social power. In A. Guinote & T. K. Vescio (Eds.), *The social psychology of power* (pp. 177–208). New York, NY: Guilford Press.

Keltner, D., Van Kleef, G. A., Chen, S., & Kraus, M. W. (2008). A reciprocal influence model of social power: Emerging principles and lines of inquiry. *Advances in Experimental Social Psychology, 40,* 151–192.

Kipnis, D. (1974). *The powerholders.* Chicago, IL: University of Chicago Press.

Kipnis, D. (1984). The use of power in organizations and in interpersonal settings. *Applied Social Psychology Annual, 5,* 179–210.

Klocke, U. (2007). How to improve decision making in small groups: Effects of dissent and training interventions. *Small Group Research, 38,* 437–468.

Larson, J. R. Jr. (2010). *In search of synergy in small group performance* New York, NY: Psychology Press.

Larson, J. R. Jr., Christensen, C., & Abbott, A. S., & Franz, T. M. (1996). Diagnosing groups: Charting the flow of information in medical decision-making teams. *Journal of Personality and Social Psychology, 71,* 315–330.

Latané, B. (1981). The psychology of social impact. *American Psychologist, 36,* 343–356.

Latané, B. (1996). Strength from weakness: The fate of opinion minorities in spatially distributed groups. In E. Witte & J. Davis (Eds.), *Understanding group behavior: Consensual action by small groups* (Vol. 1, pp. 193–219). Mahwah, NJ: Erlbaum.

Latané, B., & Darley, J. M. (1970). *The unresponsive bystander: Why doesn't he help?* New York, NY: Appleton-Century-Crofts.

Latané, B., & Harkins, S. (1976). Cross-modality matches suggest anticipated stage fright a multiplicative power function of audience size and status. *Perception & Psychophysics, 20,* 482–488.

Latané, B., & L'Herrou, T. (1996). Spatial clustering in the conformity game: Dynamic social impact in electronic groups. *Journal of Personality and Social Psychology, 70,* 1218–1230.

Latané, B., & Wolf, S. (1981). The social impact of majorities and minorities. *Psychological Review, 88,* 438–453.

Lawler, E. J. (1975). An experimental study of factors affecting the mobilization of revolutionary coalitions. *Sociometry, 38,* 163–179.

Lawler, E. J., Ford, R. S., & Blegen, M. A. (1988). Coercive capability in conflict: A test of bilateral deterrence versus conflict spiral theory. *Social Psychology Quarterly, 51,* 93–107.

Lawler, E. J., & Yoon, J. (1996). Commitment in exchange relations: Test of a theory of relational cohesion. *American Sociological Review, 61,* 89–108.

Leaper, C., & Ayres, M. M. (2007). A meta-analytic review of gender variations in adults' language use: Talkativeness, affiliative speech, and assertive speech. *Personality and Social Psychology Review, 11,* 328–363.

Le Bon, G. (1960). *The crowd* (translation of *Psychologie des foules.*). New York, NY: Viking Press. (Original work published in 1895)

Levine, J. M. (1980). Reaction to opinion deviance in small groups. In P. B. Paulus (Ed.), *Psychology of group influence* (pp. 375–429). Mahwah, NJ: Erlbaum.

Lewin, K., Lippitt, R., & White, R. (1939). Patterns of aggressive behavior in experimentally created "social climates." *Journal of Social Psychology, 10,* 271–299.

MacDonald, G., & Leary, M. R. (2005). Why does social exclusion hurt? The relationship between social and physical pain. *Psychological Bulletin, 131,* 202–223.

MacKay, C. (1841). *Memoirs of extraordinary popular delusions.* London, UK: Bentley.

MacNeil, M. K., & Sherif, M. (1976). Norm change over subject generations as a function of arbitrariness of prescribed norms. *Journal of Personality and Social Psychology, 34,* 762–773.

Maio, G. R., & Haddock, G. (2007). Attitude change. In A. W. Kruglanski & E. T. Higgins (Eds.), *Social psychology: Handbook of basic principles* (2nd ed., pp. 565–586). New York, NY: Guilford Press.

Martin, R., & Hewstone, M. (2008). Majority versus minority influence, message processing and attitude change: The source-context-elaboration model. *Advances in Experimental Social Psychology, 40,* 237–326.

Matz, D. C., & Wood, W. (2005). Cognitive dissonance in groups: The consequences of disagreement. *Journal of Personality and Social Psychology, 88,* 22–37.

McDougall, W. (1920). *The group mind: A sketch of the principles of collective psychology with some attempt to apply them to the interpretation of national life and character.* New York, NY: Putnam.

McPherson, M., Smith-Lovin, L., & Cook, J. M. (2001). Birds of a feather: Homophily in social networks. *Annual Review of Sociology, 27,* 415–444.

Milgram, S. (1963). Behavioral study of obedience. *Journal of Abnormal and Social Psychology, 67,* 371–378.

Milgram, S. (1974). *Obedience to authority.* New York, NY: Harper & Row.

Milgram, S. (1992). *The individual in a social world: Essays and experiments* (2nd ed.). New York, NY: McGraw-Hill.

Miller, D. T., & Morrison, K. R. (2009). Expressing deviant opinions: Believing you are in the majority helps. *Journal of Experimental Social Psychology, 45,* 740–747.

Miller, D. T., & Prentice, D. A. (1996). The construction of social norms and standards. In E. T. Higgins & A. W. Kruglanski (Eds.), *Social psychology: Handbook of basic principles* (pp. 799–829). New York, NY: Guilford Press.

Mischel, W. (1977). On the future of personality measurement. *American Psychologist, 32,* 246–254.

Morrison, K. R., & Miller, D. T. (2008). Distinguishing between silent and vocal minorities: Not all deviants feel marginal. *Journal of Personality and Social Psychology, 94,* 871–882.

Moscovici, S. (1985). Social influence and conformity. In G. Lindzey & E. Aronson (Eds.), *Handbook of social psychology* (Vol. 2, 3rd ed., pp. 397–412). New York, NY: Random House.

Moscovici, S. (1994). Three concepts: Minority, conflict, and behavioral styles. In S. Moscovici, A. Mucchi-Faina, & A. Maass (Eds.), *Minority influence* (pp. 233–251). Chicago, IL: Nelson-Hall.

Moscovici, S., & Personnaz, B. (1980). Studies in social influence. V. Minority influence and conversion behavior in a perceptual task. *Journal of Experimental Social Psychology, 16,* 270–282.

Nail, P. R., & MacDonald, G. (2007). On the development of the social response context model. In A. R. Pratkanis (Ed.), *The science of social influence: Advances and future progress* (pp. 193–221). New York, NY: Psychology Press.

Nemeth, C. J. (1986). Differential contributions of majority and minority influence. *Psychological Review, 93,* 23–32.

Newcomb, T. M. (1943). *Personality and social change.* New York, NY: Dryden.

Newcomb, T. M., Koenig, K., Flacks, R., & Warwick, D. (1967). *Persistence and change: Bennington College and its students after 25 years.* New York, NY: Wiley.

Nowak, A., Vallacher, R. R., & Miller, M. E. (2003). Social influence and group dynamics. In T. Millon, M. J. Lerner, & I. B. Weiner (Eds.), *Handbook of psychology: Social psychology* (Vol. 5, pp. 383–418). Hoboken, NJ: Wiley.

Onnela, J., & Reed-Tsochas, F. (2010). Spontaneous emergence of social influence in online systems. *Proceedings of the National Academy of Sciences, 107,* 18375–18380.

Packer, D. J. (2008). Identifying systematic disobedience in Milgram's obedience experiments: A meta-analytic review. *Perspectives on Psychological Science, 3,* 301–304.

Phillips, K. W. (2003). The effects of categorically based expectations on minority influence: The importance of congruence. *Personality and Social Psychology Bulletin, 29,* 3–13.

Prapavessis, H., & Carron, A. V. (1997). Sacrifice, cohesion, and conformity to norms in sport teams. *Group dynamics: Theory, research, and practice, 1,* 231–240.

Pratkanis, A. R. (2007a). An invitation to social influence research. In A. R. Pratkanis (Ed.), *The science of social influence: Advances and future progress* (pp. 1–15). New York, NY: Psychology Press.

Pratkanis, A. R. (2007b). Social influence analysis: An index of tactics. In A. R. Pratkanis (Ed.), *The science of social influence: Advances and future progress* (pp. 17–82). New York, NY: Psychology Press.

Prislin, R., Brewer, M., & Wilson, D. J. (2002). Changing majority and minority positions within a group versus an aggregate. *Personality and Social Psychology Bulletin, 28,* 640–647.

Prislin, R., & Crano, W. D. (2012). A history of social influence research. In A. W. Kruglanski & Stroebe, W. (Eds.), *Handbook of the history of social psychology* (pp. 321–339). New York, NY: Psychology Press.

Raafat, R. M., Chater, N., & Frith, C. (2009). Herding in humans. *Trends in Cognitive Sciences, 13,* 420–428.

Raven, B. H. (1992). A power/interaction model of interpersonal influence: French and Raven thirty years later. *Journal of Social Behavior and Personality, 7,* 217–244.

Reno, R. R., Cialdini, R. B., & Kallgren, C. A. (1993). The transsituational influence of social norms. *Journal of Personality and Social Psychology, 64,* 104–112.

Ridgeway, C. L. (1978). Conformity, group-oriented motivation, and status attainment in small groups. *Social Psychology, 41,* 175–188.

Ridgeway, C. L. (2006). Status construction theory. In P. J. Burke (Ed.), *Contemporary social psychological theories* (pp. 301–323). Palo Alto, CA: Stanford University Press.

Roethlisberger, F. J., & Dickson, W. J. (1934). *Studies in industrial research: Technical vs. social organization in an industrial plant.* Boston, MA: Harvard University Press.

Russell, A. M., & Fiske, S. T. (2010). Power and social perception. In A. Guinote & T. K. Vescio (Eds.), *The social psychology of power* (pp. 231–250). New York, NY: Guilford Press.

Sabini, J., Garvey, B., & Hall, A. L. (2001). Shame and embarrassment revisited. *Personality and Social Psychology Review, 27,* 104–117.

Schachter, S. (1951). Deviation, rejection, and communication. *Journal of Abnormal and Social Psychology, 46,* 190–207.

Schultz, P. W., Nolan, J. M., Cialdini, R. B., Goldstein, N. J., & Griskevicius, V. (2007). The constructive, destructive, and reconstructive power of social norms. *Psychological Science, 18,* 429–434.

Seashore, S. E. (1954). *Group cohesiveness in the industrial work group.* Ann Arbor, MI: Institute for Social Research.

Sherif, M. (1936). *The psychology of social norms.* New York, NY: Harper & Row.

Sighele, S. (1891). *La folla delinquente.* Torino, Italy: Bocca.

Singer, E. (1990). Reference groups and social evaluations. In M. Rosenberg & R. H. Turner (Eds.), *Social psychology: Sociological perspectives* (pp. 66–93). New Brunswick, NJ: Transaction.

Smith, P. K., Dijksterhuis, A., & Wigboldus, D. H. J. (2008). Powerful people make good decisions even when they consciously think. *Psychological Science, 19*(12), 1258–1259.

Spears, R., Lea, M., & Postmes, T. (2007). CMC and social identity. In A. N. Joinson, K. Y. A. McKenna, T. Postmes, & U-D. Reips (Eds.), *The Oxford handbook of internet psychology* (pp. 253–269). Oxford, UK: Oxford University Press.

Stasser, G. (1992). Information salience and the discovery of hidden profiles by decision-making groups: A "thought experiment." *Organizational Behavior and Human Decision Processes, 52,* 156–181.

Suls, J., Martin, R., & Wheeler, L. (2002). Social comparison: Why, with whom, and with what effect? *Current Directions in Psychological Science, 11,* 159–163.

Swift, E. J. (1918). *Psychology and the day's work: A study in the application of psychology to daily life.* New York, NY: Scribner.

Tanis, M., & Postmes, T. (2005). A social identity approach to trust: Interpersonal perception, group membership and trusting behavior. *European Journal of Social Psychology, 35,* 413–424.

Tarde, G. (1892). Les crimes des foules. *Actes du Troisième Congrès International d'Anthropologie Criminellee* (pp. 63–88). Bruxelles, Belgium: F. Hayez.

Thye, S. R. (2000). A status value theory of power in exchange relations. *American Sociological Review, 65,* 407–432.

Tiedens, L. Z., Unzueta, M. M., & Young, M. J. (2007). An unconscious desire for hierarchy? The motivated perception of dominance complementarity in task partners. *Journal of Personality and Social Psychology, 93,* 402–414.

Tyler, T. R. (2005). Introduction: Legitimating ideologies. *Social Justice Research, 18,* 211–215.

Vallacher, R. R., & Nowak, A. (2007). Dynamical social psychology: Finding order in the flow of human experience. In A. W. Kruglanski & E. T. Higgins (Eds.), *Social psychology: Handbook of basic principles* (2nd ed., pp. 734–758). New York, NY: Guilford Press.

van Ginneken, J. (2007). *Mass movements in Darwinist, Freudian, and Marxist perspective: Trotter, Freud, and Reich on war, revolution and reaction, 1900–1933.* Apeldoorn, The Netherlands: Het Spinhuis.

Venkatesh, B., & Goyal, S. (1998). Learning from neighbors. *Review of Economic Studies, 65,* 595–621.

Weaver, K., Garcia, S. M., Schwarz, N., & Miller, D. T. (2007). Inferring the popularity of an opinion from its familiarity: A repetitive voice can sound like a chorus. *Journal of Personality and Social Psychology, 92,* 821–833.

Weber, M. (1946). The sociology of charismatic authority. In H. H. Gert & C. W. Mills (Trans. & Eds.), *From Max Weber: Essay in sociology* (pp. 245–252). New York, NY: Oxford University Press. (Original work published in 1921)

Whatley, M. A., Webster, J. M., Smith, R. H., & Rhodes, A. (1999). The effect of a favor on public and private compliance: How internalized is the norm of reciprocity? *Basic and Applied Social Psychology, 21,* 251–259.

White, R. K., & Lippitt, R. (1968). Leader behavior and member reaction in three "social climates." In D. Cartwright & A. Zander (Eds.), *Group dynamics: Research and theory* (3rd ed., pp. 318–335). New York, NY: Harper & Row.

Whyte, W. F. (1943). *Street corner society.* Chicago, IL: University of Chicago Press.

Wilder, D. A. (1977). Perception of groups, size of opposition, and social influence. *Journal of Experimental Social Psychology, 13,* 253–268.

Williams, K. D. (2007). Ostracism. *Annual Review of Psychology, 58,* 425–452.

Winter, D. G. (2010). Power in the person: Exploring the motivational underground of power. In A. Guinote & T. K. Vescio (Eds.), *The social psychology of power* (pp. 113–140). New York, NY: Guilford Press.

Wittenbaum, G. M., Hollingshead, A. B., & Botero, I. C. (2004). From cooperative to motivated information sharing in groups: Moving beyond the hidden profile paradigm. *Communication Monographs, 71,* 286–310.

Yukl, G. A. (2006). *Leadership in organizations.* Upper Saddle River, NJ: Prentice Hall.

Yukl, G., Kim, H., & Falbe, C. (1996). Antecedents of influence outcomes. *Journal of Applied Psychology, 81,* 309–317.

CHAPTER 15

Close Relationships

MARGARET S. CLARK AND NANCY K. GROTE

WHAT IS A CLOSE RELATIONSHIP?

When asked, "With whom do you have close relationships?" people do not ask, "What is meant by close?" Instead they name specific people or categories of people considered to be friends, kin, or romantic partners. Yet, for scientific purposes it is important to specify, conceptually, what we mean by "close." Researchers have suggested a variety of definitions.

Closeness can be thought of as interdependence with people having more frequent, more diverse and stronger impacts on one another's thoughts, feelings, and actions having the closer relationships and those relationships in which such impacts persist over longer periods of time being especially close (Berscheid, Snyder, & Omoto, 1989; Rusbult & Van Lange, 2012). Such a definition does include many of the parent-child and romantic relationships and friendships about which people think when they think of close relationships. Yet it also includes relationships that would not be described as close in common language. For example, this definition includes bitter enemies who fight about almost everything, day in and day out. It also excludes some relationships people describe as close. For instance, it excludes the relationship between a mother and her adult child, each of whom cares deeply about the other's welfare but who currently live on opposite sides of the country and are leading relatively independent lives. They *would* get on a plane in an instant *if* one of them needed the other's support but that hasn't been necessary recently.

Importantly, closeness has also been defined in other ways that do exclude bitter enemies and that do include people living largely independent lives who care deeply

about one another. For example, some define closeness in terms of intimacy with people being considered closer the more they understand, validate, and care for one another (Reis & Patrick, 1996; Reis & Shaver, 1988), as the extent to which a partner and that partner's attributes are considered a part of the self (Aron, Aron, Tudor, & Nelson, 2004) or as the extent to which one is committed to a relationship defined as intending to stay in the relationship for whatever reason, be it satisfaction, lack of alternatives, past investments, or social or personal norms (Rusbult, Coolsen, Kirchner, & Clarke, 2006). There is no one right definition. Rather different ones are useful for different purposes.

In this chapter, we define closeness in terms of members being responsive to one another's welfare in terms of providing support and inclusion *and* in terms of them facilitating their own receipt of such care by expecting, seeking, desiring and accepting responsiveness from the partner (Clark & Mills, 2012; Mills, Clark, Ford, & Johnson, 2004; Reis, Clark, & Holmes, 2004).

Responsive, communal, close relationships can be mutual as often occurs in relationships we call friendships or romantic relationships, or they can be asymmetric to varying degrees with one person providing most care and the other accepting and seeking most care as may occur between a mother and infant or an adult child and frail, older parent. *Both* monitoring a partner's needs and providing responsiveness *and* seeking and accepting responsiveness contribute, we suggest, to feeling close.

Notably relationships deemed close in terms of this definition almost always will overlap, empirically, with heightened levels of interdependence, inclusion of other in the self and, very often, commitment to a partner.

329

Responsiveness is an interpersonal process. We personally think it is best to think of closeness in terms of interpersonal process and to further explore both intra- and interpersonal processes that support (or detract from) responsiveness if one is to fully understand high- (and low-) quality interpersonal processes. Whereas much past work has suggested that high-quality close relationships can be defined in terms of their stability (persistence across time), individual ratings of satisfaction, and/or absence of conflict, we suggest that use of such markers is insufficient because they provide little information regarding the functional significance of relationships for their members. They further provide no hint as to why a relationship persists or is characterized by high satisfaction or low conflict. Moreover, we believe that relationships can persist without much responsiveness taking place in those relationships, that high satisfaction can occur in just one partner and not the other or in relationships characterized by largely independent lives, and that low conflict can signal bad things (e.g., one partner's fear of the other) as well as good things about the relationship (e.g., a smoothly functioning responsive relationship.)

What Is Responsiveness? What Forms Can It Take?

Responsiveness to a partner refers to any actions a person takes with the goal of promoting a partner's welfare. It involves fostering a partner's healthy dependence upon the self (Reis et al., 2004). Responsiveness can take many forms. Most obviously one can provide help to another person when the person has a clear need. For instance, one can give a friend a ride to a train station, or instructions for setting up his computer, or advice on which job to accept. However, responsiveness takes many other forms as well. It includes taking note of a partner's goals and supporting the partner in attaining his or her goals including, at times, simply giving the partner time and space to reach goals and staying out of the person's way during the partner's goal pursuit (Feeney, 2004). It can involve including partners in activities such as inviting them to join one at a dinner party, going to the movies or even including the other in a conversation or a ball tossing game (Aron, Norman, Aron, McKenna, & Heyman, 2000; Williams, 2006). It can involve celebrating a partner's accomplishments (Gable, Gonzaga, & Strachman, 2006). It can be largely symbolic as when one tells a partner that one likes or loves the partner, sends a card, or affirms the partner's identity by nodding one's head in agreement as they express an idea (Drigotas, 2002; Swann, 1987). Sacrifice, forgiveness, and stoically putting up with a partner's unpleasant behavior

without reacting negatively (Rusbult, Hannon, Stocker, & Finkel, 2005; Whitton, Stanley, & Markman, 2002) can all be responsive behaviors as can suppressing one's own desires and behaviors if doing so benefits the partner. For instance, one might not eat the last piece of chocolate when one knows one's partner would love to consume it. Behaviors that might, on the surface, seem negative can even be responsive if the underlying motivation and effect is to promote the partner's welfare. For instance, if one's partner wishes to lose weight and has been struggling with efforts to do so, hiding that last piece of chocolate would be responsive. What all these actions have in common is that they are aimed at promoting one's partner's welfare.

Noncontingently giving responsiveness to and accepting responsiveness from a partner without feeling indebted to that partner are the hallmarks of close relationships. Each contributes to feelings of being close. That is why, even in largely asymmetric communal relationships (e.g., that between a parent and a very young child) both members of the relationship can feel close to the other. The parent reaps that feeling from providing responsiveness; the child reaps the feeling from being the recipient of responsiveness. Of course, in mutual communal relationships a feeling of closeness derives both from giving and from being the recipient of responsive actions.

Whereas there are individual differences in terms of how responsive people are to others (in general) and in terms of how much responsiveness they may elicit from others (in general), most variability in responsiveness occurs between relationships (Clark & Lemay, 2010). Almost everyone has close relationships in which they give and receive a great deal of noncontingent responsiveness and other relationships in which little noncontingent responsiveness occurs.

People have implicit hierarchies of relationships ordered in terms of the amount of felt responsibility they assume for others (i.e., the extent to which they would spend time, energy, and money) to benefit the other. These hierarchies determine whose welfare will be promoted over whose in the event of conflicts, as we can't meet everyone's needs all the time (Mills et al., 2004; Reis et al., 2004).

To Whom Are We Attracted for Responsive Relationships?

In thinking about to whom we wish to be responsive, liking for the other may be the first answer that comes to mind. That is, one might reasonably expect that we are responsive to those whom we like. Liking certainly is a factor in forming close relationships, however, the answer is more complex.

One major factor determining to whom we wish to be most responsive or closest is kinship. The degree of felt closeness to other varies with genetic relationship. People feel most responsiveness toward and expect most responsiveness from those with whom they have the closest biological ties. Among those relationships, some research further suggests that it is toward females that we both receive most responsiveness and toward whom we direct most responsiveness. For instance, we provide more responsiveness to and expect more responsiveness from mothers relative to fathers, aunts relative to uncles, and sisters relative to brothers (Monin, Clark, & Lemay, 2008).

Attachment theory suggests that parents are hardwired to form attachment bonds (which lead to noncontingent responsiveness) with their infants and infants are also hardwired to elicit noncontingent responsiveness from their caretakers (Bowlby, 1969). Mothers experience surges in oxytocin associated with the birth of their children and lactation is also associated with surges in oxytocin that appear to help bond them to infants (Feldman, Weller, Zagoory-Sharon, & Levine, 2007). Infants spontaneously cry when distressed eliciting care from caretakers. Most culture also dictate high levels of responsiveness to kin. Indeed, there are laws dictating responsiveness to certain kin. Parents, for instance, cannot neglect children without legal consequences.

Beyond kinship many factors have been shown to lead to the formation of close relationships and, in turn, to responsiveness within those relationships. One important (but often overlooked) factor is simply the number of preexisting close relationships one has with others. Close relationships involving mutual responsiveness fulfill peoples' need to belong (Baumeister & Leary, 1995) and provide a sense of security to people. When these relationships exist one is not solely responsible for one's needs. Other people "have one's back."

Thus, an important impetus to forming close relationships is simply a lack of a currently sufficient number of current close relationship partners to make one feel secure and to support one's welfare. When one starts a new school, moves to a new location, has experienced a recent divorce or the loss through death of a loved one, the drive to form and the likelihood of forming new close relationships should be greater. Supporting this idea research has shown that reminding people of social rejections from a current partner, on average, increases their interest in meeting new people (Maner, DeWall, Baumeister, & Schaller, 2007, Studies 1 and 2; Williams & Sommer, 1997). On the other hand, commitment to current close relationship partners decreases both attention and attraction to new potential partners (Johnson & Rusbult, 1989; Lydon, Fitzsimons, & Naidoo, 2003; Maner, Gailliot, & Miller, 2009; Maner, Rouby, & Gonzaga, 2008).

Yet another way in which existing bonds may decrease attraction to and approach toward new partners is through a person's worries that forming new bonds may disappoint or distress existing relationship partners. People feel less committed to romantic partners when they believe that other close relationship partners disapprove of the relationship (Cox, Wexler, Rusbult, & Gaines, 1997; Lehmiller & Agnew, 2006) and approval of relationships from one's existing, broader, social network of partners has been shown to predict relationship persistence (Sprecher & Felmlee, 1992).

Many other factors promote the formation of close relationships as well. Some have to do with qualities of the potential partner. We are, for example, attracted to physically attractive others (Eastwick & Finkel, 2008). Physical attractiveness itself seems to consist in having features that are similar to the average of many faces (Langlois, 1990). Enhanced attraction toward such faces exists even among young children (Hoss & Langlois, 2003). From an evolutionary perspective, we may desire attractive romantic partners because attractiveness signals (or at least did at one time) health and a lack of threat of contagion, and fertility (Langlois, 1990; Thornhill & Gangestad, 1999). Beyond this, research suggests that people believe that what is beautiful is good, meaning that people associate physical beauty with positive personality traits such as intelligence, popularity, and kindness (Dion, Berscheid, & Walster, 1972). Many of these inferences may be based on an initial desire to form close bonds with attractive persons and to be communally responsive to them leading to projection of those feelings onto the attractive partner (Lemay, Clark, & Greenberg, 2010). So, too, may such inferences be based on the fact that when people perceive partners to be attractive, they treat them better, which brings out the best in those partners. In other words, attraction toward physically attractive partners can create a self-fulfilling prophecy in that people desiring relationships with them treat them well, which elicits objectively more desirable behavior from them (Snyder, Tanke, & Berscheid, 1977). Finally, we may prefer attractive partners to others because those partners reflect positively on us. When we are paired with such people, other people may think better of us (Sigall & Landy, 1973).

A special form of physical attractiveness appears to arise from having baby-faced features: big eyes, a small chin, a round face, and so on. These features appear to elicit judgments of physical attractiveness and responsiveness from others (Berry & McArthur, 1985). However, attraction to adults with such features appears to be moderated by how stressful one's environment is. Adults' attraction toward baby-faced persons may be limited to times of low stress. When we encounter high stress, more adult faces seem to be preferred presumably because in such times we need more care and perhaps are less likely to dispense care (Pettijohn & Tesser, 2005).

One more powerful determinant of being attracted to others and, ultimately, forming close, responsive relationships with others is mere physical proximity. We come into contact with others who are physically close to us and we are more likely to form close responsive relationships with such people (Bossard, 1932; Festinger, Schachter, & Back, 1950). That fact is unsurprising and might be considered mundane. However, what *is* surprising is how much difference very small distances in physical proximity can make in determining the formation of close relationships. We are less likely to form close relationships with someone whose apartment is two doors away than with someone whose apartment is next door (Festinger et al., 1950) and less likely to form relationships with students seated next to us in class than with students sitting in the same row and more likely to form relationships with them than someone sitting in a different row (Back, Schmukle, & Egloff, 2008). This may occur as a result of people's desire to protect themselves from rejection (Mac-Donald & Leary, 2005). If one chats with someone seated next to you, it will not seem as though one has intentionally sought that person out and thus, if they seem uninterested in pursuing an interaction, one is likely to be less embarrassed than if one had gone to some trouble to seek the other person out. This same principle may account for another why two additional factors have been shown to be important determinants of attraction—knowing that a potential partner likes you (Feingold, 1988; Little, Burt, & Perett, 2006) and the "value" of a partner's attributes roughly matching the value of one's own attributes (Berscheid, Dion, Walster, & Walster, 1971; Gold, Ryckman, & Mosley, 1984). Partners who already like you or whose "market value" seems to match one's own should also be perceived to be less likely to reject you.

Many other factors seem to determine approach to others as well. For instance, we like those who are similar to us in attitudes, race, socioeconomic status, education, and activity preferences (e.g., Byrne, 1971; Klohnen & Luo, 2003; Newcomb, 1961; Singh, Ng, Ong, & Lin, 2008). Similarity even in terms of simply sharing birth dates and names increases liking (Jones, Pelham, Carvallo, & Mirenberg, 2004). We also like those who are familiar to us (Moreland & Beach, 1992; Moreland & Zajonc, 1982), those whose attributes remind us of people whom we've liked in the past (Andersen & Chen, 2002; Andersen, Reznik, & Manzella, 1996), and those who don't outperform us in performance domains that are important to us (Tesser, 1988). Moreover, feelings of physical warmth have been shown to be linked to judging relationship partners more positively (Williams & Bargh, 2008; Zhong & Leonardelli, 2008).

Once We Are Attracted to Another Person, How Do We Initiate and Develop Close Relationships?

Some relationships, most notably those with kin, are normatively assumed to be communal relationships and usually do not require an initiation phase. As already noted new parents are expected to be (and likely are hardwired to be) responsive to infants from the moment of birth, and infants seem built, with their baby faces, instincts to nurse, and cries of distress to seek care from proximal others from birth. Preferences for the familiar and the similar likely support these almost instant communal relationships with kin.

Yet when we consider relationships other than those with kin, forming close relationships requires a more complex "dance" of relationship initiation. Following initial attraction toward others forming communal relationships involves presenting oneself as an attractive partner to the person to whom one is attracted while simultaneously continuing to evaluate that partner and protecting the self from rejection (Beck & Clark, 2010; Clark & Beck, 2011). Perhaps the most important self-presentational thing one can do to initiate a relationship is to display oneself as being willing to benefit the other on a noncontingent basis and being willing to accept benefits offered again on a noncontingent basis. If one offers noncontingent benefits *and* if the other is interested in a communal relationship, not only will the other accept the benefits, but the other will respond with increased attraction toward you (Clark & Mills, 1979, Study 1). If the other is not interested the offer will not be accepted and liking is likely to drop (Clark & Mills, 1979). However, then one can move on to other possible relationships.

Thus, to initiate close responsive relationships one must attend to opportunities to respond to the potential partner's needs, desires, and goals (Clark, Mills, & Powell,

1986), respond without requesting repayment and see if the other accepts and shows signs of increased liking. If they are available and desirous of a close relationship they are likely to do just that (Clark & Mills, 1979, Study 2). Indeed, early in a relationship people do seem especially likely to offer help to others (relative to seeking it) (Beck & Clark, 2009b), and especially likely to "bend over backward" to appear not to be keeping track of just who has contributed what to a relationship lest responsiveness appear to be contingent (Clark, 1984; Clark, Mills, & Corcoran, 1989). Importantly, whereas efforts to self-present as a desirable communal relationship partner are important to forming close relationships, trying too hard to display one's positive attributes in general, paradoxically, may backfire (Canevello & Crocker, 2010) as it may suggest that one is primarily concerned with the self, not the partner and further may suggest that the other is too "relationally self-focused" (too preoccupied with the self and what the other is thinking of the self) (Clark, Graham, Williams, & Lemay, 2008), and insufficiently concerned with the partner's welfare. Instead, Canevello and Crocker (2010) have shown that having compassionate goals in the sense that one is focused on the other's welfare, promotes relationship growth in terms of the partner liking the person having those goals and, in turn, desiring a relationship.

If one offers benefits to another noncontingently, one has entered what we call a socially diagnostic situations or, in other words, a situation in which that other will respond either with acceptance and increased liking or, possibly, by declining the offer and with decreased liking (Clark & Mills, 1979, Study 2). In order to initiate relationships it is important to enter such situations in order to initiate close relationships, something not everyone is willing to do (Beck & Clark, 2009a).

Importantly, as noted earlier, a mutual communal relationship involves not only providing responsiveness to a partner but also seeking and accepting responsiveness from a partner. Typically, this requires revealing vulnerabilities to partners, something that requires dropping or lessening self-protective strategies. People are hesitant to do this prior to the relationship progressing to some extent. Thus, whereas it is important, revealing vulnerabilities and seeking and accepting help in relationship initiation likely comes *after* offering responsiveness—a claim that is supported by the fact that early in relationships but *not* in established relationships people offer more support than they seek (Beck & Clark, 2009b). Still, for relationships to develop, this step must be taken.

People can take this step by directly asking for support, by more openly expressing their emotions (Clark, Fitness,

& Brissette, 2001) and by openly and directly expressing needs and desires. All these behaviors facilitate relationship initiation in two ways. First, they provide powerful signals to partners that one trusts the partner and that one is willing to risk some dependence upon them. Second, they communicate important information to the potential partner regarding ways in which that potential partner can be appropriately responsive. A set of studies that illustrates the importance of being open to receiving responsiveness and of sending signals regarding one's welfare has been reported by Graham, Huang, Clark, and Helgeson (2008). These studies reveal that students' willingness to express negative emotions indicative of needs elicits support as well as the development of more friendships during the first semester of college, the development of more intimacy in the closest of those friendships, and the receipt of more support from roommates as reported independently by those roommates.

MAKING A COMMITMENT

Whereas some close relationships start out at day one with a commitment (as when a child is born and parents devote themselves to the child's care without question and with the intent to do so for so long as they are able), most other close, communal relationships do not start out with a commitment. However, at some point a commitment, explicit or implicit, must be made to having a relationship in which responsiveness is given and received at some level. That commitment consists of a decision to stay in the relationship. It is accompanied, ideally, with a drop in efforts to strategically self-present as a desirable communal partner, a drop in deliberations about whether to pursue the relationship, and a drop in self-protection. As the decision is made that the relationship is "here to stay," these things ideally are replaced with simply attending to one another's welfare and being appropriately responsive, conveying one's own state of welfare to the partner, seeking and accepting appropriate responsiveness and, importantly, when neither person has pressing needs, engaging in mutually enjoyable activities while self-conscious awareness of the self and other as individuals fades to the background.

Importantly, relationship researchers have established that committing to a relationship is associated with many relationship benefits. Committed people are more likely than others to, for instance, put up with partner's negative behaviors without responding in kind—what Rusbult has termed *accommodation* (Rusbult, Bissonette, Arriaga, & Cox, 1998), to make sacrifices for partners (Van Lange et al., 1997), to forgive partners (Rusbult et al., 2005), and to see potential rivals as less attractive (Johnson & Rusbult, 1989; Maner et al., 2008). They shift from deliberating about the relationship to implementing the norms that are appropriate to the relationship.

Once Established, What Does a Close Relationship, Ideally, Look Like?

Members of high-quality mutual friendships, romantic relationships, and family relationships trust each other, feel secure with each other, and derive satisfaction from nurturing each other. They understand, validate, and care for each other. They keep track of each other's needs (Clark et al., 1986), help each other (Clark, Ouellette, Powell, & Milberg, 1987), and feel good when they have been able to help their partners (Williamson & Clark, 1989, 1992), and bad when they do not (Williamson, Pegalis, Behan, & Clark, 1996). They celebrate each other's successes (Gable, Reis, Impett, & Asher, 2004). They respond to one another's distress and even anger with accommodation and support (Finkel & Campbell, 2001; Rusbult, Verette, Whitney, Slovik, & Lipkus, 1991) rather than with reciprocal expressions of distress and anger or with defensiveness (Gottman, 1979). They express their emotions to their partners (Clark et al., 2001; Feeney, 1995, 1999). They turn to one another for help (Simpson, Rholes, & Nelligan, 1992). They are willing to forgive one another's transgressions (McCullough, 2000). Further, members of such relationships are likely to hold positive illusions about partners that, in turn, bring out the best in those partners (Murray & Holmes, 1997; Murray, Holmes, Dolderman, & Griffin, 2000; Murray, Holmes & Griffin, 1996a, 1996b) and to possess cognitive structures in which even their partner's apparent faults are linked to virtues (Graham & Clark, 2008; Murray & Holmes, 1993).

Finally, members of such relationships appear ready to engage in active relationship protecting processes such as not being attentive to attractive alternatives to their relationship (Maner et al., 2009), and viewing their own relationship as being better than those of others (Johnson & Rusbult, 1989; Simpson, Gangestad, & Lerma, 1990; Van Lange & Rusbult, 1995). All these things contribute to a sense of intimacy between partner (Reis & Patrick, 1996; Reis & Shaver, 1988) and relationship members having the sense that their relationships are both safe havens (Collins & Feeney, 2000) and secure bases from which they can venture out and explore their worlds and pursue their goals (Feeney, 2004, 2007).

Relationship researchers do not have a single name for what we are describing as a high-quality relationship. Rather several terms currently in use describe successful close relationships as discussed here. They have been called communal relationships (Clark & Mills, 1979, 2012), responsive relationships (Reis et al., 2004), intimate relationships (Reis & Patrick, 1996; Reis & Shaver, 1988), and secure relationships (Mikulincer & Shaver, 2007). From the perspective of this chapter, the exact terminology is not that important—an understanding of the interpersonal processes characterizing high-quality relationship *is* important.

Variability in the Strength of Well-Functioning Close Relationships

Not all well-functioning responsive relationships are just alike in the attributes and processes described. We have already pointed out that although most close relationships are characterized by mutual and even levels of assumed responsibility for partner welfare, some close relationships are asymmetrical in responsibility such as those between a parent and young child, a child and an elderly parent who needs care, or a person and a disabled friend.

These relationships also vary in what is known as *communal strength* or the degree to which members do assume responsibility for partner welfare (Mills et al., 2004). As noted, people have hierarchies of what we call *communal relationships*. By this we mean that people have sets of relationships with others about whose needs they care and about whose needs they strive to be responsive in a non-contingent fashion (Clark & Mills, 2012; Mills et al, 2004). These relationships vary from weak to strong with strength referring to the degree of responsibility the person believes he or she ought to assume for the other's welfare. One end of the hierarchy is anchored by relationships in which the person feels a low degree of responsibility for the partner's needs (e.g., a relationship with an acquaintance for whom the person might provide directions or the time of day with no expectation of compensation). Such relationships are not considered to be close. The other end of the hierarchy is anchored by relationships in which the person assumes tremendous responsibility for the other's needs (e.g., a parent-child relationship in which a parent would do just about anything at any cost to ensure the child's welfare). These relationships are considered the closest relationships (or strongest communal relationships) people have.

Figure 15.1 depicts one hypothetical person's hierarchy of communal relationships. Communal relationships, from weak to strong, are depicted on the x-axis. The costs one is willing to incur to meet the other's needs (noncontingently) are depicted on the y-axis. The dashed line in

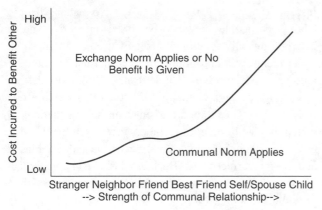

Figure 15.1 One hypothetical person's hierarchy of communal relationships

the figure depicts the costs the person is willing to incur to benefit the other on a communal basis.

Beneath the implicit cost line, benefits are given and accepted on a communal need basis. Thus, for instance, strangers give one another the time of day, neighbors take in one another's mail on a temporary basis, friends throw birthday parties for one another and travel to one another's weddings, and parents spend years raising children and tremendous amounts of money to support those children.

Above the cost line benefits are generally not given or even considered. When they are given, they are given on an exchange basis. Consider, for instance, a relationship partner who needs a house. To give a house to another person is costly and is a benefit that falls above the cost line for most relationships such as those with acquaintances, neighbors, or friends. Under most circumstances this means that this benefit will not be given (or asked for) in such relationships. The topic simply will not come up. However, a person might sell his house to a friend in an economic exchange in which parties agree that the money and the house are of equal value. Neighbors might agree to provide each other's child with rides to and from soccer practice (following a rule of equality—half the days one person drives; half the days the other drives), and so forth. These are not interchanges that contribute to closeness in the sense in which we use that term in this chapter.

Recognizing the existence of hierarchies of communal relationships raises some additional points relevant to the nature of high-quality close relationships. As we said earlier, close relationships, generally, are characterized by assumed, non-contingent responsibility for a partner's needs. Here we add that the level of responsibility actually assumed on the part of a caregiver or expected on the part of a person in need (in the absence of true emergencies) ought also to be appropriate to the location of

that relationship in its members' hierarchies of relationships if a close relationship is to be considered a high-quality close relationship. If the costs involved in meeting the need all fall beneath the implicit cost boundary shown in Figure 15.1, the responsiveness ought to be present. If costs exceed the boundary, benefits should not be given, except for emergencies or in instances in which both members wish to strengthen the communal nature of the relationship. This means that, giving a benefit that falls *above* the implicit cost boundary might harm the quality of the relationship. So, too, may asking for too costly a benefit or implying the existence of too strong a communal relationship by self-disclosing too much (given the communal strength of the relationship) (Chaiken & Derlega, 1974; Kaplan, Firestone, Degnore, & Morre, 1974) hurt the relationship.

Thus, in thinking about the nature of high-quality close relationships, it is not sufficient to assume that more responsiveness always makes for better close relationships. Members of relationships must implicitly agree on the strength of the communal relationship they have or desire and their actions should fall in the appropriate bounds. A casual friend ought not give one an extravagant present. It exceeds the appropriate level of responsiveness to needs. A young child ought not assume a great deal of communal responsibility for a parent. Indeed, a young child consistently feeling compelled to comfort a troubled parent would be not be seen as a child with a high quality relationship with that parent.

Numbers of Close Relationships a Person Can Have, Including a Close Relationship With Self

There is a limit to the number of close responsive relationships a person can have. We cannot be responsive to all people's needs; we do not need everyone to be responsive to our needs. People generally have few strong communal relationships, more moderately strong ones, more casual communal relationships and many, many weak communal relationships. Their communal relationships tend to fall in a pattern such as that displayed in Figure 15.2. The relationships falling at the top of the triangle are the ones to which we generally apply the term close in lay language.

Importantly, people place themselves in their own hierarchy of communal relationships and they generally place themselves quite high in that hierarchy. This means that taking care of themselves is important to them and generally is more important than taking care of many other people. Still, many people also have a few others who are tied with them in the hierarchy or even placed above them in the hierarchy (e.g., a spouse or a child).

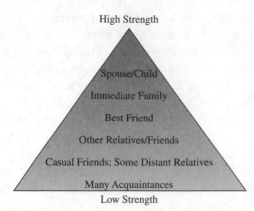

Figure 15.2 Patterning in which people's communal relationships (in western societies) typically fall

Hierarchies not only suggest the degree of responsibility people feel for close others' welfares, they also suggest whose needs will be placed above whose, in the event that two close relationship partners' needs arise at the same time and that a person simply cannot respond to both. For instance, if one's mother's birthday party and a casual friend's birthday party fell on the same day and at the same time, a person would generally attend the party of the person with whom they felt stronger communal ties or, in other words, to the person highest in their communal hierarchy.

Abilities and fortitudes necessary to pull off closeness. This chapter has focused on becoming attracted to others and forming close relationships with others. It is important to note that not all people are able to achieve this sort of closeness in relationships. Indeed, we would say that much, perhaps even the majority, of the social psychological literature on close relationships has focused on impediments to forming and maintaining close relationships. We do not review that literature here. Yet it is worth briefly commenting upon the abilities and fortitudes that appear necessary to "pull off" well-functioning close relationships.

First, there is wide consensus that having positive views about the self and others as well as trust in others is absolutely central to "risking" becoming involved in close relationships and to succeeding in them (Murray & Holmes, 2011; Murray, Holmes & Collins, 2006). Being rejected hurts (Williams, 2007). Revealing vulnerabilities opens one up to possible exploitation. Without faith that another will provide responsiveness to one and without faith that another will accept one's responsive overtures, little support will be sought or given. Individuals who lack such faith have been called, variously, low in self-esteem (Murray et al., 2000), low in communal orientation (Clark et al., 1987), rejection sensitive (Downey & Feldman, 1996), or

insecure (Shaver & Mikulincer, 2012). No matter what the label, such people appear to be so self-protective and to be so chronically relationally self-focused that they think about themselves and implications of partner or potential partners for themselves (Clark et al., 2008), overreacting to the slightest sign or thought that the other might reject or hurt them. Thus they fail to enter or create situations in which they will find out that others care about them (Beck & Clark, 2009a,b), they view others in negatively biased and often incorrect ways (Beck & Clark, 2011), they react to others' anxiety by withdrawing from them rather than providing support (Simpson et al., 1992) and when faced with any partner threat they often strike out at the partner in defensive but relationship-defeating ways (Murray, Bellavia, Rose, & Griffin, 2003).

In contrast, having confidence in others' possible positive regard for the self is central to being able to drop self-focus and initiate relationships. Having confidence in a particular other's extant positive regard for the self is central to building and committing to a particular relationship. It allows one to let self-concerns fade to the background when opportunities to support one's partner arise and to enact responsiveness without fear of it being wrong, or rejected, or producing inequities in the relationship. So, too, can one's fear of rejection fade to the background when one needs support to maintain one's own welfare, which allows one to express emotions, self-disclose, and ask for support. Finally, it allows one to jump on and take advantage of joint opportunities to pursue mutually enjoyable activities and goals in the relationship. One can engage in dancing, an enjoyable conversation, or an athletic activity together without being focused either on the self or the partner but rather on the activity itself (Clark et al., 2008). This is something that attachment theorists might call exploring the world freely as a result of having the secure base that an attachment figure can provide (Feeney, 2004).

The important point is that successful close relationships require not only knowing implicitly or explicitly what the norms of close relationships are (something we believe most people do know), but also having trust in others' positive regard for the self—trust that provides the fortitude one needs to venture forth into relationships, risk dependence, and follow those norms without fear (Murray & Holmes, 2011).

CONCLUDING COMMENTS

In this chapter we have set forth some ideas about what a close relationship is, what determines the desire for a close relationship, how one might initiate a close relationship, and, following commitment to a close relationship, what processes characterize a high-quality close relationship. We have also touched on the strength of such relationships and the place of any given close relationship within a person's broader set of close relationships. Finally, we have briefly commented on what might prevent the establishment of a close relationship or harm one's ability to commit to or maintain close relationships.

It is important to note that whereas we can sketch out the nature of close, intimate, relationships in a short chapter such as this, there is now a large and thriving literature in psychology on normatively close relationships (e.g., friendships and romantic relationships), which discusses the intra- and interpersonal processes in such relationships in far more depth than could be done here. There are also several good textbooks describing the nature and functioning of close relationships (e.g., Bradbury & Karney, 2010; Miller, 2012; Regan, 2011) as well as more extensive general reviews of work on close relationships (e.g., Clark & Lemay, 2010). We urge the reader to explore this topic further by examining these rich resources.

REFERENCES

Andersen, S. M., & Chen, S. (2002). The relational self: An interpersonal social-cognitive theory. *Psychological Review*, *109*, 619–645.

Andersen, S. M., Reznik, I., & Manzella, I. M. (1996). Eliciting facial affect, motivation, and expectancies in transference: Significant other presentations in social relationships. *Journal of Personality and Social Psychology*, *71*, 1108–1129.

Aron, A., Aron, E. N., Tudor, M., & Nelson, G. (2004). Close relationships as including the other in the self. *Journal of Personality and Social Psychology*, *60*, 241–253.

Aron, A., Norman, C. C., Aron, E. N., McKenna, C., & Heyman, R. E. (2000). Couples' shared participation in novel and arousing activities and experienced relationship quality. *Journal of Personality and Social Psychology*, *78*, 273–284.

Back, M. D., Schmukle, S. C., & Egloff, B. (2008). Becoming friends by chance. *Psychological Science*, *19*, 439–440.

Baumeister, R. F., & Leary, M. R (1995). The need to belong: Desire for interpersonal attachments as a fundamental human motivation. *Psychological Bulletin*, *117*, 497–529.

Beck, L. A., & Clark, M. S. (2010). What constitutes a healthy communal marriage and why relationship stage matters. *Journal of Family Theory and Review, 2*, 299–315.

Beck, L. A., & Clark, M. S. (2009a). Choosing to enter or avoid diagnostic social situations *Psychological Science*, *20*, 1175–1181.

Beck, L. A., & Clark, M. S. (2009b). Offering more support than we seek. *Journal of Experimental Social Psychology*, *45*, 267–270.

Beck, L. A. & Clark, M. S. (2011). Looking a gift horse in the mouth as a defense against Increasing intimacy. *Journal of Experimental Social Psychology*, *4*, 676–679.

Berry, D. S., & McArthur, L. Z. (1985). Some components and consequences of a babyface. *Journal of Personality and Social Psychology*, *48*, 312–323.

Berscheid, E., Dion, K., Walster, E., & Walster, G. W. (1971). Physical attractiveness and dating choice: A test of the matching hypothesis. *Journal of Experimental Social Psychology*, *7*, 173–189.

Berscheid, E., Snyder, M., & Omoto, A. M. (1989). The relationship closeness inventory: Assessing the closeness of interpersonal relationships. *Journal of Personality and Social Psychology*, *57*, 792–807.

Bossard, J. H. S. (1932). Residential propinquity as a factor in marriage selection. *American Journal of Sociology*, *38*, 218–224.

Bowlby, J. (1969). *Attachment and loss: Vol. I Attachment*. New York, NY: Basic Books.

Bradbury, T. N., & Karney, B. R. (2010). *Intimate relationships*. New York, NY: Norton.

Byrne, D. (1971). *The attraction paradigm*. New York, NY: Academic Press.

Canevello, A., & Crocker, J. (2010). Creating good relationships: Responsiveness, relationship quality, and interpersonal goals. *Journal of Personality and Social Psychology*, *99*, 78–106.

Chaiken, A. L., & Derlega, V. J. (1974). Liking for the norm-breaker in self-disclosure. *Journal of Personality*, *42*, 117–129.

Clark, M. S. (1984). Record keeping in two types of relationships. *Journal of Personality and Social Psychology*, *47*, 549–557.

Clark, M. S., & Beck, L. A. (2011). Initiating and evaluating social relationships: A task central to emerging adults. In F. Fincham & M. Cui (Eds.), *Romantic relationships in emerging adulthood*. New York, NY: Cambridge University Press.

Clark, M. S., Fitness, J., & Brissette, I. (2001). Understanding people's perceptions of relationships is crucial to understanding their emotional lives. In G. Fletcher & M. S. Clark (Eds.), *Blackwell handbook of social psychology: Interpersonal processes* (pp. 253–278). Oxford, UK: Blackwell.

Clark, M. S., Graham, S. M., Williams, E., & Lemay, E. P. (2008). Understanding relational focus of attention may help us to understand relational phenomena. In J. Forgas & J. Fitness (Eds.), *Social relationships: Cognitive, affective and motivational processes* (pp. 131–146). New York, NY: Psychology Press.

Clark, M. S., & Lemay, E. P. (2010). Close relationships. In S. T. Fiske, D. T. Gilbert, & L. Gardner (Eds.), *Handbook of social psychology*. (Vol. 2, 5th ed., pp. 898–940). Hoboken, NJ: John Wiley & Sons.

Clark, M. S., & Mills, J. (1979). Interpersonal attraction in exchange and communal relationships. *Journal of Personality and Social Psychology*, *37*, 12–24.

Clark, M. S., & Mills, J. (2012). Communal (and exchange) relationships. In P. A. M. Van Lange, A. W. Kruglanski, & E. T. Higgins (Eds.), *Handbook of theories of social psychology* (pp. 232–250). Thousand Oaks, CA: Sage.

Clark, M. S., Mills, J., & Corcoran, D. (1989). Keeping track of needs and inputs of friends and strangers. *Personality and Social Psychology Bulletin*, *15*, 533–542.

Clark, M. S., Mills, J., & Powell, M. C. (1986). Keeping track of needs in communal and exchange relationships. *Journal of Personality and Social Psychology*, *51*, 333–338.

Clark, M. S., Ouellette, R., Powell, M. C., & Milberg, S. (1987). Recipient's mood, relationship type and helping. *Journal of Personality and Social Psychology*, *53*, 94–103.

Collins, N. L., & Feeney, B. C. (2000). A safe haven: An attachment theory perspective on support seeking and caregiving in intimate relationships. *Journal of Personality and Social Psychology*, *78*, 1053–1073.

Cox, C. L., Wexler, M. O., Rusbult, C. E., & Gaines, S. O. (1997). Prescriptive support and commitment processes in close relationships. *Social Psychology Quarterly*, *60*, 79–90.

Dion, K., Berscheid, E., & Walster, E. (1972). What is beautiful is good. *Journal of Personality and Social Psychology*, *24*, 285–290.

Downey, G., & Feldman, S. I. (1996), Implications of rejection sensitivity for intimate relationships. *Journal of Personality and Social Psychology*, 70, 1327–1343.

Drigotas, S. M. (2002). The Michelangelo phenomenon and personal well-being. *Journal of Personality*, 70, 59–77.

Eastwick, P. W., & Finkel, E. J. (2008). Sex differences in mate preferences revisited. Do people know what they initially desire in a romantic partner? *Journal of Personality and Social Psychology*, 94, 245–264.

Feeney, B. C. (2004). A secure base: Responsive support of goal strivings and exploration in adult intimate relationships. *Journal of Personality and Social Psychology*, 87, 631–648.

Feeney, B. C. (2007). The dependency paradox in close relationships: Accepting dependence promotes independence. *Journal of Personality and Social Psychology*, 92, 268–285.

Feeney, J. A. (1995). Adult attachment and emotional control. *Personal Relationships*, 2, 143–159.

Feeney, J. A. (1999). Adult attachment, emotional control, and marital satisfaction. *Personal Relationships*, 6, 169–185.

Feldman, R., Weller, A., Zagoory-Sharon, O., & Levine, A. (2007). Evidence for a neuroedocrinological foundation of human affiliation: Plasma oxytocin levels across pregnancy and the postpartum period predict mother-infant bonding. *Psychological Science*, 18, 965–970.

Festinger, L, Schachter, S., & Back, K. (1950). Social processes in informal groups: A study of human factors in housing. Oxford, UK: Harper.

Feingold, A. (1988). Mathing for attractiveness in romantic partners and same sex friends: A metaanalysis and theoretical critique. *Psychological Bulletin*, 104, 226–235.

Finkel, E. J., & Campbell, W. K. (2001). Self-control and accommodation in close relationships. An interdependence analysis. *Journal of Personality and Social Psychology*, 81, 263–277.

Gable, S. L., Gonzaga, G., & Strachman, A. (2006). Will you be there for me when things go right? Social support for positive events *Journal of Personality and Social Psychology*, 91, 904–917.

Gable, S. L., Reis, H. T., Impett, E. A., & Asher, E. R. (2004). What do you do when things go right? The intrapersonal and interpersonal benefits of sharing positive events. *Journal of Persoanlity and Social Psychology*, 87, 228–245.

Gold, J. A., Ryckman, R. M., & Mosley, N. Z. (1984). Romantic mood induction and attraction to a dissimilar other: Is love blind? *Personality and Social Psychology Bulletin*, 10, 358–368.

Gottman, J. M. (1979). *Marital interaction: Experimental investigations*. New York, NY: Academic Press.

Graham, S. M., & Clark, M. S. (2008). Self-esteem and the organization of valenced information about others: The "Jekyll and Hyde"-ing of relationship partners. *Journal of Personality and Social Psychology*, 90, 652–665.

Graham, S. M., Huang, J. Y., Clark, M. S., & Helgeson, V. S. (2008). The positives of negative emotions: Willingness to express negative emotion promotes relationships. *Personality and Social Psychology Bulletin*, 34, 394–406.

Hoss, R. A., & Langlois, J. H. (2003). Infants prefer attractive faces. In O. Pascalis & A. Slater (Eds.), *The development of face processing in infancy and early childhood: Current perspectives* (pp. 27–38). Hauppauge, NY: Nova.

Johnson, D. J., & Rusbult, C. E. (1989). Resisting temptation: Devaluation of alternative partners as a means of maintaining commitment in close relationships. *Journal of Personality and Social Psychology*, 57, 967–980.

Jones, J. T., Pelham, B. W., Carvallo, M., & Mirenberg, M. C. (2004). How do I love thee? Let me count the Is: Implicit egoism and interpersonal attraction. *Journal of Personality and Social Psychology*, 87, 665–683.

Kaplan, K. J., Firestone, I. J., Degnore, R., & Morre, M. (1974). Gradients of attraction as a function of disclosure probe intimacy and setting formality: On distinguishing attitude oscillation from attitude change—Study one. *Journal of Personality and Social Psychology*, 30, 638–646.

Klohnen, E. C., & Luo, S. (2003). Interpersonal attraction and personality: What is attractive–self similarity, ideal similarity, complementrity or attachment security. *Journal of Personality and Social Psychology*, 85, 709–722.

Langlois, J. H. (1990). Attractive faces are only average. *Psychological Science*, 1, 115–121.

Langlois, J. H., & Roggman, L. A. (1990). Attractive faces are only average. *Psychological Science*, 1, 115–121.

Lehmiller, J. J., & Agnew, C. R. (2006.) Marginalized relationships: The impact of social disapproval on romantic relationship commitment. *Personality and Social Psychology Bulletin*, 32, 40–51.

Lemay, E. P., Clark, M. S., & Greenberg, A. (2010). What is beautiful is good because what is beautiful is desired. Physical attractiveness stereotyping as projection of interpersonal goals. *Personality and Social Psychology Bulletin*, 36, 339–353.

Little, A. C., Burt, D. M., & Perett, D. (2006). Assortative mating for perceived facial and personality traits. *Personality and Individual Differences*, 40, 973–984.

Lydon, J. E., Fitzsimons, G. M., & Naidoo, I. (2003). Devaluation versus enhancement of attractive alternatives: A critical test using the calibration paradigm. *Personality and Social Psychology Bulletin*, 29, 349–359.

MacDonald, G., & Leary, M. R. (2005). Why does social exclusion hurt? The relationship between social and physical pain. *Psychological Bulletin*, 131, 202–223.

Maner, J. K., DeWall, C. N., Baumeister, R. F., & Schaller, M. (2007). Does social exclusion motivate interpersonal reconnection? Resolving the "porcupine problem." *Journal of Personality and Social Psychology*, 92, 42–55.

Maner, J. K., Gailliot, M. T., & Miller, S. I. (2009). The implicit cognition of relationship maintenance: Inattention to attractive alternatives. *Journal of Experimental Social Psychology*, 92, 174–179.

Maner, J. K., Rouby, D. A., & Gonzaga, G. C. (2008). Automatic inattention to attractive alternatives: The evolved psychology of relationship maintenance. *Evolution and Human Behavior*, 29, 343–349.

McCullough, M. E. (2000). Forgiveness as human strength: Theory, measurement, and links to well-being. *Journal of Social and Clinical Psychology*, 19, 43–55.

Mikulincer, M., & Shaver, P. R. (2007). *Attachment in adulthood: Structure, dynamics, and change*. New York, NY: Guilford Press.

Mills, J., Clark, M. S., Ford, T. E., & Johnson, M. (2004). Measurement of communal strength. *Personal Relationships*, 11, 213–230.

Miller, R. (2012). *Intimate relationships* (6th ed.). New York, NY: McGraw-Hill.

Monin, J. K., Clark, M. S., & Lemay, E. P. (2008). Expecting more responsiveness from and feeling more responsiveness to female than to male family members. *Sex Roles*, 95, 420–441.

Moreland, R., & Beach, S. R. (1992). Exposure effects in the classroom: The development of affinity among students. *Journal of Experimental Social Psychology*, 28, 255–276.

Moreland, R., & Zajonc, R. (1982). Exposure effects in person perception: Familiarity, similarity & attraction. *Journal of Experimental Social Psychology*, 18, 395–415.

Murray, S. L., Bellavia, G. M., Rose, P., & Griffin, D. W. (2003). Once hurt, twice hurtful: How perceived regard regulates daily marital interactions. *Journal of Personality and Social Psychology*, 84, 126–147.

Murray, S. L., & Holmes, J. G. (2011). *Interdependent minds: The dynamics of close relationships*. New York, NY: Guilford Press.

Murray, S. L., & Holmes, J. G. (1993). Seeing virtues in faults: Negativity of the transformation of interpersonal narratives in close relationships. *Journal of Personality and Social Psychology*, 65, 707–722.

Murray, S. L., & Holmes, J. G. (1997). A leap of faith? Positive illusions in romantic relationships. *Personality and Social Psychology Bulletin*, 23, 586–604.

Murray, S. L., Holmes, J., & Collins, N. (2006). Optimizing assurance: The risk regulation system in relationships. *Psychological Bulletin*, 132, 641–666.

Murray, S. L., Holmes, J. G., Dolderman, D., & Griffin, D. (2000). What the motivated mind sees: Comparing friends' perspectives to married partners' views of each other. *Journal of Experimental Social Psychology*, 36, 600–620.

Murray, S. L., Holmes, J. G., & Griffin, D. (1996a) The benefits of positive illusions: Idealization and the construction of satisfaction in close relationships. *Journal of Personality and Social Psychology*, 70, 79–98.

Murray, S. L., Holmes, J. G., & Griffin, D. (1996b). The self-fulfilling nature of positive illusions in romantic relationships: Love is not blind, but prescient. *Journal of Personality and Social Psychology*, 71, 1155–1180.

Newcomb, T. M. (1961). *The acquaintance process*. New York, NY: Holt, Rinehart, & Winston.

Pettijohn, T. F., & Tesser, A. (2005). Threat and choices: When eye size matters. *The Journal of Social Psychology*, 145, 547–570.

Regan, P. (2011). *Close Relationships*. New York, NY: Routledge, Taylor Francis.

Reis, H. T., Clark, M. S., & Holmes, J. G. (2004). Perceived partner responsiveness as an organizing construct in the study of intimacy and closeness. In D. J. Mashek & A. P. Aron (Eds.), *Handbook of closeness and intimacy* (pp. 201–225). Mahwah, NJ: Erlbaum.

Reis, H. T., & Patrick, B. C. (1996). Attachment and intimacy: Component processes. In E. T. Higgins & A. W. Kruglanski (Eds.), *Social psychology: Handbook of basic principles*. New York, NY: Guilford Press.

Reis, H. T., & Shaver, P. (1988). Intimacy as an interpersonal process. In W. W. Duck (Ed.), *Handbook of personal relationships*. (pp. 367–391). New York, NY: John Wiley & Sons.

Rusbult, C. E., Bissonette, V. L., Arriaga, X. B., & Cox, C. L. (1998). Accommodation processes during the early years of marriage. In T. N. Bradbury (Ed.), *The developmental course of marital dysfunction*. (pp. 74–113). New York, NY: Cambridge University Press.

Rusbult, C. E., Coolsen, M. K., Kirchner, J. L., & Clarke, J. A. (2006). In A. Vangelisti & D. Perlman (Eds.), *The Cambridge handbook of personal relationships* (pp. 615–635). New York, NY: Cambridge University Press.

Rusbult, C. E., Hannon, P. A., Stocker, S. L., & Finkel, E. J. (2005). Forgiveness and relational repair. In E. L. Worthington Jr. (Ed.), *Handbook for forgiveness* (pp. 185–206). New York, NY: Brunner-Routledge.

Rusbult, C. E., & Van Lange, P. A. M. (2012). Interdependence theory. In A. W. Kruglanski, E. T. Higgins, & P. A. M. Van Lange (Eds.), *Handbook of theories of social psychology*. New York, NY: Sage.

Rusbult, C. E., Verette, J., Whitney, G., Slovik, L., & Lipkus, I. (1991). Accommodation processes in close relationships: Theory and preliminary empirical evidence. *Journal of Personality and Social Psychology*, 60, 53–78.

Shaver, P. R. & Mikulincer, M. (2012). Attachment theory. In P. A. M. Van Lange, A. W. Kruglanski, & E. T. Higgins (Eds.) *Handbook of Theories of Social Psychology, Vol. 2*, Thousand Oaks, CA: Sage Publications Ltd.

Sigall, H., & Landy, D. (1973). Radiating beauty: Effects of having a physically attractive partner on persona perception. *Journal of Personality and Social Psychology*, 28, 218–224.

Simpson, J. A., Rholes, W. S., & Nelligan, J. S. (1992). Support seeking and support giving within couples in an anxiety-provoking situation: The role of attachment styles. *Journal of Personality and Social Psychology*, 62, 434–446.

Simpson, J. A., Gangestad, S. W., & Lerma, M. (1990). Perception of physical attractiveness: Mechanisms involved in the maintenance of romantic relationships. *Journal of Personality and Social Psychology*, 59, 1192–1201.

Singh, R., Ng, R., Ong, E. L., & Lin, P. K. F. (2008). Different mediators for the age, sex and attitude similarity effects in interpersonal attraction. *Basic and Applied Social Psychology*, 30, 1–17.

Snyder, M., Tanke, E. O., & Berscheid, E. (1977). Social perception and interpersonal behavior: On the self-fulfilling nature of social stereotypes. *Journal of Personality and Social Psychology*, 35, 656–666.

Sprecher, S., & Felmlee, D. (1992). The influence of parents and friends on the quality and stability of romantic relationships: A three-wave longitudinal investigation. *Journal of Marriage and the Family*, 34, 888–900.

Swann, W. B. (1987). Identity negotiation: Where two roads meet. *Journal of Personality and Social Psychology*, 53, 1038–1051.

Tesser, A. (1988). Toward a self-evaluation maintenance model of social behavior. In L. Berkowitz (Ed.), *Advances in Experimental Social Psychology* (Vol. 21, pp. 181–227), San Diego, CA: Academic Press Inc.

Thornhill, R., & Gangestad, S. W. (1999). Facial attractiveness. *Trends in Cognitive Sciences*, 3, 452–460.

Van Lange, P. A. M., & Rusbult, C. E. (1995). My relationship is better than—and not as bad as—yours is: The perception of superiority in close relationships. *Personality and Social Psychology Bulletin*, 21, 32–44.

Van Lange, P. A. M., Rusbult, C. E., Drigotas, S. M., Arriaga, X. B., Witcher, B. S., & Cox, C. L. (1997). Willingness to sacrifice in close relationships. *Journal of Personality and Social Psychology*, 72, 1373–1395.

Whitton, S., Stanley, S., & Markman, H. (2002). Sacrifice in romantic relationships: An exploration of relevant research and theory. In A. L. Vangelisti, H. T. Reis, & M. A. Fitzpatrick (Eds.), *Stability and change in relationships* (pp. 156–181). Cambridge, MA: Cambridge University Press.

Williams, K. D. (2006). Cyberball: A program for use in research on interpersonal ostracism and acceptance. *Behavior Research Methods*, 38, 174–180.

Williams, K. D. (2007). Ostracism. *Annual Review of Psychology*, 58, 425–452.

Williams, K. D., & Sommer, K. L. (1997). Social ostracism by coworkers: Does rejection lead to loafing or compensation? *Personality and Social Psychology Bulletin*, 23, 693–706.

Williams, L. E., & Bargh, J. A. (2008). Experiencing physical warmth promotes interpersonal warmth. *Science*, 322, 606–607.

Williamson, G. M., & Clark, M. S. (1989). Providing help and desired relationship type as determinants of changes in moods and self-evaluations. *Journal of Personality and Social Psychology*, 56, 722–734.

Williamson, G. M., & Clark, M. S. (1992). Impact of desired relationship type on affective reactions to choosing and being required to help. *Personality and Social Psychology Bulletin*, 18, 10–18.

Williamson, G. M., Pegalis, I., Behan, A., & Clark, M. S. (1996). Affective consequences of refusing to help in communal and exchange relationships. *Personality and Social Psychology Bulletin*, 22, 34–47.

Zhong, C., & Leonardelli, G. (2008). Cold and lonely: Does social exclusion literally feel cold? *Psychological Science*, 19, 838–842.

CHAPTER 16

Prejudice

MONICA BIERNAT AND KELLY DANAHER

The study of prejudice has a long and rich history in psychology, one that aptly demonstrates the application of theory to a real-world, persistent, social problem. In using the term *prejudice*, we generally have in mind a "negative attitude toward a group or toward members of the group" (Stangor, 2009, p. 2). But, as will become clear below, prejudice can have seemingly positive components (as in benevolent attitudes expressed toward women, Glick & Fiske, 1996; Jackman, 1994), and can be context-specific (as indicated in negativity only toward "out of role" behavior; Eagly & Karau, 2002).

Prejudice is part of the triumvirate of concepts used in theorizing about intergroup relations, with *stereotyping* and *discrimination* completing the picture. Like most modern researchers, we conceptualize stereotypes as "beliefs about the personal attributes of a group of people" (Ashmore & Del Boca, 1981, p. 16), and stereotyping as the application of those beliefs to individual group members. Discrimination is typically *behavioral* in nature, and the research focus is primarily on negative behavioral treatment of groups and their members. In this chapter, we attempt to review dominant perspectives on understanding prejudice, but these perspectives often have implications for stereotyping and discrimination as well.

Prejudice has been a major focus of psychological research over the past century, and its popularity as an area of study continues to grow. Figure 16.1 reports the results of a recent search of the PscyInfo database, in which we tracked peer-reviewed journal articles with "prejudice" or "prejudicial attitude" as keywords, and then as title words. The first relevant journal article appeared in 1903. From that date through 2010, 4,814 journal articles used "prejudice" as a keyword, and 1,379 used "prejudice" in their

titles.[1] Other than the slow start to the psychology's interest in prejudice over the past century, what is perhaps most remarkable is the focus on this area in the past decade—more than half the referenced journal articles in the entire database were published between 2001 and 2010.

Approaches to prejudice have varied in focus and method, and as suggested by Duckitt (1992), have been responsive to social and historical contexts. Dovidio (2001) identified three "waves" of thinking that have predominated prejudice research. Initial theorizing approached prejudice as an individual difference (e.g., authoritarian personality; Altemeyer, 1981), with "prejudiced personalities" as the culprits of negative attitudes and intergroup hostilities. These personality theories gave way to explanations of prejudice that stressed normal psychological processes rooted in the socio-cultural structures of society and cognitive functioning. In recent years—the third wave—research on prejudice has taken on an air of multidimensionality, with models taking into account individual differences, cognitive, motivational, and affective mechanisms, all existing within and interacting with a particular sociocultural context. In the current chapter, we attempt to advance this "third wave" by outlining major theoretical perspectives that have guided psychological research since Allport's (1954) seminal work, *The Nature of Prejudice*.

---

[1]Undoubtedly, these counts include some false positives, as when prejudice is used in a legal sense ("without prejudice"), as a general form of negativity toward or bias against something other than social groups, and when Jane Austen's famous book is referenced. But we assume these false alarms are randomly distributed across the time period.

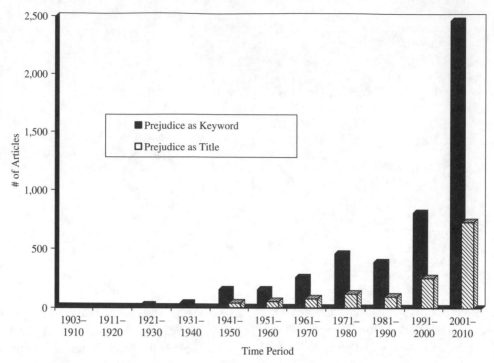

Figure 16.1 Number of peer-reviewed journal articles between 1903 and 2010 containing the words "prejudice" or "prejudicial attitude" as keywords and titles, by decade (data from PsycInfo)

The literature reviewed in this chapter reflects the current complex state of prejudice research. We have classified the models we review below in terms of a major guiding theoretical orientation (e.g., norms, motivations, evolutionary perspectives), but these often incorporate multiple levels of analysis or integrative frameworks. Current research also illuminates the targets of prejudice as well as the interactions between perpetrators and targets. And of course psychologists have long been concerned with reducing prejudice; in this chapter, we consider major classes of approaches to improving intergroup relations.

Because of the diversity and magnitude of the literature on prejudice, our review is necessarily selective. We also chose not to provide much coverage of measurement issues, despite the growing interest in the field in implicit attitudes and their measurement via various response-latency, evaluative priming, and physiological techniques (see Correll, Judd, Park, & Wittenbrink, 2010, for a review). Nonetheless, we hope to describe some of the major theoretical and empirical approaches in the field. An overview of the theories we review, grouped roughly by overarching approach, appears in Table 16.1.

Undoubtedly, much prejudice research has been conducted in reaction to concerns of equality. We take on this tradition in the next section by elaborating on models of prejudice reduction. We end by considering the perspective of the targets of prejudice, focusing on how and when

prejudice is perceived and the consequences of stereotyping and prejudice for individual performance.

MODELS OF PREJUDICE

We begin our review of the prejudice literature by elaborating on some of the major perspectives and models of prejudice that have dominated the field in recent years (see Table 16.1). Our goal is to describe modern research and ideas while at the same time respecting the historical backdrop against which these modern views developed.

Intergroup Approaches

A number of theories in the prejudice literature highlight the importance of intergroup differentiation—an us/them orientation—as key to the expression of prejudice. An important field study by Sherif and Sherif (1953) led to the development of Realistic Conflict Theory (RCT; Levine & Campbell, 1972; Sherif, 1966), which posits that prejudice is a product of resource conflict between two groups (for details, see Dovidio et al., this volume).

Whereas Realistic Conflict Theory suggests that intergroup conflict is necessary for prejudice, Tajfel, Billig, Bundy, and Flament (1971) recognized the importance of mere ingroup versus outgroup categorization as a precursor to prejudice. To test this idea, Tajfel and colleagues

TABLE 16.1 Overview of Models of Prejudice Reviewed in This Chapter

Intergroup Approaches:

Realistic conflict (Sherif, 1966)

Social Identity Theory; Self-Categorization Theory (Tajfel & Turner, 1979; Turner et al., 1987)

Infrahumanization (Leyens et al., 2000)

Normative Approaches:

Group norm theory and modern variants (Blanchard et al., 1994; Crandall et al., 2002; M. Sherif & C. Sherif, 1953 Stangor et al., 2001)

Aversive racism (Gaertner & Dovidio, 1986)

Motivations to control/avoid prejudice (Dunton & Fazio, 1997; Plant & Devine, 1998)

Evolutionary Approaches:

Principle of coalitional exploitation (Kurzban & Leary, 2001)

Social dominance (Pratto et al., 1994; Sidanius & Pratto, 1993)

Sociofunctional threat-based approach and other evolutionary threats (Cottrell & Neuberg, 2005; Park et al., 2007; Schaller et al., 2003)

Subordinate male target hypothesis (Navarrete et al., 2010; Sidanius & Veniegas, 2000)

Motivational Approaches:

Integrated threat (W. Stephan & C. Stephan, 2000)

Identity threat and Social Identity Theory (Ellemers et al., 1999; Tajfel & Turner, 1986)

Terror management theory (Greenberg et al., 1990)

System justification (Jost & Banaji, 1994)

Dual-process motivational model (Duckitt & Sibley, 2009)

Justification-suppression model (Crandall & Eshleman, 2003)

Complex Content of Prejudice:

Ambivalence (sexism, Glick & Fiske, 1996; Nadler & Morrow, 1959; racism, Katz et al., 1986)

Intergroup emotions (Mackie & Smith, 2002)

Stereotype content model (Fiske et al., 2002)

developed the *minimal groups paradigm* in which participants were assigned to groups ostensibly based on a perception task (dot-estimation or painting preferences). The simple division of participants into arbitrary groups, with no intergroup interaction, was sufficient to produce ingroup favoritism, as measured in a point-allocation task whereby rewards and punishments were distributed to group members and later exchangeable for money. Indeed, participants in these studies were inclined to divide points so as to maximize the difference between ingroup and outgroup allocations rather than merely to maximize ingroup benefit. This paradigm demonstrated that the mere categorization of ingroup versus outgroup may be sufficient to produce outgroup derogation and ingroup favoritism (see Rothbart & Lewis, 1994).

Expanding on the minimal groups paradigm, Tajfel and Turner (1979) developed Social Identity Theory (SIT). Accounting for both cognitive and motivational aspects of group identification, SIT posited that people come to perceive themselves as psychologically belonging to a group and in turn strive to maintain positive regard toward the group. Self Categorization Theory (SCT; Turner, 1981; Turner, Hogg, Oakes, Reicher, & Wetherell, 1987), developed by Turner and colleagues to more fully account for cognitive mechanism underlying identity, argues that when an ingroup identity becomes sufficiently salient, depersonalization occurs such that people come to view themselves and act as group members (interchangeable with other ingroup members). Taken together, these theories suggest that context-defined ingroup identities structure intergroup relations with people striving to maintain *positive in-group distinctiveness* (see also Dovidio et al., this volume).

Research has since demonstrated that this has implications for differential ingroup versus outgroup treatment beyond point allocations in the minimal group studies. For example, the linguistic intergroup bias model suggests that language used to describe an ingroup versus outgroup member's actions differs, such that negative ingroup and positive outgroup action are described with more abstract language (Maass, Salvi, Arcuri, & Semin, 1989). In addition, SIT researchers have repeatedly demonstrated that threats to the ingroup can lead to outgroup derogation (e.g., Branscombe & Wann, 1994; see section on "motivational approaches" below).

SIT and SCT established a theoretical understanding of ingroup identity and intergroup relations, yet the theories did not distinguish between ingroup preference and outgroup derogation. As seen in the minimal groups paradigm, participants allocated points to increase the difference between their own group and the other group; both ingroup favoritism and outgroup derogation were acting to produce intergroup discrimination. However, ingroup favoritism and outgroup derogation are distinct phenomenon with different underlying mechanisms (Brewer, 1999). This leads to the question: Is prejudice due to ingroup positivity or outgroup negativity?

Research points to both, but suggests that one does not necessitate the other (Brewer, 1979; Paladino & Castelli, 2008; Perdue, Dovidio, Gurtman, & Tyler, 1990). According to the positive-negative asymmetry model (Otten & Mummendey, 2000; Wenzel & Mummendey, 1996), whether ingroup favoritism or outgroup derogation occurs depends on the valence of the outcomes at hand. For example, minimal group members favored the ingroup's "product" (a poster created to advertise a theatre performance) when evaluations of the ingroup and outgroup posters were made on positive attributes (Wenzel & Mummendey, 1996). But when allocating negative outcomes (ratings on negative attributes), ingroup favoritism diminished, with the outgroup and ingroup receiving equal evaluations. Decreases in preferential treatment of the ingroup presumably occur because negative outcomes increase processing effort, which in turn increases awareness of intergroup norms that the ingroup should not be unfairly privileged (Otten & Mummendey, 2000; Wenzel & Mummendey, 1996).

Other research indicates that contextual variables moderate the extent to which ingroup favoritism occurs. For example, as group status increases, intergroup bias increases: Members of high-status groups tend to show more ingroup favoritism and outgroup derogation than do members of low-status groups (Bettencourt, Dorr, Charlton, & Hume, 2001; Mullen, Brown, & Smith, 1992), although this status effect may be limited to experimentally created (as opposed to "real") groups. In addition, communication context and intergroup motives qualify group status effects (Scheepers, Spears, Doosje, & Manstead, 2006). For example, in the presence of other ingroup members, those in low-status groups are more likely to show ingroup favoritism when change in status is possible.

Although outgroup derogation and ingroup preference are distinct phenomena, *infrahumanization*—perceiving the ingroup (compared to the outgroup) as more fully capturing the essence of humanity—involves both outgroup derogation and ingroup preference (Leyens et al., 2000). According to this perspective, the ingroup is viewed as superior to the outgroup because the ingroup is more uniquely human than the outgroup. That is, the "human essence" characterizes the ingroup more so than the outgroup.

What does it mean to be uniquely human? Human essence is operationalized as experiencing secondary emotions, those emotions (e.g., affection, pride, remorse) that are internally caused and nuanced, and less intense than basic, primary emotions (e.g., joy, sadness, and anger; Leyens et al., 2000). Primary emotions are animalistic in that they are displayed across species; they also develop early in life, and tend to be automatic, brief, and of sudden occurrence. Secondary emotions, on the other hand, are uniquely human; they are "more invisible, more cognitive, more moral, less intense, longer in time, and appearing later in age" (p. 189). Leyens et al. (2001) found that although primary emotions are attributed equally to the ingroup and outgroup, secondary emotions—both negative and positive—are more likely to be attributed to the ingroup than the outgroup. Returning to a simplified view of intergroup hostility, the infrahumanization perspective suggests that the differential attribution of secondary emotions to the ingroup occurs regardless of status differentials and conflict, though some degree of identification with the ingroup is necessary (Leyens, 2009; Leyens et al., 2001).

Infrahumanization has important consequences for intergroup conflict (Demoulin, Pozo, & Leyens, 2009). For example, the more Northern Irelanders infrahumanized the less likely they were to forgive the outgroup (Catholics for Protestants; Protestants for Catholics) for intergroup transgressions (Tam et al., 2007). In addition, outgroups that do express secondary emotions may nonetheless be treated more negatively than ingroups who do the same (Vaes, Paladino, Castelli, Leyens, & Giovanazzi, 2003). In one study, "lost e-mails" were sent to researchers from different universities throughout Belgium (Vaes et al., 2003, Study 1). The e-mail, meant for another person, opened with a statement containing either a primary emotion ("I'm beside myself with rage") or a secondary emotion ("I'm filled with indignation"). The sender was ostensibly an ingroup member (a researcher from the same university) or an outgroup member (a researcher from a private company). E-mail responses from the participants were coded for formality, with formal language reflecting a desire to maintain distance from the e-mailer. Responses to the e-mail did not differ for ingroup and outgroup targets when primary emotions were expressed. But when secondary emotions were expressed, responses used less formal language, espousing more solidarity, when the sender was an ingroup rather than an outgroup member. Expression of secondary emotions by the outgroup also instigates outgroup avoidance relative to expression of secondary emotions by the ingroup (Vaes et al., 2003, Study 4).

An ingroup-outgroup distinction is central to the intergroup perspectives reviewed in this section. The differential treatment of the ingroup compared to the outgroup is a product of basic us/them categorizations—even those based on minimal group definitions—that lead to attempts to maintain positive distinctiveness of the ingroup and view the ingroup as more essentially human.

Normative Approaches

The importance of norms in understanding prejudice was recognized at least as early as Sherif and Sherif's (1953) classic volume, *Groups in Harmony and Tension*. They wrote: "[T]he factors leading individuals to form attitudes of prejudice are not piecemeal. Rather, their formation is functionally related to becoming a group member—to adopting the group and its values (norms) as the main anchorage in regulating experience and behavior" (p. 218).

Allport (1954) was less certain about this "group-norm theory of prejudice," arguing instead that "prejudice is ultimately a problem of personality formation and development... no individual would mirror his group's attitude unless he had a personal need, or personal habit, that leads him to do so" (p. 39). Still, Allport recognized that groups norms matter and that indeed "the major influences upon the individual may be collective" (p. 39).

Early research documenting the importance of norms included Prothro's (1952) study of anti-Semitic and anti-Negro prejudice in Louisiana. Although authoritarianism or the "prejudiced personality" was a dominant framework for understanding prejudice at the time, Prothro noted that about 41% of his sample simultaneously reported *anti*-Black and *pro*-Jewish attitudes. Instead of focusing on personality to understand prejudice, Prothro (1952) argued that, "situational, historical, and cultural factors appear to be of considerable, perhaps major, import" (p. 108). Similarly, in a comparison of southern and New England white respondents, Pettigrew (1959) found little regional difference in authoritarianism but strong differences in anti-Black prejudice. Furthermore, it was among southern respondents "whose positions in the social structure should be associated with conformity to the culture's dictates...: females, political party identifiers, church attenders, and the upwardly mobile" who "proved to be more intolerant of Negroes than their counterparts" (p. 34).

Norms play an important role in a more modern theoretical perspective, Gaertner and Dovidio's (1986, 2000) theory of *aversive racism*. This was one of the "new racism" theories that emerged in the 1980s (along with modern racism, McConahay, Hardee, & Batts, 1981; symbolic racism, Kinder & Sears, 1981; and ambivalent racism perspectives, Katz, Wackenhut, & Hass, 1986). In contrast to old-fashioned "dominative" forms of racism (see Kovel, 1970), aversive racists "support public policies that, in principle, promote racial equality and ameliorate the consequences of racism,... regard themselves as nonprejudiced and nondiscriminatory; but, almost unavoidably, possess negative feelings and beliefs about blacks" (Gaertner & Dovidio, 1986, p. 62). The normative context determines whether the egalitarian or negative feelings are expressed: "Because aversive racists are very concerned about their egalitarian self-images, they are strongly motivated in interracial contexts to avoid acting in recognizably unfavorable or normatively inappropriate ways" (p. 66).

Thus, in structured normative situations, where expectations for appropriate behavior are clear, aversive racists should express positivity toward and egalitarian treatment of Blacks. But in normatively ambiguous or unstructured environments, anti-Black sentiment may be expressed. Much support for this contextual prediction has accumulated over the years. For example, Whites gave equal help to Black and White fellow students who were struggling with a difficult task (a situation that clearly calls for help-giving), but discriminated against Blacks who requested help after they had failed to try hard at the task (a situation where *not* giving help may be justified; Frey & Gaertner, 1986). In a study simulating undergraduate admissions, no race bias was found in evaluations of very strong or very weak applicants, but Blacks were less likely to be admitted than Whites when applicant quality was mixed (Hodson, Dovidio, & Gaertner, 2002).

In these normatively unstructured situations, Whites can maintain a sense of the self as nonprejudiced by attributing their behavior to nonracial causes. Recent theorizing from an aversive racism perspective suggests that this pattern is particularly characteristic of individuals who score low in explicit measures of racial prejudice (consistent with the self-image as egalitarian) but who nonetheless show evidence of implicit racial prejudice (consistent with the lurking, perhaps early-learned "negative feelings"; see Dovidio, 2001). Indeed, an interesting line of research suggests that interactions with such "aversive racists" are experienced more negatively by Blacks than interactions with Whites who hold explicit and implicit racial attitudes (Dovidio, 2001; Penner et al., 2009).

Individual differences are also incorporated in another normative approach that considers people's effort to control prejudiced responding. Plant and Devine (1998) have suggested that in this modern-day normative climate, individuals may be motivated by *extrinsic* reasons to avoid being (or appearing) prejudiced, as well as *intrinsic* factors, both of which are measurable via self-report (see also Dunton & Fazio, 1997). That is, some individuals may be motivated "to comply with nonprejudiced social norms and to avoid disapproval from others," whereas others "may be internally motivated to respond without prejudice in order to behave in accordance with personally held nonprejudiced beliefs" (Plant & Devine, 2009, p. 641). These motivations may differ in the extent to which they contribute to the self-regulation of prejudice, with those high in external motivation doing what they can to reduce "detectable" prejudice so as not to appear prejudiced to others, whereas those high in intrinsic motivation seek to eliminate any prejudice, detectable or not (Plant & Devine, 2009). Indeed, self-regulation of prejudice may operate in part such that individuals attempt to match their actual responses and behaviors in interracial interactions with normative standards or goals, thereby reducing any discrepancies between how they "should" behave and how they "would" behave (Monteith, 1993; Monteith & Mark, 2009).

Normative influence on prejudice has also been demonstrated in a number of studies that involve exposing individuals to information about the attitudes of relevant others. For example, respondents completing an on-campus survey reported more antiracist sentiment after hearing the opinion of a peer who was antiracist, and more condoning of racism after exposure to a racist peer (Blanchard, Crandall, Brigham, & Vaughn, 1994), and exposure to feedback about the consensual beliefs of a peer group about the stereotypes of African Americans moved individuals' own endorsement of stereotypes in the direction of that feedback (Stangor, Sechrist, & Jost, 2001). Across 105 different social groups, Crandall, Eshleman, and O'Brien (2002) found that personal prejudice toward the groups correlated extremely highly ($r = .96$) with judgments of the normative appropriateness of being prejudiced toward those groups ("definitely OK to have negative feelings about this group"). These researchers conclude, "Social norms are remarkably strong predictors of expressed prejudice—to ask about the norms regarding prejudice is, in practical terms, the same as asking people how they personally feel" (Crandall et al., 2002, p. 374).

In sum, normative approaches stress the influence of others' beliefs on the individual's experience and expression of prejudice. Norms establish which contexts are appropriate for expression of negative attitudes, as well as *which groups* are or should be targets of prejudice. Intrinsic and extrinsic motivations to avoid prejudice both originate in societal standards of prejudice expression, with those who are intrinsically motivated having successfully internalized those norms.

Evolutionary Approaches

Perhaps an even broader perspective on the nature of prejudice considers distal, evolutionary mechanisms, which contribute to modern-day intergroup bias. One might trace ingroup favoritism, for example, to the advantages offered by small coalitional groups in early human history: protection from threats and access to opportunities that facilitated reproductive fitness (e.g., Brewer & Caporael, 2006; Cosmides, Tooby, & Kurzban, 2003). Indeed, prejudice toward broad social outgroups—such as those based on racial and ethnic group membership—may be based

in "coalitional exploitation" (Kurzban & Leary, 2001): "Human beings possess a complex coalitional psychology, a set of domain-specific cognitive systems that are designed to foster cooperation within a group for the purpose of exploiting those who are not part of the group" (p. 195).

Other aspects of group life, such as the development of dominance hierarchies, may also be evolutionarily based and relevant for intergroup prejudice. Social dominance theory (SDT), for example, suggests that "many forms of group-based oppression, plus the culturally shared justifications for them (in, for example, religions) are as pervasive as they are because they have been of survival value for the human group throughout its evolutionary history" (Sidanius & Pratto, 1993, p. 173). From this perspective, institutions and individuals develop hierarchy-enhancing and -legitimizing ideologies that promote the superiority of some groups over others and legitimize discrimination. Furthermore, conflict between groups is minimized via consensus on these ideologies (e.g., belief in meritocracy, the Protestant work ethic, social Darwinism), though dominants tend to endorse hierarchy-enhancing ideologies more than do subordinates (e.g., see Pratto, Sidanius, & Levin, 2006; Pratto, Sidanius, Stallworth, & Bertram, 1994; Sidanius, Pratto, Martin, & Stallworth, 1991).

A variety of threats relevant to group life may also have resulted in specific adaptations through evolutionary history that contribute to specific *kinds* of prejudices (e.g., see Cottrell & Neuberg, 2005; Kurzban & Leary, 2001). For example, prejudice toward people with physical disabilities may be linked to the threat of disease (Kurzban & Leary, 2001; Park, Faulkner, & Schaller, 2003). Because many contagious diseases have a visible physical manifestation, "psychological mechanisms that attended to and precipitated avoidant reactions to these cues would have been adaptive" (Park et al., 2003, p. 68). Thus, one might predict disgust and avoidance in reaction to these cues. This adaptation may also produce oversensitization and false positives, such that disgust, avoidance, and prejudice are triggered in response to physical anomalies that are *not* contagious (e.g., severed limbs; obesity; cancer; see Park, Schaller, & Crandall, 2007). For example, Park et al. (2007) found that participants implicitly associated fat people with disease, particularly after the threat of pathogens was made salient.

Additionally, prejudice toward and exclusion of groups such as the poor and the elderly may be based in those groups' lack of capital (social and economic resources), typically favored in cooperative relationships (Kurzban & Leary, 2001). Unpredictability (as evidenced in groups such as the mentally ill) and evidence of cheating (as in the case of criminals) may also threaten cooperative relationships and lead to avoidance and rejection. This perspective suggests that humans have developed an adaptation for cooperation that also results in "discriminate sociality": avoidance of "interactions with individuals who are poor partners for social exchange" or "pose a social cost greater than their potential social benefit" (Kurzban & Leary, 2001, p. 192).

Potential dangers from intergroup contact in early human history—aggression, injury—may also have contributed to a cognitive adaptation that supports aggression-related beliefs about outgroup members. Associations between outgroups and traits indicating "danger" may be particularly salient in modern life when individuals feel vulnerable in some way. Indeed, a recent line of research by Schaller and colleagues suggests that dimly lit or darkened environments are especially conducive to the activation of stereotypic associations of Blacks as dangerous (aggressive, hostile, threatening), particularly among individuals who generally tend to view the world as a dangerous place (Schaller, Park, & Mueller, 2003; see also Cottrell & Neuberg, 2005).

Further theorizing suggests that outgroup *men* are particularly likely to be the agents of outgroup bias: "The potential for dramatic zero-sum imbalances between successful and unsuccessful male coalitions would have created a strong selection pressure for a suite of *male-specific* psychological mechanisms that motivate aggression toward, and dominance of, other social groups" (Navarrete, McDonald, Molina, & Sidanius, 2010, p. 934). For the same reasons, outgroup men are more likely to be the *targets* of prejudice as well. The *subordinate male target hypothesis* suggests that men are more biased than women, particularly toward subordinate outgroup men, a pattern supported in attitudinal survey data (see Sidanius & Veniegas, 2000). According to this perspective, women may also be prejudiced toward outgroup males, but for different reasons. For women, selection pressures may have shaped fear-based motivation, namely, fear of sexual coercion. Navarrete et al. (2010) found that in women, anti-Black prejudice and fear of Black men (but not White men) were predicted by perceived vulnerability to sexual coercion. Among men, aggression was a strong predictor of anti-Black bias, particularly among those high in social dominance orientation. These researchers suggest that "intergroup bias is primarily directed at males and is motivated by separate psychological systems between men and women that reflect the selection pressures that shaped these systems" (Navarrete et al., 2010, p. 936).

The evolutionary perspective offers a broad lens through which to understand basic features of human (and nonhuman) intergroup behavior. Central to this perspective is the idea that cognitive structures that contribute to prejudice have evolved in response to environmental challenges in our evolutionary past. Natural selection is thus a distal motivational underpinning that contributes to prejudice toward specific marginalized groups and outgroups more generally. Though sometimes challenged by perspectives that highlight more proximal predictors and moderators of prejudice, the evolutionary approach has become an important piece of the prejudice puzzle.

Motivational Approaches

Motivation figures in a number of theoretical approaches to prejudice, and indeed, considering it a separate type of perspective may be misleading (Yzerbyt, 2010). Motivation is clearly relevant to cognitive and intergroup approaches, in that epistemic needs such as the desire for understanding and control may lead to biases that maintain stereotyping and prejudice (e.g., Tajfel, 1982). It is also relevant to evolutionary approaches, which highlight distal reproductive fitness motives, and to normative approaches in which the need to belong may contribute to the following of group norms (e.g., Haslam et al., 1996). Recent theorizing suggests that prejudice be conceptualized using a "core motives" approach, whereby the needs "to know, to belong, and to have positive value" contribute to prejudice directed toward outgroups (Yzerbyt, 2010, p. 156; see also Yzerbyt & Demoulin, 2010). Despite this overlap with other perspectives, in this section we consider those approaches that specifically highlight "hot" factors that contribute to the experience and expression of prejudice, such as threat and motivated ideology.

Integrated threat theory offers a taxonomy of threats and fears relevant to prejudice and discrimination (W. Stephan & Stephan, 2000). These include realistic threats (as when groups contribute for economic resources; see Levine & Campbell, 1972), symbolic threats (such as value differences; see Biernat, Vescio, Theno, & Crandall, 1996), intergroup anxiety (e.g., tension caused by anticipated intergroup contact; see Britt, Boniecki, Vescio, Biernat, & Brown, 1996; Shelton & Richeson, 2006), and negative stereotypes (e.g., beliefs that groups are lazy or hostile). Each of these factors has been found to predict prejudice toward a variety of groups (see Riek, Mania, & Gaertner, 2006). In each case, the assumption is that prejudice serves to reduce whatever threat is perceived.

Self- and collective-esteem (or identity) threats have perhaps been examined most often in the literature, guided largely by the premise of social identity theory (SIT) that people strive to maintain or enhance a positive social identity, and that this can be accomplished, in part, by favorably distinguishing important ingroups from outgroups (i.e., engaging in ingroup bias; Tajfel & Turner, 1986; see Ellemers, Spears, & Doosje, 1999). There is considerable evidence that threats to one's group status or identity contribute to prejudice (e.g., see Ellemers et al., 1999). There is also evidence that threats to individual self-esteem promote the expression of prejudice. For example, Fein and Spencer (1997) found that following failure feedback on an intellectual task, non-Jewish participants denigrated a Jewish job applicant more so than did those who received success feedback and/or evaluated a non-Jewish applicant. That is, the self-esteem threat of failure led to derogation of an outgroup target. But the broader literature reveals inconsistent findings on this point. Some have suggested that it is those high in self-esteem who feel more free to express their prejudices than those low in self-esteem (Aberson, Healy, & Romero, 2000); in the SIT literature itself, the self-esteem hypothesis has been questioned (Abrams & Hogg, 1988).

But research evidence seems to be more clear about how engaging in prejudice or discrimination can enhance self-esteem. In Fein and Spencer's (1997) failure feedback study, those who engaged in outgroup denigration showed a subsequent increase in self-esteem; denigration mediated the threat—self-esteem relationship (Fein & Spencer, 1997, Study 3). In a very different sample—Dutch and Turkish preadolescents living in the Netherlands—derogation of the outgroup relative to the ingroup was also associated with increases in collective self-esteem, at least among those highly identified with their ethnic ingroup (Verkuyten, 2007; see also Rubin & Hewstone, 1998, and Aberson et al., 2000, for a review).

Beyond self-esteem, other "threats" have also been linked to prejudice, including existential concerns raised by awareness of own mortality. For example, mortality salience has been found to enhance anti-Jewish sentiment among Christian respondents (Greenberg et al., 1990), and anti-German sentiment among Italians (Castano, Yzerbyt, Paladino, & Sacchi, 2002). Terror management theory suggests that the existential terror caused by awareness of one's own mortality prompts attempts to bolster and defend one's cultural worldviews and self-esteem. Derogation of outgroups—whose worldviews may differ from one's own—may serve a means of worldview defense in response to this existential threat (see Greenberg, Landau, Kosloff, & Solomon, 2009, for a review).

Individuals may also be motivated toward prejudice and stereotyping by system justifying beliefs (e.g., Jost & Banaji, 1994; Jost, Banaji, & Nosek, 2004). Pressures exist to perceive the existing societal system—including its hierarchical structure—as just and legitimate. Prejudice toward low-status groups may be a means of justifying this structure, and stereotypes of high-status relative to low-status groups as intelligent and agentic (i.e., deserving of their status) may serve this purpose as well. The system may also be perceived as just or legitimate if one engages in complementary stereotyping. For example, perceiving the poor as "happy" and the rich as "miserable" may contribute to a perception of the current social structure as legitimate (Kay & Jost, 2003). Recent research suggests that those who perceive status differences between groups, or for whom the status quo is threatened, are particularly likely to engage in this kind of "complementary stereotyping," and such complementarity also predicts stronger perceptions of the legitimacy of the social system (see Kay, Jost, & Young, 2005; see also Dovidio et al., this volume).

Other approaches have highlighted the importance of perceived threats to the social order in promoting prejudice. Duckitt and his colleagues have suggested two paths by which such threats and personality traits combine to affect a variety of sociopolitical attitudes, including prejudice (Duckitt, 2001; Sibley & Duckitt, 2009). In their dual-process motivational model, a first path to prejudice is based in Right Wing Authoritarianism (RWA; Altemeyer, 1988), which "expresses the value or motivational goal of establishing and maintaining societal security, order, cohesion, and stability" (Sibley & Duckitt, 2009, p. 101). RWA itself derives from both personality factors (e.g., low openness and high conscientiousness) and socialization within dangerous or threatening environments. Those high in RWA are particularly sensitive to social threats (danger, unpredictability) and respond with heightened prejudice toward outgroups. A second path to prejudice is based in Social Dominance Orientation (SDO; Pratto et al., 1994), which develops from a different set of personality factors (e.g., low agreeableness) and socialization contexts that emphasize group dominance and competition. These give rise to a view of the world as a "ruthlessly competitive jungle" and heightened sensitivity to threats to group dominance, and subsequently to increased outgroup prejudice (Sibley & Duckitt, 2009, p. 102). In this dual process motivational model, personality and contextual factors contribute to different ideological systems, which motivate threat-consistent interpretations of the environment and promote prejudice expression.

At the same time, individuals may also be motivated toward *lower* expressions of prejudice when made aware that their state of privilege over outgroups is illegitimate. For example, in one study, framing of racial inequality in terms of White privilege (e.g., "White Americans can easily rent or purchase housing in any area where they can afford to live") led to lower levels of racism than did the same content framed in terms of Black disadvantage (e.g., "Black Americans often have difficulty renting or purchasing housing, even in areas where they can afford to live" (Powell, Branscombe, & Schmitt, 2005, p. 511). Furthermore, this effect was mediated by the experience of collective guilt (Branscombe, Doosje, & McGarty, 2002), suggesting that reduced expression of prejudice served to lessen an uncomfortable affective state. Others have also posited that awareness of illegitimate intergroup inequality may lead to negative self- and other-directed affect, including guilt, and that the discomfort created by these emotions prompts lesser reports of prejudice (Czopp & Monteith, 2003; Dovidio et al., 2004).

The Justification-Suppression Model (JSM; Crandall & Eshleman, 2003) offers an integrative perspective on prejudice that is fundamentally motivational in nature. The JSM suggests a distinction between "true" prejudice and "expressed" prejudice, with justification and suppression processes mediating the relationship between the two. According to this model, a conflict exists between people's desire "to express an emotion" (their prejudices) and "to maintain values and self-concepts that conflict with prejudice" (Crandall & Eshleman, 2003, p. 414). Genuine prejudice is described as "an affective reaction that has motivational force" and pushes for expression (p. 417), but expression is blocked by suppression processes and/or released by justification processes.

Suppression processes include the effects of social norms, discussed earlier in this chapter—in many situations, expression of prejudice may not be tolerated, either by external audiences or the self—as well as egalitarian value systems and the experience of empathy (Galinsky & Moskowitz, 2000). Justification processes, on the other hand, allow for the release of suppressed prejudices "without suffering external or internal sanction" (p. 425). These include beliefs that preserve the status quo (e.g., belief in a just world, Lerner, 1977; right wing authoritarianism, Adorno, Frenkel-Brunswick, Levinson, & Sanford, 1950; Altemeyer, 1988), as well as those that "celebrate" hierarchy (e.g., social dominance orientation, Pratto et al., 1994; system justification, Jost & Banaji, 1994). Thus, individual differences that historically have been considered "causes" of prejudice are conceptualized in the Justification-Suppression Model as "justifiers" that allow prejudice expression. Other justification factors include stereotypes themselves; again, rather than causing prejudice, negative outgroup stereotypes may serve to justify derogation of the group (see Tajfel & Turner, 1979) and validate their lesser privilege relative to others (Jost & Banaji, 1994; Kay & Jost, 2003).

These perspectives overlap with those reviewed in previous sections, but they highlight the importance of proximal "hot" mechanisms—self- and group- protection, emotions, and the affective force of prejudice itself—in understanding intergroup attitudes. Individuals face a variety of threats to group- or self-esteem, and prejudice may be a response that reduces these threats. At the same time, guilt may reduce the expression of prejudice, especially when high-status group members recognize the illegitimacy of their status. Individuals may also be motivated to justify the status quo, and derogation of low status groups, along with complementary stereotyping, may meet this need. Models such as Duckitt's (2001) dual-process motivational model and the Justification-Suppression Model stress the importance of motivations in supporting and deterring prejudice expression.

Complexity and Differentiation of Prejudices

A number of models of prejudice suggest a more nuanced view of the prejudice construct, one that goes beyond the definition of prejudice as merely "negative attitudes" or "negative feelings" toward groups. Research on sexism in particular has drawn attention to the fact that prejudice against women is about more than antipathy. High levels of interpersonal contact, intimacy, and interdependence between the sexes may preclude a tendency for men to simply dislike women (Eagly & Diekman, 2005; Glick & Fiske, 1996). Indeed, women typically are viewed more favorably than men by both women and men, a pattern labeled the "women are wonderful" effect (Eagly & Mladinic, 1989), observed on both explicit and implicit measures of gender attitudes (e.g., Rudman & Goodwin, 2004).

For Eagly and her colleagues, prejudice is better defined as an "attitude in context," and rests on the principle of role incongruity: "Prejudice often results from the mismatch between beliefs about the attributes typically possessed by members of a social group (that is, their stereotype) and beliefs about the attributes that facilitate success in valued social roles . . . such incongruity . . . does not necessarily lead to a generalized hostile attitude toward the mismatched individual but rather to a decline in evaluation relative to a matched individual in the context of the particular role" (Eagly & Diekman, 2005, p. 19). Thus, for example, prejudice against female leaders may be based not in antipathy per se, but on the perception that women do not "fit" the leadership role as well as men (Eagly & Karau, 2002; see also Heilman, 1983).

Another perspective regarding sexism proposes that attitudes toward women may reflect *ambivalence* (Glick & Fiske, 1996, 2001; Nadler & Morrow, 1959). Ambivalent sexism incorporates both hostile and benevolent components: Hostile sexism may fit more classic definitions of prejudice and reflect antipathy toward women, especially as they move into roles typically occupied by men. But benevolent sexism is "a set of interrelated attitudes toward women that are sexist in terms of viewing women stereotypically and in restricted roles but that are subjectively positive in feeling tone (for the perceiver)" (Glick & Fiske, 1996, p. 491). Despite this seeming positivity, benevolent sexism is ultimately patronizing in nature (see Jackman, 1994). Indeed, in a cross-nation study, levels of *both* benevolent and hostile sexism predicted negative societal outcomes for women (Glick & Fiske, 2001).

A different kind of ambivalence is typically considered in approaches to understanding *racism*, and specifically White Americans' attitudes toward Black Americans. Myrdal's (1944) "American dilemma" described the contradiction between Americans' support for values of equality and tolerance and the poor treatment and status of Blacks in society. Katz and Hass (1988) formalized the ambivalence construct by describing conflict between humanitarian/egalitarian values, which promote genuinely pro-Black sentiment, and individualistic/Protestant work ethic (PWE) values, which promote anti-Black sentiment. Indeed, the priming of egalitarian values led to increased endorsement of pro-Black attitudes, while the priming of PWE values led to increased endorsement of anti-black attitudes (Katz & Hass, 1988). These two values and corresponding sets of attitudes may co-exist, but the ambivalence may create a "high vulnerability to emotional tension" when made salient (Katz et al., 1986, p. 45). To reduce this tension, an amplified response, in the direction of the dominant feeling state, may result. For example, White students rated a Black teammate who was responsible for team success at a Trivia Challenge more favorably than a comparable White teammate, but a Black teammate who was responsible for team failure more negatively than a comparable White teammate (Hass, Katz, Rizzo, Bailey, & Eisenstadt, 1991). Ambivalent attitudes are also featured in other approaches to understanding racism (see Jones, 1997), including aversive racism theory, reviewed above (Gaertner & Dovidio, 1986), and symbolic and modern racism theories (McConahay, 1986; Sears, 1988).

The complexity of prejudice is also reflected in two recent general models of outgroup attitudes, both of which incorporate nuanced emotions as precursors of prejudice (for a review, see Mackie & Smith, 2002). Intergroup emotions theory is based on the core premise that because group identity is an important aspect of the self, group-level emotions ("the emotions that people experience when they identify with a group or think of themselves in terms of a particular social identity") arise as people appraise events in terms of their relevance for the ingroup (Smith, Seger, & Mackie, 2007, p. 431). For example, three key types of emotional responses to outgroups include fear, anger, and disgust. Fear may be based in perceptions of threat to the integrity of the ingroup, anger in the perception that the outgroup is making illegitimate demands on the ingroup, and disgust in the perception that the outgroup violates important norms (see Devos, Silver, Mackie, & Smith, 2002). These emotions form the basis for "multiple types of prejudice," and prompt different behavioral responses, including confrontation in the case of anger; avoidance in the cases of fear and disgust (Smith & Mackie, 2010, p. 138; see also Cottrell & Neuberg, 2005).

Similarly, the Stereotype Content Model (SCM) highlights complexity in attitudes toward different groups, positing four unique types of emotions, behavior tendencies, and underlying stereotypes that typify reactions to outgroups (Cuddy, Fiske, & Glick, 2007; Fiske, Cuddy, Glick, & Xu, 2002). According to the SCM, there are two main underlying dimensions of stereotype content: perceived competence and warmth. The placement of social groups along these two dimensions depends on perceived status and competitiveness of the groups: Higher status leads to perceptions of greater competence, while greater competition leads to perceptions of less warmth (Fiske et al., 2002). Outgroup stereotypes often have a mixed evaluative content on these two dimensions—groups may be seen as high on one dimension but low on the other. For example, high-status, competitive groups (e.g., rich people, feminists) tend to be described in terms of competence rather than warmth, whereas the reverse is true for low-status, non-competitive groups (e.g., housewives, elderly people; Fiske et al., 2002).

If these stereotype dimensions are crossed to produce four quadrants, two of them (high competence and high warmth; low competence and low warmth) result in univalent stereotypes (positive and negative, respectively). Positive stereotype content is tied to the emotion of *admiration* and may particularly characterize ingroups and reference groups. Uniformly negative stereotype content may be associated with the emotion of *contempt*, and include groups such as poor Blacks, poor Whites, and welfare recipients (Fiske et al., 2002). The other two quadrants of the warmth-competition matrix characterize groups with mixed stereotype content. Groups perceived as high in warmth but low in competence (e.g., the elderly and disabled) produce the paternalistic emotion of *pity*. Groups perceived as low in warmth but high in competence (e.g., Asians and Jews) may prompt admiration that is tinged with *envy*.

More recently, Cuddy and her colleagues (2007) have extended the SCM into the behavioral domain, offering the BIAS model (Behaviors from Intergroup Affect and Stereotypes). This model suggests that competence and warmth perceptions are tied to behaviors that vary on two dimensions: *Facilitation-harm*, and *activity-passivity*. Perceptions of warmth are tied to *active* behaviors that vary in terms of facilitation and harm: High warmth triggers active facilitation of targets (e.g., helping), and low-warmth perceptions trigger active harm (e.g., verbal harassment). Competence perceptions are hypothesized to lead to *passive* behaviors that also vary on the facilitation-harm dimension, with high-competence perceptions prompting passive facilitation (e.g., choosing to work with a group member assumed to be smart) and low-competence perceptions prompting passive harm (e.g., ignoring, avoiding eye contact).

The SCM and BIAS models offer an integrative perspective that links underlying beliefs about the social relations between groups (status/competitiveness) to cognitive content, emotions, and behavior. A key theme in this and other approaches reviewed in this section is that prejudice is multifaceted and complex, and may often include more than simple outgroup antipathy. This has led to increased attempts to measure prejudice in terms of varied emotional content, but has not eliminated the more traditional tendency to use valenced attitudinal statements to capture the prejudice construct.

Summary

The models of prejudice reviewed here have examined the psychological mechanisms that contribute to the experience and expression of prejudice (see Table 16.1). We began our review by considering intergroup approaches, which focus on how ingroup-outgroup distinctions may prompt intergroup bias, including the perception of own group as more "essentially human" than outgroups. Our review of normative approaches outlined the importance of what others think or condone as factors shaping one's own prejudices. Next, we discussed evolutionary perspectives, which examine how distal evolutionary environments may have contributed to modern-day cognitive adaptations that promote prejudice. We then outlined research suggesting that various motivational forces—including intergroup threats, esteem needs, mortality activated anxiety, ideologies, and conflicts between prejudice and suppression forces—as contributors to prejudice. We concluded this section by reviewing models of prejudice that define the construct in more complex and nuanced ways, incorporating ambivalence and more differentiated emotional states than mere negativity.

The proliferation of psychological theory and research on prejudice in psychology is remarkable. Each approach offers its own underlying accounting of prejudice processes, yet each is part of an overall story. We hope that it is obvious from the reviewed literature that prejudice cannot be reduced to a single explanation. In fact, our categorization of each theory and empirical finding as reflecting one of the broad approaches described above is somewhat simplistic, as modern perspectives often incorporate multiple mechanisms and recognize, if only tacitly, the contributions of individual differences, cognition, motivation, and situational cues to prejudice. These models suggest that prejudice is a complex construct, prompted in part by "normal" psychological processes such as categorization, ingroup preference, and protective reactions to threat. The outputs of these processes may vary, however, depending on the history of relations between groups and the immediate situational context.

As researchers, we have a fairly good handle on the variety of factors that matter for prejudice, and how and why they matter. A number of broad frameworks, including theories reviewed here, have provided needed elaboration and integration of these basic principles. Furthermore, research that examines how prejudice plays out at the microlevel, in actual intergroup interaction, offers some needed precision about the prejudice process. In one intriguing line of research, Richeson and Shelton and their colleagues have characterized interracial interaction as a stressor for both Blacks and Whites, with Whites being concerned about appearing racist and Blacks concerned about being the targets of racism (Richeson & Shelton, 2007; Trawalter, Richeson, & Shelton, 2009). These concerns trigger effortful self-regulatory processes that may ultimately interfere with smooth functioning in interracial encounters, as cognitive resources are depleted and negative affect results. This work provides important links to literatures outside of the prejudice domain (stress and coping, self-regulation), which may offer further benefits for understanding the individual, dyadic, and group-level processes that contribute to prejudice.

REDUCING PREJUDICE

Accompanying most discussions of prejudice are considerations of how prejudice might be reduced. Can groups and individuals be led to have more favorable attitudes toward each other? Can intergroup bias be reduced and intergroup harmony increased? These issues are addressed in some detail in the chapter by Dovidio and colleagues on social conflict, harmony, and integration, which appears in this volume. Below we briefly review some of the models highlighted in that chapter (such as intergroup contact and common group identity models), as well as other approaches to reducing intergroup prejudice.

Intergroup Contact Theory

Researchers have long recognized the possibility that bringing groups together may provide an important means of reducing negative intergroup attitudes (for a review, see Pettigrew & Tropp, 2006). Intergroup contact theory was formalized, however, by Allport (1954), who outlined the "optimal conditions," under which contact between groups could reduce prejudice. The conditions included equal status between members of the interacting groups, common goals, a spirit of cooperation rather than competition in the setting, and "sanctioned . . . institutional support (i.e., . . . law, custom, or local atmosphere)" of the contact (p. 281).

In a recent meta-analysis, Pettigrew and Tropp (2006) examined more than 500 relevant studies on contact, and reported a modest overall effect size of $r = -.215$ between intergroup contact and prejudice. This effect increased in studies where Allport's "optimal conditions" were met, $r = -.287$. Other findings from the meta-analysis suggest that the effects of contact, while modest, are broad: "Not only do attitudes toward the immediate participants usually become more favorable, but so do attitudes toward the entire outgroup, outgroup members in other situations, and even outgroups not involved in the contact" (p. 766).

Extensions of intergroup contact theory have considered that simply *imagining* intergroup contact may result in improved intergroup attitudes (Turner, Crisp, & Lambert, 2007). In one study, participants who were asked to "take a minute to imagine yourself meeting an elderly

stranger for the first time" later reported increased preference for conversing with an elderly person in an upcoming task, compared to those who were led to merely "think about the elderly" (Turner et al., 2007, Study 2). Additionally, the vicarious experience of contact—via a friend's contact experiences with outgroup members—can affect one's own attitudes as well (Wright, Aron, McLaughlin-Volpe, & Ropp, 1997). This "extended contact hypothesis" suggests that "knowledge that an in-group member has a close relationship with an out-group member can lead to more positive intergroup attitudes" (p. 73).

Although considerable evidence points to the benefits of intergroup contact, some concerns about this approach have been raised. First, meta-analytic results indicate that the effects of contact on prejudice reduction are somewhat weaker for members of racial/ethnic minority groups ($r = -.18$) than for members of racial/ethnic majority groups ($r = -.24$; Tropp & Pettigrew, 2005). Second, contact differentially predicts perceptions of injustice and support for policies designed to redress injustice: In national surveys of South Africans, interracial contact predicted increased perceptions of racism and increased support for governmental policies such as affirmative action among White respondents, but contact *decreased* racism perceptions and policy support among Black respondents (Dixon, Durrheim, & Tredoux, 2007; see also Saguy, Tausch, Dovidio, & Pratto, 2009).

Such findings suggest that contact may have the unintended consequence of weakening minority group members' concerns about discrimination and their support for social change. Wright and Lubensky (2009) have outlined two models of social change: the *prejudice-reduction* model, which has dominated others' (and our own) discussion of prejudice, and the *collective action* model, which has focused on "transforming the political orientations of members of historically disadvantaged groups in order to motivate them to challenge the status quo" (Dixon, Tropp, Durrheim, & Tredoux, 2010, p. 79). Both may be desirable, but the latter may increase the likelihood of conflict, not harmony, between groups. Describing this conflict, Dixon et al. (2010) issue this warning: "Psychologists' tendency to treat intergroup conflict as the problem and intergroup harmony as the solution is at best simplistic . . . short-term conflict sometimes lays the foundation for longer-term justice in historically unequal societies" (p. 80).

The Common Ingroup Identity Model and Extensions

Acknowledging the important role of categorization in intergroup bias, the common ingroup identity model proposes that by shifting to a "higher level of inclusiveness"—to category definitions that combine (formerly) distinct groups into a common encompassing category—prejudice can be reduced (Gaertner & Dovidio, 2000, p. 46; Gaertner, Dovidio, Anastasio, Bachman, & Rust, 1993). Pro-ingroup bias might extend to others to the extent that group members previously thought of as "them" become part of "us." For example, an early laboratory study documented that when two three-person groups of decision makers were led to think of themselves as a single group (via a joint seating arrangement and new group name), compared to two separate groups, intergroup bias was significantly reduced: Participants reported less differentiation between the ingroup and (former) outgroup in terms of liking and perceived value, and were less likely to select an original ingroup member as the group leader (Gaertner, Mann, Murrell, & Dovidio, 1989). Field and survey studies have also documented that perceptions of common ingroup identity predict low levels of ingroup bias (e.g., see Gaertner et al., 1993), and increased support for policies targeted at intergroup cooperation (e.g., Beaton, Dovidio, & Léger, 2008).

However, some problems have been noted with this approach (see Dovidio, Gaertner, & Saguy, 2009; Dovidio et al., this volume). One is that the creation of superordinate identities may provide only a temporary fix; it may be difficult to overcome preexisting and socially important categorizations such as race and sex (Hewstone, 1996). Another is that individuals may be resistant to attempts to combine their group identity with that of another group. This may constitute a threat to group distinctiveness and result in heightened levels of intergroup bias in an attempt to reestablish a positive group identity (Deschamps & Brown, 1983; Hornsey & Hogg, 2000; Tajfel & Turner, 1979). Minority group members may be particularly likely to respond negatively to a unifying common ingroup identity in that such a categorization may reflect an assimilationist rather than multicultural or "dual identity" perspective (Dovidio, Gaertner, & Kafati, 2000; Huo & Molina, 2006). In response to these issues, common ingroup identity scholars have recently suggested taking a more nuanced and complex view of the effects of commonality, focusing on its consequences for both majority and minority group members, the nature of the historical context, and prospects for intergroup relations over time (see Dovidio et al., this volume).

A related perspective suggests that intergroup bias can also be reduced by emphasizing *crossed-categorizations* (Crisp, 2010; Crisp & Hewstone, 2000, 2007). That is, rather than recategorizing at a higher level of inclusiveness, two (or more) distinct group identities could be crossed to highlight intersections: Race and gender might be crossed to create Black female, Black male, White female, and White male subgroups in a given context. The individual could therefore think of the self as sharing at least one ingroup identity with most others in the setting (excepting the "double outgroup"). A number of studies have indicated that shared identity created by the experience of crossed-categorization reduces intergroup bias (Crisp & Hewstone, 2000; Vanbeselaere, 1987). Of course, the double outgroup—such as "Black males" for a White female perceiver—may receive a larger dose of prejudice than others, but additional cross-categorizations could be sought that would bring the outgroup into an ingroup category. Still, as Crisp (2010) notes, many subgroup identities are correlated, as is the case in Northern Ireland, where religion predicts neighborhood, politics, and soccer team preference. In these correlated cases, bias against double outgroups may be particularly strong, especially among those high in subgroup identification and when the salience of subgroup categories is high (see Crisp, 2010, for a review).

Perspective Taking and Empathy Approaches

Taking the perspective of others is one means of inducing empathy, a feeling of sympathy or "tenderheartedness" toward the other (Batson, 1991). A number of studies have documented that feelings of empathy toward members of stigmatized groups can reduce expressions of bias toward those groups as a whole. For example, Batson et al. (1997) found that perspective-taking instructions induced empathy toward individual stigmatized others, which led to improved attitudes toward the relevant group as a whole: people with AIDS, the homeless, and murderers, even when these attitudes were measured 1 to 2 weeks after the empathy induction. In another study, individuals led to take the perspective of a heroin addict later allocated more funds to a drug-treatment agency (Batson, Chang, Orr, & Rowland, 2002). Induced perspective taking also increased favorable attitudes toward African Americans, regardless of whether the target individual confirmed or disconfirmed racial stereotypes (Vescio, Sechrist, & Paolucci, 2003). Writing an essay from the perspective of another person—an elderly man, or an outgroup member in a "minimal groups" procedure—led to reduced stereotyping and intergroup bias (Galinsky & Moskowitz, 2000; see also Weyant, 2007). Explicit instructions to "be empathic" while reading about discriminatory treatment of Blacks also led to increased favorability toward

Blacks (Stephan & Finlay, 1999) as did instructions to "focus on your feelings" (versus "focus on your thoughts") while watching a video depicting discrimination (Esses & Dovidio, 2002).

There is some debate about the precise mechanisms by which perspective taking has its effects. Batson (1991) suggests that perspective taking creates empathic arousal, and this other-focused arousal directly prompts altruistic responses toward the target. Others have highlighted the role of positive emotions more generally. For example, in their study of racial attitudes, Esses and Dovidio (2002) found that focusing on feelings enhanced emotional positivity (e.g., feelings of respect), which, in turn, enhanced willingness to engage in future contact with Blacks. Others have suggested a more egoistic path; that perspective taking leads to a merging of self and the other, or inclusion of other in the self (Davis, Conklin, Smith, & Luce, 1996), a mechanism central to the extended intergroup contact hypothesis described above (Wright et al., 1997). Indeed, Galinsky and Moskowitz (2000) found that those who took the perspective of an elderly man in their essays reported increased overlap in the traits that characterized the self and the elderly, and this overlap predicted reduced stereotyping of the elderly. It may well be the case that empathic arousal and self-other overlap jointly contribute to the reduced prejudice expressed by those who take the perspective of others.

As a caveat to the benefits of perspective taking, we must note that empathy does not ensure morality (Batson, Klein, Highberger, & Shaw, 1995). Indeed, empathy may lead to injustice, to the extent that resources and benefits may be preferentially allocated to those toward whom empathy has been induced (Batson et al., 1995). But positive attitudes toward groups are not zero-sum in nature; one group need not suffer because attitudes improve toward another. In this sense, empathy induction may be among the most viable methods for improving intergroup attitudes. Other approaches that emphasize the role of self-relevant emotions (such as collective guilt) in reducing prejudice may also hold promise (Stewart, Latu, Branscombe, & Denney, 2010).

"(Un)consciousness Raising" Strategies

Any reader of the prejudice literature will be aware of the tremendous attention devoted in the past 15 years or so to measuring intergroup attitudes using various response latency measures (e.g., the Implicit Association Test, Greenwald, McGhee, & Schwartz, 1998; evaluative priming techniques, Fazio, Jackson, Dunton, & Williams,

1995; Wittenbrink, 2007), projective techniques (e.g., the Affect Misattribution Procedure; Payne, Cheng, Govorun, & Stewart, 2005), and physiological indicators (see Correll et al., 2010, for a review). A number of researchers, particularly those who have focused on measuring prejudice using such implicit methods, have examined various "(un)consciousness-raising" strategies to reduce bias (Banaji, 2001, p. 136). This phrase generally refers to reducing prejudice by increasing awareness of it, but here we highlight a variety of lab-based interventions that appear to modify implicit attitudes. We define implicit attitudes as "introspectively unidentified (or inaccurately identified) traces of past experience that mediate favorable or unfavorable feeling, thought, or action toward social objects" (Greenwald & Banaji, 1995, p. 8).

One might conceptualize implicit attitudes as relatively enduring; for example, they may be learned early in life and operate at a level that reduces the likelihood of change (Wilson, Lindsey, & Schooler, 2000). But a variety of studies suggest that these attitudes can be altered via conditioning, awareness, control, and a variety of other methods (for a review, see Blair, 2002). For example, classical conditioning techniques, in which positive images (or words) are paired with stigmatized groups can improve implicit attitudes toward groups. For example, Karpinski and Hilton (2001, Study 3) paired positive words with either the term "elderly" or "youth," and found that implicit attitudes toward the elderly improved in the former condition. Olson and Fazio (2006) paired photos of Blacks with positive words and images and Whites with negative words and images and found reduced evidence of implicit race prejudice relative to a condition in which participants viewed the same stimuli in an unpaired format. Although little is known about the longer-term effects of such training, Olson and Fazio (2006, Study 3) documented a reduction in race prejudice after a 2-day delay between conditioning and measurement of racial attitudes.

Simply presenting positive images of stigmatized group members may reduce implicit bias as well. For example, after being presented with famous admired Black exemplars (e.g., Denzel Washington) and famous disliked White exemplars (e.g., Jeffrey Dahmer), White respondents showed reduced evidence of implicit race bias—even after 24 hours—relative to a control condition and a condition in which disliked Blacks and admired Whites were presented (Dasgupta & Greenwald, 2001). Viewing a film of Blacks in a positive stereotypic context (a family barbecue) reduced implicit race bias relative to a condition in which Blacks were viewed in a negative stereotypic context (a gang-related incident; Wittenbrink,

Judd, & Park, 2001). Mental imagery may produce similar effects: Imagining "what a strong woman is like" reduced implicit stereotyping (associating men with strength and women with weakness) compared to control imagery or no imagery conditions (Blair, Ma, & Lenton, 2001; see also Hugenberg, Blusiewicz, & Sacco, 2010).

Other kinds of explicit training have been shown to reduce implicit (and explicit stereotyping). "Just saying no" to stereotypes—responding "no" when stereotypic pairings of group names and trait terms were exhibited—reduced implicit stereotyping toward the groups "skinheads" and "the elderly" (Kawakami, Dovidio, Moll, Hermsen, & Russin, 2000). Similarly, training in making counterstereotypic associations (such as describing women as strong rather than sensitive) led to reductions in hiring bias against women (Kawakami, Dovidio, & van Kamp, 2007). Such practice effects are consistent with Devine's (1989) suggestion that reducing automatic stereotyping effects is akin to breaking a bad habit. Furthermore, even practicing "approach" behaviors—pulling a joystick toward (rather than away from) the self when photos of Blacks were shown reduced implicit prejudice against Blacks (Kawakami, Phills, Steele, & Dovidio, 2007). Recent work additionally suggests that training in making situational rather than dispositional attributions for behavior (e.g., attributing an African American's lateness to work to a faulty alarm clock rather than irresponsibility) led to reduced implicit racial stereotyping (Stewart, Latu, Kawakami, & Meyers, 2010).

Whether these kinds of procedures and other interventions are viable methods of prejudice reduction in the "real world" is not clear. In their excellent review of "what works" in prejudice reduction, Paluck and Green (2009) note that the "quick fixes" of the lab may be informative, but they "eliminate larger institutions and social processes in which interventions are embedded—which may fundamentally change the impact and intervening psychological processes of the intervention" (pp. 349–350). Experimental research conducted in the field, including studies of cooperative learning, media effects (reading or watching films or TV with prejudice relevant content), discussion groups, and multicultural education/diversity training may provide more practical guidance for reducing prejudice, but these interventions are often atheoretical in their approach (see Paluck & Green, 2009, for a broad review; see Hite & McDonald, 2006, for a review of diversity training effects).

Still, these approaches have promise for informing the various theoretical model described earlier in the paper. For example, a yearlong field experiment in Rwanda examined the effects of a radio soap opera "designed to promote reconciliation" between Hutus and Tutsis in the wake of the 1994 genocide that decimated the Tutsi ethnic minority population (Paluck, 2009, p. 574). Those exposed to this program (relative to a control group that heard an alternative health-related soap opera) showed favorable changes in their perceptions of social norms (e.g., regarding intermarriage, trust, and dissent), increases in empathy toward others, and increased cooperative behavior in groups, but no changes in their personal beliefs about violence, intermarriage, and trust. These findings point to the importance of social norms and social influence, perhaps magnified in this setting because participants listened to the radio in groups. Paluck (2009) concluded, "to change prejudiced behavior it may be more fruitful to target social norms than personal beliefs" (p. 582), a sentiment that echoes Sherif and Sherif's (1953) emphasis on "the group and its values (norms) as the main anchorage in regulating experience and behavior" (p. 218).

BEING THE TARGET OF PREJUDICE

Although the prejudice literature tends to focus on the perpetrator's perspective, research exploring the target's perspective has burgeoned since Goffman's (1963) classic, *Stigma: Notes on the Management of Spoiled Identity*. Goffman focused on a variety of stigmatizing conditions, including "tribal stigma of race, nation, and religion," which provoke "varieties of discrimination" in majority group members (pp. 4–5). Goffman described the consequences of stigmatization, including feelings of isolation, as well as alignment with social groups that bring value to the self (see also Crocker & Major, 1989).

Modern considerations of the target's perspective tend to focus on different kinds of threats to social identity that any individual might experience depending on the situational context (Branscombe, Ellemers, Spears, & Doosje, 1999; Ellemers, Spears, & Doosje, 2002). But members of negatively stereotyped groups that are frequently the targets of prejudice may be most likely to encounter situations that make these social identity threats relevant (Shapiro & Neuberg, 2007; Steele & Aronson, 1995).

Stereotype Threat

Stereotype threat theory is perhaps the dominant modern perspective on the experiences of targets of prejudice. Stereotype threat is a situationally activated state in which a target fears fulfilling a negative stereotype associated with his or her group membership (Steele, 1997; Steele & Aronson, 1995). Stereotype threat does not take shape in overt behavior or expressed attitudes toward the target but rather holds sway as a "threat in the air" (Steele, 1997). In initial demonstrations of this phenomenon, stereotype threat was activated through situational reminders associating the participant's race (Steele & Aronson, 1995) or gender (Spencer, Steele, & Quinn, 1999) with negative performance stereotypes. For example, Black and White participants were told that a test was "diagnostic" of their ability, or in another study, participants were asked to report their race prior to taking the test. These situational triggers were sufficient to decrease the performance of Blacks relative to Whites and relative to conditions in which test diagnosticity was not emphasized or race was not made salient. That is, reminders of negative group stereotypes in a given context triggered stereotype-consistent performance patterns. Steele and Aronson (1995) theorized that stereotype threat "is a predicament that can beset the members of any group about whom a negative stereotype exists" (p. 797). In accordance with predictions, stereotype threat effects have been found for marginalized groups other than those based on race and gender, including homosexuals (Bosson, Haymovitz, & Pinel, 2004), those low in socioeconomic status (Croizet & Claire, 1998), and the elderly (Levy, 1996), and even for members of high-status groups (e.g., White men in the domain of athletics, Stone, Perry, & Darley, 1997; and Whites in academic domains when compared with Asians, Aronson et al., 1999).

Stereotype threat research has flourished since the seminal work of Steele and Aronson (1995), with some 300 peer-reviewed journal articles published in the past 15 years. But only recently have psychologists begun to understand the underlying processes by which situational triggers of threat prompt under performance. Initial attempts that focused on anxiety, measured through self-report, as a mediating mechanism yielded mixed results (Spencer et al., 1999). However, research exploring indirect measures of anxiety (such as nonverbal behavior) has since indicated that anxiety does in fact mediate the threat-underperformance relationship (Blascovich, Spencer, Quinn, & Steele, 2001; Bosson et al., 2004). Further supporting the role of anxiety, test difficulty has been found to moderate stereotype threat effects, with members of negatively stereotyped groups performing well on easy tasks but poorly on difficult tasks when threats are triggered (Ben-Zeev, Fein, & Inzlicht, 2005; O'Brien & Crandall, 2003). Other mediating mechanisms, including activation of negative thoughts (Beilock, Rydell, & McConnell,

2007; Cadinu, Maass, Rosabianca, & Kiesner, 2005), increases in stereotype accessibility (Rydell, McConnell, & Beilock, 2009), decrements in working memory (Schmader & Johns, 2003) and thought suppression (Logel, Iserman, Davies, Quinn, & Spencer, 2009; McGlone & Aronson, 2007), have been identified.

Accounting for this plethora of mediating mechanisms, Schmader and colleagues (Schmader, Johns, & Forbes, 2008) proposed an "integrated process model," which highlights the role of disruptions in *working memory* as a key contributor to stereotype threat effects. Through stress-induced arousal, self- and performance-relevant monitoring, and/or suppression of negative thoughts and feelings, stereotype threat disrupts working memory, in turn impairing performance (Beilock et al., 2007; Schmader & Johns, 2003). Many performance outcomes measured in the stereotype threat literature rely on working memory, defined as "a limited-capacity executive process that coordinates cognition and controls behavior to achieve performance goals in the presence of . . . information that competes for attention" (Schmader et al., 2008, p. 340). For example, Schmader and Johns (2003) found that decrements in working memory accounted for the relationship between stereotype threat and math scores for women.

In addition to performance decrements in the immediate context, stereotype threat may produce other downstream effects, including disengagement with the performance domain. For example, following stereotype threat, effort put toward practicing decreases (Stone, 2002), and disidentification from or avoidance of the task domain increases (Davies, Spencer, Quinn, & Gerhardstein, 2002; Osborne & Walker, 2006; Steele, 1997). This research suggests that stereotype threat can lead members of negatively stereotyped groups to disassociate from the threatening context, harm the ability to learn new material (Rydell, Rydell, & Boucher, 2010), and even interfere on tasks that are irrelevant to stereotypes, after the threat inducing stereotype is no longer applicable (Inzlicht & Kang, 2010). The latter may occur because coping with stereotype threat results in depletion of self-regulatory resources, producing *stereotype threat spillover* that extends to other stereotype-irrelevant tasks involving self-control, such as eating restraint (Inzlicht & Kang, 2010).

With such detrimental outcomes associated with stereotype threat, researchers have explored numerous methods for decreasing its effects. Methods tend to focus on reappraisals of the performance context. For example, framing tests as a challenge can buffer against negative performance decrements (Alter, Aronson, Darley, Rodriguez, & Ruble, 2010). Similarly, viewing intelligence as a malleable construct had positive effects for members of negatively stereotyped groups (Aronson, Fried, & Good, 2002; Good, Aronson, & Inzlicht, 2003). Attributing anxiety to something in the context (Good et al., 2003), or framing arousal as something that facilitates test performance (Jamieson, Mendes, Blackstock, & Schmader, 2010) can also reduce the likelihood of stereotype threat effects. Other methods are as simple as making test takers aware of stereotype threat (Johns, Schmader, & Martens, 2005), or providing high-achieving role models (McIntyre, Paulson, & Lord, 2003). Stereotype threat-induced performance decrements can also be ameliorated by diverting thoughts of the self away from the stereotyped identity. Self-affirming—restoring one's sense of self as a "good, virtuous, and efficacious" person (Cohen, Garcia, Apfel, & Master, 2006, p. 313), or reminding targets of a more positively stereotyped identity (Gresky, Ten Eyck, Lord, & McIntyre, 2005; McGlone & Aronson, 2007; Rydell et al., 2009) have helped to maintain performance in the face of stereotype threat.

In sum, stereotype threat research suggests that societal prejudice can have pernicious effects even when there is no negative treatment or expression of negativity toward stigmatized group members in the immediate context (see also Adams, Garcia, Purdie-Vaughns, & Steele, 2006). Moreover, the targets themselves do not have to believe the stereotypes to be true; targets need only be aware of the negative beliefs associated with their group to experience the burden of stereotype threat.

Perceiving Prejudice

Research on the target's perspective examines when targets are likely to perceive or experience discrimination and the consequences of doing so. The responses of targets of prejudice may range from being highly sensitive to conditions reflecting prejudice (Crocker & Major, 1989) to minimizing or denying that prejudice has occurred (Crosby, 1984; Taylor, Wright, Moghaddam, & Lalonde, 1990). Both situational and individual difference variables contribute to when targets of prejudice are likely to perceive prejudice. Members of historically oppressed groups tend to perceive discrimination more readily than members of high-status or nonoppressed groups (e.g., Adams, Tormala, & O'Brien, 2006; Rodin, Price, Bryson, & Sanchez, 1990). But a number of factors influence this perception, including the "fit" between an incident and prototypes of discrimination (Inman & Baron, 1996; O'Brien, Kinias, & Major, 2008). Other factors affecting the perception of discrimination include the clarity of cues

suggesting discrimination has occurred (Crocker, Voelkl, Testa, & Major, 1991; Inman, 2001; Kaiser & Miller, 2001), the expectation that discrimination may occur (Kaiser, Vick, & Major, 2006), and individual differences in "stigma consciousness" (Pinel, 1999), group identification (Branscombe, Schmitt, & Harvey, 1999), and status-justifying beliefs (Jost & Banaji, 1994).

What are the consequences of perceiving prejudice? There has been a history of debate on this question: One line of argument suggests that perceiving prejudice and discrimination has negative psychological and physical consequences; another suggests that perceptions of discrimination can be an adaptive mechanism for dealing with prejudice.

The former perspective is based in findings that perceptions of discrimination are related to negative mental and physical health outcomes (Clark, Anderson, Clark, & Williams, 1999; Klonoff, Landrine, & Campbell, 2000; Landrine, Klonoff, Gibbs, Manning, & Lund, 1995). In a meta-analysis, Pascoe and Smart Richman (2009) found that perceiving discrimination is related to higher levels of mental illness (e.g., depression, anxiety, and paranoia), and lower levels of general well-being (e.g., self-esteem, life satisfaction, and perceived quality of life). They reported an overall effect size of $r = -.16$ between perceived discrimination and mental health, with recent discrimination having a stronger effect than lifetime discrimination ($r = -.25$ and $r = -.15$, respectively), and $r = -.13$ between perceived discrimination and physical health. Health decrements may occur via self-control; perceptions of prejudice may lower self-control, which leads to increases in unhealthy and decreases in healthy behaviors. Additionally, perceived discrimination may increase stress responses including anger, self-reported stress, and negative emotions (Pascoe & Smart Richman, 2009). The multitude of hypothesized moderating variables (e.g., social support, coping style, group identification) and diversity of measures used to capture perceptions of discrimination and health indicate the complicated nature of the discrimination-health relationship (Williams & Mohammed, 2009). Although the relationship is not strong, it may be one of many factors contributing to racial disparities in health (U.S. Department of Health and Human Services, 2000; Williams & Mohammed, 2009).

Additionally, research based in social identity theory (Tajfel & Turner, 1979) suggests that attributing negative outcomes to prejudice has negative consequences when the prejudicial actions are perceived to be pervasive (Schmitt & Branscombe, 2002; Schmitt, Branscombe, & Postmes, 2003). This is because discriminatory actions directed toward a minority group member imply differential treatment that extends beyond the immediate circumstance (Schmitt & Branscombe, 2002; Schmitt, Branscombe, Kobrynowicz, & Owen, 2002). In one study, women who were rejected in the immediate context tended to attribute that rejection to prejudice "because of who I am," though men did not show this pattern, presumably because discriminatory behavior is not expected to generalize across situations when one belongs to a high status group (Schmitt & Branscombe, 2002). Other research suggests that experiences or perceptions of discrimination are harmful when such events are caused by someone who has power over the target (Barreto, Ellemers, & Fiske, 2010), when the act is appraised as highly threatening and the self as incapable of dealing with the act (Kaiser, Major, & McCoy, 2004), and when individual mobility is believed to exist (Foster & Tsarfati, 2005), presumably because women blame themselves rather than the unfairness of the social structure.

This research suggests that perceiving discrimination to generalize beyond a single circumstance has negative implications for well-being. But at the same time, attributing a negative outcome to a single discriminatory experience can be adaptive (Major & Sawyer, 2009; Schmitt, Branscombe, & Postmes, 2003). For example, Schmitt et al. (2003) found that women who attributed negative feedback to a single case of discrimination reported higher self-esteem than did women who attributed negative feedback to pervasive discrimination. The self-protective consequences of perceiving prejudice were identified by Crocker and Major (1989), who argued that by blaming negative outcomes on the prejudice of others rather than oneself, self-esteem may be buffered. For example, in one study, the more women blamed rejection on discrimination, the higher their self-esteem (Major, Kaiser, & McCoy, 2003). In situations of *attributional ambiguity,* "an uncertainty about whether the outcomes one receives are indicative of one's personal deservingness or of social prejudices that others have against one's social group," the attribution to prejudice may buffer well-being (Major, Quinton, & McCoy, 2002, p. 258).

Additional research suggests that there may be other circumstance in which perceiving discrimination can have positive consequences. According to the rejection-identification model, perceiving discrimination may increase minority group members' identification with the marginalized identity, which in turn buffers the negative effects of perceiving discrimination (Branscombe et al., 1999; Schmitt et al., 2002; Schmitt, Spears, & Branscombe, 2003). The long-term outcomes of perceiving pervasive

discrimination may also be positive. At the beginning of a daily diary study, women and ethnic minorities who reported discrimination as pervasive reported low levels of active coping and more behavioral disengagement compared to those reporting discrimination to not be pervasive (Foster, 2009). But one month into the study, this effect reversed, with those perceiving discrimination to be pervasive reporting more active coping and less behavioral disengagement than those perceiving low levels of pervasive discrimination.

Of course, another positive long-term consequence of perceiving discrimination is the possibility of social or institutional change (Crosby, 1993; Czopp, Monteith, & Mark, 2006). Yet those who *claim* discrimination may face some immediate costs: being viewed as troublemakers or whiners (see Kaiser & Miller, 2001; Swim & Hyers, 1999), even by fellow ingroup members (Garcia, Reser-Horstman, Amo, Redersdorff, & Branscombe, 2005). This potential for reprimands does not go unnoticed by targets of discrimination (Stangor, Swim, Van Allen, & Sechrist, 2002). In one study, women were less likely to confront sexism in a mock interview when doing so jeopardized chances for imagined social gains (a "high-pressure interview" for a prestigious job compared to an interview for a less prestigious position; Shelton & Stewart, 2004). Compliance with gender norms may also contribute to women avoiding confronting prejudice, even when reporting a desire to confront (Hyers, 2007). Some research has explored factors that increase the likelihood that prejudice will be confronted. For example, women high in optimism report more willingness to confront a sexist evaluator (Sechrist, 2010).

Perceiving discrimination can have negative consequences (decrements in mental and physical health) as well as positive consequences (increased identification with the stigmatized group) for the individual target of prejudice. We reviewed research suggesting that perceiving prejudice to be pervasive can be detrimental to targets, but that viewing a negative outcome as reflecting a single case of discrimination can buffer self-esteem. Finally, although perceiving discrimination may be the initial trigger that prompts social change, claiming discrimination and confronting prejudice may be limited by realistic concerns about social cost.

SUMMARY AND CONCLUSIONS

We approached our review of the prejudice literature by focusing on three distinct, yet interrelated, bodies of research: Models of prejudice, approaches to reducing prejudice, and consequences for the targets of prejudice. Each of these areas continues to attract intense research attention; indeed, as Figure 16.1 suggests, research psychologists have had much more to say about prejudice in the past decade than in all of the preceding 90-year period.

The models of prejudice we reviewed address different levels of analysis and incorporate different meta-theoretical perspectives as they attempt to shed light on the prejudice phenomenon. These meta-theoretical perspectives include emphases on categorization into ingroup and outgroup, normative structure, distal evolutionary mechanisms, and motivation, broadly defined. As noted throughout our review, there is much overlap across these boundaries, and many modern perspectives attempt to incorporate multiple and complex mechanisms that support (and sometimes reduce) prejudice. For example, Duckitt's (2001) dual process motivational model highlights the joint roles of personality, ideology, information processing, and group-based threat in promoting prejudice. Social identity and self-categorization theories emphasize intergroup categorization and the attendant motivations that arise as groups strive to maintain positive distinctiveness in particular normative contexts (Tajfel & Turner, 1979; Turner et al., 1987). The Justification-Suppression Model (Crandall & Eshleman, 2003) conceptualizes prejudice as a motivational force that seeks expression, and is encouraged by justificatory beliefs and situations but "held in" by suppressive factors.

We also considered more complex views of the very construct of prejudice. From these perspectives, prejudice is more than antipathy or negativity toward groups. Instead, prejudice may be tied to rejection of "out of role" behavior (Eagly & Diekman, 2005), and may be ambivalent in nature, incorporating both hostile/negative and seemingly benevolent/positive components (Glick & Fiske, 1996; Katz & Hass, 1988). Prejudice may also be expressed via a variety of emotions, including pity, fear, disgust, and anger (Fiske et al., 2002; Mackie & Smith, 2002). These perspectives challenge researchers to incorporate more complex and nuanced measures of prejudice in their attempts to understand intergroup attitudes.

Prejudice reduction approaches have often drawn from the models described earlier, and in other cases have been based in the implicit assumptions that prejudice is a *learned response* that can be altered through exposure and practice (e.g., see Devine, 1989). Contact theory (Allport, 1954) suggests that bringing groups together—at least under a set of optimal conditions—may improve intergroup attitudes. Recent meta-analytic results confirm a positive benefit of intergroup contact, even when those exemplary contact conditions are *not* met (Pettigrew & Tropp, 2006). The common group identity model and its variants (dual identity, crossed-categorization) build on intergroup perspectives that emphasize the importance of us/them categorization in promoting prejudice (Crisp & Hewstone, 2007; Dovidio et al., 2009; Gaertner & Dovidio, 2000). By changing the boundaries—including the outgroup in the ingroup—prejudice can be reduced. Empathy approaches build on the importance of emotion and motivation in prompting prejudice, but seek to create positive emotions—tenderheartedness and sympathy—by simply inviting us to take the perspective of the other (Batson et al., 1997; Galinsky & Moskowitz, 2000). The various "unconsciousness raising" strategies we reviewed are based on the assumption that prejudiced reactions can be retrained, by changing our image of the category, or just saying "no" to stereotypes (e.g., Blair et al., 2001; Kawakami et al., 2000).

Each of these strategies has its limits. For example, contact may be more beneficial for majority than for minority group members, common ingroup identities may threaten group distinctiveness and harm minority interest in collective action to improve their lot, empathy may prompt unfairness if the targets of empathy are overbenefitted relative to others, and short-term imagery and training strategies may not extend beyond the lab. But each approach has shown some benefits for prejudice reduction, as has some research conducted in the field (see Paluck & Green, 2009, for a review). Relying on the impact of social norms as forces that can reduce prejudice holds promise as well (e.g., Paluck, 2009; Stangor et al., 2001).

Much of our review focused on the experience of prejudice from the perpetrators' perspective, but we also highlighted two key themes in recent considerations of the *targets* of prejudicial treatment. Stereotype threat may be activated in any situation that makes a negative stereotype of one's group salient; concern about confirming those stereotypes may prompt a cycle of underperformance and domain disidentification that paradoxically confirms the stereotype (Steele, 1997; Steele & Aronson, 1995). When and how prejudice is perceived have also been the subject of much investigation. When members of stigmatized groups receive negative outcomes, there is some ambiguity about whether that treatment was due to discrimination or not. Individual differences and situational factors contribute to whether prejudice is labeled as such, and the consequences of perceiving prejudice are complex and often contradictory. This line of work suggests that targets of prejudice face a variety of negative consequences, but perceiving prejudice may also buffer against self-esteem threats and provide some impetus toward collective action and social change (Dixon et al., 2010; Wright & Lubensky, 2009).

Our review of the prejudice literature was necessarily selective, and we have ignored a number of important areas of inquiry. For example, we did not review developmental approaches to prejudice, which emphasize early learning, social-cognitive development, peer socialization, and situational norms as contributors to prejudicial attitudes (Aboud, 2008; Bigler & Liben, 2007). We also did not address the large literature on stereotype development and change, or the processes by which stereotypes are applied to individual others, nor did we consider the nuances of particular varieties of entrenched prejudices (e.g., racism, sexism, heterosexism, ageism). We gave short shrift as well to the distinction between explicit and implicit prejudice, and between modern or subtle and more blatant prejudice (see the Petty et al. chapter in this volume for more detail about implicit and explicit attitudes).

Nonetheless, we hope our review provides some organization of key themes in the prejudice literature, and suggests avenues for additional theory and research. Despite advances in civil rights in the United States and elsewhere over the past century, one need not look far to see that prejudice and discrimination remain intractable problems throughout the world. The continuing, indeed growing, interest of psychologists in addressing these problems is heartening.

REFERENCES

Aberson, C. L., Healy, M., & Romero, V. (2000). Ingroup bias and self-esteem: A meta-analysis. *Journal and Social Psychology Review, 4*, 157–173. doi: 10.1207/S15327957

Aboud, F. E. (2008). A social-cognitive developmental theory of prejudice. In S. M. Quintana & C. McKown (Eds.), *Handbook of race, racism, and the developing child* (pp. 55–71). Hoboken, NJ: Wiley.

Abrams, D., & Hogg, M. A. (1988). Comments on the motivational status of self-esteem in social identity and intergroup discrimination. *European Journal of Social Psychology, 18*, 317–334. doi: 10.1002/ejsp.2420180403

Adams, G., Garcia, D. M., Purdie-Vaughns, V., & Steele, C. M. (2006). The detrimental effects of a suggestion of sexism in an instruction situation. *Journal of Experimental Social Psychology, 42*, 602–615. doi: 10.1016/j.jesp.2005.10.004

Adams, G., Tormala, T. T., & O'Brien, L. T. (2006). The effect of self-affirmation on perception of racism. *Journal of Experimental Social Psychology, 42*, 616–626. doi: 10.1016/j.jesp.2005.11.001

Adorno, T. W., Frenkel-Brunswick, E., Levinson, D. J., & Sanford, R. N. (1950). *The authoritarian personality*. Oxford, UK: Harpers.

Allport, G. W. (1954). *The nature of prejudice*. Oxford, UK: Addison-Wesley.

Altemeyer, B. (1981). *Right-wing authoritariansim*. Winnipeg, Manitoba, Canada: University of Manitoba Press.

Altemeyer, B. (1988). *Enemies of freedom: Understanding right-wing authoritarianism*. San Francisco, CA: Jossey-Bass.

Alter, A. L., Aronson, J., Darley, J. M., Rodriguez, C., & Ruble, D. N. (2010). Rising to the threat: Reducing stereotype threat by reframing the threat as a challenge. *Journal of Experimental Social Psychology, 46*, 166–171. doi: 10.1016/j.jesp.2009.09.014

Aronson, J., Fried, C. B., & Good, C. (2002). Reducing the effects of stereotype threat on African American college students by shaping theories of intelligence. *Journal of Experimental Social Psychology, 38*, 113–125. doi: 10.1006/jesp.2001.1491

Aronson, J., Lustine, M. J., Good, C., Keough, K., Steele, C. M., & Brown, J. (1999). When white men can't do math: Necessary and sufficient factors in stereotype threat. *Journal of Experimental Social Psychology, 35*, 29–46. doi: 10.1006/jesp.1998.1371

Ashmore, R. D., & Del Boca, F. K. (1981). Conceptual approaches to stereotypes and stereotyping. In D. L. Hamilton (Ed.), *Cognitive processes in stereotyping and intergroup behavior* (pp. 1–35). Hillsdale, NJ: Erlbaum.

Banaji, M. R. (2001). Implicit attitudes can be measured. In H. L. Roediger III, J. S. Nairne, I. Neath, & A. Surprenant (Eds.), *The nature of remembering: Essays in honor of Robert G. Crowder* (pp. 117–150). Washington, DC: American Psychological Association.

Barreto, M., Ellemers, N., & Fiske, S. T. (2010). "What did you say, and who do you think you are?" How power differences affect emotional reactions to prejudice. *Journal of Social Issues, 66*, 477–492. doi: 10.1111/j.1540–4560.2010.01657.x

Batson, C. D. (1991). *The altruism question: Toward a social psychological answer*. Hillsdale, NJ: Erlbaum.

Batson, C. D., Chang, J., Orr, R., & Rowland, J. (2002). Empathy, attitudes and actions: Can feeling for a member of a stigmatized group motivate one to help the group? *Personality and Social Psychology Bulletin, 28*, 1656–1666. doi: 10.1177/014616702237647

Batson, C. D., Klein, T. R., Highberger, L., & Shaw, L. L. (1995). Immorality from empathy-inducted altruism: When compassion and justice conflict. *Journal of Personality and Social Psychology, 68*, 1042–1054. doi: 10.1037/0022–3514.68.6.1042

Batson, C. D., Polycarpou, M. P., Harmon-Jones, E., Imhoff, H. J., Mitchener, E. C., Bednar, L. L., . . . Highberger, L. (1997). Empathy and attitudes: Can feeling for a member of a stigmatized group improve feelings toward the group? *Journal of Personality and Social Psychology, 72*, 105–118.

Beaton, A. M., Dovidio, J. F., & Léger, N. (2008). All in this together? Group representations and policy support. *Journal of Experimental Social Psychology, 44*, 808–817. doi: 10.1016/j.jesp.2007.07.002

Beilock, S. L., Rydell, R. J., & McConnell, A. R. (2007). Stereotype threat and working memory: Mechanisms, alleviation, and spillover. *Journal of Experimental Social Psychology, 136*, 256–276. doi: 10.1037/0096–3445.136.2.256

Ben-Zeev, T., Fein, S., & Inzlicht, M. (2005). Arousal and stereotype threat. *Journal of Experimental Social Psychology, 41*, 174–181. doi: 10.1016/j.jesp.2003.11.007

Bettencourt, B. A., Dorr, N., Charlton, K., & Hume, D. L. (2001). Status difference and in-group bias: A meta-analytic examination of the effects of status stability, status legitimacy, and group permeability. *Psychological Bulletin, 127*, 520–542. doi: 10.1037//0033–2909.127.4.520

Biernat, M., Vescio, T. K., Theno, S. A., & Crandall, C. S. (1996). Values and prejudice: Toward understanding the impact of American values on outgroup attitudes. In C. Seligman, J. M. Olson, & M. P. Zanna (Eds.), *The psychology of values: The Ontario symposium, Vol. 8. The Ontario symposium on personality and social psychology* (pp. 153–189). Hillsdale, NJ: Erlbaum.

Bigler, R. S., & Liben, L. S. (2007). Developmental intergroup theory: Explaining and reducing children's social stereotyping and prejudice. *Current Directions in Psychological Science*, *16*, 162–166. doi: 10.1111/j.1467–8721.2007.00496.x

Blair, I. V. (2002). The malleability of automatic stereotypes and prejudice. *Personality and Social Psychology Review*, *6*, 242–261. doi: 10.1207/S15327957PSPR0603_8

Blair, I. V., Ma, J. E., & Lenton, A. P. (2001). Imagining stereotypes away: The moderation on implicit stereotypes through mental imagery. *Journal of Personality and Social Psychology*, *81*, 828–841. doi: 10.1037/0022–3514.81.5.828

Blanchard, F. A., Crandall, C. S., Brigham, J. C., & Vaughn, L. A. (1994). Condemning and condoning racism: A social context approach to interracial settings. *Journal of Applied Psychology*, *79*, 993–997. doi: 10.1037/0021–9010.79.6.993

Blascovich, J., Spencer, S. J., Quinn, D., & Steele, C. (2001). African Americans and high blood pressure: The role of stereotype threat. *Psychological Science*, *12*, 225–229. doi: 10.1111/1467–9280.00340

Bosson, J. K., Haymovitz, E. L., & Pinel, E. C. (2004). When saying and doing diverge: The effects of stereotype threat on self-reported versus non-verbal anxiety. *Journal of Experimental Social Psychology*, *40*, 247–255. doi: 10.1016/S0022–1031(03)00099–4

Branscombe, N. R., Doosje, B., & McGarty, C. (2002). Antecedents and consequences of collective guilt. In D. M. Mackie & E. R. Smith (Eds.), *From prejudice to intergroup emotions: Differentiated reactions to social groups* (pp. 49–66). Philadelphia, PA: Psychology Press.

Branscombe, N. R., Ellemers, N., Spears, R., & Doosje, B. (1999). The context and content of social identity threat. In N. Ellemers, E. Spears, & B. Doosje (Eds.), *Social identity: Context, commitment, content* (pp. 35–58). Oxford, UK: Blackwell Science.

Branscombe, N. R., Schmitt, M. T., & Harvey, R. D. (1999). Perceiving pervasive discrimination among African Americans: Implications for group identification and well-being. *Journal of Personality and Social Psychology*, *77*, 135–149. doi: 10.1037/0022–3514.77.1.135

Branscombe, N. R., & Wann, D. L. (1994). Collective self-esteem consequences of outgroup derogation when a valued social identity is on trial. *European Journal of Social Psychology*, *24*, 641–657. doi: 10.1002/ejsp.2420240603

Brewer, M. B. (1979). In-group bias in the minimal intergroup situation: A cognitive-motivational analysis. *Psychological Bulletin*, *86*, 307–324. doi: 10.1037/0033–2909.86.2.307

Brewer, M. B. (1999). The psychology of prejudice: Ingroup love or outgroup hate. *Journal of Social Issues*, *55*, 429–444. doi: 10.1111/0022–4537.001260022–4537.00126

Brewer, M., & Caporael, L. R. (2006). An evolutionary perspective on social identity: Revisiting groups. In M. Schaller, J. A. Simpson, & D. T. Kenrick (Eds.), *Evolution and social psychology* (pp. 143–161). Madison, CT: Psychological Press.

Britt, T. W., Bonjecki, K. A., Vescio, T. K., Biernat, M., & Brown, L. M. (1996). Intergroup anxiety: A person x situation approach. *Personality and Social Psychology Bulletin*, *22*, 1177–1188. doi: 10.1177/01461672962211008

Cadinu, M., Maass, A., Rosabianca, A., & Kiesner, J. (2005). Why do women underperform under stereotype threat? Evidence for the rold of negative thinking. *Psychological Science*, *16*, 572–578. doi: 10.1111/j.0956–7976.2005.01577.x

Castano, E., Yzerbyt, V., Paladino, M. P., & Sacchi, S. (2002). I belong, therefore, I exist: Ingroup identification, ingroup entitativity, and ingroup bias. *Personality and Social Psychology Bulletin*, *28*, 135–143. doi: 10.1177/0146167202282001

Clark, R., Anderson, N. B., Clark, V. R., & Williams, D. R. (1999). Racism as a stressor for African Americans: A biopsychosocial model. *American Psychologist*, *54*, 805–816. doi: 10.1037/0003–066X.54.10.805

Cohen, G. L., Garcia, J., Apfel, N., & Master, A. (2006). Reducing the racial achievement gap: A social-psychological intervention. *Science*, *315*, 1307–1310. doi: 10.1126/science.1128317

Correll, J., Judd, C. M., Park, B., & Wittenbrink, B. (2010). Measuring prejudice, stereotypes, and discrimination. In J. F. Dovidio, M. Hewstone, P. Glick, & V. M. Esses (Eds.), *The SAGE handbook of prejudice, stereotyping, and discrimination* (pp. 508–525). Thousand Oaks, CA: Sage.

Cosmides, L., Tooby, J., & Kurzban, K. (2003). Perceptions of race. *Trends in Cognitive Science*, *7*, 173–179. doi: 10.1016/S1364–6613(03)00057–3

Cottrell, C. A., & Neuberg, S. L. (2005). Different emotional reactions to different groups: A sociofunctional threat-based approach to "prejudice." *Journal of Personality and Social Psychology*, *88*, 770–789. doi: 10.1037/0022–3514.88.5.770

Crandall, C. S., & Eshleman, A. (2003). A justification-suppression of the expression and experience of prejudice. *Psychological Bulletin*, *129*, 414–446. doi: 10.1037/0033–2909.129.3.414

Crandall, C. S., Eshleman, A., & O'Brien, L. (2002). Social norms and the expression and suppression of prejudice: The struggle for internalization. *Journal of Personality and Social Psychology*, *82*, 359–378. doi: 10.1037/0022–3514.82.3.359

Crisp, R. J. (2010). Prejudice and perceiving multiple identities. In J. F. Dovidio, M. Hewstone, P. Glick, & V. M. Esses (Eds.), *The SAGE handbook of prejudice, stereotyping, and discrimination* (pp. 508–525). Thousand Oaks, CA: Sage.

Crisp, R. J., & Hewstone, M. (2000). Crossed categorization and intergroup bias: The moderating roles of intergroup and affective context. *Journal of Experimental Social Psychology*, *36*, 357–383. doi: 10.1006/jesp.1999.1408

Crisp, R. J., & Hewstone, M. (2007). Multiple social categorization. In M. P. Zanna (Ed.), *Advances in experimental social psychology* (pp. 163–254). San Diego, CA: Elsevier Academic Press.

Crocker, J., & Major, B. (1989). Social stigma and self-esteem: The self-protective properties of stigma. *Psychological Review*, *96*, 608–630. doi: 10.1037/0033–295X.96.4.608

Crocker, J., Voelkl, K., Testa, M., & Major, B. (1991). Social stigma: The affective consequences of attributional ambiguity. *Journal of Personality and Social Psychology*, *60*, 218–228. doi: 10.1037/0022–3514.60.2.218

Croizet, J.-C., & Claire, T. (1998). Extending the concept of stereotype and threat to social class: The intellectual underperformance of students from low socioeconomic backgrounds. *Personality and Social Psychology Bulletin*, *24*, 588–594. doi: 10.1177/0146167298246003

Crosby, F. (1984). The denial of personal discrimination. *American Behavioral Scientist*, *27*, 371–386. doi: 10.1177/000276484027003008

Crosby, F. (1993). Why complain? *Journal of Social Issues*, *49*, 169–184.

Cuddy, A. J. C., Fiske, S. T., & Glick, P. (2007). The BIAS map: Behaviors from intergroup affect and stereotypes. *Journal of Personality and Social Psychology*, *92*, 631–648. doi: 10.1037/0022–3514.92.4.631

Czopp, A. M., & Monteith, M. J. (2003). Confronting prejudice (literally): Reactions to confrontations of racial and gender bias. *Personality and Social Psychology Bulletin*, *29*, 532–544. doi: 10.1177/0146167202250923

Czopp, A. M., Monteith, M. J., & Mark, A. Y. (2006). Standing up for a change: Reducing bias through interpersonal confrontation. *Journal of Personality and Social Psychology*, *90*, 784–803. doi: 10.1037/0022–3514.90.5.784

Dasgupta, N., & Greenwald, A. G. (2001). On the malleability of automatic attitudes: Combating automatic prejudice with images of admired and disliked individuals. *Journal of Personality and Social Psychology*, *81*, 800–814. doi: 10.1037/0022–3514.81.5.800

Davies, P. G., Spencer, S. J., Quinn, D. M., & Gerhardstein, R. (2002). Consuming images: How television commercials that elicit stereotype threat can restrain women academically and professionally. *Personality and Social Psychology Bulletin*, *28*, 1615–1628. doi: 10.1177/014616702237644

Davis, M. H., Conklin, L., Smith, A., & Luce, C. (1996). Effects of perspective taking on the cognitive representation of persons: A merging of self and other. *Journal of Personality and Social Psychology*, *70*, 713–726. doi: 10.1037/0022–3514.70.4.713

Demoulin, S., Pozo, B. C., & Leyens, J. P. (2009). Infrahumanization: The differential interpretation of primary and secondary emotions. In S. Demoulin, J. P. Leyens, & J. Dovidio (Eds.), *Intergroup misunderstandings: Impact of divergent social realities* (pp. 153–171). New York, NY: Psychology Press.

Deschamps, J. C., & Brown, R. (1983), Superordinate goals and intergroup conflict. *British Journal of Social Psychology*, *22*, 189–195.

Devine, P. G. (1989). Stereotypes and prejudice: Their automatic and controlled components. *Journal of Personality and Social Psychology*, *56*, 5–18. doi: 10.1037//0022–3514 .56.1.5

Devos, T., Silver, L. A., Mackie, D. M., & Smith, E. R. (2002). Experiencing intergroup emotions. In D. M. Mackie & E. R. Smith (Eds.), *From prejudice to intergroup emotions: Differentiated reactions to social groups* (pp. 111–134). New York, NY: Psychology Press.

Dixon, J., Durrheim, K., & Tredoux, C. (2007). Intergroup contact and attitudes toward the principle and practice of racial equality. *Psychological Science*, *18*, 867–872. doi: 10.1111/j.1467–9280 .2007.01993.x

Dixon, J., Tropp, L. R., Durrheim, K., & Tredoux, C. (2010). "Let them eat harmony": Prejudice-reduction strategies and attitudes of historically disadvantaged groups. *Current Direction in Psychological Science*, *19*, 76–80. doi: 10.1177/0963721410363366

Dovidio, J. F. (2001). On the nature of contemporary prejudice: The third wave. *Journal of Social Issues*, *57*, 829–849. doi: 10.1111/0022– 4537.002440022–4537.00244

Dovidio, J. F., Gaertner, S. L., & Kafati, G. (2000). Group identity and intergroup relations: The common ingroup identity model. In S. Thye, E. J. Lawler, M. Macy, & H. Walker (Eds.), *Advances in group processes* (Vol. 17, pp. 1–35). Stamford, CT: JAI Press.

Dovidio, J. F., Gaertner, S. L., & Saguy, T. (2009). Commonality and the complexity of "we": Social attitudes and social change. *Personality and Social Psychology Review*, *13*, 3–20. doi: 10.1177/ 1088868308326751

Dovidio, J. F., ten Vergert, M., Stewart, T. L., Gaertner, S. L., Johnson, J. D., Esses, V. M.,...Pearson, A. R. (2004). Perspective and prejudice: Antecedents and mediating mechanisms. *Personality and Social Psychology Bulletin*, *30*, 1537–1549. doi: 10.1177/ 0146167204271177

Duckitt, J. (1992). Psychology and prejudice: A historical analysis and integrative framework. *American Psychologist*, *47*, 1182–1193. doi: 10.1037/0003–066X.47.10.1182

Duckitt, J. (2001). A dual-process cognitive-motivational theory of ideology and prejudice. In M. P. Zanna (Ed.), *Advances in experimental social psychology* (pp. 41–113). San Diego, CA: Academic Press.

Duckitt, J., & Sibley, C. G. (2009). A dual-process motivational model of ideology, politics, and prejudice. *Psychological Inquiry*, *20*, 98–109. doi: 10.1080/10478400903028540

Dunton, B. C., & Fazio, R. H. (1997). An individual difference measure of motivation to control prejudice reactions. *Personality and Social Psychology Bulletin*, *23*, 316–326. doi: 10.1177/0146167297233009

Eagly, A. H., & Diekman, A. B. (2005). What is the problem? Prejudice as an attitude-in-context. In J. F. Dovidio, P. Glick, & L. A. Rudman (Eds.), *On the nature of prejudice: Fifty years after Allport* (pp. 19–35). Malden, MA: Blackwell.

Eagly, A. H., & Karau, S. J. (2002). Role congruity theory of prejudice toward female leaders. *Psychological Review*, *109*, 573–598. doi: 10.1037/0033–295X.109.3.573

Eagly, A. H., & Mladinic, A. (1989). Gender stereotypes and attitudes toward women and men. *Personality and Social Psychology Bulletin*, *15*, 543–558. doi: 10.1177/0146167289154008

Ellemers, N., Spears, R., & Doosje, B. (1999). *Social identity: Context, commitment, content*. Oxford, UK: Blackwell Science.

Ellemers, N., Spears, R., & Doosje, B. (2002). Self and social identity. *Annual Review of Psychology*, *53*, 161–186. doi: 10.1146/annurev .psych.53.100901.135228

Esses, V. M., & Dovidio, J. F. (2002). The role of emotions in determining willingness to engage in intergroup contact. *Personality and Social Psychology Bulletin*, *28*, 1202–1214. doi: 10.1177/ 01461672022812006

Fazio, R. H., Jackson, J. R., Dunton, B. C., & Williams, C. J. (1995). Variability in automotive activation as an unobtrusive measure of racial attitudes: A bona fide pipeline? *Journal of Personality and Social Psychology*, *69*, 1013–1027. doi: 10.1037/0022–3514 .69.6.1013

Fein, S., & Spencer, S. J. (1997). Prejudice as self-image maintenance: Affirming the self through derogating others. *Journal of Personality and Social Psychology*, *73*, 31–44. doi: 10.1037/0022–3514.73.1.31

Fiske, S. T., Cuddy, A. J. C., Glick, P., & Xu, J. (2002). A model of (often mixed) stereotype content: Competence and warmth respectively follow from perceived status and competition. *Journal of Personality and Social Psychology*, *82*, 878–902. doi: 10.1037/ 0022–3514.82.6.878

Foster, M. D. (2009). Perceiving pervasive discrimination over time: Implications for coping. *Psychology of Women Quarterly*, *33*, 172–182. doi: 10.1111/j.1471–6402.2009.01487.x

Foster, M. D., & Tsarfati, E. M. (2005). The effects of meritocracy beliefs on women's well-being after first-time gender discrimination. *Personality and Social Psychology Bulletin*, *31*, 1730–1738. doi: 10.1177/0146167205278709

Frey, D. L., & Gaertner, S. L. (1986). Helping and the avoidance of inappropriate interracial behavior: A strategy that perpetuates a non-prejudiced self-image. *Journal of Personality and Social Psychology*, *50*, 1083–1090. doi: 10.1037/0022–3514.50.6.1083

Gaertner, S. L., & Dovidio, J. F. (1986). The aversive form of racism. In J. F. Dividio & S. L. Gaertner (Eds.), *Prejudice, discrimination, and racism* (pp. 61–89). San Diego, CA: Academic Press.

Gaertner, S. L., & Dovidio, J. F. (2000). *Reducing intergroup bias: The common ingroup identity model*. New York, NY: Psychology Press.

Gaertner, S. L., Dovidio, J. F., Anastasio, P. A., Bachman, B. A., & Rust, M. C. (1993). The common ingroup identity model: Recategorization and the reduction of intergroup bias. In W. Stroebe & M. Hewstone (Eds.), *European review of social psychology* (Vol. 4, pp. 1–26). Orlando, FL: Academic Press.

Gaertner, S. L., Mann, J., Murrell, A., & Dovidio, J. F. (1989). Reducing intergroup bias: The benefits of recategorization. *Journal of Personality and Social Psychology*, *57*, 239–249. doi: 10.1037/0022– 3514.57.2.239

Galinsky, A. D., & Moskowitz, G. B. (2000). Perspective-taking: Decreasing stereotype expression, stereotype accessibility, and in-group favoritism. *Journal of Personality and Social Psychology*, *78*, 708–724. doi: 10.1037/0022–3514.78.4.708

Garcia, D. M., Reser-Horstman, A., Amo, R. B., Redersdorff, S., & Branscombe, N. R. (2005). Perceivers' responses to in-group and out-group members who blame a negative outcome on discrimination. *Personality and Social Psychology Bulletin*, *31*, 769–780. doi: 10.1177/0146167204271584

Glick, P., & Fiske, S. T. (1996). The ambivalent sexism inventory: Differentiating hostile and benevolent sexism. *Journal of Personality and Social Psychology*, *70*, 491–512. doi: 10.1037/0022–3514 .70.3.491

Glick, P., & Fiske, S. T. (2001). An ambivalent alliance: Hostile and benevolent sexism as complementary justification for gender inequality. *American Psychologist, 56*, 109–118. doi: 10.1037/0003–066X.56.2.109

Goffman, E. (1963). *Stigma: Notes on the management of spoiled identity*. Englewood Cliffs, NJ: Prentice-Hall.

Good, C., Aronson, J., & Inzlicht, M. (2003). Improving adolescents' standardized test performance: An intervention to reduce the effects of stereotype threat. *Journal of Applied Developmental Psychology, 24*, 645–662. doi: 10.1016/j.appdev.2003.09.002

Greenberg, J., Landau, M., Kosloff, S., & Solomon, S. (2009). How our dreams of death transcendence breed prejudice, stereotyping, and conflict: Terror management theory. In T. D. Nelson (Ed.), *Handbook of prejudice, stereotyping, and discrimination* (pp. 309–332). New York, NY: Psychology Press.

Greenberg, J., Pyszczynski, T., Solomon, S., Rosenblatt, A., Veeder, M., Kirkland, S., & Lyon, D. (1990). Evidence for terror management theory II: The effects of mortality salience on reactions to those who threaten or bolster the cultural worldview. *Journal of Personality and Social Psychology, 58*, 308–318. doi: 10.1037/0022–3514.58.2.308

Greenwald, A. G., & Banaji, M. R. (1995). Implicit social cognition: Attitudes, self-esteem, and stereotypes. *Psychological Review, 102*, 4–27. doi: 10.1037/0033–295X.102.1.4

Greenwald, A. G., McGhee, D. E., & Schwartz, J. L. K. (1998). Measuring individual differences in implicit cognition: The implicit association test. *Journal of Personality and Social Psychology, 74*, 1464–1480. doi: 10.1037/0022–3514.74.6.1464

Gresky, D. M., Ten Eyck, L. L., Lord, C. G., & McIntyre, R. B. (2005). Effects of salient multiple identities on women's performance under mathematics stereotype threat. *Sex Roles, 53*, 703–716. doi: 10.1007/s11199–005–7735–2

Haslam, S. A., Oakes, P. J., McGarty, C., Turner, J. C., Reynolds, K. J., & Eggins, R. A. (1996). Stereotyping and social influence: The mediation of stereotype applicability and sharedness by the views of in-group and out-group members. *British Journal of Social Psychology, 35*, 369–397.

Hass, R. G., Katz, I., Rizzo, N., Bailey, J., & Eisenstadt, D. (1991). Cross-racial appraisal as related to attitude ambivalence and cognitive complexity. *Personality and Psychology Bulletin, 7*, 83–92.

Heilman, M. E. (1983). Sex bias in work settings: The lack of fit model. *Research in Organizational Behavior, 5*, 269–298.

Hewstone, M. (1996). Contact and categorization: Social psychological interventions to change intergroup relations. In C. N. Macrae, C. Stangor, & M. Hewstone (Eds.), *Stereotypes and stereotyping* (pp. 323–368). New York, NY: Guilford Press.

Hite, L. M., & McDonald, K. S. (2006). Diversity training pitfalls and possibilities: An exploration of small and mid-size US organizations. *Human Resource Development International, 9*, 365–377. doi: 10.1080/13678860600893565

Hodson, G., Dovidio, J. F., & Gaertner, S. L. (2002). Processes in racial discrimination: Differential weighting of conflicting information. *Personality and Social Psychology Bulletin, 28*, 460–471. doi: 10.1177/0146167202287004

Hornsey, M. J., & Hogg, M. A. (2000). Subgroup relations: A comparison of mutual intergroup differentiation and common ingroup identity models of prejudice reduction. *Personality and Social Psychology Bulletin, 26*, 242–256. doi: 10.1177/0146167200264010

Hugenberg, K., Blusiewicz, R. L., & Sacco, D. F. (2010). On malleable and immalleable subtypes: Stereotyping malleability in one subtype does not spill over to other prominent subtypes. *Social Psychology, 41*, 124–130. doi: 10.1027/1864–9335/a000018

Huo, Y., & Molina, L. E. (2006). Is pluralism a viable model of diversity? The benefits and limits of subgroup respect. *Group Processes & Intergroup Relations, 9*, 359–376. doi: 10.1177/1368430206064639

Hyers, L. L. (2007). Resisting prejudice every day: Exploring women's assertive responses to anti-Black racism, anti-semitism, heterosexism, and sexism. *Sex Roles, 56*, 1–12. doi: 10.1007/s11199–006–9142–8

Inman, M. L. (2001). Do you see what I see?: Similarities and differences in victims' and observers' perceptions of discrimination. *Social Cognition, 19*, 521–546. doi: 10.1521/soco.19.5.521.19912

Inman, M. L., & Baron, R. S. (1996). Influence of prototypes on perceptions of prejudice. *Journal of Personality and Social Psychology, 70*, 727–739. doi: 10.1037/0022–3514.70.4.727

Inzlicht, M., & Kang, S. K. (2010). Stereotype threat spillover: How coping with threats to social identity affects aggression, eating, decision making, and attention. *Journal of Personality and Social Psychology, 99*, 467–481. doi: 10.1037/a0018951

Jackman, M. R. (1994). *The velvet glove: Paternalism in gender, class, and race relations*. Berkeley: University of California Press.

Jamieson, J. P., Mendes, W. B., Blackstock, E., & Schmader, T. (2010). Turning the knots in your stomach into bows: Reappraising arousal improves performance on the GRE. *Journal of Experimental Social Psychology, 46*, 208–212. doi: 10.1016/j.jesp.2009.08.015

Johns, M., Schmader, T., & Martens, A. (2005). Knowing is half the battle: Teaching stereotype threat as a means of improving women's math performance. *Psychological Science, 16*, 175–179. doi: 10.1111/j.0956–7976.2005.00799.x

Jones, J. M. (1997). *Prejudice and racism* (2nd ed.). New York, NY: McGraw-Hill.

Jost, J. T., & Banaji, M. R. (1994). The role of stereotyping in system-justification and the production of false consciousness. *British Journal of Social Psychology, 33*, 1–27.

Jost, J. T., Banaji, M. R., & Nosek, B. A. (2004). A decade of system justification theory: Accumulated evidence on conscious and unconscious bolstering of the status quo. *Political Psychology, 25*, 881–919. doi: 10.1111/j.1467–9221.2004.00402.x

Kaiser, C. R., Major, B., & McCoy, S. K. (2004). Expectations about the future and the emotional consequences of perceiving prejudice. *Personality and Social Psychology Bulletin, 30*, 173–184. doi: 10.1177/0146167203259927

Kaiser, C. R., & Miller, C. T. (2001). Reacting to impending discrimination: Compensation for prejudice and attribution to discrimination. *Personality and Social Psychology Bulletin, 27*, 1357–1367. doi: 10.1177/01461672012710011

Kaiser, C. R., & Miller, C. T. (2003). Derogating the victim: The interpersonal consequences of blaming events on discrimination. *Group Processes & Intergroup Relations, 6*, 227–237. doi: 10.1177/13684302030063001

Kaiser, C. R., Vick, S. B., & Major, B. (2006). Prejudice expectations moderate preconscious attention to cues that are threatening to social identity. *Psychological Science, 17*, 332–338. doi: 10.1111/j.1467–9280.2006.01707.x

Karpinski, A., & Hilton, J. L. (2001). Attitudes and the implicit association test. *Journal of Personality and Social Psychology, 81*, 774–788. doi: 10.1037/0022–3514.81.5.774

Katz, I., & Hass, R. G. (1988). Racial ambivalence and American value conflict: Correlational and priming studies of dual cognitive structures. *Journal of Personality and Social Psychology, 55*, 893–905. doi: 10.1037/0022–3514.55.6.893

Katz, I., & Wackenhut, J., & Hass, R. G. (1986). Racial ambivalence, value duality, and behavior. In J. F. Dovidio & S. L. Gaertner (Eds.), *Prejudice, discrimination, and racism* (pp. 35–59). San Diego, CA: Academic Press.

Kawakami, K., Dovidio, J. F., Moll, J., Hermsen, S., & Russin, A. (2000). Just say no (to stereotypic): Effects of training in the negation of stereotypic associations on stereotype activation. *Journal of Personality and Social Psychology, 78*, 871–888. doi: 10.1037/0022–3514.78.5.871

Kawakami, K., Dovidio, J. F., & van Kamp, S. (2007). The impact of counterstereotypic training and related correction processes on the application of stereotypes. *Group Processes & Intergroup Relations, 10*, 139–156. doi: 10.1177/1368430207074725

Kawakami, K., Phills, C. E., Steele, J. R., & Dovidio, J. F. (2007). (Close) distance makes the heart grow fonder: Improving implicit racial attitudes and interracial interactions through approach behaviors. *Journal of Personality and Social Psychology*, *92*, 957–971. doi: 10.1037/0022–3514.92.6.957

Kay, A. C., & Jost, J. T. (2003). Complementary justice: Effects of "poor but happy" and "poor but honest" stereotype exemplars on system justification and implicit activation of the justice motive. *Journal of Personality and Social Psychology*, *85*, 823–837. doi: 10.1037/0022–3514.85.5.823

Kay, A. C., Jost, J. T., & Young, S. (2005). Victim derogation and victim enhancement as alternate routes to system justification. *Psychological Science*, *16*, 240–246. doi: 10.1111/j.0956–7976.2005.00810.x

Kinder, D. R., & Sears, D. O. (1981). Prejudice and politics: Symbolic racism versus racial threats to the good life. *Journal of Personality and Social Psychology*, *40*, 414–431. doi: 10.1037/0022–3514.40.3.414

Klonoff, E. A., Landrine, H., & Campbell, R. (2000). Sexist discrimination may account for well-known gender difference in psychiatric symptoms. *Psychology of Women Quarterly*, *24*, 93–99. doi: 10.1111/j.1471–6402.2000.tb01025.x

Kovel, J. (1970). *White racism: A psychohistory*. New York, NY: Pantheon Books.

Kurzban, R., & Leary, M. R. (2001). Evolutionary origins of stigmatization: The functions of social exclusion. *Psychological Bulletin*, *127*, 187–208. doi: 10.1037/0033–909.127.2.187

Landrine, H., Klonoff, E. A., Gibbs, J., Manning, V., & Lund, M. (1995). Physical and psychiatric correlates of gender discrimination: An application of the schedule of sexist events. *Psychology of Women Quarterly*, *19*, 473–492. doi: 10.1111/j.1471–6402.1995.tb00087.x

Lerner, M. J. (1977). The justice motive: Some hypotheses as to its origins and forms. *Journal of Personality*, *45*, 1–52.

Levine, R. A., & Campbell, D. T. (1972). *Ethnocentrism: Theories of conflict, ethnic attitudes, and group behavior*. Oxford, UK: John Wiley & Sons.

Levy, B. (1996). Improving memory in old age through implicit self-stereotyping. *Journal of Personality and Social Psychology*, *71*, 1092–1107. doi: 10.1037/0022–3514.71.6.1092

Leyens, J. P. (2009). Retrospective and prospective thoughts about infrahumanization. *Group Processes & Intergroup Relations*, *12*, 807–817. doi: 10.1177/1368430209347330

Leyens, J. P., Paladino, P. M., Rodriguez-Torees, R., Vaes, J., Demoulin, S., Rodriguez-Perez, A., & Gaunt, R. (2000). The emotional side of prejudice: The attribution of secondary emotions to ingroups and outgroups. *Personality and Social Psychology Review*, *4*, 186–197. doi: 0.1207/S15327957PSPR0402_06

Leyens, J. P., Rodriguez-Perez, A., Rodriguez-Torres, R., Gaunt, R., Paladino, M. P., Vaes, J., & Demoulin, S. (2001). Psychological essentialism and the differential attribution of uniquely human emotions to ingroups and outgroups. *European Journal of Social Psychology*, *31*, 395–411. doi: 10.1002/ejsp.50

Logel, C., Iserman, E. C., Davies, P. G., Quinn, D. M., & Spencer, S. J. (2009). The perils of double consciousness: The role of thought suppression in stereotype threat. *Journal of Experimental Social Psychology*, *45*, 299–312. doi: 10.1016/j.jesp.2008.07.016

Maass, A., Salvi, D., Arcuri, L., & Semin, G. R. (1989). Language use in intergroup contexts: The linguistic intergroup bias. *Journal of Personality and Social Psychology*, *57*, 981–993. doi: 10.1037/0022–3514.57.6.981

Mackie, D. M., & Smith, E. R. (2002). *From prejudice to intergroup emotions: Differentiated reactions to social groups*. New York, NY: Psychology Press.

Major, B., Kaiser, C. R., & McCoy, S. K. (2003). It's not my fault: When and why attributions to prejudice protect self esteem. *Personality and Social Psychology Bulletin*, *29*, 772–781. doi: 10.1177/0146167203029006009

Major, B., Quinton, W. J., & McCoy, S. K. (2002). Antecedents and consequences of attributions to discrimination: Theoretical and empirical advances. In M. P. Zanna (Ed.), *Advances in experimental social psychology* (pp. 251–330). San Diego, CA: Academic Press.

Major, B., & Sawyer, P. J. (2009). Attributions to discrimination: Antecedents and consequences. In T. D. Nelson (Ed.), *Handbook of prejudice, stereotyping, and discrimination* (pp. 89–11). New York, NY: Psychology Press.

McConahay, J. B. (1986). Modern racism, ambivalence, and the modern racism scale. In J. F. Dividio & S. L. Gaertner (Eds.), *Prejudice, discrimination, and racism* (pp. 91–125). San Diego, CA: Academic Press.

McConahay, J. B., Hardee, B. B., & Batts, V. (1981). Has racism declined in America? It depends on who is asking and what is asked. *Journal of Conflict Resolution*, *25*, 563–579.

McGlone, M. S., & Aronson, J. (2007). Forewarning and forearming stereotype-threatened students. *Communication Education*, *56*, 119–133. doi: 10.1080/03634520601158681

McIntyre, R. B., Paulson, R. M., & Lord, C. G. (2003). Alleviating women's mathematics stereotype threat through salience of group achievements. *Journal of Experimental Social Psychology*, *39*, 83–90. doi: 10.1016/S0022–1031(02)00513–9

Monteith, M. J. (1993). Self-regulation of prejudiced responses: Implications for progress in prejudice-reduction efforts. *Journal of Personality and Social Psychology*, *65*, 469–485. doi: 10.1037/0022–3514.65.3.469

Monteith, M. J., & Mark, A. Y. (2009). The self-regulation of prejudice. In T. D. Nelson (Ed.), *Handbook of prejudice, stereotyping, and discrimination* (pp. 507–523). New York, NY: Psychology Press.

Mullen, B., Brown, R., & Smith, C. (1992). Ingroup bias as a function of salience, relevance, and status: An integration. *European Journal of Social Psychology*, *22*, 103–122. doi: 10.1002/ejsp.2420220202

Myrdal, G. (1944). *An American dilemma*. Oxford, UK: Harper.

Nadler, E. B., & Morrow, W. R. (1959). Authoritarian attitudes toward women, and their correlates. *The Journal of Social Psychology*, *49*, 113–123.

Navarrete, C. D., McDonald, M. M., Molina, L. E., & Sidanius, J. (2010). Prejudice at the nexus of race and gender: An outgroup male target hypothesis. *Journal of Personality and Social Psychology*, *98*, 933–945. doi: 10.1037/a0017931

O'Brien, L. T., & Crandall, C. S. (2003). Stereotype threat and arousal: Effects on women's math performance. *Personality and Social Psychology Bulletin*, *29*, 782–789. doi: 10.1177/0146167203029006010

O'Brien, L. T., Kinias, Z., & Major, B. (2008). How status and stereotypes impact attributions to discrimination: The stereotype-asymmetry hypothesis. *Journal of Experimental Social Psycology*, *44*, 405–412. doi: 10.1016/j.jesp.2006.12.003

Olson, M. A., & Fazio, R. H. (2006). Reducing automatically activated racial prejudice through implicit evaluative conditioning. *Personality and Social Psychology Bulletin*, *32*, 421–433. doi: 10.1177/0146167205284004

Osborne, J. W., & Walker, C. (2006). Stereotype threat, identification with academics, and withdrawal from school: Why the most successful students of colour might be most likely to withdraw. *Educational Psychology*, *26*, 563–577. doi: 10.1080/01443410500342518

Otten, S., & Mummendey, A. (2000). Valence-dependent probability of ingroup favouritism between minimal groups: An integrative view on the positive-negative asymmetry in social discrimination. In D. Capozza & R. Brown (Eds.), *Social identity processes: Trends in theory and research* (pp. 33–48). Thousand Oaks, CA: Sage.

Paladino, M., & Castelli, L. (2008). On the immediate consequences of intergroup categorization: Activation of approach and avoidance motor behavior toward ingroup and outgroup members. *Personality and Social Psychology Bulletin*, *34*, 755–768. doi: 10.1177/0146167208315155

Paluck, E. L. (2009). Reducing ingroup prejudice and conflict using the media: A field experiment in Rwanda. *Journal of Personality and Social Psychology*, 96, 574–587. doi: 10.1037/a0011989

Paluck, E. L., & Green, D. P. (2009). Prejudice reduction: What works? A review and assessment of research and practice. *Annual Review of Psychology*, 60, 339–367. doi: 10.1146/annurev.psych.60.110707.163607

Park, J. H., Faulkner, J., & Schaller, M. (2003). Evolved disease-avoidance processes and contemporary anti-social behavior: Prejudicial attitudes and avoidance of people with physical disabilities. *Journal of Nonverbal Behavior*, 27, 65–87. doi: 10.1023/A:1023910408854

Park, J. H., Schaller, M., & Crandall, C. S. (2007). Pathogen-avoidance mechanisms and the stigmatization of obese people. *Evolution and Human Behavior*, 28, 410–414. doi: 10.1016/j.evolhumbehav.2007.05.008

Pascoe, E. A., & Smart Richman, L. (2009). Perceived discrimination and health: A meta-analytic review. *Psychological Bulletin*, 135, 531–554. doi: 10.1037/a0016059

Payne, B. K., Cheng, C. M., Govorun, O., & Stewart, B. (2005). An inkblot for attitudes: Affect misattribution as implicit measurement. *Journal of Personality and Social Psychology*, 89, 277–293. doi: 10.1027/1618-3169.56.5.329

Penner, L. A., Dovidio, J. F., Edmondson, D., Dailey, R. K., Markova, T., Albrecht, T. L., & Gaertner, S. L. (2009). The experience of discrimination and black-white health disparities in medical care. *Journal of Black Psychology*, 35, 180–203. doi: 10.1177/0095798409333585

Perdue, C. W., Dovidio, J. F., Gurtman, M. B., & Tyler, R. B. (1990). Us and them: Social categorization and the process of intergroup bias. *Journal of Personality and Social Psychology*, 59, 475–486. doi: 10.1037/0022-3514.59.3.475

Pettigrew, T. F. (1959). Regional differences in anti-Negro prejudice. *The Journal of Abnormal and Social Psychology*, 59, 28–36. doi: 10.1037/h0047133

Pettigrew, T. F., & Tropp, L. R. (2006). A meta-analytic test of intergroup contact theory. *Journal of Personality and Social Psychology*, 90, 751–783. doi: 10.1037/0022-3514.90.5.751

Pinel, E. C. (1999). Stigma consciousness: The psychological legacy of social stereotype. *Journal of Personality and Social Psychology*, 76, 114–128. doi: 10.1037/0022-3514.76.1.114

Plant, E. A., & Devine, P. G. (1998). Internal and external motivation to respond without prejudice. *Journal of Personality and Social Psychology*, 75, 812–832. doi: 10.1037/0022-3514.75.3.811

Plant, E. A., & Devine, P. G. (2009). The active control of prejudice: Unpacking the intentions guiding control efforts. *Journal of Personality and Social Psychology*, 96, 640–652. doi: 10.1037/a0012960

Powell, A. A., Branscombe, N. R., & Schmitt, M. T. (2005). Inequality as ingroup privilege or outgroup disadvantage: The impact of group focus on collective guilt and interracial attitudes. *Personality and Social Psychology Bulletin*, 31, 508–521. doi: 10.1177/0146167204271713

Pratto, F., Sidanius, J., & Levin, S. (2006). Social dominance theory and the dynamics of intergroup relations: Taking stock and looking forward. *European Review of Social Psychology*, 17, 271–320. doi: 10.1080/10463280601055772

Pratto, F., Sidanius, J., Stallworth, L. M., & Bertram, F. (1994). Social dominance orientation: A personality variable predicting social and political attitudes. *Journal of Personality and Social Psychology*, 67, 741–763. doi: 10.1037/0022-3514.67.4.741

Prothro, E. T. (1952). Ethnocentrism and anti-Negro attitudes in the deep south. *Journal of Abnormal and Social Psychology*, 47, 105–108. doi: 10.1037/h0060676

Richeson, J. A., & Shelton, J. N. (2007). Negotiating interracial interactions: Costs, consequences, and possibilities. *Current Directions in Psychological Science*, 16, 316–320. doi: 10.1111/j.1467–8721.2007.00528.x

Riek, B. M., Mania, E. W., & Gaertner, S. L. (2006). Intergroup threat and outgroup attitudes: A meta-analytic review. *Personality and Social Psychology*, 10, 336–353. doi: 10.1207/s15327957

Rodin, M. J., Price, J. M., Bryson, J. B., & Sanchez, F. J. (1990). Asymmetry in prejudice attribution. *Journal of Experimental Social Psychology*, 26, 481–504. doi: 10.1016/0022–1031(90)90052-N

Rothbart, M., & Lewis, S. H. (1994). Cognitive processes and intergroup relations: A historical perspective. In P. G. Devine, D. L. Hamilton, & T. M. Ostrom (Eds.), *Social cognition: Impact on social psychology* (pp. 347–382). San Diego, CA: Academic Press.

Rubin, M., & Hewstone, M. (1998). Social identity theory's self-esteem hypothesis: A review and some suggestions for clarification. *Personality and Social Psychology Review*, 2, 40–62. doi: 10.1207/s15327957

Rudman, L. A., & Goodwin, S. A. (2004). Gender differences in automatic in-group bias: Why do women like women more than men like men? *Journal of Personality and Social Psychology*, 87, 494–509. doi: 10.1037/0022–3514.87.4.494

Rydell, R. J., McConnell, A. R., & Beilock, S. L. (2009). Multiple social identities and stereotype threat: Imbalance, accessibility, and working memory. *Journal of Personality and Social Psychology*, 96, 949–966. doi: 10.1037/a0014846

Rydell, R. J., Rydell, M. T., & Boucher, K. L. (2010). The effect of negative performance stereotypes on learning. *Journal of Personality and Social Psychology*, 99, 883–896. doi: 10.1037/a0021139

Saguy, T., Tausch, N., Dovidio, J. F., & Pratto, F. (2009). The irony of harmony: Intergroup contact can produce false expectations for equality. *Psychological Science*, 20, 114–121. doi: 10.1111/j.1467–9280.2008.02261.x

Schaller, M., Park, J. H., & Mueller, A. (2003). Fear of the dark: Interactive effects of beliefs about danger and ambient darkness on ethnic stereotypes. *Personality and Social Psychology Bulletin*, 29, 637–649. doi: 10.1177/0146167203029005008

Scheepers, D., Spears, R., Doosje, B., & Manstead, A. S. R. (2006). Diversity in in-group bias: Structural factors, situational features, and social functions. *Journal of Personality and Social Psychology*, 90, 944–960. doi: 10.1037/0022–3514.90.6.944

Schmader, T., & Johns, M. (2003). Converging evidence that stereotype threat reduces working memory capacity. *Journal of Personality and Social Psychology*, 85, 440–452. doi: 10.1037/0022–3514.85.3.440

Schmader, T., Johns, M., & Forbes, C. (2008). An integrated process model of stereotype threat effects on performance. *Psychological Review*, 115, 336–356. doi: 10.1037/0033-295X.115.2.336

Schmitt, M. T., & Branscombe, N. R. (2002). The internal and external causal loci of attributions to prejudice. *Personality and Social Psychology Bulletin*, 28, 620–628. doi: 10.1177/0146167202288006

Schmitt, M. T., Branscombe, N. R., Kobrynowicz, D., & Owen, S. (2002). Perceiving discrimination against one's gender group has different implications for well-being in women and men. *Personality and Social Psychology Bulletin*, 28, 197–210. doi: 10.1177/0146167202282006

Schmitt, M. T., Branscombe, N. R., & Postmes, T. (2003). Women's emotional responses to the pervasiveness of gender discrimination. *European Journal of Social Psychology*, 33, 297–312. doi: 10.1002/ejsp.147

Schmitt, M. T., Spears, R., & Branscombe, N. R. (2003). Constructing a minority group identity out of shared rejection: The case of international students. *European Journal of Social Psychology*, 33, 1–12. doi: 10.1002/ejsp.131

Sears, D. O. (1988). Symbolic racism. In P. A. Katz & D. A. Taylor (Eds.), *Eliminating racism: Profiles in controversy. Perspectives in social psychology* (pp. 53–84). New York, NY: Plenum Press.

Sechrist, G. B. (2010). Making attributions to and plans to confront gender discrimination: The role of optimism. *Journal of Applied*

Social Psychology, *40*, 1678–1707. doi: 10.1111/j.1559–1816 .2010.00635.x

Shapiro, J. R., & Neuberg, S. L. (2007). From stereotype threat to stereotype threats: Implications of a multi-threat framework for causes, moderators, mediators, consequences, and interventions. *Personality and Social Psychology Review*, *11*, 107–130. doi: 10.1177/ 1088868306294790

Shelton, J. N., & Richeson, J. A. (2006). Ethnic minorities' racial attitudes and contact experiences with white people. *Cultural Diversity and Ethnic Minority Psychology*, *12*, 149–164. doi: 10.1037/ 1099–9809.12.1.149

Shelton, J. N., & Stewart, R. E. (2004). Confronting perpetrators of prejudice: The inhibitory effects of social costs. *Psychology of Women Quarterly*, *28*, 215–223. doi: 10.1111/j.1471–6402.2004.00138.x

Sherif, M. (1966). *Group conflict and cooperation: Their social psychology*. London, UK: Routledge and Kegan Paul.

Sherif, M., & Sherif, C. W. (1953). *Groups in harmony and tension; an integration of studies of intergroup relations*. Oxford, UK: Harper & Brothers.

Sibley, C. G., & Duckitt, J. (2009). Big-five personality, social worldview, and ideological attitudes: Further test of a dual process cognitive-motivational model. *Journal of Social Psychology*, *149*, 545–561. doi: 10.1080/00224540903232308

Sidanius, J., & Pratto, F. (1993). The inevitability of oppression and the dynamics of social dominance. In P. M. Sniderman, P. E. Tetlock, & E. D. Carmines (Eds.), *Prejudice, politics, and the American dilemma* (pp. 173–211). Palo Alto, CA: Stanford University Press.

Sidanius, J., Pratto, F., Martin, M., & Stallworth, L. M. (1991). Consensual racism and career track: Some implications of social dominance theory. *Political Psychology*, *12*, 691–721. doi: 10.2307/3791552

Sidanius, J., & Veniegas, R. C. (2000). Gender and race discrimination: The interactive nature of disadvantage. In S. Oskamp (Ed.), *Reducing prejudice and discrimination. The Claremont symposium on applied social psychology* (pp. 47–69). Mahwah, NJ: Erlbaum.

Smith, E. R., & Mackie, D. M. (2010). Affective processes. In J. F. Dovidio, M. Hewstone, P. Glick, & V. M. Esses (Eds.), *The SAGE handbook of prejudice, stereotyping, and discrimination* (pp. 508–525). Thousand Oaks, CA: Sage.

Smith, E. R., Seger, C. R., & Mackie, D. M. (2007). Can emotions be truly group level? Evidence regarding four conceptual criteria. *Journal of Personality and Social Psychology*, *93*, 431–446. doi: 10.1037/0022–3514.93.3.431

Spencer, S. J., Steele, C. M., & Quinn, D. M. (1999). Stereotype threat and women's math performance. *Journal of Experimental Social Psychology*, *35*, 4–28. doi: 10.1006/jesp.1998.1373

Stangor, C. (2009). The study of stereotyping, prejudice, and discrimination within social psychology: A quick history of theory and research. *Handbook of prejudice, stereotyping, and discrimination* (pp. 1–22). New York, NY: Psychology Press.

Stangor, C., Sechrist, G. B., & Jost, J. T. (2001). Changing racial beliefs by providing consensus information. *Personality and Social Psychology Bulletin*, *27*, 486–496. doi: 10.1177/0146167201274009

Stangor, C., Swim, J. K., Van Allen, K. L., & Sechrist, G. B. (2002). Reporting discrimination in public and private contexts. *Journal of Personality and Social Psychology*, *82*, 69–74. doi: 10.1037/ 0022–3514.82.1.69

Steele, C. M. (1997). A threat in the air: How stereotypes shape intellectual identity and performance. *American Psychologist*, *52*, 613–629. doi: 10.1037/0003–066X.52.6.613

Steele, C. M., & Aronson, J. (1995). Stereotype threat and the intellectual test performance of African Americans. *Journal of Personality and Social Psychology*, *69*, 797–811. doi: 10.1037/0022–3514.69.5.797

Stephan, W. G., & Finlay, K. (1999). The role of empathy in improving intergroup relations. *Journal of Social Issues*, *55*, 729–743. doi: 10.1111/0022–4537.001440022-4537.00144

Stephan, W. G., & Stephan, C. W. (2000). An integrated threat theory of prejudice. In S. Oskamp (Ed.), *Reducing prejudice and discrimination* (pp. 23–34). Mahwah, NJ: Erlbaum.

Stewart, T. L., Latu, I. M., Branscombe, N. R., & Denney, H. T. (2010). Yes we can! Prejudice reduction through seeing (inequality) and believing (in social change). *Psychological Science*, *21*, 1557–1562. doi: 10.1177/0956797610385354

Stewart, T. L., Latu, I. M., Kawakami, K., & Meyers, A. C. (2010). Consider the situation: Reducing automatic stereotyping through situational attribution training. *Journal of Experimental Social Psychology*, *46*, 221–225. doi: 10.1016/j.jesp.2009.09.004

Stone, J. (2002). Battling doubt by avoiding practice: The effects of stereotype threat on self-handicapping in white athletes. *Personality and Social Psychology Bulletin*, *28*, 1667–1678. doi: 10.1177/ 014616702237648

Stone, J., Perry. Z. W., & Darley, J. M. (1997). "White men can't jump": Evidence for the perceptual confirmation of racial stereotypes following a basketball game. *Basic and Applied Social Psychology*, *19*, 291–306. doi: 10.1207/15324839751036977

Swim, J. K., & Hyers, L. L. (1999). Excuse me—What did you say?!: Women's public and private responses to sexist remarks. *Journal of Experimental Social Psychology*, *35*, 68–88. doi: 10.1006/jesp .1998.1370

Tajfel, H. (1982). Social psychology of intergroup relations. *Annual Review of Psychology, 33*, 1–39. doi: 10.1146/annurev.ps.33.020182 .000245

Tajfel, H., Billig, M. G., Bundy, R. P., & Flament, C. (1971). Social categorization and intergroup behavior. *European Journal of Social Psychology*, *1*, 149–178. doi: 10.1002/ejsp.2420010202

Tajfel, H., & Turner, J. C. (1979). An integrative theory of intergroup conflict. In W. G. Austin, & S. Worchel (Eds.), *Social psychology of intergroup relations* (pp. 33–48). Monterey, CA: Brooks/Cole.

Tajfel, H., & Turner, J. C. (1986). The social identity theory of intergroup behavior. In S. Worschel & W. G. Austin (Eds.), *Psychology of intergroup relations*. Chicago, IL: Nelson-Hall.

Tam, T., Hewstone, M., Cairns, E., Tausch, N., Maio, G., & Kenworthy, J. (2007). The impact of intergroup emotions on forgiveness in northern Ireland. *Group Processes & Intergroup Relations*, *10*, 119–136. doi: 10.1177/1368430207071345

Taylor, D. M., Wright, S. C., Moghaddam, F. M., & Lalonde, R. N. (1990). The personal/group discrimination discrepancy: Perceiving my group, but not myself, to be a target for discrimination. *Personality and Social Psychology Bulletin*, *16*, 254–262. doi: 10.1177/0146167290162006

Trawalter, S., Richeson, J. A., & Shelton, J. N. (2009). Predicting behavior during interracial interactions: A stress and coping approach. *Personality and Social Psychology Review, 13*, 243–268.

Tropp, L. R., & Pettigrew, T. F. (2005). Relationships between intergroup contact and prejudice among minority and majority status groups. *Psychological Science*, *16*, 951–957. doi: 10.1111/j.1467– 9280 .2005.01643.x

Turner, J. C. (1981). Towards a cognitive redefinition of the social group. *Current Psychology of Cognition*, *1*, 93–118.

Turner, R. N., Crisp, R. J., & Lambert, E. (2007). Imagining intergroup contact can improve intergroup attitudes. *Group Processes and Intergroup Relations*, *10*, 427–441.

Turner, J. C., Hogg, M. A., Oakes, P. J., Reicher, S. D., & Wetherell, M. S. (1987). *Rediscovering the social group: A self-categorization theory*. Cambridge, MA: Basil Blackwell.

U.S. Department of Health and Human Services, COSMOS Corporation. (2000). *Assessment of state minority health infrastructure and capacity to address issues of health disparity* (Contract No. 282–98–0017). Retrieved from http://minorityhealth.hhs.gov/assets/ pdf/checked/1/OMHHealthDisparityFRSept00.pdf

Vaes, J., Paladino, M. P., Castelli, L., Leyens, J. P., & Giovanazzi, A. (2003). On the behavioral consequences of infrahumanization: The implicit role of uniquely human emotions in intergroup relations. *Journal of Personality and Social Psychology*, *85*, 1016–1034. doi: 10.1037/0022-3514.85.6.1016

Vanbeselaere, N. (1987). The effects of dichotomous and crossed social categorizations upon intergroup discrimination. *European Journal of Social Psychology*, *17*, 143–156. doi: 10.1002/ejsp.2420170203

Verkuyten, M. (2007). Religious group identification and inter-religious relations: A study Turkish-Dutch Muslims. *Group Processes & Intergroup Relations*, *10*, 341–357. doi: 10.1177/1368430207078695

Vescio, T. K., Sechrist, G. B., & Paolucci, M. P. (2003). Perspective taking and prejudice reduction: The meditational role of empathy arousal and situational attributions. *European Journal of Social Psychology*, *33*, 455–472. doi: 10.1002/ejsp.163

Wenzel, M., & Mummendey, A. (1996). Positive-negative asymmetry of social discrimination: A normative analysis of differential evaluation of in-group and out-group on positive and negative attributes. *British Journal of Social Psychology*, *35*, 493–507.

Weyant, J. M. (2007). Perspective taking as a means of reducing negative stereotyping of individuals who speak English as a second language. *Journal of Applied Social Psychology*, *37*, 703–716. doi: 10.1111/j.1559-1816.2007.00181.x

Williams, D. R., & Mohammed, S. A. (2009). Discrimination and racial disparities in health: Evidence and needed research. *Journal of Behavioral Medicine*, *32*, 20–47. doi: 10.1007/s10865-008-9185-0

Wilson, T. D., Lindsey, S., & Schooler, T. Y. (2000). A model of dual attitudes. *Psychological Review*, *107*, 101–126. doi: 10.1037/0033-295X.107.1.101

Wittenbrink, B. (2007). Measuring attitudes through priming. In B. Wittenbrink & N. Schwarz (Eds.), *Implicit measures of attitudes* (pp. 17–58). New York, NY: Guilford Press.

Wittenbrink, B., Judd, C. M., & Park, P. (2001). Spontaneous prejudice in context: Variability in automatically activated attitudes. *Journal of Personality and Social Psychology*, *81*, 815–827. doi: 10.1037/0022-3514.81.5.815

Wright, S. C., Aron, A., McLaughlin-Volpe, T., & Ropp, S. A. (1997). The extended contact effect: Knowledge of cross-group friendships and prejudice. *Journal of Personality and Social Psychology*, *73*, 73–90. doi: 10.1037/0022-3514.73.1.730022-3514.73.1.73

Wright, S. C., & Lubensky, M. E. (2009). The struggle for social equality: Collective action versus prejudice reduction. In S. Demoulin, J. Leyens, & J. F. Dovidio (Eds.), *Intergroup misunderstanding: Impact of divergent social realities* (pp. 291–310). New York, NY: Psychology Press.

Yzerbyt, V. Y. (2010). Motivational processes. In J. F. Dovidio, M. Hewstone, P. Glick, & V. M. Esses (Eds.), *The SAGE handbook of prejudice, stereotyping, and discrimination* (pp. 508–525). Thousand Oaks, CA: Sage.

Yzerbyt, V., & Demoulin, S. (2010). Intergroup relations. In S. T. Fiske, D. T. Gilbert, & G. Lindzey (Eds.), *Handbook of social psychology* (pp. 1024–1083). Hoboken, NJ: Wiley.

CHAPTER 17

Persuasion and Attitude Change

RICHARD E. PETTY, S. CHRISTIAN WHEELER, AND ZAKARY L. TORMALA

Attitudes refer to the general and relatively enduring evaluations people have of other people, objects, or ideas. These overall evaluations can be positive, negative, or neutral, and can vary in their extremity. For example, one individual might view exercise in a mildly positive way, whereas another might be wildly positive, and another might be somewhat negative. Individuals can hold attitudes about very broad or abstract constructs (e.g., freedom) as well as very concrete and specific things (e.g., a particular brand of chewing gum). Attitudes are of interest because they often drive behavior. That is, people tend to act favorably toward things they like (e.g., purchase, marry) and unfavorably toward things they do not like.

BACKGROUND ISSUES

Before turning to our primary focus on the processes involved in changing attitudes, we address some important background issues on the nature and structure of attitudes. We cover such topics as whether attitudes are based on cognition or emotion, whether attitudes are stored in memory or constructed as needed, whether attitudes are consequential or not, and differences between automatic and deliberative evaluations. Following this, we describe ways to change attitudes that involve relatively high versus low amounts of thinking, and the consequences of these different strategies.

Bases of Attitudes

Attitudes can be based on different types of information. One popular conceptualization, the tripartite theory, holds that there are three primary types of information on which attitudes can be based (Rosenberg & Hovland, 1960; Zanna & Rempel, 1988): cognitions or beliefs (e.g., "This car gets 10 miles per gallon"), affect or feelings (e.g., "Owning this car makes me happy"), and actions or behavior (e.g., "I have always driven this brand of car"). Interestingly, people are not necessarily aware of the bases of their attitudes. For example, people can believe that their attitudes are based primarily on cognition when they are in fact based on affect, and both real and perceived bases of attitudes influence how people respond to persuasive messages (See, Petty, & Fabrigar, 2008). In particular, it is generally more effective to change attitudes that are actually based or perceived to be based on emotion with emotional strategies than with more cognitively rational ones and vice versa (Edwards, 1990; Fabrigar & Petty, 1999; see also Maio & Olson, this volume). It is also noteworthy that attitudes have been shown to have some genetic basis, and highly heritable attitudes can be more resistant to change than less heritable attitudes (e.g., Olson, Vernon, Harris, & Jang, 2001).

Attitude Storage Versus Construction

Implied in our definition of attitudes is the notion that attitudes are stored in memory. However, some researchers have argued that attitudes are not stored in memory and instead are newly constructed, when requested, based on salient beliefs, emotions, and behaviors (Schwarz & Bohner, 2000; Wilson & Hodges, 1992). This perspective is rooted primarily in the finding that attitude reports are susceptible to a variety of contextual biases that influence the attitudes reported (see Schwarz, 1999).

Although attitude reports are clearly influenced by the immediate context, a strict constructivist view of attitudes seems implausible for a number of reasons. First, as we review below, research has demonstrated that individuals experience aversive arousal when they violate their existing attitudes (e.g., Elliot & Devine, 1994), and individuals are often motivated to defend their attitudes in the face of counterattitudinal appeals (e.g., Ditto & Lopez, 1992; Petty & Cacioppo, 1979a). These findings make little sense if people didn't have stored attitudes in memory. Furthermore, research has delineated the conditions under which motivated defense versus attitude construction processes will operate (e.g., Fazio, Zanna, & Cooper, 1977). Second, attitudes can be automatically activated under response conditions that would make spontaneous construction seem unlikely (Bargh, Chaiken, Govender, & Pratto, 1992), though people can also have automatic evaluative reactions to specific objects (e.g., abstract paintings) they have never seen (Duckworth, Bargh, Garcia, & Chaiken, 2002). In the latter instances, people could be retrieving reactions to salient features of the object (e.g., colors, shapes). Third, it would seem to be functionally maladaptive for individuals to store a lot of attitude-relevant beliefs for attitude reconstruction in the absence of summary evaluative representations (Lingle & Ostrom, 1981). Fourth, research has uncovered structural properties of attitudes (e.g., certainty) that can influence their persistence across a variety of contexts (see Petty & Krosnick, 1995).

If there were no stored attitudes, and evaluations were simply constructed anew each time the attitude object was encountered, many of the processes described in this chapter would have little theoretical utility, or at a minimum they would be theories of attitude construction. In our view, the strict constructivist approach does not seem prudent. In this chapter, attitudes are conceptualized as stored constructs that can be retrieved from memory with more or less difficulty upon encountering the attitude object.

In using this conceptualization, we do not mean to imply that attitudes are not susceptible to context effects or are never constructed. Most obviously, when individuals do not have attitudes about a particular attitude object, they can simply construct an attitude when asked for one (Converse, 1970). Also, when individuals are instructed to think about their attitude before reporting it, they may sometimes selectively focus on a subset of attitude-relevant information (Wilson, Dunn, Kraft, & Lisle, 1989). Similarly, individuals might report different attitudes when contextual variables like conversational norms or social desirability concerns operate (Schwarz & Bohner, 2000). However, the fact that contextual variables can sometimes influence attitude reports is not tantamount to establishing that there are no stored evaluations for any attitude objects. Rather, attitude construction processes likely occur mostly when no stored evaluation is readily accessible or contextual factors contribute to current attitude reports by modifying or shading a retrieved global evaluation (Petty, Priester, & Wegener, 1994). And, even though virtually everyone has many stored attitudes, there are also individual differences in the extent to which people engage in evaluation and form attitudes, called differences in "need to evaluate" (Petty et al., 2006).

Attitude Strength

Although we define attitudes as relatively enduring constructs, attitudes can certainly change over time. Attitudes can change from being nonexistent to having some valence, or can change from one valence to another. Attitudes are fruitfully conceptualized as falling along a continuum from nonattitudes to strong attitudes (see Converse, 1970). Strong attitudes are those that influence thought and behavior, are persistent over time, and are resistant to change (Krosnick & Petty, 1995). Many indicators of attitude strength have been identified including attitude accessibility (e.g., Fazio, 1995), certainty (e.g., Petty, Briñol, Tormala, & Wegener, 2007), ambivalence (Priester & Petty, 1996), and others (see Visser, Bizer, & Krosnick, 2006, for a review of attitude strength variables). Though it is intuitively appealing to assume that attitude strength variables are manifestations of a single latent construct, intercorrelations among the various attitude strength variables are often somewhat low. Furthermore, the search for a limited number of underlying attitude strength factors has yielded inconclusive results (see Eagly & Chaiken, 1998). Nevertheless, it seems reasonable that the many strength variables will ultimately boil down to a relatively few critical dimensions that are most important for producing the major strength consequences (e.g., making the attitude resistant to change).

Measurement of Attitudes

Researchers have developed a multitude of ways to measure attitudes (see Eagly & Chaiken, 1993). Measurement of attitudes is important for determining what people's current attitudes are and whether or not they have changed. A longstanding distinction about attitude measures is whether the measure is a direct or an indirect one (Petty & Cacioppo, 1981). Direct attitude measures are those that simply ask the respondent to report his or her attitude. Included in this category are attitude measurement devices such as the classic Thurstone (1928) scale and the popular semantic differential (Osgood, Suci, & Tannenbaum, 1957), which involves rating one's evaluation as good-bad, or favorable-unfavorable. Indirect attitude measures, on the other hand, are those that do not directly ask the individual to report his or her attitude. Instead, the individual's attitude is inferred from his or her judgments, reactions, or behaviors. These measures do not make it obvious that attitudes are being assessed. Included in this category are a wide variety of methods such as using physical behaviors (e.g., seating distance or eye contact) or gauging the evaluation that automatically comes to mind using reaction times procedures such as the evaluative priming measure (Fazio, Jackson, Dunton, & Williams, 1995) or the implicit association test (Greenwald, McGhee, & Schwartz, 1998; for reviews, see Petty, Fazio, & Briñol, 2009; Wittenbrink & Schwarz, 2007). Direct and indirect measurement methods typically exhibit modest positive correlations (Dovidio, Kawakami, & Beach, 2000).

Direct and indirect measurement methods differ in the extent to which it is obvious that an attitude is being assessed, but such measures can also differ in other ways. Typical direct measures allow some time for making an attitude report whereas some indirect measures aim to tap more spontaneous evaluations. Indirect measures that attempt to assess an automatic attitude are often referred to as implicit measures whereas direct measures that allow for some deliberation are often referred to as explicit measures. When defined in this way, implicit measures are sometimes said to assess implicit (automatic) attitudes, whereas explicit measures are said to assess explicit (deliberative) attitudes.

Much research has focused on the utility of implicit and explicit measures for predicting behavior. Often, explicit and implicit measures lead to the same conclusion about a person's attitude and in these cases would predict the same behavioral outcomes (cf., Greenwald, Poehlman, Uhlmann, & Banaji, 2009). When the two measures yield different attitudes, the explicit attitude measure tends to be better in predicting deliberative behaviors (e.g., jury voting) whereas the implicit attitude measure tends to be better in predicting spontaneous behavior (e.g., seating distances; Dovidio et al., 2000; Dovidio, Kawakami, Johnson, Johnson, & Howard, 1997). Vargas, von Hippel, and Petty (2001) argued that this is because the information processing conditions of attitude measurement (spontaneous or deliberate) matched the information processing conditions of behavioral assessment, and this assessment compatibility fostered higher correlations (Ajzen & Fishbein, 1977). Fazio's (1990) MODE model suggests that automatic attitudes will influence behavior when motivation and opportunity to evaluate the consequences of actions are low, but less-accessible attitudes can influence behavior when motivation and opportunity are high. Generally, implicit and explicit measures each serve as independent predictors of behavior, suggesting that they both provide input into most action (Greenwald et al., 2009). We return to the utility of implicit and explicit measures of attitudes at the end of this chapter.

Implicit Versus Explicit Attitudes

Historically, most research on attitudes concerned people's explicit likes and dislikes as assessed with deliberative (direct) measures, but much recent research has also explored the notion of automatic (implicit) attitudes assessed with implicit measures. Although there are a number of different definitions of implicit attitudes (e.g., see Greenwald & Banaji, 1995; Wilson, Lindsey, & Schooler, 2000), two aspects have assumed the most importance. First, implicit attitudes are said to come to mind automatically on the mere presentation of the attitude object. These automatic evaluative reactions can differ from the more deliberative assessments that people provide when asked to think about their attitudes.

A second feature concerns awareness. That is, attitudes have been called implicit if people were not aware of what their attitudes are, where they came from, or what effects they have. Because people are often unaware of the causes and effects of their attitudes—even when they can easily report the evaluations themselves—these forms of awareness are not good candidates for distinguishing implicit from explicit attitudes (Petty, Wheeler, & Tormala, 2003). The question of whether people are invariably aware of what their attitudes are (e.g., do I like ice-cream?) has generated some controversy. Some have argued that there is no compelling evidence that people lack awareness of their evaluations (e.g., Fazio & Olson, 2003). Instead, some researchers suggest that people are generally aware of their evaluations, but that evaluative responses can arise from different processes: (1) automatic attitude activation or associative processes, and (2) more reflective or propositional processes (Gawronski & Bodenhausen, 2006).

The MODE model (Fazio, 1990) suggests that implicit measures of attitudes such as the evaluative priming measure tap a stored, underlying automatic evaluative association, whereas explicit self-report measures tap that association plus additional downstream processes (e.g., contextual factors) that can modify expression of that attitude. The meta-cognitive model (MCM; Petty, Briñol & DeMarree, 2007) assumes attitude objects can be linked in memory to both positive and negative evaluations (see Cacioppo, Gardner, & Berntson, 1997), which can be linked to stored validity tags (i.e., an assessment of whether the evaluation is correct or not). In this framework, implicit measures tap the links between the attitude object without respect to the validity tags whereas deliberative (explicit) measures also consider the perceived validity of the evaluative associations along with any contextual factors operating (see also Gawronski & Bodenhausen, 2006).

ATTITUDE CHANGE: AN OVERVIEW

Now that we have examined some important definitional and conceptual issues surrounding the attitude concept, we turn to a discussion of attitude change processes. In the remainder of this chapter we describe the fundamental processes of attitude change that have been proposed by social psychologists in the modern era. The study of attitude change is one of the oldest in social psychology and so many different theories and effects have been uncovered over the past 50 years that it can be challenging to understand them all (see Briñol & Petty, 2012, for a history of the field).

The focus of theories of attitude change to date has been on understanding how to produce change in explicit or deliberative attitudes, though research is accumulating rapidly on methods of changing implicit or automatic attitudes. In general, each technique that has changed deliberative attitudes has also changed automatic attitudes, though some techniques might work a bit better in one domain than the other (Rydell & McConnell, 2006; Rydell, McConnell, Mackie, & Strain, 2006; see Briñol, Petty, & McCaslin, 2009, for a review). Because the

change techniques are generally similar across the two kinds of measures, we make no further differentiation in discussing them. In general, an attitude change technique is deemed effective to the extent that it modifies either a person's self-report of attitudes or the attitude assessed with a more indirect or implicit measure. For example, if a person is neutral toward an abstract symbol prior to the change treatment, but is more favorable afterward, attitude change was deemed to be successful.

To organize the different theories of attitude change, we rely on the key ideas from contemporary dual process models of social judgment (Chaiken & Trope, 1999). The two such models that are most popular for understanding attitude change are the elaboration likelihood model (ELM; Petty & Cacioppo, 1986) and the heuristic-systematic model (HSM; Chaiken, Liberman, & Eagly, 1989). These theories provide a meta-framework from which to understand the moderation and mediation of attitude change effects, and explain how the same variable (e.g., source credibility, emotion) can have different effects on attitude change in different situations (e.g., increasing attitude change in one situation but decreasing it in another), and produce the same effect by different processes in different situations. The key idea in the dual process theories is that some processes of attitude change require relatively high amounts of mental effort, whereas other processes require relatively little mental effort. The notion that some judgment processes use higher degrees of thought than others is also a core feature of the many dual systems models of judgment (Petty & Briñol, 2006) as well as theories that rely on just one overall judgment process (Kruglanski & Thompson, 1999).

Petty and Cacioppo (1981) reasoned that most of the major theories of attitude change were not necessarily competitors or contradictory, but operated in different circumstances. Later in this chapter we use the idea that different processes of persuasion require different amounts of thought to organize the major theories of persuasion. Although the ELM and HSM stem from somewhat different traditions, the theories have many similarities and can generally accommodate the same empirical results, though the explanatory language and sometimes the assumed mediating processes vary (Petty & Wegener, 1998). After describing the Elaboration Likelihood Model and reviewing some prominent factors determining whether people tend to exert high or low amounts of mental effort in a persuasion situation, we next describe the specific persuasion processes that tend to require relatively low versus high amounts of mental effort.

The Elaboration Likelihood Model of Persuasion

The Elaboration Likelihood Model (ELM; Petty & Briñol, 2012; Petty & Cacioppo, 1986) is a theory about the processes responsible for attitude change and the strength of the attitudes that result from those processes. A key construct in the ELM is the elaboration likelihood continuum, which refers to how motivated and able people are to assess the central merits of an issue or a position. The more motivated and able people are to assess the central merits of an issue or position, the more likely they are to effortfully scrutinize all available issue-relevant information. Thus, when the elaboration likelihood is high, people will assess issue-relevant information in relation to knowledge that they already possess, and arrive at a reasoned (though not necessarily unbiased) attitude that is well articulated and bolstered by supporting information (*central route*). When the elaboration likelihood is low, however, then information scrutiny is reduced and attitude change can result from a number of less resource demanding processes that do not require as much effortful evaluation of the issue-relevant information (*peripheral route*). Attitudes that are changed by low-effort processes are postulated to be weaker (e.g., not as impactful on behavior) than attitudes that are changed the same extent by high-effort processes.

In addition to the elaboration continuum and the various associated processes, two other ELM notions are noteworthy. First, the ELM postulates a tradeoff between the impact of high- and low-effort processes on judgments along the elaboration continuum, such that as the impact of high-effort processes on judgments increases, the impact of low-effort processes on judgments decreases. This tradeoff hypothesis implies that at most points along the continuum, various change processes can co-occur and jointly influence judgments. It also implies that movement in either direction along the continuum tends to enhance the relative impact of one or the other process (e.g., effortful scrutiny for merit versus reliance on a counting heuristic) on judgments.

Another important ELM notion is the *multiple roles hypothesis*, which refers to the idea that any given variable can influence attitudes by different processes at different points along the elaboration continuum. For example, if a pleasant television show makes you feel happy, this happiness might make you develop a positive attitude toward the products featured in the commercials shown during the show. But the mechanism by which this happens can vary depending on the overall extent of elaboration. When elaboration is low (e.g., high distraction), happiness could

affect judgments by serving as a simple associative cue (e.g., if I feel good, I must like it). On the other hand, if elaboration is high, happiness could affect judgments by biasing the thoughts that come to mind (Petty, Schumann, Richman, & Strathman, 1993) or affecting confidence in one's thoughts (Briñol, Petty, & Barden, 2007). If elaboration is not constrained to be high or low, being happy can affect the extent of processing of the message arguments. In particular, if the message is counterattitudinal or unpleasant in some way, being happy reduces message processing (Bless, Bohner, Schwarz, & Strack, 1990). But if the message is uplifting and pleasant, happiness can increase message processing over neutrality (Wegener, Petty, & Smith, 1995). Other variables similarly can serve in different roles depending on the overall elaboration likelihood.

Determinants and Dimensions of Elaboration

According to the ELM, for high-effort processes to influence attitudes, people must be both motivated and able to think. There are many variables capable of affecting the extent of thinking and thereby influencing whether attitude change is likely to occur via the high- or low-effort processes to be described shortly. Some motivational and ability variables are part of the persuasion situation whereas others can be considered aspects of the recipient of persuasion. Some variables affect mostly the amount of information processing activity that takes place whereas others tend to influence the direction or valence of the thinking. Still other variables affect how confident people are in the thoughts they had.

One of the most important variables influencing a person's motivation to think is the perceived personal relevance or importance of the communication (Petty & Cacioppo, 1979b; Petty, Cacioppo, & Haugtvedt, 1992). When personal relevance is high, people are more influenced by the substantive arguments in a message and are less impacted by peripheral processes (Petty, Cacioppo, & Goldman, 1981). There are many ways to render a message self-relevant, such as including many first person pronouns (Burnkrant & Unnava, 1989), or matching the message to a person's self-conception (Petty, Wheeler, & Bizer, 2000). For example, framing a message as intended for extraverts rather than introverts increases message processing among extraverts (Wheeler, Petty, & Bizer, 2005). Other variables that increase motivation to think include telling people that they are individually accountable for message scrutiny (Tetlock, 1983), violating their expectancies in some way (e.g., Maheswaran & Chaiken, 1991), or inducing conflict about the attitude including implicit conflict between individuals' automatic and deliberative attitudes (Briñol, Petty, & Wheeler, 2006).

It is also important to consider individual differences in people's motivation to think. People who enjoy thinking (i.e., those high in need for cognition; Cacioppo & Petty, 1982) tend to form attitudes on the basis of the quality of the arguments in a message rather than on peripheral cues (see Cacioppo, Petty, & Morris, 1983). Low need for cognition individuals will engage in thinking, however, if they are sufficiently motivated to do so such as when they are told that the message is simple to understand (See, Petty, & Evans, 2009).

Among the important variables influencing a person's ability to process issue-relevant arguments is message repetition. Moderate message repetition provides more opportunities to scrutinize the arguments (e.g., Cacioppo & Petty, 1979). On the other hand, presenting the message too fast (Smith & Shaffer, 1991) or presenting distractions can reduce message scrutiny (e.g., Petty, Wells, & Brock, 1976). Individual differences also affect the ability to think about a persuasive communication. For example, as general knowledge about a topic increases, people become more able (and perhaps more motivated) to think about issue-relevant information (Wood, Rhodes, & Biek, 1995).

Of course, in most communication settings, a confluence of factors determines the extent of information processing rather than one variable acting in isolation. Although the effects of single variables on information processing have been studied extensively, there is relatively little work examining possible interactions among variables (cf., Petty, Cacioppo, & Heesacker, 1981).

Relatively Objective Versus Biased Information Processing

The variables we have discussed, such as distraction or need for cognition, tend to influence information processing activity in a relatively objective manner. All things being equal, distraction tends to disrupt whatever thoughts a person is having (Petty et al., 1976). Similarly, individuals with a high need for cognition are more motivated to think in general than people low in need for cognition (Petty, Briñol, Loersch, & McCaslin, 2009). They are not more motivated to think certain kinds of thoughts over others. Some variables, however, are selective in their effects on thinking. For example, when people are highly motivated to think, a positive mood tends to encourage positive thoughts and/or discourage negative thoughts (Petty et al., 1993) and expert sources tend to encourage

favorable rather than unfavorable interpretations of message arguments (Chaiken & Maheswaran, 1994).

The ELM accommodates both relatively objective and relatively biased information processing and assumes that motivation is relatively objective when no apriori judgment is preferred. In contrast, a motivated bias can occur whenever people prefer one judgment over another (see also Kruglanski, 1990). A wide variety of motivations can determine which particular judgment is preferred in any given situation. For example, if the motive for autonomy (Brehm, 1966) is aroused, people will prefer to hold whatever judgment is forbidden or wish to not hold whatever judgment is demanded. If balance motives (Heider, 1958) are operating, people would prefer to adopt the position of a liked source but distance themselves from a disliked source. Importantly, these and other biasing motives could have an impact on judgments by either the central or the peripheral route. For example, invocation of the need for autonomy could lead to simple rejection of a forbidden position without much thought or through active counterarguing of the position.

The ELM holds that biased processing can occur even if no specific judgment is preferred. This is because ability factors can also determine bias. For example, some people might simply possess more biased knowledge compared to other people. If so, their ability to process the message objectively can be compromised. The recipients with a biased store of knowledge might be better able to see the flaws in opposition arguments and the merits in their own side versus recipients with more balanced knowledge (cf., Lord, Ross, & Lepper, 1979). In addition, variables in the persuasion situation can bias retrieval of information even if what is stored is completely balanced and no motivational biases are operating. For example, a positive mood can increase access to positive material in memory (e.g., Bower, 1981). In general, biases in processing a persuasive message are amplified when the message contains information that is ambiguous or mixed rather than clearly strong or weak (Chaiken & Maheswaran, 1994).

Finally, just because some motivational or ability factor produces biased information processing, a biased judgment will not necessarily result. This is because people sometimes attempt to correct for factors they believe could have unduly biased them (e.g., Petty & Wegener, 1993; Wilson & Brekke, 1994). People not only correct their judgments to render them more accurate, but they can also be motivated to correct by motives for fairness, self-enhancement, and others (e.g., McCaslin, Petty, & Wegener, 2010; see Wegener & Petty, 1997, for a review).

Assessing Information Processing

Persuasion researchers have identified a number of ways to assess the extent to which persuasion is based on effortful consideration of information. Perhaps the most popular procedure to assess the amount of objective information processing has been to vary the quality of the arguments in a message and to gauge the extent of message processing by the size of the argument quality effect on attitudes and valenced thoughts (e.g., Petty et al., 1976). Greater argument quality effects suggest greater objective scrutiny of the message. If the message processing is biased, however, the size of the argument quality effect could be attenuated compared to objective processing (Nienhuis, Manstead, & Spears, 2001; Petty & Cacioppo, 1986). This is because when engaged in biased processing, people may fail to appreciate the merits or demerits of the arguments (e.g., seeing strengths in even weak arguments that agree with you).

When biased processing is an issue, there are other means to gauge the extent of thinking, such as assessing the mere number of issue-relevant thoughts generated (Petty, Ostrom, & Brock, 1981). High elaboration conditions are associated with more thoughts. Also, correlations between valenced message-relevant thoughts and postmessage attitudes tend to be greater when argument scrutiny is high (e.g., Chaiken, 1980; Petty & Cacioppo, 1979b) though as described shortly, other variables can affect this correlation such as the confidence people have in their thoughts (Petty, Briñol, & Tormala, 2002). Finally, high-message elaboration can produce longer reading or exposure times than more cursory analyses, though longer reading times might sometimes reflect daydreaming rather than careful message scrutiny (see Wegener, Downing, Krosnick, & Petty, 1995).

RELATIVELY LOW EFFORT PROCESSES OF ATTITUDE CHANGE

We have now seen that a multitude of variables can determine whether the attitude change context is likely to be one of relatively high- or low-cognitive effort and whether the processing is relatively objective or biased. We now turn to more specific processes of persuasion and first focus on some of the relatively low effort processes that can determine whether attitudes will change. Then, we turn to higher-effort processes. The low-effort mechanisms of attitude change vary in the extent to which they require conscious processing, ranging from those relying on automatic associations to those positing simple inferences.

Associative Processes

Attitudes can be impacted by associations that develop between attitude objects and positive or negative stimuli (i.e., objects and feelings), or even by mere observations of those associations. Examples of these processes include conditioning, affective priming, and mere exposure.

Conditioning

One way to produce attitude change in the absence of effortful scrutiny is to associate an attitude object that is initially neutral (e.g., a new product) with stimuli that already have positive or negative meaning. Considerable research has demonstrated that when an initially neutral stimulus immediately precedes another stimulus that already has positive or negative associations, the neutral stimulus can come to be positively or negatively evaluated itself. For example, attitudes toward words, people, and products have been influenced by their association with pleasant or unpleasant odors, temperatures, sounds, shock, photographs, and so on (e.g., Staats, Staats, & Crawford, 1962; Zanna, Kiesler, & Pilkonis, 1970). Furthermore, attitudes can be influenced by the contraction of certain muscles associated with positive and negative experiences (e.g., Cacioppo, Priester, & Berntson, 1993). Consistent with the classification of conditioning as a relatively low effort process, conditioning effects have been found to be particularly likely when effortful processing is at a minimum (Field, 2000).

Recent work has attempted to separate conditioning into two types—classical and evaluative. The former is based on the early work by the famous Russian physiologist, Pavlov, who taught dogs to salivate at the sound of a bell by associating it with food. This type of conditioning is based on individuals learning that good or bad things follow the stimulus to be conditioned. When the good or bad things stop, the conditioning effects extinguish over time. In contrast, in evaluative conditioning (Martin & Levey, 1994), awareness of the pairing of the CS and UCS is unnecessary, which may explain why the conditioned response in evaluative conditioning tends not to extinguish when the UCS is no longer presented (see de Houwer, Thomas, & Baeyens, 2001, for a review). Recent research suggests that evaluative conditioning might even be reliant on relatively simple misattribution inferences similar to the self-perception and heuristic processes that are described shortly (see Jones, Fazio, & Olson, 2009).

Affective Priming

Another process that relies on simple associations between stimuli is affective priming. In this method, also known as "backward conditioning," presentation of positively or negatively valenced stimuli immediately precedes rather than follows presentation of target stimuli. These presentations influence evaluations of previously neutral target stimuli. For example, Krosnick, Betz, Jussim, and Lynn (1992) found that subliminal presentation of positive or negative pictures (e.g., smiling people versus snakes) made subsequent evaluations of unfamiliar target individuals more favorable or unfavorable, respectively. Consistent with classification of this change mechanism as a low-effort process, these effects were unaffected by cognitive load (e.g., Hermans, Crombez, & Eelen, 2000) and more likely to occur when the initial affective stimuli is processed only minimally or not at all (e.g., when presented subliminally; Murphy & Zajonc, 1993). One method (i.e., the Affect Misattribution Procedure) relies on this mechanism to assess individuals' attitudes indirectly. For example, if people are presented with a stimulus about which their attitudes are unknown (e.g., a picture of the President of the United States), followed by an unfamiliar target (e.g., an unfamiliar symbol), ratings of the unfamiliar target can be used to infer attitudes toward the preceding stimulus (see Payne, Cheng, Govorun, & Stewart, 2005).

Mere Exposure

Research has also shown that the mere repeated exposure of an object can make one's attitude toward that object more favorable, even if one does not recognize the object as having been encountered previously (Zajonc, 1968). Kunst-Wilson and Zajonc (1980), for instance, repeatedly presented participants with a series of polygon images, and found that even though participants could not recognize which images they had seen before, and which they had not, they expressed significantly greater preferences for those they had seen. Some researchers have argued that even when a stimulus cannot be consciously identified as having been encountered, its previous exposure might make it easier to process. That is, prior exposures could create a perceptual fluency (Jacoby, Kelley, Brown, & Jasechko, 1989) that becomes attached to the stimulus or confused with a positive evaluation of the stimulus. These feelings of fluency and familiarity—the mechanisms thought to be responsible for mere exposure effects—have also influenced attitudes and persuasion even when they do not stem from prior exposure. For instance, messages written in easy-to-read fonts or more clear color combinations are sometimes evaluated more favorably than those written in difficult-to-read or unclear fonts (Alter & Oppenheimer, 2009, for reviews; see Schwarz, 2004).

As with other low-effort processes, the influence of mere exposure on attitudes appears to be increased when the repeated object is low in meaning or presented subliminally (see Bornstein, 1989, for a review). Similarly, the mere exposure effect appears to be decreased as conscious processing increases, such as when evaluation apprehension is induced (Kruglanski, Freund, & Bar-Tal, 1996). When meaningful stimuli are presented (e.g., familiar words or persuasive messages), repeated exposure has been found to accentuate the dominant reaction (e.g., Cacioppo & Petty, 1989), whether this is positive or negative.

Inference-Based Processes

People sometimes base their attitudes on simple inferences that do not require extensive thinking. We discuss some of these inferences next.

Balance

According to balance theory (Heider, 1958), certain cognitive states are associated with pleasantness whereas other states are associated with unpleasantness. Specifically, balance within the elements of an attitudinal system exists when people agree with others they like (or with whom they are closely associated) and disagree with others they dislike (or with whom they are dissociated). Because imbalance is an uncomfortable state, people want to eliminate it as quickly as possible. In many cases, the easiest way to restore balance is to alter one's evaluation of an inconsistent element in the attitude system (Rosenberg & Abelson, 1960). Unlike the effortful restoration of cognitive consistency associated with dissonance reduction (Festinger, 1957; see subsequent discussion), the alteration of evaluations need not be effortful according to balance theory. Aside from the general preference for balanced relationships among people, objects, and attitudes, people also prefer positivity in these relationships (Cacioppo & Petty, 1981; Miller & Norman, 1976). Importantly, the changes people make to ensure balance and positivity do not require thoughtful consideration of the central merits of the attitude objects in the system (see Insko, 1984, for further discussion).

Attribution

At a general level, attribution theory addresses the inferences people make about themselves and others after witnessing behaviors and the situational constraints surrounding those behaviors (e.g., Jones & Davis, 1965). In some cases, these inferences involve attitudes, such as when individuals infer their own or someone else's attitudes on the basis of their behavior with respect to an attitude object (e.g., if a person donates money to a presidential candidate, it is reasonable to infer favoritism toward the candidate). Although some attributional processes require effortful cognitive activity (see Gilbert, 1998, for a review), others produce relatively quick and simple inferences (e.g., inferring that you like a certain TV program because you smile when you watch it).

According to Bem's (1972) *self-perception theory*, when people are not attuned to their internal states, they can infer their own attitudes from their own behaviors just as they might do when inferring the attitudes of others. Self-perception is more likely to operate under relatively low-effort conditions. For example, Taylor (1975) conducted a study in which women evaluated the photographs of men under high- or low personal relevance conditions. Participants also received false physiological feedback about their heart rate responses toward some of the men (see Valins, 1966). The women inferred attitudes from their ostensible physiological reactions to a greater extent when personal relevance was low than when it was high (see also Wood, 1982). This implies that self-perception processes are more likely to operate when the likelihood of thinking about the attitude object is relatively low rather than high.

Attribution theory has also contributed to attitude change research in other ways. In one application called the *overjustification effect*, people come to devalue previously enjoyed activities (e.g., running) when they are given overly sufficient rewards for engaging in them (e.g., Lepper, Greene, & Nisbett, 1973). Furthermore, attribution theory has shed light on the processes by which inferences about a message source can affect attitudes. For example, Eagly, Chaiken, and Wood (1981) argued that when people are exposed to a persuasive communication, their expectancies regarding the position that the source of the communication will take have an important impact on their acceptance of that source's position. If the communicator advocates a position that violates self-interest, he or she is perceived as more trustworthy than when a position consistent with self-interest is taken. When the source is seen as trustworthy, the position can be accepted with relatively little scrutiny. However, when the position is seen as possibly invalid, effortful scrutiny of the information is increased (Priester & Petty, 1995).

Heuristics

The heuristic/systematic model of persuasion (HSM; Chaiken et al., 1989) suggests that when people are engaged in relatively little thinking, they can evaluate persuasive information in terms of stored heuristics, or simple decision rules, based on prior experiences or observations. One such heuristic is that "experts are correct." People rely on simple heuristics more when they are relatively unmotivated or unable to engage in extensive thought (e.g., low need for cognition or low personal relevance; Chaiken, 1980; Petty, Cacioppo, & Goldman, 1981). Chaiken et al. (1989) proposed that the use of heuristics depends on their availability (i.e., the heuristic must be stored in memory), accessibility (i.e., it must be activated from memory), and applicability to the judgment at hand. Although this is an intriguing proposition, little research has been conducted examining these aspects of heuristics.

Heuristics can stem from many places such as the communicator or the message itself. One message-based heuristic is that "length implies strength." Thus, when thinking is low, people tend to be more persuaded the more information that is presented, regardless of whether that information is strong or weak. When thinking is high, however the merits of information are examined, more good arguments lead to more persuasion whereas more weak arguments lead to less persuasion (Petty & Cacioppo, 1984).

An intriguing set of studies by Schwarz and colleagues (1991) has suggested that people infer that different numbers of arguments are available depending on how easy or difficult it is to generate them. In one study, participants were asked to rate how assertive they were after recalling either 6 or 12 examples of their own assertive behavior. People rated themselves as more assertive after retrieving 6 rather than 12 examples. This result was surprising because a straightforward application of the availability heuristic would have suggested that people generating 12 instances would judge themselves to be more assertive than those generating only 6. Schwarz and colleagues reasoned, however, that people also considered the ease with which the thoughts could be retrieved from memory (see Schwarz, 2004, for a review). The easier it was to generate information in favor of something, the more supportive information people inferred there to be. Thus, inferences about the amount of information available, rather than the actual amount of information generated, drove judgments. Furthermore, because a heuristic was involved, this mechanism was proposed to operate most strongly when people were relatively unmotivated or unable to think.

Many variables have now been shown to be capable of serving as simple cues. Although many of these variables operate by invoking learned heuristics, some of them can also impact attitudes through some other peripheral process (e.g., classical conditioning). Nevertheless, the heuristic concept has been very useful and has sparked a great deal of persuasion research.

Priming

Another low-effort means by which attitudes can be shifted is through priming (i.e., presenting one concept with the goal of activating related concepts). This method does not create or modify associations between attitude objects and valenced stimuli, nor does it necessarily rely on inferences. Rather, priming procedures can shift attitudes by activating constructs related to attitudes, which then alter the attitude itself. For example, exposure to situations can affect the private expression of attitudes. In one experiment (Berger, Meredith, & Wheeler, 2008), people who were assigned to cast their vote in schools versus other locations such as churches, were more likely to support raising the state sales tax to fund education.

Social construct primes, such as stereotypes, can also shift attitudes. For example, those primed with the "skinhead" stereotype subsequently reported more racist attitudes (Kawakami, Dovidio, & Dijksterhuis, 2003) than those primed with a nonrelevant concept. These effects are especially pronounced among those who have inconsistent or uncertain self-views. For instance, in one study, participants primed with the African-American stereotype (versus control) reported more stereotype-consistent attitudes (e.g., liking rap music), especially if they were ambivalent regarding stereotype traits (e.g., believed that African Americans were both lazy and industrious; DeMarree, Morrison, Wheeler, & Petty, 2011). Similarly, participants primed with goal-relevant words (e.g., regarding thirst) were subsequently more persuaded by advertisements targeting that goal, but only when they were already motivated to pursue that goal (Strahan, Spencer, & Zanna, 2002). Hence, primes, whether situations, social constructs, or goals, can lead people to hold more prime-consistent attitudes. One mechanism by which this can occur is by people incorporating the primed material into their current self-conception. Once people come to view themselves as like the primed concept, relevant attitudes and behaviors will follow (Wheeler, DeMarree, & Petty, 2007).

RELATIVELY HIGH-EFFORT PROCESSES OF ATTITUDE CHANGE

In addition to the low-effort attitude change mechanisms just described, attitudes can also be formed and changed

through relatively high-effort processes. According to dual-process formulations, these high-effort processes tend to impact persuasive outcomes when motivation and ability to think are relatively high, such as when the issue is of high personal relevance, few distractions are present, and so forth.

Message Learning/Reception

Early information-processing theories of attitude change held that persuasion was contingent upon a sequence of stages: attention, comprehension, learning, acceptance, and retention of the information in a persuasive communication (Hovland, Janis, & Kelley, 1953). McGuire (1968) later modified this model and focused on just two core processes—reception and yielding. Variables could influence persuasive outcomes by affecting either of these processes, and variables might affect each process in different ways. For example, having higher intelligence might increase the likelihood of message reception and learning but decrease the likelihood of yielding to the message.

Despite the intuitive appeal of the learning model, considerable research has demonstrated that attitudes and message recall are often weakly related at best (e.g., see Eagly & Chaiken, 1993, for a review). Stated simply, this is because two people might each be able to remember an argument, but evaluate it quite differently. Attitudes correlate more strongly with learning and recall when people are not evaluating information online at the time of exposure. For example, when people have nonevaluative processing goals (e.g., Hastie & Park, 1986), or when they are the type of people who do not spontaneously engage in evaluation (low in their "need to evaluate;" Jarvis & Petty, 1996), the attitude-recall correlation is higher (Tormala & Petty, 2001). Under these conditions, when people are asked to report their attitudes, they are forced to first retrieve what information relevant to the attitude object they can from memory, and then base their attitudes on the evaluative implications of this information.

Expectancy/Value Formulations

Following the findings that attitude change and information recall were not consistently related, researchers shifted toward approaches that attempted to gauge individual's idiosyncratic reactions to the information presented. Expectancy value theories propose that attitudes reflect an individual's subjective assessment of the desirability of the consequences with which an attitude object is linked and the likelihood that those consequences will come about (see Bagozzi, 1985, for a review).

Theory of Reasoned Action

A particularly influential model, the *theory of reasoned action* (Fishbein & Ajzen, 1975), posited that attitudes were a multiplicative function of the desirability and likelihood of the consequences associated with an object or issue, summed across all consequences. For example, the attitude toward a political candidate could be predicted by the expectancy that the candidate will enact a certain policy if elected and the desirability of that policy, summed across all relevant policies. This theory implies that attitude change should follow changes in perceptions of the likelihood or desirability of the consequences associated with a position (see Fishbein & Ajzen, 2010). In fact, a number of studies indicate that persuasive messages and contextual variables such as a person's emotions can produce attitude change by changing the perceived likelihood or desirability of salient beliefs (e.g., Albarracín & Wyer, 2001; DeSteno, Petty, Rucker, Wegener, & Braverman, 2004; Wegener, Petty, & Klein, 1994).

Although some researchers have proposed that all attitude change occurs via the thoughtful consideration of likelihood and desirability assessment (Fishbein & Middlestadt, 1995), as we described previously, attitude change can also occur via multiple low effort processes. Additionally, even likelihood and desirability assessments could be made this way. For example, under low-elaboration conditions, individuals are prone to automatically believe whatever they hear (Gilbert, 1991) and perceive stimuli positively (Cacioppo et al., 1997). Repeated exposure appears to magnify these propensities. Thus, repeated exposure to a piece of information increases perceptions of its validity (e.g., Arkes, Boehm, & Xu, 1991) and desirability (Zajonc, 1968).

However, it seems likely that the retrieval and integration of likelihood and desirability assessments of multiple salient beliefs would typically require effort and would occur primarily when individuals have the ability and motivation to do so. In support of this reasoning, expectancy-value processes tend to account for more variance in attitudes when motivation (e.g., the need for cognition; Wegener et al., 1994) and ability (e.g., topic-relevant knowledge; Lutz, 1977) to think are high.

Information Integration

In addition to specifying the primary components of attitudes, attitude theorists have also attempted to specify the means by which these components are combined to influence attitudes. The expectancy-value formulation of Fishbein and Ajzen (1975) is additive. That is, attitudes are postulated to be the sum of the likelihood × desirability products for each salient attribute associated with the attitude object. However, other theorists have proposed that beliefs are combined by an averaging function. In Anderson's (1971) *information integration theory* formulation, each salient belief is weighted by the individual's assessment of the importance of that piece of information and a weighted average of beliefs then best predicts the person's attitude. This model has proven efficacious in explaining the impact of different information on resulting attitudes or summary judgments.

The flexibility of the averaging account in accommodating the data, however, is simultaneously its greatest strength and weakness. By adjusting the weighting parameter of the initial attitude or beliefs in a post hoc fashion, the model can accommodate nearly any finding. Distinguishing the averaging account from additive accounts can be exceedingly difficult, and convincing crucial tests have yet to emerge. At present, there is some suggestion that people are more likely to use an adding integration rule when thinking is at the low end of the elaboration continuum but an averaging rule when elaboration is higher (Betsch, Plessner, Schwieren, & Guetig, 2001; Petty & Cacioppo, 1984).

Cognitive Response Approach

A third approach touting the view that individuals' own reactions to a message are more important than memory for the message itself is the *cognitive response approach* (e.g., Brock, 1967; Greenwald, 1968; Petty et al., 1981). According to this formulation, when exposed to a persuasive message, people reflect on it with respect to their preexisting knowledge and prior attitude (if they have one), considering information not contained in the message itself. Three aspects of people's thoughts have proven important.

Content of Thoughts

Perhaps the most important dimension of thoughts for persuasion is the overall valence of the thinking. Researchers typically categorize thoughts as favorable, unfavorable, or neutral, and then compute an overall valence index (e.g., positive thoughts minus negative thoughts; see Mackie, 1987). Persuasion is likely to be effective to the extent that the message elicits mostly favorable thoughts (e.g., "If we raise taxes, the roads will improve and reduce my commute time") and few unfavorable thoughts (e.g., "If we raise taxes, I'll have less money to go out to dinner"). On the other hand, people can resist messages to the extent that they generate mostly unfavorable thoughts and few favorable thoughts.

As noted earlier, particular thoughts can be facilitated by external variables. For example, if people are forewarned that a speaker is trying to persuade them, they typically become motivated to counterargue the anticipated message in advance of receiving it and this undermines the effectiveness of the appeal (e.g., Petty & Cacioppo, 1979a). In a classic series of studies on resistance to change, McGuire (1964) demonstrated that people could be motivated to resist an upcoming counterattitudinal message, which ordinarily would be effective, by initially giving them an easy to counterargue communication prior to the stronger attack. The underlying logic of this *inoculation approach* to resistance is that a small dose of an attacking virus (i.e., a weak challenge to the person's attitude that is refuted) motivates the person to build up antibodies (i.e., counterarguments), which can be used against subsequent attacks.

Amount of Thoughts

Another aspect of thinking is the amount of valenced thoughts generated. As noted earlier, a number of variables affect how much people are motivated (e.g., personal relevance) or able (e.g., distraction) to think about a persuasive communication. As people generate more positive thoughts to a message, persuasion is increased and the more unfavorable thoughts (counterarguments) they generate to a message, persuasion is decreased. Conversely, the more positive thinking can be reduced, persuasion is reduced, and the more negative thinking can be interfered with, the more persuasion is increased (e.g., Petty et al., 1976).

Confidence in Thoughts

A third aspect of thought also influences persuasion. According to the *self-validation hypothesis* (Petty et al., 2002), people vary in the extent to which they have confidence or doubt about the validity of the thoughts that they have generated to a persuasive message. Thoughts in which people have confidence have a large impact on attitude change whereas thoughts in which people have low confidence do not. This research suggests that favorable thoughts increase persuasion primarily when people have confidence in them. Similarly, unfavorable thoughts decrease persuasion mostly when people have confidence in them. When confidence in thoughts is low, they do not predict attitudes well even under high-elaboration conditions. People can even have so much doubt about their thoughts that they tend to form an attitude that is opposite to what their thoughts imply (Briñol & Petty, 2009). Although people tend to be more confident in thoughts

that point to likely rather than unlikely consequences, confidence is conceptually and empirically distinct from the likelihood component from expectancy-value theories (Petty et al., 2002).

The self-validation idea is part of a growing body of work in social psychology on meta-cognition, or people's thoughts about their thoughts or thought processes (Briñol & DeMarree, 2012). One of the first meta-cognitive studies relevant to the use of thoughts was described earlier—on ease of retrieval. The self-validation idea provides one explanation for this phenomenon. In a series of studies, Tormala, Petty, and Briñol (2002) found that when it was easy to generate thoughts, people assumed that these thoughts were more valid than when generating them was difficult and thus they relied on them more. Furthermore, consistent with the idea that ease or retrieval effects can stem from a relatively high effort meta-cognitive process rather than a lower effort availability heuristic process, the ease effects were greater when the likelihood of thinking was high rather than low.

Self-validation mechanisms can also account for numerous other variables. For example, in one study (Briñol & Petty, 2003), people who were nodding their heads in a "yes" (vertical) fashion while listening to a message reported more confidence in their thoughts than people who were nodding their heads in a "no" (horizontal) fashion. As a result, when processing a compelling message that elicited mostly favorable thoughts, people nodding yes were more persuaded than people nodding no (see also Wells & Petty, 1980). However, when processing a specious message that elicited mostly unfavorable thoughts, people nodding yes were less persuaded than people nodding no. Other variables that have been shown to affect the perceived validity of thoughts and thus their use are source expertise, feelings of power, emotions, self-affirmations, body postures, and many others. These variables tend to affect thought confidence when conditions favor high rather than low-effort thinking and the experience of confidence follows or is contiguous with rather than precedes thought generation (see Briñol & Petty, 2009, for a review).

Self-Persuasion With No Message

Self-persuasion can occur even in the absence of an external message. Persuasion in the absence of a message can occur when individuals are asked to actively present or generate their own messages or even when individuals are simply permitted to engage in sustained thought about an attitude object.

Role Playing

Early research on role playing in persuasion found it to be an effective tool to increase persuasion as well as the resistance and persistence of the resulting attitudes. In one of the earliest role-playing demonstrations, Janis and King (1954) examined the differential effects of having people actively present persuasive arguments to others versus passively hearing arguments presented by others. Results indicated that participants who actively generated and presented messages were typically more persuaded than those who passively listened to messages. This effect has been replicated numerous times.

A number of mechanisms have been proposed to account for these role-playing effects. Janis (1968) proposed a biased scanning explanation whereby individuals, in the process of supporting an attitudinal position, recruit consistent beliefs while inhibiting inconsistent beliefs. Furthermore, people tend to generate information that is especially persuasive to themselves (Greenwald & Albert, 1968). The self-generated information might seem particularly compelling to people because of the enhanced effort involved in generation over passive exposure (Festinger, 1957), or, the arguments might seem more compelling simply because they are associated with the self (Perloff & Brock, 1980), or people have more confidence in them (Briñol & Petty, 2009). Recent research has demonstated that self-generation of arguments is more effective in producing self-persuasion when the intended target of the arguments is the self rather than another person if the topic is counterattitudinal, but when the topic is proattitudinal, it is more effective if the intended target is another person rather than the self (Briñol, McCaslin, & Petty, in press).

Mere Thought

Some research has indicated that attitude polarization can also occur when individuals simply engage in extensive thought about an attitude object (see Tesser, Martin, & Mendolia, 1995, for a review). Polarization following thought requires attitude-consistent knowledge (e.g., Chaiken & Yates, 1985); otherwise, thought leads to attitude moderation. The attitudinal consequences of mere thought are dependent on the subset of information, which is the focus of the thought. For example, when participants are instructed to analyze the reasons for their attitudes, they often focus on those that are easiest to verbalize (Wilson et al., 1989). Consequently, they may often overemphasize the cognitive component of their attitudes to the neglect of the affective (emotional) component leading to a momentary attitude shift. Such impact of that limited subset of information on attitude judgments can lead to suboptimal decision making (e.g., Wilson & Schooler, 1991). In addition to structural components of thoughts, the mere thought effect also depends on metacognitive properties such as thought confidence. Clarkson, Tormala, and Leone (2011) found that when individuals find it easy to think (e.g., because enough time is provided), they feel more confident about their thoughts and show the polarization effect. When it is more difficult to think, thought confidence is reduced and the polarization effect attenuates or even reverses.

Self-Persuasion as a Result of Dissonance Processes

We have seen that self-persuasion can occur when people are prompted to think by a persuasive message, by a role-playing exercise, or by simply being asked to think. Attitude change can also occur when a person's own behavior motivates him or her to think. A common assumption of many persuasion theories is that individuals have a default motivation of accuracy (i.e., wanting to hold correct attitudes). However, the ELM and other persuasion theories also hold that a variety of biasing motivations can sometimes distort objective processing. The motive to be consistent is the most studied, and the theory of cognitive dissonance is the most influential of the consistency theories. In its original formulation (Festinger, 1957), dissonance was described as a feeling of aversive arousal akin to a drive state experienced by an individual who simultaneously held two conflicting cognitions. The resulting aversive arousal was hypothesized to instigate attempts to restore consonance among the relevant cognitions. Attempts to restore consistency typically involved very active thinking about the attitude object, and the end result of this thinking was often a change in the person's attitude.

Dissonance Effects

A large body of research using different experimental paradigms has supported the essence of dissonance theory (see Harmon-Jones & Mills, 1999). Some experimental procedures used to create dissonance include inducing people to comply with a counterattitudinal request (the induced compliance paradigm, e.g., Cooper & Fazio, 1984), undergoing harsh initiations to join a group that turns out to be uninteresting (the effort justification paradigm, e.g., Aronson & Mills, 1959), and choosing between two different but equally desirable products (the free choice paradigm, e.g., Brehm, 1956). In these instances, people become more favorable toward the initially counterattitudinal behavior, the uninteresting group, and the chosen product.

A number of studies have supported the hypothesis that physiological arousal follows from situations thought to induce cognitive dissonance (Elkin & Leippe, 1986) and that such arousal is subjectively unpleasant (Elliot & Devine, 1994). When the arousal can be plausibly misattributed to some unrelated environmental agent (rather than to the true dissonance-arousing event), dissonance-based attitude change fails to occur (Zanna & Cooper, 1974). However, evidence for the mediational role of arousal in eliciting dissonance-based attitude change is equivocal. Although initial work suggested that individuals must directly resolve the cognitive inconsistency by changing their attitudes, generating cognitions to make the dissonant elements more consistent (i.e., bolstering), or minimizing the importance of the dissonant cognitions (i.e., trivializing), some research has suggested that dissonance can be reduced (at least temporarily) by engaging in virtually any activity that distracts one from the dissonance (e.g., watching a comedy, Cooper, Fazio, & Rhodewalt, 1978; or affirming the self, Steele, 1988).

Clarifying Dissonance Effects

Early research supported the hypothesis that dissonance was experienced when a person had insufficient justification for violating a belief or attitude (e.g., Festinger & Carlsmith, 1959). Since its original formulation, however, many researchers have imposed limiting conditions on the basic dissonance predictions. For example, some researchers asserted that commitment to the behavior was necessary to elicit dissonance (e.g., Brehm & Cohen, 1962). Some research also indicated that cognitive inconsistency per se was neither necessary nor sufficient to generate dissonance. Cooper and Fazio (1984) concluded that for dissonance to be aroused, an individual must be responsible for negative consequences. Similarly, even a proattitudinal behavior can arouse dissonance if it has unintended, aversive consequences (Scher & Cooper, 1989). Moreover, if the individual does not feel responsibility for the discrepant action because the consequences were unforseeable (e.g., Cooper, 1971), dissonance fails to obtain.

Three additional attempts at clarifying dissonance theory implicate the self as the essential component in eliciting dissonance. Steele's self-affirmation theory suggests that dissonance results from any threat to viewing oneself as "adaptively and morally adequate" (Steele, 1988, p. 262). Aronson (1969) has argued that dissonance is based on inconsistency between one's self-view and one's actions (e.g., I am a good person and did a bad deed). A third alternative is the Self-Standards Model of dissonance (Stone & Cooper, 2001), which places the other theories under a single conceptual umbrella by suggesting that dissonance results from the violation of salient normative or ideographic self-standards. The flexibility associated with these different ways of interpreting dissonance findings affords greater explanatory breadth, but comes with a cost. Specifically, this flexibility makes it difficult to accurately predict when any given individual will experience dissonance.

Finally, an influential nondissonance alternative has been proposed to account for the findings of dissonance researchers. As described earlier, self-perception theory (Bem, 1972) holds that individuals often infer their attitudes from their own behavior. Initially, self-perception theory was a formidable opponent to the dissonance view because it was able to account for many of the results attributed to dissonance mechanisms. However, it later became apparent that self-perception was a different phenomenon, which operated in different settings and was not simply an alternative explanation for cognitive dissonance. For instance, in contrast to dissonance, which operates when people engage in strongly counterattiudinal action, self-perception processes appear to operate more when one's behavior is contrary to an attitude, but not so far from it (Fazio et al., 1977).

In closing our discussion of dissonance theory it is notable that specific criticisms of various aspects of dissonance theory research continue to arise. Notably, however, these newer criticisms tend to apply only to particular studies or paradigms (e.g., see Chen & Risen, 2010; Zentall, 2010) and thus do not undermine the dissonance framework in general. Thus, the theory remains viable today.

MULTIPLE ROLES FOR VARIABLES

We have now described the low- and high-effort processes that can determine persuasion and some of the variables that influence these processes. Notably, however, most of the variables that we have considered are not relegated to just one process. Rather, in accord with the multiple roles postulate of the ELM, variables operate differently to influence attitudes at different points along the elaboration continuum. Consider source expertise. Expertise is most often thought of as a simple cue that affects attitudes in response to a message without much thinking. And, indeed, expertise can serve in this role when thinking is low (Chaiken, 1980; Petty et al., 1981). However, expertise takes on other roles at other points along the elaboration continuum. When thinking is high, expertise can be analyzed as an argument or can bias the thoughts that come to mind (Chaiken & Maheswaran, 1994). Learning of the source's expertise after processing a message can affect confidence in one's thoughts in response to the message (Tormala, Briñol, & Petty, 2006). If the source is revealed prior to a message and people are uncertain as to whether the message warrants processing, they may decide to do so based on the source (Clark, Evans, & Wegener, 2011; Priester & Petty, 1995). Notably, the impact of source expertise on attitudes depends on the mechanism involved. For example, the effect of expertise under high-elaboration conditions can be equivalent to, or even exceed, its impact under low elaboration conditions, though the mechanism is different. Furthermore, the impact of increasing source expertise can even be negative under some conditions (Tormala et al., 2006), as when expertise enhances confidence in negative thoughts in response to weak arguments.

The power of the multiple roles idea is that many variables can serve in these same roles under the same conditions. For example, a variable like happiness, though different from source credibility, affects attitudes in exactly the same ways (e.g., serving as a simple cue when the likelihood of thinking is low, biasing thinking when the likelihood is high). And, just as in the case of expertise, whether happiness is good or bad for persuasion depends on the mechanism involved.

WHAT HAPPENS WHEN ATTITUDES CHANGE?

Contemporary theories of persuasion agree that the more thought that goes into forming a new attitude, the stronger that attitude will be: the more it will persist over time, resist attempts at change, and guide further thought and behavior (Petty, Haugtvedt, & Smith, 1995). Thus, the processes by which variables produce attitude change are important to understand not only for the initial effects produced, but also because these processes help to elucidate the long-term consequences of persuasion.

Another aspect of attitude change that is important is understanding whether a persuasion technique has produced a change in deliberative attitudes, automatic attitudes, or both. Originally, researchers assumed that once an attitude changed, the old attitude disappeared and was replaced with a new one. Contemporary theorists have

a more complex view. For example, according to what is called a *dual attitudes* approach (Wilson et al., 2000), when attitudes change, the original attitude does not actually disappear. Instead, it becomes implicit and persists in memory along with the new attitude, which is considered the explicit attitude. The dual attitudes model is depicted schematically in the top panel of Figure 17.1. This model represents a case where a person with an initially negative attitude toward a racial group subsequently becomes positive. Whereas the newer (explicit) attitude affects controlled responses (e.g., deliberative attitude measures and behaviors), the older (now implicit) attitude affects responses that individuals are not motivated or able to control (e.g., automatic attitude measures; spontaneous behaviors; see Dovidio et al., 1997; and Greenwald & Banaji, 1995).

An alternative view is provided by the Meta-Cognitive Model (MCM; Petty, Briñol, & DeMarree, 2007) described earlier. The MCM provides a more dynamic picture of the relationship between the old and new attitudes, suggesting that both can simultaneously impact responding under certain circumstances. In short, the MCM, like the dual attitudes model, holds that when an attitude changes, the prior evaluation remains in memory, and because it is consciously rejected, can be considered implicit (i.e., people deny currently holding this attitude; Petty, Tormala, Briñol, & Jarvis, 2006). However, the MCM proposes that when a new attitude is acquired, the old attitude takes on a "false" or "no" tag that must also be activated if the old attitude is to be suppressed. The bottom panel

Dual Attitudes Model

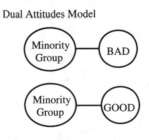

Meta-Cognitive Model

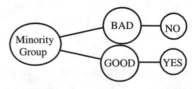

Figure 17.1 Dual attitudes model (top panel) and Meta-Cognitive Model (bottom panel) depiction of conflicting implicit and explicit attitudes

of Figure 17.1 presents a depiction of a person who was initially unfavorable toward a minority group and then became favorable. According to this framework, to the degree that the false tag is accessible, the newer attitude will guide responses. The prior attitude will have an impact, however, if it was never fully rejected (i.e., no "false" tag was developed), if the false tag cannot be retrieved (e.g., is low in accessibility), or if the tag is retrieved but the prior attitude's influence cannot be inhibited. In the MCM, when current and prior evaluations conflict people will act as if they are ambivalent, though they may not be aware of the source of the conflict (see Petty, Briñol, & Johnson, 2012, for a review).

WHAT HAPPENS WHEN ATTITUDES RESIST CHANGE?

Although most of the literature on attitudes and persuasion has focused on understanding mechanisms driving successful attitude change, researchers periodically have explored resistance to change as well. As noted earlier, McGuire's inoculation theory (1964) represents one of the earliest attempts to better understand resistance, suggesting that practice in counterarguing weak arguments helps to bolster or strengthen attitudes against future stronger attacks. More recent work in this domain suggests that people's meta-cognitive appraisals of their own resistance experiences can have important implications for their attitudes and future behavior. In particular, research suggests that people can appraise their own success at resisting a persuasive message and adjust their attitude certainty accordingly, becoming more or less certain of their original attitudes than they were to begin with (Petty, Tormala, & Rucker, 2004; Tormala 2008). When people are impressed with their resistance, because they resisted easily or withstood a strong attack, they become more certain of their initial attitudes. In contrast, when people are unimpressed with their resistance, because they believe that they struggled to resist or resisted by illegitimate means, they become less certain of their attitudes (Tormala et al., 2006). Moreover, when attitude certainty is affected following resistance to persuasion, the attitudes can become more or less predictive of future behavior or open to future change.

Ultimately, whether people become more or less certain of their attitudes following an encounter with a persuasive message depends on numerous situational appraisals—including whether people believe they considered both sides of the issue in question (Rucker, Petty,

& Briñol, 2008), whether people believe they gave the message or issue a great deal or too little thought (Barden & Petty, 2008; Wan, Rucker, Tormala, & Clarkson, 2010), whether people evaluated the message or topic in a way that fits their preferred evaluative style (Tormala, Clarkson, & Henderson, 2011), and others. The certainty arising from these various appraisals is as consequential as the certainty that arises from more structural features of attitudes (e.g., actually engaging in more thinking; see Petty, Briñol, Tormala, & Wegener, 2007).

CONCLUSIONS

The goal of this chapter has been to present an organizing framework for understanding the psychological processes responsible for attitude change. After making some distinctions about implicit versus explicit attitudes and attitude strength, we divided the theoretical processes responsible for modifying attitudes into those that emphasize effortful thinking about the central merits of the attitude object from those that rely on less cognitively demanding processes. This framework facilitates understanding and prediction of what variables affect attitudes and in what general situations. In addition, this framework helps to place the various mini-theories of attitude change in their proper domains of operation. Finally, recognition of an elaboration continuum permits understanding and prediction of the strength of attitudes (i.e., changes resulting from considerable mental effort are more persistent, resistant, and predictive of behavior than changes produced by low mental effort; Petty et al., 1995).

Although a multitude of processes are involved in changing attitudes, we have a reasonably good understanding of what these processes are, and when they operate. Yet, despite the considerable progress that has been made in understanding attitude change, much work remains to be done. First, greater appreciation is needed for the view that any one variable is capable of multiple roles in the persuasion process. Second, one of the most exciting new domains of inquiry is the interplay between automatic and deliberative attitudes. For example, under what conditions are each likely to guide action? Are some attitude change processes more likely to impact automatic attitudes whereas others are more likely to change deliberative attitudes? Work on the topic of automatic attitudes is in the early stages, but the next decade promises to provide more definitive answers to these and other questions.

REFERENCES

Ajzen, I., & Fishbein, M. (1977). Attitude-behavior relations: A theoretical analysis and review of empirical research. *Psychological Bulletin*, *84*, 888–918.

Albarracín, D., & Wyer, R. S. (2001). Elaborative and nonelaborative processing of a behavior-related communication. *Personality and Social Psychology Bulletin*, *27*, 691–705.

Alter, A. L., & Oppenheimer, D. M. (2009). Uniting the tribes of fluency to form a metacognitive nation. *Personality and Social Psychology Review, 13*, 219–235.

Anderson, N. H. (1971). Integration theory and attitude change. *Psychological Review*, *78*, 171–206.

Arkes, H. R., Boehm, L. E., & Xu, G. (1991). Determinants of judged validity. *Journal of Experimental Social Psychology*, *27*, 576–605.

Aronson, E. (1969). The theory of cognitive dissonance: A current perspective. In L. Berkowitz (Ed.), *Advances in experimental social psychology* (Vol. 4, pp. 1–34). San Diego, CA: Academic Press.

Aronson, E., & Mills, J. (1959). The effects of severity of initiation on liking for a group. *Journal of Abnormal and Social Psychology*, *59*, 177–181.

Bagozzi, R. P. (1985). Expectancy-value attitude models: An analysis of critical theoretical issues. *International Journal of Research in Marketing*, *2*, 43–60.

Barden, J., & Petty, R. E. (2008). The mere perception of elaboration creates attitude certainty: Exploring the thoughtfulness heuristic. *Journal of Personality and Social Psychology*, *95*, 489–509.

Bargh, J. A., Chaiken, S., Govender, R., & Pratto, F. (1992). The generality of the automatic attitude activation effect. *Journal of Personality and Social Psychology*, *62*, 893–912.

Bem, D. J. (1972). Self-perception theory. In L. Berkowitz (Ed.), *Advances in experimental social psychology* (Vol. 6, pp. 1–62). New York, NY: Academic Press.

Berger, J., Meredith, M., & Wheeler, S. C. (2008). Contextual priming: Where people vote affects how they vote. *Proceedings of the National Academy of Science*, *105*(26), 8846–8849.

Betsch, T., Plessner, H., Schwieren, C., & Guetig, R. (2001). I like it but I don't know why: A value-account approach to implicit attitude formation. *Personality and Social Psychology Bulletin*, *27*, 242–253.

Bless, H., Bohner, G., Schwarz, N., & Strack, F. (1990). Mood and persuasion: A cognitive response analysis. *Personality and Social Psychology Bulletin*, *16*, 331–345.

Bornstein, R. F. (1989). Exposure and affect: Overview and meta-analysis of research, 1968–1987. *Psychological Bulletin, 106*, 265–289.

Bower, G. H. (1981). Mood and memory. *American Psychologist*, *36*, 129–148.

Brehm, J. W. (1956). Postdecision changes in the desirability of alternatives. *Journal of Abnormal and Social Psychology*, *52*, 384–389.

Brehm, J. W. (1966). *A theory of psychological reactance*. San Diego, CA: Academic Press.

Brehm, J. W., & Cohen, A. R. (1962). *Explorations in cognitive dissonance*. New York, NY: Wiley.

Briñol, P., & DeMarree, K. G. (Eds.). (2012). *Social metacognition*. New York, NY: Psychology Press.

Briñol, P., McCaslin, M. J., & Petty, R. E. (in press). Self-generated persuasion: Effects of the target and direction of arguments. *Journal of Personality and Social Psychology*.

Briñol, P., & Petty, R. E. (2003). Overt head movements and persuasion: A self-validation analysis. *Journal of Personality and Social Psychology, 84*, 1123–1139.

Briñol, P., & Petty, R. E. (2009). Persuasion: Insights from the self-validation hypothesis. In M. P. Zanna (Ed.), *Advances in Experimental Social Psychology, 41*, 69–118. New York, NY: Elsevier.

Briñol, P., & Petty, R. E. (2012). The history of attitudes and persuasion research. In A. Kruglanski & W. Stroebe (Eds.), *Handbook of the history of social psychology* (pp. 285–320). New York, NY: Psychology Press.

Briñol, P., Petty, R. E., & Barden, J. (2007). Happiness versus sadness as a determinant of thought confidence in persuasion: A self-validation analysis. *Journal of Personality and Social Psychology, 93*, 711–727.

Briñol, P., Petty, R. E., & McCaslin, M. J. (2009). Changing attitudes on implicit versus explicit measures: What is the difference? In R. E. Petty, R. H. Fazio, & P. Briñol (Eds.), *Attitudes: Insights from the new implicit measures* (pp. 285–326). New York, NY: Psychology Press.

Briñol, P., Petty, R. E., & Wheeler, S. C. (2006). Discrepancies between explicit and implicit self-concepts: Consequences for information processing. *Journal of Personality and Social Psychology*, *91*, 154–170.

Brock, T. C. (1967). Communication discrepancy and intent to persuade as determinants of counterargument production. *Journal of Experimental Social Psychology*, *3*, 296–309.

Burnkrant, R. E., & Unnava, R. (1989). Self-referencing: A strategy for increasing processing of message content. *Personality and Social Psychology Bulletin*, *15*, 628–638.

Cacioppo, J. T., Gardner, W. L., & Berntson, G. G. (1997). Beyond bipolar conceptualizations and measures: The case of attitudes and evaluative space. *Personality and Social Psychology Review*, *1*, 3–25.

Cacioppo, J. T., & Petty, R. E. (1979). Effects of message repetition and position on cognitive response, recall, and persuasion. *Journal of Personality and Social Psychology*, *37*, 97–109.

Cacioppo, J. T., & Petty, R. E. (1981). Effects of extent of thought on the pleasantness ratings of P-O-X triads: Evidence for three judgmental tendencies in evaluating social situations. *Journal of Personality and Social Psychology, 40*, 1000–1009.

Cacioppo, J. T., & Petty, R. E. (1982). The need for cognition. *Journal of Personality and Social Psychology*, *42*, 116–131.

Cacioppo, J. T., & Petty, R. E. (1989). Effects of message repetition on argument processing, recall, and persuasion. *Basic and Applied Social Psychology*, *10*, 3–12.

Cacioppo, J. T., Petty, R. E., & Morris, K. J. (1983). Effects of need for cognition on message evaluation, recall, and persuasion. *Journal of Personality and Social Psychology*, *45*, 805–818.

Cacioppo, J. T., Priester, J. R., & Berntson, G. G. (1993). Rudimentary determinants of attitudes II: Arm flexion and extension have differential effects on attitudes. *Journal of Personality and Social Psychology, 65*, 5–17.

Chaiken, S. (1980). Heuristic versus systematic information processing in the use of source versus message cues in persuasion. *Journal of Personality and Social Psychology*, *39*, 752–766.

Chaiken, S., Liberman, A., & Eagly, A. H. (1989). Heuristic and systematic processing within and beyond the persuasion context. In J. S. Uleman & J. A. Bargh (Ed.), *Unintended thought* (pp. 212–252). New York, NY: Guilford Press.

Chaiken, S., & Maheswaran, D. (1994). Heuristic processing can bias systematic processing: Effects of source credibility, argument ambiguity, and task importance on attitude judgment. *Journal of Personality and Social Psychology*, *66*, 460–473.

Chaiken, S., & Trope, Y. (1999). *Dual-process theories in social psychology*. New York, NY: Guilford.

Chaiken, S., & Yates, S. M. (1985). Affective-cognitive consistency and thought-induced attitude polarization. *Journal of Personality and Social Psychology*, *49*, 1470–1481.

Chen, M. K., & Risen, J. L. (2010). How choice affects and reflects preferences: Revisiting the free-choice paradigm. *Journal of Personality and Social Psychology*, *99*(4), 573–594.

Clark, J. K., Evans, A. T., & Wegener, D. T. (2011). Perceptions of source efficacy and persuasion: Multiple mechanisms for source effects on attitudes. *European Journal of Social Psychology*, *41*, 596–607.

Clarkson, J. J., Tormala, Z. L., & Leone, C. (2011). A self-validation perspective on the mere thought effect. *Journal of Experimental Social Psychology*, *47*, 449–454.

Converse, P. E. (1970). Attitudes and non-attitudes: Continuation of a dialogue. In E. R. Tufte (Ed.), *The quantitative analysis of social problems* (pp. 168–189). Reading, MA: Addison-Wesley.

Cooper, J. (1971). Personal responsibility and dissonance: The role of foreseen consequences. *Journal of Personality and Social Psychology*, *18*, 354–363.

Cooper, J., & Fazio, R. H. (1984). A new look at dissonance theory. In L. Berkowitz (Ed.), *Advances in experimental social psychology* (Vol. 17, pp. 229–266). New York, NY: Academic Press.

Cooper, J., Fazio, R. H., & Rhodewalt, F. (1978). Dissonance and humor: Evidence for the undifferentiated nature of dissonance arousal. *Journal of Personality and Social Psychology*, *36*, 280–285.

de Houwer, J., Thomas, S., & Baeyens, F. (2001). Associative learning of likes and dislikes: A review of 25 years of research on human evaluative conditioning. *Psychological Bulletin*, *127*, 853–869.

DeMarree, K. G., Morrison, K. R., Wheeler, S. C., & Petty, R. E. (2011). Self-ambivalence and resistance to subtle self-change attempts. *Personality and Social Psychology Bulletin*, *37*, 674–686.

DeSteno, D., Petty, R. E., Rucker, D. D., Wegener, D. T., & Braverman, J. (2004). Discrete emotions and persuasion: The role of emotion-induced expectancies. *Journal of Personality and Social Psychology*, *86*, 43–56.

Ditto, P. H., & Lopez, D. F. (1992). Motivated skepticism: Use of differential decision criteria for preferred and nonpreferred conclusions. *Journal of Personality and Social Psychology*, *63*, 568–584.

Dovidio, J. F., Kawakami, K., & Beach, K. R. (2000). Implicit and explicit attitudes: Examination of the relationship between measures of intergroup bias. In A. Tesser & N. Schwarz (Eds.), *Blackwell handbook of social psychology: Intrapersonal processes*. Oxford, UK: Blackwell.

Dovidio, J. F., Kawakami, K., Johnson, C., Johnson, B., & Howard, A. (1997). On the nature of prejudice: Automatic and controlled processes. *Journal of Experimental Social Psychology*, *33*, 510–540.

Duckworth, K. L., Bargh, J. A., Garcia, M., & Chaiken, S. (2002). The automatic evaluation of novel stimuli. *Psychological Science*, *13*, 513–519.

Eagly, A. H., & Chaiken, S. (1993). *The psychology of attitudes*. Fort Worth, TX: Harcourt, Brace, Jovanovich.

Eagly, A. H., & Chaiken, S. (1998). Attitude structure and function. In D. T. Gilbert, S. T. Fiske, & G. Lindzey (Eds.), *The handbook of social psychology* (Vol. 1, pp. 269–322). New York, NY: McGraw-Hill.

Eagly, A. H., Chaiken, S., & Wood, W. (1981). An attribution analysis of persuasion. In J. H. Harvey, W. J. Ickes, & R. F. Kidd (Ed.), *New direction in attribution research* (Vol. 3, pp. 37–62). Hillsdale, NJ: Erlbaum.

Edwards, K. (1990). The interplay of affect and cognition in attitude formation and change. *Journal of Personality and Social Psychology*, *59*, 202–216.

Elkin, R. A., & Leippe, M. R. (1986). Physiological arousal, dissonance, and attitude change: Evidence for a dissonance-arousal link and a "don't remind me" effect. *Journal of Personality and Social Psychology*, *51*, 55–65.

Elliot, A. J., & Devine, P. G. (1994). On the motivational nature of cognitive dissonance: Dissonance as psychological discomfort. *Journal of Personality and Social Psychology*, *67*, 382–394.

Fabrigar, L. R., & Petty, R. E. (1999). The role of the affective and cognitive bases of attitudes in susceptibility to affectively and cognitively based persuasion. *Personality and Social Psychology Bulletin*, *25*, 363–381.

Fazio, R. H. (1990). Multiple processes by which attitudes guide behavior: The MODE model as an integrative framework. In M. P. Zanna (Ed.), *Advances in experimental social psychology* (Vol. 23, pp. 75–109). San Diego, CA: Academic Press.

Fazio, R. H. (1995). Attitudes as object-evaluation associations: Determinants, consequences, and correlates of attitude accessibility. In R. E. Petty & J. A. Krosnick (Ed.), *Attitude strength: Antecedents and consequences* (pp. 247–282). Mahwah, NJ: Erlbaum.

Fazio, R. H., Jackson, J. R., Dunton, B. C., & Williams, C. J. (1995). Variability in automatic activation as an unobtrusive measure of racial attitudes: A bona fide pipeline? *Journal of Personality and Social Psychology, 69*, 1013–1027.

Fazio, R. H., & Olson, M. A. (2003). Implicit measures in social cognition research: Their meaning and uses. *Annual Review of Psychology, 54*, 297–327.

Fazio, R. H., Zanna, M. P., & Cooper, J. (1977). Dissonance and self-perception: An integrative view of each theory's proper domain of application. *Journal of Experimental Social Psychology, 13*, 464–479.

Festinger, L. (1957). *A theory of cognitive dissonance*. Evanston, IL: Row, Peterson.

Festinger, L., & Carlsmith, J. M. (1959). Cognitive consequences of forced compliance. *Journal of Abnormal and Social Psychology*, *58*, 203–210.

Field, A. P. (2000). I like it, but I'm not sure why: Can evaluative conditioning occur without conscious awareness? *Consciousness & Cognition: An International Journal*, *9*, 13–36.

Fishbein, M., & Ajzen, I. (1975). *Belief, attitude, intention, and behavior*. Reading, MA: Addison-Wesley.

Fishbein, M., & Ajzen, I. (2010). *Predicting and changing behavior: The reasoned action approach*. New York, NY: Psychology Press.

Fishbein, M., & Middlestadt, S. (1995). Noncognitive effects on attitude formation and change: Fact or artifact? *Journal of Consumer Psychology*, *4*, 181–202.

Gawronski, B., & Bodenhausen, G. V. (2006). Associative and propositional processes in evaluation: An integrative review of implicit and explicit attitude change. *Psychological Bulletin*, *132*(5), 692–731.

Gilbert, D. T. (1991). How mental systems believe. *American Psychologist*, *46*, 107–119.

Gilbert, D. T. (1998). Person perception. In D. Gilbert, S. Fiske, & G. Lindzey (Eds.), *Handbook of social psychology* (Vol. 2, pp. 89–150). New York, NY: McGraw-Hill.

Greenwald, A. G. (1968). Cognitive learning, cognitive response to persuasion, and attitude change. In A. G. Greenwald, T. C. Brock, & T. M. Ostrom (Eds.), *Psychological foundations of attitudes* (pp. 147–170). New York, NY: Academic Press.

Greenwald, A. G., & Albert, R. D. (1968). Acceptance and recall of improvised arguments. *Journal of Personality and Social Psychology*, *8*, 31–34.

Greenwald, A. G., & Banaji, M. R. (1995). Implicit social cognition: Attitudes, self-esteem, and stereotypes. *Psychological Review*, *102*, 4–27.

Greenwald, A. G., McGhee, D. E., & Schwartz, J. L. K. (1998). Measuring individual differences in implicit cognition: The implicit association test. *Journal of Personality and Social Psychology*, *74*, 1464–1480.

Greenwald, A. G., Poehlman, A. T., Uhlmann, E. L., & Banaji, M. R. (2009). Understanding and using the implicit associaiton test: III. Meta-analysis of predictive validity. *Journal of Personality and Social Psychology*, *97*(1), 17–41.

Harmon-Jones, E., & Mills, J. (1999). *Cognitive dissonance: Progress on a pivotal theory in social psychology*. Washington, DC: American Psychological Association.

Hastie, R., & Park, B. (1986). The relationship between memory and judgment depends on whether the judgment task is memory-based or on-line. *Psychological Review*, *93*, 258–268.

Heider, F. (1958). *The psychology of interpersonal relations*. New York, NY: Wiley.

Hermans, D., Crombez, G., & Eelen, P. (2000). Automatic attitude activation and efficiency: The fourth horseman of automaticity. *Psychologica Belgica*, *40*, 403–422.

Hovland, C. I., Janis, I. L., & Kelley, H. H. (1953). *Communication and persuasion: Psychological studies of opinion change*. New Haven, CT: Yale University Press.

Insko, C. A. (1984). Balance theory, the Jordan paradigm, and the Wiest tetrahedron. In L. Berkowitz (Ed.), *Advances in experimental social psychology* (Vol. 18, pp. 89–140). Orlando, FL: Academic Press.

Jacoby, L. L., Kelley, C. M., Brown, J., & Jasechko, J. (1989). Becoming famous overnight: Limits on the ability to avoid unconscious influences of the past. *Journal of Personality and Social Psychology*, *56*, 326–338.

Janis, I. L. (1968). Attitude change via role playing. In R. Abelson, E. Aronson, W. McGuire, T. Newcomb, M. Rosenberg, & P. Tannenbaum (Eds.), *Theories of cognitive consistency: A sourcebook* (pp. 810–818). Chicago, IL: Rand McNally.

Janis, I. L., & King, B. T. (1954). The influence of role playing on opinion change. *Journal of Abnormal and Social Psychology*, *49*, 211–218.

Jarvis, W. B. G., & Petty, R. E. (1996). The need to evaluate. *Journal of Personality and Social Psychology, 70*, 172–194.

Jones, C. R., Fazio, R. H., & Olson, M. A. (2009). Implicit misattribution as a mechanism underlying evaluative conditioning. *Journal of Personality and Social Psychology, 96*, 933–948.

Jones, E. E., & Davis, K. E. (1965). From acts to dispositions: The attribution process in person perception. In L. Berkowitz (Ed.), *Advances in experimental social psychology* (Vol. 2, pp. 219–266). New York, NY: Academic Press.

Kawakami, K., Dovidio, J. F., & Dijksterhuis, A. (2003). Effect of social category priming on personal attitudes. *Psychological Science*, *14*(4), 315–319.

Krosnick, J. A., Betz, A. L., Jussim, L. J., & Lynn, A. R. (1992). Subliminal conditioning of attitudes. *Personality and Social Psychology Bulletin*, *18*, 152–162.

Krosnick, J. A., & Petty, R. E. (1995). Attitude strength: An overview. In R. E. Petty & J. A. Krosnick (Eds.), *Attitude strength: Antecedents and consequences* (pp. 1–24). Hillsdale, NJ: Erlbaum.

Kruglanski, A. W. (1990). Motivations for judging and knowing: Implications for causal attribution. In E. T. Higgins & R. M. Sorrentino (Eds.), *Handbook of motivation and cognition: Foundations of social behavior* (Vol. 2, pp. 333–368). New York, NY: Guilford Press.

Kruglanski, A. W., Freund, T., & Bar-Tal, D. (1996). Motivational effects in the mere-exposure paradigm. *European Journal of Social Psychology*, *26*, 479–499.

Kruglanski, A. W., & Thompson, E. P. (1999). Persuasion by a single route: A view from the Unimodel. *Psychological Inquiry*, *10*, 83–109.

Kunst-Wilson, W. R., & Zajonc, R. B. (1980). Affective discrimination of stimuli that cannot be recognized. *Science, 207*, 557–558.

Lepper, M. R., Greene, D., & Nisbett, R. E. (1973). Undermining children's intrinsic interest with extrinsic reward: A test of the "overjustification" hypothesis. *Journal of Personality and Social Psychology*, *28*, 129–137.

Lingle, J. H., & Ostrom, T. M. (1981). Principles of memory and cognition in attitude formation. In R. E. Petty, T. M. Ostrom, & T. C. Brock (Eds.), *Cognitive responses in persuasion* (pp. 399–420). Hillsdale, NJ: Erlbaum.

Lord, C. G., Ross, L., & Lepper, M. R. (1979). Biased assimilation and attitude polarization: The effects of prior theories on subsequently considered evidence. *Journal of Personality and Social Psychology*, *37*, 2098–2109.

Lutz, R. J. (1977). An experimental investigation of causal relations among cognitions, affect, and behavioral intention. *Journal of Consumer Research*, *3*, 197–208.

Mackie, D. M. (1987). Systematic and nonsystematic processing of majority and minority persuasive communications. *Journal of Personality and Social Psychology*, *53*, 41–52.

Maheswaran, D. J., & Chaiken, S. (1991). Promoting systematic processing in low-motivation settings: Effect of incongruent information on processing and judgment. *Journal of Personality and Social Psychology*, *61*, 13–33.

Martin, D. G., & Levey, A. B. (1994). The evaluative response: Primitive but necessary. *Behavioral Research Therapy*, *32*, 305–310.

McCaslin, M. J., Petty, R. E., & Wegener, D. T. (2010). Self-enhancement and theory-based correction processes. *Journal of Experimental Social Psychology, 46*, 830–835.

McGuire, W. J. (1964). Inducing resistance to persuasion: Some contemporary approaches. In L. Berkowitz (Ed.), *Advances in experimental social psychology* (Vol. 1, pp. 191–229). New York, NY: Academic Press.

McGuire, W. J. (1968). Personality and attitude change: An information-processing theory. In A. G. Greenwald, T. C. Brock, & T. M. Ostrom (Ed.), *Psychological foundations of attitudes* (pp. 171–196). New York, NY: Academic Press.

Miller, C. E., & Norman, R. M. G. (1976). Balance, agreement, and attraction in hypothetical social situations. *Journal of Experimental Social Psychology*, *12*, 109–119.

Murphy, S. T., & Zajonc, R. B. (1993). Affect, cognition, and awareness: Affective priming with optimal and suboptimal exposures. *Journal of Personality and Social Psychology, 64*, 723–739.

Nienhuis, A. E., Manstead, A. S. R., & Spears, R. (2001). Multiple motives and persuasive communication: Creative elaboration as a result of impression motivation and accuracy motivation. *Personality and Social Psychology Bulletin, 27*, 118–132.

Olson, J. M., Vernon, P. A., Harris, J. A., & Jang, K. L. (2001). The heritability of attitudes: A study of twins. *Journal of Personality and Social Psychology*, *80*(6), 845–860.

Osgood, C. E., Suci, G. J., & Tannenbaum, P. H. (1957). *The measurement of meaning*. Urbana: University of Illinois Press.

Payne, B. K., Cheng, C. M., Govorun, O., & Stewart, B. (2005). An inkblot for attitudes: Affect misattribution as implicit measurement. *Journal of Personality and Social Psychology*, *89*, 277–293.

Perloff, R. M., & Brock, T. C. (1980). And thinking makes it so: Cognitive responses to persuasion. In M. Roloff & G. Miller (Ed.), *Persuasion: New directions in theory and research* (pp. 67–100). Beverly Hills, CA: Sage.

Petty, R. E., & Briñol, P. (2006). Understanding social judgment: Multiple systems and processes. *Psychological Inquiry*, *17*, 217–223.

Petty, R. E., & Briñol, P. (2012). The elaboration likelihood model. In P. A. M. Van Lange, A. Kruglanski, & E. T. Higgins (Eds.), *Handbook of theories of social psychology* (Vol. 1, pp. 224–245). London, UK: Sage.

Petty, R. E., Briñol, P., & DeMarree, K. G. (2007). The meta-cognitive model (MCM) of attitudes: Implications for attitude measurement, change, and strength. *Social Cognition*, *25*, 657–686.

Petty, R. E., Briñol, P., & Johnson, I. (2012). Implicit ambivalence. In B. Gawronski & F. Strack (Eds.), *Cognitive consistency: A fundamental principle in social cognition* (pp. 178–201). New York, NY: Guilford Press.

Petty, R. E., Briñol, P., Loersch, C., & McCaslin, M. J. (2009). The need for cognition. In M. R. Leary & R. H. Hoyle (Eds.), *Handbook of individual differences in social behavior* (pp. 318–329). New York, NY: Guilford Press.

Petty, R. E., Briñol, P., & Tormala, Z. L. (2002). Thought confidence as a determinant of persuasion: The self-validation hypothesis. *Journal of Personality and Social Psychology, 82*, 722–741.

Petty, R. E., Briñol, P., Tormala, Z. L., & Wegener, D. T. (2007). The role of meta-cognition in social judgment. In A. W. Kruglanski & E. T. Higgins (Eds), *Social psychology: Handbook of basic principles* (2nd ed., pp. 254–284). New York, NY: Guilford Press.

Petty, R. E., & Cacioppo, J. T. (1979a). Effects of forewarning of persuasive intent and involvement on cognitive responses. *Personality and Social Psychology Bulletin, 5*, 173–176.

Petty, R. E., & Cacioppo, J. T. (1979b). Issue-involvement can increase or decrease persuasion by enhancing message-relevant cognitive responses. *Journal of Personality and Social Psychology, 37*, 1915–1926.

Petty, R. E., & Cacioppo, J. T. (1981). *Attitudes and persuasion: Classic and contemporary approaches*. Dubuque, IA: Brown.

Petty, R. E., & Cacioppo, J. T. (1984). The effects of involvement on responses to argument quantity and quality: Central and peripheral routes to persuasion. *Journal of Personality and Social Psychology, 46*, 69–81.

Petty, R. E., & Cacioppo, J. T. (1986). The elaboration likelihood model of persuasion. In L. Berkowitz (Ed.), *Advances in experimental social psychology* (Vol. 19, pp. 123–205). New York, NY: Academic Press.

Petty, R. E., Cacioppo, J. T., & Goldman, R. (1981). Personal involvement as a determinant of argument-based persuasion. *Journal of Personality and Social Psychology, 41*, 847–855.

Petty, R. E., Cacioppo, J. T., & Haugtvedt, C. (1992). Involvement and persuasion: An appreciative look at the Sherifs' contribution to the study of self-relevance and attitude change. In D. Granberg & G. Sarup (Ed.), *Social judgment and intergroup relations: Essays in honor of Muzifer Sherif* (pp. 147–175). New York, NY: Springer-Verlag.

Petty, R. E., Cacioppo, J. T., & Heesacker, M. (1981). Effects of rhetorical questions on persuasion: A cognitive response analysis. *Journal of Personality and Social Psychology, 40*, 432–440.

Petty, R. E., Briñol, P., Tormala, Z. L., & Wegener, D. T. (2007). The role of meta-cognition in social judgment. In A. W. Kruglanski & E. T. Higgins (Eds), *Social psychology: Handbook of basic principles* (2nd ed., pp. 254–284). New York, NY: Guilford Press.

Petty, R. E., Fazio, R. H., & Briñol, P (Eds.) (2009). *Attitudes: Insights from the new implicit measures*. New York, NY: Psychology Press.

Petty, R. E., Haugtvedt, C. P., & Smith, S. M. (1995). Elaboration as a determinant of attitude strength. In R. E. Petty & J. A. Krosnick (Eds.), *Attitude strength: Antecedents and consequences* (pp. 93–130). Mahwah, NJ: Erlbaum.

Petty, R. E., & Krosnick, J. A. (1995). *Attitude strength: Antecedents and consequences*. Mahwah, NJ: Erlbaum.

Petty, R. E., Ostrom, T. M., & Brock, T. C. (1981). *Cognitive responses in persuasion*. Hillsdale, NJ: Erlbaum.

Petty, R. E., Priester, J. R., & Wegener, D. T. (1994). Cognitive processes in attitude change. In R. S. Wyer & T. K. Srull (Eds.), *Handbook of social cognition*, (2nd ed., Vol. 2, pp. 69–142). Hillsdale, NJ: Erlbaum.

Petty, R. E., Schumann, D. W., Richman, S. A., & Strathman, A. J. (1993). Positive mood and persuasion: Different roles for affect under high- and low-elaboration conditions. *Journal of Personality and Social Psychology, 64*, 5–20.

Petty, R. E., Tormala, Z. L., Briñol, P., & Jarvis, W. B. G. (2006). Implicit ambivalence from attitude change: An exploration of the PAST model. *Journal of Personality and Social Psychology, 90*, 21–41.

Petty, R. E., Tormala, Z. L., & Rucker, D. D. (2004). Resisting persuasion by counterarguing: An attitude strength perspective. In J. T. Jost, M. R. Banaji, & D. A. Prentice (Eds.), *Perspectivism in social psychology: The yin and yang of scientific progress* (pp. 37–51). Washington, DC: American Psychological Association.

Petty, R. E., & Wegener, D. T. (1993). Flexible correction processes in social judgment: Correcting for context induced contrast. *Journal of Experimental Social Psychology, 29*, 137–165.

Petty, R. E., & Wegener, D. T. (1998). Attitude change: Multiple roles for persuasion variables. In D. T. Gilbert, S. T. Fiske, & G. Lindzey (Eds.), *The handbook of social psychology* (Vol. 1, pp. 323–390). New York, NY: McGraw-Hill.

Petty, R. E., Wells, G. L., & Brock, T. C. (1976). Distraction can enhance or reduce yielding to propaganda: Thought disruption versus effort justification. *Journal of Personality and Social Psychology, 34*, 874–884.

Petty, R. E., Wheeler, S. C., & Bizer, G. B. (1999). Is there one persuasion process or more? Lumping versus splitting in attitude change theories. *Psychological Inquiry, 10*, 156–162.

Petty, R. E., Wheeler, S. C., & Bizer, G. B. (2000). Attitude functions and persuasion: An elaboration likelihood approach to matched versus mismatched messages. In G. R. Maio & J. M. Olson (Eds.), *Why we evaluate: Functions of attitudes* (pp. 133–162). Mahwah, NJ: Lawrence Erlbaum.

Petty, R. E., Wheeler, S. C., & Tormala, Z. L. (2003). Persuasion and attitude change. In T. Millon & M. J. Lerner (Eds.), *Handbook of psychology: Volume 5: Personality and social psychology* (pp. 353–382). Hoboken, NJ: Wiley.

Priester, J. R., & Petty, R. E. (1995). Source attributions and persuasion: Perceived honesty as a determinant of message scrutiny. *Personality and Social Psychology Bulletin, 21*, 637–654.

Priester, J. M., & Petty, R. E. (1996). The gradual threshold model of ambivalence: Relating the positive and negative bases of attitudes to subjective ambivalence. *Journal of Personality and Social Psychology, 71*, 431–449.

Rosenberg, M. J., & Abelson, R. P. (1960). An analysis of cognitive balancing. In C. I. Hovland & M. J. Rosenberg (Eds.), *Attitude organization and change: An analysis of consistency among attitude components* (pp. 112–163). New Haven, CT: Yale University Press.

Rosenberg, M. J., & Hovland, C. I. (1960). Cognitive, affective, and behavioral components of attitudes. In C. I. Hovland & M. J. Rosenberg (Eds.), *Attitude organization and change: An analysis of consistency among attitude components* (pp. 1–14). New Haven, CT: Yale University Press.

Rucker, D. D., Petty, R. E., & Briñol, P. (2008). What's in a frame anyway? A meta-cognitive analysis of the impact of one versus two sided message framing on attitude certainty. *Journal of Consumer Psychology, 18*, 137–149.

Rydell, R. J., & McConnell, A. R. (2006). Understanding implicit and explicit attitude change: A systems of reasoning analysis. *Journal of Personality and Social Psychology, 91*, 995–1008.

Rydell, R. J., McConnell, A. R., Mackie, D. M., & Strain, L. M. (2006). Of two minds: Forming and changing valence-inconsistent implicit and explicit attitudes. *Psychological Science, 17*, 954–958.

Scher, S. J., & Cooper, J. (1989). Motivational basis of dissonance: The singular role of behavioral consequences. *Journal of Personality and Social Psychology, 56*, 899–906.

Schwarz, N. (1999). Self-reports: How the questions shape the answers. *American Psychologist, 54*, 93–105.

Schwarz, N. (2004). Meta-cognitive experiences in consumer judgment and decision making. *Journal of Consumer Psychology, 14*, 332–348.

Schwarz, N., Bless, H., Strack, F., Klumpp, G., Rittenauer-Schatka, H., & Simons, A. (1991). Ease of retrieval as information: Another look at the availability heuristic. *Journal of Personality and Social Psychology, 61*, 195–202.

Schwarz, N., & Bohner, G. (2000). The construction of attitudes. In A. Tesser & N. Schwarz (Eds.), *Blackwell handbook of social psychology: Intrapersonal processes*. Oxford, UK: Blackwell.

See, Y. H. M., Petty, R. E., & Evans, L. M. (2009). The impact of perceived message complexity and need for cognition on information processing and attitudes. *Journal of Research in Personality*, *43*, 880–889.

See, Y. H. M., Petty, R. E., & Fabrigar, L. R. (2008). Affective and cognitive meta-bases of attitudes: Unique effects on information interest and persuasion. *Journal of Personality and Social Psychology*, *94*, 938–955.

Smith, S. M., & Shaffer, D. R. (1991). Celerity and cajolery: Rapid speech may promote or inhibit persuasion through its impact on message elaboration. *Personality and Social Psychology Bulletin*, *17*, 663–669.

Staats, A. W., Staats, C. K., & Crawford, H. L. (1962). First-order conditioning of meaning and the parallel conditioning of a GSR. *Journal of General Psychology, 67*, 159–167.

Steele, C. M. (1988). The psychology of self-affirmation: Sustaining the integrity of the self. In L. Berkowitz (Ed.), *Advances in experimental social psychology* (Vol. 21, pp. 261–302). New York, NY: Academic Press.

Stone, J., & Cooper, J. (2001). A self-standards model of cognitive dissonance. *Journal of Experimental Social Psychology, 37*, 228–243.

Strahan, E. J., Spencer, S. J., & Zanna, M. P. (2002). Subliminal priming and persuasion: Striking while the iron is hot. *Journal of Experimental Social Psychology*, *38*(6), 556–568.

Taylor, S. E. (1975). On inferring one's attitude from one's behavior: Some delimiting conditions. *Journal of Personality and Social Psychology, 31*, 126–131.

Tesser, A., Martin, L., & Mendolia, M. (1995). The impact of thought on attitude extremity and attitude-behavior consistency. In R. E. Petty & J. A. Krosnick (Eds.), *Attitude strength: Antecedents and consequences* (pp. 73–92). Mahwah, NJ: Erlbaum.

Tetlock, P. E. (1983). Accountability and the complexity of thought. *Journal of Personality and Social Psychology*, *45*, 74–83.

Thurstone, L. L. (1928). The measurement of opinion. *Journal of Abnormal and Social Psychology*, *22*, 415–430.

Tormala, Z. L. (2008). A new framework for resistance to persuasion: The resistance appraisals hypothesis. In W. D. Crano & R. Prislin (Eds.), *Attitudes and attitude change* (pp. 213–234). New York, NY: Psychology Press.

Tormala, Z. L., Briñol, P., & Petty, R. E. (2006). When credibility attacks: The reverse impact of source credibility on persuasion. *Journal of Experimental Social Psychology*, *42*, 684–691.

Tormala, Z. L, Clarkson, J. J., & Henderson, M. D. (2011). Does fast or slow evaluation foster greater certainty? *Personality and Social Psychology Bulletin*, *37*, 422–434.

Tormala, Z. L., & Petty, R. E. (2001). On-line versus memory-based processing: The role of "need to evaluate" in person perception. *Personality and Social Psychology Bulletin*, *27*, 1599–1612.

Tormala, Z. L., Petty, R. E., & Briñol, P. (2002). Ease of retrieval effects in persuasion: A self-validation analysis. *Personality and Social Psychology Bulletin*, *28*, 1700–1712.

Valins, S. (1966). Cognitive effects of false heart-rate feedback. *Journal of Personality and Social Psychology, 4*, 400–408.

Vargas, P. T., von Hippel, W., & Petty, R. E. (2001). It's not just what you think, it's also how you think: Implicit attitude measures tapping biased information processing. In S. E. Heckler & S. Shapiro (Eds.), *Proceedings of the society for consumer psychology winter conference* (pp. 82–88). Tempe, AZ: Society for Consumer Psychology.

Visser, P. S., Bizer, G. Y., & Krosnick, J. A. (2006). Exploring the latent structure of strength-related attitude attributes. In M. P. Zanna (Ed.), *Advances in experimental social psychology* (Vol. 38, pp. 1–67). San Diego, CA: Academic Press.

Wan, E. W., Rucker, D. D., Tormala, Z. L., & Clarkson, J. J. (2010). The effect of regulatory depletion on attitude certainty. *Journal of Marketing Research*, *47*, 531–541.

Wegener, D. T., Downing, J., Krosnick, J. A., & Petty, R. E. (1995). Measures and manipulations of strength-related properties of attitudes: Current practice and future directions. In R. E. Petty & J. A. Krosnick (Eds.), *Attitude strength: Antecedants and consequences* (pp. 455–487). Mahwah, NJ: Erlbaum.

Wegener, D. T., & Petty, R. E. (1997). The flexible correction model: The role of naive theories of bias in bias correction. In M. P. Zanna (Ed.), *Advances in experimental social psychology* (Vol. 29, pp. 141–208). San Diego, CA: Academic Press.

Wegener, D. T., Petty, R. E., & Klein, D. J. (1994). Effects of mood on high elaboration attitude change: The mediating role of likelihood judgments. *European Journal of Social Psychology*, *24*, 25–43.

Wegener, D. T., Petty, R. E., & Smith, S. M. (1995). Positive mood can increase or decrease message scrutiny: The hedonic contingency view of mood and message processing. *Journal of Personality and Social Psychology*, *69*, 5–15.

Wells, G. L., & Petty, R. E. (1980). The effects of overt head movement on persuasion: Compatibility and incompatibility of responses. *Basic and Applied Social Psychology*, *1*, 219–230.

Wheeler, S. C., DeMarree, K. G., & Petty, R. E. (2007). Understanding the role of the self in prime-to-behavior effects: The active self account. *Personality and Social Psychology Review, 11*, 234–261.

Wheeler, S. C., Petty, R. E., & Bizer, G. Y. (2005). Self- schema matching and attitude change: Situational and dispositional determinants of message elaboration. *Journal of Consumer Research*, *31*, 787–797.

Wilson, T. D., & Brekke, N. (1994). Mental contamination and mental correction: Unwanted influences on judgments and evaluations. *Psychological Bulletin*, *116*, 117–142.

Wilson, T. D., Dunn, D. S., Kraft, D., & Lisle, D. J. (1989). Introspection, attitude change, and attitude-behavior consistency: The disrupting effects of explaining why we feel the way we do. *Advances in Experimental Social Psychology*, *22*, 287–343.

Wilson, T. D., & Hodges, S. D. (1992). Attitudes as temporary constructions. In L. L. Martin & A. Tesser (Eds.), *The construction of social judgments* (pp. 37–65). Hillsdale, NJ: Erlbaum.

Wilson, T. D., Lindsey, S., & Schooler, T. Y. (2000). A model of dual attitudes. *Psychological Review*, *107*, 101–126.

Wilson, T. D., & Schooler, J. W. (1991). Thinking too much: Introspection can reduce the quality of preferences and decisions. *Journal of Personality and Social Psychology*, *60*, 181–192.

Wittenbrink, B., & Schwarz, N. (Eds.). (2007). *Implicit measures of attitudes*. New York, NY: Guilford Press.

Wood, W. (1982). Retrieval of attitude-relevant information from memory: Effects on susceptibility to persuasion and on intrinsic motivation. *Journal of Personality and Social Psychology*, *42*, 798–910.

Wood, W., Rhodes, N., & Biek, M. (1995). Working knowledge and attitude strength: An information processing analysis. In R. E. Petty & J. A. Krosnick (Eds.), *Attitude strength: Antecedents and consequences* (pp. 283–313). Mahwah, NJ: Erlbaum.

Zajonc, R. B. (1968). Attitudinal effects of mere exposure. *Journal of Personality and Social Psychology Monograph Supplements*, *9*, 1–27.

Zanna, M. P., & Cooper, J. (1974). Dissonance and the pill: An attribution approach to studying the arousal properties of dissonance. *Journal of Personality and Social Psychology*, *29*, 703–709.

Zanna, M. P., Kiesler, C. A., & Pilkonis, P. A. (1970). Positive and negative attitudinal affect established by classical conditioning. *Journal of Personality and Social Psychology*, *14*, 321–328.

Zanna, M. P., & Rempel, J. K. (1988). Attitudes: A new look at an old concept. In D. Bar-Tal & A. W. Kruglanski (Eds.), *The social psychology of knowledge* (pp. 315–334). Cambridge, UK: Cambridge University Press.

Zentall, T. R. (2010). Justification of effort by humans and pigeons: Cognitive dissonance or contrast? *Current Directions in Psychological Science*, *19*, 296–300.

CHAPTER 18

Emotion Regulation Effectiveness: What Works When

GAL SHEPPES AND JAMES J. GROSS

Consider the fear a student may experience while giving a presentation for a class assignment. Observing the frightened student, we might notice that his fear response involves a change across various external and internal domains. This change is manifested in a fearful facial expression, which involves a widening of the eyes; increased autonomic arousal, which includes sweating and increased heart rate; increased activation in limbic brain regions including the amygdala; a strong negative subjective experience of dread; racing negative cognitions about threat and failure; and a desire to flee.

Clearly, in this example the fear response seems to be dominant but is it unchangeable? In the following sections we begin by briefly outlining what makes a given situation emotional. We then discuss how emotions develop in these special situations. Following that we discuss *emotion regulation*, which refers to the ways in which emotions can be altered or controlled. In doing so, we discuss past and present conceptions of emotion regulation with an emphasis on a process model of emotion regulation (Gross & Thompson, 2007). We then suggest additional relevant factors that determine the effectiveness of different emotion regulation strategies. These factors are arranged in

a new framework to which we give direct empirical evidence. We conclude by offering future directions for better understanding emotion regulation.

EMOTION GENERATION

Emotions play a vital part in our lives. We may experience fear prior to an important test and surprise followed by happiness when we receive a better grade than we expected. At the same time we can also experience sadness when our best friend tells us he she received a poor grade or switch to experiencing anger or even genuine disgust (Chapman, Kim, Susskind, & Anderson, 2009) if we perceive the grading of that exam to be fundamentally unfair.

The Modal Model of Emotion

Though clearly central in our lives, emotions are invoked in unique circumstances and are not experienced all of the time. What are these unique circumstances in which emotions are called into being? From an evolutionary perspective, emotions are induced in order to prepare the organism and to produce a certain response that will create circumstances that are advantageous to the organism (Damasio, 1999). Specifically, emotions are generated

This chapter draws on and updates previous reviews by Gross (1998a,b, 2001, 2002), Gross and Thompson (2007), and Gross, Sheppes, and Urry (2011). The authors would like to thank Mayra Burguera for assistance.

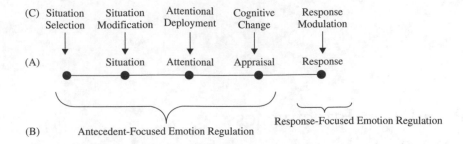

(A) Components of emotion generation. (B) Antecedent-focused versus response-focused emotion regulation strategies. (C) Five emotion regulation families.

Figure 18.1   The process model of emotion regulation (reprinted from Sheppes and Gross, 2011)

when a certain situation is attended to, given a valenced meaning, and this evaluation gives rise to a coordinated set of experiential, behavioral and physiological responses (Gross, 1998a, 1998b, 2001, 2002). Going back to the student who is giving a presentation, fear would be generated if the student attends to the presentation situation and appraises it as potentially harmful, leading to the experience of fear, as well as behavioral (e.g., facial expressive behavior, Ekman, 1992) and physiological (e.g., increased sympathetic activation, Kreibig, 2010) responses.

In Figure 18.1, we present in schematic form the situation-attention-meaning-response sequence that constitutes an emotional response. We use a rather abstract definition here—which we refer to as the "modal model" of emotion—because emotions form such a heterogeneous category that it is difficult to make generalizations that apply to all cases. For example, emotions can vary in their intensity, ranging from mild to overwhelming panic-like responses. Emotions can also vary in their duration or other temporal characteristics. For example, some emotions like sadness have a wave-like pattern rising and subsiding fairly slowly, whereas other emotions like disgust or fear have a burst-type pattern with fast rise time to peak and also a fast decline (Davidson, 1998). Despite these fundamental differences between emotions, we wish to emphasize three common features for different emotional episodes.

Common Features of Emotion

First, emotions arise when a situation is construed as being relevant to one or more of an individual's personal strivings or active goals (Scherer, Schorr, & Johnstone, 2001). Some of these goals may be biologically based (e.g., securing food). Others may be culturally derived (e.g., avoiding familial shame). Some of these goals may be

social (e.g., helping an elderly person in the street). Others may be self-focused (e.g., wanting to behave according to one's ideals). Because many goals are usually active at any one time, the most dominant goal will dictate which emotion—if any—will be activated, and to what degree that emotion will be activated. Whatever the details of the emotion-generating goals that are active at a particular point in time, and whatever the details of the situation the individual faces, it is ultimately the situational-meaning-in-relation-to-a-goal that gives rise to an emotion. As either the goals or the individual's construal of the situation change, so too will the emotion.

A second common feature is that emotions are multi-faceted, embodied phenomena that involve loosely-coupled changes in the domains of subjective experience, behavior, and peripheral physiology (Mauss, Levenson, McCarter, Wilhelm, & Gross, 2005). The experiential component of emotion, which is also defined as *feeling*, is a private state or an internal representation of the changes invoked by the emotional unfolding (Damasio, 1999). The behavioral component of emotion includes changes in activity in muscles of the face and body, and in what one says, as well as more general changes in basic motivational states such as the likelihood of approaching or withdrawing from something in the environment (Frijda, 1986). The peripheral physiological component of emotion includes the autonomic and neuroendocrine responses that putatively provide metabolic support for anticipated and actual behavioral responses (Levenson, 1999).

A third common feature is that emotions play out in ways that are sensitive to the particular details of a given internal or external environment. This means that, under some circumstances, emotions can take full control (Frijda, 1986). For example, walking around the streets of Paris, your dominant goal may be sightseeing. But if a stranger pulls a knife and asks for all of your money, your dominant goal quickly becomes to survive, and fear takes over. In this case, the emotion-related goal (survival) has overridden the non–emotion-related goal (sightseeing). However, emotions do not always trump other goal-driven processes (i.e., processes related to meeting active goals like sightseeing in the example above that are unrelated to the emotion-generating goals). This means that emotions can be and often are adjusted to suit our needs in a given situation. It is this third common feature of emotion that permits us to change modify or in other words regulate our emotions (see Gross, Sheppes, & Urry, in press, for a relevant review on the distinction between emotion generation and emotion regulation).

EMOTION REGULATION: PAST AND PRESENT

Emotion regulation has now emerged as an independent field of study within affective science (Gross, 2007; Koole, van Dillen, & Sheppes, 2011). However, to appreciate the scope of problems addressed by this field, it is helpful to consider two major historical antecedents (Gross, 1999).

Historical Antecedents to the Contemporary Study of Emotion Regulation

The first important influence on contemporary emotion regulation research is Sigmund Freud's (1894/1962) conception of defensive mechanisms. Freud argued that individuals have a flexible defensive apparatus that employs diverse mental operations to ward off differing levels of negative experiences, unacceptable drives, and threats from conscious experience. A major premise in Freud's psychoanalytic theory is that some negative content might threaten the integrity of the self-concept if it were available to awareness. Therefore, various unconscious defense mechanisms were needed to keep these unacceptable mental contents from entering awareness. Since Freud's times the study of defensive mechanisms has had its ups and downs, but in recent years there have been important experimental accounts that support these basic tenets (see Cramer, 2008, for a review).

In contrast to the subconscious role of defensive mechanisms in the psychoanalytic approach, a second important influence on current emotion regulation theorizing comes from the study of stress and coping (e.g., Carver & Scheier, 1994; Folkman & Lazarus, 1985). In this literature, conscious appraisals are given a central role in determining one's initial construal of events in the environment and subsequent reactions to these events. Specifically, appraisals are divided into *primary appraisals* when a certain event or encounter is construed on dimensions such as relevance to one's well being, positivity, or how negative/stressful an event is. *Secondary appraisals* refer to how an individual evaluates the coping resources and options to address a particular event. In the stress and coping literature, emotion generation is the result of specific primary appraisals. Coping is divided into *problem focused coping*, which refers to doing something to directly change or influence the environment that causes distress, and *emotion focused coping* (most directly related to modern emotion regulation), which refers to efforts to manage the distress caused by a particular event. In the 1960s, Lazarus did groundbreaking work on emotion-focused coping by showing that appraising a disgusting film in an intellectual manner reduces disgust related experience and physiological arousal (Speisman, Lazarus, Mordkoff, and Davison, 1964). In more modern times influential studies by Cheng (2001) have shown that individuals who use problem focused coping strategies for controllable situations and who switch to emotion focused coping in uncontrollable situations show more adaptive long term adaptation.

The Contemporary Study of Emotion Regulation

The modern study of emotion regulation has benefited from both the psychoanalytic and stress and coping literatures. Nevertheless, by conducting rigorous experimental studies that make it possible to expose the underlying mechanisms of specific regulatory strategies, and by investigating the role of specific emotions rather than general stress, this emerging field has increased our understanding of the processes that influence which emotions we have, when we have them, and how we experience or express these emotions (Gross, 1998a). A key idea in this field is that emotion regulation is defined by the activation of a goal to modify the emotion-generative process, and involves the motivated recruitment of one or more processes to influence emotion generation (Gross et al., 2011). Whether we consult our own experiences, or the empirical literature, it is clear that emotions may be regulated in many different ways (Gross, Richards, & John, 2006).

One important point of difference across emotion regulation episodes is whether the emotion-regulatory goal is activated in the individual who is having (or is likely to have) an emotion episode, or in someone else. An example of the first type of emotion regulation episode—which we refer to as *intrinsic emotion regulation*—is when someone tries not to think about something that is upsetting. An example of the second type of emotion regulation episode—which we refer to as *extrinsic emotion regulation*—is when a friend calms us down by putting an upsetting situation in perspective. Although extrinsic emotion regulation remains important in adulthood it is perhaps the most dominant form of emotion regulation in infancy where parents have a crucial role in helping infants to develop an ability to regulate their emotions (Macklem, 2008).

A second point of difference across emotion regulation episodes is whether the motivation to engage in emotion regulation is *hedonic* (to feel less negative or more positive in the near term) or *instrumental* (to achieve one's long-term goals) (Tamir, 2009). In some cases these two types of goals are congruent; for example, when someone tries to decrease fear and anxiety because it makes her jittery in the moment and at the same time it can hurt her long-term health. At other times these goals can compete, when, for example, one wants to avoid a dreaded situation in order to feel relief in the short run, but in the long run this perpetuates the situation.

A third point of difference across emotion regulation episodes is whether the emotion-regulatory goal is *explicit* or *implicit* (Bargh, Gollwitzer, Lee-Chai, Barndollar, & Trotschel, 2001; Mauss, Cook, & Gross, 2007). Sometimes, this goal is explicit. That is, the goal is deliberate and consciously perceived, such as when an individual decides to try to direct his attention toward the exit sign when among a big crowd in an effort to calm down. At other times, this goal is implicit. That is, the goal is activated outside of an individual's awareness, such as when an individual unconsciously stands next to the exit sign and feels calm while there. Implicit emotion regulation is perhaps the rule rather than the exception. That is, in many real life situations we regulate in an automatic fashion without consciously pondering how we should go about our emotions. These automated and habitual implicit processes offer an efficient regulatory option, demonstrated in forming a strong goal that is persistent in the face of obstacles, that is reenacted after disruption (Bargh et al., 2001; Williams, Bargh, Nocera, & Gray, 2009).

Finally, emotions can be *down-regulated* where the goal is to decrease a certain emotion response, *maintained* where the goal is to prolong a given emotional response, or *up-regulated* where the goal is to increase an emotional response. Although the obvious examples of down-regulation refer to decreasing negative emotions, and maintaining and up-regulation refer to positive emotions, there are many instances where one's instrumental goals are to down-regulate positive emotions or maintain or up-regulate negative emotions (Tamir, 2009). For example, when a person is on a diet they might try to reduce their joy when eating high caloric food, or when people wish to avoid certain dangers they might prefer to maintain or even up-regulate their fear levels (Tamir & Ford, 2009). Though clearly important, in the present chapter we will focus on down regulation of negative emotions, which have been central in studies in emotion regulation.

THE PROCESS MODEL OF EMOTION REGULATION

To create a framework for analyzing emotion regulation processes, we have found it useful to consider which parts of the emotion-generative process are primary targets of an active goal to influence emotion. To examine this dimension of variation, we take the emotion generation model depicted in Figure 18.1 as a starting point. Emotion regulatory acts are, from this perspective, seen as having their primary impact on different stages of the emotion generative process (Gross, 2001). In Figure 18.1, we highlight five points in the emotion-generative process at which individuals can regulate their emotions, corresponding to five families of emotion regulation processes: situation selection, situation modification, attentional deployment, cognitive change, and response modulation. In the sections that follow, we elaborate on each of these families.

Situation Selection

Situation selection refers to efforts an individual makes to influence the situation he will encounter, with a view to increasing (or decreasing) the likelihood that certain emotions will arise. Situation selection may best be captured in the classic conceptualization of choosing between *approaching* and *avoiding* a situation. Seminal work by Kurt Lewin (1943)—one of the founders of social psychology—suggests that many situations are uncertain in the rewards and risks they offer. Therefore, individuals experience conflicts between approaching and avoiding a certain situation.

Going back to our fearful student who is required to present to others, this situation offers uncertainty about the probability of reward (receiving a positive feedback from the instructor) or risk (being too anxious at the talk to an extent that impairs its fluency). In this case our student can choose to regulate his fear by avoiding the situation altogether if he does not show up for the presentation. Avoidance functions as a strong regulatory option that intersects the emotion generative process at the earliest point. Nevertheless, it can be clearly maladaptive if generalized, as will be elaborated below (Campbell-Sills & Barlow, 2007).

Situation Modification

Situation modification refers to attempting to change the external features of a situation in a way that will alter one's emotional response to that situation. That is, even when one approaches or engages in a given situation, regulatory options that concentrate on changing certain characteristics of the external situation are possible.

Classic examples of situation modification include some forms of *safety signals or behaviors* (Barlow, 1988) and *problem-focused coping* (Folkman & Lazarus, 1985). Safety signals or behaviors refer to external objects individuals use in fearful situations in order to decrease anxiety. For example, our fearful student from the example above can decide to come to the presentation with papers that include a verbatim transcript of his talk. Note that these papers can offer relief simply by being there even if the student does not end up using them. Problem-focused coping, which was described earlier, refers to strategies individuals use to deal with the cause of a certain problem. For example, our fearful student may decide to come to the presentation early and adjust the placement of the podium in a way that feels more comfortable.

Attentional Deployment

In the first two families of emotion regulation processes (situation selection, situation modification), there is a focus on external change of the actual situation. However, the third family of regulatory processes, which we refer to as attentional deployment, involves a shift to an internal emotion regulation process that plays out in one's mind. Specifically, attentional deployment refers to directing attention in such a way that the emotion-response trajectory is altered. In this third stage, we refer to regulatory options that take place after an emotional situation has been encountered. There are several attentional regulation options.

Distraction is a broad name for different emotion regulation options that involve diverting attention away from an emotional situation. For example distraction can refers

to either shifts of overt gaze from emotional features to nonemotional features (Dunning & Hajcak, 2009; Hajcak, Dunning, & Foti, 2009) or to performing a secondary task like trying to remember a 7-digit number that is provided (McRae et al., 2010; Van Dillen & Koole, 2007) to creating neutral thoughts (Sheppes & Meiran, 2007, 2008). Distraction has been considered to be an emotion regulation strategy that provides fast and relatively effortless relief from emotional responses but it may become maladaptive in the long run (see McCaul, & Malott, 1984, for conceptual convergence in the realm of pain regulation).

Another classic attentional strategy is *thought suppression*, which involves efforts not to think about a certain emotional content (Wegner, 1994). Suppressing one's thoughts is an effortful process that can be successful at times, but can backfire by "ironically" making the suppressed content more accessible in one's mind especially under stress or when cognitive resources are limited.

Rumination is another emotion regulation strategy that involves directing attention inward, focusing on negative aspects of the self in an abstract, passive and repetitive way (Nolen-Hoeksema, Wisco, & Lyubomirsky, 2008; Watkins 2008). Rumination could be viewed as asking big why questions (e.g., Why am I sad? Why do these bad things happen to me?) about the causes of negative events without a translation into a concrete way to deal with things. Two decades of research suggest that this form of self-focus is largely maladaptive and is a strong risk factor for mood and anxiety disorders. Specifically, individuals who ruminate as a way to regulate negative mood are more likely to develop a depressive episode that is stronger and longer in duration, relative to individuals who do not ruminate (Nolen-Hoeksema, 1991).

In recent years, influential accounts from eastern philosophy and Buddhism have introduced *mindfulness* as an additional form of attentional regulation. Mindfulness involves attending to emotional experiences by focusing on immediate here and now aspects with an orientation of curiosity, openness and acceptance (Bishop et al., 2004). Mindfulness has proven to be an adaptive way to regulate negative emotions and have been incorporated in cognitive treatments of anxiety and depression (Goldin, Ramel, & Gross, 2009).

To provide a clear example of each, again consider our fearful student. He could distract his attention by diverting his gaze from the fear provoking audience to his computer screen, or think about neutral calming thoughts. He could also suppress fearful thoughts by trying not to think about potential failure, or he could try to ruminate and focus inward in trying to understand why he is so preoccupied with potential criticism. Being mindful of the scary situation, the student could focus on momentary changes in his thinking by embracing such thoughts in an open and accepting way.

Cognitive Change

Cognitive change refers to altering a situation's meaning in a way that influences the emotions that situation will produce. In this fourth stage of the process model, we refer to changing the meaning of the original appraisal of an emotional event.

The most studied regulation strategy is *cognitive reappraisal,* which involves construing an emotional event in non-emotional terms (Gross, 2001, 2002; Gross & Thompson, 2007). Within the reappraisal category, there are several ways in which emotional appraisals can be modified. Self-focused reappraisal involves internal focusing in decreasing the sense of personal meaning of the situation through detachment and situation-focused reappraisal includes external focusing in reinterpreting the emotional contents as neutral (Ochsner et al., 2004). Interestingly, self-focused reappraisal allows asking why questions (e.g., why bad things happen) from a distance (i.e., from a third-person perspective), resulting in an effective way to engage in self-focus that is different from maladaptive rumination (Kross & Ayduk, 2008; Kross, Ayduk, & Mischel, 2005). As will be elaborated below, reappraisal has been found to be an effective emotion regulation strategy. Returning to our fearful student, he could reappraise the frightening situation by thinking that this presentation provides an opportunity to learn and improve his oral skills.

Response Modulation

Response modulation refers to targeting one or more of the experiential, behavioral, or physiological components of an activated emotion response for change. In this final stage of the process model, experiential, behavioral, and physiological emotional response tendencies have been launched and regulation targets a change in one of these response systems that have been sufficiently evolved.

One form of response modulation that targets the behavioral response tendency is *expressive suppression*, which involves inhibiting emotion-expressive facial behavior (Richards & Gross, 1999, 2000). A second response modulation strategy that targets the physiological emotional response tendency is *bio-feedback*. In general biofeedback refers to the broad category of consciously noticing changes in physiological activation. Some specific forms

of biofeedback were found to be effective in modulating sympathetic arousal for example through controlled breathing (Philippot, Chapelle, & Blairy, 2002) or progressive muscle relaxation (Pawlow & Jones, 2002). A third response modulation regulatory option that targets a change in experiential emotional response tendency is *acceptance* which involves allowing oneself to experience an emotion by adopting an open and curious approach, without controlling, inhibiting or elaborating on its consequences (Levitt, Brown, Orsillo, & Barlow, 2004).

Going back for the last time to our fearful student, even after the fear response was created he can still keep his face calm via suppression so that he no longer appears fearful, or try to slow down his breathing via biofeedback, or accept his fearful responses with an open approach. As will be elaborated below expressive suppression has been found to be a relatively maladaptive and effortful emotion regulation strategy, whereas biofeedback and acceptance are considered both effective emotion regulation strategies that are also applied in psychosocial interventions for various mood and anxiety disorders.

EMOTION REGULATION EFFECTIVENESS

Now that we have a basic understanding of the different regulatory options individuals have when dealing with their emotions, it is important to consider which emotion regulation strategies may be more effective than others. When we refer to *effectiveness* in this context, we mean how successful a regulatory strategy is at decreasing emotional intensity per unit effort expended. In other contexts, effectiveness could refer to other targets, including emotion magnification, or qualitative changes in emotion. Clearly, understanding the benefits and costs of different emotion regulation strategies could help us to improve well-being, and assess and treat individuals who engage in maladaptive emotion regulation strategies. Yet predicting which emotion regulation strategy would be effective is a hard task as it requires taking into account many factors. In what follows we begin with predictions that derive from the process model of emotion regulation regarding different emotion regulation strategies. We then provide a new conceptual framework that builds on the process model but elaborates on it by including other important factors.

Predicting Effectiveness Using the Process Model

As noted earlier, the process model of emotion regulation categorizes different emotion regulation strategies according to the point in which they influence the emotion generative process. According to the process model, the five different families of emotion-regulatory processes (situation selection, situation modification, attentional deployment, cognitive change, response modulation, depicted in Figure 18.1[B]) may be distinguished according to when in the emotion-generative process they have their primary impact. However, at a broader level, this model also distinguishes between *antecedent-focused strategies* that start operating early in the emotion-generative process, before response tendencies are fully activated, and *response-focused strategies* that start operating later on, after emotion response tendencies are more fully activated (see Figure 18.1[C]).

The emphasis placed on the developing emotional response signals the importance that this conception of emotion generation and emotion regulation places on the effectiveness of regulation strategies. In this context, a major feature of the process model is that antecedent-focused strategies are thought to be generally more effective than response-focused strategies. This is because antecedent-focused strategies divert the emotional trajectory quite early, before emotional response tendencies are fully developed, whereas response-focused strategies must overcome a well-developed suite of inter-related emotion processes (e.g., Gross, 2001).

Empirical Tests of the Process Model's Predictions

To date, one of the main ways that this hypothesis has been tested is by pitting *cognitive reappraisal* (i.e., construing an emotional situation in nonemotional terms), which is an antecedent-focused strategy, against *expressive suppression* (i.e., inhibiting emotion-expressive behavior), which is a response-focused strategy. The basic logic of this comparison is that reappraisal that alters the emotional trajectory early on, should be a more effective regulation strategy than suppression, which intervenes later, and thus has to combat a higher intensity emotional response.

Results from a large number of studies have demonstrated the relative costs of suppression relative to reappraisal in affective, cognitive, and social domains. Affectively, suppression relative to reappraisal does not result in a reduction of negative emotional experience (see Gross 2002 for a review), increases sympathetic nervous system arousal (Gross, 1998b; Gross & Levenson, 1993, 1997) that when chronically prolonged may be associated with various health adversities such as coronary heart disease (e.g., Diamond, 1982) and cancer (e.g., Temoshok,

1987), and increases activation in emotion-generative brain regions (Goldin, McRae, Ramel, & Gross, 2008). Cognitively, suppression but not reappraisal results in poorer memory for the emotion-eliciting situation, possibly due to the resource depletion associated with higher levels of cognitive effort (see Richards, 2004, for a review). Socially, individuals interacting with people who are engaging in suppression but not reappraisal show increased physiological responses that may reflect the diverse effects and uneasiness associated with the communication with a nonresponsive partner (Butler, Egloff, Wilhelm, Smith, Erickson, & Gross, 2003).

In more recent studies, these basic differences between antecedent-focused reappraisal and response-focused suppression have been extended to other important fields. For example, in behavioral economics, reappraisal but not suppression efficiently reduces the experience of fear and disgust, which results in lower levels of emotion-related biases on rational decision making (Heilman, Crisan, Houser, Miclea & Miu, 2010). In the emotional eating domain, which studies how emotion and emotion regulation relates to food consumption, regulating negative mood with suppression but not reappraisal leads to increased food intake of high caloric foods, which is associated with binge-eating episodes (Evers, Stok, & de Ridder, 2010). In an academic setting according to some accounts, suppression contributes to cognitive deficits that cause academic performance decrements related to stereotype threat (i.e., the experience of anxiety in a situation where a person has the potential to confirm a negative stereotype about their social group. Steele & Aronson, 1995), and reappraisal can eliminate these negative consequences (Johns, Inzlicht, & Schmader, 2008).

Expanding Our Conception of Emotion Regulation Effectiveness

These findings provide compelling evidence that reappraisal and suppression have different consequences. These findings also provide initial evidence in support of the basic effectiveness hypothesis according to which antecedent regulation strategies (e.g., reappraisal) that start operating early before emotional response tendencies are fully activated are more effective than response focused strategies (e.g., suppression) that fight off a strong emotional response. However, there seem to be additional factors that influence the effectiveness of regulation strategies. In our new account (described earlier), we elaborate and add to the original process model three important factors.

First, regulation strategies can differ in their ability to modulate an emotional response because of their underlying operation and the cognitive effort involved in achieving this modulation. The five regulatory families in the process model of emotion regulation suggest that for example attentional strategies (like distraction) operate differently from cognitive change strategies (like reappraisal). Therefore, instead of predicting differential effectiveness based on a broad categorization (antecedent versus response-focused strategies) we can put reappraisal (or any other regulation strategy) under a magnifying glass and see what are the unique characteristics and resources required in trying to change the semantic meaning or interpretation of an original emotional appraisal.

Second, the emotional intensity one is facing is likely to affect the effectiveness of some regulation strategies. Before addressing this issue it is important to clarify a confusion regarding the definition of antecedent response strategies. One may think that antecedent response strategies *must* operate before emotional response tendencies are substantially activated. However, consider the reappraisal options for our fearful student. Though our student can definitely create reappraisals before the talk and before he feels very afraid (see earlier), we can easily imagine an alternative option where the student starts to talk, becomes significantly anxious, and only then tries to reappraise his fear. This latter sort of case is in fact discussed in theoretical elaborations of the process model (see Gross, 1998; Gross & Thompson, 2007). That is, according to the process model, emotion generation is a dynamic process that involves repeated cycles through the emotion-generative process. If emotions arise as a result of these multiple iterating cycles, it should be possible to engage in emotion regulation at various points as an emotion episode unfolds over time. That is, reappraisal (or any other strategy) may be engaged either under low levels of emotional intensity, in one of the first few emotion-generative cycles, or under high levels in emotional intensity, in one of the later emotion-generative cycles. Nevertheless, the issue of whether reappraisal or any other regulation strategy would be differentially effective when applied under low or high emotional intensity remained open until recently.

The third factor that can be important for effectiveness is the goal one has in mind. That is, some emotion regulation strategies can provide fast relief and thus be effective in the short run, however, these strategies when generalized can actually have long-term costs. One example, which we will elaborate on later, is distraction. Although distraction blocks or modulates an emotional response quickly it can be maladaptive in the long run especially in situations where prolonged attentional disengagement can be problematic (see also Roth & Cohen, 1986; Suls & Fletcher, 1985). In the section below we elaborate and provide evidence for these three factors in predicting the effectiveness of regulation strategies (see also Sheppes & Gross, 2011, for a complete account).

AN EXPANDED VIEW OF EMOTION REGULATION EFFECTIVENESS

In our expanded framework, we take into account three major factors in order to predict the effectiveness of regulation strategies. The first and central factor is the underlying operating mechanism and the cognitive resources required for modulation. The second factor is the emotional intensity one is facing when regulating. Emotional intensity can range from a zero point where there is no indication of an emotion to a maximum degree, which varies for different emotion types, situations, and contexts (Reisenzein, 1994). For present purposes, intensity is best understood as the magnitude of activation in the coordinated response systems that constitute emotion, and we can evaluate the effectiveness of different regulation strategies under different emotional intensities. The third factor is whether a regulation strategy is effective in the short or long run.

Underlying Mechanisms and Cognitive Resources

The basic logic of our framework derives from a consideration of when and how emotion-generative processes are altered via emotion-regulatory processes. Our account borrows heavily from information processing theories, which argue that people have limited cognitive capacity to execute mental operations (e.g., Pashler, 1998). The constraints posed by limited capacity and cognitive resources dictates a continuous competition between different sources of information for dominance, and consequently for determining the final output or response of the cognitive system.

This competition among different sources of information occurs at two major processing stages (e.g., Hubner, Steinhauser, & Lehle, 2010; Johnston & Heinz, 1978; Pashler, 1998). At the early stage, incoming perceptual information competes to capture selective attention, and a filtering mechanism determines which stimuli gain access to the next stage, where more elaborated semantic analysis occurs. Resolution of conflict via the early filtering mechanism requires minimal resources. At the late stage, different types of representations compete at the semantic level to affect the final response. Resolution of conflict at this stage requires more mental effort because more information is gathered about the nature of the stimuli in question (Johnston & Heinz, 1978).

How might these considerations apply to emotion regulation? We propose that emotion-generative and emotion-regulatory processes can compete at both early and late processing stages. To provide concrete examples we chose two emotion regulation strategies.

The early selection strategy that was chosen was *distraction,* which involves diverting attention away from an emotional situation by loading working memory with independent neutral contents (see Ochsner & Gross, 2005; Van Dillen & Koole, 2007). In distraction, the neutral contents that are called to mind are independent from, and not in conflict with, the emotional contents (e.g., thinking about errands in the presence of a distressing situation). Therefore, distraction involves replacing existing emotional information with independent neutral information. Furthermore, incoming emotional information competes with emotion-regulatory processes at an early processing stage before stimuli are represented in working memory for further semantic evaluative processing. That is, distraction prevents the affective meaning of a stimulus from being processed by blocking it via a strong early selection filter (see Figure 18.2[A]).

The late selection strategy that was chosen was *cognitive reappraisal*, which entails attending to the emotional stimulus and reinterpreting the meaning of this stimulus in a way that alters its emotional impact (e.g., Gross, 1998a; Ochsner & Gross, 2008). In reappraisal, the basic emotional representation functions as the building block of the neutral reinterpretation. Therefore, the reinterpreted neutral representation is, by definition, associatively linked to the emotional representation (e.g., the process of reinterpreting a distressing situation requires directly relating to the distressing situation). Consequently, in reappraisal, existing and incoming emotional information is modified via a dependent neutral reinterpretation and a semantic conflict exists between the emotion-generative and emotion-regulatory representations. That is, in reappraisal, emotional information passes the early attentional stage, and is provided elaborated semantic meaning before it is modified via a weak late selection filter that requires increased cognitive resources to operate (see Figure 18.2[B]; see also Kalisch, Wiech, Herrmann, & Dolan, 2006, for a related categorization of distraction and reappraisal). The result here would be that under some circumstances that are described below, late selection

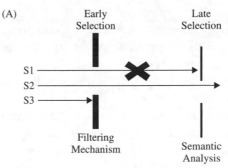

Distraction's Underlying Operation

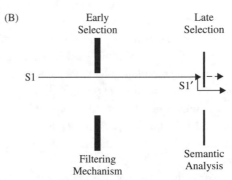

Reappraisal's Underlying Operation

The thickness of each filter reflects its strength, and is inversely related to its use of cognitive resources. Thus, the early filter is stronger and uses less resources than the late filter. The thickness of each arrow represents its relative strength, with thicker arrows inducing stronger influence on the final response, which is represented in the right side of the figure. (A) Operation of distraction. Existing emotional information (arrow S1) is being replaced (indicated by the X notation) by a strong independent neutral stream of information (thick arrow S2) that is dominating the final response. In addition, incoming emotional information is filtered out at an early selection phase (the arrow S3 is blocked by the strong early filter). (B) Operation of reappraisal. In reappraisal, existing and incoming emotional information are treated in the same way (indicated by a single S1 notation for both types of emotional information). High intensity existing and incoming emotional information (thick arrow S1) are not fully modified by a dependent neutral interpretation (thin arrow S1′) via the late selection filter. As a result, emotional information passes through the late selection filter (indicated by a dashed arrow that passes through the late selection filter and affects the response). Therefore, the dependent neutral reinterpretation of the emotional information (thin arrow S1′) only partially affects the final response and is being outweighed by the strong emotional information.

Figure 18.2 Underlying operation of distraction and reappraisal (reprinted from Sheppes and Gross, 2011)

strategies may not be always successful at blocking emotional information.

Level of Emotional Intensity

The second factor one needs to take into account is the emotional intensity one is facing when trying to regulate an emotion. The simplest possibility is that the stronger the emotional impulse, the harder it is to regulate it. However, our model predicts that the later the emotion-regulatory process occurs, the more likely it is to be affected by the level of emotional intensity. Emotion regulation strategies that operate at an early stage (*early selection strategies*) like distraction should be relatively unaffected by the level of emotional intensity because they replace existing and incoming emotional information with minimal effort. Therefore, we would expect these strategies to operate quickly and efficiently. By contrast, emotion regulation strategies that operate at a late stage (*late selection strategies*) like reappraisal should be affected by the level of emotional intensity because they require effort to modify existing and incoming emotional information. Therefore, under conditions of low emotional intensity reappraisal is likely to successfully modulate emotional responding via the weak late selection filter. However, under high levels of emotional intensity, the weak late selection filter is likely to only partially block emotional information, which results in emotional responding that passes that filter and affects the final response (see Figure 18.2[B]).

It is important to note that we do not argue that all emotional intensity levels could be successfully modified with early selection strategies. Clearly, there are levels of emotional intensity that are overwhelmingly high where distraction or any other regulatory strategy is likely to fail. In our account this is represented in emotional information that is so strong that it passes the strong early-selection filter and the weak late selection filter and ends up dominating the final response.

Short-Term Versus Long-Term Effectiveness

The third factor that one needs to consider is whether a given regulation strategy is effective in the short term versus the long term. When we described emotion regulation earlier, we referred to whether the motivation to engage in regulation is hedonic or instrumental. Some regulatory strategies may operate quickly and provide short-term relief from negative affect and thus satisfy one's hedonic goals, but they can be maladaptive and incongruent with one's long-term instrumental goals. That is, in many situations one needs to engage with an emotional event and understand it so that if encountered again that emotional situation would have less impact. For example, if our student does not engage with his fear and understand it, he is likely to experience fear every time he has to give a speech. In fact, according to a recent model of affective

adaptation, emotional adjustment occurs when a person attends to an emotional event and explains it (Wilson & Gilbert, 2008).

Accordingly, our account suggests that early selection strategies like distraction are likely to offer short-term relief at a long-term cost, because in distraction the affective meaning is blocked from processing and it does not allow elaborated processing and consequential understanding of the emotional event (Campbell-Sills & Barlow, 2007). Thus, distraction can be considered as a "bandage" regulation strategy that can stop the "bleeding" but not offer actual remedy. At the same time, our account predicts that adaptive late selection regulation strategies like reappraisal might have short-term costs but long-term benefits. Despite the increased effort associated with implementing reappraisal under high emotional intensity, reappraisal may facilitate long-term adaptation, because it involves attending an emotional event and understanding it.

Not all ways of engaging with and understanding of an emotional event are beneficial in the long run. Rumination, for example, involves a repetitive and passive engagement with emotional events does not result in better understanding and thus does not result in affective adaptation (see below and also see Watkins, 2008, for a review). Furthermore, there are some cases where engaging and understanding an emotional event, even via adaptive strategies like reappraisal, does not facilitate achievement of one's instrumental goals. There are goals that are simply unrealistic, unattainable, or that may not be as important as we think. In such cases engaging and understanding may not be the best regulatory option. Put differently, in these situations it is better to disengage from a certain goal and to move on to concentrate on something else (Watkins, in press). In these cases early selection strategies may offer better long-term benefit.

EMPIRICAL TESTS OF THE EXPANDED FRAMEWORK

Our framework makes clear predictions regarding the effectiveness of early selection distraction versus late selection reappraisal. Early selection distraction is expected to provide short-term relief from high (and low) emotional intensity stimuli with minimal effort, but it is also expected to be noneffective in the long run. By contrast, late selection reappraisal is expected to be successful at modifying low levels of emotional intensity, but to only partially modify high emotional stimuli and its operation would require substantial effort. Nevertheless, reappraisal can be adaptive in the long run.

Effects of Early-Selection Distraction

Consistent with our framework, our findings indicate that distraction is equally effective in attenuating negative affect under low and high levels of emotional intensity (Sheppes & Meiran, 2007). Support for distraction's engagement of early-selection processes was demonstrated by impaired memory for emotional details of the sadness-inducing film (Sheppes & Meiran, 2007, 2008). This result indicates that once distraction is operating, the regulatory process blocks incoming emotional information at an early encoding phase, thereby preventing elaborated processing.

Furthermore, in a recent study we provided direct support for distraction's early selection operation (Thiruchselvam, Blechert, Sheppes, Rydstrom, & Gross, 2011). Utilizing the excellent temporal resolution of electroencephalography (EEG) and event related potentials (ERPs) we showed that distraction modulated an ERP component (late positive potential; see Hajcak, MacNamara, & Olvet, 2010, for a review) that is sensitive to processing emotionally arousing information, at an early point before emotional information is provided elaborated processing. Crucially, even under high levels of emotional intensity, distraction did not result in increased recruitment of cognitive control resources, indicative of the relative minimal resource requirement in the operation of the strong early filtering mechanism in distraction (Sheppes, Catran, & Meiran, 2009; Sheppes & Meiran, 2008).

Last, our framework predicts that distraction would prove noneffective in the long run. In the ERP study mentioned above, we were able to show that emotional stimuli that were previously distracted resulted in an increased emotional responding when subjects were reexposed to these stimuli again. These findings are also consistent with a study performed by Kross and Ayduk (2008) that showed that although distraction attenuated sad mood in the short run, it did not lead to changes in the way negative experiences are evaluated and responded to in the long run.

Effects of Late-Selection Reappraisal

In sharp contrast to the consistent effects of distraction at low versus high levels of emotional intensity, reappraisal had different effects under low versus high levels of emotional intensity (Sheppes & Meiran, 2007).

Specifically, under low levels of emotional intensity, reappraisal modulated negative emotional experience relative to a control condition in which participants responded naturally. Reappraisal also eliminated semantic activation of sadness-related memory concepts, erasing the faster reaction times usually seen for sadness versus neutral words in a lexical decision task. However, under high levels of emotional intensity, reappraisal resulted in higher negative affect and in impaired ability to regulate sadness, manifested in slow and limited recall of happy autobiographical memories.

The notion that in reappraisal incoming emotional information passes the early filter and is provided elaborated semantic meaning prior to being modified is supported by finding intact memory for emotional information that was presented after participants began using reappraisal (Richards & Gross, 2000; Sheppes & Meiran, 2007, 2008). In addition, in the ERP study described above (Thiruchselvam et al., 2011), we found that reappraisal modulated the LPP at a late point long after emotional information was provided elaborated processing. Furthermore, reappraisal's increased recruitment of the effortful late selection filter when reinterpreting high-intensity levels of existing and new emotional information was demonstrated by showing that reappraisal resulted costly expenditure of self-control resources (Sheppes & Meiran, 2008).

In addition, when operating under high emotional intensity, reappraisal also resulted in increased physiological sympathetic activation (increased skin conductance and reduced finger temperature), which has previously been interpreted as reflecting the increased monitoring demand that characterizes a strong semantic conflict (Sheppes et al., 2009). Last, our framework predicts that though reappraisal results in short-term costs it can nevertheless pay off in the long run. The reason is that an emotional stimulus that was reinterpreted via reappraisal would change in a way that it would become less intense upon reexposure. In the aforementioned ERP study we showed that emotional stimuli that were previously reappraised resulted in reduced emotional processing on reexposure indicative of emotional adaptation.

Applications to Other Forms of Emotion Regulation

Our framework holds that the effectiveness of emotion regulation strategies is determined by taking onto account three major factors. This framework can be applied for other emotion regulation strategies other than distraction and reappraisal.

For example, other strategies like avoidance should have the same characteristics as distraction. Avoidance that is a situation selection strategy is considered an early selection strategy according to our framework because it does not allow any processing of emotional materials. Accordingly, avoidance is expected to be effective in providing short-term relief with minimal effort. Nevertheless, avoidance has clear long-term costs as it does not allow emotional adaptation. In fact, avoidance is considered a key player in maintaining anxiety symptoms, and psychological interventions that reduce avoidance using repeated exposure improve anxiety symptomatology.

Strategies such as rumination are expected to be noneffective because they involve allowing emotional materials to be attended to and in the late semantic meaning phase negative content is being elaborated and magnified. For that reason, rumination is considered to be maladaptive in the short as well as in the long run.

Strategies such as thought suppression and expressive suppression are also considered maladaptive for a somewhat different reason. The reason is related to the way the emotional information is blocked by the early filter, which is ineffective. Wegner (1994) has suggested that suppression involves trying *not* to think a certain thought without forming a substitute of what to actively think about (termed feature negative). Forming a feature negative of not thinking or expressing something is considered to be effortful and it may be that in this case the content that is tried to be suppressed ends up passing the early filter and affecting the final response. In that sense distraction is different from thought suppression because it allows actively thinking about something else. Indeed Wegner, Schneider, Carter, and White (1987) have shown that giving subjects a focused distraction instruction resulted in eliminating the maladaptive rebound effects associated with thought suppression. In a similar way it may be that part of the reason why expressive suppression is maladaptive and biofeedback is considered an adaptive regulatory strategy is due to suppression being a feature negative strategy (i.e., do *not* show emotional facial expressions) and biofeedback involving an active feature positive substitute (e.g., focus on your breathing).

EXTENSIONS AND FUTURE RESEARCH DIRECTIONS

In this chapter, we defined how emotion develops in a series of stages and how emotion regulation strategies can target each of these unfolding stages. We also discussed the factors that influence when emotion regulation strategies will be effective. Our starting point is the process model of emotion regulation (Gross & Thompson, 2007), which holds that antecedent regulation strategies that are initiated before the emotion generative response is sufficiently developed should be more effective than response focused strategies that try to fight off a well-established emotional response. There have been multiple demonstrations in support of this model showing that reappraisal (an antecedent response focused strategy) is more effective than expressive suppression (response-focused strategy).

Elaborating on this conception, in this chapter we argue that the effectiveness of regulation strategies depends on three factors (see Sheppes & Gross, in press, for elaboration). These factors are: the resources required by the underlying regulatory strategy; the emotional intensity of the impulse one is regulating; and whether a strategy targets a short-term or long-term goal. We show that distraction blocks emotional information at an early processing stage with a minimal effort. For these reasons, distraction provides short-term relief with minimal effort but it can prove to be maladaptive in the long run. By contrast, reappraisal is a late selection strategy that allows emotional information to be attended and provided meaning before it is being modulated by a late selection filter. For these reasons, reappraisal is effective in the context of a low-intensity emotional response, but it becomes costly and effortful in the context of a high-intensity emotional response. Nevertheless, because reappraisal allows elaborated processing it can prove useful in the long run.

It is clear that emotion regulation is a young field that is developing rapidly (see Gross, 2010). It is therefore safe to assume that new and more sophisticated models are likely to emerge as the field matures. We acknowledge that there are many other factors that are likely to be important in determining the effectiveness of regulation strategies. In the following sections, we point to several of the factors we believe are important to consider as the field develops.

Gender Differences in Emotion Regulation

On an individual difference level, certain strategies could be more effective for certain people relative to others. For example, we have not discussed gender differences: whether certain strategies are more effective for men or women (see McRae, Ochsner, Mauss, Gabrieli, & Gross, 2008). In order to appreciate gender differences in emotion regulation, one needs to also evaluate gender differences in emotion generation. Though the popular belief is that women show more emotional reactivity than men, empirical findings have been mixed. Specifically, while women consistently display more emotional facial expressions than men (Brody, 1997), differences between genders in other emotional response systems including subjective self-reports (when self-report biases are controlled), peripheral psychophysiology, and neural activation in the amygdala are not consistently found (see McRae et al., 2008, for discussion). Studies that target gender differences in emotion regulation have been relatively rare.

Related to the present focus, McRae and colleagues (2008) have conducted a neuroimaging study in order to investigate gender differences in cognitive reappraisal. This study did not find differences in effectiveness in self-report measures but interesting neural differences evinced. Specifically, relative to women, men showed less prefrontal activations and greater emotional modulation in the amygdala. These findings suggest that neurally men may show a more efficient profile of cognitive reappraisal demonstrated in less effort exerted and more emotional modulation. Nevertheless, this study also found that women relative to men showed greater activity in reward brain regions, suggesting that women may use positive emotions in the service of regulating negative emotions. Future studies are needed in order to more fully investigate gender differences in other emotion regulation strategies.

Emotion Regulation Effectiveness and Psychopathology

Another clearly important domain where individual differences in emotion regulation are crucial is in the study of psychopathology. Disrupted emotion generation and emotion regulation are a hallmark for most of the psychiatric disorders. Central features in the diagnosis of mood and anxiety disorders include disrupted emotional reactivity. Nevertheless, the nature of disrupted emotional reactivity is not always simple.

For example, in the depression literature, there are three competing accounts regarding differences in emotion generation. Specifically, some accounts argue that depressed individuals show heightened negative affect, others argue for decreased positivity and yet a third recent account suggests that severe depression involves emotional numbing with dampened negative and positive affect (see Rottenberg, 2005, for a review). Within the emotion regulation domain, individuals who rely on strategies such as rumination are at high risk to develop depressive episodes that tend to be prolonged and more severe relative to

individuals who use strategies like distraction (see Nolen-Hoeksema et al., 2008, for a review). In anxiety disorders, a common regulatory deficit involves an impaired ability to disengage from threatening information (see Cisler & Koster, 2010, for a recent review). In a similar vein, in posttraumatic stress disorder, regulatory impairments are manifested in an imbalance between intense and uncontrolled reexperiencing of the traumatic event with impaired regulatory efforts to overly avoid and dissociate (see Foa & Kozak, 1986; Nemeroff et al., 2006, for reviews). Recently, new emotion regulation have been applied to develop novel clinical interventions for anxiety and depression (Campbell-Sills & Barlow, 2007), but further research is clearly needed.

Culture and Emotion Regulation

Expanding the focus still further, emotion regulation has been important in the study of culture. In order to understand cultural differences in emotion regulation, differences in emotion generation should be accounted for. As with the gender literature, differences between cultures in emotion generation are not trivial. For example, in a recent important study, Chentsova-Dutton and Tsai (2010) have shown that cultural differences in emotion reactivity depend on the target of self-focus. Specifically, when individuals focused on individual aspects of their self (which is central in European independent cultures), European-American individuals showed greater emotional reactivity than Asian Americans. However, when individuals focused on relational self-aspects (which is central in Asian interdependent cultures) a reversed pattern emerges.

In the emotion regulation domain it was shown that expressive suppression, which is considered to be generally maladaptive in western cultures, was less disadvantageous in Eastern Asians whose culture norms involve minimizing facial expressions in public (Butler, Lee, & Gross, 2007). Recently, emotion regulation frameworks have been further extended to understand and aid conflict resolution between countries (Halperin, Sharvit, & Gross, in press). More work is clearly needed to understand how cultural processes shape emotion generation and emotion regulation processes.

REFERENCES

Bargh, J. A., Gollwitzer, P. M., Lee-Chai, A., Barndollar, K., & Trotschel, R. (2001). The automated will: Nonconscious activation and pursuit of behavioral goals. *Journal of Personality and Social Psychology, 81*(6), 1014–1027.

Barlow, D. H. (1988). *Anxiety and its disorders: The nature and treatment of anxiety and panic*. New York, NY: Guilford Press.

Bishop, S. R., Lau, M., Shapiro, S., Carlson, L., Anderson, N. D., Carmody, J.,...Devins, G. (2004). Mindfulness: A proposed operational definition. *Clinical Psychology: Science and Practice, 11*(3), 230–241.

Brody, L. R., (1997). Gender and emotion: Beyond stereotypes. *Journal of Social Issues, 53,* 369–393.

Butler, E. A., Egloff, B., Wilhelm, F. W., Smith, N. C., Erickson, E. A., & Gross, J. J. (2003). The social consequences of expressive suppression. *Emotion, 3,* 48–67.

Butler, E. A., Lee, T. L., & Gross, J. J. (2007). Emotion regulation and culture: Are the social consequences of emotion suppression culture-specific? *Emotion, 7*(1), 30–48.

Campbell-Sills, L., & Barlow, D. H. (2007). Incorporating emotion regulation into conceptualizations and treatments of anxiety and mood disorders. In J. J. Gross (Ed.), *Handbook of Emotion Regulation* (pp. 542–559). New York, NY: Guilford Press.

Carver, C. S., & Scheier, M. F. (1994). Situational coping and coping dispositions in a stressful transaction. *Journal of Personality and Social Psychology, 66,* 184–195.

Chapman, H. A., Kim, D. A., Susskind, J. M., & Anderson, A. K. (2009). In bad taste: Evidence for the oral origins of moral disgust. *Science, 323,* 1222–1226.

Cheng, C. (2001). Assessing coping flexibility in real-life and laboratory settings: A multimethod approach. *Journal of Personality and Social Psychology, 80,* 814–833.

Chentsova-Dutton, Y. E., & Tsai, J. L. (2010). Self-focused attention and emotional reactivity: the role of culture. *Journal of Personality and Social Psychology, 98,* 507–519.

Cisler, J. M., & Koster, E. H. W. (2010). Mechanisms of attentional biases towards threat in anxiety disorders: An integrative review. *Clinical Psychology Review, 30,* 203–216.

Cramer, P. (2008). Seven pillars of defense mechanism theory. *Social and Personality Psychology Compass, 2,* 1963–1981.

Damasio, A. R. (1999). *The feeling of what happens: Body and emotion in the making of consciousness*. New York, NY: Harcourt Brace.

Davidson, R. J. (1998). Affective style and affective disorders: Perspectives from affective neuroscience. *Cognition and Emotion, 12,* 307–330.

Diamond, E. L. (1982). The role of anger and hostility in essential hypertension and coronary disease. *Psychological Bulletin, 92,* 410–433.

Dunning, J. P., & Hajcak, G. (2009). See no evil: Directing visual attention within unpleasant images modulates the electrocortical response. *Psychophysiology, 46*(1), 28–33.

Ekman, P. (1992). Facial expressions of emotion: New findings, new questions. *Psychological Science, 3*(1), 34–38.

Evers, C., Stok, F. M., & de Ridder, D. T. D. (2010). Feeding your feelings: Emotion regulation strategies and emotional eating. *Personality and Social Psychology Bulletin, 36,* 792–804.

Foa, E. B., & Kozak, M. J. (1986). Emotional processing of fear: Exposure to corrective information. *Psychological Bulletin, 99,* 20–35.

Folkman, S., & Lazarus, R. S. (1985). If it changes it must be a process: Study of emotion and coping during three stages of a college examination. *Journal of Personality and Social Psychology, 48*(1), 150.

Freud, S., (1962). The neuro-psychoses of defense. In J. Strachey (Ed. and Trans.), *The standard edition of the complete works of Sigmund Freud* (Vol. 3, pp. 45–61). London, UK: Hogarth Press. (Original work published 1894)

Frijda, N. H. (1986). The current status of emotion theory. *Bulletin of the British Psychological Society, 39,* A75–A75.

Goldin, P. R., McRae, K., Ramel, W., & Gross, J. J. (2008). The neural bases of emotion regulation: Reappraisal and suppression of negative emotion. *Biological Psychiatry, 63,* 577–586.

Goldin, P., Ramel, W., & Gross, J. (2009). Mindfulness meditation training and self-referential processing in social anxiety disorder: Behavioral and neural effects. *Journal of Cognitive Psychotherapy, 23*(3), 242–257.

Gross, J. J. (1998a). The emerging field of emotion regulation: An integrative review. *Review of General Psychology, 2,* 271–299.

Gross, J. J. (1998b). Antecedent and response focused emotion regulation: divergent consequences for experience, expression and physiology. *Journal of Personality and Social Psychology, 74,* 224–237.

Gross, J. J. (1999). Emotion regulation: Past, present, future. *Cognition and Emotion, 13,* 551–573.

Gross, J. J. (2001). Emotion regulation in adulthood: Timing is everything. *Current Directions in Psychological Science, 10,* 214–219.

Gross, J. J. (2002). Emotion regulation: Affective, cognitive, and social consequences. *Psychophysiology, 39,* 281–291.

Gross, J. J. (Ed.) (2007). *Handbook of emotion regulation*. New York, NY: Guilford Press.

Gross, J. J. (2010). The future's so bright, I gotta wear shades. *Emotion Review, 2*(3), 212–216.

Gross, J. J., & Levenson, R. W. (1993). Emotional suppression: Physiology, self-report, and expressive behavior. *Journal of Personality and Social Psychology, 64,* 970–986.

Gross, J. J., & Levenson, R. W. (1997). Hiding feelings: The acute effects of inhibiting positive and negative emotions. *Journal of Abnormal Psychology, 106,* 95–103.

Gross, J. J., Sheppes, G., & Urry, H. L. (2011). Emotion generation and emotion regulation: A distinction we should make (carefully). *Cognition and Emotion, 25,* 765–781.

Gross, J. J., Richards, J. M., & John, O. P. (2006). Emotion regulation in everyday life. In D. K. Snyder, J. A. Simpson, & J. N. Hughes (Eds.), *Emotion regulation in couples and families: Pathways to dysfunction and health*. Washington, DC: American Psychological Association.

Gross, J. J., & Thompson, R. A. (2007). Emotion regulation: conceptual foundations. In J. J. Gross (Ed.), *Handbook of Emotion Regulation* (pp. 3–24). New York, NY: Guilford Press.

Hajcak, G., Dunning, J. P., & Foti, D. (2009). Motivated and controlled attention to emotion: Time-course of the late positive potential. *Clinical Neurophysiology, 120*(3), 505–510.

Hajcak, G., MacNamara, A., & Olvet, D. M. (2010). Event-related potentials, emotion, and emotion regulation: An integrative review. *Developmental Neuropsychology, 35,* 129–155.

Halperin, E., Sharvit, K., & Gross, J. J. (in press). Emotion and emotion regulation in intergroup conflict: An appraisal based framework. In D. Bar-Tal (Ed.), *Intergroup conflicts and their resolution: Social psychological perspectives*. New York, NY: Psychology Press.

Heilman, R. M., Crisan, L. G., Houser, D., Miclea, M., & Miu, A. C. (2010). Emotion regulation and decision making under risk and uncertainty. *Emotion, 10,* 257–265.

Hubner, R., Steinhauser, M., & Lehle, C. (2010). A dual-stage two-phase model of selective attention. *Psychological Review, 117,* 759–784.

Johns, M. J., Inzlicht, M., & Schmader, T. (2008). Stereotype threat and executive resource depletion: Examining the influence of emotion regulation. *Journal of Experimental Psychology: General, 137,* 691–705.

Johnston, W. A., & Heinz, S. P (1978). Flexibility and capacity demands of attention. *Journal of Experimental Psychology: General, 107,* 420–435.

Kalisch, R., Wiech, K., Herrmann, K., & Dolan, R. J. (2006). Neural correlates of self-distraction from anxiety and a process model of cognitive emotion regulation. *Journal of Cognitive Neuroscience, 18,* 1266–1276.

Kreibig, S. D. (2010). Autonomic nervous system activity in emotion: A review. *Biological Psychology, 84*(3), 394–421.

Koole, S. L., Van Dillen, L. F., & Sheppes, G. (2011). The self regulation of emotion. In K. D. Vohs & R. F. Baumesiter (Eds), *Handbook of self regulation: Research, theory, and applications* (pp. 22–40). New York, NY: Guilford Press.

Kross, E., Ayduk, O., & Mischel, W. (2005). When asking "why" does not hurt: Distinguishing rumination from reflective processing of negative emotions. *Psychological Science, 16,* 709–715.

Kross, E., & Ayduk, O. (2008). Facilitating adaptive emotional analysis: Distinguishing distanced-analysis of depressive experiences from immersed-analysis and distraction. *Personality and Social Psychology Bulletin, 34,* 924–938.

Levenson, R. W. (1999). The intrapersonal functions of emotion. *Cognition & Emotion, 13*(5), 481–504.

Levitt, J. T., Brown, T. A., Orsillo, S. M., & Barlow, D. H. (2004). The effects of acceptance versus suppression of emotion on subjective and psychophysiological response to carbon dioxide challenge in patients with panic disorder. *Behavior Therapy, 35*(4), 747–766.

Lewin, K. (1943). Defining the "field at a given time." *Psychological Review, 50,* 292–310.

Macklem, G. L. (2008). Parenting and emotion regulation. *Practitioner's guide to emotion regulation in school-aged children* (pp. 42–62). New York, NY: Springer.

Mauss, I. B., Cook, C. L., & Gross, J. J. (2007). Automatic emotion regulation during anger provocation. *Journal of Experimental Social Psychology, 43*(5), 698–711.

Mauss, I. B., Levenson, R. W., McCarter, L., Wilhelm, F. H., & Gross, J. J. (2005). The tie that binds? Coherence among emotion experience, behavior, and physiology. *Emotion, 5,* 175–190.

McCaul, K. D., & Malott, J. M. (1984). Distraction and coping with pain. *Psychological Bulletin, 95,* 516–533.

McRae, K., Hughes, B., Chopra, S., Gabrieli, J. J. D., Gross, J. J., & Ochsner, K. N. (2010). The neural correlates of cognitive reappraisal and distraction: An fMRI study of emotion regulation. *Journal of Cognitive Neuroscience, 22,* 248–262.

McRae, K., Misra, S., Prasad, A., Pereira, S., & Gross, J. J. (2010). Bottom-up and top-down emotion generation: Implications for emotion regulation. *Manuscript submitted for publication.*

McRae, K., Ochsner, K. N., Mauss, I. B., Gabrieli, J. J. D., & Gross, J. J. (2008). Gender differences in emotion regulation: An fMRI study of cognitive reappraisal. *Group Processes & Intergroup Relations, 11*(2), 143–162.

Nemeroff, C. B., Bremner, J. D., Foa, E. B., Mayberg, H. S., North, C. S., & Stein, M. B. (2006). Posttraumatic stress disorder: A state-of-the-science review. *Journal of Psychiatric Research, 40,* 1–21.

Nolen-Hoeksema, S. (1991). Responses to depression and their effects on the duration of depressive episodes. *Journal of Abnormal Psychology, 100,* 569–582.

Nolen-Hoeksema, S., Wisco, B. E., & Lyubomirsky, S. (2008). Rethinking rumination. *Perspectives on Psychological Science, 3*(5), 400.

Ochsner, K. N., & Gross, J. J. (2005). The cognitive control of emotion. *Trends in Cognitive Sciences, 9,* 242–249.

Ochsner, K. N., & Gross, J. J. (2008). Cognitive emotion regulation. *Current Directions in Psychological Science, 17*(2), 153–158.

Ochsner, K. N., Ray, R. D., Cooper, J. C., Robertson, E. R., Chopra, S., Gabrieli, J. D. E., . . . Gross, J. J. (2004). For better or for worse: neural systems supporting the cognitive down- and up-regulation of negative emotion. *NeuroImage, 23*(2), 483–499.

Pashler, H. (1998). *The psychology of attention.* Cambridge, MA: MIT Press.

Pawlow, L. A., & Jones, G. E. (2002). The impact of abbreviated progressive muscle relaxation on salivary cortisol. *Biological Psychology, 60*(1), 1–16.

Philippot, P., Chapelle, G., & Blairy, S. (2002). Respiratory feedback in the generation of emotion. *Cognition & Emotion, 16*(5), 605–627.

Reisenzein, R. (1994). Pleasure-arousal theory and the intensity of emotions. *Journal of Personality and Social Psychology, 67,* 525–539.

Richards, J. M. (2004). The cognitive consequences of concealing feelings. *Current Directions in Psychological Science, 13,* 131–134.

Richards, J. M., & Gross, J. J. (1999). Composure at any cost? The cognitive consequences of emotion suppression. *Personality and Social Psychology Bulletin, 25*(8), 1033–1044.

Richards, J. M., & Gross, J. J. (2000). Emotion regulation and memory: The cognitive costs of keeping one's cool. *Journal of Personality and Social Psychology, 79*(3), 410–424.

Roth, S., & Cohen, L. (1986). Approach, avoidance, and coping with stress. *American Psychologist, 41,* 813–819.

Rottenberg, J. (2005). Mood and emotion in major depression. *Current Directions in Psychological Science, 14,* 167–170.

Scherer, K. R., Schorr, A., & Johnstone, T. (2001). *Appraisal processes in emotion: Theory, methods, research.* New York, NY: Oxford University Press.

Sheppes, G., Catran, E., & Meiran, N. (2009). Reappraisal (but not distraction) is going to make you seat: physiological evidence for self control effort. *International Journal of Psychophysiology, 71,* 91–96.

Sheppes, G., & Gross, J. J. (2011). Is timing everything? Temporal considerations in emotion regulation. *Personality and Social Psychology Review, 15,* 319–331.

Sheppes, G., & Meiran, N. (2007). Better late than never? On the dynamics of on-line regulation of sadness using distraction and cognitive reappraisal. *Personality and Social Psychology Bulletin, 33,* 1518–1532.

Sheppes, G., & Meiran, N. (2008). Divergent cognitive costs for online forms of reappraisal and distraction. *Emotion, 8,* 870–874.

Speisman, J. C., Lazarus, R. S., Mordkoff, A., & Davison, L. (1964). Experimental reduction of stress based on ego-defense theory. *Journal of Abnormal and Social Psychology, 68,* 367–380.

Steele, C. M., & Aronson, J. (1995). Stereotype threat and the intellectual test performance of African Americans. *Journal of Personality and Social Psychology, 69*(5), 797–811.

Suls, J., & Fletcher, B. (1985). The relative efficacy of avoidant and nonavoidant coping strategies: A meta-analysis. *Health Psychology, 4,* 249–288.

Tamir, M. (2009). What do people want to feel and why? Pleasure and utility in emotion regulation. *Current Directions in Psychological Science, 18,* 101–105.

Tamir, M., & Ford, B. Q. (2009). Choosing to be afraid: Preferences for fear as a function of goal pursuit. *Emotion, 9,* 488–497.

Temoshok, L. (1987). Personality, coping style, emotion and cancer: Toward an integrative model. *Cancer Surveys, 6,* 545–567.

Thiruchselvam, R., Blechert, J., Sheppes, G., Rydstrom, A., & Gross, J. J. (2011). The temporal dynamics of emotion regulation: An EEG study of distraction and reappraisal. *Biological Psychology, 87,* 84–92.

Van Dillen, L. F., & Koole, S. L. (2007). Clearing the mind: A working memory model of distraction from negative mood. *Emotion, 7,* 715–723.

Waktins, E. (in press). Dysregulation in level of goal and action identification across psychological disorders. *Clinical Psychology Review.*

Watkins, E. R. (2008). Constructive and unconstructive repetitive thought. *Psychological Bulletin, 134*(2), 163–206.

Wegner, D. M. (1994). Ironic processes of mental control. *Psychological Review, 101*(1), 34–52.

Wegner, D. M., Schneider, D. J., Carter, S. R., & White, T. L. (1987). Paradoxical effects of thought suppression. *Journal of Personality and Social Psychology, 53*(1), 5–13.

Williams, L. E., Bargh, J. A., Nocera, C., & Gray, J. R. (2009). On the unconscious regulation of emotion: Nonconscious reappraisal goals modulate emotional reactivity. *Emotion, 9,* 847–854.

Wilson, T. D., & Gilbert, D. T. (2008). Explaining away: A model of affective adaptation. *Perspectives on Psychological Science, 3,* 370–386.

CHAPTER 19

Justice Theory and Research:
A Social Functionalist Perspective

LINDA J. SKITKA AND DANIEL C. WISNESKI

Social systems cannot function without some degree of agreement on the norms and principles that regulate relationships among individuals. One widely invoked solution to the problem of social regulation is to focus on fairness and justice, or as Hospers (1961) suggests, "getting what one deserves: what could be simpler?" (p. 433). Perhaps a more appropriate question, however, is: What could be more complex? For example, what criteria should be used to decide who deserves scarce resources? What is a just income distribution? How much of the public purse should be spent on defense, to stimulate the economy, or to aid the poor? Should taxes be fixed or progressive? When people fail to live up to cooperative social norms, should they be punished, and if so, how severely? Who should be entrusted to make these decisions and how should those chosen make decisions in ways that ensure that people will accept and abide by them, even when those decisions go against the immediate interests of those affected?

There are a variety of ways to summarize the vast psychological literature that has grown to address these and related questions in psychology. The approach taken here will be to describe five functionalist metaphors of human nature that researchers have relied on at different times to help guide theoretical explanations about how

people make judgments and choices (e.g., Tetlock, 2002). Like most other psychological theories, theories of justice often rest on implicit and sometimes explicit functionalist assumptions about human motivations and goals. In other words, theorists generally assume that people do not think, feel, and act as they do without reasons. Instead, theorists often assume that people think, feel, and act as they do because it serves some kind of end. Researchers' assumptions about the ends people are attempting to achieve can play an important role in shaping theory and research.

There are at least five functionalist metaphors that have guided justice theory and research in social psychology: people as lay or intuitive (1) economists, (2) politicians, (3) scientists, (4) prosecutors, and (5) theologians. These functionalist metaphors are similar to Lakatos' concept of "hard-core" assumptions that guide science (Lakatos, 1978), and influence what research questions are considered interesting and important, how these questions are structured, the relevant data observed or collected, and how the results of scientific investigations are interpreted. The goal of this chapter is to review (a) how these social functional metaphors have guided justice theorizing and research, (b) the major discoveries associated with of these approaches to justice research, (c) the boundary conditions of each approach, (d) how insights gleaned from one approach might fruitfully inform other programs of research, and finally, (e) a functional pluralism model of justice that theoretically integrates and unifies these different lines of inquiry.

Many thanks to Christopher Bauman, Brittany Hanson, William C. McCready, G. Scott Morgan, and Elizabeth Mullen for helpful comments on earlier versions of this manuscript.

THE INTUITIVE ECONOMIST

The intuitive economist metaphor characterizes social life as a series of negotiated exchanges, in which people rely on subjective cost-benefit analyses to guide their behavior and to understand both themselves and others. Theories guided by the intuitive economist metaphor vary in the degree to which they assume that people are motivated by rational self-interest. At one end of the continuum are models positing that people are solely motivated by their immediate and rational self-interests. At the other end are models positing that a Hobbesian war of "all against all" is curtailed by the human realization that participating in social cooperation and fair exchange maximizes individuals' interests in the long run. In this view, complete and total self-interest is bounded and constrained by people's recognition that they must engage in social cooperation.

Theories inspired by the intuitive economist metaphor focus on distributive justice, that is, "the fairness of the distribution of the conditions and goods that affect individual well-being" (Deutsch, 1985, p. 1). Examples of theories based on the intuitive economist view of human nature include various versions of equity theory including more recent versions in behavioral economics (e.g., Adams; 1963, 1965; Homans, 1958, 1961; Konow, 2003; Walster, Berscheid, & Walster, 1976), social exchange theory (e.g., Blau, 1964; Homans, 1958; Thibaut & Kelley, 1959), and theories of relative deprivation (e.g., Crosby, 1976, 1982; Folger, 1984, 1986; Stouffer, Suchman, Devinney, Star, & Williams, 1949; see also Walker & Smith, 2002).

One particularly influential program of justice research inspired primarily by the idea of humans as intuitive economists is equity theory (Adams, 1963, 1965; Homans, 1958, 1961; Walster et al., 1976). Equity theory extended a central thesis of Aristotelian ethics that fair outcomes are those that are divided into parts consistent with the merits of those participating in an exchange. Equity theorists argue that people expect that a balance should be maintained between the ratio of people's outcomes to their contributions or inputs and the outcome/contribution ratios of those with whom they interacts. In other words, equity theory posits that people perceive that they have been treated fairly when the two proportions presented in Figure 19.1 are equal.

Equity theorists and researchers are also particularly interested in the consequences of injustice, which occurs when the ratio of people's outcomes to contributions is less or more than a comparison other's. The further an outcome is from the expected reward given a relevant social

$$\frac{Outcomes_{Self}}{Inputs_{Self}} = \frac{Outcomes_{Other}}{Inputs_{Other}}$$

Figure 19.1 The equity formula: Exchanges are perceived as fair when the proportion of one's own outcomes to inputs equals the proportion of a comparison other's outcomes to inputs.

comparison, the more distressing the injustice. When people feel inequity-based distress, they engage in efforts to restore actual or psychological equity. Inequity distress can be resolved in a number of different ways, including increasing or decreasing contributions to the exchange relationship (e.g., working harder if one is overpaid, or reducing effort if one is underpaid), subjectively recalibrating impressions of one's own contributions and outcomes or those of the comparison other, or leaving the exchange relationship (Walster et al., 1976). Two core discoveries of research inspired by equity theory are that fairness and favorability are distinguishable constructs, and that social comparisons are critically important factors that affect people's perceptions of fairness, topics we review next.

Fairness Versus Favorability

Outcome fairness refers to the degree that an outcome is consistent with, or can be justified by, a standard of deservingness (e.g., outcomes are proportional to inputs) whereas outcome favorability refers to whether one receives a positive or negative result (Kulik & Ambrose, 1992; Stepina & Perrewe, 1991). From a purely self-interested point of view, receiving more pay than one's peers for similar levels of effort should be experienced as pleasurable—lots of reward for little cost or investment; what's not to love? One key insight of research guided by a view of people as intuitive economists, however, was the discovery that fairness is an important boundary condition on pure selfishness. Even though people respond more strongly to under- than over-benefit (Greenberg, 1982), they do not respond to overbenefit with pleasure, but with distress instead (e.g., Austin & Walster, 1974). For example, husbands and wives who feel either under- or overbenefited relative to their spouses report higher levels of depression and other forms of distress than those who report more equitable and balanced relationships (e.g., Shafer & Keith, 1980; Sprecher, 1986). People also experience elevated levels of cardiovascular activity (Vermunt & Steensma, 2003) and serum lipids (Richards, Hof, & Alvarenga, 2000) when treated unfairly, variables that could ultimately affect people's health outcomes (Greenberg, 2011).

Receiving more or less than is deserved leads people to attempt to restore equity by subsequently increasing or decreasing their contributions to an exchange relationship (e.g., the exchange of work for pay in an employee/employer relationship, Adams, 1963; Adams & Freedman, 1976; Adams & Jacobsen, 1964; Adams & Rosenbaum, 1962; Greenberg, 1982; Pritchard, Dunnette, & Jorgenson, 1972). People also react negatively to a mismatch between valence of contributions and outcomes (such as cheating to win a race), much as they do to an imbalance of their input/output ratios relative to other's input/output ratios. In short, it is particularly unfair for negative inputs to yield positive outcomes or vice versa (Feather, 1994, 1999, 2008).

In further support of the idea that there is something special about fairness that does not reduce to favorability, a meta-analysis of the effects of outcome fairness and outcome favorability manipulations and measures on outcome satisfaction found that outcome fairness explained 43% whereas outcome favorability explained 19% of the variance in outcome satisfaction judgments. Outcome fairness also explains significantly more variation in organizational commitment, organizational citizenship, and task satisfaction than does outcome favorability (Skitka, Winquist, & Hutchinson, 2003).

Research in behavioral economics also supports the claim that concerns about fairness constrain self-interested behaviors. For example, when people are given control of scarce and therefore valuable resources (e.g., they are asked to imagine they have the only supply of snow shovels in the context of a major storm), they do not raise the prices of the shovels. Although people clearly recognize that raising prices is personally advantageous, it is nonetheless perceived as unfair (Kahneman, Knetsch, & Thaler, 1986). Similarly, when people are given an endowment (e.g., $10) and are given the opportunity either to share or not share it with another participant (in what is called a "dictator game"), nearly all participants give a portion—typically half—to the other participant, even under conditions in which they are completely anonymous and will never meet the other participant (see Bolton, Katok, & Zwick, 1998; Henrich et al., 2004, for reviews). Likewise, third parties punish "dictators" who fail to share their endowments with recipients, and the degree of punishment corresponds to the degree of the dictator's selfishness (Fehr & Fischbacher, 2004).

In summary, outcome favorability and fairness are psychologically distinct constructs, with distinct consequences. Concerns about fairness also serve as an important constraint on unconstrained self-interest.

The Importance of Social Comparison

Another important discovery of the intuitive economist approach is the important role of social comparisons in how people make justice judgments. One of the earliest empirical examples of the importance of social comparison information in shaping people's perceptions of fairness came from studies of American soldiers during World War II. Samuel Stouffer and colleagues asked soldiers among other things, "[H]ave you gotten a square deal in the Army?" (Stouffer et al., 1949). Soldiers' responses were not determined by rank, promotion rates, or their actual likelihoods of being promoted, but were instead based most strongly on how they felt they were treated relative to those immediately around and similar to them. Although in many cases certain classes of soldiers (e.g., the military police or MPs) had fewer opportunities for promotion and other positive outcomes than others (e.g., the Air Corp), the MPs were nonetheless more satisfied and felt their treatment in the army was quite fair, in part because the MPs compared their outcomes with other MPs (many of whom were also not promoted), instead of comparing themselves with soldiers in the Air Corp (who were more frequently promoted). In short, the Stouffer studies were important because they discovered that people's perceptions of fairness are influenced not only by their rewards and punishments, but also by whether people's rewards and punishments are proportional to those of similar others.

A substantial body of subsequent work further revealed the importance of comparison others on the degree to which people recognize when they are the targets of fair or unfair treatment. Although historically discriminated against groups have little difficulty recognizing that there is group-level discrimination, they nonetheless do not tend to see themselves as being individual victims, which Crosby (1982, 1984) labeled as the "denial of personal discrimination." For example, although employed women are victims of pay discrimination in objective terms, they nonetheless express no more dissatisfaction with their pay than do men, even though they understand that women as a class are being discriminated against. When making group level social comparisons (i.e., comparing women's treatment to men's), women can recognize they are at a disadvantage. However, because women tend to compare their lots with other women, it is more difficult for them to recognize when they are the personal victims of discrimination. These results have subsequently been replicated across a wide range of different historically discriminated against groups (Crosby, 1982, 1984, 2003;

see also Operario & Fiske, 2001; Taylor, Wright, Moghaddam, & LaLonde, 1990).

In summary, people use social comparison information to judge whether they are fairly or unfairly treated. Moreover, to understand people's fairness judgments, one has to have a clear understanding of people's choice of comparison. One unfortunate side effect of the tendency to compare one's lot with similar others, however, is that it can inadvertently facilitate the persistence of group-level inequities (Crocker & Major, 1989).

Empirical and Conceptual Boundary Conditions of the Intuitive Economist

The intuitive economist and equity theory dominated justice theory and research from the mid-1950s through the late 1970s or early 1980s. A major strength of equity theory was the clarity of its core proposition that just outcomes are ordinally related to individual contributions. In a perfectly just system, those who contribute more get more. That said, considerable debate began to emerge about the precise form of the equity formula, such as whether it is best represented by an additive or ratio model (e.g., Mellers, 1986; Messick & Sentis, 1979) and how people quantify contributions and outcomes. For example, Deutsch's (1985) concern remains as much of an issue now as it was several decades ago, specifically that equity theory "assumes a common currency underlying diverse rewards and costs, which permits addition, subtraction, and division. Such a psychological currency, of course, has not yet been identified, and it is still an unsolved problem of how to add such rewards as a good dinner, a mediocre concert, and a kiss" (p. 25).

Other scholars objected to the intuitive economist as the dominant guiding metaphor for justice research on different grounds. They argued that theories based on assumptions that people are like intuitive economists are problematic because they implicitly reify capitalistic and individualistic values at the expense of other important human values and belief systems (e.g., Bakan, 1966; Sampson, 1975).

Another core challenge for equity theory was the empirical finding of robust gender differences in both how people allocate resources and what kind of allocations they perceive as fair. Women are more likely to allocate material rewards equally rather than equitably, and to rate equal allocations as more fair than equitable ones (e.g., Major & Adams, 1983; Major, Bylsma, & Cozzarelli, 1989; Major & Deaux, 1982; Watts, Messé, & Vallacher, 1982).

In a related vein, evidence also emerged that the distributive rules people use to allocate resources or judge the fairness of outcome distributions are context dependent. People at times allocate resources equally or according to need, rather than proportionally. Deutsch (1985), Lerner (1974), Leventhal (1976b), and Sampson (1975) provided similar theoretical accounts for the contingencies that predict when people are more likely to allocate resources according to equity, equality, or need rules and when perceivers are most likely to perceive allocations based on each of these principles as more fair. They predicted that in cooperative relationships in which economic productivity is the dominant goal, people should be more likely to see equity as more fair than either equality or need. When the dominant goal orientation is to facilitate solidarity and group harmony, equality should be seen as more fair than either equity or need. Finally, when fostering personal development and individual welfare, need-based distributions will be seen as most fair.

Consistent with these predictions, equitable distributions are preferred and seen as more fair than need or equality when participants are focused on productivity (e.g., Deutsch, 1975, 1985). Equal allocations are preferred over equitable ones in contexts that emphasize partnerships (Lerner, 1977), when working to help out a friend (Leung & Park, 1986), and when instructions motivate allocators to have the goal of enhancing group solidarity and harmony (Leventhal, Michaels, & Sanford, 1972; Mikula, 1974). Need emerges as a stronger distributive norm than either equity or equality in contexts that emphasize minimizing suffering (e.g., Lerner, Miller, & Holmes, 1976; Leventhal, 1976b; Schwartz, 1975), and in more intimate than distant relationships (e.g., Lamm & Schwinger, 1980; Schwinger, 1980).

Taken together, these representative findings made it increasingly clear that even though equity theory has many strengths, it nonetheless is not a complete theory of justice. Equity concerns are instead best understood as one of several concerns or distributive rules that people use when thinking about the problem of how to distribute outcomes fairly.

In summary, an intuitive economist portrait of human motivation, nearly by definition, focuses researchers and theorists on questions of distributive justice, to the neglect of considering the possibility that people weigh other considerations besides costs/benefits and material interests as important to how they decide if they have been treated fairly. Increasing concern about anomalous findings that could not be easily explained by equity or other theories guided by the intuitive economist metaphor, as well as increasing discomfort with the intuitive economist metaphor itself, led theorists and researchers to begin to look for new ideas. They began to consider the possibility that people's fairness reasoning is shaped as much or more by characteristics of procedures and interactional treatment as is it by outcome considerations. Although one can partially explain the effects of procedural fairness on people's reasoning by relying on bounded self-interest, procedural justice research began to focus more on power, decision control, and status explanations instead. In short, the intuitive economist ceded to the intuitive politician as a dominant metaphor guiding justice theory and research.

THE INTUITIVE POLITICIAN

If people are like intuitive politicians, they should be motivated to be in a position to influence others, to accumulate the symbols, status, and prestige that go along with influence and power, and to be thought well of by the social groups and individuals to whom they are accountable (Tetlock, 2002). Intuitive politicians' motivation is rooted in "the knowledge that one is under the evaluative scrutiny of important constituencies in one's life who control valuable resources and who have some legitimate right to inquire into the reasons behind one's opinions or decisions. This knowledge activates the goal of establishing or preserving a desired social identity vis-à-vis these constituencies" (p. 454).

Thinking about motivation in more political than economic terms leads to different kinds of research questions and hypotheses about why people care about fairness and what should influence their fairness reasoning. Accordingly, justice theory and research began to emphasize people's needs about control and status. This shift was first marked in the mid-1970s with the development of process control theory (e.g., Thibaut & Walker, 1975), which explained people's concern with fairness through the lens of people's desires for power and decision control. Another shift occurred in the mid-to-late 1980s when theories began to focus more on people's needs for status and standing than on needs for control (e.g., Lind & Tyler, 1988).

Decision Control: Power in the Form of Voice

One of the first theories of procedural fairness focused on the importance of decision control, primarily in the form of having an opportunity for voice in decision making. Specifically, Thibaut and Walker (1975) were interested in people's fairness perceptions of situations in which conflicts between two parties were to be decided by a disinterested authority. They reasoned that adversarial procedures that allow opportunities for affected parties to present their case would be seen as more fair than inquisitorial procedures that provide no decision control to participants.

Given the emphasis process control theory placed on getting desired outcomes, one could argue that the theory is premised more on an intuitive economist than politician guiding metaphor (e.g., Shapiro & Brett, 2005; Tyler & Blader, 2000; Van Prooijen et al., 2008). Thibaut and Walker (1975), however, argued that people are motivated more by needs for control and to ensure fairness, than with maximizing their outcomes. Consistent with this idea, the most frequent explanation that people provide for their desire to go to trial is not the desire to win or to minimize transaction costs, but is to "tell my side of the story" (Lind, Kanfer, & Earley, 1990; MacCoun, 2005; MacCoun, Lind, Hensler, Bryant & Ebener, 1988). Although there continue to be debates about whether voice effects are motivated more by control needs or utility maximization, the consensus opinion seems to be that that voice can and does serve both needs simultaneously (see Shapiro & Brett, 2005, for a review).

Research has generally validated the importance of providing voice in enhancing perceptions of both procedural fairness and outcome satisfaction (e.g., Folger, 1977; Lind et al., 1990; Lind & Tyler, 1988; Shapiro & Brett, 1993; Tyler, Rasinski, & Spodick, 1985; Van den Bos, 2005). Even autocratic procedures are perceived as more fair if they incorporate opportunities for voice (Folger, Cropanzano, Timmerman, & Howes, 1996; Sheppard, 1985). Among other things, people are more willing to accept negative outcomes when they are the result of procedures that include opportunities for voice (the "fair process effect.")[1] Evidence for the fair process effect has been found in laboratory experiments (e.g., Folger, Rosenfield, Grove, & Cockran, 1979; Greenberg, 1987, 1993; Lind et al., 1980, 1990; Van den Bos, Wilke, Lind, & Vermunt, 1997) as well as correlational field studies conducted in the courts, citizen-police encounters, public policy decision making, police officer evaluations of the fairness

---

[1] Van den Bos (2005) extended the term "fair process effect" to refer to all effects of procedural fairness, rather than Folger et al.'s (1979) more narrow definition of the fair process effect as referring to the positive effect of voice on willingness to accept non-preferred outcomes. We are retaining the Folger et al. (1979) narrower definition to maintain greater conceptual specificity.

of their assignment decisions, and more (e.g., Farmer, Beehr, & Love, 2003; Lind, Kulik, Ambrose, de Vera Park, 1993; Tyler, 1994; Tyler et al., 1985; Tyler & Caine, 1981; Tyler & Degoey, 1995; Tyler & Folger, 1980; Tyler & Huo, 2002). A meta-analysis indicated that variation in opportunities for voice explained an estimated 2% of the variance in measures of performance and 4% of the variance in turnover (variables often measured behaviorally; Skitka et al. 2003). Variables usually measured with self-reports revealed even stronger effects for voice: voice explained 9%, 12%, 8%, 27%, and 46% in the variance respectively in affective reactions to decisions, organizational citizenship, organizational commitment, decision acceptance, and task satisfaction across studies (Skitka et al., 2003).

Although voice appears to have effects on a host of variables, not all studies find support for the fair process effect and some studies find evidence of fair process effect reversals (i.e., that fair procedures lead to lower levels of satisfaction with negative outcomes, not higher levels). For example, an opportunity to voice one's views is helpful in groups in when the degree of conflict of opinions is high rather than low, because having some opportunities for voice allows participants and leaders to learn where all group participants' stand. Continued opportunities for voice, however, and repetition of competing points of view increases conflict and decreases satisfaction with both the process and the outcome it yields (Peterson, 1999). In other words, too much voice over time can be a bad thing, especially in groups with conflicting points of view.

Moreover, voice only increases perceived fairness and satisfaction when people have a direct connection to the decision being made, such as when the decision is personally relevant and important. Voice has no effect when decisions are not particularly important or personally relevant to the participant (Van den Bos & Spruijt, 2002), and when people feel they do not have anything useful to contribute to decision making (Brockner et al., 1998). Similarly, voice does not ameliorate the negative effects of having an important aspect of one's identity challenged or threatened (the "identity violation effect," Mayer, Greenbaum, Kuenzi, & Shteynberg, 2009). Finally, although fair procedures often increase people's satisfaction with unfavorable and negative outcomes, fair procedures do not lead people to judge distributively unfair (inequitable) outcomes as fair or satisfactory (e.g., Van den Bos et al., 1997, 1998).

Other research finds either no evidence of a fair process effect (e.g., Mullen & Nadler, 2008; Skitka, 2002;

Skitka, Bauman, & Lytle, 2009; Skitka & Mullen, 2002) or finds fair process effect reversals (e.g., Bauman & Skitka, 2009) when people have strong moral attachments to outcomes. Other reversals of the fair process effect emerge when people are given voice when they have been led not to expect it (Van den Bos, Vermunt, & Wilke, 1996), or are prompted to directly compare their outcomes with the procedures that yield them (Van den Bos, 2002). Negative effects for voice have been attributed to a "frustration effect" that emerges when opportunities for voice nonetheless yield unfavorable or unfair outcomes (e.g., Bauman & Skitka, 2009; Folger, 1977; Kulik & Clark, 1993; Renn, 1998), an effect that may be especially likely to emerge when outcomes are framed in terms of losses rather than gains (Cropanzano, Paddock, Rupp, Bagger, & Baldwin, 2007).

The Importance of Standing, Respect, and Status

Other theorists guided by the intuitive politician metaphor have focused less on decision control and more on the importance of fairness in the maintenance and stability of long-term relationships (e.g., Bies, 1987; cf. Bies, 2005; Bies & Moag, 1986; Lind & Tyler, 1988; Tyler & Bies, 1990, Tyler & Blader, 2003; Tyler & Lind, 1992).[2] This theoretical approach is based on the assumption that people care more about being valued by important authorities and peers than by the material outcomes of a specific encounter or exchange. Similar to theorists inspired by the intuitive economist metaphor, these theorists argue that people's long-term interests are best served by cooperating with others. However, trusting one's fate to others comes with attendant risks, including possible neglect and exploitation. Although other process dimensions matter as well (e.g., the neutrality of the procedure

---

[2]There is some controversy about whether interactional justice (defined as the fairness of one's interpersonal treatment, Bies & Moag, 1986) and procedural fairness defined in terms of dignity processes (e.g., Lind & Tyler, 1988; Tyler & Lind, 1992) represent the same or different constructs. Bies at one point concurred that these constructs were essentially the same thing (Tyler & Bies, 1990). A later meta-analytic review concluded that these variables were highly overlapping but nonetheless distinguishable constructs (Colquitt, Conlon, Wesson, Porter, & Ng, 2001), and Bies (2005) now argues that these constructs should be treated as separate facets. At this juncture, however, we see the cost of treating these constructs separately to theoretical parsimony to be greater than the gain in theoretical or empirical precision of treating them differently given how much the constructs conceptually and empirically overlap.

and trustworthiness of authorities, e.g., Leventhal, 1976a), people are theorized to be especially attuned to information that they have good status and standing with group members and authorities. Standing and status affirmation are communicated by "dignity processes" such as polite, dignified, and respectful treatment (Lind & Tyler, 1988; Tyler & Lind, 1992).

Consistent with theoretical predictions, being treated with greater dignity, respect, and propriety not only increases people's perceptions of procedural fairness, but also facilitates decision acceptance (e.g., Skarlicki & Folger, 1997; Williams, 1999). Dignity processes also affect a host of other relevant organizational variables including organizational commitment (e.g., LaVelle et al., 2009; McFarlin & Sweeney, 1992; Seigel, Post, Brockner, Fishman, & Garden, 2005), trust in supervisors (e.g., Folger & Konovsky, 1989), extra-role citizenship behavior (e.g., Blader & Tyler, 2009; LaVelle et al., 2009; Moorman, 1991; Moorman & Bryne, 2005), job satisfaction (Diekman, Sondak & Barsness, 2007; cf. McFarlin & Sweeney, 1992), successful management of work-life conflict (Seigel et al., 2005), and stress (Vermunt & Steensma, 2003, 2005).

In addition to these organizational outcomes, the relationship between fair procedural treatment and status and standing concerns has also received strong support. For example, people spontaneously mention issues about treatment and lack of respect more than they do specific outcomes when asked to recall specific instances of injustice or unfairness (Lupfer, Weeks, Doan, & Houston, 2000; Mikula, Petri, & Tanzer, 1990). People react especially negatively when they feel they have been disrespected (MacCoun, 2005; Miller, 2001; cf. Vermunt, Van der Kloot, & Van der Meer, 1993). Moreover, dignity process variables and voice have stronger effects when social identity needs are particularly strong (Brockner, Tyler, & Cooper-Schneider, 1992; Huo, Smith, Tyler, & Lind, 1996; Platow & Von Knippenberg, 2001; Smith, Thomas, & Tyler, 2006; Wenzel, 2001, 2004), participants are of low rather than high status (Chen, Brockner, & Greenberg, 2003), status concerns are primed (Van Prooijen, Van den Bos, & Wilke, 2002), people are higher in interdependent self-construal (Brockner, Chen, Mannix, Leung, & Skarlicki, 2000; Holmvall & Bobocel, 2008) or higher in the need to belong (De Cremer & Alberts, 2004), and in cultures that place a higher value on interdependence than independence (Brockner et al., 2000). People treated with greater procedural fairness also experience gains in self-esteem (e.g., cf. Brockner et al., 1998; Koper, Van Knippenberg, Bouhuijs, Vermunt, & Wilke, 1993; Shroth &

Shah, 2000; Tyler, 1999; Tyler, Degoey, & Smith, 1996; Van den Bos, Bruins, Wilke, & Dronkert, 1999), and a sense of self-other merging with relevant authorities (De Cremer, Tyler, & Den Ouden, 2005). In summary, people care about procedurally fair treatment in part because being treated with dignity and respect serves their needs to feel valued and like they have status and standing vis-à-vis authorities and the group.

Empirical and Conceptual Boundary Conditions of the Intuitive Politician

Although research inspired by the intuitive politician metaphor has generated considerable interest in both social psychology and organizational behavior studies of justice, there are nonetheless some limitations to some of the claims made by this theoretical approach as well as anomalies that are difficult to explain in terms of the motives of the intuitive politician.

For example, researchers inspired by the intuitive politician guiding metaphor often claim that procedures are more important to people's justice reasoning than are the outcomes people receive (e.g., Lind & Tyler, 1988; Tyler & Blader, 2003). These claims are sometimes interpreted to mean that theories of distributive justice are outmoded or are not particularly relevant. It is important to acknowledge that claims about the relative importance of procedures over outcomes are based on comparisons of procedures and favorable or unfavorable, but not necessarily fair or unfair, outcomes (Fortin, 2008). For example, most tests of the relative importance of procedural and outcome variables on people's perceptions of fairness do not provide participants with social comparison information that allows them to make a clear judgment of whether their outcomes are fair. It is not surprising then, that procedural fairness might appear to have a stronger influence than "outcome fairness," given that participants are making judgments in a social vacuum and without relevant information they need to make an outcome fairness judgment (i.e., social comparisons). Two of the few studies that provided participants with relevant social comparison information found results that were inconsistent with the claim that procedural fairness is more important to people's justice reasoning than distributive fairness (Van den Bos et al., 1997, 1998).

Similarly, a meta-analysis of more than 80 studies that included measures or manipulations of procedural fairness variables as well as outcome fairness or favorability revealed that (a) there is little evidence of the fair process effect when the criterion is outcome fairness rather than outcome favorability; (b) outcome fairness has stronger effects than outcome favorability, and equally or stronger effects as procedural fairness variables on a host of outcome measures; and (c) manipulations of outcome fairness and favorability have stronger effects on perceptions of procedural fairness than the converse (Skitka et al., 2003). Outcome fairness is therefore as, if not more, influential than procedural fairness.

These conclusions should not be interpreted to mean that procedural fairness is irrelevant to how people think about fairness. One of the most important tests of any complete theory of justice is a demonstration of the relative power of justice considerations—procedural or distributive—relative to other motives. Discovering that procedural fairness concerns do not reduce to material self-interest is important validation of the role that procedural fairness concerns play in social life. Discovering the importance of procedures on how people think about fairness does not, however, persuasively diminish the importance people also attach to concerns about distributive justice (Greenberg, 1990).

Distributive justice theorists and researchers took considerable pains to distinguish between fair and favorable outcomes and to prove that people's outcome fairness judgments were based on something unique to fairness, rather than based on violated expectations (e.g., Austin & Walster, 1974; Fisk & Young, 1985). Procedural justice researchers, however, have not made similar efforts to establish the discriminant validity of judgments of procedural fairness. The few studies that have tested expectations in the context of procedural fairness research have found reversals of the fair process effect when providing voice violated participants' preexisting expectations (i.e., instead of voice leading to increased perceptions of procedural fairness and decision acceptance, it led to decreased perceptions of procedural fairness and decision acceptance; Kanfer et al., 1987; Van den Bos et al., 1996). More research is needed that tests whether procedural fairness effects are really about fairness rather than favorability or unfavorability, or expected versus unexpected interpersonal treatment.

Given the emphasis placed on social comparison information and deservingness in the intuitive economist approach to justice research, the amount of theoretical and empirical attention to social comparisons when people judge the fairness of procedures has also been surprisingly thin. The limited available evidence suggests that people do weigh whether people deserve to be treated with dignity and respect (Heuer, Blumenthal, Douglas, & Weinblatt, 1999; Sunshine & Heuer, 2002). Moreover,

people make ample use of social comparison information about how others are treated when making judgments of procedural fairness as well (Grienberger, Rutte, & Van Knippenberg, 1997; Lytle, 2010; Van den Bos et al., 1996), results that confirm the central (but neglected) role that consistency plays in people's judgments of procedural fairness (e.g., Crosby & Franco, 2003; Leventhal, 1976b; Lytle, 2010).

Finally, some argue that this field of inquiry promotes the positive social benefits of procedural fairness as a means of ensuring social cooperation and compliance without considering the possible ways that creating a false consciousness of fairness without substance amounts to appeasing the masses without any concern whatsoever for treating them with real fairness and justice (Fortin & Fellenz, 2008; MacCoun, 2005). The perils of encouraging blind obedience and compliance in the context of already overly socialized tendencies to respect authority are well known (e.g., Milgram, 1974). As MacCoun (2005) noted,

> The neglect of the dark side of procedural justice is unfortunate. As a psychological dynamic, procedural fairness is clearly a double-edged sword. Our poignant desire for voice and dignity makes it possible to promote cooperation and tolerance in a diverse society facing uncertainty, scarcity, and inevitable conflicts of interest. But these same needs leave us potentially vulnerable to manipulation and exploitation by those who control resources and the processes for distributing them. (p. 193)

More research is clearly needed to explore the potential "dark side" of procedural justice, and researchers should be sensitive to not only the positive implications of procedural fairness, but the negative implications as well.

In summary, the intuitive politician has been an incredibly generative metaphor that has dominated most justice theory and research for the past 20 to 30 years. Although a number of areas need further research inquiry, the shift from the intuitive economist to the intuitive politician nonetheless has led to a number of important discoveries. People do care about status and socioemotional aspects of social exchange and not just material gain. Some procedural justice theorists, however, struggled to find a way to understand mounting experimental evidence that both outcomes and procedures seem to matter to people's fairness reasoning and that their relative effects depend on the availability or salience of different kinds of information. Models based on the intuitive scientist guiding metaphor were therefore invoked to provide potentially a more natural account for information processing effects than do theories based on the intuitive economist or politician.

THE INTUITIVE SCIENTIST

Theories inspired by the intuitive scientist focus on the cognitive processes that give rise to different kinds of judgments, and in particular to the cognitive shortcuts people tend to take when processing information. Because people have limited capacity to process information, they depend on automatic processes and various mental shortcuts to more efficiently and easily navigate their way through the buzz and confusion of everyday life (Fiske & Taylor, 1984). The intuitive scientist approach to justice reasoning suggests that people make fairness judgments relying on the same kind of cognitive heuristics and shortcuts they use to make other kinds of judgments. The most influential justice theory that takes the intuitive scientist perspective—fairness heuristic theory, and in its most recent incarnation, uncertainty management theory—is reviewed next.

Fairness Heuristic and Uncertainty Management Theories

Similar to many other theories, fairness heuristic theory starts with a motivational premise, in this case, that people are especially motivated to manage uncertainty about the potential for being exploited in their social exchange relationships (Lind, 2001; Lind et al., 1993; Van den Bos & Lind, 2002). Information about procedures and outcomes serve the heuristic function of managing people's uncertainty about others' motives and are therefore considered relatively interchangeable. Thus, in the absence of relevant information to judge the fairness of outcomes, people rely on procedural information. In the absence of information about procedural fairness or dignity processes, people rely on outcome information. Being treated either distributively or procedurally fairly serves as a heuristic proxy for trust. Neither source of information, however, is predicted by fairness heuristic theory to be as important as having direct knowledge that authorities or others can be trusted.

Uncertainty management theory primarily differs from fairness heuristic theory in the emphasis placed on trust as driving people's uncertainty management concerns. Uncertainty management theory posits a broader existential role for uncertainty management, regardless of whether uncertainty is specific to trust in relevant authorities (Lind & Van den Bos, 2002; Van den Bos, 2001; Van den Bos & Lind, 2002). Fair treatment is theorized in uncertainty management theory as a remedy for all kinds of uncertainty (e.g., about the self, about the future), and not just uncertainty specific to trust in authorities.

Consistent with fairness heuristic and uncertainty management theories, the effects of dignity process variables and voice are weaker when uncertainty is not salient (Van den Bos, 2001), when people have more rather than less trust in an authority (Van den Bos et al., 1998; Van Dijke & Verboon, 2010; Yang, Mossholder, & Peng, 2009), and when social comparison information about others' outcomes is available (Van den Bos et al., 1997; see also Blader, 2007; De Cremer, Brebels, & Sedikides, 2008; Jones & Martens, 2008; Van den Bos & Miedema, 2000, for other forms of support).

In summary, the intuitive scientist guiding metaphor has played a recent role in shaping theory and research on the psychology of justice and fairness, but the intuitive scientist approach to justice research has not received as much empirical attention as the economic and politician models. The long-term viability of the intuitive scientist as a guiding metaphor in justice research has yet to be fully tested, and remains an area for further theoretical development and research.

THE INTUITIVE PROSECUTOR

In addition to studying questions of distributive and procedural justice, some justice researchers have focused their attention on questions of retributive justice—that is, the psychological processes that explain how justice relates to punishing people who violate social, legal, or moral norms. Retributive justice researchers found it more useful to draw on the notion that people approach transgressions in ways that resemble intuitive prosecutors than as intuitive economists, politicians, scientists, or theologians. The core functionalist premise of the intuitive prosecutor is that people are motivated to vigorously defend their commitment to social systems, norms, and rules that they see as integral to their view of the way the world either works, or the way they believe it should work. Violations of these rules of appropriate conduct cause harm to both individual victims as well as the broader social fabric (Tetlock, 2002). Among the core questions of interest in the study of retributive justice has been whether people as intuitive prosecutors are primarily concerned with (and therefore motivated by) the desire to deter future transgressions, compensate victims, or punish perpetrators.

Even though people often say they are motivated by other concerns, numerous studies find that people show a clear preference for punishment based in retribution and just deserts over deterrence (e.g., Carlsmith, 2006; Carlsmith & Darley, 2008; Carlsmith, Darley, & Robinson,

2002; Darley, Carlsmith, & Robinson, 2000; Van Prooijen, 2010). Punitive reactions are also driven by a sense of moral outrage. In other words, people are not rationally and dispassionately applying principles of rewards and punishments as much as they are emotionally striking out at those who disrupt the social order and harm others (Darley, 2009; Darley & Pittman, 2003). Punitive responses are especially likely when (a) offences are intentional rather than unintentional (Darley & Pittman, 2003), (b) people are high in chronic or situationally primed concerns about social threat (Tetlock et al., 2007), (c) the perpetrator has low rather than high moral status (Carlsmith & Sood, 2009), (d) people have been recently exposed to examples of unpunished transgressions (Goldberg, Lerner, & Tetlock, 1999; Lerner, Goldberg, & Tetlock; 1998; Tetlock et al., 2007), (e) people are socially aware and connected to others (e.g., when high in interdependent self-construal, Gollwitzer & Bucklein, 2007), and (f) among those for whom the intuitive prosecutor mind-set is more chronically activated (e.g., political conservatives; Carroll, Perkowitz, Lurigio, & Weaver, 1987; Skitka & Tetlock, 1992, 1993).

One reason why people are motivated to respond punitively to transgressors may be that they expect hedonic benefit or catharsis from vengeance. Exacting revenge, however, is not sufficient to derive psychological benefit from punishing transgressors: People need to believe that transgressors understand their punishment is a direct consequence of a specific transgression (Gollwitzer & Denzler, 2009; Gollwitzer, Meder, & Schmitt, 2011). There are also ironic effects for revenge-seeking: people who seek vengeance end up ruminating more about the transgression, and therefore experience more negative affect than those without an opportunity for vengeance (Carlsmith, Wilson, & Gilbert, 2008).

Theories of retributive justice tend to include explicit propositions about factors that make it more or less likely for people to adopt this particular mind-set: In other words, there is considerable evidence that the intuitive prosecutor mind-set has several "on" and "off" buttons (Alicke, 2000). For example, some researchers have recently begun to explore the degree people can be prompted to care about restorative justice and rehabilitation instead of retribution (e.g., Okimoto & Wenzel, 2009; Wenzel, Okimoto, Feather, & Platow, 2008). These researchers find that (a) when transgressors are seen as questioning shared community values, the goal of punishment can shift to restoring justice by reaffirming those values instead of degrading the offender (Wenzel & Thielman, 2006) and (b) dispute resolution processes that

focus on shared identity and bilateral communication between victim and offender—in addition to appropriate punishment—are perceived by people to be fairer than dispute resolution processes that focus on retribution and punishment alone (Okimoto, Wenzel, & Feather, 2009).

In summary, although the majority of justice researchers have tended to focus on the allocation of positive material and socioemotional resources or goods, there has been increasing attention to the psychology of retributive justice and the allocation of punishment. Punishment, however, is only one negatively valenced resource. It would be interesting for future justice research to explore how people think about the fair distribution of other negative resources. For example, we know a great deal about how people think about the benefits of social cooperation, but little about how the costs, should be distributed (see, however, Sondak, Neale, & Pinkley, 1995). What fairness considerations loom as most important, for example, when deciding where to locate landfills, nuclear waste dumps, or halfway homes for sexual offenders?

We turn next to a review of justice theory and research motivated by the idea that people are like intuitive theologians, including justice world theory and recent theories that posit a contingency role for moral concerns as shaping people's concerns about fairness. These theoretical approaches share some commonalities with theory and research inspired by the intuitive prosecutor, including positing important roles for moral emotions and a focus on explaining how people react to violations of justice norms and beliefs.

THE INTUITIVE THEOLOGIAN

Research guided by the intuitive theologian metaphor posits that people are motivated by concerns about morality and immorality, and questions of fundamental right and wrong. According to this view, conceptions of morality are not arbitrary social constructions, but are instead experienced as fundamental truths about the social world. People's moral values therefore "provide reassuringly absolute answers to unsettling questions about the meaning of existence and the ends to which we should devote our lives" (Tetlock, 2002, p. 458).

According to the intuitive theologian view, the particular challenges of group living (e.g., aggression, competition, cooperation, deception, and the undermining role of self-interest) led to adaptation through natural selection of human capacities to care about morality and justice independent of self-interest, power, status, or uncertainty management needs. People who learned to manage the balance between competition and cooperation, develop conceptions of moral right and wrong, and punish those who broke contracts or other justice arrangements, had a clear adaptive advantage over those who failed to develop traits that allowed them to manage these challenges (see Robinson, Kurzban, & Jones, 2007, for a detailed review). In short, a working definition of justice and what it means to people could reasonably start with the adaptive functions of morality, righteousness, virtues, and ethics rather than with self-interest, status, or other nonmoral motivations.

A variety of current theories of justice postulate that people's concerns with fairness reflect moral concerns, rather than serving as a proxy for people's nonmoral needs and goals. These perspectives range from those positing that moral concerns lay at the core of when and why people care about justice to more contingent approaches that suggest people's justice reasoning is sometimes motivated by moral concerns, even if at other times other concerns (e.g., economic, relational) might play roles as well. We review these approaches in turn next.

Just World Theory and the Justice Motive

Just world theory is premised on the notion that one of the fundamental dilemmas facing children during development is whether to seek immediate satisfaction for their needs versus delaying gratification (Lerner, 1975, 1980). Developing children ultimately design what Lerner called the personal contract, that is, a sense of entitlement. Children learn that if they give up and are willing to do certain things, desired outcomes come to them in the end. The concern with getting what one deserves develops eventually into the concern for fairness and the belief that others should get what they deserve as well (otherwise referred to as the justice motive, Lerner, 1987). People become so invested in the notion that what happens to people is a consequence of something about them, that any information or instance that contradicts this belief, such as being the random victim of a violent crime, causes considerable distress. This distress in turn leads people to generate justifications for why victims must have deserved their plight.

Consistent with just world theory predictions, willingness to delay gratification and to commit to long-term goals is correlated with increased concerns about deservingness, as well as individual differences in a belief in a just world (Braband & Lerner, 1974; Hafer, 2000a; Hafer, Bégue, Choma, & Dempsey, 2005; Lerner, 1977,

1980; Lerner et al., 1976; Long & Lerner, 1974). A now rather vast amount of research has also tested the prediction that having a stronger justice motive is associated with greater victim blaming (see Furnham, 2003; Hafer & Bégue, 2005, for recent reviews). When there is little hope of fully addressing a victim's plight, people cope by reinterpreting and rationalizing the harm to victims by believing it was somehow deserved (Reichle & Schmitt, 2002), engaging in denial, avoidance and psychological distancing (Drout & Gaertner, 1994; Hafer, 2000b), focusing more on the victimization than the cause of the victimization (Correia & Vala, 2003), or even by distorting their memory of what happened to victims (Callan, Kay, Davidenko, & Ellard, 2009).

A belief in a just world may serve as a buffer against a wide array of threats beyond fears of exploitation in social exchange or reactions to innocent victims. Because people higher in a belief in a just world work actively to compensate for or justify their fate (e.g., by self-blaming or downplaying the injustice; see Bulman & Wortman, 1977; Dalbert, 1998), belief in a just world can provide an effective coping strategy in the face of misfortune. For example, flood victims who were higher in just-world belief had less depression, anxiety, insecurity, hostility, and paranoid thinking than those with weaker beliefs in a just world (e.g., Otto, Boos, Dalbert, Schops, & Hoyer, 2006; see also Bulman & Wortman, 1977; Dalbert, 1998, 2001, 2002, for examples in other contexts of misfortune, such as being the victim of a severe accident).

Just world theory has been very generative and has received considerable empirical support. For the most part, however, just world theory does not provide predictions or guidance that help resolve some of the core debates in the justice literature, such as when and why dignity process concerns might matter to people's fairness reasoning, and when outcome considerations might matter more; it simply posits that the justice motive is at the root of people's concerns with justice, whether those concerns are related to procedures or outcomes.

One could argue that even Lerner's personal contract is still overly focused on the notion that people are primarily concerned with getting what they want rather than concerns specifically with fairness, even if it involves deferring gratification and incorporating beliefs about deservingness. According to other moral theorists, however, if people are like intuitive theologians, then people's concern about fairness—at least at times—is based on feelings of obligation, duty, and morality, not various personal wants or needs (deferred or otherwise). We review these theoretical perspectives next.

"Deonance Theory"

Folger and colleagues use the term *deonance theory* as a description for the meta-theoretical position that one can better understand why people care about justice, and therefore behave justly, more from the view of the intuitive theologian than from either an intuitive economist, politician, or scientist perspective (Cropanzano & Stein, 2009; Folger, 2001; Folger, 2011). Although presented as a theory, we prefer to consider it a meta-theory, or an alternative way of representing the intuitive theologian as a guiding metaphor, largely because "deonance theory" is not a formal theory with testable if-then propositions. Consistent with this interpretation of deonance theory, research cited as supporting or testing deonance theory to date has relied upon indirect evidence rather on theoretically derived hypothesis testing.

For example, deonance theorists cite evidence against the hegemony of self-interest or relational motives that indicate people are willing to sacrifice some profit to punish others who intentionally violate fairness norms (Kahneman et al., 1986; Turillo, Folger, Lavelle, Umphress, & Gee, 2002) as support for the theory. These results are clearly inconsistent with a theory arguing that rational self-interest governs people's behavior, because the majority of the participants in these studies sacrifice maximizing their own gain to punish unfair behavior. Moreover, because participants do not know each other and never meet face-to-face, it is difficult to attribute these results to something about people's needs to be accepted or valued by the group. The results do make sense, however, if justice is a morally motivated response that can trump people's desires to maximize their material or socio-emotional utilities, even if these studies test deonance theory indirectly and negatively (the results are inconsistent with nondeonance perspectives) rather than directly and positively (testing specific predictions, and finding positive evidence in support of deonance theory predictions). Taken together, deonance theorists' critical analysis of previous perspectives on justice and focus on the alternative guiding metaphor of the intuitive theologian has played a useful role in motivating more research that takes ethics and morality seriously as possible motivational underpinnings of people's concern with justice.

Most justice theorists appear to be wedded to one or another guiding assumption about human nature, and therefore what explains why people care and how they reason about fairness. There have, however, been a number of recent attempts to provide some integration across different guiding metaphors to generate more complex and contingent explanations for how people think about fairness, and that incorporate a role for morality as one motivational basis for these concerns. We turn next to a brief review of two theories that have taken this approach: the accessible identity and contingency models of justice.

Contingency Models of Morality

The contingency model of justice (an updated version of the accessible identity model, or AIM, Skitka, 2003) argues that people will sometimes be concerned about maximizing material gain; other times they will be more concerned about their social status and standing in the group; yet other times, they will be motivated to live up to or defend personal conceptions of the moral good (Skitka, Aramovich, Lytle, & Sargis, 2009). This constitutes a contingency model about when the concerns of the intuitive theologian are likely to dominate people's justice reasoning. How people define what is fair or unfair and the factors that weigh most heavily in their fairness judgments should vary as a function of which perceptual frame of reference they currently see as most relevant to their current situation. The AIM version of this theory organized contingency predictions around different aspects of the self—that is, people's material, social, and personal/moral identities (Skitka, 2003). The contingency version leaves open whether the self is integral to when people care about fairness, making the role of the self a testable proposition rather than a guiding assumption of the model. The contingency model posits that the economist, politician, and theologian can serve as functional schemas or mind-sets as a function of which point of view is either situationally activated or more chronically accessible to perceivers at any given time (Skitka et al., 2009).

Two predictions of the contingency model (Skitka et al., 2008) will be reviewed here: The authority independence and litmus test hypotheses. The authority independence hypothesis is that when people's moral convictions are at stake, they are more likely to believe that duties and rights follow from the greater moral purposes underlying rules, procedures, and authority dictates, than from the rules, procedures or authorities themselves (Skitka et al., 2008; Skitka & Mullen, 2008; see also Kohlberg, 1976). Moral beliefs are not by definition anti-establishment or anti-authority; they just are not dependent on establishment, convention, rules, or authorities. Instead, when people take a moral perspective, they focus more on their ideals, and the way they believe things "ought" or "should" be done, than on a duty to comply with authorities.

The litmus test hypothesis is that people's personal moral beliefs affect not only their perceptions of decisions and willingness to comply with authorities, but also their perceptions of authorities' legitimacy. When people have moral certainty about what outcome authorities and institutions should deliver, they do not need to rely on standing perceptions of legitimacy as proxy information to judge whether the system works—in these cases, they can simply evaluate whether authorities get it "right." "Right" decisions indicate that authorities are appropriate and work as they should. "Wrong" answers signal that the system is somehow broken and is not working as it should. In short, the litmus test hypothesis predicts that people use their sense of morality as a benchmark to assess not only outcome fairness, but also procedural fairness and authorities' legitimacy.

Consistent with these predictions, voice and dignity process variables have weak or no effects on people's perceptions of outcome fairness, decision acceptance, and other related variables when people have a moral investment in outcomes (e.g., Bauman & Skitka, 2009; Skitka, 2002, 2009; Skitka & Houston, 2001; Skitka & Mullen, 2002). Instead, people primarily care that the morally correct outcome is achieved. Procedural fairness concerns play a more significant role in people's justice reasoning only when people do not have a vested moral interest in outcomes (Bauman & Skitka, 2009; Skitka & Houston, 2001). In support of the litmus test hypothesis, people use whether authorities get it "right" to inform their judgments about both procedural fairness (Skitka, 2002; Skitka & Mullen, 2008) and authorities' legitimacy (Skitka et al., 2009).

In summary, even though contingency models of justice still posit roles for the intuitive economist and politician, these models also (a) rely on the intuitive theologian as a guiding metaphor, and (b) do not reduce all concerns about justice to one or another kind of instrumentality or utility maximization. Given most intuitive theologian approaches to justice theory and research is relatively new, however, they have yet to receive the same degree of empirical and theoretical scrutiny as the other guiding metaphors. With additional research, the boundary conditions and limitations of theories based on the intuitive theologian metaphor will be identified, much as we have discovered the limitations and boundary conditions on people as intuitive economists, politicians, scientists, and prosecutors. That said, we concur with Greenberg (2011) who concluded that "any approach to justice that ignores the role of morality is surely incomplete."

PUTTING IT TOGETHER: A FUNCTIONAL PLURALISM MODEL OF JUSTICE

Although there have been a number of attempts to integrate the theoretical and empirical insights across different social functionalist approaches for the psychology of justice (e.g., Cropanzano et al., 2001; Lind, 2001; Lind & Van den Bos, 2002; McFarlin & Sweeney, 1992; Schroeder, Steel, Woodrell, & Bembenek, 2003; Skitka, 2003; Skitka et al. 2009; Törnblom & Vermunt, 2007; Van den Bos & Lind, 2002), for the most part researchers adopt a single approach as "the" way to study the psychology of fairness.

We argue that there is sufficient evidence in support of each approach to justice that they each need to be taken seriously when explaining when, why, and how people care about justice. Theoretical integration is the only way to move the field forward. Rather than remain wedded to a monistic account about how concerns about fairness shape people's thoughts, feelings, and behavior, we therefore build on the contingency models discussed earlier and propose a functional pluralism model of justice instead—a model that incorporates the predictions of all five social functionalist guiding metaphors reviewed here.

The adaptive challenges people confront in their everyday lives require the ability to move fluidly between different goal states or motives. For example, people have to resolve the problems of (a) competing for scarce resources, such as wages or jobs (the economist), (b) how to get along with others and secure their standing in important groups (the politician), (c) making useful inferences about others' goals, behavior, and trustworthiness (the scientist), (d) defending themselves and others from harm (the prosecutor), and (e) building a meaningful sense of existence (the theologian). In short, the functional pluralism model's position is that people are economists, politicians, scientists, prosecutors, *and* theologians, not just one or another of these options. Which homunculus will be steering the ship at any given time (so to speak), depends on the current goal orientation of the actor and the salience of various situational cues that could activate one or another of these mind-sets (e.g., Higgins, 1996; Mischel & Shoda, 1995).

Based on previous theory and research, we already have some idea of the conditions that will predict when one or another mind-set is most likely to dominate fairness reasoning. For example, people are most likely to take a material or economic perspective when (a) their basic material needs and goals are not being met or are under threat (e.g., Abramson & Inglehart, 1995; Cropanzano et al., 2001; Maslow, 1993), (b) material losses or gains are explicitly primed, (c) the relational context is defined primarily in market pricing terms (e.g., when shopping, negotiating the price of car, paying rents, tithing, e.g., Fiske, 1991), and (c) the goal of the social system is to maximize productivity (Deutsch, 1985; Lerner, 1977; Leung & Park, 1986).

Existing research also provides some clues about when people are more likely to take the intuitive politician perspective when thinking about fairness. Specifically, people should be more like intuitive politicians in their fairness reasoning when: (a) their material needs are at least minimally satisfied (e.g., Abramson & Inglehart, 1995; Maslow, 1993), (b) their needs to belong, for status, and inclusion, are not being met or are under threat (e.g., Cropanzano et al., 2001; De Cremer & Blader, 2006; Maslow, 1993), (c) the potential for significant relational losses or gains are made especially salient, (d) the dominant goal of the social system is to maximize group harmony or solidarity (e.g., Deutsch, 1985), (e) people's interdependency concerns are primed (e.g., Holmvall & Bobocel, 2008), and (f) accountability demands are high (Tetlock, 2002).

Although further research is still needed to test the full implications of how the intuitive scientist metaphor guides justice reasoning, the current literature suggests that people should be motivated to engage in causal analysis of their situation and whether it is fair or unfair when they are confronted with negative and unexpected events (e.g., Taylor, 1982; Weiner, 1985). According to uncertainty management and fairness heuristic theory, people should also be motivated by the intuitive scientist when they are feeling especially (a) uncertain, and (b) information about the trustworthiness of others is not directly available. These hypotheses are also consistent with the prediction that people should be more likely to behave more like intuitive scientists than intuitive economists, politicians, prosecutors, or theologians when they are dealing with strangers than with familiar others, whose trustworthiness is known.

There also are likely to be circumstances when people will adopt the intuitive prosecutor mind-set. Specifically, people are more likely to be guided by the prosecutor when they perceive a norm violation to be: (a) offensive to shared moral values, (b) widespread and routinely unpunished (Goldberg et al., 1999; Lerner et al., 1998; Tetlock et al., 2007), (c) intentional (Darley & Pittman, 2003), (d) threatening to the social order or society at large (Gollwitzer & Bucklein, 2007), or (e) transgressors exhibit a weak understanding of the connections between the punishment and perpetrators' specific offense (Gollwitzer

et al., 2011; Gollwitzer & Denzler, 2009), or lack of sincere evidence of reform (Skitka & Tetlock, 1993).

Existing theory and research also provides suggestions about when people will be most likely to take on the mind-set of the theologian. Specifically, people should be more likely to use a moral frame of reference for evaluating fairness when (a) their material and social needs are minimally satisfied (Maslow, 1993), (b) people have a moral stake in the outcomes being decided (e.g., whether abortion is or is not legal; e.g., Skitka, 2002; Skitka et al., 2009; Skitka & Mullen, 2002); (c) moral emotions are aroused, such as moral outrage, guilt or shame (Haidt, 2003; Mullen & Skitka, 2006), (d) there is a real or perceived threat to people's conceptions of moral order (core beliefs about right and wrong) and not just to normative conventions (e.g., arbitrary rules and laws) (e.g., Skitka, 2002; Tetlock, 2002), (e) people's sense of personal moral authenticity is questioned or undermined (e.g., Zhong & Liljenquist, 2006), or (f) people are reminded of their mortality (e.g., Jonas, Schimel, Greenberg, & Pyszczynski, 2002).

Implications and Directions for Future Research

Hastorf and Cantril (1954) conducted a study that is often cited as providing the case for the value of social psychology. Specifically, they studied Dartmouth and Princeton students' perceptions of an actual football game played in 1951 between the Dartmouth Indians and the Princeton Tigers. It was a particularly rough game with many penalties. The Princeton quarterback had to leave the game with a broken nose and a concussion in the second quarter of the game; the Dartmouth quarterback's leg was broken in a backfield tackle in the third quarter. One week after the game, students who saw the game, as well as a sample of students who viewed a film of it were queried. Despite seeing the same game, Princeton and Dartmouth participants viewed it very differently. The Princeton students "saw" the Dartmouth team make over twice as many rule infractions as the Dartmouth students, whereas the Dartmouth students "saw" a reverse pattern of infractions. Sixty-nine percent of Princeton students described the game as "rough and dirty," whereas a majority of Dartmouth students felt that even though the Dartmouth team played rough, the play was generally "clean" and "fair." These results indicated that people actively constructed different realities as a function of their perspective; as Hastorf and Cantril (1954) put it: "there is no such 'thing' as a 'game' existing 'out there' in its own right which people merely 'observe.' The game 'exists' for a person and is experienced by him only insofar as certain happenings have significances in terms of his purpose" (p. 133).

Hastorf and Cantril's (1954) findings and other similar research results led psychologists and other scholars to the realization that people do not react to each other's actions in a stimulus-response pattern without the mediating influence of interpretation. People's interpretations of their social worlds and human interactions are mediated through their *understanding* of what social interactions mean (Blumer, 1969). Similarly, a guiding premise of the functional pluralism theory of justice is that there is not an objective reality or set of circumstances that are fair or unfair. People do not always interpret social interactions like football games, performance evaluations, negotiations of the price of a car or home, social policies, or their intimate relationships from similar perspectives. Instead, people actively construct their perceptions of fairness and unfairness, and these active constructions are influenced by different fairness norms and the various goals, needs, expectations, and histories people carry with them into their social interactions.

In addition to regrounding justice theory in classic conceptions of symbolic interactionism, a functional pluralism theory of justice can account for the mundane reality that people often disagree about whether a given situation was handled fairly or unfairly. Until people arrive at some consensus about the nature of the judgment to be made and the goals they wish to achieve in a given context, it is not surprising that they approach the same situation with very different conceptions of fairness. The notion that people are likely to approach the same situation from different perspectives and that these perspectives shape the fairness norms or considerations they apply to it, suggests that future research should extend beyond the study of how individuals in isolation make fairness judgments. Future research should begin to explore how people socially negotiate and arrive at consensus about how to make decisions fairly and whether fairness has been achieved in specific circumstances.

In a related vein, a truism of early theories of distributive justice is that people do not make justice judgments in social vacuums (e.g., Homans, 1958, 1961; Stouffer et al., 1949). Instead, justice judgments are inherently *social* judgments and require social comparison information. The social aspect of deciding whether something is fair or unfair may go beyond relying on available comparisons to see if others received outcomes proportional to inputs, similar treatment, or opportunities for voice. Instead, people's natural fairness reasoning may rely more on active gathering of social information. People are likely to attempt to seek social consensus about how others interpret a given situation and whether they too see it as fair or unfair before deciding whether an event amounts to an injustice and whether to act on these judgments. Moreover, it will be interesting to explore whether active influence attempts that frame issues in more in intuitive economic, politician, scientist, prosecutor, or theologian terms differentially affect concessions to others' views that a given situation is fair or unfair (Skitka, 2003).

Finally, although previous theory and research provides some grounds for making predictions about when each functional set of justice assumptions will be most likely to influence how people reason about fairness, it is important to note that these functional metaphors have fuzzy and indeterminate boundaries. Some situations are likely to prompt more than one set of concerns or mind-sets. Serious transgressions, for example, are likely to activate concerns consistent with both the intuitive prosecutor and the intuitive theologian. Some of the most interesting possibilities for future research will be to explore what happens when different justice relevant goals and mind-sets come into conflict. Among other things, when people feel unjustly treated according to one subjective mind-set, they may be highly motivated to find evidence in support of being treated fairly using another mind-set, in part to stave off the risks of social conflict and strife. Also, it will be interesting to test how effective different kinds of functional trade-offs might be in leading to a perception of fairness. It might be the case, for example, that deciding to serve a greater moral purpose might balance the pain of economic or socioemotional losses associated with a given allocation decision. Expanding the theoretical scope of justice to acknowledge the reality that people have many needs and concerns and that they have developed complicated conceptions of justice and morality in an effort to cope with the many challenges of social coordination opens the door to a host of new and fascinating research questions.

REFERENCES

Abramson, P. R., & Inglehart, R. (1995). *Value change in global perspective.* Ann Arbor: University of Michigan Press.

Adams, J. S. (1963). Toward an understanding of inequity. *Journal of Abnormal Psychology, 67,* 422–436.

Adams, J. S. (1965). Inequity in social exchange. In L. Berkowitz (Ed.), *Advances in experimental social psychology* (Vol. 2, pp. 267–299). New York, NY: Academic Press.

Adams, J. S., & Freedman, S. (1976). Equity theory revisited: Comments and annotated bibliography. In L. Berkowitz & E. Walster (Eds.), *Advances in experimental social psychology* (pp. 43–90). New York, NY: Academic Press.

Adams, J. S., & Jacobsen, P. R. (1964). Effects of wage inequities on work quality. *Journal of Abnormal and Social Psychology, 69,* 19–25.

Adams, J. S., & Rosenbaum, W. B. (1962). The relationship of worker productivity to cognitive dissonance about wage inequities. *Journal of Applied Psychology, 46,* 161–164.

Alicke, M. D. (2000). Culpable control and the psychology of blame. *Psychological Bulletin, 126,* 556–574.

Austin, W., & Walster, E. (1974). Reactions to confirmations and disconfirmations of expectancies of equity and inequity. *Journal of Personality and Social Psychology, 2,* 208–216.

Bakan, D. (1966). *The duality of human existence.* Chicago, IL: Rand McNally.

Bauman, C. W., & Skitka, L. J. (2009). Moral conflict and procedural justice: Moral mandates as constraints to voice effects. *Australian Journal of Psychology, 61,* 40–49.

Bies, R. J. (1987). Beyond "voice": The influence of decision-maker justification and sincerity on procedural fairness judgments. *Representative Research in Social Psychology, 17,* 3–14.

Bies, R. J. (2005). A procedural justice and interactional justice conceptually distinct? In J. Greenberg & J. A. Colquitt (Eds.), *Handbook of organizational justice* (pp. 85–112). Mahwah, NJ: Erlbaum.

Bies, R. J., & Moag, J. S. (1986). Interactional justice: Communication criteria of fairness. In B. Shepphard (Ed.), *Research on negotiation in organizations* (pp. 43–55). Greenwich, CT: JAI Press.

Blader, S. (2007). What determines people's fairness judgments? Identification and outcomes influence procedural fairness evaluations under uncertainty. *Journal of Experimental Social Psychology, 43,* 986–994.

Blader, S., & Tyler, T. R. (2009). Testing and extending the group engagement model: Linkages between social identity, procedural justice, economic outcomes, and extra role behavior. *Journal of Applied Psychology, 94,* 445–464.

Blau, P. M. (1964). *Exchange and power in social life.* New York, NY: Wiley.

Blumer, H. (1969). *Symbolic interactionism: Perspective and method.* Berkeley: University of California Press.

Bolton, G. E., Katok, E., & Zwick, R. (1998). Dictator game giving: Rules of fairness versus acts of kindness. *International Journal of Game Theory, 27,* 269–299.

Braband, J., & Lerner, M. J. (1974). "A little time and effort"... Who deserves what from whom? *Personality and Social Psychology Bulletin, 1,* 177–179.

Brockner, J., Chen, Y., Mannix, E. A., Leung, K., & Skarlicki, D. P. (2000). Culture and procedural fairness: When the effects of what you do depend on how you do it. *Administrative Science Quarterly, 45,* 138–159.

Brockner, J., Heuer, L., Seigel, P. A., Wiesenfeld, B., Martin, C., & Grover, S. (1998). The moderating effect of self-esteem in reaction to voice: Converging evidence from five studies. *Journal of Personality and Social Psychology, 75,* 394–407.

Brockner, J., Tyler, T. R., & Cooper-Schneider, R. (1992). The influence of prior commitment to an institution on reactions to perceived unfairness: The higher they are, the harder they fall. *Administrative Science Quarterly, 37,* 241–261.

Bulman, R. J., & Wortman, C. B. (1977). Attributions of blame and coping in the "real world": Severe accident victims react to their lot. *Journal of Personality and Social Psychology, 35,* 351–363.

Callan, M. J., Kay, A. C., Davidenko, N., & Ellard, J. H. (2009). The effects of justice motivation on memory for self- and other-relevant events. *Journal of Experimental Social Psychology, 45,* 614–623.

Carlsmith, K. M. (2006). The roles of retribution and utility in determining punishment. *Journal of Experimental Social Psychology, 4,* 437–451.

Carlsmith, K. M., Darley, J. M., & Robinson, P. H. (2002). Why do we punish?: Deterrence and just desserts as motives for punishment. *Journal of Personality and Social Psychology, 83,* 284–299.

Carlsmith, K. M., & Darley, J. M. (2008). Psychological aspects of retributive justice. *Advances in Experimental Social Psychology, 40,* 193–236.

Carlsmith, K. M., & Sood, A. M. (2009). The fine line between interrogation and retribution. *Journal of Experimental Social Psychology, 45,* 191–196.

Carlsmith, K. M., Wilson, T. D., & Gilbert, D. T. (2008). The paradoxical effects of revenge. *Journal of Personality and Social Psychology, 95,* 1316–1324.

Carroll, J., Perkowitz, W., Lurigio, A., & Weaver, K. (1987). Sentencing goals, causal attributions, and personality. *Journal of Personality and Social Psychology, 52,* 107–118.

Chen, Y., Brockner, J., & Greenberg, J. (2003). When is it a "pleasure to do business with you?" The effects of status, outcome favorability, and procedural fairness. *Organizational Behavior and Human Decision Processes, 92,* 1–21.

Colquitt, J. A., Conlon, D. E., Wesson, M. J., Porter, C. O. L. H., & Ng, K. Y. (2001). Justice at the millennium: A meta-analytic review of 25 years of organizational justice research. *Journal of Applied Psychology, 86,* 425–445.

Correia, I., & Vala, J. (2003). When will a victim be secondarily victimized? The effect of observer's belief in a just world, victim's innocence, and persistence of suffering. *Social Justice Research, 16,* 379–400.

Crocker, J., & Major, B. (1989). Social stigma and self-esteem: The self-protective properties of stigma. *Psychological Review, 96,* 608–630.

Cropanzano, R., Byrne, Z. S., Bobocel, D. R., & Rupp, D. E. (2001). Moral virtues, fairness hueristics, social entities, and other denizens of organizational justice. *Journal of Vocational Behavior, 58,* 164–209.

Cropanzano, R., Paddock, L., Rupp, D. E., Bagger, J., & Baldwin, A. (2007). How regulatory focus impacts the process-by-outcome interaction for perceived fairness and emotions. *Organizational Behavior and Human Decision Processes, 105,* 36–51.

Cropanzano, R., & Stein, J. H. (2009). Organizational justice and behavioral ethics: Promises and prospects. *Behavioral Ethics Quarterly, 19,* 193–233.

Crosby, F. J. (1976). A model of egotistical relative deprivation. *Psychological Review, 83,* 85–113.

Crosby, F. J. (1982). *Relative deprivation and the working woman.* New York, NY: Oxford University Press.

Crosby, F. J. (1984). The denial of personal discrimination. *American Behavioral Scientist, 27,* 371–386.

Crosby, F. J. (2003). Affirmative action: Psychological data and the policy debates. *American Psychologist, 58,* 93–115.

Crosby, F. J., & Franco, J. (2003). The ivory tower and the multicultural world. *Personality and Social Psychology Review, 7,* 362–373.

Dalbert, C. (1998). Belief in a just world, well-being, and coping with an unjust fate. In L. Montada & M. J. Lerner (Eds.), *Responses to victimizations and belief in a just world* (pp. 87–105). New York, NY: Plenum Press.

Dalbert, C. (2001). *The justice motive as a personal resource: Dealing with challenges and critical life events.* New York, NY: Plenum Press.

Dalbert, C. (2002). Beliefs in a just world as a buffer against anger. *Social Justice Research, 15,* 123–145.

Darley, J. M. (2009). Morality in the law: The psychological foundations of citizens' desire to punish transgressions. *Annual Review of Law and Social Science, 5,* 1–23.

Darley, J. M., Carlsmith, K. M., & Robinson, P. M. (2000). Incapacitation and just deserts as motives for punishment. *Law and Human Behavior, 24,* 659–683.

Darley, J. M., & Pittman, T. S. (2003). The psychology of compensatory and retributive justice. *Personality and Social Psychology Review, 7*, 324–336.

De Cremer, D., & Alberts, H. J. E. M. (2004). When procedural fairness dos not influence how positive I feel: The effects of voice and leader selection as a function of belongingness. *European Journal of Social Psychology, 34*, 333–344.

De Cremer, D., & Blader, S. L. (2006). Why do people care about procedural fairness? The importance of belongingness in responding and attending to procedures. *European Journal of Social Psychology, 36*, 211–228.

De Cremer, D., Brebels, L., & Sedikides, C. (2008). Uncertain about what? Procedural fairness effects as a function of general uncertainty and belongingness uncertainty. *Journal of Experimental Social Psychology, 44*, 1520–1525.

De Cremer, D., Tyler T. R., & Den Ouden, N. (2005). Managing cooperation via procedural fairness: The mediating influence of self-other merging. *Journal of Economic Psychology, 26*, 393–406.

Deutsch, M. (1975). Equity, equality, and need: What determines which value will be used as the basis of distributive justice? *Journal of Social Issues, 31*, 137–149.

Deutsch, M. (1985). *Distributive justice: A social psychological perspective*. New Haven, CT: Yale University Press.

Diekman, K. A., Sondak, H., & Barsness, Z. I. (2007). Does fairness matter more to some than others? The moderating role of workplace status on the relationship between procedural fairness perceptions and job satisfaction. *Social Justice Research, 20*, 161–180.

Drout, C. E., & Gaertner, S. L. (1994). Gender differences in reactions to female victims. *Social Behavior and Personality, 22*, 267–277.

Farmer, S. J., Beehr, T. A., & Love, K. G. (2003). Becoming an undercover police officer: A note on fairness perceptions, behavior and attitudes. *Journal of Organizational Behavior, 24*, 373–387.

Feather, N. T. (1994). Attitudes toward high achievers and reactions to their fall: Theory and research concerning tall poppies. In M. P. Zanna (Ed.), *Advances in experimental social psychology* (Vol. 26, pp. 1–73). San Diego. CA: Academic Press.

Feather, N. T. (1999). Judgments of deservingness: Studies in the psychology of justice and achievement. *Personality and Social Psychology Review, 3*, 86–107.

Feather, N. T. (2008). Perceived legitimacy of a promotion decision in relation to deservingness, entitlement, and resentment in the context of affirmative action and performance. *Journal of Applied Social Psychology, 38*, 1230–1254.

Fehr, E., & Fischbacher, U. (2004). Third-party punishment and social norms. *Evolution and Human Behavior, 25*, 63–87.

Fisk, R. P., & Young, C. E. (1985). Disconfirmation of equity expectations: Effects on consumer satisfaction with services. *Advances in Consumer Research, 12*, 340–345.

Fiske, A. P. (1991). *Structures of social life: The four elementary forms of human relations*. New York, NY: Free Press.

Fiske, S. T., & Taylor, S. E. (1984). *Social cognition*. New York, NY: McGraw-Hill.

Folger, R. (1977). Distributive and procedural justice: Combined impact of "voice" and improvement on experienced inequity. *Journal of Personality and Social Psychology, 35*, 108–119.

Folger, R. (1984). Perceived injustice, referent cognitions, and the concept of comparison level. *Representative Research in Social Psychology, 14*, 88–108.

Folger, R. (1986). A referent cognitions theory of relative deprivation. In J. M. Olson, C. P. Herman, & M. P. Zanna (Eds.), *Social comparison and relative deprivation: The Ontario symposium* (Vol. 4, pp. 33–55). Hillsdale, NJ: Erlbaum.

Folger, R. (2001). Fairness as deonance. In S. W. Gilliland, D. D. Steiner, & D. P. Skarlicki (Eds.), *Research in social issues in management* (pp. 3–31). Greenwich, CT: Information Age.

Folger, R. (2011). Behavioral ethics: A deontic perspective. In D. De Cremer & A. Tenbrunsel (Eds.), *Behavioral business ethics: Shaping an emerging field*. London, UK: Taylor & Francis.

Folger, R., Cropanzano, R., Timmerman, T. A., & Howes, J. C. (1996). Elaborating procedural fairness: Justice becomes both simpler and more complex. *Personality and Social Psychology Bulletin, 22*, 435–431.

Folger, R., & Konovsky, R. (1989). Effects of procedural and distributive justice on reactions to pay raise decisions. *Academy of Management Journal, 32*, 115–130.

Folger, R., Rosenfield, D., Grove, J., & Cockran, L. (1979). Effects of "voice" and peer opinions on responses to inequity. *Journal of Personality and Social Psychology, 45*, 268–273.

Fortin, M. (2008). Perspectives on organizational justice: Concept clarification, social context integration, time and links with morality. *International Journal of Management Reviews, 10*, 93–126.

Fortin, M., & Fellenz, M. R. (2008). Hypocrisies of fairness: Toward a more reflexive ethical base in organizational justice research and practice. *Journal of Business Ethics, 78*, 415–433.

Furnham, A. (2003). Belief in a just world: Research progress over the past decade. *Personality and Individual Differences, 34*, 795–817.

Goldberg, J. H., Lerner, J. S., & Tetlock, P. E. (1999). Rage and reason: The psychology of the intuitive prosecutor. *European Journal of Social Psychology, 29*, 781–795.

Gollwitzer, M., & Bucklein, K. (2007). Are "we" more punitive than "me"? Self-construal styles, justice-related attitudes, and punitive judgments. *Social Justice Research, 20*, 457–478.

Gollwitzer, M., & Denzler, M. (2009). What makes revenge sweet: Seeing the offender suffer or delivering a message? *Journal of Experimental Social Psychology, 45*, 840–844.

Gollwitzer, M., Meder, M., & Schmitt, M. (2011). What gives victims satisfaction when they seek revenge? *European Journal of Social Psychology, 41*, 364–374.

Greenberg, J. (1982). Approaching equity and avoiding inequity in groups and organizations. In J. Greenberg & R. L. Cohen (Eds.), *Equity and justice in social behavior* (pp. 79–103). New York, NY: Academic Press.

Greenberg, J. (1987). Reactions to procedural injustice in payment distributions: Do the means justify the ends? *Journal of Applied Psychology, 72*, 55–61.

Greenberg, J. (1990). Organizational justice: Yesterday, today, and tomorrow. *Journal of Management, 16*, 399–432.

Greenberg, J. (1993). The social side of fairness. Interpersonal and informational classes of organizational justice. In R. Cropanzano (Ed.), *Justice in the workplace: Approaching fairness in human resource management* (pp. 79–103). Hillsdale, NJ: Erlbaum.

Greenberg, J. (2011). Organizational justice: The dynamics of fairness in the workplace. In S. Zedeck (Ed.), *Handbook of industrial and organizational psychology* (pp. 271–327). Washington DC: American Psychological Association.

Grienberger, I. V., Rutte, C. G., & Van Knippenberg, A. F. M. (1997). Influence of social comparisons of outcomes and procedures on fairness judgments. *Journal of Applied Psychology, 82*, 913–919.

Hafer, C. L. (2000a). Investment in long-term goals and commitment to just means drive the need to believe in a just world. *Personality and Social Psychology Bulletin, 26*, 1059–1073.

Hafer, C. L. (2000b). Do innocent victims threaten the belief in a just world? Evidence from a modified Stroop task. *Journal of Personality and Social Psychology, 79*, 165–173.

Hafer, C. L., & Bégue, L. (2005). Experimental research on just-world theory: Problems, developments, and future challenges. *Psychological Bulletin, 131*, 128–167.

Hafer, C. L., Bégue, L., Choma, B. L., & Dempsey, J. L. (2005). Belief in a just world and commitment to long-term deserved outcomes. *Social Justice Research, 18*, 30–38.

Haidt, J. (2003). The moral emotions. In R. J. Davidson, K. R. Scherer, & H. H. Goldsmith (Eds.), *Handbook of affective sciences* (pp. 852–870). New York, NY: Oxford University Press.

Hastorf, A., & Cantril, H. (1954). They saw a game: A case study. *Journal of Abnormal and Social Psychology, 49,* 129–134.

Henrich, J., Boyd, R., Bowles, S., Camerer, C., Fehr, E., & Gintis, H. (2004). *Foundations of human sociality: Economic experiments and ethnographic evidence from fifteen small-scale societies.* New York, NY: Oxford University Press.

Heuer, L., Blumenthal, E., Douglas, A., & Weinblatt, T. (1999). A deservingness approach to respect as a relationally based fairness judgment. *Personality and Social Psychology Bulletin, 25,* 1279–1292.

Higgins, E. T. (1996). Self-discrepancy theory. In L. Berkowitz (Ed.), *Advances in experimental social psychology* (Vol. 22, pp. 93–136). New York, NY: Academic Press.

Holmvall, C. M., & Bobocel, D. R. (2008). What fair procedures say about me: Self-construals and reactions to procedural fairness. *Organizational Behavior and Human Decision Processes, 105,* 147–168.

Homans, G. (1958). Social behavior as exchange. *American Journal of Sociology, 62,* 597–606.

Homans, G. (1961). *Social behaviour: Its elementary forms.* London, UK: Routledge & Kegan Paul.

Hospers, J. (1961). *Human conduct.* New York, NY: Harcourt, Brace, & Janvonowich.

Huo, Y. J., Smith, H. J., Tyler, T. R., & Lind, E. A. (1996). Superordinate identification, subgroup identification, and justice concerns: Is separatism the problem; is assimilation the answer? *Psychological Science, 7,* 40–45.

Jonas, E., Schimel, J., Greenberg, J., & Pyszczynski, T. (2002). The scrooge effect: Evidence that mortality salience increases prosocial attitudes and behavior. *Personality and Social Psychology Bulletin, 28,* 1342–1353.

Jones, D. A., & Martens, M. L. (2008). The mediating role of overall fairness and the moderating role of trust certainty in justice-criteria relationships: The formation and use of heuristics in the workplace. *Journal of Organizational Behavior, 30,* 1025–1051.

Kahneman, D., Knetsch, J. L., & Thaler, R. H. (1986). Fairness and the assumptions of economics. *Journal of Business, 59,* s285–s300.

Kanfer, R., Sawyer, J., Earley, P. C., & Lind, E. A. (1987). Participation in task evaluation procedures: The effects of influential opinion expression and knowledge of evaluative criteria on attitudes and performance. *Social Justice Research, 1,* 235–249.

Kohlberg, L. (1976). Moral stages and moralization: The cognitive developmental approach. In Lickona, T. (Ed.), *Moral development and behavior: Theory, research and social issues.* New York, NY: Holt, Rinehart, & Winston.

Konow, J. (2003). Which is the fairest one of all? A positive analysis of justice theories. *Journal of Economic Literature, 16,* 1188–1239,

Koper, G., Van Knippenberg, D., Bouhuijs, F., Vermunt, R., & Wilke, H. (1993). Procedural justice and self-esteem. *European Journal of Social Psychology, 23,* 313–325.

Kulik, C. T., & Ambrose, M. L. (1992). Personal and situational determinants of referent choice. *Academy Management Review, 17,* 212–237.

Kulik, C. T., & Clark, S. C. (1993). Frustration effects in procedural justice research: The case of drug-testing legislation. *Social Justice Research, 6,* 301–324.

Lakatos, I. (1978). *The methodology of scientific research programmes: Philosophical papers* (Vol. 1). Cambridge, MA: Cambridge University Press.

Lamm, J., & Schwinger, T. (1980). Norms concerning distributive justice: Are needs taken into consideration in allocation decisions? *Social Psychology Quarterly, 43,* 425–429.

LaVelle, J. J., Brockner, J., Konovsky, M. A., Price, K., Henley, A., Taneja, A., & Vinekar, V. (2009). Commitment, procedural fairness, and organizational citizenship behavior: A multifoci analysis. *Journal of Organizational Behavior, 30,* 337–357.

Lerner, J. S., Goldberg, J., & Tetlock, P. (1998). Sober second thought: The effects of accountability, anger, and authoritarianism on attributions of responsibility. *Personality and Social Psychology Bulletin, 24,* 563–574.

Lerner, M. J. (1974). The justice motive: "Equity" and "parity" among children. *Journal of Personality and Social Psychology, 29,* 539–550.

Lerner, M. J. (1975). The justice motive of social behavior: Introduction. *Journal of Social Issues, 31,* 1–19.

Lerner, M. J. (1977). The justice motive: Some hypotheses as to it origins and forms. *Journal of Personality, 45,* 1–52.

Lerner, M. J. (1980). *The belief in a just world: A fundamental delusion.* New York, NY: Plenum Press.

Lerner, M. J. (1987). Integrating societal and psychological rules of entitlement: The basic task of each social actor and the fundamental problem for the social sciences. *Social Justice Research, 1,* 107–121.

Lerner, M. J., Miller, D. T., & Holmes, J. G. (1976). Deserving and the emergence of forms of justice. In L. Berkowitz & E. Walster (Eds.), *Advances in experimental social psychology* (pp. 133–162). New York, NY: Academic Press.

Leung, K., & Park, H. J. (1986). Effects of interactional goal on choice of allocation rules: A cross-national study. *Organizational Behavior and Human Decision Processes, 37,* 111–120.

Leventhal, G. S. (1976a). The distribution of rewards and resources in groups and organizations. In L. Berkowitz & E. Walster (Eds.), *Advances in experimental social psychology, 9,* 91–131. New York, NY: Academic Press.

Leventhal, G. S. (1976b). Fairness in social relationships. In J. W. Thibaut, J. T. Spence, & R. C. Carsa (Eds.), *Contemporary topics in social psychology.* Morristown, NJ: General Learning Press.

Leventhal, G. S., Michaels, J. W., & Sanford, C. (1972). Inequity and interpersonal conflict: Reward allocation and secrecy about reward as methods of preventing conflict. *Journal of Personality and Social Psychology, 23,* 88–102.

Lind, E. A. (2001). Fairness heuristic theory: Justice judgments as pivotal cognitions in organizational relations. In J. Greenberg & R. Cropanzano (Eds.), *Advances in organizational justice* (pp. 56–88). Stanford, CA: Stanford University Press.

Lind, E. A., Kanfer, R., & Earley, P. C. (1990). Voice, control, and procedural justice: Instrumental and noninstrumental concerns in fairness judgments. *Journal of Personality and Social Psychology, 59,* 952–959.

Lind, E. A., Kulik, C. T., Ambrose, M., & de Vera Park, M. V. (1993). Individual and corporate dispute resolution: Using procedural fairness as a decision heuristic. *Administrative Science Quarterly, 38,* 224–251.

Lind, E. A., Kurtz, S., Musanté, L., Walker, L., & Thibaut, J. (1980). Procedure and outcome effects on reactions to adjudicated resolution of conflicts of interest. *Journal of Personality and Social Psychology, 39,* 19–29.

Lind, E. A., & Tyler, T. R. (1988). *The social psychology of procedural fairness.* New York, NY: Plenum Press.

Lind, E. A., & Van den Bos, K. (2002). When fairness works: Toward a general theory of uncertainty management. In B. M. Staw & R. M. Kramer (Eds.), *Research in organizational behavior* (Vol. 24, pp. 181–233). Boston, MA: Elsevier.

Long, G. T., & Lerner, M. J. (1974). Deserving the "personal contract" and altruistic behavior by children. *Journal of Personality and Social Psychology, 29,* 551–556.

Lupfer, M. B., Weeks, K. P., Doan, K. A., & Houston, D. A. (2000). Folk conceptions of fairness and unfairness. *European Journal of Social Psychology, 30,* 405–428.

Lytle, B. L. (2010). *Types of social comparison and procedural fairness.* (Doctoral dissertation). University of Illinois at Chicago.

MacCoun, R. J. (2005). Voice, control, and belonging: The double-edged sword of procedural fairness. *Annual Review of Law and Social Science, 1,* 171–201.

MacCoun, R. J., Lind, E. A., Hensler, D. R., Bryant, D. L., & Ebener, P. (1988). *Alternative adjudication: An evaluation of the New Jersey automobile arbitration program.* Santa Monica, CA: RAND.

Major, B., & Adams, J. B. (1983). Role of gender, interpersonal orientation, and self-presentation in distributive-justice behavior. *Journal of Personality and Social Psychology, 45,* 598–608.

Major, B., Bylsma, W. H., & Cozzarelli, C. (1989). Gender differences in distributive justice preferences: The impact of domain. *Sex Roles, 21,* 487–497.

Major, B. & Deaux, K. (1982). Individual differences in justice behavior. In J. Greenberg & R. L. Cohen (Eds.), *Equity and justice in social behavior* (pp. 43–76). New York, NY: Academic Press.

Maslow, A. H. (1993). *The farther reaches of human nature.* New York, NY: Penguin Books.

Mayer, D. M., Greenbaum, R. L., Kuenzi, M., & Shteynberg, G. (2009). When do fair procedures not matter? A test of the identity violation effect. *Journal of Applied Social Psychology, 94,* 142–161.

McFarlin, D. B., & Sweeney, P. D. (1992). Distributive and procedural justice as predictors of satisfaction with personal and organizational outcomes. *Academy of Management Journal, 35,* 626–637.

Mellers, B. A. (1986). "Fair" allocations of salaries and taxes. *Journal of Experimental Psychology: Human Perception and Performance, 12,* 80–91.

Messick, D. M., & Sentis, K. P. (1979). Fairness and preference. *Journal of Experimental Social Psychology, 15,* 418–434.

Mikula, G. (1974). Nationality, performance, and sex as determinants of reward allocation. *Journal of Personality and Social Psychology, 29,* 435–440.

Mikula, G., Petri, B., & Tanzer, N. (1990). What people regard as unjust. *European Journal of Social Psychology, 22,* 133–149.

Milgram, S. (1974). *Obedience to authority.* New York, NY: Harper & Row.

Miller, D. T. (2001). Disrespect and the experience of injustice. *Annual Review of Psychology, 52,* 527–553.

Mischel, W., & Shoda, Y. (1995). A cognitive-affective system theory of personality: Reconceptualizing situations, dispositions, dynamics, and invariance in personality structure. *Psychological Review, 102,* 246–268.

Moorman, R. H. (1991). Relationship between organizational justice and organizational citizenship behaviors: Do fairness perceptions influence employee citizenship? *Journal of Applied Psychology, 76,* 845–855.

Moorman, R. H., & Bryne, Z. S. (2005). How does organizational justice affect organizational citizenship behavior? In J. Greenberg & J. A. Colquitt (Eds.), *Handbook of Organizational Justice* (pp. 355–382). Mahwah, NJ: Erlbaum.

Mullen, E., & Nadler, J. (2008). Moral spillovers: The effect of moral violations on deviant behavior. *Journal of Experimental Social Psychology, 44,* 1239–1245.

Mullen, E., & Skitka, L. J. (2006). Exploring the psychological underpinnings of the moral mandate effect: Motivated reasoning, identification, or affect? *Journal of Personality and Social Psychology, 90,* 629–643.

Okimoto, T. G., & Wenzel, M. (2009). Punishment as restoration of group and offender values following a transgression: Value consensus through symbolic labeling and offender reform. *European Journal of Social Psychology, 39,* 346–367.

Okimoto, T. G., Wenzel, M., & Feather, N. T. (2009). Beyond retribution: Conceptualizing restorative justice and exploring its determinants. *Social Justice Research, 22,* 156–180.

Operario, D., & Fiske, S. T. (2001). Ethnic identity moderates perceptions of prejudice: Judgments of personal versus group discrimination and evaluations of subtle versus blatant bias. *Personality and Social Psychology Bulletin, 27,* 550–561.

Otto, K., Boos, A., Dalbert, C., Schops, D., & Hoyer, J. (2006). Post-traumatic symptoms, depression, and anxiety of flood victims: The impact of a belief in a just world. *Personality and Individual Differences, 40,* 1075–1084.

Peterson, R. S. (1999). Can you have too much of a good thing? The limits of voice for improving satisfaction. *Personality and Social Psychology Bulletin, 25,* 313–324.

Platow, M. J., & Von Knippenberg, D. A. (2001). A social identity analysis of leadership endorsement: The effects of leader in-group prototypicality and distributive intergroup fairness. *Personality and Social Psychology Bulletin, 27,* 1508–1519.

Pritchard, R. D., Dunnette, M. D., & Jorgenson, D. 0. (1972). Effects of perceptions of equity and inequity on worker performance and satisfaction, *Journal of Applied Psychology, 56,* 75–94.

Reichle, B., & Schmitt, M. (2002). Helping and rationalization as alternative strategies for restoring belief in a just world: Evidence from longitudinal change analyses. In M. Ross & D. T. Miller (Eds.), *The justice motive in everyday life* (pp. 127–148). New York, NY: Cambridge University Press.

Renn, R. W. (1998). Participation's effect on task performance: Mediating roles of goal acceptance and procedural justice. *Journal of Business Research, 41,* 115–125.

Richards, J. C., Hof, A., & Alvarenga, M. (2000). Serum lipids and their relationships with hostility and angry affect and behaviors in men. *Health Psychology, 19,* 393–398.

Robinson, P. H., Kurzban, R., & Jones, O. D. (2007). The origins of shared intuitions of justice. *Vanderbilt Law Review, 60,* 1634–1688.

Sampson, E. E. (1975). On justice as equality. *Journal of Social Issues, 31,* 45–64.

Schroeder, D. A., Steel, J. E., Woodrell, A. J., & Bembenek, A. F. (2003). Justice within social dilemmas. *Personality and Social Psychology Review, 7,* 394–387.

Schwartz, S. (1975). The justice of need and the activation of humanitarian norms. *Journal of Social Issues, 31,* 111–136.

Schwinger, T. (1980). Just allocation of goods: decisions among three principles. In G. Mikula (Ed.), *Justice and social interaction* (pp. 95–125). New York, NY: Springer Press.

Seigel, P. A., Post, C., Brockner, J., Fishman, A. Y., & Garden, C. (2005). The moderating influence of procedural fairness on the relationship between work-life conflict and organizational commitment. *Journal of Applied Psychology, 90,* 13–24.

Shafer, R. B., & Keith, P. M. (1980). Equity and depression among married couples. *Social Psychology Quarterly, 43,* 430–435.

Shapiro, D. L., & Brett, J. M. (1993). Comparing three processes underlying judgments of procedural fairness: A field study of mediation and arbitration. *Journal of Personality and Social Psychology, 65,* 1167–1177.

Shapiro, D. L., & Brett, J. M. (2005). What is the role of control in organizational justice? In J. Greenberg & J. A. Colquitt (Eds.), *Handbook of organizational research* (pp. 155–178). Mahwah, NJ: Erlbaum.

Sheppard, B. H. (1985). Justice is no simple matter: The case for elaborating our model of procedural fairness. *Journal of Personality and Social Psychology, 49,* 953–962.

Shroth, H. A., & Shah, P. P. (2000). Procedures: Do we really want to know them? An examination of the effects of procedural justice on self-esteem. *Journal of Applied Psychology, 85,* 462–471.

Skarlicki, D. P., & Folger, R. (1997). Retaliation in the workplace. *Journal of Applied Psychology, 82,* 434–443.

Skitka, L. J. (2002). Do the means always justify the ends or do the ends sometimes justify the means? A value protection model of justice reasoning. *Personality and Social Psychology Bulletin, 28,* 588–597.

Skitka, L. J. (2003). Of different minds: An accessible identity model of justice reasoning. *Personality and Social Psychology Review, 7,* 286–297.

Skitka, L. J. (2009). Exploring the "lost and found" of justice theory and research. *Social Justice Research, 22,* 98–116.

Skitka, L. J., Aramovich, N., Lytle, B. L., & Sargis, E. (2009). Knitting together an elephant: an integrative approach to understanding the psychology of justice reasoning. In D. R. Bobocel, A. C. Kay, M. P. Zanna, & J. M. Olson (Eds.), *The psychology of justice and legitimacy: The Ontario symposium* (Vol. 11, pp. 1–26). Philadelphia, PA: Psychology Press.

Skitka, L. J., Bauman, C. W., & Mullen, E. (2008). Morality and justice: An expanded theoretical perspective and review. In K. A. Hedgvedt & J. Clay-Warner (Eds.), *Advances in group processes, Vol. 25* (pp. 1–27). Bingley, UK: Emerald Group.

Skitka, L. J., Bauman, C. W., & Lytle, B. L. (2009). The limits of legitimacy: Moral and religious convictions as constraints on deference to authority. *Journal of Personality and Social Psychology, 97,* 567–578.

Skitka, L. J., & Houston, D. (2001). When due process is of no consequence: Moral mandates and presumed defendant guilt or innocence. *Social Justice Research, 14,* 305–326.

Skitka, L. J., & Mullen, E. (2002). Understanding judgments of fairness in a real-world political context: A test of the value protection model of justice reasoning. *Personality and Social Psychology Bulletin, 28,* 1419–1429.

Skitka, L. J., & Mullen, E. (2008). Moral convictions often override concerns about procedural fairness: A reply to Napier and Tyler. *Social Justice Research, 21,* 529–546.

Skitka, L. J., & Tetlock, P. E. (1992). Allocating scarce resources: A contingency model of distributive justice. *Journal of Experimental Social Psychology, 28,* 491–522.

Skitka, L. J., & Tetlock, P. E. (1993). Providing public assistance: Cognitive and motivational processes underlying liberal and conservative policy preferences. *Journal of Personality and Social Psychology, 65,* 1205–1223.

Skitka, L. J., Winquist, J., & Hutchinson, S. (2003). Are outcome fairness and outcome favorability distinguishable psychological constructs? A meta-analytic review. *Social Justice Research, 16,* 309–341.

Smith, H. J., Thomas, T. R., & Tyler, T. R. (2006). Concrete construction employees: When does procedural fairness shape self-evaluations? *Journal of Applied Social Psychology, 3,* 644–663.

Sondak, H., Neale, M. A., & Pinkley, R. L. (1995). The negotiated allocation of benefits and burdens: The impact of outcome valence, contribution, and relationship. *Organizational Behavior and Human Decision Processes, 64,* 249–260.

Sprecher, S. (1986). The relation between inequity and emotions in close relationships. *Social Psychology Quarterly, 49,* 309–321.

Stepina, L. P., & Perrewe, P. L. (1991). The stability of comparative referent choice and feelings of inequity: A longitudinal field study. *Journal of Organizational Behavior, 12,* 185–200.

Stouffer, S. A., Suchman, E. A., DeVinney, L. C., Star, S. A., & Williams, R. M. Jr. (1949). *The American soldier: Adjustment during army life* (Vol.1). Princeton, NJ: Princeton University Press.

Sunshine, J., & Heuer, L. (2002). Deservingness and perceptions of procedural justice in citizen encounters with the police. In M. Ross & D. T. Miller (Eds.), *The justice motive in everyday life* (pp. 397–416). New York, NY: Cambridge University Press.

Taylor, D. M., Wright, S. C., Moghaddam, F. M., & LaLonde, R. N. (1990). The personal/group discrimination discrepancy: Perceiving my group, but not myself, to be a target of discrimination. *Personality and Social Psychology Bulletin, 16,* 254–262.

Taylor, S. E. (1982). Social cognition and health. *Personality and Social Psychology Bulletin, 8,* 549–562.

Tetlock, P. E. (2002). Social functionalist frameworks for judgment and choice: Intuitive politicians, theologians, and prosecutors. *Psychological Review, 109,* 451–471.

Tetlock, P. E., Visser, P. S., Singh, R., Polifroni, M., Scott, A., Elson, S. B., & Mazzocco, P. (2007). People as intuitive prosecutors: The impact of social-control goals on attributions of responsibility. *Journal of Experimental Social Psychology, 43,* 195–209.

Thibaut, J., & Kelley, H. H. (1959). *The social psychology of groups.* New York, NY: Wiley.

Thibaut, J., & Walker, L. (1975). *Procedural justice: A psychological analysis.* Hillsdale, NJ: Erlbaum.

Törnblom, K. Y., & Vermunt, R. (2007). Towards an integration of distributive justice, procedural justice, and social resource theories. *Social Justice Research, 20,* 312–335.

Turillo, C. J., Folger, R., Lavelle, J. J., Umphress, E. E., & Gee, J. O. (2002). Is virtue its own reward? Self-sacrificial decisions for the sake of fairness. *Organizational Behavior and Human Decision Processes, 89,* 839–865.

Tyler, T. R. (1994). Psychological models of the justice motive. *Journal of Personality and Social Psychology, 67,* 850–863.

Tyler, T. R. (1999). Why people cooperate with organizations: An identity-based perspective. *Research on Organizational Justice, 21,* 201–246.

Tyler, T. R., & Bies, R. J. (1990). Beyond formal procedures: The interpersonal context of procedural justice. In J. S. Carroll (Ed.), *Applied social psychology and organizational settings* (pp. 77–98). Hillsdale, NJ: Erlbaum.

Tyler, T. R., & Blader, S. (2000). *Cooperation in groups: Procedural justice, social identity, and behavioral engagement.* New York, NY: Psychology Press.

Tyler, T. R., & Blader, S. (2003). The group engagement model: Procedural justice, social identity, and cooperative behavior. *Personality and Social Psychology Review, 7,* 349–361.

Tyler, T. R., & Caine, A. (1981). The influence of outcomes and procedures on satisfaction with formal leaders. *Journal of Personality and Social Psychology, 41,* 642–655.

Tyler, T. R., & DeGoey, P. (1995). Collective restraint in social dilemmas: Procedural justice and social identification effects on support for authorities. *Journal of Personality and Social Psychology, 69,* 482–497.

Tyler, T. R., DeGoey, P., & Smith, H. (1996). Understanding why the justice of group procedures matter: A test of the psychological dynamics of the group-value model. *Journal of Personality and Social Psychology, 70,* 913–930.

Tyler, T. R., & Folger, R. (1980). Distributional and procedural aspects of satisfaction with citizen-police encounters. *Basic and Applied Social Psychology, 1,* 281–292.

Tyler, T. R., & Huo, Y. J. (2002). *Trust in the law: Encouraging public cooperation with the police and courts.* New York, NY: Sage.

Tyler, T. R., & Lind, E. A. (1992). A relational model of authority in groups. In M. P. Zanna (Ed.), *Advances in Experimental Social Psychology, 25,* 115–191. San Diego, CA: Academic Press.

Tyler, T. R., Rasinski, K. A., & Spodick, N. (1985). Influence of voice on satisfaction with leaders: Exploring the meaning of process control. *Journal of Personality and Social Psychology, 48,* 72–81.

Van den Bos, K. (2001). Uncertainty management: The influence of uncertainty salience on reactions to perceived procedural fairness. *Journal of Personality and Social Psychology, 80,* 931–941.

Van den Bos, K. (2002). Assimilation and contrast in organizational justice: The role of primed mindsets in the psychology of the fair process effect. *Organizational Behavior and Human Decision Processes, 89,* 866–880.

Van den Bos, K. (2005). What is responsible for the fair process effect? In J. Greenberg & J. A. Colquitt (Eds.), *Handbook of organizational justice: Fundamental questions about fairness in the workplace* (pp. 273–300). Mahwah, NJ: Erlbaum.

Van den Bos, K., Bruins, J., Wilke, H. A. M., & Dronkert, E. (1999). Sometimes unfair procedures have nice aspects: On the psychology of the fair process effect. *Journal of Personality and Social Psychology, 77,* 324–336.

Van den Bos, K., & Lind, E. A. (2001). The psychology of own versus others' treatment: Self-oriented and other-oriented effects on perceptions of procedural fairness. *Personality and Social Psychology Bulletin, 27,* 1324–1333.

Van den Bos, K., & Lind, E. A. (2002). Uncertainty management by means of fairness judgments. *Advances in Experimental Social Psychology, 34,* 1–60.

Van den Bos, K., & Miedema, J. (2000). Toward understanding why fairness matters: The influence of mortality salience on reactions to procedural fairness. *Journal of Personality and Social Psychology, 79,* 355–366.

Van den Bos, K., & Spruijt, N. (2002). Appropriateness of decisions as a moderator of the psychology of voice. *European Journal of Social Psychology, 32,* 57–72.

Van den Bos, K., Vermunt, R., & Wilke, H. A. M. (1996). The consistency of rule and the voice effect: The influence of expectations on procedural fairness judgments and performance. *European Journal of Social Psychology, 72,* 95–104.

Van den Bos, K., Wilke, H. A. M., Lind, E. A., & Vermunt, R. (1997). How do I judge my outcome when I do not know the outcome of others? The psychology of the fair process effect. *Journal of Personality and Social Psychology, 72,* 1034–1046.

Van den Bos, K., Wilke, H. A. M., Lind, E. A., & Vermunt, R. (1998). Evaluating outcomes by means of the fair process effect: Evidence for different processes in fairness and satisfaction judgments. *Journal of Personality and Social Psychology, 74,* 1493–1503.

Van Dijke, M., & Verboon, P. (2010). Trust in authorities as a boundary condition to procedural justice effects on tax compliance. *Journal of Economic Psychology, 31,* 80–91.

Van Prooijen, J. W. (2010). Retributive versus compensatory justice. Observers' preference for punishing in response to criminal offenses. *European Journal of Social Psychology, 40,* 72–85.

Van Prooijen, J. W., De Cremer, D., Van Beest, I., Ståhl, T., Van Dijke, M., & Van Lange, P. A. M. (2008). The egocentric nature of procedural justice: Social value orientation as moderator of reactions to decision-making procedures. *Journal of Experimental Social Psychology, 44,* 1303–1315.

Van Prooijen, J. W., Van den Bos, K., & Wilke, H. A. M. (2002). Procedural justice and status: Status salience as antecedent of procedural fairness effects. *Journal of Personality and Social Psychology, 83,* 1353–1361.

Vermunt, R., & Steensma, H. (2003). Physiological relaxation: Stress reduction through fair treatment. *Social Justice Research, 16,* 135–149.

Vermunt, R., & Steensma, H. (2005). How can justice be used to manage stress in organizations? In J. Greenberg & J. A. Colquitt (Eds.), *Handbook of organizational justice* (pp. 385–410). Mahwah, NJ: Erlbaum.

Vermunt, R., Van der Kloot, W. A., & Van der Meer, J. (1993). The effect of procedural and interactional criteria on procedural fairness judgments. *Social Justice Research, 6,* 183–194.

Walker, I., & Smith, H. J. (2002). Fifty years of relative deprivation research. In I. Walker & H. J. Smith (Eds.), *Relative deprivation: Specification, development, and integration* (pp. 1–13). New York, NY: Cambridge University Press.

Walster, E., Berscheid, E., & Walster, G. W. (1976). New directions in equity research. In L. Berkowitz & E. Walster (Eds.), *Advances in experimental social psychology* (Vol. 9, pp. 1–43). New York, NY: Academic Press.

Watts, B. L., Messé, L. A., & Vallacher, R. R. (1982). Toward understanding sex differences in pay allocation: Agency, communion, and reward distribution behavior. *Sex Roles, 8,* 1175–1187.

Weiner, B. (1985). An attributional theory of achievement motivation and emotion. *Psychological Review, 92,* 548–573.

Wenzel, M. (2001). Justice and identity: The significance of inclusion for perceptions of entitlement and the justice motive. *Personality and Social Psychology Bulletin, 26,* 157–176.

Wenzel, M. (2004). Social identification as a determinant of concerns about individual-, group-, and inclusive justice. *Social Psychology Quarterly, 67,* 70–87.

Wenzel, M., Okimoto, T. G., Feather, N. T., & Platow, M. J. (2008). Retributive and restorative justice. *Law and Human Behavior, 32,* 375–389.

Wenzel, M., & Thielman, I. (2006). Why we punish in the name of justice: Just desert versus value restoration and the role of social identity. *Social Justice Research, 19,* 450–470.

Williams, S. (1999). The effects of distributive and procedural justice on performance. *Journal of Psychology, 133,* 183–193.

Yang, J., Mossholder, K. W., & Peng, T. K. (2009). Supervisory procedural justice effects: The mediating roles of cognitive and affective trust. *Leadership Quarterly, 20,* 143–154.

Zhong, C. B., & Liljenquist, K. (2006). Washing away your sins: Threatened morality and physical cleansing. *Science, 8,* 1451–1452.

CHAPTER 20

Social Conflict, Harmony, and Integration

JOHN F. DOVIDIO, SAMUEL L. GAERTNER, ELENA WRIGHT MAYVILLE,
AND SYLVIA PERRY

SOCIAL CONFLICT, HARMONY, AND INTEGRATION

Intergroup relations, which are frequently characterized by distrust and competition, are often fragile. Even a single incident can ignite intense intergroup conflict. For example, in 1914 the assassination of Archduke Ferdinand of Austria, who was the heir to the throne of Austria-Hungary, triggered World War I. Eighty years later, the assassination of Juvénal Habyarimana, the President of Rwanda, set off the Rwandan genocide, in which approximately 800,000 people were murdered (mainly Tutsis by Hutus) in the next 100 days. The present chapter considers the psychological basis of intergroup bias and conflict and how greater understanding of these psychological processes may aid in the reduction of bias and promote reconciliation and social integration.

In this chapter, first we present a brief historical overview of empirical and theoretical emphases in the social psychological study of intergroup relations. Second, we discuss basic cognitive, motivational, interpersonal, and social influence—often normal and generally functional processes—that can contribute to intergroup bias and social conflict. Third, we explore how intergroup interactions can both reflect and reinforce intergroup bias. Fourth, we consider how the processes that, if left unmanaged, contribute to intergroup bias can be redirected to improve intergroup attitudes and promote social integration. Finally, we conclude the chapter by outlining future directions and practical implications.

BRIEF HISTORICAL BACKGROUND ON INTERGROUP RELATIONS

The study of intergroup relations, although currently one of the most popular and active areas, came relatively late to social psychology. Brewer and Brown (1998) observed, "A casual sampling of the first recognizable textbooks of social psychology, which appeared in the first three decades of the twentieth century, reveals that it [the topic of intergroup relations] was seldom, if ever, considered a legitimate field of inquiry" (p. 554). Nevertheless, as early as the turn of the 20th century, sociologists recognized the importance of groups to the identity and existence of human beings (Cooley, 1902). Sumner (1906), for example, is credited with coining the terms *ingroup* and *outgroup*. Social conflict and bias were also prominent in Freudian applied psychodynamic theory, which suggested that prejudice was a form of displaced hostility arising from unfulfilled basic needs.

Beginning in the late 1920s and 1930s, social psychologists developed greater interest in intergroup bias and conflict, particularly in the measurement of prejudice (Bogardus, 1925) and stereotypes (Katz & Braly, 1933). In addition, some of Freud's ideas about displaced aggression were incorporated by Dollard, Sears, and colleagues (1939) in their work on the Frustration-Aggression Hypothesis to explain extreme manifestations of social bias, such as lynchings, and Adorno, Frenkel-Brunswik, Levinson, and Sanford (1950) borrowed theoretically from Freud in their classic work on the authoritarian personality. This line of research continued to focus the field of psychology on developing ways of conceptualizing the roots of social conflict in abnormal human qualities.

Sociological theories, in contrast, emphasized the role of large-scale social and structural dynamics in intergroup relations. These theories considered the dynamics of race relations largely in functional, economic, class-based terms—often to the exclusion of individual influences (see Bobo, 1999). Nevertheless, in the late 1950s and early 1960s both sociological and psychological approaches converged to recognize the importance of understanding the impact of group functions and collective identities on race relations (see Bobo).

Beginning in the late 1960s and in the 1970s, two dominant strands of research emerged within social psychology that, in complementary ways, emphasized general processes in human social cognition and motivation as key dynamics in social bias and conflict. One development was the shift in focus from individual differences in intergroup bias to general mechanisms underlying social bias and conflict. From this perspective, prejudice, stereotyping, and bias were conceived as outcomes of normal cognitive processes associated with simplifying and storing the overwhelming quantity and complexity of information people encounter daily (see Hamilton, 1981).

The other major development in the study of intergroup relations had its origins in European social psychology. Henri Tajfel's work innovatively investigated the role of category-based perceptions and collective identity, as opposed to individual identity, on group and intergroup behavior. Social identity theory (Tajfel & Turner, 1979; see also Hogg, 2006) is currently one of the most comprehensive and generative perspectives in the study of intergroup relations, conflict, and integration.

This chapter builds directly on the foundation of research traditions in social cognition, social identity, and functional relations between groups to understand not only the causes of social bias and conflict but also to develop strategies and interventions for promoting integration and reconciliation.

SOCIAL COGNITION, CATEGORIZATION, AND IDENTITY

This section reviews basic processes and mechanisms that contribute to the development and maintenance of intergroup bias and conflict: (a) social cognition and categorization, and (b) social identity.

Social Cognition and Social Categorization

Psychological research on social cognition highlighted the distinction between perceiving and thinking about others as unique individuals or as members of social categories and groups (Brewer, 1988; Fiske, Lin, & Neuberg, 1999). Brewer's (1988) dual-process model, for example, distinguished between two types of processing. One type of processing is *person-based*. Person-based processing is bottom-up and data-driven, involving the piecemeal acquisition of information that begins "at the most concrete level and stops at the lowest level of abstraction required by the prevailing processing objectives" (Brewer, 1988, p. 6). The other type of processing is *category-based*. It represents top-down processing, in which the external reality is perceived and experienced in a way that is influenced by category-based, subjective impressions. Category-based processing is more likely to occur than person-based processing because social information is typically organized around social categories (Brewer, 1988). Category-based processes appear to be a fundamental social process, perhaps rooted in humans' evolutionary heritage. Other primates, such as the rhesus macaque, also attend strongly to group membership within their species in their social encounters (Mahajan et al., 2011).

Categorizing people or objects into groups, which often occurs rapidly and automatically, profoundly affects people's perceptions, cognitions, feelings, and behavior (see Dovidio & Gaertner, 2010). When people are seen as members of social categories, members of the same group are perceived to be more similar than before, and distinctions between members of different categories become exaggerated (Tajfel, 1969). Furthermore, these similarities and differences are often viewed as inherent to the nature of the groups (see Yzerbyt & Demoulin, 2010) and generalize to additional dimensions (e.g., character traits) beyond those facets that differentiated the categories originally (Allport, 1954).

Recognition of one's membership in some groups (ingroups) but not others (outgroups) arouses further biases. Cognitively, people process information about ingroup members more deeply than information about outgroup members (Van Bavel, Packer, & Cunningham, 2008), perceive ingroup members as more heterogeneous than outgroup members (Boldry, Gaertner, & Quinn, 2007), retain information in a more detailed fashion for ingroup than outgroup members (Park & Rothbart, 1982), have better memory for information about ways ingroup members are similar and outgroup members are dissimilar to the self (Wilder, 1981), and remember less positive information about outgroup members than ingroup members (Howard & Rothbart, 1980). Additionally, people are better at recognizing and remembering the facial features of people who are members of their group (Hehman, Mania, & Gaertner, 2010; Meissner & Brigham, 2001). They are also more accurate at perceiving expressions of emotion displayed by ingroup than outgroup members (Elfenbein & Ambady, 2002; Young & Hugenberg, 2010).

In addition, people differ fundamentally in how they react to others and interpret others' actions based on group membership. People spontaneously experience more positive affect toward ingroup than outgroup members (Otten & Moskowitz, 2000; Otten & Wentura, 1999) and value the lives of ingroup members more (Pratto & Glasford, 2008). Although traditional examinations of intergroup relations have primarily focused on attitudes and beliefs about ingroup versus outgroup members, a recent meta-analysis of studies of racial attitudes and discrimination demonstrated that emotional bias, or differential feelings toward outgroup compared to ingroup members, predicted discrimination twice as strongly as did stereotypes and beliefs (Talaska, Fiske, & Chaiken, 2008).

Individuals are also more generous and forgiving in their attributions about the behaviors of ingroup members relative to outgroup members. Positive behaviors and successful outcomes are more likely to be attributed to internal, stable characteristics of ingroup members (e.g., she is helpful) than outgroup members (e.g., she walked across the street holding the old man's hand), whereas negative outcomes are more likely to be ascribed to the personalities of outgroup members (e.g., she is hostile) than ingroup members (e.g., she slapped the girl; Hewstone, 1990). Moreover, people are not only less accurate in reading the emotions of outgroup members, they are also systematically inaccurate: People are more likely to perceive a hostile face as belonging to an outgroup member (Dunham, 2011) and are more likely to misperceive neutral facial expressions as conveying anger for outgroup than ingroup members (Hugenberg & Bodenhausen, 2004).

In part because people anticipate outgroup members to display bias toward their group (Judd, Park, Yzerbyt, Gordijn, & Muller, 2005), they show a preference for ingroup members who show bias against outgroup members (Castelli, Tomelleri, & Zogmaister, 2008). In fact, expressing biases toward members of another group enhances the social connection among members of the ingroup (Clark & Kashima, 2007).

Categorization also has immediate effects on behavioral orientations toward others. Upon social categorization, people exhibit a "physical readiness" to approach ingroup members and avoid outgroup members (Paladino & Castelli, 2008). In terms of social relations and behavioral outcomes, people are more cooperative and trusting of ingroup than outgroup members (see Gaertner & Dovidio, 2000; Voci, 2006), as well as influenced more by their actions (Platow et al., 2007). Furthermore, individuals display more positive forms of social behavior toward ingroup than outgroup members. They exercise more personal restraint when using endangered resources shared with ingroup members than with others (Kramer & Brewer, 1984), and are more generous in their reward allocations with ingroup than outgroup members (Mullen, Brown, & Smith, 1992). Individuals also show greater empathy toward ingroup members in need than toward outgroup members (Piliavin, Dovidio, Gaertner, & Clark, 1981), and this empathy more strongly predicts helping behavior when the other person is an ingroup member than an outgroup member (Stürmer, Snyder, & Omoto, 2005).

In general, people spontaneously think more positively and deeply about ingroup members than about outgroup members, show greater emotional connection to ingroup members, and react more positively to ingroup members. Thus the sense of belonging to a group has deep psychological and social significance.

Social Identity

Social identity theory (Tajfel & Turner, 1979) and self-categorization theory (J. Turner, 1985; see also Onorato & Turner, 2001) view the distinction between personal identity and social identity as a critical one. According to social identity theory, a person's experience of identity varies along a continuum that ranges at one extreme from the self as a separate individual with personal motives, goals, and achievements, to the self as the embodiment of a social collective or group. At the individual level, one's personal welfare and goals are most salient and important. At the group level, the goals and achievements of the group are merged with one's own (see Brown & Turner, 1981), and the group's welfare is paramount. Social identity theory is relevant not only to prejudice (see Biernat's & Danaher's chapter in this volume) but also to more general intergroup dynamics. Intergroup relations begin when people think about themselves as group members rather than solely as distinct individuals.

Self-categorization theory (Turner, Hogg, Oakes, Reicher, & Wetherell, 1987; see also Hogg, 2010a), which evolved from social identity theory, further emphasizes that when people have a salient social identity they think of themselves and other ingroup members mainly in terms of a group prototype, the standard of what a member of that group should be. When social identity is salient, "people come to perceive themselves as more interchangeable exemplars of a social category than as unique personalities defined by their individual differences from others" (Turner et al., 1987, p. 50). People see themselves and other ingroup members as similar in fundamental ways and experience "depersonalized attraction" to other ingroup members—attraction based on group membership than on individual qualities (Hogg & Hains, 1996). This sense of solidarity and like-mindedness makes people feel secure and reduces the uncertainty they experience when thinking about or interacting with members of other groups (Hogg, 2010b).

Illustrating the dynamics of the distinction between personal and social identity, Verkuyten and Hagendoorn (1998) found that when individual identity was emphasized, individual differences in authoritarianism were the major predictor of Dutch students' prejudice toward Turkish migrants. Other research has shown that, when personal identity is salient, other individual differences can predict bias as well. Lower levels of openness to experience and agreeableness, two basic dimensions of personality, predict greater intergroup bias (Sibley & Duckitt, 2008; see also Duckitt, 2001). In contrast, when social identity (i.e., national identity) was made salient by Verkuyten and Hagendoorn, ingroup stereotypes and standards primarily predicted prejudiced attitudes; individual differences were no longer a significant factor. Thus, whether personal or collective identity is more salient critically shapes how a person perceives, interprets, evaluates, and responds to situations and to others.

In social identity theory, Tajfel and Turner (1979) further proposed that a person's need for positive identity may be satisfied by membership in prestigious social groups. The basic human drive in social identity theory is that people want to feel good about themselves. One way to achieve this end is to join social groups that are socially valued; another is to increase the perceived worth of the social groups to which one already belongs. To the extent that people are motivated to regard themselves positively, they will also be motivated to differentiate themselves from outsiders by perceiving as much difference as possible between their ingroup and those groups to which they do not belong (Tajfel & Turner, 1979).

This need for positive distinctiveness also motivates social comparisons that favorably differentiate ingroup from outgroup members, particularly when self-esteem has been challenged. Within social identity theory, successful intergroup discrimination is thus presumed to restore, enhance, or elevate one's self-esteem (see Rubin & Hewstone, 1998).

Drawing from social identity theory and self-categorization theory, intergroup emotion theory (Mackie, Devos, & Smith, 2000) proposes that a salient social identity also arouses corresponding group-based emotions. These emotions are functional, reflecting and signaling the significance of an event for one's group. Both the intensity and nature of the emotion experienced vary as a function of ingroup identification. For instance, after male English soccer fans watched their team lose, those who identified less with the team felt anger, not sadness, while those who identified more with the group felt sadness, not anger (Crisp, Heuston, Farr, & Turner, 2007).

Haslam and Reicher (2007) have applied the principles of social identity theory and self-categorization theory to theorizing about the perpetrators of historical atrocities, considering, for example, the actions of prominent Nazis during the Holocaust. They concluded that it was not blind obedience or extreme conformity that accounted for the Nazis' cooperation to commit genocide. Instead, it was the sense of moral superiority, coupled with the sense of identification with a like-minded group that had a true hatred for Jews, homosexuals, and gypsies, that led individual members of the Nazi party to actively and creatively engage in human atrocities.

Although social categorization generally leads to intergroup bias, Oakes (2001) notes that social categorization is not solely responsible for initiating social biases. Categorization is a necessary but not sufficient cause of intergroup bias. The nature of that bias—whether it is based on ingroup favoritism or extends to derogation and negative treatment of the outgroup—depends on a number of factors, such as whether the structural relations between groups and associated social norms foster and justify hostility or contempt (Mummendey & Otten, 2001). However, different treatment of ingroup versus outgroup members, whether rooted in favoritism for one group or derogation of another (see Biernat & Danaher's chapter in this volume), can lead to different expectations, perceptions, and behavior toward ingroup versus outgroup members that can ultimately create a self-fulfilling prophecy. In the next section, we examine how these different expectations, perceptions, and behaviors systematically influence intergroup interactive processes.

INTERGROUP INTERACTION PROCESSES

Intergroup biases affect not only how people unilaterally respond in assessing and evaluating others but also influence interactions with members of another group (i.e., intergroup interactions). In this section of the chapter, we first consider the psychological forces that influence the nature and outcomes of interactions of two people from different groups, and then we examine interactions between the memberships of different groups.

Interactions Between Individuals From Different Groups

Interactions between representatives of different groups are systematically shaped by intergroup biases in expectations, perceptions, and attributions in ways that often reinforce or exacerbate intergroup biases. These biases occur as people (a) anticipate the interaction, (b) contingently respond in these encounters, and (c) reflect on and assess the interaction.

Anticipating Interaction

As we noted earlier, group-based biases influence what people expect of others. People generally assume that ingroup members share their attitudes and beliefs more than outgroup members do (Robbins & Krueger, 2005), and sometimes expect outgroup members to have a contrasting perspective (Mullen, Dovidio, Johnson, & Copper, 1992). Perhaps as a consequence, people are less trusting of outgroup than ingroup members (Foddy, Platow, & Yamagishi, 2009). Individuals are particularly vigilant to cues of bias from outgroup members (Vorauer, 2006). In general, people not only perceive ingroup members more favorably, they also have negative expectations about how outgroup members will treat them.

Group-based biases shape how people perceive others, as well as how they believe they are perceived by others (i.e., meta-perceptions). Vorauer, Main, and O'Connell (1998) demonstrated that people's meta-perceptions can have a substantial impact on intergroup relations. Specifically, they found that White Canadians and Aboriginal Canadians believed that the other group had a negative stereotype of their group (i.e., perceived negative meta-stereotypes), which produced negative expectations for their interaction. In addition, negative meta-perceptions can motivate the avoidance of intergroup interaction altogether. Shelton and Richeson (2005) found that both Whites and Blacks were personally interested in

intergroup interaction, but they avoided these interactions because they anticipated that their overtures would be rejected by members of the other group.

Intergroup contact is one of the most robust predictors of positive intergroup understanding, empathy, and relations (see Biernat & Danaher, this volume; Pettigrew & Tropp, 2006, 2008), yet both Whites and Blacks regularly fail to engage each other, despite their personal interest, because they expect members of the other group to react negatively. The uncertainty and negative expectations associated with intergroup interaction (W. Stephan & C. Stephan, 1985, 2000) often lead to the avoidance of intergroup contact (Plant, 2004; Plant & Butz, 2006). Moreover, these effects may often be greater among low-prejudiced Whites, who may be more invested in having these interactions, than among high-prejudiced Whites (Shelton, Richeson, & Bergsieker, 2009).

In summary, whereas social categorization systematically biases intergroup perceptions in ways that enhance the evaluation of the ingroup and often disparages members of outgroups, the mere anticipation of interaction introduces additional dynamics creating divergent group perspectives. People not only enter interactions with more negative perceptions of outgroup members than ingroup members, but they also believe that outgroup members have negative perceptions of them. These meta-perceptions, however, typically underestimate the interest in and the desire of members of the other group to engage in positive intergroup contact and overestimate the negativity of their perceptions. As a consequence, people experience high levels of anxiety in anticipation of intergroup contact and avoid these interactions. The avoidance of intergroup interactions, in turn, reinforces intergroup misunderstandings and divergent perspectives. Avoiding contact with members of other groups limits the opportunities for people to correct their misperceptions of the characteristics of members of other groups (Miller, 2002) and of the ways that members of other groups view them.

Intergroup Perspectives on Interaction

Social categorization biases further influence how individuals evaluate interactions with outgroup members. When contact does occur, anxiety influences attentional processes (Trawalter, Todd, Baird, & Richeson, 2008), sensitizing interactants to cues of bias or potential threat (Vorauer, 2006), particularly when interactants are focusing on their different group memberships (Vorauer & Sasaki, 2011). This vigilance, which occurs more strongly among members of stigmatized groups, increases sensitivity to subtle cues of prejudice. Sue and colleagues (2007; see also Sue, 2010) characterize some of the cues perceived by members of stigmatized groups as "microaggressions." Microaggressions are "the brief and commonplace daily verbal, behavioral, and environmental indignities, whether intentional or unintentional, that communicate hostile, derogatory, or negative racial, gender, sexual orientation and religious slights and insults to the target person or group" (Sue et al., 2007, p. 271). Importantly, microaggressions frequently occur in ways outside the awareness of perpetrators, who will often express surprise or even offense when confronted with the idea that the action was biased. In addition, anxiety is cognitively taxing (Vorauer, Martens, & Sasaki, 2009), which reduces the capacity for people to regulate their behavior and allows typically inhibited thoughts, such as stereotypes, to intrude on and shape people's behavior. These intrusions can increase the likelihood that microaggressions will occur.

These anxiety-related processes can have both immediate and longer-term effects on dyadic and group relations. Pearson et al. (2008), for example, showed that intergroup interactions are substantially more fragile than intragroup exchanges. Whereas a slight (1-second) delay in audiovisual feedback between interactants over closed-circuit television, which was imperceptible to participants, had no detrimental affect on same-race dyadic relations, it had a significant adverse effect on cross-race dyadic interactions. Of particular importance was how this delay led participants in cross-race interactions to perceive their rapport more negatively, compared to participants in a control condition. Participants in cross-race, but not same-race interactions became more anxious as a function of the delay, and they perceived more anxiety in their partner. However, it was the perception of partner's anxiety, not their personally experienced anxiety, that primarily mediated the lower level of rapport. These effects were symmetrical for both White and Black interactants. Thus, perceived anxiety carries surplus meaning in cross-race interaction that disrupts rapport-building. Moreover, these processes, which have been studied primarily in initial interactions between strangers, have persistent effects across time (West, Pearson, Dovidio, Shelton, & Trail, 2009).

People also have a tendency to attribute problems in intergroup interactions to inherent group differences. For example, Paolini, Harwood, and Rubin (2010) demonstrated in one study that when White Australians had a negative, compared to positive, interaction with an ethnic minority confederate, the White Australians mentioned the confederate's group membership more quickly and more often. In a second study, these authors found that American young adults rated age as more salient when the valence of recent intergenerational contact was negative, compared to when it was positive, and that this effect persisted over time. Thus, for two different forms of group relations on different continents, individuals were more likely to see difficulties in their interpersonal interactions due to the different group membership of their partner.

These biases tend to persist because people may sometimes view experiences with individuals that disconfirm their expectations as an exception. Rather than revise their view of the outgroup as a whole, people may engage in subtyping. Subtyping occurs when outgroup members who disconfirm a stereotype are confined to a new category that is subordinate to the original group, thereby preserving and even strengthening the stereotype (e.g., Hewstone, Macrae, Griffiths, & Milne, 1994). However, subtyping occurs less frequently under certain conditions, such as when the outgroup member disconfirming the group stereotype is seen as a more typical outgroup member (e.g., Kunda & Oleson, 1997) or when the characteristics that distinguish the subtype from the general stereotype are more variable and distributed across people rather than clustered consistently in a subset of individuals (Deutsch & Fazio, 2008).

In intergroup interactions, groups are rarely of equal social status or power. In fact, much of the research on intergroup interaction involves encounters between majority and minority group members. Although both majority and minority group members are vulnerable to many of the same processes contributing to the persistence of intergroup bias, there also may be distinctive influences.

Not only do majority and minority group members bring different values, identities, and experiences to intergroup interactions, but also these different perspectives can shape perceptions of and reactions to the nature of the contact. Blumer (1958) proposed that group status is a fundamental factor in the extent of and type of threat that different groups experience. Surveys reveal, for example, that Blacks show higher levels of distrust and greater pessimism about intergroup relations than do Whites (Dovidio, Gaertner, Kawakami, & Hodson, 2002). Majority group members tend to perceive intergroup interactions as more harmonious and productive than do minority group members (S. Gaertner, Rust, Dovidio, Bachman, & Anastasio, 1996) but, because they value the humanity of their group more (Lammers & Stapel, 2011), they also tend to perceive subordinate and minority groups as unfairly encroaching on their rights and prerogatives (Bobo, 1999).

In addition, majority and minority group members have different preferences for the ultimate outcomes of intergroup contact. Members of high-status, majority groups are motivated to be accepted, whereas members of low-status, minority groups seek empowerment (Shnabel, Nadler, Canetti-Nisim, & Ullrich, 2008). In interracial interactions, Whites are motivated to be liked, whereas Blacks have the goal to be respected (Bergsieker, Shelton, & Richeson, 2010). Interactions that satisfy these different motivations are more effective at creating more positive exchanges, more favorable intergroup attitudes, and greater commitment to intergroup reconciliation. Also, whereas minority group members often tend to want to retain their cultural identity, majority group members may favor the assimilation of minority groups into one single culture (a traditional "melting pot" orientation)—the dominant culture.

Berry (1997) presents four forms of cultural relations in pluralistic societies that represent the intersection of "yes, no" responses to two relevant questions. First, are cultural identities of value, and to be retained? Second, are positive relations with the larger society of value, and to be sought? These combinations reflect four adaptation strategies for intergroup relations: (1) integration, when cultural identities are retained and positive relations with the larger society are sought; (2) separation, when cultural identities are retained but positive relations with the larger society are not sought; (3) assimilation, when cultural identities are abandoned and positive relations with the larger society are desired; and (4) marginalization, when cultural identities are abandoned and are not replaced by positive identification with the larger society.

Research in the area of immigration suggests that immigrant groups and majority groups have different preferences for these different types of group relations (Verkuyten, 2006). For example, van Oudenhoven, Prins, and Buunk (1998) found in the Netherlands that Dutch majority group members preferred an assimilation of minority groups (in which minority group identity was abandoned and replaced by identification with the dominant Dutch culture), whereas Turkish and Moroccan immigrants most strongly endorsed integration (in which they would retain their own cultural identity while also valuing the dominant Dutch culture). These preferences also apply to the preferences of Whites and minorities about racial and ethnic group relations in the United States, with Whites preferring assimilation and racial and ethnic minorities favoring pluralistic integration

(Dovidio, Gaertner, & Kafati, 2000; Ryan, Hunt, Weible, Peterson, & Casas, 2007).

These findings have practical as well as theoretical implications for intergroup conflict. According to the Interactive Acculturation Model (Bourhis, Montreuil, Barrette, & Montaruli, 2009), immigrants' adjustment is worse and intergroup relations more strained when acculturation ideologies of members of the host society and of immigrants diverge (see also Plaut, Thomas, & Goren, 2009; see also Peeters & Oerlemans, 2009). By contrast, Zagefka and Brown (2002), for instance, demonstrated that the more group members (either immigrants to Germany or native-Germans) perceived the acculturation ideology of outgroup members as compatible to their own, the less biased and more tolerant they were toward the other group (see also Pfafferott & Brown, 2006).

Whereas the current section has focused on interactions between individual members of different groups, which are fragile and can lead to divergent perspectives that can, without maliciousness, exacerbate social conflict, the next section considers interactions between groups collectively. Specifically, the next section reviews the role of functional relations between groups on the nature of intergroup relations and conflict.

Functional Relations Between Groups

In general, intergroup relations tend to be less positive than interpersonal relations. Insko, Schopler, and their colleagues have demonstrated a fundamental *individual-group discontinuity effect* in which groups are greedier and less trustworthy than individuals (Insko et al., 2001). As a consequence, relations between groups tend to be more competitive and less cooperative than those between individuals. Feelings of intergroup threat are a robust predictor of intergroup bias and conflict (Riek, Mania, & Gaertner, 2006).

In sociology as well as psychology, theories based on functional relations often point to competition as a fundamental cause of intergroup prejudice and conflict, as well as the nature of the group-based emotions that are experienced (Cottrell & Neuberg, 2005; Smith & Mackie, 2005). Realistic group conflict theory (Bobo, 1999; Campbell, 1965; Sherif, 1966), for example, posits that perceived group competition for resources produces efforts to reduce the access of other groups to the resources. This process was illustrated in classic work by Muzafer Sherif and his colleagues (Sherif, Harvey, White, Hood, & Sherif, 1961). In 1954, Sherif and his colleagues conducted a field study on intergroup conflict in an area adjacent to Robbers

Cave State Park in Oklahoma (USA). In this study, 22 12-year-old boys attending summer camp were randomly assigned to two groups (who subsequently named themselves Eagles and Rattlers). Over a period of weeks they became aware of the other group's existence, engaged in a series of competitive activities that generated overt intergroup conflict, and ultimately participated in a series of cooperative activities designed to ameliorate conflict and bias.

To permit time for group formation (e.g., norms and a leadership structure), the two groups were kept completely apart for 1 week. During the second week the investigators introduced competitive relations between the groups in the form of repeated competitive athletic activities such as tug-of-war, baseball, and touch football, with the winning group receiving prizes. As expected, the introduction of competitive activities generated derogatory stereotypes and conflict among these groups. These boys, however, did not simply exhibit benign forms of ingroup favoritism in the way that is frequently observed in laboratory studies. Rather, there was genuine hostility between the two groups. Each group conducted raids on the other's cabins that resulted in the destruction and theft of property. The boys carried sticks, baseball bats, and socks filled with rocks as potential weapons. Fistfights broke out between members of the groups, and food and garbage fights erupted in the dining hall. In addition, group members regularly exchanged verbal insults (e.g., "ladies first") and name-calling (e.g., "sissies," "stinkers," "pigs," "bums," "cheaters," and "communists").

During the third week, Sherif and his colleagues arranged intergroup contact under neutral, noncompetitive conditions. These interventions did not calm the ferocity of the exchanges, however. Mere intergroup contact was not sufficient to change the nature of the relations between the groups. Only after the investigators altered the functional relations between the groups by introducing a series of superordinate goals—ones that could not be achieved without the full cooperation of both groups and which were successfully achieved—did the relations between the two groups become more harmonious.

The nature of the intergroup interactions between the two groups of boys exemplifies the role of functional relations between groups in determining intergroup attitudes (Sherif et al., 1961). When groups are competitively interdependent, the interplay between the actions of each group results in positive outcomes for one group and negative outcomes for the other. Thus, in the attempt to obtain favorable outcomes for themselves, the actions of the members of each group are also realistically

perceived to be calculated to frustrate the goals of the other group. Therefore, a win-lose, zero-sum competitive relation between groups can initiate mutually negative feelings and stereotypes toward the members of the other group. In contrast, a cooperatively interdependent relation between members of different groups can reduce bias (Esses, Jackson, Dovidio, & Hodson, 2005).

Functional relations do not have to involve explicit competition with members of other groups to generate biases. In the absence of any direct evidence, people typically presume that members of other groups are competitive and will hinder the attainment of one's goals (Fiske, 2000). Moreover, feelings of interdependence on members of one's *own* group may be sufficient to produce bias. Either intragroup cooperation or intergroup competition may stimulate intergroup bias (see Rabbie & Lodewijkx, 1996). Indeed, dependence on ingroup members independently generates intergroup bias (L. Gaertner & Insko, 2000). Perhaps as a consequence of feelings of outcome dependence, increasing opportunities for interaction among ingroup members increases intergroup bias (L. Gaertner & Schopler, 1998), whereas increasing interaction between members of different groups (S. Gaertner et al., 1999) or even inducing the anticipation of future interaction with other groups (Insko et al., 2001) decreases intergroup bias.

There may be evolutionary reasons for competition between groups. According to social dominance theory (Sidanius & Pratto, 1999), because of the evolutionary advantage of hierarchical relations, groups are hierarchically organized within societies and are motivated to maintain their higher status and power over other groups. People who more strongly endorse this ideology—those higher in social dominance orientation (SDO)—believe more strongly that group hierarchies are inevitable and desirable, see the world as involving greater zero-sum competition between groups for resource, and are particularly sensitive to threats posed by other groups (Costello & Hodson, 2011). From the perspective of social dominance theory, most forms of group conflict and oppression are manifestations of this predisposition (see Biernat & Danaher's chapter in this volume for a discussion of the relationship of SDO to prejudice).

Though symbolic and realistic threats to group identity are independent factors, they can operate reciprocally or even jointly to cause increased intergroup bias. In terms of reciprocal relations, not only do psychological biases produce perceptions of competition and motivate actual competition between groups, competition between groups itself further increases bias and distrust. When people perceive outgroup members as a threat, they tend to derogate and discriminate against them more directly (Esses, Dovidio, Jackson, & Armstrong, 2001). Thus, psychological biases and actual competition often reinforce each other to escalate intergroup biases.

With respect to complementary influences, W. Stephan and his colleagues (e.g., W. Stephan, Renfro, Esses, Stephan, & Martin, 2005; see W. Stephan & Stephan, 2000) have found that personal negative stereotypes, realistic group threat, and symbolic group threat all predict discrimination against other groups (e.g., immigrants), and each accounts for a unique portion of the effect. Riek and colleagues (2006) performed a meta-analysis of 34 studies that further found that intergroup bias was related to both realistic threat ($r = .42$) and symbolic threat ($r = .45$), and these effects remained significant ($rs = .13$ and $.19$, respectively) when controlling for each other, as well as for anxiety and stereotypes.

Individual-level biases and collective biases may also have separate and additive influences. Bobo and his colleagues (see Bobo, 1999, for a review) have demonstrated that group threat and personal prejudice can contribute independently to discrimination against other groups. The independence of these effects points to the importance of considering each of these perspectives for a comprehensive understanding of intergroup bias, while at the same time reinforcing the theoretical distinctions among the hypothesized underlying mechanisms.

In addition to processes relating to one's immediate group interests, system justification theory (see Jost, Banaji, & Nosek, 2004) posits that people not only want to hold favorable attitudes about themselves and their own groups, but they also want to hold favorable attitudes about the overarching social order (system justification). System justification relates to the processes that people engage in to maintain and reinforce the current social structure (see also Biernat & Danaher's chapter in this volume).

This process of system justification has obvious advantages for members of high status or dominant groups, but system justification theory also makes the counterintuitive prediction that members of disadvantaged groups will also support the current social system, thereby justifying its legitimacy. When people see the current social system as fair and are dependent on it, they tend to see the way society *is now* as the way it *should be* (Kay et al., 2009). For example, Southern Italians, who have been traditionally lower in status than Northern Italians, also endorsed negative stereotypes of their group, particularly when they were more conventional and politically conservative (Jost, Burgess, & Mosso, 2001).

To summarize thus far, from a social psychological perspective intergroup bias and conflict is rooted in basic processes of cognition (social cognition and categorization), identity and motivation (needs for self-esteem, certainty, and control), functional relations between groups (perceived competition and zero-sum outcomes), and the reinforcement of divergent perspectives in intergroup interactions. Although these processes generally promote bias and conflict, understanding these psychological dynamics can inform strategies and interventions to reduces bias and conflict and promote integration and reconciliation between groups.

PROMOTING INTEGRATION AND RECONCILIATION

Each of the processes we discussed in the previous section, when left unmanaged, facilitate intergroup bias and social conflict. Nevertheless, these are general principles and mechanisms that, when appropriately directed and structured, can significantly improve intergroup relations. Biernat and Danaher, in their chapter on prejudice in this volume, discuss in detail how intergroup encounters that are structured around the principles of contact theory (Allport, 1954; Pettigrew & Tropp, 2006, 2011) can reduce intergroup bias. In this section we focus on two aspects of the dynamics that, in part, underlie the effectiveness of intergroup contact for reducing prejudice but have substantial impact on intergroup relations generally. These complementary strategies, which build on processes discussed earlier in this chapter, are (a) social categorization and identity, and (b) functional relations between groups.

Social Categorization and Identity

Although thinking about people in terms of their group membership may be the cognitive "default," people are able to think about others in terms of their individual qualities when they are so motivated (Fiske, 1998, 2000). In addition, people can think of themselves and others as members of different groups at different times. The process of social categorization, although fundamental to human perception, cognition, and social functioning, is fluid. The salience of different social identities varies in different contexts. Thus, even though it may be difficult to alter basic cognitive and motivational principles, it may be possible to combat bias by understanding, managing, and redirecting these processes.

In the remainder of this section, we review two ways to do this: decategorization/personalization and recategorization. *Decategorization* refers to influencing whether people identify themselves primarily as group members or as distinct individuals (Miller, 2002; Wilder, 1986). *Recategorization*, like decategorization, is designed to alter group boundaries but by redefining rather than by eliminating group categorization (S. Gaertner & Dovidio, 2000, 2009). We first turn to decategorization and the related process of personalization.

Decategorization and Personalization

Based on the assumption that the categorization of people into different groups, specifically the ingroup and an outgroup, forms the foundation for bias, the goal of *decategorization* (see Wilder, 1981, 1986) is to weaken the salience of group boundaries. Specifically, decategorization interventions encourage people from different groups to regard one another primarily as distinct individuals and interact in interpersonal (i.e., "me" and "you") rather than group-based (i.e., "we" versus "they") modes of relating to one another. In addition, if decategorization occurs through personalized interactions in which information about each other's unique qualities is exchanged, intergroup bias will be further reduced by undermining the validity of the outgroup stereotypes (Brewer & Miller, 1984; Miller, 2002; Miller, Brewer, & Edwards, 1985). Criss-crossing category memberships by forming new subgroups, each composed of members from former subgroups, changes the pattern of who is "in" and who is "out" and weaken original group boundaries, leading to decategorization (Crisp & Hewstone, 2006; see also Biernat & Danaher's chapter in this volume). Decategorization reduces intergroup bias in part by improving attitudes toward others previously categorized as outgroup members but also by producing less favorable responses to those who were previously perceived as members of one's ingroup (S. Gaertner, Mann, Murrell, & Dovidio, 1989).

In contrast to Wilder's individuation/decategorization approach, *personalization* (Brewer & Miller, 1984) involves receiving self-relevant, more intimate information about members of the outgroup. In general, individuals may be less likely to self-disclose to outgroup members than ingroup members (Stephan, Stephan, Wenzel, & Cornelius, 1991), which has the unfortunate result of limiting the amount of personal information explored in intergroup interactions and thus limits opportunities for making meaningful connections. Thus, personalization involves perceiving outgroup members in a more individuated and differentiated way but further includes a focus on information about an outgroup member that is relevant to the self. With personalized interaction, an individual's characteristics rather than their group memberships become primarily salient and can thereby undermine group stereotypes as a source of information about members of that group (Brewer & Miller, 1984; Miller, 2002), producing more positive attitudes toward their group as a whole. Consistent with this reasoning, Turner, Hewstone, and Voci (2007) found that self-disclosure in intergroup contact is associated with more positive intergroup attitudes and perceptions of the outgroup as more heterogeneous.

A number of other experimental studies demonstrate that personalization produces more positive attitudes toward an outgroup as a whole, not just to those involved in the personalized interaction, as long as people continue to think about each other to some degree in terms of their group memberships (see Miller, 2002). In Miller et al. (1985), for example, intergroup contact that permitted more personalized interactions (e.g., when interaction was person-focused rather than task focused) resulted not only in more positive attitudes toward those outgroup members present but also to other outgroup members viewed on a videotape. Thus, these conditions of intergroup contact reduced bias in both an immediate and generalizable fashion.

Whereas decategorization is designed to degrade group boundaries entirely and personalization attempts to make group membership secondary to personal connections between individuals, another approach allows group boundaries to be maintained. This alternative framework acknowledges the difficulty of eliminating perceptions of group identities and, instead of attempting to degrade group boundaries, seeks to change perceptions of the relationship between the groups while emphasizing the positive distinctiveness of each group.

Recategorization

Recategorization involves replacing the original categorization of members of different groups with an overriding shared identity. This approach builds upon the principles of social categorization and social identity theory discussed earlier in this chapter. The key idea of the Common Ingroup Identity Model is that factors that induce members of different groups to recategorize themselves as members of the same, more inclusive group can reduce intergroup bias through cognitive and motivational processes involving ingroup favoritism

The Common Ingroup Identity Model

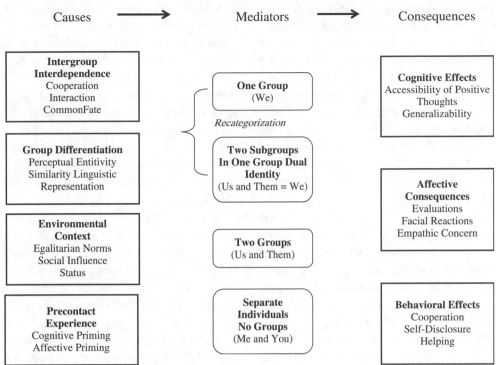

Figure 20.1 Hypothesized processes in the Common Ingroup Identity Model

(S. Gaertner & Dovidio, 2000, 2009). Thus, the more positive beliefs, feelings, and behaviors usually reserved for ingroup members are extended or redirected to former outgroup members because of their recategorized ingroup status. Consequently, recategorization dynamically changes the conceptual representations of the different groups from an "us" versus "them" orientation to a more inclusive, superordinate connection: "we."

Figure 20.1 presents the general framework and specifies the causes and consequences of a common ingroup identity. Specifically, it is hypothesized that the different types of intergroup interdependence and cognitive, perceptual, linguistic, affective, and environmental factors (listed on the left) can either independently or in concert alter individuals' cognitive representations of the aggregate (listed in the center). In addition, common ingroup identity may be achieved by increasing the salience of existing common superordinate memberships (e.g., a school, a company, a nation) or categories (e.g., students; Gómez, Dovidio, Huici, Gaertner, & Cuardrado, 2008) or by introducing factors (e.g., common goals or fate; see S. Gaertner et al., 1999) that are perceived to be shared by the memberships. These resulting cognitive representations (i.e., one group, two subgroups within one group [a dual

identity], two groups, or separate individuals) are then proposed to result in the specific cognitive, affective and overt behavioral consequences (listed on the right).

For instance, cooperative intergroup interaction improves outgroup attitudes and reduces bias between members of different groups through its effect on creating a more inclusive, common identity. Once former outgroup members are regarded as ingroup members, it is proposed that they would be accorded the benefits of ingroup status heuristically. There would likely be more positive thoughts, feelings, and behaviors (listed on the right) toward these former outgroup members by virtue of categorizing them now as ingroup members.

Experimental evidence of intergroup attitudes in support of the Common Ingroup Identity Model comes from research using both ad hoc and real groups, with children as well as adults, and in the United States (e.g., see S. Gaertner & Dovidio, 2000; Houlette et al., 2004; Nier, Gaertner, Dovidio, Banker, & Ward, 2001) as well as in other countries (e.g., Guerra et al., 2010). Recategorization in terms of a common ingroup identity can reduce even very robust and fundamental biases. For example, Hehman et al. (2010) demonstrated that grouping faces in terms of participants' own university versus another university eliminated the greater accuracy that Whites typically have for identifying White faces over Black faces.

Common identity also promotes intergroup forgiveness and trust. Wohl and Branscombe (2005) showed that increasing the salience of Jewish students' "human identity," in contrast to their "Jewish identity," increased their perceptions of similarity between Jews and Germans, as well as their willingness to forgive Germans for the Holocaust and their willingness to associate with contemporary German students. A shared superordinate identity has also been shown to affect responsiveness to others. Kane, Argote, and Levine (2005) found that group members were more accepting of a newcomer's innovation when the newcomer shared a superordinate identity with them than when the newcomer did not, and that the strength of superordinate group identification was positively related to the extent to which group members accepted the innovative solution. Also, people are more responsive to the needs of former outgroup members perceived within a common ingroup identity across a range of situations (Dovidio et al., 1997), including emergency situations (Levine, Prosser, Evans, & Reicher, 2005).

However, efforts to induce a common identity can sometimes be met with resistance that can increase bias between members of the original groups. People are motivated to maintain the positive distinctiveness of their group relative to other groups (Tajfel & Turner, 1979). Furthermore, when the integrity of one's group identity is threatened, people are motivated to reestablish positive and distinctive group identities and thereby maintain relatively high levels of intergroup bias (Brown & Wade, 1987) or show increased levels of bias (see Jetten, Spears, & Postmes, 2004, for a review). Consistent with this reasoning, introducing interventions such as emphasizing similarity or overlapping boundaries between the groups (Dovidio et al., 1997; Jetten, Spears, & Manstead, 1997) or shared identity (Hornsey & Hogg, 2000) can exacerbate intergroup bias as a way of reaffirming positive distinctiveness. This effect is particularly likely to occur among people who value their original group highly, such as those more highly identified with their original group (Crisp, Walsh, & Hewstone, 2006), and when the initiative to form a superordinate identity is perceived to come from an outgroup rather than an ingroup member (Gómez et al., 2008).

However, within the context of the Common Ingroup Identity Model, the development of a common ingroup identity does not necessarily require each group to forsake its less inclusive group identity. Social identities are complex; every individual belongs to multiple groups simultaneously (Brewer, 2000). Thus, depending on their degree of identification with different categories and contextual factors that make particular identities more salient, individuals may activate one or more of these identities simultaneously (Roccas & Brewer, 2002) as well as sequentially (J. Turner et al., 1987). As depicted by the "subgroups within one group" (i.e., a dual identity) representation, it is possible for members to conceive of two groups (for example, science and art majors) as distinct units within the context of a superordinate (i.e., university identity) social entity. Morrison and Chung (2011) found that participants who were induced to identify themselves as "European American," a dual identity, exhibited less bias toward U.S. minority groups than did participants to identify themselves as "White."

It is also important to recognize that the successful induction of a common ingroup identity does not necessarily eliminate social biases entirely; it may simply redirect them. When recategorization occurs and a superordinate group identity is established, other outgroups groups at the same level of inclusiveness are likely to be recognized as relevant comparison groups. Because of the need to establish, maintain, or enhance the positive distinctiveness of the superordinate identity, biases toward these groups are likely to be aroused (Mummendey, Klink, & Brown, 2001). For example, Kessler and Mummendey (2001) found, consistent with the Common Ingroup Identity Model, that East Germans who recategorized West Germans and East Germans within the superordinate national identity of "Germans" displayed reduced bias toward West Germans. However, they also became more biased over time toward members of other countries relative to those who continued to use the East-West German categorization scheme. Kessler and Mummendey noted that "recategorization is a two-edged process: Although it reduces conflict at the subgroup level, it may initiate conflict at the common ingroup level" (p. 1099).

In addition, a common identity may sometimes be more effective for promoting social harmony (improved intergroup attitudes) than social change toward equality (either through the actions of the majority or collective action by minorities). If common identity reduces attention to structural inequality as it promotes positive attitudes toward members of the outgroup, it can have consequences for group members' expectations regarding intergroup relations and hierarchy. Specifically, such outcomes may inflate perceptions of the fairness of the advantaged group among disadvantaged-group members and thus produce optimism about prospects of equality and relax their motivation to take direct action for social change (Saguy, Tausch, Dovidio, & Pratto, 2009).

Saguy et al., for example, found that stronger feelings of positive connections between Arabs and Jews in Israel was associated with Arabs' more positive attitudes toward Jews and with reduced awareness of inequality between Jews and Arabs. Improved attitudes also were associated with increased perceptions of Jews as fair. Moreover, both perceptions of Jews as fair and reduced awareness of inequality were associated with reduced support for social change. Thus, through its effects on the way disadvantaged-group members viewed social inequality and members of the other group, contact was associated with a *decrease* in support for social change. Results of the study of Muslims in India (Saguy, Tausch, Dovidio, Pratto, & Singh, 2011) replicated these findings (see also Wright & Lubensky, 2009).

As explored in this section, decategorization, personalization, and recategorization have all been shown to decrease intergroup bias and social conflict by producing changes in personal and collective identity. These approaches focus primarily on how people conceive of others. In the next section, we discuss the role of functional relations between groups. Whereas intergroup competition typically creates and reinforces intergroup bias and conflict, cooperation between members of different groups can facilitate positive relations. Cooperation is a key element of contact theory for the reduction of prejudice (see Biernat & Danaher, this volume), but it is also an important factor for intergroup dynamics more broadly.

Functional Relations

Consistent with functional theories of intergroup relations, changing the nature of interdependence between members of different groups from perceived competition to cooperation significantly improves intergroup attitudes (Cook, 1985; Slavin & Cooper, 1999). The *jigsaw classroom* is one particularly effective strategy that has been used in schools (Aronson, 2004). This strategy, in which each participant has a valuable piece of the information that (like a jigsaw piece) is needed to obtain the total correct solution, is designed to replace competitive aspects of classrooms with a cooperative one. Putting students into an interdependent, cooperative relationship and acknowledging the value of each student's different contribution improved their level of liking, degree of friendship, self-esteem, and academic performance. The jigsaw classroom remains a popular and effective intervention today (Aronson, 2004).

Recent empirical and theoretical work has also integrated elements of social categorization and identity processes with functional relations perspectives. As reviewed earlier, one of the fundamental premises of social identity theory is that people are motivated to maintain the positive distinctiveness of their social identity. Interventions that threaten the integrity of collective identity, such as attempts to degrade group boundaries, can sometimes arouse resistance and exacerbate bias. Recognizing the potential of identity threat to arouse intergroup bias, Hewstone and Brown (1986) introduced a different categorization-based framework for reducing intergroup bias, the Mutual Intergroup Differentiation Model. In this model, Hewstone and Brown posited that intergroup relations will be harmonious when group identities remain *mutually differentiated,* rather than threatened by extinction, but maintained in the context of cooperative intergroup interaction. Thus, relative to the decategorization strategies, this perspective proposes that maintaining group distinctiveness within a cooperative intergroup relationship should be associated with low levels of intergroup threat and, consequently, with lower levels of intergroup bias. In addition, the salience of intergroup boundaries provides an associative mechanism through which changes in outgroup attitudes that occur during intergroup contact can generalize to the outgroup as a whole. Because the most recent research has focused on the hypothesis that to be effective for reducing bias contact should be *intergroup* contact, with category memberships salient, they no longer refer to their approach as the Mutual Intergroup Differentiation Model but prefer to label it simply as intergroup contact theory (see Brown & Hewstone, 2005).

According to Brown and Hewstone's (2005) framework, opportunities for intergroup contact (quantity of contact) are important in that these encounters increase the possibility of forming close (high quality) friendships with outgroup members. The salience of the friend's outgroup membership and the perceived typicality of the friend as a member of that group moderate the amount of anxiety experienced with other members of the group and perspective-taking and empathy for the group. Less intergroup anxiety and greater cognitive and affective empathy, in turn, mediate more positive attitudes toward the outgroup.

Supportive of Brown and Hewstone's (2005) approach, several studies have demonstrated that the effects of positive contact produce more generalized reductions in bias toward the outgroup when people are aware of the intergroup, rather than interpersonal, nature of the interaction (see Kenworthy, Turner, Hewstone & Voci, 2005; Pettigrew, 1998). Evidence in support of this approach (see also Brown & Hewstone, 2005) comes from the results of an experiment by Brown and Wade (1987) in which work teams composed of students from two different faculties engaged in a cooperative effort to produce a two-page magazine article. When the representatives of the two groups were assigned separate roles in the team task (one group working on figures and layout, the other working on text), the contact experience had a more positive effect on intergroup attitudes than when the two groups were not provided with distinctive roles (see also Dovidio, Gaertner, & Validzic, 1998; Ensari & Miller, 2002; Voci & Hewstone, 2003).

The mutual intergroup differentiation/intergroup contact theory perspective further proposes that in addition to the salience of social categories, the perceived typicality of outgroup members is a critical moderator of the extent to which positive intergroup contact can reduce bias toward the outgroup as a whole. Rothbart and John (1985) suggested, and subsequent research has demonstrated, that the more representative (prototypical) of his or her group a person is perceived to be, the greater the likelihood that impressions about that person will generalize to change perceptions of the group overall (Wilder, Simon, & Faith, 1996). Although people tend to make stronger generalizations from a member to the group for stereotype-consistent than stereotype-inconsistent impressions (Johnson, Ashburn-Nardo, Spicer, & Dovidio, 2008), typicality plays an important role in changing group stereotypes.

The relationship between exposure to counterstereotypic group members and amount of stereotype change for the social group is mediated by the degree of perceived typicality of the group members (Hewstone, Hassebrauck, Wirth, & Waenke, 2000). In addition, typicality has been shown to moderate the effects of contact with outgroup members. With respect to group stereotypes, more change occurs when people are presented with counterstereotypic information about representative than nonrepresentative group members (Weber & Crocker, 1983). In terms of attitudes toward the outgroup, cooperation more effectively reduces prejudice when the partner is perceived as more typical of the group (Brown, Eller, Leeds, & Stace, 2007). The moderating effect of typicality, however, occurs primarily when the outgroup is perceived as homogeneous rather than heterogeneous (Brown, Vivian, & Hewstone, 1999). Perceptions of typicality reduce the likelihood that group members who demonstrate counterstereotypic qualities will be seen as exceptions, which can be discounted, or as representing a subtype of the group, leaving the overall group stereotype intact and outgroup evaluation largely unaffected.

CONCLUSION

In this chapter, we have examined the fundamental psychological processes related to intergroup relations, group conflict, social harmony, and intergroup integration. Intergroup bias and conflict are complex phenomena having historical, cultural, economic, as well as psychological roots. A debate about whether a societal, institutional, intergroup, or individual level of analysis is most appropriate, or a concern about which model of bias or bias reduction accounts for the most variance, may thus be not only futile but may distract scholars from a more fundamental mission—developing a comprehensive model of social conflict, harmony, and integration.

We propose that understanding how structural, social, and psychological mechanisms *jointly* shape intergroup relations can have both valuable theoretical and practical implications. Theoretically, individual-difference, functional, and collective identity approaches can be viewed as complementary rather than competing explanations for social conflict and harmony (see Figure 20.2). Functional relations within and between groups and social identity can influence both perceptions of intragroup and intergroup support or threat, as well as the nature of group representations. For instance, greater dependence on ingroup members can strengthen the perceived boundaries, fostering representations as members of different groups and increasing perceptions of threat (L. Gaertner & Insko, 2000). Empirically, self-interest, realistic group threat, and identity threat independently affect intergroup relations adversely (Bobo, 1999; Esses et al., 2001; Stephan & Stephan, 2000). Perceptions of functional relations and group representations can also mutually influence one another. Perceptions of competition or threat increase the salience of different group representations and decrease the salience of superordinate group connections, whereas stronger inclusive representations of the groups can decrease perceptions of intergroup competition.

Similarly, within the social categorization approach, researchers have posited that decategorization/ personalization and recategorization processes each play a role in the reduction of bias over time (Pettigrew, 1998), and also that these processes can facilitate each other reciprocally (S. Gaertner & Dovidio, 2009; Hewstone, 1996). Within an alternating sequence of categorization processes, mutual differentiation may emerge initially to neutralize threats to original group identities posed by the recategorization and decategorization processes. Once established, mutual differentiation can facilitate the subsequent recognition and acceptance of a salient

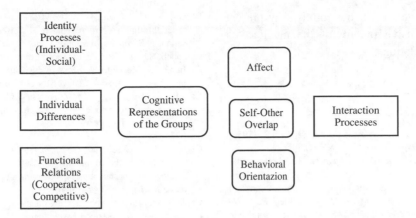

Salient identity, individual differences, and functional relations influence how the groups are perceived (e.g., as one common group or different groups, which shapes the ways people feel about, think about, and act toward members of other groups). The nature and outcomes of the interactions between members of different groups or between the groups collectively then can reduce or exacerbate bias, produces cyclical changes: They can alter the salience and meaning of different identities and the ways people conceive of the functional relations between groups.

Figure 20.2   Overview of influences shaping intergroup interaction processes

superordinate identity and recategorization, which would have previously stimulated threats to the distinctiveness of group identities.

Reductions in perceived threat, increased perceptions of intergroup support, and more inclusive representations (either as a superordinate group or as a dual identity), in turn, can activate group- and individual-level processes that can reduce intergroup conflict (see Figure 20.2). In addition, people may come to see respect for difference and diversity not only as beneficial for solving complex problems but also, eventually, as an integral aspect of group common identity (Jans, Postmes, & van der Zee, 2011).

Pragmatically, understanding the nature of bias and conflict can suggest ways in which these forces can be harnessed and redirected to promote social harmony. Given the different perspectives, needs, and motivations of majority (high-status) and minority (low-status) groups, interventions based on these principles need to be considered carefully. Nevertheless, understanding the multilevel nature of prejudice and discrimination is an essential step for finding solutions—which may need to be similarly multifaceted. These principles may be applied to reduce social conflict and facilitate the integration of groups as disparate as corporations and stepfamilies (S. Gaertner, Bachman, Dovidio, & Banker, 2001) and more generally to meet the challenge of managing immigration successfully—in ways that facilitate the achievement and well-being of immigrants and that produce the cooperation

and support of residents of the receiving country (Esses et al., 2001).

In addition, these approaches may be applied integratively to reduce international tensions and improve national relations (Kelman, 2005, 2010; Staub, 2008). Kelman (2005), for example, described the activities and outcomes of a program of workshops designed to improve Palestinian-Israeli relations and to contribute to peace in the Middle East. These workshops require Palestinian and Israeli participants, working within a common workshop identity, to search for solutions that satisfy the needs of both parties. This structure changes relations between the groups from competition to cooperation and facilitates the development of mutually differentiated national identities within a common goal, and permits the type of personalized interaction that can enhance social harmony. Thus, a strategic and reflective application of basic social psychological principles can have significant practical benefits in situations of long-standing conflict.

In conclusion, the issues related to social conflict, harmony, and integration are complex indeed. As a consequence, approaches to understanding these processes need to address the issues at different levels of analysis and to consider structural as well as psychological factors. This diversity of perspectives produces a complicated and sometimes apparently inconsistent picture of the nature of intergroup relations. However, rather than viewing these approaches as competing positions, we suggest that they often reflect different perspectives on a very large issue.

No single position is definitive, but jointly they present a relatively comprehensive picture of the multifaceted nature of intergroup relations.

REFERENCES

Adorno, T., Frenkel-Brunswik, E., Levinson, D., & Sanford, R. (1950). *The authoritarian personality.* New York, NY: Harper.

Allport, G. W. (1954). *The nature of prejudice.* Cambridge, MA: Addison-Wesley.

Aronson, E. (2004). Reducing hostility and building compassion: Lessons from the jigsaw classroom. In A. G. Miller (Ed.), *The social psychology of good and evil* (pp. 469–488). New York, NY: Guilford Press.

Bergsieker, H. B., Shelton, J. N., & Richeson, J. A. (2010). To be liked versus respected: Divergent goals in interracial interaction. *Journal of Personality and Social Psychology, 99,* 248–264.

Berry, J. W. (1997). Immigration, acculturation, and adaptation. *Applied Psychology: An International Review, 46,* 5–34.

Blumer, H. (1958). Race prejudice as a sense of group position. *Pacific Sociological Review, 1,* 3–7.

Bobo, L. D. (1999). Prejudice as group position: Microfoundations of a sociological approach to racism and race relations. *Journal of Social Issues, 55,* 445–472.

Bogardus, E. (1925). Measuring social distance. *Journal of Applied Sociology, 9,* 299–308.

Boldry, J. G., Gaertner, L., & Quinn, J. (2007). Measuring the measures: A meta-analytic investigation of the measures of outgroup homogeneity. *Group Processes and Intergroup Relations, 10,* 147–178.

Bourhis, R. Y., Montreuil, A., Barrette, G., & Montaruli, E. (2009). Acculturation and immigrant/host community relations in multicultural settings. In S. Demoulin, J. P. Leyens, & J. F. Dovidio (Eds.), *Intergroup misunderstanding: Impact of divergent social realities* (pp. 39–61). New York, NY: Psychology Press.

Brewer, M. B. (1988). A dual process model of impression formation. In T. S. Srull & R. S. Wyer (Eds.), *Advances in social cognition: Vol. I: A dual process model of impression formation* (pp. 1–36). Hillsdale, NJ: Erlbaum.

Brewer, M. B. (2000). Reducing prejudice through cross-categorization: Effects of multiple social identities. In S. Oskamp (Ed.), *Reducing prejudice and discrimination: The Claremont symposium on applied social psychology* (pp. 165–183). Mahwah, NJ: Erlbaum.

Brewer, M. B., & Brown, R. J. (1998). Intergroup relations. In D. T. Gilbert, S. T. Fiske, & G. Lindzey (Eds.), *The handbook of social psychology* (Vol. 2, pp. 554–594). New York, NY: McGraw-Hill.

Brewer, M. B., & Miller, N. (1984). Beyond the contact hypothesis: Theoretical perspectives on desegregation. In N. Miller & M. B. Brewer (Eds.), *Groups in contact: The psychology of desegregation* (pp. 281–302). Orlando, FL: Academic Press.

Brown, R., Eller, A., Leeds, S., & Stace, K. (2007). Intergroup contact and intergroup attitudes: A longitudinal study. *European Journal of Social Psychology, 37,* 692–703.

Brown, R., & Hewstone, M. (2005). An integrative theory of intergroup contact. In M. P. Zanna (Ed.), *Advances in experimental social psychology* (Vol. 37, pp. 255–343). San Diego, CA: Academic Press.

Brown, R. J., & Turner, J. C. (1981). Interpersonal and intergroup behavior. In J. C. Turner & H. Giles (Eds.), *Intergroup behavior* (pp. 33–64). Chicago, IL: University of Chicago Press.

Brown, R. J., & Wade, G. (1987). Superordinate goals and intergroup behavior: The effect of role ambiguity and status on intergroup attitudes and task performance. *European Journal of Social Psychology, 17,* 131–142.

Brown, R. J., Vivian, J., & Hewstone, M. (1999). Changing attitudes through intergroup contact: The effects of group membership salience. *European Journal of Social Psychology, 29,* 741–764.

Campbell, D. T. (1965). Ethnocentric and other altruistic motives. In D. Levine (Ed.), *Nebraska symposium on motivation* (Vol. 13, pp. 283–311). Lincoln: University of Nebraska Press.

Castelli, L., Tomelleri, S., & Zogmaister, C. (2008). Implicit ingroup metafavoritism: Subtle preference for ingroup members displaying ingroup bias. *Personality and Social Psychology Bulletin, 34,* 807–818.

Clark, A. E., & Kashima, Y. (2007). Stereotypes help people connect with others in the community. A situated functional analysis of the stereotype consistency bias in communication. *Journal of Personality and Social Psychology, 93,* 1028–1039.

Cook, S. W. (1985). Experimenting on social issues: The case of school desegregation. *American Psychologist, 40,* 452–460.

Cooley, C. (1902). *Human nature and the social order.* New York, NY: Scribner's.

Costello, K., & Hodson, B. (2011). Social dominance-based threat reactions to immigrants in need of assistance. *European Journal of Social Psychology, 41,* 220–231.

Cottrell, C. A., & Neuberg, S. L. (2005). Different emotional reactions to different groups: A sociofunctional threat-based approach to "prejudice." *Journal of Personality and Social Psychology, 88,* 770–789.

Crisp, R. J., Heuston, S., Farr, M. J., & Turner, R. N. (2007). Seeing red or feeling blue: Differentiated intergroup emotions and ingroup identification in soccer fans. *Group Processes and Intergroup Relations, 10,* 9–26.

Crisp, R. J., & Hewstone, M. (2006). (Eds.), *Multiple social categorization: Processes, models, and applications.* Philadelphia, PA: Psychology Press.

Crisp, R. J., Walsh, J., & Hewstone, M. (2006). Crossed categorization in common ingroup contexts. *Personality and Social Psychology Bulletin, 32,* 1204–1218.

Deutsch, R., & Fazio, R. H. (2008). How subtyping shapes perception: Predictable exceptions to the rule reduce attention to stereotype-associated dimensions. *Journal of Experimental Social Psychology, 44,* 1020–1034.

Dollard, J., Doob, L., Miller, N. E., Mowrer, O., & Sears, R. (1939). *Frustration and aggression.* New Haven, CT: Yale University Press.

Dovidio, J. F., & Gaertner, S. L. (2010). Intergroup bias. In S. T. Fiske, D. Gilbert, & G. Lindzey (Eds.), *Handbook of social psychology* (Vol. 2, 5th ed., pp. 1084–1121). New York, NY: Wiley.

Dovidio, J. F., Gaertner, S. L., & Kafati, G. (2000). Group identity and intergroup relations: The common in-group identity model. In S. R. Thye, E. J. Lawler, M. W. Macy, & H. A. Walker (Eds.), *Advances in group processes* (Vol. 17, pp. 1–34). Stamford, CT: JAI Press.

Dovidio, J. F., Gaertner, S. L., Kawakami, K., & Hodson, G. (2002). Why can't we just get along? Interpersonal biases and interracial distrust. *Cultural Diversity & Ethnic Minority Psychology, 8,* 88–102.

Dovidio, J. F., Gaertner, S. L., & Saguy, T. (2009). Commonality and the complexity of "we": Social attitudes and social change. *Personality and Social Psychology Review, 13,* 3–20.

Dovidio, J. F., Gaertner, S. L., & Validzic, A. (1998). Intergroup bias: Status, differentiation, and a common ingroup identity. *Journal of Personality and Social Psychology, 75,* 109–120.

Dovidio, J. F., Gaertner, S. L., Validzic, A., Matoka, K., Johnson, B., & Frazier, S. (1997). Extending the benefits of re-categorization: Evaluations, self-disclosure and helping. *Journal of Experimental Social Psychology, 33,* 401–420.

Duckitt, J. (2001). A dual-process cognitive-motivational theory of ideology and prejudice. In M. P. Zanna, (Ed.), *Advances in experimental social psychology* (Vol. 33, pp. 41–113). New York, NY: Academic Press.

Dunham, Y. (2011). An angry = outgroup effect. *Journal of Experimental Social Psychology, 47,* 668–671.

Elfenbein, H. A., & Ambady, N. (2002). On the universality and cultural specificity of emotion recognition: A meta-analysis. *Psychological Bulletin, 128,* 203–235.

Ensari, N., & Miller, N. (2002). The outgroup must not be so bad after all: The effects of disclosure, typicality, and salience on intergroup bias. *Journal of Personality and Social Psychology, 83,* 313–329.

Esses, V. M., Dovidio, J. F., Jackson, L. M., & Armstrong, T. M. (2001). The immigration dilemma: The role of perceived group competition, ethnic prejudice, and national identity. *Journal of Social Issue, 57,* 389–412.

Esses, V. M., Jackson, L. M., Dovidio, J. F., & Hodson, G. (2005). Instrumental relations among groups: Group competition, conflict, and prejudice. In J. F. Dovidio, P. Glick, & L. A. Rudman (Eds.), *On the nature of prejudice: Fifty years after Allport* (pp. 227–243). Malden, MA: Blackwell.

Fiske, S. T. (1998). Stereotyping, prejudice, and discrimination. In D. T. Gilbert, S. T. Fiske, & G. Lindzey (Eds.), *The handbook of social psychology* (Vol. 2, 4th ed., pp. 357–411). New York, NY: McGraw-Hill.

Fiske, S. T. (2000). Interdependence and the reduction of prejudice. In S. Oskamp (Ed.), *Reducing prejudice and discrimination* (pp. 115–135). Hillsdale, NJ: Erlbaum.

Fiske, S. T., Lin, M., & Neuberg, S. L. (1999). The continuum model: Ten years later. In S. Chaiken & Y. Trope (Eds.), *Dual process theories in social psychology* (pp. 231–254). New York, NY: Guilford Press.

Foddy, M., Platow, M. J., & Yamagishi, H. (2009). Group-based trust in strangers: The role of stereotypes and expectations. *Psychological Science, 20,* 419–422.

Gaertner, L., & Insko, C. A. (2000). Intergroup discrimination in the minimal group paradigm: Categorization, reciprocation, or fear? *Journal of Personality and Social Psychology, 79,* 77–94.

Gaertner, L., & Schopler, J. (1998). Perceived ingroup entitativity and intergroup bias: An interconnection of self and others. *European Journal of Social Psychology, 28,* 963–980.

Gaertner, S. L., Bachman, B. A., Dovidio, J. D., & Banker, B. S. (2001). Corporate mergers and stepfamily marriages: Identity, harmony, and commitment. In M. A. Hogg & D. Terry (Eds.), *Social identity in organizations* (pp. 265–288). Oxford, UK: Blackwell.

Gaertner, S. L., & Dovidio, J. F. (2000). *Reducing intergroup bias: The common ingroup identity model.* Philadelphia, PA: Psychology Press.

Gaertner, S. L., & Dovidio, J. F. (2009). A common ingroup identity: A categorization-based approach for reducing intergroup bias. In. T. Nelson (Ed.), *Handbook of prejudice* (pp. 489–506). New York, NY: Psychology Press.

Gaertner, S. L., Dovidio, J. F., Rust, M. C., Nier, J., Banker, B., Ward, C. M., ... Houlette, M. (1999). Reducing intergroup bias: Elements of intergroup cooperation. *Journal of Personality and Social Psychology, 76,* 388–402.

Gaertner, S. L., Mann, J. A., Murrell, A. J., & Dovidio, J. F. (1989). Reduction of intergroup bias: The benefits of recategorization. *Journal of Personality and Social Psychology, 57,* 239–249.

Gaertner, S. L., Rust, M. C., Dovidio, J. F., Bachman, B. A., & Anastasio, P. A. (1996). The contact hypothesis: The role of a common ingroup identity on reducing intergroup bias among majority and minority group members. In J. L. Nye & A. M. Brower (Eds.), *What's social about social cognition?* (pp. 230–360). Newbury Park, CA: Sage.

Gómez, A., Dovidio, J. F., Huici, C., Gaertner, S. L., & Cuardrado, I. (2008). The other side of we: When outgroup members express common identity. *Personality and Social Psychology Bulletin, 34,* 1613–1626.

Guerra, R., Rebelo, M., Monteiro, M. B., Riek, B. M., Maia, E. W., Gaertner, S. L., & Dovidio, J. F. (2010). How should intergroup contact be structured to reduce bias among majority and minority group children? *Group Processes and Intergroup Relations, 13,* 445–460.

Hamilton, D. L. (1981). Stereotyping and intergroup behavior: Some thoughts on the cognitive approach. In D. L. Hamilton (Ed.), *Cognitive processes in stereotyping and intergroup behavior* (pp. 333–353). Hillsdale, NJ: Erlbaum.

Haslam, S. A., & Reicher, S. (2007). Beyond the banality of evil: Three dynamics of an interactionist social psychology of tyranny. *Personality and Social Psychology Bulletin, 33,* 615–622.

Hehman, E., Mania, E. W., & Gaertner, S. L. (2010). Where the division lies: Common ingroup identity moderates the cross-race facial-recognition effect. *Journal of Experimental Social Psychology, 46,* 445–448.

Hewstone, M. (1990). The "ultimate attribution error"? A review of the literature on intergroup attributions. *European Journal of Social Psychology, 20,* 311–335.

Hewstone, M. (1996). Contact and categorization: Social psychological interventions to change intergroup relations. In C. N. Macrae, C. Stangor, & M. Hewstone (Eds.), *Stereotypes and stereotyping* (pp. 323–368). New York, NY: Guilford Press.

Hewstone, M., & Brown, R. J. (1986). Contact is not enough: An intergroup perspective on the "Contact Hypothesis." In M. Hewstone & R. Brown (Eds.), *Contact and conflict in intergroup encounters* (pp. 1–44). Oxford, UK: Basil Blackwell, Oxford.

Hewstone, M., Hassebrauck, M., Wirth, A., & Waenke, M. (2000). Pattern of disconfirming information and processing instructions as determinants of stereotype change. *British Journal of Social Psychology, 39,* 399–411.

Hewstone, M., Macrae, C. N., Griffiths, R. J., & Milne, A. B. (1994). Cognitive models of stereotype change: 5. Measurement, development, and consequences of subtyping. *Journal of Experimental Social Psychology, 30,* 505–526.

Hogg, M. A. (2006). Social identity theory. In P. J. Burke (Ed.), *Contemporary social psychological theories* (pp. 111–136). Palo Alto, CA: Stanford University Press.

Hogg, M. A. (2010a). Self-categorization theory. In J. M. Levine & M. A. Hogg (Eds.), *Encyclopedia of group processes & intergroup relations* (pp. 728–731). Thousand Oaks CA: Sage.

Hogg, M. A. (2010b). Human groups, social categories, and collective self: Social identity and the management of self-uncertainty. In R. Arkin, K. C. Oleson, & P. J. Carroll (Eds.), *Handbook of the uncertain self* (pp. 401–420). New York, NY: Psychology Press.

Hogg, M. A., & Hains, S. C. (1996). Intergroup relations and group solidarity: Effects of group identification and social beliefs on depersonalized attraction. *Journal of Personality and Social Psychology, 70,* 295–309.

Hornsey, M. J., & Hogg, M. A. (2000). Subgroup relations: A comparison of mutual intergroup differentiation and common ungroup identity models of prejudice reduction. *Personality and Social Psychology Bulletin, 26,* 242–256.

Houlette, M., Gaertner, S. L., Johnson, K. M., Banker, B. S., Riek, B. M., & Dovidio, J. F. (2004). Developing a more inclusive social identity: An elementary school intervention. *Journal of Social Issues, 60,* 35–56.

Howard, J. M., & Rothbart, M. (1980). Social categorization for ingroup and out-group behavior. *Journal of Personality and Social Psychology, 38,* 301–310.

Hugenberg, K., & Bodenhausen, G. V. (2004). Ambiguity in social categorization: The role of prejudice and facial affect in race categorization. *Psychological Science, 15,* 342–345.

Insko, C. A., Schopler, J., Gaertner, L., Wildschut, T., Kozar, R., Pinter, B., ... Montoya, M. R. (2001). Interindividual-intergroup discontinuity reduction through the anticipation of future interaction. *Journal of Personality and Social Psychology, 80,* 95–111.

Jans, L., Postmes, T., & van der Zee, K. (2011). The induction of shared identity: The positive role of individual distinctiveness for groups. *Personality and Social Psychology Bulletin, 37,* 1130–1141.

Jetten, J., Spears, R., & Manstead, A. S. R. (1997). Strength of identification and intergroup differentiation: The influence of group norms. *European Journal of Social Psychology, 27,* 603–609.

Jetten, J., Spears, R., & Postmes, T. (2004). Intergroup distinctiveness and differentiation: A meta-analytic integration. *Journal of Personality and Social Psychology, 86,* 862–879.

Johnson, J. D., Ashburn-Nardo, L., Spicer, V., & Dovidio, J. F. (2008). The role of Blacks' discriminatory expectations in their prosocial orientations toward whites. *Journal of Experimental Social Psychology, 44,* 1498–1505.

Jost, J. T., Banaji, M., & Nosek, B. A. (2004). A decade of system justification theory: Accumulated evidence of conscious and unconscious bolstering of the *status quo. Political Psychology, 25,* 881–919.

Jost, J. T., Burgess, D., & Mosso, C. O (2001). Conflicts of legitimation among self, group, and system: The integrative potential of system justification theory. In J. T. Jost & B. Major (Eds.), *The psychology of legitimacy: Emerging perspectives on ideology, justice, and intergroup relations* (pp. 363–388). New York, NY: Cambridge University Press.

Judd, C. M., Park, B., Yzerbyt, V., Gordijn, E. H., & Muller, D. (2005). Attributions of intergroup bias and outgroup homogeneity to ingroup and outgroup others. *European Journal of Social Psychology, 35,* 677–704.

Kane, A. A., Argote, L., & Levine, J. M. (2005). Knowledge transfer between groups via personnel rotation: Effects of social identity and knowledge quality. *Organizational Behavior and Human Decision Processes, 96,* 56–71.

Katz, D., & Braly, K. (1933). Racial stereotypes in one hundred college students. *Journal of Abnormal and Social Psychology, 28,* 280–290.

Kay, A. C., Gaucher, D., Peach, J. M., Laurin, K., Friesen, J., Zanna, M. P., & Spencer, S. J. (2009). Inequality, discrimination, and the power of the status quo: Direct evidence for a motivation to see the way things are as the way they should be. *Journal of Personality and Social Psychology, 97,* 421–434.

Kelman, H. C. (2005). Building trust among enemies: The central challenge for international conflict resolution. *International Journal of Intercultural Relations, 29,* 639–650.

Kelman, H. C. (2010). Interactive problem solving: Changing political culture in the pursuit of conflict resolution. *Peace and Conflict: Journal of Peace Psychology, 16,* 389–413.

Kenworthy, J. B., Turner, R. N., Hewstone, M., & Voci, A. (2005). Intergroup contact: When does it work, and why? In J. F. Dovidio, P. Glick, & L. A. Rudman (Eds.), *On the nature of prejudice: Fifty years after Allport* (pp. 278–292). Malden, MA: Blackwell.

Kessler, T., & Mummendey, A. (2001). Is there any scapegoat around? Determinants of intergroup conflict at different categorization levels. *Journal of Personality and Social Psychology, 81,* 1090–1102.

Kramer, R. M., & Brewer, M. B. (1984). Effects of group identity on resource utilization in a simulated commons dilemma. *Journal of Personality and Social Psychology, 46,* 1044–1057.

Kunda, Z., & Oleson, K. C. (1997). When exceptions prove the rule: How extremity of deviance determines the impact of deviant examples on stereotypes. *Journal of Personality and Social Psychology, 72,* 965–979.

Lammers, J., & Stapel, D. A. (2011). Power increases dehumanization. *Group Processes & Intergroup Relations, 14,* 113–126.

Levine, M., Prosser, A., Evans, D., & Reicher, S. (2005). Identity and emergency intervention: How social group membership and inclusiveness of group boundaries shape helping behavior. *Personality and Social Psychology Bulletin, 31,* 443–453.

Mackie, D. M., Devos, T., & Smith, E. R. (2000). Intergroup emotions: Explaining offensive action tendencies in an intergroup context. *Journal of Personality and Social Psychology, 79,* 602–616.

Mahajan, N., Martinez, M. A., Gutierrez, N. L., & Diesendruck, G., Banaji, M. R., & Santos, L. R. (2011). The evolution of intergroup bias: Perceptions and attitudes in rhesus macaques. *Journal of Personality and Social Psychology, 100,* 387–405.

Meissner, C. A., & Brigham, J. C. (2001). Thirty years of investigating the own-race bias in memory for faces: A meta-analytic review. *Psychology, Public Policy, and Law, 7,* 3–35.

Miller, N. (2002). Personalization and the promise of contact theory. *Journal of Social Issues, 58,* 387–410.

Miller, N., Brewer, M. B., & Edwards, K. (1985). Cooperative interaction in desegregated settings: A laboratory analog. *Journal of Social Issues, 41*(3), 63–79.

Morrison, K. R., & Chung, A. C. (2011). "White" or "European American"? Self-identifying labels influence majority group members' interethnic attitudes. *Journal of Experimental Social Psychology, 47,* 165–170.

Mullen, B., Brown, R. J., & Smith, C. (1992). Ingroup bias as a function of salience, relevance, and status: An integration. *European Journal of Social Psychology, 22,* 103–122.

Mullen, B., Dovidio, J. F., Johnson, C., & Copper, C. (1992). Ingroup-outgroup differences in social projection. *Journal of Experimental Social Psychology, 28,* 422–440.

Mummendey, A., Klink, A., & Brown, R. (2001). Nationalism and patriotism: National identification and out-group rejection. *British Journal of Social Psychology, 40,* 159–172.

Mummendey, A., & & Otten, S. (2001). Aversive discrimination. In R. Brown & S. L. Gaertner (Eds.), *Blackwell handbook of social psychology: Intergroup processes* (pp. 112–132). Malden, MA: Blackwell.

Nier, J. A., Gaertner, S. L., Dovidio, J. F., Banker, B. S., & Ward, C. M. (2001). Changing interracial evaluations and behavior: The effects of a common group identity. *Group Processes and Intergroup Relations, 4,* 299–316.

Oakes, P. (2001). The root of all evil in intergroup relations? Unearthing the categorization process. In R. Brown & S. L. Gaertner (Eds.), *Blackwell handbook of social psychology: Intergroup processes* (pp. 3–21). Oxford, UK: Blackwell.

Onorato, R. S., & Turner, J. C. (2001). The "I," "me," and the "us": The psychological group and self-concept maintenance and change. In C. Sedikides & M. B. Brewer (Eds.), *Individual self, relational self, collective self* (pp. 147–170). Philadelphia, PA: Psychology Press.

Otten, S., & Moskowitz, G. B. (2000). Evidence for implicit evaluative in-group bias: Affect-based spontaneous trait inference in a minimal group paradigm. *Journal of Experimental Social Psychology, 36,* 77–89.

Otten, S., & Wentura, D. (1999). About the impact of automaticity in the minimal group paradigm: Evidence from affective priming tasks. *European Journal of Social Psychology, 29,* 1049–1071.

Paladino, M-P., & Castelli, L. (2008). On the immediate consequences of ingroup categorization: Activation of approach and avoidance motor behavior toward ingroup and outgroup members. *Personality and Social Psychology Bulletin, 34,* 755–768.

Paolini, S., Harwood, J., & Rubin, M. (2010). Negative intergroup contact makes group memberships salient: Explaining why intergroup conflict endures. *Personality and Social Psychology Bulletin, 26,* 1723–1738.

Park, B., & Rothbart, M. (1982). Perception of out-group homogeneity and levels of social categorization: Memory for the subordinate attributes of in-group and out-group members. *Journal of Personality and Social Psychology, 42,* 1051–1068.

Pearson, A. R., West, T. V., Dovidio, J. F., Powers, S. R., Buck, R., & Henning, R. (2008). The fragility of intergroup relations. *Psychological Science, 19,* 1272–1279.

Peeters, M. C. W., & Oerlemans, W. G. M. (2009). The relationship between acculturation orientations and work-related well-being: Differences between ethnic minority and majority employees. *International Journal of Stress Management, 16,* 1–24.

Pettigrew, T. F. (1998). Intergroup contact theory. *Annual Review of Psychology, 49,* 65–85.

Pettigrew, T. F., & Tropp, L. R. (2006). A meta-analytic test of intergroup contact theory. *Journal of Personality and Social Psychology, 90,* 751–783.

Pettigrew, T. F., & Tropp, L. R. (2008). How does contact reduce prejudice? A meta analytic test of three mediators. *European Journal of Social Psychology, 38,* 922–934.

Pettigrew, T. F., & Tropp, L. R. (2011). *When groups meet: The dynamics of intergroup contact.* New York, NY: Psychology Press.

Pfafferott, I., & Brown, R. (2006). Acculturation preferences of majority and minority adolescents in Germany in the context of society and family. *International Journal of Intercultural Relations, 30,* 703–171.

Piliavin, J. A., Dovidio, J. F., Gaertner, S. L., & Clark, R. D., III. (1981). *Emergency intervention.* New York, NY: Academic Press.

Plant, E. A. (2004). Responses to interracial interactions over time. *Personality and Social Psychology Bulletin, 30,* 1458–1471.

Plant, E. A., & Butz, D. A. (2006). The causes and consequences of an avoidance-focus for interracial interactions. *Personality and Social Psychology Bulletin, 32,* 833–846.

Platow, M. J., Voudouris, N. J., Coulson, M., Gilford, N., Jamieson, R., Najdovski, L., . . . Terry, L. (2007). In-group reassurance in a pain setting produces lower levels of physiological arousal: Direct support for a self-categorization analysis of social influence. *European Journal of Social Psychology, 37,* 649–660.

Plaut, V. C., Thomas, K. M., & Goren, M. J. (2009). Is multiculturalism or color blindness better for minorities? *Psychological Science, 20,* 444–446.

Pratto, F., & Glasford, D. E. (2008). Ethnocentrism and the value of human life. *Journal of Personality and Social Psychology, 95,* 1411–1428.

Rabbie, J. M., & Lodewijkx, H. F. M. (1996). A behavioral interaction model: Toward an integrative theoretical framework for studying intra- and intergroup dynamics. In E. H. Witte & J. H. Davis (Eds.), *Understanding group behavior, Vol. 2: Small group processes and interpersonal relations. Understanding group behavior* (pp. 255–294). Hillsdale, NJ: Erlbaum.

Riek, B. M., Mania, E. W., & Gaertner, S. L. (2006). Intergroup threat and outgroup attitudes: A meta-analytic review. *Personality and Social Psychology Review, 10,* 336–353.

Robbins, J. M., & Krueger, J. I. (2005). Social projection to ingroups and outgroups: A review and meta-analysis. *Personality and Social Psychology Review, 9,* 32–47.

Roccas, S., & Brewer, M. (2002). Social identity complexity. *Personality and Social Psychology Review, 6,* 88–106.

Rothbart, M., & John, O. P. (1985). Social categorization and behavioral episodes: A cognitive analysis of the effects of intergroup contact. *Journal of Social Issues, 41* (3), 81–104.

Rubin, M., & Hewstone, M. (1998). Social identity theory's self-esteem hypothesis: A review and some suggestions for clarification. *Personality and Social Psychology Review, 2,* 40–62.

Ryan, C. S., Hunt, J. S., Weible, J. A., Peterson, C. R., & Casas, J. F. (2007). Multicultural and colorblind ideology, stereotypes, and ethnocentrism among Black and White Americans. *Group Processes and Intergroup Relations, 10,* 617–637.

Saguy, T., Tausch, N., Dovidio, J. F., & Pratto, F. (2009). The irony of harmony: Intergroup contact can produce false expectations for equality. *Psychological Science, 20,* 114–121.

Saguy, T., Tausch, N., Dovidio, J. F., Pratto, F., & Singh, P. (2011). Tension and harmony in intergroup relations. In P. R., Shaver & M. Mikulincer (Eds.), *Understanding and reducing aggression, violence, and their consequences* (pp. 333–348). Washington, DC: American Psychological Association.

Shelton, J. N., & Richeson, J. A. (2005). Intergroup contact and pluralistic ignorance. *Journal of Personality and Social Psychology, 88,* 91–107.

Shelton, J. N., Richeson, J. A., & Bergsieker, H. (2009). Interracial friendship development and attributional biases. *Journal of Social and Personal Relationships, 26,* 179–193.

Sherif, M. (1966). *Group conflict and cooperation: Their social psychology.* London: Routledge and Kegan Paul.

Sherif, M., Harvey, O. J., White, B. J., Hood, W. R., & Sherif, C. W. (1961). *Intergroup conflict and cooperation: The Robbers Cave experiment.* Norman: University of Oklahoma Book Exchange.

Shnabel, N., Nadler, A., Canetti-Nisim, D., & Ullrich, J. (2008). The role of acceptance and empowerment in promoting reconciliation from the perspective of the needs-based model. *Social Issues and Policy Review, 2,* 159–186.

Sibley, C. G., & Duckitt, J. (2008). Personality and prejudice: A meta-analysis and theoretical review. *Personality and Social Psychology Review, 12,* 248–279.

Sidanius, J., & Pratto, F. (1999). *Social dominance: An intergroup theory of social hierarchy and oppression.* New York, NY: Cambridge University Press.

Slavin, R., & Cooper, R. (1999). Improving intergroup relations: Lessons learned from cooperative learning programs. *Journal of Social Issues, 55,* 647–663.

Smith, E. R., & Mackie, D. M. (2005). Aggression, hatred, and other emotions. In J. F. Dovidio, P. Glick, & L. A. Rudman (Eds.), *On the nature of prejudice: Fifty years after Allport* (pp. 361–376). Malden, MA: Blackwell.

Staub, E. (2008). Promoting reconciliation after genocide and mass killing in Rwanda—and other postconflict settings: Understanding the roots of violence, healing, shared history, and general principles. In A. Nadler, T. E. Malloy, & J. D. Fisher (Eds.), *The social psychology of intergroup reconciliation* (pp. 395–422). New York, NY: Oxford University Press.

Stephan, W. G., Renfro, C. L., Esses, V. M., Stephan, C. W., & Martin, T. (2005). The effects of feeling threatened on attitudes toward immigrants. *International Journal of Intercultural Relations, 29,* 1–19.

Stephan, W. G., & Stephan, C. W. (1985). Intergroup anxiety. *Journal of Social Issues, 41,* 157–175.

Stephan, W. G., & Stephan C. W. (2000). An integrated threat theory of prejudice. In S. Oskamp (Ed.), *Reducing prejudice and discrimination* (pp. 23–45). Hillsdale, NJ: Erlbaum.

Stephan, W. G., Stephan, C. W., Wenzel, B., & Cornelius, J. (1991). Intergroup interaction and self-disclosure. *Journal of Applied Social Psychology, 21,* 1370–1378.

Stürmer, S., Snyder, M., & Omoto, A. M. (2005). Prosocial emotions and helping: The moderating role of group membership. *Journal of Personality and Social Psychology, 88,* 532–546.

Sue, D. W. (2010). *Microaggressions in everyday life: Race, gender, and sexual orientation.* Hoboken, NJ: Wiley.

Sue, D. W., Capodilupo, C. M., Torino, G. C., Bucceri, J. M., Holder, A. M. B., Nadal, K. L., & Esquilin, M. (2007). Racial microaggressions in everyday life: Implications for clinical practice. *American Psychologist, 62,* 271–286.

Sumner, W. G. (1906). *Folkways.* New York, NY: Ginn.

Tajfel, H. (1969). Cognitive aspects of prejudice. *Journal of Social Issues, 25*(4), 79–97.

Tajfel, H., & Turner, J. C. (1979). An integrative theory of intergroup conflict. In W. G. Austin & S. Worchel (Eds.), *The social psychology of intergroup relations* (pp. 33–48). Monterey, CA: Brooks/Cole.

Talaska, C. A., Fiske, S. T., & Chaiken, S. (2008). Legitimating racial discrimination: Emotions, not beliefs, best predict discrimination in a meta-analysis. *Social Justice Research, 21*, 263–296.

Trawalter, S., Todd, A. R., Baird, A. A., & Richeson, J. A. (2008). Attending to threat: Race-based patterns of selective attention. *Journal of Experimental Social Psychology, 44*, 1322–1327.

Turner, J. C. (1985). Social categorization and the self-concept: A social cognitive theory of group behavior. In E. J. Lawler (Ed.), *Advances in group processes* (Vol. 2, pp. 77–122). Greenwich, CT: JAI Press.

Turner, J. C., Hogg, M. A., Oakes, P. J., Reicher, S. D., & Wetherell, M. S. (1987). *Rediscovering the social group: A self-categorization theory*. Oxford, UK: Basil Blackwell.

Turner, R. N., Hewstone, M., & Voci, A. (2007). Reducing explicit and implicit outgroup prejudice via direct and extended contact: The mediating role of self-disclosure and intergroup anxiety. *Journal of Personality and Social Psychology, 93*, 369–388.

Van Bavel, J. J., Packer, D. J., & Cunningham, W. A. (2008). The neural substrates of in-group bias. *Psychological Science, 19*, 1131–1139.

van Oudenhoven, J. P., Prins, K. S., & Buunk, B. (1998). Attitudes of minority and majority members towards adaptation of immigrants. *European Journal of Social Psychology, 28*, 995–1013.

Verkuyten, M. (2006). Multicultural recognition and ethnic minority rights: A social identity perspective. In W. Stroebe & M. Hewstone (Eds.), *European review of social psychology* (Vol. 17, pp. 148–184). Hove, E. Sussex, UK: Psychology Press.

Verkuyten, M., & Hagendoorn, L. (1998). Prejudice and self-categorization: The variable role of authoritarianism and in-group stereotypes. *Personality and Social Psychology Bulletin, 24*, 99–110.

Voci, A. (2006). The link between identification and in-group favouritism: Effects of threat to social identity and trust-related emotions. *British Journal of Social Psychology, 45*, 265–284.

Voci, A., & Hewstone, M. (2003). Intergroup contact and prejudice toward immigrants in Italy: The mediational role of anxiety and the moderational role of group salience. *Group Processes and Intergroup Relations, 6*, 37–54.

Vorauer, J. D. (2006). An information search model of evaluative concerns in intergroup interaction. *Psychological Review, 113*, 862–886.

Vorauer, J., Main, K., & O'Connell, G. (1998). How do individuals expect to be viewed by members of lower status groups?: Content and implications of meta-stereotypes. *Journal of Personality and Social Psychology, 75*, 917–937.

Vorauer, J. D., Martens, V., & Sasaki, S. J. (2009). When trying to understand detracts from trying to behave: Effects of perspective taking in intergroup interaction. *Journal of Personality and Social Psychology, 96*, 811–827.

Vorauer, J. D., & Sasaki, S. J. (2011). In the worst rather than the best of times: Effects of salient intergroup ideology in threatening intergroup interactions. *Journal of Personality and Social Psychology, 101*, 307–320.

Weber, R., & Crocker, J. (1983). Cognitive processes in the revision of stereotypic beliefs. *Journal of Personality and Social Psychology, 45*, 961–977.

West, T. V., Pearson, A. R., Dovidio, J. F., Shelton, J. N., & Trail, T. (2009). Superordinate identity and intergroup roommate friendship development. *Journal of Experimental Social Psychology, 45*, 1266–12772.

Wilder, D. A. (1981). Perceiving persons as a group: Categorization and intergroup relations. In D. L. Hamilton (Ed.), *Cognitive processes in stereotyping and intergroup behavior* (pp. 213–257). Hillsdale, NJ: Erlbaum.

Wilder, D. A. (1986). Social categorization: Implications for creation and reduction of intergroup bias. In L. Berkowitz (Ed.), *Advances in experimental social psychology* (Vol. 19, pp. 291–355). Orlando, FL: Academic Press.

Wilder, D. A., Simon, A. F., & Faith, M. (1996). Enhancing the impact of counterstereotypic information. Dispositional attributions for deviance. *Journal of Personality and Social Psychology, 71*, 276–287.

Wohl, M. J. A., & Branscombe, N. R. (2005). Forgiveness and collective guilt assignment to historical perpetrator groups depend on level of social category inclusiveness. *Journal of Personality and Social Psychology, 88*, 288–303.

Wright, S. C., & Lubensky, M. (2009). The struggle for social equality: Collective action vs. prejudice reduction. In S. Demoulin, J. P. Leyens, & J. F. Dovidio (Eds.), *Intergroup misunderstandings: Impact of divergent social realities* (pp. 291–310). New York, NY: Psychology Press.

Young, S. G., & Hugenberg, K. (2010). Mere social categorization modulates identification of facial expressions of emotion. *Journal of Personality and Social Psychology, 99*, 964–977.

Yzerbyt, V., & Demoulin, S. (2010). Intergroup relations. In S. T. Fiske, D. Gilbert, & G. Lindzey (Eds.), *Handbook of social psychology* (Vol. 2, 5th ed., pp. 1024–1083). New York, NY: Wiley.

Zagefka, H., & Brown, R. (2002). The relationship between acculturation strategies, relative fit, and intergroup relations: Immigrant-majority relations in Germany. *European Journal of Social Psychology, 32*, 171–188.

CHAPTER 21

Aggression

C. NATHAN DEWALL, CRAIG A. ANDERSON, AND BRAD J. BUSHMAN

AGGRESSION

This chapter provides an overview of classic and contemporary aggression research. We begin by providing operational definitions of aggression and related constructs, followed by a discussion of the forms and functions of aggression. Next, we review theoretical perspectives that have influenced aggression researchers over the years. We then discuss the development of aggressive behavior, including its continuity over time. Later sections discuss the emergence of individual differences that predispose people to behave aggressively, situational factors that increase aggression, and the roles of emotion, cognition, and arousal in influencing aggression. The final section discusses research on how to prevent aggression and violence.

Definitions of Aggression, Violence, and Antisocial Behavior

Laypeople and researchers often use the term *aggression* differently. Laypeople may describe a salesperson who tries hard to sell merchandise as aggressive. The salesperson does not, however, want to harm potential customers. Most social psychologists define human aggression as any behavior intended to harm another person who does not want to be harmed (Baron & Richardson, 1994; Bushman & Huesmann, 2010). This definition includes three important features. First, aggression is a behavior—you can see it. Aggression is not an emotion, such as anger.

Aggression is not a thought, such as mentally rehearsing a murder. You cannot behave aggressively by thinking, nor can you behave aggressively by feeling. A person can only behave aggressively by *doing* something. Second, aggression is intentional (not accidental), and the intent is to cause harm. For example, a dentist might intentionally give a patient a shot of Novocain (and the shot hurts!), but the goal is to help rather than to harm the patient. Third, the victim must be motivated to avoid the harm. Most people naturally wish to avoid harm from others, but this is not always the case. People who derive sexual pleasure from being beaten, choked, slapped, or spanked are not victims of aggression because they wish to experience harm from another person. Suicide is typically not considered a form of aggression because people inflict pain on themselves (and therefore are not sufficiently motivated to avoid the harm), though clinical researchers have begun to consider suicide as a form of self-aggression (McCloskey & Berman, 2003). People can behave aggressively without causing harm to others. For example, if a husband swings a bat at his wife and misses, he has still behaved aggressively even though he did not cause physical harm to his wife.

Laypeople and researchers also differ in their use of the term *violence*. A meteorologist might call a storm *violent* if it has intense winds, rain, thunder, and lightning. When researchers use the term, *violence* refers to aggression that has as its goal extreme physical harm, such as injury or death. The U.S. Federal Bureau of Investigation (FBI) classifies four crimes as "violent": homicide, aggravated assault, forcible rape, and robbery. Some criminologists define violence as an act that has a high probability of causing harm requiring medical attention. However, most aggression researchers would classify less serious acts as violence, such as slapping someone across the face with tremendous force. And some researchers classify some extreme forms of verbal aggression as emotional violence. In general, all violent acts are aggressive acts, but not all aggressive acts are violent (only those that are likely to cause extreme physical harm).

Antisocial behavior is a term that researchers have used in casual and somewhat inconsistent ways (though clinicians have offered more precise definitions). In general, it refers to behavior that either damages interpersonal relationships or is culturally undesirable. Aggression is often equated with antisocial behavior (e.g., American Psychiatric Association, 2000). Others have pointed out, however, that aggression is often a social as well as an antisocial strategy, in that it is a way that people seek to manage their social lives, such as by influencing the behavior of others so as to get their way (Tedeschi & Felson, 1994). Littering, cheating, stealing, and lying are behaviors that qualify as antisocial but may or may not involve aggression.

Aggression varies in its forms and functions. By forms we mean how the aggressive act is expressed, such as physically (e.g., hitting, kicking, stabbing, shooting) or verbally (e.g., yelling, screaming, swearing, name calling). In *displaced aggression*, a substitute aggression target is used (e.g., Marcus-Newhall, Pedersen, Carlson, & Miller, 2000). The substitute target is innocent of any wrong doing and just happens to be in wrong place at the wrong time. For example, a man is berated by his boss at work but does not retaliate. When he gets home, he yells at his daughter instead. In *triggered displaced aggression* the substitute target is not entirely innocent, but the target commits a minor or trivial offense (Pedersen, Gonzales, & Miller, 2000). For example, the man berated by his boss might yell at his daughter because she forgot to clean her room. Triggered displaced aggression is especially likely to occur when the aggressor ruminates about the initial offense (Bushman, Bonacci, Pedersen, Vasquez, & Miller, 2005), and when the aggressor does not like the substitute target, such as when the target is an outgroup member or has a personality flaw (e.g., Pedersen, Bushman, Vasquez, & Miller, 2008).

People displace aggression for two main reasons. First, directly aggressing against the source of provocation is often unfeasible because the source is unavailable (e.g., the provoker has left the area), or because the source is an intangible entity (e.g., hot temperature). Second, fear of retaliation or punishment from the provoker inhibits direct aggression. For example, the man who was berated by his boss is reluctant to retaliate because he does not want to lose his job.

Different forms of aggression are expressed directly or indirectly. With *direct aggression*, the victim is physically present. With *indirect aggression*, the victim is absent. For example, physical aggression can be direct (e.g., hitting a person in the face) or indirect (e.g., burning a person's house down while they are on holiday). Likewise, verbal aggression can be direct (e.g., screaming in a person's face) or indirect (e.g., spreading rumors behind a person's back). Males are more likely than females to use direct aggression, whereas females are more likely than males to use indirect aggression (e.g., Lagerspetz, Bjorkqvist, & Peltonen, 1988).

Aggressive acts may also differ in their function or motivation. Consider two examples. In the first example, a husband finds his wife and her lover together in bed. He takes his rifle from the closet, and shoots and kills both individuals. In the second, a "hitman" uses a rifle to kill another person for money. The form of aggression is the same in both examples (i.e., physical aggression caused by shooting and killing victims with a rifle). However, the motives appear quite different. In the first example, the husband appears to be motivated by anger. He is enraged when he finds his wife making love to another man, so he shoots them both. In the second example, the "hitman" appears to be motivated by money. The "hitman" probably does not hate his victim. He might not even know his victim, but he kills the person anyway for the money.

To capture different functions or motives for aggression, psychologists make a distinction between reactive aggression (also called *hostile, affective, angry, impulsive,* or *retaliatory* aggression) and proactive aggression (also called *instrumental* aggression; e.g., Buss, 1961). *Reactive aggression* is "hot," impulsive, angry behavior that is motivated by a desire to harm someone. *Proactive aggression* is "cold," premeditated, calculated behavior that is motivated by some other goal (obtaining money, restoring one's image, restoring justice). Some researchers have argued that it is difficult (if not impossible) to distinguish between reactive and proactive aggression because they are highly correlated and because motives are often mixed (Bushman & Anderson, 2001). For example, what if the husband who finds his wife making love to another man instigates a deadly plan to slowly poison both individuals? Would this be reactive or proactive aggression? It has elements of both types. Therefore, although the reactive/proactive distinction has proven useful, it is important to realize that this dichotomy cannot account for all aggressive acts.

An alternative approach is to characterize aggressive acts on multiple dimensions, including: how much the primary and the ultimate goal is to harm the victim versus benefit the perpetrator; amount of hostile or agitated affect present; and how much consequences were considered (Anderson & Huesmann, 2003).

Theoretical Perspectives

Since its inception, the aggression literature has enjoyed a rich set of theoretical perspectives. These theories have offered frameworks from which hypotheses regarding the causes and consequences of aggression could be tested. Although each theory is distinct, several theories share a considerable degree of overlap. In what follows, we review seven main theories that have guided aggression research. They are reviewed largely in the chronological order in which they were formulated.

Frustration-Aggression Theory

In 1939, psychologists from Yale University published an important book titled *Frustration and Aggression* (Dollard, Doob, Miller, Mowrer, & Sears, 1939). In this book, partially as a reaction to the spreading influence of Freud's theory, the authors proposed that aggression resulted from frustration. They defined frustration as the blocking of goal directed behavior, such as when someone crowds in front of you in line. Their theory was summarized in two bold statements on the book's first page: (1) "the occurrence of aggressive behavior always presupposes the existence of frustration," and (2) "the existence of frustration always leads to some form of aggression" (Dollard et al., 1939, p. 1). In their view, frustration depended on an "expected" or "hoped for" goal being denied, and was not simply absence of achieving a goal. It was the first systematic theory of aggression, and was heavily influenced by psychoanalytic theory. It fit with essentialist perspectives of that historical period that argued that constructs must have certain characteristics and properties.

Frustration-aggression theory enjoyed early empirical support as a theory of aggression. In one classic paper, Hovland and Sears (1940) argued that people experience tremendous frustration when their goal for financial stability is thwarted. This frustration, they argued, will cause people to behave aggressively. To test this hypothesis, Hovland and Sears examined the association between the value of cotton in the U.S. South and the number of African Americans who were murdered through lynching in the U.S. South. The value of cotton was chosen as a proxy of frustration because, at that period in U.S. history, lower cotton prices thwarted Southerners' goal of having financial stability. Consistent with frustration-aggression theory, there was a significant negative correlation between the price of cotton and the number of African Americans who were lynched, suggesting a relationship between experiencing greater frustration and more frequent acts of aggression and violence.

Several other studies have found support for frustration-aggression theory. When people's desire to get to their destination on time is thwarted, they are more likely to behave aggressively (Novaco, 1991). Unemployment, which frustrates a person's goal for financial stability, is also associated with greater aggression (Catalano, Novaco, & McConnell, 2002). More recent work has replicated and extended this pattern of results in Germany by showing that merely expecting to be unemployed in the future is enough to increase aggressive inclinations (Fischer, Greitemeyer, & Frey, 2008).

This theory seemed to explain a large amount of everyday occurrences of aggression, but it readily became apparent to the authors that not every frustration led to observable aggression. Miller (1941), one of the original authors, was the first to revise the theory. He explained that frustrations actually stimulate a number of different inclinations besides an inclination to aggress, such as an inclination to escape or to find a way around the obstacle to the goal. The inclination that eventually dominates, he theorized, is the one that is most successful in reducing frustration. In other words, people learn through experience to respond to frustrations with aggressive or nonaggressive responses. This idea opened the door for learning theory explanations of aggression.

Learning Theories

The earliest learning theory explanations for individual differences in human aggressiveness focused on operant and, to a lesser extent, classical conditioning processes. *Operant conditioning theory*, developed by behaviorists such as Edward Thorndike and B. F. Skinner, proposes that people are more likely to repeat behaviors that have been rewarded and are less likely to repeat behaviors that have been punished. *Classical conditioning theory*, developed by Ivan Pavlov, proposes that through repeated pairing of an unconditioned stimulus with a conditioned stimulus, the unconditioned stimulus eventually elicits a response similar to that elicited by the conditioned stimulus. For example, dogs that hear a bell (conditioned stimulus) every time they receive meat powder (unconditioned stimulus) will eventually salivate when they hear the bell alone (conditioned response). Research showed that children could be taught to behave aggressively through *positive reinforcement*—adding pleasure (Cowan & Walters, 1963) or *negative reinforcement*—subtracting pain (Patterson, Littman, & Bricker, 1967). Children not only learn to behave aggressively, they also learn to discriminate between situations when aggression pays and when it does not. Through stimulus generalization they apply what they have learned to new situations (Sears, Whiting, Nowlis, & Sears, 1953). Taken together these processes explained how aggressive behavior could be learned (Eron, Walder, & Lefkowitz, 1971).

By the early 1960s, it became clear that conditioning by itself could not fully explain individual differences in aggression. Bandura theorized that the more powerful learning processes in understanding social behavior (including aggression) were *observational learning* or *imitation* (also called *social learning*) (e.g., Bandura, 1977) in which people learn how to behave aggressively by observing and imitating others. In several classic experiments, he showed that young children imitated specific aggressive acts they observed in aggressive models, for example, hitting a "bobo" doll that they had seen an actor hit. Furthermore, he developed the concept of *vicarious learning* of aggression by showing that children were especially likely to imitate models that had been rewarded for behaving aggressively (Bandura, 1965; Bandura, Ross, & Ross, 1963). Bandura argued that imitation was the key to social learning. The idea is that people do not just imitate the specific social behaviors they see, but they make cognitive inferences based on the observations, and these inferences lead to generalizations in behavior. What is important is how the child interprets social events, and how competent the child feels in responding in different ways (Bandura, 1986). These cognitions provide a basis for stability of behavior tendencies across a variety of situations. Watching one parent hit the other parent not only increases a child's likelihood of hitting, but it also increases the child's belief that hitting is okay when someone provokes you.

Other work has supported social learning theory by showing that reinforcing people for behaving aggressively not only increases their sense of reward they receive from aggression, but it also increases their feelings of confidence that they have what it takes to successfully carry out an aggressive act (Perry, Perry, & Rasmussen, 1986).

Excitation-Transfer Theory

Excitation-transfer theory (Zillmann, 1979) assumes that physiological arousal, however produced, dissipates slowly. If two arousing events are separated by a short amount of time, some of the arousal caused by the first event may transfer to the second event and add to the arousal caused by the second event. In other words, arousal from the first event may be misattributed to the second event. If the second event is related to anger (or any other emotional state), then the additional arousal should make the person even angrier. The notion of excitation transfer also suggests that anger may be extended over long periods of time, if the person has attributed their heightened arousal to anger. Thus, even after the arousal has dissipated the observer may remain ready to aggress for as long as the self-generated label of anger persists.

In one experiment, participants completed a task meant to increase their arousal (i.e., riding an exercise bike) or not to increase their arousal (i.e., threading discs onto a wire) (Zillmann & Bryant, 1974). Afterward, participants were insulted or not insulted by a confederate and then had the opportunity to behave aggressively toward the confederate by giving him electric shocks. Participants who were both aroused and provoked behaved more aggressively than all other participants, presumably because they "transferred" their initial levels of arousal from the bicycle to the provoking situation.

According to excitation-transfer theory, one reason why people behave aggressively is that they transfer their arousal from one situation to another person, making them more reactive. This line of reasoning jibes with earlier drive theories, which stated that arousal energizes behavioral tendencies in conjunction with a person's learning history (Hebb, 1955). Within the context of aggression, experiencing arousal, regardless of its initial relation to aggression, can energize later aggressive behavioral tendencies toward another person.

Information-Processing Theories

The introduction of ideas from cognitive psychology into theorizing about aggression was given another boost in the early 1980s with the formulation of two cognitive information-processing models. One model focused particularly on scripts, beliefs, and observational learning (Huesmann, 1982). In a play or movie, scripts tell actors or actresses what to say and do. In memory, *scripts* define situations and guide behavior: The person first selects a script to represent the situation and then assumes a role in the script. One example is a restaurant script (i.e., enter restaurant, go to table, look at menu, order food, eat food, pay for food, leave tip, exit restaurant; see Abelson, 1981). People learn scripts by direct experience or by observing others (e.g., parents, siblings, peers, mass media characters).

The second model focused particularly on perceptions and attributions (Dodge, 1980). *Attributions* are the explanations people make about why others behave the way they do. For example, if a person bumps into you, a hostile attribution would be that the person did it on purpose to hurt you. Meta-analytic evidence suggests that having a hostile attribution bias is a reliable predictor of aggression (Orobio de Castro, Veerman, Koops, Bosch, & Monshouwer, 2002).

Cognitive Neoassociation Theory

Berkowitz (1989, 1990) proposed that aversive events such as frustrations, provocations, loud noises, uncomfortable temperatures, and unpleasant odors, produce negative affect. Negative affect produced by unpleasant experiences automatically stimulates various thoughts, memories, expressive motor reactions, and physiological responses associated with *both* fight and flight tendencies. The fight associations give rise to rudimentary feelings of anger, whereas the flight associations give rise to rudimentary feelings of fear. Furthermore, cognitive neoassociation theory assumes that cues present during an aversive event become associated with the event and with the thoughts, memories, expressive motor reactions, and physiological responses triggered by the event. In short, the theory includes the learning mechanisms identified by the learning tradition. It also is directed primarily at explaining affective aggression.

Cognitive neoassociation theory also includes higher order cognitive processes, such as appraisal and attribution processes. If people are motivated to do so, they may use higher order cognitive processes to further analyze their situation. For example, they might think about how they feel, make causal attributions for what led them to feel this way, and consider the consequences of acting on their feelings. This more deliberate thought produces more clearly differentiated feelings of anger, fear, or both. It can also suppress or enhance the action-tendencies associated with these feelings.

Cognitive neoassociation theory not only subsumes the frustration-aggression hypothesis, but it also provides a causal mechanism for explaining why aversive events increase aggressive inclinations, that is, via negative affect.

General Aggression Model

The General Aggression Model (GAM; Anderson & Bushman, 2002; DeWall, Anderson, & Bushman, 2011) integrates these previous theories in into a parsimonious, unified framework. It simultaneously incorporates biological, personality development, social processes, basic cognitive processes (e.g., perception, priming), short-term and long-term processes, and decision processes into understanding aggression.

GAM argues for a flexible understanding of aggression based on a knowledge structure approach (Bushman & Anderson, 2001). Knowledge structures refer to how people perceive their environment, other people, expectations regarding how likely various outcomes are to occur, knowledge and beliefs about how people typically respond in various situations, and how much people believe they can respond to a variety of events. GAM focuses heavily on how the development and use of knowledge structures influence both early (e.g., basic visual perception) and downstream (e.g., attributions, judgments, decisions, and behaviors) psychological processes (e.g., Wegner & Bargh, 1998).

GAM emphasizes three critical stages in understanding a single episodic cycle of aggression: (1) person and situation inputs, (2) present internal states (i.e., cognition, arousal, affect, including brain activity), and (3) outcomes of appraisal and decision-making processes. A feedback loop influences future cycles of aggression, which produce a violence escalation cycle (Anderson, Buckley, & Carnagey, 2008). See Figures 21.1 and 21.2 for illustrations of the basic tenets of GAM and the violence escalation cycle, respectively.

GAM argues that different forms of aggression can be distinguished in terms of proximate and ultimate goals. Proximate goals provide the most direct guiding force behind aggression and violence. In contrast, ultimate goals provide an explanation as to how a certain behavior may aid the organism in satisfying goals for survival and reproduction (see Tooby & Cosmides, 1992). Angry people may behave aggressively due to a proximal goal of wanting to feel better (e.g., Bushman, Baumeister, & Phillips, 2001), but their aggression may also function to protect themselves or close others from threat, thereby increasing the likelihood that their genes will be passed on to future generations.

Using the knowledge structure approach, GAM can categorize any violent or aggressive behavior according to four dimensions. The first dimension is how much hostile or agitated affect is present. The second dimension is how much a specific thought, feeling, or action has become automatized. The third dimension is how much the primary (ultimate) goal is to harm the victim compared to benefitting the perpetrator. The fourth dimension is

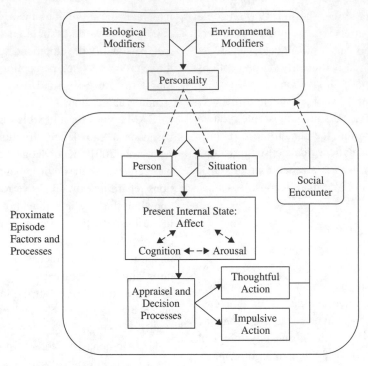

Figure 21.1 General aggression model

how much the perpetrator considers the consequences of committing the aggressive act.

I³ Theory

I³ Theory (pronounced "I-cubed theory") is the most recent of the reviewed theoretical perspectives on

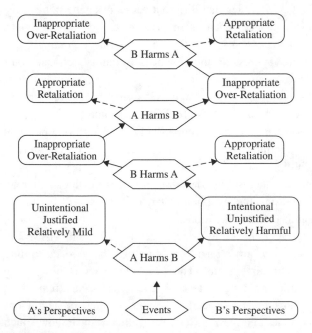

Figure 21.2 The violence escalation cycle

From Anderson & Carnagey, 2004. Reprinted by permission.

aggression (Finkel, 2008; Finkel & Eckhardt, in press). I³ Theory is a new, broad meta-theory of aggression that imposes theoretical coherence on the massive number of established risk factors for aggression. Of the reviewed theories, it gives the most emphasis to self-control processes. Specifically, I³ Theory emphasizes the underlying *process* (or processes) through which risk factors promote aggression.

I³ Theory identifies three processes: *I*nstigation, *I*mpellance, and *I*nhibition (with the italicized vowels representing the three *I*s in I³ Theory). Instigating factors are discrete social dynamics that frequently increase an aggressive urge. Examples of instigating factors are social rejection and provocation. Impellors are factors that predispose people to experience strong aggressive urges in the presence of an instigator. Examples of impelling factors are dispositional anger and physical aggressiveness. Inhibiting factors refer to individual difference or situational features that diminish the likelihood of an aggressive urge being translated into an actual aggressive act. Examples of inhibiting factors are having adequate self-control resources or energy and high levels of relationship commitment.

Using conceptual and statistical tools of moderation as a guiding framework, I³ Theory examines how the instigating, impelling, and inhibiting factors combine additively and interactively to increase or decrease the likelihood of aggression. According to I³ Theory, aggression should be most likely to occur when instigators and impellors are high and when inhibiting factors are low. For example, an instigating factor such as provocation may increase aggression primarily among people who are high in an impelling factor such as trait anger. The interaction between provocation and trait anger may be especially pronounced among people who lack inhibition, such as people who have low levels of self-control resources to override an aggressive urge. The implication is that high instigating and impelling factors increase the strength of the aggressive urge and a lack of inhibiting factors provides a weak tendency to override the urge, thereby leading people to behave aggressively.

DEVELOPMENT OF AGGRESSION AND STABILITY OVER TIME

When are people the most aggressive in their lives? Multiple longitudinal studies have shown that people are more aggressive between ages 1 and 3 than at any other time in their lives (e.g., Cote, Vaillancourt, LeBlanc, Nagin, & Tremblay, 2006; Tremblay et al., 2004). Tremblay (2000) has shown that in daycare settings, one out of four interactions that children have involves aggression. That frequency of aggression in one's daily interactions exceeds the amount of aggression among prison inmates and gang members. (To be sure, aggression at daycare results in lower levels of injuries compared to aggression in prison and between gang members.) Aggression declines substantially after age 3, which is when children learn to inhibit their aggression. Although aggression tends to decline with age, a small subset of people continue to behave aggressively as they become older. The majority of violent crimes in the United States are committed by people who are between the ages of 15 and 30 (U.S. Department of Justice, 2011).

Although absolute frequency of aggression tends to decrease as people grow older, relative frequency is very stable over time. Aggressive children tend to become aggressive adolescents, and aggressive adolescents tend to become aggressive adults (see Bushman & Huesmann, 2010, for a review). The consistency of aggression over time is approximately the same as intelligence, explaining approximately 36% of a person's aggressive behavior over a 10-year period (Olweus, 1979). That is, if a researcher wants to predict another person's aggression in 10 years, around a third of the variance in that person's aggression can be predicted from his or her current level of aggression. Thus, people tend to become less aggressive as they mature, but their aggression rate relative to others of the same age will remain relatively consistent over time.

INDIVIDUAL DIFFERENCES

Individual difference factors refer to dispositions that people bring with them to situations. They include sex, personality traits, attitudes, beliefs, values, and genetic predispositions. They are generally enduring features of the person, remaining consistent over time and across different situations.

Sex differences in aggression. Males are generally more aggressive than females. These gender differences emerge in early childhood and persist over the lifespan, especially for extremely violent crimes (e.g., Loeber & Hay, 1997). But females also show an assortment of aggressive behaviors. Young girls show levels of relational aggression and indirect aggression that exceed levels shown by young boys (Crick & Grotpeter, 1995; Rys & Bear, 1997). Although men generally show higher levels of physical aggression compared to women, these gender differences disappear under conditions of high provocation (Bettencourt & Miller, 1996).

Narcissism and self-esteem. Self-views can also influence aggression. Intuitively, one might expect that having positive self-views would reduce the chances that a person would behave aggressively against others, whereas people with negative self-views would behave aggressively to make themselves feel better. Contradicting this intuitive prediction, people with extremely high and unstable *positive self-views* are at greatest risk of behaving aggressively. People with unstable high self-esteem report heightened levels of anger and hostility (Kernis, Grannemann, & Barclay, 1989). People scoring highly on narcissism, a personality trait marked by inflated and grandiose positive self-views, behave very aggressively in response to provocation, an effect that is especially pronounced among people with high self-esteem (Bushman & Baumeister, 1998; Bushman et al., 2009). People high in narcissistic entitlement, who believe they deserve respect and special treatment from others, also behave very aggressively and antisocially (e.g., blasting strangers with intense and prolonged blasts of noise, stealing candy from small children) (Campbell, Bonacci, Shelton, Exline, & Bushman, 2004). These findings suggest that extremely high and unstable positive self-views predispose people to behave aggressively.

Trait anger. Of the many individual difference variables that predispose people to behave aggressively, few are more reliable and potent than trait anger. People who are high in trait anger, compared to those low in trait anger, are hypersensitive to provocation. When provoked, high trait anger people express heightened intentions to behave aggressively (Bettencourt, Talley, Benjamin, & Valentine, 2006). They show elevated levels of systolic and diastolic blood pressure (Suls & Wan, 1993). And they show increased activation in the left dorsal anterior cingulate cortex, which is a region implicated in the experience of anger and physical pain (Denson, Pedersen, Ronquillo, & Nandy, 2009).

Trait self-control, executive functioning, and IQ. Self-control, defined as overriding an impulse to remain in agreement with personal and social standards for appropriate responding (Baumeister, Heatherton, & Tice, 1994), is intimately linked to aggression. In their influential book *A General Theory of Crime*, Gottfredson and Hirschi (1990) argue that poor self-control is among the strongest predictors of crime. Indeed, meta-analytic findings have shown that poor self-control has an average correlation of $r = .27$ on criminal behavior, leading researchers to suggest that poor self-control qualifies as "one of the strongest known correlates of crime" (Pratt & Cullen, 2000, p. 952). Psychological studies have also shown that individual differences in self-control processes reliably predict aggression. Children with better self-control tend to behave less aggressively as young adults (Moffitt et al., 2011). Adolescents with better self-control report engaging in fewer acts of intimate partner violence (Finkel, DeWall, Slotter, Oaten, & Foshee, 2009). College students with better self-control report having fewer aggressive conflicts toward strangers and close relationship partners (Derefinko, DeWall, Metze, Walsh, & Lynam, 2011; Tangney, Baumeister, & Boone, 2004).

Executive functioning is quite similar to trait self-control, in that both primarily involve overriding automatic urges to remain in agreement with standards for what is appropriate in a given situation. Low executive functioning is associated with greater aggression (Hawkins & Trobst, 2000; Stevens, Kaplan, & Hesselbrock, 2003). The average size of effect regarding the relationship between low executive functioning and higher aggression is "medium" to "large" (Morgan & Lilienfeld, 2000).

Relatively little research has investigated the relationship between intelligence and aggression, but existing research suggests that lower intelligence is associated with higher aggression. Children with a low intelligence quotient tend to display higher levels of aggression (e.g.,

Lynam, Moffitt, & Stouthamer-Loeber, 1993). The relationship between low intelligence and higher aggression may also depend on self-control. In one study, children with low verbal intelligence were more likely to be rated as highly aggressive, especially those children with poor self-control (Ayduk, Rodriguez, Mischel, Shoda, & Wright, 2007).

Five-Factor Model. Perhaps the most widely established model of personality is the Five-Factor Model (FFM; e.g., Goldberg, 1993), which argues that personality can be explained in terms of five broadly defined personality traits: neuroticism (i.e., negative affect and emotions, emotional instability), extraversion (i.e., positive emotions and behaviors such as sociability), conscientiousness (i.e., being adept at impulse control), agreeableness (i.e., being affiliative and prosocial), and openness to experience (i.e., curiosity, fantasy). Of these five personality traits, three are most reliably related to aggression: neuroticism (positive relation), conscientiousness (negative relation), and agreeableness (negative relation) (Caprara, Barbaranelli, & Zimbardo, 1996; Egan, 2009; Hines & Saudino, 2008; Miller, Lynam, & Leukefeld, 2003). Other work has shown that combinations of these three personality traits provide the strongest predisposition toward aggression. For example, a combination of high neuroticism, low agreeableness, and low conscientiousness is associated with elevated levels of aggressive and violent behavior (Blonigen & Krueger, 2007). Many of these basic personality effects on aggression and violence are mediated by their effects on aggressive emotions and aggressive attitudes (Barlett & Anderson, in press).

Psychopathy/conduct disorder. Psychopathy is a disorder marked by being callous and unemotional (primary factor) and impulsive/antisocial (secondary factor) (Hare et al., 1990). Thus, psychopaths tend to engage in cold, calculated, unemotional, and premeditated proactive aggression (Nouvion, Cherek, Lane, Tcheremissine, & Lieving, 2007). Despite the stereotype of the psychopathic murderer, most people who commit murder are not psychopathic (Williamson, Hare, & Wong, 1987). Because most murders occur as a result of fits of rage, they tend not to fit the profile of the psychopath. Nonetheless, psychopathic traits can be considered a risk factor for aggression.

Testosterone. Both males and females have testosterone, but males have about 10 times more of it. Testosterone levels peak during puberty and decline while people are in their mid-twenties—the age group that commits the most violent crimes (U.S. Department of Justice, 2011). Testosterone is robustly associated with higher aggression. People with elevated testosterone levels tend to show heightened levels of a variety of types of aggression (Archer, 1991). In addition, higher testosterone levels have the long-term effect of changing a person's body to become more adept at dominating others through aggression, such as by increasing physical strength and height (Cosmides & Tooby, 2006). When people experience dominance over others, their testosterone also tends to increase (e.g., Gladue, Boechler, & McCaul, 1989).

Genetic predispositions. There are two significant lines of evidence that demonstrate the role of genetics in predisposing people to behave aggressively. First, aggression is heritable. Research shows that heritability explains between 26% and 32% of aggression in children (Tuvblad, Raine, Zheng, & Baker, 2009). These findings offer some explanation regarding why aggression and antisocial behavior appear to "run in families."

Second, people who have various single nucleotide polymorphisms (SNPs) appear predisposed to aggression. Two of the most widely studied genes are a polymorphism in the promoter of the monoamine oxidase A gene (MAOA) and genetic variations in the serotonin transporter gene (5-HT). The MAOA gene is sometimes referred to as the "warrior gene" because of its robust relationship to aggression and antisocial behavior, whereas the 5-HT gene helps transport the "feel good" serotonin transmitter. When people do not feel good, they are more prone to behave aggressively. In one illustrative study, provoked male participants with the low expression allele of the MAOA gene, compared to provoked male participants with the high expression allele, doled out significantly more amounts of hot sauce to someone who expressed dislike for spicy foods (McDermott, Tingley, Cowden, Frazzetto, & Johnson, 2009).

Furthermore, environmental factors interact with the MAOA gene in producing violence-prone individuals. One study examined the interaction between alleles of the MAOA gene and childhood maltreatment on later antisocial outcomes (Caspi et al., 2002). For all antisocial outcomes, the association between maltreatment and antisocial behavior was conditional on the MAOA genotype. Just 12% of the sample had both the genetic risk (low-activity MAOA levels) and maltreatment, but they accounted for 44% of the total convictions for violent crime. In the absence of maltreatment, the genotypic risk factor did not manifest itself behaviorally.

SITUATIONAL FACTORS

Aggression does not occur in a vacuum. Features of the situation also influence aggression. This section reviews evidence regarding the importance of situational factors in predicting aggression.

Social rejection. People have a fundamental need for positive and lasting relationships (Baumeister & Leary, 1995). A growing body of work has shown that experimental manipulations of social rejection increase aggressive behavior against the rejectors and even against innocent bystanders (e.g., see DeWall & Bushman, 2011, for a review). A case study of 15 school shooters indicated that social rejection was present in all but two cases, more than any other risk factor (Leary, Kowalski, Smith, & Phillips, 2003). Overall, findings clearly point to social rejection as a situational factor that causes people to engage in direct and displaced aggression.

Violent media. Violent media are ubiquitous. People watch violent movies, play violent video games, and witness violent actions on television shows more today than ever before. Exposure to violent media, compared to nonviolent media, causes people to behave more aggressively and less prosocially (e.g., see Anderson et al., 2010, for a review). The overall effect size for the relationship between media violence and aggression exceeds the effect size for the link between homework and academic achievement, passive smoking and lung cancer, and calcium intake and bone mass, among several others (Bushman & Anderson, 2001). Exposure to violent media also causes people to become desensitized to violence (Bailey, West, & Anderson, 2011; Bartholow, Bushman, & Sestir, 2006; Carnagey, Anderson, & Bushman, 2007). Moreover, this desensitization to violence mediates the relationship between exposure to violent media and aggression (Engelhardt, Bartholow, Kerr, & Bushman, in press). People generally have strong inhibitions against behaving aggressively. Exposure to violence decreases these inhibitions, making people numb to the violence and therefore increases the likelihood of aggression.

Provocation. Social rejection is one form of interpersonal provocation. Another type of interpersonal provocation that increases aggression is insult or ego-threat. When people experience provocation, they are more likely to behave aggressively (see Bettencourt et al., 2006, for a review). Indeed, provocation is perhaps the most important single cause of aggression (Anderson & Bushman, 2002).

Aggressive cues. Psychologists have devoted their attention primarily to the effect of one type of aggressive cue—a weapon—on aggression. People own weapons for many reasons, including self-defense and sporting events (e.g., hunting, competitive shooting). Being in the presence of weapons is also enough to increase aggressive behavior. In one classic experiment, participants were given the opportunity to behave aggressively toward another person while in the presence of either two weapons (i.e., a rifle and a revolver) or two badminton rackets (Berkowitz & LePage, 1967). Exposure to weapons, compared to badminton rackets, caused participants to behave more aggressively toward an annoying person. Weapons did not increase aggression toward a person who was not annoying. Further research has shown that exposure to weapons increases aggressive cognition (Anderson, Benjamin, & Bartholow, 1998).

Alcohol. Alcohol intoxication is involved in at least 50% of all violent crimes (e.g., Innes, 1988). Laboratory experiments have shown that alcohol intoxication increases aggression among both men and women (Giancola et al., 2009). In naturalistic field studies, acute alcohol consumption is involved in at least one-third of murders, aggravated assaults, forcible rapes, and intimate partner violence incidents (Greenfeld & Henneberg, 2001). Simply seeing alcohol-related stimuli is enough to increase aggressive cognition and behavior (Bartholow & Heinz, 2006). Alcohol does not cause everyone to become aggressive. Instead, it reduces inhibitions, increasing aggression among people who are generally predisposed to behave aggressively (Giancola, 2000). Thus, alcohol consistently causes people to behave more aggressively inside and outside the laboratory, but this increased aggression is most reliably present in people who are predisposed to behave aggressively.

Physical pain. Physical pain increases aggression in humans (e.g., Berkowitz, Cochran, & Embree, 1981) and nonhuman animals (e.g., O'Kelly & Steckle, 1939). In one investigation, participants who kept one hand in a bucket of painfully cold water, compared to those who kept a hand in a bucket of warm water, behaved more aggressively toward an innocent bystander (Berkowitz et al., 1981).

Hot temperatures. Hot temperatures reliably increase aggression. Actual hot temperatures increase aggressive thoughts, angry feelings, and aggressive behaviors (e.g., Anderson, 1989, 2001). For example, major league pitchers hit more batters with their pitches on hot days than on cooler days (Reifman, Larrick, & Fein, 1991), riots occur more frequently in hotter temperatures than in cooler temperatures (Carlsmith & Anderson, 1979), hotter geographical regions have more violence than do cooler geographical regions (Anderson, 1989), and violent crimes (but not nonviolent crimes) are higher during hotter years than during cooler years, and during hotter summers than during cooler summers (Anderson, Bushman, & Groom,

1997), even after potential confounding variables are controlled (e.g., poverty, age). People need not experience hot temperatures directly to increase aggression-related outcomes. For example, priming people with words related to hot temperatures, compared to words related to cold temperatures or neutral words, increases their aggressive thoughts and hostile perceptions (DeWall & Bushman, 2009).

Intangible entities (e.g., bad odors, noise). Many times people experience unpleasantness due to intangible entities, such as bad odors and noise. Although a person cannot behave aggressively toward these intangible entities, these triggers can increase aggression. For example, participants who sat in a room filled with a putrid odor (i.e., ammonium sulfide), compared to only a mildly unpleasant odor (i.e., ethyl mercoptan), gave more intense electric shocks to punish a confederate's errors on a learning task (Rotton, Frey, Barry, Milligan, & Fitzpatrick, 1979). Similar relationships between foul odors and aggression have been observed in relation to secondhand smoke (Jones & Bogat, 1978) and air pollution (Rotton & Frey, 1985).

Exposure to noxious noise also increases aggression. As with the relationship between alcohol and aggression, exposure to noxious noise does not increase aggressive for everyone. When people feel a lack of control over the noise, they tend to behave quite aggressively (Geen & McCown, 1984). When control over the noise is restored, aggression diminishes (Warburton, Williams, & Cairns, 2006). The relationship between noxious noise and aggression is most pronounced when people are exposed to other situational events known to increase aggression, such as provocation (Donnerstein & Wilson, 1976) and violent media (Geen & O'Neal, 1969).

Ego depletion. Just as self-control, impulsivity, and executive functioning can differ between people, they can also differ within people. The limited resource model of self-control argues that people have a finite capacity to exert self-control (Baumeister, Bratslavsky, Muraven, & Tice, 1998). When people exert self-control on an initial task, it saps their self-control resources, leading to subpar performance on subsequent self-control tasks. This effect, dubbed *ego depletion*, is closely linked to aggression. When people experience an aggressive urge, they use self-control to override it. In the absence of the required self-control control resources needed to override the aggressive urge, people tend to behave aggressively.

Ego depletion increases aggression toward both strangers (DeWall, Baumeister, Stillman, & Gailliot, 2007) and romantic relationship partners (Finkel et al., 2009). Crucially, ego depletion only increases aggression when an aggressive urge has been stimulated, suggesting that self-control resources are needed to override such urges.

Anonymity. To have anonymity means that people's thoughts, feelings, and actions are not publicly associated with their identity. When people's identities are hidden, they behave more aggressively than when their actions are publicly associated with their identity (Diener, Fraser, Beaman, & Kelem, 1976). For example, wearing a hood covering one's face caused participants to deliver more intense shocks to another person compared to participants who wore no hood (Zimbardo, 1969). Outside of the laboratory, anonymity also increases extreme violence. In a study of 500 violent attacks in Northern Ireland, 41% (206) occurred when the perpetrator hid his or her identity (Silke, 2003). One reason why anonymity increases aggression is that people experience a state of deindividuation, which is characterized by a loss of restraints that normally curb behaviors when people are seen or attended to as individuals (Zimbardo, 1969).

EMOTION, COGNITION, AND AROUSAL

Whereas the previous sections focused on individual difference and situational factors that may influence aggression, the current section reviews evidence regarding internal states that can increase or decrease aggression. Specifically, we focus on the relationship between emotion, cognition, and arousal on aggression.

Emotion. How people feel influences their likelihood to behave aggressively. Many situational factors that increase aggressive behavior also increase negative and aggressive affect. Exposure to violent media and hot temperatures, for example, increase aggressive feelings (Anderson et al., 2010; Anderson, Anderson, & Deuser, 1996). Social rejection can also increase anger (Leary, Twenge, & Quinlivan, 2006). Anger is commonly regarded as a precursor to aggression, but it increases aggression primarily through reducing inhibitions, increasing attention to aggressive cues, and serving as an information cue about potential threats (see Berkowitz, 2001).

Whereas dominant theories of aggression have focused primarily on emotional states that increase aggression (e.g., Anderson & Bushman, 2002; Berkowitz, 1990), there is some research on the role of emotions in lowering aggression. Empathy, defined as taking another person's perspective and having concern for him or her, relates to lower aggression (Giancola, 2003). Gratitude also reduces aggression, especially in situations in which

people experience provocation (DeWall, Lambert, Pond, Kashdan, & Fincham, 2012).

How people expect to feel is also crucial in predicting their aggressive behavior. Recent theoretical and meta-analytic work suggests that how people expect to feel may be a more reliable predictor of their behavior than how they currently feel (Baumeister, Vohs, DeWall, & Zhang, 2007). For example, angered people who believe that they can improve their mood tend to behave quite aggressively, but angered people who believe that they cannot change their mood do not (Bushman et al., 2001). Like a moth drawn to flame, angered people who chronically believe that expressing anger extinguishes negative feelings are most likely to choose to play violent video games (Bushman & Whitaker, 2010).

Motivational direction – approach versus avoidance – also helps explain how emotion influences aggression. Aggression is an approach-related behavior and therefore approach-related emotional states (even those that are positive) may increase aggression. In contrast, avoidance-related emotional states (even those that are negative) may decrease aggression. These predictions have been confirmed in several studies (e.g., see Carver & Harmon-Jones, 2009, for a review). For example, anger increases activation in the left prefrontal cortex and increases aggression, whereas anxiety increases activation in the right prefrontal cortex and decreases aggression (see Carver & Harmon-Jonesfor a review). Other work has shown that disgust sensitivity, an emotion marked by behavioral avoidance, is associated with lower levels of aggression (Pond et al., 2012).

Thus, the aggression literature is at an exciting transitional point in terms of understanding the relationship between emotion and aggression. Whereas the majority of previous aggression research has focused on negative emotions, recent research has emphasized the importance of anticipated emotions, emotions that mitigate against aggression, and considering the motivational direction of an emotion instead of its valence.

Cognition. Like unpleasant feelings (e.g., anger, frustration), aggressive cognitions hold a prominent place in many theories of aggression. A number of external triggers (e.g., guns, alcohol, temperature, media violence) heighten accessibility of aggressive thoughts. Aggressive thoughts, in turn, increase the likelihood of aggressive behaviors, either through simple priming (Bartholow, Anderson, Carnagey, & Benjamin, 2005), their place in aggressive behavioral scripts (e.g., Huesmann, 1998), or by biasing their interpretation of others' behaviors (e.g., Dodge, 1986).

Arousal. Arousal, whether it is physiological or psychological, is closely linked to aggression. As noted above, arousal plays a crucial role in excitation-transfer theory (Zillmann, 1979). When people are aroused, they rely on dominant action tendencies. In cases where people have experienced provocation, for example, arousal is associated with higher levels of aggression (Geen & O'Neal, 1969). Crucially, how people become aroused is irrelevant to whether they will behave aggressively. Arousal helps explain why certain individual difference and situational factors increase aggression. When people watch pornography or masturbate, for example, they become aroused, which in turn increases their aggression and antisocial tendencies (Ariely & Loewenstein, 2006; Donnerstein & Barrett, 1978; Jaffe, Malamuth, Feingold, & Feshbach, 1974). If arousal is excessive, it is perceived as unpleasant, and may increase aggression in the same way as other aversive events, by increasing negative affect or by priming aggressive cognitions.

Although the relationship between arousal and aggression may appear clear, there is also some evidence that *lower* levels of arousal may relate to higher aggression. Theoretically, people with lower levels of arousal may lack an inhibitory force that can reduce the likelihood of aggression (Raine, 1996). In one study, men who showed diminished sensitivity to their wives' expressions of happiness (an indicator of reduced arousal) perpetrated more violence compared to men who showed high sensitivity to their spouse's emotional expressions (Marshall & Holtzworth-Munroe, 2010). People who show diminished arousal to a stressful situation are also most likely to be imprisoned criminals or are generally aggressive (Brennan et al., 1997; Raine, 1996).

These findings suggest a somewhat complicated portrait of the relationship between arousal and aggression. Higher state levels of arousal, whether experienced through diverse activities such as riding an exercise bike or masturbating, can increase aggression. But lacking a normal arousal response to stressful or emotion-provoking situations (i.e., low trait arousal) can also increase one's risk for engaging in aggressive or antisocial behavior, much like being desensitized to violence via scenes of violence in the mass media.

INTERACTIONS AMONG RISK FACTORS

In the previous sections on individual difference and situational risk factors, we focused on the overall effects on aggression and violence. However, in many cases—too

many to describe in one summary chapter—one risk or protective factor can moderate the effect of another risk factor. These moderating effects show up as statistical interactions. In some cases, the interactions are between biological factors and family environments. For example, the maltreatment in childhood increases the likelihood of antisocial personality disorder in adulthood, but this effect is significantly stronger among those who have the genotype that confers low MAOA activity (Kim-Cohen et al., 2006).

In other cases, life experiences interact with situational factors. For example, one study examined hunting experience on the classic weapons effect on aggression (Bartholow et al., 2005). Based on GAM's knowledge structure approach, the authors hypothesized that college-age males who grew up in a family hunting tradition would have more sophisticated and accurate knowledge about hunting weapons and assault weapons than their nonhunting counterparts. When primed with photos of hunting weapons versus assault weapons, these knowledge structure differences may moderate the weapons effect on accessibility of aggressive cognitions and aggressive behavior. All of these predictions were supported. Hunters, compared to nonhunters, reported more detailed and specific information about guns. Furthermore, hunting experience interacted with gun type (hunting versus assault weapons) in predicting affective and cognitive reactions to guns. Hunting guns were more likely than assault guns to prime aggressive thoughts among nonhunters, whereas assault guns were more likely than hunting guns to prime aggressive thoughts among hunters. As can be seen in Figure 21.3, for hunters the photos of assault guns yielded greater aggression than photos of

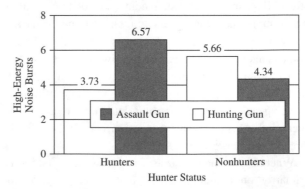

Figure 21.3 Aggressive behavior (number of high-energy noise bursts directed at the opponent) as a function of hunter status and weapon prime

From Bartholow, B. D., Anderson, C. A., Carnagey, N. L., & Benjamin, A. J. (2005). Interactive effects of life experience and situational cues on aggression: The weapons priming effect in hunters and nonhunters. *Journal of Experimental Social Psychology, 41*, 48–60.

hunting guns, whereas the opposite pattern occurred for nonhunters. In sum, the life experiences of hunters (typically, happy outings hunting with Dad and other friends and family) influences one's beliefs, affective reactions, and scripts regarding guns, which in turn influences the effect of different types of gun photos.

The point is that there are numerous moderating effects in the aggression and violence literature, and they can occur between various types of risk factors for aggression. Many more remain to be discovered. A comprehensive model of human aggression, one that encompasses everything from basic biological processes to complex social systems, aids greatly in directing future research in the discovery of new moderator effects.

REDUCING AGGRESSION

Most aggression treatment programs can be divided into one of two broad categories, depending upon whether aggression is viewed as proactive or reactive (see Berkowitz, 1993, pp. 358–370). Recall that proactive aggression is cold-blooded, premeditated, and serves as a means to some other end, whereas reactive-aggression is hot-blooded, impulsive, and is an end in itself. Both types of treatment programs focus on personal (e.g., beliefs and attitudes about the effectiveness of aggression in solving problems) and situational factors (e.g., provocation, frustration) to reduce angry internal states. Once people are calm, they make less hostile cognitive appraisals, and behave in a less impulsive, nonaggressive manner.

People may resort to aggression because it is the easiest way for them to get what they want in the short run. Negotiating, inducing guilt, compromising, ingratiating, and other ways of influencing others all require considerable skills and self-control, whereas aggression does not. People may therefore turn to aggression as a seemingly rational and appealing way of pursuing their goals.

Therapists who view aggression as proactive (instrumental) behavior concentrate on teaching aggressive people that they will satisfy their goals more effectively using nonaggressive means. This approach to reducing aggression uses *behavior modification* learning principles that focus on reinforcing nonaggressive behaviors. One example is the approach used by the Oregon Social Learning Center (e.g., Patterson, Reid, Jones, & Conger, 1975). In this approach, parents play a key role in forming aggressive tendencies in their children by doing things like nagging them, failing to reward desirable behavior,

and inconsistently punishing undesirable behavior. Thus, parents are involved in the treatment plan.

The treatment is based on a contract the therapist makes with the aggressive child. The contract specifies the rewards the child will receive if he or she complies with the contract. For example, the child might earn 1 point for listening to parents, and lose 1 point for swearing at someone. The points can be exchanged for privileges (e.g., playing video games, favorite treats). If the first contract is successful, a second contract is negotiated that includes new behaviors. The program is effective in reducing aggression in about one of three children.

Another effective program is social skills training, in which people learn about the verbal and nonverbal behaviors involved in social interactions (e.g., Pepler, King, Craig, Byrd, & Bream, 1995). For example, they are taught how to make "small talk" in social settings, how to maintain good eye contact during a conversation, and how to "read" the subtle cues contained in social interactions. By learning how to interact better with others, people do not have to resort to aggression to get what they want.

Having prosocial role models, even virtual ones, also helps (e.g., Spivey & Prentice-Dunn, 1990). Just as exposure to violent models in the media can increase aggression, exposure to prosocial models in the media can decrease aggression and increase cooperation (e.g., Saleem & Anderson, 2012; for a meta-analytic review see Mares & Woodard, 2005).

Other approaches to reducing aggression focus on dampening emotional reactivity using relaxation and cognitive-behavioral techniques (for a meta-analytic review see DiGiuseppe & Tafrate, 2003). Most relaxation-based techniques involve deep breathing, visualizing relaxing images (e.g., a peaceful meadow), or tightening and loosening muscle groups in succession. For example, people can practice relaxing after imagining or experiencing a provocative event. In this way, they learn to calm down after they have been provoked.

Cognitive-based treatments focus on how an event is appraised or interpreted. When provocative events occur, people talk to themselves (in their minds), a process called *self-instructional training* (e.g., Novaco, 1975). When preparing for a provocation, people rehearse statements such as: "If I find myself getting upset, I'll know what to do." When confronting the provocation, people rehearse statements such as: "Stay calm. Just continue to relax." To cope with arousal and agitation that arises following provocation, people rehearse statements such as: "My muscles are starting to feel tight. Time to relax and slow things down." If the conflict is resolved, people rehearse statements such as: "That wasn't as hard as I thought." If the conflict is not resolved, people rehearse statements such as: "These are difficult situations, and they take time to work out." Research shows that it is especially helpful to combine relaxation and cognitive techniques (e.g., Novaco, 1975). Other reappraisal training programs have proven effective with a general college student population (e.g., Barlett & Anderson, 2011).

CONCLUSION

Why do people behave aggressively? For nearly a century, psychologists have sought to answer this question by developing sophisticated theories of aggression, examining the development of aggression over time, identifying individual differences and situational factors that increase aggression, considering the roles of emotion, cognition, and arousal in influencing aggression, and designing interventions to reduce aggression. This chapter reviewed classic and contemporary aggression research that has searched for answers as to why people behave aggressively. By understanding the causes of aggression, researchers and laypersons will have a better understanding of how to prevent aggression.

REFERENCES

Abelson, R. P. (1981). Psychological status of the script concept. *American Psychologist, 36,* 715–729.

American Psychiatric Association. (2000). *Diagnostic and statistical manual of mental disorders* (4th ed.). Washington, DC: Author.

Anderson, C. A. (1989). Temperature and aggression: Ubiquitous effects of heat on the occurrence of human violence. *Psychological Bulletin, 106,* 74–96.

Anderson, C. A. (2001). Heat and violence. *Current Directions in Psychological Science, 10,* 33–38.

Anderson, C. A., Anderson, K. B., & Deuser, W. E. (1996). Examining an affective aggression framework: Weapon and temperature effects on aggressive thoughts, affect, and attitudes. *Personality and Social Psychology Bulletin, 22,* 366–376.

Anderson, C. A., Benjamin, A. J., & Bartholow, B. D. (1998). Does the gun pull the trigger? Automatic priming effects of weapon pictures and weapon names. *Psychological Science, 9,* 308–314.

Anderson, C. A., Buckley, K. E., & Carnagey, N. L. (2008). Creating your own hostile environment: A laboratory examination of trait aggression and the violence escalation cycle. *Personality and Social Psychology Bulletin, 34,* 462–473.

Anderson, C. A., & Bushman, B. J. (2002). Human aggression. *Annual Review of Psychology, 53,* 27–51.

Anderson, C. A., Bushman, B. J., & Groom, R. W. (1997). Hot years and serious and deadly assault: Empirical tests of the heat hypothesis. *Journal of Personality and Social Psychology, 73,* 1213–1223.

Anderson, C. A., & Carnagey, N. L. (2004). Violent evil and the general aggression model. In A. Miller (Ed.), *The social psychology of good and evil* (pp. 168–192). New York, NY: Guilford.

Anderson, C. A., & Huesmann, L. R. (2003). Human aggression: A social-cognitive view. In M. A. Hogg & J. Cooper (Eds.), *Handbook of Social Psychology* (pp. 296–323). London: Sage.

Anderson, C. A., Shibuya, A., Ihori, N., Swing, E. L., Bushman, B. J., Sakamoto, A., . . . Saleem, M. (2010). Violent video game effects on aggression, empathy, and prosocial behavior in Eastern and Western countries. *Psychological Bulletin, 136,* 151–173.

Ariely, D., & Loewenstein, G. (2006). The heat of the moment: The effect of sexual arousal on sexual decision making. *Journal of Behavioral Decision Making, 19,* 87–98.

Archer, J. (1991). The influence of testosterone on human aggression. *British Journal of Psychology, 82,* 1–28.

Ayduk, O., Rodriguez, M. L., Mischel, W., Shoda, Y., & Wright, J. (2007). Verbal intelligence and self-regulatory competencies: Joint predictors of boys' aggression. *Journal of Research in Personality, 41,* 374–388.

Bailey, K., West, R., & Anderson, C. A. (2011). The association between chronic exposure to video game violence and affective picture processing: An ERP study. *Cognitive, Affective, and Behavioral Neuroscience, 11,* 259–276.

Bandura, A. (1965). Influence of models' reinforcement contingencies on the acquisition of imitative responses. *Journal of Personality and Social Psychology, 1,* 589–595.

Bandura, A. (1977). *Social learning theory.* New York, NY: Prentice Hall.

Bandura, A. (1986). *Social foundations of thought and action: A social cognitive theory.* Englewood Cliffs, NJ: Prentice-Hall.

Bandura, A., Ross, D. & Ross, S. A. (1963). Vicarious reinforcement and imitative learning. *Journal of Abnormal and Social Psychology, 67,* 601–607.

Bandura, A., Ross, D., & Ross, S. A. (1961). Transmission of aggression through imitation of aggressive models. *Journal of Abnormal and Social Psychology, 63,* 575–582.

Barlett, C. P., & Anderson, C. A. (2011). Re-appraising the situation and its impact on aggressive behavior. *Personality and Social Psychology Bulletin, 37,* 1564–1573.

Barlett, C. P. & Anderson, C. A. (in press). Direct and indirect relations between the Big 5 personality traits and aggressive behavior. *Personality and Individual Differences,*

Baron, R. A., & Richardson, D. R. (1994). *Human aggression* (2nd ed.). New York, NY: Plenum Press.

Bartholow, B. D., Anderson, C. A., Carnagey, N. L., & Benjamin, A. J. (2005). Interactive effects of life experience and situational cues on aggression: The weapons priming effect in hunters and nonhunters. *Journal of Experimental Social Psychology, 41,* 48–60.

Bartholow, B. D., Bushman, B. J., & Sestir, M. A. (2006). Chronic violent video game exposure and desensitization: Behavioral and event-related brain potential data. *Journal of Experimental Social Psychology, 42,* 532–539.

Bartholow, B. D., & Heinz, A. (2006). Alcohol and aggression without consumption: Alcohol cues, aggressive thoughts, and hostile perception bias. *Psychological Science, 17,* 30–37.

Baumeister, R. F., Bratslavsky, E., Muraven, M., & Tice, D. M. (1998). Ego depletion: Is the active self a limited resource? *Journal of Personality and Social Psychology, 74,* 1252–1265.

Baumeister, R. F., Heatherton, T. F., & Tice, D. M. (1994). *Losing control: How and why people fail at self-regulation.* San Diego, CA: Academic Press.

Baumeister, R. F., & Leary, M. R. (1995). The need to belong: Desire for interpersonal attachments as a fundamental human motivation. *Psychological Bulletin, 117,* 497–529.

Baumeister, R. F., Vohs, K. D., DeWall, C. N., & Zhang, L. (2007). How emotion shapes behavior: Feedback, anticipation, and reflection, rather than direct causation. *Personality and Social Psychology Review, 11,* 167–203.

Berkowitz, L. (1989). Frustration-aggression hypothesis: Examination and reformulation. *Psychological Bulletin, 106*, 59–73.

Berkowitz, L. (1990). On the formation and regulation of anger and aggression: A cognitive-neoassociationistic analysis. *American Psychologist, 45*, 494–503.

Berkowitz, L. (1993). *Aggression: Its causes, consequences, and control.* New York, NY: McGraw-Hill.

Berkowitz, L. (2001). Affect, aggression and antisocial behavior. In R. J. Davidson, K. R. Scherer, & H. H. Goldsmith (Eds.), *Handbook of affective sciences* (pp. 804–823). New York, NY: Oxford University Press.

Berkowitz, L., Cochran, S., & Embree, M. C. (1981). Physical pain and the goal of aversively stimulated aggression. *Journal of Personality and Social Psychology, 40*, 687–700.

Berkowitz, L., & LePage, A. (1967). Weapons as aggression-eliciting stimuli. *Journal of Personality and Social Psychology, 7*, 202–207.

Bettencourt, B. A., & Miller, N. (1996). Gender differences in aggression as a function of provocation: A meta-analysis. *Psychological Bulletin, 119*, 422–447.

Bettencourt, B. A., Talley, A., Benjamin, A. J., & Valentine, J. (2006). Personality and aggressive behavior under provoking and neutral conditions: A meta-analytic review. *Psychological Bulletin, 132*, 751–777.

Blonigen, D. M., & Krueger, R. F. (2007). Personality and violence: The unifying role of structural models of personality. In I. Waldman, D. J. Flannery, & A. T. Vazsonyi (Eds.), *The Cambridge handbook of violent behavior* (pp. 288–305). Cambridge, UK: Cambridge University Press.

Brennan, P. A., Raine, A., Schulsinger, F., Kirkegaard-Sorensen, L., Knop, J., Hutchings, B., . . . Mednick, S. A. (1997). Psychophysiological protective factors for male subjects at high risk for criminal behavior, *American Journal of Psychiatry, 154*, 853–855.

Bushman, B. J., & Anderson, C. A. (2001). Media violence and the American public: Scientific facts versus media misinformation. *American Psychologist, 56*, 477–489.

Bushman, B. J., & Baumeister, R. F. (1998). Threatened egotism, narcissism, self-esteem, and direct and displaced aggression: Does self-love or self-hate lead to violence? *Journal of Personality and Social Psychology, 75*, 219–229.

Bushman, B. J., Baumeister, R. F. & Phillips, C. M. (2001). Do people aggress to improve their mood? Catharsis beliefs, affect regulation opportunity, and aggressive responding. *Journal of Personality and Social Psychology, 81*, 17–32.

Bushman, B. J., Baumeister, R. F., Thomaes, S., Ryu, E., Begeer, S., & West, S. G. (2009). Looking again, and harder, for a link between low self-esteem and aggression. *Journal of Personality, 77*, 427–446.

Bushman, B. J., Bonacci, A. M., Pedersen, W. C., Vasquez, E. A., & Miller, N. (2005). Chewing on it can chew you up: Effects of rumination on triggered displaced aggression. *Journal of Personality and Social Psychology, 88*, 969–983.

Bushman, B. J., & Huesmann, L. R. (2010). Aggression. In S. T. Fiske, D. T. Gilbert, & G. Lindzey (Eds.), *Handbook of social psychology* (Vol. 2, 5th ed., pp. 833–863). Hoboken, NJ: Wiley.

Bushman, B. J., & Whitaker, J. L. (2010). Like a magnet: Catharsis beliefs attract angry people to violent video games. *Psychological Science, 21*, 790–792.

Buss, A. H. (1961). *The psychology of aggression.* New York, NY: Wiley.

Campbell, W. K., Bonacci, A. M., Shelton, J., Exline, J. J., & Bushman, B. J. (2004). Psychological entitlement: Interpersonal consequences and validation of a self-report measure. *Journal of Personality Assessment, 83*, 29–45.

Caprara, G., Barbaranelli, C., & Zimbardo, P. (1996). Understanding the complexity of human aggression. *European Journal of Personality, 10*, 133–155.

Carlsmith, J. M., & Anderson, C. A. (1979). Ambient temperature and the occurrence of collective violence: A new analysis. *Journal of Personality and Social Psychology, 37*, 337–344.

Carnagey, N. L., & Anderson, C. A., Bushman, B. J. (2007). The effect of video game violence on physiological desensitization to real-life violence. *Journal of Experimental Social Psychology, 43*, 489–496.

Carver, C. S., & Harmon-Jones, E. (2009). Anger is an approach-related affect: Evidence and implications. *Psychological Bulletin, 135*, 183–204.

Catalano, R. F., Novaco, R., & McConnell, W. (2002). Layoffs and violence revisited. *Aggressive Behavior, 28*, 233–247.

Caspi, A., McClay, J., Moffitt, T. E., Mill, J., Martin, J., Craig, I. W., . . . Poulton, R. (2002). Role of genotype in the cycle of violence in maltreated children. *Science, 297*, 851–854.

Cosmides, L., & Tooby, J. (2006). Origins of domain specificity: The evolution of functional organization. In Bermudez, J. L. (Ed.), *Philosophy of psychology: Contemporary readings* (pp. 539–555), New York, NY: Routledge.

Cote, S., Vaillancourt, T., LeBlanc, J., Nagin, D. W., & Tremblay, R. E. (2006). The development of physical aggression from toddlerhood to pre-adolescence: A nation wide longitudinal study of Canadian children. *Journal of Abnormal Child Psychology, 34*(1), 71–85.

Cowan, P. A., & Walters, R. A. (1963). Studies of reinforcement of aggression: I. Effects of scheduling. *Child Development, 34*, 543–551.

Crick, N. R., & Grotpeter, J. K. (1995). Relational aggression, gender, and social-psychological adjustment. *Child Development, 66*, 710–722.

Denson, T. F., Pedersen, W. C., Ronquillo, J., & Nandy, A. S. (2009). The angry brain: Neural correlates of anger, angry rumination, and aggressive personality. *Journal of Cognitive Neuroscience, 21*, 734–744.

Derefinko, K., DeWall, C. N., Metze, A. V., Walsh, E. C., & Lynam, D. R. (2011). Do different facets of impulsivity predict different types of aggression? *Aggressive Behavior, 37*, 223–233

DeWall, C. N., Anderson, C. A., & Bushman, B. J. (2011). The general aggression model: Theoretical extensions to violence. *Psychology of Violence, 1*, 245–258.

DeWall, C. N., Baumeister, R. F., Stillman, T. F., & Gailliot, M. T. (2007). Violence restrained: Effects of self-regulation and its depletion on aggression. *Journal of Experimental Social Psychology, 43*, 62–76.

DeWall, C. N., & Bushman, B. J. (2009). Hot under the collar in a lukewarm environment: Hot temperature primes increase aggressive cognition and biases. *Journal of Experimental Social Psychology, 45*, 1045–1047.

DeWall, C. N., & Bushman, B. J. (2011). Social acceptance and rejection: The sweet and the bitter. *Current Directions in Psychological Science, 20*, 256–260.

DeWall, C. N., Lambert, N. M., Pond, R. S., Kashdan, T. B., & Fincham, F. D. (2012). A grateful heart is a nonviolent heart: Cross-sectional, experience sampling, longitudinal, and experimental evidence. *Social Psychological and Personality Science, 3*, 232–280.

Diener, E., Fraser, S. C., Beaman, A. L., & Kelem, R. T. (1976). Effects of deindividuation variables on stealing among Halloween trick-or-treaters. *Journal of Personality and Social Psychology, 33*, 178–183.

DiGiuseppe, R., & Tafrate, R. C. (2003). Anger treatment for adults: A meta-analytic review. *Clinical Psychology: Science & Practice, 10*, 70–84.

Dodge, K. A. (1980). Social cognition and children's aggressive behavior. *Child Development, 51*, 620–635.

Dodge, K. A. (1986). Social information processing variables in the development of aggression and altruism in children. In C. Zahn-Waxler, M. Cummings, & M. Radke-Yarrow (Eds.), *The* development of altruism and aggression: Social and biological origins (pp. 280–302). New York: Cambridge University Press.

Dollard, J., Doob, L., Miller, N., Mowrer, O., & Sears, R. 1939. *Frustration and aggression.* New Haven, CT: Yale University Press.

Donnerstein, E., & Barrett, G. (1978). Effects of erotic stimuli on male aggression toward females. *Journal of Personality and Social Psychology, 36,* 180–188.

Donnerstein, E., & Wilson, D. W. (1976). Effects of noise and perceived control on ongoing and subsequent aggressive behavior. *Journal of Personality and Social Psychology, 34,* 774–781.

Egan, V. (2009). The "Big Five": Neuroticism, extraversion, openness, agreeableness and conscientiousness as an organisational scheme for thinking about aggression and violence. In M. McMurran & R. Howard (Eds.), *Personality, personality disorder, and risk of violence: An evidence-based approach* (pp. 63–84). Chichester, UK: Wiley.

Ellison, C. G., & Anderson, K. L. (2001). Religious involvement and domestic violence among U.S. couples. *Journal for the Scientific Study of Religion, 40,* 269–286.

Engelhardt, C. R., Bartholow, B. D., Kerr, G. T., & Bushman, B. J. (in press). This is your brain on violent video games: Neural desensitization to violence predicts increased aggression following violent video game exposure. *Journal of Experimental Social Psychology.*

Eron, L. D., Walder, L. O., & Lefkowitz, M. M. (1971). *The learning of aggression in children.* Boston, MA: Little, Brown.

Finkel, E. J. (2008). Intimate partner violence perpetration: Insights from the science of self-regulation. In J. P. Forgas & J. Fitness (Eds.), *Social relationships: Cognitive, affective, and motivational processes* (pp. 271–288). New York, NY: Psychology Press.

Finkel, E. J., DeWall, C. N., Slotter, E. B., Oaten, M., & Foshee, V. A. (2009). Self-regulatory failure and intimate partner violence perpetration. *Journal of Personality and Social Psychology, 97,* 483–499.

Finkel, E. J., & Eckhardt, C. I. (in press). Intimate partner violence. In J. A. Simpson & L. Campbell (Eds.), *The Oxford handbook of close relationships.* New York, NY: Oxford University Press.

Fischer, P., Greitemeyer, T., & Frey, D. (2008). Self-regulation and selective exposure: The impact of depleted self-regulation resources on confirmatory information processing. *Journal of Personality and Social Psychology, 94,* 382–395.

Fuller, R. (2001). *Spiritual, but not religious: Understanding unchurched America.* New York, NY: Oxford University Press.

Gaertner, L., Iuzzini, J., O'Mara, E. M. (2008). When rejection by one fosters aggression against many: Multiple-victim aggression as a consequence of social rejection and perceived groupness. *Journal of Experimental Social Psychology, 44,* 958–970.

Gallup, G., & Lindsay, D. M. (1999). *Surveying the religious landscape: Trends in US beliefs.* Harrisburg, PA: Morehouse.

Galovski, T., Blanchard, E. B., & Veazey, C. (2002). Intermittent explosive disorder and other psychiatric co-morbidity among court-referred and self-referred aggressive drivers. *Behaviour Research and Therapy, 40,* 641–651.

Garbe, C. M., & Kemble, E. D. (1993). Effects of novel odor exposure on maternal aggression in mice. *Bulletin of the Psychonomic Society, 31,* 571–573.

Geen, R. G., & McCown, E. J. (1984). Effects of noise and attack on aggression and physiological arousal. *Motivation and Emotion, 8,* 231–241.

Geen, R. G., & O'Neal, E. C. (1969). Activation of cue-elicited aggression by general arousal. *Journal of Personality and Social Psychology, 11,* 289–292.

Giancola, P. R. (2000). Executive functioning: A conceptual framework for alcohol-related aggression. *Experimental and Clinical Psychopharmacology, 8,* 576–597.

Giancola, P. R. (2003). The moderating effects of dispositional empathy on alcohol-related aggression in men and women. *Journal of Abnormal Psychology, 112,* 275–281.

Giancola, P. R., Levinson, C. A., Corman, M. D., Godlaski, A. J., Morris, D. H., Phillips, J. P., & Holt, J. C. D. (2009). Men and women, alcohol and aggression. *Experimental and Clinical Psychopharmacology, 17,* 154–164

Gladue, B. A., Boechler, M., & McCaul, K. D. (1989). Hormonal responses to competition in human males. *Aggressive Behavior, 17,* 313–326.

Goldberg, L. R. (1993). The structure of phenotypic personality traits. *American Psychologist, 48*(1), 26–34.

Gottfredson, M. R., & Hirschi, T. (1990). *A general theory of crime.* Stanford, CA: Stanford University Press.

Greenfeld, L. A., & Henneberg, M. A. (2001). Victim and offender self-reports of alcohol involvement in crime. *Alcohol Health & Research World, 25,* 20–31.

Hare, R. D., Harpur, T. J., Hakstian, A. R., Forth, A. E., Hart, S. D., & Newman, J. P. (1990). The Revised Psychopathy Checklist: Descriptive statistics, reliability, and factor structure. *Psychological Assessment: A Journal of Consulting and Clinical Psychology, 2,* 338–341.

Hawkins, K. A., & Trobst, K. K. (2000). Frontal lobe dysfunction and aggression: conceptual issues and research findings. *Aggression and Violent Behavior: A Review Journal, 5,* 147–157.

Hebb, D. O. (1955). Drives and the C.N.S. (conceptual nervous system). *Psychological Review, 62,* 243–254.

Hines, D. A., & Saudino, K. J. (2008). Personality and intimate partner aggression in dating relationships: The role of the "Big Five." *Aggressive Behavior, 34,* 593–604.

Hovland, C., & Sears, R. (1940). Minor studies of aggression: VI. Correlation of lynchings with economic indices. *Journal of Psychology, 9,* 301–310.

Huesmann, L. R. (1982). Information processing models of behavior. In N. Hirschberg & L. Humphreys (Eds.), *Multivariate applications in the social sciences* (pp. 261–288). Hillsdale, NJ: Erlbaum.

Huesmann, L. R. (1998). The role of social information processing and cognitive schema in the acquisition and maintenance of habitual aggressive behavior (pp. 73–109). In R. G. Geen & E. Donnerstein (Eds.), *Human aggression: Theories, research, and implications for policy* (pp. 73–109). New York, NY: Academic Press.

Innes, C. A. (1988). *Drug use and crime.* Washington, DC: U.S. Department of Justice.

Jaffe, Y., Malamuth, N., Feingold, J., & Feshbach, S. (1974). Sexual arousal and behavioral aggression. *Journal of Personality and Social Psychology, 30,* 759–764.

Jones, J., & Bogat, G. (1978) Air pollution and human aggression. *Psychological Reports, 43,* 721–722.

Kernis, M. H., Grannemann, B. D., & Barclay, L. C. (1989). Stability and level of self-esteem as predictors of anger arousal and hostility. *Journal of Personality and Social Psychology, 56,* 1013–1023.

Kim-Cohen, J., Caspi, A., Taylor, A., Williams, B., Newcombe, R., Craig, I. W., & Moffitt, T. E. (2006). *MAOA,* maltreatment, and gene-environment interaction predicting children's mental health: New evidence and a meta-analysis. *Molecular Psychiatry, 11,* 903–913.

Lagerspetz, K. M., Bjorkqvist, K., & Peltonen, T. (1988). Is indirect aggression typical of females? Gender differences in aggressiveness in 11- to 12-year-old children. *Aggressive Behavior, 14,* 403–414.

Leary, M. R., Kowalski, R. M., Smith, L., & Phillips, S. (2003). Teasing, rejection, and violence: Case studies of the school shootings. *Aggressive Behavior, 29,* 202–214.

Leary, M. R., Twenge, J. M., & Quinlivan, E. (2006). Interpersonal rejection as a determinant of anger and aggression. *Personality and Social Psychology Review, 10,* 111–132.

Loeber, R., & Hay, D. (1997). Key issues in the development of aggression from childhood to early adulthood. *Annual Review of Psychology, 48,* 371–410.

Lynam, D., Moffitt, T., & Stouthamer-Loeber, M. (1993). Explaining the relation between IQ and delinquency: Class, race, test motivation, school failure, or self-control? *Journal of Abnormal Psychology, 102,* 187–196.

Marcus-Newhall, A., Pedersen, W. C., Carlson, M., & Miller, N. (2000). Displaced aggression is alive and well: a meta-analytic review. *Journal of Personality and Social Psychology, 78,* 670–689.

Mares, M. L., & Woodard, E. (2005). Positive effects of television on children's social interactions: A meta-analysis. *Media Psychology, 7,* 301–322.

Marshall, A. D., & Holtzworth-Munroe, A. (2010). Recognition of wives' emotional expressions: A mechanism in the relationship between psychopathology and intimate partner violence perpetration. *Journal of Family Psychology, 24,* 21–30.

McCloskey, M. S., & Berman, M. E. (2003). Alcohol intoxication and self-aggressive behavior. *Journal of Abnormal Psychology, 112,* 306–311.

McDermott, R., Tingley, D., Cowden, J., Frazzetto, G., & Johnson, D. D. P. (2009). Monoamine oxidase A gene (MAOA) predicts behavioral aggression following provocation. *Proceedings of the National Academy of Sciences, 106,* 2118–2123.

Miller, N. (1941). The frustration-aggression hypothesis. *Psychological Review, 48,* 337–342.

Miller, J. D., Lynam, D., & Leukefeld, C. (2003). Examining antisocial behavior through the lens of the five factor model of personality. *Aggressive Behavior, 29,* 497–514.

Milner, B. (1995). Aspects of human frontal lobe function. In H. Jasper, S. Riggio, & P. Goldman-Rakic (Eds.), *Epilepsy and the functional anatomy of the frontal lobe* (pp. 67–84). New York, NY: Raven Press.

Moffitt, T. E., Arseneault, L., Belsky, D., Dickson, N., Hancox, R. J., Harrington, H., . . . Caspi, A. (2011). A gradient of childhood self-control predicts health, wealth, and public safety. *PNAS Proceedings of the National Academy of Sciences of the United States of America, 108,* 2693–2698.

Morgan, A. B., & Lilienfeld, S. O. (2000). A meta-analytic review of the relation between antisocial behavior and neuropsychological measures of executive function. *Clinical Psychology Review, 20,* 113–136.

Novaco, R. W. (1975). *Anger control: The development and evaluation of an experimental treatment.* Lexington, MA: Heath.

Novaco, R. (1991). Aggression on roadways. In Baenninger R, editor. *Targets of violence and aggression.* (pp. 253–326). Amsterdam, The Netherlands: North-Holland.

Nouvion, S. O., Cherek, D. R., Lane, S. D., Tcheremissine, O. V., & Lieving, L. M. 2007. Human proactive aggression: association with personality disorders and psychopathy. *Aggressive Behavior 33,* 552–562.

O'Kelly, K. E., & Steckle, L. C. (1939). A note on long-enduring emotional responses in the rat. *Journal of Psychology, 8,* 125–131.

Olweus, D. (1979). The stability of aggressive reaction patterns in males: A review. *Psychological Bulletin, 86,* 852–875.

Orobio de Castro, B., Veerman, J. W., Koops, W., Bosch, J. D., & Monshouwer, H. J. (2002). Hostile attribution of intent and aggressive behavior: A meta-analysis. *Child Development, 73,* 916–934.

Patterson, G. R., Littman, R. A., & Bricker, W. (1967). Assertive behavior in children: A step toward a theory of aggression. *Monographs of the Society for Research in Child Development, 32,* 1–43.

Patterson, G. R., Reid, J. G., Jones, R. R., & Conger, R. E. (1975). *A social learning approach to family intervention.* Eugene, OR: Catalia.

Pedersen, W. C., Bushman, B. J., Vasquez, E. A., & Miller, N. (2008). Kicking the (barking) dog effect: The moderating role of target attributes on triggered displaced aggression. *Personality and Social Psychology Bulletin, 34*(10), 1382–1395.

Pedersen, W. C., Gonzales, C., & Miller, N. (2000). The moderating effect of trivial triggering provocation on displaced aggression. *Journal of Personality & Social Psychology, 78,* 913–27.

Pepler, D. J., King, G., Craig, W., Byrd, B., & Bream, L. (1995). The development and evaluation of a multisystem social skills group training programs for aggressive children. *Child & Youth Care Forum, 24,* 297–313.

Perry, D. G., Perry, L. C., & Rasmussen, P. (1986). Cognitive social learning mediators of aggression. *Child Development, 57,* 700–711.

Pond, R. S., DeWall, C. N., Lambert, N. M., Deckman, T., Bonser, I., & Fincham, F. D. (2012). Repulsed by violence: Disgust sensitivity buffers trait, behavioral, and daily aggression. *Journal of Personality and Social Psychology, 102,* 175–188.

Pratt, T. C., & Cullen, F. T. (2000). The empirical status of Gottfredson and Hirschi's general theory of crime: A meta-analysis. *Criminology, 38,* 931–964.

Raine, A. (1996). Autonomic nervous system factors underlying disinhibited, antisocial, and violent behavior: Biosocial perspectives and treatment implications. In C. F. Ferris & T. Grisso (Eds.), *Understanding aggressive behavior in children* (pp. 46–59). New York, NY: New York Academy of Sciences.

Reifman, A., Larrick, R., & Fein, S. (1991). Temper and temperature on the diamond: the heat-aggression relationship in major league baseball. *Personality and Social Psychology Bulletin, 17,* 580–585.

Rotton, J., & Frey, J. (1985). Air pollution, weather, and violent crimes: Concomitant time-series analysis of archival data. *Journal of Personality and Social Psychology, 49,* 1207–1220.

Rotton, J., Frey, J., Barry, T., Milligan, M., & Fitzpatrick, M. (1979). The air pollution experience and physical aggression. *Journal of Applied Social Psychology, 9,* 397–412.

Rys, G. S., & Bear, G. G. (1997). Relational aggression and peer relations: Gender and developmental issues. *Merrill-Palmer Quarterly, 43,* 87–106.

Saleem, M., & Anderson, C. A. (2012). The good, the bad, and the ugly of electronic media. Chapter to appear in J. Dvoskin, J. L. Skeem, R. W. Novaco, & K. S. Douglas (Eds.) (pp. 83–101), *Applying Social Science to Reduce Violent Offending.*

Sears, R. R., Whiting, J. W., Nowlis, V., & Sears, P. S. (1953). Some childrearing antecedents of aggression and dependency in young children. *Genetic Psychology Monographs, 47,* 135–236.

Silke, A. (2003). Deindividuation, anonymity and violence: Findings from Northern Ireland. *Journal of Social Psychology, 143/4,* 493–499.

Spivey, C. B., & Prentice-Dunn, S. (1990). Assessing the directionality of deindividuated behavior: Effects of deindividuation, modeling, and private self-consciousness on aggressive and prosocial responses. *Basic and Applied Social Psychology, 11,* 387–403.

Stevens, M., Kaplan, R., & Hesselbrock, V. (2003). Executive-cognitive functioning in the development of antisocial personality disorder. *Addictive Behaviors, 28,* 285–300.

Suls, J., & Wan, C. K. (1993). The relationship between trait hostility and cardiovascular reactivity: A quantitative review and analysis. *Psychophysiology, 30,* 615–626.

Tangney, J., Baumeister, R. F., & Boone, A. L. (2004). High self-control predicts good adjustment, less pathology, better grades, and interpersonal success. *Journal of Personality, 72,* 271–322.

Tedeschi, J. T., & Felson, R. B. (1994). *Violence, aggression, and coercive actions.* Washington, DC: American Psychological Association.

Tooby, J., & Cosmides, L. (1992). The psychological foundations of culture. In J. Barkow, L. Cosmides, & J. Tooby (Eds.), *The adapted mind* (pp. 19–136). New York, NY: Oxford University Press.

Tremblay, R. E. (2000). The development of aggressive behavior during childhood: What have we learned in the past century. *International Journal of Behavioral Development, 24,* 129–141.

Tremblay, R. E., Nagin, D. S., Seguin, J. R., Zoccolillo, M., Zelazo, P., Boivin, M., . . . Japel, C. (2004). Physical aggression during early childhood: Trajectories and predictors. *Pediatrics, 114* (1), e43–e50.

Tuvblad, C., Raine, A., Zheng, M., & Baker, L. A. (2009). Genetic and environmental stability differs in reactive and proactive aggression. *Aggressive Behavior, 35,* 437–452.

U.S. Department of Justice, Bureau of Justice Statistics. (2011). Homicide trends in the United States. Retrieved May 7, 2011, from http://bjs.ojp.usdoj.gov/content/homicide/homtrnd.cfm

Warburton, W. A., Williams, K. D., & Cairns, D. R. (2006). When ostracism leads to aggression: The moderating effects of control deprivation. *Journal of Experimental Social Psychology, 42,* 213–220.

Wegner, D. M., & Bargh, J. A. (1998). Control and automaticity in social life. Chapter in D. Gilbert, S. Fiske, & G. Lindzey (Eds.), *The handbook of social psychology* (pp. 446–496). New York, NY: McGraw-Hill.

Williamson, S., Hare, R. D., & Wong, S. (1987). Violence: Criminal psychopaths and their victims. *Canadian Journal of Behavioural Science, 19,* 454–462.

Zillmann, D. (1979). *Hostility and aggression.* Hillsdale, NJ: Erlbaum.

Zillmann, D., & Bryant, J. (1974). Effect of residual excitation on the emotional response to provocation and delayed aggressive behavior. *Journal of Personality and Social Psychology, 30,* 782–791.

Zimbardo, P. G. (1969). The human choice: Individuation, reason, and order vs. deindividuation, impulse, and chaos. In W. J. Arnold & D. Levine (Eds.), *Nebraska symposium on motivation* (pp. 237–307). Lincoln: University of Nebraska Press.

CHAPTER 22

Altruism and Prosocial Behavior

MARK SNYDER AND PATRICK C. DWYER

Prosocial behavior occurs when a person acts in a manner that benefits another person or a group of people. Altruism is a kind of prosocial motivation, such that a person is led to engage in prosocial action by the selfless goal of increasing another person's welfare (Batson, 1991). Although altruistically motivated prosocial behavior has been shown to occur, instances of prosocial behavior need not be altruistic to be considered prosocial. Indeed, the psychological study of prosocial behavior covers a broad range of phenomena, which people may engage in for a variety of reasons. From serving as volunteers in communities at home and abroad to voting and participating in the political process, from donating blood to getting involved in neighborhood groups, from coming to the aid of disaster victims to going "above and beyond" one's required duties in the workplace, from intervening in an unforeseen emergency to participating in a large-scale social movement, there are many ways in which people can and do take action to benefit others.

As these examples suggest, prosocial behavior may be considered as both an individual and a collective phenomenon (Snyder & Omoto, 2007). Instances of interpersonal (i.e., one-to-one) helping, in which one person provides assistance to another, comprise one kind of prosocial behavior. The classic example of this kind of prosocial behavior is assistance delivered spontaneously to a stranger during an unforeseen emergency. Investigations into interpersonal helping dominated research on prosocial behavior for many years (Dovidio, Piliavin, Schroeder, & Penner, 2006).

More recently, however, psychologists have turned their attention to other kinds of prosocial behaviors, extending beyond the interpersonal domain to include larger groups of people, and extending beyond spontaneous responses to unforeseen events to address forms of helping that are planned and sustained over longer periods of time. Consider, for example, instances of volunteering, blood donation, and disaster relief. Although all involve the actions of individuals, the societal benefits of these phenomena arise out of the aggregated consequences of many people's actions, and may involve considerable amounts of deliberate planning and coordination between and among helpers and organizers of helping efforts (Snyder & Omoto, 2008).

Cooperation within and between groups represents another kind of prosocial behavior, and is an important ingredient for a well-functioning society (Sullivan, Snyder, & Sullivan, 2008). Although it, too, typically occurs voluntarily, and at the will of the people involved, cooperation also differs from one-to-one helping and more collective forms of prosocial behavior, such as volunteering. Cooperation generally involves two or more people working together as more-or-less equal partners. These dynamics are different from the behaviors mentioned earlier, in which the lines between "helper" and "recipient" are more clearly drawn (Dovidio et al., 2006).

In spite of the wide variety of forms that prosocial behavior can take, and the fact that such actions are often highly socially valued, it is important to note that an individual's prosocial attitudes and beliefs don't necessarily translate into prosocial actions. For example, a large gap exists between the number of people who believe in the positive value of volunteerism and the number who

The National Science Foundation has supported the preparation of this manuscript.

actually volunteer on a regular basis; this discrepancy has been referred to as the "problem of inaction" (Snyder, 1993). Similarly, although voting is central to the democratic process, and the right to vote is widely valued among citizens, rates of voting in national elections are notoriously low. Indeed, the absence of prosocial behavior sometimes seems more remarkable than its presence, as is suggested by the fairly regular occurrence of reports in the media of unresponsive bystanders during emergencies. Ironically, it was incidents such as these, in which people failed to engage in prosocial behavior, that prompted a flood of research in the 1960s and 1970s on when and why people do (and don't) help others in such situations (e.g., Darley & Latané, 1968).

This tendency toward inaction, as opposed to action, points to a potentially important role that motivation plays in leading people to behave prosocially (Snyder & Omoto, 2007). Accordingly, psychologists have devoted considerable time and effort to understanding what moves people to engage in these behaviors, identifying sources of prosocial motivation that are internal, such as personal needs and drives, and external, such as situational demands and social norms. Moreover, different kinds of prosocial behavior have been shown to arise out of different sources of prosocial motivation. For example, whereas investigations into interpersonal prosocial behavior often have focused on the role of external influences, investigations into collective prosocial behavior have largely focused on the role of internal sources of motivation, due to the fact that they are often planned out in advance and unfold over a longer period of time.

INTERPERSONAL PROSOCIAL BEHAVIOR

In addressing the question of when people will engage in one-to-one helping, social psychologists often have embraced a situationist tradition, which can be traced back to Kurt Lewin's discussion of "channel factors" and the research that he and his co-workers conducted on the extent to which aspects of the immediate social situation are responsible for guiding and directing behaviors (Ross & Nisbett, 1991). The popularity of this approach to understanding human social behavior has also been bolstered by claims of low levels of correspondence between some dispositions and their behavioral expressions (e.g., Hartshorne & May, 1928; Mischel, 1968; Newcomb, 1929). As a result, there exists an enormous literature on the powerful influence of situational variables on prosocial behavior.

Situational Influences

Much of this research has examined the phenomenon of bystander intervention in emergency situations. According to Latané and Darley (1970), whether a person will intervene depends on a series of sequential decisions; they must first notice that something is wrong, then define the situation as an emergency, then decide to take personal responsibility, then choose how to intervene, and finally determine to implement that course of action. Aspects of the surrounding situation can influence the outcome of each of these decisions, thus affecting whether a person will help. For example, the more vivid and attention getting an incident is, the more likely people are to help because they are more likely to recognize that something is wrong and to define it as an emergency. Piliavin, Piliavin, and Broll (1976) found that those who witnessed a person stumble and fall down the stairs were approximately seven times more likely to help than those who only witnessed the person rubbing their ankle in the aftermath of the incident.

Even if a person notices an event and defines it as an emergency, contextual features can also influence the extent to which they take personal responsibility for helping. Darley and Latané (1968) provided evidence of this in a line of research inspired by a tragic event that occurred in Queens, New York, in the mid-1960s. In the wake of the murder of a young woman named Kitty Genovese, the news media attributed inaction on the part of the numerous people who witnessed the incident to aspects of their dispositions, such as alienation and indifference. However, Darley and Latané hypothesized that features of the social situation, not bystanders' personalities, were responsible for their inaction. In particular, they proposed that diffusion of responsibility occurs in the presence of other bystanders, such that as the number of onlookers increases the likelihood of any one of them intervening decreases.

Support for this hypothesis has been found across several studies. In one experiment, participants overheard another person (actually a confederate) having a seizure (Darley & Latané, 1968). Participants were led to believe that they were the only person witnessing the emergency, that one other person was also witnessing it, or that four other people were also witnessing it. The presence of others decreased participants' feelings of personal responsibility and speed of responding. Whereas 85% of participants who believed they alone were witnessing the seizure eventually intervened, only 62% intervened when one other person was present. When four other people were present, only 31% of participants intervened.

Moreover, potentially relevant features of personality—such as alienation, Machiavellianism, need for approval, and authoritarianism—predicted neither speed nor likelihood of help.

Another demonstration of the powerful influence of situational forces on helping is offered by Darley and Batson (1974), who conducted a field experiment involving a staged emergency. Participants were seminary students who were asked to walk across campus to deliver a speech about the Good Samaritan. The situational variable of time press was manipulated, such that participants were told either (a) that they were late and should hurry to the other building, (b) that they should simply go right over, or (c) that they were probably early but might as well go over anyway, even if it means that they end up having to wait. While walking across campus, all participants encountered a "victim" slumped in a doorway in an alley, with head down and eyes closed.

The victim, who was actually a confederate, and who was blind to experimental condition, rated each participant on the amount of help offered. Darley and Batson (1974) found that participants who were in a hurry were significantly less likely to offer help than those who were not. Whereas 63% of the students offered help in the "low hurry" condition, this number dropped to 45% in the "intermediate hurry" condition. A mere 10% of the seminary students in the "high hurry" condition stopped to offer help. Through their demonstration that a seemingly minor aspect of the social situation can have a big effect on the people's behavior, Darley and Batson's (1974) work also highlights Lewin's situationist concept of the "channel factor." In this case, time press can be considered a channel factor, or stimulus–response pathway, the inputs for which are small situational factors, and which in turn elicit large behavioral effects (Ross & Nisbett, 1991). The important point here is not simply that situations influence prosocial behavior, but that they do so in a manner that is consistent, large, and consequential.

Social Norms

In addition to considerations of how specific others behave in one's immediate social environment, more general social rules or norms can also be powerful determinants of prosocial behavior. According to social learning theory (e.g., Bandura, 1977), people learn how to behave through observing the behavior of others, and using it as a model for their own behavior. Therefore, people may engage in prosocial behavior because previous social learning has taught them that they ought to do so, and that doing

so is the appropriate response. With regard to one-to-one helping, researchers have focused much of their attention on the motivational influences of social norms relating to reciprocity and social responsibility.

Reciprocity Norm

The norm of reciprocity concerns obligations of repayment for past favors that a person has received. Specifically, it states that people should help those who have helped them, and avoid injuring those who have helped them (Gouldner, 1960). Moreover, this norm dictates that those whom a person has helped are obligated to return the favor, so that helping others becomes one way to increase the likelihood of receiving help for oneself in the future. According to Gouldner, the norm of reciprocity serves to regulate an individual's relationships with others and plays a role in maintaining social stability. The norm of reciprocity is so widespread that Gouldner suggested it to be a universal rule that is present in all societies.

Reciprocation of prosocial acts has been demonstrated in many studies. Much of this research has adopted an experimental procedure devised by Regan (1971), who examined the effect of an initial favor on a participant's level of compliance with a confederate's request. Specifically, Regan found that participants were more likely to comply with a confederate's request to purchase raffle tickets, the proceeds from which would be used to build a new gymnasium at his school, when the confederate bought them a soft drink earlier, compared to when they had not. The pressure to reciprocate has even been found to lead people to send Christmas greeting cards to complete strangers simply because they sent them one first (Kunz & Woolcott, 1976). Using a variation of Regan's procedure, Whatley, Webster, Smith, and Rhodes (1999) found that the reciprocity effect occurred whether the confederate who initially performed the favor would find out that the favor had been returned by the participant, suggesting that participants had internalized the norm. Considering the strength of this social norm, it may not be surprising that salespeople often take advantage of it by giving potential customers a "free gift" immediately prior to making a sales pitch (Cialdini, 1993).

But how much reciprocation is enough to maintain equitable social relations? Research by Zhang and Epley (2009) suggests that it depends on whether you ask the giver or receiver of a prosocial act because different psychological processes underlie each person's decision about how much to reciprocate. They proposed that people assess the value of a prosocial act in a self-centered manner, such that favor givers attend more to the costs they incur and favor receivers attend more to the benefits they receive. Therefore, givers base their expectations about how much reciprocation they should receive on the costs of the action they performed, and receivers base their expectations about how much reciprocation they should give on the benefits they received.

Zhang and Epley (2009) found support for this hypothesized asymmetry across several experiments. For example, in one of their experiments, participants were randomly assigned to recall a recent favor that they either performed for, or that they received from, a friend, colleague, or neighbor. They were then asked to indicate how much they expected the recipient of their favor to spend on a thank-you gift, or, if they had been on the receiving end of the favor, how much they would spend on a thank-you gift for the person who had done them a favor. In each instance, participants were also asked to estimate how beneficial they felt the favor was to the recipient, and how costly it was to the benefactor. The time taken to make these estimations was also measured.

The results of this experiment revealed that the recalled cost of the favor predicted the size of the thank-you gift expected by favor givers, but not the size of the gift that favor receivers reported they would actually provide. However, the recalled benefit of the favor predicted the size of the thank-you gift that receivers would provide, but not the size of the gift that was expected by favor givers. Moreover, favor givers were quicker to estimate the costs of the favor than the benefits and favor receivers were quicker to estimate the benefits than the costs, suggesting that differential attention paid to cost versus benefit information may be the psychological mechanism underlying the gap between expected and actual reciprocity. Thus, the results of Zhang and Epley's (2009) study suggest that this differential use of costs versus benefits by givers and receivers of prosocial acts represents an important challenge to the harmonious and efficient management of prosocial exchanges.

Social Responsibility Norm

The social responsibility norm proscribes that people should help those who are dependent on them (Berkowitz, 1972). In several studies, Berkowitz and Daniels (1963, 1964) found that participants who believed that a peer's evaluation of them was dependent on their task performance worked harder on the task than those who were told that their performance would not affect the peer's evaluation. This occurred despite the fact that doing so would bring no additional benefits to the participant, suggesting that it was increased feelings of responsibility for

the dependent person that enhanced participants' motivation in the high dependency condition. Similarly, Clark (1975) found that participants were more likely to help a person who had dropped a book if the other person was walking with the aid of crutches (high dependency) than if that person was walking in a normal manner (low dependency).

However, several boundary conditions have been found to limit the influence of the social responsibility norm. For example, adherence to the social responsibility norm increases as attractiveness of the recipient increases, and decreases as liking for the recipient decreases (Daniels & Berkowitz, 1963). Also, as we previously noted, diffusion of responsibility increases as the number of bystanders in an emergency situation increases, thereby decreasing the likelihood that an individual will intervene (Darley & Latané, 1968). Therefore, the influence of the social responsibility norm may be best viewed as a general rule that can be regulated by characteristics of persons and of situations (Dovidio et al., 2006).

A person's attribution of the cause of another person's dependency can also determine whether help is given, such that a dependent person who is seen as responsible for his or her own plight will receive less help than one who is not regarded as responsible (Weiner, 1980, 1986). For example, Piliavin, Rodin, and Piliavin (1969) found that passengers on a subway were more likely to help a person who had staggered forward and collapsed if the person was ill (low responsibility) than if the person was drunk (high responsibility). Similarly, Greitemeyer, Rudolph, and Weiner (2003) found that participants were less willing to console a person whose romantic partner had recently broken up with them if the person was responsible for the separation (i.e., if they had a history of betraying their partner) than if they were not responsible. Interestingly, even a member of the participant's family was less likely to be consoled than a casual acquaintance if the family member was judged to be responsible for their plight and the acquaintance was not.

Mood

Through their experiences of helping others, as well as their observations of others who do so, people may learn of mood-enhancing rewards that can be garnered through taking such actions. Adopting a social-learning theory perspective, Cialdini, Baumann, and Kenrick (1981) suggested that people gradually acquire knowledge of these kinds of benefits of helping throughout the process of socialization. Such gratifications may arise out of a person's adherence to the aforementioned social norms (Salovey, Mayer, & Rosenhan, 1991). For example, a child may receive praise from adults as a result of following the norm of social responsibility, or may have the positive experience of being paid back for their good deeds, as a result of the norm of reciprocity. According to Cialdini et al., the majority of adults come to view prosocial behavior as a rewarding experience due to repeated pairings of prosocial acts with positive consequences during socialization. Research by Cialdini and Kenrick (1976) has shown that older children, who presumably have had more exposure to such pairings, were more likely to help when experiencing a negative mood than were younger children, perhaps because the older children were more likely to have learned that helping could make them feel better.

Negative Moods

Due to the rewarding consequences of helping, particularly with regard to mood regulation, psychologists have focused on the potential for negative mood states to motivate prosocial behavior. In particular, the motivational consequences of one kind of mood state, empathic arousal, have received much attention. Empathic arousal is an emotional response generated as a result of witnessing another person's distress. One-to-one helping has been shown to be more likely to occur to the extent that an individual feels empathic arousal, although the nature of one's motivation to help (i.e., whether or not it is truly altruistic) is determined by the manner in which this arousal is interpreted (Dovidio et al., 2006).

If empathic arousal is personally distressing or elicits sadness or guilt, then helping may be motivated by the selfish desire to reduce this negative state; in fact, this effect has been repeatedly demonstrated in research guided by diverse theoretical perspectives on arousal-helping relations (Dovidio, 1984). For example, the "arousal: cost-reward" model suggests that witnessing another person in need elicits an aversive state of personal distress, which the witness attempts to reduce through helping, and does so in a manner that incurs as few net costs as possible (Dovidio, Piliavin, Gaertner, Schroeder, & Clark, 1991).

Moreover, even when a witness's negative state is not attributable to the plight of the person in distress, it can still motivate helping. Cialdini, Darby, and Vincent (1973) found that feelings of guilt or sadness elicited in one situation, through having participants accidentally either destroy a researcher's data or witness someone else do so, led to increased helping in an unrelated situation (i.e., when compared to a neutral-mood control group). In their negative state relief model, Cialdini and his colleagues (1987) propose that people learn of the esteem-enhancing

functions of helping through experience, and that the goal of helping is to improve the helper's situation by relieving their negative mood.

However, Cialdini et al. (1987) also suggest that helping will not occur if another means of eliminating one's negative state precedes the opportunity to help. And, in fact, Cialdini et al. (1973) found that, if sad or guilty participants were first relieved of their negative moods through the receipt of either money or praise, then they did not help more than control participants. Because they involve considerations of fleeting states of arousal, the negative state relief and arousal: Cost-reward models are particularly well suited to explaining why people engage in instances of episodic or short-term, rather than long-term, forms of prosocial action.

Empathy-Altruism Hypothesis

In addition to its role in motivating self-oriented forms of prosocial action, an emotional response to a person in need may also lead to an other-oriented, altruistic motivation to help. Batson (1991) proposed that when this response accompanies a sense of attachment to the other person (e.g., due to taking that person's perspective), empathic concern is elicited, and this other-oriented emotional response produces an altruistic motivation to attend to the other person's needs. Support for the empathy-altruism hypothesis has been provided by many studies spanning several decades, through an empirical approach that has largely focused on ruling out alternative, egoistic explanations for helping in various experimental situations.

For example, many studies pitting the empathy-altruism hypothesis against the egoistic negative state relief model have provided evidence in favor of altruistically motivated helping. Empathic concern, which is typically induced through taking the perspective of a person in need, has been found to elicit helping even when a person believes that their mood is temporarily fixed by a drug (Schroeder, Dovidio, Sibicky, Matthews, & Allen, 1988), and even when they believe their mood will be improved in some other way (Batson et al., 1989). Moreover, people experiencing empathic concern were more likely to help when they were given an opportunity to specifically relieve the main problem causing the beneficiary's distress, as opposed to an unrelated problem. These findings do not support the negative state relief model, which predicts that both types of helping will be equally likely, as they are both opportunities for reducing one's own distress. Although people can and often do help others for self-serving reasons, these findings suggest that altruism, too, is a part of the human repertoire.

Humans' capacity for altruism appears, however, to be limited. Batson's (1991) proposal that empathic concern requires a sense of attachment to a person in need has generated research on the boundary conditions of empathy-induced helping. For example, its potential to motivate helping appears to depend on whether or not the person in need is a member of one's ingroup. Stürmer, Snyder, and Omoto (2005) found that empathy was a stronger predictor of helping when the recipient was an ingroup member than when the recipient was an outgroup member. When the recipient was an outgroup member, higher levels of liking for the person was the connection that increased helping. These findings suggest that appeals to empathy may only be effective in motivating prosocial behavior when the appeal is made on the behalf of an ingroup member.

Positive Moods

The experience of positive affective states, such as happiness and joy, has been shown to facilitate helping across a number of studies. Isen and Levin (1972), for example, found that people for whom a positive mood state had been induced, either by receiving cookies while studying in the library or by unexpectedly finding a dime in the coin return slot of a public telephone, were more helpful than control participants. Other means of inducing a positive mood, such as sunny weather (e.g., Cunningham, 1979) and pleasant fragrances (e.g., Baron, 1997) have produced the same effect. More recently, it has been shown that the experience of elevation, a positive emotion elicited by witnessing another person perform a good deed, can lead to increases in prosocial behavior (Schnall, Roper, & Fessler, 2010). The regular and reliable appearance of findings such as these has led some to state that "there is hardly a more consistent finding in the psychological literature that that which demonstrates the effects of positive affect on altruism" (Rosenhan, Salovey, & Hargis, 1981, p. 899).

Interestingly, empathizing with the positive mood of another person, such as focusing on their experience of happiness or joy, tends to inhibit helping (Salovey et al., 1991). For example, Rosenhan et al. (1981) had participants take part in an "imagination experiment," in which they listened to a scenario in which they would be sent on a holiday vacation in Hawaii (i.e., self-oriented positive affect), their friend would be sent on a holiday vacation in Hawaii (i.e., other-oriented positive affect), or an affectively neutral control condition. Participants were later given an opportunity to help the experimenter's friend by completing an unrelated set of multiple-choice questions. Results revealed that participants in the self-oriented positive affect condition were more helpful than those in the

control condition, but participants in the other-oriented positive affect condition were *less* helpful than controls. Whereas positive affect for the self facilitates helping, positive affect for another person actually appears to inhibit it.

COLLECTIVE PROSOCIAL BEHAVIOR

Looking beyond instances of one-to-one helping between individuals, psychologists have also invested considerable time and energy attempting to understand more collective forms of prosocial behavior. Although behaviors such as volunteering, donating blood, and participating in disaster relief efforts are clearly prosocial (in that they extend benefits to other people), they also differ from interpersonal helping in important ways. For example, these behaviors are often aimed at benefiting groups of people who share a common need (Dovidio et al., 2006). Furthermore, although each of these behaviors involves the actions of individuals, their benefits arise out of the aggregated consequences of many people's actions (Snyder & Omoto, 2008). Unlike instances of one-to-one helping, the efforts of a single individual engaging in one of these kinds of prosocial behavior (i.e., a single volunteer, blood donor) would probably not be enough to meet the need. Moreover, these kinds of behaviors are often carried out by groups of people working in concert. Volunteerism, for example, often involves teams of people working together, and this is further evidence of its collective nature. Also, unlike interpersonal prosocial behavior, which typically involves spontaneous responses to unforeseen events, instances of collective prosocial behavior are generally planned in advance and sustained over longer periods of time. Because greater levels of planning and deliberation precede the initiation of collective prosocial behavior, psychologists have given greater consideration to the personal reasons and motives that lead people to engage in them.

Personal Motives

The notion that prosocial action can be enacted for different reasons, which may vary from person to person, is a central tenet of the functional approach to prosocial motivation (Clary & Snyder, 1991). Research adopting this approach has examined the motivations of those who engage in volunteerism (Clary et al., 1998; Omoto & Snyder, 1995). Several motives have been identified for volunteerism, such as expressing humanitarian values, making new friends, gaining greater understanding, boosting one's self-esteem, and obtaining career-related benefits. When it comes to initiating involvement in volunteer work, individuals are more likely to do so to the extent that they feel it will fulfill personally relevant motives. Clary, Snyder, Ridge, Miene, and Haugen (1994), for example, showed participants videotaped advertisements that were either motive-matched or motive-mismatched after having them indicate the volunteer motives that were most important to them. Individuals who viewed a recruitment message that matched personally relevant motives judged the advertisements as more persuasive and were more likely to volunteer in the future than individuals exposed to motivationally mismatched messages.

Research on volunteerism has demonstrated the importance of personal motives, not only in leading a person to become a volunteer, but also in guiding and sustaining their involvement over time. Once involved in volunteer service, people are more likely to be satisfied with the experience of volunteering and less likely to experience burnout to the extent that their own motives are being fulfilled (e.g., Omoto, Snyder, & Martino, 2000). Matching of motives to experiences has also been shown to facilitate decisions to maintain volunteer service over time (e.g., Clary et al., 1998). In these ways, a person's reasons for getting involved sets the stage for the unfolding process of volunteerism.

The role of personal motives has also been emphasized in attempts to understand other forms of collective prosocial behavior, such as participation in social movements. In his theory of social movement participation, Klandermans (1997) distinguishes between three motives for involvement, each a function of perceptions of different types of costs and benefits associated with participation, and each involving considerations of the self and others to differing degrees. Perceptions of the positive social changes that the movement seeks comprise the "collective" motive. The expected reactions of family, friends and associates to one's participation comprise the "normative" motive. Individual costs and benefits derived from participation comprise the "reward" motive. Empirical studies have shown that these three motives are engaged in social movement participation in a variety of different contexts (e.g., Klandermans & Oegema, 1987).

Identity

Involvement in prosocial action may be seen not just as something that someone does, but also as a part of who someone is, that is, as a part of their identity. For instance, for people who donate their time as volunteers, the role of "volunteer" may over time become a defining part of who they are. Finkelstein, Penner, and Brannick (2005) found that hospice volunteers who more strongly identified themselves as a volunteer spent more time volunteering per week and had a longer duration of volunteer service. The implications of identity for prosocial behavior have also been considered with regard to people's decisions to become blood donors. The work of Piliavin and Callero (1991) has demonstrated that for some people, donating blood becomes a defining part of who they are, and that identification with the role of blood donor is a factor that sustains blood-donation behavior over time.

Further, researchers adopting a social identity approach (Tajfel & Turner, 1986) have considered the role of collective identification in motivating and sustaining prosocial action. This approach focuses on the degree to which people see themselves in terms of particular group memberships. With regard to social movement participation, Stürmer, Simon, Loewy, and Jorger (2003) have shown that, among members of a disadvantaged group, willingness to become involved on behalf of that group increases as collective identification with the group also increases. The work of Stürmer and colleagues has also demonstrated that this collective identification pathway to social movement participation operates independently of a separate pathway concerned with the personal costs and benefits of participation. As Snyder and Omoto (2007) point out, this distinction between pathways reflects the broader theme that engagement in prosocial action involves considerations of both self (e.g., concern with personal rewards and costs) and others (e.g., identification with the group).

Personality

Psychologists seeking to uncover the features of individuals that lead to prosocial behavior have investigated the influence of enduring personality traits. In general, these kinds of dispositional influences have been shown to be better predictors of collective prosocial behavior, which is often planned in advance and sustained over time, as opposed to interpersonal prosocial behavior, which typically arises in spontaneous instances (Batson, 1998).

Prosocial Personality

Some researchers have sought to identify constellations of traits that make up a "prosocial personality" that may dispose people to behave in prosocial fashion of many forms. One example of these efforts is the work of Penner and colleagues, who suggest there are two important dimensions of prosocial personality (Penner, Fritzsche, Craiger,

& Freifeld, 1995). The first of these dimensions, which they term other-oriented empathy, assesses the extent to which a person is predisposed to be concerned for the welfare of others, and to feel a sense of personal responsibility to care for those in need. The second dimension, labeled helpfulness, assesses a person's subjective history of engaging in prosocial acts. Whereas other-oriented empathy primarily concerns prosocial cognitions and affects, helpfulness primarily concerns prosocial behavioral tendencies. Across several studies, correlations of .25 to .40 have been observed between these two dimensions (Penner et al.), and associations between both dimensions and a range of more thoughtful and deliberative kinds of prosocial behavior have been demonstrated (Borman, Penner, Allen, & Motowidlo, 2001; Davis, 1994; Davis et al., 1999; Eisenberg & Miller, 1987; Penner & Fritzsche, 1993).

Big Five

Researchers of prosocial behavior have also focused their attention on the influence of the Big Five personality dimensions, which include openness to experience, conscientiousness, extraversion, agreeableness, and neuroticism (Costa & McCrae, 1992). Of the five, agreeableness has been singled out as a significant determinant of prosocial behavior (Graziano & Eisenberg, 1997). Agreeableness is associated with higher levels of dispositional empathy (Ashton, Paunonen, Helmes, & Jackson, 1998; Penner et al., 1995), and its role in promoting prosocial behaviors such as volunteerism has been demonstrated in many studies (e.g., Caprara, Alessandri, Giunta, Panerai, & Eisenberg, 2010; Carlo, Okun, Knight, & de Guzman, 2005; Graziano, Habashi, Sheese, & Tobin, 2007; Smith & Nelson, 1975). Of the remaining four of the Big Five, conscientiousness has also been shown to have implications for prosocial behavior. A meta-analysis by Lodi-Smith and Roberts (2007) revealed a small but significant positive association between conscientiousness and volunteerism. Also, in a survey study of blood donors, Ferguson (2004) found that higher levels of conscientiousness were modestly associated with more regular donations.

Self-Esteem

The influence of self-esteem on prosocial behavior has also been examined, in order to see whether engaging in prosocial behavior can serve the purpose of maintaining or enhancing an individual's self-esteem. In support for this notion, Brown and Smart (1991) found that people with high, but not low, self-esteem behaved more prosocially after a threat to self-esteem was delivered (i.e., in the form of false failure feedback following an intelligence test). These results are concordant with research suggesting that people with high and low self-esteem respond differently to negative outcomes, with highs actively coping and lows passively accepting (Brown & Gallagher, 1992). Additionally, considerations of the recipients of prosocial acts have also taken self-esteem into account. In their Threat to Self-Esteem Model of receiving help, Nadler and Fisher (1986) suggest that if a person considers him- or herself to be capable of dealing with a crisis on their own, then receiving help may be viewed as threatening in that it is inconsistent with this view. This proposition is supported by the research of Nadler (1987), which shows that people with high self-esteem are less willing to receive help from others who are similar to them, because doing so would threaten their sense of competence and self-worth.

Biological and Environmental Origins of Prosociality

The distinction between prosocial behavior, which is defined in terms of its social consequences (i.e., the benefits to the recipient) and the concept of altruism, which is defined in terms of its psychological causes (i.e., the other-oriented motivations of the helper) is largely sufficient for the work of the social psychologist, for whom both of these variables are relatively well observable among the individuals they study, namely human beings. In addressing the biological bases of prosocial behavior, however, we take a slightly different perspective, for much of the work in this area is conducted by biologists and evolutionary theorists. Because these researchers are attempting to understand the physical bases of prosocial action, and because they work with a number of different species— the motives of which are often inaccessible to scientists— altruism, for them, has a distinct meaning. Evolutionary theorists and geneticists view altruism as an action that is costly for the helper and that offers benefits not for a particular individual, but rather for a particular gene pool. From this perspective, an altruistic act is one that is thought to increase the likelihood that other members of the helper's species will survive, reproduce, and pass on their *genes* (Dovidio et al., 2006).

Evolutionary Perspectives

This understanding of evolution as taking place at the level of genes, not individuals, helps reconcile the evolutionary paradox of prosocial behavior, and thereby provides an answer to the question of how prosocial behavior would evolve through natural selection when it is costly to the beneficiary (Rushton, 1980). Hamilton (1964) was among the first to take "a gene's point of view," and proposed the concept of inclusive fitness, which was concerned with the survival of common genes, rather than simply the number of direct descendants an individual had, as in Darwin's concept of individual fitness. This principle of inclusive fitness is of central importance to several contemporary evolutionary theories with implications for prosocial behavior.

Kin selection theory suggests that the more genetically related two individuals are, the more willing each will be to help the other (Smith, 1964). This theory has been supported by much empirical work, including a study of helping between squirrels (conducted by Sherman, 1981), which revealed that the extent to which squirrels helped each other varied in proportion to their genetic relatedness. For example, more closely related squirrels were less likely to chase each other from territories they "owned," but were more likely to assist each other when animals had intruded on one another's territory (i.e., through helping chase the intruding animal away).

This association between relatedness and helping has also been observed in human participants. A study by Borgida, Conner, and Manteufal (1992) found that living kidney donors were significantly more likely to donate if the recipient was a relative than a nonrelative. Further evidence for kin selection theory is provided by Burnstein, Crandall, and Kitayama (1994), who found that, as the likelihood that a relative will produce offspring decreases (e.g., due to advanced age), so does the likelihood of particularly risky forms of help being offered to them, such as rescuing them from a fire.

Whereas kin selection theory can explain help that is directed toward one's relatives, the culturally widespread norm of reciprocity is useful in explaining why individuals help nonrelated others. Reciprocal altruism centers on the economic notion of trade (Cosmides & Tooby, 1992). That is, prosocial actions delivered to another individual, even an unrelated one, represent an evolutionarily successful strategy if reciprocal benefits are exchanged in return. Such alliances are known to develop between unrelated vervet monkeys. A field study by Seyfarth and Cheney (1984) demonstrated that, among unrelated monkeys, offering to help groom another monkey served the function of increasing the likelihood that that monkey would be responsive to solicitations for aid in the future. As Cosmides and Tooby point out, however, when the opportunity for "cheating," or not returning the favor, exists, indiscriminate helping will not be selected for. Their research suggests that humans have evolved a set of related skills and abilities that allow them to make relatively accurate judgments about what other persons will do in the future—whether they are likely

to reciprocate or to cheat—before they expend the energy and suffer the costs associated with offering to help.

These processes proposed by contemporary evolutionary theory—kin selection and reciprocal altruism—offer compelling arguments for how helping that is directed at both relatives and nonrelatives could provide an individual (or, more precisely, their genes) with an evolutionary advantage (Dovidio et al., 2006). They also seem to suggest that individual differences in prosocial tendencies may be caused by genetic differences between people (Rushton, 1980). When one considers the range among individuals in the amount of prosocial behavior they exhibit alongside the variety of genetic material that is the basis for natural selection, it is tempting to speculate that people's willingness to help others is biologically based. In an attempt to address this possibility, researchers have used behavioral genetic techniques to determine how much of the variation in prosocial tendencies is due to heredity and how much is attributable to environmental factors.

Behavioral Genetics

A common approach used in assessing heritability involves studies of monozygotic and dizygotic twins. Whereas monozygotic (MZ) twins share 100% of their genetic material, dizygotic (DZ) twins share, on average, only 50% of their genes. Assuming that common environments are roughly equal for MZ and DZ twins, if the correlation between scores on a trait for MZ twins is higher than the correlation between scores for DZ twins, then the difference is thought to be attributable to genetics (e.g., Rushton, 1980). Falconer's (1981) estimate of heritability, which is widely used in the field of behavioral genetics, is obtained through doubling the difference between MZ and DZ twin correlations.

Rushton and associates (i.e., Rushton, Fulker, Neale, Nias, & Eysenck, 1986) were among the first to attempt to determine the heritability of prosocial tendencies using this procedure. As part of their study, they had pairs of twins complete questionnaires assessing prosocial tendencies (i.e., "altruism," "empathy," and "nurturance"). Whereas the correlations for these three scales among MZ twins were .53, .54, and .49, among DZ twins they were .25, .20, and .14, leading Rushton and colleagues to conclude that approximately 50% of the variance on each of these scales was due to genetic influence, and that very little, if any, of the variance was due to shared environmental effects (e.g., family cultural practice, parents' child rearing style). Rather, the remaining nongenetic variance was due to environmental factors unique to the individual (e.g., an illness, a chance friendship). The results of most twin studies converge on the finding that both genes and environment contribute to prosociality, with environmental influences typically being of the nonshared type (Knafo & Israel, 2010).

However, some twin studies have linked individual differences in prosocial tendencies to both shared and non-shared environmental factors (e.g., Krueger, Hicks, & McGue, 2001). Knafo and Plomin (2006) suggest that the discrepancy between the results of this more recent work and those of Rushton and his colleagues could have resulted from either sampling error, due to relatively small sample size, or the use of a modified version of the self-reported altruism scale used by Rushton et al. Whereas items on the Rushton et al. scale pertain primarily to actions taken to benefit strangers, Krueger and his colleagues also included items pertaining to actions taken that were intended to benefit friends and acquaintances. Perhaps this difference in the operationalization of prosocial behavior is what led to discrepant results among these studies. Doing good deeds for friends and acquaintances is a behavior that is heavily socialized, to an even greater degree than doing so for strangers, and perhaps this is why environmental influences accounted for more of the variance in the modified measure.

Behavioral geneticists have also investigated the development of prosocial behavior, and in particular how genetic and environmental influences on prosocial behavior change as children grow up. In a study of child and adolescent pairs of twins, Scourfield, John, Martin, and McGuffin (2004) examined prosocial behavior as reported by participants' parents and teachers. Among the behaviors that parents and teachers were asked to report were the degree to which a participant is "considerate of other people's feelings" or is "helpful if someone is hurt, upset, or feeling ill" (Scourfield et al., p. 928). Scourfield and colleagues found that as age increased, genetic influences on prosocial behavior increased and influences of the shared environment decreased. Compared to the adolescent participants they studied, genetic influences accounted for less of the variance in prosocial behavior among children (27% versus 47%), and effects of the shared environment accounted for more of the variance among children (7% versus 21%).

A similar pattern of results emerged in a more recent study by Knafo and Plomin (2006). In addition to using a substantially larger number of participants (i.e., 9,424 pairs of twins), these researchers conducted a longitudinal assessment of prosocial behavior, gathering parent and teacher ratings of the same participants at different points in time. They, too, found that as children grew older, the influence of the shared environment decreased and the influence of genetic factors increased. This same pattern of findings has emerged in numerous studies, and has been generalized to other cultures using cross-cultural methods. In a sample of 2- to 9-year-old South Korean twins, Hur and Rushton (2007) observed the same tendency of increasing genetic effects and decreasing effects of shared environment as children grow up.

How can we account for this pattern of increase in genetic influence and decrease in shared environmental influence? After all, one might expect that the continuous presence of the familial environment and other social forces during childhood might eventually begin to override the effects of genetics, and not the other way around. As Knafo and Plomin (2006) point out, however, this pattern of results makes sense when one considers that children are not passive recipients of these social influences. Rather, aspects of a child's temperament, which is significantly genetically determined (Clark & Watson, 1999), may influence his or her environment either through eliciting certain responses from others or because it leads the child to deliberately create or select certain environments. Because intrinsic individual differences in prosocial behavior may play out in an individual's environment in this manner, these kinds of gene-environment correlations could serve to inflate the heritability estimate in these studies.

Empathic Origins

The empirical evidence that we have reviewed suggests a clear contribution of genetic factors to prosocial behavior. These findings, however, raise the question of *how* genetic predispositions are translated into altruistic action. It has been suggested that emotions, particularly the emotional response of empathy, may represent one mechanism through which genes can have this effect. This is because the part of the brain that affects emotion, the limbic system, evolved much earlier than that involved in judgment and cognition (Dovidio et al., 2006). In fact, the limbic system dates back so far in evolutionary history that the capacity for empathy may have been present among our most primitive ancestors. Further, and as previously noted, a substantial amount of research has documented a positive relation between the experience of empathy and willingness to engage in prosocial behavior (Batson & Oleson, 1991).

However, as Dovidio and colleagues (2006) point out, just because a clear and consistent relation between empathic emotionality and prosocial behavior has been observed does not, by itself, prove that genes are responsible for prosocial behavior, for empathy could also arise through socialization processes. Rather, a firm biological basis for empathy itself also needs to be established. Recent research suggests that, in addition to limbic system activity, "mirror neurons" may provide further evidence of a neural basis for empathy (Preston & de Wall, 2002). Mirror neurons are found throughout the brain, and have been shown to track the actions, emotions, and even intentions of other people. They provide a "brain-to-brain link," which allows humans to not only understand the emotional state of others, but also to "catch" their feelings and empathize with them (Goleman, 2006). Thus, mirror neurons offer further support for a biological basis for empathy, which may influence prosocial behavior.

Although research suggests a genetic basis for altruism and prosocial behavior, genes do not appear to cause prosocial behavior directly. Rather, genetic factors may predispose people to be better able to tune in to the emotional state of others and to experience empathic emotionality at the plight of another, which then leads to greater likelihood of their acting prosocially. The notion that prosocial behavior has a heritable component is congruent with behavioral genetic research showing that much of the individual variability in other behaviors is also attributable to genes (Plomin, DeFries, McClearn, & McGuffin, 2008). The importance of the environment in determining prosocial behavior must not be overlooked, however. Research by Liew et al. (2003), for example, suggests that an individual's innate capacity for empathy can be moderated by environmental factors relating to parental expressivity of emotion. Not only have environmental factors been shown to influence the development of prosocial behavior, the effect of genes often play out in an individual's social environment, and prosocial behavior may therefore arise as a result of the interplay of genetics and environment.

Attachment and Caregiving

Psychologists have also begun to examine the linkages between attachment security and prosocial values and behaviors (e.g., Gillath et al., 2005; Mikulincer et al., 2001; Mikulincer et al., 2003). According to attachment theory, experiences with early caregivers influence the operation of the attachment behavioral system, resulting in different levels of attachment security among different people (Bowlby, 1969/1982). If caregivers are available and responsive, an adequate sense of attachment security will arise, such that the individual will have a sense that others will be supportive during times of need. However,

if caregivers are not available and responsive, a sense of attachment security will not be achieved, for the individual will develop a sense that others will not be there for them when they need support.

Insecurely attached individuals can be categorized according to whether they adopt either of two major kinds of secondary strategies for regulating distress (Mikulincer & Shaver, 2005). Individuals high in attachment anxiety exhibit strategies associated with the hyperactivation of the attachment behavioral system, such as compulsively seeking closeness and security from others, being overly sensitive to signals of rejection and loss, and ruminating on personal deficiencies, threats to relationships, and worst-case scenarios. Individuals high in attachment avoidance exhibit strategies associated with the deactivation of the attachment behavioral system, such as inhibiting desires for proximity, keeping a distance from others, and suppressing or discounting distressing cognitions about negative personal and relationship outcomes. People who score low on the orthogonal dimensions of avoidance and anxiety are considered securely attached.

In addition to the attachment behavioral system, Bowlby (1973) proposed that humans possess a complementary caregiving behavioral system. Whereas the purpose of the attachment system is the achievement of protection and security through facilitating proximity to supportive others, the caregiving system functions to provide protection and security to others in times of need. Thus, a support provider's caregiving system is complementary to a support seeker's attachment system, in that both systems operate to achieve the same goal. Moreover, because a person may alternate between needing and providing support, the interplay between these two systems can be considered within individuals (Mikulincer & Shaver, 2005). Bowlby proposed that an individual's caregiving system will only become active if the individual's attachment system is not activated, because activation of the attachment system interferes with the activation of the caregiving system. If a person's security is jeopardized, he or she will be more concerned with achieving support for him or herself, and will therefore not be concerned with others' needs. Only when secure, and not concerned with vulnerability, will a person attend to another's needs. Therefore, attachment security should increase, and insecurity decrease, the likelihood of prosocial behavior.

Gillath et al. (2005) have placed volunteerism in an attachment-theoretical framework. In two cross-sectional studies across three countries, they examined the relation between attachment insecurity and volunteerism. They found that greater levels of avoidant attachment were negatively associated with altruistic motives for volunteering and level of engagement in volunteer activities. Although anxious attachment was unrelated to amount of volunteer engagement, it was associated with more selfish reasons for volunteering. Mikulincer, Shaver, Gillath, and Nitzberg (2005) have also found that higher avoidance scores predicted less willingness to help a distressed person in need, but that momentary activation of a sense of attachment security increases willingness to help. These findings suggest that the beneficial impacts of attachment security may extend beyond one's intimate relationships with family members and peers to other forms of prosocial behavior (Lopez, 2009).

Community Connections

Whereas considerations of the immediate context have guided research addressing when people will help in relatively spontaneous emergency situations, attempts at understanding why people choose to engage in more sustained forms of collective prosocial behavior have involved considerations of broader, more diffuse, community contexts. In particular, a sense of psychological connection with a larger community has been shown to foster collective prosocial behavior. Those with a stronger psychological sense of community are more likely to get involved in community organizations and neighborhood groups, and vote and participate in political activities (Snyder & Omoto, 2007). Community concerns can also motivate an individual to serve as a volunteer in his or her community, as well as sustain volunteers' services over time (Omoto & Snyder, 1995). In addition, the experience of volunteerism may also have the reciprocal effect of bolstering an individual's sense of community connection, which in turn may influence participation in other forms of collective prosocial behavior (Omoto & Snyder, 2002).

COOPERATION

Cooperation involves "behaviors undertaken by individuals and groups of individuals in the service of a shared and collective goal and to promote collective well-being," and is vitally important for the effective functioning of organizations, societies, and other collectives (Sullivan et al., 2008, p. 3). An additional feature of cooperation is that it typically occurs voluntarily, and at the will of the individuals involved. Therefore, as with interpersonal and collective forms of prosocial behavior, psychologists have attempted to understand factors that motivate cooperation.

However, and as the above definition suggests, cooperation also differs from the previously examined forms of prosocial behavior in important ways.

Dovidio et al. (2006) have suggested two ways in which cooperation differs from the kinds of prosocial behavior that we have already discussed. First, cooperation involves two or more people coming together to work interdependently toward a shared and collective goal. Not only are competing goals absent, but a common goal also exists, such that individuals and groups are motivated to coordinate their actions to bring about an outcome that is mutually valued and beneficial to both parties. In doing so, individuals and groups function as more-or-less equal partners. These dynamics are different from the forms of prosocial behavior that we have already addressed, in which the lines between "helper" and "recipient" are more clearly drawn.

Secondly, whereas the research on prosocial behavior that we have addressed to this point has largely relied on the *individual* level of analysis, attempts to understand cooperation have broadened out to consider factors at the *group* level of analysis (Penner, Dovidio, Piliavin, & Schroeder, 2005). Specifically, investigations into factors that motivate cooperation within and between collectives have considered influences at the individual level of analysis (e.g., social value orientation) and at the group level of analysis (e.g., leadership), as well as influences that blend individual and group levels of analysis (e.g., social identity).

Social Value Orientation

At an individual level of analysis, the primary construct that has been examined with regard to cooperation is social value orientation, which refers to a person's preferences for different patterns of resource distribution between the self and others (Van Lange, 1999). This construct was originally identified by Messick and McClintock (1968), who sought to understand the wide amount of variation in people's choices in social dilemmas and conflicts in which an individual's narrow self-interest is at odds with the broader interest of the collective (Dawes, 1980). In a social dilemma, self-interested motives are elicited because acting contrary to the group's best interest (i.e., going it alone) can result in personal gains, independent of the actions of other group members. However, because everyone in a social dilemma will be better off if everyone else cooperates, the motivation to act in the collective interest is also elicited. Many social problems, such as energy conservation, involve this kind of motivational conflict, and can thus be thought of as social dilemmas.

Social value orientation has been conceptualized in terms of interdependence theory (Kelley & Thibaut, 1978), which suggests that people do not always act in accordance with rational self-interest. Rather, people's motives in social interactions may involve considerations of others' outcomes, in addition to their own, as well as considerations of relations between the two. Building on these foundations, Van Lange (1999) proposed three different social value orientations, which differ in the extent to which they weigh different kinds of outcomes for the self and others. Individuals with a "prosocial" orientation prefer an equal distribution of resources, and seek to maximize the joint outcomes for themselves and others. Alternatively, two "proself" orientations were also proposed, displayed by "individualists" and "competitors." Whereas individualists seek to maximize personal gains, with little regard for the outcomes of others, competitors seek to maximize their relative advantage over others.

Classification according to social value orientation is determined by a person's series of choices about how to distribute resources between themselves and a stranger. Participants never actually meet this other person, but are told that they are making similar decisions. Moreover, participants are in a situation in which each person's outcomes are presumably influenced by both sets of decisions. A review of 47 separate studies, involving a total of 8,862 participants, revealed that 50% of people were classified as prosocials, 24% as individualists, and 13% as competitors, with the remaining 13% unable to be classified as having a consistent social value orientation (Au & Kwong, 2004).

Evidence for the influence of social value orientation on cooperation can be found in research on social dilemmas, such as Van Lange's (1999) finding that prosocials were more cooperative in a Prisoner's Dilemma game than individualists, who in turn were more cooperative than competitors. Mirroring this pattern of results, a recent meta-analysis of 82 studies examining the relation between social value orientation and cooperation in social dilemmas revealed that overall, prosocials cooperated more than proselfs, and that, among proselfs, individualists cooperated more than competitors (Balliet, Parks, & Joireman, 2009).

Leadership

The influence of leadership in promoting and sustaining prosocial behavior, especially its role in facilitating cooperation among members of a group, has been examined. Tyler (2002) has identified two major types of motivation that leaders can draw on in order to do so. On the one hand, leaders can tap into people's motivations to obtain external rewards and avoid punishments from others. For example, leaders may reward efforts to cooperate among group members, and punish those who fail to cooperate. Although the use of rewards and punishments has been shown to influence cooperation within collectives, their impact on behavior is only modest, and the implementation of incentive and sanctioning systems can be impractical to organizations (Tyler, 2008). On the other hand, leaders can also appeal to a person's attitudes and values, which can in turn motivate behavior. In these cases, because cooperation occurs independently of external rewards and punishments, individuals' behavior is internally motivated. According to Tyler (2002), with regard to promoting cooperation within groups, there are distinct advantages to leadership using this latter approach.

Researchers have also considered the influence of leadership on prosocial behaviors in workplace settings. Much of this work has focused on organizational citizenship behaviors (OCBs), discretionary activities that a person chooses to undertake, which promote organizational effectiveness, and which go above and beyond the duties they are expected to carry out as part of their job description (Organ, 1988). In particular, researchers have found that higher levels of transformational leadership by those in charge are associated with increases in organizational citizenship behaviors among subordinates (Podsakoff, MacKenzie, Moorman, & Fetter, 1990; Purvanova, Bono, & Dzieweczynski, 2006). Transformational leaders motivate employees by linking work to an employee's values so that they see their work as a reflection of themselves, by increasing employee confidence, and by increasing identification and cohesion among teams of employees (Arnold, Turner, Barling, Kelloway, & McKee, 2007; Bass, 1999; Bono & Judge, 2004; Burns, 1978; Shamir, House, & Arthur, 1993).

Social Identity

A person's social identity can be thought of as the "social glue" that holds groups of people together (Van Vugt & Hart, 2004), and it has been shown to motivate individuals to act in cooperative ways for the benefit of group (Snyder & Omoto, 2007; Tyler, 2008). Of foundational importance to theories of social identity is the notion that humans have a pervasive tendency to categorize each other into groups (Allport, 1954). Social identity theory (Tajfel & Turner, 1986) proposes that an individual's social identity is determined by their group memberships, and is different from their personal identity, which is determined by their interpersonal relationships and by features of their personality. Moreover, social identity theory proposes that people have a need to positively differentiate ingroup from outgroup, so that a positive social identity is established.

The notion of intergroup social comparison, which is central to social identity theory, hinges on an individual's identification with an ingroup. In this way, the social identity construct lies at the intersection of personal and social processes, and social identity theory can therefore be seen as providing a conceptual bridge between the individual and the group levels of analysis (Brewer, 2001). Although individuals' social identities are personally important to them, due to their collective nature they are not entirely "reducible" to the individual level of analysis. Intergroup comparisons are also both personal and collective in nature, in that they concern how *we* (i.e., my entire group) compare to *them* (i.e., their entire group), rather than how an individual ingroup member compares to an individual outgroup member.

Social Identity and Cooperation Within Groups

Social categorization and identification have consequences for cooperation within groups. In particular, the "merging" of individual and group through social identity motivates the individual to behave in ways that are beneficial to the group, such that group memberships can render self-interest and group-interest as interchangeable (Tyler, 2008). For example, Tajfel, Billig, Bundy, and Flament (1971) employed a "minimal group" paradigm (in which groups were only distinguishable by an arbitrary classification) to demonstrate that a pro-ingroup bias could be elicited in the absence of actual conflict or competition, either historical or in the immediate situation. These dynamics can be interpreted as an individual's attempt to give the ingroup an advantage, which increases its relative value compared to the outgroup, and satisfies the individual's desire for positive distinctiveness. Brewer's (1979) review of research employing the minimal group paradigm suggests that such desire for positive self-regard typically takes the form of ingroup favoritism rather than outgroup derogation.

Because group memberships contribute to individuals' identities, people are more likely to engage in behaviors that benefit the groups they belong to (Tyler, 2008). For example, Worchel, Rothgerber, Day, Hart, and Butemeyer (1998) examined individual productivity within groups from the perspective of social identity theory. Across three experiments, they found that group members work harder for groups identified as ingroups. They also found that, as the importance of a group membership to participants' social identities increased, individual productivity increased. Related research has shown that the more group members experience their group as part of the self, the more their level of cooperation increases (De Cremer & Stouten, 2003), and the more loyal group members become, even when an individual's outcomes could be improved by leaving the group (Van Vugt & Hart, 2004). Studies of the influence of heightened ingroup identification on cooperation within groups have revealed similar findings, such that enhanced identification with one's group increases intragroup cooperation in a social dilemma (e.g., De Cremer & Stouten, 2003; De Cremer & Van Vugt, 1998, 1999; Kramer & Brewer, 1984).

Social Identity and Cooperation Between Groups

The consequences of social identity for cooperation between groups are quite different from the effects of social identity on intragroup cooperation. Whereas social identity binds members of a group together, it can also be seen as pulling members of different groups apart, setting the stage for competition and hostility between groups. Evidence of this can be seen in the perceptual consequences of categorization, where differences between members of separate categories are exaggerated and differences between members of the same category are minimized (Tajfel, 1959; Taylor, 1981). Tajfel and Wilkes (1963) found that even categorizing a physical object, such as a line, as a member of a group was enough for people to exaggerate perceived differences between groups. Moreover, as feelings of connection with one's ingroup increase, bias toward outgroups also increases (Kessler & Mummendey, 2001). This pattern of effects provides one perspective on why it is generally harder to get groups to cooperate than individuals (Schopler & Insko, 1992).

However, according to Dovidio, Gaertner, and Esses (2008), social identity processes that lead to intergroup conflict can be redirected to enhance intergroup cooperation. (Also see chapter by Dovidio et al. in this volume.) A specific strategy for doing so is provided by the common ingroup identity model (Gaertner & Dovidio, 2000). Because intergroup hostility arises out of the tendency to categorize others, categorization processes are the target of this strategy. In particular, the process of *recategorization* is emphasized, such that broadening the boundaries of the ingroup alters the basis for categorization. Rather than having members of different groups think of themselves as separate, recategorization occurs through emphasizing a common superordinate group membership. Former outgroup members who are recategorized as members of a superordinate ingroup tend to be evaluated more favorably (Gaertner, Mann, Murrell, & Dovidio, 1989).

In addition to producing more favorable judgments of outgroup members, inducing a common identity has also been shown to lead to enhanced intergroup helping and cooperation (Dovidio et al., 2008). For example, Dovidio et al. (1997) manipulated aspects of an intergroup contact situation such that participants, who were initially separated into two groups, were led to either maintain the two-group representation or to abandon it for a superordinate one-group recategorization. Results revealed that, when participants were later asked to provide help to someone who was originally an outgroup member, the typical pattern of ingroup favoritism with regard to help giving was significantly reduced for participants who were led to create a common group identity. Similar patterns have been reported by researchers using the social dilemma paradigm (e.g., De Cremer & Van Vugt, 1998; Wit & Kerr, 2002). Wit and Kerr (2002), for example, found that participants behaved more cooperatively in a social dilemma when a common group membership was emphasized, as compared to when personal or subgroup identities were emphasized.

Consequences of Cooperation

The definition of cooperation that we offered earlier also emphasizes its consequences, including its potential for promoting collective well being. Past research is suggestive of this positive role of cooperation in intergroup relations. Evidence that working cooperatively toward superordinate goals can lead to harmonious intergroup relations comes from Sherif's classic series of field studies of boys' summer camps (e.g., Sherif, 1958). Similarly, Worchel, Andreoli, and Folger (1977) found that, whereas intergroup liking decreased when groups were in competition, liking increased when groups worked cooperatively towards a common goal. Additionally, research suggests that the compatibility of group goals overrides the importance of dispositional characteristics of group members, such as inter-individual sources of hostility. Bobo (1983) tested this proposition in the context of Black-White relations and found that, even though Whites may hold positive attitudes toward Blacks, hostile orientations toward Blacks will arise if they are perceived as challenging the goals and resources of Whites. Findings such as these have led psychologists to suggest that eliciting intergroup cooperation through the coordination of goal relations between different groups may be a particularly promising approach promoting harmonious intergroup relations (Cohen & Insko, 2008). Further evidence that prosocial behavior can influence intergroup dynamics has been

offered by Brown (2011), who found that participation in community service led to reductions in college students' levels of social dominance orientation (Sidanius & Pratto, 1999), or the extent to which a person prefers hierarchical (i.e., unequal) relations between groups.

CONCLUSION

The tradition of psychological theory and research on prosocial behavior has been both broad in scope and rich in its emphases. Classic work in the area, such as the bystander intervention research of the 1960s and 1970s, has revealed much about when people will, and will not, help others, and appropriately these studies are mainstays of psychology textbooks (e.g., Latané & Darley, 1970). Although this emphasis on one-to-one (i.e., interpersonal) helping, as when one person responds to the spontaneous plight of another, has dominated the study of prosocial behavior for many years, theory and research has since broadened from this initial focus. Over the years, psychologists increasingly have considered a wider range of actions that people perform to benefit others and society. Collective forms of prosocial behavior, such as volunteerism and participation in social movements, which offer societal benefits through the aggregated consequences of many people's actions, have received greater attention, along with the dynamics of cooperation within and between collectives, in which individuals and groups operate as more or less equal partners in pursuit of shared goals. Our perspective on prosocial behavior involves considerations of processes at multiple levels of analysis, from the biological bases of prosocial tendencies to the interpersonal dynamics that occur within helper-recipient dyads to the larger social contexts within which many kinds of prosocial behavior are carried out (for a related perspective, see Penner et al., 2005).

Within each of these areas of emphasis, psychological investigators have identified a range of factors that may lead a person to engage in prosocial behavior. Among these, a compelling case has been made for the existence of altruism as a truly selfless motivation with the ultimate goal of improving another person's welfare (Batson, 1991). However, whether motivated by self- or other-oriented concerns, or some combination of the two, it is still important to remember that prosocial action is beneficial to its recipients and to society (Dovidio et al., 2006). Consider the findings of Omoto and Snyder (1995), which suggest that volunteers who serve for more self-oriented reasons are those most likely to stick with their volunteer work over time, continuing to benefit themselves, the recipients, and society through their activities. Although the actions of these individuals may not be considered as truly altruistic, they may in fact be more prosocial in their consequences, in that ultimately the volunteers, their recipients, and society stand to gain more as a result of those actions. This recognition of the convergence of interests of self, other, and society may allow us to move beyond the longstanding debate regarding whether human nature is inherently altruistic or self-interested.

REFERENCES

Allport, G. W. (1954). *The nature of prejudice*. Cambridge, MA: Addison-Wesley.

Arnold, K. A., Turner, N., Barling, J., Kelloway, E. K., & McKee, M. C. (2007). Transformational leadership and psychological well-being: The mediating role of meaningful work. *Journal of Occupational Health Psychology, 12*, 193–203.

Ashton, M. C., Paunonen, S. V., Helmes, E., & Jackson, D. N. (1998). Kin altruism, reciprocal altruism, and the Big Five personality factors. *Evolution and Human Behavior, 1*, 243–255.

Au, W. T., & Kwong, Y. Y. (2004). Measurements and effects of social-value orientation in social dilemmas: A review. In R. Suleiman, D. V. Budescu, I. Fischer, & D. M. Messick (Eds.), *Contemporary research on social dilemmas* (pp. 71–98). New York, NY: Cambridge University Press.

Balliet, D., Parks, C. D., & Joireman, J. (2009). Social value orientation and cooperation: A meta-analysis. *Group Processes and Intergroup Relations, 12*, 533–547.

Bandura, A. (1977). *Social learning theory*. Englewood Cliffs, NJ: Prentice Hall.

Baron, R. A. (1997). The sweet smell of . . . helping: Effects of pleasant and ambient fragrances on prosocial behavior in shopping malls. *Personality and Social Psychology Bulletin, 23*, 498–503.

Bass, B. M. (1999). Two decades of research and development in transformational leadership. *European Journal of Work and Organizational Psychology, 8*, 9–32.

Batson, C. D. (1991). *The altruism question: Toward a social-psychological answer*. Hillsdale, NJ: Erlbaum.

Batson, C. D. (1998). Altruism and prosocial behavior. In D. T. Gilbert, S. T. Fiske, & G. Lindzey (Eds.), *The handbook of social psychology* (4th ed., Vol. 2, pp. 282–315). New York, NY: McGraw-Hill.

Batson, C. D., Batson, J. G., Griffitt, C. A., Barrientos, S., Brandt, J. R., Sprengelmeyer, P., & Bayly, M. J. (1989). Negative-state relief and the empathy-altruism hypothesis. *Journal of Personality and Social Psychology, 56*, 922–933.

Batson, C. D., & Oleson, K. C. (1991). Current status of the empathy–altruism hypothesis. In M. S. Clark (Ed.), *Review of personality and social psychology: Vol. 12. Prosocial behavior* (pp. 62–18). Newbury Park, CA: Sage.

Berkowitz, L. (1972). Social norms, feelings, and other factors affecting helping behavior and altruism. In L. Berkowitz (Ed.), *Advances in experimental social psychology* (Vol. 6, pp. 63–108). New York, NY: Academic Press.

Berkowitz, L., & Daniels, L. R. (1963). Responsibility and dependency. *Journal of Abnormal and Social Psychology, 66*, 429–436.

Berkowitz, L., & Daniels, L. R. (1964). Affecting the salience of the social responsibility norm: Effect of past help on the responses to dependency relationships. *Journal of Abnormal and Social Psychology, 68*, 275–281.

Bobo, L. (1983). Whites' opposition to busing: Symbolic racism or realistic group conflict? *Journal of Personality and Social Psychology, 45*, 1196–1210.

Bono, J. E., & Judge, T. A. (2004). Personality and transformational and transactional leadership: A meta-analysis. *Journal of Applied Psychology, 89*, 901–910.

Borgida, E., Conner, C., & Manteufal, L. (1992). Understanding living kidney donation: A behavioral decision-making perspective. In S. Spacapan & S. Oskamp (Eds.), *Helping and being helped* (pp. 183–212). Newbury Park, CA: Sage.

Borman, W. C., Penner, L. A., Allen, T. D., & Motowidlo, S. J. (2001). Personality predictors of citizenship performance. *International Journal of Selection and Assessment, 9*, 52–69.

Bowlby, J. (1973). *Attachment and loss: Vol. 2. Separation: Anxiety and anger*. New York, NY: Basic Books.

Bowlby, J. (1982). *Attachment and loss: Vol. 1. Attachment* (2nd ed.). New York, NY: Basic Books. (Original ed. 1969)

Brewer, M. B. (1979). In-group bias in the minimal intergroup situation: A cognitive motivational analysis. *Psychological Bulletin, 86*, 307–324.

Brewer, M. B. (2001). The many faces of social identity: Implications for political psychology. *Political Psychology, 22*, 115–125.

Brown, J. D., & Gallagher, F. M. (1992). Coming to terms with failure: Private self-enhancement and public self-effacement. *Journal of Experimental Social Psychology, 28*, 3–22.

Brown, J. D., & Smart, S. A., (1991). The self and social conduct: Linking self representations to prosocial behavior. *Journal of Personality and Social Psychology, 60*, 368–375.

Brown, M. A. (2011). Learning from service: The effect of helping on helpers' social dominance orientation. *Journal of Applied Social Psychology, 41*, 850–871.

Burns, J. M. (1978). *Leadership*. New York, NY: Harper & Row.

Burnstein, E., Crandall, C., & Kitayama, S. (1994). Some neo-Darwinian decision rules for altruism: Weighing cues for inclusive fitness as a function of the biological importance of the decision. *Journal of Personality and Social Psychology, 67*, 773–789.

Caprara, G. V., Alessandri, G., Di Giunta, L., Panerai, L., & Eisenberg, N. (2010). The contribution of agreeableness and self-efficacy beliefs to prosociality. *European Journal of Personality, 24*, 36–55.

Carlo, G., Okun, M. A., Knight, G. P., & de Guzman, M. R. T. (2005). The interplay of traits and motives on volunteering: Agreeableness, extraversion, and prosocial value motivation. *Personality and Individual Differences, 38*, 1293–1305.

Cialdini, R. B. (1993). *Influence: Science and practice* (3rd ed.). New York, NY: HarperCollins.

Cialdini, R. B., Baumann, D. J., & Kenrick, D. T. (1981). Insights from sadness: A three-step model of the development of altruism as hedonism. *Developmental Review, 1*, 207–223.

Cialdini, R. B., Darby, B. K., & Vincent, J. E. (1973). Transgression and altruism: A case for hedonism. *Journal of Experimental Social Psychology, 9*, 502–516.

Cialdini, R. B., & Kenrick, D. T. (1976). Altruism as hedonism: A social development perspective on the relationship of negative mood state and helping. *Journal of Personality and Social Psychology, 34*, 907–914.

Cialdini, R. B., Schaller, M., Houlihan, D., Arps, K., Fultz, J., & Beaman, A. L. (1987). Empathy-based helping: Is it selflessly or selfishly motivated? *Journal of Personality and Social Psychology, 52*, 749–758.

Clark, L. A., & Watson, D. (1999). Temperament: A new paradigm for trait psychology. In L. A. Pervin & O. P. John (Eds.), *Handbook of personality: Theory and research* (2nd ed., pp. 399–423). New York, NY: Guilford Press.

Clark, R. D. (1975). The effects of reinforcement, punishment and dependency on helping behavior. *Personality and Social Psychology Bulletin, 1*, 596–599.

Clary, E. G., & Snyder, M. (1991). A functional analysis of altruism and prosocial behavior: The case of volunteerism. In M. S. Clark (Ed.), *Review of personality and social psychology: Vol. 12. Prosocial behavior* (pp. 119–148). Newbury Park, CA: Sage.

Clary, E. G., Snyder, M., Ridge, R. D., Copeland, J., Stukas, A. A., Haugen, J., & Miene, P. (1998). Understanding and assessing the motivations of volunteers: A functional approach. *Journal of Personality and Social Psychology, 74*, 1516–1530.

Clary, E. G., Snyder, M., Ridge, R. D., Miene, P. K., & Haugen, J. A. (1994). Matching messages to motives in persuasion: A functional approach to promoting volunteerism. *Journal of Applied Social Psychology, 24*, 1129–1146.

Cohen, T. R., & Insko, C. A. (2008). War and peace: Possible approaches to reducing intergroup conflict. *Perspectives on Psychological Science, 3*, 87–93.

Cosmides, L., & Tooby, J. (1992). Cognitive adaptations for social exchange. In J. H. Barkow & L. Cosmides (Eds.), *The adapted mind: Evolutionary psychology and the generation of culture* (pp. 193–228). London, UK: Oxford University Press.

Costa, P. T. Jr., & McCrae, R. R. (1992). *Revised NEO Personality Inventory (NEO-PI-R) and NEO Five-Factor Inventory (NEO-FFI) professional manual*. Odessa, FL: Psychological Assessment Resources.

Cunningham, M. R. (1979). Weather, mood, and helping behavior: Quasi experiments with the sunshine samaritan. *Journal of Personality and Social Psychology, 37*, 1947–1956.

Daniels, L. R., & Berkowitz, L. (1963). Liking and response to dependency relationships. *Human Relations, 16*, 141–148.

Darley, J. M., & Batson, C. D. (1974). From Jerusalem to Jericho: A study of situational and dispositional variables in helping behavior. *Journal of Personality and Social Psychology, 27*, 100–108.

Darley, J. M., & Latané, B. (1968). Bystander intervention in emergencies: Diffusion of responsibility. *Journal of Personality and Social Psychology, 8*, 377–383.

Davis, M. H. (1994). *Empathy: A social psychological approach*. Madison, WI: Brown and Benchmark.

Davis, M. H., Mitchell, K. V., Hall, J. A., Lothert, J., Snapp, T., & Meyer, M. (1999). Empathy, expectations, and situational preferences. Personality influences on the decision to participate in volunteer helping behaviors. *Journal of Personality, 67*, 469–503.

Dawes, R. M. (1980). Social dilemmas. *Annual Review of Psychology, 31*, 169–193.

De Cremer, D., & Stouten, J. (2003). When do people find cooperation most justified? The effect of trust and self-other merging in social dilemmas. *Social Justice Research, 16*, 41–52.

De Cremer, D., & Van Vugt, M. (1998). Collective identity and cooperation in a public goods dilemma: A matter of trust or self-efficacy? *Current Research in Social Psychology, 3*, 1–11.

De Cremer, D., & Van Vugt, M. (1999). Social identification effects in social dilemmas: A transformation of motives. *European Journal of Social Psychology, 29*, 871–893.

Dovidio, J. F. (1984). Helping behavior and altruism: An empirical and conceptual overview. In L. Berkowitz (Ed.), *Advances in experimental social psychology* (Vol. 17, pp. 361–427). New York, NY: Academic Press.

Dovidio, J. F., Gaertner, S. L., & Esses, V. M. (2008). Cooperation, common identity, and intergroup contact. In B. A. Sullivan, M. Snyder, & J. L. Sullivan (Eds.), *Cooperation: The political psychology of effective human interaction* (pp. 143–160). Malden. MA: Blackwell.

Dovidio, J. F., Gaertner, S. L., Validzic, A., Matoka, A., Johnson, B., & Frazier, S. (1997). Extending the benefits of recategorization: Evaluations, self-disclosure, and helping. *Journal of Experimental Social Psychology, 33*, 401–420.

Dovidio, J. F., Piliavin, J. A., Gaertner, S. L., Schroeder, D. A., & Clark, R. D. III. (1991). The arousal: Cost-reward model and the process of intervention: A review of the evidence. In M. S. Clark (Ed.), *Review of personality and social psychology: Vol. 12. Prosocial behavior* (pp. 86–118). Newbury Park, CA: Sage.

Dovidio, J. F., Piliavin, J. A., Schroeder, D. A., & Penner, L. A. (2006). *The social psychology of prosocial behavior*. Mahwah, NJ: Erlbaum.

Eisenberg, N., & Miller, P. (1987). The relation of empathy to prosocial and related behaviors. *Psychological Bulletin, 101*, 91–119.

Falconer, D. S. (1981). *Introduction to quantitative genetics* (2nd ed.). London, UK: Longman.

Ferguson, E. (2004). Conscientiousness, emotional stability, perceived control and the frequency, recency, rate and years of blood donor behavior. *British Journal of Health Psychology, 9*, 293–314.

Finkelstein, M. A., Penner, L. A., & Brannick, M. T. (2005). Motive, role identity, and prosocial personality as predictors of volunteer activity. *Social Behavior and Personality, 33*, 403–418.

Gaertner, S. L., & Dovidio, J. F. (2000). *Reducing intergroup bias: The common ingroup identity model*. Philadelphia, PA: Psychology Press.

Gaertner, S. L., Mann, J., Murrell, A., & Dovidio, J. F. (1989). Reducing intergroup bias: The benefits of recategorization. *Journal of Personality and Social Psychology, 57*, 239–249.

Gillath, O., Shaver, P. R., Mikulincer, M., Nitzberg, R. E., Erez, A., & van Izendoorn, M. H. (2005). Attachment, caregiving, and volunteering: Placing volunteerism in an attachment-theoretical framework. *Personal Relationships, 12*, 425–446.

Goleman, D. (2006). The healing power of relationships. *International Herald Tribune*. October 11.

Gouldner, A. (1960). The norm of reciprocity: A preliminary statement. *American Sociological Review, 25*, 161–178.

Graziano, W. G., & Eisenberg, N. (1997). Agreeableness: A dimension of personality. In R. Hogan, J. A. Johnson, & S. R. Briggs (Eds.), *Handbook of personality psychology* (pp. 795–824). San Diego, CA: Academic Press.

Graziano, W. G., Habashi, M. M., Sheese, B. E., & Tobin, R. M. (2007). Agreeableness, empathy, and helping: A person X situation perspective. *Journal of Personality & Social Psychology, 93*, 583–599.

Greitemeyer, T., Rudolph, U., & Weiner, B. (2003). Whom would you rather help: An acquaintance not responsible for her plight or a responsible sibling? *Journal of Social Psychology, 143*, 331–340.

Hamilton, W. D. (1964). The genetical evolution of social behavior. *Journal of Theoretical Biology, 7*, 1–16.

Hartshorne, H., & May, M. A. (1928). *Studies in the nature of character, vol. I, studies in deceit*. New York, NY: Macmillan.

Hur, Y-M., & Rushton, J. P. (2007). Genetic and environmental contributions to prosocial behavior in 2- and 9-year-old South Korean twins. *Biology Letters, 3*, 664–666.

Isen, A. M., & Levin, P. F. (1972). Effect of feeling good on helping: Cookies and kindness. *Journal of Personality and Social Psychology, 21*, 384–388.

Kelley, H. H., & Thibaut, J. W. (1978). *Interpersonal relations: A theory of interdependence*. New York, NY: Wiley.

Kessler, T., & Mummendey, A. (2001). Is there any scapegoat around? Determinants of intergroup conflicts at different categorization levels. *Journal of Personality and Social Psychology, 81*, 1090–1102.

Klandermans, B. (1997). *The social psychology of protest*. Oxford, UK: Blackwell.

Klandermans, B., & Oegema, D. (1987). Potentials, networks, motivations, and barriers: Steps towards participation in social movements. *American Sociological Review, 52*, 519–531.

Knafo, A., & Israel, S. (2010). Genetic and environmental influences on prosocial behavior. In M. Mikulincer & P. R. Shaver (Eds.), *Prosocial motives, emotions, and behavior: The better angels of our nature* (pp. 149–167). Washington, DC: American Psychological Association.

Knafo, A., & Plomin, R. (2006). Prosocial behavior from early to middle childhood: Genetic and environmental influences on stability and change. *Developmental Psychology, 42*, 771–786.

Kramer, R. M., & Brewer, M. B. (1984). Effects of group identity on resource use in a simulated commons dilemma. *Journal of Personality and Social Psychology, 46*, 1044–1057.

Krueger, R. F., Hicks, B. M., & McGue, M. (2001). Altruism and antisocial behavior: Independent tendencies, unique personality correlates, distinct etiologies. *Psychological Science, 12*, 397–402.

Kunz, P. R., & Woolcott, M. (1976). Season's greetings: From my status to yours. *Social Science Research, 5*, 269–278.

Latané, B., & Darley, J. M. (1970). *The unresponsive bystander: Why doesn't he help?* New York, NY: Appleton-Century-Crofts.

Liew, J., Eisenberg, N., Losoya, S. H., Fabes, R. A., Guthrie, I. K., & Murphy, B. C. (2003). Children's physiological indices of empathy and their socioemotional adjustment: Does caregivers' expressivity matter? *Journal of Family Psychology, 17*, 584–597.

Lodi-Smith, J., & Roberts, B. W. (2007). Social investment and personality: A meta-analysis of the relationship of personality traits to investment in work, family, religion, and volunteerism. *Personality and Social Psychology Review, 11*, 68–86.

Lopez, F. G. (2009). Adult attachment security: The relational scaffolding of positive psychology. In C. R. Snyder & S. J. Lopez (Eds.), *Oxford handbook of positive psychology* (pp. 405–416). New York, NY: Oxford University Press.

Messick, D. M., & McClintock, C. G. (1968). Motivational bases of choice in experimental games. *Journal of Experimental Social Psychology, 4*, 1–25.

Mikulincer, M., Gillath, O., Halevy, V., Avihou, N., Avidan, S., & Eshkoli, N. (2001). Attachment theory and reactions to others' needs: Evidence that activation of the sense of attachment security promotes empathic responses. *Journal of Personality and Social Psychology, 81*, 1205–1224.

Mikulincer, M., Gillath, O., Sapir-Lavid, Y., Yaakobi, E., Arias, K., Tal-Aloni, L., & Bor, G.. (2003). Attachment theory and concern for others' welfare: Evidence that activation of the sense of secure base promotes endorsement of self-transcendence values. *Basic and Applied Social Psychology, 25*, 299–312.

Mikulincer, M., & Shaver, P. R. (2005). Attachment security, compassion, and altruism. *Current Directions in Psychological Science, 14*, 34–38.

Mikulincer, M., Shaver, P. R., Gillath, O., & Nitzberg, R. E. (2005). Attachment, caregiving, and altruism: Boosting attachment security increases compassion and helping. *Journal of Personality and Social Psychology, 85*, 817–839.

Mischel, W. (1968). *Personality and assessment*. New York, NY: Wiley.

Nadler, A. (1987). Determinants of help seeking behavior: The effects of helper's similarity, task centrality and recipient's self-esteem. *European Journal of Social Psychology, 17*, 57–67.

Nadler, A., & Fisher, J. D. (1986). The role of threat to self-esteem and perceived control in recipient reaction to help: Theory development and empirical validation. In L. Berkowitz (Ed.), *Advances in experimental social psychology* (Vol. 19, pp. 81–122). San Diego, CA: Academic Press.

Newcomb, T. M. (1929). *Consistency of certain extrovert-introvert behavior patterns in 51 problem boys*. New York, NY: Columbia University, Teachers College, Bureau of Publications.

Omoto, A. M., & Snyder, M. (1995). Sustained helping without obligation: Motivation, longevity of service, and perceived attitude change among AIDS volunteers. *Journal of Personality and Social Psychology, 68*, 671–686.

Omoto, A. M., & Snyder, M. (2002). Considerations of community: The context and process of volunteerism. *American Behavioral Scientist, 45*, 846–867.

Omoto, A. M., Snyder, M., & Martino, S. C. (2000). Volunteerism and the life course: Investigating age-related agendas for action. *Basic and Applied Social Psychology, 22*, 181–198.

Organ, D. W. (1988). *Organizational citizenship behavior: The good soldier syndrome*. Lexington, MA: Lexington Books.

Penner, L. A., Dovidio, J. F., Piliavin, J. A., & Schroeder, D. A. (2005). Prosocial behavior: Multilevel perspectives. *Annual Review of Psychology, 56*, 365–392.

Penner, L. A., & Fritzsche, B. A. (1993). Magic Johnson and reactions to people with AIDS: A natural experiment. *Journal of Applied Social Psychology, 23*, 1035–1050.

Penner, L. A., Fritzsche, B. A., Craiger, J. P., & Freifeld, T. R. (1995). Measuring the prosocial personality. In J. Butcher & C. D. Spielberger (Eds.), *Advances in personality assessment* (Vol. 10, pp. 147–163). Hillsdale, NJ: Erlbaum.

Piliavin, I. M., Rodin, J., & Piliavin, J. A. (1969). Good Samaritanism: An underground phenomenon? *Journal of Personality and Social Psychology, 13*, 289–299.

Piliavin, J. A., & Callero, P. L. (1991). *Giving blood: The development of an altruistic identity*. Baltimore, MD: Johns Hopkins University Press.

Piliavin, J. A., Piliavin, I. M., & Broll, L. (1976). Time of arrival at an emergency and likelihood of helping. *Personality and Social Psychology Bulletin, 2*, 273–276.

Plomin, R., DeFries, J. C., McClearn, G. E., & McGuffin, P. (2008). *Behavioral genetics* (5th ed.). New York, NY: Worth.

Podsakoff, P. M., MacKenzie, S. B., Moorman, R. H., & Fetter, R. (1990). Transformational leader behaviors and their effects on followers' trust in leader, satisfaction, and organizational citizenship behaviors. *Leadership Quarterly, 1*, 107–142.

Preston, S. D., & de Wall, F. B. M. (2002). Empathy: Its ultimate and proximate bases. *Behavioral and Brain Sciences, 25*, 1–72.

Purvanova, R. K., Bono, J. E., & Dzieweczynski, J. (2006). Transformational leadership, job characteristics, and organizational citizenship performance. *Human Performance, 19*, 1–22.

Regan, D. T. (1971). Effect of a favor on liking and compliance. *Journal of Experimental Social Psychology, 7*, 627–639.

Rosenhan, D. L., Salovey, P., & Hargis, K. (1981). The joys of helping: Focus of attention mediates the impact of positive affect on altruism. *Journal of Personality and Social Psychology, 40*, 899–905.

Ross, L., & Nisbett, R. E. (1991). *The person and the situation*. New York, NY: McGraw-Hill.

Rushton, J. P. (1980). *Altruism, socialization, and society*. Englewood Cliffs, NJ: Prentice-Hall.

Rushton, J. P., Fulker, D. W., Neale, M. C., Nias, D. K. B., & Eysenck, H. J. (1986). Altruism and aggression: The heritability of individual differences. *Journal of Personality and Social Psychology, 50*, 1192–1198.

Salovey, P., Mayer, J. D., & Rosenhan, D. L. (1991). Mood and helping: Mood as a motivator of helping and helping as a regulator of mood. In M. S. Clark (Ed.), *Review of personality and social psychology: Vol. 12. Prosocial behavior* (pp. 215–237). Newbury Park, CA: Sage.

Schnall, S., Roper, J., & Fessler, D. M. T. (2010). Elevation leads to altruistic behavior. *Psychological Science, 21*, 315–320.

Schopler, J., & Insko, C. A. (1992). The discontinuity effect in interpersonal and intergroup relations: Generality and mediation. In W. Stroebe & M. Hewstone (Eds.), *European review of social psychology* (Vol. 3, pp. 121–151). New York, NY: Wiley.

Schroeder, D. A., Dovidio, J. F., Sibicky, M. E., Matthews, L. L., & Allen, J. L. (1988). Empathic concern and helping behavior: Egoism or altruism? *Journal of Experimental Social Psychology, 24*, 333–353.

Scourfield, J., John, B., Martin, N., & McGuffin, P. (2004). The development of prosocial behavior in children and adolescents: A twin study. *Journal of Child Psychology and Psychiatry, 45*, 927–935.

Seyfarth, R. M., & Cheney, D. L. (1984). Grooming, alliances and reciprocal altruism in vervet monkeys. *Nature, 308*, 541–543.

Shamir, B., House, R. J., & Arthur, M. B. (1993). The motivational effects of charismatic leadership: A self-concept based theory. *Organizational Science, 4*, 577–594.

Sherif, M. (1958). Superordinate goals in the reduction of intergroup conflict. *The American Journal of Sociology, 63*, 349–356.

Sherman, P. W. (1981). Kinship demography, and Belding's ground squirrel nepotism. *Behavioral Ecology and Sociobiology, 17*, 313–323.

Sidanius, J., & Pratto, F. (1999). *Social dominance: An intergroup theory of social hierarchy and oppression*. New York, NY: Cambridge University Press.

Smith, B. M., & Nelson, L. D. (1975). Personality correlates of helping behavior. *Psychological Reports, 37*, 307–310.

Smith, J. M. (1964). Group selection and kin selection. *Nature, 201*, 1145–1147.

Snyder, M. (1993). Basic research and practical problems: The promise of a "functional" personality and social psychology. *Personality and Social Psychology Bulletin, 19*, 251–264.

Snyder, M., & Omoto, A. M. (2007). Social action. In A. W. Kruglanski & E. T. Higgins (Eds.), *Social psychology: A handbook of basic principles* (pp. 940–961). New York, NY: Guilford Press.

Snyder, M., & Omoto, A. M. (2008). Volunteerism: Social issues perspectives and social policy implications. *Social Issues and Policy Review, 2*, 1–36.

Stürmer, S., Simon, B., Loewy, M., & Jorger, H. (2003). The dual pathway model of social movement participation: The case of the fat acceptance movement. *Social Psychology Quarterly, 66*, 71–82.

Stürmer, S., Snyder, M., & Omoto, A. M. (2005). Prosocial emotions and helping: The moderating role of group membership. *Journal of Personality and Social Psychology, 88*, 532–546.

Sullivan, B. A., Snyder, M., & Sullivan, J. L. (2008). *Cooperation: The political psychology of effective human interaction*. Malden, MA: Blackwell.

Tajfel, H. (1959). Quantitative judgment in social perception. *British Journal of Psychology, 50*, 16–29.

Tajfel, H., Billig, M. G., Bundy, R. P., & Flament, C. (1971). Social categorization and intergroup behavior. *European Journal of Social Psychology, 1*, 149–178.

Tajfel, H., & Turner, J. C. (1986). The social identity theory of intergroupbehavior. In S. Worchel & W. G. Austin (Eds.), *Psychology of intergroup relations* (2nd ed., pp. 7–24). Chicago, IL: Nelson-Hall.

Tajfel, H., & Wilkes, A. L. (1963). Classification and quantitative judgment. *British Journal of Psychology, 54*, 101–114.

Taylor, S. E. (1981). A categorization approach to stereotyping. In D. Hamilton (Ed.), *Cognitive processes in stereotyping and intergroup behavior* (pp. 88–114). Hillsdale, NJ: Erlbaum.

Tyler, T. R. (2002). Leadership and cooperation in groups. *American Behavioral Scientist, 45*, 769–782.

Tyler, T. R. (2008). The psychology of cooperation. In B. A. Sullivan, M. Snyder, & J. L. Sullivan (Eds.), *Cooperation: The political psychology of effective human interaction* (pp. 105–122). Malden. MA: Blackwell.

Van Lange, P. A. M. (1999). The pursuit of joint outcomes and equality in outcomes: An integrative model of social value orientation. *Journal of Personality and SocialPsychology, 77*, 337–349.

Van Vugt, M., & Hart, C. M. (2004). Social identity as social glue: The origins of group loyalty. *Journal of Personality and Social Psychology, 86*, 585–598.

Weiner, B. (1980). A cognitive (attribution)-emotion-action model of motivated behavior: An analysis of judgments of help-giving. *Journal of Personality and Social Psychology, 39*, 186–200.

Weiner, B. (1986). *An attributional theory of motivation and emotion*. New York, NY: Springer-Verlag.

Whatley, M. A., Webster, J. M., Smith, R. H., & Rhodes, A. (1999). The effect of a favor on public and private compliance: How internalized is the norm of reciprocity? *Basic and Applied Social Psychology, 21*, 251–259.

Wit, A. P., & Kerr, N. L. (2002). "Me versus just us versus us all" categorization and cooperation in nested social dilemmas. *Journal of Personality and Social Psychology, 83*, 616–637.

Worchel, S., Andreoli, V. A., & Folger, R. (1977). Intergroup cooperation and intergroup attraction: The effect of previous interaction and outcome of combined effort. *Journal of Experimental Social Psychology, 13*, 131–140.

Worchel, S., Rothgerber, H., Day, E. A., Hart, D., & Butemeyer, J. (1998). Social identity and individual productivity within groups. *British Journal of Social Psychology, 37*, 389–413.

Zhang, Y., & Epley, N. (2009). Self-centered social exchange: Differential use of costs versus benefits in prosocial reciprocity. *Journal of Personality and Social Psychology, 97*, 796–810.

CHAPTER 23

Evolutionary Social Psychology

JON K. MANER AND ANDREW J. MENZEL

Residents of areas with historically high levels of infectious disease tend to be low in extraversion and openness to new experiences. Women call their fathers less often and for shorter periods of time during the most fertile times of their menstrual cycle. Fathers spend more time and money caring for children that closely resemble them. Allowing people to gossip leads them to behave more cooperatively.

These research findings, and many others like them, are difficult to explain with most traditional social psychological theories. However, they were all predicted from the perspective of evolutionary psychology (Alvergne, Faurie, & Raymond, 2010; Lieberman, Pillsworth, & Haselton, 2011; Piazza & Bering, 2008; Schaller & Murray, 2008). An evolutionary perspective implies that many of people's thoughts, feelings, and behaviors are caused, in part, by biological mechanisms that have been shaped by thousands of generations of evolution. From romantic relationships, friendship, and altruism to fear, violence, and prejudice, the principles of evolutionary psychology provide a deeper understanding of virtually all the important topics in social psychology (see Buss, 2005; Gangestad & Simpson, 2007; Kenrick, Maner, & Li, 2005).

SOME HISTORY ABOUT EVOLUTIONARY PSYCHOLOGY

Since Charles Darwin published *On the Origin of Species* and *The Descent of Man*, scientists have recognized that the human body is a product of biological evolution. However, it was not until the 1970s that scientists began to seriously explore the possibility that biological evolution also influences human psychology and behavior. E. O. Wilson's book *Sociobiology* (1975) ushered in the perspective of evolutionary psychology—an approach in which psychologists use what they know about human biological evolution to inform their understanding of the contemporary human mind. A relative newcomer on the social psychology scene, evolutionary psychology has become a major explanatory force that unites into one conceptual framework many diverse findings within the field.

Early on, evolutionary psychology was colored by controversy. Many people thought that, although evolution might underlie human physical characteristics (like opposable thumbs and upright posture), it was less obvious how evolution provides a foundation for psychology and behavior. At the time, most psychological research and theorizing relied heavily on explanations involving unconstrained learning—a "blank slate" view of the mind in which behavior and cognition are products only of reinforcement and learning. Even early connectionist models growing out of the cognitive revolution of the 1960s were based primarily on this approach. The notion that human behavior is constrained by relatively innate biological processes did not conform to the zeitgeist view of the mind as a blank slate, and many doubted that the more ultimate perspective of evolutionary psychology could produce testable hypotheses about human behavior. If one cannot observe human evolution directly, how could one ever know whether a pattern of cognition and behavior was produced by evolution (see Conway & Schaller, 2002; Schmitt & Pilcher, 2004)?

Nevertheless, evolutionary approaches have generated a large number of new findings and ideas, as hundreds of social psychological studies have tested evolutionarily informed hypotheses about the whole range of social psychological phenomena, from altruism to xenophobia (e.g., Griskevicius et al., 2007; Navarrete et al., 2009; Schaller & Murray, 2008). In the following sections, we outline some of the basic assumptions and conceptual tools of an evolutionary approach, and detail a subset of relevant empirical findings.

WHAT IS EVOLUTIONARY SOCIAL PSYCHOLOGY?

Evolutionary psychology is not limited to any particular domain of scientific inquiry. It is not a single theory or a single hypothesis. Instead, evolutionary psychology is an overarching meta-theoretical perspective. It comprises a set of assumptions that govern how scientists approach questions about psychological phenomena (Ketelaar & Ellis, 2000). Evolutionary psychology asserts that cognition is produced in part by underlying biological processes, and that human biology and psychology have been shaped by a long history of evolutionary forces in ancestral environments. These assertions are scientifically noncontroversial, and are based on a vast foundation of knowledge within the biological sciences. Evolutionary psychology asserts that the human mind has been shaped in ways designed to help people face important adaptive challenges. When applied to the conceptual landscape of social psychology, these assumptions focus scientific inquiry on specific kinds of research questions and generate specific kinds of answers to those questions.

The broad perspective of evolutionary psychology provides a set of conceptual tools that can be used to deduce specific mid-level theories and hypotheses about social psychological phenomena. It is these theories and hypotheses (not the overarching perspective of evolution) that offer specific predictions pertaining to social psychological phenomena. Rarely do evolutionary psychologists frame their research questions in terms of broad considerations like survival and reproduction. Rather, research questions tend to be framed so that they test mid-level theories that provide a more specific portrait of the influences of evolution on psychology and behavior. Tinbergen

(1963) distinguished between historical evolutionary hypotheses (concerned with questions such as when mammalian females shifted from laying eggs to bearing live young) and functional evolutionary hypotheses (concerned with questions such as the functional implications of how males versus females invest in their offspring). Evolutionary psychology is generally concerned with the latter level of analysis (Kenrick, Griskevicius, Neuberg, & Schaller, 2010).

Partly because its assumptions are rooted in the biological sciences (rather than the social sciences), evolutionary social psychology has sometimes been incorrectly viewed as an *alternative* to the basic assumptions of social psychology. An evolutionary approach, however, is quite consistent with the defining themes of social psychology (Neuberg, Kenrick, & Schaller, 2010). Evolutionary social psychology, for example, incorporates the power of the situation, assuming that proximate triggers for action typically lie in the immediate social context. Evolutionary social psychology is also an interactionist perspective, in recognizing that thoughts, feelings, and behavior emerge as an interactive function of variables inside the person (e.g., individual differences, specific motives) and the situation (e.g., salient situational variables). Thus, an evolutionary perspective is not meant to replace traditional social psychological perspectives. Far from it. The perspective of evolutionary psychology supplements traditional approaches by providing a deeper explanatory framework that helps explain psychological phenomena in terms of their root causes.

For critics of an evolutionary approach, the notion that biology constrains thought and behavior often conjures images of genetic determinism—a picture in which psychology is determined at birth by a genetic blueprint. Quite the contrary. As evolutionary psychologists are quick to point out, an evolutionary perspective rejects any simplistic "nature *versus* nurture" approach to the causes of social behavior. Rather, it acknowledges, and seeks to unpack, the fascinating and dynamic interactions among evolved psychological mechanisms, developmental processes, learning, and culture. When asked the question: "Where does evolution have its effects?" an evolutionary psychologist would be remiss in not mentioning genes, but clearly the answer is far more complex. Our evolutionary heritage unfolds as we learn and grow, interact with our culture, and develop knowledge structures based on our experiences (Nettle, 2009). Research in the emerging field of epigenetics offers evidence that experience and environmental cues can affect the expression of genetic information (Holliday, 2006; Scott-Phillips, Dickins, & West,

2011). By incorporating this perspective of nature *via* nurture, an evolutionary approach replaces both a blank slate view and a genetic determinist view with a view of the mind as a coloring book: some of the basic foundations of the human mind are predetermined, just as the lines in a coloring book are already written in. But the richness of human experience, learning, and culture are needed to color in those lines to make an actual human being (Kenrick, Nieuweboer, & Buunk, 2010).

Thus, an evolutionary approach does not imply that human behaviors are robotically determined by instinctive mechanisms over which people have no conscious control (e.g., Barrett, Frederick, Haselton, & Kurzban, 2006). People can and often do exercise control over fundamental emotional and motivational inclinations such as anger, fear, and sexual arousal. Indeed, some have argued that self-control itself reflects a set of evolved processes (Baumeister, DeWall, Ciarocco, & Twenge, 2005). Furthermore, most psychological mechanisms reflect flexible trade-offs, determined in interaction with current environmental conditions and past learning experiences (Kenrick, Li, & Butner, 2003). Contrary to a common misperception, an evolutionary perspective does not discount the role of social learning. The capacity for learning is itself based on a set of evolutionary adaptations (Moore, 2004), and many specific psychological processes that are rooted in evolved mechanisms are still responsive to cultural context and social learning histories (Kurzban, Tooby, & Cosmides, 2001; Maner et al., 2005). Rather than being "hardwired" to act in certain ways, the human mind evolved to be adept at learning those elements of the social environment that are relevant to solving evolutionarily fundamental challenges, and to respond flexibly when those elements come into play.

IMPORTANT ASSUMPTIONS OF AN EVOLUTIONARY APPROACH

Some individual organisms have characteristics that enable them, compared to other members of their species, to more successfully exploit the prospects and avoid the perils presented by their environment. As a consequence, these organisms tend to be more successful at reproducing and thus transmitting their genes into future generations. Over many generations of differential reproductive success, this process—*natural selection*—produces organisms possessing those characteristics that previously conferred relatively high reproductive fitness.

The mind has also been shaped by the process of *sexual selection*, which refers to the process whereby some organisms are better able to compete with members of their own sex over access to potential mating partners. In some cases, traits that are selected for because they enhance reproductive success may be neutral with respect to survival or they may even hinder survival. A classic example is the peacock's tail: A peacock's tail draws attention and is physically unwieldy, thus making the bird more vulnerable to predation. However, an ornate tail enhances the peacock's attractiveness to potential mating partners. This example highlights the critical importance of *trade-offs* in evolutionary processes. A trait that improves reproductive fitness in one way can work against reproductive fitness in another.

Tradeoffs can be found throughout the animal kingdom, including humans. For example, testosterone is a hormone closely linked to status-striving, dominance behaviors, and muscle development. Status, dominance, and muscularity make men attractive to women, thus increasing their potential reproductive success. However, the greater muscle mass associated with testosterone requires more energy to maintain. Moreover, testosterone suppresses a person's immune system; higher levels of testosterone are linked with higher likelihoods of infection (Lassek & Gaulin, 2009). Thus, testosterone illustrates a trade-off, in that it makes men more attractive to women, but imposes costs on the individual's immune system.

REPRODUCTIVE FITNESS IS THE ENGINE THAT DRIVES EVOLUTION

Evolutionary approaches begin with the assumption that many social psychological processes have been shaped by evolution to serve some function. The *ultimate* function of evolved psychological processes is to promote reproduction—the perpetuation of genes into subsequent generations. This does not mean that every thought or behavior directly promotes reproductive success. First, not all psychological and behavioral processes reflect evolved mechanisms. Many processes can reflect byproducts of evolved mechanisms. What television shows people like to watch, the languages they speak, and whether they prefer chocolate or vanilla ice cream have not been specifically designed by evolution, though they may reflect byproducts of underlying evolved mechanisms. Second, even processes that have been designed through evolution to serve some function do not necessarily enhance reproduction in a direct sense. Although successful reproduction requires mating, successful reproduction involves a diverse array of other challenges including protecting oneself from predators and other forms of physical harm, avoiding contagious diseases, avoiding rejection and social exclusion, navigating status hierarchies, caring for one's offspring, and so on (Kenrick et al., 2002; Kenrick, Becker, Butner, Li, & Maner, 2003; Tooby & Cosmides, 1990a).

Reproductive fitness is not defined by the production of offspring but by the successful reproduction of genes. Actions that have implications for the survival and reproduction of close genetic relatives, therefore, have indirect implications for one's own reproductive fitness (this illustrates the concept of *inclusive fitness*; Hamilton, 1964). Under certain conditions, for instance, some birds have a better chance of perpetuating their genes by helping their siblings raise offspring than by mating on their own (Trivers, 1985). People and other animals may also enhance their own reproductive fitness by performing behaviors that promote the survival and reproduction of close kin (Burnstein, Crandall, & Kitayama, 1994; Faulkner & Schaller, 2007; Hrdy, 1999), even if it means putting their own survival at risk (Sherman, 1977). Consequently, evolutionary analyses apply not only to the small set of behaviors bearing directly on sex and mating, but also altruism, coalition formation, and a wide range of human social cognition and behavior.

Adaptations Are "Designed" to Solve Recurrent Social Problems

The physical and psychological characteristics produced through natural and sexual selection are known as *adaptations*. Adaptations are features of an organism that were selected because they enhanced the reproductive fitness of the organism's ancestors. Adaptations are designed to solve specific adaptive challenges that arose consistently in ancestral environments. In this chapter, we focus on (a) adaptive problems defined by the recurring threats and opportunities presented by human social ecologies; (b) the cognitive, emotional, and behavioral mechanisms that evolved to help ancestral humans solve those challenges (Tooby & Cosmides, 1990b).

What kinds of recurring social problems did early humans face? Like many other social species, humans often must avoid sources of harm including harm from predators, intrasexual rivals, and members of hostile outgroups (Haas, 1990; Marks & Nesse, 1994; Öhman & Mineka, 2001). Humans must also avoid contact with sources of disease. This includes pathogens potentially carried by other people (Ewald, 1994; Neuberg, Kenrick, & Schaller, 2011). In order to reproduce, humans must solve challenges pertaining to the formation of new romantic and sexual relationships (Li & Kenrick, 2006; Symons, 1979).

Like the (relatively few) mammals that include long-term pair-bonding as a predominant mating strategy, humans must solve challenges associated with maintaining and protecting long-term romantic relationships (Kenrick & Trost, 1997). Like other animals that invest heavily in offspring, humans must also solve problems related to child rearing (Bowlby, 1969; Bugental, 2000). Like other highly social species, humans must solve problems associated with forming and maintaining lasting coalitions of allies (de Waal & Luttrell, 1988; Isaac, 1978). Additionally, many human social structures are organized hierarchically, thus requiring humans to solve problems associated with the attainment of social status and dominance (van Vugt, 2006).

These broad classes of problems can each be divided into hierarchically linked subproblems. For instance, maintaining coalitions of allies requires people to solve the problem of successful social exchange. Individuals must be able to identify individuals with traits that facilitate or hinder successful exchange, detect people who might be cheaters or nonreciprocators, discourage cheating and free-riding, and so on (Buchner, Bell, Mehl, & Musch, 2009; Cosmides & Tooby, 2005; Cottrell, Neuberg, & Li, 2007). To solve challenges associated with forming new romantic partnerships, individuals must also solve myriad subproblems including the ability to discriminate between individuals according to their fertility, parental potential, genetic quality, and degree of kinship (Lie, Simmons, & Rhodes, 2010; Lieberman, Tooby, & Cosmides, 2007; Singh, 1993). Most adaptations are designed to solve these kinds of specific sub-problems.

Adaptations Are Functionally Specialized and Domain-Specific

Traditional psychological theories presume that the mind reflects an information processor designed to encode and integrate many different forms of information according to the same basic rules, similar to a computer with a single operating system. In contrast, most evolutionary approaches presume that natural selection produces a large number of relatively specialized, domain-specific psychological mechanisms, similar to the range of different software applications one can run on a computer (Cosmides & Tooby, 2005). In fact, both viewpoints are right. Some mental processes are domain-general, in the sense that they work the same way across many different domains. The ability to exert self-control over one's own behavior, for example, appears to work the same way regardless of whether one is dieting, presenting oneself in a particular way to others, or studying (Muraven & Baumeister, 2000).

Above and beyond such general processes, however, many mental phenomena operate in ways that are quite specific (Klein, Cosmides, Tooby, & Chance, 2002). Just as computer software comes in many different packages, some designed to process text, others designed to organize information into a spreadsheet, others designed to interface with the Web, and so on, many mental processes are designed to serve highly specific functions (Barrett & Kurzban, 2006; Cosmides & Tooby, 1992; Fodor, 1983; Kurzban & Aktipis, 2007; Sherry & Schacter, 1987).

Functionally specific psychological mechanisms can perform more effectively than a single all-purpose information-processing system (Cosmides & Tooby, 2005). Mechanisms that serve specific functions are better equipped to deal with the huge influx of information from the environment, because they are designed to process only a narrow and specific portion of that information. Human threat-avoidance mechanisms, for example, are built to associate fear with natural sources of threat such as snakes, spiders, and angry faces. Because snakes, spiders, and angry people have posed threats throughout evolutionary history, some of their meaning comes already built into the cognitive system (Kaschak & Maner, 2009). As a result, people are especially efficient at learning to fear those things (Öhman & Mineka, 2001). This specificity may have a cost. The lethality of contemporary dangers (car accidents, heart disease) may be underestimated because they do not match ancestrally recurrent dangers.

Thus, a view of the mind as domain-specific implies that psychological mechanisms that govern cognition and behavior in one social domain may be very different from those that govern cognition and behavior in other social domains (Ackerman & Kenrick, 2008; Kenrick, Sundie, & Kurzban, 2008; Neuberg & Cottrell, 2006). The focus on recurrent fitness-relevant problems encourages attention not only to specific underlying processes, but to the specific *content* of those processes (e.g., whether a social exchange process involves sharing information among friends, trading food between members of different groups, or helping a family member in a fistfight). The result is a set of hypotheses that are often more highly specific and nuanced than those deduced from other perspectives in psychology.

EVOLUTIONARY SOCIAL PSYCHOLOGY BY DOMAINS

The bottom line of evolution by natural selection is differential reproductive success. Successful reproduction involves a diverse array of tasks—making friends, negotiating status hierarchies, forming and maintaining long-term relationships, and taking care of one's children. Adaptationist reasoning—bolstered by cognitive, behavioral, and neurophysiological evidence—suggests that much of human behavior may be organized around a fairly limited set of fundamental motives, each linked to a particular adaptive challenge posed by ancestral environments. Based on several recent reviews (Buss, 1999; Fiske, 1992; Kenrick et al., 2002; Kenrick, Becker, et al., 2003), we organize the remainder of our discussion around five key domains of social life—coalition formation, status, self-protection, mating, and parental care. We consider evidence for some of the cognitive and behavioral mechanisms that may have evolved to help people succeed in each of these domains.

Coalition Formation and Cooperation

Humans are a social species with a fundamental need for belonging (Baumeister & Leary, 1995). For most of human history, our ancestors lived in small highly interdependent groups (Sedikides & Skowronski, 1997). Successful cooperation among group members greatly increased each person's probability of surviving, prospering, and eventually reproducing (Ackerman & Kenrick, 2009). Conversely, exclusion from the social group imposed heavy costs, as ostracized individuals were unlikely to mate or even survive. The evolutionary literature on social affiliation has important implications for understanding cooperation, ostracism, prosocial behavior, exchange, reciprocity, and the psychology of kinship.

Alliances With Kin

Little research in traditional social psychology has focused on the differences between interactions among kin versus non-kin (Daly, Salmon, & Wilson, 1997). However, there are important differences between these kinds of relationships. Research with humans and other species, for example, suggests substantially lower thresholds for engaging in various types of cooperative behavior among individuals who are genetically related (e.g., Ackerman, Kenrick, & Schaller, 2007; Burnstein et al., 1994). Inclusive Fitness Theory (Hamilton, 1964) predicts that people will preferentially align themselves with kin because a benefit shared with a kin member implies indirect genetic benefits to oneself. For example, if one's assistance to a sister allows her to have two additional children that is genetically equivalent to the helper having a child of his or her own. Each child contains roughly half of the parent's genes, and each nephew or niece contains one quarter. Thus, by helping relatives survive and reproduce, individuals increase the proliferation of their own genes.

The logic of inclusive fitness provides an explanation for one form of altruism—nepotism—the preferential allocation of resources to genetically related individuals. Evidence of nepotistic altruism is found widely across the animal kingdom (Holmes & Sherman, 1983; Suomi, 1982). Similarly, monozygotic (identical) twins are more cooperative than dizygotic twins (Segal & Hershberger, 1999). This aligns with inclusive fitness theory because monozygotic twins share all of their genes, while dizygotic twins share half. The tendency to help genetically related kin is bolstered under conditions that have direct implications for the kin member's survival and reproductive fitness (Burnstein et al., 1994; Stewart-Williams, 2008).

The evolved psychology of kinship even has important implications for prosocial behavior among total strangers. As with many other animals, ancestral humans were often unable to directly identify kin—one cannot "see" genes—but instead inferred kinship implicitly on the basis of cues such as familiarity and similarity (Lieberman et al., 2007; Park, Schaller, & Van Vugt, 2008). For instance, facial similarity promotes trust and cooperation (Krupp, DeBruine, & Barclay, 2008). Emotions may also serve as heuristic cues to kinship. Empathy likely evolved as part of a system for aiding kin in distress (Maner & Gailliot, 2007; Preston & de Waal, 2002), and thus kinship may be connoted by the experience of empathy. Despite the origin of empathy, empathy can promote prosocial behavior even when the empathy is elicited by nonkin (Hoffman, 1981; Park et al., 2008). Indeed, prosocial behavior among strangers is mediated by the release of oxytocin, a hormone closely linked with empathy, trust, and parent-infant social bonding (Morhenn, Park, Piper, & Zak, 2008). This suggests that the often-observed relation between empathy and helping behavior among strangers may be rooted, in part, in the evolved psychology of kinship.

Alliances With Nonkin

Why would people form coalitions with nonkin? Theories of reciprocal altruism provide one answer (Axelrod & Hamilton, 1981; Trivers, 1971). According to these theories, our ancestors would have benefited from cooperating with others to the extent that those people were likely to reciprocate. In this way, each member of reciprocal exchange relationship reaps benefits in the long term. Indeed, whereas close kin cooperate with relatively less

regard for past reciprocation, sharing between progressively less related individuals becomes more linked to a history of reciprocal sharing (e.g., Fiske, 1992; Trivers, 1971). Across societies, the norm of reciprocal exchange is universal (Brown, 1991; Fiske, 1992).

Because future interactions are uncertain, people cooperate with group members based on the *probability* that those group members will reciprocate. Hence, it behooves people to attend carefully to signs that a member of one's group will not reciprocate or that he or she is likely to draw more resources from the group than he or she is willing or able to give back. Indeed, evidence suggests that people are vigilant to potential deceit and evidence of social cheating (Cosmides, Tooby, & Barkow, 1992; Mealey, Daood, & Krage, 1996; Oda & Nakajima, 2010). Conversely, recent evolutionary analyses of what attributes people most value in group members highlight the universal value placed on trustworthiness (Cottrell et al., 2007).

Social Exclusion and Social Anxiety

What happens when people's need for social belonging is thwarted? Being excluded can be distressing and can precipitate neurophysiological responses resembling physical pain (Eisenberger, Lieberman, & Williams, 2003; MacDonald & Leary, 2005). This response to ostracism makes sense from the standpoint that throughout much of evolutionary history, being excluded from one's group spelled disastrous consequences, even death. Social exclusion can promote a variety of psychological changes aimed at restoring a person's level of social belonging (Maner, DeWall, Baumeister, & Schaller, 2007; Maner, Miller, Schmidt, & Eckel, 2010). When threatened with social exclusion, people become attuned to other people in ways that foster social connection (DeWall, Maner, & Rouby, 2009; Gardner, Pickett, & Brewer, 2000), although negative and antisocial responses to exclusion have been observed (e.g., DeWall, Twenge, Gitter, & Baumeister, 2009; Leary, Twenge, & Quinlivan, 2006).

Evolutionary considerations suggest that social anxiety—the tendency to anticipate and fear negative social evaluation—may have been designed to help people avoid social exclusion (Buss, 1990; Maner, 2009). Anxiety leads people to avoid doing potentially embarrassing things and taking social risks, and thus helps people avoid negative social attention and potential rejection. Thus, extreme social anxiety can cause problems, but moderate social anxiety facilitates functional cognitive and behavioral responses to the threat of social exclusion.

Status

Like the social structures of many other species, human societies are organized hierarchically, with some individuals enjoying higher status than others (Eibl-Eibesfeldt, 1989). Social status refers to one's position in a social hierarchy, such that people high in status have greater influence over others and greater access to group resources. Even in face-to-face interactions between complete strangers, relative status differences emerge quickly and spontaneously, often on the basis of very limited social information (Fisek & Ofshe, 1970).

Links Among Status, Dominance, and Prestige

Having high social status is associated with an array of rewards such as group assets, friends, mates, respect, praise, admiration, happiness, and health (Eibl-Eibesfeldt, 1989; Keltner, Gruenfeld, & Anderson, 2003). Status also brings reproductive success; across species, high-status individuals have more success than low-status individuals in mating and providing care to offspring (e.g., Ellis, 1995; Sadalla, Kenrick, & Venshure, 1987). Having status may also increase the likelihood that one's mate will be willing and able to devote time and energy to caring for one's offspring (Eibl-Eibesfeldt, 1989).

Dominance and prestige provide two different ways to climb the social hierarchy (Henrich & Gil-White, 2001). They are associated with different postures, emotional states, and behavioral outcomes (Cheng, Tracy, & Henrich, 2010). Dominance involves influencing other people via force or intimidation. In many nonhuman primates this involves physical force, and so depends largely on physical size and fighting ability. Dominance in humans depends less on physical force, and more on enlisting allies and manipulating rewards and punishments in order to influence other people. Prestige, on the other hand, comes from having expertise, knowledge, or wisdom in a domain that is useful to the group. The difference lies in whether status is attained through force (dominance) or through knowledge and expertise (prestige).

Because there are many benefits to having high status, some have argued that status-striving is a fundamental human motive (McClelland, 1975), and many behaviors are designed to help an individual gain status. For example, people will sometimes behave prosocially as a means of achieving high social status (Flynn & Reagans, 2006). Males, in particular, occasionally use violence as a means of increasing their status (Archer, 1994; Griskevicius et al., 2009). Females also aggress to gain or maintain status, but they are more likely to use forms of indirect aggression such as gossip (Björkqvist, Österman, & Lagerspetz, 1994). Although many studies note that people present themselves to others in ways designed to increase their own status (Allen, Madison, Porter, Renwick, & Mayes, 1979; Bushman, 1993), an evolutionary analysis provides a deeper explanation as to why people often are so motivated to achieve status. For both sexes, advantages of status included access to material resources and extended social alliances. These advantages, in turn, translated into increased reproductive success: resources could be invested in one's offspring and allies can assist in caring for and protecting one's offspring.

The evolutionary literature on status has also been applied to the study of leadership (van Vugt, 2006). Ingroup interactions, members do not always work together seamlessly. Group leaders possess status and influence by virtue of their leadership position. Thus, leaders can coordinate groups to manage fundamental challenges such as protecting themselves from rival outgroups, acquiring resources, and defusing conflicts within the group. However, recent evolutionarily inspired work has noted that there may also be a fundamental motivational conflict between leaders and their followers (van Vugt, Hogan, & Kaiser, 2008). Leaders are given power, defined in terms of their ability to control group resources and influence people (see Keltner et al., 2003), whereas followers lack power. Van Vugt and colleagues (2008) proposed that this power asymmetry results in a basic ambivalence in the relationship between leaders and followers. Followers need leaders to achieve their goals, but giving up some of their power makes them vulnerable to exploitation. Consequently, followers may be motivated to decrease the power gap between themselves and leaders. Conversely, leaders may be motivated to increase the power gap between themselves and followers, and to use their power for personal gain. This motivational conflict may have negative consequences for group functioning, as leaders sometimes use their power in corrupt and selfish ways (e.g., Kipnis, 1972; Maner & Mead, 2010).

Gender Differences in Fitness Payoffs for Status-Striving

From an evolutionary perspective, males gain an additional set of reproductive benefits from status-striving. Women, due to their high level of parental investment, tend to be highly selective in choosing their long-term mates, and place a premium on the social status of long-term romantic partners (Sadalla et al., 1987). High-status men are able to offer their mates relatively greater protection and access to resources, both of which were useful in caring for offspring. Consequently, males are, compared with females, more motivated to seek high levels of social dominance (Hill & Hurtado, 1996), more likely to take risks that could potentially increase their status (Hill & Buss, 2010), and more likely to worry about possible loss of status (Daly & Wilson, 1988; Maner, Miller, Schmidt, & Eckel, 2008). Status provides access to resources and safety from threats, thus it is not surprising that females also form status hierarchies. However, females are less likely than males to risk life and limb to gain status, preferring to befriend high-status females or use gossip to aggress against rivals (Crick & Grotpeter, 1995).

Self-Protection

The need to protect oneself from harm is perhaps the most fundamental human motivation. Ancestral humans frequently confronted threats from members of hostile outgroups (Baer & McEachron, 1982) and intragroup competition over status and material resources led to recurrent threats from ingroup members (Daly & Wilson, 1988). Moreover, some threats take the form of contagious disease, and are transmitted via interpersonal contact (Kurzban & Leary, 2001; Park, Schaller, & Crandall, 2007). Thus, threats can come from many sources in the social environment and, consequently, psychological mechanisms are designed specifically to help people detect and avoid those threats (see Öhman & Mineka, 2001, for a review).

The Evolved Fear Module

Psychological processes are sensitively tuned to evolutionarily relevant cues in the environment that signal the presence of possible threat (Haselton & Nettle, 2006). An angry facial expression, for example, often signals that a person is inclined toward aggressive behavior (Parkinson, 2005). Indeed, expressions of anger are culturally universal—they are recognized the world over as a sign of impending threat (Ekman, 1982). Consequently, people attend to angry faces and quickly and accurately detect angry faces in a variety of visual search tasks (e.g., Becker, Kenrick, Neuberg, Blackwell, & Smith, 2007).

The effects of natural selection can be seen in the process by which people learn to associate particular kinds of stimuli with threat. To the extent that particular threats have posed recurrent dangers to humans throughout history, people may be adept at learning to fear those threats. In a series of classical conditioning experiments, people were submitted to electric shocks while they viewed images of threatening stimuli—ancestrally dangerous stimuli such as snakes and spiders, as well as more contemporary threat stimuli such as guns and knives (see Gerdes, Uhl, & Alpers, 2009; Öhman & Mineka, 2001). People demonstrated more efficient conditioned fear responses to stimuli such as snakes and spiders—stimuli that have posed physical threats to humans throughout history—than they did to guns, knives, or broken electrical outlets, even though the latter arguably present more immediate and common dangers to people in modern society.

These findings illustrate the interaction between evolution and learning. They fit with Seligman's (1971) preparedness theory, which suggests that people come biologically prepared to learn particular associations—those with bearing on important adaptive opportunities or threats—with a high degree of efficiency. Indeed, people do not come into the world preprogrammed with a store of ready-to-use knowledge at their disposal. Rather, people are born into the world biologically prepared to learn certain things more efficiently than others.

Intergroup Processes

Anthropological excavations have unearthed cave drawings depicting warfare, skulls with multiple fractures, and skeletons with flint arrowheads lodged deep in the bone (Thorpe, 2003; Wendorf, 1968). These findings indicate that throughout evolutionary history, people were threatened by members of hostile outgroups (Baer & McEachron, 1982; Daly & Wilson, 1988). Consequently, a variety of self-protective processes are selectively directed at protecting oneself from outgroup members. For example, self-protective goals can lead people to see anger in the faces of outgroup members, even when those faces are perceived as neutral in other contexts (Maner et al., 2005). Although people tend to remember the faces of outgroup members less well than the faces of ingroup members, that pattern is reversed when the outgroup members display an angry facial expression (Ackerman et al., 2006). Moreover, the presentation of one angry-looking outgroup member leads people to see subsequent outgroup members as more threatening; the same does not hold true for perceptions of ingroup members (Shapiro et al., 2009). Thus, people display forms of vigilance to members of coalitional outgroups as sources of physical danger.

Cottrell and Neuberg (2005) proposed an evolutionarily inspired "sociofunctional" theory of intergroup prejudice. Their approach emphasized the domain-specificity of intergroup processes, hypothesizing that prejudice is not a generalized negative evaluation of outgroups, but rather a set of domain-specific evaluative mechanisms that reflect the existence of different forms of outgroup threat. That is, different outgroups are perceived to pose different kinds of threat, which evoke highly specific emotional and behavioral responses. For example, participants associated gay men with a threat to their health, and experienced the related emotion of disgust. In contrast, their stereotypes about African-American men were related to violence and threats to physical safety. Therefore, African-American men elicited fear, an emotion adapted for dealing with physical threats. Some groups are thought to pose threats to the security of one's economic resources; other groups are perceived as posing threats to physical safety; some groups are perceived to increase the threat of contagion, and so on. In each case, the specific type of perceived threat evokes a highly specific pattern of emotion (anger, fear, disgust, pity) and behavior (avoidance, ostracism, aggression). And in each case, the pattern of psychological responses maps onto forms of recurrent intergroup threat faced by humans throughout history.

Vigilance toward sources of outgroup threat is exacerbated by contextual cues that, throughout history, have signaled increased vulnerability to forms of harm. In a number of studies, for example, recent research has examined the implications of ambient darkness on outgroup prejudice (Schaller, Park, & Mueller, 2003). Darkness affords greater susceptibility to harm, and tends to evoke fear and anxiety. As a result, being in the dark can increase vigilance toward members of outgroups that are heuristically associated with physical threat. Compared with control participants, for example, participants seated in a dark laboratory room were more likely to endorse stereotypes linking African-American men with danger.

Research on racial prejudice provides another excellent illustration that evolution works via the constraints it places on learning (i.e., "nature via nurture"; Ridley, 2003). Humans, like other primates, tend to be xenophobic, favoring their own group over other groups (Holloway, 1974). Toward that end, people possess basic mechanisms for parsing people into coalitional categories of "us" and "them," and for rapidly learning whatever cues reliably make that distinction. The specific cues used for this purpose, however, are highly variable, implying that coalitional distinctions depend importantly on local learning environments (Kurzban et al., 2001). Although much of the recent prejudice research in the United States focuses on prejudice toward particular racial groups, an evolutionary perspective provides a wider lens with which to conceptualize intergroup processes. From an evolutionary perspective, ethnic and racial distinctions provide only one of many possible characteristics that people may use to define the boundaries between ingroup and outgroup (Gaertner & Insko, 2000; Tajfel, 1970).

Disease Avoidance

In many industrialized countries antibiotics, vaccines and other medical advances have dramatically reduced the likelihood that infection with pathogens leads to death. However, infection had disastrous consequences for the infected individual throughout most of human evolutionary history. As a result, humans possess a number of emotional and cognitive mechanisms designed to help avoid contact with potential sources of contagion.

The emotion of disgust plays a key role in promoting adaptive avoidance of potential contagion (Rozin & Fallon, 1987). Disgust serves as a rich source of information signaling that a substance, food, or person potentially harbors disease. Disgust responses are deeply rooted in human biology and have a profound influence on learning. For example, taste aversion can be conditioned to novel tastes with just a single exposure; this is highly functional because it helps isolate the food most likely to have caused illness (Garcia & Koelling, 1966).

Researchers have shown that concerns about disease lead people to display vigilance to other people who display cues that are heuristically associated with disease, even though those cues may not be truly indicative of disease (e.g., Ackerman et al., 2009; Kurzban & Leary, 2001). Physical abnormalities or disabilities, for example, promote avoidance of people as if they were a source of contagious infection (Park, Faulkner & Schaller, 2003). These false positives are indicative of a disease-avoidance mechanism adaptively tuned to err on the side of caution. In support of this adaptationist view of disgust, recent research indicates that individuals prone to experiencing disgust are less likely to have recent infections than individuals relatively low in disgust sensitivity (Stevenson, Case, & Oaten, 2009).

An intriguing set of evolutionary hypotheses pertains to disease avoidance mechanisms that emerge at particular points in a woman's menstrual cycle. Fessler and colleagues have argued that, although avoidance of contagion is important for both men and women, infection presents a particularly pernicious problem for women (Fessler, 2002; Fessler & Navarrete, 2003). So that their body does not reject an unborn offspring, women's immune systems are suppressed when likelihood of pregnancy is high. Fessler hypothesized that women are most likely to experience disgust and avoid the eliciting stimulus when their immune system is compromised. He tested this hypothesis by examining disgust and avoidance of potential pathogens in women across their menstrual cycle. They observed an increase in sensitivity to disgusting stimuli in the luteal phase of the menstrual cycle—the period immediately following possible fertilization in which the immune system is suppressed (Fessler, 2001).

Mating

Because reproductive success is the engine that drives evolutionary processes, and because success in mating is essential for reproductive success, the vestiges of human evolution are highly apparent in the way people approach challenges involved in mating (Buss, 1989; Miller, 2000). Evolutionary research on mating can be organized into two primary domains: relationship selection and relationship maintenance. Relationship selection refers to a person's choice of potential partners, and the priority they place on long-term, committed relationships and short-term, casual sexual relationships. Relationship maintenance refers to processes involved in helping people protect their long-term relationships; this includes avoiding the temptation of attractive relationship alternatives and warding off intrasexual competitors.

Relationship Selection

Virtually all human societies have some form of institutionalized long-term bonding such as marriage (Daly & Wilson, 1983). At the same time, people often engage in short-term casual sexual relationships, with little or no intention of staying together for the long term (Marshall & Suggs, 1971). Decisions about which type of relationship to pursue—long term or short term—depend in part on an individual's sociosexual orientation (Jackson & Kirkpatrick, 2007; Simpson & Gangestad, 1991). Sociosexual orientation refers to a person's general inclination to pursue committed long-term relationships and/or short-term sexual relationships. An orientation toward short-term mating is referred to as being sociosexually unrestricted, whereas an orientation toward long-term mating is referred to as being sociosexually restricted.

There is variability in sociosexuality both among individuals (with some people being more unrestricted than others) and between the sexes. On average, men tend to be somewhat more unrestricted than women; they are relatively more inclined to pursue short-term sexual relationships and to desire sex without commitment. Women, in contrast, are relatively more inclined to seek long-term commitment (Hald & Høgh-Olesen, 2010; Simpson & Gangestad, 1991). Evolutionary theorists have attributed sex differences to differences in minimum obligatory parental investment (Trivers, 1972). Because human females, like other mammalian females, incubate their young, they are required to make a more substantial investment of time and resources than males are. Thus, throughout evolutionary history, the benefit-to-cost ratio of casual sex has been lower for women than for men (although new forms of birth control have changed some of the costs of casual sex). As such, women tend to be relatively more cautious and choosy in selecting their partners (e.g., Buss & Schmitt, 1993).

A complete account of sex differences in sociosexuality takes into consideration not only how the sexes differ on average, but also how individuals interact with each other and actually decide on which type of relationship to pursue (Gangestad, Haselton, & Buss, 2006a). Indeed, there is substantial variability within each sex with regard to people's romantic strategies. Kenrick, Li, and Butner (2003) suggested that each sex bases its decisions of which strategy (short term versus long term) to pursue on an implicit comparison of sex ratios in the local environment. Sex ratios can be thought of as a comparison of opposite-sex people (i.e., available mates) to same-sex people (i.e., intrasexual competitors). In any local environment, a strategy becomes more desirable to the extent that there are more available mates responding to that strategy, and fewer same-sex competitors using that strategy.

Evolutionary analyses also provide a basis for predicting sex differences in the types of characteristics valued in short-term and long-term partners (Li & Kenrick, 2006). With regard to short-term relationships, both men and women are highly attentive to the physical attractiveness of a potential partner (Maner, Gailliot, Rouby, & Miller, 2007). Physical attractiveness can signal a number of characteristics relevant to reproductive fitness. Highly symmetrical people, for example, typically are judged to be attractive, and symmetry can signal the presence of a strong immune system and a person's overall level of genetic fitness (Gangestad & Thornhill, 1997). Mating with an attractive man should increase the likelihood that a woman will have more genetically fit offspring (Scheib, Gangestad, & Thornhill, 1999). Moreover, a man's physical attractiveness often signals his level of social dominance (e.g., via markers of testosterone; Cunningham, Barbee, & Pike, 1990). Women tend to prefer dominant men (Buss, 1989), particularly when that dominance is targeted toward strangers or rivals (Lukaszewski & Roney, 2010).

Features signaling health, youth, and fertility are related to perceptions of female attractiveness (Buss &

Schmitt, 1993). For example, a low waist-to-hip ratio, meaning the hips are wider than the waist, is a valid indicator of a woman's ability to bear children. Men from cultures around the world find this body type attractive (Singh, Dixson, Jessop, Morgan, & Dixson, 2010). Even men blind from birth, with no visual cultural influence on preferences, tend to prefer women with a low waist-to-hip ratio (Karremans, Frankenhuis, & Arons, 2010). From an evolutionary perspective, men have an evolved preference for fertile, healthy, young mates because such a preference would have increased the likelihood that a male ancestor would have fathered healthy offspring and, in turn, successfully passed his genes on to subsequent generations (Singh, 1993).

The characteristics people value in long-term mates are somewhat different than what they seek in short-term mates. When considering marriage partners, for example, there is evidence that women tend to prefer status and access to resources somewhat more than men do, and men tend to prefer physical attractiveness somewhat more than women do (e.g., Buss, 1989; Sprecher, Sullivan, & Hatfield, 1994). Evolutionary theorists have suggested that these sex differences reflect the fact that men and women have faced somewhat different adaptive problems (Symons, 1979). Because fertility peaks in a woman's early- to mid-twenties, and drop off rapidly after age 30, men from around the world may be especially drawn to women displaying physical markers of sexual maturity and youth (Singh, 1993; Singh et al., 2010). Male reproductive potential, on the other hand, is not as constrained by fertility as it is by the ability to provide resources. Thus, women may be especially attentive to cues signaling a man's status in the social hierarchy and his ability to provide resources to her and her offspring (Buss, 1989; Maner, DeWall, & Gailliot, 2008; Sadalla, et al., 1987).

Research grounded in traditional psychological theories often look for characteristics that everyone, regardless of sex, would look for in a relationship partner. Kindness and similarity are two commonly desired traits, and an evolutionary perspective sheds light on the boundary conditions of this finding. Kindness is a characteristic that both sexes value in a partner, but the situation is somewhat complex. Women who are motivated to find a mate tend to conspicuously help others to signal their benevolence, prosocial orientation, and maternal skill (Griskevicius et al., 2007). However, men primed with a mating motive do not increase public acts of kindness, perhaps because women find it more attractive when a man preferentially targets his kindness toward her and her offspring (Lukaszewski & Roney, 2010).

Many people are similar to their romantic partner in personality and beliefs, and this similarity predicts the quality and length of the relationship (Gonzaga, Campos, & Bradbury, 2007). However, similarity in the physical domain can be an indicator that the relationship partners share genes and thus are more likely to produce offspring with genetic abnormalities. To navigate this mating challenge, humans appear to have an implicit bias to find faces that indicate genetic overlap less attractive as romantic relationship partners (Lie et al., 2010).

Relationship Maintenance

Because human infants are helpless and slow to develop, sustained input from both parents helps to ensure the offspring's survival (Hrdy, 1999). Although human mating arrangements vary from culture to culture, all include long-term relationships in which both the male and female contribute to the offspring's welfare (Daly & Wilson, 1983). From both social psychological and evolutionary perspectives, the maintenance of long-term relationships serves key social affiliation and child-rearing functions that enhance reproductive success (Hazan & Diamond, 2000).

Humans, like many other sexually reproducing species, sometimes display a tendency toward polygamy and may be disinclined from maintaining romantic relationships that are completely monogamous (Barash & Lipton, 2001; Betzig, 1985). One challenge, therefore, involves the temptation of desirable relationship alternatives. For people who are already in a romantic relationship, attention to other desirable people can threaten people's satisfaction with and commitment to their existing romantic partnership (Johnson & Rusbult, 1989; Miller, 1997). Evolutionary theories help generate predictions about which particular members of the opposite sex might threaten one's commitment to a current relationship partner. Theories of short-term mating suggest that both men and women place a premium on the physical attractiveness of extra-pair relationship partners (Gangestad & Thornhill, 1997). Consequently, highly attractive members of the opposite sex can threaten one's commitment to a current partner, and psychological mechanisms designed to reduce threats posed by relationship alternatives tend to focus selectively on the attractiveness of alternative partners. For example, people in committed romantic relationships sometimes "devalue" alternative partners by judging alternatives as being less physically attractive than single people do (Simpson, Gangestad, & Lerma, 1990). Negative evaluations of alternative partners can help reduce perceived relationship threat and aid in maintaining commitment to one's current partner. In addition, because relationship alternatives threaten people's commitment, people sometimes display attentional biases such that, as soon as physically attractive alternatives are perceived, people's attention is repelled and they look away (Maner, Gailliot, & Miller, 2009).

The emotion of romantic love has been conceptualized as an adaptation designed to help people maintain commitment to a long-term relationship (Frank, 1988, 2001). When experiencing romantic love, people show less interest in alternative partners and report more satisfaction and commitment to their current partner (Gonzaga, Keltner, Londahl, & Smith, 2001). Consistent with this literature, priming people with thoughts and feelings of love for their partner helps them suppress thoughts about the attractiveness of relationship alternatives (Gonzaga, Haselton, Smurda, Davies, & Poore, 2008) and stay inattentive to attractive relationship alternatives (Maner, Rouby, & Gonzaga, 2008).

Generally, psychological mechanisms help people protect their long-term relationships, but those mechanisms are sensitive to the costs and benefits of staying in a relationship. For example, if a couple has offspring, it raises the threshold for decisions to leave a relationship for an alternative mate (Rasmussen, 1981). On the other hand, the availability of desirable alternatives tends to lower the decision threshold to leave a relationship (Kenrick, Li, & Butner, 2003).

Preventing infidelity by one's partner is another challenge people face in maintaining a long-term relationship. Warding off romantic rivals and preventing one's partner from engaging in extra-pair relationships is a key part of ensuring one's own reproductive success (Buss & Shackelford, 1997; Haselton & Gangestad, 2006). Just as some psychological processes help maintain commitment to a relationship, psychological processes also help one prevent partner infidelity (Shackelford, Goetz, Buss, Euler, & Hoier, 2005; Sheets, Fredendall, & Claypool, 1997).

The threat of infidelity may promote adaptive cognitive processes designed to ward off potential intrasexual rivals. An evolutionary perspective is useful for identifying the specific types of relationship rivals that might be most appealing to one's mate. As mentioned previously, people tend to seek out extra-pair mates who are physically attractive. Consequently, when primed with the threat of infidelity, members of both sexes attend vigilantly to same-sex interlopers who are physically attractive (Maner, Miller, Rouby, & Gailliot, 2009).

Despite this similarity between men and women, there also is evidence for sex differences in jealousy. Buss,

Larsen, Westen, and Semmelroth (1992) proposed that, although both sources of infidelity invoke jealousy in both sexes, men respond more strongly when their partner appears to be sexually attracted to others, whereas women are relatively more sensitive to emotional infidelity (see also Becker, Sagarin, Guadagno, Millevoi, & Nicastle, 2004; Sagarin, 2005; Schützwohl, 2008). From an evolutionary perspective, this sex difference reflects innate jealousy modules designed to deal with sex-specific challenges related to paternal uncertainty (for men) and paternal investment (for women) (Buss, 2002). Because fertilization occurs within women, men can never be certain that they are the father of their mate's offspring. As a result, the prospect of a woman's sexual infidelity may be particularly distressing for a man because it could lead him to invest time and resources to raising another man's offspring. In contrast to men, women are certain of their maternity; thus, sexual infidelity should be somewhat less disconcerting for women than for men. Women, however, have faced a different threat—having their long-term mate direct limited resources toward other women. As a consequence, a man's emotional infidelity may be particularly distressing because it can indicate a high likelihood of him diverting resources to other women and their offspring.

The evolutionary approach to sex differences in jealousy is not universally accepted. Many researchers have criticized it on methodological and theoretical grounds. First, some have argued that methods designed to assess sex differences in jealousy (e.g., forcing people to choose which type of infidelity is more distressing) overestimate the size of the sex difference because, in fact, both types of infidelity tend to be highly distressing to both sexes (e.g., Harris, 2003, 2005). In addition, researchers have questioned whether the sex difference reflects different evolved mechanisms in men and women, or simply differences in the inferences men and women make based on the kind of infidelity. DeSteno and Salovey (1996), for example, suggested the "double-shot" hypothesis: a woman might think that her husband's emotional attachment to another woman indicates he is probably having sex with her, too, and thus this double shot of infidelity is particularly distressing. Thus, even if one acknowledges the existence of sex differences in jealousy, there is still debate about the underlying cause.

Parental Care

Human offspring require a period of parental care much longer and more intensive than other species, even close genetic relatives such as chimpanzees and bonobos.

(Geary, 2000; Hrdy, 1999). The desire to nurture offspring, however, varies among parents along factors predicted by an evolutionary perspective. The amount of child nurturance depends on the perceived genetic relatedness to the parent, likelihood that parental investment would increase the offspring's reproductive success, and the opportunity costs of investing (Alexander, 1979; Daly & Wilson, 1980).

Evolutionary selection is not limited to a single generation of differential reproductive success. Evolution is driven by the propagation of genes throughout a population over a series of generations. Fitness is ultimately measured by the reproductive success of one's offspring because every child contains half of each parent's genes. Therefore, evolutionary psychologists theorized that humans would possess psychological mechanisms that promote the survival *and* reproductive success of one's offspring. However, there are subtle distinctions that factor into parental care. Consider the following: Mothers tend to invest more in their offspring than fathers do. Maternal grandparents tend to invest more than paternal grandparents do. Biological parents invest more in their children than stepparents do, and are 40 times less likely to abuse them (Daly & Wilson, 1985) and up to several hundred times less likely to kill them than stepparents are (Daly & Wilson, 1988; Harris, Hilton, Rice, & Eke, 2006).

The likelihood of genetic relatedness predicts these differences in parental investment. Only women can be completely sure which offspring are theirs; men can never be certain. Thus, it makes sense that mothers invest more than fathers, and that relatives on the mother's side invest more than relatives on the father's side. Paternal uncertainty may also explain why fathers report more emotional closeness to children that show more facial resemblance, which indicates genetic relatedness (Alvergne, Faurie, & Raymond, 2010). Additionally, because investing in unrelated offspring is unwise from a reproductive standpoint, it makes sense from an evolutionary perspective that the behavior of stepparents toward stepchildren is not on par with that of biological parents toward their own children.

Male offspring have higher variability in reproductive success than females. Therefore, investment in male children has a greater potential return *and* risk than investment in female offspring (Daly & Wilson, 1988; Trivers & Willard, 1973). As discussed earlier, there is rarely a shortage of males willing to mate with a female because of the relatively low obligatory investment of males in offspring. Therefore, a male typically needs to compete against other males to gain access to mates. In addition, whereas females are physically limited to having children

at a relatively slow rate across a shorter reproductive life span, males are not constrained by internal gestation and menopause. Rather, male reproductive success varies greatly. Men at the bottom of a status hierarchy may have no mates or offspring while those at the top have been known to sire up to several hundred children (e.g., Betzig, 1992; Daly & Wilson, 1988). Because of this differential in risk and return, it may benefit a family with abundant resources to invest in sons, but for resource-poor families to allocate what they have to their daughters (Trivers & Willard, 1973). In support of this reasoning, a study of families in North America found differences in investment patterns between low- and high-income families (Gaulin & Robbins, 1991). Low-income mothers were more likely to breastfeed their daughters than their sons, whereas the opposite pattern was true for mothers of affluent families. Low-income mothers also had another child sooner if the first was a son, whereas high-income mothers had another child sooner if the first was a daughter.

Finally, the benefits of parental investment are weighed against the reproductive advantages of alternative uses of time and resources. Because men are not constrained by childbearing and nursing, the pursuit of other mating relationships is a more viable option to them than it is for women. Indeed, tribal evidence from Africa shows that among the Aka pygmies, men of high status have more wives and spend less time on parenting than men of low status do (Hewlett, 1991).

CURRENT ZEITGEISTS WITHIN EVOLUTIONARY SOCIAL PSYCHOLOGY

Each year, the field of evolutionary social psychology sees significant new advances in theory and method. Here we briefly outline a few trends in contemporary evolutionary psychology. Evolution, learning, and culture shape the cognition and behavior of individuals, yet they are occasionally erroneously perceived to be alternative explanations. An evolutionary perspective predicts that these factors are inextricably linked and interact in complex ways (e.g., Kenrick et al., 2010; Schaller, Norenzayan, Heine, Yamagishi, & Kameda, 2010). Evolved psychological mechanisms work in conjunction with learning, and that learning occurs within a rich context of cultural information. Researchers have begun to deliver on the promise of an integrative evolutionary psychology by examining directly the interaction of evolution and culture (Tooby & Cosmides, 1992). For example, several lines of research suggest that people's mating strategies are adaptively tuned to the prevalence of disease-causing pathogens in the environment (Gangestad et al., 2006). In more pathogen-rich environments (e.g., hot and humid areas near the equator), people place greater value on the physical attractiveness of potential romantic partners, as attractiveness can signal the strength of a person's immune system (Gangestad & Buss, 1993). In addition, higher levels of polygymy are found in pathogen-rich environments because, in such environments, it may be more reproductively advantageous for a woman to become the second wife of an attractive man with a strong immune system than to become the first wife of a less fit man (Low, 1990). Such findings suggest that aspects of the physical environment interact with evolved biological mechanisms to produce different normative mating patterns, which can emerge in the form of large-scale differences among cultures. Similarly, using an evolutionary analysis, Schaller and Murray (2008) showed that basic units of personality such as sociosexual orientation, extraversion, and openness to experience vary predictably with the prevalence of pathogens in local cultural environments. New cross-cultural research is providing unique opportunities to examine the environmental and cultural contingencies that influence the here-and-now manifestation of evolved mental processes (Henrich et al., 2006; Marlowe et al., 2008).

One source of debate involves the distinction between "evoked" and "transmitted" culture. Evoked culture refers to the process through which ecological variables directly activate genetic mechanisms, as in the mating-related examples above. Transmitted culture instead refers to the process through which cultural norms travel from individual to individual via learning processes (e.g., imitation, mimicry, and storytelling; e.g., Tomasello, Kruger, & Ratner, 1993). Although there is little doubt that both systems work together in producing culture (Norenzayan, 2006; see also Henrich & Gil-White, 2001; Richerson & Boyd, 2005), it is less clear exactly how they work together, and what aspects of cultural variation are evoked versus transmitted. Research today is attempting to address these issues (Nettle, 2009; Schmitt, 2011).

A second (and related) set of new developments pertains to the conceptual integration of situational and evolutionary causes (Kenrick et al., 2010). Whereas traditional psychological theories tend to focus on proximate factors within the person or immediate situation, evolutionary theories tend to focus on background factors that help explain the underlying functions of particular psychological mechanisms. New evolutionarily inspired research bridges these two approaches by considering not only how particular cognitive mechanisms are linked to the recurrent adaptive challenges encountered by humans living in social groups, but also how immediate psychological factors (e.g., temporarily activated motives, individual differences, acute biological processes) shape adaptive social cognition.

For example, researchers have begun to document a number of interesting changes that occur across women's menstrual cycles. During ovulation (their peak period of fertility) women dress more attractively, act in flirtatious ways, and seek out men displaying cues to high genetic fitness (Haselton & Gangestad, 2006; Penton-Voak et al., 1999). Women at the peak of their reproductive fertility are even more likely to cheat on their current partner, so long as the man they are cheating with is more sexually attractive than their current partner (Pillsworth & Haselton, 2006). Other recent research is integrating social psychological theories of priming with evolutionary theories of adaptive psychological processes. Findings from these priming studies suggest that the temporary activation of important goal states promotes the engagement of adaptive psychological processes ultimately designed to enhance reproductive success (Ackerman, Becker, et al., 2009; Griskevicius, Cialdini, & Kenrick, 2006; Griskevicius, Goldstein, et al., 2006; Maner et al., 2005; Maner, DeWall, et al., 2007).

CLOSING REMARKS

Darwin's theory of evolution by natural selection is likely the grandest of unifying theories in the life sciences. And it has great integrative potential for social psychology. Embracing an evolutionary perspective, however, does not challenge the findings of traditional social psychology; nor does it mean that social psychologists should send their laboratory participants home, march off to a remote part of the globe to live with a tribe of hunter-gatherers, dig up australopithecine bones, or commune with chimpanzees. Embracing an evolutionary explanation does not mean giving up research on ongoing phenomenology or learning processes or culture. In fact, because we carry around with us the vestiges of ancestral adaptations, one of the best ways to gather evidence regarding the adaptive significance of human behavior is to study contemporary humans in modern environments (Buss & Kenrick, 1998).

How "ultimate" do one's explanations for behavior need to be? When searching for causes, one can in theory go as far back as the beginning of life or the Big Bang. However, such an explanation would hardly be useful.

A more satisfactory stop-point is one that connects current causes to their adaptive function—the particular way in which behaviors served ancestral survival and reproduction. A causal explanation that simply points to "differential reproduction" would, by this reasoning, be going a step too far up the causal ladder. It would fail to distinguish the explanation for a bird's hollow skeletal structure from sharks' ability to sense prey by generating electromagnetic fields. We want to understand the particulars—how is it that these very different adaptations solved specific challenges posed by the organism's ecology. A more useful level of explanation would, for example, connect the bird's lightweight bones to intrinsic flight constraints set by an animal's strength to weight ratio, and a hammerhead's uniquely shaped head to its need to sweep the ocean floor in search of prey hiding under the sand. Being able to lift one's body into the air and finding hidden prey were different needs that birds' and sharks' physical design features were differentially adapted to solve. Thus, an adaptationist account seeks to explain how an animal's cognitive and behavioral mechanisms are connected to the specific demands and opportunities its ancestors regularly confronted.

The debate is no longer about nature *or* nurture. Both genes and learning play a strong role in shaping people's behavior. Only by spanning the continuum from proximate to ultimate levels of explanation will psychologists be able to paint a full picture of a psychological phenomenon. Considering multiple levels of causation leads to a depth of understanding not possible by considering only one level of analysis at a time. For example, experimental social psychological studies suggest that nonverbal indicators of social dominance increase the sexual attractiveness of males, but not females (e.g., Sadalla et al., 1987). Comparative studies conducted with other species indicate a link between an animal's testosterone level and his or her social rank (e.g., Rose, Bernstein, & Holaday, 1971). Physiological studies indicate that males typically produce more testosterone than do females (Mazur & Booth, 1998). Correlational studies indicate that individuals with high testosterone also exhibit more antisocially competitive behavior, particularly when other paths to social success are blocked (Dabbs & Morris, 1990). Together, these and other sources of evidence provide a whole network of findings that fit together to tell a compelling story about sexual selection and gender differences (Geary, 1998). No one source of data is superior to the others, and none is superfluous—each is necessary to understand a complicated but ultimately sensible natural process. Though data from psychological studies are not by themselves sufficient, they are, in alliance with data from other disciplines and methods, necessary for complete explanations of behavior.

REFERENCES

Ackerman, J. M., Becker, D. V., Mortensen, C. R., Sasaki, T., Neuberg, S. L., & Kenrick, D. T. (2009). A pox on the mind: Disjunction of attention and memory in the processing of physical disfigurement. *Journal of Experimental Social Psychology, 45,* 478–485.

Ackerman, J. M., & Kenrick, D. T. (2008). The costs of benefits: Help-refusals highlight key trade-offs of social life. *Personality & Social Psychology Review, 12,* 118–140.

Ackerman, J. M., & Kenrick, D. T. (2009). Cooperative courtship: Helping friends raise and raze relationship barriers. *Personality and Social Psychology Bulletin, 35,* 1285–1300.

Ackerman, J. M., Kenrick, D. T., & Schaller, M. (2007). Is friendship akin to kinship? *Evolution & Human Behavior, 28,* 365–374.

Ackerman, J. M., Shapiro, J. R., Neuberg, S. L., Kenrick, D. T., Becker, D. V., Griskevicius, V., . . . Schaller, M. (2006). They all look the same to me (unless they're angry): From outgroup homogeneity to outgroup heterogeneity. *Psychological Science, 17,* 836–840.

Alexander, R. D. (1979). *Darwinism and human affairs.* Seattle: University of Washington Press.

Allen, K. M., Madison, D. L., Porter, L. W., Renwick, P. A., & Mayes, B. T. (1979). Organizational politics: Tactics and characteristics of its actors. *California Management Review, 22,* 77–83.

Alvergne, A., Faurie, C., & Raymond, M. (2010). Are parents' perceptions of offspring facial resemblance consistent with actual resemblance? Effects of parental investment. *Evolution and Human Behavior, 31,* 7–15.

Archer, J. (1994). Introduction: Male violence in perspective. In J. Archer (Ed.), *Male violence* (pp. 1–22). New York, NY: Routledge.

Axelrod, R., & Hamilton, W. D. (1981). The evolution of cooperation. *Science, 211,* 1390–1396.

Baer, D., & McEachron, D. L. (1982). A review of selected sociobiological principles: Application to hominid evolution I: The development of group structure. *Journal of Social & Biological Structures, 5,* 69–90.

Barash, D. P., & Lipton, J. E. (2001). *The myth of monogamy: Fidelity and infidelity in animals.* New York, NY: Henry Holt.

Barrett, H. C., Frederick, D. A., Haselton, M. G., & Kurzban, R. (2006). Can manipulations of cognitive load be used to test evolutionary hypotheses? *Journal of Personality and Social Psychology, 91,* 513–518.

Barrett, H. C., & Kurzban, R. (2006). Modularity in cognition: Framing the debate. *Psychological Review, 113,* 628–647.

Baumeister, R. F., DeWall, C. N., Ciarocco, N. J, & Twenge, J. M. (2005). Social exclusion impairs self-regulation. *Jounral of Personality and Social Psychology, 88,* 589–604.

Baumeister, R. F., & Leary, M. R. (1995). The need to belong: Desire for interpersonal attachments as a fundamental human motivation. *Psychological Bulletin, 117,* 497–529.

Becker, D. V., Kenrick, D. T., Neuberg, S. L., Blackwell, K. C., & Smith, D. M. (2007). The confounded nature of angry men and happy women. *Journal of Personality and Social Psychology, 92,* 179–190.

Becker, V. D., Sagarin, B. J., Guadagno, R. E., Millevoi, A., & Nicastle, L. D. (2004). When the sexes need not differ: Emotional responses to the sexual and emotional aspects of infidelity. *Personal Relationships, 11,* 529–538.

Betzig, L. (1985). *Despotism and differential reproduction: A Darwinian view of history.* New York, NY: Aldine de Gruyter.

Betzig, L. (1992). Roman polygyny. *Ethology and Sociobiology, 13,* 309–349.

Björkqvist, K., Österman, K., & Lagerspetz, K. (1994). Sex differences in covert aggression among adults. *Aggressive Behavior, 20,* 27–33.

Bowlby, J. (1969). *Attachment and loss: Vol. 1. Attachment.* New York, NY: Basic Books.

Brown, D. E. (1991). *Human universals.* New York, NY: McGraw-Hill.

Buchner, A., Bell, R., Mehl, B., & Musch, J. (2009). No enhanced recognition memory, but better source memory for faces of cheaters. *Evolution and Human Behavior, 30,* 212–224.

Bugental, D. B. (2000). Acquisition of the algorithms of social life: A domain-based account. *Psychological Bulletin, 126,* 187–219.

Burnstein, E., Crandall, C., & Kitayama, S. (1994). Some neo-Darwinian decision rules for altruism: Weighing cues for inclusive fitness as a function of the biological importance of the decision. *Journal of Personality and Social Psychology, 67,* 773–389.

Bushman, B. J. (1993). Human aggression while under the influence of alcohol and other drugs: An integrative research review. *Current Directions in Psychological Science, 2,* 148–152.

Buss, D. M. (1989). Conflict between the sexes: Strategic interference and the evocation of anger and upset. *Journal of Personality & Social Psychology, 56,* 735–747.

Buss, D. M. (1989). Sex differences in human mate preferences: Evolutionary hypotheses tests in 37 cultures. *Behavioral and Brain Sciences, 12,* 1–49.

Buss, D. M. (1990). The evolution of anxiety and social exclusion. *Journal of Social and Clinical Psychology, 9,* 196–210.

Buss, D. M. (1999). Evolutionary psychology: A new paradigm for psychological science. In D. H. Rosen & M. C. Luebbert (Eds.), *Evolution of the psyche. Human evolution, behavior and intelligence* (pp. 1–33). Westport, CT: Praeger/Greenwood.

Buss, D. M. (2002). Human mate guarding. *Neurendocrinology Letter Special Issue, 23,* 23–29.

Buss, D. M. (2005). *The handbook of evolutionary psychology.* Hoboken, NJ: Wiley.

Buss, D. M., & Kenrick, D. T. (1998). Evolutionary social psychology. In D. T. Gilbert, S. T. Fiske, & G. Lindzey (Eds.), *Handbook of social psychology* (Vol. 2, 4th ed., pp. 982–1026). New York, NY: McGraw-Hill.

Buss, D. M., Larsen, R. J., Westen, D., & Semmelroth, J. (1992). Sex differences in jealousy: Evolution, physiology, and psychology. *Psychological Science, 3,* 251–255.

Buss, D. M., & Schmitt, D. P. (1993). Sexual strategies theory: A contextual evolutionary analysis of human mating. *Psychological Review, 100,* 204–232.

Buss, D. M., & Shackelford, T. K. (1997). From vigilance to violence: Mate retention tactics in married couples. *Journal of Personality and Social Psychology, 72,* 346–361.

Cheng, J. T., Tracy, J. L., & Henrich, J. (2010). Pride, personality, and the evolutionary foundations of human social status. *Evolution and Human Behavior, 5,* 334–347.

Conway, L. G., & Schaller, M. (2002). On the verifiability of evolutionary psychological theories: An analysis of the psychology of scientific persuasion. *Personality and Social Psychology Review, 6,* 152–166.

Cosmides, L., & Tooby, J. (1992). Cognitive adaptations for social exchange. In J. Barkow, L. Cosmides, & J. Tooby (Eds.), *The adapted mind* (pp. 163–228). New York, NY: Oxford University Press.

Cosmides, L., & Tooby, J. (2005). Neurocognitive adaptations designed for social exchange. In D. M. Buss (Ed.), *The handbook of evolutionary psychology.* New York, NY: Wiley.

Cosmides, L., Tooby, J., & Barkow, J. (1992). Evolutionary psychology and conceptual integration. In J. Barkow, L. Cosmides, & J. Tooby (Eds.), *The adapted mind: Evolutionary psychology and the generation of culture.* New York, NY: Oxford University Press.

Cottrell, C. A., & Neuberg, S. L. (2005). Different emotional reactions to different groups: A sociofunctional threat-based approach to "prejudice." *Journal of Personality and Social Psychology, 88,* 770–789.

Cottrell, C. A., Neuberg, S. L., & Li, N. P. (2007). What do people desire in others? A sociofunctional perspective on the importance of different valued characteristics. *Journal of Personality and Social Psychology, 92,* 208–231.

Crick, N. R., & Grotpeter, J. K. (1995). Relational aggression, gender, and social psychological adjustment. *Child Development, 66,* 710–722.

Cunningham, M. R., Barbee, A. P., & Pike, C. L. (1990). What do women want? Facialmetric assessment of multiple motives in the perception of male facial physical attractiveness. *Journal of Personality and Social Psychology, 59,* 61–72.

Dabbs, J. Jr., & Morris, R. (1990). Testosterone, social class, and antisocial behavior in a sample of 4,462 men. *Psychological Science, 1,* 209–211.

Daly, M., Salmon, C., & Wilson, M. (1997). Kinship: The conceptual hole in psychological studies of social cognition and close relationships. In J. A. Simpson & D. T. Kenrick (Eds.), *Evolutionary social psychology* (pp. 265–296). Mahwah, NJ: Erlbaum.

Daly, M., & Wilson, M. (1980) Discriminative parental solicitude: A biological perspective. *Journal of Marriage & Family, 42,* 277–288.

Daly, M., & Wilson, M. I. (1983). *Sex, evolution and behavior: Adaptations for reproduction* (2nd ed.). Boston, MA: Willard Grant Press.

Daly, M., & Wilson, M. I. (1985). Child abuse and other risks of not living with both parents. *Ethology & Sociobiology, 6,* 197–210.

Daly, M., & Wilson, M. (1988). *Homicide.* Hawthorne, NY: Aldine de Gruyter.

DeSteno, D. A., & Salovey, P. (1996). Evolutionary origins of sex differences in jealousy? Questioning the "fitness" of the model. *Psychological Science, 7,* 367–372.

de Waal, F. B. M., & Luttrell, L. M. (1988). Mechanisms of social reciprocity in three primate species: Symmetrical relationship characteristics or cognition? *Ethology and Sociobiology, 9,* 101–118.

DeWall, C. N., Maner, J. K., & Rouby, D. A. (2009). Social exclusion and early-stage interpersonal perception: Selective attention to signs of acceptance. *Journal of Personality and Social Psychology, 96,* 729–741.

DeWall, C. N., Twenge, J. M., Gitter, S. A., & Baumeister, R. F. (2009). It's the thought that counts: The role of hostile cognition in shaping aggressive responses to social exclusion. *Journal of Personality and Social Psychology, 96,* 45–59.

Eibl-Eibesfeldt, I. (1989). *Human ethology.* New York, NY: Aldine deGruyter.

Eisenberger, N. I., Lieberman, M. D., & Williams, K. D. (2003). Does rejection hurt? An fMRI study of social exclusion. *Science, 302,* 290–292.

Ekman, P. (1982). *Emotion in the human face* (2nd ed.). Cambridge, UK: Cambridge University Press.

Ellis, L. (1995). Dominance and reproductive success among nonhuman animals. *Ethology and Sociobiology, 16,* 257–333.

Ewald, P. W. (1994). *Evolution of infectious disease.* New York, NY: Oxford University Press.

Faulkner, J., & Schaller, M. (2007). Nepotistic nosiness: Inclusive fitness and vigilance of kin members' romantic relationships. *Evolution and Human Behavior, 28,* 430–438.

Fessler, D. M. T. (2001). Luteal phase immunosuppression and meat eating. *Rivista di Biologia/Biology Forum 94* (3), 403–426.

Fessler, D. M. T. (2002). Reproductive immunosuppression and diet: An evolutionary perspective on pregnancy sickness and meat consumption. *Current Anthropology, 43* (1), 19–39, 48–61.

Fessler, D. M. T., & Navarrete, C. D. (2003). Meat is good to taboo: Dietary proscriptions as a product of the interaction of psychological mechanisms and social processes. *Journal of Cognition and Culture,* *3*(1), 1–40.

Fisek, M. H., & Ofshe, R. (1970). The process of status evolution. *Sociometry, 33,* 327–346.

Fiske, A. P. (1992). The four elementary forms of sociality: Framework for a unified theory of social relations. *Psychological Review, 99,* 689–723.

Flynn, F. J., & Reagans, R. E. (2006). Helping one's way to the top: Self-monitors achieve status by helping others and knowing who helps whom. *Journal of Personality and Social Psychology, 91,* 1123–1137.

Fodor, J. A. (1983). *The modularity of mind an essay on faculty psychology.* Cambridge, MA: MIT Press.

Frank, R. H. (1988). *Passions within reason: The strategic role of the emotions.* New York, NY: Norton.

Frank, R. H. (2001). Cooperation through emotional commitment. In R. M. Nesse (Ed.), *Evolution and the capacity for commitment* (pp. 57–76). New York, NY: Sage.

Gaertner, L., & Insko, C. (2000). Intergroup discrimination in the minimal group paradigm: categorization, reciprocation, or fear? *Journal of Personality and Social Psychology, 79,* 77–94.

Gangestad, S. W., & Buss, D. M. (1993). Pathogen prevalence and human mate preferences. *Ethology and Sociobiology, 14,* 89–96.

Gangestad, S. G., Haselton, M. G., & Buss, D. M. (2006a). Evolutionary foundations of cultural variation: Evoked culture and mate preferences. Target article. *Psychological Inquiry, 17,* 75–95.

Gangestad, S. G., Haselton, M. G., & Buss, D. M. (2006b). Toward an integrative understanding of evoked and transmitted culture: The importance of specialized psychological design. *Psychological Inquiry, 17,* 138–151.

Gangestad, S. W., & Simpson, J. A. (2007). *The evolution of mind: Fundamental questions and controversies.* New York, NY: Guilford Press.

Gangestad, S. W., & Thornhill, R. (1997). The evolutionary psychology of extra-pair sex: The role of fluctuating asymmetry. *Evolution and Human Behavior, 18,* 69–88.

Garcia, J., & Koelling, R. A. (1966). Relation of cue to consequence in avoidance learning. *Psychonomic Science, 4,* 123–124.

Gardner, W. L., Pickett, C. L., & Brewer, M. B. (2000). Social exclusion and selective memory. How the need to belong influences memory for social events. *Personality and Social Psychology Bulletin, 26,* 486–496.

Gaulin, S., & Robbins, C. (1991). Trivers-Willard effect in contemporary North American society. *American Journal of Physical Anthropology, 85,* 61–69.

Geary, D. C. (1998). *Male, female: The evolution of human sex differences.* Washington, DC: American Psychological Association.

Geary, D. C. (2000). Evolution and proximate expression of human paternal investment. *Psychological Bulletin, 126,* 55–77.

Gerdes, A. B. M., Uhl, G., & Alpers, G. W. (2009). Spiders are special: Fear and disgust evoked by pictures of arthropods. *Evolution and Human Behavior, 30,* 66–73.

Gonzaga, G. C., Campos, B., & Bradbury, T. (2007). Similarity, convergence, and relationship satisfaction in dating and married couples. *Journal of Personality and Social Psychology, 93,* 34–48.

Gonzaga, G. C., Haselton, M. G., Smurda, J., Davies, M., & Poore, J. C. (2008). Love, desire, and the suppression of thoughts of romantic alternatives. *Evolution and Human Behavior, 29,* 119–126.

Gonzaga, G. C., Keltner, D., Londahl, E. A., & Smith, M. D. (2001). Love and the commitment problem in romantic relations and friendship. *Journal of Personality and Social Psychology, 81,* 247–262.

Griskevicius, V., Cialdini, R. B., & Kenrick, D. T. (2006). Peacocks, Picasso, and parental investment: The effects of romantic motives on creativity. *Journal of Personality and Social Psychology, 91,* 63–76.

Griskevicius, V., Goldstein, N. J., Mortensen, C. R., Cialdini, R. B., & Kenrick, D. T. (2006). Going along versus going alone: When fundamental motives facilitate strategic (non)conformity. *Journal of Personality and Social Psychology, 91,* 281–294.

Griskevicius, V., Tybur, J. M., Gangestad, S. W., Perea, E. F., Shapiro, J. R., & Kenrick, D. T. (2009). Aggress to impress: Hostility as an evolved context-dependent strategy. *Journal of Personality and Social Psychology, 96,* 980–994.

Griskevicius, V., Tybur, J. M., Sundie, J. M., Cialdini, R. B., Miller, G. F., & Kenrick, D. T. (2007). Blatant benevolence and conspicuous consumption: When romantic motives elicit strategic costly signals. *Journal of Personality and Social Psychology, 93,* 85–102.

Haas, J. (1990). *The anthropology of war.* New York, NY: Cambridge University Press.

Hald, G. M., & Høgh-Olesen, H. (2010). Receptivity to sexual invitations from strangers of the opposite gender. *Evolution and Human Behavior, 31,* 453–458.

Hamilton, W. D. (1964). The genetical evolution of social behavior: I & II. *Journal of Theoretical Biology, 7,* 1–32.

Harris, C. R. (2003). A review of sex differences in sexual jealousy, including self-report data, psychophysiological responses, interpersonal violence, and morbid jealousy. *Personality and Social Psychology Review, 7,* 102–128.

Harris, C. R. (2005). Male and female jealousy, still more similar than different: Reply to Sagarin (2005). *Personality and Social Psychology Review, 9,* 76–86.

Harris, G. T., Hilton, N. Z., Rice, M. E., & Eke, A. W. (2006). Children killed by genetic parents versus stepparents. *Evolution and Human Behavior, 28,* 85–95.

Haselton, M. G., & Gangestad, S. W. (2006). Conditional expression of women's desires and men's mate guarding across the ovulatory cycle. *Hormones and Behavior, 49,* 509–518.

Haselton, M. G., & Nettle, D. (2006). The paranoid optimist: An integrative evolutionary model of cognitive biases. *Personality and Social Psychology Review, 10,* 47–66.

Hazan, C., & Diamond, L. M. (2000). The place of attachment in human mating. *Review of General Psychology, 4,* 186–204.

Henrich, J., & Gil-White, F. J. (2001). The evolution of prestige: Freely conferred deference as a mechanism for enhancing the benefits of cultural transmission. *Evolution and Human Behavior, 22,* 165–196.

Henrich J., McElreath, R., Barr, A., Ensminger, J., Barret, C., Bolyanatz, A., . . . Ziker, J. (2006). Costly punishment across human societies. *Science, 312,* 1767–1770.

Hewlett, B. S. (1991). *Intimate fathers: The nature and context of Aka pygmy paternal infant care.* Ann Arbor: University of Michigan Press.

Hill, K., & Hurtado, A. M. (1996). *Ache life history.* Hawthorne, NY: Aldine deGruyter.

Hill, S. E., & Buss, D. M. (2010). Risk and relative social rank: Positional concerns and risky shifts in probabilistic decision-making. *Evolution and Human Behavior, 31,* 219–226.

Hoffman, M. (1981). Is altruism part of human nature? *Journal of Personality and Social Psychology, 40,* 121–137.

Holliday, R. (2006). Epigenetics: A historical overview. *Epigenetics, 1,* 76–80.

Holloway, R. L. (1974). On the meaning of brain size. A review of H. J. Jerison's 1973 evolution of the brain and intelligence. *Science, 184,* 677–679.

Holmes, W. G., & Sherman, P. W. (1983). Kin recognition in animals. *American Scientist, 71,* 46–55.

Hrdy, S. H. (1999). *Mother nature: A history of mothers, infants, and natural selection.* New York, NY: Pantheon.

Isaac, G. (1978). The food-sharing behavior of protohuman hominids. *Scientific American, 238,* 90–108.

Jackson, J. J., & Kirkpatrick, L. A. (2007). The structure and measurement of human mating strategies: Toward a multidimensional model of sociosexuality. *Evolution and Human Behavior, 28*, 382–391.

Johnson, D. J., & Rusbult, C. E. (1989). Resisting temptation: Devaluation of alternative partners as a means of maintaining commitment in close relationships. *Journal of Personality and Social Psychology, 57*, 967–980.

Karremans, J. C., Frankenhuis, W. E., & Arons, S. (2010). Blind men prefer a low waist-to-hip ratio. *Evolution and Human Behavior, 31*, 182–186.

Kaschak, M. P., & Maner, J. K. (2009). Embodiment, evolution, and social cognition: An integrative framework. *European Journal of Social Psychology, 39*, 1236–1244.

Keltner, D., Gruenfeld, D. H., & Anderson, C. (2003). Power, approach, and inhibition. *Psychological Review, 110*, 265–284.

Kenrick, D. T., Becker, D. V., Butner, J., Li, N. P., & Maner, J. K. (2003). Evolutionary cognitive science: Adding what and why to how the mind works. In J. Fitness & K. Sterelny (Eds.), *From mating to mentality: Evaluating evolutionary psychology* (pp. 13–38). New York, NY: Psychology Press.

Kenrick, D. T., Griskevicius, V., Neuberg, S. L., & Schaller, M. (2010). Renovating the pyramid of needs: Contemporary extensions built upon ancient foundations. *Perspectives in Psychological Science, 5*, 292–314.

Kenrick, D. T., Li, N. P., & Butner, J. (2003). Dynamical evolutionary psychology: Individual decision-rules and emergent social norms. *Psychological Review, 110*, 3–28.

Kenrick, D. T., Maner, J. K., Butner, J., Li, N. P., Becker, D. V., & Schaller, M. (2002). Dynamical evolutionary psychology: Mapping the domains of the new interactionist paradigm. *Personality and Social Psychology Review, 6*, 347–356.

Kenrick, D. T., Maner, J. K., & Li, N. P. (2005). Evolutionary social psychology. In D. Buss (Ed.), *The handbook of evolutionary psychology.* Hoboken, NJ: Wiley.

Kenrick, D. T., Nieuweboer, S., & Buunk, A. P. (2010). Universal mechanisms and cultural diversity: Replacing the blank slate with a coloring book. In M. Schaller, S. Heine, A. Norenzayan, T. Yamagishi, & T. Kameda (Eds.), *Evolution, culture, and the human mind* (pp. 257–272). Mahwah, NJ: Erlbaum.

Kenrick, D. T., Sundie, J. M., & Kurzban, R. (2008). Cooperation and conflict between kith, kin, and strangers: Game theory by domains. In C. Crawford & D. Krebs (Eds.), *Foundations of Evolutionary Psychology* (pp. 353–370). New York, NY: Erlbaum.

Kenrick, D. T., & Trost, M. R. (1997). Evolutionary approaches to relationships. In S. Duck (Ed.), *Handbook of personal relationships: Theory, research, and interventions* (pp. 151–177). Chichester, UK: Wiley.

Ketelaar, T., & Ellis, B. J. (2000). Are evolutionary explanations unfalsifiable? Evolutionary psychology and the Lakatosian philosophy of science. *Psychological Inquiry, 11*, 1–21.

Kipnis, D. (1972). Does power corrupt? *Journal of Personality & Social Psychology, 24*, 33–41.

Klein, S. B., Cosmides, L., Tooby, J., & Chance, S. (2002). Decisions and the evolution of memory: Multiple systems, multiple functions. *Psychological Review, 109*, 306–329.

Krupp, D. B., DeBruine, L. M., & Barclay, P. (2008). A cue of kinship promotes cooperation for the public good. *Evolution and Human Behavior, 29*, 49–55.

Kurzban, R., & Aktipis, C. A. (2007). Modularity and the social mind: Are psychologists too self-ish? *Personality and Social Psychology Review, 11*, 131–149.

Kurzban, R., & Leary, M. R. (2001). Evolutionary origins of stigmatization: The functions of social exclusion. *Psychological Bulletin, 127*, 187–208.

Kurzban, R., Tooby, J., & Cosmides, J. (2001). Can race be erased? Coalitional computation and social categorization. *Proceedings of the National Academy of Sciences, 98*, 15387–15392.

Lassek, W. D., & Gaulin, S. J. C. (2009). Costs and benefits of fat-free muscle mass in men: Relationship to mating success, dietary requirements, and native immunity. *Evolution and Human Behavior, 30*, 322–328.

Leary, M. R., Twenge, J. M., & Quinlivan, E. (2006). Interpersonal dejection as a determinant of anger and aggression. *Personality and Social Psychology Review, 10*, 111–132.

Li, N. P., & Kenrick, D. T. (2006). Sex similarities and differences in preferences for short-term mates: What, whether, and why. *Journal of Personality and Social Psychology, 90*, 468–489.

Lie, H. C., Simmons, L. W., & Rhodes, G. (2010). Genetic dissimilarity, genetic diversity, and mate preferences in humans. *Evolution and Human Behavior, 31*, 48–58.

Lieberman, D., Pillsworth, E. G., & Haselton, M. G. (2011). Kin affiliation across the ovulatory cycle: Females avoid fathers when fertile. *Psychological Science, 22*, 13–18.

Lieberman, D., Tooby, J., & Cosmides, L. (2007). *The architecture of human kin detection. Nature, 445*, 727–731.

Low, B. S. (1990). Marriage systems and pathogen stress in human societies. *American Zoologist, 30*, 325–339.

Lukaszewski, A. W., & Roney, J. R. (2010). Kind toward whom? Mate preferences for personality traits are target specific. *Evolution and Human Behavior, 31*, 29–38.

MacDonald, G., & Leary, M. R. (2005). Why does social exclusion hurt? The relationship between social and physical pain. *Psychological Bulletin, 131*, 202–223.

Maner, J. K. (2009). Anxiety: Proximate processes and ultimate functions. *Social and Personality Psychology Compass, 3*, 798–811.

Maner, J. K., DeWall, C. N., Baumeister, R. F., & Schaller, M. (2007). Does social exclusion motivate interpersonal reconnection? Resolving the "porcupine problem." *Journal of Personality and Social Psychology, 92*, 42–55.

Maner, J. K., DeWall, C. N., & Gailliot, M. T. (2008). Selective attention to signs of success: Social dominance and early stage interpersonal perception. *Personality and Social Psychology Bulletin, 34*, 488–501.

Maner, J. K., & Gailliot, M. T. (2007). Altruism and egoism: Prosocial motivations for helping depend on relationship context. *European Journal of Social Psychology, 37*, 347–358.

Maner, J. K., Gailliot, M. T., & Miller, S. L. (2009). The implicit cognition of relationship maintenance: Inattention to attractive alternatives. *Journal of Experimental Social Psychology, 45*, 174–179.

Maner, J. K., Gailliot, M. T., Rouby, D. A., & Miller, S. L. (2007). Can't take my eyes off you: Attentional adhesion to mates and rivals. *Journal of Personality and Social Psychology, 93*, 389–401.

Maner, J. K., Kenrick, D. T., Neuberg, S. L., Becker, D. V., Robertson, T., Hofer, B., . . . Schaller, M. (2005). Functional projection: How fundamental social motives can bias interpersonal perception. *Journal of Personality and Social Psychology, 88*, 63–78.

Maner, J. K., & Mead, N. L. (2010). The essential tension between leadership and power: When leaders sacrifice group goals for the sake of self-interest. *Journal of Personality and Social Psychology, 99*, 482–497.

Maner, J. K., Miller, S. L., Rouby, D. A., & Gailliot, M. T. (2009). Intrasexual vigilance: The implicit cognition of romantic rivalry. *Journal of Personality and Social Psychology, 97*, 74–87.

Maner, J. K., Miller, S. L., Schmidt, N. B., & Eckel, L. A. (2008). Submitting to defeat: Social anxiety, dominance threat, and decrements in testosterone. *Psychological Science, 19*, 264–268.

Maner, J. K., Miller, S. L., Schmidt, N. B., & Eckel, L. A. (2010). The endocrinology of exclusion: Rejection elicits motivationally tuned changes in progesterone. *Psychological Science, 21*, 581–588.

Maner, J. K., Rouby, D. A., & Gonzaga, G. (2008). Automatic inattention to attractive alternatives: the evolved psychology of relationship maintenance. *Evolution & Human Behavior, 29*, 343–349.

Marks, I. M., & Nesse, R. M. (1994). Fear and fitness: An evolutionary analysis of anxiety disorders. *Ethology and Sociobiology, 15*, 247–261.

Marlowe, F. W., Berbesque, J. C., Barr, A., Barrett, C., Bolyanatz, A., Cardenas, J. C., ... Tracer, D. (2008). More "altruistic" punishment in larger societies. *Proceedings of the Royal Society Biology, 275*, 587–590.

Marshall, D. S., & Suggs, R. G. (1971). *Human sexual behavior: Variations in the ethnographic spectrum*. New York, NY: Basic Books.

Mazur, A., & Booth, A. (1998). Testosterone and dominance in men. *Behavioral and Brain Sciences, 21*, 353–397.

McClelland, D. C. (1975). *Power: The inner experience*. Oxford, UK: Irvington.

Mealey, L., Daood, C., & Krage, M. (1996). Enhanced memory for faces of cheaters. *Ethology and Sociobiology, 17*, 119–128.

Miller, G. F. (2000). *The mating mind: How sexual choice shaped the evolution of human nature*. New York, NY: Doubleday.

Miller, R. S. (1997). Inattentive and contented: Relationship commitment and attention to alternatives. *Journal of Personality and Social Psychology, 73*, 758–766.

Moore, B. R. (2004). The evolution of learning. *Biological Review, 79*, 301–335.

Morhenn, V. B., Park, J. W., Piper, E., & Zak, P. J. (2008). Monetary sacrifice among strangers is mediated by endogenous oxytocin release after physical contact. *Evolution and Human Behavior, 29*, 375–383.

Muraven, M. R., & Baumeister, R. F. (2000). Self-regulation and depletion of limited resources: Does self-control resemble a muscle? *Psychological Bulletin, 126*, 247–259.

Navarrete, C. D., Olsson, A., Ho, A., Mendes, W., Thomsen, L., & Sidanius, J. (2009). Fear extinction to an outgroup face: The role of target gender. *Psychological Science, 20*, 155–158.

Nettle, D. (2009). Beyond nature versus culture: Cultural variation as an evolved characteristic. *Journal of the Royal Anthropological Institute, 15*, 223–240.

Neuberg, S. L., & Cottrell, C. A. (2006). Evolutionary bases of prejudices. In M. Schaller, J. A. Simpson, & D. T. Kenrick (Eds.), *Evolution and social psychology* (pp. 163–187). New York, NY: Psychology Press.

Neuberg, S. L., Kenrick, D. T., & Schaller, M. (2010). Evolutionary social psychology. In S. T. Fiske, D. T. Gilbert, & G. Lindzey (Eds.), *Handbook of social psychology* (5th ed.). New York, NY: Wiley.

Neuberg, S. L., Kenrick, D. T., & Schaller, M. (2011). Human threat management systems: Self-protection and disease avoidance. *Neuroscience and Biobehavioral Reviews, 35*, 1042–1051.

Norenzayan, A. (2006). Evolution and transmitted culture. *Psychological Inquiry, 17*, 123–128.

Oda, R., & Nakajima, S. (2010). Biased face recognition in the Faith Game. *Evolution and Human Behavior, 31*, 118–122.

Öhman, A., & Mineka, S. (2001). Fears, phobias, and preparedness: Toward an evolved module of fear and fear learning. *Psychological Review, 108*, 483–522.

Park, J. H., Faulkner, J., & Schaller, M. (2003). Evolved disease-avoidance processes and contemporary anti-social behavior: Prejudicial attitudes and avoidance of people with physical disabilities. *Journal of Nonverbal Behavior, 27*, 65–87.

Park, J. H., Schaller, M., & Crandall, C. S. (2007). Pathogen-avoidance mechanisms and the stigmatization of obese people. *Evolution and Human Behavior, 28*, 410–414.

Park, J., Schaller, M., & Van Vugt, M. (2008). The psychology of human kin recognition: Heuristic cues, erroneous inferences, and their implications. *Review of General Psychology, 12*, 215–235.

Parkinson, B. (2005). Do facial movements express emotions or communicate motives? *Personality and Social Psychology Review, 9*, 278–311.

Penton-Voak, I. S., Perrett, D. I., Casteles, D. L., Kobayashi, T., Burt, D. M., Murray, L. K., & Minamisawa, R. (1999). Female preference for male faces changes cyclically. *Nature, 399*, 741–742.

Piazza, J., & Bering, J. M. (2008). Concerns about reputations via gossip promote generous allocations in an economic game. *Evolution and Human Behavior, 29*, 172–178.

Pillsworth, E. G., & Haselton, M. G. (2006). Male sexual attractiveness predicts differential ovulatory shifts in female extra-pair attraction and male mate retention. *Evolution and Human Behavior, 27*, 247–258.

Preston, S. D., & de Waal, F. B. M. (2002). Empathy: Its ultimate and proximate bases. *Behavioral and Brain Sciences, 25*, 1–71.

Rasmussen, D. R. (1981). Pair bond strength and stability and reproductive success. *Psychological Review, 88*, 274–290.

Richerson, P. J., & Boyd, R. (2005). *Not by genes alone: How culture transformed human evolution*. Chicago, IL: University of Chicago Press.

Ridley, M. (2003). *Nature via nurture: Genes, experience, and what makes us human*. New York, NY: HarperCollins.

Rose, R. M., Bernstein, I. S., & Holaday, J. W. (1971). Plasma testosterone, dominance rank, and aggressive behavior in a group of male rhesus monkeys. *Nature, 231*, 366.

Rozin, P., & Fallon, A. (1987). A perspective on disgust. *Psychological Review, 94*, 23–41.

Sadalla, E. K., Kenrick, D. T., & Venshure, B. (1987). Dominance and heterosexual attraction. *Journal of Personality and Social Psychology, 52*, 730–738.

Sagarin, B. J. (2005). Reconsidering evolved sex differences in jealousy: Comment on Harris (2003). *Personality & Social Psychology Review, 9*, 62–75.

Schaller, M., & Murray, D. R. (2008). Pathogens, personality and culture: Disease prevalence predicts worldwide variability in sociosexuality, extraversion, and openness to experience. *Journal of Personality and Social Psychology, 95*, 212–221.

Schaller, M., Norenzayan, A., Heine, S. J., Yamagishi, T., & Kameda, T. (2010). *Evolution, culture, and the human mind*. New York, NY: Psychology Press.

Schaller, M., Park, J. H., & Mueller, A. (2003). Fear of the dark: Interactive effects of beliefs about danger and ambient darkness on ethnic stereotypes. *Personality and Social Psychology Bulletin, 29*, 637–649.

Scheib, J. E., Gangestad, S. W., & Thornhill, R. (1999). Facial attractiveness, symmetry, and cues of good genes. *Proceedings of the Royal Society of London, B, 266*, 1913–1917.

Schmitt, D. P. (2011). Psychological adaptation and human fertility patterns: Some evidence of human mating strategies and evoked sexual culture. *Biosocial Foundations of Family Processes, 3*, 161–170.

Schmitt, D. P., & Pilcher, J. J. (2004). Evaluating evidence of psychological adaptation: How do we know one when we see one? *Psychological Science, 15*, 643–649.

Schützwohl, A. (2008). The crux of cognitive load: Constraining deliberate and effortful decision processes in romantic jealousy. *Evolution and Human Behavior, 29*, 127–132.

Scott-Phillips, T. C., Dickins, T. E., & West, S. A. (2011). Evolutionary theory and the ultimate-proximate distinction in the human behavioral sciences. *Perspectives on Psychological Science, 6*, 38–47.

Sedikides, C., & Skowronski, J. J. (1997). The symbolic self in evolutionary context. *Personality and Social Psychology Review, 1*, 80–102.

Segal, N. L., & Hershberger, S. L. (1999). Cooperation and competition in adolescent twins: Findings from a prisoner's dilemma game. *Evolution and Human Behavior, 20,* 29–51.

Seligman, M. E. P. (1971). Phobias and preparedness. *Behavior Therapy, 2,* 307–320.

Shackelford, T. K., Goetz, A. T., Buss, D. M., Euler, H. A., & Hoier, S. (2005). When we hurt the ones we love: Predicting violence against women from men's mate retention. *Personal Relationships, 12,* 447–463.

Shapiro, J., Ackerman, J., Neuberg, S. L., Maner, J. K., Becker, D. V., & Kenrick, D. T. (2009). Following in the wake of anger: When not discriminating is discriminating. *Personality & Social Psychology Bulletin, 35,* 1356–1367.

Sheets, V. L., Fredendall, L. L., & Claypool, H. M. (1997). Jealousy evocation, partner reassurance and relationship stability: An exploration of the potential benefits of jealousy. *Evolution and Human Behavior, 18,* 387–402.

Sherman, P. W. (1977). Nepotism and the evolution of alarm calls. *Science, 197,* 1246–1253.

Sherry, D. F., & Schacter, D. L. (1987). The evolution of multiple memory systems. *Psychological Review, 94,* 439–454.

Simpson, J. A., & Gangestad, S. W. (1991). Individual differences in sociosexuality: Evidence for convergent and discriminant validity. *Journal of Personality and Social Psychology, 67,* 870–883.

Simpson, J. A., Gangestad, S. W., & Lerma, M. (1990). Perception of physical attractiveness: Mechanisms involved in the maintenance of romantic relationships. *Journal of Personality and Social Psychology, 59,* 1192–1201.

Singh, D. (1993). Adaptive significance of waist-to-hip ratio and female attractiveness. *Journal of Personality and Social Psychology, 65,* 293–307.

Singh, D., Dixson, B. J., Jessop, T. S., Morgan, B., & Dixson, A. F. (2010). Cross-cultural consensus for waist-hip ration and women's attractiveness. *Evolution and Human Behavior, 31,* 176–181.

Sprecher, S., Sullivan, Q., & Hatfield, E. (1994). Mate selection preferences: Gender differences examined in a national sample. *Journal of Personality and Social Psychology, 66,* 1074–1080.

Stevenson, R., Case, T. I., & Oaten, M. J. (2009). Frequency and recency of infection and their relationship with disgust and contamination sensitivity. *Evolution and Human Behavior, 30,* 363–368.

Stewart-Williams, S. (2008). Human beings as evolved nepotists: Exceptions to the rule and effects of cost of help. *Human Nature, 19,* 414–425.

Suomi, S. J. (1982). Sibling relationships in nonhuman primates. In M. E. Lamb & B. Sutton-Smith (Eds.), *Sibling relationships.* Mahwah NJ: Erlbaum.

Symons, D. (1979). *The evolution of human sexuality.* New York, NY: Oxford University Press.

Tajfel, H. (1970). Experiments in intergroup discrimination. *Scientific American, 223,* 96–102.

Thorpe, I. N. (2003). Anthropology, archaeology, and the origin of warfare. *World Archaeology, 35,* 145–165.

Tinbergen, N. (1963). On the aims and methods of ethology. *Zeitschrift für* Tierpsychologie, *20,* 410–433.

Tomasello, M., Kruger, A. C., & Ratner, H. H. (1993). Cultural learning. *Behavioral and Brain Sciences, 16,* 495–552.

Tooby, J., & Cosmides, L. (1990a). On the universality of human nature and the uniqueness of the individual: The role of genetics and adaptation. *Journal of Personality, 58,* 17–67.

Tooby, J., & Cosmides, L. (1990b). The past explains the present: Emotional adaptations and the structure of ancestral environments. *Ethology and Sociobiology, 11,* 375–424.

Tooby, J., & Cosmides, L. (1992). The psychological foundations of culture. In J. Barkow, L. Cosmides, & J. Tooby (Eds.), *The adapted mind: Evolutionary psychology and the generation of culture.* New York, NY: Oxford University Press.

Trivers, R. (1971). The evolution of reciprocal altruism. *Quarterly Review of Biology, 46,* 35–37.

Trivers, R. L. (1972). Parental investment and sexual selection. In B. Campbell (Ed.), *Sexual selection and the descent of man* (pp. 136–179). Chicago, IL: Aldine-Atherton.

Trivers, R. L. (1985). *Social evolution.* Menlo Park, CA: Benjamin/ Cummings.

Trivers, R. L., & Willard, D. E. (1973). Natural selection of parental ability to vary the sex ratio of offspring. *Science, 197,* 90–92.

van Vugt, M. (2006). Evolutionary origins of leadership and followership. *Personality and Social Psychology Review, 10,* 354–371.

van Vugt, M., Hogan, R., & Kaiser, R. (2008). Leadership, followership, and evolution: Some lessons from the past. *American Psychologist, 63,* 182–196.

Wendorf, F. (1968). Site 117: A Nubian final Palaeolithic graveyard near Jebel Sahaba, Sudan. In F. Wendorf (Ed.), *The prehistory of Nubia* (Vol. 2, pp. 954–1040). Dallas, TX: Southern Methodist University Press.

Wilson, E. O. (1975). *Sociobiology: The new synthesis.* Cambridge, MA: Harvard University Press.

CHAPTER 24

Culture and Social Psychology

JOAN G. MILLER AND J. PATRICK BOYLE

During much of its past, psychology represented a culturally grounded enterprise that took into account the constitutive role of cultural meanings and practices in human development. Yet, as historical accounts make clear (Jahoda, 1993), this attention to culture was muted during the 20th century, with psychology dominated by an idealized physical science model of explanation. This has given rise to the enigma that psychologists find it "difficult to keep culture in mind," noted by Cole (1996):

> On the one hand, it is generally agreed that the need and ability to live in the human medium of culture is one of the central characteristics of human beings. On the other hand, it is difficult for many academic psychologists to assign culture more than a secondary, often superficial role in the constitution of our mental life. (p. 1)

From this type of perspective, which dominates the field, culture is seen as at most affecting the display of individual psychological processes, but not as affecting qualitatively their form.

However, although culture remains in a peripheral role in the contemporary discipline, recent years have seen a reemergence of interest in cultural approaches and an increased recognition of their importance to psychological theory. As reflected in the interdisciplinary perspective of cultural psychology (e.g., Cole, 1990; Greenfield, 1997; J. G. Miller, 1997; Shweder, 1990), human development occurs in historically grounded social environments that are structured by cultural meanings and practices. Cultural meanings and practices are themselves understood to be dependent on the subjectivity of communities of intentional agents. By affecting individuals' understandings and intentions, cultural meanings and practices, in turn, are recognized to have a qualitative impact on the development

of psychological phenomena and to be integral to the formulation of basic psychological theory.

The goal of this chapter is to highlight some of the insights for understanding social psychology emerging from a consideration of the cultural grounding of psychological processes. The first section of the chapter considers factors that have contributed to the downplaying of culture in mainstream social psychology and the assumptions that guided some of the earliest research in the traditions of cross-cultural psychology. In the second section, consideration is given to key conceptual developments underlying cultural psychology, recent empirical findings that illustrate the existence of cultural variation in basic social psychological processes, and challenges for future theory and research. In conclusion, consideration is given to the multiple contributions of a cultural perspective in psychology.

APPROACHES TO CULTURE IN MAINSTREAM SOCIAL PSYCHOLOGY AND IN EARLY CROSS-CULTURAL PSYCHOLOGY

The present section provides an overview of shifts in the role accorded to culture in psychological theory over time. It also outlines some of the changing conceptual understandings and disciplinary practices that are affecting these shifts.

Downplaying of Culture in Mainstream Social Psychology

Signs of the peripheral theoretical role accorded to cultural considerations in social psychology may be seen in its being downplayed in major social psychological publications. Textbooks typically either leave the construct of culture theoretically undefined, treat it as the same as the objective environment or social ecology, or approach it in an eclectic way that lacks conceptual clarity. Likewise, basic theory tends to be presented without any reference to cultural considerations. Culture is treated merely as a factor that influences the universality of certain psychological effects but not as a process that must be taken into account to explain the form of basic psychological phenomena. An example of such a stance can be found in Kruglanski and Higgins's (2007) handbook on basic principles of social psychology in which most of the references made to culture occur within a chapter on culture by Chiu and Hong (2007) or on six pages of a chapter by Oyserman (2007) on social identity and self-regulation. Except for a one-page citation, no reference is made to culture in the 12 chapters devoted to the cognitive system, despite the chapters in this section addressing issues of basic theory on which there has been extensive cultural research, such as causal explanation, prediction, expectancy, knowledge activation, and principles of social judgment. In the following discussion, we argue that this downplaying of culture reflects to a great degree the tendency to conceptualize situations in culture-free terms, the embrace of an idealized natural-science model of explanation, and the default assumption of cultural homogeneity that dominates the field.

Culture-Free Approach to Situations

A key contribution of social psychology—if not its signature explanatory feature—is its recognition of the power of situations to impact behavior. Such a stance is reflected, for example, in a series of classic studies. Salient examples include the Milgram conformity experiment, which demonstrated that to conform with the orders of an experimenter, individuals were willing to inflict a harmful electric shock on a learner (Milgram, 1963), and the prison experiment of Zimbardo and his colleagues (Haney, Banks, & Zimbardo, 1973), which demonstrated that individuals who had been thrust into the role of guards in a simulated prison behaved abusively toward individuals in the role of prisoners. It also may be seen in recent lines of inquiry on such topics as individuals' limited conscious access to their cognitive processes, priming effects, and the mere exposure effect (Bargh, 1996; Bornstein, Kale, & Cornell, 1990). Social psychological work of this type has shown that contexts affect behavior in ways that do not depend on conscious mediation and that may even violate individuals' conscious expectations and motivational inclinations.

Supplementing this focus on the power of situations to affect behavior, it has also been documented that individual differences influence the meaning accorded to situations. This attention to individual differences is evident not only in work on personality processes but also in the attention given to cognitive and motivational schemas as sources of individual variability in behavior. Individual difference dimensions, however, typically are accorded a secondary role to situational influences within social psychological theory. They are believed to affect the display of certain basic psychological dimensions, but they are not often implicated in normative models of psychological phenomena (Ross & Nisbett, 1991).

The crucial point is that the approach to situations that dominates social psychological inquiry treats contexts as presenting objective information that can be known through inductive or deductive information processing without the need for cultural input. No consideration is given to the possibility that culture is necessarily implicated in the definition of situations or that cultural presuppositions constitute prerequisites of what is considered objective knowledge. It is assumed that variability in judgment arises from differences in the information available to individuals or from differences in their information processing abilities, resulting in certain judgments being more or less cognitively adequate or veridical than others (Nisbett & Ross, 1980). Evidence that individuals from different cultural backgrounds maintain contrasting systems of belief, value, or meaning—and that they interpret situations in contrasting ways—tends to be assimilated to an individual difference dimension. Such evidence is viewed as implying that individual differences in attitudes, understandings, or available information may relate to cultural group membership, but not as implying that there is a need to give any independent weight to cultural meanings and practices per se in the construction of basic psychological theory.

Natural Science Ideals of Explanation

The tendency to downplay the importance of culture in social psychological theory also derives from the field's embrace of an idealized physical-science model of explanation. Although social psychology makes use of multiple normative models of scientific inquiry, it has typically treated physical science models of scientific inquiry as the ideal approach. This has affected both the goals and methods of inquiry in ways that have tended to marginalize cultural approaches.

In terms of explanatory goals, the foremost aim of psychological explanation has been to identify universal laws of behavior. Adopting the criteria of parsimony and of predictive power as the hallmarks of a successful explanation, psychological inquiry has been conceptualized as involving the identification of deep structural explanatory mechanisms that (it is assumed) underlie overt behavior. Higgins and Kruglanski (1996) outline this vision for social psychological inquiry:

> A discovery of lawful principles governing a realm of phenomena is a fundamental objective of scientific research.... A useful scientific analysis needs to probe beneath the surface. In other words, it needs to get away from the "phenotypic" manifestations and strive to unearth the "genotypes" that may lurk beneath.... We believe in the scientific pursuit of the non-obvious. But less in the sense of uncovering new and surprising phenomena than in the sense of probing beneath surface similarities and differences to discover deep underlying structures. (p. vii)

From this perspective, the assumption is made that fundamental psychological processes are timeless, ahistorical, and culturally invariant, with the principles of explanation in the social sciences no different from those in the natural or physical sciences.

Based on the current physical-science view of explanation, cultural considerations tend to be regarded as noise; consequently, they are held constant in order to focus on identifying underlying processes. According to this perspective, an explanation that identifies a process as dependent on culturally specific assumptions is regarded as deficient. To discover that a phenomenon is culturally bound is to suggest that the phenomenon has not as yet been fully understood and that it is not yet possible to formulate a universal explanatory theory that achieves the desired goals of being both parsimonious and highly general.

Another consequence of the present physical-science model of explanation is that social psychology has tended to privilege laboratory-based methods of inquiry and to be dismissive of what is perceived to be the inherent lack of methodological control of cultural research. Skepticism surrounds the issue of whether sufficient comparability can be achieved in assessments made in different cultural contexts to permit valid cross-cultural comparisons. Serious concerns are also raised about methodological weaknesses inherent in the qualitative methods that are frequently involved in assessment of cultural meanings and practices. In particular, because such measures are at times based on analyses undertaken by a single ethnographer or similar methods, measures used in cultural assessment are seen as characterized by limited reliability and validity, as well as by heavy reliance on interpretive techniques.

Default Assumption of Cultural Homogeneity

Finally, the downplaying of the importance of cultural considerations in social psychology also stems from the tendency to assume a universalistic cultural context in recruitment of research participants and in formulation of research questions. This type of stance has led to skewed population sampling in research. As critics (Reid, 1994) have charged, the field has proceeded as though the cultural context for human development is homogeneous; consequently, research has adopted stances that treat middle-class European-American research populations as the default or unmarked subject of research:

> Culture...has been assumed to be homogenous, that is, based on a standard set of values and expectations primarily held by White and middle-class populations.... For example, in developmental psychology, children means White children (McLoyd, 1990); in psychology of women, women generally refers to White women (Reid, 1988). When we mean other than White, it is specified. (p. 525)

In this regard, a review conducted of more than 14,000 empirical articles in psychology published between 1970 and 1989 yielded fewer than 4% centering on African Americans (Graham, 1992).

However, it is not only these skewed sampling practices but also the resulting skewed knowledge base brought to bear in inquiry that contributes to the downplaying of the importance of cultural considerations. Commonly, research hypotheses are based on investigators' translations of observations from their own experiences into testable research hypotheses. In doing this, however, researchers from non–middle-class European-American backgrounds frequently find themselves having to suppress intuitions or concerns that arise from their own cultural experiences. As reflected in the following account by a leading indigenous Chinese psychologist (Yang, 1997), the present type of stance may give rise to a sense of alienation among individuals who do not share the so-called mainstream cultural assumptions that presently dominate the field:

> I found the reason why doing Westernized psychological research with Chinese subjects was no longer satisfying or rewarding to me. When an American psychologist, for example, was engaged in research, he or she could spontaneously let his or her American cultural and philosophical orientations and ways of thinking be freely and effectively reflected in choosing a research question, defining a concept,

constructing a theory and designing a method. On the other hand, when a Chinese psychologist in Taiwan was conducting research, his or her strong training by over learning the knowledge and methodology of American psychology tended to prevent his or her Chinese values, ideas, concepts and ways of thinking from being adequately reflected in the successive stages of the research process. (p. 65)

It has been suggested, in this regard, that to broaden psychological inquiry to be sensitive to aspects of self emphasized in Chinese culture, greater attention would need to be paid to such presently understudied concerns as filial piety, impression management, relationship harmony, and protection of face (Hsu, 1963, 1985; Yang, 1988; Yang & Ho, 1988). Taking issues of this type into account, researchers in the area of social attribution, for example, have highlighted the understandings of causality entailed in the Buddhist concept of *yuan*, a concept that entails the idea of cooperative causes and that contrasts with the more unitary and fixed perspective on causality emphasized in Western cultural traditions (Chang & Holt, 1991). As defined by Soothill and Hodous (1968), "(*yuan*)...is the circumstantial, conditioning, or secondary cause, in contrast with the direct or fundamental cause...the direct cause is the seed, and *yuan* is the soil, rain, and the sunshine" (p. 440). The cultural emphasis on *yuan*, evidence suggests, is related not only to the greater emphasis given by East Asian as compared with U.S. populations to contextual factors in social attribution (e.g., Morris & Peng, 1994) but also to their tendencies to take more information into account before making causal attributions (Choi, Dalal, Kim-Prieto & Park, 2003).

As a consequence of its tendency to privilege considerations emphasized in European-American cultural contexts, psychology in many cases has focused on research concerns that have a somewhat parochial character, as Moscovici (1972) has argued in appraising the contributions of social psychology:

> The real advance made by American social psychology was...in the fact that it took for its theme of research and for the content of its theories the issues of its own society. Its merit was as much in its techniques as in translating the problems of American society into socio-psychological terms and in making them an object of scientific inquiry. (p. 19)

In proceeding with a set of concepts that are based on a relatively narrow set of cultural experiences, psychological research then has tended to formulate theories and research questions that lack adequate cultural inclusiveness and instead are based on the experiences of highly select populations.

Summary

Social psychological inquiry has tended to downplay cultural factors, given its tendencies to accord no independent explanatory force to cultural factors and to embrace a natural-science model of explanation. In both its sampling practices and consideration of research questions, social psychology has privileged a middle-class European-American outlook that gives only limited attention to diverse cultural and subcultural populations.

Early Research in Cross-Cultural and Sociocultural Psychology

Although cultural considerations have tended to be accorded little importance in social psychological theory, there exists a long-standing tradition of research in cross-cultural psychology as well as in the sociocultural-historical tradition of work on culture and thought. Empirical work from these perspectives are extensive enough to fill the six-volume first edition of the *Handbook of Cross-Cultural Psychology* (Triandis & Lambert, 1980), as well as numerous textbooks and review chapters (e.g., Berry, Poortinga, Segall, & Dasen, 1992; Brislin, 1983; Cole & Scribner, 1974). Brief consideration is given here to some of the major traditions of work in cross-cultural psychology, of work on culture and personality, and on individualism/collectivism, as well to early work in the sociocultural-historical tradition.

Culture and Personality

Work on culture and personality constituted an interdisciplinary perspective that generated great interest and inspired extensive research throughout the middle years of the 20th century (e.g., LeVine, 1973; Shweder, 1979a, 1979b; Wallace, 1961; J. W. Whiting & Child, 1953; B. B. Whiting & Whiting, 1975). Although many of the assumptions of this perspective were challenged, and interest in this viewpoint diminished after the 1980s, work in culture and personality has served as a foundation for later work on culture and the development of self.

Some of the earliest work in the tradition of culture and personality adopted a critical case methodology to test the generality of psychological theories. For example, in a classic example of this approach, Malinowski tested the universality of the Oedipus complex against case materials from the Trobriand Islands (1959). Likewise, in another early example, Mead provided evidence that adolescence does not invariably involve the patterns of psychosocial conflict that were once assumed in psychological theory to be universal (1928, 1939).

Other work in culture and personality developed models that portrayed culture as an integrated entity that conformed to the dominant pattern of individual personality held by members of the culture. Applying this model to an analysis of Japan, Benedict (1946) traced broad consistencies that characterized Japanese values, social institutions, national policy, and interpersonal relations. Similar types of assumptions characterized national character studies, such as in work identifying an assumed "authoritarian" personality that was viewed as characteristic of the German psyche and as contributing to the emphasis on obedience to authority observed in Nazi Germany (Fromm, 1941).

Still a third thrust of work on culture and personality forwarded a personality–integration-of-culture model (Kardiner, 1945; Whiting & Child, 1953). From this viewpoint, individual personality structures were regarded as adapted to cultural meanings and practices, which, in turn, were regarded as adapted to the demands of particular ecological settings. It was assumed that individuals come over time to be socialized to behave in ways that fit their culture. In a groundbreaking program of research that stands as one of the most influential contributions of this school of thought, the Six Culture study tested these relations in an investigation that involved conducting behavioral observations of parenting and child behavior in everyday contexts in a worldwide sampling of cultures (J. W. Whiting & Whiting, 1975). As one example of the many findings from the Six Culture project, cultures with complex socioeconomic systems, characterized by such features as occupational specialization, a central government, social stratification, and a priesthood, were observed to give rise to differences in the daily routines and roles that parents assigned to children, and to tendencies for the children to develop personality dispositions that were characterized by domineering and aggressive tendencies.

In terms of criticisms, concerns were raised about the determinism of treating culture as a reflection of individual personality, as well as regarding what was viewed as an overly socialized conception of the person—a conception that treated the individual as merely passively conforming to prevailing norms (Shweder, 1979a, 1979b). Additionally, it was argued that work in culture and personality overestimated the thematic nature of cultural forms, as well as failed to take into account the limited longitudinal stability and cross-situational consistency of personality. For example, evidence suggested that what had been interpreted as a difference in personality between cultural populations in fact could be explained in normative terms—as individuals responding to the behavioral

expectations of different everyday cultural settings (B. B. Whiting & Edwards, 1988).

Individualism-Collectivism

Constituting one of the most influential and long-standing traditions of research in cross-cultural psychology, work on individualism-collectivism is associated with the early theoretical work of investigators such as Hofstede and Triandis (Hofstede, 1980; Triandis, 1972, 1989, 1996) and has been applied to explain behavioral variation on a worldwide scale. Thus, these constructs have been invoked in explaining such diverse phenomena, among others, as values (Hofstede, 1980; S. H. Schwartz, 1994), cognitive differentiation (Witkin & Berry, 1975), and modernity (Inkeles, 1974).

In recent years, researchers have shown increased interest in the constructs of individualism and collectivism as a consequence of these constructs being linked to the distinction drawn by Markus and Kitayama (1991) between independent versus interdependent modes of self-construal. In introducing the contrast between independent versus interdependent self-construal, Markus and Kitayama did not adopt all of the assumptions of the individualism-collectivism framework, as developed by early cross-cultural psychologists. They were concerned with the cultural psychological agenda of identifying insights for basic psychological theory of cultural variation, rather than with the cross-cultural agenda of applying existing psychological theories in diverse cultural contexts (for discussion of distinction between cross-cultural and cultural psychology, see Miller, 1997; Shweder, 1990). A cross-cultural psychologist might use the variation provided by differing social environments to test claims made in existing psychological theories, such as assessing whether, as predicted by attachment theory, less secure modes of attachment are associated with kibbutz living arrangements, which involve early separation of the child from their parents (e.g., Sagi & van Ijzendoom, 1994). In contrast, a cultural psychologist would focus on conducting research that seeks to culturally broaden existing psychological theories, such as demonstrating that attachment theory assumes a qualitatively distinctive form in a culture such as Japan, with its emphasis on amae (e.g., Rothbaum, Weisz, Pott, Miyake, & Morelli, 2000). However, in part as a reflection of the interest in the distinction between independent versus interdependent self-construals introduced by Markus and Kitayama (1991), the number of investigators concerned with individualism and collectivism has grown in recent years. Many investigators draw on this framework to further the cultural psychological agenda of broadening basic psychological theory (e.g., Greenfield & Cocking, 1994; Greenfield & Suzuki, 1998), while other investigators draw on the framework to further the original agenda of theorists such as Triandis to develop a universal, ecologically based framework to explain psychological variation on a worldwide scale (e.g., Oyserman, Coon, & Kemmelmeier, 2002).

In terms of limitations, work on individualism/ collectivism as well as on other related broad dichotomies, such as that between interdependent vs. independent self-construal (e.g., Markus & Kitayama, 1991) or between Easterners and Westerners (e.g., Nisbett, 2003) has been criticized for its stereotypical portrayal of these two cultural systems (e.g., Dien, 1999; J. G. Miller, 2002, 2004). Methodological criticisms have also been directed at the widespread use of attitudinal scale measures in work in this tradition (e.g., Kitayama, 2002), with theorists noting the many problems associated with the limited ability of individuals to report on their culture and with the inattention to everyday cultural practices, artifacts, and routines.

Sociocultural-Historical Approaches to Culture and Thought

Inspired by Vygotsky and other Soviet investigators (e.g., Vygotsky, 1929, 1934/1987, 1978; Luria, 1928, 1976), theorists in the early sociocultural-historical tradition assumed that culture has a formative influence on the emergence of thought. Rather than viewing development as proceeding independently of cultural learning, cultural learning was assumed to be necessary for development. Vygotskiian theory and related sociocultural-historical approaches emphasized the importance of tool use in extending cognitive capacities. From this perspective, cognitive development was seen as involving the internalization of the tools provided by the culture. Among the key cultural tools assumed to transform minds were literacy and formal schooling, through their assumed effects of providing exposure to abstract symbolic resources and giving rise to modes of reasoning that are relatively decontextualized and not directly tied to practical activity (e.g., Goody, 1968).

The earliest traditions of research undertaken by sociocultural historical theorists resembled those of Piagetian researchers in both their methods and their findings. After making minor modifications, experimental tests were administered to diverse cultural populations, that were selected to provide a contrast in the cultural processes thought to influence cognitive development, such as literacy and schooling (e.g., Bruner, Olver, & Greenfield, 1966; Cole, Gay, Glick, & Sharp, 1971). Early results revealed that individuals who were illiterate or who lacked formal education scored lower in cognitive development, failing to show such features as abstract conceptual development or propositional reasoning, which appeared as end points of cognitive development in Western industrialized contexts. Such findings supported a "primitive versus modern mind" interpretation of cultural differences, in which it was assumed that the cognitive development of certain populations remains arrested at lower developmental levels (Greenfield & Bruner, 1969).

Later experimental research in the socioculturalhistorical tradition challenged these early conclusions about global differences in thought and about the transformative impact of cultural tools on minds. Programs of cross-cultural research were undertaken that focused on unpacking the complex cognitive processes that are tapped in standard cognitive tests (Cole & Scribner, 1974). Also, processes such as memory were assessed in the context of socially meaningful material, such as stories, rather than merely in decontextualized ways, such as through the presentation of words. These and similar modifications showed that cognitive performance varied depending on features of the task and that cultural differences did not remain stable. In a landmark program of such research, Scribner and Cole (1981) conducted research among the Vai tribal community as a way of assessing the impact of literacy on thought independently of the effects of schooling. Although formal schooling enhanced performance on tests of cognitive achievement, it had limited generality to everyday domains of thought (Sharp, Cole, & Lave, 1979).

Overall, early work in the sociocultural-historical tradition established a strong foundation for contemporary cognitive research in cultural psychology. Whereas early findings suggested that culture had the effect of arresting the rate of cognitive development or the highest levels of cognitive development attained, this finding was qualified as conclusions pointed to the need for a more contextually based view of cognition. The initial image of global cultural differences in thought, linked to an image of a primitive versus modern mind, gave way to a view of common basic cognitive competencies.

Summary

In sum, early research in cross-cultural psychology and in the sociocultural-historical tradition laid a groundwork for contemporary research in cultural psychology. This early research, however, tended to remain in a relatively peripheral role in the discipline and not to impact fundamentally on psychological theory. Thus, in particular, work on culture and personality never challenged the universality of psychological theories. Work on individualism and collectivism was concerned with developing parameters that affected the level of development of particularly psychological phenomena, but not the nature of the psychological phenomena themselves. Although early research in the sociocultural-historical tradition approached cognitive processes as culturally dependent, it tended not to go beyond a contextually based view of cognition and claims of universal cognitive competencies in its implications for psychological theory.

Insights and Challenges of Cultural Psychology

Cultural psychology represents an eclectic interdisciplinary perspective that has many roots. In many (but not all) cases, investigators associated with some of these traditions of research in cross-cultural psychology moved toward a cultural psychological outlook in response to the perceived limitations of some of the conceptual frameworks and goals of their earlier research. Thus, for example, many leading investigators associated with culture and personality, such as individuals who worked on the Six Culture project (B. B. Whiting & Whiting, 1975), as well as those associated with early work in the sociocultural-historical tradition on culture and thought, are at the forefront of contemporary work in cultural psychology. Research in cultural psychology has also drawn from disciplinary perspectives outside psychology. Thus, within psychological and cognitive anthropology, many investigators moved in a cultural psychological direction both from a concern that some of the early theories of culture and personality were parochial and needed to be formulated in more culturally grounded terms and from a sense that to understand culture requires attention to psychological and not merely anthropological considerations (e.g., Lutz & White, 1986; T. Schwartz, White, & Lutz, 1992; Shore, 1996; Strauss & Quinn, 1997). Thus, for example, arguments were made that to avoid an oversocialized conception of the person as merely passively conforming to cultural expectations required taking into account the subjectivity of intentional agents (e.g., Strauss, 1992). In another major research tradition, interest developed in cultural work within sociolinguistics. Thus, in work on language learning, it was recognized that individuals come to acquire not only the code of their language but also the meaning systems of their culture through everyday language use (e.g., Heath, 1983; P. Miller, 1986;

Ochs & Schieffelin, 1984). Likewise, it came to be understood that everyday discourse contexts serve as a key context of cultural transmission.

Key Conceptual Premises

The perspective of cultural psychology is defined conceptually by its view of culture and psychology as mutually constitutive phenomena. From this perspective, cultural processes are seen as presupposing the existence of communities of intentional agents who contribute meanings and form to cultural beliefs, values, and practices. Psychological functioning is seen as dependent on cultural mediation, as individuals participate in and come to acquire, as well as create, and transform the shared meaning systems of the cultural communities in which they participate. It is this monistic assumption of psychological and cultural processes as mutually dependent—not the type of methodology adopted—that is central to cultural psychology. Thus, for example, whether an approach employs qualitative versus quantitative methods or comparative versus single cultural analysis does not mark whether the approach may be considered as within the tradition of cultural as compared with cross-cultural psychology.

Active Contribution of Meanings to Experience

A core assumption underlying cultural psychology is linked to the insight of the Cognitive Revolution regarding the importance of meanings in mediating behavior (Bruner, 1990). Individuals go beyond the information given as they contribute meanings to experience, with these meanings in turn influencing individuals' affective, cognitive, and behavioral reactions. The cultural implications of this cognitive shift were not appreciated immediately within psychology. Rather, as Bruner (1990) observes in presenting a brief history of the field, there was a tendency for many years to emphasize the autonomous self-construction of knowledge—independently of cultural transmission. The cultural implications of the Cognitive Revolution were also not apparent for many years because of the ascendance of information-processing accounts of cognition, which stress the automatic processing of information rather than the more active and creative processes of meaning making. Nonetheless, although this image of an active constructivist agent for many years was not linked with cultural viewpoints, it formed a valuable theoretical basis for cultural psychology. The recognition that an act of interpretation mediates between the stimulus and the response established a theoretical basis on which investigators could draw as they began to appreciate the cultural aspects of meanings and these meanings' impact on thought and behavior.

Symbolic Views of Culture

The development within anthropology of symbolic views of culture (Geertz, 1973; Sahlins, 1976; Shweder & LeVine, 1984) also contributed to the emergence of cultural psychology in that it highlighted the need to go beyond the prevailing tendency to treat culture merely in ecological terms as an aspect of the objective environment. Ecological views of culture have value in calling attention to the adaptive implications of features of the context (Bronfenbrenner, 1979). However, they also are limited in treating the context exclusively in objective terms, as presenting affordances and constraints that are functional in nature. In such frameworks, which have tended to be adopted in both mainstream and cross-cultural psychology, culture is seen as nonessential to the interpretation or construction of reality. In contrast, within symbolic approaches, cultural systems are understood as bearing an indeterminate or open relationship to objective constraints rather than being fully determined by adaptive contingencies. Within symbolic approaches to culture, cultural meanings are seen as serving not merely to represent reality, as in knowledge systems, or as serving a directive function, as in systems of social norms. Rather, they assume constitutive or reality-creating roles. In this latter role, cultural meanings serve to create social realities, whose existence rests partly on these cultural definitions (Shweder, 1984). This includes not only cases in which culturally based social definitions are integral to establishing particular social institutions and practices (e.g., marriage, graduation) but also cases in which such definitions form a key role in creating psychological realities. Thus, it is increasingly recognized that aspects of psychological functioning (e.g., emotions) depend, in part, for their existence on cultural distinctions embodied in natural language categories, discourse, and everyday practices. For example, the Japanese emotional experience of amae (Doi, 1973; Yamaguchi, 2001) presupposes not only the concepts reflected in this label but also norms and practices that support and promote it. As an emotional state, amae involves a positive feeling of depending on another's benevolence. At the level of social practices, amae is evident not only in caregiver-child interactions in early infancy (Doi, 1973, 1992), but also in the everyday interactions of adults, who are able to presume that their inappropriate behavior will be accepted by their counterparts in close relationships (Yamaguchi, 2001).

The significance of a symbolic view of culture for the development of cultural psychology was in its complementing the attention to meaning-making heralded by the cognitive revolution. It became clear not only were meanings in part socially constructed and publicly based, but they also could not be purely derived merely by inductive or deductive processing of objective information. In this way, culture became an additional essential factor in psychological explanation, rather than merely a focus on objective features of the context and subjective features of the person.

Incompleteness Thesis

Finally, and most critically, the theoretical grounding of cultural psychology emerged from the realization of the necessary role of culture in completion of the self, an insight that has been termed the incompleteness thesis (Geertz, 1973; Wertsch, 1995). This stance does not assume the absence of innate capacities or downplay the impact of biological influences as a source of patterning of individual psychological processes. However, without making the assumption that psychological development is totally open in direction, with no biological influences either on its initial patterning or on its subsequent developmental course, this stance calls attention to the essential role of culture in the emergence of higher-order psychological processes. Individuals are viewed not only as developing in culturally specific environments and utilizing culturally specific tools, but also as carrying with them, in their language and meanings systems, culturally based assumptions through which they interpret experience. Although there has been a tendency within psychology to treat this culturally specific input as noise that should be filtered out or controlled in order to uncover basic features of psychological functioning, the present considerations suggest that it is omnipresent and cannot be held constant or eliminated. Rather, it is understood that the culturally specific meanings and practices that are essential for the emergence of higher-order psychological processes invariably introduce a certain cultural-historical specificity to psychological functioning. As Geertz (1973) once noted:

> We are . . . incomplete or unfinished animals who complete or finish ourselves through culture—and not through culture in general but through highly particular forms of it. (p. 49)

From the present perspective, it is assumed that whereas an involuntary response may proceed without cultural mediation, culture is necessary for the emergence of higher-order psychological processes. Wertsch (1995) articulates this point:

> Cultural, institutional, and historical forces are 'imported' into individuals' actions by virtue of using cultural tools, on the one hand, and sociocultural settings are created and recreated through individuals' use of mediational means, on the other. The resulting picture is one in which, because of the role cultural tools play in mediated action, it is virtually impossible for us to act in a way that is not socioculturally situated. Nearly all human action is mediated action, the only exceptions being found perhaps at very early stages of ontogenesis and in natural responses such as reacting involuntarily to an unexpected loud noise. (p. 160)

Thus, for example, whereas involuntary physiological reactions may be elicited by situational events, whether they become interpreted and experienced in emotional terms depends in part on such input as culturally based theories regarding the nature, causes, and consequences of emotions, cultural routines for responding to emotions, natural language categories for defining emotions, and a range of other sociocultural processes.

This assumption of the interdependence of psychological and cultural processes represents the central idea of cultural psychology. Notably, the term *cultural psychology* was selected by theorists to convey this central insight that psychological processes need to be understood as always grounded in particular sociocultural-historical contexts that influence their form and patterning, just as cultural communities depend for their existence on particular communities of intentional agents. The present considerations then lead to the expectation that qualitative differences in modes of psychological functioning will be observed among individuals from cultural communities characterized by contrasting self-related sociocultural meanings and practices.

Summary

Among the key conceptual insights giving rise to cultural psychology were the emergence of a view of the individual as actively contributing meanings to experience and an understanding of culture as a symbolic system of meanings and practices that cannot be explained exclusively in functional terms as mapping onto objective adaptive constraints. Crucial to the field's development was that it also came to be recognized that higher-order psychological processes depend for their emergence on individuals' participation in particular sociocultural contexts, and thus that culture is fundamental to the development of self.

Select Overview of Empirical Research in Cultural Psychology

The present section reviews studies in social psychology that embody this core insight regarding the cultural grounding of psychological processes, an insight that is central to the many traditions of work in cultural psychology (e.g., Cole, 1990, 1996; Markus et al., 1996; J. G. Miller, 1997; Shweder, 1990; Shweder et al., 1998). While the overview is selective in the range of research it considers as well as in its focus on work in social psychology, the overview serves to illustrate ways in which cultural research is offering new insights into the cultural grounding of psychological phenomena. Consideration here is given to sample cultural psychological research on core substantive topics in social psychology. In each case, the work reviewed identifies variability in basic psychological processes.

Social Attribution

In early groundbreaking work on social attribution, Shweder and Bourne (1984) challenged the completeness of contemporary social psychological theories of social attribution. It was documented that, as compared with European-Americans, Hindu Indians place significantly greater emphasis in person description on actions versus abstract traits, with their person descriptions more frequently making reference to the context. Thus, for example, their investigation revealed that whereas European-Americans are more likely to describe a friend by saying she is friendly, Indians are more likely to describe the friend by saying she brings cakes to my family on festival days. This type of cultural difference was not explicable in terms of the types of ecological or individual psychological factors that had been emphasized in previous studies, such as variation in schooling, literacy, socioeconomic status, linguistic resources, or capacities for abstract thought. Rather, the trends were demonstrated to reflect the contrasting cultural conceptions of the person and related sociocultural practices emphasized in Hindu Indian versus European-American cultural communities.

Subsequent cross-cultural developmental research on social attribution demonstrated that these types of cultural considerations give rise to variation in the paths and endpoints of development (J. G. Miller, 1984, 1987). It was documented that whereas European-American children show an age increase in their reference to traits (e.g., "she is aggressive") but no age-related change in their reference to contextual considerations, Hindu Indian children show an age increase in their references to the social context (e.g., "there are bad relations between our families") but no age increase in their references to traits. This type of work has been extended to understanding the development of theory of mind, with cultural work calling into question claims that theory of mind understandings develop spontaneously toward an endpoint of trait psychology (Lillard, 1998; Wellman & Miller, 2008).

The research has also been extended to the domain of autobiographical memory, with work by Qi Wang and her colleagues documenting that the age of first autobiographical memories are earlier among the U.S. than among Chinese populations, and that the content of these memories vary in ways that reflect cross-cultural differences observed in social attribution (Han, Leichtman & Wang, 1998; Wang, 2001, 2004; Wang & Leichtman, 2000). Thus, whereas the autobiographical memories of U.S. children and adults tend to be focused on the self's unique perspective, the autobiographical memories of Chinese children and adults tend to focus on everyday social routines and to include more information about social relations.

In other lines of work on social attribution and cognition, cultural research is calling into question the universality of various attribution tendencies long assumed to be basic to all psychological functioning. Thus, for example, it has been demonstrated that Japanese college students tend to maintain weaker beliefs in attitude-behavior consistency than do Australian college students (Kashima, Siegal, Tanaka, & Kashima, 1992), while being less prone than are North American college students to show cognitive dissonance biases—that is, tendencies to distort attitudes and beliefs to make them more congruent with behavior (Heine & Lehman, 1997; Hoshino-Browne, Zanna, Spencer, Zanna, Kitayama & Lackenbauer, 2005; Kitayama, Snibbe, Markus & Suzuki, 2004). Also, relative to European-Americans, East Asians have been found to be less prone to the fundamental attributional error (Ji, Peng, & Nisbett, 2000), a tendency to treat behaviors as correspondent with dispositions. Likewise, reflecting their sensitivity to context, Japanese show less vulnerability than do Americans to the correspondence bias, a tendency to infer corresponding attitudes in a person whose behavior is constrained (Masuda & Kitayama, 2004). It has also been found that Chinese, as compared with Americans, are less influenced by the response alternatives presented on rating scales when reporting on unobservable behavior, an effect seen as reflecting the emphasis in collectivist cultures on monitoring of behavior to avoid inappropriate conduct (Ji, Schwarz & Nisbett, 2000).

Cognitive Styles and Perception

Extending this earlier attributional work, a line of research has also developed to support the claim that cultural variation exists at the level of core epistemological presuppositions that impact on basic perceptual processes. In particular, the claim has been made by Nisbett and his colleagues that East Asian outlooks embody a holistic viewpoint that approaches thought in a dialectical way that makes little use of formal logic, whereas Western outlooks embody an analytic viewpoint that focuses attention on objects and that relies on rules and formal logic (Nisbett, 2003; Nisbett, Peng, Choi, & Norenzayan, 2001; Peng & Nisbett, 1999). These contrasting outlooks are seen as having their origins historically in markedly different social and cultural systems that existed in Ancient Greek and Chinese society, which were characterized by contrasting emphases on aspects such as personal agency versus social harmony, and on free debate versus social control. In terms of implications for psychology, holistic as compared with analytic thought is shown to impact on logic as well as on basic perceptual processes.

In terms of logic, the contrast is drawn between dialectical outlooks associated with Chinese and other East Asian cultural perspectives that emphasize seeking a "middle way" between opposing positions that might otherwise appear as seeming contradictions, in contrast to an analytic outlook that constitutes a lay version of Aristotelian logic and emphasizes resolving apparently contradictory positions to derive one assumed correct outlook. Reflecting this type of contrast, experimental research has demonstrated that when presented with different types of arguments, Chinese, as compared with U.S. participants, preferred dialectical over classical Western arguments (Peng & Nisbett, 1999; see also Ji, Nisbett, & Su, 2001). Also, when presented with apparently contradictory propositions, Chinese were moderately accepting of both positions while Americans adopted more polarized outlooks. These contrasting perspectives have also been shown to affect knowledge related to the self. Thus, for example, research has shown that contradictory self-knowledge is more accessible among Japanese and Chinese than among Euro-Americans (Spencer-Rodgers, Boucher, Mori, Wang, & Peng, 2009; Spencer-Rodgers, Williams, & Peng, 2010). Notably, recent research is also pointing to a culturally variable preference for holistic as compared with analytic modes of thought (Buchtel & Norenzayan, 2008) and suggesting that the emphasis on holistic thinking found in East Asian cultures leads to a greater cultivation of expert forms of intuitive thinking, such as meditation practices, than found in the West (Buchtel & Norenzayan, 2009).

The contrast in analytic as compared with holistic thinking is also viewed as giving rise to shifts in perception, with East Asian populations more sensitive to contextual features of their environment than are Euro-Americans. For example, in experimental research, Japanese and Americans were shown animated vignettes of underwater scenes and in a subsequent recognition test asked to judge whether they had been previously shown specific objects that were now presented in either a new or in their original settings (Masuda & Nisbett, 2001). Only the responses of Japanese were affected by the contextual information, with Japanese respondents more accurate when they saw objects in their original setting as compared with a novel setting, and U.S. respondents unaffected by this contextual manipulation. These same types of culturally based perceptual differences have also been shown to affect the phenomena of change blindness, a phenomenon in visual perception in which large changes occurring in full view in a visual scene are not noticed (Simons & Rensink, 2005). Whereas research on change blindness has established that Americans are more sensitive to changes in focal objects than to objects in the periphery or context, cultural research demonstrates that the opposite trend occurs among East Asians, who are more sensitive to contextual change information than to focal object changes (Masuda & Nisbett, 2006). Work on visual perception also documents that European-Americans are spontaneously more attentive to using part-object cues in perceptual inference than are Asian Americans (Ishii, Tsukasaki, & Kitayama, 2009). Similar types of cultural differences in perception have been documented on the framed-line test (Kitayama, Duffy, Kawamura, & Larsen, 2003). This task involves involves presenting individuals first with a square frame within which is printed a vertical line, and next with a second square frame of the same or different size, and asking the participants to draw a line that either is the same absolute length as in the first frame (absolute task) or that is of the same proportion relative to the height of the surrounding frame (relative task). Cultural differences are found to occur, with Americans performing better on the absolute task and Japanese performing better on the relative task.

Recent work in this tradition has also focused on identifying the mechanisms underlying these types of perceptual differences, such as variation in allocation of attention. Researchers utilizing a visual change detection task found that East Asians are better than Americans at detecting color changes when a set of colored blocks is expanded to cover a wide region and are worse than Americans when it is shrunk in size (Boduroglu, Shah, & Nisbett, 2009). Such findings support the claim that relative to Americans, East Asians tend to allocate their attention more broadly, which may be related to their overall greater context sensitivity.

Recent work has also traced this type of difference to features of the physical and cultural environment. A study that involved presenting both U.S. and Japanese college students with photographs of locations in cities in the United States, as well as in Japan, revealed that in both cultural groups the Japanese scenes tended to be seen as including more elements than did the U.S. scenes, providing support for the claim that cultural variation in patterns of attention relate to contrasting affordances of the physical context (Miyamoto, Nisbett, & Masuda, 2006). The same types of cultural differences have been found in research that involved comparing drawings of landscape pictures as well as photographs taken by U.S. and East Asian college students, as well as that analyzed styles found in Western as compared with East Asian art, with East Asian artistic products characterized by greater context inclusiveness and less object centeredness than Western artistic products (Masuda, Gonzalez, Kwan, & Nisbett, 2008).

Self-Processes

In the area of the self-concept, psychological research is challenging the long-standing assumption that individuals spontaneously engage in self-maintenance strategies that are oriented toward self-enhancement, and that self-esteem is universally fundamental to psychological well-being (Heine, Lehman, Markus & Kitayama, 1999). Open-ended attributional research on self-description has documented that whereas the open-ended self-descriptions of U.S. adults emphasize positive attributes (Herzog, Franks, Markus, & Holmberg, 1998), those of Japanese adults emphasize either weakness or the absence of negative self-characteristics (e.g., I'm poor at math, I'm not selfish). Research has also documented that whereas the scores of Americans on measures of self-esteem tend to be higher than the scale midpoints—an indication of a tendency toward self-enhancement—those of Japanese tend to be at or slightly below the scale midpoint, an indication of a tendency to view the self as similar to others (E. Diener & Diener, 1995).

In a growing body of research, investigators are also examining the boundaries of this cultural difference in self-enhancement and associated processes. Thus, for example, research that has utilized a modified version of the Implicit Association Test (Greenwald & Farnham, 2000) among Japanese and American populations indicates that the cultural difference in self-enhancement does not tend to occur when assessed on an implicit level or in a context that does not involve emotional interdependence, but does occur at an explicit level (Kitayama & Uchida, 2003). The growing body of work conducted on this topic also indicates that self-enhancement among East Asians does not tend to occur with methods that involve directly comparing oneself to the average other, though is evident in methods in which separate judgments of self and others are made (Hamamura, Heine, & Takemoto, 2007; Heine & Hamamura, 2007; Rose, Endo, Windschitl, & Suls, 2008). However, whereas this recent work provides some indication that some level of tactical self-enhancement is universal, it supports the claim of marked cross-cultural differences in the prominence of self-enhancement and in its impact on behavior (Heine, Kitayama, & Hamamura, 2007).

One of the most far-reaching implications of this type of research is that it calls into question the centrality of self-esteem in psychological functioning in collectivist cultural communities, and suggests that other types of self-processes may be more central in everyday adaptation in such contexts. In this regard, cross-national survey research has shown that self-esteem is more closely associated with life satisfaction in individualist than in collectivist cultures (E. Diener & Diener, 1995). In contrast, a concern with maintaining relationship harmony shows a stronger relationship with life satisfaction in collectivist than in individualist cultures (Gabrenya & Hwang, 1996). These contrasting patterns of interrelationship distinguish everyday socialization practices and have adaptive consequences. Thus, for example, Chinese as well as Japanese mothers tend to be more self-critical of their children's academic performance than are U.S. mothers (Crystal & Stevenson, 1991), with this stance implicated in the tendencies of Chinese and Japanese versus U.S. mothers to place greater emphasis on their children's exerting effort to achieve academically (Stevenson & Lee, 1990). Research has also shown that whereas North Americans persist less on tasks after failure than after success, Japanese persist more after failure (Heine et al., 2001). This cultural difference is seen as resulting from the greater tendencies of Japanese to experience negative feedback as constructive rather than as a threat to their self-esteem, given their lesser tendencies to self-enhance.

Cultural research on the self is also challenging psychological theory in the domain of self-consistency. Social psychological theory has long assumed that individuals are inherently motivated to maintain a consistent view of the self and that such consistency is integral to psychological well-being. This stance is evident not only in classic theories of cognitive dissonance (Festinger, 1957), but also in more recent work on attribution. For example, work on self-verification has shown that individuals tend to prefer information that is consistent rather than inconsistent about themselves (Swann, Wenzlaff, Krull, & Pelham, 1992), as well as that autobiographical memories are structured in ways that preserve a consistent sense of self (Ross, 1989). In addition, work on psychological health has suggested that having an integrated and consistent view of self has adaptive value (Jourard, 1965; Suh, 2000).

A growing body of attributional research in Asian cultures, however, suggests in these cultures that the self tends to be experienced as more fluid than is typically observed in U.S. populations. Work on self-description has demonstrated, for example, that the self-descriptions of Japanese but not of Americans tend to vary as a function of the presence of others (Kanagawa, Cross, & Markus, 2001). Likewise, experimental research has documented that cognitive dissonance effects tend not to be observed among Japanese as compared with Canadian populations (Heine & Lehman, 1997), and that consistency across situations shows a much weaker relationship to psychological well-being among Korean as compared with American populations (Suh, 2000).

Emotions

Emotions provide a particularly challenging area for cultural research because they involve not merely cognition but also behavioral action tendencies and somatic reactions. Notably, as suggested in the following discussion, culture affects the expression of emotions and their form, as well as their role in mental health outcomes.

One influence of cultural processes on emotion occurs in the degree of an emotion's elaboration or suppression. It has been documented that cultural meanings and practices affect the extent to which particular emotions are hypercognized (in the sense that they are highly differentiated and implicated in many everyday cultural concepts and practices) versus hypocognized (in that there is little cognitive or behavioral elaboration of them; Levy, 1984). Even universal emotions play contrasting roles in individual experience in different cultural settings. For example, whereas in all cultures both socially engaged feelings (e.g., friendliness, connection) and socially disengaged feelings (e.g., pride, feelings of superiority) may exist; however, among Japanese only socially engaged feelings are linked with general positive feelings, whereas among Americans both types of emotions have positive links (Kitayama, Markus, & Kurokawa, 2000; Kitayama, Mesquita, & Karasawa, 2006).

Cross-cultural differences have also been observed in emotion categories as well as in individuals' appraisals of emotions. Variation in emotion concepts has been documented not only in the case of culturally specific categories of emotion, such as the concept of amae among the Japanese (Russell & Yik, 1996; Wierzbicka, 1992), but also among such assumed basic emotions as anger and sadness (Russell, 1991, 1994). For example, Turkish adults make different appraisals of common emotional experiences than do Dutch adults, whose cultural background is more individualist (Mesquita, 2001). Thus, as compared with Dutch adults, Turkish adults tend to categorize emotions as more grounded in assessments of social worth, as more reflective of reality than of the inner subjective states of the individual, and as located more within the self-other relationship than confined within the subjectivity of the individual. In addition, research documents that a relationship exists between dialectical reasoning and emotional experience, with Japanese, as compared with Americans, more prone to report experiencing both positive and negative emotions simultaneously about the same experience (Miyamoto, Uchida, & Ellsworth, 2010; Spencer et al., 2010).

Notably, work on culture and emotions is also providing evidence of the open relationship that exists between physiological and somatic reactions, social relationships, and emotional experiences. For example, research has revealed that although Minangkabu and U.S. men show the same patterns of autonomic nervous system arousal to voluntary posing of prototypical emotion facial expressions, they differ in their emotional experiences (Levenson, Ekman, Heider, & Friesen, 1992). Whereas Americans tend to interpret their arousal in this type of situation in emotional terms, Minangkabu tend not to experience emotion in such cases, because it violates their culturally based assumptions that social relations constitute an essential element in emotional experience. Likewise, it has been shown that Japanese show a greater tendency than do Americans to infer emotions based on relationships rather than on oneself (Uchida, Townsend, & Markus, 2009).

Cultural influences on the mental health consequences of affective arousal are also being documented. For example, various somatic experiences—such as fatigue, loss of appetite, or agitation—that are given a psychological interpretation as emotions by European-Americans tend not to be interpreted in emotional terms but rather as purely physiological events among individuals from various Asian, South American, and African cultural backgrounds (Shweder, Much, Mahapatra, & Park, 1997). Notably, such events tend to be explained as originating in problems of interpersonal relationships, thus requiring some form of nonpsychological form of intervention for their amelioration (Rosaldo, 1984; White, 1994).

Motivation, Morality, and Attachment

Whereas early cross-cultural research on motivation was informed exclusively by existing theoretical models, such as Rotter's framework of internal versus external locus of control (Rotter, 1966), recent work suggests that motivation may assume socially shared forms. This kind of focus, for example, is reflected in the construct of secondary control, which has been identified among Japanese populations, in which individuals are seen as demonstrating agency via striving to adjust to situational demands (Morling, 2000; Morling, Kitayama, & Miyamoto, 2002, 2003; Weisz, Rothbaum, & Blackburn, 1984). Likewise, research in India is pointing to the existence of joint forms of control, in which the agent and the family or other social groups are experienced as together equally important in bringing about certain outcomes (Sinha, 1990).

In another related area of work on motivation, research is highlighting the positive affective associations linked with social expectations. For example, behavioral research has documented that Asian-American children experience greater intrinsic motivation for an anagrams task that has been selected for them by their mothers than for one that they have freely chosen (Iyengar & Lepper, 1999). In contrast, European-American children experience greater intrinsic motivation when they have selected such a task for themselves.

Support for the view that agency is compatible with meeting social expectations may also be seen in attribution research, which has shown that Indian adults report wanting to help as much and deriving as much satisfaction from helping when acting to fulfill norms of reciprocity as compared with when acting in the absence of such normative expectations (J. G. Miller & Bersoff, 1994). Indians also associate a sense of choice with the fulfillment of role-related interpersonal responsibilities and social expectations to meet the needs of family and friends tend to be more fully internalized among Indians than among Americans (J. G. Miller, Das, & Chakravarthy, 2011). Although these types of findings support the assertion made by self-determination theorists that in all cultures agency involves individuals coming subjectively to experience their actions in terms of internalized motivational factors (Chirkov, Ryan, Kim, & Kaplan, 2003), they underscore the need in work on self-determination theory to recognize that cultural variation exists in the affective meanings of duty and in the degree to which acting out of a sense of role based duty rather than only out of psychological motives, such as values or felt importance, is experienced in agentic ways.

In turn, research in the domain of morality with both Hindu Indian populations (Shweder, Mahapatra, & Miller, 1990) and among orthodox religious communities within the United States (Jensen, 1997) has documented forms of morality based on concerns with divinity that are not encompassed by existing psychological theories of morality (e.g., Kohlberg, 1971; Turiel, 1983). Furthermore, work on moralities of community (J. G. Miller, 1994, 2001; Snarey & Keljo, 1991) has documented the individualistic cultural assumptions that inform Gilligan's morality of caring framework (Gilligan, 1982). This research reveals that in collectivist cultural settings responsibilities to meet the needs of family and friends tend to be regarded as role related duties rather than, as assumed by Gilligan, self-chosen commitments.

In terms of relationship research, a growing cross-cultural literature on attachment is suggesting that some of the observed variation in distribution of secure versus nonsecure forms of attachment arises, at least in part, from contrasting cultural values related to attachment, rather than from certain cultural subgroups having less adaptive styles of attachment. For example, research conducted among Puerto Rican families suggests that the greater tendency of children to show highly dependent forms of attachment reflects the contrasting meanings that they place on interdependent behavior. An analysis of open-ended responses of mothers revealed that compared with European-American mothers, Puerto Rican mothers viewed dependent behavior relatively positively as evidence of the child's relatedness to the mother. Suggesting that present dimensions of attachment may not be fully capturing salient concerns for Puerto Rican mothers, this work further demonstrated that Puerto Rican mothers spontaneously emphasized other concerns—such as display of respect and of tranquillity—that are not tapped by present attachment formulations.

In other research, work on attachment among Japanese populations highlights the greater emphasis on indulgence of the infant's dependency and on affectively based rather than informationally oriented communication in Japanese versus American families (Rothbaum, Kakinuma, Nagaoka, & Azuma, 2007; Rothbaum, Weisz, Pott, Miyake, & Morelli, 2000, 2001). In contrast to the predictions of attachment theory, however, such forms of parenting are not associated with maladaptive outcomes; rather, these parenting styles have positive adaptive implications in fitting in with the cultural value placed on *amae*, an orientation that involves being able to depend on the other person's good will and that plays a central role in close relationships throughout the life cycle (for related claims see also, Carlson & Harwood, 2003; Harwood, Miller, & Irizarry, 1995).

Summary

Work in cultural psychology is not only documenting cultural variability in psychological outcomes, but is also focused on uncovering respects in which this variation highlights the implicit cultural underpinnings of existing psychological effects. We have seen the existence of contrasting culturally based cognitive styles, as well as extensive cultural variation in basic psychological processes involving the self, emotions, motivation, morality, and attachment.

New Directions and Challenges

Not only has there been a dramatic increase in the number of culturally based investigations being undertaken in social psychology in recent years, but this work is proceeding in new directions. Brief consideration is given here to identifying some of these new directions as well as to pinpointing both longstanding and new challenges of social psychological work in cultural psychology.

Within and Between Cultural Variation

A valuable new direction of cultural work in social psychology is to give greater attention to within- and between-culture variation linked to regional, cultural, as well as socioeconomic differences. Such work is pointing to varieties of individualism and collectivism as well as to the impact of differential resources and experiences on cultural outlooks.

In terms of within-culture variation, greater attention is being given to regional variation. For example, variations in cultural perspectives occur within the United States that reflect the historical experiences and outlooks that develop in particular areas (Kitayama, Conway, Pietromonaco, Park, & Plaut, 2010). In this regard, for example, Nisbett and Cohen have documented the concerns with a culture of honor in southern and western parts of the United States and shown its widespread impact on attitudes and behavior (Nisbett & Cohen, 1996). In work on psychological well-being conducted among a nationally representative sample of midlife Americans, Plaut and her colleagues have also identified distinct regional concerns, such as a concern in New England with not being socially constrained, as compared with a concern with personal growth and feeling cheerful and happy in the Southwest (Plaut, Markus, & Lachman, 2002; Markus, Plaut, & Lachman, 2004).

Increasingly researchers are also attending to variation linked to socioeconomic status. For example, ethnographic research conducted among European-Americans has documented that within lower-class and working-class communities there tends tend to be a "hard defensive" type of individualism, which stresses the adoption of abilities to cope in harsh everyday environments, in contrast with the "soft" individualism found in upper middle class contexts, which stresses the cultivation of individual uniqueness and gratification (Kusserow, 1999). Research also suggests that lower SES individuals, as compared to higher SES individuals, are more prone to act in a prosocial manner (Piff, Kraus, Cote, Cheng, & Keltner, 2010), have a reduced sense of personal control (Kraus, Piff, & Keltner, 2009), are more cognizant of others in their social environment (Kraus & Keltner, 2009), place greater emphasis on contextual considerations, and are more empathically accurate (Kraus, Cote, & Keltner, 2010). The claim has also been made that the modes of agency emphasized within working class communities resemble those found in collectivist cultures in focusing more on social and relational styles than do the models of agency found within middle class communities in the United States (Snibbe & Markus, 2005; Stephens, Markus, & Townsend, 2007).

Greater attention is also being given in recent years to expanding research beyond the simple comparisons of Asian and North American populations. This is seen, for example, in work that has shown that Central and East Europeans, like East Asians, tend to be more holistic than are U.S. populations (Varnum, Grossmann, Katunar, Nisbett, & Kitayama, 2008), and that southern Italians, who culturally are relatively more interdependent, tend to reason in a more holistic way than do northern Italians (Knight & Nisbett, 2007).

In terms of challenges, while this attention to within- and between cultural diversity represents a valuable direction to continue to pursue in future work, it is also valuable to approach it with more culturally grounded theoretical understandings and in terms of new dimensions. For example, while there may be similarities on certain psychological dimensions between the responses of working class individuals within the United States and the responses of various collectivist populations, marked differences distinguish these subgroups and thus they should not be regarded as equivalent or identical in outlook. As a way of theoretically sharpening existing explanatory

frameworks, it is crucial to continue to extend consideration of cultural variation beyond comparisons of Asian and North American populations and between contrasts on such well-worn dimensions as analytic/holistic thought or interdependent versus independent self-construal, a distinction that continues to be emphasized (Varnum, Grossmann, Kitayama, & Nisbett, 2010). For example, to the extent that holistic thinking is found not only in East Asian cultural communities, but is also evident in India as well as in various European cultural groups, theories that explain the origins of these modes of thought in terms of historical traditions linked to Greek and Chinese thought will be shown to be limited in explanatory force. Also, to the extent that communities are understood in more culturally nuanced ways, it will be possible to identify more subtle and dynamic differences distinguishing different cultural and subcultural viewpoints.

Priming and Process Accounts of Culture

One of the newest directions of cultural research in social psychology is the effort to tap culturally based processes by means of priming, a procedure that involves implicit memory effects in which exposing someone to a stimulus influences their responses to a later stimulus. This type of effort increasingly has been adopted in efforts to prime individualism and collectivism directly (Oyserman & Lee, 2008). For example, widely used primes developed by Brewer and Gardner (1996) ask participants to read a paragraph describing a trip made either alone or with others and to circle either first-person singular pronouns (in the individualistic priming condition) or plural pronouns (in the collectivist priming condition). The typical finding is for the effects of primed individualism and collectivism to parallel differences observed in cross-national comparisons undertaken between individualistic and collectivist populations. As an example, whereas Hong Kong students preferred a compromise choice when primed with collectivism (Briley & Wyer, 2002), they preferred a choice based on their personal preferences when primed with individualism.

In other approaches to priming research, priming focuses not on dimensions associated directly with individualism/collectivism but with the specific behavioral or cognitive processes believed to underlie a given effect. For example, in recent work, the assumption that differences in compassion explain the tendency for lower-class individuals to be more altruistic than upper-class individuals was experimentally supported by manipulating participants' experiences of compassion and assessing their tendencies to help another person in distress (Piff et al.,

2010). Supporting the study hypotheses, results indicated that upper class participants exhibited greater compassion in the compassion condition than in the baseline condition.

Notably, culturally based work on priming is seen, by some theorists as providing support for a situated cognition or a dynamic social constructivist view of cultural variation, in calling into question claims of fixed global differences in cultural outlook (Oyserman, Sorensen, Reber, & Chen, 2009: Weber & Morris, 2010). This work is also significant more generally, in empirically identifying mediators and moderators of any observed effects.

However, while priming represents a productive new direction for cultural research in social psychology, it is also vital to underscore its limitations and the need to go beyond current priming approaches to tap culture in more process-oriented terms. For example, the demonstration in priming work that cultural differences are contextually dependent may represent a corrective to models that portray the impact of culture on psychological processes in overly generalized ways. However, as critiques have argued (Miller, 2002), priming approaches to culture tend to be adopted in ways that reduce culture to a mere contextual effect. As also has been noted (Markus & Kitayama, 2010), it is vital to understand the contrasting cultural meanings associated with global constructs such as independence and interdependence, as well as to better understand what is likely to be the contrasting cultural knowledge elicited by priming techniques. More generally, it is crucial to avoid the tendency, assumed in certain recent social psychological research on cultural priming, to assume that priming is a means of directly "measuring" culture. In addition, it should not be assumed that culture can be measured by utilizing attitudinal scale measures, given the understanding of culture as socially shared meanings and practices rather than as individual psychological tendencies (e.g., Markus & Kitayama, 2010; Miller, 1997; Shweder & LeVine, 1984).

Cultural Neuroscience

Finally, one of the newest directions of recent cultural research is to understand the neurological correlates of culturally variable psychological phenomena (e.g., Ambady & Bharucha, 2009; Chiao & Ambady, 2007). One of the contributions of this type of work is to identify the neurological correlates of known cross-cultural differences. For example, recent cross-cultural research comparing the performance of American and East Asian college students on simple visuospatial tasks has found that activation in the frontal and parietal brain regions, which are known to be associated with attentional control, were more strongly activated during culturally nonpreferred as compared with culturally preferred judgments. This work provides evidence on a neurological level of cross-cultural differences observed in behavior, while demonstrating that culture moderates activation in brain networks (Hedden, Ketay, Aron, Markus, & Gabrieli, 2008).

Work in cultural neuroscience is also providing unique insight into neural plasticity. For example, consistent with cross-cultural differences observed on a behavioral level, it has been shown that U.S. adults show more engagement of object-processing areas in the ventral visual cortex than do Chinese young adults when assessed on a visuospatial task (Gutchess, Welsh, Boduroglu, & Park, 2006). However, this cultural difference is magnified with aging, with elderly Singaporeans displaying larger deficits in object processing brain areas than do elderly Americans (Chee et al., 2006). Providing insight into the relative contributions of biological and experiential factors in human aging, this research provides neurological support for a "use it or lose it" view of cognitive aging (Park & Huang, 2010) and highlights the unique role that cultural research can play in understanding brain-behavior relationships.

However, even with the contemporary widespread enthusiasm for this type of research and the respect that it gains in the larger discipline through linking cultural work to natural science visions of psychology (Kagan, 2007), challenges exist in the adoption of neuroscience techniques. Neuroscience techniques in many cases serve only to provide evidence that is congruent with known psychological findings while adding little if any new theoretical insights. It is also critical to recognize the extent to which many contemporary programs of research in neuroscience are circular in their conclusions, if not in cases deterministic. Thus, for example, Miller and Kinsbourne (2011) point out how recent claims by Chiao et al. (2009) to be able "to predict how individualistic or collectivist a person is across cultures" (p. 2813) by reference to patterns of brain activation are based on a circular process of inference. In particular, their conclusions depend on past cross-cultural findings related to the attributional differences they seek to predict. Additionally, neurological evidence is frequently applied in a deterministic way to argue for the biological bases of psychological phenomena, including cross-cultural differences, without taking into account respects in which brain imagining is unable to explain meaning.

Summary

Cultural research in social psychology is extending into a range of new directions, with this work giving more attention both to between and within-culture variation in outlooks, exploring ways that priming techniques can provide insight into the contextual dependence of culturally influenced psychological effects, and expanding an understanding of brain-behavior relationships through work in cultural neuroscience. However, challenges remain in going beyond views of culture that remain overly global and stereotypical, and in identifying theoretical frameworks that can incorporate new methodologies while still providing creative new insights into the cultural grounding of basic psychological processes.

CONCLUSION

In conclusion, the present examination of culture in social psychological theory highlights the importance of recognizing that culture is part of human experience and needs to be an explicit part of psychological theories that purport to predict, explain, and understand that experience. What work in cultural psychology aims to achieve, and what it has already accomplished in many respects, is more than to lead investigators to treat psychological findings and processes as limited in generality. Rather than leading to an extreme relativism that precludes comparison, work in this area holds the promise of leading to the formulation of models of human experience that are increasingly culturally inclusive. By calling attention to cultural meanings and practices that form the implicit context for existing psychological effects, and by broadening present conceptions of the possibilities of human psychological functioning, work in cultural psychology is contributing new constructs, research questions, and theoretical insights to expand and enrich basic psychological theory.

REFERENCES

Ambady, N., & Bharucha, J. (2009). Culture and the brain. *Current Directions in Psychological Science, 18*, 342–345.

Bargh, J. A. (1996). Automaticity in social psychology. In E. T. Higgins & A. Kruglanski (Eds.), *Social psychology: Handbook of basic principles* (pp. 169–183). New York, NY: Guilford Press.

Benedict, R. (1946). *The chrysanthemum and the sword*. Boston, MA: Houghton Mifflin.

Berry, J. W., Poortinga, Y. H., Segall, M. H., & Dasen, P. R. (1992). *Cross-cultural psychology: Research and applications*. Cambridge, UK: Cambridge University Press.

Boduroglu, A., Shah, P., & Nisbett, R. (2009). Cultural differences in allocation of attention in visual information processing. *Journal of Cross-Cultural Psychology, 40*, 349–360.

Bornstein, R. F., Kale, A. R., & Cornell, K. R. (1990). Boredom as a limiting condition on the mere exposure effect. *Journal of Personality and Social Psychology, 42*, 239–247.

Brewer, M. B., & Gardner, W. (1996). Who is this "we"? Levels of collective identity and self representations. *Journal of Personality and Social Psychology, 71*, 83–93.

Briley, D. A., & Wyer, R. S. (2002). The effect of group membership salience on the avoidance of negative outcomes: Implications for social and consumer decisions. *Journal of Consumer Research, 29*, 400–415.

Brislin, R. W. (1983). Cross-cultural research in psychology. *Annual Review of Psychology, 34*, 363–400.

Bronfenbrenner, U. (1979). *The ecology of human development: Experiments by nature and design*. Cambridge, MA: Harvard University Press.

Bruner, J. S. (1990). *Acts of meaning*. Cambridge, MA: Harvard University Press.

Bruner, J. S., Olver, R. R., & Greenfield, P. M. (1966). *Studies in cognitive growth: A collaboration at the Center for Cognitive Studies*. New York, NY: Wiley.

Buchtel, E., & Norenzayan, A. (2008). Which should you use, intuition or logic? Cultural differences in injunctive norms about reasoning. *Asian Journal of Social Psychology, 11*, 264–273.

Buchtel, E., & Norenzayan, A. (2009). Thinking across cultures: Implications for dual processes. In J. Evans & K. Frankish (Eds.), *In two minds: Dual processes and beyond* (pp. 217–238). New York, NY: Oxford University Press.

Carlson, V. J., & Harwood, R. L. (2003). Attachment, culture, and the caregiving system: The cultural patterning of everyday experiences among Anglo and Puerto Rican mother-infant pairs. *Infant Mental Health Journal, 24*, 53–73.

Chee, M. W. L., Goh, J. O. S., Venkatraman, V., Tan, J. C., Gutchess, A., Sutton, B., ... Park, D. (2006). Age-related changes in object processing and contextual binding revealed using *fMR* adaptation. *Journal of Cognitive Neuroscience, 18*, 495–507.

Chang, H., & Holt, G. R. (1991). The concept of yuan and Chinese interpersonal relationships. In S. Ting-Toomey & F. Korzenny (Eds.), *Cross-cultural interpersonal communication* (pp. 29–57). Newbury Park, CA: Sage.

Chiao, J. Y., & Ambady, N. (2007). Cultural neuroscience: Parsing universality and diversity across levels of analysis. In S. Kitayama & D. Cohen (Eds.), *Handbook of cultural psychology* (pp. 237–254). New York, NY: Guilford Press.

Chiao, J. Y., Harada, T., Komeda, H., Li, Z., Mano, Y., Saito, D., ... Lidaka, T. (2009). Neural basis of individualistic and collectivist views of self. *Human Brain Mapping, 30*, 2813–2820.

Chirkov, V., Ryan, R., Kim, Y., & Kaplan, U. (2003). Differentiating autonomy from individualism and independence: A self-determination theory perspective on internalization of cultural orientations and well-being. *Journal of Personality and Social Psychology, 84*, 97–110.

Chiu, S. Y., & Hong, Y. Y., (2007). Cultural processes: Basic principles. In A. W. Kruglanski & E. T. Higgins (Eds.), *Social psychology: Handbook of basic principles* (2nd ed., pp. 807–825). New York, NY: Guilford Press.

Choi, I., Dalal, R., Kim-Prieto, C., & Park, H. (2003). Culture and judgment of causal relevance. *Journal of Personality and Social Psychology, 84*, 46–59.

Cole, M. (1990). Cultural psychology: A once and future discipline? In J. J. Berman (Ed.), *Nebraska symposium on motivation: Vol. 38. Cross-cultural perspectives* (pp. 279–335). Lincoln: University of Nebraska Press.

Cole, M. (1996). *Cultural psychology: A once and future discipline*. Cambridge, MA: Harvard University Press.

Cole, M., Gay, J., Glick, J., & Sharp, D. W. (1971). *The cultural context of learning and thinking*. New York, NY: Basic Books.

Cole, M., & Scribner, S. (1974). *Culture and thought: A psychological introduction*. New York, NY: Wiley.

Crystal, D. S., & Stevenson, H. W. (1991). Mothers' perceptions of children's problems with mathematics: Across-national comparison. *Journal of Educational Psychology, 83*, 372–376.

Dien, D. S. (1999). Chinese authority-directed orientation and Japanese peer-group orientation: Questioning the notion of collectivism. *Review of General Psychology, 3*, 372–385.

Diener, E., & Diener, M. (1995). Cross-cultural correlates of life satisfaction and self-esteem. *Journal of Personality & Social Psychology, 68*, 653–663.

Diener, E., Diener, M., & Diener, C. (1995). Factors predicting the subjective well-being of nations. *Journal of Personality Psychology, 69*, 851–864.

Doi, T. (1973). *Anatomy of dependence.* Tokyo, Japan: Kodansha International Press.

Doi, T. (1992). On the concept of *amae. Infant Mental Health Journal, 13*, 7–11.

Festinger, L. (1957). *A theory of cognitive dissonance.* Stanford, CA: Stanford University Press.

Fromm, E. (1941). *Escape from freedom.* New York, NY: Farrar & Rinehart.

Gabrenya, W. K. Jr., & Hwang, K.-K. (1996). Chinese social interaction: Harmony and hierarchy on the good earth, *The handbook of Chinese psychology* (pp. 309–321). Hong Kong: Oxford University Press.

Geertz, C. (1973). *The interpretation of cultures.* New York, NY: Basic Press.

Gilligan, C. (1982). *In a different voice: Psychological theory and women's development.* Cambridge, MA: Harvard University Press.

Goody, J. (Ed.). (1968). *Literacy in traditional societies.* New York, NY: Cambridge Press.

Graham, S. (1992). Most of the subjects were White and middle class: Trends in published research on African Americans in selected APA journals, 1970–1989. *American Psychologist, 47*, 629–639.

Greenfield, P. M. (1997). Culture as process: Empirical methods for cultural psychology. In J. W. Berry, Y. H. Poortinga, & J. Pandey (Eds.), *Handbook of cross-cultural psychology: Vol. 1. Theory and method* (2nd ed., pp. 301–346). Boston, MA: Allyn & Bacon.

Greenfield, P. M., & Bruner, J. S. (1969). Culture and cognitive growth. In D. A. Goslin (Ed.), *Handbook of socialization theory and research* (pp. 633–657). Chicago, IL: Rand-McNally.

Greenfield, P. M., & Cocking, R. R. (Eds.). (1994). *Cross-cultural roots of minority child development.* Hillsdale, NJ: Erlbaum.

Greenfield, P. M., & Suzuki, L. (1998). Culture and human development: Implications for parenting, education, pediatrics, and mental health. In I. E. Sigel & K. A. Renninger (Eds.), *Handbook of child psychology* (Vol. 4, pp. 1059–1109). New York, NY: Wiley.

Greenwald, A. G., & Farnham, S. D. (2000). Using the implicit association test to measure self-esteem and self-concept. *Journal of Personality and Social Psychology, 79*, 1022–1038.

Gutchess, A. H., Welsh, R. C., Boduroglu, A., & Park, D. C. (2006). Cultural differences in neural function associated with object processing. *Cognitive, Affective, and Behavioral Neuroscience*, 102–109.

Hamamura, T., Heine, S. J., & Takemoto, T. R. S. (2007). Why the better-than-average effect is a worse-than-average measure of self-enhancement: An investigation of conflicting findings from studies of East Asian self-evaluations. *Motivation and Emotion, 31*, 247–259.

Han, J. J., Leichtman, M. D., & Wang, Q. (1998). Autobiographical memory in Korean, Chinese, and American children. *Developmental Psychology, 34*, 701–713.

Haney, C., Banks, C., & Zimbardo, P. (1973). Interpersonal dynamics in a simulated prison. *International Journal of Criminology and Penology, 1*, 69–97.

Harwood, R. L., Miller, J. G., & Irizarry, N. L. (1995). *Culture and attachment: Perceptions of the child in context.* New York, NY: Guilford Press.

Heath, S. B. (1983). *Ways with words: Language, life, and work in communities and classrooms.* Cambridge, UK: Cambridge University Press.

Hedden, T., Ketay, S., Aron, A., Markus, H. R., & Gabrieli, J. D. E. (2008). Cultural influences on neural substrates of attentional control. *Psychological Science, 19*, 12–17.

Heine, S., & Hamamura, T. (2007). In search of East Asian self-enhancement. *Personality and Social Psychology Review, 11*, 1–24.

Heine, S., Kitayama, S., Lehman, D., Takata, T., Ide, E., Leung, C., & Matsumoto, H. (2001). Divergent consequences of success and failure in Japan and North America: An investigation of self-improving motivations and malleable selves. *Journal of Personality and Social Psychology, 81*, 599–615.

Heine, S., Kitayama, S., & Hamamura, T. (2007). Inclusion of additional studies yields different conclusions: Comment on Sedikides, Gaertner, & Vevea (2005) Journal of Personality and Social Psychology. *Asian Journal of Social Psychology, 10*, 49–58.

Heine, S. J., & Lehman, D. R. (1997). Culture, dissonance, and self affirmation. *Personality & Social Psychology Bulletin, 23*, 389–400.

Heine, S. H., Lehman, D. R., Markus, H. R., & Kitayama, S. (1999). Is there a universal need for positive self-regard? *Psychological Review, 106*, 766–794.

Herzog, A. R., Franks, M. M., Markus, H. R., & Holmberg, D. (1998). Activities and well-being in older age: Effects of self concept and educational attainment. *Psychology & Aging, 13*, 179–185.

Higgins, E. T., & Kruglanski, A. W. (1996). *Social psychology: Handbook of basic principles.* New York, NY: Guilford Press.

Hofstede, G. (1980). *Culture's consequences.* Beverly Hills, CA: Sage.

Hoshino-Browne, E., Zanna, A. S., Spencer, S., Zanna, M., Kitayama, S., & Lackenbauer, S. (2005). On the cultural guises of cognitive dissonance: The case of *Easterners and Westerners. Journal of Personal and Social Psychology, 89*(3), 294–310.

Hsu, F. L. K. (1963). *Clan, caste and club.* New York, NY: van Nostrand.

Hsu, F. L. K. (1985). The self in cross-cultural perspective. In A. J. Marsella, G. DeVos, & F. L. K. Hsu (Eds.), *Culture and self: Asian and western perspectives* (pp. 24–55). London, UK: Tavistock.

Inkeles, A. (1974). *Becoming modern: Individual change in six developing countries.* Cambridge, MA: Harvard University Press.

Ishii, K., Tsukasaki, T., & Kitayama, S. (2009). Culture and visual perception: Does perceptual inference depend on culture? *Japanese Psychological Research, 51*, 103–109.

Iyengar, S. S., & Lepper, M. R. (1999). Rethinking the value of choice: A cultural perspective on intrinsic motivation. *Journal of Personality & Social Psychology, 76*, 349–366.

Jahoda, G. (1993). *Crossroads between culture and mind: Continuities and change in theories of human nature.* Cambridge, MA: Harvard University Press.

Jensen, L. A. (1997). Different worldviews, different morals: America's culture war divide. *Human Development, 40*, 325–344.

Ji, L.-J., Peng, K., & Nisbett, R. E. (2000). Culture, control, and perception of relationships in the environment. *Journal of Personality and Social Psychology, 78*, 943–955.

Ji, L.-J., Nisbett, R. E., & Su, Y. (2001). Culture, change, and prediction. *Psychological Science, 12*, 450–456.

Ji, L.-J., Schwarz, N., & Nisbett, R. E. (2000). Culture, autobiographical memory, and behavioral frequency reports: Measurement issues in cross-cultural studies. *Personality & Social Psychology Bulletin, 26*, 585–593.

Jourard, S. M. (1965). *Personal adjustment: An approach through the study of healthy personality.* New York, NY: Macmillan.

Kagan, J. (2007). A trio of concerns. *Perspectives on Psychological Science, 2*, 361–376.

Culture and Social Psychology **525**

Kanagawa, C., Cross, S. E., & Markus, H. R. (2001). "Who am I?": The cultural psychology of the conceptual self. *Personality and Social Psychology Bulletin, 27,* 1557–1564.

Kardiner, A. (1945). *Psychological frontiers of society.* New York, NY: Columbia University Press.

Kashima, Y., Siegal, M., Tanaka, K., & Kashima, E. S. (1992). Do people believe behaviours are consistent with attitudes? Towards a cultural psychology of attribution processes. *British Journal of Social Psychology, 31,* 111–124.

Kitayama, S. (2002). Culture and basic psychological processes: Toward a system view of culture: Comment on Oyserman et al. (2002). *Psychological Bulletin, 128*(1), 89–96.

Kitayama, S., Conway, L. G., Pietromonaco, P., Park, H., & Plaut, V. C. (2010). Ethos of independence across regions in the United States: The production-adoption model of cultural change. *American Psychologist, 65,* 559–574.

Kitayama, S., Duffy, S., Kawamura, T., & Larsen, J. T. (2003). Perceiving an object and its context in different cultures: A cultural look at new look. *Psychological Science, 14,* 201–206.

Kitayama, S., Markus, H. R., & Kurokawa, M. (2000). Culture, emotion, and well-being: Good feelings in Japan and the United States. *Cognition & Emotion, 14,* 93–124.

Kitayama, S., Mesquita, B., & Karasawa, M. (2006). Cultural affordances and emotional experience: Socially engaging and disengaging emotions in Japan and the United States. *Journal of Personality and Social Psychology, 91,* 890–903.

Kitayama, S., Snibbe, A. C., Markus, H. R., & Suzuki, T. (2004). Is there any "free" choice? Self and dissonance in two cultures. *Psychological Science, 15,* 527–533.

Kitayama, S., & Uchida, Y. (2003). Explicit self-criticism and implicit self-regard: Evaluating self and friend in two cultures. *Journal of Experimental Social Psychology, 39,* 476–482.

Knight, N., & Nisbett, R. E. (2007). Culture, class and cognition: Evidence from Italy. *Journal of Cognition and Culture, 7,* 283–291.

Kohlberg, L. (1971). From is to ought: How to commit the naturalistic fallacy and get away with it in the study of moral development. In T. Mischel (Ed.), *Cognitive development and epistemology* (pp. 151–236). New York, NY: Academic Press.

Kraus, M. W., Cote, S., & Keltner, D. (2010). Social class, contextualism, and empathic accuracy. *Psychological Science, 21,* 1716–1723.

Kraus, M. W., & Keltner, D. (2009). Signs of socioeconomic status: A thin-slicing approach. *Psychological Science, 99*–106.

Kraus, M. W., Piff, P. K., & Keltner, D. (2009). Social class, the sense of control, and social explanation. *Journal of Personality and Social Psychology, 97,* 992–1004.

Kruglanski, A. W., & Higgins, E. T. (Eds.). (2007). *Social Psychology: Handbook of Basic Principles* (2nd ed.). New York, NY: Guilford Press.

Kusserow, A. S. (1999). De-homogenizing American individualism: Socializing hard and soft individualism in Manhattan and Queens. *Ethos, 27,* 210–234.

Levenson, R. W., Ekman, P., Heider, K., & Friesen, W. V. (1992). Emotion and autonomic nervous system activity in the Minangkabau of West Sumatra. *Journal of Personality and Social Psychology, 62,* 972–988.

LeVine, R. A. (1973). *Culture, behavior and personality.* Chicago, IL: Aldine.

Levy, R. I. (1984). Emotion, knowing, and culture. In R. A. Shweder & R. A. LeVine (Eds.), *Culture theory: Essays on mind, self, and emotion* (pp. 214–237). Cambridge, UK: Cambridge University Press.

Lillard, A. (1998). Ethnopsychologies: Cultural variations in theories of mind. *Psychological Bulletin, 123,* 1–32.

Luria, A. R. (1928). The problem of the cultural development of the child. *Journal of Genetic Psychology, 35,* 493–506.

Luria, A. R. (1976). *Cognitive development: Its cultural and social foundations.* Cambridge, MA: Harvard University Press.

Lutz, C., & White, G. (1986). The anthropology of emotions. *Annual Review of Anthropology, 15,* 405–436.

Ma, H. K. (1988). The Chinese perspective on moral judgment development. *International Journal of Psychology, 23,* 201–227.

Ma, H. K. (1989). Moral orientation and moral judgment in adolescents in Hong Kong, Mainland China, and England. *Journal of Cross-Cultural Psychology, 20,* 152–177.

Malinowski, B. (1959). *Sex and repression in savage society.* New York, NY: Meridian Books.

Markus, H. R., & Kitayama, S. (1991). Culture and the self: Implications for cognition, emotion, and motivation. *Psychological Review, 98,* 224–253.

Markus, H. R. & Kitayama, S. (2010). Culture and selves: A cycle of mutual constitution. *Perspectives on Psychological Science, 5,* 420–430.

Markus, H. R., Kitayama, S., & Heiman, R. J. (1996). Culture and "basic" psychological principles in social psychology: Handbook of basic principles (pp. 857–913). New York, NY: Guilford.

Markus, H. R., Plaut, V. C., & Lachman, M. E. (2004). Well-being in America: Core features and regional patterns. In O. G. Brim, C. D. Ryff, & R. C. Kessler (Eds.), *How healthy are we?: A national study of well-being at midlife* (pp. 614–650). Chicago, IL: University of Chicago Press.

Masuda, T., Gonzalez, R., Kwan, L., & Nisbett, R. (2008). Culture and aesthetic preference: Comparing the attention to context of East Asians and Americans. *Personality and Social Psychology Bulletin, 34,* 1260–1275.

Masuda, T., & Kitayama, S. (2004). Perceiver-induced constraint and attitude attribution in Japan and the US: A case for the cultural dependence of the correspondence bias. *Journal of Experimental Social Psychology, 40,* 409–416.

Masuda, T., & Nisbett, R. E. (2001). Attending holistically versus analytically: Comparing the context sensitivity of Japanese and Americans. *Journal of Personality and Social Psychology, 81,* 922–934.

Masuda, T., & Nisbett, R. A. (2006). Culture and change blindness. *Cognitive Science, 30,* 381–399.

McLoyd, V. (1990). The impact of economic hardship on black families and children: Psychological distress, parenting, and socioemotional development. *Child development: Special issue: Minority children, 61,* 311–346.

Mead, M. (1928). *Coming of age in Samoa.* New York, NY: Morrow.

Mead, M. (1939). *From the South Seas.* New York, NY: Morrow.

Mesquita, B. (2001). Emotions in collectivist and individualist contexts. *Journal of Personality and Social Psychology, 80,* 68–74.

Milgram, S. (1963). The behavioral study of obedience. *Journal of Abnormal and Social Psychology, 67,* 467–472.

Miller, J. G. (1984). Culture and the development of everyday social explanation. *Journal of Personality & Social Psychology, 46,* 961–978.

Miller, J. G. (1987). Cultural influences on the development of conceptual differentiation in person description. *British Journal of Developmental Psychology, 5,* 309–319.

Miller, J. G. (1994). Cultural diversity in the morality of caring: Individually oriented versus duty-based interpersonal moral codes. *Cross-Cultural Research, 28,* 3–39.

Miller, J. G. (1997). Theoretical issues in cultural psychology. In J. W. Berry, Y. H. Poortinga, & J. Pandey (Eds.), *Handbook of cross-cultural psychology: Vol. 1. Theory and method* (2nd ed., pp. 85–128). Boston, MA: Allyn & Bacon.

Miller, J. G. (2001). Culture and moral development. In D. Matsumoto (Ed.), *The handbook of culture and psychology* (pp. 151–169). New York, NY: Oxford University Press.

Miller, J. G. (2002). Bringing culture to basic psychological theory: Beyond individualism and collectivism: Comment on Oyserman et al. (2002). *Psychological Bulletin, 128,* 97–109.

Miller, J. G. (2004). Culturally sensitive research questions and methods in social psychology. In C. Sansone, C. C. Morf, & A. T. Panter (Eds.), *The Sage handbook of methods in social psychology* (pp. 93–116). Thousand Oaks, CA: Sage.

Miller, J. G., & Bersoff, D. M. (1994). Cultural influences on the moral status of reciprocity and the discounting of endogenous motivation [Special issue]. *Personality and Social Psychology Bulletin: The self and the collective, 20,* 592–602.

Miller, J. G., Das, R., & Chakravarthy, S. (2011). Culture and the role of choice in agency. *Journal of Personality and Social Psychology, 101,* 46–61.

Miller, J. G., & Kinsbourne, M. (2011). Culture and neuroscience in developmental psychology: Contributions and challenges. *Child Development Perspectives, 6,* 35–41.

Miller, P. (1986). Teasing as language socialization and verbal play in a white working-class community. In B. B. Schieffelin & E. Ochs (Eds.), *Language socialization across cultures* (pp. 199–212). New York, NY: Cambridge University Press.

Miyamoto, Y., Nisbett, R. E., & Masuda, T. (2006). Culture and the physical environment: Holistic versus analytic perceptual affordances. *Psychological Science, 17,* 113–119.

Miyamoto, Y., Uchida, Y., & Ellsworth, P. C. (2010). Culture and mixed emotions: Co-occurrence of positive and negative emotions in Japan and the United States. *Emotion, 10,* 404–415.

Morling, B. (2000). "Taking" an aerobics class in the U.S. and "Entering" an aerobics class in Japan: Primary and secondary control in a fitness context. *Asian Journal of Social Psychology, 3,* 73–85.

Morling, B., Kitayama, S., & Miyamoto, Y. (2002). Cultural practices emphasize influence in the United States and adjustment in Japan. *Personality and Social Psychology Bulletin, 28,* 311–323.

Morling, B., Kitayama, S., & Miyamoto, Y. (2003). American and Japanese women use different coping strategies during normal pregnancy. *Personality and Social Psychology Bulletin, 29,* 1533–1546.

Morris, M. W., & Peng, K. (1994). Culture and cause: American and Chinese attributions for social and physical events. *Journal of Personality and Social Psychology, 67,* 949–971.

Moscovici, S. (1972). Society and theory in social psychology. In J. Israel & H. Tajfel (Eds.), *The context of social psychology: A critical assessment* (pp. 17–69). New York, NY: Academic Press.

Nisbett, R. E. (2003). *The geography of thought: How Asians and westerners think differently—and why.* New York, NY: Free Press.

Nisbett, R. E., & Cohen, D. (1996). *Culture of honor: The psychology of violence in the South.* Boulder, CO: Westview Press.

Nisbett, R. E., Peng, K., Choi, I., & Norenzayan, A. (2001). Culture and systems of thought: Holistic versus analytic cognition. *Psychological Review: Special Issue, 108,* 291–310.

Nisbett, R. E., & Ross, L. (1980). *Human inference: Strategies and shortcomings of social judgment.* Englewood Cliffs, NJ: Prentice Hall.

Ochs, E., & Schieffelin, B. B. (1984). Language acquisition and socialization: Three developmental stories and their implications. In R. A. Shweder & R. A. LeVine (Eds.), *Culture theory: Essays on mind, self, and emotion* (pp. 276–320). Cambridge, UK: Cambridge University Press.

Oyserman, D. (2007). Social identity and self-regulation. In A. W. Kruglanski & E. T. Higgins (Eds.), *Social psychology: Handbook of basic principles* (2nd ed., pp. 432–453). New York, NY: Guilford Press.

Oyserman, D., Coon, H., & Kemmelmeier, M. (2002). Rethinking individualism and collectivism: Evaluation of theoretical assumptions and meta-analyses. *Psychological Bulletin, 128,* 3–72.

Oyserman, D., & Lee, S., (2008). Does culture influence what and how we think? Effects of priming individualism and collectivism. *Psychological Bulletin, 134*(2), 311–342.

Oyserman, D., Sorensen, R., Reber, R., & Chen, S. X. (2009). Connecting and separating mind-sets: Culture as situated cognition. *Journal of Personality and Social Psychology, 97*(2), 217–235.

Park, D. C., & Huang, C.-M. (2010). Culture wires the brain: A cognitive neuroscience perspective. *Perspectives on Psychological Science, 5,* 391–400.

Peng, K., & Nisbett, R. E. (1999). Culture, dialectics, and reasoning about contradiction. *American Psychologist, 54*(9), 741–754.

Piff, P., Kraus, M., Cote, S., Cheng, B. H., & Keltner, D. (2010). Having less, giving more: The influence of social class on prosocial behavior. *Journal of Personality and Social Psychology, 99,* 771–784.

Plaut, V. C., Markus, H. R., & Lachman, M. E. (2002). Place matters: Consensual features and regional variation in American well-being and self. *Journal of Personality and Social Psychology, 83*(1), 160–184.

Reid, P. T. (1988). Racism and sexism: Comparisons and conflicts. In P. Katz & D. Taylor (Eds.), *Eliminating racism: Profiles in controversy* (pp. 203–221). New York, NY: Plenum Press.

Reid, P. T. (1994). The real problem in the study of culture. *American Psychologist, 49*(6), 524–525.

Rosaldo, M. A. (1984). Toward an anthropology of self and feeling. In R. A. Shweder & R. A. LeVine (Eds.), *Culture theory: Essays on mind, self, and emotion* (pp. 137–157). New York, NY: Cambridge University Press.

Rose, J. P., Endo, Y., Windschitl, P. D., & Suls, J. (2008). Cultural differences in unrealistic optimism and pessimism: The role of egocentrism and direct versus indirect comparison measures. *Personality and Social Psychology Bulletin, 34*(9), 1236–1248.

Ross, L., & Nisbett, R. (1991). *The person and the situation: Perspectives of social psychology.* New York, NY: McGraw-Hill.

Ross, M. (1989). Relation of implicit theories to the construction of personal histories. *Psychological Review, 96,* 341–357.

Rothbaum, F., Kakinuma, M., Nagaoka, R., & Azuma, H. (2007). Attachment and AMAE: Parent-child closeness in the United States and Japan. *Journal of Cross-Cultural Psychology, 38,* 465–486.

Rothbaum, F., Weisz, J., Pott, M., Miyake, K., & Morelli, G. (2000). Attachment and culture: Security in the United States and Japan. *American Psychologist, 55,* 1093–1104.

Rothbaum, F., Weisz, J., Pott, M., Miyake, K., & Morelli, G. (2001). Deeper into attachment and culture. *American Psychologist, 56,* 827–828.

Rotter, J. G. (1966). Generalized expectancies for internal versus external locus of control of reinforcement. *Psychological Monographs: General and Applied, 80* (Whole No. 609).

Russell, J. A. (1991). Culture and the categorization of emotions. *Psychological Bulletin, 110,* 426–450.

Russell, J. A. (1994). Is there universal recognition of emotion from facial expression? A review of the cross-cultural studies. *Psychological Bulletin, 115,* 102–141.

Russell, J. A., & Yik, M. S. M. (1996). Emotion among the Chinese. In M. H. Bond (Ed.), *The handbook of Chinese psychology* (pp. 166–188). Hong Kong: Oxford University Press.

Sagi, A., & van Ijzendoom, M. H. (1994). Sleeping out of home in a kibbutz communal arrangement: It makes a difference for infant-mother attachment. *Child Development, 65,* 992–1004.

Sahlins, M. (1976). *Culture and practical reason.* Chicago, IL: University of Chicago Press.

Schwartz, S. H. (1994). Beyond individualism and collectivism: New cultural dimensions of values. In U. Kim, H. C. Triandis, C. Kagitcibasi, S.-C. Choi, & G. Yoon (Eds.), *Individualism and collectivism: Theory, method, and applications* (pp. 85–122). Newbury Park, CA: Sage.

Schwartz, T., White, G. M., & Lutz, C. (Eds.). (1992). *New directions in psychological anthropology*. Cambridge, UK: Cambridge University Press.

Scribner, S., & Cole, M. (1981). *The psychology of literacy*. Cambridge, MA: Harvard University Press.

Sharp, D., Cole, M., & Lave, C. (1979). Education and cognitive development: The evidence from experimental research. *Monographs of the Society for Research on Child Development, 44*(1–2).

Shore, B. (1996). *Culture in mind: Cognition, culture and the problem of meaning*. New York, NY: Oxford University Press.

Shweder, R. A. (1979a). Rethinking culture and personality theory part I: A critical examination of two classical postulates. *Ethos*, 255–278.

Shweder, R. A. (1979b). Rethinking culture and personality theory: Pt 2. A critical examination of two more classical postulates. *Ethos, 7*, 255–278.

Shweder, R. A. (1984). Anthropology's romantic rebellion against the enlightenment, or there's more to thinking than reason and evidence. In R. A. Shweder & R. A. LeVine (Eds.), *Culture theory: Essays on mind, self, and emotion* (pp. 27–66). Cambridge, UK: Cambridge University Press.

Shweder, R. A. (1990). Cultural psychology: What is it? In J. W. Stigler, R. A. Shweder, & G. Herdt (Eds.), *Cultural psychology: Essays on comparative human development* (pp. 27–66). New York, NY: Cambridge University Press.

Shweder, R. A., & Bourne, E. J. (1984). Does the concept of the person vary cross-culturally? In R. A. Shweder & R. A. Levine (Eds.), *Culture theory: Essays on mind, self, and emotion* (pp. 158–199). New York, NY: Cambridge University Press.

Shweder, R. A., Goodnow, J., Hatano, G., LeVine, R. A., Markus, H., & Miller, P. (1998). The cultural psychology of development: One mind, many mentalities. In W. Damon (Ed.), *Handbook of child psychology* (Vol. 1, pp. 865–937). New York, NY: Wiley.

Shweder, R. A., & LeVine, R. A. (1984). *Culture theory: Essays on mind, self, and emotion*. Cambridge, UK: Cambridge University Press.

Shweder, R. A., Mahapatra, M., & Miller, J. G. (1990). Culture and moral development. In J. W. Stigler, R. A. Shweder, & G. Herdt (Eds.), *Cultural psychology: Essays on comparative human development* (pp. 130–204). New York, NY: Cambridge University Press.

Shweder, R. A., Much, N. C., Mahapatra, M., & Park, L. (1997). The "big three" of morality (autonomy, community, divinity) and the "big three" explanations of suffering. In A. M. Brandt (Ed.), *Morality and health* (pp. 119–169). New York, NY: Routledge.

Simons, D. J., & Rensink, R. A. (2005). Change blindness: Past, present, and future. *Trends in Cognitive Sciences, 9*, 16–20.

Sinha, D. (1990). The concept of psycho-social well being: Western and Indian perspectives. *National Institute of Mental Health and Neurosciences Journal, 8*, 1–11.

Snarey, J., & Keljo, K. (1991). In A Gemeinschaft voice: The cross-cultural expansion of moral development theory, *Handbook of moral behavior and development, Vol. 1: Theory* (pp. 395–424). Hillsdale, NJ: Erlbaum.

Snibbe, A. C., & Markus, H. R. (2005). You can't always get what you want: Educational attainment, agency, and choice. *Journal of Personality and Social Psychology, 88*, 703–720.

Soothill, W. E., & Hodous, L. (1968). *The dictionary of Chinese Buddhist terms*. London, UK: Kegan Paul.

Spencer-Rodgers, J., Boucher, H., Mori, S., Wang, L., & Peng, K. (2009). The dialectical self-concept: Contradiction, change, and holism in East Asian cultures. *Personality and Social Psychology Bulletin, 35*, 29–44.

Spencer-Rodgers, J., Peng, K., & Wang, L. (2010). Dialecticism and the co-occurrence of positive and negative emotions across cultures. *Journal of Cross-Cultural Psychology, 41*, 109–115.

Spencer-Rodgers, J., Williams, M. J., & Peng, K. (2010). Cultural differences in expectations of change and tolerance for contradiction:

A decade of empirical research. *Personality and Social Psychology Review, 14*(3), 296–312.

Stephens, N. M., Markus, H. R., & Townsend, S. M. (2007). Choice as an act of meaning: The case of social class. *Journal of Personality and Social Psychology, 93*, 814–830.

Stevenson, H. W., & Lee, S.-Y. (1990). Contexts of achievement: A study of American, Chinese, and Japanese children. *Monographs of the Society for Research in Child Development*. Chicago, IL: University of Chicago Press.

Strauss, C. (1992). What makes Tony run? Schemas as motives reconsidered, *Human motives and cultural models* (pp. 197–224). New York, NY: Cambridge University Press.

Strauss, C., & Quinn, N. (1997). *A cognitive theory of cultural meaning*. New York, NY: Cambridge University Press.

Suh, E. (2000). Culture, identity consistency, and subjective well-being. Manuscript submitted for publication, University of California, Irvine.

Swann, W. B., Wenzlaff, R. M., Krull, D. S., & Pelham, B. W. (1992). Allure of negative feedback: Self-verification strivings among depressed persons. *Journal of Abnormal Psychology, 101*, 293–306.

Triandis, H. C. (1972). *The analysis of subjective culture*. New York, NY: Wiley.

Triandis, H. C. (1989). The self and social behavior in differing cultural contexts. *Psychological Review, 96*, 506–520.

Triandis, H. C. (1996). The psychological measurement of cultural syndromes. *American Psychologist, 51*, 407–415.

Triandis, H. C., & Lambert, W. E. (Eds.). (1980). *Handbook of cross-cultural psychology: Vol. I: Perspectives*. Boston, MA: Allyn & Bacon.

Turiel, E. (1983). *The development of social knowledge: Morality and convention*. Cambridge, UK: Cambridge University Press.

Uchida, Y., Townsend, S. M., & Markus, H. R. (2009). Emotions as within or between people? Cultural variation in lay theories of emotion expression and inference. *Personality and Social Psychology Bulletin, 35*, 1427–1439.

Varnum, M. E. W., Grossmann, I., Katunar, D., Nisbett, R. E., & Kitayama, S. (2008). Holism in a European cultural context: Differences in cognitive style between Central and East Europeans and Westerners. *Journal of Cognition and Culture, 8*(3–4), 321–333.

Varnum, M. E. W., Grossmann, I., Kitayama, S., & Nisbett, R. E. (2010). The origin of cultural differences in cognition: The social orientation hypothesis. *Psychological Science, 19*, 9–13.

Vygotsky, L. S. (1929). The problem of the cultural development of the child, Pt 2. *Journal of Genetic Psychology, 36*, 414–436.

Vygotsky, L. S. (1978). *Mind in society: The development of higher psychological processes*. Cambridge, MA: Harvard University Press.

Vygotsky, L. S. (1987). *Thinking and speech*. New York, NY: Plenum Press. (Original work published 1934)

Wallace, A. F. C. (1961). *Culture and personality*. New York, NY: Random House.

Wang, Q. (2001). Culture effects on adults' earliest childhood recollection and self-description: Implications for the relation between memory and self. *Journal of Personality and Social Psychology, 81*, 220–233.

Wang, Q. (2004). The emergence of cultural self-constructs: Autobiographical memory and self-description in European American and Chinese children. *Developmental Psychology, 40*(1), 3–15.

Wang, Q., & Leichtman, M. D. (2000). Same beginnings, different stories: A comparison of American and Chinese children's narratives. *Child Development, 71*, 1329–1346.

Weber, E., & Morris, M. W. (2010). Culture and judgment and decision making: The constructivist turn. *Perspectives on Psychological Science, 5*, 410–419.

Weisz, J. R., Rothbaum, F. M., & Blackburn, T. C. (1984). Standing out and standing in: The psychology of control in America and Japan. *American Psychologist, 39*, 955–969.

Wellman, H. M., & Miller, J. G. (2008). Including deontic reasoning as fundamental to theory of mind. *Human Development, 51*, 105–135.

Wertsch, J. V. (1995). Sociocultural research in the copyright age. *Culture and Psychology, 1*, 81–102.

White, G. M. (1994). Affecting culture: Emotion and morality in everyday life. In S. Kitayama & H. R. Markus (Eds.), *Emotion and culture: Empirical studies of mutual influence* (pp. 219–240). Washington, DC: American Psychological Association.

Whiting, B. B., & Edwards, C. P. (1988). *Children of different worlds: The formation of social behavior.* Cambridge, MA: Harvard University Press.

Whiting, B. B., & Whiting, J. W. (1975). *Children of six cultures: A psycho-cultural analysis.* Cambridge, MA: Harvard University Press.

Whiting, J. W., & Child, I. (1953). *Child training and personality.* New Haven, CT: Yale University Press.

Wierzbicka, A. (1992). Talking about emotions: Semantics, culture and cognition. *Cognition and Emotion, 6*, 285–319.

Witkin, H. A., & Berry, J. W. (1975). Psychological differentiation in cross-cultural perspective. *Journal of Cross-Cultural Psychology, 6*, 4–87.

Yamaguchi, S. (2001). Culture and control orientations. In D. Matsumoto (Ed.), *The handbook of culture and psychology* (pp. 223–243). New York, NY: Oxford University Press.

Yang, K.-S. (1997). Indigenizing westernized Chinese psychology. In M. H. Bond (Ed.), *Working at the interface of culture: Eighteen lives in social science.* London, UK: Routledge.

Yang, K.-S. (1988). Chinese filial piety: A conceptual analysis. In K. S. Yang (Ed.), *The psychology of the Chinese people: An indigenous perspective* (pp. 39–73). Taipei, Taiwan: Kuei-Kuan. (In Chinese)

Yang, K.-S., & Ho, D. Y. F. (1988). The role of the *yuan* in Chinese social life: A conceptual and empirical analysis. In A. C. Paranjpe, D. Y. F. Ho, & R. W. Rieber (Eds.), *Asian contributions to psychology* (pp. 263–281). New York, NY: Praeger.

Author Index

Dolderman, D., 334, 336
Doll, J., 286
Dollard, J., 429, 451
Domhoff, G. W., 75
Donenberg, G. R., 52
Donnellan, M., 169
Donnellan, M. B., 10, 184–187, 205
Donnerstein, E., 458, 460
Donovan, S., 106
Doob, L., 429, 451
Doosje, B., 343, 344, 348, 349, 355, 358
Dorr, N., 344
Dossche, D., 148
Dotson, D., 77
Douglas, A., 414
Douglas-Palumberi, H., 204
Dovidio, J. D., 443
Dovidio, J. F., 229, 317, 341, 343, 345, 349, 350, 352–355, 359, 371, 378, 383, 430, 431, 433–443, 467, 470–472, 474–476, 478, 480, 481
Downey, G., 165, 168, 336
Downs, D. L., 247, 248, 252
Doyle, A. E., 30
Drigotas, S. M., 330, 334
Driscoll, P., 35, 38
Dronkert, E., 413
Drout, C. E., 417
Duan, C., 236
Duckitt, J., 296, 341, 343, 348, 349, 359, 432
Duckworth, K. L., 370
Duff, K. J., 235
Duffy, G., 284
Duffy, S., 517
Duke, M., 74
Dulaev, I., 200
Duncan, L. E., 212
Dunham, Y., 431
Dunn, D. S., 370, 381
Dunnette, M. D., 409
Dunning, D., 260
Dunning, J. P., 395
Dunton, B. C., 277, 343, 345, 354, 371
Duong, D., 144, 150
Durantini, M. R., 296
Durbin, C. E., 185, 204
Duregger, C., 59

Durkheim, E., 249
Durrheim, K., 352, 360
Dutton, J. E., 213
Dweck, C. S., 168, 169, 171, 174–176
Dyce, J. A., 146
Dye, D. A., 80
Dykas, M. J., 52
Dzieweczynski, J., 479

Eagle, M. N., 50, 52, 54, 56, 57
Eagly, A. H., 275, 288, 291, 313, 341, 349, 350, 359, 370–372, 377, 378
Earl, A. N., 296
Earley, P. C., 411, 414
Eastwick, P. W., 331
Eaton, A. A., 287
Eaton, N. R., 152
Eaves, L., 290
Eaves, L. J., 15
Ebbesen, E. B., 226
Ebener, P., 411
Eberhardt, J. L., 237
Ebner-Priemer, U. W., 149
Ebstein, R. P., 9, 19, 20, 30
Eccles, J., 189
Eckel, L. A., 492, 494
Edelmann, R. J., 263
Edelstein, R. S., 168
Edmonds, G., 205, 207
Edmonds, G. W., 207
Edmondson, D., 345
Edvardsen, J., 12
Edwards, A. L., 256
Edwards, C. P., 511
Edwards, J., 34
Edwards, K., 291, 369, 438
Eelen, P., 376
Egan, V., 456
Egger, J., 191
Eggins, R. A., 347
Egloff, B., 332, 397
Ehlert, U., 33
Ehrenreich, B., 267
Eibl-Eibesfeldt, I., 233, 493
Eichler, W. C., 141, 149, 150
Eid, M., 149
Eidelman, S., 123, 315
Ein-Dor, T., 57
Einstein, A., 43

Eisen, S. A., 15
Eisenberg, N., 205, 474, 477
Eisenberger, N. I., 317, 492
Eisenstadt, D., 350
Eke, A. W., 499
Ekman, P., 392, 494, 519
Eley, T. C., 15, 204
Elfenbein, H. A., 431
Elizur, Y., 30
Elkin, R. A., 382
Ellard, J. H., 417
Ellemers, N., 343, 348, 355, 358
Ellenberger, H., 45
Eller, A., 442
Elliot, A. J., 147, 209, 262, 370, 382
Ellis, B. J., 488
Ellis, L., 493
Ellsworth, P. C., 241, 519
Elms, A. C., 320, 321
Elson, S. B., 416, 420
Embree, M. C., 458
Emde, R. N., 44, 57
Emersen, E., 52
Emerson, R. W., 87, 305
Emery, N. J., 36
Emmons, R. A., 209, 255
Endo, Y., 518
English, E., 267
Ennis, R., 282
Ensari, N., 442
Ensminger, J., 500
Epley, N., 170, 235, 469, 470
Epstein, A., 113
Epstein, R. M., 193
Epstein, S., 94–99, 101, 103–111, 113–115, 129, 131, 163
Erber, R., 260
Erdelyi, M. H., 44, 46, 53, 56
Erez, A., 206, 209, 477
Erickson, E. A., 397
Erickson, T. M., 148
Erikson, E. H., 49, 210, 252, 266
Eron, L. D., 452
Eshkoli, N., 477
Eshleman, A., 343, 346, 349, 359
Eskritt, M., 234
Esquilin, M., 434
Esses, V., 285
Esses, V. M., 278–280, 288, 294, 296, 349, 354, 436, 437, 442, 443, 480, 481

Subject Index